L MORRISON

Children in a Changing World

Development and Social Issues

Second Edition

Children in a Changing World

Development and Social Issues
Second Edition

Edward F. Zigler
Yale University

Matia Finn Stevenson
Yale University

Brooks/Cole Publishing Company
Pacific Grove, California

Brooks/Cole Publishing Company
A Division of Wadsworth, Inc.
©1993, 1987 by Edward F. Zigler and Matia Finn Stevenson.

Printed in the United States of America

10   9   8   7   6   5   4   3

Library of Congress Cataloging-in-Publication Data
Zigler, Edward
      Children in a changing world : development and social issues /
    Edward F. Zigler, Matia Finn Stevenson.—2nd ed.
          p.   cm.
      Rev. ed. of: Children, development and social issues. ©1987.
      Includes bibliographical references (p.   ) and indexes.
      ISBN 0-534-14238-9
1. Child development.   2. Developmental psychology.   I. Finn
        Stevenson, Matia.   II. Zigler, Edward.   Children,
        development and social issues.   III. Title.
      HQ767.9.Z54 1992
      305.23'1—dc20   91-43130
                                                                            CIP

Sponsoring Editor: *Vicki Knight*
Project Development Editors: *Bob Cunningham and Pat Gadban*
Marketing Representative: *Ira Zuckerman*
Editorial Assistant: *Heather L. Graeve*
Production Editor: *Penelope Sky*
Manuscript Editor: *Robin L. Witkin*
Permissions Editor: *Marie DuBois*
Interior and Cover Design: *Roy R. Neuhaus*
Cover Photo: *David Young-Wolff/Photo Edit*
Art Coordinator: *Cloyce J. Wall*
Interior Illustration: *Publication Services*
Photo Editors: *Ruth Minerva, Nancy Shammas, and Larry Molmud*
Photo Researcher: *Gail Meese/Meese Photo Research*
Typesetting: *TSI Graphics*
Printing and Binding: *Arcata Graphics/Hawkins*

For Ima
and
For Bernice

About the Authors

Edward F. Zigler earned his Ph.D. from the University of Texas at Austin. At Yale University, he is former chairman of the Department of Psychology and currently Sterling Professor of Psychology, head of the psychology section of the Child Study Center, and Director of the Bush Center in Child Development and Social Policy. He is the author, coauthor, and editor of numerous scholarly publications and has conducted extensive investigations on topics related to normal child development and to psychopathology and mental retardation.

Dr. Zigler regularly testifies as an expert witness before congressional committees and has served as a consultant to a number of cabinet-rank officers. He was one of the planners of Project Head Start; President Carter later named him chair of the fifteenth anniversary of the project. From 1970 to 1972, Dr. Zigler was the first director of the U.S. Office of Child Development (now the Administration for Children, Youth and Families) and Chief of the Children's Bureau.

Dr. Zigler's many honors include awards from the U.S. Department of Health, Education, and Welfare, the American Psychological Association, the American Academy of Pediatrics, the Society for Research in Child Development, The American Academy of Child and Adolescent Psychiatry, the American Academy on Mental Retardation, and the American Orthopsychiatric Association.

Matia Finn Stevenson earned her Ph.D. from Ohio State University. She is a Research Scientist at Yale University, with a joint appointment at the Department of Psychology and the Child Study Center of the School of Medicine. She is also a member of the faculty and Associate Director of the Bush Center in Child Development and Social Policy. She is a former editor of *The Networker,* a newsletter on child and family policy issues.

Dr. Finn Stevenson has done extensive research in child development, children's services, parent training, and work–family life issues. In her current research she is focusing on the involvement of schools in child care and social support programs. She is the author and coauthor of many scholarly publications, the most recent of which are related to child care and welfare, parental leave policies, and family support programs.

Dr. Finn Stevenson has been an advisor on domestic policy issues to the staff of the White House Office of Policy Development and a consultant to the Connecticut legislature's Committee on Work and Family, the Committee on Education and Labor, the U.S. House of Representatives, and the U.S. Senate Subcommittee on Children, Youth, Families, Alcohol, and Drug Abuse. She regularly advises school districts and state departments of education on programs and services for children and serves as a consultant to policy makers at the state and federal levels.

Preface

T he study of child development has undergone major transformations in the past few decades. Discoveries have been made and research methods refined; many assumptions about the developmental capabilities of children have been challenged; and issues that were not previously considered are being investigated. Children are now regarded as actively shaping their own environment, influencing others as well as being affected by them. Child development specialists recognize that human existence at any period of life occurs within a social context. Accordingly, studies must include the settings in which children live and the dynamics that govern social relationships. Research is as likely to be conducted in a child care center, classroom, or playground as in the laboratory, and often includes family life.

Also new is the effort by an increasing number of researchers to apply their findings to the health, education, and welfare of children and their families; to improve children's lives by developing public policies and making adjustments in the workplace. Due to changes in demography, in the economy, and in family life, many children are growing up poor, and many are in single-parent families. Divorce, teen parenthood, and child care are other conditions that affect children.

In writing this book, our goals were:

1. To describe major developments in the field;
2. to emphasize the effects on children of recent societal changes;
3. to help students appreciate research and theory; and
4. to show that basic knowledge has practical applications.

Social issues approach   We emphasize two themes: (1) Children develop within the family *and* in a social context. (2) Our research knowledge should be used to develop programs and policies that enhance the quality of life of children and their families. We introduce this perspective in Chapter 1 and return to it in every chapter in social issues sections, where we examine ways of integrating research and social policy. We encourage students to think critically about the conditions in which children live, and about policies that have been or can be developed for their benefit. We suggest that the needs of children can be addressed not only by government officials, but also by educators, business leaders, and social scientists.

Research   Although we emphasize social issues, we provide a comprehensive and rigorous view of research and its applications. We communicate the excitement of researchers accumulating basic knowledge. We present different theoretical viewpoints and, noting current questions, describe the techniques researchers use to find the answers. We also stress the continuing importance of classic studies, making sure that students gain insight into the history and evolution of the discipline.

New to This Edition

Social scientists are increasingly aware of the importance of cross-cultural studies to our understanding of children's development. This theme is reflected in our new title, *Children in a Changing World*. Throughout, we include studies of children in other countries, and also focus on cultural diversity in the United States.

Several new topics reflect emerging areas of research, including the Human Genome Project, legal implications of protecting the unborn child, how children learn the meanings of words, and the development of self-esteem in minority group children.

We also added concrete examples, based on the lives of real children and adults, to give students a sense of the relevance of research to everyday life.

Organization

Within each chronologically ordered chapter, we present the material topically, so instructors can use either approach. In Part I we review the history of the field, and introduce the social issues focus and research methodology. In Part II we present the biological foundations of child development and discuss prenatal development. Parts III through VI, on infancy, early childhood, middle childhood, and adolescence, contain chapters on physical, cognitive, social, and emotional development.

In each chapter we continue developmental themes from one section to the next. Instructors who use a chronological approach will assign Chapters 1–16 in order. Those who prefer a topical approach can assign Chapters 1–4 as a general introduction; followed by Chapters 5, 8, 11, and 14, on physical development; then Chapters 6, 9, 12, and 15, on cognitive development; and Chapters 7, 10, 13, and 16, on social and emotional development.

We convey the coherence of development concretely, by pointing out how increasing skills of one kind affects growth in another area. For example, in Chapters 5 and 8 we discuss the connection between physical growth and social and cognitive development. In Chapter 13 we consider how cognitive growth underlies a child's changing understanding of people and social relations.

In the first edition, research on atypical development was separated from the main discussion and placed at the end of each Part. In this edition, we integrate the atypical development studies into several chapters, thus providing a better appreciation of the range of development. In Chapter 3 we consider, among other topics, genetic explanations of autism and schizophrenia. In Chapter 5, where we discuss physical development during infancy, we describe babies who have physical and developmental disabilities. In Chapter 12, on cognitive development during middle childhood, we focus on learning disabled children. In Chapter 15 we discuss both IQ tests and mental retardation.

Special Features

Each chapter contains the following distinct features:

Discussion of Social Issues: We look at selected social policies and programs, stressing our responsibility as a society to monitor their implementation.

A *Closer Look* and *Feature:* We conduct in-depth discussions of current research findings on topics that are referred to in the text, highlighting specific studies.

Learning from Other Cultures: We consider the development of children in various cultural groups in the United States, and examine cross-cultural studies.

Additional pedagogical aids are chapter opening outlines and chapter summaries; color photo essays; a glossary; a bibliography; and name and subject indexes.

Supplementary Materials

We completely revised the supplementary materials that accompany this edition of the book, working with Alice Carter and Nancy Hall to create an integrated package that includes not only an *Instructor's Guide* and test questions, but also a range of teaching tools. Included for every chapter are *lecture launchers,* ideas for material not covered in the text; a *list of readings* instructors may suggest to students; *overhead transparencies* on selected topics; and *video segments,* covering topics that are often challenging to convey to students (for example, the "Strange Situation" experiment).

All the questions in the test bank are new; they were developed by several contributors and reviewed by instructors.

The accompanying *Study Guide* for students is also entirely new. For each chapter it includes review points, practice questions, suggested topics for independent research, and suggested readings.

Acknowledgments

We are grateful to Gwenn Fishcer, who typed and proofread the entire book. Although word processing eases the task somewhat, her efforts were considerable. We thank Sharen Petti, for preparing the indexes, and Betsy Beacom, Theresa Claire, Karen Sampara, and Ellie Kamezie for their editorial and research assistance. We appreciate the contributions of Steven Reznick, Margo Malakof, and Sharvari Dixit Munkur, who reviewed several chapters and provided suggestions. We are also grateful to Alice Carter and Nancy Hall, who collaborated with us on the supplementary materials, and to Marion Glick, for her helpful suggestions.

At Brooks/Cole Publishing Company, Vicki Knight helped us in many ways throughout our writing of the second edition and coordinated the complicated process of producing it. We appreciate her efforts and advice, and those of our production editor, Penelope Sky. We also acknowledge the contributions of Robert Cunningham and Pat Gadban.

We thank the following colleagues, who reviewed the manuscript and made valuable comments and suggestions: Kenneth Beauchamp, University of the Pacific; David Carroll, University of Wisconsin, Superior; Karen Edwards, Tennessee Joint Legislative Committee on Children and Youth; David Elkind, Tufts University; Joline N. Jones, Worcester State College; Mary S. Link, Miami University; Kathleen McCluskey-Fawcett, University of Kansas; John Rieser, Vanderbilt University; and Robert Rycek, University of Nebraska at Kearney.

Finally, and most importantly, we extend our thanks and appreciation to our families. Without their help, encouragement, and patience, this book would never have gotten off the ground.

Edward F. Zigler
Matia Finn Stevenson

Brief Contents

Contents

2   The Study of Child Development   **40**

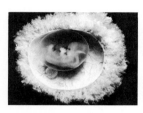

PART II
The Beginning of Life   74

3 Our Biological Heritage   76

4   Prenatal Development and Birth   **114**

7   Social and Emotional Development During Infancy   **240**

10   Social and Emotional Development During the Preschool Years   346

PART V
The Middle Childhood Years   **384**

11 Physical Development During Middle Childhood   **386**

PART VI
Adolescence   488

14 Physical Development During Adolescence   490

15 Cognitive Development During Adolescence   **518**

I Children in a Changing World

1 Children and Social Change

2 The Study of Child Development

P art I is an overview of the goals of child development research. In Chapter 1, we briefly discuss the influence of 17th- and 18th-century philosophers and 19th- and 20th-century scientific researchers. We show that present-day research emphasizes social policy; child development researchers are increasingly sensitive to the influence of their work on decisions in educational and other policy areas. You will see that the kinds of topics investigated today—such as the effects of infant day care on development or the effects of computer use on children's learning, motivation, and social behavior—reflect a modern interest in studying children within the social context. Such research both contributes to our knowledge and increases our ability to use that knowledge to help children become productive members of society.

In Chapter 2, we describe the major theories on child development developed in the 20th century. Scientists moved from studying one child at a time to studying large groups of children, their parents, and others with whom the children interact. You will learn about sophisticated techniques for collecting and analyzing data, and about how our understanding of child development benefits from contributions by researchers from such disciplines as genetics and ethnology.

1 Children and Social Change

Why Study Children?

Myths about child development abound. You may have heard your parents commenting on how today's children are growing up: "Kids have it all compared to when I was a kid." "When we were growing up, we were poor: It didn't hurt me." "Unless the mother stays home to raise her children, they'll have problems."

Although we may believe some of these statements, research shows a different picture. In this chapter you will be introduced to the field of child development and you will learn about some early ideas that have contributed to our understanding of how children develop. You will also be introduced to current directions in research and their contributions to social policy issues. And you will learn about the impact that changes in society can have on children and their parents. But first, it is important to ask the question, Why study children?

The study of child development was once considered important because it furthered our understanding of the nature of the adult. Such popular sayings as "The child is the father of the man" and "As the twig is bent, so grows the tree" attest to the belief that the experiences of infancy and childhood contribute to adult personality and behavior. Understanding the child can help us understand who we are and how we got to be that way. However, researchers today believe that studying children can also lead to ways of enhancing their development and improving their lives.

Perhaps you want to study child development because you are a parent or hope to be one some day. Or perhaps this study can help you in a career as a teacher or pediatrician or a judge who handles custody cases. Whatever your reasons, you will find that the study of children is intriguing and filled with useful information for everyday life.

A Brief History of Child Development

The modern era of research began in the late 1880s, when the study of children began to take shape as a scientific endeavor. However, interest in the nature of children has ancient roots. Scholars and philosophers throughout the ages have suggested ways to rear and educate our young, and these views continue to influence child psychology and education.

The Influence of Locke, Rousseau, and Darwin

The writings of philosophers John Locke and Jean-Jacques Rousseau and of the great English humanist Charles Darwin have had a profound impact on child development.

John Locke English philosopher John Locke (1632–1704) saw a child as an incomplete adult, governed by strong urges and desires that need to be controlled. Believing that environment played a crucial role in the child's growth and development, he advocated structured and constant supervision in order to appropriately mold the child's development.

John Locke (1632–1704)

As children grow up they are influenced by many people whom they affect in turn. This 6-year-old listens as her grandfather explains how onions grow.

At the time of Locke's writing, most scholars held that heredity largely determined the differences between human beings. But Locke believed that education and experience were fundamental determinants of development. He proposed that at birth, the child's mind was a **tabula rasa,** or blank slate, receptive to all types of learning. Thus, education and guidance were essential during childhood. The goal of education was to enhance self-discipline and self-control. Locke advised parents and educators to teach self-discipline as early as possible so children would learn to deny themselves the satisfaction of their own desires.

Jean-Jacques Rousseau   Rousseau (1712–1778), the French philosopher who wrote almost a century after Locke, also believed in the critical importance of environmental experiences. However, he argued that children did not need strict supervision or structured education. Rather, Rousseau saw a child as a "noble savage" who possesses an intuitive knowledge of right and wrong but encounters pitfalls because of restrictions imposed by society. His views were set forth in his book *Emile* (1762), in which a tutor describes a boy's growth and development. Like many progressive educators of the 1960s, Rousseau suggested that children be allowed to explore the world and use the environment to suit their needs and interests.

In contrast to Locke's notion of the tabula rasa, Rousseau regarded children as having abilities and interests that change as they grow and learn about the world. The task of adults, therefore, is to provide children with opportunities to explore and to learn, and to follow their lead as they explore their surroundings.

Locke and Rousseau obviously held strongly contrasting views about the nature of the child and the role of education. These views were the precursors of a fundamental division among researchers referred to as the *nature–nurture controversy;* that is, the debate about whether human traits are genetically endowed or wholly shaped by experience. We now know that children do not enter the world with a "blank slate" but are born with highly structured brains and sensory and perceptual capabilities. The idea of a child as a "noble savage" is also not plausible. Today the prevailing view is that both heredity (nature) and experience (nurture) influence development. Thus, Locke and Rousseau contributed to our understanding of children and encouraged the study of childhood, even though their writings were not based on scientific study.

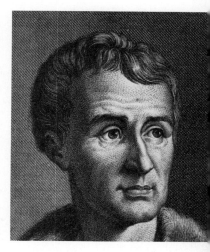

Jean-Jacques Rousseau (1712–1778)

Charles Darwin A scientific approach to the study of children did not emerge until the 19th century, when Charles Darwin's work on the principles of natural selection and evolution focused scientists' interest on the development of human beings. In fact, the publication of *On the Origin of Species* (1859) is considered the most important force in establishing child study as a scientific endeavor.

Before Darwin, plant and animal species were seen as either God's creation or mutations; each species was distinct. Darwin put forth the notion of an evolutionary process, arguing that human beings are not set apart from other species. Rather, there is continuity among and within species, and the transmission of traits occurs through heredity. Although Darwin was considered a revolutionary, his thesis sparked an interest in the study of any possible link between human beings and such species as apes and between the biological makeup of adults and children. Scientists began to see children as interesting objects for the study of human development. Darwin's interest in the study of children also lent credibility to child development as a field worthy of scientific effort. After the publication of *On the Origin of Species*, "man was not to be understood by the analysis of his adult function," writes William Kessen (1965), " . . . rather, man was to be understood by the study of his origins—in nature and in the child." Such questions as "When does consciousness begin?" and "How can we know the world of the infant?" were derived from Darwin's views on the origins of human beings and were, according to Kessen, to dominate child psychology for many years.

Charles Darwin's On the Origin of Species *launched the study of children as a scientific endeavor. Earlier philosophers had considered children's development and behavior, but their writings were based on speculation, not scientific evidence.*

Early Observational Studies: Baby Biographies

Observation was one of the first methods used to study and understand child development. Carefully recorded observations were compiled into day-to-day accounts of children's development known as **baby biographies.** These records became popular largely because Darwin used this method to observe and study his son. Darwin's baby biography, written in 1840–1841 and published in 1877, objectively recorded the reflexes and sensory abilities of the newborn infant.

Several other infant biographies were published in the late 19th and early 20th centuries. They highlighted many significant aspects of psychological development and paved the way for later discoveries of normal and universal patterns of development.

G. Stanley Hall and Early Experimental Studies

As interest in children as objects of scientific study grew, the study of child development became more systematic and sophisticated. Increasingly, the studies focused on large groups of children. Many researchers contributed to making this study increasingly more objective and scientific. The most notable was G. Stanley Hall (1846–1924), a co-founder of the American Psychological Association and the founder of child and adolescent psychology as subareas of general psychology.

G. Stanley Hall (1846–1924) is credited with developing the questionnaire as a method of collecting data about large groups of people.

Hall is a giant in early experimental research on child development. Like Darwin and other earlier scientists, Hall investigated the child's mind because he believed that understanding child development was crucial to understanding adult behavior. However, unlike his predecessors whose ideas were based largely on speculation or on observation of one child, Hall generalized about development and then attempted to support his generalizations by collecting representative data from a large number of subjects.

To collect information from a large group, Hall developed a tool known as the questionnaire. Primarily by using these questionnaires, he was able to obtain children's views on numerous topics. He then collated the responses and interpreted the overall significance of his findings. The questionnaire has become an important tool for researchers, although it is limited to studies of children who have language skills.

Numerous researchers in many different countries and disciplines have continued Hall's work. In Chapter 2 we introduce the most important of these researchers and their findings. Now, however, we want to discuss a new and important emphasis that has developed among dedicated modern researchers—the emphasis on social policy.

Why Focus on Social Policy?

Researchers in numerous disciplines are beginning to believe that their work should focus on contemporary social problems as well as generate knowledge. In developmental psychology, in particular, researchers are realizing that their study of children and their families has social application (Gallagher, 1989; Bevan, 1982; Takanishi, 1981). Hence, many child development researchers are concerned about the welfare and development of American children and are attempting to resolve social problems that affect them and their families.

Our focus in this book is on these new directions. We combine our discussions of the research on developmental processes from the prenatal period through adolescence with highlights of social policy issues. Researchers' involvement in social policy stems, in part, from the adverse conditions facing children, which have been brought about by rapid changes in family life, demography, the economy, and technology. In many ways some of these changes have contributed to opportunities unheard of 20 or 30 years ago, such as greater access to education and information and more choices of occupation and lifestyle (Hetherington, 1989). At the same time, however, social changes have brought attendant stresses on family life. A key question for child development researchers is, What can we do to counteract the negative effects of change in family life?

Development of Interest in Social Policy

A number of developments have stimulated researchers' interest in the social policy arena. First, during the late 1960s and 1970s, federal and state governments committed substantial resources to the development of social programs. This enabled social scientists to participate in the policy process by designing and evaluating programs aimed at improving children's lives. Through their participation, researchers refined their methodologies and increased their understanding of the factors that affect child development. Indeed, several social programs (for example, Project Head Start, which we will discuss later in the book) served as "natural laboratories."

Second, our knowledge of child development has increased substantially, and researchers are beginning to realize how that knowledge can influence decisions made on behalf of children. Thus more scholars feel they must share their knowl-

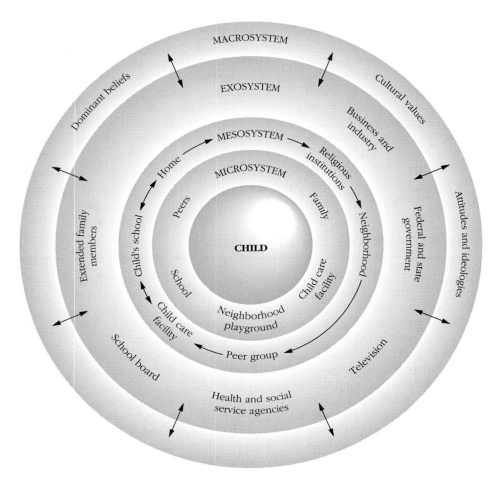

Figure 1.1 *Urie Bronfenbrenner's ecological model of child development has had a tremendous influence on current studies, which examine the child's development within the immediate social setting (the family), as well as within the more remote social settings, such as the school, the workplace, and the mass media.*

edge with parents, educators, physicians, judges, and policymakers, who can influence the lives of children (Stipek & McCroskey, 1989).

Finally, as we will see in Chapter 2, researchers have begun examining social factors that influence children (Kessen & Cahan, 1986). Such factors (see Figure 1.1) include the immediate social setting (the family) as well as larger, more remote social systems, such as the school, the community, the government, and even the mass media (Bronfenbrenner, 1986, 1979), most notably, television, over which children and parents have little control.

Childhood Social Indicators

Hand-in-hand with this line of inquiry, researchers have also compiled an index of **childhood social indicators.** These indicators are measures of changes or constancies in the conditions of children's lives, and in the health, achievement, behav-

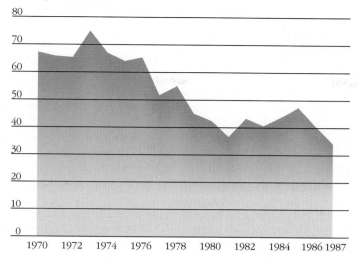

Index of Social Health

Figure 1.2 *At the Fordham Institute for Innovation in Social Policy, researchers developed an index of social health for children by combining national statistics for each of six social problems: infant mortality, child abuse, number of children in poverty, teen suicide, drug and alcohol abuse, and school dropout rates. The higher the incidence of these problems, the lower the index. You can see that except for 1973, each year since 1970 has been increasingly hard for children.*

Source: *The Index of Social Health 1989: Measuring the Social Well-Being of the Nation.* (Focus: The social health of children and youth.) © Marc L. Miringoff, 1989.

ior, and well-being of the children (Zill et al., 1983; Parke & Peterson, 1981; Sheldon & Parke, 1975).

Infant mortality, child abuse, the number of children living in poverty, and high school dropout rates are examples of the indicators used to gauge well-being. As you can see in Figure 1.2, the well-being of children declined dramatically between 1970 and 1987, the latest year for which figures are available (Miringoff, 1989).

Another measure of well-being is derived from statistics on mental health disorders. According to a report published by the Committee for the Institute of Medicine (1989), at least 12% of children under age 18 (7.5 million children) have a diagnosable mental illness and many other children exhibit broader indicators of dysfunction, including substance abuse, teen pregnancy, and school dropout. Similar findings are noted in a Children's Defense Fund report (1990), which cites such disorders as depression and suicide among an increasing number of children.

That so many children are affected by mental health disorders suggests that this is a nationwide problem. It is difficult to estimate the costs involved, but recent analyses indicate that just treating mentally and emotionally disturbed children can cost as much as $1.5 billion a year (Rice, 1990). In addition, indirect costs are borne by families, the schools, the juvenile justice system, and other social institutions that have to make special services available to these children (Office of Technology Assessment, 1986).

What factors contribute to the large number of children with mental health disorders? More research is needed to unravel the causes and determinants of such disorders. However, over the past few years, evidence has pointed to a variety of biological, psychological, social, and environmental factors. In some cases, interaction among these factors exacerbates the child's vulnerability to mental disorders.

Recent studies also suggest that social and environmental risk factors are implicated in the onset of mental dysfunction in increasing numbers of children (Tuma, 1989). These risk factors include poverty, physical or sexual abuse, marital discord, and a variety of other factors related to instability in the family environment (Tuma, 1989). Children who experience only one of these risk factors may not suffer serious consequences than children who experience no risk factor. However, the more risk factors or stressors present in their lives, the greater the probability of a damaging outcome (Rutter, 1979b).

In addition, such risk factors as poverty often compound other problems. Consider premature or low-birth-weight infants. They may experience central nervous system difficulties that inhibit their ability to develop normally. These difficulties may be overcome if the infants are reared in stable, supportive family environments. But if they are raised in unstable, low-income families where the parents have no support systems and are concerned about lack of money, decent housing, and access to health care, the difficulties present at birth may result in developmental delays and learning problems (Sameroff et al., 1987).

These findings are of considerable concern. A significant number of children are trying to cope with potentially damaging experiences stemming from difficult family conditions (National Commission on Children, 1990), which often result from recent changes within our society. In the following discussion we explore some of these changes.

Growing Up in the 1990s

Changes in Family Life

One significant change in society is the transformation of the family structure and the roles and responsibilities of family members. Childrearing has become more difficult, creating stress-filled lives for both children and adults.

Fragmentation and isolation of the family   The growing number of single-parent families (Figure 1.3) is particularly disturbing because of the associated stresses that impact both parents and children. Single-parent families are generally characterized by female heads of household, poverty, and the presence of young children (U.S. Bureau of the Census, 1988). One out of every four children in this country lives in a single-parent family; among blacks, the number is one out of every two (National Center for Children in Poverty, 1990).

Another change is the relative isolation and lack of social support that many families experience. People today move frequently in search of jobs or for other reasons (Mintz & Kellogg, 1988; Packard, 1972). As a result, many families no longer live near enough to their friends and relatives to have their support and assistance. For example, many parents have no one to turn to if they need help with child care.

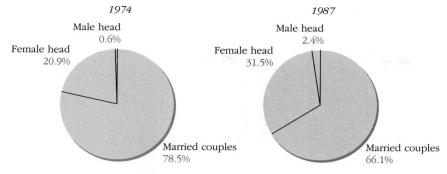

Distribution of Children in Young Families by Family Type
(March 1974 and March 1987)

1974

Male head
0.6%

Female head
20.9%

Married couples
78.5%

1987

Male head
2.4%

Female head
31.5%

Married couples
66.1%

Figure 1.3 *Distribution of children in young families by family type (March 1974 and March 1987)*
Source: *Vanishing Dreams: The Growing Economic Plight of America's Young Families.* Children's Defense Fund and Center for Labor Market Studies, Northeastern University. © 1988 CDF.

Access to a support system is important because it can often lessen the negative consequences of stress (Gore, 1980; Garmezy, 1985).

Poverty   An increasing number of families are also experiencing serious economic problems; many live in poverty. This is due in part to the increase in single-parent families whose median annual income is $4500 if the mother does not work and only $9000 more if she does (U.S. Department of Labor, 1988a). For single-parent families that are a product of divorce, the father's failure to pay child support is a major reason for poverty (Hetherington, Stanley-Hagan, & Anderson, 1989). Another contributing factor is the decline in the real value of family income. According to a report by the Economic Policy Council (1986), between 1973 and 1984, weekly wages, adjusted for inflation, declined by 10.1%. Reischauer (1987), in an analysis of the U.S. job market, found that only one out of three jobs pays enough to keep a family of four above the poverty line.

Thus, many wives have had to join the labor force to augment the family income. But even among two-income families, median family income, adjusted for inflation, declined by 3.1% between 1973 and 1984 (Economic Policy Council, 1986). Hence, many women have several jobs. For example, according to a recent study by the Bureau of Labor Statistics (1990), 5.9% of women working full-time had more than one job in 1989 as compared to 2.2% in 1970 (see Figure 1.4). Explaining this increase, Kilborn (1990) notes that these women are often single parents who need extra income to keep the family above the poverty line.

The decline in family income and the increase in the number of poor families affects adults as well as children. However, the consequences are particularly serious for children because a significant percentage of poor families have young children. According to the U.S. Bureau of the Census (1988), the poverty rate among the general population is actually declining, but it has almost doubled among young families in the past 20 years (Figure 1.5). As you can see in Figure 1.6, the number of families on welfare is rising in every state but Louisiana, Wisconsin, and Mississippi.

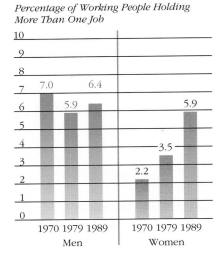

Percentage of Working People Holding More Than One Job

Figure 1.4 *An increasing number of women, needing the additional income, are holding more than one job.*

Source: Based on data from the Bureau of Labor Statistics, 1990. Copyright © 1990 by The New York Times Company. Reprinted by permission.

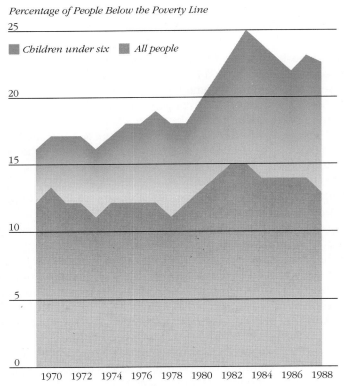

Percentage of People Below the Poverty Line

■ *Children under six*   ■ *All people*

Figure 1.5 *The rate of poverty in all families is declining, but in the past 20 years it has almost doubled among families with children under 6 years old.*

Source: Based on U.S. Bureau of the Census 1970–1988 statistics. National Center for Children in Poverty, 1990. Reprinted by permission.

A record 1 out of 16 families is on welfare. Currently, 32.6% of families in which one parent is age 25 or under are poor; the figure is 21.6% of families in which one parent is age 30 or under. In Figure 1.7 you can see that the drop in family income has been especially significant among young black and Hispanic families.

The ramifications of living in poverty are numerous, including assaults on children's physical and mental health. Margolin and Farran (1983) found that a drop in family income often leads to poor health care. Several other studies indicate that there is a powerful, although indirect, link between poverty and mental health disorders. The conclusion is that poverty is a major risk factor in such disorders (Rutter, 1979b; Albee, 1986). There is also a link between poverty and educational failure. At one time mental dysfunction, low achievement in school, and other social problems were assumed to be negative traits found among poor children. Today, however, researchers realize that the major problems associated with poverty stem from environmental stresses and feelings of powerlessness and frustration (Albee, 1986). Also, there is a high incidence of lack of prenatal care, low-birth-weight babies, poor nutrition, lack of housing, and exposure to environmental hazards such as lead poisoning. These factors all place children at risk for developmental problems (Committee for the Institute of Medicine, 1989).

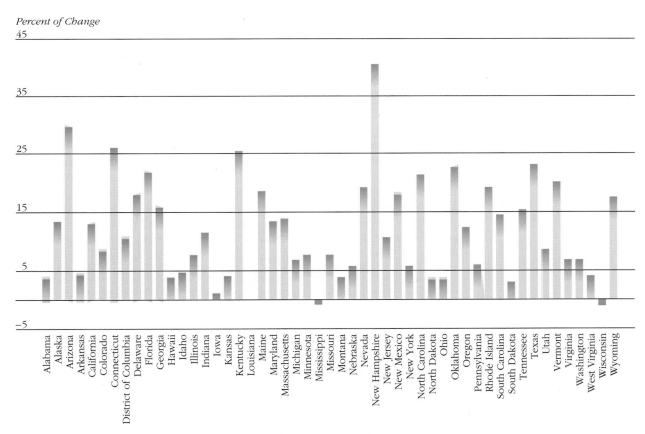

Figure 1.6 *Percentage of change in the number of families living on welfare from July 1989 to November 1990.*
Source: Data from a report by the American Welfare Association, 1991.

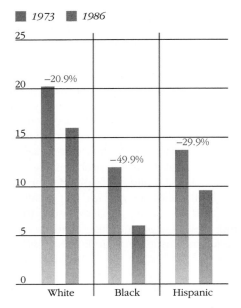

Median Annual Earnings of Heads of Young
Families, by Race, in Thousands of Dollars

Figure 1.7 *Decrease in median annual earnings of heads of
young families by race from 1973 to 1986.*
Source: *Vanishing Dreams: The Growing Economic Plight of America's
Young Families.* Children's Defense Fund and Center for Labor Market
Studies, Northeastern University © 1988 CDF.

Children living in poverty may not necessarily suffer from any problems, but
they are *at risk* for developing them. The National Commission on Children, made
up of 36 members appointed by the president and the U.S. Congress and serving as a
forum on behalf of children, highlights the risks associated with poverty. According
to the Commission's recent report (1990), poor children are often resilient and have
support from parents and other caring adults that shields them from the consequences of poverty. However, many poor children in America are in double jeopardy:

> [Poor children] have the most health problems and the least access to [health] care.
> They are growing up in families that experience the most stress, yet receive the least
> social support. They are at the highest risk for educational failure, and they often attend
> the worst schools. They are in the greatest danger of following paths that jeopardize
> their futures, yet they enjoy the fewest legitimate job opportunities. (p. 36)

These stressful conditions are just a few examples of the changed circumstances that affect many poor children. The pervasiveness of drugs in our society and
the lack of health care and housing are other examples.

But it is not only poor children who confront potentially damaging conditions.
Children from all segments of society face problems arising from such changes in
family life as marital discord, maternal employment, and the lack of child care
services. (We will discuss these issues later in the chapter.) Although many families
are affected by these changes, U.S. social policies have not kept pace with their
needs. Thus our society is in a state of disequilibrium (Hoffman, 1989).

This disequilibrium creates hardships for families. Many of these children find it increasingly difficult to cope with the demands of school, family, and peer relationships. And because these problems involve economic realities, traditions, and institutional structures, solutions may come about rather slowly (Zeitlin, 1989).

Nevertheless, child development researchers have helped enhance family life in at least two ways. First, they have helped policymakers and the public realize that many children are growing up under conditions that are potentially damaging to their development. Second, researchers study children's responses to these conditions. These studies enrich our understanding of child development and help explain why some children can cope with difficulties while others cannot (Garmezy, 1985). Researchers also develop useful ways to intervene and prevent problems.

The following discussion illustrates the use of scientific research in dealing with social problems by focusing on two major societal changes that have had a profound impact on family life.

Working mothers   The growing number of women in the labor force is especially evident among women with children.

For women with school-age children, full-time employment has been relatively common for about two decades; over 70% of these women now work outside the home (Hoffman, 1989). More recent and even more pronounced, however, is the increase in the labor force among women with infants and preschool children. In 1950 only 11.9% of women with children under age 6 worked outside the home; by

A CLOSER LOOK

Not All Poor Families Are Alike

Although poor families generally have fewer economic resources than other families, not all poor families are alike. Let's look at Lillian and Bob, who got married when they were 18. A year later, Andrea was born. Bob was working at the local supermarket and taking evening courses at the community college. After Andrea's birth, Lillian quit her job as a receptionist in a real estate office to care for her baby.

Over the past ten years, Lillian and Bob have had two more children, Jack and Bob Jr. Bob received a two-year degree from the community college and went on to a university for his B.A. in business and marketing. With Bob working and studying and Lillian raising the children, stress built up within the family. Eventually, Bob and Lillian divorced. Bob pays child support as agreed in the divorce settlement, but Lillian is really struggling to make ends meet. She is looking for a job but has limited skills and has not worked for ten years. In addition, if she finds employment, she wonders how much child care will cost for the three children and if she can afford it.

Brenda is 19 and lives in a housing project with her two young children, ages 2 and 4. Brenda did not complete high school and has no means of support, except for monies she receives from the government-sponsored programs Aid to Families with Dependent Children and Food Stamps. Brenda's life is much the same as her mother's was when she was Brenda's age. In fact, Brenda grew up in the same housing project. She doesn't think about the future and spends most of her time watching television and looking after the kids. Now Brenda's next-door neighbor just told her that, according to new welfare regulations, when her younger child is 3, she will have to look for a job or enroll in a job training program.

As you can see from these two examples, some families become poor because of divorce, unemployment, or the disability of one or both parents. Their stay in poverty is usually brief, and they are quickly able to rebound economically and emotionally. Other families experience longer spells of disability or unemployment and, in the process, gradually lose all their savings as well as their ability to cope with their lives. For these families, escaping from poverty becomes increasingly difficult. Some families are formed in poverty. These families include single-parent households in which the mother has never married and families in which

(continued)

1987 the figure had risen to 56.8% (U.S. Department of Labor, 1988). What is even more significant is that mothers are returning to work shortly after giving birth. In the 1950s it was unusual for a woman to work during her baby's first year, and even a decade ago, only 30% of women with infants age 1 or under were working outside the home. Today, 52% of these mothers are in the labor force (U.S. Department of Labor, 1988).

Research has shown that maternal employment does not necessarily have a negative effect on children (Hoffman, 1989; Greenberger, 1989). The family's attitude toward the mother's employment seems to be the significant factor. Also, in many two-income families an inordinate amount of stress arises because the working mothers have not abdicated their traditional responsibilities for family life and childrearing. Often these women may have no one to help share such responsibilities; they may be single, or their husbands may not be willing to share the household duties (Hochschild, 1989). As a result, many mothers feel guilty about working outside the home (Moen & Dempster, 1987).

Fathers are also having difficulties. In a survey of working parents, researchers found that close to 40% of both men and women experience severe stress in trying to manage work and family responsibilities (Friedman, 1987). The children only get to see their parents for a limited time, and during this time the parents are further stressed by trying to accomplish too much. This, in turn, further disturbs the children.

A CLOSER LOOK

(continued)

one or both parents have neither the education nor the skills to escape from poverty. Children in such families are apt to stay in poverty throughout their childhood and eventually to form their own families, still in poverty.

Poor families also differ in the type of assistance they need. Some families are able to care for their children; they only need better-paying jobs to escape poverty and ensure that their children do not suffer from its consequences. Other families need better-paying jobs and additional services and support. According to the National Center for Children in Poverty (1990), poor families can be helped by such services as specialized job training, basic education, and English language instruction for parents, as well as by access to health care and transportation, and by assistance in paying for child care services. To protect children in other poor families, safer housing in less-impoverished neighborhoods, intensive mental health services, and drug or alcohol treatment programs are essential.

We know how to improve the lives of children from poor families. Schorr and Schorr (1988) and Price et al. (1988) note that a number of existing programs can reduce risk factors for children in poverty. However, current poli-

cies and programs fall short of what is needed. Programs known to be effective often remain at a demonstration stage; that is, they are not replicated and disseminated widely. In addition, many successful programs serve only a small percentage of eligible families; a nutrition program known as the Supplemental Food Program for Women, Infants and Children (WIC), which we will describe in Chapter 4, serves less than half the eligible population.

One problem is a lack of public funds to serve more children. In addition, we need to decide how to invest the limited amount of public funds. Knowing that a growing number of American children are living in persistent poverty, how would you, if you were a legislator, decide to appropriate public funds?

In their book *Within Our Reach: Breaking the Cycle of Disadvantage* (1988), Schorr and Schorr discuss the nation's commitment—or lack thereof—to policies that aid the disadvantaged. In their defense of such a commitment, the authors list several types of intervention programs that can alter the living conditions of many poor children and they also present "five pillars" upon which "a new national commitment" must be built. The five pillars are as follows:

• A public acknowledgment that high-risk children can be

These findings give us a direction for social policy. For example, we may conclude—in the absence of data to the contrary—that maternal employment can be damaging to children. As a result, we would attempt to enable mothers to stay home until their children reach adolescence. However, the data indicate that such problems may arise from the difficulties associated with both parents working *and* raising children. In that case our policy direction would call for services designed to make the dual role of the parents less stressful. Indeed, this is the direction taken in many European countries with working mothers. (This subject is discussed more fully in Chapter 7.)

In many nations, social change—specifically, the increase in the number of mothers in the labor force—has given rise to special services designed to facilitate family life. These services, which may include maternity and paternity leave and child care, enable parents to stay home to look after their young children or go to work assured that their children are well cared for (Zigler & Frank, 1988; Kamerman & Kahn, 1988).

The United States, however, has no comprehensive family policy, nor are there sufficient child care facilities to accommodate the infants, preschool, and school-age children of working mothers (National Research Council, 1990).

The lack of good quality, affordable child care facilities is one of the major social problems of our time. As you will see in later chapters, there is a great deal of concern about the effects of child care on child development. The lack of child care

A CLOSER LOOK

helped by systematic intervention early in life, and that such intervention programs must offer continuity of care, a "broad spectrum of services," and skilled staffs.
- A public understanding that paying for prevention is ultimately much cheaper than paying for the consequences of unemployment, neglected health, and other problems experienced by the disadvantaged.
- A willingness of the public and private sectors to allocate funds needed to implement programs and policies shown to benefit those in need.

- A shift in societal attitude toward those who work at "breaking the cycle of disadvantage," so that talented, committed people will want to go into the social services field and will be appropriately rewarded.
- An awareness that social policy must be aimed at long-term improvements rather than short-term solutions.

Do you agree with Schorr and Schorr's agenda? How do you think we might go about changing the attitudes of the American public in favor of this agenda?

Percentage Distribution of Children by the Duration of Poverty During the First Ten Years of Childhood by Family Type, 1970-1982

Family type	Never poor	Short-term poor (1–3 years)	Medium-term poor (4–5 years)	Long-term poor (7–10 years)
Always in a married-couple family	80.0%	13.6%	4.4%	2.0%
Some years in a single-parent family	32.8	40.7	14.7	11.7
Always in a single-parent family	6.7	11.9	20.8	60.6

Source: Ellwood, D.T., (1989). Unpublished manuscript. Cited in National Center for Children in Poverty, 1990. Reprinted by permission of the author.

services is a source of great anxiety for parents. When they are unable to find or afford good quality care, parents may place their children in facilities that can be potentially damaging. For example, parents may enroll their infants or preschool children in a facility that does not have enough adult staff to look after and interact with each child. Or parents may enroll their children in facilities where the staff has no training in child development. Staff training is an important aspect of quality care. Recent studies have found that trained child care providers are more likely than their untrained counterparts to relate to children in positive ways, to interact with them, and to provide activities that enhance child development (National Research Council, 1990).

Child care facilities for older children are also in short supply. As a result, parents often leave their children at home alone or with older brothers or sisters. Several million children between 6 and 12 years of age come home each day to an empty house (Children's Defense Fund, 1990). These children are known as **children in self-care** or **latchkey children** because they carry their house keys on chains around their necks. Reports of these children encountering burglars or being victimized are not uncommon. One study examining causes of fires in Detroit during a particular period discovered that one-sixth of all the fires involved an unattended child (Smock, 1977).

Research on latchkey children is relatively new, and researchers disagree about the effects. Some researchers claim that leaving children alone is of no consequence (Rodman et al., 1985) and may promote independence. Other researchers have found that children who are left alone too long or too often grow up scared. Long and Long (1983) studied 1000 current and former latchkey children and their parents. When the former latchkey children discussed their experiences, over one-

 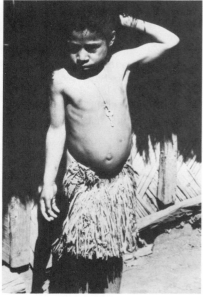

Children in different parts of the world face similar situations. In Columbus, Ohio, a "latchkey" child returns home. Children also carry keys in Southern Highlands, Papua, New Guinea, where mothers work in the fields and their huts are kept padlocked.

The increase in the number of children in out-of-home care is one of the major societal changes of our times.

third said they were still afraid to be alone. The Longs suspect that these adults are carrying into adulthood fears they suffered as children. The children currently left alone said that their biggest fear is that someone will break into their home. Their second biggest fear is being hurt by an accident or a fire.

Latchkey children face other problems as well. In a recent Harris poll (1987), 51% of the teachers interviewed reported that being left alone for part of the day is the most critical factor undermining some children's school performance. According to a report by the Alan Guttmacher Institute (1981), teen pregnancies often result when children are unsupervised after school. Richardson et al. (1989) have interviewed over 5000 latchkey children in the largest study of its kind. They found a greater prevalence of delinquency and drug and alcohol abuse among these children than among children who were in supervised programs before and after school.

A recent major study shows that supervised before- and after-school programs help prevent delinquency and substance abuse in school-age children.

Divorce Divorce also contributes to the changes in family life. The number of divorces per year seems to be leveling off; nevertheless, divorce continues to affect 40% to 50% of all American children (Glick & Lin, 1986).

Despite the large number of children involved in divorce, few researchers have examined its impact. Mavis Hetherington and Judith Wallerstein and their colleagues have found that divorce is not a single event, but a sequence of experiences, each one a transition requiring adjustments (Hetherington, Stanley-Hagan, & Anderson, 1989). The transitions include (1) a shift from the family life before the divorce; (2) disequilibrium and disorganization immediately following the divorce; (3) experimentation with a variety of coping mechanisms, living arrangements, and relationships; and (4) eventual reorganization and attainment of equilibrium.

At least during the periods immediately before and after the divorce, families become increasingly disorganized and there are marked changes in the management of children. Hence, the children often encounter inconsistent discipline and diminished communication and nurturance (Hetherington, Cox, & Cox, 1982). In other words, children in some divorced families receive little, if any, parental attention (Furstenberg, 1988).

Divorce and the transition periods following it are painful to almost all children (Levitin, 1979; Wallerstein & Kelly, 1979). Even those who eventually recognized their parents' divorce as constructive initially underwent considerable stress. Even though so many children are involved in divorce and even though it has become socially acceptable, these developments do not alleviate its pain (Rofes, 1980).

In addition, some children who appear to adapt well in the early stages of the divorce and family disorganization display delayed negative effects, often several years later (Wallerstein & Corbin, 1991; Wallerstein et al., 1988). How well children cope with divorce is related to several factors:

1. Age. The preschool child is more susceptible to the emotional and psychological problems associated with the divorce and the post-divorce period than is the older child.
2. Sex and birth order. Boys suffer for longer periods than girls and exhibit more behavioral problems and difficulties in their relationships with their mothers, other adults, and peers.
3. Siblings. Only children experience more distress and psychological problems during the early stages of post-divorce than do children with siblings.
4. Psychological status of the custodial parent and availability and involvement of the noncustodial parent (Camara & Resnick, 1989; Hetherington, Cox, & Cox, 1982; Wallerstein & Kelly, 1980).

Parents also undergo emotional, psychological, and economic stresses after divorce. Often their distress is so acute that they fail to give their children sufficient attention and recognize their painful experiences. Many parents confide in their children, especially in the older ones, burdening them with information and problems they do not understand. In addition, both parents are likely to be depressed for about a year after the divorce and to have difficulties adjusting to their own lives. Hetherington and her colleagues (1982) found that mothers are often depressed in part because the children become disobedient and disturbed, especially once the mother has found a job. The divorced father appears to be even more depressed than the mother during the first year after divorce.

Custody battles The most tragic and vulnerable children of divorce are those involved in legal battles between their parents over custody issues and visitation rights. Legal battles can continue indefinitely because the courts can modify any decision on any issue. A parent's rage against an ex-spouse can also continue for many years and is often expressed in litigation over the child.

The courts are directed to make custody decisions on the basis of the child's best interests; however, putting this principle into practice is not always easy. Judges and lawyers are often unable to determine what the child's best interests are. And they have little help since few psychologists or mental health professionals see the court as an arena of interest. When the courts do have access to psychological services, they are often staffed by people who are not trained to work with children (Wallerstein & Kelly, 1979). Goldstein, Freud, and Solnit (1973, 1979) provide guidelines for decisions on custody issues. They recommend resolving decisions in accelerated proceedings, giving decisions final effect, and making them irreversible. In addition, the courts should award full control of the children to one parent.

Not all psychologists agree with these recommendations. Some researchers argue that a child needs both parents (Benedek & Benedek, 1977). Some studies point out that children can actually gain some stability and protection from the inevitable parental upsets that arise from divorce if they have contacts with several adults and if their relationship with one parent is not stressful (Santrock, Warshak, & Elliott, 1982). Wallerstein and Corbin (1991) and Johnson, Kline, and Tschann (1989) found that joint custody does not have negative effects on children whose parents' divorce was amicable. However, in bitter divorces children were psychologically worse off if the courts forced them to divide their time between parents.

Stepfamilies   Another source of potential problems and anxiety is the remarriage of one or both parents. Divorce and subsequent remarriage are so prevalent that a significant portion of children spend at least part of their childhood living in stepfamilies, also referred to as **blended families, reconstituted families,** and **new extended families.**

Living in a stepfamily environment can be an enriching experience, but it can also be a source of stress, at least in the early adjustment period (Fishman & Hamel, 1981). But even when the children are able to adjust to their new circumstances, they sometimes anger the original family members over issues of loyalty. For example, a 10-year-old girl's parents had been divorced since she was 2 years old. Soon after the divorce, both her parents remarried, and she developed a close relationship with her father and stepmother. She visited them every two weeks during the year and for a couple of months during the summer. She considered her stepmother's parents to be her grandparents. The girl's mother became angry whenever she mentioned that she had visited her "grandparents" and insisted that her daughter refrain from addressing them in that way. Imagine this child's conflict, being pulled one way by her feelings for her father's family and another way by her feelings for her mother.

Besides questions of loyalty that may arise, children in stepfamilies are also often confused about values and lifestyles. They have to know what is expected of them in two different homes, and they have to adapt to modes of discipline that may be different (Jacobson, 1979). The same is true of children of divorce in general, whether or not their parents remarry.

Changes in Demography

Another fundamental change in society has been in the makeup and balance of the U.S. population (what we refer to as *demography*). Because of the unusually high birth rates during the two decades after World War II (referred to as the *baby boom*), the current decline in birth rate, and increased longevity, the composition of our population has changed considerably. In fact, our society has become an aging one, with few children, a plethora of young adults, and mounting numbers of older individuals.

Let us paint a more graphic picture of the situation. Between 1980 and 1989, the number of children aged 18 and under *declined* by 690,000. During this same period, the number of young and middle-aged adults increased, as did the number of people 65 years and older. In 1980 there were 25.5 million individuals aged 65 or older; by 1989 that figure had increased to close to 31 million, an increase of almost 6 million. The significance is not only that there are fewer children now than there were two decades ago, but that there are also so many more older persons (Levitan & Conway, 1990).

How can we explain this change in demographic trends? There are more young adults because they are the postwar baby boom children who have become adults. The increase in the number of older individuals is attributable to better nutrition and medical advances. More people today live to old age than was true several decades ago, and this trend is expected to continue into the next century (U.S. Bureau of the Census, 1984).

FEATURE

Societal Changes in Other Countries

Traditional family life in the United States is undergoing a series of changes. Sometimes these challenges to family life seem uniquely American, but they are not. Investigating social change abroad, Sorrentino (1990) noted that during the past few decades, the same changes have occurred in almost all developed countries: the decline in fertility rates, the aging of the population, erosion of the institution of marriage, and the rapid increase in out-of-wedlock births. Indeed, Sorrentino contends that in some countries, the changes are even more pronounced than in the United States. Denmark and Sweden, for example, have higher numbers of unmarried couples living together. Larger drops in fertility rates have occurred in Holland, Japan, Denmark, and Canada than in the United States; life expectancy in these countries is also increasing so their populations are fast becoming composed of primarily older individuals.

According to Sorrentino's study, published by the Bureau of Labor Statistics, the United States leads in the number of single-parent households. There are so many single parents because of the high rate of divorce and because young, American parents who have never been married are more likely to live without a partner. In many countries couples who live together, even if they are not married, are included with married couples as constituting a household, and they receive benefits as such. In addition, social policies in many other countries recognize the changes in family life, whereas U.S. policies do not.

In the accompanying table you can see how the United States fares when compared to other nations: 19th in infant mortality rate, 29th in low-birth-weight deliveries.

The United States is not among the 70 nations worldwide that provide medical care and financial assistance to all pregnant women, not among the 61 nations that insure or provide basic medical care to all workers and their dependents, not among the 63 nations that provide a family allowance to workers and their children, and not among the 17 industrialized nations that have paid maternity/parenting leave programs.

U.S. Ranking in Childhood Social Indicators

Indicator	U.S. rank[a]	Some of the countries we trail
Infant mortality rate (1988)	19th	Singapore, Hong Kong, Spain, and Ireland
Mortality rate for children younger than 5 (1988)	21st	Japan, Singapore, New Zealand, and East Germany

But why is the number of children declining? This is explained by an over-whelming trend toward later marriage and childbearing. Two decades ago fewer than 20% of women and 30% of men in the 25- to 29-year-old age group had never married; in 1988 close to 30% of these women and more than 40% of these men had never married (U.S. Bureau of the Census, 1988). In the same period the average age at which a woman has her first child has risen. In addition, an increasing number of couples have been choosing not to have children or to have fewer children (U.S. Bureau of the Census, 1988).

Many factors account for these demographic trends. The women's movement, which began in the 1960s, made an increasing number of women aware of their career potential; thus many women are choosing a career first and marriage and motherhood later. The use of effective contraceptives, the high cost of raising children, and the prevailing pessimism about economic conditions are also cited as reasons for the decrease in the birth rate (Dowd, 1983). Most people still become parents, however; according to the U.S. Bureau of the Census (1988), 86% of all women under 40 have given birth at least once. But families today tend to have an average of only 1.8 children (Levitan & Conway, 1990). Figure 1.8 shows the decline in family size since 1950.

FEATURE

U.S. Ranking in Childhood Social Indicators

Indicator	U.S. rank[a]	Some of the countries we trail
Low-birth-weight births (1988)	29th	Austria, Hong Kong, East Germany, and West Germany
Proportion of 1-year-old children fully immunized against polio (latest reported year)	15th	Poland, Jordan, Czechoslovakia, and Chile
Number of school-age children per teacher (1986)	19th	Libya, East Germany, Lebanon, and Cuba
Childhood poverty (1979–1982)	8th (among 8 industrialized countries studied)	Switzerland, Sweden, Norway, West Germany, Canada, the United Kingdom, and Australia
Mathematical achievement of eighth-grade students (1981–1982)	12th (among 18 nations studied)	Japan, Hungary, and England
Expenditures on elementary and secondary education as a percentage of the gross domestic product (1985)	14th (among 16 countries studied)	Italy, France, Japan, West Germany, and Canada
Teen pregnancy rates (1985)	6th (among 6 nations studied)	Canada, England and Wales, France, the Netherlands, and Sweden

Source: SOS America! A Children's Defense Budget, Children's Defense Fund. © 1990 CDF.
[a]When the U.S. nonwhite population's rate is compared with other nations' overall rates, the United States lags behind 48 other countries, including Albania, Oman, Botswana, Tunisia, and Sri Lanka.

Children per Woman of Childbearing Age (15 to 44)

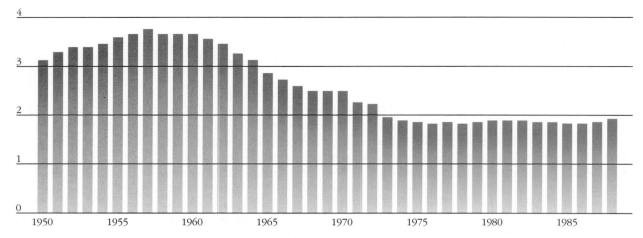

Figure 1.8 *The number of children per woman of childbearing age has been declining since the 1950s.*
Source: Based on statistics from the U.S. Census Bureau and the National Center for Health Statistics.

LEARNING FROM OTHER CULTURES

Population Policies in China

The decline in the number of children as a portion of the U.S. population will undoubtedly have some consequences for children and society as well. Some potential consequences of demographic change are becoming evident in China, which is in the midst of a *natural experiment*.

Population growth in the People's Republic of China was reaching crisis proportions. To contain this growth, the government has actively encouraged families to have only one child by initiating a vigorous program that combines persuasion with economic incentives and penalties. Billboards in major cities proclaim, "It is better to have one child only!" One-child families receive extra health care and school subsidies, extra grain rations, and a large plot of land for growing produce for private sale. Families with more than one child lose privileges, which severely curtails their financial and social status. There have even been reports of abortions in families that already have a child and are afraid of the economic consequences of having another (Kristof, 1989).

China has been successful in slowing its rapid population growth. An increasingly larger portion of children have no siblings. Studies are now trying to determine the effect of this trend on the child, the family, and society. The question is not whether the number of children should be limited, but how best to identify and combat the negative aspects of this policy on the development of the next generation. Researchers point out that if families continue to have only one child for the next 30 years, the next generation will grow up with no brothers or sisters, and their children will have no aunts or uncles.

In an effort to contain its population growth, the People's Republic of China has taken steps to ensure that families have only one child each. This billboard advertises the advantages of a single-child family. Researchers question the possible effects of a generation growing up with no siblings.

Thus far, studies on Chinese children indicate that single children demonstrate superior intellectual abilities, especially those living in urban areas (Falbo, 1990). However, these studies also show that the children display a higher incidence of negative social behaviors. In one study comparing siblings and only children, the single children were rated as disrespectful to elders, less cooperative, and lacking in self-care skills (Ching, 1982). According to this study and others (for example, Bronfenbrenner, 1970), children develop social traits largely by interacting with older children. Siblings form the child's first play group. The more children are involved in play situations with children of various ages, the greater the training they receive in mutual cooperation.

In China the ramifications of a large number of single-child families are extensive. The Chinese constitution gives children the primary responsibility for care of their aged parents. Thus, although retired workers receive pensions, there may be financial problems associated with having only one child. Also, the traditional Chinese emphasis on having a son to carry on the family name poses a potential obstacle. What if the one child is a girl? In a study of 100 pregnant women in China who were screened to determine the sex of the unborn child, over 60% of those carrying a girl chose to abort the fetus, as compared to 2% of those carrying a boy (*Chinese Medical Journal,* 1975). The idea of electing to have an abortion on the basis of the child's sex may be unthinkable to many Americans, but this option may appear differently to a Chinese couple who only has one opportunity to have a son. Imagine the social consequences of having future generations made up primarily of males! This could be the case if girls continue to be aborted.

In an attempt to resolve this problem, the law has been changed. The new laws are designed to help families make a better transition from what tradition dictates to what current policies require. A young couple can now live with their maternal in-laws rather than with their paternal in-laws; a woman can retain her family name;

and parents can give their child the maternal surname, thereby giving families with a daughter a sense of continuity. But even so, if the parents have no siblings, each would want the child to have his or her family name. Thus, these changes, although helpful in intent, may have little practical effect.

What impact will a declining number of children have on U.S. society? What role will children have in a society where they will be outnumbered by so many older individuals? As their numbers decline, will children, particularly those in need, receive better services? Will parents and taxpayers be more interested in the children, or will the needs of the young conflict with the goals of adults?

It is not easy to answer these questions or to predict what life will be like for these children as adults in the 21st century. Some researchers contend that as the smaller cohorts of children start entering the job market as adults, reduced competition for entry-level jobs will increase their market value, employment, and earnings. This, in turn, will give them a sense of confidence about the future. With improved earnings and prospects, they may marry earlier and produce more children. In due course, so the argument goes, the rise in fertility would produce an improved climate of opinion toward children and improved conditions for them.

This prediction is not very convincing because it assumes that young adults, influenced by improved economic conditions, will revert to early marriage and childbearing. However, many middle-class women would rather build a career. Of course, the middle class is only one group in our society, and many women must work just to keep their families above the poverty line. In either case, however, women may defer childbearing until they have gained a secure foothold in the working world. And, if these women have children, they will tend to have fewer children since it is difficult to work and raise more than one or two children.

Numerous studies show that although motherhood is still an important role for many women, so is a career (Daniels & Weingarten, 1982). In addition, recent analyses of fertility trends indicate that the postwar baby boom has been an unusual phenomenon (Ryder, 1978). Indeed, it is often referred to as the "age of ultradomesticity" (Hewlett, 1986). The United States now fits the general reproductive pattern prevalent in most modern developed countries; this pattern is characterized by small families (Levitan & Conway, 1990). Therefore, a sharp upturn in childbearing is highly unlikely. Of course, for the next few years as the baby boom generation continues to have children, there will be some increase in the actual number of newborns. But this will be a temporary phenomenon in a long-term decline.

On the basis of this prediction, let us consider a likely scenario. Young people will be hired for entry-level jobs, but there will be few opportunities for promotion. Higher-level jobs will be held by the Baby Boomers, who will not retire until after the year 2000. In addition, these young people will be competing with older workers for jobs. Thus today's children can probably look forward to a static income as adults in the 21st century.

Once they reach adulthood, they will have to shoulder a heavy burden. These relatively few adults will have to produce the nation's cadre of professional, administrative, technical, skilled, and unskilled workers. In addition to ensuring their own children's well-being, they will have to provide security and social services for the increasing percentage of older individuals (Bane, 1976; Committee on Economic Development, 1988). Thus every child today, and every child born in the near future, will be a scarce resource and precious asset as an adult in the 21st century.

Technological Advances

Growing up with televisions and computers Technological advances have given rise to other changes in society. From the perspective of child development, the most significant advances are television and the computer. Although they provide new opportunities, they have changed the way children are growing up, what they are exposed to and at what age, and the way they are taught.

Research on the effects of the computer on children's learning, motivation, and social behavior is still in its infancy (Lepper & Gurtner, 1989), in part because home and school computer use have become commonplace only in the past five to ten years (Becker & Sterling, 1987). Research on children and television, however, is more extensive.

Child nurturing and television Television is ubiquitous in American society and in most other industrialized societies. The TV set is on for several hours each day as children are growing up. In many cases television enters their lives long before such institutions as school. Six- and seven-month-old infants are already attentive to television (Hollenbeck & Slaby, 1979). Thus television becomes as much of a socializing agent as parents and peers.

Children also spend a great deal of time watching television at an early age. Estimates of children's viewing time vary widely, from 11 to 28 hours a week. In fact, American children spend more time watching television than in any other activity (Nielson, 1988; Murray, 1980). Thus children must learn to organize their experiences in relation to the social environment of the home, school, and neighborhood and to the ever-present TV screen.

Parents, educators, and psychologists acknowledge the potential benefits of television, but they are also concerned about any negative effects. Public concern generally focuses on program content (Huston et al., 1987), most of which is violent. According to numerous correlational and experimental studies, heavy TV viewing is consistently associated with aggressive behavior in children and adults (Friedrich-

Television is a socializing agent as much for children as for teenagers and adults. Television enters the lives of many children before they start school.

Cofer & Huston, 1986; Huesmann & Eron, 1986). Many of these studies are compiled in *Television and Behavior: Ten Years of Scientific Progress and Implications for the 1980s* (Pearl et al., 1982), a report submitted to the U.S. surgeon general. Although the television industry and some researchers (such as Freedman, 1986) dispute these findings, the American Psychological Association (1985) and numerous other organizations have concluded that a link exists between TV violence and aggressive behavior in children.

Of course, there may be other explanations for aggressive behavior in children. For example, aggressive children may simply prefer more violent shows and may tend to view them more often. Aggressive children may also imitate parents who are also prone to violent or aggressive behavior and who may also prefer violent TV shows. Jerome and Dorothy Singer (1980a,b) have found that children who are heavy viewers of action adventures or cartoons depicting violence are more likely to exhibit aggressive behavior than children who are not heavy viewers of these programs. Furthermore, the Singers have noted that neither the preferential viewing explanation nor the parental aggression pattern explanation account for such behavior.

Television commercials   Because children spend so much time watching television, they are a target market for advertisers of toys, cereals, candy, sport clothes, and other goods. Parents have been particularly concerned with TV advertising, because children are captive audiences and the commercials shown during children's viewing times tend to promote unhealthy eating habits by advertising sugar-filled cereals, candy, and soft drinks (Finn, 1977). In addition, children below age 8 do not understand the persuasive intent of an advertisement and are particularly vulnerable. Older children are more aware of the intent behind a commercial, but they too are easily persuaded (Huston, Watkins, & Kunkel, 1989). These conclusions are substantiated by the huge amounts of advertising dollars that corporations spend on television commercials targeting children.

Children are extremely attentive to commercials. Television producers attempt to create fast-paced, action-packed adventures (Singer, 1981) that so engross the viewers that they look forward to the next event. Once viewer anticipation builds to a peak, they run a series of commercials. Television advertisers presuppose viewers will remain "glued" to the program and be unable to avoid the commercials. Many adults, however, tend to get up or avert their gaze, read, or mentally tune out the commercials (Singer, 1981). But preschool and elementary school children, in particular, usually do not have such discriminating strategies. They respond equally to commercials and to TV shows.

Also, young children are not able to judge the relative worth of the products being advertised. Through commercials, children are encouraged to develop an attitude of "continuous consumption" (Baecher, 1983). Commercials usually depict "new and improved" versions of just about everything, leading to the feeling that every new product is an improvement and worth having, while every old product is only worth replacing. New toys, designer jeans, and name-brand athletic shoes are soon discarded in favor of different toys, jeans, and sneakers. So effective are the commercials in encouraging children's buying that **Action for Children's Television (ACT)**—a group of parents who monitor and try to change television's impact on children—considers TV commercials a far greater problem than TV violence. According to ACT officials, up to three times as many commercials air when shows are targeted to a young audience, particularly Saturday mornings, than when they are geared to an adult audience (Condry, Bence, & Scheib, 1987).

The effects of television on family interaction Television's impact also extends into family life. When TV sets first came on the market in the late 1940s, a major marketing push was that television would bring the family together in the home (Maccoby, 1964). Television may increase the time that family members spend at home watching programs, but it is essentially a noninteractive activity because very little conversation can occur. The potential exists for increasing interaction among family members by stimulating discussion about programs. But most often television is used in ways that intentionally reduce family interaction. Parents, especially of young children, use television as a babysitter; it removes some of the burden of having to provide entertainment or specific educational experiences (Parke, 1978). As Bronfenbrenner (1970) observes:

> The primary danger of the television screen lies not so much in the behavior it produces—although there is danger there—as in the behavior that it prevents: the talks, the games, the family festivities and arguments through which the child's learning takes place and through which his character is formed. Turning on the television set can turn off the process that transforms children into people.

Television as a learning tool We do not want to create the impression that there are no advantages to watching television. Used appropriately, it can be a learning tool. Preschool children can learn social skills from slow-action TV shows, such as *Mister Rogers' Neighborhood*, that encourage viewer involvement (Stein & Friedrich, 1975; Singer & Singer, 1976). Preschool children who watch *Sesame Street* develop improved vocabulary and prereading skills (Rice et al., 1987). Older children benefit from programs that are informative as well as entertaining. Although such programs are relatively rare (Huston, Watkins, & Kunkel, 1989), *Reading Rainbow* and *Wonderworks* (Kerkman et al., 1987) are good examples. You will see in Chapter 10 that just as some TV shows promote aggression in children, other shows enhance prosocial behavior.

The introduction of television has also contributed to great progress in mass communication. Just over a century ago, many people had to rely on word of mouth to get information; only a small percentage of the population could read and write (Siegel & White, 1982). Today, increased educational opportunities and almost universal access to radio and television expose the average citizen to more information than ever before. More people read more books, magazines, and newspapers, and they hear and see actual and fictional events on radio and television. This tremendous increase in the availability of information is due to the popular media in general and television in particular.

Television versus reading Television is only one aspect of the popular media that affects the development of children. Books and comics are also influential (Maccoby, 1964). Books are particularly important because they promote reading and writing, contribute to knowledge, and stimulate imagination. In a few printed words children can become privy to moments of joy and agony, of heroism and bewilderment, that often become fixed in their memory. They can share the experiences of heroes and heroines and learn about societal pressures and customs, religion, economics, and love. A story has been likened to the flare of a match, bringing faces out of the darkness.

This is also true of television. But television as a medium of communication is fundamentally different from other media because viewers remain essentially passive. Words and images are presented on the screen. The material comes so rapidly that there is no time to talk or reflect on it. Only in sports programs does the "instant replay" allow the viewer to go over the event and think about it for a moment, perhaps seeing some new aspect.

In contrast, readers can review a sentence or paragraph or an earlier page. They can take time to piece together the words and images. Reading, and listening to the radio, stimulates the imagination. The reader must actively participate by translating the words into images. Thus it is much harder mental work than watching television, but it is also very rewarding.

Because TV viewing is a passive activity, researchers suggest that excessive viewing may alter children's capacity for sustained attention and deliberate thought. In a review of the research on television's impact on children's reading skills, Beentjes and Van der Voort (1988) found that more than three hours of television viewing per day is likely to slow the academic progress of children with a high IQ and that viewing of cartoons and situational comedies inhibits reading ability. Teachers also report that students are impatient with long presentations. If we compare textbooks published two decades ago with those published today, we can see a dramatic decrease in the number of words used to convey information and an increase in illustrations and pictures (Tower et al., 1979).

From Problem to Solution: Addressing Children's Needs

The changes we have described in the way children are growing up today make it clear that there are more opportunities for children than ever before, but there are also more problems and stresses. We have described only some of the difficulties confronting children and families. Other social problems, which will be discussed in the following chapters, are listed in Table 1.1. Students of child development and society in general need to recognize these problems that endanger the well-being of American children.

According to a number of studies, children from every segment of society risk experiencing difficult life conditions. Consider, for example, the *Martha's Vineyard Child Health Survey* (Garrison & Earls, 1982). This work is unusual in that it looked at an entire community of seemingly "normal" families who had not seen a psychiatrist or a social worker, who were not on welfare, and who had not been identified as having problems. This study included 400 preschool children. According to the researchers, a significant number of these children exhibited psychiatric and behavioral disorders that stemmed from chronic, continual stress. Among the families reporting stress-producing difficulties that affect children, the most prevalent worry was financial security, followed by housing, work, marriage, and health problems.

Family Support Programs

Several types of programs have been developed to address contemporary problems faced by children and families. Many of these programs have proved effective (Schorr & Schorr, 1988). We can group some of these programs under the general heading of *family support programs*. They are different from previous efforts to help children because they regard child development as occurring in the context of the family; any attempts to help children thus include helping to strengthen families. Many of these programs, which range from information and referral services for

TABLE 1.1   One Day in the Lives of America's Children

17,051	women get pregnant.
2,795	of them are teenagers.
1,106	teenagers have abortions.
372	teenagers miscarry.
1,295	teenagers give birth.
689	babies are born to women who have had inadequate prenatal care.
719	babies are born at low birth weight (less than 5 pounds, 8 ounces).
129	babies are born at very low birth weight (less than 3 pounds, 5 ounces).
67	babies die before 1 month of life.
105	babies die before their first birthday.
27	children die from poverty.
3	children die from child abuse.
10	children die from guns.
30	children are wounded by guns.
6	teenagers commit suicide.
135,000	children bring guns to school. A child is safer in Northern Ireland than on the streets of America.
7,742	teens become sexually active.
623	teenagers get syphilis or gonorrhea.
211	children are arrested for drug offenses.
437	children are arrested for drinking or drunken driving.
1,512	teenagers drop out of school.
1,849	children are abused or neglected.
3,288	children run away from home.
1,629	children are in adult jails.
2,556	children are born to unmarried women.
2,989	see their parents divorced.
34,285	people lose jobs.
100,000	children are homeless.

Source: *SOS America!: A Children's Defense Budget,* p. 5, Children's Defense Fund. © 1990 CDF.

child care to such support groups as Parents Without Partners (Weiss, 1988, 1983), are grass-roots, self-help programs (Whittaker & Garbarino, 1983); that is, they are initiated and supported by the people they serve. The family support program movement is still relatively new, yet many researchers see it as the wave of the future. The movement will probably have a major impact on the health, development, and well-being of American families because its programs represent families solving their own problems (Zigler & Weiss, 1985).

The services rendered and populations served by family support programs vary. They are committed to providing emotional, informational, and instrumental assistance to family members, thus enabling them to cope with their problems. Thus these programs exemplify a primary prevention strategy aimed at mental health disorders (Caplan, 1974; Price et al., 1988). The programs help family members withstand stress and ward off severe dysfunction.

The Role of Government

Taking its lead from the family support movement, the U.S. government may develop new policies in this decade that facilitate the nurturing of children. Most people regard government social policies as aimed solely at the poor. However, by enacting laws pertaining to child care and parental leave (which are relevant to everyone), the government can help support all families.

Still, government support is especially significant to poor families. Public assistance originated in the Social Security Act of 1935, which focused on alleviating economic insecurity by providing publicly supported sources of income to economically deprived groups. Because of the overwhelming need for assistance during the Depression, the act singled out particular groups to receive aid first: the aged, the blind, and children in fatherless homes. Currently, large numbers of children in families with an income below the poverty level, and often with a single parent, receive support from the government program known as Aid to Families with Dependent Children (AFDC). This support includes food stamps and health care because adequate nutrition and health care are essential to growth and development. Without this support, these children's lives would be substantially different.

A few years ago Americans had a clear demonstration of how important government support is to children and families in need. When the president and the U.S. Congress drastically reduced federal monies for social services in 1981, many programs for children were severely curtailed. For example, Aid to Families with Dependent Children was slashed by $1 billion; the funding cut and the enactment of more stringent eligibility requirements removed hundreds of thousands of children from the program and reduced benefits for thousands more. What are the results? According to reports from Catholic Charities (one of the largest private agencies serving families in need), requests for emergency shelter for families and children nearly tripled between 1981 and 1983 (Harvey, 1983). Thus there are many more families without homes. According to the same reports, requests for emergency food also tripled during this period. The demand for food assistance was so enormous that Catholic Charities had to limit each family to three days of food per week. So because of the $1 billion cut in the AFDC program, many families with children entered the ranks of the homeless. Since cuts in social services continue to dominate social policies in the 1990s, the problems of children in poverty and of hunger and homelessness only grow worse (National Center for Children in Poverty, 1990).

The family support act   For the past few years a wide-ranging debate has ensued over ways to reduce the number of homeless, hungry children. Rather than provide additional money to AFDC, the federal government decided to change the nature of welfare services by implementing the Family Support Act. Enacted by the U.S. Congress in 1988 and now being implemented at the state level, this law calls for stronger work, education, and training requirements for AFDC recipients. It strengthens the enforcement of child support payments in divorce cases and also extends Medicaid and child care assistance to families during the transition from welfare to work.

It is too early to tell if the act will be successful, although child development researchers are planning to monitor its effects. One initial concern is that each state must provide AFDC recipients with training, education, and money for child care so that the children are supervised while their mothers are in training or in the workplace. And even though the funding for child care services was increased in 1990, it is still not enough. Thus children may not be receiving good quality care, because there is a close link between the cost of care and its quality (National Research Council, 1990). The question is, will we be jeopardizing the development of children by expecting their parents to place them in low-cost child care facilities that may be of low quality as well?

The integration of child development research and social policy   Before any government activity is initiated, policymakers should ask how it will affect children and families.

Any government policies facilitating family life could be based on the social indicators discussed earlier in the chapter. These policies could also take into account several basic concepts drawn from research on child development. Although these concepts are open to debate and criticism, they are generally accepted by researchers and scholars in the field, and thus could guide policy development. The research on child care is one example. Researchers are still debating the effects of child care, but they agree that as long as children are in good quality care they will not be adversely affected. On the other hand, poor quality care will probably have a negative impact (National Center for Clinical Infant Programs, 1988).

Another principle derived from research—that of *integrity and continuity*— states that children and families benefit if the family's integrity and continuity are maintained. This principle is not new. Researchers have known that young children need the presence of a loving adult who takes care of them *over time*.

Even with this knowledge, some government policies tend to foster the family's breakup. The foster care program is one such policy. Because of poor family conditions, such as a severely depressed mother or physical abuse and neglect, children are placed with foster parents. The intent is to care for the children *temporarily* by removing them from the family until the situation improves. Foster care parents are encouraged not to develop long-term attachments with the children. In fact, prospective foster parents only become eligible to participate in the program after authorities are convinced that they have no intention of adopting a child. Often the children are moved from one home to another to discourage emotional attachment. Although the foster care program is a temporary solution, some children spend their entire childhood moving from one foster care home to another (Children's Defense Fund, 1990). This approach is both detrimental and costly. Wouldn't it be better to prevent the family life from deteriorating? For example, home visitors might routinely visit homes to see if the parents and children need help *before* conditions worsen (Zigler & Finn, 1982). If the family situation is hopeless, the children should become eligible for adoption after some period so they can begin life anew. In Connecticut, the Family Support Service program provides 24-hour in-home assistance for families in which the child is at risk of foster care placement (Adnopoz, Grigsby, & Nagler, 1991).

These solutions may seem simple and straightforward. Unfortunately, some modifications in the foster care program took place only after enactment of the 1980 Adoption Assistance and Child Welfare Act. However, the foster care program remains problematic, with an even greater number of children in the system today than a decade ago (U.S. Congress, House Select Committee on Children, Youth and Families, 1989).

Why does the government allow children to be hurt emotionally and psychologically? Policymakers are often not aware that their programs harm children. Their expertise is in the policy process and in fiscal and management matters, not in child development. Therefore, child development researchers have a dual role: to generate knowledge about psychological processes and child development, and to integrate that knowledge with social policy by helping policymakers develop programs on the basis of principles drawn from child development research (Zigler & Finn-Stevenson, in press; Garwood et al., 1989; Masters, 1983).

The Role of Business and Industry

Although the role of the government in facilitating family life is clear, there are limitations on the extent to which government can provide for the nation's children. There is only so much money to go around. Obviously, then, support for children and families must come from the private sector. Perhaps an alliance should be formed with executives in business and industry who can institute changes that might have a positive effect on families.

For example, the private sector can help children and families in that area where work and family life overlap. With working mothers the norm, and with the increase in single-parent families, the impact of the workplace on family life has become a relevant issue. According to several recent studies, work and family life are interdependent (Levitan & Conway, 1990; Brim & Abeles, 1975; Kanter, 1977). The interplay between these two worlds and its effects on the child concern developmental psychologists.

As we noted earlier, life for dual-career and single-parent families can be stressful. These families need to make child care arrangements for infants and preschoolers and to find after-school programs for older children. School vacations and days when children are ill require still other solutions. Since family stability and other family concerns affect worker satisfaction and productivity (Kanter, 1977), it is in the best interests of the private sector to offer services and benefits that can help their employees' families.

Although the private sector's role has been slow in developing, several attempts have been made to accommodate family needs. These attempts include changes in the work structure to allow flexible work arrangements and part-time job opportunities (Bureau of National Affairs, 1988). Under the Pregnancy Disability Act of 1978, businesses that have a general medical leave policy are required by law to provide women with a leave of absence to give birth (Bureau of Business Practice, 1979). These leaves are generally for six weeks; however, an increasing number of companies are offering more liberal policies. Some firms even enable parents to take several months off with a guarantee that they will not lose their jobs (Trczinski & Finn-Stevenson, 1991). Although several states have enacted family leave policies and some companies voluntarily provide these leaves, the United States lags far behind many other countries in developing policies that encourage the nurturing of infants and young children.

Some U.S. companies have on-site child care centers or subsidize the cost of child care. Company-based child care centers have been successful for such corporations as Stride-Rite in Boston and Champion International in Stamford, Connecticut. Often, however, parents prefer to leave their children in facilities near home. Also, not all corporations can afford to operate such facilities. Another, less expensive answer would be for several businesses to cooperate in the financial support of a child care center.

Several cities use zoning regulations to ensure that businesses help with child care. In San Francisco, for example, an ordinance requires developers either to provide space for child care or to contribute to a child care fund. In Seattle, zoning rules for building projects require new buildings to include space for child care (Kyle, 1987).

Industry can help facilitate family life in many other ways (Child Care Action Campaign, 1989; Economic Policy Council, 1986). Often child development researchers help business and industry executives plan and implement these projects. Moreover, some researchers are investigating whether changes implemented in the workplace really benefit children. Do parents who take advantage of flexible working arrangements actually spend more time with their children? Do such changes in work schedules reduce stress in parents? Given the option of maternity leaves, do parents use them?

The School of the 21st Century

School administrators increasingly realize that successfully educating children requires more than academic courses. Hence many schools have been implementing programs designed to teach children interpersonal problem-solving skills (see Chapter 13). Numerous schools have also implemented programs designed to prevent emotional and behavioral problems and to address mental health needs (Comer, 1988; 1991).

In addition to extra academic programs, school officials are offering child care and family support programs, some beginning at the birth of the child. The School of the 21st Century program (Zigler, 1987) includes two major components; all-day child care for children ages 3, 4, and 5, and before- and after-school and vacation care for children from kindergarten through age 12. The program also includes three outreach services. A home visitation program begins at the child's birth and extends through age 3. A parent-educator visits the child's home several times during the year, teaches the parents about child development, and assesses the child to determine if he or she needs any special preventive services. Also included is an information and referral service and a service that provides support to family day care providers in the neighborhood of the school.

The School of the 21st Century was developed in response to the country's lack of child care services and to the fact that many children are in poor quality child care settings or left alone at home. The program is voluntary, used only by parents who need child care, and supported by parental fees for service. To ensure low-income children's access to the program, a sliding-scale fee system allows the parents to pay for the service according to their financial ability.

The program has been successfully implemented in numerous parts of the country. In Missouri, Wyoming, Colorado, and Kansas, the program began because of an apparent need for child care in certain communities. Financial resources were either solicited or made available by the school board. In other states, such as Connecticut and Kentucky, the state legislature appropriated funds to initiate the program statewide or in certain schools.

These variations in the School of the 21st Century program indicate a trend to use the public school as a means to reach out to families. These initiatives also demonstrate a growing realization that if children are to succeed academically, their needs and those of their parents must be addressed; and children must be reached earlier. You will see in Chapter 10, for example, that in addition to providing child care and family support programs, many schools provide preschool services to children from economically disadvantaged families.

Providing nonacademically oriented services is not without problems, however. In the School of the 21st Century program, for example, the school has to extend its hours of operation to accommodate the needs of working parents, and it also has to stay open year-round. Nevertheless, by overcoming these obstacles, schools are indicating their commitment to change.

The Role of Advocates

Changes in the way that government, industry, or the schools operate to benefit children and families cannot occur in the absence of *advocacy*. When a problem exists, some individual or group must see to it that the public becomes aware of the problem and that change takes place. Advocacy has been practiced as long as people have cared for and protected one another. Advocacy can be defined as a combination of acting in behalf of one's own interests, pleading the cause of others, and defending or maintaining a cause (Zigler, 1984; Blom, Keith, & Tomber, 1984).

The need for adults to become advocates for children is obvious: children are unable to act for themselves. Child advocacy has a general aim: to prevent or change conditions that are harmful or undesirable for children and families.

In contrast to advocates representing business concerns, child advocates are not well organized. Often competition exists among groups that represent different issues. However, child advocates are now realizing that working together in greater numbers and forming coalitions (Zigler & Finn, 1981) enables them to achieve their goals. Any interested individual can be a child advocate. Researchers and other professionals who deal with children increasingly find that they cannot remain aloof from the search for solutions to children's problems. Parents, too, form an important element of child advocacy.

What is child advocacy?   Essentially, child advocates monitor the conditions of children's lives to ensure that needed improvements are made. Such improvements often require government intervention. Part of the advocacy process involves educating the general public and policymakers about children's needs. This aspect of advocacy is important because human beings seldom act unless they have a sense of a problem's immediacy (Zigler & Finn, 1981). The researchers' role is especially important here. They can provide expert testimony to government officials and can disseminate their findings in scholarly journals and in popular newspapers and magazines (McCall et al., 1981; McCall, Gregory, & Murray, 1984; Muenchow & Gilfillan, 1983).

A number of child advocacy groups work in child care; these groups inform policymakers of various issues that can result in poor quality child care, such as staff turnover, low staff wages, and lack of training. Working in conjunction with child development researchers, these groups disseminate the results of research about the effects of child care. Advocates challenge federal and state policymakers and business executives to work together to build a child care system in America that can meet the diverse needs of working families and their children (Zigler & Lang, 1990).

Action for children's television   Child advocates have focused on numerous other important issues such as child abuse and neglect, physical punishment, health care, and the special needs of poor and handicapped children. In their attempts to better children's lives, advocates direct their efforts to Congress and state and federal governments, as well as to the courts, public schools, and various social service agencies.

Action for Children's Television (ACT) exemplifies the importance of child advocates. For over 30 years ACT has struggled with the television industry and with policymakers who have the power to regulate the industry about the types of programs, scheduling, and amount and kind of advertising viewed by children. One result is a recent law that limits commercials on children's programs and compels broadcasters to offer more educational programming or risk losing their license.

It has been a long, difficult struggle for ACT. The television industry has powerful advocates and a lot more money. Nonetheless, ACT members persist in conveying their concerns to the public. Americans are beginning to view the television industry as unresponsive to its audience's needs but acquiescent to its advertisers, which are the source of its profits. ACT members and other child advocates hope that the industry will now capitalize on the medium's potential as a learning tool by allocating more time to educational programs.

Summary

We began this chapter by briefly considering why people study child development. Although child development did not gain the status of a science until this century, human beings have long been interested in the nature of the child and in how best to train and educate children. Philosophers like Locke and Rousseau provided direction and guidance, but a more objective study did not emerge until the 19th century. This study was made possible by a growth in the discipline of biology, which began to investigate scientifically the evolution of the human organism.

We then learned why present-day researchers are increasingly studying social policy issues in an effort to find solutions for the contemporary social problems that affect American children. We explored new directions in child development research, including the conditions under which children live and the possible effects on development. We looked at childrearing issues and concerns in the 1990s and beyond by highlighting social changes and trends that influence family life. During the past two decades children have faced stressful conditions that threaten to undermine their development. These problems stem from the isolation and fragmentation of the family, poverty, the high incidence of divorce, and the fact that working parents cannot find quality, affordable child care facilities. Additional problems have surfaced from such technological changes as the introduction of television. Although television offers numerous benefits, research findings indicate that violence depicted on television can lead to aggressive behavior, that TV advertising is directed more at children than at any other group, and that there is cause for concern about intellectual and social development of children exposed to television for a substantial part of their lives.

The solutions to some of these problems lie in our ability to support and facilitate family life. This can be achieved in several ways. The government can help ease stress in family life by basing government policies and programs on social indicators and on principles drawn from child development research. Schools also have a role in providing child care and family support services, and that role now begins with the birth of the child. Because of school officials' interest in addressing the needs of children and preparing them to perform well in school, schools in the 21st century are likely to offer a range of services that extends well beyond traditional academic subjects.

The private sector can also facilitate family life by introducing changes in the workplace. Researchers can help business executives plan and implement such changes and then can investigate whether these changes actually benefit children. Finally, advocates bring about changes in family life through public or private initiatives and monitor the conditions of children.

2 The Study of Child Development

The Goal of Child Development Research

A University of Virginia research psychologist is testifying before the U.S. Congress, providing the results of a five-city study on the conditions of child care centers to Senator Edward Kennedy, chairman of the Senate Labor Committee, and Senator Christopher Dodd, chairman of the Subcommittee on Children, Youth, Families, Drug and Alcohol Abuse. Her testimony, and that of other researchers, has convinced policymakers that a national child care policy is needed to increase the number of quality child care facilities.

Many researchers in psychology, education, and other disciplines related to human development are concerned about children's welfare and want to give direction to child and family policies. They regard their knowledge as an indispensable tool, and they see their goal as understanding the process of development by studying the changes that occur in children as they mature.

In the course of their work, researchers devise scientific methods to study children of different ages and backgrounds. They also develop theoretical frameworks that can explain behavior and behavioral changes. As they strive to accumu-

A CLOSER LOOK

The Concept of Childhood

Ideas about the nature of the child and concepts of childhood are reflected in the way children are treated, in the concerns adults have for them, and in the policies created for their benefit. Every age has had its perceptions of the meaning and place of childhood in the social order. In fact, today's concept of childhood is peculiar to the technological societies of this century and was virtually nonexistent at other times. Children were not always seen as they are now.

Philippe Aries (1962), who has studied changes in the way children were perceived through the ages, notes that during the Middle Ages "infancy" lasted until age 6 or 7. After that, children were simply assimilated into the adult world.

In contrast, in the 20th century childhood is seen as a special period of the life cycle (Larrabee, 1960). As you saw in Chapter 1, children today are growing up under adverse conditions that affect their development and well-being. Although some childhood conditions need to be improved, historically children have experienced worse conditions, depending on the popular concept of childhood and the value adults attached to children.

A Brief History of Childhood

Not much is known about children in Europe before the 18th century; writings about them are relatively skimpy. Philippe Aries's (1962) account of the lives of European children in the Middle Ages, which is essentially based on such fragmentary data as paintings of the period, speculates about how the medieval child was viewed.

The documentation available after 1700 shows that before the enactment of certain social reforms, young children suffered a great deal. First, there appears to have been no special emotional attachment to children; most were unwanted. Before 1750 children in Europe were born in great numbers. Women could be expected to give birth to as many as 10 or 12 infants, most of whom died at birth or in early childhood. About two-thirds of infants and children died before age 5 (Kessen, 1965). Since the chances of survival were so slim for their children, parents found it difficult to establish an emotional attachment; infants who did live were often abandoned in the streets or simply neglected. This abandonment and neglect was so rampant that authorities in France and England instituted increasingly stricter penalties for infanticide. As a result, parents abandoned their children in orphanages or foundling homes, instead of in the streets. It is difficult to imagine the enormity of this problem. Consider that for every three births recorded in Paris in the 18th century, one baby was left in a foundling home (Kessen, 1965). Moreover, 90% of all children left in orphanages in several large European cities died at an early age (Kessen, 1965).

Children of the 19th century suffered from different problems than modern children. Conflicting views of child-

late an organized, systematic body of knowledge about child development and behavior, researchers focus on such broad questions as how do children acquire the capacity to think? or how do they feel, perceive, and interact with others, or acquire language skills? Beyond questions about specific developmental processes, researchers are also concerned with influences on these developmental processes. For example, they may engage in research to help clarify the role genes play in determining individual differences or to determine to what extent variations may be related to observable differences in experience or environment.

No single study ever attempts to answer such complex questions. Rather, researchers synthesize the findings of many studies that look at related and more circumscribed behaviors. For instance, to understand how the child grows as a social being, able to benefit from and contribute to interactions with other people, we would study the relationship between the newborn infant and mother. This research would look at differences between infants and young children whose mothers work and those whose mothers stay home; different childbearing practices in various cultures would be investigated to determine cultural effect on development. Or, to better understand why some children grow up to become happy, productive members of society while others become unhappy or disturbed adults, researchers might analyze family relationships of mentally ill children; they might

A CLOSER LOOK

hood were rooted in the self-interest of adults. Religious leaders and middle-class parents were concerned with the child's moral redemption, and they resorted to several methods to "break their will," considered essential to salvation. Letters from mothers of that period reveal that they felt they had to resort to severe punishment to "keep the children in line." Although kind and rational at times, parents generally believed that firm discipline would produce an upright citizen (Scarr, 1984).

Poor children, on the other hand, were regarded as economic assets and were exploited by their parents and by employers. They worked long hours in dreadful conditions and often died young:

> It must be borne in mind that it is in this district [of England] that the regular hours of a full day's labour are 14 and occasionally 16; and the children have to walk a mile or two at night without changing their clothes . . . there are very few [mines] . . . where the main roadways exceed a yard in height . . . so that in such places the youngest child cannot work without the most constrained posture. The ventilation, besides, in general is very bad, and the drainage worse. . . . The ways are so low that only little boys can work in them, which they do naked and often in mud and water, dragging sledge-tubs by the girdle and chain. (From a speech by the Earl of Shaftesbury, June 7, 1842, as quoted in Kessen, 1965.)

The exploitation of children was not as rampant in America. In the United States, less than 20% of the children

under age 13 living in urban areas were employed during the late 19th century. Their working conditions were also horrendous, but not as grim as those in England and Wales, where children and often pregnant women worked in mines and factories six days a week. The number of employed children in America decreased steadily during the early part of the 20th century, and by the 1940s, only 1% of young children were employed. In many rural areas, however, children either assumed a great deal of work around the house or farm or were apprenticed or rented out to another farm for labor.

The decrease in the number of young children put to work in the late 19th and early 20th centuries reflects changes in public attitudes. As advances in health care and medicine helped children survive their childhood, general interest in them improved as well. American and European child labor laws ensured that young children did not work in factories and mines.

Another milestone was the introduction of compulsory schooling. A 1933 report of the U.S. Office of Education indicates that between 1870 and 1915 the total number of American pupils aged 5 to 17 increased from 7 to 20 million (White, 1982). Thus childhood became a period protected for learning. Early in this century, however, adolescents from poor homes still had to work and many could not read or write. Nevertheless, children were increasingly recognized

(continued)

examine the characteristics of abused children; or they might assess the impact of stress or poverty on development. The more knowledge they accumulate, the more likely researchers are to refine their understanding of development and change their theoretical formulations.

In this chapter you will learn about the major child development theories and the scientific techniques used. At the outset, however, it is important to discuss a few of the field's historical highlights. As you will recall from Chapter 1, the earliest scientific studies were baby biographies. Then, early in this century, G. Stanley Hall developed the questionnaire to collect information from large groups of children. The next major achievement was the intelligence test.

Historical Highlights

The Testing Movement

At the request of the French Ministry of Public Education, Alfred Binet, a psychologist, and Theodore Simon, a physician, developed an intelligence test (1905). They were to study how to teach mentally retarded children in French public schools.

A CLOSER LOOK

(continued)

as needing education and protection. The view of childhood as a unique and special period is an unmistakable feature of our society (Larrabee, 1960), which has become more child-centered since the early 1900s.

The two decades following World War II were perhaps the greatest period of child-centeredness in U.S. society. There was a very high birth rate, a phenomenon referred to as the *postwar baby boom*. The persuasive arguments of researchers and childrearing experts, such as Bowlby (1951) and Spock (1968), who wrote of the importance of the mother and of the pleasures of childrearing, fueled the strong child and family orientation. Also, most white, middle-class families could be supported by the husband's income so the mother could stay home and care for the children.

Since the early 1970s, however, our society has moved away from its focus on the child and the family. There is ample evidence that children are no longer adequately cared for, and there are strong indications of a general devaluation of children and childrearing. For example, the number of reported cases of child abuse is increasing each year (U.S. Department of Health & Human Services, 1988; see also Chapter 10). Child labor, although prohibited by laws enacted over 50 years ago, appears to be making a comeback. Numerous reports indicate that children, often as young as 11, are working in factories and garment industry sweatshops (Freitag, 1990). As we saw in Chapter 1, and will see in

the social issues sections of subsequent chapters, many other indicators point to the general neglect of children.

In his book *Our Endangered Children: Growing Up in a Changing World*, Packard (1983) examines the actual setting in which a child is likely to grow up today and its impact on the child. For the majority of children, being young may mean, among other things:

- Wondering if your parents are going to split up
- Living in a single-parent family
- Having to adjust to newcomers in your home in case of the remarriage of one or both of your parents
- Being taken care of by a caregiver, usually outside the home
- Being left alone in an empty house
- Having relatively little contact with adults
- Sitting in front of the TV set most of the time when you are not in school
- Being lonely a lot of the time
- Having parents who are self-absorbed, uncertain about their role in life or about the future, or experiencing a great deal of stress.

Obviously, these problems are different from those historically encountered by children. Today's problems represent a new kind of adversity; as Packard writes, the new ways children are growing up "promote a sense of insecurity that may lie behind a seemingly cheerful countenance. They often add [up] to a poor foundation for adult life."

Binet and Simon set out to develop a method of distinguishing normal from subnormal intelligence so children could be placed in regular public schools or in special schools. Before Binet and Simon's endeavors, such decisions were often based on subjective, biased information. To secure a more objective measurement, Binet and Simon devised a series of short, simple tests. Children were asked to define words or to complete a sentence with the appropriate word (for example, "The weather is clear, the sky is *blue*"). Binet and Simon first gave each test to a large number of normal children. The age at which roughly 75% of normal children passed a test defined the mental age required by the test. Children were considered subnormal if their mental age, as determined from the entire series of tests, was markedly below their chronological (or actual) age.

Lewis Terman (1916), one of G. Stanley Hall's students (see Chapter 1), worked on the Binet-Simon tests, adapted them for use in America, and added other questions. Eventually, researchers suggested that the most meaningful measure of intelligence was the *intelligence quotient*, or *IQ*, which is the ratio of mental age to chronological age. Since Terman worked at Stanford University, his new test was labeled the *Stanford-Binet test*. This test was quick, easy to administer, and provided an indication of children's ability to succeed in school. That is, children who did well on the test also did well in school, suggesting that the test did measure intellectual ability. As we will see in Chapter 15, intelligence tests are still being administered. However, during the past few decades, the test has come under heavy criticism (Weinberg, 1989; Cronbach, 1975). Researchers now understand that although these tests can predict children's school performance, they are not measures of intelligence. *Intelligence* refers to many other aspects of behavior as well, so the IQ test score alone does not encompass what is meant by intelligence in many contexts.

The Increasing Popularity of Child Study

The study of children interested scientists, parents, and educators (Siegel & White, 1982). Another of Hall's students, Arnold Gesell (1880–1961), is well known both for his contributions to the field and for his theory of maturation, which greatly influenced parents and educators. Maturational theories emphasize that the child's development is decided from within; it unfolds according to a predetermined timetable. Gesell believed that both heredity and environment shape development; however, environment is decidedly secondary because it does not give rise to the basic progressions of behavior, which are determined by inherent maturational mechanisms.

Gesell's notions of development were derived from observing many children and documenting behaviors among full-term, preterm, and impaired infants. He believed such documentation would help show the course of children's growth and provide a framework for a standardized diagnostic tool.

Gesell was the first to film observations, which enabled him to later study and analyze the children's activities. On the basis of his observations, he determined age standards for development in motor, visual, and language skills and social behavior. Gesell concluded that certain *orderly stages of development* formed a *universal* and *invariant sequence* (Gesell & Thompson, 1934). The stages were universal because, within a given range, they occurred in all children observed. And they were invariant because each stage set the conditions for the next one. That is, the child first crawls and then walks; no child ever follows the reverse pattern. Gesell set out to determine which changes formed orderly patterns of growth and which appeared less regular and subject to greater degrees of individual variation. If development is orderly, he reasoned, it must follow a well-defined path. Understanding how this developmental path unfolds gives meaning to children's behavior at different ages.

Thus Gesell believed that development depended on a naturally unfolding process. According to his notion of *maturational readiness*, when children are sufficiently mature, they will benefit from training; children who are not ready require far more effort and time for learning. Gesell's position is critical because it does not acknowledge environmental input or the role of learning (Crain, 1985). Nevertheless, parents and educators found his concept attractive; it provided some concrete guidelines on such issues as toilet training and discipline. Parents also relied on Gesell's idea of behavioral stages, which reflected his belief that development was the result of forces of growth. Some forces were dominant at one age, whereas others were dominant at another age. Gesell labeled each age: the "terrible twos," the "conforming threes," the "lively fours" (Gesell & Ilg, 1942); this procedure helped parents understand and predict children's behaviors at different ages. Thus the mother of a 2-year-old who continuously disobeys can take some comfort in the realization that all parents experience difficulty with 2-year-olds and that this stage of development will pass.

Child study during Gesell's time, the early 1900s, emphasized collecting large amounts of data and providing direction and guidance for parents and others who work with children. Gesell established one of the first child development research centers at Yale University in 1911. During the 1920s many such centers and "laboratory schools" were established in universities across the country. The purpose of these centers was to understand how children develop, to use this understanding to facilitate childrearing and education, and to train the increasing number of teachers needed to accommodate the growing numbers of schoolchildren.

The scientists at these laboratories did not always share Gesell's belief in the theory of maturation. For example, at the Iowa Child Welfare Research Center, a lab school established in 1917, Harold Skeels (see Chapter 7) studied children raised in institutions. His research led him to challenge the view that environment does not affect development.

The existence of these centers and lab schools provided opportunities for an increasing number of scientists to concentrate on child development research. Many researchers at these centers, such as Myrtle McGraw (1940) and Mildred Parten (1932), conducted classic studies on motor development and play. Their work, based on large groups of children, lent scientific credibility to the field. Indeed, by the early 1930s, interest in child development became so great that research appeared with increasing frequency in psychological journals; the study of child development had become firmly established in America as a science.

The maturational theory was extremely popular in the early 1900s, but there were other theoretical viewpoints as well. Sigmund Freud's psychoanalytic theory and John B. Watson's emphasis on behaviorism were also popular during the early 1900s and continued to exert enormous influence on developmental research and childrearing practices after World War II.

We have given you a glimpse of some historical highlights in child development so you can appreciate how the field has grown. Numerous other changes occurred as the study of children became a more popular and increasingly sophisticated scientific endeavor. Whereas the early part of the 1900s was characterized by the accumulation of large stores of descriptive data, by midcentury, researchers began testing theories of development.

Theories of Child Development

What Is a Theory?

A theory can be defined as a *statement or set of statements offered to explain a phenomenon.* It is a way of organizing ideas to provide a more complete understanding of what the data indicate in a piecemeal fashion. A theory's importance may lie more in its ability to provide direction for further research than in its correctness (Zigler, 1963).

Indeed, we rely on theories to provide direction for action in everyday life. We use the word *theory* to mean a "hunch." On television, for instance, a detective formulates a theory based on the available facts or clues. She has what she thinks is an explanation for the mystery under investigation. Likewise, a mechanic working on a car that does not run listens to the engine; on the basis of an initial examination and of his experience and knowledge, he offers his theory of what is wrong with the car. On the basis of their theories, both the detective and the mechanic can pursue a course of action that either proves or disproves their explanations; at any rate, it will bring them closer to a solution. Without a theory, neither the detective nor the mechanic would be able to decide what to do next.

Testability   Scientific theories are similar to theories used in everyday life. They differ in the phenomena they explain, and they are governed by a set of rules. One rule is *testability,* which means that a theory can be subjected to proof or disproof; that is, it must be stated in such a way that it can be tested by observable events. If a theory appears to explain a phenomenon but can never be put to a test, then its value is limited.

In theory testing the scientist first tests a *hypothesis,* or specific prediction derived from the theory. The scientist does not assume that the hypothesis is true or that it can be proved. Rather, there are different *levels of certainty*; at best, the scientist hopes that the research findings will *support* the hypothesis. Vasta (1979) provides an example in which researchers test the hypothesis that infants smile less in the presence of strangers than when they are with familiar people. The researchers select a number of infants and observe them, documenting how often they smile when they are with their parents and when they are with strangers. Even if the researchers find that all the infants tested smile less in the presence of strangers, they still cannot claim that the hypothesis is absolutely correct. Rather, they can say only that their findings *support* the hypothesis. Absolute proof could only be established by testing *all* infants under the same circumstances. This requirement may seem absurd; after all, all the infants in the study did smile less in the presence of a stranger. Bear in mind, however, that the study involved only a sample of infants. Also, experiments do not usually yield such clear-cut results. In a real study, some of the infants would smile less, in which case the scientist must make a decision, on the basis of statistics, about whether the evidence is adequate to accept or to reject the hypothesis.

The uses of theories   Numerous child development theories have emerged during the 20th century. Today, theories attempt to explain limited aspects of behavior, such as smiling and grasping in an infant. Earlier theories, however, were ambitious attempts to explain everything related to developmental phenomena. Many theories, such as the psychoanalytic theory, do not meet the testability requirement. In other words, they are stated in a way that cannot be tested. From a scientific perspective, such theories cannot be considered true theories but rather are said to provide a "frame of reference" (Zigler, 1963). Despite being pretheoretical in nature, however, these theories have had a significant influence on child development research. Indeed, scientists welcome theories and conjectures in order to test them with available instruments and methods.

Major theories in child development   We can divide theories of development into several general categories. For example, *epigenetic theories* explain development and behavior on the basis of the interaction between the environment and genetic inheritance. *Environmental theories* explain behavior and development on the basis of past experience and learning. Both epigenetic and environmental theories can be further categorized based on the aspect of development they focus on—thinking and learning or personality and social behavior. Variations in perspective can lead to markedly different interpretations of development. To date, no one theory has been found to be the only correct explanation, but all theories are useful in helping construct a picture of development.

To highlight the varied and rich resource of knowledge provided by child development theories, we present several major theoretical approaches. By way of introduction, we will consider only some major points, the theories behind them, and the factors that led to the emergence of these theories.

The Psychoanalytic Theory

Sigmund Freud (1856–1939) developed the *psychoanalytic theory* in Vienna. The impact of Freud's theory has been so widespread that few people do not recognize his name. The psychoanalytic theory is generally referred to as a *biological theory of personality* because it focuses on biological drives as manifested within the social context.

Sigmund Freud (1856–1939)

Freud, a physician and neurologist by training, was influenced by the work of fellow physician Josef Breuer, who successfully treated a patient using hypnosis. Freud was extremely impressed by this treatment, which he later called the "talking cure." He began to treat his own patients in a similar way, but he replaced hypnosis with free association. That is, he encouraged his patients to talk freely about whatever came to mind. Freud compiled careful notes on the traumatic experiences and events that had been repressed into his patients' unconscious memory. On the basis of this information, he developed his theory of personality development and psychoanalysis as a method of treating emotional disorders.

With novel techniques like brain imaging, which permits the study of the brain while it performs specific tasks, researchers are developing new ways to understand the mind and treat mental disorders. Freud, however, was a pioneer, the first scientist to explore the human mind by probing the unconscious. Although his theory is no longer studied or used to the extent it once was, Freud has had a significant influence on the field of psychiatry. In addition, his theory encouraged researchers in child development to examine such issues as guilt and sexuality and their relationship to development and behavior (Gay, 1990).

Freud noted that human personality is made up of the id, the ego, and the superego. The *id*, which is present at birth, is a force of energy guided by instincts and directed toward satisfying basic needs and desires; the id inevitably causes the newborn infant unresolved tensions as he or she struggles to deal with reality. To cope with reality, the *ego* emerges to regulate desires, modulate frustrations, and guide thought and behavior. During early childhood, the *superego* emerges. It represents societal values and traditions communicated to the child by adults.

The id, the ego, and the superego are concepts that Freud developed to explain the biological (id), psychological (ego), and social (superego) components of development. According to Freud, the emergence of the ego and superego parallel stages of psychosexual development (see Table 2.1). During these stages, what is gratifying to the id changes. At birth, and through the first year of life, the id focuses on the *oral zone*, and the infant seeks gratification through stimulation of the mouth by sucking or chewing. During the second and third years, the focus is on the *anal zone*, and the id derives gratification from the anal musculature. Freud believed that this stage is complete once toilet training is successful.

From ages 3 to 5, the *phallic zone*, or genital region, is the focus of id gratification. During the *latency period* (6 years to puberty), however, there is a reduced focus on the genital area, and sexual drives become dormant. Thus the child can

TABLE 2.1   Freud's Stages of Psychosexual Development

The Oral Stage	During this stage, which encompasses the first year of life, the id focuses on sensual pleasure. Thus infants suck the breast or a bottle, from which food is given, as well as their thumb or pacifier, and tend to pick up objects and mouth them just for the sheer pleasure that such oral stimulation brings.
The Anal Stage	During this stage, which starts at about 1 year and lasts until about 3 years of age, pleasure is derived not from oral stimulation but from the rectum. Hence children enjoy either retaining or expelling feces, and toilet training becomes a battleground between parents and children, each wanting to control the other. The parents feel obligated to toilet train the child, whereas the child often wants to control his or her own bodily functions. Eventually the child minds the parents in an effort to please them.
The Phallic Stage	Freud considered this stage, which lasts from age 3 to about age 6, to be a critical period during which pleasure is derived from the genitals. Hence children are seen fondling their sexual organs, and they are curious about their peers' and parents' genitals as well. Boys experience sexual desires for their mothers as they undergo the Oedipus conflict, but because they admire and fear their fathers, they eventually repress their feelings for their mothers and identify with their fathers. Girls experience the Electra conflict, which involves sexual feelings toward their fathers, and they eventually resolve it by identifying with their mothers.
The Latency Stage	This stage occurs from age 6 until puberty. It is characterized by latent sexual feelings. During this period children are no longer distracted by any sexual desires and spend time mastering a variety of tasks and acquiring different interests.
The Genital Stage	During this last period of psychosexual development, the focus is once again on pleasure derived from the genital area. This period begins at the same time as puberty and lasts through adulthood. It is characterized by efforts toward sexual maturity as individuals seek to find someone of the opposite sex with whom to share sexual pleasures.

expend efforts on learning and acquiring social skills. Finally, during adolescence, in the *genital period* sexual desires awaken, and the individual seeks to find someone with whom to share sexual pleasures.

Freud believed that each stage of development is critical to the developing child. Any unresolved crisis or conflict occurring in any stage would give rise to personality problems that might persist throughout life. Thus the personality can become fixated at any given psychosexual stage. For example, if the id doesn't receive sufficient satisfaction during the oral stage, it may be reluctant to leave that stage until satisfaction is obtained. This *negative fixation*, according to Freud, can result in manifestations of oral-stage processes in adult life. On the other hand, the id may receive too much satisfaction during the oral stage and want to retain oral-stage satisfaction later in life, beyond the appropriate time. Freud referred to this occurrence as *positive fixation*. He believed such fixations, whether negative or positive, could lead to personality problems. For example, a child whose parents were overly strict in their demands during toilet training seeks satisfaction later in life through undue retention as a mode of personality functioning. Freud believed such *anal retentive* personalities show signs of selfishness as adults. Similarly, an adult who derives oral gratification by chewing tobacco or eating may be manifesting fixations that occurred during the oral stage.

The Psychosocial Theory

A number of Freud's contemporaries and students developed theories on the basis of their own observations. Erik Erikson (1903–   ), for example, developed his *psychosocial theory*, which emphasizes lifelong emotional development and focuses on instinctive drives as they relate to society. According to Erikson, personality develops in steps that are predetermined by the individual's readiness to be driven toward and to interact with the social environment. His theory is similar to Freud's in its focus on the person's need to resolve conflicts. However, Erikson believes that conflicts can develop at any stage, including adulthood and old age, and these conflicts do not necessarily result from problems in infancy or early childhood (Erikson, 1963).

The crux of Erikson's theory is that human development consists of the progressive resolution of conflicts between needs and social demands. He theorizes that an individual progresses through eight stages (see Table 2.2). During each stage, the person resolves specific crises before progressing to the next set of problems. Failure to resolve problems at any stage can result in psychological disorders.

Erik Erikson (1903–   )

These eight stages, described in more detail in the chapters on social development (Chapters 7, 10, 13, and 16), begin with the stage of *trust versus mistrust* during infancy. For ego identity to emerge, the infant must develop a sense of trust in herself and in the world. Such trust is predicated on the sense that there are people in the infant's world who can be counted on to provide comfort and care. However, the amount of care given is not as important as the overall quality of the relationship between infant and caretaker and the feeling transmitted to the infant that her actions do indeed have meaning. If the infant cries, for example, someone should respond to her cries and attempt to feed her or otherwise comfort her. If the infant's needs are not attended to, she will not develop a sense of trust and the feeling that the world is a safe place. The subsequent psychosocial stages of development are autonomy versus shame, initiative versus guilt, industry versus inferiority, and identity versus role confusion, which occur during childhood and adolescence. Intimacy versus isolation, generativity versus stagnation, and ego integrity versus despair occur during young adulthood, adulthood, and old age.

TABLE 2.2 Erikson's Stages of Psychosocial Development

Stage 1 *Trust versus Mistrust,* *First Year of Life*	The infant's relationship with his mother is crucial during this stage; the infant acquires a sense of trust and the knowledge that he is loved when he is cared for in a predictable, warm, and sensitive manner. If the infant's world is chaotic and unpredictable, and his parents' affection and care cannot be counted on, he develops a sense of mistrust and feels anxious and insecure in his interactions with others. These basic attitudes of trust or mistrust are acquired over about a year through the infant's experiences with his primary caregiver.
Stage 2 *Autonomy versus* *Shame and Doubt,* *Age 2 to 3*	Once the child is able to walk, run, climb, and talk, she begins to explore her world and acquires a sense of independence, at times becoming adamant. If parents nurture the child's attempts to become an independent individual and allow her to explore her world, while making sure she does not hurt herself, the child develops a sense of autonomy and a feeling that she is competent. If, on the other hand, parents are overprotective, stifling her attempts to explore her surroundings, or critical, she develops shame, doubt, and uncertainty about herself and her capabilities.
Stage 3 *Initiative versus* *Guilt,* *Age 3 to 6*	After the child has gained a relatively secure sense of autonomy, he is ready to take initiative in his activities. He explores, plans, and works for goals, thus acquiring a sense of purpose and direction. Parents must encourage the child's initiatives. If they do not allow him to take initiative or if they downgrade his activities, he develops a sense of guilt for his attempts at independence.
Stage 4 *Industry versus* *Inferiority,* *Age 6 to 12*	During this stage the child becomes responsible for homework and other assignments; she develops an awareness that tasks can be accomplished through industry, or that they can be failed. If parents reinforce the child's efforts with praise and reward, she develops a sense of industry and curiosity and is eager to learn. If the child's work is downgraded, she develops low self-esteem and a sense of inferiority and inadequacy, often withdrawing from attempts to learn new skills. At this stage, parents are only one source of influence on the child's development. The child is also influenced by peers, teachers, and other adults she comes in contact with.
Stage 5 *Identity versus Role* *Confusion,* *Age 12 to 18*	During this stage the individual is in a transition phase of his life. No longer a child, and preparing for life as an adult, the adolescent undergoes what Erikson calls a "physiological revolution" and must come to grips with an identity crisis. In the process of trying to form an identity, the adolescent experiments with different options. The danger during this stage is role confusion, because the adolescent may not be able to piece together a coherent sense of self from the many possible roles.
Stage 6 *Intimacy versus* *Isolation, Young* *Adulthood*	Once she develops a sense of personal identity and is comfortable with it, the individual can begin to establish intimate relationships with other people. Forming close relationships and committing herself to another person, the individual feels gratified. However, intimate relationships are also fraught with dangers. The individual can be rejected, or the relationship may

(continued)

TABLE 2.2 *(continued)*

Stage 6 *Intimacy versus* *Isolation, Young* *Adulthood*	fail through disagreement, disappointment, or hostility. Individuals who focus on the negative possibilities of intimate relationships may be tempted not to take a chance on becoming close to another person and instead withdraw from social contact, thereby becoming isolated, or establishing only superficial relationships.
Stage 7 *Generativity versus* *Stagnation,* *Middle Age*	Erikson regards generativity as emanating from marriage, parenthood, and a sense of working productively and creatively. Having a sense of accomplishment in adult life means giving loving care to others and regarding contributions to society as valuable. Working, getting married, and bearing and rearing children in and of themselves are not sufficient to give an individual a sense of generativity. He must also enjoy his work and his family. If he does not enjoy his work and cares little for other people, he acquires a sense of stagnation, a sense that he is going nowhere and doing nothing important.
Stage 8 *Integrity versus* *Despair, Old Age*	Toward the end of life, the individual reflects on her past accomplishments and the kind of person she has been. She looks back on life either with a sense of integrity and satisfaction or with despair. If earlier crises have been successfully met, the individual realizes that her life has had meaning, and she is ready to face death. If earlier crises have not been resolved successfully, the individual feels despair as she realizes that she has no time now to start another life and try out alternative roads to integrity. Individuals who have a sense of despair are not ready to face death and feel bitterness about their lives.

The Learning Theories

Behaviorism Psychoanalytic theorists look for the unconscious motives that drive human behavior, but *behaviorists* examine only those behaviors that can be seen and measured. Behaviorism, also known as *traditional learning theory*, maintains that through learning, human beings and animals change and advance in their development. Learning theorists emphasize different aspects of learning. Despite their diversity, however, they agree that all behavior, with the exception of basic reflexes, is learned.

American psychologist John B. Watson (1878–1958) developed an extreme view of this approach. Often referred to as the father of behaviorism, Watson adhered to John Locke's view that the infant's mind is a tabula rasa to be entirely shaped by learning. He described the newborn as a "lively squirming bit of flesh, capable of making few simple responses," and he noted that parents take this "raw material and begin to fashion it to suit themselves" (Watson, 1928). Watson argued that if he were given a group of infants, he could turn each child into any kind of adult—a lawyer, a doctor, an artist, or a beggar—depending on the environment and experiences he exposed the child to. Watson was convinced that thought and emotions were acquired through learning. He conducted a number of experiments to show that many fears could be acquired and then eliminated through *conditioning*, which is the process of learning a particular response to particular stimuli.

B.F. Skinner (1904–1990), in his laboratory.

On the basis of his views, Watson suggested a "sensible" way of treating children. Unlike modern developmental psychologists, Watson discouraged emotional dependency between parents and children:

> Treat them as though they were young adults. Let your behavior always be objective and kindly and firm. Never hug and kiss them, never let them sit on your lap. If you must, kiss them once on the forehead when you say goodnight. Shake hands with them in the morning. Give them a pat on the head if they have made an extraordinarily good job of a difficult task. (Watson, 1928)

Learning theorists contend that all learning takes place through conditioning. There are two basic kinds of conditioning: classical and operant. **Classical conditioning,** demonstrated earlier in this century by Russian physiologist Ivan Pavlov, is a kind of learning in which involuntary responses, such as glandular secretions and muscle reflexes, can become learned reactions to environmental events. This learning happens by a process of association.

If an individual is frightened by an experience, for instance, events associated with that experience will tend to arouse fear later, even though those events are harmless. For example, if a doctor wearing white gives a baby a painful injection, the baby may later associate someone else wearing white with that painful experience.

A second kind of learning is **operant conditioning,** in which the organism operates on the environment to produce a change that will lead to a reward. Our understanding of operant conditioning comes primarily from the work of Harvard psychologist B. F. Skinner (1953, 1957). In his book *Walden Two* (1948), Skinner envisioned a utopian society that totally controls behavior. He believed that the child's development is learned and can be changed and shaped by environmental influences. According to Skinner, learning occurs through operant conditioning, which is based on the individual's tendency to repeat a behavior if it is rewarded or reinforced and to discontinue the behavior if it is punished or fails to be reinforced. Learning theorists who employ operant conditioning use principles of reward and punishment to shape or modify behavior. Table 2.3 contains a summary of the

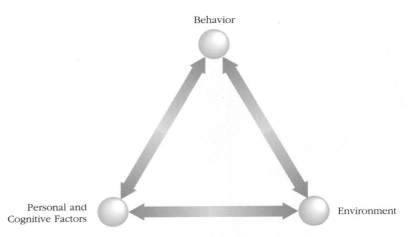

Figure 2.1 *According to Bandura there is a reciprocal relationship between such personal and cognitive factors as intelligence and self-control, behavior, and the environment.*
Source: Albert Bandura, *Social Foundations of Thought and Action: A Social Cognitive Theory,* © 1986, p. 24. Adapted by permission of Prentice Hall, Englewood Cliffs, New Jersey.

principles of operant conditioning. (See Chapter 6 for further discussion of classical and operant conditioning.)

Considerable controversy surrounds traditional learning theories. For example, how much human behavior is learned and how much is innate? Learning theorists disagree with maturational theorists such as Gesell, who postulated that there is a genetically predetermined timetable for development; important events such as walking and talking generally appear on schedule for most children, regardless of their learning experiences. Researchers have learned over the years that genetic factors alone do not determine development. However, are people controlled by rewards and punishments to the extent suggested by learning theorists like Skinner? Both genetic predispositions and environmental experiences are now known to influence behavior. Nevertheless, learning theorists have made and continue to

TABLE 2.3 Summary of Basic Principles of Operant Conditioning

Principle	Characteristic procedure and its effect on behavior
Reinforcement	Presentation or removal of an event after a response that increases the frequency of the response.
Punishment	Presentation or removal of an event after a response that decreases the frequency of the response.
Extinction	No longer presenting a reinforcing event after a response that decreases the frequency of the previously reinforced response.
Stimulus control	Reinforcing the response in the presence of one discrimination stimulus but not in the presence of another. This training procedure increases the frequency of the response in the presence of the former stimulus and decreases the frequency of the response in the presence of the other stimulus.

Source: Alan Kazdin, "Learning theory and behavioral approaches," in Melvin Lewis (Ed.), *Child and Adolescent Psychiatry: A Comprehensive Textbook.* © 1991, Williams & Wilkins Co., Baltimore.

Albert Bandura (1925–   )

make important contributions to the field of child development, and they encourage a scientific approach to its study (Skinner, 1987).

Social learning theory   Social learning theory is an outgrowth of behaviorism. One leading theorist in this area is Albert Bandura (1977) of Stanford University, who employed principles of both classical and operant conditioning to explain how children learn social behaviors. Bandura believes that children learn not only through their experience but also through observation. The reciprocal relationship among behavior, environmental influences, and cognition is a key factor in how children learn (Bandura, 1986). That is, such personal factors as intelligence and thought processes affect behavior and vice versa, and environmental influences influence behavior as well as thought processes (see Figure 2.1).

Bandura also differed from behaviorists in his position that rewards for learning do not have to be concrete, such as a piece of candy, but instead may be social responses such as attention, affection, and praise. He contends that learning occurs in the social context and a child who is smiled at and praised for work or good conduct learns that behaving in certain ways brings rewards.

Social learning theorists differ further from behaviorists in regarding children as actively contributing to their learning. For example, they contend that children learn language, or ways of dealing with aggression, by observing and imitating models like parents and teachers. The children are active in this process because they *choose* models they want to identify with and imitate.

Theories of Cognitive Development

Although for many years psychoanalytic and learning theories dominated psychology, many developmental psychologists are now interested in cognition. **Cognition** refers to the way in which humans gain knowledge through perception, memory, and thought processing. The cognitive approach regards children as spontaneously active individuals who construct their own knowledge of the world. Thus, development is not a series of cumulative changes; rather the mind undergoes a series of reorganizations. With each reorganization, the child moves to a higher level of psychological functioning.

Two theoretical orientations have dominated the study of cognitive development: Jean Piaget's theory of genetic epistemology and information processing. Although traditionally researchers adhered to one approach or the other, current studies are influenced by theoretical formulations incorporating elements of both theories (Small, 1990).

Piaget's genetic epistemology   For over half a century, Jean Piaget (1896–1980) wrote extensively on cognitive development; he is considered one of the most influential theorists of our time. Yet American psychologists did not accept his beliefs until the 1960s and 1970s. Piaget lived in Switzerland, where he studied philosophy, logic, and the biological sciences. For a time he worked in Alfred Binet's laboratory in France, where he helped develop intelligence tests. One of his tasks was to question children in order to establish what children know at different ages. He became interested not so much in the answers they gave as in the reasoning they used to arrive at the answers. He found that their reasoning seemed to change depending on their age. Thus he discovered that how people understand the world changes with their development.

In 1929 Piaget began to systematically observe his own three children, keeping detailed records of their activities from birth. On the basis of his observations, he developed his theory of cognitive development.

Piaget referred to his work as *genetic epistemology*. Epistemology is the study of the nature of knowledge. Piaget argued that all knowledge comes from action and

Jean Piaget (1896–1980)

FEATURE

Lev Vygotsky

A contemporary of Piaget and Werner, Lev Vygotsky (1896–1934) emphasized sociocultural influences on development. Although he died in 1934, his ideas are enjoying increased attention today as more developmental psychologists acknowledge the importance of culture in child development (Rogoff & Morrelli, 1989).

Vygotsky believed that the child's ability to think and talk occurs within and is influenced by interactions with people. A key idea is the *zone of proximal development*, which underscores his belief that some tasks that are difficult to achieve alone can be mastered if the child is guided by an individual who is already skilled at the task. According to Vygotsky, the ZPD may be conceptualized as having a lower and upper limit. The lower limit is what the child is capable of doing alone; the upper limit is what the child can accomplish with guided instruction and practice. The goal in the interaction between the child and the "instructor" (for example, a parent, a teacher, or a skilled peer) is

to teach the upper limit of the ZPD. Say that a 3-year-old is helping his mother bake cookies. She teaches him by explaining the process as she does most of the work. He watches and she gives him small tasks that she knows he can do, such as measuring a cup of flour or mixing the dough. After several times, the mother gradually reduces her explanations and demonstrations, and the child becomes increasingly able to perform the task alone. Once achieved, this goal becomes the foundation of a new ZPD as the child learns more complicated tasks. Two important elements are necessary here: the child must be motivated to learn a skill and the instructor must recognize the child's capabilities and adjust the teaching situation accordingly.

In addition to his emphasis on sociocultural influences and his notion of the zone of proximal development, which has been applied to classroom teachings, Vygotsky wrote about the relationship between language and thought, an issue covered in Chapter 9.

that human beings actively acquire knowledge. That is, from the moment of birth, people explore the environment; through these explorations, they learn, and their views of the environment change.

Piaget revolutionized developmental psychology in large part because he asserted that children know less than adults and that their ability to reason differs according to their developmental stage. According to Piaget (1952), an underlying organization of thought, referred to as **cognitive structures,** exists in the individual and is tied to stages in intellectual development. These stages are as follows: the sensorimotor period (birth to age 2); the preoperational period (2–7 years); the concrete operations period (7–12 years); and formal operations period (12 years and over).

Piaget contended that these stages (described in Chapters 6, 9, 12, and 15, on cognitive development) emerge in a constant order of succession. Neither heredity nor the environment explains their progressive development. Rather, cognitive development is based on interaction between individual genetic potential (an inherited trait) and the experiences the child encounters (environmental factors).

Cognitive theorist Heinz Werner (1890–1964) also emphasized the interaction of the individual with the environment. The major theme of Werner's theory is the *orthogenetic principle* (Werner, 1948), which stipulates that in physical and psychological development an individual moves from a global, undifferentiated state to one of higher differentiation and integration. Werner made an analogy between the development of the embryo and psychological development, and he saw behavioral responses and skills as increasingly organized into hierarchies in a process called *hierarchic integration.*

Like Piaget, Werner believed that all children pass the same developmental milestones in the same way. He stressed that human development reveals both change and stability; that is, people go through an ordered sequence of stages characterized by different ways of understanding the environment. During each stage there is adaptive change and organizational stability. By *adaptive change*, Werner meant that with progressive development children perceive things differently and change the way they behave. By *organizational stability*, Werner meant that even though these changes occur, children retain a basic inborn organization. He noted that throughout their life people are organized and have some degree of competence; their inborn organization and competence are the basis for changes in behavior.

The information-processing approach   Information processing includes several theories of cognitive development. Although information-processing theories vary, they have numerous assumptions in common. First, the mind is seen as a system for storing and retrieving information, much like a computer. Second, individuals process information from the environment. As the information is processed, it is transformed. For example, information initially in a visual code may eventually be transformed into a verbal code. Finally, there are limitations on an individual's capacity to process information. Young children, for instance, are limited because they have an insufficient or uneven attention span or a limited memory.

As you can see in Figure 2.2, the information-processing model has several major components: environmental input, sensory registers and perceptual processes, and short- and long-term memory. Children detect information in the environment by using their sensory and perceptual processes. They store the information and later transform and retrieve it from memory. Hence, there is a constant flow

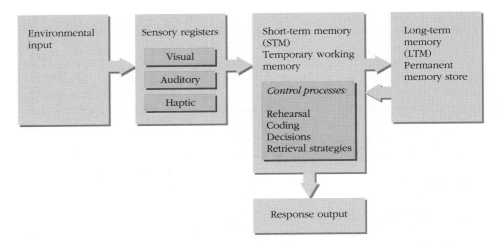

Figure 2.2 *According to the information-processing model, the human mind functions much like a computer: information (or input) from the environment is picked up by the sensory registers; it is processed and stored and can later be retrieved from short- and long-term memory.*
Source: Allen Beechel, illustration on p. 82, in R.C. Atkinson and R.M. Shiffrin, "The control of short-term memory," *Scientific American, 255,* 82–90. Copyright © 1971 by Scientific American, Inc. All rights reserved.

between sensory and perceptual processes and memory. (This simplified explanation will be fleshed out in the chapters on cognitive development.)

Sources of Ideas and Evidence

We have just introduced several major theories that have dominated developmental psychology at different times. Each one has contributed to the understanding of development, and as more knowledge was acquired, new theories evolved. Thus theories are important because they give researchers the opportunity to test their hypotheses; in this way, knowledge and understanding of child development continue to be refined. In this section we describe theories that have developed within various approaches to child development research.

The Cross-Cultural Approach

The cross-cultural approach enables researchers to apply knowledge gained about other cultures to the overall understanding of human behavior. This approach is based on studies conducted by psychologists who study children in different societies and by anthropologists who study how children learn to behave in ways that are acceptable in their culture.

American anthropologist Margaret Mead contributed a great deal to our understanding of the effects of culture on development. Her work, although discounted by some (Freeman, 1983) who regard it as idealized and somewhat inac-

Studying children from different cultures helps us understand how children learn to behave in ways that are acceptable in their particular environment.

curate, is significant because it encourages researchers to recognize that multiple considerations exist in the study of child development. Intrigued by the traditional Western view of adolescence as a time of extreme emotional stress due to the physical changes of puberty, Mead (1928) visited the island of Samoa where she found adolescence to be uneventful. She concluded that for the Samoans, "adolescence represented no period of crisis or stress but was instead an orderly developing of a set of slowly maturing interests and activities." Mead discerned that Western culture harbors many stresses that contribute to emotional difficulties during adolescence and that the physical changes of puberty alone do not account for these difficulties.

Cross-cultural studies have also verified some theories of development. For example, cross-cultural researchers (namely, Cole et al., 1971; Scribner, 1976; Rogoff, Gauvain, and Ellis, 1984) have scrutinized Piaget's theory of cognition. They want to know if children all over the world experience the same stages of cognitive growth described by Piaget and in the same sequence. This question is important, because Piaget based his theory in large part on his observations of his own children and Western European children. Although Piaget's stages of cognitive growth are universal, cross-cultural studies have shown that children progress through these stages at different rates, depending on their experiences.

These studies are also used to provide direction for research and to study other issues. For example, in studying language development, we see that initial speech progresses from one or two words to increasingly longer and more grammatically complex sentences. According to one theory, an innate process guides the way all human beings learn to speak. Another explanation is that common speech patterns result from characteristics of the native language. Using a cross-cultural approach, the researcher can examine speech patterns of children from different countries to determine whether they all make similar progress in acquiring their language. The researcher can thus determine whether an innate process is at work or whether language development reflects the characteristics of a particular language.

Using the same methods that they apply to studying distant cultures, some anthropologists are now focusing on cultures within the United States. Michael Moffat (1989), for example, studied sexuality among students in a co-ed dormitory at Rutgers University and published his findings in his book *Coming of Age in New Jersey*. Although the majority of cross-cultural studies are conducted by American scientists doing fieldwork in other countries, Nigerian anthropologist John Ogbu came to the United States to study Americans.

Studying minority-group children in the United States Ogbu and other anthropologists and developmental psychologists have begun to systematically study minority-group children in the United States.

The United States is made up of peoples of numerous cultural backgrounds. Nevertheless, researchers have only recently started to look at the context within which minority-group children develop. Historically, researchers tended to compare the behaviors and skills of minority-group children with those of white, middle-class children who constitute the majority culture. Inherent in this approach is the erroneous assumption that the practices of the majority culture are appropriate and conducive to children's development and those of the minority cultures are not (Ogbu, 1982). However, researchers now are examining aspects of the minority cultures, such as peer relations among minority-group children who live in socially segregated neighborhoods (see Chapter 16), acquisition of English as a second

The experiences of children in ethnic minority groups are now being taken into account in the study of child development.

language among Hispanic children (see Chapter 12), and the differences in cultural values between Native American children and white, middle-class children (see Chapter 13).

The Behavioral-Genetic Approach

Whereas the cross-cultural approach enhances our appreciation of external cultural and experiential factors in development, the behavioral-genetic approach focuses on individual biological characteristics in determining psychological development.

This approach examines the extent to which genes contribute to the development of behavioral traits. Recall that learning theorists, for example, believe that only the environment is at work, whereas maturational theorists believe that genetic factors predetermined development. Most psychologists now think that development and behavior are the product of the interaction between these forces; however, this interaction is very complex, so the relationship between genetic and environmental factors remains baffling (Plomin, 1989).

Some researchers note that behavior tendencies such as aggression are transmitted genetically. Although aggression *may* have a genetic link, a host of other factors related to the child, the family, and the community also influence aggression (Parke & Slaby, 1983). For example, children can learn aggression by observing the behavior of their parents or of television actors. Some children contribute to the process by arousing anger and aggression in their parents. For instance, some infants cry more than others, or sleep less, thus eliciting very different responses from their caretakers. Such infants create, in effect, different environments, thereby encountering and learning aggression. This example gives you some idea of the complexity of the interaction between genetic traits and experiential factors that results in development.

The Comparative Approach

In the comparative approach the researcher examines an aspect of human behavior in relation to similar behaviors in other species, such as monkeys or dogs. When Harry Harlow and his University of Wisconsin colleagues raised rhesus monkeys in the laboratory as orphans (Harlow, 1971, 1963), they were using the comparative approach. This research was full of surprising findings, as you will see in Chapter 7, when we discuss how these monkeys came to regard robots covered with terry cloth as the mothers they never knew and how they grew up to be cruel and abusive parents to their own offspring. The key question is, can we draw any conclusions between these studies on monkeys and children who grow up with no opportunities for interactions with adults? Many times the comparisons are only theoretical and difficult to apply to humans; however, this research does provide ideas for further child development research and possible theoretical explanations for development. For example, Harlow's work with monkeys helped researchers study the characteristics of parents and children in families where child abuse occurs (Ainsworth, 1980). In many cases abused children have difficulty relating to other people. This finding was also established with animal studies.

Ethologists contribute to our understanding of human development by studying the behavior of other species. For example, they identified a critical period, almost immediately after birth, during which newborn chicks follow the first prominent object near them, usually their mother. This photograph shows Konrad Lorenz (1903–   ) with some of the ducklings that were imprinted to him. Although a similar phenomenon has not been found among humans, researchers have investigated a possible critical period during which mothers and infants become attached.

The Ethological Approach

The ethological approach is closely related to the comparative approach, because ethologists study behavior in many species. This approach focuses on the evolutionary origins of behavior and emphasizes behaviors that occur in the natural environment. Ethologists try to identify what determines development in an individual and to find out the evolutionary influences involved.

The ethological approach provides observational methods that enhance the study of human development. It is often used in studies related to social signals, play behavior, and the mother-infant relationship. One example of this approach is research on imprinting. *Imprinting* is the process that seems to be responsible for bonding in some bird species. Almost immediately after birth, there is a critical period when newborn chicks will follow the first prominent object they see, usually their mother. This period of following results in a unique attachment to that object.

John Bowlby (1969, 1980, 1989) is famous for his application of the ethological approach to child development research. Bowlby noted that infants of different species exhibit several *species-typical behaviors* that help them stay close to their mother. Crying is an example. When infants cry, their mother attends to their needs. Such behaviors, according to Bowlby, have an evolutionary survival value; they tend to keep the mother close and thereby help avoid accidents and attacks from predators. Bowlby also described the phases of the mother-infant attachment process and the importance of attachment to later development. His ideas are supported by research on rhesus monkeys and on human infants (Ainsworth, 1973), and by case studies he conducted on hospitalized and orphaned children (Bowlby, 1969). Bowlby's research is described in more detail in Chapter 7.

The Ecological Approach

Another source of knowledge is the ecological approach, in which the organism is studied in its natural environment. The roots of the concept of ecology are in biology, specifically that branch dealing with the relations of living organisms to their surroundings, habits, and modes of life. Extending this definition to child development, the ecological approach involves the study of children in the context of their natural environment: the home, the school, and the community.

This approach is not entirely new to child development research. Some years ago Barker and Wright (1951, 1955) attempted to describe in concrete detail the conditions of life and behavior of a single boy, in *One Boy's Day*, and of all the children in a community, in *Midwest and Its Children*. Today, the ecological approach is enjoying a resurgence, in part because researchers are arguing that laboratory-based research has not produced sufficient gains in our understanding of human development (Bronfenbrenner, 1977). Studying children in their natural setting is not a simple matter, however. Researchers are now working to refine their research techniques for use in real-world circumstances. And they are suggesting that psychologists integrate findings from different types of research (such as laboratory-based, ecological, and so on) in order to understand development (Weisz, 1978).

Dimensions of Child Development Research

Research Evidence versus Personal Knowledge

Hypotheses derived from theories of development or from investigations in other disciplines are tested through research. Although in this book we rely primarily on research evidence, it is only one way to learn about and understand children. We can also understand children by observing and working with them. Through these observations and experiences, we can draw conclusions about their behavior and development. However, these conclusions cannot be generalized to all children, because each of us defines behaviors differently. For example, if you see a child take a toy from another child, you may define that behavior as assertiveness, whereas someone else may define it as aggressiveness. In other words, we cannot always agree on a particular aspect of children's behavior, and we may not be able to figure out why we disagree (Moore & Cooper, 1982).

Knowledge derived from formal research is explicit and open to examination. Every aspect of the information-gathering process in each research study should be conducted according to scientific definitions and rules and should be described in detail so that other scientists can verify whether the methods used were valid.

Types of Research

Child development research can be classified in various ways, such as on the basis of its purpose, on the ultimate use of its findings, or on the basis of its methodology. The categorization of research as applied or basic is based on its purpose or ultimate use. *Applied research* is designed to meet society's needs or provide information that could be put to immediate use (Zigler & Finn-Stevenson, in press). For example, more and more children are sent outside the home for care, and it is important to know the effect of that care on them; thus, research on day care is applied research. *Basic research*, on the other hand, is motivated by the desire to expand human knowledge and understanding of human beings and the environment.

Basic and applied research studies are not two separate, distinct categories. Although they may be somewhat different, they are at each end of the same continuum and thus overlap and contribute to each other. This reciprocity is especially evident in child development research. For example, studies on child abuse are applied because they are conducted in response to the problem of widespread child abuse in the United States. The research tries to determine why inappropriate interaction patterns develop between abusive parents and their children; thus this research is of immediate social relevance. In studying the development of attachment in families where abuse occurs, however, Ainsworth (1973) drew on Harlow's basic research work with rhesus monkeys (1961, 1963). Harlow provided evidence that rhesus monkeys will cling both to their surrogate mothers, which emit frightening noises, and to their real mothers, who physically abuse them. These findings have important implications for child abuse research and support Ainsworth's (1980) applied research findings that abused children want to be with their abusive parents.

In this example you can see how Harlow's basic research overlapped and contributed to the applied research on the social problem of child abuse. There are also numerous examples of applied research adding to our store of basic knowledge.

Methods for Research with Children

Researchers employ many different research methods, depending on the kind of information they want, the ultimate intent of their research, and their orientation.

The normative method *Normative studies* provide information about the sequence of behaviors and the "average" age when they appear. On the basis of these studies, researchers have established norms for gross motor development, fine motor development, language skills, mental development, and social and personal aspects of behavior. Normative studies focus on when and to what extent developmental processes occur. Researchers want to know when during development a behavior typically appears and how much of the behavior occurs in the population. Normative studies have shown, for example, that on the average, a baby will sit by the age of 6 months and begin walking without assistance at around 12 months. However, extensive individual differences are associated with each behavior, so it is normal for a baby to begin to walk at 9 months or at 15 months. Since normative studies only provide an average age, some children will fall below the average and others will be above the average. This qualification is especially important to point out to parents who tend to judge the behavior and progress of their children according to the established norm without realizing that individual differences exist.

The observational method   As we learned in Chapter 1, observational research techniques are not new to child development research. Today, however, as research begins to focus on children in their natural setting, interest in these techniques has revived. Using the observational method, researchers hope to acquire ecological validity.

This method requires researchers to collect information as they watch their subjects and record their behavior. Videotape recordings facilitate observation and let researchers repeatedly view the behavior under study.

The accuracy of the facts (behaviors, events) that are gathered, compiled, and analyzed is paramount. Two factors are built into the research to ensure accuracy. *Reliability* ensures objectivity and entails defining the behavior to be studied, specifying what counts and does not count, and training the observers to record all their observations accurately. *Validity* refers both to the behavior under study and to the sample of subjects under study. To be valid, the behavior must be related to the psychological processes it is said to be related to. And conclusions are valid only if the subjects are representative of the larger population. If, for instance, the subjects are a group of children, the sample must include both sexes, various ethnic groups, and other characteristics of children in the general population to whom the findings apply, or, to use the terminology of research, to whom the findings are *generalized*. The need for reliability and validity are important, no matter what method is used.

The experimental method   Experimental studies are used to answer questions about the causes of behavior. Consider an example provided by Moore and Cooper (1982) in which a researcher wanted to test the hypothesis that viewing TV shows portraying violence causes high levels of aggression in the play of 4-year-old children. To test this hypothesis, a sample of children would be randomly assigned to one of two viewing conditions: a violent TV show and a nonviolent TV show. *Random assignment* ensures the inclusion of both aggressive and nonaggressive children in the two viewing conditions. The two groups of children would then view the TV shows for perhaps two or three 15-minute segments, after which they would be observed playing. Researchers would record and compare instances of aggressive and nonaggressive play and later determine if the children who watched the violent TV show displayed more aggressive play behavior than those who watched the nonviolent show.

In designing a study like this, researchers must try to control as many aspects as possible. Thus since boys are generally more aggressive in their play than girls, researchers would ensure that the groups have equal numbers of boys. The selection of available toys and materials is also important. Both groups should have the same toys, because different toys may elicit different levels of aggressive behavior. Obviously, it is hard to establish the comparability of the groups in a natural environment. Thus experimental studies are often conducted in laboratory settings, where the researcher can control the environment. Variables under control in research studies are referred to as independent and dependent variables. The researcher selects the *independent variables* in order to study their effect on the *dependent variable,* which is the behavior under study. So in our example, the independent variable is TV violence and the dependent variable is the play behavior of 4-year-old children.

Conducting studies in laboratory settings enables the researcher to consider all existing variables. In our example we noted that care should be taken to select toys appropriately and to distribute the same toys to both groups. When researchers fail to acknowledge a variable (referred to as the *extraneous variable*) or to control it, then they cannot be absolutely sure that the independent variable caused the effects on the dependent variable. In a well-designed experimental study that minimizes the extraneous variable's influence, any change in the dependent variable may be attributed to the independent variable, and the experiment is said to have *internal validity.* However, if sources of invalidity are present—for example, if there is a possibility that the extraneous variable causes the changes in the dependent variable—then the experiment is said to be *confounded* and may not be valid.

Experiments outside the laboratory   Although experiments conducted in the laboratory are important, they are limited, especially in child development research. They are carried out in artificial settings, thus making any general statements based on the findings highly questionable. In fact, the use of laboratory research has led some critics to claim that the field of child development constitutes a "science of the strange behavior of a child in a strange situation with a strange adult" (Bronfenbrenner, 1977). To overcome these limitations, researchers often use either the field experiment or the natural experiment. In the *field experiment,* research is conducted in a natural setting, but the researcher controls the environment by deliberately introducing a change. Field experiments in child development research are conducted in nursery schools, child care centers, or schools. The advantage of a field experiment over a laboratory experiment is that the researcher still maintains control over the independent variable and the findings are more readily applied to other children because the experiment took place in a natural setting.

In some instances a change can occur in a child's life that is not due to research intervention. In these instances, referred to as *natural experiments,* the researcher may capitalize on the natural change to draw conclusions. For example, television was introduced in a Canadian town, so children who had never seen TV now began to watch it. This situation provided a naturally occurring experiment that enabled researchers to determine the effects of TV on children. By measuring the children's aggressive play behavior before and after their exposure, the researchers demonstrated that aggression increased after the introduction of television. Although the research appears more applicable to all children because children were introduced to the independent variable in their natural setting, we cannot be absolutely sure of the findings because the researchers had no control over what the children watched on television, how long they watched it, and so on.

The correlational method   In correlational studies the researcher assesses the extent to which variables appear to be related. The two most common correlational relationships are *positive* and *negative*. For example, a positive correlation exists between children's height and weight; that is, as children's height increases so does their weight. A negative correlation exists between children's age and the amount of time they spend with an adult caretaker; that is, as children's age increases, the number of hours spent with a caretaker decreases.

Correlations range from −1.00 to +1.00, with +1.00 being a perfectly positive correlation and −1.00 a perfectly negative correlation. Thus a correlation of +0.25 indicates a weak positive relationship and a correlation of −0.80 indicates a strongly negative correlation. Perfect correlations are relatively rare. Even in the instance of children's height and weight, rarely will a group of children arranged by height fall into exactly the same order if arranged by weight. Thus the correlation must be determined through statistics. A correlation is determined to be *statistically significant* if the relationship between the variables is greater than would occur by chance, even though it might not be a perfect correlation.

Also remember that correlations do not establish causes; they simply describe patterns of variations. Thus a positive correlation between height and weight does

Project Head Start began in 1965 as part of the national "war on poverty," and has since become a natural laboratory where researchers learn effective interventions.

not indicate that one variable caused the other. For example, there is a positive correlation between the number of churches and the number of crimes; that is, as the number of churches increases, so does the number of crimes. But that does not mean that one variable caused the other. A third variable, say, an increase in population, may be involved in both the increase in the number of churches and the increase in the number of crimes.

Longitudinal research Another important tool in developmental research—although a difficult one to implement—is the longitudinal study. Longitudinal research is a research perspective rather than a methodology; it may involve an experimental or a correlational study.

The major advantage is that longitudinal studies enable researchers to study changes in an individual's behavior over time, thus gaining valuable information about the stability or instability of the behavior. An example would be a study on the following question: Do children with good language skills at an early age continue to show high competence in linguistic skills as they grow older? Another advantage of longitudinal studies is their usefulness in evaluating environmental effects on development. They enable researchers to address such questions as, do different childrearing practices have long-term influences on children's behavior? What are the effects of day care on child development?

Although valuable in such research, longitudinal studies have several major disadvantages. First, they are difficult to undertake because of the large amounts of money involved. Second, they require a great deal of time to find answers to problems that often need a quick solution. A case in point is research on child care. Longitudinal studies on child care are important to establish the effects on infants and children of spending a large portion of the day away from their parents and home. Ideally, researchers would study children over several years. However, an increasing number of parents are using child care. Thus more immediate information is desperately needed on child care's effects in order to plan social policies that help families.

A third disadvantage is the difficulty of finding people willing to commit themselves or their children to long-term participation in the study. When people are willing to make such a commitment, researchers should ask whether they may be representative of the larger population or whether they are better educated, more curious, or perhaps more cooperative than most people. A fourth disadvantage is subject attrition; some subjects will invariably drop out of the study. Although attrition is a possibility in any research study, it is more of a problem in a longitudinal study simply because of the long time period involved.

The fifth disadvantage is the phenomenon of repeat testing. Because of the need to administer numerous tests and take measurements at regular intervals, subjects may become "test-wise," improving their ability to answer questions correctly. Thus, any improvement in test scores may be simply the result of practice in taking tests rather than of any change in the individual.

Finally, there is the problem of historical events. A variety of events and circumstances may take place that the researcher finds difficult or impossible to control. Changes in social values and attitudes and economic conditions are likely to affect the subjects. For example, in a longitudinal study examining the relationship between discipline techniques and later social behavior, very different effects might result from strict parental control if the study takes place during a permissive social climate rather than during a period of rigid moral values (Vasta, 1979).

Cross-sectional studies To overcome the disadvantages of the longitudinal approach, some researchers rely on *cross-sectional studies*. These studies examine developmental questions by comparing groups of subjects at different age levels rather than by following the same individual for many years (Vasta, 1979). This design produces information in less time than longitudinal studies. However, it is subject to the *cohort effect*. This effect arises when a researcher, wishing to investigate changes in behavior over time, studies a group of individuals at different ages. If differences among the individuals are observed, these differences might be a function of age. However, the subjects also differ in another important characteristic—generation. For example, subjects who are 60 years old and have lived through the Depression and World War II probably have had very different experiences and have very different values from 20-year-old participants who have not experienced economic difficulties or war. Thus cross-sectional studies do not allow for the examination of behavioral changes as they occur in one individual over time; rather, they focus on differences among individuals at the time of the study.

Researchers often use a combined longitudinal and cross-sectional approach, in which several groups of subjects of different ages are studied over several years. The research might begin with groups at ages 1, 3, and 5. An initial assessment of the dependent variables would demonstrate any developmental differences in performance in these three age levels (a cross-sectional approach). If these subjects are studied over a longer period (a longitudinal approach), several years of data would be amassed on each subject, thus permitting an in-depth examination of the individual's behavior. The result would be comparison data at different age levels. In many ways, therefore, the combined longitudinal and cross-sectional approach is an excellent tool for addressing a wide range of questions concerning development (Vasta, 1979).

Retrospective research The *retrospective approach* is also an alternative to the longitudinal study. It attempts to link an individual's current behavior with events that occurred earlier in life. A questionnaire or structured interview is used to uncover various aspects of the individual's life. The researcher examines correlations between earlier events and current behaviors and developmental problems to try to identify possible relationships (Vasta, 1979). Naturally, these hypothetical relationships can never be tested directly. But this approach can provide a basis for further research with other individuals; it also helps researchers understand determinants of behavior. For example, in attempting to discover causes of learning disabilities, researchers may examine events that occurred before or during the birth of the children in question. They may find that a significant percentage of the mothers underwent prolonged labor and difficulties during childbirth. This finding might encourage further investigation of developmental delays in infants to see how such delays affect learning and may also lead to earlier identification of learning disabilities.

Case histories A retrospective research study may involve a *case history*, which is an account of the development of a particular child. The case history was devised as a method of assessing a child in order to apply scientific principles to that child's training and care. Typically prepared for a child with psychological or other problems, the case history is a compilation of relevant facts about the child, which is used by case workers to gain a better perspective on possible problems and to find solutions. Data are obtained from as many sources as possible, including direct observation; interviews with parents, caretakers, teachers, physicians, and other adults the child interacts with; and results of psychological testing.

As a scientific method, the case history has disadvantages. It is often subjective and may include only those events the recorder regards as pertinent. Also, the subjects of case histories cannot be considered representative of a population of children as a whole, because they are likely to be children receiving or in need of psychological treatment. Nonetheless, the case history provides a rich source of data from which to draw hypotheses for further investigation.

Ethical Considerations

Any research study involving human participants is generally subject to approval by an independent review board before work can begin. The board examines the proposed procedures to ensure that they will not harm the subjects and ensures that the researcher only involves subjects who are informed of the research and willing to participate.

The difficulty in applying these standards to children is obvious. The Society for Research in Child Development established the following ethical standards for conducting research with children:

- Each child must be fully informed about the purposes of the study and the procedures to be employed.
- If the child is too young to understand the aims and purposes of the research, parental consent must be secured.
- Each child may withdraw at any time during the study.
- The child will not be subjected to any harmful treatment during the research.
- All information about individual participants obtained in the research will be kept confidential.
- No matter how young the child, he or she has rights that supersede the investigator's rights.

Today researchers employ these standards to protect children's rights, but this was not always true.

Although the review procedure is now mandated by law, an ethical course of action is not always clear. Consider an investigation of the hypothesis that premature infants may become abused children because they are difficult to soothe and may frustrate and anger their parents. Should the investigator inform the parents of the hypothesis, thus sensitizing them to the fact that there might be something wrong with their relationship to their newborn baby? Or should the investigator proceed, masking the central question of the study and thereby deceiving the parents? Will there be any long-term harm or benefits to the parents and children of pursuing either action? If you were the researcher, what would you do?

Consider another dilemma in studies examining the potential benefits of a new treatment or program. To evaluate the effectiveness of the new treatment, researchers must study some subjects who receive the treatment and others who do not, often referred to as the *control group*. If the treatment proves effective, is the researcher obliged to provide the treatment to the control group after the study is completed? Would it be fair not to?

This issue arose in a recent study that examined the effects of early intervention (Infant Health and Development Programs, 1990). The study assigned premature infants to either an experimental group or a control group. The experimental group received extensive home visitation services; during these visits, the parents received support and instruction on ways to interact with their babies. During the second and third year of the program, the experimental-group infants attended a special child care program, and their caregivers received specific training about effective ways to interact with the children and enhance their development. The control-group infants, who had not received any services, and the experimental group were tested to see if the experimental group had benefited from the intensive services provided over the three-year period. The researchers found that the experimental infants benefited from the intervention and, as a result, were more likely to lead normal, productive lives.

No doubt the experimental-group parents were grateful for the opportunity their babies had to participate in the study. But how do you think the control parents felt? Should the researchers offer them the same opportunity?

These are sensitive issues and there is no single answer. Since most researchers strive to uphold children's rights, and are required to do so by law, we may argue that, because the research potentially benefits everyone, some amount of risk may be worth the eventual progress. This argument over the costs and benefits of research is seldom easy to settle. Therefore, researchers rely on the independent review board procedure so other scientists can have input on such difficult ethical questions. Combining the judgments of several researchers may not necessarily lead to more ethical decisions. In addition, review board members are not necessarily child psychologists and may be unaware of potential psychological risks to children, depending on their age, entailed in certain studies (Thompson, 1990). At the very least, the review board procedure reminds researchers of their work's ethical implications.

The Application of Research to Practice

Research findings are useful because they enhance our understanding of children and are applicable to everyday life. However, you need to remember several issues as you reflect on the research described in this book.

Multiple causes of behavior   When a research study identifies a phenomenon as a causal factor, it is tempting to think of it as the *only* cause for the behavior being studied. However, a child's behavior and development are not that simple. Most behaviors of interest to child development professionals have multiple causes. Even though the researcher must isolate those causes in order to study each one independently, it is generally understood that causes rarely function in isolation in a child's natural environment.

Norms of behavior   Most researchers emphasize the importance of recognizing individual differences. However, most research is directed at establishing norms of behavior; that is, what is generally true for *most* children *most* of the time, or what can be expected of children at a given age, or how children may react in certain situations. Such generalizations do not necessarily apply to all children in all circumstances. This raises the question, are research studies useful? Admittedly, we usually get to know children as individuals, in which case research generalizations may not always be appropriate.

However, there are many instances when we can consider children collectively. For example, a decision on what to include in an elementary or secondary school curriculum is based on what research has found about the cognitive capabilities of children of different ages and about how children function in a group setting such as a classroom. Thus research knowledge complements our understanding of development and enhances the validity of our decisions about and for children.

The uses of research Many professionals—such as teachers, nurses, pediatricians, and child psychologists—rely on evidence from child development research.

The following chapters discuss social issues that affect children's behavior and development, such as changes in family life like divorce and factors in the social environment like television. Even government policies have an indirect effect on a child's growth and behavior. For example, government officials must decide how many children can be safely cared for by one day-care worker. They must also decide on intervention programs for handicapped children and set standards for children's health and nutrition. Such decisions, however, will not be beneficial unless they are based on the results of child development research. For example, a policymaker may make an arbitrary decision that a single child-care worker can safely care for 15 preschool children. In the physical sense one caregiver may be able to look after a group of 15 children. The policymaker may assume that in case of fire these children will be able to run out of the building. But what about the psychological ramifications of such a decision? The single, most important determinant in a child's development is interaction with adults. Can one child-care worker give sufficient attention and warmth to all 15 children? Thus this one example gives you an idea how important child development research is for government decisions.

Summary

Child development is a multifaceted field of complementary approaches. In this chapter we introduced you to the field of child development by examining its relatively brief history and the theories and research methods used to explain development.

Two principal questions concerning child development research are "How do children change as they grow and develop, and what factors influence these changes?" To develop their hypotheses to answer these questions, researchers rely on information from other disciplines and on different theories of development. These theories are based on different assumptions and focus on different aspects of development. No one theory provides an adequate explanation of development; but taken together, they help construct a picture of development and provide direction for research.

Child development researchers use various methods to confirm their hypotheses and ideas derived from theories or research in other disciplines. We described several research strategies used to convey the spirit and current status of research. We also mentioned scientific safeguards required for specific types of research to ensure useful results.

Each research method has its advantages and limitations. For this reason scientists have to rely on multiple studies and research methods. Also, studies are not planned or interpreted as isolated pieces of work. Research plans are influenced in many ways by previous studies. Researchers have to interpret their results within the framework of an ongoing program and a discipline to which many other scientists are contributing. By extending or challenging existing findings, they contribute to the advancement of knowledge.

Advancing knowledge is one purpose of child development research. Another is to apply research findings to practical situations in ways that benefit children, their parents, and other caregivers. The importance of applied research and the relevance of child development studies to present-day problems is obvious. The difficult conditions of life that most children face were described in Chapter 1. Child development research today focuses on the effect these changes will have on children's development.

II The Beginning of Life

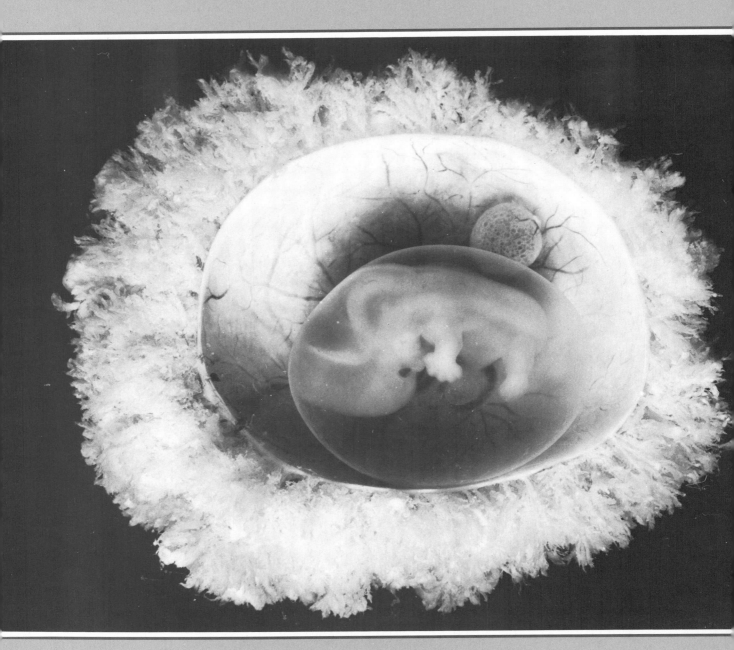

3 Our Biological Heritage

4 Prenatal Development and Birth

I n this unit we discuss a remarkable process: the beginning of human life. Because there are no breaks in nature, human development is continuous. Yet the examination of certain aspects of the prenatal period will help us understand the whole process.

One family we discuss is Arlene and Steve; they have a child with Down's syndrome. They wonder what their chances are of having another child with the same disorder and are thinking about talking to a genetic counselor. Heather and Matthew are planning the birth of their first child. They want to know if the warnings about the hazards to prenatal life are really true. They have read that smoking, for example, is harmful to the unborn baby. Yet Heather points out that her mother smoked when she was pregnant and Heather turned out fine. Does this mean that the warnings about smoking during pregnancy are unfounded?

The information these families seek is discussed in the next two chapters. In Chapter 3 we study the genetic factors controlling the process of development and the interaction between genetic and environmental factors that influences the emergence of physical and behavioral characteristics. We look at various genetic disorders and the progress that has been made in detecting and treating them. In Chapter 4 we describe the stages of prenatal development and the birth process. You will learn that external factors, such as smoking and other environmental influences, can affect normal growth processes and permanently alter the child's appearance and functioning.

3 Our Biological Heritage

Many developmental characteristics that unfold from the time children are born until they reach maturity are predictable. Infants are expected to attempt to sit up during the first few months of life, later to take their first step, and eventually to walk. Despite the predictability of development and the similarities in the way children grow and develop, each child is unique in physical appearance and in every other characteristic as well. Even children in the same family rarely look or behave exactly alike. In some families one child may have features from both parents, whereas another may resemble either the mother or the father. And then there is the child who bears no resemblance to either parent. What accounts for such variations?

Since parents transmit hereditary material to their children, why aren't all children born to the same parents exactly the same? The answer lies in the complex process by which hereditary information passes from parent to offspring through the genes. There are so many possible combinations of genes that children in the same family inevitably inherit quite different characteristics.

Genes influence the emergence and nature of every human trait from eye color to intelligence. They account for our susceptibility to many diseases and, in part, determine whether our offspring will be born with physical or mental abnormalities. Because so much of human growth and development is based on genetic heritage, an understanding of genetics is an integral aspect of child development study. Some researchers believe that understanding genetic factors in development is the key to understanding how individual variation develops (Scarr-Salapatek, 1975; Plomin, 1989). In this chapter, then, we present the mechanisms that enable hereditary transmission and see how problems can occur in the process. Although a vast amount of physical growth and development, and some aspects of psychological development, are mapped out in a child's unique genetic makeup, environmental factors before and after birth also play an important role. However, neither heredity nor environment alone determines development. Rather, human development is the result of complex transactions between genetic and environmental factors. Now let's examine several concepts that help explain the relationship between genetic and environmental factors as they interact to influence development.

Gene/Environment Transactions

Each individual's development is the process by which a genotype is expressed as a phenotype (Scarr-Salapatek, 1975). A **genotype** is the individual's genetic makeup, the pattern of genes that makes each individual unique. A **phenotype** is the individual's observable or measurable characteristic. A given genotype, that which the individual inherits, can give rise to many different phenotypes, or observable characteristics. Some genes, such as those for hair texture or eye color, are directly expressed as phenotypes. But some characteristics, such as intelligence or personality traits, are influenced by the genes and subject to environmental influence as well. Thus, depending on the environment, different phenotypes can develop from the same genotype. This can happen because the genotype does not fix development; it sets limits, or boundaries, within which an individual's abilities can vary. These boundaries may be viewed as the individual's potential; whether the individual realizes that potential depends on environmental circumstances and how the person responds to them (Plomin & Daniels, 1987). Researchers call this the **range**

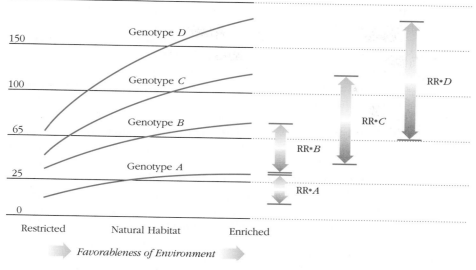

Mean Phenotypic IQ

Favorableness of Environment

Figure 3.1 *The intellectual reaction ranges of several genotypes in favorable and unfavorable environments. RR indicates the reaction range of phenotypic IQ. Genotype A is not part of the normal reaction range.*
Source: Irving I. Gottesman, 1963, in Norman R. Ellis (Ed.), *The Handbook of Mental Deficiency: Psychological Theory and Research*, New York: McGraw-Hill.

of reaction; that is, the individual's genotype establishes a range within which he or she will realize the potential for certain characteristics.

Children vary in the way they respond to conditions in the environment and to different life experiences. For example, if four children with genotypes *A, B, C,* and *D* are put in either an unstimulating, restrictive environment or in a stimulating environment, under a similar condition (the stimulating environment), a child with genotype *D* will always perform better on intellectual tasks than children with genotypes *C, B,* and *A* (see Figure 3.1). This is because child *D* has the widest range of reaction for intelligence among the four children. Child *A,* on the other hand, has the most limited range of reaction and thus scores below average in intelligence, regardless of the environment. Even in the most favorable and stimulating environment, child *A* will not perform well on intellectual tasks. The same may be true of other traits and abilities. For instance, a child may try desperately to excel in music, and her parents may spend an enormous amount of money on music lessons, but if she has not inherited the genes or set of genes that enable her to excel musically, no amount of practice and training will make her a musical prodigy.

Thus it may appear that the genotype simply sets the limits on the development of a characteristic, while the environment determines the extent to which the characteristic will develop to its full potential. The developmental process is more complex, however; it entails a constant transaction between genetic and environmental factors (Plomin, DeFries, & Fulker, 1988). Consider, for example, irritability as a trait. Some infants are apparently born genetically predisposed to being irritable and are often referred to as "difficult" babies. If a difficult baby has parents who also tend to be irritable, their presence may foster that trait in the baby. However, if the baby's parents are calm, the extent to which the baby's irritability is expressed will be reduced (Scarr & McCartney, 1983). The environment, in this case the baby's parents, influences the extent to which the genotype may be expressed. However, genes are not always passive; they can also influence the environment. Let us consider an extremely irritable baby born to relatively calm parents. Such a baby would be difficult to soothe and may continually cry to the point where his parents are so tired and frustrated that they become abusive. Here the baby's genetic predisposition contributed to his environmental experiences, namely, the way his parents reacted to him. This notion of complex gene/environment transaction is referred to as the *transactional model of development* (Sameroff & Chandler, 1975; Scarr & McCartney, 1983).

In addition, the extent to which an individual's genotype is expressed in the phenotype depends on the timing of environmental influences. This is known as a **critical period;** that is, different environmental factors or experiences at different points during development can have differing effects on development (Gottlieb, 1976). You will see in Chapter 4, for example, that during certain periods of pregnancy, the fetus is especially vulnerable to such environmental factors as drugs ingested by the mother, resulting in the birth of a baby with physical or behavioral abnormalities.

Canalization

Although some genetic factors are subject to environmental influence, others follow a prescribed genetic course; thus their expression in behavior is not likely to differ much on the basis of environmental differences. In other words, some behaviors are inevitable, regardless of environmental influence. The term **canalization** (or **preparedness**) describes such behaviors.

A highly canalized characteristic is difficult to modify; however, less canalized characteristics can be modified and are vulnerable to environmental influence. For example, walking, like talking, is a highly canalized behavior since all normal infants learn to walk. Although certain personality and mental characteristics may also be inherited, they are less highly canalized because they are subject to the child's environmental conditions.

A behavior is said to be canalized if it is easily learned:

> What is inherited is ease of learning rather than fixed instinctive patterns. The species early, almost intuitively, learns the essential behaviors for its survival. . . . Human beings *learn* to talk, but they *inherit* structures that make this inevitable, except under the most peculiar circumstances. (Washburn & Hamburg, 1965)

The genetic endowment a child is born with should be viewed as his or her potential. The extent to which this genetic potential will be realized depends on environmental experiences and a complex transaction between genetic and environmental factors. Thus both a sound genetic makeup and a favorable environment are necessary for healthy development. Both factors affect the individual in so many ways that it is impossible to estimate which one has the greater influence (Lewontin, 1982; Plomin, 1989). Now let's examine how genetic information is transmitted from parent to child.

Transmission of Genetic Information

Mendel's work   Our understanding of how genetic information is transmitted has been facilitated by the work of an Austrian monk, Gregor Mendel (1822–1884), called the "father of modern genetics." During Mendel's time, scientists attempted to understand the process of inheritance by studying complex animal species. Inheritance was thought of as the blending of a fluid, possibly blood, which the parents passed to the child. Even today this idea persists among some people who have no knowledge of genetics; the expression *blood relative* is rooted in this premise.

Mendel chose to study the simple traits of the garden pea plant and obtained significant results. He demonstrated that in hereditary transmission no mixing or blending of blood or any other fluid occurs; instead, hereditary material is attached to an entity, later referred to as the **gene.**

Homozygotes and heterozygotes   From principles derived from Mendel's work, known as Mendel's laws of inheritance, we have learned that for any given gene there are two **alleles,** or alternative forms of the gene. A child receives one allele from the mother and one from the father. If both alleles give the same hereditary direction for the determination of a trait, the child is said to be **homozygous** for that trait. If the alleles are different, the child is said to be **heterozygous** for that trait. Alleles do not blend; rather, they behave in a pattern of **dominance** and **recessiveness.** In a heterozygous condition, one allele will dominate the other. The dominant allele determines the phenotype, or observable characteristic associated with a particular trait. The recessive allele, which is present but not observable, may reappear in successive generations. The dominant allele is usually symbolized by a capital letter, say, *H,* whereas the recessive allele is symbolized by a lowercase letter, in this case *h.* The homozygous child for that trait will be *HH* or *hh,* whereas the heterozygous child will be *Hh.*

Let us assume that *H* is the dominant allele for hair texture and signifies curly hair and that *h* signifies straight hair. A child who inherits two dominant alleles will thus be *HH;* that is, she will have curly hair. A child who inherits a dominant allele from one parent and a recessive allele from the other will be *Hh.* But, since curly hair *(H)* is the dominant trait, she will also have curly hair. In the case of a child who has either one or both parents with curly hair, the hereditary transmission of the trait appears obvious. However, two curly-haired parents may have a child with straight hair. Is something other than heredity at work here? Not at all. In this case both parents are heterozygous for hair texture, or *Hh;* thus their phenotypes are curly hair since it is the dominant allele. However, each of them contributed a recessive allele *h* for straight hair to their child, who was born homozygous, or *hh,* for that particular trait. Since a number of combinations of alleles are possible, even siblings do not always share the same characteristics.

Applying Mendel's laws   Mendel's laws of inheritance have also helped scientists understand how certain abnormal conditions and diseases are passed from parent to offspring. Let us look at how a condition known as **albinism** is passed through the genes. The albino individual is born with almost white hair, no skin pigmentation, and pink retinas. For our example, let us use *A* to represent the allele for normal skin pigmentation and *a* to represent the allele for albinism. Albinism is caused by a *recessive allele.* An albino child would be *aa.* The parents of an albino

Gregor Mendel is often called the father of modern genetics.

child may also be albino *aa,* or they may be heterozygous *Aa* for albinism, meaning that they have a normal skin pigmentation but are carriers of the recessive allele for albinism. Thus each parent passed a recessive allele to the child. However, because each parent has one dominant allele for skin pigmentation, their phenotype is normal skin pigmentation (see Figure 3.2). If both parents carry a recessive gene for albinism, they have 1 chance in 4 of having an albino child. There is also a chance that two of their children will carry the recessive gene. However, if two albino adults (both would have to be *aa*) have children, all their children will be albinos, since the only possible allele the children can receive from either parent is *a.*

Many other disorders, some life-threatening, are passed on to children by parents who each have the recessive allele. **Phenylketonuria (PKU)** is caused by a recessive gene *p,* which leads to the absence of a certain enzyme needed to convert the protein phenylalanine, found in milk, into tyrosine. Since milk is the basic diet of infants, phenylpyruvic acid accumulates in the PKU infant's body, causing damage to the central nervous system and resulting in mental retardation. Infants with phenylketonuria appear normal at birth, but with the gradual buildup of the acid, they become mentally retarded.

Approximately 1 out of 20 individuals carries the recessive allele for phenylketonuria. Fortunately, hospitals in the United States are required to routinely check newborns for PKU. Once detected, PKU infants can begin dietary therapy to prevent the damaging effects of the disease. The PKU test—a simple heel prick in which a few drops of blood are drawn for analysis—is usually conducted twice, during the first and sixth weeks after birth, to ensure accurate results.

Our ability to prevent the mental retardation associated with PKU demonstrates the importance of environmental factors in gene expression. If PKU is detected shortly after birth, a PKU infant can be given a special diet that will prevent the accumulation of toxic substances hindering the normal development of cells in the central nervous system. Time is of critical importance. Placing an affected PKU child on a proper diet will be of no use once brain damage occurs; hence, the need for early detection. A PKU infant who receives a proper diet at the crucial period may appear no different from a person having the normal allele. The child must stay on a restricted diet for several years. Initially, PKU children resumed a normal diet at age 5 or 6, when brain development was complete. However, new studies suggest that they should remain on a restricted diet until adolescence to prevent loss of IQ and cognitive skills sometimes seen among children who were taken off the diet too early (Berry et al., 1990).

The infant diagnosed and treated for PKU will lead a normal life. However, although an environmental factor (dietary therapy) has prevented full expression of the genotype, the environment has not altered the individual's genes. That is, the infant's genotype remains homozygous *(pp)* for the recessive gene even though the infant has escaped the dire effects of the disease. This individual is referred to as a **phenocopy,** one whose phenotype (gene expression) has been environmentally altered so that it mimics the phenotype usually associated with another specific genotype. A phenocopy individual may appear normal and function normally but could still transmit the defective recessive gene to an offspring.

There is also a reverse side to the phenocopy phenomenon. Using our PKU example, a woman with PKU who has escaped brain damage because of early detection and treatment is likely, if she marries a person with the dominant allele in a homozygous condition *(PP),* to have a child who also has the dominant trait, although in a heterozygous condition *(Pp).* This child will not have PKU. However, one side effect of the PKU will remain; when the PKU woman is pregnant, she will have a high concentration of toxic substances in her uterus. This is because even though she has been treated for PKU, she still has an abnormal metabolism. These

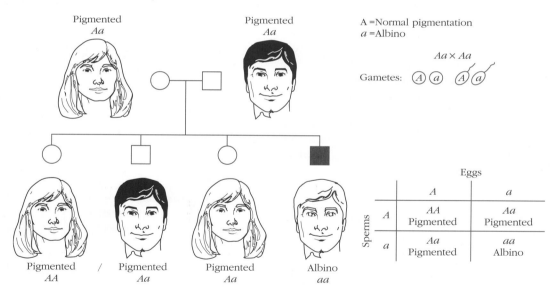

Figure 3.2 *Monohybrid cross in the human. A common form of albinism is inherited as a simple Mendelian recessive. At left is a representation of a simple mating and pedigree in which the parents are both heterozygotes. At right is a Punnett square illustrating the same cross. In such a cross the chance is 3 to 1 for a normal offspring at any one birth. By no means does the figure mean that one out of four offspring must be albino in such a family.*

Source: Norman V. Rothwell, *Human Genetics,* © 1977, p. 16. Reprinted by permission of Prentice-Hall, Inc., Englewood Cliffs, New Jersey.

toxic substances will not harm her, but they will cause brain damage in her unborn child. Although not genetically programmed to suffer from PKU, this child will still suffer mental retardation (Lenke & Levy, 1980).

Such damage can be prevented if the phenocopy woman is treated before conception and throughout pregnancy (Lenke & Levy, 1982). However, some PKU individuals who have been treated as children may not know that their future offspring will be at risk for brain damage. Physicians are now searching for women who have been diagnosed and treated for this condition since 1961 (when the PKU screening test was first developed). With a concerted educational campaign, they can be alerted to their need for treatment before they conceive (Brody, 1990). Treatment must begin before conception, because the potential damage to the fetus occurs before a woman even knows she is pregnant.

The example of the PKU phenocopy demonstrates the complex relationship between heredity and the environment. There are many other such examples; rarely is either heredity or the environment the sole determining factor in the expression of a trait or a characteristic. In an increasing number of cases, children with hereditary defects and their parents can be spared a great deal of suffering if their environment is altered in time to prevent the expression of the defective gene. However, there is still no treatment for some conditions, such as albinism.

Complex Gene Activity

Not all gene activity follows the simple, straightforward Mendelian model of inheritance. Although human beings acquire many traits and diseases through this classic single-gene heredity pattern, in most cases transmission of hereditary information

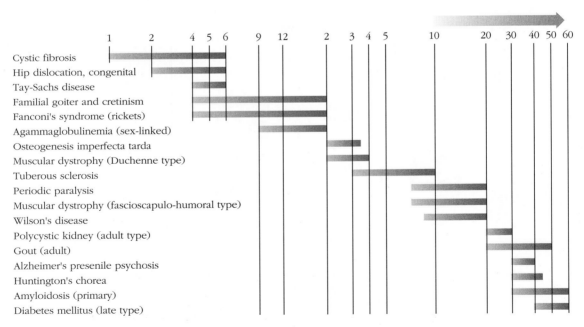

Figure 3.3 *Age ranges of genetic abnormalities.*

Source: Aposhian, V., "The use of DNA for gene therapy—The need, experimental approach, and implications," in *Perspectives in Biology and Medicine,* Vol. 14, No. 1, Autumn 1970, p. 100, fig. 2 © 1970 by University of Chicago Press. All rights reserved.

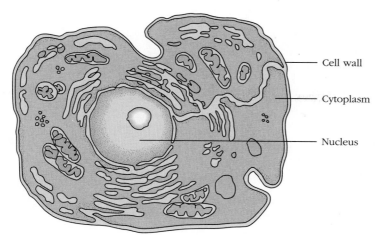

Cell wall

Cytoplasm

Nucleus

Figure 3.4 *The basic parts of a human cell.*

follows a multifactorial model of inheritance. This model is characterized by complex gene activity involving the action of many genes in the transmission of a trait, the influence of some genes over others, and the influence of environmental factors (Novitski, 1977; Scarr & McCartney, 1983).

When a number of genes act together to transmit a trait, the phenomenon is known as **polygenetic inheritance** (*poly* means "many"). One gene is insufficient to produce the trait in question; but acting in concert, the genes give the individual a predisposition toward the trait. When activated by certain environmental conditions, the predisposition then appears as an inherited trait. In yet another phenomenon called **pleiotropy,** a single gene can influence more than one trait.

Some genes, known as **modifier genes,** influence the actions or observable characteristics of other genes. For example, children with phenylketonuria have differing levels of phenylalanine, even though they have identical genes for phenylketonuria. This is because modifier genes determine variations in the amounts of phenylalanine produced. You can see how complicated gene activity can be. Furthermore, the effects of many genes do not appear until later in life, as is the case with baldness and certain genetically inherited diseases such as Huntington's disease (see Figure 3.3).

Genes and Chromosomes

The chemical nature of genes   So far we have been considering the basic principles involved in hereditary transmission. Now we are going to examine more specifically the chemical nature of genes and their relationship to cells in the human body. The human body is made up of billions of **cells,** which are packets of life substances. Most cells have specialized functions: brain cells for intelligence and memory, heart cells for rhythmic contraction, and so on. Despite their specialized functions, all cells have similar, basic component parts (see Figure 3.4): an outer membrane known as the **cell wall,** which contains fluid called the **cytoplasm,** and a special compact structure known as the **nucleus.** The nucleus, which floats in the center of each cell, contains the genes and other structures directing the manufacture and traffic of substances within the cell.

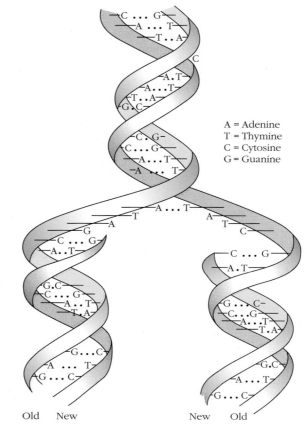

A = Adenine
T = Thymine
C = Cytosine
G = Guanine

Old   New   New   Old

Figure 3.5 *Replication of DNA.*

There are several types of genes; each type has a different function. For example, **structural genes** guide the manufacture of material (protein) that goes into the cell's structural organization. **Operator genes** turn protein synthesis on and off in nearby structural genes. **Regulator genes** produce molecules that tell all genes when to turn on and off. Individual differences are largely due to the regulatory genes, which modify the genes' basic biochemical processes (Novitski, 1977). The cell's genetic material is the basis for an amazingly complex, self-regulating system that produces effects in the body, interprets feedback, and reacts with new effects. This process continues throughout the life cycle of the organism. When even one gene is defective, the child will be affected with physical or developmental deviations associated with that gene.

The genes are found within the nucleus on long, tiny fibers called **chromatin.** When a cell is preparing to divide into two cells, the chromatin fibers contract into short, tightly coiled threads. If we stain this cell in a laboratory procedure, the threads will become highly visible under a microscope; hence, their name **chromosome** from the Greek words *chromo,* meaning "color" and *soma,* meaning "body."

As recently as 1956, scientists thought that human beings, like chimpanzees, had 48 chromosomes in each cell. Because of improvements in staining techniques, the number of chromosomes in a normal human cell is now established at 46. Each chromosome holds hundreds of thousands of genes; and each gene has a specific place, called the **gene locus,** where it appears on every chromosome of that type. Thus if we look at another cell containing a duplicate chromosome, we would find the same genes on the same loci. Every chromosome will have different gene loci, bearing genes that influence a different set of traits.

DNA The most important component of the chromosome is **DNA,** or **deoxyribonucleic acid,** which controls the biological inheritance of all living things. Often referred to as the alphabet of life, DNA contains a genetic code that directs the operational functioning of **RNA,** or **ribonucleic acid.** The RNA brings the instructions from DNA in the cell's nucleus to its cytoplasm, where the instructions are carried out. These instructions govern the organism's development. Since our bodies are made of protein, the DNA contains instructions for a specific type of protein chain.

The organism grows and develops as cells duplicate themselves. Let us see what happens to DNA during the process. DNA consists of a pair of intertwined coils of indefinite length composed of sugar phosphate molecules. The two chains are linked together by chemical bonds that come off one of four bases: **adenine, thymine, cytosine,** or **guanine.** These bonds may be arranged in any order along one or two coils, but the guanine can only link with cytosine, and adenine can only link with thymine (see Figure 3.5). Thus the sequence on one chain determines the sequence on the other.

These four bases are units of information—the letters of the alphabet, if you will—that direct the synthesis of proteins that are vital to the cell's metabolism and development. Each protein consists of a specific combination of amino acids arranged in a particular order. Three letters in a code—that is, a series of three bases—spell a single amino acid. A series of such three-letter codes, arranged in a specific order on part of the DNA coil, makes up a sentence that translates into a complete protein or a complete chain of a multiple protein. A section of code is what we call a gene. A gene segment of DNA is shown in Figure 3.6. Thus genetic information is coded by the ordering, or arrangement, of the chemical steps at different locations on the chromosome. The particular order of these steps gives each gene its special character.

The Beginning of Life and Cell Division

Life begins when a sperm cell from the father penetrates and fuses with the **ovum** cell (the egg) from the mother. Once penetration occurs, the now-fertilized ovum is known as the **zygote.** From the moment of fertilization, the zygote's cells rapidly multiply by cell division and eventually develop into the embryo, then the fetus, and, at birth, the child.

The sperm and ovum cells are different from other cells in the body. They are known as **germ cells** or **gametes** or, because of their function, as reproductive cells. All other cells, called **somatic** or **body cells,** make up the muscles, the bones, and the various systems of the body. These two types of cells differ in the number of chromosomes they contain and in the process by which they divide. Gametes have 23 chromosomes each. Somatic cells have 23 *pairs* of chromosomes, or 46 chromosomes.

Somatic cells divide by *mitosis,* in which each chromosome in the nucleus duplicates itself. The resulting two sets of 46 chromosomes move to opposite sides of the cell. The cell separates, and two new cells are formed (see Figure 3.7). In the process of human development, the somatic cells form by mitosis; each cell contains 46 chromosomes identical to those found in the zygote. The zygote has a complete set of chromosomes, because both the egg and the sperm that formed it contained exactly half as many chromosomes as the somatic cells. Their joining gave the zygote 46 chromosomes.

The egg and sperm developed only half the number of chromosomes through a process known as **meiosis.** Meiosis is slightly different in sperm cells than in egg cells; however, for illustration purposes, we use the production of sperm cells. The premeiotic sperm cell has 46 chromosomes, as do somatic cells. These chromosomes duplicate themselves as the cell divides once, producing two new cells; both cells divide, producing four cells in all. Each cell will become a mature sperm cell.

After the first division, the new cells divide again, but this time the chromosomes do not duplicate themselves. Instead, as the nucleus in each cell divides, each *part* of the chromosome pair migrates to opposite sides of the dividing nucleus. When cell division is complete, four cells stand where there was only one cell, and each cell contains 23 *single* chromosomes (see Figure 3.8.).

Meiosis is the same in the female, but the final result is one egg. Since three of the egg cells are stunted and have very little cytoplasm, they do not survive. The surviving egg, however, retains a great deal of cytoplasm, making it one of the largest cells in the human body.

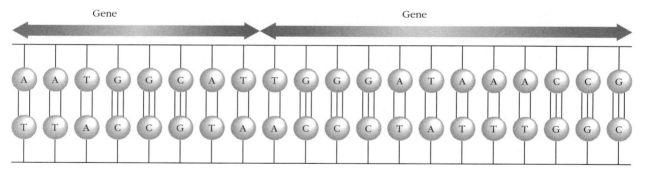

Figure 3.6 *A gene segment of DNA. While the DNA exists in the form of a double helix, it is basically a linear molecule. When viewed as "untwisted," one nucleotide pair follows another in a linear order. A gene is a segment of a DNA molecule, and the difference between any two genes resides in the sequence of the base pairs contained in each. There is no set way in which the base pairs must occur in a gene. This fact makes possible an endless variety of genes that may be of different lengths. This figure is greatly simplified; in actuality, no gene would be composed of so few nucleotide pairs.*
Source: From Norman V. Rothwell, *Human Genetics,* © 1977, p. 214. Reprinted by permission of Prentice-Hall, Inc. Englewood Cliffs, New Jersey.

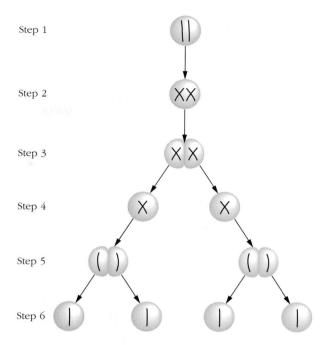

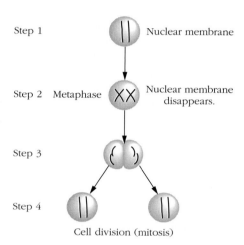

Cell division (mitosis)

Step 1:   Shows the single cell with the pair of chromosomes we are following.
Step 2:   The chromosomes split longitudinally, making a total of two pairs.
Step 3:   The chromosome pairs separate; the cell nucleus and the cell itself begin to divide.
Step 4:   One chromosome member of each pair is now found in a new cell. We note that there are two cells from the original single cell. This whole process of cell division continues an infinite number of times to constitute finally all the cells in the human body.

Figure 3.7 *Cell division by mitosis.*

Source: From p. 19 of *Know Your Genes* by Aubrey Milunsky, M.D. Copyright © 1977 by Aubrey Milunsky, M.D. Reprinted by permission of Houghton Mifflin Company. All rights reserved.

Step 1:   Shows one cell with a pair of chromosomes.
Step 2:   The chromosomes split longitudinally and begin to pair off.
Step 3:   The cell nucleus begins to divide.
Step 4:   The cell nucleus (and the cell that it occupies) has divided into two new nuclei, each containing a pair of chromosomes.
Step 5:   The two chromosomes in each new nucleus now begin to move apart as the cell and its nucleus divide.
Step 6:   A new cell and nucleus are formed, each with only one chromosome from the preceding cell. We can see that, from the original cell with a pair of chromosomes, there are four cells each with a single chromosome. These are the sperm cells (or eggs, if in the ovary) and they obviously contain 23 chromosomes, which is half of the original number. When a sperm with 23 chromosomes and an egg with 23 chromosomes meet in fertilization, a single cell is constituted with 46 chromosomes. We have therefore received half our chromosomes (and therefore genes) from our father and half from our mother.

Figure 3.8 *Cell division by meiosis.*

Source: From p. 18 of *Know Your Genes* by Aubrey Milunsky, M.D. Copyright © 1977 by Aubrey Milunsky, M.D. Reprinted by permission of Houghton Mifflin Company. All rights reserved.

Genetic Variability

During the first meiotic division, each pair of chromosomes lines up lengthwise, so they resemble parallel pairs. While the pairs are lined up, some sections of each chromosome may break away and attach themselves to adjacent chromosomes. This phenomenon, known as **crossing over,** is essentially a reshuffling of the genes. The chromosomes are altered because genes are exchanged between pairs of chromosomes, and the characteristics of these genes are now carried on different chromosomes. This random reshuffling, which is generally regarded as an important factor in genetic variability, can occur any time a sperm or egg cell is produced. Stern (1975) estimates that if a man produces 1 trillion sperm cells in his lifetime, this number represents about one sixty-million-trillion-trillionth of the total number of possible combinations of genes in a cell containing 23 chromosome pairs! And you wonder why you are so different from your brothers and sisters!

Sex Chromosomes

Each cell nucleus contains 22 chromosomes from the sperm and 22 chromosomes from the ovum known as **autosomes.** Both males and females have autosomes, and each pair of autosomes determines the same trait. But the 23rd chromosome differs in the sperm and the ovum. In the sperm, or in males, the 23rd chromosome is XY; in the ovum, or in females, the 23rd chromosome is XX. An X chromosome is five times as long as a Y and therefore carries more genes. According to recent research, just one gene or a few genes on the Y chromosome actually determine that the fetus will be a male; this particular gene or genes are triggered during the seventh week of pregnancy when sexual differentiation occurs (Page et al., 1990).

The mother is XX, so the 23rd chromosome she contributes to the offspring is always X. However, the father can contribute either X or Y; thus the zygote has a chance of being XY or XX—that is, male or female. So the father determines the child's sex. Because the father can contribute an X or Y, we may assume that for each conception, there is an equal chance of having a boy or a girl. Yet in fact slightly fewer girls are born (for every 106 boys, 100 girls are born) (Lerner & Libby, 1976). More males are actually conceived, but the male embryo is more vulnerable, so more males are miscarried (Lips, 1988).

Because some genes on the X chromosome have no equivalent genes on the shorter Y chromosome, sex-linked (or X-linked) recessive disorders can occur. Males have only one X chromosome; therefore, if the recessive allele for a particular defect is present, the sex-linked defect will always appear because there is no equivalent allele on the Y chromosome to counteract its effect. In females, however, the defect will be expressed only if the matching allele on the other X chromosome is also defective.

Sex-linked recessive disorders follow a pattern of transmission that makes them skip generations before they recur. One classic example of a sex-linked recessive disease is **hemophilia,** often referred to as the "bleeding disease." Hemophiliacs lack the factor necessary for blood clotting and thus bleed excessively, either spontaneously or from cuts and bruises. This disease appears to skip generations because a female who inherits the recessive gene from either her mother or father usually has a dominant allele on her X chromosome that counteracts the effects of the defective gene. Thus she becomes a carrier, but her health is not impaired. When she bears children, however, she is likely to pass the defective gene on to some of her sons and daughters. Daughters who receive the defective gene will probably be unaffected carriers as well. But any son who inherits the gene will definitely have hemophilia, because his Y chromosome does not contain a locus for that gene, and its action therefore cannot be counteracted. A father with hemophilia will not pass the defective gene to his son, since the son will only receive the Y chromosome. But all his daughters are likely to be unaffected carriers and will pass the defective gene on to their children. As a result, the man's grandson will be a hemophiliac. There is only a remote chance that the man's daughters will receive the recessive gene from him and from the mother and thus be homozygous for that gene and affected by hemophilia.

Sex chromosome abnormalities   Sex chromosome abnormalities can be identified using a pictorial arrangement known as a **karyotype.** In this process the chromosomes are photographed, the pictures are enlarged, and then the chromosomes are cut out and arranged into pairs according to length. A quick glance at the karyotype enables geneticists to detect such abnormalities as missing, broken, or additional chromosomes and to identify many genetic diseases.

Chromosomes photographed in their original positions (right), and arranged according to size and shape on a standard karyotype (left).

Ordinarily, the formation of sperm and ovum cells is a smooth process; the genes are properly segregated and distributed on the chromosomes. However, on rare occasions, cells form that do not have a normal number of sex chromosomes. That is, there may be no sex chromosome or an extra one. When an abnormal cell joins with a normal cell or with an abnormal cell, the resulting zygote will either have too few or too many sex chromosomes. A child born as a result of this union will have certain atypical physical and mental characteristics.

One such abnormality is the absence of the sex chromosome X (XO instead of XX), known as **Turner's syndrome.** Women having Turner's syndrome are intellectually normal but have several physical abnormalities. They remain short in stature and often have short fingers and unusually shaped mouths and ears. In addition, because their bodies do not produce female hormones, they are sterile and have incompletely developed breasts. However, estrogen treatments can help these women look more normal.

Sex chromosome abnormalities also occur in males. An example is **Klinefelter's syndrome,** in which the afflicted male has an extra X chromosome. These XXY men are sterile, of excessive height, and may have female characteristics such as developed breasts. In yet another sex chromosome abnormality, some men have an extra Y chromosome, so they are XYY. They, too, are sterile and tend to be tall.

In addition to the physical abnormalities of XXY and XYY males, some research indicates that they tend to have psychosocial problems: they are often impulsive, even violent, and are likely to be in mental institutions or in prison (Jacobs, 1968; Hook, 1973). These findings are controversial, however; some researchers note that the prevalence of XXY and XYY males among criminals is no higher than in the general population (Baroankar & Shah, 1974; Witkin et al., 1976). Other researchers note that although children with sex chromosome abnormalities are at risk for psychosocial problems, a supportive family environment can minimize the abnormality's negative effects. This conclusion is the result of a study of a group of 46 infants with sex chromosome abnormalities (including XXY and XYY) and a control group of normal infants (Bender, Linden, & Robinson, 1987). The researchers followed the children in both groups annually through early adolescence. A relatively high percentage of the abnormal infants living in dysfunctional families exhibited psychosocial problems, but this was not the case among the normal children reared in dysfunctional families. In contrast, the abnormal children reared in nurturant and supportive families did not differ significantly in psychosocial functioning from the control children. Thus, although children born with sex chromosome abnormalities are at risk for being unable to function within a social setting, a supportive family can be a protective factor that enables them to lead relatively normal lives.

Another sex chromosome abnormality is the *Fragile X syndrome*. Here, the X chromosome is constricted and often breaks. It is found among boys more often than girls (perhaps because the second X chromosome in girls negates the disorder's damaging effects). The majority of children born with this disorder suffer from mental retardation and a variety of behavior problems (Largo & Schinzel, 1985).

Mutations   Genetic variability can also result from **mutations** (changes in a gene) in the arrangements of the genes or in the quantity of chromosomal material. **Somatic mutations** affect body cells after cell division has begun; **germinal mutations** affect the gametes. As a result of germinal mutation, a child may have an allele that neither of his parents carried. A newborn child stands a chance of 1 in 25 of carrying a mutation not passed on by either parent. In this case the departure from the normal is genetic in that hereditary material is associated with the change but is not necessarily inherited. Although the abnormality may arise in a parent's gamete and be transmitted to the offspring, it often goes no further.

A large number of the mutations present in a population will be recessive with lethal effects on the developing embryo and fetus. If mutations do not result in death before or at birth, they may cause the child's early death or gross maldevelopment. Scientists do not entirely understand why mutations occur but note that some are due to **mutant genes.** These genes increase the rate of mutations in individuals who carry them. In addition, environmental factors such as high temperatures, chemicals, and radiation can lead to gene mutation. Radiation, for example, can occur naturally or can result from human action as in X rays, nuclear accidents, or atomic fallout. Exposure to radiation during pregnancy is associated with high rates of abnormalities, including mental retardation and leukemia (Milunsky, 1977).

Down's syndrome   An example of a mutation involving chromosome anomalies is **Down's syndrome,** which occurs in approximately 1 out of 500 births and involves abnormalities related to chromosome 21. Arlene and Steve's firstborn has Down's syndrome and, like other children with the condition, he has some associated physical characteristics: a folding of the skin of the upper eyelid, flattened face, small ears, and small stature. He can see well, but some Down's syndrome children suffer an assortment of abnormalities affecting vision and such internal organs as the heart, lungs, and thyroid and many have varying levels of mental retardation.

Arlene and Steve had never suspected that they would have a Down's syndrome child. After Joey was born, they found out that recent research on chromosome 21 has shown that its genes are linked not only to Down's syndrome, but also

Down's syndrome varies in severity. Some children are able to learn and lead productive lives.

to a susceptibility among normal individuals to cancer, Alzheimer's disease, congenital heart defects, and vision problems (Kolata, 1989).

The relationship of Down's syndrome to a deviation in the 21st chromosome was discovered in 1959. This was the first time that a specific chromosome was linked to a disease. Since this discovery, research has established that Down's syndrome individuals may have one of their 21st chromosomes translocated to another chromosome. In **translocation** part of the chromosome attaches itself to another chromosome, usually number 13, 14, 15, or 22. Although the 46 chromosomes are present, they are not arranged in the correct order. **Nondisjunction** of a chromosome occurs in other cases of Down's syndrome; as a result, the individuals will have an extra chromosome, or part of another chromosome, on chromosome 21. Researchers speculate that the chromosomes may have failed to separate during meiosis in the egg, so the individual has 47 instead of the normal 46 chromosomes.

The incidence of Down's syndrome is related to maternal age; the older the mother at the time of conception, the greater the risk of having a Down's syndrome child. The incidence of Down's syndrome rises from 1 in 3000 for mothers in their twenties to 1 in 280 for mothers aged 35 to 40, to 1 in 40 for mothers aged 40 to 45. At birth, the human female carries all the potential egg cells she will ever produce. These cells are vulnerable to such environmental agents as viruses, radiation, and chemicals that can damage the chromosomes or interfere with the process of meiosis. The older a fertile woman is, therefore, the more time such environmental factors have had to operate to the detriment of the cells. The incidence of other anomalies—for example, the XXY Klinefelter's anomaly—is also known to increase with maternal age (Novitski, 1977). However, Down's syndrome can occur among younger mothers as well. In fact, Arlene was 25 when she gave birth to Joey.

The gene advantage and natural selection   All forms of life change during the process of **evolution.** When we say humanity has evolved, we mean that the human species has changed over time. Evolution is a constant process of natural selection; organisms that survive have genetic characteristics that help them adapt to the environment. The more adaptive the organism is, the more likely it is to reproduce. Less-adaptive organisms will eventually be wiped out. Thus in different parts of the world people have similar genetic characteristics, a phenomenon known as **population gene pools.** Their genes have persisted because they help the individuals adapt to and survive in a particular environment. These gene pools may explain, for example, physical differences among people of different ethnic and racial groups.

Certain genetic diseases associated with gene mutations occur with greater frequency among certain populations or ethnic groups. Often this occurs because the gene mutation, although detrimental, has some advantage in a particular environment. The best example is the genetic mutation causing **sickle-cell anemia,** a hereditary disease that mostly attacks blacks but also affects some Greeks, Italians, and other people living near the Mediterranean Sea. It causes 100,000 deaths yearly. An individual who is homozygous for this gene produces abnormal hemoglobin, which causes distortion in blood cells that are exposed to the low oxygen levels that occur in some blood vessels. Since the condition often results in early death, the process of natural selection keeps it typically at a very low level within a population. However, as many as 30% of some African populations may carry this potentially harmful gene in a recessive allele paired with a normal allele. Scientists suspected, therefore, that some environmental factor was responsible for the high incidence of the detrimental gene. Researchers discovered that the frequency of this potentially harmful gene parallels the incidence of malaria; the greater the incidence of malaria in a particular geographical region, the greater the incidence of the sickle-cell gene. Further investigations revealed another interesting fact: an infant who is heterozygous for the gene, and who thus produces both normal and sickle-cell hemoglobin in the red blood cells, has a much better chance of resisting malaria than does a child of a normal genotype who produces only normal hemoglobin. Researchers concluded that for some reason the malarial parasite has greater difficulty in invading a red blood cell containing both kinds of hemoglobin. Thus in malarial regions the mutation actually has a selective advantage.

While the sickle-cell trait does not protect adults from malaria, small children with the trait have a greater chance of surviving the first malaria attack. They then develop antibodies against future attacks. Thus in malarial regions individuals carrying the defective gene have a higher rate of survival than those who do not carry the defective gene and hence die of malaria. In this way the high frequency of the gene in the population is maintained. This would not be the case in nonmalarial areas, where the sickle-cell gene serves no adaptive function.

This advantage explains why certain black populations were able to live in malaria-laden regions of Africa that proved fatal to many European settlers. The

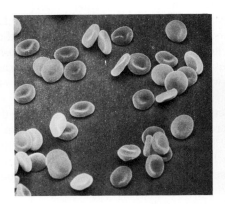 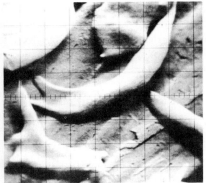

Normal red blood cells (left), and sickled red blood cells (right).

sickle-cell example also provides a dramatic illustration of the interaction between genes and the environment.

In parts of the world where the sickle-cell gene serves no adaptive function, early detection of the condition is imperative. The sickle-cell disease is potentially fatal and has been associated with 20% of U.S. infant mortality cases. However, recent medical advances have occurred in the management of the disease. Scientists recommend giving an infant with sickle-cell anemia oral penicillin until age 5 to prevent the serious bacterial infections associated with the disorder (Kinney & Ware, 1988). In addition, parents must be taught to be alert to early signs of infections, which can be quickly prevented.

Do You Know Your Genes?

The many possibilities now available for treating or managing genetically transmitted diseases make it even more important to know one's genotype and the chances of passing on a defective gene before conceiving a child.

Since Joey has Down's syndrome, Arlene and Steve are concerned that they might have other children with a genetic disorder, so they plan to discuss their concerns with a genetic counselor. Usually, couples seek genetic counseling when they suspect problems. Most people, however, do not know if they carry harmful

---

A CLOSER LOOK

The Human Genome Project

Many diseases, as well as physical and mental disorders, are related to genes, and the research on their role in disease is progressing so rapidly that it seems as if the identification of yet another gene that can be linked to a particular disease or disorder happens almost daily. This progress owes much to the Human Genome Project, an ambitious 15-year enterprise supported by several billion dollars in government funds and involving geneticists in the United States and abroad. This project is designed to encourage the exchange of information among researchers in order to accelerate the understanding of genetics.

The project is an effort to *map* the genes (that is, to find their location on the chromosomes) and then *sequence* them to determine their order (Cook-Deegan, 1990). Mapping and sequencing the genes is a first step in finding the gene responsible for a disease or disorder. Scientists hope eventually to identify diseases that can be diagnosed prenatally and to determine an individual's susceptibility to a particular health problem or mental illness. Besides working on the identification of genetically related diseases, scientists in the Human Genome Project are trying to trace the link between genes and behavior.

Some scientists are concerned that the project, which seeks to decipher the complete code of genes forming the blueprint for a human being, is far too ambitious and will result in huge amounts of data that researchers will be unable to interpret. Proponents contend that, despite the difficulty of the effort, it will enhance understanding of the genes' role in the development of physical and mental diseases and help prevent such diseases.

We may be close to the day when we can request a personalized genetic map with all our individual weaknesses, and perhaps strengths, clearly demarcated. The potential benefits of genetic mapping in terms of disease prevention are obvious, but there is a dark side as well. How might a person react on finding out that he is susceptible to an untreatable genetic disease? How might a person react to news that a relative is susceptible to a genetic disease? Would an individual feel guilty knowing that she is not susceptible to an inherited disease but that her sibling is? Beyond these individual problems, people with known susceptibility to an untreatable genetic disease may be discriminated against by insurance companies or employers. Insurers now rely primarily on blood tests and health examinations to decide whether to insure an individual. In the future will they want a genetic map? These issues may emerge in the decade ahead as more knowledge becomes available. As a society, we may need to develop guidelines for effectively incorporating and dealing with the explosion of information expected from genetic research.

---

genes. Couples having a child with a hereditary disease know at least about that one gene, but this first clue may be too late to avert a tragedy. Yet knowledge exists that can help determine the risk of bearing a child with a genetic disease.

Hereditary disease and ethnic groups   The chance that a child will be born with, or be the carrier of, a hereditary disorder is partially related to the parents' ethnic origin. As you can see in Table 3.1, some ethnic groups are more susceptible than others to particular inherited diseases. Phenylketonuria and cystic fibrosis are found mostly in whites and are rare among blacks and Asians, whereas sickle-cell anemia tends to strike blacks.

Tay-Sachs disease, a disorder causing brain destruction, blindness, and eventually death in early childhood, occurs almost exclusively among Ashkenazi Jews (who are of Eastern European descent) but not among Sephardic Jews (of Spanish origin). However, any of these diseases could occur, through intermarriage or mutation, in any ethnic group. Tay-Sachs disease, for example, is found in children who are not Jewish, although it is at least 100 times less frequent. Knowledge about one's country of origin or ethnic group is crucial, therefore, for establishing the potential risk of carrying the genes for certain diseases. If two individuals of the same ethnic group marry, the likelihood that their offspring will be affected by a genetic disease peculiar to that group increases, because they may both carry a recessive gene for that disease.

Genetic counseling   When couples, such as Arlene and Steve, are faced with a problem they believe is genetic in origin, their best course is to obtain more information before having a child. They can obtain such information through genetic counseling programs, which help family members understand the genetic and medical implications of disorders. In this way the couple is better able to decide whether to pursue pregnancy.

Unfortunately, most individuals who seek genetic counseling already have a child with a genetic disorder. Some couples, however, are aware of a genetic disorder within their families. What genetic diseases prompt people to seek counseling? According to one study, approximately 50% seek genetic counseling for defects determined by a single gene, such as PKU; another 20% do so for chromosome anomalies, mostly Down's syndrome; and another 20% for congenital defects with polygenetic or unknown genetic causes. Families rarely seek genetic advice because they anticipate problems from exposure to environmental factors, such as radiation, that are known to mutate genes (Novitski, 1977).

The explosion of information on the genetic link to disease may cause counseling to increase in the future. The genetic counseling procedure involves making a detailed pedigree, listing all known relatives, their ages, countries of origin, and reproductive histories, including any instances of stillbirths, miscarriages, and neonatal deaths (Milunsky, 1977). Sometimes the pedigree shows the course of inheritance of a specific disorder. Even in these cases, however, the couples must be educated in the *principles of probability;* that is, the likelihood of having a child with the disorder. For example, a counselor may tell a couple that, since they are both heterozygous for a special trait, there is 1 chance in 4 that they will have a child with that disorder. If the couple has already given birth to a child with the disease, they will often assume that their next three children will be born normal. But this is not the case. For *each* pregnancy there is a 1-to-4 chance that offspring will be born with a defect; thus there is risk each time a pregnancy is planned, no matter how many normal or abnormal children have been born. Also, counselors give statistical prob-

TABLE 3.1   Selected Genetic Disorders in Some Ethnic Groups

If you are	The chance is about	That
black	1 in 10	you are a carrier of sickle-cell anemia.
	7 in 10	you have an intolerance to milk (e.g., develop diarrhea).
black and male	1 in 10	you have a hereditary predisposition to develop hemolytic anemia after taking sulfa or other drugs.
black and female	1 in 50	
	1 in 4	you have or will develop high blood pressure.
white	1 in 25	you are a carrier of cystic fibrosis.
	1 in 80	you are a carrier of phenylketonuria.
Jewish (Ashkenazic)	1 in 30	you are a carrier of Tay-Sachs disease.
	1 in 100	you are a carrier of familial dysautonomia, a central nervous system disorder characterized by mental retardation, motor incoordination, and frequent convulsions.
Italian-American or Greek-American	1 in 10	you are a carrier of thalassemia, a form of anemia.
Armenian or Jewish (Sephardic)	1 in 45	you are a carrier of familial Mediterranean fever, a disorder characterized by frequent spells of fever and arthritis.
Afrikaaner (white South African)	1 in 330	you may have porphyria, a metabolism disorder.
Asian	close to 100%	you will have milk intolerance as an adult.

Source: Table from p. 63 of *Know Your Genes* by Aubrey Milunsky, M.D. Copyright © 1977 by Aubrey Milunsky, M.D. Reprinted by permission of Houghton Mifflin Company. All rights reserved.

abilities that apply to whole populations; they cannot predict with certainty that a particular couple will conceive a child with a genetic disorder. Once the genetic counselors tell couples the risks involved, each couple must make decisions on the basis of this information.

As yet, there are not enough genetic counseling programs to accommodate the increasing numbers of couples who will need them. This issue has arisen in relation to a test recently developed to identify the gene linked to **cystic fibrosis.** The test, conducted during pregnancy, is designed to let people know what their chances are of having a child with cystic fibrosis (Lemna et al., 1990). Although cystic fibrosis is the most frequent severe genetic disease of childhood in the United States, no successful treatment exists. One out of 20 or 30 individuals are carriers, and the incidence of affected children is in the range of 1 out of 2000 (among blacks, the incidence is 1 out of 20,000; among Asians, 1 out of 100,000). The disorder, inherited as a recessive trait, is a malfunction of the exocrine glands. CF patients produce excess amounts of mucus, get chronic lung infections, and are frequently hospitalized. Their average life expectancy is 27 years.

Physicians hail the development of the CF test as a major medical break-through that can eventually lead to prevention of the disease. Yet the test is different from other genetic tests. In the PKU example given earlier, screening is done after birth and treatment is given to the affected children. The CF test is designed to let parents know their chances of giving birth to a baby suffering from the disease. Prospective parents told that they *might* have a child with cystic fibrosis will need to have the support of professionals, family, and friends to cope with the news and make informed decisions. Should they take the chance and have the baby? If the baby is born with the disease, will they feel that they could have prevented the suffering that they and the child will experience? If they decide to end the pregnancy and then find out that the child would have been born normal, how will they feel? Obviously, if genetic testing is to be widespread, a network of helping professionals must also be available to support parents who undergo the tests.

Genetic screening   The cystic fibrosis test is an example of a prenatal test designed to identify risk for a particular disease. Other tests, conducted after birth, seek to identify newborns with a particular genetic disease. The screening tests for PKU and sickle-cell anemia are examples of tests routinely given to all infants at birth.

Screening is only the first step in the detection of a genetic disease; it should not be interpreted as a diagnosis. Although screening tests are designed to discover infants with specific disorders, these tests actually detect only a primary finding in a disorder (Novitski, 1977). The finding may also be present in other disorders or may be unrelated to any genetic disorders. For example, the PKU test detects high levels of phenylalanine (hyperphenylalaninemia), not specifically PKU. Although some infants with hyperphenylalaninemia have PKU, others may have it in association with another condition, or it may be an isolated, transient finding of no clinical significance (Baer, 1977). Only additional tests can help determine the specific genetic disorder. Thus more specific diagnostic tests and treatments should follow genetic screening.

Phenylketonuria was the first genetic disease for which large populations were screened; sickle-cell anemia was the second. Now Tay-Sachs and other, even rarer genetic diseases have been added to the list. There are still several problems associated with genetic screening. Ironically, one problem arises from the simplicity of the tests. Screening for rare disorders can be conducted in geographic areas that lack the medical capacity for any follow-up diagnostic testing. For example, shortly after PKU screening began, some infants without PKU were put on low-phenylala-nine diets because of aberrations detected in a single screening test. Frequently, these infants had no follow-up evaluation to determine whether they truly had PKU.

DISCUSSION OF SOCIAL ISSUES

Detecting Genetic Disorders and Genetic Engineering

In addition to screening tests to detect genetic abnormalities after birth, other tests can discover genetic abnormalities during pregnancy. The latest such test, which can be conducted as early as the ninth week of pregnancy, is the **chorion biopsy** (or

chorionic villus sampling). It involves taking a sample of the chorion, which is the outer membrane of the amniotic sac that protects the developing fetus. The chorion is composed of cells outside the fertilized egg and contains the same genetic material as the embryo. *Within a few days,* examination and biopsy of the chorion can reveal the sex of the unborn baby as well as such genetic abnormalities as Down's syndrome. This test is a significant medical advance. If parents elect to abort the abnormal embryo, the abortion can take place early in pregnancy with relatively little risk to the mother. Also, receiving the test results so quickly relieves expectant parents of undue stress and anxiety. In about 1% of cases, however, a chorion biopsy can lead to spontaneous abortion.

Another test, **amniocentesis,** samples the amniotic fluid, which also contains genetic information about the unborn child. Obstetricians withdraw the fluid by inserting a needle through the abdomen into the amniotic sac in the uterus. (Figure 3.9 shows both amniocentesis and the chorion biopsy.) Then the fluid is examined to detect any genetic abnormalities; this test can also tell the child's sex. Physicians can only perform amniocentesis after the 10th week of pregnancy; usually the test is done between the 16th and 18th weeks. The parents receive the results in approximately three weeks. If the mother elects to abort the fetus on the basis of the test results, there is considerably more risk to her health because it must be done during the fifth month of pregnancy.

This test may also affect the fetus. In the first long-term study on the procedure's effects, researchers in England followed two groups of children matched for maternal age and other factors. One group included children whose mothers had had amniocentesis, and the other consisted of children whose mothers had not. Measuring the two groups on a variety of developmental tests at 4 days, 6 months, 4 years, and 7 years, the researchers found that children whose mothers had had amniocentesis developed more frequent ear infections and middle-ear abnormalities than children in the other groups (Finegan et al., 1990). Although scientists need to replicate the study before drawing any definitive conclusions, removal of some amniotic fluid during pregnancy appears to lead to pressure changes in the fetal ear that result in abnormalities in anatomical development.

In a third prenatal test, **alpha-fetoprotein screening,** physicians draw blood from the pregnant woman and test it to see if the fetus is suffering from neural tube defects. Such defects, which lead to mental retardation, occur in 1 out of 1000 live births and are among the most common birth defects in the United States. When a fetus has a neural tube defect, large amounts of alpha-fetoprotein pour out of the fetal blood and eventually enter the mother's bloodstream. Pregnant women who have high levels of alpha-fetoprotein in their blood are then given a sonogram and amniocentesis to confirm that there is a problem. A **sonogram** gives a detailed picture of the fetus through high-frequency sound waves. Before amniocentesis, physicians use a sonogram to determine the position of the fetus. Thus they can avoid a fetal injury when inserting the needle into the uterus.

Physicians also use the sonogram in conjunction with other prenatal tests where they have to know the fetus's position. Recent advances indicate that the sonogram can be used as the first fetal warning signal. For example, fetuses with Down's syndrome exhibit two telltale signs in the sonogram: the fetal thigh bones are slightly shorter than usual, and an extra roll of skin appears on the back of the neck. Since a sonogram is safer than amniocentesis, physicians recommend that women at risk for giving birth to a Down's syndrome child have a sonogram first. If abnormalities are revealed, amniocentesis can then confirm the disorder's existence.

Another recently developed procedure—the analysis of the mother's blood to detect the fetus's sex—might ultimately revolutionize the approach to prenatal testing (Lo et al., 1989). Using this new procedure, researchers found Y chromosome genes (which can only be found in males) in a pregnant woman's bloodstream, thus proving the presence of fetal cells in the mother's blood. At present, the test only detects the sex of the fetus. Eventually, however, researchers hope to use a simple blood test to detect a range of genetic diseases. This breakthrough would certainly lead to safer methods of prenatal testing.

Such medical advances in prenatal diagnosis can further our ability to prevent and treat genetic diseases. But the increasing use of such diagnostic tests, and the likelihood that they will become increasingly simpler—and, therefore, more prevalent—means that more women will be facing difficult choices. They will have to decide whether to take prenatal tests; if they do, they must then face yet other decisions on how to act on the results (Kolata, 1987). The increased use of the tests has also produced major medical, moral, religious, and legal controversies. One argument against the widespread use of such tests focuses on the procedures' risks to the mother and unborn child. However, some researchers contend that the benefits far outweigh the risks (Fuchs, 1980). There is also the important moral question of denying life to the fetus because of its physical or mental defects. Parents who discover that their child will be born with a defect may decide to abort the fetus. We might argue that an abortion is warranted when severe mental and physical abnormalities would otherwise result. But the question is, How severe must a defect be to warrant an abortion? Although chorion biopsy and amniocentesis can detect genetic

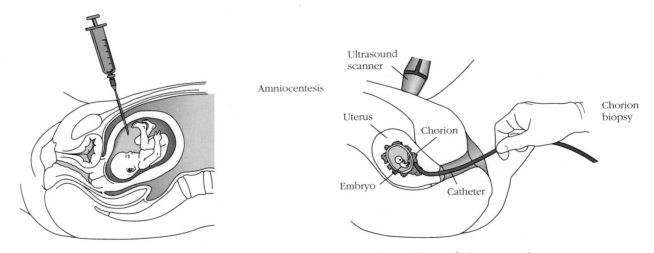

Figure 3.9 *Amniocentesis and chorion biopsy procedures. These techniques examine the chromosomal makeup of the embryo and fetus when some abnormality is suspected. In amniocentesis (top), a large needle is inserted into the woman's abdomen until it penetrates the uterus. A small amount of amniotic fluid is removed and examined for the presence of abnormalities. In the chorion biopsy (bottom), a small piece of the chorion is removed and its cells are examined. In both procedures, ultrasound waves help determine the position of the fetus in the uterus.*

abnormalities, they cannot tell anything about their severity. Consider Down's syndrome, which is associated with varying levels of mental retardation. If given appropriate, stimulating experiences and adequate medical attention, some Down's syndrome children function relatively well once they reach school age. Should all Down's syndrome fetuses be aborted?

Even if we resolve the abortion issue, there are still other problems. For example, when the physician performs an abortion rather late in pregnancy, as may happen with women who have had amniocentesis, there is the possibility of a live birth. When an abortion becomes a birth, who must decide what procedures are in the infant's best interest and who is financially responsible? These questions arise because infants born of abortion are injured in the process. As a result, legal scholars are asking whether the parents or society, on behalf of a seriously injured infant, can make a claim of "wrongful life" against the hospital. Also, a child's life now may be continued outside the womb by artificial life-support systems even if that baby is extremely premature. When an abortion results in the live birth of a child with genetic abnormalities, should doctors withhold life-prolonging intervention? These are not easy issues to resolve; some physicians refuse to perform amniocentesis because it might lead to an abortion.

Other ethical problems are associated with advances in **genetic engineering,** a research activity entailing the manipulation of genes. Given the progress in genetic engineering, researchers project that physicians may be able to restore to normal the genes responsible for many diseases described in this chapter. Perhaps PKU can be prevented by synthesizing the genetic code for the missing enzyme and adding it to the cell. Perhaps cystic fibrosis can be prevented by transplanting a normal gene from a healthy cell. This is still speculative, but you can see that such techniques may yield enormous benefits.

Genetic engineering also entails some potential dangers as well. One example is **cloning,** an asexual form of reproduction in which all progeny are identical. Again, this type of research has many potential benefits, such as greater understanding of chromosomes and their relationship to growth and disease. However, many people oppose both gene manipulation and cloning, noting that a laboratory-created organism might escape to the environment, with potentially dire consequences. Others fear that cloning will result in the creation of a super race that could take over the world. Because these fears are not altogether unfounded, genetic engineering must be conducted within government guidelines and regulations. With sufficient safeguards, such research can be useful.

Safeguards are also needed for other techniques, notably, the detection of genetic diseases during pregnancy. Despite the value of such techniques, they can be powerful tools for tampering with a population's genetic pool. The blood test that reveals the sex of the fetus falls into this realm. It can lead to the development of safer means of prenatal diagnosis, but will some parents want to abort a fetus when they discover it is a boy, and not the girl they were hoping for? Most couples would not choose to abort a fetus on the basis of its sex, but some people might (remember the discussion on China in Chapter 2). You can imagine the drastic social changes that would result, not to mention the decrease in genetic variability (Etzioni, 1977). All these factors must be considered as we forge ahead with advances in genetic research.

Heredity and Behavior

The study of genetics provides valuable information on physical growth and development and the etiology and nature of some abnormalities. Such research also helps explain variations in human behavior. For many years developmental psychologists have sought to determine how much genetic or environmental factors contribute to different behavioral characteristics. Is human behavior determined by a person's genetic heredity (nature) or by upbringing (nurture)? This question led to the nature-nurture controversy. Many researchers took extreme positions on this issue. Some emphasized the exclusive role of genetic heredity, whereas others emphasized only the role of learning and experience. The question is meaningless, however, when posed in this either/or manner (Anastasi, 1958; Plomin, 1989). Although there are no genes for behavior, at a molecular level genes act on the development and maintenance of structures that do have consequences for behavior (Scarr-Salapatek, 1975). The inheritance of behavioral traits follows a multifactorial pattern, involving the action of many genes and the interaction between heredity and the environment.

Researchers are now attempting to ascertain how and to what extent genetic and environmental factors interact to affect development. They also want to discover how this interaction differs for specific behavioral traits.

Methods of Studying Heredity and Behavior

To learn more about the influence of genetic and environmental factors on development, researchers employ different kinds of studies.

Animal studies   Researchers can more easily control the environment of animals because their behavior is not nearly as complex as human behavior. As a result, the

A CLOSER LOOK

Alcoholism Is Linked to Genetic Abnormality

In recent research on alcoholism, scientists found a form of a gene in an overwhelming majority of alcoholics under study. Although the structure is not necessarily a gene for alcoholism, it seems to be closely associated with the disease and may play a significant role in addictive behavior.

Alcoholism triggers increased dopamine output, so Blum et al. (1990) focused on a gene that dictates the structure in the brain known as the *d2 dopamine receptor*. Of the alcoholics studied, 77% had a slight abnormality in their d2 receptors, whereas only 25% of the nonalcoholic control group had such an abnormality. The researchers theorize that individuals with an abnormal receptor need to consume more alcohol to increase the amount of dopamine acting on the receptor, and that this leads to the disease.

More studies are needed to establish the genetic link between the genes and alcohol; however, the notion that

there may be a genetic basis to addictive behavior is not new. Researchers have known for some time that alcoholism runs in families; twin and adoption studies have confirmed this (Bohman, Sigvardsson, & Cloninger, 1982). Plomin (1989) notes that alcohol use and abuse are good examples of how genes influence behavior; no matter how strong the genetic propensity for alcoholism is, the genes do not drive a person to drink. Yet, Plomin adds, once individuals with a propensity for alcoholism drink, they lack the brakes; that is, the physiological and/or psychological factors that make most people want to stop drinking after a certain point of intoxication. Research on a genetic link to alcoholism also increases the likelihood that scientists will find a way to prevent the disease that often devastates the lives of alcoholics and their children.

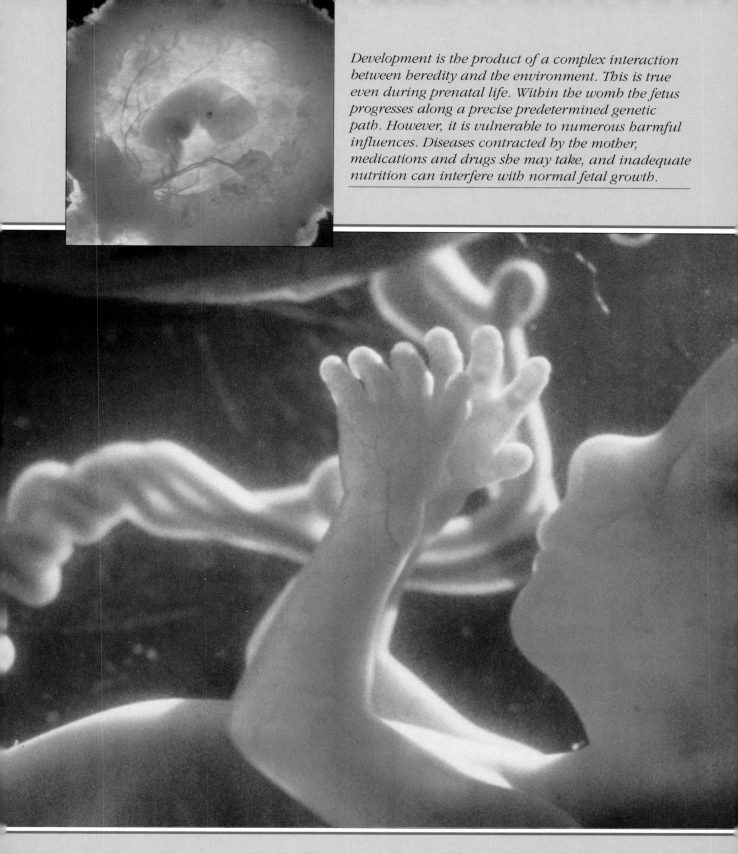

Development is the product of a complex interaction between heredity and the environment. This is true even during prenatal life. Within the womb the fetus progresses along a precise predetermined genetic path. However, it is vulnerable to numerous harmful influences. Diseases contracted by the mother, medications and drugs she may take, and inadequate nutrition can interfere with normal fetal growth.

Prenatal Life and Birth

Pregnancy, labor, and birth are natural biological processes. Nevertheless, how a woman experiences them may depend on her cultural background. In our society, a pregnant woman is advised to have regular medical checkups, which helps the physician monitor the health of the fetus.

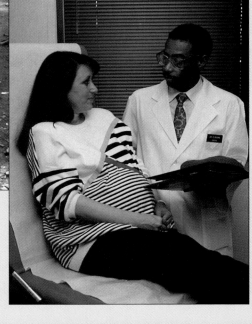

When the fetus is at risk for atypical development or a genetic abnormality is suspected, ultrasound provides a picture of the baby in the womb. The physician can then proceed with other tests that may be required, such as amniocentesis.

The birth process is normal for most infants and mothers. Labor proceeds without complications, the baby's heartbeat is strong, and the baby is born vaginally. In some cases, however, a caesarian section is necessary, but does not usually result in any problems for the mother or baby.

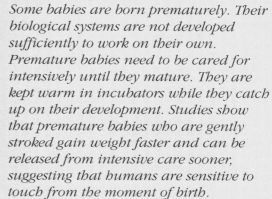

Some babies are born prematurely. Their biological systems are not developed sufficiently to work on their own. Premature babies need to be cared for intensively until they mature. They are kept warm in incubators while they catch up on their development. Studies show that premature babies who are gently stroked gain weight faster and can be released from intensive care sooner, suggesting that humans are sensitive to touch from the moment of birth.

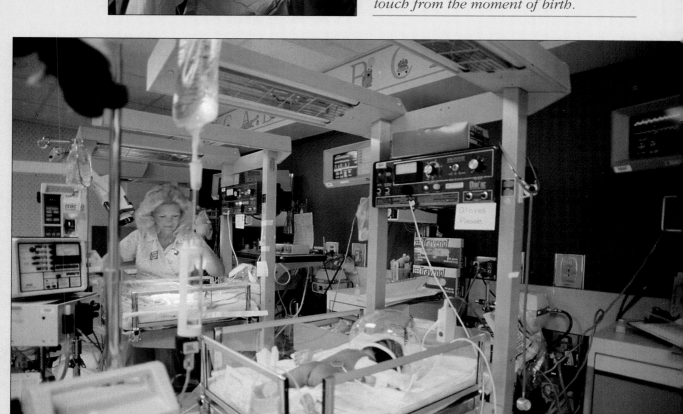

Breastfeeding is recommended because of the immunologic properties of the mother's milk. In some societies, other women support the new mother as she attempts to breastfeed, which is not a new task if she has grown up watching her own siblings breastfeed. But in our society, many women have not been exposed to this practice, and they may not have relatives living close by to advise them.

Having a new baby is a joyous experience for the entire family. However, caring for the newborn is often difficult, especially for first-time parents. In some cultures, new parents depend on the advice and support of family and friends. In our society, the new mother may not live near her parents or other relatives, so parent educators may visit on a regular basis to provide assistance. Parent educators not only help with the physical care of the baby, they also explain psychological development and show parents how to interact with their child effectively.

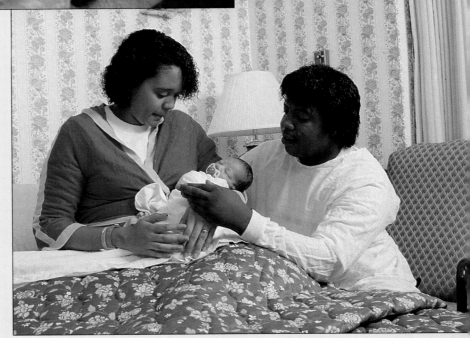

genetic contributions to behavior can be more easily understood through animal studies. Although the results of such studies cannot be directly applied to humans, animal studies are important. This research demonstrates the different ways in which genetic inheritance may be expressed in various environmental settings.

One technique used is **selective breeding,** in which scientists mate animals evidencing similarity on a particular trait. Studies using this technique have been conducted to assess whether emotionality or learning ability are inherited traits. Several classic studies illustrate how researchers ascertained a genetic influence on behavioral traits. Tyron (1942) gave 19 trials in a complex maze to 142 rats. Some rats learned the maze quickly and made few errors; they were identified as "bright" rats. Other rats, identified as "dull," learned slowly and made many errors. The "bright" rats were then mated with each other, as were the "dull" rats, and their offspring were tested in the maze. The experiment was repeated for eight generations. The differences between the two groups in errors made while running the maze became greater with each generation. Since each new generation had no prior experience in running the maze, Tyron attributed the difference between the bright and dull groups to genetic inheritance.

Tyron's experiment demonstrates the relationship between heredity and learning ability. However, in a subsequent study, Searle (1949) tested rats from the twenty-second generation of Tyron's rats for about 30 different traits, such as emotionality, activity levels, discrimination learning, and performance on Tyron's maze. Searle confirmed Tyron's findings on the original maze, but when he tested the rats on other mazes, he found that the bright and dull rats differed not only in their performance but also in such other traits as emotionality. Perhaps this emotional difference (or some other difference) in the rats affected their ability to perform.

Other animal studies demonstrate the effects of environment on such behavioral traits as learning ability and emotionality. Fuller (1967), for example, studied the learning ability of two breeds of dogs reared in different environments. He raised some pups from each breed normally and others in isolation, deprived of any environmental stimulation. Fuller found that although the effects of isolation differed according to the breed, dogs reared alone generally demonstrated a poorer learning ability. Moreover, the experience of isolation hindered the dogs *emotionally* but not intellectually. As a result, they were unable to perform. When these dogs became emotionally stronger, their performance improved.

In another study on the effects of the environment, Cooper and Zubek (1958) reared strains of "bright" and "dull" rats in two different environments. One group had an enriched environment, including considerable sensory stimulation using balls and tunnels. The second group had a restricted environment containing only a food box and water pan. On testing the rats for maze learning, researchers found that the enriched environment helped "dull" rats but not "bright" ones; the restricted environment had no effect on "dull" rats, but it hurt the performance of "bright" rats. Thus this study clearly demonstrates that researchers can alter behavioral traits by changing the environment, and that developmental characteristics are the result of interaction between genetic and environmental factors.

Many other animal studies have helped demonstrate a point made earlier in the chapter: that is, the organism inherits a range of modifiability or a range of reaction. Each genotype specifies a range of phenotypes that are possible under certain environmental circumstances. If the range of reaction is narrow for a particular trait, environmental factors will have little or no influence on its development. But if the range of reaction is broad, the environmental influence will be significant.

Twin studies   Researchers have used studies of twins and adopted children to determine the extent to which genetic and environmental factors contribute to human traits. The idea behind twin studies is that two people with identical genes might be expected to have identical traits if those traits are largely genetically determined. Pairs of people with identical genes are known as *identical*, or **monozygotic twins**, since they develop from a single (*mono*) fertilized egg (*zygote*) and thus share the exact genotype. If one twin possesses a genetic trait, the identical partner will also possess it. The similarity between the twins is called **intrapair concordance**.

A second type of twins, known as *fraternal*, or **dizygotic twins**, develops simultaneously in the womb but from two separate eggs fertilized by two separate sperm; the twins are no more similar than two siblings born at different times. Twin studies capitalize on the innate difference between monozygotic and dizygotic twin types by investigating whether the concordance rate for monozygotic twins for a given trait will be significantly higher than the concordance rate for dizygotic twins. Researchers interpret a higher monozygotic concordance rate as strong evidence that the trait has a significant genetic influence.

Researchers assume that environmental factors are the same for twins of each type as long as they grow up in the same home and experience the same family life. If identical twins show more resemblance on some traits than fraternal twins, scientists assume that genetic factors influence that trait. Some researchers, however, have questioned these assumptions, asking whether parents perhaps treat identical twins exactly alike. If this is the case, then how can we be sure that the genes, and not the environmental circumstances, determine a particular trait under investigation? To determine how parents actually relate to twins, Lytton (1976) observed mothers of identical and fraternal twins. Mothers of identical twins responded to them in a similar way, whereas mothers of fraternal twins did not. However, the mothers' responses related to the children's behavior. Since identical twins behave in a sim-

Concordance in identical twins.

ilar way, then it is not surprising that they elicit similar responses from their mothers. Similar findings from other studies showed that even when mothers mistook the zygosity of their twins, they nonetheless responded to the behavior of the twins, thinking, for example, that they were fraternal when they were identical (Scarr, 1968; Plomin, DeFries, & McClearn, 1989).

Researchers have also studied monozygotic twins reared apart, and therefore under different environmental circumstances. Thus, any similarities found in these twins would largely be due to genetic factors. These studies are harder to execute, however, because it is often difficult to find a large sample of identical twins who were separated at birth. In these studies researchers often find that the twins' environments are similar, so that even though they did not grow up together, they still share a similar background.

The most useful studies are of monozygotic twins who grew up in widely different environments. Here, the research of Thomas Bouchard and his colleagues (1981, 1990) is important. Bouchard leads the Minnesota Study of Twins Reared Apart, one of the best-known research projects on twins. Twins have come from all over the world to Minneapolis to be studied. Sets of twins who meet for the first time at the testing site are given a number of intelligence tests, personality tests, and physical examinations, during which their heart rates and brain wave patterns are tested. Bouchard and his team also conduct extensive interviews to determine the twins' interests, values, and the kinds of families in which they grew up.

Adoption studies   Adoption studies are another avenue for investigating genetic and environmental influences on behavior. Three groups are suitable for study: the adopted children as adults, the biological parents, and the adoptive parents. This three-way comparison is very instructive, because the biological parents are related to the adopted child genetically but do not share the same environment, whereas the adoptive parents share the same environment but are not genetically related. Significant similarities between the adopted child and the biological parents would point to hereditary influences, whereas similarities between the adopted child and the adoptive parents could only be due to chance or to the influence of a shared environment.

There is one problem, however. Adoption agencies attempt to place children with adoptive parents who are similar in physical and other characteristics to the biological parents. This practice may dilute any findings on the relative influence of genes and the environment.

Consanguinity studies   In other studies researchers examine as many relatives in a family as possible to discover the degree to which they share a particular trait and whether the closeness of the relationship (for example, whether they are first or second cousins) affects the degree of similarity.

Heredity and Intelligence

Using various combinations of the study types noted in this section, researchers have accumulated vast amounts of data that address the question: How much does heredity affect behavior? Most research has focused on intellectual abilities, personality, and mental illness. Let us examine some of the research.

Studies of the extent to which heredity influences intelligence have given rise to a great deal of controversy, in part because many studies rely on IQ scores as a measure of intelligence, even though the validity of IQ tests is questionable. (IQ

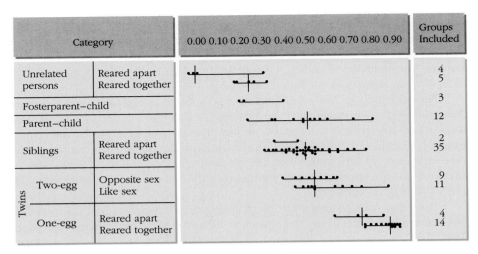

Category		0.00 0.10 0.20 0.30 0.40 0.50 0.60 0.70 0.80 0.90	Groups Included
Unrelated persons	Reared apart		4
	Reared together		5
Fosterparent–child			3
Parent–child			12
Siblings	Reared apart		2
	Reared together		35
Twins — Two-egg	Opposite sex		9
	Like sex		11
Twins — One-egg	Reared apart		4
	Reared together		14

Figure 3.10 *Correlation coefficients for "intelligence" test scores from 52 studies. Some studies reported data for more than one relationship category; some included more than one sample per category, giving a total of 99 groups. Over two-thirds of the correlation coefficients were derived from IQs, the remainder from special tests (for example, Primary Mental Abilities). Midparent/child correlation was used when available; otherwise mother/child correlation was used. Correlation coefficients obtained in each study are indicated by dark circles; medians are shown by vertical lines intersecting the horizontal lines that represent the ranges.*

Source: From "Genetics and Intelligence: A Review," Erlenmeyer-Kimling, L. and Jarvik L. F., from *Science,* Vol. 142, Fig. 1, p. 1478, 13 December 1963. Copyright © 1963 by the American Association for the Advancement of Science.

testing is discussed in detail in Chapter 15.) Nevertheless, the studies are important; they demonstrate that although performance on IQ tests is highly influenced by heredity, intellectual characteristics are malleable. Thus environmental factors also have a significant impact on intellectual performance.

The evidence that performance on intelligence tests has a genetic component comes from numerous studies based on the rationale that if heredity influences intellectual performance, there should be a greater similarity in IQ scores among individuals with more genes in common. In a summary of over 50 different studies involving 30,000 correlations, Erlenmeyer-Kimling and Jarvik (1963) found that the greater the genetic similarity between individuals, the more likely they were to have similar IQ scores. Other reviews of the research drew similar conclusions (Bouchard & McGue, 1981).

Recall that a correlation coefficient estimates how two measures—in this case, scores and genetic similarity—vary together. As you can see in Figure 3.10 the correlation of IQ scores for unrelated persons is small, but it increases as genetic similarity between subjects increases. Thus for dizygotic twins the correlation is quite high, but for monozygotic twins it is still higher. So it is obvious that genetic heredity is an important factor in intellectual performance.

But how important is heredity? One method of determining the relative importance of both heredity and the environment is the **heritability ratio,** a mathematical estimate of the proportion of trait variance having genetic causes. The

TABLE 3.2   Correlations in Intelligence of Monozygotic (MZ) and Dizygotic (DZ) Twins and Heritabilities (H) Found in a Number of Twin Studies

Author of study	Date	Country	MZ	DZ	H
Von Verschuer	1930	Germany	*	*	.62
Day	1932	U.S.	.92	.61	.80
Stocks and Karn	1933	England	.84	.65	.54
Newman et al.	1937	U.S.	.90	.62	.74
Gottschaldt	1939	Germany	*	*	.82
Wictorin	1952	Sweden	.89	.72	.61
Husén	1953	Sweden	.90	.70	.67
Blewett	1954	England	.76	.44	.57
Thurstone et al.	1955	U.S.	*	*	.65
Zazzo	1960	France	.90	.60	.75
Vandenberg	1962	U.S.	.74	.56	.41
Nichols	1965	U.S.	.87	.63	.65
Huntley	1966	England	.83	.66	.50
Partanen et al.	1966	Finland	.69	.42	.51
Schoenfeldt	1969	U.S.	.80	.48	.62

Source: Reprinted with permission of Macmillan Publishing Company from *Encyclopedia of Education,* Lee C. Deighton, Editor in chief, Volume 5, page 125. Copyright © 1970 by Crowell Collier and Macmillan Publishing Company, Inc., a Maxwell Macmillan Co.

heritability ratio is a population statistic that applies to a trait distributed in a given population. Researchers calculate this statistic by comparing identical twins who were separated early in life and lived under different environmental circumstances. If the identical twins are raised apart but nevertheless resemble each other in a trait, the evidence is strong that that trait is influenced by genetic heredity, and the heritability ratio would be high. If they do not resemble each other on a particular trait, this would provide evidence for the importance of environmental influences on that trait and the heritability ratio would be low.

You can see in Table 3.2 that the heritability ratio for IQ scores varies according to different studies, but it is clear that for the population studied, variability has a substantial genetic factor. If the genetic factor is important, then the correlation between the IQ scores of identical twins reared apart should remain high. Indeed, summaries of studies reveal that this is the case (Vandenberg, 1971). In a recent study comparing IQ test results of identical and fraternal twins reared apart, Bouchard and his colleagues (1990) report a 70% heritability estimate, by far the highest estimate for the heritability of intelligence. Critics point out this finding may be due in part to the relatively small size of the sample Bouchard studied (Beckwith et al., 1990). Plomin (1990) contends that the estimated heritability of IQ is not likely to be more than 50%.

Indeed, limitations to other studies using the heritability ratio become evident when the raw data are examined. Consider a study of the IQ scores of different sets of identical twins reared apart since infancy (Newman, Freeman, & Holzinger, 1937). In one case of twin girls, the researchers found significant differences in IQ scores. They noted that one twin lived in an isolated, rural area where she received only a minimal education. The other twin lived in a more stimulating environment and received a college education. In the same study the researchers found a difference of only one IQ point between identical twin boys, even though one twin was raised by a farmer of modest means, and the other by a well-to-do physician.

TABLE 3.3 Twin Correlations for Tests of Specific Cognitive Abilities

Ability	Number of studies	Twin correlations Identical	Fraternal
Verbal comprehension	27	0.78	0.59
Verbal fluency	12	0.67	0.52
Reasoning	16	0.74	0.50
Spatial visualization	31	0.64	0.41
Perceptual speed	15	0.70	0.47
Memory	16	0.52	0.36

Source: Plomin, R. (1990). *Nature and nurture: An introduction to human behavioral genetics.* Pacific Grove, CA: Brooks/Cole, Table 4.3, page 78. (Based on data from Nichols, 1978, p. 163.)

Depending on which set of twins we choose, we could argue that the environment makes a difference (as in the case of the first set) or that heredity is the more important factor (as in the second set).

The research method used and the statistic being compared can also affect results. For example, some correlational studies highlight the genetic influence on intelligence, but they use IQ scores (which tend to illustrate the effects of the environment) as a measure of intelligence. Several studies of adopted children illustrate this point. Skodak and Skeels (1949) examined the IQ scores of 100 adopted children who were tested at repeated intervals for 16 years. Educational level, which is related to the IQ score, was available for both the biological and adoptive parents. As they grew older, the adopted children's IQ scores correlated more highly with the educational level of their biological parents than with that of their adoptive parents. In fact, in a later analysis of the data, Honzik (1957) showed that the correlation found for adopted children and their biological parents was similar to that found for children (who were *not* adopted) and their parents (see Figure 3.11). These findings support the argument that the genetic influence on intelligence is significant. However, when researchers only looked at the IQ scores found in these same studies, they noted that the environment was a determinant. The mean IQs of 63 biological mothers of the adopted children was 86. The mean IQs of their children, tested at adolescence, was 106, a 20-point difference. Rarely will children have exactly the same IQ as their biological parents, but a 20-point difference is substantial enough to suggest that environment is a key determinant of intelligence.

Researchers who have begun to examine genetic influences on specific cognitive skills such as verbal comprehension, reasoning, and memory have also noted the role of genes in intelligence. Several reviews of such studies conclude that although there is much to be learned about the role of heredity in specific cognitive abilities, many such abilities appear (as you can see in Table 3.3) to be significantly influenced by the genes (DeFries, Vandenberg, & McClearn, 1976; Plomin, 1988).

In summary, although different types of studies document that genetic factors make a significant contribution to individual differences in performance on intelligence tests and cognitive skills, environmental factors clearly play a major role (Plomin, 1989). Stimulating environments can dramatically enhance the intellectual development and performance of some infants and children, whereas restricted environments that deprive children of tactile and verbal stimulation can hinder this development. (This subject is discussed further in Chapters 5, 6, and 9.)

Inheritance of Personality Traits

A variety of studies have sought to determine whether genetics influences personality traits. Personality, which is defined as an individual's overall pattern of behavior, is difficult to study. Unlike some physical traits that have specific and easily defined characteristics, personality encompasses a diversity of behavioral traits present in varying degrees and combinations. Nevertheless, researchers have found that genes play a significant role in some dimensions of personality, namely, sociability, activity level, and emotionality. The individual does not inherit a specific personality trait, but rather a general way of responding to the environment.

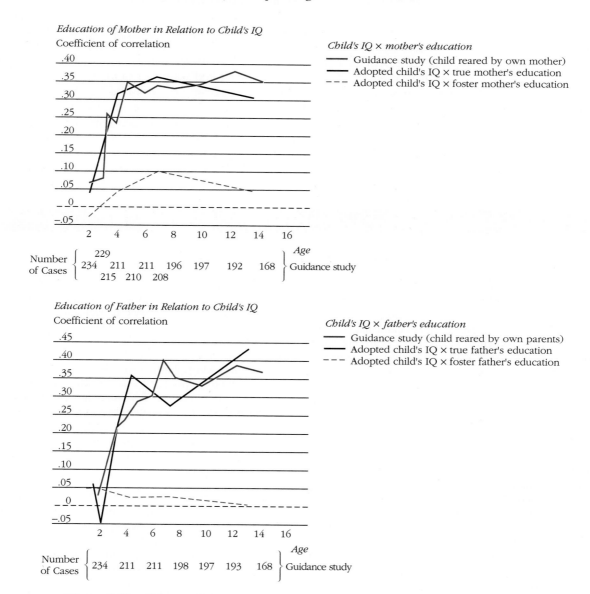

Figure 3.11 *Genetic influence on intelligence.*

Source: From "Intellectual resemblance of adopted children to true and adopted parents and of children to their own parents" by Marjorie P. Honzik from *Child Development,* 28 (2) p. 219, Fig. 2 and p. 222, Fig. 4. Copyright © 1957 by The Society for Research in Child Development, Inc.

For example, researchers have found that there appears to be a genetic influence (Henderson, 1982) on introversion/extroversion, which denotes the extent of a person's sociability, although not to the same extent as with cognitive abilities (Plomin, 1989). Introverted individuals are withdrawn and inhibited; extroverted individuals are outgoing and appear self-confident. A person's temperament—whether calm or irritable, easygoing or difficult—also appears to be genetically determined (Thomas, Chess, & Birch, 1968) and can be noticed within a few moments of birth.

In discussing twins who were part of the Minnesota study, Holden (1980) notes that although some identical twins have been reared in different parts of the world and experienced vastly different cultural and religious upbringings, they have remarkably similar personality profiles. In one case study of identical twin males separated in infancy, one grew up in Trinidad and the other in Europe. Researchers found that both men had similar interests and capabilities. Both had quick tempers and liked the same foods. They also exhibited a number of idiosyncracies, such as fidgeting with rubber bands and reading magazines from back to front.

Several other pairs of twins studied by the Minnesota team showed surprising similarities that were difficult to explain. For example, one pair of twin men had sons named James Alan and James Allan. Both men had married and divorced women named Linda and remarried women named Betty. A pair of twin women had sons named Richard Andrew and Andrew Richard and daughters named Catherine Louise and Karen Louise!

A CLOSER LOOK

Mental Disorders: A Genetic Link

One of the most dramatic advances in the quest to identify genetic influence on behavior has been in psychopathology. Recent findings suggest that hereditary factors play a significant role in schizophrenia and autism in particular (Plomin, 1989, 1986). However, environmental factors are important as well. Researchers now examine a variety of factors—genetic, psychological, environmental, and sociological—to determine the etiology of mental disorders (Cicchetti, 1989).

Schizophrenia

Schizophrenia is a psychiatric illness characterized by serious loss of contact with reality and a marked deterioration in the ability to function. The term *schizophrenia* literally means "split mind." However, schizophrenics do not have a "split personality," another distinct psychiatric disorder. Schizophrenics suffer from delusions, hallucinations, and severe disordering of their thought processes, which make them unable to think straight and evidence bizarre behaviors.

There are several types of schizophrenia, and they all have similar features and symptoms. Each type is diagnosed on the basis of the predominating symptoms, which can include deep apathy and the inability to muster an interest in the social world, paranoia, delusions of persecution or grandeur, and hallucinations. Typically, schizophrenics experience auditory rather than visual hallucinations; they hear voices of people they believe are attempting to control or harm them or who are divulging certain information to which no one else is privy (Maxmen, 1985).

At times schizophrenics have brief episodes of relief from the symptoms of their disease. During these periods, they appear to be relatively normal. Still, most of the time their behavior is so bizarre that they become increasingly distant and remote to outsiders. They gradually retreat into the self, dwelling on their own thoughts and becoming socially isolated and mistrustful of others. Often they believe that everyone is "out to get" them (Maxmen, 1985).

Causes of Schizophrenia

What causes such disabling disturbances in thought and behavior? Researchers and clinicians are not sure, noting that schizophrenia is perhaps the most baffling of all mental disorders. Although the etiology remains a mystery, some advances have been made. For example, researchers had thought that dysfunction in the family and pathological interaction between the individual and the parents caused schizophrenia. Today they note that, although the stress of living in dysfunctional families can trigger the disorder, there is likely

Researchers have also been surprised to find that identical twins who have had the least contact with one another are the most alike (Farber, 1981). This could be due to the fact that identical twins who are reared together often want to assert their own individualities and may downplay their similarities. Identical twins raised apart do not have to assert their individualities in this way, and thus their similarities are more pronounced (Farber, 1981; Lewontin, Rose, & Kamin, 1984).

Longitudinal studies of twins and adopted children have documented another interesting finding. When the children are tested over time, heritability ratios increase substantially as the children grow and develop (Plomin, 1989). Researchers had thought that with age, the opportunity for environmental influence would increase and the heritability ratios would decrease. But for many traits this is not necessarily so. For example, in an adoption study that followed 300 families over the years, researchers found that children whose biological mothers were emotionally disturbed seemed to be emotionally normal at age 7; but by age 17, they began to show signs of emotional distress, even though their adoptive parents did not evidence any emotional problems (Willerman & Cohen, 1989).

In summarizing findings on the role of genes in behavior, Plomin (1989) notes that significant genetic influences were found for other aspects of behavior, including delinquency and crime, alcoholism, and mental disorders. Thus we can no longer assume that behavior is not affected by genetic influence. Indeed, according to Plomin, we should "ask not what is heritable; [we should] ask instead what is not heritable" (p. 111). Remember, however, that this chapter is on our biological her-

A CLOSER LOOK

to be a biological explanation as well. Schowalter and Anyan (1979) cite evidence that people inherit the tendency to become schizophrenic. Researchers have established this hypothesis on the basis of studies revealing that, although schizophrenia may occur in 1% of the general population, it occurs in 12% of children with one schizophrenic parent and in 35% to 44% of children whose parents are both schizophrenic. However, it is the vulnerability to the disease that is inherited, since even in identical twins schizophrenia may be present in one but not in the other (Plomin, 1989). For individuals who have inherited a great vulnerability to schizophrenia, even mild environmental stress can trigger the disorder. For those who have inherited only some vulnerability, much greater stress is required to produce the condition (Asarnow, Asarnow, & Strandberg, 1989; Zubin & Spring, 1977).

Besides the genetic link associated with schizophrenia, the brain chemistry of schizophrenic adolescents differs from that of normal adolescents, especially in how the brain handles dopamine (a chemical that transmits signals in the brain). Dopamine is present in excessive amounts among schizophrenics. Treatment with drugs that block the action of dopamine seems to work. In addition, recent studies using scanning instruments have shown that schizophrenics often have an enlarged cavity in the interior of the brain as well as

other abnormalities, such as unusual electrical impulses or decreased blood flow (Willerman & Cohen, 1989; Shapiro, 1981). Although these findings clearly point to the biological nature of the disorder, more research is needed before the precise role of biological factors is known.

Autism

Researchers are also attempting to find a genetic link to autism. Leo Kanner (1942) first identified autism over 40 years ago. It occurs in about 1 out of every 2500 children and is characterized by numerous symptoms, such as the inability to establish emotional and social relationships. Autistic children are unresponsive to their social environment; they seem to have no interest in being with other children or playing with them. They may also actively avoid being with people, preferring instead to be alone. Kanner (1942) presents a case study of a 6-year-old autistic boy, Frederick W., whose mother described him as

> . . . a child [who] has always been self-sufficient. I could leave him alone and he'd entertain himself very happily, walking around, singing. I have never known him to cry in demanding attention. . . . He doesn't want me to touch him or to put my arms around him.

(continued)

itage and emphasizes the genetic influence on development. Later chapters will focus on the crucial role of the environment. As Gedo (1990) notes, "Nature and nurture are both aspects of a single process. . . . Every adaptive challenge draws on our biological resources and our development in a human environment" (p. 6).

Summary

A child's development is largely programmed by genes. However, genetic factors alone do not determine the course of child development, because they do not operate in a vacuum. Rather, they interact with and are influenced by environmental factors. Genetic endowment can be seen as a potentiality. Realizing this genetic potential depends on factors in the environment.

Genes are carried on 46 chromosomes, half of which come from the mother and half from the father. The mechanisms underlying gene functioning are very complex. Each gene occurs in two alternative forms called alleles, which behave in a pattern of dominance and recessiveness to determine the observable characteristic of a trait. Physical characteristics, such as eye color and hair texture, and certain abnormal conditions and diseases, such as albinism and PKU, are established by this pattern of dominance and recessiveness.

Although a single gene transmits some characteristics and diseases, most human traits are determined by a complex interaction of many different genes. Gene activity is further complicated by biological and environmental factors, such as

A CLOSER LOOK

(continued)

Autistic children also fail to acquire normal language skills. Some are functionally mute. Others learn to speak, but have bizarre speech patterns that are essentially noncommunicative. They seem to be speaking to themselves even if other people are present. They may mechanically repeat a sentence or two they have heard, a condition called *echolalia*, or they may repeat, over and over, certain songs, commercials, or slogans. Some autistic children obsessively count numbers or repeatedly ask nonsensical questions such as, "Am I first, am I second, am I third?" without any apparent desire for an answer (Stewart & Gath, 1978).

Numerous studies also indicate that over 50% of autistic children are mentally retarded, having IQ scores of less than 50 (Ando & Yoshimura, 1979; Barry & James, 1978; Schopler & Dalldorf, 1980). However, some often have special talents. In discussing the handicaps and talents of some autistic children, Caparulo and Cohen (1977) describe James who did not speak until he was 5 years old but was able to complete complicated puzzles designed for much older children. At age 5, James made his first statement, looking up to the sky and saying that it looked like a flower. He had a fascination with numbers and would read encyclopedias and talk in detail about what he had read.

Early Symptoms of Autism

Despite their abnormal behaviors, autistic children have normal physical and motor development so the disorder often remains undiagnosed until late infancy or early childhood. Recent research has shown that the behavioral and emotional disturbances of childhood autism are apparent as early as the first three or four months of life, especially to the parents. Whereas normal babies of this age establish frequent eye contact with their parents and other caretakers and smile at them and seem happy and content to be in close physical contact with them, autistic infants seem content to be alone and hold themselves rigidly when they are being held.

Causes of Autism

At one time researchers considered the disorder to be a form of emotional or social withdrawal stemming from environmental factors. Child development professionals, such as Bruno Bettelheim (1967), noted that autism is the child's response to negative experiences in the home, and that this social withdrawal is a way of avoiding any further painful interpersonal experiences.

In support of the environmental explanation, Bettelheim (1967) and others (Eisenberg & Kanner, 1956) stated that parents of autistic children seem to be colder and more

the mother's age and experiences after birth, that modify the phenotypical expression of the genotype. In addition, gene mutations can lead to a variety of abnormalities. The survival of mutations depends on how adaptive that mutant characteristic is to the environment; for example, sickle-cell anemia, when carried as a recessive trait, has proved adaptive in regions with a high incidence of malaria but destructive in other areas.

Because of the survival of mutations with an adaptive advantage in certain geographic areas, some genetic diseases occur in greater frequencies among some ethnic groups. Genetic counseling, screening, and prenatal detection of genetic diseases are among the mechanisms available to prevent genetic deviations in development. However, these procedures harbor several ethical problems. For example, should a fetus with a genetic disease be aborted? These procedures can also detect the child's sex. Will parents who want a boy choose to abort a female fetus? If so, what would be the consequences for society as a whole?

Although we know a great deal about hereditary transmission and the causes and detection of many genetic diseases, we know very little about the genetic processes involved in behavioral traits. Several genes or unrelated chromosomes converge to create specific patterns of behavior. The inheritance of behavioral traits follows a multifactorial pattern involving the action of many genes and an interaction between heredity and the environment. Numerous animal studies have established this pattern. Other studies have used twins, adopted children, and relatives to investigate genetic contributions to such traits as intelligence, personality, and mental disorders.

A CLOSER LOOK

emotionally detached than parents of children suffering from other developmental disturbances. However, empirical studies have failed to establish a link between parental characteristics and childhood autism (Rutter, 1971; Reichter & Schopler, 1976). In a study that compared the functioning of mothers of autistic children and mothers of normal children, Rodrigue, Morgan, and Geffken (1990) found that the mothers of autistic children felt less competent as parents and were less able to cope with stress than were the mothers of normal children. However, given the unresponsiveness of their children, this finding is hardly surprising. In that same study, the researchers also interviewed mothers of Down's syndrome children and they, too, reported feeling less competent.

Researchers have since abandoned the environmental explanation in favor of a biological hypothesis, explaining that autism stems from one or several problems related to brain dysfunction. Such dysfunction, which may be caused by an assault to prenatal development, results in the child's inability to comprehend sound or make any sense out of what is being said. Thus researchers explain the child's failure to establish social relationships as stemming from abnormalities in the central nervous system (Young & Cohen, 1979).

Although the biological explanation of autism is far from complete, several recent findings provide forceful evidence of possible organic damage. For example, more than 25% of autistic children in some studies develop seizures during late infancy (Lotter, 1978). Research has also linked autism to maternal rubella (Chess, 1977) and to metabolic conditions such as Celiac's disease (Coleman, 1978). Some studies have also demonstrated a possible genetic factor (Folstein & Rutter, 1978). In addition, some researchers point out that the disorder is more likely to occur among boys than among girls. For every girl diagnosed as autistic, three to four boys are diagnosed with the disorder (Lord, Schopler, & Revicki, 1982). Finally, while it is unusual to find more than one autistic child in a family, there are families with autism, language disorders, and other developmental disabilities in siblings and relatives, a fact suggesting some genetic contribution to the disorder (Caparulo & Cohen, 1982). However, as Schopler and Mesibov (1984) point out, none of the mechanisms identified exist in all autistic children, but "the evidence indicates . . . that a number of biologic factors, acting singly or in combination are most likely to produce the autistic syndrome."

4 Prenatal Development and Birth

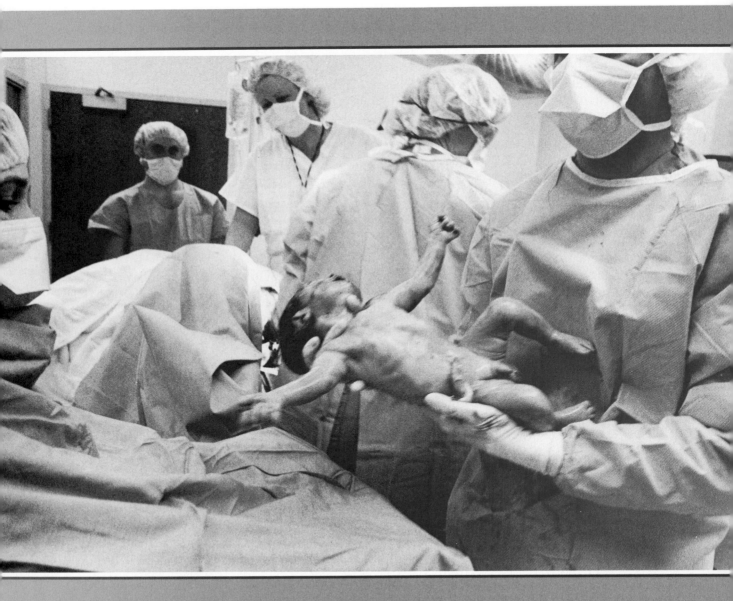

Heather just found out that she is pregnant, and she can't wait to share the news with her husband, Matthew. They have been trying to conceive for about eight months, and in preparation, they have been reading just about every book and magazine article on pregnancy. The more they read, the more amazed they are at how the baby develops from a single cell formed when the ovum is fertilized by a sperm. Indeed, this remains the greatest miracle of nature. The whole process takes only about 266 days. During this time the single cell becomes a complex structure of many millions of cells, each highly developed to perform a specialized function. At birth, the baby is 6 billion times heavier than the egg from which it came!

Growth during the prenatal period is remarkably regular and predictable. Changes occur in a fixed order at a fixed time. Although there is a great deal of information about what happens inside the uterus during gestation, very little is known about why the baby develops as it does. How do cells "know" that they are to become brain cells or the face or feet? What we do know is that the genes and chromosomes we studied in Chapter 3 control fetal development. As human beings, we are what our parents' genes have made us. But not entirely! The baby's environment both before and after birth can modify the effects of heredity considerably. During the prenatal period, the fetus is vulnerable to a variety of environmental factors that can influence the course of development. Many factors are related to the mother's physical condition, emotional well-being, diet, or the drugs she takes during pregnancy. Heather knows this and wants to do all she can to ensure the health of her baby. Still, she is skeptical of some of the advice she is being given.

In this chapter we look at the stages of prenatal development and examine the factors that affect the course of embryonic and fetal growth and the newborn baby's subsequent development. We also study some environmental and family factors at birth and after birth that can result in complications, including current issues like fetal development during the drug age. In addition, we discuss the social aspects of pregnancy and birth and the circumstances surrounding conception. Finally, we examine the failure to conceive and some causes of and treatments for infertility.

Prenatal Development

Conception

About once each month, on approximately the fourteenth day of a woman's 28-day menstrual cycle, a mature *ovum*, or egg cell, is released from the ovary and arrives in the fallopian tube (see Figure 4.1). If a man's sperm penetrates the ovum, their nuclei join, the ovum is fertilized, and pregnancy begins. Although this process appears simple, it is not. Before fertilization can occur, semen, which contains the sperm, must be deposited in the female's vagina at the time of the male orgasm. Most semen leaks back out of the vagina. The remaining sperm face a difficult journey to reach the egg. They must make their way past the cervix to the outer part of the fallopian tube. Many die before completing their journey, killed by an acidic secretion that covers the vagina and cervix and is hostile to sperm. (Some women worry that the acidity of their vaginal secretion may be the cause of their failure to conceive, but this is not the case.) Successful sperm escape the effects of the vaginal secretion by reaching the fallopian tube within a few minutes.

Of the millions of sperm deposited in the vagina, only a few hundred reach their destination. Because so many sperm do not survive this journey, a sufficient number must be deposited in the vagina for conception to occur. Thus, if the male is

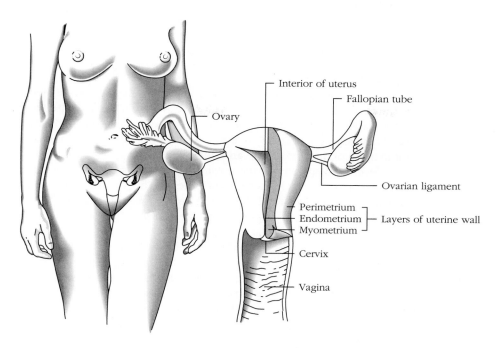

Figure 4.1 *The female reproductive system.*

infertile—either his sperm is abnormal or he has a low sperm count—it will be difficult to achieve conception.

The sperm that do arrive at the outer end of the fallopian tube undergo a process called **capacitation,** which produces enzymes that enable the sperm to dissolve the outer membrane of the egg cell and penetrate its center. The successful sperm is very highly selected; once a sperm penetrates the egg cell, the egg changes its outer membrane so that penetration by other sperm cannot occur. In this way multiple fertilization is avoided.

A CLOSER LOOK

Infertility

About one out of five couples who want to have children cannot conceive, and the number of infertile couples (those who fail to conceive within a year of trying) may be increasing (Mishell & Davajan, 1986; Hendershot & Placek, 1981). In part, this increase is due to delayed childbearing, since it becomes more difficult for a woman to conceive as she ages (Booher, 1990). Although physicians can link infertility to problems in either the man or the woman, they cannot determine the cause in 10% to 20% of such cases. Causes of male infertility include too few sperm, abnormally shaped sperm, or low sperm motility, which means that the sperm have a

hard time moving up the vaginal tract to meet the egg cell. Female infertility may be due to the ovary's failure to produce egg cells, the secretion of a mucus hostile to sperm, or blocked fallopian tubes that prevent the egg from passing down to the uterus. Although fertility experts can fairly easily diagnose a problem like blocked fallopian tubes, they sometimes need months to pinpoint the cause or causes of infertility; and in some cases the problem is never solved.

Infertility can be emotionally traumatic for both partners, especially since fewer babies are available for adoption.

(continued)

The timing of fertilization is precise. The egg cell lives for about 24 hours after entering the fallopian tube, and the sperm, once deposited, can only survive for about 48 hours. For conception to occur, therefore, intercourse should take place within two days of ovulation.

Immediately on fertilization, the ovum, now known as the *zygote,* begins to divide and to travel from the fallopian tube to the uterus, where it implants itself into the **decidua,** the thickened lining of the uterine wall (see Figure 4.2). Thereafter, rapid growth and development occur, so that by 8 weeks, a recognizable embryonic baby is present in a bag of fluid called the **amniotic sac.** This sac is formed by two membranes that develop from cells on the outside of the fertilized egg. The outer membrane is the **chorion;** it encloses the inner membrane, or **amnion,** which contains the **amniotic fluid.** This fluid serves as a protective support enabling the fetus to safely move and change positions within the uterus.

Stages of Prenatal Development

The nine months in utero are divided into three periods corresponding to the organism's developmental stage: the period of the ovum, the period of the embryo, and the period of the fetus. As you can see in Table 4.1 (p. 121), the organism undergoes a number of changes during these periods.

A CLOSER LOOK

(continued)

Although it is not always possible to treat the causes of infertility, scientists are quickly developing new "miracle" methods that help infertile couples bear children. Soon hospitals and fertility clinics will employ these methods routinely. We are going to discuss some methods of treating or circumventing infertility. As you read about them, bear in mind two points. First, although new infertility treatment options are well publicized and offer a great deal of hope to infertile couples, they can also be a source of frustration and disappointment, because they work in only a small percentage of cases. Many procedures, such as in vitro fertilization, have a clinical success rate of only 10% to 15% (Booher, 1990). For every 100 couples who try the technique, 10 to 15 will enjoy success and most will experience deep disappointment. Second, the options are not problem-free, so they must be considered realistically.

Donor Sperm

One of the easiest ways to deal with male infertility is to inseminate the wife with sperm from an anonymous donor. At times the husband's sperm is mixed with the donor's sperm so there is always the possibility that the husband has fathered the child. The parents are advised to keep the procedure secret, even from their own obstetrician, so that they will come to believe that both the father and mother are biologically related to the baby. Although physicians have successfully employed this procedure for many years, the possibility remains that the father may reject a child to whom he is not biologically related. Also, acquired immune deficiency syndrome (AIDS) has become a problem. Although AIDS is ordinarily transmitted through sexual contact, a woman artificially inseminated with the semen of an infected donor can also become infected. Current screening techniques for AIDS are inadequate, making it hard to identify sperm donors exposed to the AIDS virus. Thus artificial insemination, which provides hope for many couples, can turn to tragedy for some couples, who also have to consider the possibility of both mother and child contracting AIDS.

In Vitro Fertilization

Women with blocked fallopian tubes are the main users of in vitro fertilization. The physician retrieves an egg by a relatively simple surgical technique. The egg is then placed in a petri dish along with the husband's sperm. (Note that a test tube is not used, despite the popular term *test-tube baby.*) When the sperm penetrates and fertilizes the egg, the physician carefully implants the egg in the uterus and hopes for a

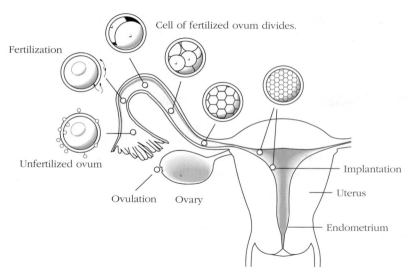

Cell of fertilized ovum divides.

Fertilization

Unfertilized ovum

Ovulation   Ovary

Implantation

Uterus

Endometrium

Figure 4.2   Fertilization and migration of the ovum from the fallopian tube to implantation in the uterine wall.

successful pregnancy. The good outcome of this procedure depends on an elaborate process of preparing the uterus for the egg. This procedure can also help couples with a low sperm count, because fertilization requires only a few sperm. Unfortunately, in vitro fertilization cannot always help even its best candidates. Costing $4500 to $6000 for each attempt, the procedure is prohibitively expensive. In addition, clinics offering in vitro fertilization are not regulated. Thus clinics with a lower-than-average success rate can continue to attract—and sometimes exploit—hopeful prospects (*New York Times*, 28 July 1988).

Egg Transplant

Recently an infertile woman in Los Angeles County gave birth to a healthy infant through yet another "miracle" of modern-day medicine and genetic engineering: an egg transplant. In this procedure a fertile female donor is inseminated with sperm from the would-be father. Five days later the physician retrieves the fertilized egg from the donor and implants it into the infertile woman's uterus, where pregnancy resumes. Scientists praise this process because it offers hope to women who are unable to ovulate and it can stem genetic diseases. According to researchers, a woman with a known genetic disease may opt for this procedure to prevent pass-

ing her genes on to her offspring (Bustillo et al., 1984). Plans are under way to open ovum-transfer centers in hospitals and fertility clinics despite objections from critics who feel the procedure poses a fundamental challenge to the concept of parenthood.

Surrogate Womb

In yet another procedure a fertile woman "rents" the use of her uterus to a couple. Sperm from the would-be father clinically inseminates the donor, who carries the baby through-out the pregnancy. After birth, the infertile couple legally adopts the infant. Surrogacy is quite expensive; the infertile couple must often pay for the donor's prenatal care and remunerate her on delivery of the child. Surrogacy also involves legal help for the adoption and for the contract that the donor must sign to give up the baby. One potential problem is breach of contract, in which the donor refuses to give up the baby once it is born; this happened in the famous case involving Baby Melissa, or Baby M. Another problem is that the baby may not be biologically related to the husband. A woman who signs a contract as a donor for a surrogate pregnancy agrees to abstain from sexual intercourse for a number of days to ensure that the right sperm penetrates her egg.

(continued)

Period of the ovum   During the **period of the ovum,** which lasts approximately two weeks from the time of conception, the zygote establishes itself in the uterine wall. Tendrils from the zygote penetrate the blood vessels in the wall, beginning a physiologically dependent relationship that continues throughout pregnancy.

Period of the embryo   The **period of the embryo** lasts from the time of the zygote's attachment to the uterine wall until the first occurrence of **ossification,** the formation of solid bone, at the end of the eighth week. This is a very hazardous time. Not all embryos are properly attached to the uterine wall. Most miscarriages (spontaneous abortions) occur during this period when the embryo can become detached from the wall and expelled. According to a recent study, 31% of embryos are aborted during the embryo period; in 22% of the cases, the miscarriage occurs without the woman even knowing she is pregnant (Wilcox et al., 1988). These spontaneous abortions occur because of abnormalities in the embryo, the uterine wall, or other life-supporting structures of the uterine environment. The pregnant woman's immune system may also be involved. In some cases that are still not completely understood, a pregnant woman with an underactive immune system

A CLOSER LOOK

(continued)
But does the woman really abstain? This is not always easy to ascertain.

Must the couple who chooses to have a child through the surrogate womb procedure accept the child as their own? In one case a handicapped baby was born, and the husband rejected it, contending that it was not his child. The surrogate mother also rejected the child, noting that she had signed a contract agreeing only to carry the baby through

pregnancy. The welfare department had blood tests made to determine the child's paternity. These tests revealed that the surrogate mother's husband had fathered the child. Thus she had breached her contract by having intercourse with her husband at a time when she had agreed to abstain. Had it been the other man's child, he would have been held legally responsible, and the welfare department would have placed an unwanted child in its father's home.

These cases are examples of ***traditional surrogacy***. In addition, there is ***gestational surrogacy***. This procedure follows the same pattern as in vitro fertilization, placing the sperm and egg of a couple wishing to have a child in a petri dish. The physician then implants the fertilized egg into the uterus of a surrogate mother. Although the child is biologically related to the mother and father, a surrogate mother gives birth to the baby. Critics see this method as a way for healthy women who can become pregnant to circumvent the inconvenience of pregnancy, perhaps for career reasons. In contrast, women unable to become pregnant are the main users of traditional surrogacy. Both forms of surrogacy are highly controversial means of solving the infertility problem. Critics have called surrogacy baby selling and a kind of prostitution. The infamous Baby M. case brought surrogacy into the national spotlight, raising the following questions about motherhood, social class, sexual politics, and ethics: Are babies a commodity that can be bought and sold? What does it mean to have women "renting" their uteruses to wealthy couples?

TABLE 4.1 Stages of Prenatal Development

	Time past conception	*Development*
Period of the ovum	1 week	Zygote (fertilized ovum) travels through fallopian tube toward uterus.
	2 weeks	After attaching itself to uterine wall, zygote becomes an embryo. Embryo now develops rapidly, and cells begin to differentiate.
Period of the embryo	3 weeks	Embryo begins to form, with distinguishable head and tail regions. Brain begins to develop. Circulatory system develops: blood cells and blood vessels appear, and heart begins to beat.
	4 weeks	Embryo is no larger than human thumbnail. Body is curled into a C-shape, with discernible limb buds and primitive vertebrae. Eyes, ears, and mouth develop. Nerves and digestive system begin to form. Circulatory system continues to develop: small vessel destined to become the heart begins to pulse. Divisions of brain become more differentiated.
	5 weeks	Beginnings of lungs appear, and hands begin to form.
	6 weeks	Head becomes larger than body. Three main parts of brain are distinguishable, and external ear appears. Hands and feet develop, and limbs are clearly discernible.
	7 weeks	Body begins to straighten, with regression of tail and development of neck. Eyelids begin to form, and muscles develop throughout body. Beginnings of cerebral cortex appear in brain.
	8 weeks	Embryo is approximately 1 inch long and begins to resemble human being, although head is about as large as rest of body. Face and features are distinguishable. Fingers, toes, and external genitals are present. By end of 8th week, embryo is a fetus and able to move about.
Period of the fetus	12 weeks	Fetus is approximately 3 inches long. Facial features become more refined, and sex of fetus is easily discernible. Reflex response to being touched is present.
	16 weeks	Fetus is approximately 4½ inches long, and body is larger in proportion to head. The mother can usually feel fetus's movements. Sucking, swallowing, and other reflexes begin. Ossification of bones continues, and joints appear.
	5 months	Hands and feet are fully developed, and fetus is capable of moving about freely within uterus. Hearing is present.
	6 months	Eyes are fully developed and can open and close, and nails, sweat glands, coarser skin, and hair develop. Lungs begin to manufacture surfactin, which prevents them from collapsing, and fetus is able to inhale and exhale.
	7 months	Fetus attains "age of viability"; if birth occurs child could survive. Lungs are able to breathe air. Fat is forming and eyes open. Central nervous system continues to develop, and brain begins to develop folds and fissures.
	9 months	Fetus spends last weeks in utero, adding 50% of its weight, although weight gain slows down as birth approaches. Brain continues to develop, as it will for several months after birth.

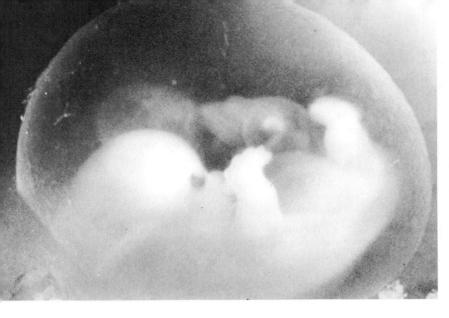

At seven weeks the embryo is already recognizable as a baby. The umbilical cord has formed and some facial features are visible.

may not have an appropriate response to a type of fetal cell called a trophoblast and may be at risk for a spontaneous abortion (Kolata, 1988).

Differentiation of important organs occurs during this period (Moore, 1982). The inner mass of the zygote differentiates into three layers. The hair, nails, a part of the teeth, the outer layer of the skin and skin glands, the nervous system, and sensory cells develop from the **ectoderm.** The muscles, skeleton, excretory and circulatory systems, and inner skin layers develop from the **mesoderm.** And the gastrointestinal tract, eustachian tubes, glands, and other organs, such as the lungs, pancreas, and liver, develop from the **endoderm.** By the end of the fourth week after conception, a small vessel destined to become the heart begins to pulse, even though at this point the embryo is no larger than a thumbnail. By the end of this period, at 8 weeks after conception, the embryo is approximately 1 inch long and beginning to resemble a human being. It is somewhat out of proportion, because its head is about as large as the rest of its body, but the face and features are recognizable, and the fingers, toes, and external genitals are present.

Several structures supporting the fetus also develop during the embryo period. The **placenta** (or afterbirth), a fleshy disc growing on part of the chorion, is made up of a large number of fingerlike projections called **villi.** The villi burrow into the uterine lining, coming to rest in the **intervillous space.** The life of the fetus depends on the placenta, which allows substances to pass from the maternal bloodstream to that of the fetus. If, for example, the mother's blood supply is reduced (due to high blood pressure, for example), the fetus will starve and will be born smaller than normal. If a serious reduction in the blood flow occurs, the fetus may die from lack of oxygen.

Substances made up of large molecules cannot pass through the placenta, which is why it is sometimes called the **placental barrier.** However, some hazardous substances, such as drugs ingested by the mother, do pass through the barrier and harm the fetus. The maternal and fetal bloodstreams do not mix. Each bloodstream is separate, and substances passing from the mother to the baby, or vice versa, must come out of one bloodstream, cross the villi, and then enter the other bloodstream.

The **umbilical cord,** which also develops during the embryo period, joins the embryo to the placenta at the abdomen (at the site of the future navel). This cord

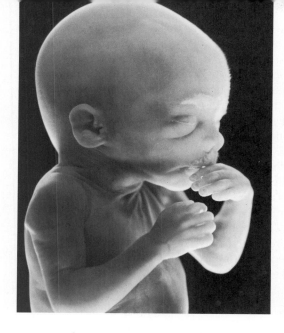
The fetus at 20 weeks.

is relatively long; in fact, at birth it is longer than the newborn baby. The cord's considerable length allows the embryo flexibility of movement. The umbilical cord consists of arteries and veins that carry blood to and from the placenta. The fetal heart can pump blood through the umbilical arteries to the placenta and receive blood back through the umbilical veins.

Another supporting structure that develops is the *amniotic sac*. It contains a liquid substance—the amniotic fluid—that supports the embryo as it moves and protects it from physical shocks.

Period of the fetus   The **period of the fetus** lasts from the beginning of the third month until birth. Muscular development occurs at a rapid rate, and various body parts become more differentiated. The central nervous system begins to develop rapidly as well and continues to develop for six months after birth (Tanner, 1978).

By the end of 16 weeks after conception, the mother usually can feel the fetus move. Its lips are well formed and can move, and its mouth can open and close. By the end of 24 weeks, its eyes are fully developed and can open and close; the fetus develops nails, sweat glands, a coarser skin, and hair (much of the hair is shed in utero, but at times shedding continues after birth). Next, there is gradual improvement and organization of the nervous and sensory systems.

At the end of 26 to 28 weeks, a time known as the **age of viability,** fetal development is sufficiently advanced so the child can survive if birth occurs. If birth occurs before that time, the nervous and respiratory systems are usually not mature enough, and the baby's survival is less likely. The age of viability is periodically revised due to medical advances in caring for premature babies. For example, some babies born at 24 weeks are now able to survive. Thus the age of viability may be changed to 24 weeks. However, extremely premature infants have poorly developed motor skills and difficulties in feeding and sleeping for several months after birth.

During the last part of pregnancy, from 28 weeks to birth at full term (usually 38 to 42 weeks after conception), the fetus experiences rapid increases in height and weight and accumulates layers of fat tissue under the skin. This fat prepares the fetus for birth, by insulating it from the changes in temperature that will occur.

Sensory Capabilities

The developing fetus appears to respond to sounds from outside the uterine environment. Thus, certain sensory capabilities such as hearing may develop before birth. By inserting a microphone into the uterus, researchers were able to document the sounds the fetus is likely to hear. Although the noises are somewhat muted, sounds from inside the mother's body, such as her heartbeat, and outside are audible. Early studies (Sontag & Wallace, 1935) and mothers' reports indicate that the fetus reacts to noise by increasing its activity level. Can the fetus hear the mother's voice? Ockleford and colleagues (1988) believe that the fetus learns to recognize its mother's voice. In tests of infants who were less than 24 hours old, the researchers found that when the infants heard tape recordings of their mothers' voices, their heart and respiration rates changed. The infants exhibited similar changes when they heard tape recordings of their fathers' voices, but the reactions were not as intense. When they listened to an unfamiliar voice, they did not exhibit any reaction (see "A Closer Look: Learning in the Womb").

Environmental Influences

Prenatal development is usually completely normal. But since many things can go wrong, the prenatal period is referred to as a *critical period*. This is a time in the process of development when the organism is especially sensitive to a particular influence. The same influence before or after the critical period has less impact on development, or even no impact.

A CLOSER LOOK

Learning in the Womb

You will learn in Chapter 5 that babies are capable of responding to their environment immediately after birth; they can even recognize and show preference for their mothers' voices. Researchers have been intrigued with whether infants learn in the womb. A relatively new body of research suggests that learning may begin even before birth.

In their study of fetal learning, Anthony DeCasper and his associates hypothesized that since the fetus hears the mother's stomach noises, heartbeat, and voice, the newborn baby may also prefer to hear these sounds. To test this hypothesis, they devised a study in which each baby was given a nipple to suck. They attached the nipple to a tape recorder so that by sucking in a pattern of longer and shorter sucks, the baby would hear the mother's voice. By sucking in a different pattern, the baby would hear some other recording, such as another woman's voice or the father's voice. A series of studies (DeCasper & Fifer, 1980; DeCasper & Spence, 1986) found that babies sucked in order to hear their mothers' voices.

In a follow-up study the researchers had 16 pregnant women read aloud part of the children's book *The Cat in the Hat*. The women, who were in the last 6½ weeks of pregnancy, read the same part of the book to their fetuses twice a day for a total of five hours per day. When the babies were born, the researchers, using their sucking test, found that the babies sucked in order to hear their mothers' reading of *The Cat in the Hat* as opposed to hearing their mothers reading of *The King, the Mice, and the Cheese*, a book that is quite different in tone. This type of study suggests that babies may be influenced by prenatal experiences.

Of course, no conclusions can be drawn on the basis of the research done so far; additional studies are needed. However, studies on fetal learning, along with animal studies, will eventually help us understand how to condition young infants. These studies will also help explain the brain's functional organization before birth and may eventually help psychologists and neurologists assess and facilitate the development of babies who are born prematurely with underdeveloped brains.

For many years researchers thought that the fetus was insulated from external influences. However, we now know that numerous environmental factors, such as drugs, chemicals, and viruses, can cross the placental barrier and damage the developing fetus. In addition, such factors as the mother's age and diet during pregnancy contribute to atypical development (see Table 4.2).

TABLE 4.2 Factors That May Affect the Fetus

Factors	Effect
Drugs	
Alcohol	Small head size, defective joints, congenital heart defects, mental retardation
Nicotine	Low birth weight, prematurity, stillbirth, spontaneous abortion, nicotine dependency at birth; associated with sudden infant death syndrome, hyperactivity, and increased respiratory infections during first year of life
Aspirin—moderate use	Relatively safe until third trimester; use then may prolong labor and lengthen clotting time for both mother and baby, increasing the risk of hemorrhage
Tetracycline	Liver, bone, and teeth damage, discolored teeth, abnormally short arms or legs, webbed hands
Thalidomide	Stunted limb growth
Tranquilizers	In first trimester, cleft palate and other birth defects, neonatal jaundice
Heroin	Low birth weight, maternal toxemia, postpartum maternal hemorrhaging (including risk of neonatal death), altered neonatal sleep patterns, fetal addiction/withdrawal, respiratory depression
Methadone	Low birth weight, hyperirritability, respiratory depression
Caffeine	Low birth weight
Marijuana	In animals: reduced growth rate, spontaneous abortion, low birth weight
LSD	Poorly understood; stillbirth, spontaneous abortion (animals: neonatal death, temporary chromosomal damage)
Diseases or medical conditions	
Rubella virus	First-trimester miscarriage, deafness, blindness, cataracts, heart malformations, various other defects
Diabetes	Maternal toxemia, abnormally large fetus, stillbirths, spontaneous abortion
Syphilis	Malformations, mental retardation, syphilitic infant, deafness, blindness, spontaneous abortion, stillbirth
Influenza	In first trimester, malformations
Gonorrhea	Blindness, gonococcal arthritis, increased risk of ectopic pregnancy
Anemia	Neonatal anemia
Herpes, type II	Neonatal death
Hormones	
Androgens	In females, masculinization of internal and/or external genitals
Estrogens	In males, less aggression and athletic skill compared to age-matched controls
Progesterone	Masculinization of female fetus
DES	In males, semen and testicular abnormalities, reduced fertility; in females, abnormal vaginal or cervical growth or cancer, miscarriage later in life
Other	
Oral contraceptives	Congenital abnormalities

The scientific study of abnormalities caused by environmental influences during the prenatal period is called **teratology,** from the Greek word *teras* meaning "monster." The environmental agents that can produce abnormalities and malformations in the developing fetus are called **teratogens.** Studying the effects of teratogens and other factors that influence human development may help eliminate some congenital defects (Wilson & Fraser, 1977). This type of study is also relevant to our discussion for two reasons. First, we need to know some causes of atypical development to gain an overall understanding of children's growth and development. Second, there are important social implications. For example, some women who live in poverty do not receive adequate medical care and nutrition during pregnancy. And an increasing number of babies are born to women who abuse drugs during pregnancy. Some of these babies may be born addicted, whereas others may suffer physical malformations or behavioral disorders that make it impossible for them to lead productive lives as adults. Knowledge of the process by which environmental factors affect fetal growth will facilitate the prevention of such problems through timely medical care, changes in living conditions, and specific interventions.

Although the risks are numerous, the odds are in favor of having a normal healthy child. Why then are some fetuses affected by adverse environmental factors while others are not? For example, Heather's physician asked her to stop smoking because it might harm her unborn child. It is difficult for Heather to quit, and when her husband expresses his concern, she reminds him that her mother smoked during her pregnancies and that her friend Diane smokes and her baby is just fine.

The effects of teratogens vary according to the genotypes of both mother and fetus; *some, but not all, individuals have a genetic predisposition to the effect of a particular teratogen or other adverse factors.* However, doctors cannot tell what the unborn baby's genetic predisposition is, with absolute certainty. Should Heather take the chance and continue smoking? What advice would you give her?

In addition, Heather should consider that environmental influences such as the mother's age can interact with a teratogen to influence development. The effects of teratogens and other adverse influences also vary depending on the developmental stage of the embryo or fetus. Teratogens only damage developing organs. Since different organs begin and end their developments at different times, their vulnerability to the teratogens will vary. The vulnerable period for the eyes, for example, is 20 to 50 days after conception; for the heart, it is 20 to 40 days after conception. Exposure to teratogens during these times will result in malformations to these organs. In general, the first three months of pregnancy are particularly vulnerable to adverse influences. Teratogens will affect the body's basic structure and form and seriously impact the nervous system.

Thus there are variations in the degree to which the influence of specific teratogens culminates in fetal abnormalities. These variations occur on a **continuum of reproductive casualty;** they range from relatively minor problems that may be noticeable after birth, such as slightly retarded growth and learning difficulties, to such major problems as severe mental retardation and physical deformity.

Experiences after birth may also determine the extent to which the effects of a teratogen or any other adverse influence will be manifest. Sameroff and Chandler (1975) refer to this notion as the **continuum of caretaking casualty;** it ranges from a stable family situation in which few adverse environmental factors exist to a poor, unstable, or dysfunctional family situation that contains several harmful factors. The interaction between the reproductive casualty continuum and the caretaking casualty continuum often determines developmental outcome. To explain this principle, Sameroff and Chandler (1975) note that approximately 10% of all children are born with some kind of handicap. In many cases, the handicaps are hardly noticeable and decrease with age, or disappear entirely, because human beings have a strong, innate, self-righting mechanism toward normal development. Negative factors in the home, however, will contribute to, and possibly increase, the severity of the handicap. For this reason, researchers are particularly concerned with poor children; many suffer from prenatal neglect and exposure to teratogens and then after birth are subjected to harmful conditions associated with poverty, such as poor sanitation, inadequate shelter, inadequate health care, and malnutrition (National Center for Children in Poverty, 1990).

Finally, whether a handicap limits a child's development often depends on the relationship with significant adults—namely, the parents, teachers, and caregivers (McGillicuddy-Delisi & Sigel, 1982). Are the parents of a congenitally blind infant caring toward her or do they reject her? Will the parents of a lethargic, unresponsive baby become anxious, frustrated, and perhaps even abusive if he fails to meet their expectations? Such possible reactions are ultimately the most important factors in how the handicap will affect the child's development (Field, 1980). Now let us examine some specific influences on the course of fetal growth and also some conditions during birth that can affect development.

Influence of Teratogens

Radiation and chemicals   Many adverse influences on development are related to the mother's condition, but other teratogens, such as radiation or chemicals, can also damage the fetus.

In Warsaw, Poland, a youngster swallows an antiradiation iodine solution as a precaution against fallout from the accident at the nuclear power station Chernobyl.

X-rays and other forms of radiation can damage both the parent's genetic material and the developing organism. The effects of radiation are cumulative; radiation builds up in the body over years. Low dosages, such as those involved in routine X-ray examinations, may not be immediately harmful to adults, but they could harm a fetus. Hence pregnant women are advised not to have any X-rays. Even a nonpregnant woman of childbearing age should take precautions in the event there is an unknown pregnancy. Thus a protective shield is used during X-ray examinations to guard against possible harmful effects.

Massive doses of radiation might kill the fetus. Lesser dosages may still cause mental or physical deformities, depending on when the exposure occurs (Moore, 1982). The dangers associated with radiation exposure became evident after the 1945 atomic bombings of Hiroshima and Nagasaki; pregnant women within 1500 meters of the blasts gave birth to stillborn babies. Those farther away and thus exposed to lesser dosages gave birth to babies who were later diagnosed as mentally retarded (Murphy, 1947).

Less conclusive connections between radiation and fetal damage occur with regard to electromagnetic fields, such as those found around high-voltage power lines and VDTs (video display terminals) used in countless offices and homes around the country. Recent studies suggest that pregnant women living near high-voltage power lines may be at an increased risk for miscarrying or giving birth to an infant with birth defects (Ahlbom et al., 1987), although it is unlikely. Pregnant women who work at VDTs for more than 20 hours a week may also be at higher risk for miscarriage, stillbirth, premature delivery, and fetal birth defects.

Some chemicals damage genetic material, whereas others may directly impact fetal development and cause malformations. Many of these chemicals are added to items commonly used at home, such as hair dyes and cleaning fluids; in addition, many women encounter potentially hazardous chemicals, such as lead compounds and asbestos, in the workplace. Because overexposure to these chemicals causes birth defects, physicians advise women to limit their use of many chemicals during pregnancy; during the first three months, they should avoid using chemicals altogether.

Industrial pollution is another threat to the unborn baby. For example, health authorities in a small Texas city have reported an unusually high number of Down's syndrome births during the past several years. A 1987 explosion at a nearby chemical plant revealed that the plant had been spewing toxic chemicals into the air and contaminating the city's principal source of water. The Occupational Safety and Health Administration (OSHA) is still investigating a possible connection between chemical pollution and the high occurrence of Down's syndrome. The plant management contends that toxic waste does not play a role in Down's syndrome. But medical literature supports the view that toxic chemicals can damage the proteins and enzymes involved in the separation of chromosomes when the egg and sperm join (Schneider, 1990). If such damage occurs, the 21st chromosome, which is responsible for Down's syndrome, would fail to separate properly and an extra chromosome would result, thus leading to the disorder.

Drugs taken by the mother Various prescription and nonprescription drugs also have deleterious effects on the developing fetus. The possible teratogenic effects of some drugs became evident following the European thalidomide disaster during the late 1950s and early 1960s. Physicians had prescribed **thalidomide** to pregnant women as a sedative or antinausea drug in early pregnancy. Many mothers who took this drug had babies with gross anatomical defects in their limbs, missing limbs, or feet and hands attached to the torso (a deformity known as **phocome-lia**).

Other drugs can also influence fetal growth. For example, iodine and acne medications are particularly dangerous because they are so commonly used that women in the first stages of pregnancy may use these drugs without knowing that they are pregnant (O'Brien & McManus, 1978). Any woman who is not actively trying to prevent pregnancy should refrain from using such drugs for the first two weeks after ovulation until she is certain she is not pregnant.

Another drug known to affect the unborn child is **DES,** or **diethylstilbestrol.** Unlike other drugs, DES has delayed effects that do not appear until the child reaches maturity. A synthetic hormone, DES was prescribed between the late 1940s and early 1960s to an estimated 2 million American women who were at risk of miscarrying. Their children appeared normal, but in the late 1960s researchers found that some adult daughters were developing vaginal deformities and cancer of the cervix.

Medication administered during labor and delivery to ease pain and sedate the mother may also affect the newborn. Several researchers found that babies whose mothers had received medication during labor and delivery tended to be more irritable and less responsive and attentive at birth than babies whose mothers remained unmedicated (Brazelton, 1961; Conway & Brackbill, 1970; Brackbill, 1979). But there is no evidence that low dosages of such medications have significant long-term effects on otherwise healthy babies. Thus the kind of medication administered, the amount, and when during labor and delivery it is administered

Thalidomide child.

may be significant factors in determining whether the baby will be adversely affected (Brackbill, McManus, & Woodward, 1985). Nevertheless, the use of pain medication during labor and delivery is controversial, in part because physicians sometimes administer it unnecessarily. Some researchers also question the wisdom of placing the baby at risk for complications that may arise as a consequence of the medication. Even if the consequences are short-term and result only in a temporarily unresponsive and irritable baby, such behavior may frustrate the parents and lead to possible problems in the parent/child relationship (Parke, O'Leary, & West, 1972).

After learning about these risks, some mothers opt for natural childbirth and attempt to avoid medication during labor and delivery. But that is not always possible. Women who need medication should not feel guilty about it; rather they should try to understand that any unresponsiveness in their baby may only be temporary.

Drug addiction   In addition to prescribed medications, other drugs taken by some pregnant women may affect the unborn child. For example, researchers suspect that cocaine use during pregnancy can cause miscarriages, stillbirths, birth defects, or long-term behavioral deficiencies in affected children (see "A Closer Look: Crack Babies"). Information about marijuana's effects on a developing fetus remains sketchy. Smoking marijuana during pregnancy, however, appears to affect

A CLOSER LOOK

Crack Babies

Use of illegal drugs in the United States increased during the 1980s and continues to increase into the 1990s. Yet cocaine use, and the use of "crack," or crystalline cocaine, in particular, are on the rise; an estimated 24 million Americans have used cocaine in some form, and about 5 million of them are regular users. Most of these individuals are between the ages of 26 and 49, a span that includes the prime childbearing years (Sussman & Levitt, 1989).

Drugs ingested during pregnancy affect the woman who takes them and her developing fetus as well. In the United States about 375,000 babies are born each year to mothers who use drugs (American Academy of Pediatrics, 1989), and many of these babies are born with serious, perhaps life-threatening, complications.

Drugs used during pregnancy affect a child's development at a very fragile time. A fetus is most vulnerable to substances ingested by its mother between 17 and 85 days after conception. Most of the organ systems are developing during this period, and drugs can impede normal development, causing birth defects or death. In the latter part of pregnancy, drug abuse may inhibit the fetus's brain growth and weight gain or may precipitate premature delivery.

Although the specific fetal effects of maternal cocaine use are not yet certain because the problem is still too new,

recent studies suggest that the drug is teratogenic, causes complications with labor and delivery, and may cause some long-term impairment in affected children. Cocaine's teratogenic nature is due in part to the fact that it constricts blood vessels; when it constricts placental blood vessels, the fetus's supply of nutrients and oxygen diminishes. Without these necessary elements, growth may be hindered or deformities may develop. In addition, cocaine use during the last trimester may cause hyperactive fetal activity, increased fetal blood pressure, or premature placental detachment from the uterus, which endangers both mother and child.

Women using cocaine during pregnancy have more complicated labors and deliveries. For instance, premature labor, which may occur as a result of maternal cocaine use during the last trimester, can result in low birth weight—the leading threat to neonatal health in the United States today. Fetuses exposed to cocaine are more likely to exhibit a high rate of distress at delivery, and stillbirths also occur more often.

These babies are at greater risk for dying of sudden infant death syndrome (see also Chapter 5); they are also more likely to contract AIDS because the mothers may have used contaminated needles.

Some cocaine-exposed infants may experience long-the fetus in much the same way as cigarette smoking does. If a pregnant woman smokes marijuana, it can lead to fetal oxygen deprivation and perhaps brain damage. Hallucinogens such as LSD have been implicated as causal agents of physical birth defects and behavioral disorders (Ostrea & Chavez, 1979). Maternal addiction to morphine, methadone, and heroin may also cause dependence in the infant. Health authorities have reported infants born to addicted mothers undergo withdrawal symptoms such as vomiting, trembling, and even death within the first few days after birth (Strauss et al., 1975). The severity of the symptoms is related to the length of the mother's addiction (Burnham, 1972). If the mother refrains from drug use for several months before birth, the baby will usually not suffer withdrawal symptoms.

In a review of studies on this subject, Jones and Lopez (1988) point out that although babies of mothers who abuse drugs are often referred to as "addicted babies," we need to consider more broadly the effects of maternal drug abuse: some drugs are addictive and result in withdrawal symptoms in the newborn baby; other drugs are toxic and can cause the baby to be sick and to be born prematurely or at a low birth weight; yet other drugs may have a teratogenic effect and result in identifiable anomalies at birth. Moreover, the mother's behavior constitutes an indirect risk that can result in harm to the baby either before or after birth (Weston et al., 1989).

A CLOSER LOOK

term problems when they interact with other children. As they grow older, they may show signs of permanent brain damage and have difficulty developing their motor, sensory, and language skills. If these children do not receive consistent developmental assistance right from the start, they will not be prepared for school and will continue to fall behind their peers throughout childhood and adolescence.

In addition, the social costs of their condition are great. For example, health care expenditures for these children are enormous. The normal delivery of an infant costs about $3000. The delivery and follow-up care of a cocaine-exposed baby can amount to $150,000, because they may need treatment by pediatricians, physical therapists, early-childhood educators, foster parents, and other specialists. According to a congressional study, a cocaine-exposed child's care can cost between $750 and $1768 per day. On the national level, preparing drug-affected children for kindergarten may cost $15 billion, or about $40,000 per child per year; many of these children will have to attend special education classes (Kadaba, 1990). Unfortunately, state and federal budgets are allocating less money for many social programs, including those benefiting children of drug-addicted mothers. As a result, these children may not receive the help they need to develop properly.

Preventing children's exposure to cocaine involves reaching their mothers before they become pregnant; the cost of a woman attending a drug treatment program is very low compared to the cost of a drug-exposed child's years of special care. The issue of infants born to women who use drugs, and particularly cocaine or crack, has received considerable publicity in recent years. Many observers question these women's fitness as mothers and even characterize their actions as criminal offenses. Since hundreds of so-called crack babies have to receive medical treatment in the hospitals where they were born, many ask whether it will even be possible to entrust them to their mothers. Often these women appear unable or unwilling to take care of their offspring. Moreover, ending an addiction to drugs, in spite of a desire to do so, can be nearly impossible to do alone, and social agencies have historically excluded pregnant women from drug treatment programs. Not until 1989 did Congress appropriate money to fund research and treatment to help pregnant women addicted to drugs.

Source: Based on reviews of the research by Chasnoff, 1989; Petitti & Coleman, 1990; American Academy of Pediatrics, 1989; Kadaba, 1990; Sussman & Levitt, 1989.

Caffeine, nicotine, and alcohol Other commonly used drugs such as caffeine (contained in coffee and some soft drinks), nicotine, and alcohol also influence fetal growth and result in spontaneous abortion, prematurity, and low-birth-weight babies (Streissguth et al., 1980a).

Although inconclusive, studies of caffeine use during pregnancy suggest a link between high caffeine consumption and birth defects. In studies reviewed by Sussman and Levitt (1989), pregnant women who ingested large amounts of caffeine—for instance, over four cups of coffee per day—appeared more likely to give birth to infants with birth defects than women who consumed little or no caffeine during pregnancy.

When a pregnant woman smokes, the nicotine and other chemicals contained in the smoke may pass through the placental barrier (U.S. Department of Health, Education and Welfare, 1979). Researchers have also established that the pregnant smoker creates a dangerous environment for her unborn child because smoking increases carbon monoxide levels in her blood, thus depriving the fetus of vital oxygen (National Research Council, 1982). The fetal heart rate increases when the mother smokes, apparently because of oxygen deprivation (Quigley et al., 1979). A study conducted in Great Britain found that women who smoked during pregnancy had a 28% greater chance of delivering a stillborn baby than nonsmokers (Bolton, 1983). According to other researchers, smoking during pregnancy may lead to premature or low-birth-weight babies (Frazier et al., 1961; Butler, Goldstein, & Ross, 1972); strong connections also appear to exist between maternal smoking and sudden infant death syndrome (Haglund & Cnattingius, 1990).

FEATURE

Father's Role in Birth Defects

Although most studies of prenatal influences on development focus on mothers, fathers may also play a role. John, Savitz, and Sandler (1991) found that children exposed to their fathers' smoking were 20% more likely to develop leukemia, lymphoma, and brain cancer than were children whose fathers did not smoke. Leading researcher Ellen Silbergeld (Silbergeld et al., in press), a toxologist at the University of Maryland in Baltimore, exposed male rats to relatively low levels of lead, equivalent to amounts encountered by men working in some factories. The male rats' offspring were born with brain defects, even though the mother rats were healthy and were not exposed to lead. Other researchers, who are looking for links between the father's occupation and birth defects, have found that welders who breathe toxic metal fumes develop abnormal sperm and that firemen exposed to toxic fumes have an increased risk of having children who are born with heart defects (Davis, 1991). Researchers are also studying links between alcohol use in fathers and low-birth-weight infants. Although still in the early stages, these studies suggest that certain substances may alter the sperm, thus leading to birth defects.

Recent research illuminates the possibility that some chemical substances may alter sperm and thus lead to birth defects in the offspring of affected men.

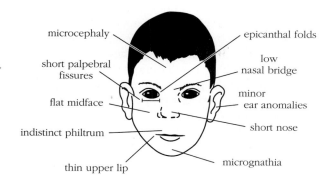

Facies in Fetal Alcohol Syndrome

microcephaly

short palpebral
fissures

flat midface

indistinct philtrum

thin upper lip

epicanthal folds

low
nasal bridge

minor
ear anomalies

short nose

micrognathia

*Physical features reflect
fetal alcohol syndrome.*

When a pregnant woman drinks alcohol, her baby may be born with **fetal alcohol syndrome (FAS).** First described in 1973 by Jones and Smith, FAS and its devastating long-term impact on development are only now beginning to be fully understood. The exact number of affected individuals is unknown, but studies estimate that more than 8000 alcohol-damaged babies are born annually (Rosenthal, 1990).

Depending on the severity of their condition, these babies may exhibit a variety of symptoms, including impaired functioning of the central nervous system (retarded mental and motor development, hyperactivity, poor attention span, and small brain size); deficiencies in height, weight, and head circumference; and a cluster of facial characteristics, such as short eye slits, a low nasal bridge, and a narrow upper lip (Streissguth et al., 1980a). Because only 20% of FAS children are born with marked facial deformities, the condition is often not diagnosed until the child fails to meet development landmarks; this may take several years.

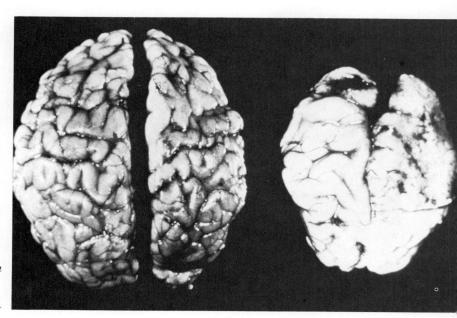

A normal brain (left) and the brain of an infant afflicted with fetal alcohol syndrome (right).

The type of damage caused by alcohol depends on when during pregnancy the woman drinks. During the first trimester, alcohol affects the fetus's bones and organs; during the last trimester when fetal weight and height gains occur, alcohol retards growth. Since the brain develops throughout pregnancy, drinking at any time during the nine months could result in brain damage (Rosenthal, 1990).

The risks of FAS and the severity of its symptoms increase the more a pregnant woman drinks (Rosett & Weiner, 1985). Drinking 1 or 2 ounces of alcohol per day results in a 10% risk; drinking 2 or more ounces per day increases the risk to 19% (Abel, 1980). Alcohol abuse is also often associated with other factors that can affect the developing fetus (such as smoking and using drugs, poor nutrition, ill health, poverty, and stress). Thus the logical question is which factor or factors are primarily responsible for the disorder's observed effects. Since the effects of drinking can be seen even when the other factors are under control, alcohol appears to be a particularly harmful substance during the prenatal period even when consumed in moderate amounts (Streissguth et al., 1980b).

Even among alcoholics, however, not every pregnant woman who drinks will have a baby born with FAS. Scientists suggest that (1) on certain days the fetus is more vulnerable to alcohol's teratogenic effects than on other days, and (2) women differ in their genetic susceptibility to having children with the syndrome. Since it is impossible to know whether there is a genetic susceptibility to alcohol's teratogenic effects, experts advise any woman who is pregnant or contemplating pregnancy not to drink at all (Rosenthal, 1990).

Men who drink alcohol may also place their offspring at risk. Although inconclusive, recent studies have suggested a connection between the father's drinking habits during the month preceding conception and low-birth-weight infants. If the mothers abstained from drinking alcohol and the fathers drank at least two drinks per day during the preconception month, their babies weighed several ounces less

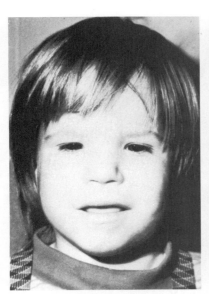

A child with fetal alcohol syndrome, at three different ages.

Many chemicals and drugs can influence the development of the fetus; physicians advise pregnant women to avoid such substances.

than babies whose parents did not drink (Sussman & Levitt, 1989). Low birth weight, as we will see later in the chapter, threatens the infant's health.

Legal Implications: Protecting the Fetus

The knowledge we are accumulating on fetal development and the factors that have a negative influence on reproductive outcome can help us develop programs to prevent birth defects. However, such knowledge also poses hard-to-resolve legal and moral questions. Consider the following examples: in Florida a woman was convicted of child abuse for using cocaine while pregnant; she was sentenced to 15 years' probation (*New York Times*, September 10, 1989). In a similar case in Michigan, a judge ordered a woman to stand trial for delivering cocaine to a minor— namely, her unborn child—through the umbilical cord (*New York Times*, February 5, 1990). In Wyoming a pregnant woman was arrested and charged with abusing her unborn child by being intoxicated. The charges were dismissed because no one could prove that the fetus was harmed.

Nationwide, there have been an increasing number of cases of women facing criminal charges for using drugs or alcohol and thereby placing their unborn babies at risk. In all but one case, charges were dismissed, primarily because most states do not consider the fetus a child, and child abuse statutes do not cover fetal abuse.

State and local authorities may amend these laws, but in the meantime a heated debate is taking place over the growing trend toward prosecution. Prosecutors contend that they are trying to prevent harm to the fetus and encourage women to seek treatment. Public health groups and women's rights advocacy groups contend that criminal sanctions are unlikely to protect the unborn. Also since many drug treatment programs exclude pregnant women, legal measures are unlikely to encourage them to seek treatment. In fact, realizing that they may be charged with child abuse if the authorities find out that they use drugs, women may avoid seeking treatment and prenatal care.

Systems set up to locate at-risk women may also have built-in inequities that defeat their purpose. Poor or minority women may be reported to authorities because of care providers' biases, while white women of a higher socioeconomic status may find their care providers more willing to "look the other way." For example, according to a study in Florida—a state that requires care providers to report to local health departments women who have used drugs or alcohol during pregnancy—black women and poor women were reported for their behavior more often than wealthier white women, even though both groups used drugs at about the same rate (Chasnoff, Landress, & Barrett, 1990).

Perhaps a better approach would be to make treatment programs more widely available to pregnant women. But if they still fail to seek treatment, would you recommend prosecution? As long as we know that drug and alcohol abuse jeopardizes fetal development, we have to take action to protect the unborn. But in doing so, would we be pitting the mother's rights against those of her fetus (Pollitt, 1990)? People will probably raise such questions as more scientific knowledge on fetal development becomes available.

Diseases of the Mother

Diseases contracted by the mother during pregnancy may also affect the fetus. Although the placenta is an effective barrier against most maternal illnesses, certain infectious diseases can be transmitted to the fetus. Infants have been born with smallpox, measles, chicken pox, mumps, scarlet fever, tuberculosis, malaria, herpes, and AIDS. The transmission of syphilis is also possible. The spirochetes of syphilitic mothers often produce such severe damage that a spontaneous abortion, or stillbirth, occurs. A surviving child is often born with physical or mental deformities. In some cases the infant may appear normal at birth and manifest a deformity several years later. Unlike many other diseases, syphilis does not affect fetuses under 18 weeks of age. Thus syphilitic transmission can be prevented by treating the mother with antibiotics early in her pregnancy (Pritchard & McDonald, 1976).

The effects of maternal diseases vary depending on when in the pregnancy they were contracted. Mumps, for example, results in a higher incidence of malformation if contracted in the first trimester. For rubella (German measles), the likelihood of fetal developmental deviations decreases from 50% if the mother contracts the disease in the first month to 17% if she contracts it in the third month. Almost no abnormalities will occur if the mother contracts rubella after the third month of pregnancy (Annis, 1978). The rubella virus can cause deafness, blindness, cataracts, heart abnormalities, and various other disorders. Some children who contract the virus in utero also appear to be mentally retarded, possibly because the resultant blindness or deafness interferes with their intellectual growth.

Even disorders that cannot be transmitted can affect the fetus. Maternal diabetes causes babies to be large and mature-looking at birth, but they are immature in their functioning. Diabetes that is not well controlled can result in a miscarriage, stillbirth, or respiratory distress that can be fatal to the newborn baby (Gellis & Hsia, 1959). The Centers for Disease Control (1990) found that babies born to insulin-dependent mothers were eight times more likely to have major malformations diagnosed during the first year of life than those born to nondiabetic mothers. In addition, if the mothers had gestational diabetes (that is, diabetes contracted during pregnancy) and did not take insulin, their babies were not at risk for malformations.

Another common maternal disorder is **toxemia,** a condition probably caused by toxic substances in the blood. Toxemia generally occurs among first-time mothers during the latter part of pregnancy and results in the swelling of the mother's limbs; in some cases it causes a dysfunction of her kidneys and circulatory system. The cause is unknown, but because of toxemia's prevalence among the poor, researchers suggest that malnutrition may play a role. When toxemia is left untreated, the mother's life is at stake (Moore, 1982). Increased rates of cerebral palsy, epilepsy, mental retardation, reading disability, and hyperactivity occur among children whose mothers had toxemia. Researchers hypothesize that by depriving the fetus of oxygen, toxemia leads to brain damage (DeMyer, 1975).

The Mother's Age

Maternal age is another factor often thought to influence reproductive outcome. For instance, mortality rates and incidences of retardation are higher in children born to mothers under 20. But these problems are not necessarily related to the mother's age (Mednick, Baker, & Sutton-Smith, 1979). According to Baldwin and Cain (1980), the intellectual deficits suffered by children of teenage parents can be explained by social and economic factors; teenage mothers are more often nonwhite, unmarried, and from lower socioeconomic backgrounds. Their difficult life circumstances have a negative impact on their children. Furthermore, a baby makes it difficult for the mother to complete school, hindering later job prospects and contributing to further economic problems. Education and support systems for a teenage mother may help her infant's intellectual development a great deal. At least one study has related how well the babies developed to their teenage mothers' personal development in education, employment, and family planning matters (Badger, 1980).

Birgitte Mednick and her colleagues (1979) suggest that inadequate medical care may be responsible for the higher mortality incidence among these infants. Statistics on infant mortality are usually based on studies of representative samples of the general population. Mednick compared the results of this type of study with studies of women receiving prenatal care from university hospitals; in the university hospital samples, the incidence of infant mortality was the same or lower for mothers aged 14 to 19 as for mothers 20 and older. This study demonstrated, therefore, that lack of prenatal care contributes to the mortality of infants of young mothers.

Until recently, women who delay childbearing until they are over age 35 were considered at risk for delivering premature, low-birth-weight babies. However, a well-controlled study of 4000 pregnancies found that older first-time mothers do not run a significantly higher risk of having premature or low-birth-weight babies, stillbirths, or neonatal deaths (Resnick, 1990). Resnick also found that older pregnant women are twice as likely to experience such complications as gestational diabetes, high blood pressure, and bleeding and rupture of the placenta. Although these conditions are potentially hazardous to the mother and fetus, they are manageable with appropriate prenatal care.

As discussed in Chapter 3, another risk associated with pregnancy in older women is giving birth to a baby suffering from a genetic disease such as Down's syndrome. But the risk is not so great that any woman over 35 should be dissuaded from having a baby.

Genetic Problems: Rh Factor

Incompatibility between the mother's blood and her infant's is another potentially hazardous problem. If the mother has Rh negative blood and the baby has inherited Rh positive blood, a reaction can occur in the mother and eventually in the fetus, culminating in a possible miscarriage. The baby may also be born mentally retarded.

The problem here is that antibodies build up in the mother's bloodstream. These antibodies treat the fetus as if it were foreign to the mother's system; they have a toxic effect on the fetus. The first baby is usually not affected, but by the second pregnancy the antibodies build up to such an extent that damage to the fetus is inevitable. If the mother receives regular prenatal examinations, however, her physician will detect her Rh negative blood characteristic and can prevent any subsequent problem through appropriate treatment; this may entail injections of Rh immune globulin or blood transfusions.

The Mother's Emotions

In the past physicians doubted that maternal emotions could affect the fetus (Ferreira, 1969). But evidence shows that an inordinate amount of psychological stress can impact the fetus and result in prematurity (Blau, 1963), prolonged pregnancy (Strean & Peer, 1956), and syndromes of restlessness and fussiness in the newborn (Turner, 1956; Sameroff & Chandler, 1975).

There is a scientific explanation for the mechanism by which the mother's psychological state influences reproductive outcome. Emotional reactions such as extreme stress result in the increase in the levels of cortisone, adrenaline, and other hormones in the maternal bloodstream (Whol, 1963). These substances pass through the placental barrier and affect the fetus. Hyperventilation, usually associated with anxiety, also has adverse effects on fetal development (Motoyama, 1966). In addition, the mother may turn to tranquilizers, alcohol, or other drugs and thus indirectly damage the fetus by failing to gain sufficient weight, or she may smoke cigarettes. All these behaviors are connected with low birth weight. McAnarney and Stevens-Simon (1990) believe that such indirect effects of maternal psychological stress or depression may have a more significant impact on fetal development than do direct effects.

Dunkel-Schetter, Lobel, and Scrimshaw (1990) conducted one of the most extensive studies on the relationship between the mother's psychological health and birth outcome. They found that stress during pregnancy affects birth weight and preterm birth. The researchers examined 130 pregnant women of diverse ethnic backgrounds, ranging in age from 18 to 42 years. Stress—measured on the basis of anxiety tests, self-reports of perceived stress, and distress caused by 22 major life events, such as death of a relative, financial pressure, and job loss—did not affect all birth outcomes. For example, stress during pregnancy had no impact on difficulty during labor or on neonatal medical complications, but it was related to birth weight and length of gestation.

Nutrition

The mother's diet and nutrition play a significant role in the growth and development of her fetus. During the prenatal period, the mother must have an adequate diet—including protein, calcium, iron and other minerals, and vitamins—to support the fetus's constantly developing body. Infants of poorly nourished mothers are more likely to be premature than infants of well-nourished mothers (Friedman & Sigman, 1980). Also, they are more likely to be of low birth weight or to die at birth or shortly after (Brozek & Schurch, 1984).

There is also an association between poor nutrition during pregnancy and impaired mental development (Pollitt & Thomson, 1977). One study found that even mild nutritional deficiencies in utero and after birth can disrupt a child's emotional stability later on (Barrett, 1982; Barrett, Radke-Yarrow, & Klein, 1982). Prenatally malnourished children were generally sadder, more withdrawn, dependent, and unfriendly than children whose mothers had adequate diets during pregnancy.

Multivitamins and neural tube defects   A recent landmark study (Milunsky et al., 1989) discovered that women who take multivitamins during the early stages of pregnancy sharply reduce the risk of having a baby with neural tube defects. Such defects, occurring at about the sixth week after conception, can cause paralysis and death and are among the most devastating neurological disorders; they affect an estimated 4000 babies each year in the United States. In the study, researchers interviewed 23,000 pregnant women, about half of whom took multivitamins containing folic acid during the first six weeks of pregnancy. The incidence of neural tube defects among babies born to these mothers was one-fourth that of babies born to women who did not take vitamin supplements. The idea that vitamin deficiencies might be implicated in these defects originated after World War II, when an unexpectedly large number of babies with neural tube defects were born to malnourished European women. Since then, researchers have been studying the role of vitamin supplements in preventing birth defects.

Malnutrition and brain growth   Malnutrition also affects brain development. Several approaches are used to study the effects of maternal malnutrition on fetal brain development. Autopsies are performed to examine the brains of animals or infants who die at birth or shortly after. Another approach is to compare newborns whose mothers are well nourished with those whose mothers are poorly nourished. (The weight of the placenta at birth sometimes helps determine the extent of dietary deprivation during pregnancy.) These studies have shown that malnutrition during the prenatal period interferes with development of the nervous system, and that the specific damage often depends on the stage during which the malnutrition occurs.

During certain periods called *growth spurts*, the brain undergoes accelerated growth. If malnutrition occurs at this time, damage will be more deleterious than if it occurs during slower brain growth. For the human organism, accelerated brain growth occurs from the latter part of the prenatal period through the first two years of life. The newborn brain is about one-quarter of its adult weight; its weight increases substantially during the next two years. Although the brain continues to grow after age 2, its growth rate is markedly decreased between age 2 and 10. At age 10, the brain has attained about 96% of its adult size (Dobbin, 1974).

During the prenatal period the brain grows mainly by cell division. Cell division continues after birth, but at a somewhat decreased rate. Between 6 months and 2 years, the increase in brain size occurs through a process called **myelination**, during which a fatty protective covering called myelin develops on nerve fibers. Autopsies of malnourished animals and children suggest that prenatal malnutrition leads to deficits in brain weight at birth and to a decrease in the number of brain cells (Kopp, 1983; Winick, Brasel, & Rosso, 1972).

Poverty, Pregnancy, and Child Development

Given the critical importance of adequate prenatal nutrition, researchers are particularly concerned about the development of poor children. Learning about or affording the healthy foods that are vital during pregnancy and the first few years of life may be difficult for their mothers. The nutritional status of poor women and children has improved in recent years, primarily due to various federal food programs such as Food Stamps, the Supplemental Food Program for Women, Infants, and Children, and the Child Care Food Program. These programs reach only a portion of the eligible population, however, so many American pregnant women and children still exhibit signs of poor nutrition (Klerman, 1991).

Infant mortality rates are also high in the United States. Traditionally used as an indicator of the population's overall health and well-being, the U.S. infant mortality rate has been decreasing over the past few years. As you can see in Table 4.3, the U.S. infant mortality rate was 10.4 in 1986; in 1987, the latest year for which figures are available, there were 10.1 infant deaths per 1000 live births. In 1987 the U.S. ranked 20th in infant mortality among industrialized nations (National Commission to Prevent Infant Mortality, 1990).

TABLE 4.3   Number of Deaths in the First Year of Life for Every 1000 Live Births (1986). The United States Lags Far Behind Many Other Countries in Caring for Its Infants, and Has One of the Highest Infant Mortality Rates.

Japan	5.2	Italy	9.8
Finland	5.9	Northern Ireland	10.2
Sweden	5.9	Austria	10.3
Switzerland	6.8	UNITED STATES (All)	10.4
Hong Kong	7.7	New Zealand	11.4
Netherlands	7.8	Israel	11.4
Canada	7.9	Greece	12.3
Norway	8.0	Czechoslovakia	13.4
France	8.0	Cuba	13.6
Denmark	8.2	Bulgaria	14.7
West Germany	8.5	Kuwait	15.7
Spain	8.5	Portugal	15.9
Ireland	8.7	Belgium	16.1
UNITED STATES (White)	8.9	Poland	17.6
Australia	8.9	Costa Rica	17.8
Scotland	8.9	UNITED STATES (Black)	18.0
East Germany	9.2	Hungary	19.1
Singapore	9.3	Chile	19.1
England and Wales	9.6		

Source: Based on data from the Department of Health and Human Services, 1986. Copyright © 1990 by The New York Times Company. Reprinted by permission.

Although we have improved the U.S. infant mortality rate, in some parts of the country it is still very high. Even more alarming is that the infant mortality rate is twice as high for black Americans as for whites, due in large part to poor nutrition and lack of prenatal care.

What is even more alarming is that the infant mortality rate is twice as high for blacks as for whites (National Center for Health Statistics, 1987; Children's Defense Fund, 1985). Studies show that poor, black pregnant women and their babies are more likely to suffer from malnutrition and inadequate health care (Children's Defense Fund, 1990; National Center for Children in Poverty, 1990). In addition, these women may not be able to pay for or find transportation to medical care. Approximately two-thirds of all infant deaths are associated with low birth weight (Institute of Medicine, 1988; Chase & Byrnes, 1983), which in turn is associated with poor nutrition during pregnancy and other prenatal factors such as smoking and lack of health care.

In spite of its high poverty rate and limited use of prenatal care, the Mexican-American population has a lower infant mortality rate than either American blacks or whites. Researchers are not sure why this group of women, whose use of prenatal care is as low as that of black, Puerto Rican, and American Indian women (see Figure 4.3, p. 142), fares as well as it does in pregnancy outcomes; suspected contributing factors are diet and social support (National Center for Health Statistics, 1990).

The WIC Program

Several years ago the government sponsored the development of a preventive health and nutrition program for pregnant women and young children. Known as the **Supplemental Food Program for Women, Infants, and Children,** and popularly referred to as **WIC,** this program provides vouchers for high-protein, iron-fortified foods to low-income pregnant women, infants, and young children up to age 5. WIC also includes nutrition education and counseling to encourage good eating habits. All participating women and children receive medical evaluations.

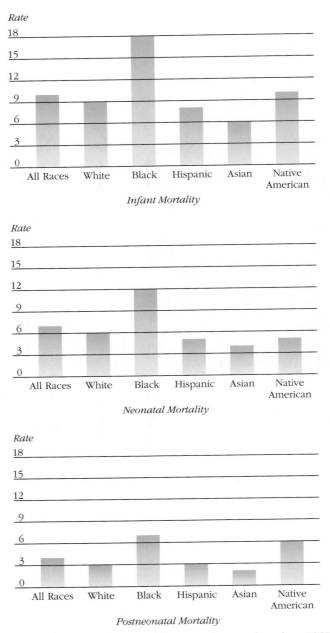

Figure 4.3 *U.S. infant mortality rates, by race, based on 1987 data from 18 reporting states and the District of Columbia.*

Source: From *Troubling Trends: The Health of America's Next Generation,* Fig. 4.1. National Commission to Prevent Infant Mortality, 1990.

WIC has been hailed as one of the most successful government health programs (U.S. House Select Committee on Children, Youth and Families, 1989; Hill, 1984). One reason for its success is that Congress appropriated enough funding to evaluate WIC's effectiveness. The role of research and evaluation is critical in social programs (Travers & Light, 1982), which are at the mercy of changing economic and political trends. Lawmakers often eliminate these programs in order to spend money for other purposes. Having research findings that document a program's success can help ensure its future.

Several studies have evaluated WIC's effectiveness. Besides demonstrating the program's success, they provided additional evidence on the important role of adequate nutrition during the prenatal period and infancy. Conducted for the Massachusetts Department of Public Health, the studies (Kotelchuck et al., 1981; 1984) compared 4000 WIC mothers with 4000 non-WIC mothers in terms of health, nutrition, and the incidence of infant mortality. Mothers participating in WIC and receiving nutritional supplements had a 21% decrease in low-birth-weight infants as compared with non-WIC mothers. Infant mortality rates decreased about 33%. Furthermore, the longer a woman participated in the program, the more the outcome of her pregnancy improved: participation for seven to nine months during pregnancy showed the most positive results. According to the researchers, "Birth weight [of offspring] increased . . . , length of gestation [time in uterus] increased . . . , and neonatal mortality was decreased" (Kotelchuck et al., 1981).

Other studies have demonstrated that children receiving WIC nutritional supplements during the prenatal period have higher cognitive functioning and behavioral adaptation five to seven years later (Hicks, Langham, & Takenaka, 1982). Researchers compared two groups of children: siblings who had received nutritional supplements for at least 3 months prenatally and up to 12 months postnatally, and those who did not receive the supplements until after the first year of life. Thus the former group received vital nutrition during the developmental stage that corresponded to an increased rate of brain growth. According to the study, early supplementation of nutrition was associated with higher levels of intellectual functioning and significantly better behavioral adjustment at home, a longer attention span, and higher grades in school. So you can see that one social program can prevent some of the effects of poverty on pregnancy and child development. Unfortunately, not all women and young children can participate in WIC. Because of limited funds, fewer than half of the eligible women, infants, and children receive WIC food supplements (U.S. House Committee on Ways and Means, 1985).

Birth

As with prenatal development, the birth process is usually normal; that is, there is no need to sedate the mother or perform surgery to facilitate the birth. The mother's labor proceeds without complications, the infant's heartbeat remains strong, and the infant is born vaginally rather than by cesarean section.

The Birth Process

The birth process has three overlapping stages. During the first stage, lasting an average of 12 to 24 hours, uterine contractions widen the cervix until it is large enough for the baby to pass through. The initially mild contractions become more intense. Since the cervix is stretched substantially, the mother experiences labor pains, which beta endorphin (a chemical secreted by the pituitary gland) may ease somewhat. Although helpful, this natural painkiller does not totally ease the discomfort. Many mothers can either control their pain through breathing techniques or request pain medication. The longer the contractions last, the more pain.

TABLE 4.4 The Apgar Scoring System

Sign	Score		
	0	*1*	*2*
Heart rate	Absent	Slow (<100)	>100
Respiratory effort	Absent	Weak cry; hyperventilation	Good; strong cry
Muscle tone	Limp	Some flexion of extremities	Good flexion
Reflex irritability (response to skin stimulation to feet)	No response	Grimace	Coughing, sneezing, crying
Color	Entire body blue or pale	Body pink, extremities blue	Entire body pink

The second stage, which lasts approximately two hours on average, begins when the baby's head starts to pass through the cervix. At this point the mother helps the baby pass through by bearing down hard, or "pushing," with her abdominal muscles. At the end of this stage, the baby is completely outside the mother's body. Finally, at the final stage, she expels the placenta and umbilical cord and the doctor or new father cuts the umbilical cord.

Evaluating the Newborn

Birth is traumatic for the infant, involving a relatively sudden change from a state of dependency to a separate existence. The newborn's condition is assessed using the **Apgar scoring system,** developed in the 1950s by physician Virginia Apgar. At one minute and five minutes after birth, the infant is rated for heart rate, respiratory effort, reflex irritability, muscle tone, and body color. A score of 0, 1, or 2 is given for each factor: the higher the score, the more favorable the baby's condition. A total Apgar score of between 7 and 10 means that the infant is in good condition; a score below 5 indicates that the infant may suffer from developmental disabilities; and a score of 3 or lower indicates that the infant's survival may be at stake and that emergency procedures are imperative (see Table 4.4).

Birthing Options

Maternal anxiety during birth may affect the birth process and the newborn. In one study, researchers found that women with high anxiety scores just before delivery have a greater likelihood of having difficulties during labor and of giving birth to children with abnormalities than women with low anxiety scores (Davies et al., 1971). Although these findings are controversial, strongly negative emotions can affect the autonomic nervous system, which controls the smooth functioning of the uterine muscles, thereby making the birth process more difficult.

Because of the possible negative effects of maternal anxiety, the mother's psychological as well as physiological well-being is important.

Natural childbirth, Lamaze, and gentle birthing Concern for the mother's psychological needs has given rise to several birthing practices: natural childbirth, the Lamaze method, and gentle birthing. The major tenet of natural childbirth, a process described in the book *Childbirth Without Fear* (Dick-Read, 1972), is that much of the pain that the mother experiences during birth is due to anxieties about the birth rather than to the physiological process itself. In **natural childbirth** the mother takes no medication during labor or takes it sparingly just before the baby is born. This reduces or eliminates the need for medication because the mother is taught to counteract her fears about the pain of childbirth. Also, she is taught physical exercises that help prepare her for relaxation during the birth.

In yet another technique—the *Lamaze method* (also referred to as *prepared childbirth*)—the mother is taught how to breathe in order to ease the pain of uterine contractions. Preparation involves an educational process in which expectant parents read relevant material, meet with medical staff and other expectant couples in group discussions, and practice exercises for proper breathing and strengthening the uterine muscles. Although a physician is in constant attendance during labor, the mother decides if she should be sedated; the father provides support and coaches her through the breathing exercises.

Most pregnant women and their husbands are introduced to natural childbirth or the Lamaze method by trained nurses or other specialists in hospitals or private clinics. Many soon-to-be parents opt for these birthing procedures, even though they may find out that a cesarean delivery is necessary. A **cesarean delivery**—surgically removing the baby from the uterus—is usually performed when labor is taking too long. This can happen when the baby is in **breech position** (the baby's legs or buttocks, rather than the head, emerge first) or in **transverse position** (the baby is lying crosswise across the uterus). A cesarean is also performed if another problem prevents the baby from passing through the cervix.

Another birthing method is **gentle birthing,** an adaptation of a method developed by the French obstetrician Frederick Leboyer. Leboyer (1975) argues that the birth process is unnecessarily traumatic for the baby. Having grown for nine months within the warm, dark, supportive uterine environment, the baby enters a cold, noisy world, full of bright lights—traditional conditions in many labor and delivery rooms. Then the baby is held upside-down by the feet and slapped on the back until doctors are sure that he or she is alive and can breathe!

Many of these "rituals" of birth are unnecessary, according to Leboyer. He advocated a gentler method of delivery in which the baby is born in a dimly lit delivery room and then gently held in warm water as if still surrounded by the amniotic fluid. Although this latter aspect of the Leboyer method is controversial, other aspects have influenced many physicians and parents. Today babies are rarely held upside-down and slapped on the back. Now they are often placed on their mother's abdomen for a few moments and gently wiped and covered with a blanket; then the umbilical cord is cut.

Birthing rooms and rooming in   An increasing number of hospitals are also changing routine medical practices that can cause undue stress during birth. For example, some hospitals have birthing rooms, which are comfortable, homelike rooms, often with soothing music and dim lights, where both labor and delivery take place. Also, many hospitals allow the mother and baby to stay together in one room, a practice called **rooming in.**

Rooming in was initiated in part as a response to the growing number of couples preferring to give birth at home or in birthing centers rather than in hospitals. Recently, even couples who value the medical care available in a hospital have insisted on being allowed to remain with their baby immediately after birth.

In part, parents' preferences for rooming in reflect the research of Klaus and Kennell (1976), who contended that there is a critical period immediately after birth during which the mother and infant "bond," or become attached, to each other.

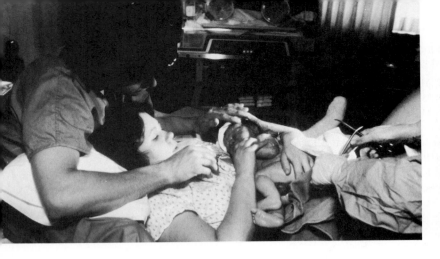

Birth is more pleasant for the entire family today than several decades ago. Most hospitals no longer remove the infant from the mother immediately after birth; instead, they allow the family to enjoy their first few hours together.

They compared mothers and babies who had extended contact after birth with mothers who were separated from their babies, according to usual hospital routines. Klaus and Kennel found differences in bonding between the two groups. Their findings, although preliminary, were extensively reported in the popular media. Many mothers who had not spent the first few hours after birth with their baby felt they had made an irrevocable mistake that might interfere with their relationship with their child. Their concerns are needless, however, because follow-up studies failed to replicate Klaus and Kennel's original findings (Lamb, 1982; Chess & Thomas, 1982). In the second edition of their book, Klaus and Kennel (1982) modified their position. A secure relationship between parent and baby is fundamental to development. But, as you will see in Chapter 6, it does not develop in a few hours or even a few days but over a longer period during which parent and baby learn to interact with each other.

Although research has not established a critical period for mother/infant bonding, that this study helped change hospital practice is significant. Rooming in often helps reduce many common anxieties that mothers experience if the baby is taken from them immediately. The mother also has a better opportunity to know and learn to care for her baby. Probably the greatest benefit of rooming in is the more immediate closeness that develops among mother, father, and infant. However, not all mothers want rooming in. Some would like their entry into parenthood to be more gradual. Others may need a few days to recover from stress and fatigue and to adjust to their new role. Hospital staff should be sensitive to these women and assume primary caretaking responsibility during the first day or two of the baby's life.

Risks to Infants During Delivery

At one time complications during childbirth were a major cause of death for infant and mother alike. Today, childbirth is relatively safe, but it still carries some risks.

In the delivery process, the two major dangers to the infant are (1) pressures on the head, which may cause some blood vessels in the brain to break, resulting in hemorrhaging, and (2) a lack of sufficient oxygen once the infant is separated from the mother. Both hemorrhaging and failure to begin breathing early enough influence the supply of oxygen to the brain's nerve cells.

During labor and delivery, lack of oxygen is a particularly serious problem. Infants generally undergo some oxygen deprivation and retention of carbon dioxide, but when it is extreme, they can suffer dire consequences. This can occur in breech birth or if the umbilical cord is squeezed or becomes tangled, depriving the infant of oxygen for an extended period. The neurons in the brain have a strong requirement for oxygen; if deprived of it, some brain cells may die. The resulting effects may range from slight brain damage to death. Children who suffer **anoxia,** a severe lack of oxygen at birth, often develop **cerebral palsy,** a condition related to a variety of motor defects, such as paralysis of the legs or arms, tremors of the face or fingers, or inability to use the vocal muscles. Some children also evidence developmental delays, become irritable, and have difficulty directing their attention. At age 3 their IQ tends to be low, although there is some evidence that IQ scores tend to increase by age 7, especially if the anoxia was mild (Corah et al., 1965).

Prematurity and Low Birth Weight

Although about 7% of all American infants are born prematurely, these infants account for 50% of newborn deaths. This fact alerts us to the vulnerability of babies born too soon. These babies are called **preterm** or **premature babies** because they have not had their full term of 38 to 42 weeks in the uterus. Infants born before the end of their 37th week are considered preterm.

At one time all low-birth-weight babies were thought to be preterm. Now doctors know that time in the uterus, not weight, defines preterm. While a preterm baby could weigh as much as 5 pounds 8 ounces and a full-term baby could weigh as little as 5 pounds, the full-term baby is physically mature enough to breathe and suck normally, whereas the preterm baby is not. However, low birth weight—under 5 pounds—in a full-term infant is considered much more serious. In a full-term baby low weight suggests impaired fetal development, due perhaps to maternal illness, smoking, poor nutrition, or some other factor. The preterm infant, on the other hand, is of low weight primarily because of premature birth. Surprisingly, the time of birth does not seem to affect the maturation of the premature infant's nervous system. That is, an infant born prematurely at 28 weeks will, 10 weeks later, be like an infant born at 38 weeks (Tanner, 1970). A variety of reflexes seem to appear on schedule whether the baby is inside or outside the uterus.

At birth, the preterm baby's biological systems are not developed enough to work on their own; the impact varies depending on the degree of prematurity and the infant's weight. Some premature babies may develop jaundice or breathing difficulties, and some may be retarded in sensory and motor development. Despite their biological immaturity, many preterm babies will catch up as they develop (Kopp & Parmelee, 1979). However, the smaller the baby is, the greater the risks involved and the more intensive the need for care. The one constant is that all preterm babies need to be cared for and kept warm in an incubator while they catch up with normal infants.

During the first few months of life, preterm and low-birth-weight babies are at risk for deviations in neurological functioning. Some may appear lethargic and may be slow to respond to environmental stimuli. In behavior these babies are similar to infants diagnosed as having organic brain damage.

Some researchers point out that the characteristics and behaviors of premature infants may be due to other related factors, such as delivery complications, inability to withstand the stresses of birth and postnatal life, or isolation in an incubator (which deprives these babies of sensory and social stimulation). Scarr-Salapatek and Williams (1973) established the importance of the last factor; prema-

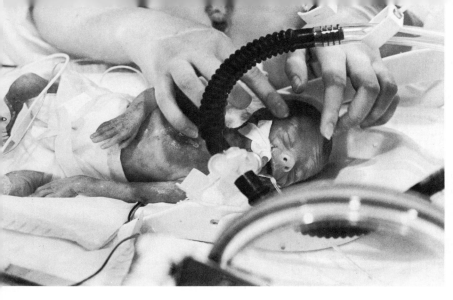

Medical technology can save smaller and smaller babies, but these children may experience developmental delays and learning disabilities. More longitudinal studies are needed, but researchers do know that if these babies receive appropriate care and stimulation they are less likely to suffer neurological or other defects.

ture infants who were held, fondled, and talked to more often gained weight faster and were more advanced developmentally than their isolated counterparts. Other studies also indicated that stimulated preterm infants are more advanced in mental development, neurological development, and sensorimotor and motor skills than unstimulated preterm infants (Rice, 1977). In addition, fewer incidences of **apnea,** or temporary cessation of breathing, occur among stimulated premature infants (Korner et al., 1975).

Mothers of Premature Infants

The parents' reaction is another important factor in the developmental outcome of preterm infants. Some researchers suggest that the affectionate bond between the mother and the premature infant may be disrupted, perhaps by the separation of the infant from the mother immediately after birth and for several weeks thereafter, or by the infant's characteristics and the parents' stress (Brown & Bakeman, 1978). Mothers of premature babies often endure strong conflicting emotions after the child's birth. Feelings of fear about the baby's condition or about her ability to care for the child alternate with feelings of hope and pride. Mothers may be disappointed when they see a small, skinny, premature infant, whose head seems too big and whose body is covered with fine hair and very delicate skin instead of the chubby, cuddly baby they anticipated. Sometimes feelings of anger and guilt alternate with moments of gratitude. These erratic mood changes can last for months after delivery (Quinn, Sostek, & Davit, 1978). Leaving the baby in the hospital compounds the problem; and regular visits to the hospital are often difficult for mothers who have other children or who must return to work.

Fathers of Premature Infants

Fathers of preterm infants have problems, too. Aside from dealing with his own worries about the infant, he has to remain the prime source of comfort and support for his wife. During the first few days after birth, the father's initial concern is also for the child's health, and he may have extensive contact with medical staff in an attempt to learn about the baby's condition. As a result, the mother may feel left out and neglected. In time, these feelings change as both parents become involved with visiting and helping care for the infant. However, both parents are under great stress and need emotional support.

This need continues after the baby leaves the hospital. Joy and relief at bringing the baby home combine with ongoing pressures and worries. Preterm babies need more attention and more feedings, and their sleep is often disrupted. Later in life, they may be no different from other babies, but for the first several months, they are sluggish and unresponsive, late to smile, and have floppy necks and heads because the muscles are not yet developed (Jason & Van der Meer, 1989). Even though these characteristics tend to diminish, if parents compare their infant's development with that of full-term babies, they become worried, frustrated, and disappointed. In addition, research indicates that parents find the cry of a preterm baby more irritating than that of a full-term baby (Thoden, Jarvenpaa, & Michelsson, 1985). Preterm babies are also more irritable and less easy to soothe (Friedman et al., 1978). Since irritability often strains the relationship between parents and infant and between mother and father (Liederman, 1983), these problems may make preterm babies vulnerable to abuse. Studies show that a fairly high proportion of abused children were born prematurely (Egeland & Brunquette, 1979).

The problems involved in having and caring for a preterm infant often lead parents to seek help. Hospital-based programs help them cope with stress and arrange for other services, such as financial aid or home visits from a public health nurse or a foster grandparent. There are also mutual support groups in which parents of preterm infants meet regularly to share experiences and knowledge. Researchers report that parents who participate in such groups tend to provide better care and to feel more at ease with their preterm babies than parents who do not participate (Friedman & Sigman, 1980; Quinn, Sostek, & Davit, 1978).

Sameroff (1975) and Belsky (1978) note that continuing disruptions in the relationship between infant and parents are often attributable to other factors in the family, as well as to individual differences in the child's responsivity and the parents' general competence. Disruptions tend to be more marked and enduring in economically deprived families because of additional daily stresses, such as unemployment and lack of adequate shelter.

If preterm babies are in middle-class homes (rather than poor), if they are exposed to sufficient stimulation, and if they are encouraged to be independent, they can overcome physical and mental problems associated with prematurity. Even babies born extremely prematurely may do well by the time they reach school age (Friedman & Sigman, 1980).

Early Intervention Programs

A recent study (Infant Health and Development Program, 1990) established the importance of intervention programs for premature and low-birth-weight infants and their parents. This study was the first national, randomized clinical trial conducted on the effects of interventions for such infants; it found that as a result of concerted efforts to help the babies, they can function better socially and achieve higher scores on intelligence tests.

The researchers conducted the study in eight geographically and demographically distinct sites to ensure that the findings could apply to the whole population. Included in the study were 985 infants who weighed less than 5.5 pounds at birth and had a gestational age of 37 weeks or less. Two-thirds of the sample weighed less than 4.4 pounds at birth and were thus considered at greater risk for developmental and health problems. The infants participated in the study from the time of their discharge from the hospital until they reached 3 years of age.

Infants in the study were assigned to one of two groups. The intervention group received high-quality pediatric follow-up care and home visits (weekly during the infants' first year, and biweekly thereafter). During these visits, the parents were taught play activities to enhance the children's cognitive and language development and social skills. The parents were also taught a series of problem-solving skills to help them better understand and interact with their babies. Intervention-group parents also attended a support group that met each month after the first year; thus the parents had an opportunity to share their concerns and to learn from other parents' experiences. At age 2, intervention-group infants began going to a child development center for at least four hours a day, five days a week, until they reached age 3. The center's staff used the same play activities the parents had been taught to use.

Infants assigned to a comparison group received only high-quality pediatric follow-up care. Findings showed that infants receiving the intervention were less likely than the comparison infants to have IQ scores in the range of mental retardation. Overall, the mean IQ scores (using the Stanford-Binet Intelligence Scale) were significantly higher for the intervention group, especially among heavier infants (weighing 4.5 to 5.5 pounds), who scored 13.2 points higher than the comparison-group infants of the same weight. Among the lighter infants (weighing less than 4.4 pounds), there was an average of 6.6 IQ points' difference between the intervention- and comparison-group infants. Also, mothers of the intervention-group infants reported fewer behavioral problems.

Researchers had previously reported similar findings on the positive effects of early intervention (e.g., Wertmann, 1980), but the Infant Health and Development study was the first large-scale, carefully controlled study on the effects of early intervention. This study provided undisputable evidence that low-birth-weight and premature infants at risk for delayed development can be helped. Nevertheless, the study raises a serious cost issue. To conduct the study over a four-year period cost approximately $33 million. A major philanthropic foundation largely underwrote the program for the purpose of documenting the effects of early intervention. Follow-up studies are now under way to determine the cost of the intervention per infant. Although the figures are not yet known, they should be high since the intervention services were intensive.

The question is, Can we provide such costly services to all premature and low-birth-weight infants? A cost analysis may show that it is cheaper in the long term to intervene during the first three years than to pay for remedial educational programs later in life. But at a time of fiscal restraint, should intervention programs be a priority at the expense of programs for children who did not have the benefit of intervention and still need remedial care? Also, since premature births are often related to such factors as poverty, poor prenatal care, and poor maternal health, wouldn't it be more cost effective to intervene during the prenatal period and prevent premature births? For policymakers and for society in general, these difficult issues need to be resolved.

Social Aspects of Pregnancy and Birth

Although pregnancy and birth are biological phenomena, they occur within a social context composed of factors that can influence a child's life. Is the child born into a loving family? Do the parents want the child? These are just a few questions that arise from the social aspects of pregnancy and birth.

Attitudes Toward Pregnancy and Childrearing

Since giving birth is a major milestone in a woman's life, pregnancy and birth precipitate a variety of emotions. Naturally, these emotions vary a great deal from woman to woman. Some women may feel that giving birth represents an essential self-fulfillment as a woman. Few women, however, do not feel at least some apprehension. The first-time mother is often concerned about whether she is competent to care for her child. Some women may feel that their own dependency needs are more important, and that requiring them to give affection and care rather than receive it is unfair. Still others may wonder how they will work out the conflicting demands of employment and family.

Fathers, too, have mixed emotions. Becoming a father makes most men feel proud, at least initially. However, they may also worry about being displaced in their wife's affection and may see the infant as a competitor. Also, in many societies, including ours, a baby is an overt symbol of the father's masculinity and virility; thus, as can also be true for a woman, the birth of his child may make a man feel more secure in his sex role. At the baby's birth, many fathers feel a sense of fulfillment as well as apprehension about their new responsibilities.

Despite these conflicting feelings, many couples are overjoyed at the birth of their baby. They find that being mutually responsible for a new human adds a new dimension to their relationship as well. Because so many couples seem genuinely delighted and happy on first having a baby, couples with troubled marriages sometimes have children in the hope that the newborn will improve the relationship. However, although a baby may enhance a marriage, he or she may also present problems and stresses that put the marriage to a severe test.

LEARNING FROM OTHER CULTURES

The Desire to Have Children

Why do people have children? To answer this question, researchers examined the motivations for having children expressed in different societies (Hoffman & Hoffman, 1963; Hoffman, 1975). They organized the responses according to a set of psychological needs, or *values*. The value of children to their parents lies in their capacity to satisfy one or more of these needs (see Table A).

TABLE A.   The Value of Children

1. Adult status and social identity (included here is the concept that motherhood is woman's major role)
2. Expansion of the self, tie to larger entity, "immortality"
3. Morality: religion, altruism, good of the group, regarding sexuality, impulsivity, virtue, character norms building
4. Primary group ties, affection
5. Stimulation, novelty, fun
6. Achievement, competence, creativity
7. Power, influence, effectance
8. Social comparison, competition
9. Economic utility

Source: "The Value of Children to Parents" by Lois Wladis Hoffman from *Proceedings of the American Philosophical Society*, 119, (6) Table 1, p. 431. Reprinted with the permission of the American Philosophical Society, 1975.

TABLE B. **Advantages of Having Children. Reported by Married Women under 40 with at Least One Child; National Sample of the United States.**

Values	Percent persons who gave such a response	Percent persons who did not give response	Total percent
Adult status and social identity	21.9	78.1	100
Expansion of the self	35.2	64.8	100
Morality	6.8	93.2	100
Primary group ties and affection	66.2	33.8	100
Stimulation and fun	60.1	39.9	100
Achievement and competence	11.0	89.0	100
Power	2.2	97.8	100
Social comparison	0.1	99.9	100
Economic utility	7.9	92.1	100
N = 1258			

Source: "The Value of Children to Parents" by Lois Wladis Hoffman from *Proceedings of the American Philosophical Society,* 119, (6) Table 2, p. 433. Reprinted with the permission of the American Philosophical Society, 1975.

The Hoffmans accumulated the values of, or reasons for, having children on the basis of answers to the following question: What would you say are the advantages or good things about having children as compared with not having children? Obviously, the reasons for having children differed in different cultures and often depended on the social climate and the economy.

In many cultures children are taken along while parents work and they learn by watching their elders.

TABLE C. Advantages of Having Children. Reported by Men with Wives under 40 with at Least One Child.

Values	Percent persons who gave such a response	Percent persons who did not give response	Total percent
Adult status and social identity	19.8	80.2	100
Expansion of the self	32.4	67.6	100
Morality	6.4	93.6	100
Primary group ties and affection	60.1	39.9	100
Stimulation and fun	55.3	44.7	100
Achievement and competence	9.5	90.5	100
Power	2.2	97.8	100
Social comparison	.3	99.7	100
Economic utility	10.1	89.9	100
$N = 358$			

Source: "The Value of Children to Parents" by Lois Wladis Hoffman from *Proceedings of the American Philosophical Society,* 119, (6) Table 1, p. 434. Reprinted with the permission of the American Philosophical Society, 1975.

In a village in India, for example, most respondents considered the advantages to be related to the children's economic utility and value. The most common reason given for having children, mostly sons, was to have someone to take care of the parents in their old age. Villagers reported that if they did not have a son to take care of them when they got older, they would starve, since the government does not provide old-age security.

Other studies also noted the economic value of children in other countries. Harway and Liss (1988) found that in Morocco, a country characterized by a wide diversity of ethnic groups, children represent security for old age, especially for the mother. But perhaps even more important, Moroccan children provide the woman with power and status, since, according to local religious custom, failure to procreate (for some reason considered solely a function of the woman) can be one ground for divorce or repudiation in marriage (Mikhail, 1979).

In the United States both men and women value children for the opportunity for nurturance they represent and because they provide stimulation and fun (see Tables B and C). In the Hoffman studies noted earlier (Hoffman & Hoffman, 1963; Hoffman, 1975), some U.S. respondents stated their reasons for having children as follows: "They bring liveliness to your life," "We love playing with them," "They're so funny," and "They bring you happiness and joy."

Learning to Be Parents

There is concern, however, about the reasons American parents give for having children, especially since some parents do not think realistically about the difficulties and constraints of childrearing. From their answers, some people evidently see the coming child simply as a pleasurable plaything and anticipate the fun of dressing the baby in cute clothes and showing it off to friends and family. Needless to say, after a few late-night feedings, messy diaper changes, and difficulties soothing a baby who may cry more often than they had anticipated, some parents become tired, angry, and disenchanted; they may vent their frustrations on the child.

Because of these immature expectations of parenting, some hospitals teach new parents how to be a parent. Courses on parenting are also offered in some elementary schools and high schools (Harman & Brim, 1980; Fitzgerald, 1974, 1981). These courses used to involve merely teaching parents the physical care of the newborn. Now, however, some health practitioners and educators are teaching about the newborn's capabilities and about basic principles of psychological development in infancy and early childhood. Why? First, there is so much useful knowledge about the newborn's capabilities. For example, immediately after birth newborns can hear and see somewhat and are able to follow objects with their eyes; this knowledge is helpful to new parents who might think the baby only sleeps and cries for the first three months of life. Second, the increase in the incidence of child abuse and neglect is so great. Some parents expect too much too early; they become angry and often abusive if these expectations are not met. For example, some parents tend to mistake normal developmental behaviors, such as the baby's throwing an object to the floor over and over again, as actions deliberately aimed against them. Such parents often retort, "He is just doing this to test me," or "He really tries to get me angry." Actually, what the baby is doing is part of an expected repertoire of developmental activities at a certain stage of life. Such developmental activities enable children to understand that they can affect the world around them. When parents understand children's developmental characteristics at different stages, they become more patient and understanding.

Most parents eventually learn to interact effectively with their children. They read books and articles and watch TV programs on childrearing, or learn from friends and relatives. At-risk parents, however, are often unable to use these resources to learn about children. They may be too distressed by difficulties in their daily lives, or they may be burdened by something in their past; as a result, they are unable to function properly and enjoy caring for their children. For children in such families to grow up normally, the parents must learn about successful parenting. Wieder (1989) notes that teaching at-risk parents—that is, simply conveying information about child development—is insufficient. Practitioners must also make the

In the early 1970s the federal government developed education for parenthood programs because many people have naive expectations about the growth and development of children. Some elementary and secondary schools offer courses in which children can learn firsthand about some of the realities of having a baby.

parents feel unique; whenever possible, they must build the parents' and children's self-esteem by pointing out the children's successes and underscoring the parents' role in helping their children achieve. In this way, practitioners put the parents in charge and reinforce effective behaviors instead of focusing on the parents' inadequacies and problems.

Summary

At the moment of conception, when the sperm cell penetrates the egg cell, the fertilized egg becomes a zygote. Cells begin to multiply rapidly and to differentiate their functions, eventually developing several membranes that protect the infant. Cell division and differentiation occur during the three developmental stages of the prenatal period: the periods of the ovum, the embryo, and the fetus.

The infant is most vulnerable to the effects of teratogens during the embryo period. Some teratogens are chemicals and drugs that cross the placenta and enter the fetal bloodstream. Because of the increased number of women using crack, a cocaine derivative, the number of "crack babies," who suffer multiple development and behavioral problems, is increasing; these babies were subjected prenatally to the effects of the drug. Other factors also influence development, such as the mother's age, health, nutritional status, and diet. The effects of teratogens and other influences vary according to the fetus's stage of development and the organs developing at the time of exposure.

The effects also vary based on the genotype of the mother and child. These effects may range from mild mental retardation and developmental delays to gross physical and mental abnormalities. If the handicap is not severe, factors arising after birth, such as the parents' reaction to the child, may determine the continuance of the abnormalities. Poor children are more likely than affluent children to suffer from the effects of teratogens and are also less likely to overcome these effects after birth. Infant mortality, which is a consequence of the effects of teratogens, is more likely to occur among poor blacks despite prevention possibilities that include adequate prenatal nutrition and medical care.

Although the birth process, which occurs in three overlapping stages, is usually a normal event, it can pose additional risks to the infant, such as a lack of oxygen and prematurity. Some premature infants suffer neurological deviations during the first few months of life and are also at risk for developmental delays and mental retardation. Yet, according to a well-controlled national study, if care providers intervene early and provide stimulating play activities, premature babies will grow up with no cognitive or behavioral handicaps. The risk that developmental deviations associated with prematurity will last is, again, greater among poor children than among the affluent.

The social context within which parents conceive and rear their children is also important to developmental outcome. There are many reasons for having children, and these reasons vary from culture to culture. Researchers note that many American parents want children because they are fun to be with. Because parents often have unrealistic expectations of children's development, they may later become angry or frustrated with them. For this reason, many schools and hospitals offer courses in parenting.

Infertility affects an increasing number of couples. Although there are different methods for overcoming failure to conceive, these methods may cause ethical and legal problems for both parents and children.

5 Physical Development During Infancy

6 Cognitive and Language Development in Infancy

7 Social and Emotional Development in Infancy

The newborn baby—so small, so wrinkled, so far to go. Sometimes it is hard to imagine that this tiny infant will someday be a full-grown person. Yet it doesn't take long before the first stretches, yawns, and gurgles suggest the person who is already there. The parents are soon caught up in the wonder of watching this tiny, apparently helpless being develop. In a relatively few months, they see a much more complex organism, with well-integrated and differentiated responses, mastering a variety of skills: clasping their finger, smiling when they smile, responding to their sounds and moods and, even without words, becoming part of the social scene. The baby is, in fact, born with sensory and perceptual abilities that enable him or her to interact with the environment from the first day of life. Between birth and age 2, the period of infancy, the baby's physical growth is so rapid that changes in size, shape, and body proportions occur almost daily (a fact any parent with a camera will gladly show you . . . as often as you like). Infancy is one of the most fascinating periods of human development, and it is also an essential period of bonding between caregiver and child.

5 Physical Development During Infancy

In this chapter we focus on the physical development and acquisition of skills that occur during infancy. You will see that physical development follows a predictable and orderly sequence governed by the genes and by interaction between genetic and environmental factors. The infant's physical development and characteristics have both a direct and indirect influence on psychological development. Once the baby acquires the ability to walk, for example, many more opportunities for learning become available. In discussing preterm and low-birth-weight babies, we have seen that the newborn's physiological characteristics influence care-giving styles and parental responses to and interaction with the child. At a later age a child's physical attributes—such as obesity, which may elicit teasing and ridicule, or attractive features, which often elicit admiration—inevitably affect self-image and emotional well-being.

Since physical development has important implications for psychological development, we discuss the progress of physical growth and the changes in physical characteristics at that stage, how these changes correspond to other aspects of development, and how they influence the child's interactions with other children and adults. In this chapter we look at physical growth during infancy and at the infant's repertoire of sensory, perceptual, and motor skills. This knowledge can lead to a more sophisticated understanding of human development. Although for most infants the course of physical growth and development proceeds smoothly, some infants are born with a physical disability or are identified as disabled shortly after birth. Information on what constitutes normal physical growth helps identify disabled infants and develop programs addressed to their special needs. Although intervention programs can significantly improve the developmental outcome for some physically disabled children, this is not always the case for all handicapping conditions or for infants born with AIDS.

Before discussing physical growth and development in infancy, let us describe the baby's characteristics during the first month of life. The newborn baby is so different from the infant he becomes even a few weeks later, and our understanding from the research on the capabilities of the newborn is so new, that the first few weeks of life deserve special emphasis. But perhaps even more important is the impact the newborn has on the family. Some of you may have children and may have attended childbirth classes and read books and other materials about the newborn. But despite all the courses and readings, you know that the first few days of parenting are an experience that cannot be totally prepared for.

The Newborn

Indeed, the baby's arrival is overwhelming for the parents as well as for the baby. Having suddenly become responsible for a tiny, dependent human being, parents face a total upheaval in their lives and a period of adjustment. The baby is brand-new and seems so vulnerable. Many parents, particularly those who have no other children, may not know how to care for the baby. Furthermore, during the first few hours or days after birth, they have no idea how the baby looks when she is content; therefore, they do not know when she is unhappy. They do not know how much she ordinarily cries, so they cannot tell whether her cries signal a potentially serious medical problem. The parents lack a baseline for the newborn's appearance and behavior (Leach, 1983).

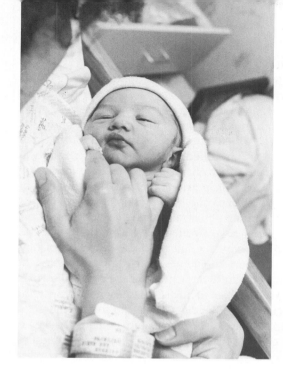

Newborn babies are seldom beautiful for the first few days after birth. Nevertheless, adults are naturally attracted to them.

The baby, who has yet to adapt to life outside the womb, must establish this baseline. During her first month or so, she will establish a pattern of sleeping, crying, eating, looking, and listening. Only after she establishes such a routine, however, do parents feel that here is a person they can understand and whose behavior they can, to an extent, predict. Some babies take longer than others to reach this stage. On the whole, mothers report that they begin to feel comfortable caring for their babies sometime between two and six weeks after birth (Leach, 1983).

In the meantime, whether or not parents feel comfortable caring for their newborn, they must look after her. The baby has few physiological needs. Essentially, she needs to be fed and kept warm, comfortable, and clean. However, fulfilling each of these needs is a new experience for many parents. The newborn is also having new experiences. She has to contend with a myriad of sensations she never encountered before: light, temperature changes, feelings of fullness and emptiness, the sensations of being held and put down, and so on. Also, existence was relatively effortless in the womb. At birth, however, the heart, circulatory system, respiratory system, and nervous system begin adapting to life outside the womb. Thus, for the first few days of life, the baby has many adjustments to make.

Characteristics of the Newborn

If you have ever seen a newborn, you have no doubt marveled at how perfect his hands, toes, and fingernails are, at how tiny he is, and at how a whole, perfectly formed human being could be so little. There are other characteristics that are amazing as well, such as his appearance and individuality. In addition, we are finding that although the newborn depends on adult care, he is actually a competent human being who is capable of survival and who can respond to environmental stimuli.

Appearance

Many adults are naturally attracted to the newborn, but her appearance right after birth often surprises them and contributes to their hesitancy and insecurity in caring for her. The newborn appears fragile, and other aspects of her appearance seem odd; she is hardly beautiful. She has a short neck, if any, and covering her body is an oily substance called **vernix caseosa,** which dries a few days after birth. Some newborns have a growth of fine-textured hair, called **lanugo,** all over their body, a bulging abdomen, and a broad, flat face. Other characteristics include disproportionately small arms, legs, and trunk and a disproportionately large head that may be misshapen. Newborns also have flexible bones and blotchy skin, and they may be prone to all sorts of conditions and appearances that, although they appear odd, are perfectly normal for newborns. They may have swollen breasts (in both male and female newborns) and swollen genitals, which result from the secretion of high levels of hormones during the prenatal period. The newborn's appearance for the first few days after birth is so odd that an adult's attraction to her is indeed surprising. However, many adults are drawn to babies of any species, especially once the babies attain the cute feature characteristics of infants. As you can see in Figure 5.1, the young—whether human or animal—have distinctive features such as large eyes, bulging forehead, small nose, and chubby cheeks. Some ethologists contend that these features trigger affectionate feelings in adults, thereby encouraging survival (Lorenz, 1971).

Individuality

Although all newborns have an unusual appearance for the first couple of weeks, they vary greatly in size, shape, degree of physical maturity, general health, and even personality traits. Some differences are the result of the prenatal experiences (Field, 1987). As Tanner (1974) notes:

> It is quite wrong to think of newborns as identical buds, from which in the fullness of time flower the variegated colors of the preschool assembly. The newborn already has had a long and very eventful history. . . . Just like the 6-year-old or the 14-year-old— although perhaps not so obviously—[newborns] represent a wide variety of degrees of physiological maturity.

Some differences are related to prenatal experiences, but many differences are also genetically determined, as we noted in Chapter 3. Some babies cannot cope with even small amounts of stress and this tendency is apparent right after birth; faced with a situation that doesn't bother most babies, these babies' hearts may beat faster and they may show other signs of distress. Freedman and Freedman (1969) found differences between Chinese-American and European-American newborns in the extent that they cried and in their ability to be calmed: Chinese-American newborns tend to be more easily calmed when crying. Freedman (1974) describes another study in which experimenters placed a cloth over the newborn's nose. American newborns of European descent and black American newborns reacted by turning their heads and attempting to swipe the cloth with their hands; whereas Chinese-American babies did not react at all: they simply continued to lie quietly with the cloth covering their nose. Other researchers have found differences depending on the newborns' sex. Moss (1967), for example, found that boys are more difficult to pacify. Phillips, King, and DuBois (1978), who had set out to prove that there was no difference in activity level between the males and females at birth,

Figure 5.1 *Features of infant humans and other mammals, such as large head, chubby cheeks, and small eyes, have a biologically adaptive function, because they may encourage nurturance in adults.*

found instead that boys are awake for longer periods and move their heads, hands, bodies, and faces more frequently. The newborns in their study had normal deliveries and were matched for birth weight and birth order. They were also wrapped in blankets of the same color to reduce the possibility of observer bias during the rating of newborn behavior.

Does the newborn baby have a personality? Determining whether the newborn exhibits personality traits right from birth would help clarify the nature-nurture question of whether personality is formed by experience or is genetically endowed. On the basis of research with twins, researchers note that personality is likely to be the result of a combination of experience and genes (Plomin, 1989). They reached the same conclusion after research with newborns. For example, newborns exhibit different temperament traits right from birth. **Temperament** refers to the individual's pattern of response to the environment; many observers describe it as the foundation upon which later personality is developed (Bates, 1987). Thus, some individuals are quiet and calm when they encounter new situations, whereas others are emotional or tense.

In one of the most extensive longitudinal studies on temperament, Thomas and Chess and their colleagues (Thomas et al., 1968; Thomas & Chess, 1977, 1984) studied a group of about 140 middle-class American children. Later in the study they included working-class children, children from different ethnic backgrounds, and neurologically impaired children. Relying primarily on parental reports of behavior, the researchers followed these children from birth through adolescence and also studied other groups of infants and children for shorter periods. Shortly after the child was born, they asked parents about their infant's behavior—for example, his or her reaction to being changed or bathed. Periodically during childhood and adolescence, they interviewed the parents about the children's behavior.

Thomas and Chess found that immediately after birth, the newborns had different ways of responding to the environment and of expressing themselves; these differences sometimes persisted throughout childhood. The researchers also established that temperamental traits among newborns, and later among children, tended to occur in clusters. As a result, they were able to categorize individuals in their study as "easy" infants, "difficult" infants, "slow-to-warm-up" infants, or infants exhibiting a mixture of traits. Table 5.1 gives their findings, which show that the child has a distinct temperament early in life. As the child grows, the temperament

TABLE 5.1   Stability of Selected Temperament Traits Over Time

Temperamental quality	Rating	2 Months	6 Months
Activity level	High	Moves often in sleep. Wriggles when diaper is changed.	Tries to stand in tub and splashes. Bounces in crib. Crawls after dog.
	Low	Does not move when being dressed or during sleep.	Passive in bath. Plays quietly in crib and falls asleep.
Rhythmicity	Regular	Has been on four-hour feeding schedule since birth. Regular bowel movement.	Is asleep at 6:30 every night. Awakes at 7:00 A.M. Food intake is constant.
	Irregular	Awakes at a different time each morning. Size of feedings varies.	Length of nap varies; so does food intake.
Distractibility	Distractible	Will stop crying for food if rocked. Stops fussing if given pacifier when diaper is being changed.	Stops crying when mother sings. Will remain still while clothing is changed if given a toy.
	Not distractible	Will not stop crying when diaper is changed. Fusses after eating, even if rocked.	Stops crying only after dressing is finished. Cries until given bottle.
Approach/Withdrawal	Positive	Smiles and licks washcloth. Has always liked bottle.	Likes new foods. Enjoyed first bath in a large tub. Smiles and gurgles.
	Negative	Rejected cereal the first time. Cries when strangers appear.	Smiles and babbles at strangers. Plays with new toys immediately.
Adaptability	Adaptive	Was passive during first bath; now enjoys bathing. Smiles at nurse.	Used to dislike new foods; now accepts them well.

tends to remain constant in quality. The shaded areas of the table represent characteristics of temperament that most clearly classify a child as easy, slow to warm up, or difficult. Easy infants adapt easily to most situations, exhibit a positive mood, enjoy being handled, and so on.

Difficult infants, on the other hand, adjust poorly to new situations and often seem distressed. They are easily frustrated and may become tense when picked up or hugged. Thomas and Chess contend that these temperamental differences are genetically endowed, since they are apparent from birth, and that they are stable

1 Year	2 Years	5 Years	10 Years
Walks rapidly. Eats eagerly. Climbs into everything.	Climbs furniture. Explores. Gets in and out of bed while being put to sleep.	Leaves table often during meals. Always runs.	Plays ball and engages in other sports. Cannot sit still long enough to do homework.
Finishes bottle slowly. Goes to sleep easily. Allows nail-cutting without fussing.	Enjoys quiet play with puzzles. Can listen to records for hours.	Takes a long time to dress. Sits quietly on long automobile rides.	Likes chess and reading. Eats very slowly.
Naps after lunch each day. Always drinks bottle before bed.	Eats a big lunch each day. Always has a snack before bedtime.	Falls asleep when put to bed. Bowel movement regular.	Eats only at mealtimes. Sleeps the same amount of time each night.
Will not fall asleep for an hour or more. Moves bowels at a different time each day.	Nap time changes from day to day. Toilet training is difficult because bowel movement is unpredictable.	Food intake varies; so does time of bowel movement.	Food intake varies. Falls asleep at a different time each night.
Cries when face is washed unless it is made into a game.	Will stop tantrum if another activity is suggested.	Can be coaxed out of forbidden activity by being led into something else.	Needs absolute silence for homework. Has a hard time choosing a shirt in a store because they all appeal to him.
Cries when toy is taken away and rejects substitute.	Screams if refused some desired object. Ignores mother's calling.	Seems not to hear if involved in favorite activity. Cries for a long time when hurt.	Can read a book while television set is at high volume. Does chores on schedule.
Approaches strangers readily. Sleeps well in new surroundings.	Slept well the first time he stayed overnight at grandparents' house.	Entered school building unhesitatingly. Tries new foods.	Went to camp happily. Loved to ski the first time.
Stiffened when placed on sled. Will not sleep in strange bed.	Avoids strange children in the playground. Whimpers first time at beach. Will not go into water.	Hid behind mother when entering school.	Severely homesick at camp during first days. Does not like new activities.
Was afraid of toy animals at first; now plays with them happily.	Obeys quickly. Stayed contentedly with grandparents for a week.	Hesitated to go to nursery school at first; now goes eagerly. Slept well on camping trip.	Likes camp, although homesick during first days. Learns enthusiastically. *(continued)*

TABLE 5.1 *(continued)*

Temperamental quality	Rating	2 Months	6 Months
	Not adaptive	Still startled by sudden, sharp noise. Resists diapering.	Does not cooperate with dressing. Fusses and cries when left with sitter.
Attention span and persistence	Long	If soiled, continues to cry until changed. Repeatedly rejects water if he wants milk.	Watches toy mobile over crib intently. "Coos" frequently.
	Short	Cries when awakened but stops almost immediately. Objects only mildly if cereal precedes bottle.	Sucks pacifier for only a few minutes and spits it out.
Intensity of reaction	Intense	Cries when diapers are wet. Rejects food vigorously when satisfied.	Cries loudly at the sound of thunder. Makes sucking movements when vitamins are administered.
	Mild	Does not cry when diapers are wet. Whimpers instead of crying when hungry.	Does not kick often in tub. Does not smile. Screams and kicks when temperature is taken.
Threshold of responsiveness	Low	Stops sucking on bottle when approached.	Refuses fruit he likes when vitamins are added. Hides head from bright light.
	High	Is not startled by loud noises. Takes bottle and breast equally well.	Eats everything. Does not object to diapers being wet or soiled.
Quality of mood	Positive	Smacks lips when first tasting new food. Smiles at parents.	Plays and splashes in bath. Smiles at everyone.
	Negative	Fusses after nursing. Cries when carriage is rocked.	Cries when taken from tub. Cries when given food she does not like.

1 Year	2 Years	5 Years	10 Years
Continues to reject new foods each time they are offered.	Cries and screams each time hair is cut. Disobeys persistently.	Has to be hand led into classroom each day. Bounces on bed in spite of spankings.	Does not adjust well to new school or new teacher; comes home late for dinner even when punished.
Plays by self in playpen for more than an hour. Listens to singing for long periods.	Works on a puzzle until it is completed. Watches when shown how to do something.	Practiced riding a two-wheeled bicycle for hours until he mastered it. Spent over an hour reading a book.	Reads for two hours before sleeping. Does homework carefully.
Loses interest in a toy after a few minutes. Gives up easily if she falls while attempting to walk.	Gives up easily if a toy is hard to use. Asks for help immediately if undressing becomes difficult.	Still cannot tie his shoes because he gives up when he is not successful. Fidgets when parents read to him.	Gets up frequently from homework for a snack. Never finishes a book.
Laughs hard when father plays roughly. Screamed and kicked when temperature was taken.	Yells if he feels excitement or delight. Cries loudly if a toy is taken away.	Rushes to greet father. Gets hiccups from laughing hard.	Tears up an entire page of homework if one mistake is made. Slams door of room when teased by younger brother.
Does not fuss much when clothing is pulled on over head.	When another child hit her, she looked surprised, did not hit back.	Drops eyes and remains silent when given a firm parental "No." Does not laugh much.	When a mistake is made in a model airplane, corrects it quietly. Does not comment when reprimanded.
Spits out food he does not like. Giggles when tickled.	Runs to door when father comes home. Must always be tucked tightly into bed.	Always notices when mother puts new dress on for first time. Refuses milk if it is not ice-cold.	Rejects fatty foods. Adjusts shower until water is at exactly the right temperature.
Eats food he likes even if mixed with disliked food. Can be left easily with strangers.	Can be left with anyone. Falls to sleep easily on either back or stomach.	Does not hear loud, sudden noises when reading. Does not object to injections.	Never complains when sick. Eats all foods.
Likes bottle; reaches for it and smiles. Laughs loudly when playing peekaboo.	Plays with sister; laughs and giggles. Smiles when he succeeds in putting shoes on.	Laughs loudly while watching television cartoons. Smiles at everyone.	Enjoys new accomplishments. Laughs when reading a funny passage aloud.
Cries when given injections. Cries when left alone.	Cries and squirms when given haircut. Cries when mother leaves.	Objects to putting boots on. Cries when frustrated.	Cries when he cannot solve a homework problem. Very "weepy" if he does not get enough sleep.

Source: Table from pages 108–9 of "The Origin of Personality," by Thomas, A., Chess, S., and Birch, H. C., *Scientific American,* August 1970. Copyright © 1970 by Scientific American, Inc. All rights reserved.

over time. That is, easy infants tend to continue to exhibit positive personality traits throughout their life, whereas difficult infants continue to be difficult. In fact, 70% of the difficult infants in the study entered psychiatric counseling or treatment in later life, whereas only 18% of the easy infants did.

It is understandable that more "difficult" infants would be found to have psychiatric problems later in life. But why would 18% of the "easy" infants also have such difficulties? This issue—that no child, regardless of temperament, is immune from problems—intrigued Thomas and Chess. After a closer look at the data, they found that the easy infants who developed problems later in life experienced a great deal of stress because they were expected to act in ways that were contrary to their temperament. Joey, for example, likes to play by himself, put together puzzles, or read. His outgoing parents encourage him to play in large groups of children and take him to parties. Whenever they see him playing alone, they call some of his friends over to play with him. You can imagine how stressful the situation must be for Joey. Thomas and Chess note that for children to develop normally and adjust to their environment, there must be a **goodness of fit,** or a good match, between the children's temperament and the demands placed on them. Parents, teachers, and other caregivers would do well to observe children and attempt to determine activities they enjoy (Thomas & Chess, 1987).

Although Thomas and Chess's work has far-reaching implications for child rearing, not all researchers agree with them. Some researchers have failed to find evidence that temperamental traits are stable over the course of development (Goldsmith & Campos, 1982). Others take issue with the reliance on parental reports, which could be influenced by parents' beliefs about what constitutes normal infant behavior (Wasserman et al., 1990).

Some researchers contend that although children may exhibit the same temperamental traits over time, this does not mean that genetic factors are involved or that environmental factors are not. For example, temperament may be related to the

---

A CLOSER LOOK

Sudden Infant Death Syndrome

Parents of newborns are normally anxious about the well-being of their child, even if they are "veterans" with other children. But nothing is more chilling than the prospect of sudden infant death syndrome (SIDS), otherwise known as crib death. Waking to find your newborn dead, without a cry or struggle, and perhaps even in the same room, is an experience of shock, grief, and often guilt for parents who wonder what they might have done.

Each year approximately 8000 American infants die, apparently the victims of SIDS. In fact, more infants die of SIDS than of cystic fibrosis, leukemia, cancer, heart disease, and child abuse combined. SIDS is the most common cause of death for infants between 1 week and 1 year of age. Not only in the United States but worldwide, 1 out of 360 infants dies of this condition. Why is this so and what can be done about it? Researchers are not yet sure, although they have a profile of the event and of the infants who are at high risk.

This profile enables us to identify infants who are at risk so that special attention can be given to them.

We now know that SIDS is more likely to occur among male rather than female infants and that the peak incidence of SIDS occurs at 8 to 9 weeks of age and between 13 and 15 weeks of age. It is also more likely to occur during the winter months among infants who have a cold or a runny nose. And, although crib death can strike any child, and most victims are well cared for and well nourished, the incidence of SIDS is higher among poor families. It is also higher among premature and low-birth-weight babies.

The health and habits of the mother are an additional factor. There is a higher incidence of SIDS in babies born to women who are seriously anemic during pregnancy, to heavy smokers as opposed to nonsmokers, and to women who use cocaine or heroin during pregnancy. Moreover, bottle-fed infants are at higher risk than breast-fed babies.

different caregiving approaches the infants elicit from birth. DeVries and Sameroff (1984) present data on infant temperament in three African societies, which suggest that each culture's childrearing patterns and maternal orientation, in addition to the infant's characteristics, contribute to temperament; thus temperament is sensitive to environmental influences. As a parent, you would no doubt enjoy caring for an easy baby, and the baby's positive response to you would encourage you to play with her more and hold her more. But if you have a baby who is likely to tense up every time you hug him, this would very likely discourage you from handling the baby too often; as a result, you might resort to avoiding physical contact (Wolff, 1971). As long as the baby continues to be difficult, your reactions to him would continue to be the same. So you can see that babies can elicit different responses from adults and these responses can eventually change the type of care the infant receives. This pattern, in turn, might influence the infant's personality.

Dependence and Competence

For several months after birth, the baby depends on adult care. She must be fed, pacified, cleansed, and protected, and she looks helpless. Appearing helpless serves an adaptive function; it elicits a protective, nurturant response from adults. Despite the newborn's prolonged dependency, she is not totally unprepared for life outside the womb. On the contrary, at birth she has remarkable capacities for dealing with the world and survival. She is able to eat, to eliminate body waste, and to regulate her body temperature, which is subject to frequent variation.

Infant reflexes   Nature ensures the newborn's survival and adaptability by equipping him with certain **reflexes,** which are specific, involuntary responses to stimuli. The baby is born with a host of reflexes (see Table 5.2, p. 170), many of which disappear after the first 2 or 3 months of life. Some reflexes are adaptive in that they

A CLOSER LOOK

Although we cannot yet prevent SIDS, it is important to continue the research to isolate its causes. There are already numerous theories to explain the condition. For example, botulism (acute food poisoning) appears to be the cause of some cases. There may also be a genetic explanation; a baby born in a family where an infant has died of SIDS is likely to wake up from sleep less often than do most other babies, suggesting that he too may be vulnerable to SIDS. Researchers are also looking into the possibility that thiamin (vitamin B1) deficiency in apparently healthy pregnant women, stemming from inadequate nutrition or a genetically related inability to metabolize the vitamin, may also be related to SIDS.

Another hypothesis is that SIDS could be related to subtle damage to the body's respiratory control center located in the brainstem. This damage usually occurs during the prenatal period and results from a drop in maternal blood pressure, maternal anemia, and cigarette smoking. It may also occur in premature babies.

Still other research is being done to investigate the possibility that apnea, that is, the temporary cessation of breathing common in premature infants, is a possible cause of SIDS. At one time it was believed that brief apneic pauses during sleep were predictive of longer, potentially fatal pauses. More recent evidence, however, suggested that apnea does not necessarily predict SIDS and that SIDS infants do not exhibit abnormal breathing patterns. Research continues in the hope that this form of infant death will be both understood and prevented.

Source: Based on research by Black, 1979; Steinschneider, 1975; Marx, 1978; Harper et al., 1981; Naeye, 1982; Guntheroth, Lohmann, & Spiers, 1990; Haglund & Cnattingius, 1990; Sussman & Levitt, 1989; Waggener, Southall, & Scott, 1990; and Foundation for the Study of Infant Deaths and British Pediatric Respiratory Group, 1990.

TABLE 5.2 Selected Newborn Reflexes

Reflex	Description	Age of disappearance
Blink	When light is flashed on infant's eyes, both eyelids close in response.	Remains
Babinski	When sole of infant's foot is stroked, toes spread out in response.	Around end of first year of life
Grasping	When finger or any other graspable object is placed in palm of hand, infant grasps it tightly.	Very strong during the first 2–3 months; then disappears around 3 or 4 months; becomes voluntary around 5 months
Moro	When infant is held upside down as if going to be dropped, throws arms out and clenches hands.	After first 4 or 5 months
Stepping	When infant is held upright with feet against flat surface, moves feet as if walking.	After 2 or 3 months
Swimming	When infant is placed horizontally in water, makes paddle-like movements.	After 2 or 3 months
Rooting	When infant is lightly touched on cheek with finger, turns head toward finger and opens mouth in attempt to suck finger.	After 2 or 3 months
Sucking	When infant encounters something suckable that can be put in mouth, sucks it.	After 3 or 4 months

help infants secure food or protect them from harm. Coughing, sucking, blinking, and crying are examples of built-in adaptive reflexes. We call them "built-in" because they are available to the infant immediately after birth and "adaptive" because they help ensure the baby's survival. The infant does not learn to suck, for example; if he did have to learn, he would be in danger of dying of starvation.

Another adaptive reflex is the **rooting reflex.** We can most readily elicit it in infants 1 or 2 weeks old by gently touching a finger to the corner of the baby's mouth and moving it slowly toward the cheek. Usually the infant will move her tongue, mouth, or head in an attempt to suck the finger. This reflex appears to be important in feeding because it can be more easily elicited when the baby is hungry. Babies who breast-feed release the nipple for a brief period, only to regain it later. It is easier for the baby to retrieve the nipple if it rubs against his mouth and cheek and the rooting reflex takes over.

The infant has other reflexes that seem to have no obvious survival value; thus researchers think they are relics left from the evolutionary past. One such reflex is the **Moro reflex,** named after Ernst Moro, the German pediatrician who first described it in 1918. Child experts also refer to it as the **startle reflex.** The reflex appears when the newborn is held in midair and suddenly released for a moment so that he almost drops, or drops about 6 inches; at this point she will throw her arms upward and clench her fingers, as if in a fist. Although of no apparent value to the human infant, the Moro reflex is very adaptive for the infant monkey, who is held by the mother next to her chest (Prechtl & Beintema, 1977). When the mother moves, the monkey's sense of sudden loss of support automatically produces the Moro reflex; that is, the monkey grasps and clings to its mother. Researchers are not positive that the Moro reflex is related to our evolutionary past, but is does appear likely. This instinctive clinging may explain the discomfort many infants display when their caretaker holds them in positions that prevent them from making full body contact. Most infants are happy when carried in a cradled position in their mother's arm, held against her chest, or held with their backs touching her chest.

Some reflexes, such as coughing and yawning, are present in the newborn and persist throughout life. Other reflexes reveal that a neurological apparatus present in the newborn is later used for important abilities. Grasping, for example, initially occurs as a reflex action when something touches the newborn's hand. By the third month of life, this reflex disappears, but the infant is able to voluntarily grasp something within his visual field. Walking is another example. The newborn has a stepping reflex for the first few days after birth; when held on a hard surface, she will step forward as if walking. This stepping reflex disappears; but later in infancy, as higher brain functions and learning take place, the child learns to walk.

Recent studies show that newborns whose stepping reflex is actively exercised increase their stepping response and walk earlier than infants who do not receive the exercise (Zelazo, Zelazo, & Kolb, 1972). However, there seems to be little value

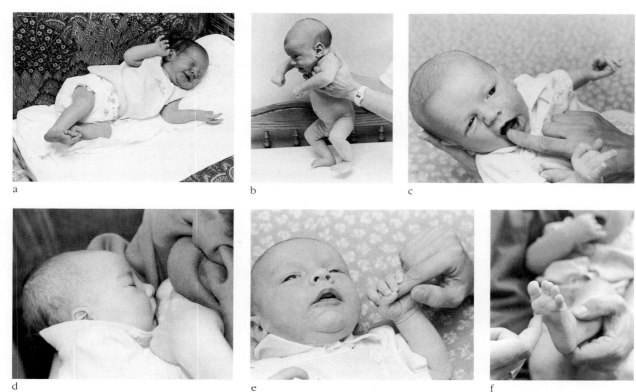

a   b   c

d   e   f

Six reflexes seen in newborn infants: (a) the Moro reflex; (b) the stepping reflex; (c) the rooting reflex; (d) the sucking reflex; (e) the grasping reflex; and (f) the Babinski reflex.

in attempting to exercise the baby's stepping reflex so that he will begin to walk early.

The study of infant reflexes helps researchers formulate and test hypotheses about infant growth and development (Thelen & Fisher, 1982). Our knowledge of infant reflexes also provides a framework for the neurological assessment of newborns, because the absence of any reflex may indicate a serious developmental disturbance (Self & Horowitz, 1979). In addition, parents can use play to elicit their infant's reflex responses. The newborn's ability to respond with reflex action depends on his state of arousal, as we see in the following section. Thus, researchers have studied the newborn's pattern of sleep and wakefulness.

Infant states Infant **states** refers to the extent to which the baby is asleep or aroused (see Table 5.3). Newborns spend most of their time asleep, but their sleep, unlike that of adults, is not regulated. Rather, infants sleep approximately three and one-half hours out of every four-hour period; over the course of the day, they undergo cycles of wakefulness and sleepiness and varying degrees of activity and sleep. Infant states are predictable and organized, alerting us to the newborn's physiological competence and the internal mechanisms (an inner clock, we might say) that regulate behavior (Berg & Berg, 1987; Schaffer, 1977).

How much time infants spend in each state varies according to the individual; some require more sleep, others less, and some are more irritable. There are also developmental changes in states. The newborn typically sleeps a total of 16 to 20 hours a day (Hutt, Lenard, & Prechtl, 1969). As the baby matures, she sleeps less but for longer periods. By the time she is approximately 6 to 12 months old, the baby

A CLOSER LOOK

Breast-Feeding

To breast-feed or bottle-feed? It's a question every prospective mother faces. Advice comes from experts, not all of whom agree and most of whom have changed their opinions over time, sometimes admonishing mothers for breast-feeding and other times encouraging them to do so (Kessen, 1965).

Breast-feeding was a common practice for centuries and still is in many rural parts of this country and certainly in most Third World countries. Before the pasteurization of milk paved the way for the substitution of cow's milk for human milk, almost all babies were breast-fed. Mothers who were wealthy enough to choose not to do so hired wet nurses. Eventually, however, bottle-feeding became the preferred practice; many mothers believed that this method was more convenient and actually more nutritionally sound for the baby, especially if infant formula was used.

Bottle-feeding may be more convenient, especially for mothers who work outside the home. However, physicians and psychologists note that mothers should attempt to breast-feed their babies, especially during the first few months, for several reasons.

At birth, infants are suddenly transferred from a regulated environment to one in which adaptation is required for survival. They must receive adequate nourishment and quickly develop immunologic mechanisms that will enable them to survive. There is increasing evidence that newborn babies can acquire these immunologic mechanisms from breast milk (Garrad, 1974; American Academy of Pediatrics, 1982). Breast milk also contains a blend of nutrients needed by the human infant (Koop, 1984). In addition, the practice of breast-feeding facilitates the development of a close psychological bond between the mother and the baby.

If there are so many obvious advantages to breast-feeding, why don't more mothers do it? Some mothers may not be physically capable of breast-feeding. Others may not be able to, because they have to work full-time and have to leave the baby in some form of substitute care. Some mothers collect ("express") their breast milk and leave it with the caretaker, but this is not always possible and the process does not appeal to everyone. Still other mothers experience

TABLE 5.3   Infant States

State	Description
Regular sleep	Eyes are closed, breathing is regular, and no movements except for sudden, generalized starts. Cannot be aroused by mild stimuli.
Irregular sleep	Eyes are closed, breathing is irregular, and muscles twitch from time to time. Still no major movements, but external stimulation such as bright light or noise can elicit smiles or pouts.
Drowsiness	Occurs either before or after sleep. Eyes may be open or closed, breathing is irregular. However, baby is highly sensitive to external stimuli.
Alert inactivity	No distressing internal and external stimuli. Awake, eyes are open, and looking at immediate environment.
Waking activity	Awake, eyes open, not alert. Seems to engage in frequent motor activity, moving whole body.
Crying	Awake, crying intensely, often kicking feet and thrashing arms.

Source: Adapted from "The Causes, Controls, and Organization of Behavior in the Neonate," by Peter H. Wolff, *Psychological Issues Monograph 17,* (Vol. V, No. 1). Copyright 1966 by International Universities Press.

A CLOSER LOOK

societal pressure to treat their breasts solely as aesthetic objects; they feel that breast-feeding deforms the breast or leads to their being less sexually appealing.

Finally, some mothers do not breast-feed simply because they do not know how. As one writer notes, "Most American babies by now have inherited grandmothers who themselves were bottle feeders. There's practically no one left who remembers the old urgencies, the old tales and ways" (Raphael, 1973, p. 57). When breast-feeding was a common practice, mothers received encouragement and instructions from nearby relatives. Today mothers are relatively isolated from relatives, and they may not have ever seen anyone breast-feed before.

The American Academy of Pediatrics believes that breast-feeding is so important for the infant's development that policies should be implemented to encourage the practice. In fact, the academy recommends that parenting education classes include instruction on the importance of breast-feeding and that the United States adopt legislation enabling all mothers to take a three-month leave of absence to care for and breast-feed their babies (American Academy of Pediatrics, 1982).

The evidence for the importance of breast-feeding is not new. "Back in 1867 a perceptive French industrialist, horrified at the 40% infant mortality rate in his district, decided to do something about it. He offered his women employees a six-week paid vacation immediately after they delivered a baby, so that they could stay home and establish a feeding routine with their newborn infants. The death rate immediately dropped from 40% to 25%" (*Scientific American*, 1867, 1967 in Raphael 1973, p. 76).

Support for breast-feeding is available from the La Leche League, an international organization that encourages and provides information about breast-feeding. Local chapters exist in many communities across the United States. At regular meetings, breast-feeding mothers exchange information and offer and receive support. It is this kind of support plus increased awareness about the benefits of breast-feeding that is needed.

sleeps through the night. However, it is not unusual for babies a year old or older to wake up at night. Some stay quietly in bed when they are awake, but others want company and cry. Worried parents often rush to the infant's bedside thinking he is hungry or wet, only to find a happy baby who is a bit bored!

Infant states influence the extent to which the baby benefits from environmental stimuli. To benefit from the environment, the infant must be in an alert, quiet state. In this state sensory pathways are open, and the infant can see, hear, and respond to touch. Obviously when the infant is in a sleep state or in a state characterized by intense crying, her attention is not directed toward outside stimuli. Often, infants use sleeping and crying to regulate the amount of stimulation they receive; they cannot cope with a lot of stimulation when they are so young.

When subjected to too much stimulation, some infants change from one state to another (Brazelton, 1976); that is, they fall asleep or begin to cry. Other infants avert their gaze, thus signaling that they can no longer cope with stimulation (for example, a playing situation with the parents). Using this research knowledge, Brazelton, a noted pediatrician who has written several books on childrearing, developed an assessment tool to examine the newborn's status. Known as the Brazelton Neonatal Behavioral Assessment Scale (Brazelton, 1973; Brazelton et al., 1979), the test assesses behavior in relation to the state the infant is in and examines the capacity for interaction. The examiner is trained to influence the infant to an optimal state and to modify the techniques used to elicit a response until the best response is produced (see Table 5.4).

Most of the scoring is done after the test items are administered at least once. The test findings also include a description of the examiner's overall impressions of the baby, a discussion of the conditions under which the test was done, and a notation of the infant's state at the time of testing. The Brazelton scale does not predict the infant's future development, but it is useful in screening for infants at risk and providing guidelines for interventions (Francis, Self, & Horowitz, 1987). Hence, this tool is sometimes used in conjunction with the Apgar scale (see Chapter 4) to assess the newborn's neurological status immediately after birth or to monitor the developmental status of premature infants.

Do babies dream while they sleep?   Since newborns spend so much time sleeping, do they dream? Obviously, the answer is elusive, because they cannot relate their experiences during sleep. However, by recording their brain activity, researchers have established that newborns spend as much as half of their sleeping hours in rapid eye movement, or **REM sleep** (Emde, Gaensbauer, & Harmon, 1976), which is characterized by rapid eye movements and fluctuations in the heart rate, blood pressure, and brain waves. Premature infants spend even more time in REM sleep. When awakened during this sleep stage, adults often report that they had been dreaming, so REM sleep is sometimes called **dream sleep** (Kryger, Roth, & Dement, 1989).

A certain amount of REM sleep is essential to optimal functioning in adults (McCarley, 1989). Although researchers do not entirely understand why, they know that adults who get little REM sleep or who are repeatedly awakened from it are irritable and disorganized the next day (Dement, 1960). Adults spend much less time in REM sleep than do infants. The percentage drops from 50% in the newborn period to only 25% in the 2- to 3-year-old child, to less than 20% in adults between ages 33 and 45 (Roffwarg, Muzio, & Dement, 1966). The distribution of the different sleep phases also changes with maturity. Adults usually spend an hour in non-REM

TABLE 5.4   The Brazelton Neonatal Behavioral Assessment Scale

		Scoring
Neurological items		
Elicited reflexes and movements	plantar grasp hand grasp ankle clonus Babinski standing automatic walking crawling tonic neck reflex Moro rooting sucking passive movements of both legs and both arms	These neurological items are rated on a 3-point scale for low, medium, and high intensity of response; asymmetry and absence are also noted.
Behavioral items		
Specific behaviors observed or elicited	focusing and following an object reaction to an auditory stimulus reaction to persons reaction to a voice reaction to a person's face and voice	These behavioral items are rated on a 9-point scale; the midpoint of the scale denotes the expected behavior of a 3-day-old normal baby.
General behaviors observed	degree of alertness motor maturity cuddliness consolability with intervention peak of excitement irritability amount of startles self-quieting activity hand-to-mouth facility number of smiles	

Source: Adapted from *Neonatal Behavioral Assessment Scale,* Clinics in Developmental Medicine (no. 50), by T. B. Brazelton, 1973, Philadelphia: JB Lippincott.

sleep before drifting into REM sleep, whereas newborns can enter REM sleep from any waking or sleeping state.

Some sleep-research experts propose that autostimulation may account for the increased time infants spend in REM sleep (Roffwarg, Muzio, & Dement, 1966). According to the **autostimulation theory,** REM sleep is a spontaneous neurological firing in the brain that stimulates higher brain centers. The high degree of REM sleep during the newborn period may thus stimulate the development of the central nervous system. As the infant matures and becomes increasingly more alert, this type of internal stimulation is less necessary because the nervous system is more mature, and the infant is more capable of processing external stimuli. Emde and his colleagues have proposed that the more external stimulation infants experience when awake, the less time they spend in REM sleep (Emde et al., 1971). For example, newly circumcised infants spend less time in REM sleep (circumcision has an extreme impact on the baby). The autostimulation theory may also explain why premature infants, whose nervous system is less mature than that of full-term infants, spend more time in REM sleep. This theory, however, is still only a theoretical explanation of the sleep patterns of babies.

Influencing the infant state   Parents often try to influence the newborn's state. Naturally, the state they most want to change is when the infant cries. It is important to quiet an unhappy baby, because a baby who cries continually can be unnerving for the parents and because the quieter and calmer the baby is, the more he is able to become acquainted with the environment (Korner, 1972), increase his body weight, and adjust to life (Stuart & Prugh, 1960).

Soothing the crying baby   Early in life, crying is a reflexive reaction to some discomfort, but as the baby matures, crying is used to communicate. There are several reasons for crying: hunger, pain, overstimulation, restlessness, or boredom. And there are various ways to soothe the baby. Feeding is one way. Another is wrapping the baby in a blanket, a practice more common in Russia and China than in the United States (Lipton, Steinschneider, & Richmond, 1965). Stimulating a restless baby—for example, walking with the baby, rocking her, introducing rhythmic sound, or clothing or unclothing her—is another way to soothe her. It results in lowered heart and respiratory rates and in the cessation of crying (Brackbill, 1971). When the baby cries because she has had too much stimulation, letting the baby rest

FEATURE

Understanding Colic

Infant colic is one of the most difficult problems parents can encounter. A colicky infant cries in a seemingly endless, inconsolable wail, sometimes creating desperation, frustration, and irritability throughout the household. This puzzling, though benign, condition occurs in 20% of all infants. Colic usually begins late in the second week of life and continues until the infant is 3 months old. Episodes of unremitting crying occur almost daily and last longer than with most newborns (Brazelton, 1962; Wessel et al., 1956). Colicky infants have a piercing cry, and when they cry, they arch their backs, clench their fists, and turn red.

In some cases colicky infants cry for much of the day or night, but typically they appear content for most of the day and do not begin to cry until late afternoon or evening, often continuing for much of the night (Adams & Davidson, 1987; Keefe, 1988).

Neither birth order, gender, ethnicity, nor social class have been found to correlate with colic (Weissbluth,

1984). Researchers have attributed the condition to allergy (Illingworth, 1985), gastrointestinal anomalies (Hewson, Oberklaid, & Menahem, 1987), and maternal stress (Carey, 1968). Some have implicated environmental factors, ranging from diet to parental smoking, although researchers have not produced strong evidence to support these notions (Forsyth, Leventhal, & McCarthy, 1985).

Colic is usually viewed as a variant of infant behavior, rather than as a disorder (St. James-Roberts, 1989); even in noncolicky infants, crying tends to peak later in the afternoon and they tend to cry more during the first 6 to 12 weeks of life (Brazelton, 1962). Colicky infants may simply be less able to regulate their ability to handle stimulation from external and internal sources as a result of normal differences in temperament and a slight physiologic immaturity.

Nevertheless, colic can be a source of great stress for parents. This is of concern, since high levels of maternal

often is soothing. Parents and caregivers can use these research findings, especially for premature infants, who are often irritable and spend more time crying.

Knowledge of ways to soothe the infant can also help reduce the incidence of physical abuse, which often occurs when adults are unable to pacify the baby (Frodi, 1985). Crying is one way the infant communicates with adults. As noted earlier, babies cry differently depending on whether they are hungry, in pain, or simply irritable. However, parents cannot always distinguish among these cries (Muller, Hollien, & Murray, 1974; Donovan & Leavitt, 1985), especially during the first few days of life when facial expressions, physical movements, and noncrying noises are unfocused and difficult to interpret. As parents become more attuned to the baby, they can better distinguish among the different cries and can tell, for example, when the crying means loneliness, discomfort, or pain (Boukydis, 1985).

Some babies, after they become used to sleeping through the night, may awaken at night and begin to cry. Moreover, parents can do little to soothe the baby; when they attend to him, he is fine, but the minute they put him back to bed he cries. Usually, parents check with the pediatrician, who finds nothing wrong with the baby. In this case the baby may awaken and, finding that he is alone in the dark, simply become bored. Pediatricians often advise parents not to pick the child up or otherwise socialize with him in these situations, but to check on him, perhaps rub his back, and then let him cry. Eventually he will adjust if parents pay no attention to his cries. But you will see in Chapter 7 that this may be a correct strategy for dealing with *older infants*. It is vitally important to always respond to the cries of infants younger than 6 months old. Newborns must learn that they can communicate their needs (White, 1988), and they learn this only if adults respond to their crying.

FEATURE

stress can lead to disturbances in the relationship between parent and infant (Crnic et al., 1983; see also Chapter 7). A recent study of colicky infants found that their mothers reported higher levels of stress associated with their infants' crying than did a comparison group of mothers of noncolicky infants (Humphrey & Hock, 1989). In another comparison between mothers of colicky infants and mothers of noncolicky infants, researchers found that mothers of colicky infants were more likely to report that their infants were bothersome, intense, and negative in mood (Sloman, Bellinger, & Kentzel, 1990). The researchers also found that at 6 months of age, infants with a history of colic had lower scores on the mental and psychomotor scales of the Bayley Scale of Infant Development. But this lag disappeared by the first birthday, which prompted the researchers to speculate that the colic had temporarily interfered with the normal pattern of mother/infant interaction, thereby contributing to temporary developmental delays.

What can parents do to alleviate colic? There is no uniformly effective treatment for colic, but parents can try some interventions. Gentle vestibular stimulation, such as taking the infant for a ride in the car or walking with the baby in an infant carrier, sometimes helps. Applications of heat to the baby's abdomen, the elimination of certain foods from the mother's diet, if she is breast-feeding (for example, garlic, caffeine, or milk), or switching to infant formula, have also helped some infants. In extreme cases the pediatrician may prescribe a mild sedative or antiflatulence medication. Parents dangerously stressed by the crying should seek relief by taking turns caring for the baby or by enlisting the help of relatives and friends. We cannot overemphasize the importance of strong social support systems. Above all, parents should be reassured that colic is not their fault and will subside with time.

Sensory and Perceptual Capabilities

Until the 1950s a newborn was considered an essentially passive, incompetent creature who simply cried, ate, and slept, and who possessed a few simple reflexes. With the surge of infancy research beginning in the 1960s, however, scientists realized that the newborn is equipped with acute senses and is capable of making immediate responses to the environment. In fact, all the senses function at birth or shortly after; the newborn can hear, see, smell, taste, and respond to touch. Most of these sensory abilities are still immature and become more refined and acute as the infant grows (Lowery, 1978). Limited perceptual ability is also present at birth; newborns pay selective attention to some aspects of their environment, such as bright lights and loud noises. There is a difference between sensory abilities and perceptual abilities. **Sensation** refers to the ability to detect a certain stimulus in the environment. **Perception** refers to the ability to process or interpret these sensations. The newborn's capabilities in both these areas are amazing, making us realize the extent and significance of prenatal physiological development.

The "amazing newborns" (Pines, 1982) and their repertoire of sensory and perceptual skills are not some new breed of baby. Babies have always had these skills. What is new is the ability to study these behaviors. It is difficult to study infants, especially newborns, since many methods developed to study children and adults depend on motor and verbal responses; therefore, they are useless when studying infants. Newborns cannot tell us what they see, and they cannot point to an object or otherwise specify a response. Still, scientists have developed research methods based on responses that the newborn and infant *can* make. They measure heart rate, rate and change of respiration, muscle contraction, and other physiological functions to determine the newborn's sensory capabilities. For example, detecting a change in the baby's respiration when she hears her mother's voice, but not when she hears other sounds, would suggest that the newborn recognizes or is sensitive to her mother's voice. Some researchers also monitor the newborn's eye movement and sucking pattern to establish an index of the effects of sensory stimuli.

In much of the research, researchers rely on habituation and dishabituation to interpret the findings. **Habituation** is a type of learning indicating that a particular stimulus has become familiar, or learned, and thus no longer elicits interest or attention. For example, if a newborn is shown an object he has not seen before, he will evidence interest by getting somewhat excited. His heart rate may increase, perhaps. After repeated exposure to the object, he will no longer be interested and will evidence no response. If, at the same time that he is shown the familiar object, he is also shown a new object, which is similar but slightly different from the first one, he may notice the difference and pay attention to the new object. This is known as **dishabituation;** it reveals that the baby can discriminate between objects and remember what he has seen in the past. We will also discuss habituation and dishabituation in Chapter 6 on cognitive development.

Many findings on newborn capabilities are relatively new. There is no overall theory that guides the research, in part because researchers have primarily sought to find appropriate methods of study (Banks & Salapatek, 1983). But the discovery of effective techniques for assessing the sensory and perceptual capacities of very young infants will eventually help researchers begin theorizing. As Acredolo and Hake (1982) note, now that researchers have breached the "methodological barriers holding back the curious," there is an "exhilarating rush toward the solution of the nature-nurture question so long at the heart of psychological and philosophical debate." In addition, researchers are also exploring the relationship between sensory and perceptual development and the development of the brain. As you will see in Chapter 6, knowledge about the infant's sensory capabilities can be used in research on cognitive development and language acquisition (Haith, 1990). Now let us discuss the sensory capabilities of the newborn.

Hearing

At birth newborns' auditory canals are filled with amniotic fluid; thus for the first day or two after birth, they may have difficulty hearing. However, as soon as the fluid left in the ear is discharged or absorbed, their hearing improves, and they can apparently hear remarkably well. Still, their hearing is not as acute as it will become later on (Hecox & Deegan, 1985). Newborns can localize sounds, and there is evidence that they are especially sensitive to high-pitched sounds, although with age, they lose this sensitivity (Aslin, 1987). Unborn babies can also respond to loud noises (Bench, 1978), because the **cochlea,** the main hearing organ, is functional about four months before birth.

Brody, Zelazo, and Chaika (1984) found that even three days after birth, newborns can distinguish between new speech sounds and those they have heard before. Newborns also seem to selectively respond to adult speech. Freedman (1971) notes that newborns respond to the sound of a female voice more often than to the sound of a bell. The newborn's selective responsivity to human speech may have an important survival value, because it plays a vital part in the development of an affectionate bond between parent and child (Hutt et al., 1968). Researchers also suggest that newborns do not have to learn to respond to the adult voice; rather, their auditory system is "prewired" for these sounds.

For example, when studying newborns and babies approximately 1 and 2 months old, researchers found that they can distinguish between such similar speech sounds as *pa* and *ba* (Eimas, 1985; Eimas & Tartter, 1979; Eimas et al., 1971). Japanese newborns can distinguish between *r* and *l,* even though Japanese adults cannot (Eimas, 1985). Although infants are born with the ability to respond to all speech sounds, they eventually tailor their speech perception to the speech sounds they hear. Hence researchers have found that at 8 months of age, infants of English-speaking parents could distinguish speech sounds in Hindi, but at 1 year of age they lost this ability and could only differentiate speech sounds of the English language (Eimas, 1985).

With a little practice, very young infants come to recognize and prefer their own mother's voice, provided, however, that the mothers speak normally. By measuring the sucking responses of 1-month-old infants, Mehler and colleagues (1978) found that the infants can distinguish the mother's voice from a stranger's. This finding held as long as the mother spoke in her usual fashion and addressed herself to the infant. When the mother simply read from a book with no intonation in her voice, the infant did not show a discriminating response to the mother's voice.

Newborns also tune into the syllabic content of the speech they hear. During a conversation, adults usually move in synchrony with the speech they hear. That is, just when the speaker changes from one syllable to the next, listeners will flex an arm, tap a finger, shift the weight of their legs, and so on (Condon & Sander, 1974). In an intriguing study researchers found that the newborn synchronizes her movements precisely to the patterns of adult speech. To illustrate this amazing phenomenon, the researchers (Condon & Sander, 1974) filmed and analyzed the newborn's movements. Their subjects, infants ranging from 12 hours old to 2 weeks old, were filmed while listening to natural speech in English and Chinese, to disconnected vowel sounds, and to tapping sounds. Analysis of the films shows that infants who were already moving when the speech began synchronized their movements to the acoustic structure of the speech. Their movements started and stopped in concert with the speech they were hearing. The researchers noted that watching the film gives the impression of a subtle sequence of ballet, so precise and definite is the interaction. They also observed synchrony of movement to speech when both English and Chinese sentences were used, even though the infants were of English-speaking parents. However, the researchers could see no synchrony when the infants heard either disconnected vowel sounds or the tapping sound. This study provides a dramatic example that the newborn is predisposed to listen selectively to human speech.

Vision

Researchers have also studied the newborn's ability to see. In fact, vision in infancy is perhaps the most widely investigated topic. As a result, researchers are acquiring increasing amounts of information about the visual world of newborn babies.

At birth the newborn's eyes are physiologically and anatomically ready to respond to many aspects of the visual field (Aslin, 1987; Gottlieb & Krasnegor, 1985; Reese & Lipsitt, 1970). Babies can also see objects as long as the objects are close-by (Lewis, Maurer, & Kay, 1978), and they can distinguish between some colors (Warner & Wooten, 1979). However, babies have poor **visual acuity,** which is the ability to detect the separate parts of an object (Banks & Salapatek, 1983), and cannot focus well at a distance (Haynes, White, & Held, 1965). Newborns, for example, cannot see objects that are, say, 40 yards away. But up close they can see better. The ability to focus improves with age as neural development becomes more advanced. While research in this area is not conclusive, researchers note that by about 1 year of age, the baby sees as clearly as adults do (Acredolo & Hake, 1982). In a summary of major studies on basic visual processes, Haith (1990) notes that newborns' acuity is in the range of 20/200 and 20/400 and reaches an adult level of 20/20 by the time the infant is 1 year old.

According to Haith (1990), the research also indicates that infants have the physiological capability to perceive color in much the same way as adults do, and that color vision is similar to that of the adult by the time the infant is 4 months old. However, the research on color perception is controversial, since it is hard to ascertain whether newborns perceive color in the same way adults do (Aslin, 1987; Teller & Bornstein, 1987).

Strategies for looking   Newborns have strategies for scanning the environment, and some parts of objects seem more interesting to them than others. However, they do not scan the environment the same way as adults do. To find out what parts of the visual target the newborn attends to, Salapatek and Kessen (1966) used an infrared camera that enabled them to see precisely where on the object the newborn's eyes were focused. When the researchers showed newborns a triangle form, they looked only at the edges, not at the whole form as an adult would do. Salapatek's later research (1969) suggests that at 2 months, infants focus on the center or internal area of the visual target and on both its edges. Salapatek (1975) also found that when newborns are shown two forms—say, two different-size triangles, one inside the

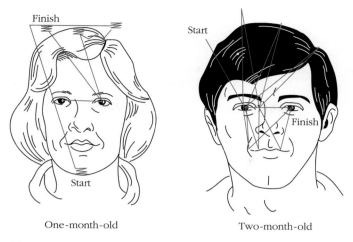

One-month-old   Two-month-old

Figure 5.2 *Scanning patterns of the newborn.*
Source: Adapted from "Visual Scanning of Triangles by the Human
Newborn" by P. Salapatek and W. Kessen, 1966, *Journal of Experimental
Child Psychology, 3.* Reprinted with permission.

other—they look only at the external form. By 2 to 3 months of age, they begin to
pay attention to the internal form as well.

On the basis of such studies, Haith (1980) found that the baby has visual
scanning rules. Let us look at what the newborn sees when his mother bends over
him. The movement of the mother's face will elicit scanning by the baby. In the
course of his searching, what he focuses on is subject to developmental changes. At
1 month of age the infant will focus on the edge of the face; that is, the hairline at the
top or side of the face. Some parents become frustrated by this phenomenon; they
feel that the baby is "looking through them," and they fail to maintain eye-to-eye
contact. By 2 months of age, the infant is now more skillful visually and will concentrate on high-contrast areas within the general outline. That is, he will look at the
eyes rather than the hairline. In Figure 5.2, you can see the difference in the scanning patterns of a 1-month-old infant and a 2-month-old infant. By 3 months of age,
the infant can find and focus on his mother's eyes rather quickly, even while the
mother is talking (Haith, Bergman, & Moore, 1977). This is a remarkable feat that
may facilitate development of a close relationship between parent and infant, since
eye-to-eye contact is an important aspect of communication and social ties (McCall,
1980).

Pattern perception   With age, infants also improve in their ability to perceive
different patterns and shapes. To establish the development of pattern perception in
infants and to find out if infants can discriminate among patterns, Fantz (1961)
measured the amount of time infants gazed at a visual target. He put the infant in a
crib facing visual stimuli (different pattern forms, as in Figure 5.3) attached to the
ceiling. An observer determined how long the infant looked at each of the stimuli. If
the infant looked longer at one form, the observer assumed that the infant preferred
that form. In this classic study, which was of infants at 2 months of age, Fantz found
that infants looked longest at a pattern of a face, next at a pattern of newsprint, and

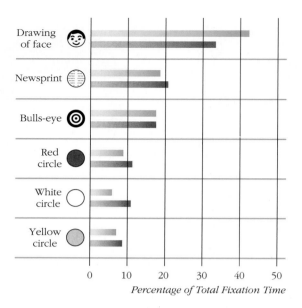

0   10   20   30   40   50
Percentage of Total Fixation Time

Figure 5.3   Visual preferences of infants. Infants would rather look at a pattern than at color, and they prefer to look at a human face rather than at a pattern such as a bull's-eye or newsprint. The black bars represent preferences of infants 2 to 3 months old, and the color bars show preferences of infants older than 3 months.

Source: Adapted from "The Origin of Form Perception," by R. L. Fantz, *Scientific American,* May 1961, p. 72, bottom. Copyright © 1961 by Scientific American, Inc. All rights reserved.

then at concentric circles (a bull's-eye). The infants preferred such patterns to non-patterned objects. In a related study (Fantz, 1963), the researcher found that at 48 hours of age infants looked longer at a colored pattern than at a plain block of color, and longer still at a circle with eyes, nose, and mouth sketched in than at a plain piece of paper. But of most interest to infants in this study was a face pattern that also moved. Therefore, for visual inspection these very young infants were selecting interesting objects, especially objects having the qualities of a human face.

In another study Fantz (1966) showed newborns and 3-month-old infants a drawing of a normal face and a drawing of a scrambled pattern. He found that newborns showed no preference for either drawing. By 3 months of age, however, they clearly preferred the pattern of a normal face, which means that by that age the face had become a meaningful visual object. When movement is included in the experimental condition—that is, when babies are presented with a facelike figure moving in front of them—newborns will turn their heads to look at it; they will not do so if shown a scrambled moving figure (Goren, Sarty, & Wu, 1975). Thus under real-life conditions, newborns may indeed be attracted to the human face (Aslin, 1987).

Depth perception   Young babies also have some idea of depth. Depth perception may be an innate mechanism, because it protects the young of any species from falling. In a classic experiment Gibson and Walk (1960) constructed a visual "cliff,"

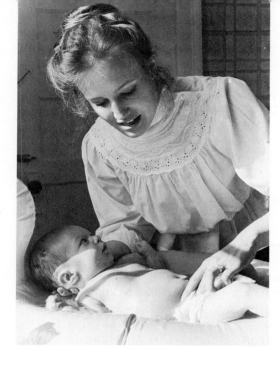

The experience of being touched has a direct and crucial effect on growth and development. Because this premature baby was massaged, he gained weight faster than other premature infants who were not massaged, even though their caloric intake was the same.

which consisted of a glass-covered board divided into two sections. On one section they set up a checkered pattern, and on the other side several feet below it, they put a clear glass surface with a checkerboard pattern. In this way they created on one side an illusion of depth. The babies in the experiment were 6 months old or older. They crawled readily on the nondeep side of the "cliff" but refused to crawl to the side of the cliff that looked deep, even though their mothers were on that side. Obviously, by 6 months of age the infants might have learned about depth perception, so we cannot be sure that depth perception is innate. However, Campos, Langer, and Krowitz (1970) studied 2- and 3-month-old infants to see if they had any depth perception. Since the infants could not crawl, the researchers placed them on their stomachs on both sides of the cliff and recorded their heart rates on the deep and nondeep sides. They found that the babies had a faster heartbeat when placed on the deep side, suggesting that perhaps the babies were distinguishing and responding to the deep side as a new experience.

Touch, Smell, and Taste

Our knowledge of the newborn's sensory capabilities extends beyond hearing and seeing. For example, newborns are responsive to touch, as exemplified by their reflex responses and by the fact that we can usually soothe crying babies by holding them or picking them up. Research shows that the experience of being touched has a direct effect on growth and development. Premature infants who are massaged, for instance, gain more weight than those who are not massaged, even though the caloric intake of the two groups is the same (Field, 1980; Scarr-Salapatek & Williams, 1973).

Research also indicates that the newborn's sense of smell is developed at birth. Lipsitt, Engen, and Kaye (1963) observed that newborns can distinguish between smells such as anise, garlic, vinegar, and phenyl alcohol. With repeated exposure to a smell, they eventually take no notice of it. But when a new smell is introduced, the babies detect the difference. So infants can smell some odors, they can remember that they have previously encountered an odor, and they can distinguish the difference between one odor and another. Other researchers found that newborns also turn away from an unpleasant odor more frequently than toward it (Rieser, Yonas, & Wilkner, 1976); but the substances used were strong-smelling. The question remains, Can the infant recognize other odors, say, his own mother's? In two studies (Cernoch & Porter, 1985; MacFarlane, 1975) researchers asked nursing mothers to wear pads inside their bras between feedings. The mother's pad was then placed on one side of the infant, and a clean pad was placed on the other side. In one of the studies (MacFarlane, 1975), even 5-day-old infants turned their heads more often toward their mother's pad than toward the clean pad. In a follow-up to that study, the researchers compared pads worn by the newborn's mother with pads worn by another nursing mother. At 2 days of age, the infants did not discriminate between the two pads, but at 6 days they spent more time facing their mother's pad than that of another mother, and at 10 days they spent even more time facing their mother's pad.

Much of the sense of taste is based on smell, so it should follow that the newborn has the ability to detect differences in flavor. This is confirmed by studies (Crook & Lipsitt, 1976) showing that infants' sucking responses differ depending on whether they are given sweet or salty solutions. Babies also prefer sweet-tasting liquids rather than bitter- or salty-tasting liquids (Haith, 1986). In addition, Lipsitt

---

FEATURE

A Quest for Superbabies

First, they played tapes directly beside her pregnant, distended abdomen. Then, even before the baby was born, they painted the walls several different colors. They hung an elaborate mobile over the crib when their daughter was finally born. Her mother insisted on reading a story each night, even though the baby was only 2 weeks old, and her father started to make word cards to place on objects throughout the house. Good parents? Of course! Somewhat anxious? Indeed! Their quest? The superbaby—a product of nurturance and stimulation galore!

Superbaby programs claim to be based on notions derived from research studies that showed that although severely deprived environments can delay development, these delays can be overcome by extra perceptual and sensory stimulation (White, 1967; White & Held, 1966). In a good example of a logical fallacy, therefore, all babies need "enriched" perceptual and sensory stimulation for normal development. Deluged by information in the popular press about the newborns' abilities, many parents feel pressured to continually stimulate their baby's senses and to provide as many experiences as early in life as possible. The older parent, who has worked for some years before deciding to

have children and has accumulated resources, is especially likely to want to do as much as possible to ensure a "good early start" for the baby. Lipsitt (1990a) refers to these parents as "trophy-child parents"; they read everything they can find having to do with raising children "right" and are obsessed with providing them with every experience possible. Such parents often continue to pressure their child to excel academically or learn to speak a second language or to play a musical instrument at an early age. As a result, the young child experiences a great deal of stress and fewer opportunities to learn through play (Elkind, 1987).

Although children may benefit by being their parents' priority, there is *no* indication that superbaby programs are effective. Certainly infants need a certain amount of stimulation to fully develop their physical skills. However, the question is not whether stimulation is or is not important. The question is, in what amounts and in what ways should stimulation be provided? Most parents are likely to play with their infants and give them toys and periods of undivided attention during the day. But beyond these natural stimulating experiences, overstimulation may actually harm some babies. In fact, Bower (1977) contends

(1977) determined that newborns would suck two different-tasting liquids at different speeds even though both these liquids had the same smell.

Interconnectedness Among the Senses

Although we have described the senses one by one for the sake of simplicity, the sensory systems do not necessarily operate in isolation from one another; rather, they work together. We expect to be able to see something we hear, which is why we turn toward the source of sound. Thus the information gained from one sense is used to "inform" other senses, a process referred to as **cross-modal transfer of information.** How the infant develops this process is the subject of some debate. Piaget (1971) argued that infants learn it through gradual associations. That is, infants learn to link vision with touch through repeated visual observation of hand movements. They learn to link vision with hearing through their efforts to locate the source of sound. Piaget also noted that there is a developmental progression in this process; infants gradually move from use of the senses in isolation to their eventual interconnectedness. Current research suggests that coordination of the senses may be present at birth; during infancy babies learn differentiation of the senses, not interconnectedness (Bower, 1974; Spelke, 1976). Much of the evidence for this theory comes from such studies as the ones discussed earlier. For example, the fact that infants turn their head and eyes toward the source of sound indicates that they use the two senses in a perceptual event and that they are sensitive to visual/sound correspondences at an early age.

FEATURE

that overstimulation could cause the baby to become temporarily withdrawn. Other researchers also found that while some babies deprived of basic environmental stimulation benefited from enrichment activities, it was too much stimulation for most infants, who sometimes became confused and irritated (White & Held, 1966).

What is the best rule of thumb? Simply have a good time together (McCall, 1980), and don't worry about exercising your baby's reflexes or stimulating her senses. Physical development will usually take care of itself. Not all activities are equally stimulating for all babies. Many studies have underscored the presence of individual differences on this dimension that may persist through life. Korner (1971), for example, found that infants differed in how much they cried, how soothable they were, and how capable they were of self-comforting behavior. Infants also differed in their capacity to take in and synthesize sensory stimuli. Some have a low sensory threshold; they are likely to cry excessively during the first few months and tend to become overwhelmed and overstimulated unless the caretaker can act as a shield and tension-reducing agent. In contrast, other infants, who have high sensory thresholds to

all sensory stimuli, require a great deal of stimulation for optimal development. Korner and others (such as Zuckerman, 1979) proposed that the low/high sensory threshold is a personality characteristic that persists beyond infancy. Honzik (1964) also described children who differed in their reactions to the environment. They were *reactive/ expressive* to the new situations or *retractive/inhibitive*. Honzik noted that this personality characteristic persisted throughout childhood and adolescence. Kagan's research (1965) also demonstrated that some children respond quickly and impulsively to problems or situations that arise, whereas others respond reflectively and with caution.

These studies suggest that there are clear-cut, extreme differences in how individuals deal with stimulation and excitement. Differences in responsivity to and synthesis of external stimuli are, in all likelihood, an expression of neurophysiological makeup (Korner, 1990). Thus there is no one way to provide a good environment for an infant. Instead, it is important to respond to the requirements of each individual.

Physical Growth and Motor Development

Physical Growth

Another amazing aspect of the development of infants is their rapid rate of physical growth. It occurs so rapidly during infancy that by the time infants approach their second birthday, parents wonder if they really ever were as small and dependent as the tiny baby they brought home from the hospital. Although all infants grow rapidly, there are individual differences in their rates of growth; some grow steadily, while others seem to grow in spurts (Lampl & Emde, 1983).

Immediately after birth infants lose weight, but after the first few days they start to gain again; weight gain during the first few months is substantial (Eichorn, 1979). On the average infants double their birth weight by the time they reach 4 months, and by the time they are 2 years of age, they have quadrupled their birth weight. Substantial gains also occur in length (height); infants more than double their length by the time they are 2 years old.

However, growth during infancy is not merely a matter of gain in weight and height. Because different parts of the body grow at different rates, babies' body proportions change as they grow older. Changes in proportions are most evident in the size of the head in relation to the total body. Newborns have a disproportionately large head, which is about one-quarter of their overall length. As the baby grows, the head becomes proportionately smaller. By the end of the first year of life, the head is one-fifth of the infant's height, and during adulthood it is one-eighth of the adult's height (see Figure 5.4). We can observe similar proportional changes in the legs. Newborns have short legs that account for only a small part of their overall height, whereas adults' legs account for about half their height.

In addition, during infancy *ossification* (the hardening of the bones, a process that began during the prenatal period) and skeletal growth continue. Legs and arms grow stronger and longer, enabling the infant to acquire new skills. For example, the newborn's legs are bent and fragile, and they are not strong enough to support the body in an upright position. Toward the end of the first year, however, the infant's legs straighten and become increasingly stronger, so that by the age of 15 months, most infants are able to stand and walk unassisted.

Three principles govern physical growth. First, growth occurs in a **cephalocaudal sequence;** that is, from head to toe. The head develops first, and then the rest of the body. This pattern of growth is followed even before birth; in the fetus the head forms first, then arm buds appear, then leg buds. Similarly, facial muscles are present before other muscles in the body. Growth also occurs on a **proximodistal direction;** that is, development first occurs at the center of the body, then at the extremities. For this reason, the baby's arms are small in proportion to the trunk of the body, which develops faster. Hands and fingers are also small in proportion to arms, because the arms, being closer to the center of the body than the fingers, develop first. The cephalocaudal and proximodistal principles of growth are illustrated in Figure 5.5 (p. 188). Additionally, as you will see in our discussion on motor development, there is a definite order in the acquisition of motor skills proceeding from the simple to the complex.

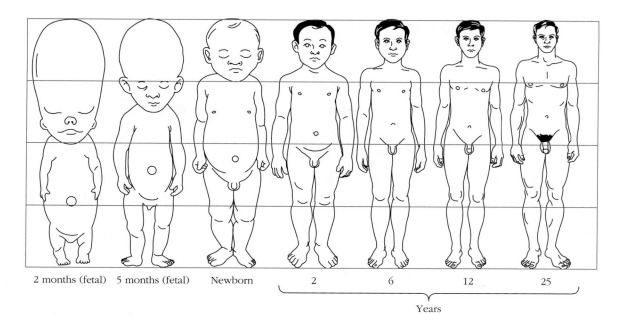

2 months (fetal)   5 months (fetal)   Newborn   2   6   12   25

Years

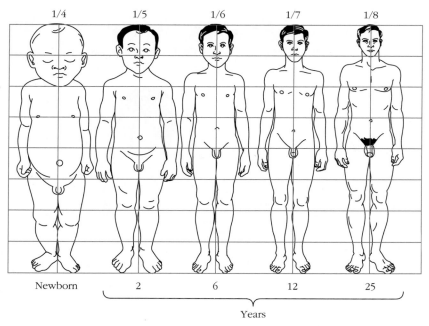

1/4   1/5   1/6   1/7   1/8

Newborn   2   6   12   25

Years

Figure 5.4 *Changes in body proportions. In the newborn, the length of the head is approximately one-fourth of the total length of the body. In the adult, it is only one-eighth. Conversely, the legs are comparatively shorter in the baby than in the adult.*
Source: Adapted from "Contrasting Characteristics of Prenatal and Post Natal Life," p. 283. Reprinted with permission of Macmillan Publishing Company from *Developmental Physiology and Aging* by Paola S. Timiras. Copyright © 1972 by Paola S. Timiras.

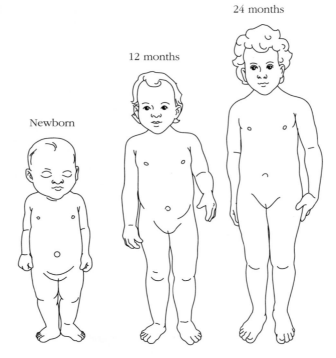

Newborn

12 months

24 months

Cephalocaudal Growth

Proximodistal Growth

Figure 5.5 *Cephalocaudal (head to toe) and proximodistal (from the center to the extremities) growth patterns.*

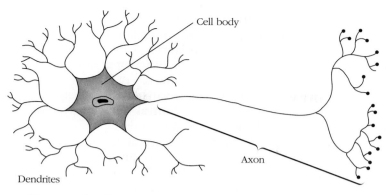

Figure 5.6 *The nerve cell, or neuron. Unlike other cells in the body, the cytoplasm in nerve cells is drawn out into dendrites and axons, which receive and send impulses.*

The Brain

Development of the brain is one of the most important aspects of physical development during infancy. Brain development also has far-reaching implications for psychological development, because the brain is the basis of intellectual functioning. The more mature the brain is, the more capable the infant is of understanding and acting on the environment and of communicating with others.

In recent years our understanding of the human brain has increased substantially as researchers systematically map its structure and growth and relate it to changes in human behavior (Lipsitt, 1986). Considerable brain growth occurs in the uterus, and the baby is born with a neural apparatus that permits a great deal of behavior. Brain growth also continues rapidly for six months after birth, which accounts for the infant's rapid behavioral development (Tanner, 1978). Then growth slows down, until by the infant's second birthday, the brain is at 75% of its adult weight.

When exposed, the brain looks rather like a walnut. Like other organs, it is made up of cells. There are two kinds of brain cells. **Neurons,** or nerve cells, receive and send impulses, or signals. **Neuroglia, or glial cells,** feed and support the nerve cells. During the prenatal period and until the baby is 6 months old, brain cells rapidly increase in number. After that, the brain matures in other ways.

Each neuron consists of a cell body, a nucleus, and cytoplasm, much as other cells in the body are constructed. In neurons, however, the cytoplasm is drawn out into large numbers of fine, wirelike dendrites and axons (see Figure 5.6). Dendrites and axons also have many branches that connect with other branches that emerge from other cells. The **dendrites** receive impulses; the **axons** send impulses. These impulses, or messages, are transmitted from one neuron to the next by chemicals. The *connecticity* of the neurons—that is, the number of connections made by the axons and dendrites with other cells—accounts for the brain's functional maturity and governs even the most basic, simple actions. Any action, even picking up a pencil, may take only a fraction of a second, but it can occur only on the basis of numerous messages that travel from the eyes to the brain and then to the hand.

Developmental changes in the brain   Different parts of the brain mature at different times. Think of the brain as having three layers: the forebrain, the midbrain, and the hindbrain. The forebrain is known as the **upper cortex;** the midbrain and hindbrain, often referred to as the **subcortex,** make up the brainstem (see Figure 5.7). Connecting the brainstem to the rest of the body is the spinal cord, which carries fibers from the brain to connect with muscles or sense organs in other parts of the body. This entire system is the **central nervous system.**

The hindbrain and midbrain are the first to develop and achieve maturity. Thus, for the first few months of life, the subcortical centers of the brain control behavior. The hindbrain, which controls vegetable functions such as breathing, is mature at birth. The midbrain, which controls emotions, state of arousal, reflexes, and vision, is somewhat mature at birth but does not achieve full maturity for several months thereafter. However, the forebrain, which is responsible for much of our intellectual behavior, speech, and motor coordination, is immature and hardly functional at birth. During the first six months of life, however, the forebrain undergoes rapid development. Its neurons increase in number, size, and connectedness. In the infant's initial repertoire of reflexes when movement is involuntary, behavior is a function of the subcortical brain. However, after the newborn period, behavior becomes a function of the upper cortex. The baby's developing capacity to control

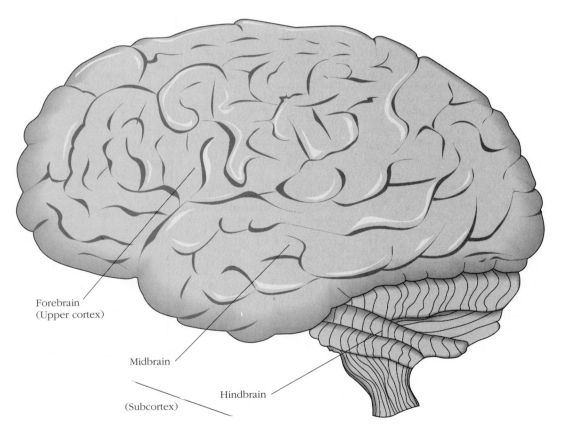

Forebrain
(Upper cortex)

Midbrain

Hindbrain

(Subcortex)

Figure 5.7   *The hierarchy of the brain. The brainstem, which is made up of the hindbrain and the midbrain, matures earlier than the forebrain, which is associated with higher mental functions.*

movement, as we describe later in this chapter, is evidence that after the first few months, behavior becomes a function of the maturing cortex.

Environmental factors also influence brain growth and can have a lasting effect on the capacity of the central nervous system. Recall that in Chapter 4 we discussed that chronic malnutrition during the prenatal period of rapid brain growth can result in fewer brain cells and, potentially, in brain damage.

DISCUSSION OF SOCIAL ISSUES

Babies with AIDS

Central nervous system complications can also occur when diseases are transmitted during the prenatal period. This is nowhere more clear than in the tragedy of infants born with AIDS.

Acquired immune deficiency syndrome, or **AIDS,** is caused by the human immunodeficiency virus (HIV). Recognized in the 1980s, AIDS has become the most serious health problem in the United States and the world. In adult AIDS victims, the immune system breaks down, leaving the victims vulnerable to fatal illnesses. This also happens to children with AIDS. Pediatric AIDS is different, however, since most infected children experience central nervous system complications, whereas such problems affect only a small number of infected adults. In addition, because AIDS attacks the immune system, infected infants do not develop antibodies to ward off such childhood diseases as polio and measles. Infants infected with AIDS also experience retarded and abnormal growth and have abnormal facial features, such as a small head, big eyes, a flat nose, and a prominent forehead.

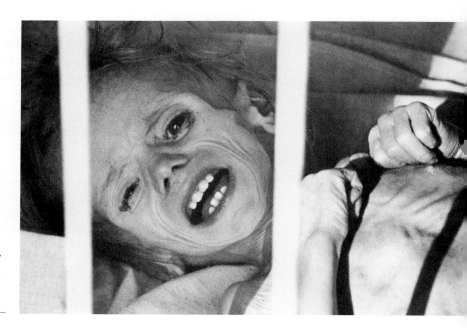

An HIV-infected baby suffers from incomplete brain development, retarded growth, and complications of the central nervous system. The prominent forehead, large protruding eyes, and flat nose are characteristic features of such babies.

Infants at risk for AIDS are those whose parents are in high-risk groups: namely, individuals with multiple sex partners, homosexuals, bisexuals, intravenous drug users who share needles, and people who have received blood transfusions. According to the American Academy of Pediatrics (1991), over 75% of pediatric AIDS cases result from perinatal (meaning before or around the time of birth) transmission, and 20% to 40% of infants born to HIV-infected women are HIV-infected. Children living in poverty and minority children make up the majority of pediatric AIDS victims: black and Hispanic children, who constitute only one-quarter of all American children, account for three-quarters of pediatric AIDS cases (Pediatric AIDS Foundation, 1990).

Seventy-five percent of babies born with AIDS die before their second birthday, although recent treatment advances are prolonging their lives. The longest surviving child, infected since birth, died at age 13 (American Academy of Pediatrics, 1991). Along with the pain of living with a terminal disease, infants with AIDS often face problems with care-giving arrangements and difficult issues of rejection by the community. Adult AIDS victims face similar problems (Musto, 1987), because many people are afraid of "catching" the virus even though medical research has established that the disease cannot be spread by casual contact. Although this rejection adds to the agony of the disease no matter what the victim's age, the issue becomes especially tragic with infants. Often AIDS infants remain in the hospital after birth because their mothers, also infected or ill with AIDS, have abandoned them or are too sick to care for them. Known as "boarder babies," some spend their entire lives in hospitals; the cost of their care ranges from $90,000 to $200,000 annually per child. Observers are also concerned because these infants do not receive the nurturing and personal attention necessary for their development.

What is being done in the United States to fight AIDS, pediatric AIDS in particular? No solutions are available, although a U.S. House Select Committee on Children, Youth and Families report (1989) called for increased spending for education, research, testing, and treatment. Controversial means of dealing with AIDS include mandatory testing for the virus and needle-exchange programs for drug addicts to try to stem the spread of the disease. Funding for research on pediatric AIDS has been more available than funding for research on adult AIDS. The research's major focus has been on inhibiting perinatal transmission of the virus, since this is the leading cause of AIDS in children. But there has been no progress, and the number of infants infected with AIDS continues to soar. The American Academy of Pediatrics (1991) estimates that the rate of pediatric AIDS is growing by 200% a year.

Motor Development

When infants are free from disease, they also acquire greater muscular movement. **Motor** is the term used to denote muscular movement, and motor development is the process through which the child acquires movement patterns and skills.

The acquisition of motor skills proceeds in a definite order, from the simple to the complex. Initially, movement is involuntary reflex action; the newborn has an impressive number of reflexes, many of which disappear as the cortex matures. Brain maturation and increases in strength during infancy eventually allow the baby to exhibit more control over a variety of differentiated movements. These new abilities are then integrated into more complex behavior patterns. For example, the baby's control over the separate movements of the legs, feet, and arms is eventually integrated into walking. Werner (1948) termed this integration of individual abilities into a complex behavior **hierarchic integration.**

Motor development also follows a cephalocaudal and proximodistal pattern. Thus a baby will first learn to lift her head, and sometime later to sit up and eventually, to stand (see Figure 5.8). To illustrate the sequential order of motor development, consider how the infant acquires the ability to walk. This ability allows her to develop new, more rapid means of locomotion (such as running) and also frees her hands from their role as supports so she can experiment with a variety of manipulative skills (Malina, 1982). The developmental changes that lead to walking are essentially a series of postural changes through which the infant gains the control necessary to maintain an upright posture, as shown in Figure 5.9. Initially, she acquires head and trunk control, which leads to the ability to roll over, sit up with support and without support, crawl, stand, climb stairs, and walk.

Most babies follow this sequence of motor development, but the age during which a particular skill emerges will vary according to the individual. Thus, some infants can walk at 12 months and others at 15 months. Of course, walking is a major milestone in the baby's development, and many parents are anxious for their infant to begin to walk. In fact, so much importance is attached to walking that many parents equate early walking with superior intelligence. However, the age at which walking begins is not an indication of how intelligent an infant is.

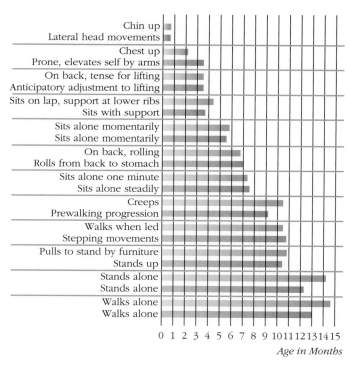

Figure 5.8 *Milestones in motor development during infancy. The bars represent data from two separate studies.*

Source: Adapted from "The Development of Motor Abilities During the First Three Years," by N. Bayley, 1936, *Monographs of the Society for Research in Child Development,* vol. 1, no. 1. Chicago, Ill.: Society for Research in Child Development, p. 16, Fig. 4. Reprinted with permission.

The Role of Maturation and the Environment

There are orderly, stable changes that occur in physical growth, neural development, and motor ability. Thus, we can describe physical development as a function of **maturation,** which refers to the orderly physiological changes in the organism over time. The sequentiality and universality of the maturational process are impressive, characterizing all species perhaps as the result of the genetic blueprint.

Scientists sometimes define maturation as a series of changes occurring independently of learning. In many respects, physical development is a function of maturation, and bodily growth and the development of motor skills are biologically determined. However, some environmental stimulation is necessary for optimal physiological and neural development. For example, when chimpanzees are raised in the dark, the neural cells in their retinas fail to develop normally, and their vision is permanently impaired (Riesen, 1947; 1958).

Figure 5.9 *Postural changes that lead to walking.*
Source: Adapted from *The First Two Years: A Study of Twenty-Five Babies,* by Mary M. Shirley, vol. 2, Fig. 1, frontispiece. Minneapolis: University of Minnesota Press, Copyright © 1933 by the University of Minnesota.

Motor Development and Childrearing Practices

An African baby in a dashiki and an American baby on his father's back. Babies who are carried in an erect position learn to keep their heads steady and have ample opportunities for experiential stimulation.

We have learned about the role of maturation and the environment in physical and motor development from several classic studies on children in other cultures. When researchers compared infants from different countries, they observed that, in general, all children experience the same sequence and schedule of motor development. This led researchers to believe that maturation plays a significant role in motor development. Consider, for example, a study of Hopi Indian infants. Some infants were reared in the traditional Hopi manner; that is, they were placed on cradleboards and swaddled so that they could not move their hands and legs. Others were allowed the freedom to move their arms and legs. There were essentially no differences in the ages during which both groups of infants began to walk; the average age at which infants in both groups walked was 15 months (Dennis, 1940).

However, in later studies, researchers found that some environmental stimulation is necessary for motor development. In one classic study Dennis (1960) studied the motor development of infants in several Iranian orphanages. The orphanages differed in the type and level of care provided to the infants. In two orphanages the infants were extremely retarded in their motor development. These orphanages did not have a sufficient number of caretakers for the children, so the infants spent most of their time lying on their backs in a crib. They drank from propped bottles; they were never placed in different positions, taken out of their cribs, or played with. At age 2, or later, the infants were taken out of their cribs and placed on the floor, usually in a sitting position; but they were not given any toys, and caretakers did not spend time with them. Because the ratio of caretakers to infants was about 1 to 8, there was not enough time for each caretaker to care for and play with each infant. In contrast, infants in another institution showed normal levels of motor development. This institution had more caretakers and the infants were held more frequently by adults; they were smiled at and held while they were fed; and they were placed in different positions. At 4 months, these infants were occasionally placed in playpens and had access to a variety of toys.

Dennis obtained similar findings when he studied infants in Lebanese orphanages. He noted that in some orphanages, infants were not receiving sufficient attention from their caretakers and were slow in acquiring motor and other skills (Dennis, 1973).

Can motor development be accelerated? When infants are given certain experiences, they can indeed develop some motor skills at a slightly faster rate. For example, Super (1981) notes that African infants sit up and walk earlier than infants in this country, because their parents prop them in a sitting position with rolled-up blankets as support. On the other hand, African infants do not necessarily crawl any earlier than American infants, because traditionally they are not placed on the ground on their stomach. So you can see that the rate of their motor development may differ depending on the infants' experiences. However, parents should interact with their baby naturally and should not attempt to hasten his sitting up or walking by propping him up for long periods. After all, it doesn't really matter if a baby begins to walk a month earlier or later, and making conscious efforts to hasten development may cause the baby and the parents undue stress (Gottlieb, 1983).

Physically disabled babies may require special experiences to help them develop motor skills. The parents of blind infants, for instance, are encouraged to give their children sound-making toys so the babies can locate the objects and attempt to crawl toward them. Because they are unable to see, these infants cannot otherwise be motivated to reach for objects or crawl toward them and their motor development can be slowed (Fraiberg, 1977). In the next section, we consider the development of blind and other physically disabled infants.

Atypical Development

The Birth of Severely Disabled Infants

In most cases physical development proceeds normally: the infant gains weight, matures physically, and acquires motor skills. But sometimes a baby is born with a physical disability or multiple handicapping conditions that may be severe enough to threaten his or her life.

Until recently nature determined the fate of most severely handicapped babies. However, now that the medical world has the skills to extend their lives, questions arise as to who has the right to determine their fate and decide whether they live or die. Consider the baby boy known only as Baby Doe, born April 9, 1982, in Bloomington, Indiana. He had an incomplete esophagus and Down's syndrome (a condition causing moderate to severe mental retardation). Advances in neonatal surgery would have enabled physicians to attach the esophagus to the stomach, thereby ensuring the baby's survival. Still the child would have remained mentally retarded. Baby Doe's parents were confronted with a difficult decision: Should they consent to an operation that would save the life of their retarded child? Or should they allow the child to die of starvation? Even though physicians advised them to the contrary, and sought a court order to proceed with the surgery, the parents chose to let the baby die. The courts upheld their decision, and Baby Doe died April 15, one week after his birth (Wallis, 1983).

In yet another example, a baby girl known as Baby Jane Doe was born with **spina bifida,** a failure of the spinal column to close, an abnormally small head, and fluid in the brain. Physicians predicted that, with conservative treatment and without a series of operations, she would die within two years. Surgery might allow her to survive into her 20s, but she would remain paralyzed and would require repeated operations. Her parents agonized over the painful decision they had to make, in the end rejecting surgery and opting instead for conservative treatment. In this case the physicians were in agreement with the parents, but the federal government sued for the release of the baby's health records so federal lawyers could determine what course of action to take.

The lawsuit over Baby Jane Doe's health records and ultimately her fate was the first time the federal government had gone to court in defense of a handicapped infant; it has generated a fierce controversy (Campbell, 1983; Sherlock, 1979). At issue are the following questions: How should society protect the rights of severely disabled infants? Who should make life-and-death decisions on their behalf? The federal government, the health profession, right-to-life organizations, and several groups serving as advocates for disabled citizens are involved in the controversy. These groups and the federal government contend that in every case of a disabled infant, physicians should do everything possible to provide treatment and prolong life.

Many physicians, however, argue that each disabled infant deserves individual attention, and that parents and physicians should make case-by-case decisions on the basis of the condition's severity and ultimate prospects for recovery (Duff, 1979; 1981). Some physicians further argue that decisions on the baby's fate should be made within the context of a "moral" community, which would include the parents, physicians, nurses, and social workers. A member of the clergy would also be involved, if the family so desired (Campbell & Duff, 1979). The task would be to support the family in its grief and to counsel the parents about decisions regarding the baby's care (Duff, 1981). Some parents who have given birth to a severely disabled baby and have written about their agony agree that, as parents, they should have the right and responsibility to decide their baby's fate (Stinson & Stinson, 1983). However, there might be cases where parents would refuse treatment clearly beneficial to the child, or where parents would make decisions that conflict with physicians' advice, as happened in the Baby Doe case. Would parents make a decision simply because they did not want the emotional and financial burden of caring for a disabled baby?

There is no easy solution to the dilemmas we face in caring for and treating severely disabled newborns (Wallis, 1983). But this is a problem society has to confront and attempt to resolve. Another related social issue concerns the improved medical technology that enables babies born with defects to survive. Some contend that such technology has contributed to a possible increase in the number of disabled infants. This theory has caused an intense argument among physicians, policymakers, and even philosophers on the following issues: As a society, should we continue to develop techniques that enable severely disabled infants to survive? Is it beneficial or potentially too costly for society to keep those infants alive? Since disabled individuals require special care and education throughout their adult years as well, any increase in the number of disabled individuals would probably place a substantial burden on society.

It is not easy to resolve the issue of whether as a society we should sustain life at any cost. Moreover, some observers question whether medical technology has contributed to an increase in the number of disabled infants. Are there, in fact, more handicapped individuals now than in the past? There are no clear-cut answers. Some people contend that over the past 25 years, the number of handicapped infants born annually has doubled. According to analyses of birth patterns in the United States, approximately 70,000 handicapped infants were born annually in the 1950s; currently the number is about 140,000 (Lyons, 1983; Newaceck, Burdetti, & Halfon, 1986).

Other observers suggest that changes in the lifestyle of American women may also be responsible for a possible increase. For example, during the past 25 years, cigarette smoking, which has an adverse influence on the developing fetus, has doubled in popularity among women of childbearing age; thus smoking may be a possible reason for an increase in the number of disabled infants. Another cause may be toxic substances in the workplace that have teratogenic effects on fetal development. These observers argue that many women, in particular pregnant women, are subjected to or subject themselves and their unborn children to adverse environmental influences. Thus, it is not surprising that many more babies are now born disabled.

Not all professionals agree that the number of disabled infants has doubled in the last 25 years. Some contend that we are now diagnosing more newborns as disabled.

Identifying the Disabled Infant

Indeed, we have made enormous advances during the past 25 years in identifying infants who may be physically or mentally disabled. Also, child development professionals now realize that the best chance for the optimal development of a disabled child depends on identifying the problem early in life and promptly referring him to professionals who can evaluate his developmental status and recommend follow-up services. Partly for this reason, Congress enacted a law in 1986 to ensure identification of infants as early as possible. The law—PL 99-457 (Part H), Services for Infants and Toddlers with Handicapping Conditions—requires all states to develop a plan addressing the special needs of all disabled children from birth to age 5 (Gallagher, 1989).

Physicians have developed several screening tests to identify these infants. These tests are not diagnostic; they only identify an infant suspected of having a disorder. The identified infant is then retested to verify the original finding. If the case warrants further care, the child receives a more formal developmental evaluation and diagnosis of the disorder (Frankenburg, 1981).

Several screening tests are routinely administered to all newborns to identify specific genetic disorders. Other tests identify subtle abnormalities and assaults to the central nervous system (Francis, Self, & Horowitz, 1987). But all these tests have limitations. Kochanek (1988) points out that they may be subject to errors. Thus it is important to consider other factors as well, such as any stressful events affecting the family, the family's size, and the available support system (see Figure 5.10), because these factors may also help determine whether the child is at developmental risk.

Some screening tests focus on a direct examination of the infant to establish her neurological status. They test, for example, a variety of reflexes, since the absence of an expected reflex, or the presence of a reflex for a longer period than normal, could be an indication of damage to the central nervous system (Prechtl, 1982). Other screening tests seek to detect behavior problems that may interfere with interactions with her caretakers. Such tests examine the baby's sensory and perceptual skills, her ability to interact with the environment and modulate the amount of environmental stimulation she is subject to, and her capacity to cope with distressing situations (Als, 1981).

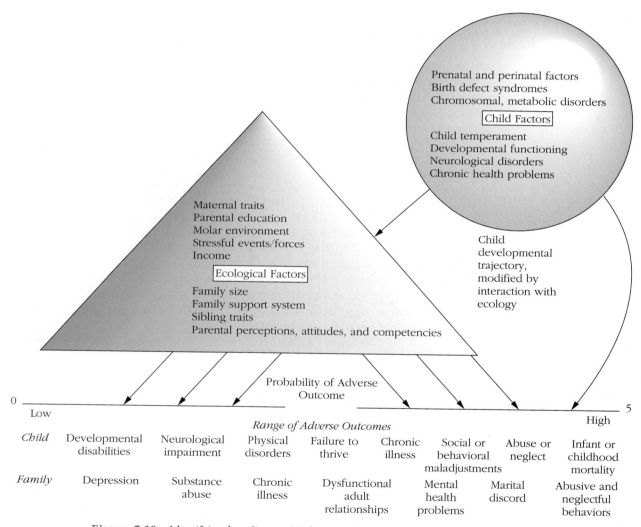

Figure 5.10 *Identifying handicapped infants and young children: a multivariate, interactional risk model.*

Source: "Point of View: Conceptualizing Screening Models for Developmentally Disabled and High Risk Children and Their Families," by T. Kochanek, *Zero to Three*, Dec. 1988. Reprinted by permission of the National Center for Clinical Infant Programs.

Infants at risk   Such screening tests, when appropriately used and interpreted, help identify infants at risk for atypical development. Kopp and Kaler (1989) note that risks compromising the newborn's development are diverse and include risks of biological origin, environmental origin, and a combination of both. While at-risk infants may not necessarily evidence a disability, they enter the world with certain vulnerabilities or with limited sensory and perceptual skills needed to benefit and learn from environmental experiences (Gorski, 1984).

Some infants considered to be at developmental risk have experienced prenatal and perinatal complications (Nelson & Ellenberg, 1979) or are born too small for their gestational age. Several of the reasons we discussed in Chapter 4, including prenatal malnutrition and the mother's smoking during pregnancy, may account for full-term, underweight babies. Infants born prematurely or postmaturely (that is, beyond the normal gestational period of 41 to 42 weeks) are also considered at risk for developmental delays or disabilities. In cases of postmaturity, the risks occur because the infants have had to rely on an old placenta functioning beyond the time for which it is naturally programmed (Gorski, 1984). Although risk events can have serious consequences for development, not all infants identified as at risk are equally vulnerable. Some recover full health and function and behave normally as early as their first year of life (Kopp & Parmelee, 1979; Kopp & Kaler, 1989). Others, especially infants whose families experience stressful life events, may be unable to overcome their disability. By identifying at-risk infants and alerting parents to some of their baby's vulnerabilities and characteristics, we may be able to prevent many problems associated with developmental risk factors (Sameroff & Chandler, 1975; Yarrow, 1979).

Developmentally disabled infants   Screening tests are also used to identify infants suffering from a developmental disability. We define *developmental disability* as a chronic disorder that can be manifest in mental or physical impairment. This disability is likely to continue indefinitely and result in substantial functional limitations on the individual's ability to learn and acquire the capacity for independent living. Mental retardation, cerebral palsy, language and learning disabilities, blindness, and deafness are among the major disorders grouped under developmental disabilities. Other disorders or diseases, such as epilepsy or cystic fibrosis, are also considered developmental disabilities if they are so severe that they impose limitations on the child's ability to learn and on his eventual capacity for self-care (Golden, 1984; Gabel & Erickson, 1980).

Visual impairments   A developmental disability may not always impose limitations on the infant's capacity for developmental progress if the infant is helped in her ability to compensate for the handicap. For example, consider infants born blind or with severe visual impairments. Many have a genetic basis for the handicap, or they may be blind because of some prenatal assault to development (Roeske, 1980). When the blindness is not associated with any other defect, blind infants seem to follow much the same sequence in motor development as sighted infants; blind infants achieve some motor milestones, such as sitting or standing, at about the same age as sighted infants. However, blind infants are delayed in their mobility patterns; as a result, they reach for objects, crawl, or walk at a later age.

Researchers have found that, whereas sighted babies begin to crawl at about 9 months, blind infants do not begin to crawl until sometime during their second year (Fraiberg, 1971; 1968; Adelson & Fraiberg, 1974). According to the researchers, mobility patterns require visual education, and the ability to see is a powerful incentive for mobility; hence, you can understand blind infants' delay in crawling and in other mobility skills.

Although blind infants are slow to acquire mobility skills, they eventually do so. Thus blindness does not affect their motor development to any great extent. They also acquire cognitive, language, and social skills in much the same sequence as sighted infants but evidence developmental delays. Selma Fraiberg (1977) notes that developmental delays in blind infants are probably due to their "experiential poverty." She suggests that parents who know that their baby is blind should attempt to help the baby compensate for the disability by providing auditory cues. For example, they should try to talk to their baby whenever they come close and provide toys and other objects that make a sound. Often, however, auditory cues alone are insufficient. The blind infant may be attracted to a toy that makes a sound, but the sound does not give the infant any information about the toy's physical properties—whether it is round or square or graspable. For this reason parents need to be taught how to use auditory and other sensory cues to promote their babies' development (Fraiberg, 1977).

Hearing impairments   The need to facilitate parents' ability to help a baby compensate for a handicap is also evident in the case of deaf infants. There are two major causes of congenital deafness: genetic deafness and rubella contracted by the mother during the first three months of pregnancy (Mindel, 1980). But deafness can also occur in premature infants or those suffering from other developmental disabilities.

Research on deaf infants is limited, in large part because if these infants do not suffer from any other developmental problems, they babble and make other vocalizations much as hearing infants do. During the first few months of life, these infants appear normal; so their deafness is not diagnosed until they are older (Meadow, 1980). Research is further limited because most studies have focused only on one aspect of development: language acquisition. As far as vocabulary, during the first 9 months of life, language development in deaf infants progresses in much the same way as in hearing infants (Lenneberg, 1967). However, deaf infants do not progress in auditory discrimination, nor can they respond to sound patterns, so after 9 months they begin to show increasingly significant deficits in their ability to learn language skills (Schlesinger & Meadow, 1972). Some deaf babies have some residual hearing and can benefit from hearing aids. If the hearing impairment is not detected, the child deteriorates in his ability to communicate and learn other cognitive skills; as a result, his parents or teachers may think he is mentally retarded. However, if caretakers detect the hearing impairment early and provide the infant with corrective hearing aids or introduce sign language, they can minimize the negative impact of the disability on his development (Wolfson, Aghamohamadi, & Berman, 1980).

Cerebral palsy   Blindness or deafness can occur as a single defect, but other handicapping conditions often accompany either disorder. This is especially the case with cerebral palsy. Cerebral palsy results from brain damage (due to oxygen deprivation, severe nutritional deficiency, radiation, or other problems) during the prenatal or perinatal period. Its characteristics may include paralysis, muscle weakness, incoordination, aberration of motor dysfunction, or other handicapping conditions. For example, some children with cerebral palsy are also mentally retarded (Molnar, 1979). Speech or hearing problems occur in 70% to 80% of these children (Love & Walthod, 1977). Besides these defects, cerebral-palsied children may also suffer from severe visual impairments, learning disabilities, and frequent seizures (Huttenlocher, 1979). But the cerebral-palsied, like other developmentally disabled people, vary greatly in the severity of their motor dysfunction and also in the extent to which they suffer from other disabilities. Some cerebral-palsied children are so severely disabled by motor dysfunction and other disorders that they need help in the activities of daily living. Others are only mildly disabled and can function independently.

These developmental disabilities represent only some of the disorders that are identifiable at birth or shortly thereafter. We discussed several genetic disorders in Chapter 3. There are still other handicapping conditions that do not become apparent until later in life. No matter what the disorder, we need to keep two points in mind:

1. Like normal infants, disabled infants are a heterogeneous group. They differ in the severity of their disability and in their temperament and ability to compensate for or overcome the disability.
2. All infants, even the disabled, are competent and active learners who should be given the opportunity to interact with and respond to the environment (Lewis, 1984).

Early Intervention Programs

These two points are inherent in the goals of numerous intervention programs that have recently been developed and implemented. The aim of early intervention programs is to prevent disorders arising from genetic or adverse influences to development and to remediate the effects of identified disorders (Hanson, 1984a).

Early intervention programs are available in most communities; they provide disabled infants and their families with access to a broad variety of services. Although PL 99-457 may ensure services for more infants who need early intervention programs, researchers and child advocates note that not all disabled and at-risk infants are referred to such programs at an early age (Kopp & Kaler, 1989). States and localities give varying levels of support to early identification and intervention

Early intervention programs for disabled infants help parents structure the environment so it is conducive to the baby's development.

efforts. Furthermore, programs vary greatly in the quality and type of services they provide, and even in the location where they provide the services. Some services are home-based; trained personnel go to the child's home. Others are both home- and center-based and may be located in a variety of settings, such as hospitals, private and public schools, and mental health and social service clinics.

In evaluating several early intervention programs, we have found that one important criterion for a successful intervention is that the program focuses on the child *and* parents. For example, we have seen that parents of blind and deaf infants have to be shown how to structure the infants' environment so it is conducive to development. Hanson (1984b) and Taft (1981) also note that, while the disabled infant needs preventive or remedial therapy to overcome the disability, the parents often need support to cope with the ramifications of the disability and of living with a disabled child. When specialists show parents how to recognize the particular needs and characteristics of their child, both infant and parents benefit significantly. Although as a society we have yet to resolve numerous considerations associated with the care and treatment of disabled infants, we have made significant strides in identifying infants with handicapping conditions and providing services for them.

Summary

Physical growth and motor development occur at a very rapid rate during infancy; infants quadruple their birth weight and more than double their height by their second birthday. During this time, they also acquire a number of motor skills and more control over their motor movement as a result of brain maturation. Thus they are able to have greater locomotion and to manipulate the environment in different ways.

Physical growth and development follow a predictable, orderly sequence governed largely by maturation. But environmental stimulation is necessary for optimal development. This becomes especially evident in the acquisition of motor skills during infancy. As studies of infants in orphanages show, those who are left alone in their crib and do not receive minimal adult contact are extremely retarded in motor development. The same is true of blind infants, who are delayed in acquiring motor skills unless they receive stimulating experiences that enable them to identify objects and persons by sound.

Infants are also born with an impressive number of skills. The surge of infancy research over the past few years has enabled scientists to document that newborns can hear, see, touch, taste, and smell on the first day of life. Publicizing the "new" capabilities of the newborn has placed pressure on some parents to provide stimulating and enriching experiences to the baby at younger and younger ages in order to develop a superbaby. The notion behind baby gym classes and infant reading programs—both part of the superbaby trend—is based on research attesting to the importance of early stimulation. Although a certain amount of environmental stimulation is indeed important, we probably cannot really alter the genetic blueprint for growth beyond the amount needed for optimal development.

Physical growth and development proceed normally in most infants. However, some are born with disabilities or are identified as disabled during their infancy. For many of these children, intervention programs help them and their families learn to cope with their disabilities.

6 Cognitive and Language Development in Infancy

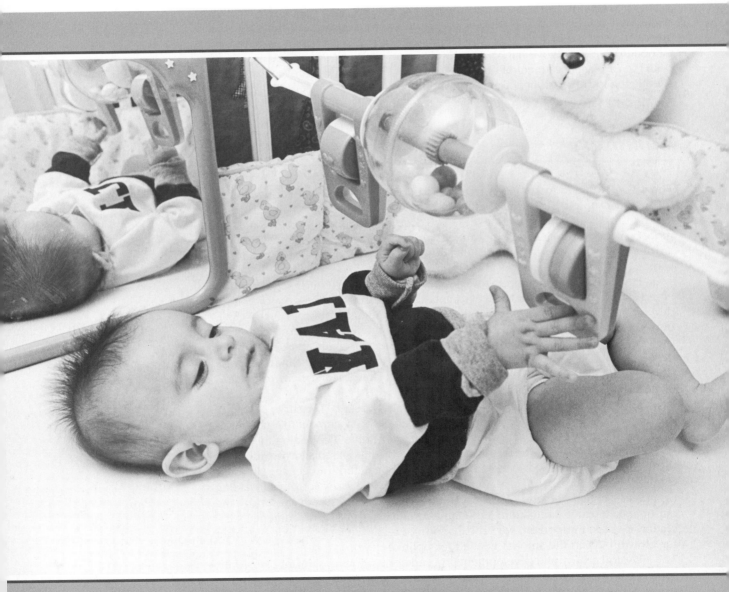

In Chapter 5 we learned that infants are more complex and responsive organisms than was once believed. They come into the world prepared with sensory and motor capabilities that help them gather information about their environment and interact with adults. These capabilities develop rapidly during the first few months of life, as the central nervous system matures.

Infants are also capable of organized intellectual behavior; within two years, they accumulate a vast amount of knowledge, including the ability to understand and speak the language they hear. In this chapter we examine what infants understand about the world they inhabit, and how that understanding develops. Researchers have made significant strides in studying cognitive and language development and in understanding infants' mental and linguistic skills. Nevertheless, a controversy surrounds these topics, stemming mostly from the nature-nurture issue. How do babies acquire the ability to think or talk? Is it through maturation or experience? Although most child development professionals agree that biological and environmental factors work together in cognitive development, they disagree over the relative importance of each. Specifically, they differ over such issues as: Will infants learn on their own as long as there is a stimulating environment, or do they need to be taught? What is a good environment that is conducive to their cognitive development?

Answers to these questions are of practical concern as well. Many infants spend a large portion of their day in child care centers or family day-care homes. Are their experiences in these settings, where people take care of them in groups, conducive to mental growth? What are the effects on cognitive development of being raised in group care? Additional concerns arise from recent claims that parents should take advantage of their infants' powerful desire to learn and teach them to read or accomplish other academic tasks, thereby giving them a head start in life and increasing their intellectual potential. Is there any scientific evidence that infants can, and should, be taught academic skills? Is there any evidence that intellectual potential can be increased? Before we try to sort out the facts and myths, we will look at research demonstrating infants' interest in the environment and their amazing ability to learn from their experiences.

Cognitive Development

Learning in Early Life

Learning is defined as a relatively permanent change in behavior brought about as a result of experience. Learning can occur in several ways: through habituation (see Chapter 5), classical conditioning, operant conditioning, observation, and imitation.

Classical conditioning   *Classical conditioning* is a form of learning in which the individual learns about relationships between events. In the early 1900s Russian physiologist Ivan Pavlov first demonstrated classical conditioning in his experiments with dogs. Realizing that dogs salivate at the sight of food, Pavlov paired various stimuli with food. For example, he would feed his dogs and also ring a bell. After several such feedings, the dogs came to associate the bell's ringing with the food. Eventually the dogs salivated when they heard the bell, even if they did not receive food. Apparently, Pavlov had conditioned their salivation reflex to respond to the bell in the same way as it responded to food.

This same phenomenon occurs with infants. When 3-week-old Emily is given a taste of sugar water, she automatically responds by sucking; this is called the *sucking reflex*. If the sugar water is repeatedly paired with ringing a bell, Emily will eventually begin to make sucking movements when she hears the bell, as if anticipating the sugar water.

In classical conditioning the *conditioned stimulus*, in this case the bell, is considered to be a neutral; that is, before the experiment, it does not produce the desired response. The *unconditioned stimulus*, the sugar water, does produce a response: sucking. The sugar water is called an unconditioned stimulus because it automatically and invariably elicits a sucking response when put on Emily's lips. If we pair the conditioned stimulus with the unconditioned stimulus several times, Emily learns to associate the bell with sugar water and begins sucking just on hearing the bell, which means that learning has taken place.

Classical conditioning helps the infant get a sense of the orderliness of his environment and anticipate events (Lipsitt, 1990b). Numerous studies have demonstrated classical conditioning in infants. And everyday examples of infants being classically conditioned abound. When she grows up, Emily will become excited on hearing the escalating sounds of her father's footsteps; when her mother feeds her, she will open her mouth and salivate as the spoon leaves the jar rather than waiting for the spoon to reach her mouth (Lipsitt, 1990b).

Researchers have attempted to determine how soon after birth infants can be conditioned and have even studied conditioning to see if it occurs before birth. Although far from conclusive, there are indications that even before birth the infant can be conditioned (Rovee-Collier, 1987). Studies on newborns and infants younger than 2 to 3 months provide evidence that classical conditioning can often occur very early in life. Indeed, one group of researchers (Blass, Granchrow, & Steiner, 1984), using tactile stimulation (stroking the infant's head) as the conditioned stimulus, found evidence that 2-hour-old infants can learn predictive relationships through classical conditioning.

The difficulty of replicating these experiments has led some researchers to question whether classical conditioning can occur in very young infants (Sameroff & Cavanaugh, 1979). In the past decade, however, researchers have become increasingly convinced that classical conditioning can occur with very young infants. They have found that certain prerequisites need to be met for successful conditioning to occur in early infancy: the infant needs to be in an awake/alert state, and the interstimulus interval—that is, the time lapse between the conditioned stimulus and the unconditioned stimulus—needs to be long enough to allow the infant to process the information. Apparently, the younger the infant, the longer the time he needs to process information (Fitzgerald & Brackbill, 1976).

In addition, the stimulus chosen in the experiments needs to be something that pleases the infant. This interesting point is based on the researchers' inability to demonstrate *aversive conditioning* in young infants. (In this situation infants are expected to learn to anticipate an unpleasant event.) The infant's response to only a pleasant stimulus may reflect an evolutionary adaptation to the environment. That is, early in life when the central nervous system is still immature, the infant strives toward self-regulation and is guided by pleasurable stimulation (Lipsitt, 1990b). Also, during the first few weeks of life, infants are protected by adult caretakers. As a result, their ability to form expectations about unpleasant or aversive events is not biologically relevant until they are slightly older and begin to move around on their own (Rovee-Collier, 1987). Hence, only studies using pleasant stimulation (for example, milk, sugar water, or stroking the infant's forehead) are likely to be successful in demonstrating classical conditioning early in infancy.

Operant conditioning Classical conditioning helps explain how the infant learns to make associations between events in the environment, but it does not explain how the infant's behavior changes. In a second type of learning—*operant*, or *instrumental, conditioning*—the infant's behavior changes as a result of the consequences of that behavior; that is, through reinforcement. Behaviors leading to reward are repeated; those leading to punishment are abandoned. This form of learning helps infants learn the contingency between their behavior and its consequences.

In operant conditioning studies, the subject first initiates an action and then experiences a consequence for initiating it. Harvard psychologist B. F. Skinner (1938) trained pigeons, for example, to push a certain bar or to peck a certain button to get food. As with classical conditioning, operant conditioning takes place during a series of trials and errors; more trials ensure the durability of the learning.

Several studies have shown that, by using a pleasant reinforcement (for instance, sweet-tasting milk or a pacifier), newborns can be taught to change the way they suck or to turn their heads in a certain sequence. Researchers choose these behaviors because infants demonstrate them early in life. By giving or withholding milk (the reinforcer), Sameroff (1968) modified infants' choice of response to a nipple (that is, whether they get fluid by squeezing the nipple between the tongue and palate or by sucking).

To illustrate how researchers study operant conditioning in infants, let us look at Sigueland's study (1968) demonstrating that newborns can learn to turn their heads in order to suck on a pacifier. The infants wore headbands that enabled the

---

A CLOSER LOOK

Learning Through Imitation

Infants and children acquire new behaviors through imitation. We have all seen children try to do what their older brother or sister does, or try to shave like Dad, or dress up like Mom. And very young children quickly learn to imitate language. But how early does true imitation (that is, modeling that leads to learning) begin?

Researchers have found that 2- and 3-week old babies can imitate lip and tongue protrusions (Meltzoff & Moore, 1977; 1983) and other facial expressions denoting happiness, sadness, and surprise (Field et al., 1982). But is this true imitation? Perhaps it is only pseudoimitation and does not represent a real effort to model the behavior. For example, if the examiner says "Ahhh" and the infant responds by saying "Ehhh," the vocalization is similar so it could be considered in the same class of behaviors. But it is still not an exact imitation. Only instances of exact imitation would help prove that infants are actually trying to imitate.

Pseudoimitation may also occur if the examiner reinforces a desired behavior. For instance, suppose the examiner hugs the baby or smiles when the baby imitates sticking out his tongue. This kind of rewarding experience is very common. Parents in particular find it hard not to reward the infant in this way. In fact, almost any time an infant appears to be imitating a behavior, adults seem elated (Stern, 1977). Their excitement may reinforce the baby who may simply have stumbled on the behavior by chance.

In addition, researchers have demonstrated only that newborns can imitate behavior that they can *already spontaneously exhibit*. Is that true imitation? Some researchers contend that it is, because they believe that babies are born with well-developed cognitive structures that enable them to acquire more and more information from the environment; thus they believe that the ability to imitate is innate. However, other researchers believe that the ability to imitate is gradually acquired over the infancy period; they argue that infants are not really imitating because they are not demonstrating their ability to learn new behaviors through imitation.

In an attempt to settle the controversy, Moshe Anisfeld (in press) reviewed 26 experiments on the topic. He found

researchers to record the number of times they turned their heads to the left or right. To establish a baseline rate, the researchers counted the number of times the infants moved their heads normally. Then, when the infants turned their heads at least 10 degrees, they were given pacifiers to suck on. The researchers found that after repeated reinforcement with a pacifier, the infants tripled the rate at which they turned their heads at least 10 degrees. Another group of infants in the same experiment were rewarded with a pacifier for not turning their heads; after repeated reinforcement, they moved their heads less frequently than did the other group of infants.

These studies show, therefore, that infants are capable of operant conditioning very early in life and that learning and maturation are interdependent processes. That is, as infants age, they become more capable of learning, a concept referred to as **learning readiness.** The younger the infant is, the more trials are required before conditioning occurs. In a study demonstrating this point, researchers reinforced infants with milk each time they turned their heads to one side or another. Newborn infants needed an average of 177 trials before they were conditioned, whereas 3-month-old infants needed an average of only 42 trials and 5-month-old infants, an average of 28 trials (Papousek, 1967).

Memory

Both operant and classical conditioning remain important methods of learning throughout a child's development. Studies demonstrating that conditioning occurs early in life indicate that young infants can learn and that they can remember, since

A CLOSER LOOK

that young infants demonstrate the ability to imitate tongue protrusion, *but not necessarily other facial gestures.* He notes that "there is nothing new in the findings [of the experiments he reviewed] to dispute the view that early imitation is distinct from the more mature imitation that occurs in the last quarter of the first year." Early imitation, according to Anisfeld, lacks the deliberateness and effort characteristic of later imitation. Later in this chapter, you will see that Jean Piaget also takes this position.

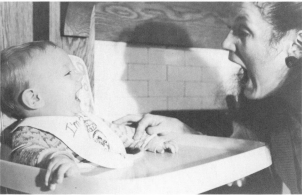

learning depends on memory. As Lipsitt (1990b) notes, "Learning is memory-dependent: a previous experience is said to leave a residual impact, such that the behavior of the organism will be altered . . . in some way by the earlier event" (p. 62).

Researchers distinguish between recognition memory and recall memory. **Recognition memory** enables us to identify something previously known (Small, 1990). For example, if you walk into class and spot someone who is familiar, you are judging that you have seen that person before, even though you cannot remember where and you do not recall the person's name. Here, a physical stimulus (the person you spot) is present. In **recall memory,** however, a physical stimulus is not present, and in some way we must generate the item and test it against memory representations (Small, 1990).

Rovee-Collier and her colleagues illustrated one technique for studying recognition memory in infants. A series of their studies (Sullivan, Rovee-Collier, & Tyne, 1979; Rovee-Collier et al., 1980; Borovsky, Hill, & Rovee-Collier, 1987) involved training infants to move a mobile that was attached to their leg by a long ribbon; each time they moved or kicked their leg, the mobile moved. Once the infants were trained to activate the mobile, researchers tested their ability to remember the experience over different lengths of time. In one study 6-week-old infants retained the learned response for a week; when they were put in the same situation, they demonstrated that they remembered their previous experiences by immediately starting to kick to activate the mobile. Other studies found that 8- to 12-week-old infants can remember learned responses for up to 2 weeks (Early, Griesler, & Rovee-Collier, 1985). At longer delays, infants do not immediately kick to activate the mobile, suggesting that forgetting has taken place.

Rovee-Collier and her colleagues further showed that when the infants are periodically given a visual reminder during the delay interval—that is, they are shown the mobile, but it is not tied to their leg—they can remember even one month after the initial training (Rovee-Collier & Fagen, 1981).

Although it is difficult to ascertain if infants can remember without reintroducing the stimulus, researchers have shown that toward the end of the first year of life, infants develop the capacity for recall memory. Ashmead and Perlmutter (1984), for example, asked parents of 7- to 11-month-old infants to keep a record of instances revealing memory behaviors. The parents recorded numerous instances of productive memory, especially in older infants. For example, a parent wrote that one day her baby kept looking at the side of her changing table. She seemed puz-

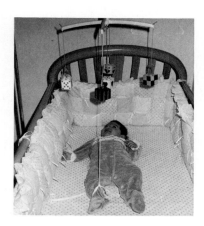

At not quite a year old, this baby shows the ability to generate simple categories: note that she chooses from among many toys those that are somewhat circular in shape.

zled, as if searching for something she couldn't find. Usually, the mother placed a bottle of baby lotion on the side of the table, but apparently on this occasion the bottle had been put elsewhere. The infant may have remembered this, because her eyes brightened when her mother showed her the baby lotion. Several formal experiments have shown that recall memory appears only in the latter half of the first year of life, perhaps because this capacity depends on the maturation of the brain (Mandler, 1984). This new capacity for recall in older infants is still rudimentary; it develops as the infants mature.

Forming Categories

Early in life, infants develop the ability to distinguish among individual objects and also to ignore differences among objects. **Categorization,** which is the ability to mentally organize information into related groupings, is a fundamental cognitive skill that requires us to ignore differences so that we can group objects. This skill greatly reduces the information load on our cognitive system (Younger, 1990) and enhances our ability to respond quickly. For example, if you are shown an assortment of different objects—an apple, a basketball, a banana, a baseball bat—it would be easier to remember them if you mentally sort them into two different categories, such as foods and nonfoods.

Although we have not perfected techniques to demonstrate categorization in infants, we can draw a general conclusion on the basis of current studies. In a review of the literature, Reznick (1989) notes that by at least the middle of the first year of life, most infants are able to detect simple categories. In one study researchers showed a group of 6-, 9-, and 12-month-old infants a mix of yellow plastic boxes and blue round balls. Six-month-old infants touched the boxes and balls rather haphazardly, but older infants first touched either the boxes or the balls, indicating that they recognized the distinction in shape (Younger & Cohen, 1986).

Younger (1990) found that the basis for simple categorization might be the ability to detect correlations among the various properties of objects. She showed 10- to 13-month-old infants pictures of different animals. Each animal had certain correlated properties: animals with a feathered tail also had ears, and animals with a

Figure 6.1 *The set of 12 habituation stimuli for the ear/feather habituation condition. The appearance of the correlated features (namely, ears and feathered tails, and antlers and furry tails) varies from animal to animal. All properties represented in the different bodies vary independently of the correlated features.*

Source: "Infants' Detection of Correlations Among Feature Categories," by B. Younger, 1990, *Child Development*, 61, p. 616. © 1990 Society for Research in Child Development, Inc.

furry tail also had antlers (see Figure 6.1). When Younger tested the infants, she found that they were sensitive to the correlated properties and used them as the basis for categorization.

At the end of their first year, infants can generate simple categories by choosing, for example, all the red toys from a mixed grouping of red and blue dolls and red and blue cars. Their ability to categorize, however, is based on perceptual similarities. For example, we may place a bed and a chair both under the heading *furniture,* and a duck and a horse under the category of *animals.* Since these items do not look alike, the infant might not recognize them initially as belonging to the same category. But a 2-year-old can categorize ducks and birds, which are more perceptually similar (see Figure 6.2) (Fenson, Cameron, & Kennedy, 1988). A study by Mandler, Fivush, and Reznick (1987) indicates that this ability may be present in infants as young as 14 months.

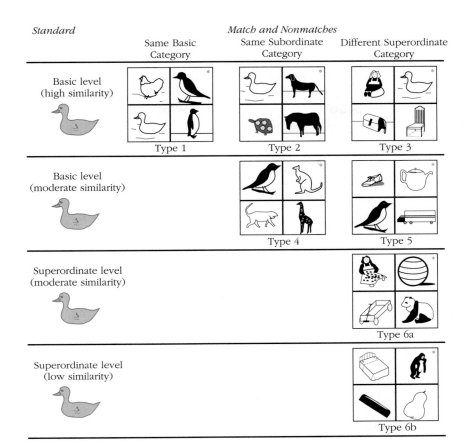

Standard	Same Basic Category	Same Subordinate Category	Different Superordinate Category

Basic level (high similarity) — Type 1, Type 2, Type 3

Basic level (moderate similarity) — Type 4, Type 5

Superordinate level (moderate similarity) — Type 6a

Superordinate level (low similarity) — Type 6b

Figure 6.2 *Infants can recognize that objects belong to the same category when the objects look similar. For example, a duck resembles a bird, so infants may group the two together. However, they cannot recognize that a duck belongs in the same category as a panda (both are animals), because the two are not perceptually similar.*

Source: "Role of Perceptual and Conceptual Similarity in Category Matching at Age 2 Years," by L. Fenson, M. S. Cameron, and M. Kennedy, 1988, *Child Development, 59.* © 1988 Society for Research in Child Development, Inc.

Approaches to Studying Cognitive Development

The infant's ability to organize information in the environment and to learn and remember events illustrate his cognitive competence. *Cognition* is defined as the act of knowing and includes learning and the acquisition of knowledge as well as thinking, imagining, creating, problem solving, and other skills associated with intellectual behavior (Flavell, 1985).

Developmental psychologists have long been interested in the study of intellectual behavior. Initially, they focused on measuring intelligence. This *psychometric approach* (which we will discuss in detail in Chapter 15) began at the turn of the century with the development of standardized intelligence tests. Although psychologists originally developed these tests for school-age children, some have also been used to test infants and toddlers.

More recently, developmental psychologists changed their approach and now study the growth in cognitive abilities and changes in the way children think.

The Information-Processing Approach

One theoretical orientation to the study of cognitive development is information processing. This approach began with the study of adult cognition and has only recently been applied to child development. Instead of attempting to measure intelligence, the information-processing approach focuses on studying the processes underlying intellectual behavior. Researchers are investigating how information is perceived, how it enters the mind, and how it is then stored, transformed, and retrieved. Thus, the research often focuses on one aspect of cognition such as memory.

As you can see in Figure 6.3, the information-processing system includes sensory registers, short-term memory, long-term memory, and control processes. The sensory registers handle information from the environment, which is stored in short-term memory where it is retained for several seconds while being processed. Then the information is stored in long-term memory, which holds memories of past experiences.

Although information-processing theories address various aspects of cognition, they all assume that the human mind is somewhat analogous to a computer in that it stores and processes information (Small, 1990). They also assume that human beings have limited information-processing abilities, and that through cognitive growth these limitations are gradually reduced. The limitations may be on our ability to pay attention, our capacity for memory, or our facility of output.

Even at birth or shortly thereafter, infants can receive information through their senses and then process that information. Recall, for example, that very young babies can differentiate among different patterns. Young infants can also differentiate between novel speech sounds and familiar sounds, such as their mother's voice. This ability to differentiate new sights and sounds indicates that at an early age infants form mental images of the stimuli they encounter.

Now we ask, how efficient is the young infant in processing information? To answer this question, researchers have looked at the infant's attention, an important aspect of cognitive development that allows the individual to focus on particular aspects of the environment and mobilize effort for learning. Researchers have focused on two measures of attention: **decrement of attention** (or *habituation*), which infants exhibit when aspects of their environment remain unchanged, and **recovery of attention** (or *dishabituation*), which infants exhibit when they notice something new in their environment. By monitoring how long it takes infants to become used to something familiar in the environment and how long it takes them to recover their attention when something new appears, researchers can determine how well infants process information.

Borenstein and Sigman's review of the literature (1986) indicates that some infants process information better than others, and that decrement and recovery of attention seem to predict cognitive competence in the early childhood years. For example, researchers gave infants two sets of pictures to look at; one set of pictures was familiar and one set was new. Infants who at 6 months of age spent most of their time looking at the new pictures (meaning that they had already habituated to the familiar ones and thus lost interest in them) were tested at ages 2 and 4 and found to

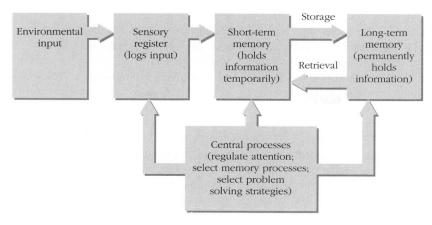

Figure 6.3 *A schematic model of the information-processing approach to cognitive development.*

do well on cognitive tests. Infants who took longer to process the information and did not habituate as fast at age 6 months did not do as well on the tests at ages 2 and 4. Thus, by focusing on the infant's attention, we may be able to predict the child's intellectual performance. Attention in infancy, in fact, has proved a better predictor of later intellectual performance than such cognitive skills as memory and problem solving, but we don't know why (Borenstein & Sigman, 1986). Also, even when we use the infant's attention, our ability to predict later intellectual performance is limited. However, these findings alert us to the fact that patterns of attention may become established as manifestations of cognition early in life, and they help identify infants who may be at risk for developing cognitive problems.

The Piagetian Approach

The information-processing approach examines only limited aspects of cognition, but the Piagetian approach, named after psychologist and philosopher Jean Piaget, provides a comprehensive theory. (We briefly discussed Piaget's work in Chapter 2.)

Piaget developed his theory on the basis of diligent, extensive observations of his own three children and later of other children. Although his work dominated developmental psychology for several decades, researchers are now finding that infants are generally more competent than Piaget had proposed (Gratch & Schatz, 1987). Piaget did not have access to the innovative experimental techniques used in current studies on infancy. And he may have underestimated the importance of perceptual learning and its role in cognitive growth (Flavell, 1985).

Despite these apparent limitations, Piaget's theory is still an important contribution to the field. Miller (1982) and others (such as Gratch & Schatz, 1987) note that Piaget's studies were the focus of thousands of follow-up studies. Piaget also helped delineate central theoretical questions about the nature of intelligence. And although new explanations for several aspects of infant development have emerged, no grand, comprehensive theory has come forth to challenge Piaget's view.

Piaget explored cognitive growth as a continuous process beginning at birth and continuing over four major stages: sensorimotor, preoperational, concrete operations, and formal operations. Each stage is associated with a specific age period: infancy, the preschool years, the school-age years, and adolescence.

According to Piaget, individuals progress from one period to the next at their own rate so the age at which a child reaches any period is relatively unimportant. What is important, however, is that these periods of mental growth occur in an invariant order, that no period is ever skipped, and that each lays the groundwork for the next. In addition, each period of cognitive development involves different *cognitive structures*. These structures provide the framework of understanding that helps people make sense of the world. For example, a 9-month-old infant's way of understanding is physical; it involves the behaviors she uses to explore and manipulate objects—grasping them, mouthing them, and so on. An 8-year-old child's understanding is different, because it entails the ability to classify objects. For instance, he understands that an object may belong to two classes of things simultaneously. That is, he can classify a wooden object with four legs and a top as a table *and* as a piece of furniture. Cognitive structures are the means by which human beings understand, code, and remember information from the environment.

A major tenet of Piaget's theory is that the individual (infant, child, or adult) is actively engaged in acquiring knowledge and constantly exploring the environment in an attempt to understand it. Advances in cognitive ability occur as individuals interact with their environment. Piaget uses the term **schema** to explain these interactions. (Some texts prefer the word **scheme**.) **Schemata** (the plural of schema) are the strategies by which the infant interacts with the environment. Initially, these schemata are innate reflexes, such as sucking and grasping. As the infant grows, however, he combines the schemata into more complex actions, until eventually they are based on mental representations rather than on reflex or motor activity.

Two inherent tendencies—**organization** and **adaptation**—govern the individual's interaction with the environment, which in turn modifies the schemata.

A CLOSER LOOK

Piaget's Sensorimotor Period

Stage 1: Reflex Activity
(Approximately Birth to 1 Month)

During Stage 1 the infant has numerous innate reflexes. Although many of these reflexes disappear after a few weeks when the brain becomes neurologically mature, other reflexes such as sucking and grasping undergo significant functional changes. Piaget regarded these latter reflexes as the building blocks of cognitive growth. They are the infant's first sensorimotor schemata, which gradually become more efficient and more voluntary. Piaget emphasized that children at any age practice the kinds of activities they are capable of carrying out. Thus, during the first month of life infants learn through sucking, looking, and grasping.

Stage 2: Primary Circular Reactions
(Approximately 1 to 4 Months)

During Stage 2 progress occurs on several major fronts. First, through repeated actions involving their bodies and the modification of these actions, infants' initial sensorimotor schemata become more refined, and they attempt to repeat actions they may have stumbled on by chance or from which they derive pleasure. That is, if an infant by chance turns over, he will repeat this activity over and over again, each time deriving pleasure from doing so. Sucking, which during Stage 1 was a reflex related to hunger and food, now occurs for the sheer pleasure of it. Infants suck just about anything, not only their bottle or a nipple, but their fingers, toys, and other objects. These repeated (hence, *circular*) actions are focused on the body (hence, *primary*).

Second, some rudimentary coordination now appears between the schemata. Whereas in the previous stage infants either grasped an object or looked at it, they now stop and look at an object while grasping it. This indicates the development of coordination between the two schemata of looking and grasping—in other words, the beginning of eye/hand coordination.

Piaget explains that the nature of the individual is to organize her experiences and to adapt herself to what she has experienced. In organizing experiences, she integrates two or more schemata into a more complex, higher-order schema. Initially the newborn will only look at an object placed in front of her, but eventually she will reach out for the object and grasp it. Infants also adapt to the environment through two other complementary processes: assimilation and accommodation. Although for the sake of clarity they are usually referred to as separate cognitive activities, Piaget noted that they are inseparable aspects of the adaptation process.

Assimilation means interpreting external objects, places, people, and events in terms of our present way of thinking. A 2-year-old playing with a large cooking pot as if it were a car, or pretending that a chip of wood floating on a shallow stream is a boat, is engaging in pretend play. Piaget would say that he is "assimilating" the pot or piece of wood to his mental concepts of what a car or boat is. In fact, he is taking in new information and interpreting it (even distorting it) to make it agree with what he already knows.

Accommodation entails changing and expanding on what we already know. For example, a 2-year-old child who sees a Great Dane for the first time may wonder why it is called a dog, because it does not look like the small dogs she has seen before. However, once she hears the Great Dane bark, she will begin to understand that although the animal is slightly different from other dogs she has seen, it is actually part of the dog classification because it behaves the way dogs generally do. Accordingly, the child accommodates to this new information and expands her concept of dogs.

Assimilation and accommodation are equally important in adapting to the environment. These mutually dependent processes result in the gradual transformation of the mind as the child adapts to the environment. Piaget believed that

A CLOSER LOOK

Object permanence Another significant change is related to object permanence. In Stage 1, the infant was not aware of any boundary between himself and objects in the environment. In the second stage, however, he realizes that objects are separate entities. When he drops a rattle, he will stare at the place where it was last—his hand. But after a few seconds he will give up and quickly forget that he even held the rattle. For the infant at this stage, out-of-sight is out-of-mind!

Stage 3: Secondary Circular Reactions (Approximately 4 to 8 Months)
Whereas the infant's actions focused on his body in Stage 2, the infant's attention now centers on objects (hence the word *secondary*). He continues to repeat his actions over and over again, but this time he does so for the results the actions bring. Again, this behavior begins by chance as the infant, in manipulating an object, brings about an unanticipated outcome. For example, he grasps and shakes a rattle, and the rattle unexpectedly responds with a sound. At first, he pauses

in wonder. Then he shakes the rattle again, and even more confidently and quickly the third time. He continues to repeat this action for a considerable time—in much the same way each time.

Object permanence Further progress also occurs in object permanence. For example, when a rattle the infant is holding drops and is then partially covered with a cloth, he recognizes the rattle and attempts to uncover it. But if the cloth completely hides the rattle, his reactions will be the same as in Stage 2—that is, out-of-sight, out-of-mind. He will not look for the rattle even if he saw you cover it with the cloth.

Stage 4: Coordination of Secondary Schemes (Approximately 8 to 12 Months)
A significant cognitive change occurs during Stage 4 as the infant clearly intends to solve a problem. Piaget gave an example of how he held a matchbox in one hand to show his
(continued)

human beings adapt to the environment because, like all biological systems, we seek equilibrium. When our store of knowledge cannot explain something we encounter, we feel a cognitive tension or disequilibrium and experience a sense of not understanding. To restore equilibrium, we must change and expand (accommodate) our view of the world. Thus, according to Piaget, equilibration is a fundamental aspect of cognitive growth because it motivates us to maintain a balance between assimilation and accommodation. Piaget believed that the principal motive of cognitive growth is our need for *equilibrium*; that is, the restoration of the harmony between reality and our view of the environment (Flavell, 1977).

The Sensorimotor Period

In Piaget's theory the sensorimotor period, which lasts in most infants from birth to age 2, is the first step in cognitive development. The infant's interactions with the environment are governed by overt sensory and motor abilities, such as seeing, touching, grasping, reaching, and sucking. Thus, thinking occurs as part of the infant's explorations of his environment. The infant learns by acting on the objects and people around him.

A CLOSER LOOK

(continued)

infant son, Laurent; before Laurent could grasp the matchbox, Piaget held a pillow in front of it. Laurent hit the pillow in an attempt to move it out of his way so he could attain his goal—grasping the matchbox. In other words he exercised one schema (hitting) as the means to exercise another schema (grasping) in order to obtain a goal (getting the matchbox). This major accomplishment—the appearance of intentional means/ends behavior—would not have occurred in a previous stage. A younger infant might have been distracted by striking the pillow repeatedly, or she might have simply given up her attempt to grasp the matchbox once an obstacle was placed in her way.

Object permanence The infant at this stage is also capable of retrieving his rattle even if it is completely hidden from view. However, object permanence is still not fully developed; the infant attempts to remove a cloth completely covering the rattle. But if the rattle is then hidden under a different cloth, the infant looks only under the original cloth. Researchers refer to this as the A-not-B error (see the accompanying figure): First, an object is covered under cloth A and the infant is allowed to retrieve it. Then, while the baby is looking, the object is placed under cloth B. But the baby, seeking to retrieve the object, still looks under cloth A where he found the object before, rather than under cloth B. This A-not-B error continues past the baby's first year of life.

Stage 5: Tertiary Circular Reactions (Approximately 12 to 18 Months)

This is the highest level of purely sensorimotor activity. As the word *circular* implies, the infant's actions are still repetitive. However, he is now actively searching for novel experiences. For this reason Stage 5 is sometimes called the stage of active experimentation. Recall, too, that at this age the infant is likely to be walking, so he has greater opportunity to explore the environment.

The infant no longer repeats his actions in exactly the same way each time, as in previous stages. Rather, he repeats them in a way that suggests that he is learning something about the *consequences* his actions have on objects. He purposely varies his movements to observe the results. For example, the infant drops his rattle. When he is given back the rattle, he drops it again and again. In Stage 3, dropping the rattle would have been done in the same way each time. In this stage, however, the infant varies how he drops objects and watches what happens. First he may drop the object with some force, later with less force, each time watching what happens as he changes his actions. Parents often think that the baby is doing this to annoy them. This may be so, but he is also learning how objects, and parents, behave when he acts on them. There is nothing more frustrating than continually picking up objects or cleaning up food the infant drops. But if parents understand that this is part of the infant's cognitive development, it may help them cope better.

To understand Piaget's views on how infants think, consider that when you think of people, objects, or events, you form a mental picture; you use these mental pictures to compare one image with another. This information is carried "in your head," so to speak. According to Piaget, infants do not have this capability. Instead, their way of representing objects is through the actions they can perform on the objects. A toy is something to hold, put in the mouth, or look at.

Gradually, as infants develop the capacity for object permanence, these motor representations become mental representations. We can define **object permanence** as the awareness that objects continue to exist even when they cannot be seen, touched, or smelled. This concept is similar to recall memory. Indeed, in Piaget's theory, both object permanence and recall memory emerge late in the first year of life.

To describe the gradual progress in cognitive development during infancy, Piaget divided the sensorimotor period into six stages; each stage builds on the preceding one (see A Closer Look: Piaget's Sensorimotor Period). In the first stage, newborns' actions are governed by reflexes; they do not differentiate between themselves and the objects. By the sixth stage, they become capable of thinking; their actions, which had been based on immediate sensory experiences, now show

A CLOSER LOOK

 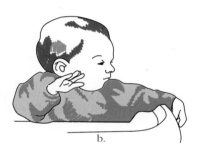 

a.   b.   c.

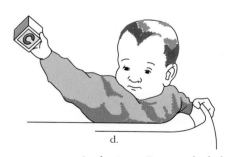  

d.   e.   f.

In the A-not-B error, the baby plays (a), drops his toy (b), looks for it (c), and retrieves it (d). He then drops the toy again, but on the other side (e). Nevertheless, he looks for it on the side where he first found it (f).

(continued)

that they think first, and that they have a mental representation of an object—even of an object that is not present.

This new ability has important real-life implications for infants and their parents, and it changes infants' behavior. For example, until about Stage 4, infants will not cry when their parents leave the room or when they cannot find a favorite toy. But beginning in Stage 4 and increasingly more so through Stage 6, they can maintain mental pictures of their parents, toys, and other objects, so they experience a keen sense of loss when their parents leave the room or when they cannot find their toy.

Their capability for representational thought also enables babies to progress in their ability to solve problems. Before this stage, they solved problems mainly by trial and error, always using action. For example, in an attempt to get something out of a small box, an infant might try sticking her finger in the box, shaking the box, and so on until eventually one of these methods works. During the final stage of the sensorimotor period, however, she does not need to try all these activities manually, because she can go over them mentally before she acts. In other words, she can reason, imagine, and invent solutions to problems.

Imitation is another example of representational thought. Through observation and imitation, infants learn about aspects of their social world and add to their repertoire of behaviors. The ability to imitate is another indication of the ability to learn. In charting the course of the infant's increased ability to imitate, Piaget noted that the younger infant, in Stage 2 or 3, is capable of repeating the actions he initiates. This may not be true imitation, however, since he started the process. Nonetheless, if he sticks out his tongue—a schema obviously within his repertoire—and if his mother imitates him by sticking out her tongue, the infant will again stick out his tongue, and so on. Later, in Stage 4, the infant becomes capable of imitating an action initiated by an adult because at this point he can modify his schemata somewhat. When his mother waves "bye-bye" and closes and opens her hand, he will attempt to imitate her by opening and closing his hand—an action that is a modification of the grasping schema.

In Stage 6 a significant advancement occurs; infants can imitate even when the person or activity being imitated is no longer present. This *deferred imitation* can

A CLOSER LOOK

(continued)
Object permanence   At this stage the infant will correctly search for an object hidden under two different cloths, but only if he sees the object being placed under the cloths. For example, if you take a rattle, cover it with your hand, and then put your hand under one cloth and then under another and finally hide the rattle under a third cloth, the infant will search for the toy by looking at your hand, or she will move one of the cloths, but she will not search any further. At this stage, according to Piaget, she cannot figure out invisible displacements. When she is about 18 months old and object

permanence is fully developed, she will be able to search for a toy that has been invisibly displaced.

Stage 6: Beginning of Representational Thought (Approximately 18 to 24 Months)
Finally, the infant reaches the stage of what we normally call *thought*. He has a fully developed notion of object permanence and is able to retain a mental image of objects or events. In Piaget's terms, he becomes capable of representational thought.

occur because the infant is capable of retaining and retrieving a mental representation of the activity. A 2-year-old may be seen reenacting some activity she observed earlier—say, her mother pointing a finger at her or waving "bye-bye." In deferred imitation the infant will point her finger or wave her hand at a doll in much the same way.

Although, as Piaget maintained, the infant's ability to imitate improves with age, recent studies indicate that the infant may be able to imitate sooner than Piaget suggested (see A Closer Look: Learning Through Imitation). Recall that in a series of studies described earlier, Meltzoff and Moore (1977; 1983) found that 2-week-old infants can imitate facial gestures, such as sticking out their tongues and making lip protrusions, that are modeled for them. Other researchers have found that even younger infants appear to imitate facial expressions (Field et al., 1982), which suggests that they have an inborn capability to match their movements to another's. But this finding has been controversial; a recent review of 26 experiments on the topic indicates that neonatal imitation is distinct from more mature imitation (Anisfeld, in press). That is, the newborns' ability to imitate does not necessarily mean that they are using imitation as a mechanism for learning, which is what occurs in infants close to age 2.

Researchers today are discovering that Piaget may have underestimated some of the infant's cognitive abilities. Still, he has provided valuable insight into the infant mind, revealing its capacity to learn and solve problems (Gratch & Schatz, 1987).

Language Development

Piaget's theory also described the gradual process by which infants acquire the ability for mental representation. This ability enables them to think about objects that are not present and heralds advances in the most remarkable of human abilities—language. Because infants have the capacity for mental representation, they can use a word to refer to an object. They can learn to respond to words and to use words as a way of organizing their experiences and perceptions (Halliday, 1975).

Theories of Language Acquisition

Language has three interrelated dimensions: semantics, syntax, and pragmatics (Bloom & Lahey, 1978). **Semantics,** which is the linguistic representation of what we know about objects and events, refers to the meaning of words and sentences. **Syntax** refers to the rules of sentence formation: the regularities of language reflected in the way we put words together. The **pragmatic** aspect refers to how we use language.

Anyone who has ever learned a second language, especially its grammar, can attest to the fact that it is not an easy task. Nevertheless, for most children language appears spontaneously, progressing from a small vocabulary at age 2 to an adult grammar and vast vocabulary by age 5. The 18-month-old generally has a small vocabulary and may use only one word at a time. By the time she enters first grade, she will have an extensive vocabulary and speak in complete, well-formed sentences. In addition, she will understand and appropriately use the basic rules of grammar.

How do children acquire the ability to speak in rich, complex sentences? Is language taught or are human beings innately disposed to acquire it? Although researchers agree that language acquisition follows a predictable course and that each child progresses through several distinct milestones, there are many disagreements about how language is acquired. Some researchers emphasize environmental influences; others point to the genetic bases of language development. However, most take a middle-of-the-road approach; that is, although the human organism is equipped to learn language, experience with language is necessary for language development. According to these researchers, there are several different approaches to language learning.

The learning theory approach Behaviorist B. F. Skinner put forth an extreme position on language *learning*. Skinner (1957) claimed that adults, through their systematic reinforcement of children's behavior, cause youngsters to learn every new skill, including language. Thus when a baby babbles or a child utters a new word, parents respond by clapping their hands, smiling, or getting excited. The baby, happy at the reaction he has managed to produce, makes the same sound or utters the same word again. The adults' reactions reinforce the vocalizations, thereby increasing their frequency. As the child grows older, the adults continue to reinforce him each time he attempts to speak correctly; they also correct him when he speaks incorrectly. Eventually, through his attempts to repeat words and sentences in the correct form and order, the child acquires the ability to speak the same way as adults.

Although more recent observers generally dismiss this extreme position, the debate continues as studies indicate that parental input may play a role in language acquisition (Rice, 1989). Studies of so-called wild children raised in isolation have shown that children fail to acquire language in the absence of adult input. Also, infants babble more when their parents reinforce their babbling by immediately touching them or smiling at them (Rheingold, Gewirtz, & Ross, 1959). Moreover, numerous recent studies have shown that parents play an important role by responding to children's language errors (that is, by correctly repeating, expanding, or recasting [phrasing the sentence differently] the children's utterances) (Bohannon & Hirsch-Pasek, 1984; Bohannon & Stanowicz, 1988; Bohannon, MacWhinney, & Snow, 1990). In addition, preschool children whose parents talk to them a great deal (that is, children with a linguistically enriched environment) and children whose parents listen to them are more verbal than children whose parents ignore them or are overly directive in communicating with them (Rice, 1989).

Considering the different ways parents respond to their children's correct and incorrect utterances as an implicit form of feedback would support the important role of the environment in language acquisition (Bohannon, MacWhinney, & Snow, 1990). All the same, the learning theory explanation does not account for many aspects of language acquisition. For example, why do infants and young children, who are just learning the language, have a unique way of speaking? They may say "no sleepy" when they mean "I am not sleepy yet." Or they may refer to "mouses" or "feets" instead of *mice* and *feet*. Obviously, the child is not simply imitating adults and repeating what she hears; instead, she is creating her own language.

The learning theory also does not explain why language develops slowly during the first two years of life and phenomenally fast during the preschool years. According to some researchers, during the preschool period children acquire about nine new words a day or one new word an hour (Markman, 1986). There also appears to be a sensitive period for language acquisition between age 2 and puberty. Children acquire language skills more easily during this time. Evidence for this critical period is available from studies showing that children acquire a second language more readily than adults. In addition, children suffering brain damage during this sensitive period can compensate for it and still learn to speak, whereas adults sustaining brain damage may lose their speech (Lenneberg, 1967).

Studies indicating abnormal language development of wild children after they have been rescued also point to a critical period for acquiring language. For example, Genie, who was isolated until age 13, never learned to speak in grammatically correct, rich sentences (see Genie: A Modern-Day Wild Child). Does this mean that there is some biological explanation for language development?

Biological orientation   Linguist Noam Chomsky of the Massachusetts Institute of Technology (1968) believes that there is a biological explanation for language acquisition. Despite differences in languages, cultures, and families, he notes that infants and children worldwide acquire very similar language skills at about the same age. To explain this phenomenon, he proposes that human beings have an innate ability to learn language and suggests that the central nervous system contains a mental structure (or module), which he calls the **language-acquisition device** (LAD). This LAD enables infants to isolate speech sounds and speech patterns from birth and to process these sounds differently from other sounds in the environment. This mental structure also triggers various speech milestones, so infants begin to babble at about 6 months, are able to produce single words at about 1 year, and can speak in short sentences at about 2 years.

The language-acquisition device helps explain the brain's innate capacity to process words and to understand the structure of language and the fundamental relationship between words. According to Chomsky, language has two levels of

---

FEATURE

Genie: A Modern-Day Wild Child

Theorists argue back and forth about whether certain skills or basic personality dimensions are learned at specific periods of life and lay the foundation for the rest of development. Much of the evidence seems to suggest that human development is more flexible and that certain learning deficiencies, whether social or cognitive, can be made up. However, some data indicate the existence of a critical period for at least some skills.

Genie, often referred to as a modern-day "wild child," was raised in isolation. During her entire childhood, she was restrained by a harness and forced to sit on a toilet or sleep in a caged crib. She was given very little to eat, and no one spoke to her; when she did make any noise, her father beat her. She was not discovered until she was

13, when her partially blind mother applied for public assistance. Attempts to rehabilitate Genie were extensive but only partially successful (Curtiss, 1977). Over the years, she learned to walk and was toilet-trained. She actually learned quite a few words and could eventually speak, but she could not ask questions and did not understand the rules of grammar. She could put words together, but her speech was telegraphic, much like an infant's. She would say, for example, "Father hit leg" rather than "My father hit my leg."

Because Genie only began learning to speak at age 13, she never completely acquired language skills. This case certainly supports the idea that there is a critical period for language acquisition.

---

structure: the **surface structure,** which is the arrangement of words (for example, the order of words in a sentence), and **deep structure,** which is the meaning, or basic relationship, between words. For example, the sentences "Marie picked up the crayon" and "The crayon was picked up by Marie" have a different surface structure, but they have the same deep structure and convey the same message. Children and adults intuitively recognize that the sentences mean the same thing. The rules that connect surface and deep structures are known as *transformational grammar.*

Eric Lenneberg (1967) also adhered to the biological explanation of language development. He proposed that the human being's ability to produce and understand language is an inherited species-specific characteristic. In his view language is based on highly specialized biological mechanisms that predispose humans toward learning language and also shape language development. These mechanisms include the articulatory system, which produces speech sounds. Animals do not have these mechanisms. Although researchers can teach apes how to use a simple sign language (Patterson, 1980) and even how to use inflection to convey meaning (Gardner & Gardner, 1986), apes cannot learn to speak, because they lack the anatomical apparatus necessary to produce speech sounds (Gardner & Gardner, 1980).

Milestones in Language Development

Lenneberg further pointed out that infants go through milestones in language development. These milestones are related to brain maturation in much the same way that milestones characteristic of motor skills development are related. Look at Figure 6.4, which lists the language milestones of an infant's first two years of life. As you can see, language development proceeds along a regular and predictable course. Although the infant does not begin to speak until some time between the ages of 12 and 18 months, he actually begins to apply himself at birth to the task of listening and responding to language.

To understand that language development begins at birth, we have to distinguish between expressive (or productive) language and receptive language. *Expressive language* refers to the ability to talk. *Receptive language* refers to other conditions necessary for language development, such as listening attentively, discriminating among sounds, and understanding what is being said. Recall that newborns are disposed to selective listening and that they are especially attentive to the human voice (DeCasper & Spence, 1986; DeCasper & Sigafoos, 1983). Two-month-old infants respond differently to their mother's voice and to another woman's voice, and they synchronize their body movements to adult speech patterns (Stern, 1985). In Chapter 7 you will learn that even though infants cannot engage in conversation by using language, they are quite adept at communicating their needs. They also learn how to take turns, a necessary aspect of any conversational exchange, and can discriminate among speech sounds. Eimas et al. (1971) found, for example, that infants raised in an English-speaking environment can distinguish between such speech sounds as *pa* and *ba.*

Can infants discriminate between speech sounds in a foreign language as well? Recent research suggests that newborns are born with the ability to discriminate among all the speech sounds of human languages. By the time they are babbling, however, they have lost the ability to discriminate and produce sounds that are not part of their acoustic environment (Eimas, 1985; Werker & LaLonde, 1988). For

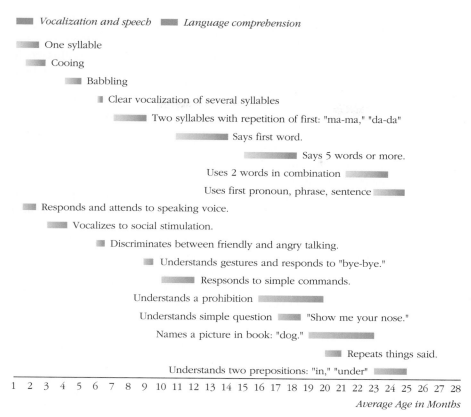

■ Vocalization and speech   ■ Language comprehension

■ One syllable

■ Cooing

■ Babbling

▌ Clear vocalization of several syllables

■ Two syllables with repetition of first: "ma-ma," "da-da"

■ Says first word.

■ Says 5 words or more.

Uses 2 words in combination ■

Uses first pronoun, phrase, sentence ■

■ Responds and attends to speaking voice.

■ Vocalizes to social stimulation.

■ Discriminates between friendly and angry talking.

■ Understands gestures and responds to "bye-bye."

■ Respsonds to simple commands.

Understands a prohibition ■

Understands simple question ■ "Show me your nose."

Names a picture in book: "dog." ■

■ Repeats things said.

Understands two prepositions: "in," "under" ■

1 2 3 4 5 6 7 8 9 10 11 12 13 14 15 16 17 18 19 20 21 22 23 24 25 26 27 28

Average Age in Months

Figure 6.4 *Some of the language milestones that occur during the first two years of life. The average ages are approximations, and the lengths of the lines show the range of ages resulting from a compilation of several studies.*
Source: Adapted by permission from *Infants: The New Knowledge About the Years from Birth to Three,* by R. B. McCall. Cambridge, Mass.: Harvard University Press. Copyright © 1979 by The McCall Children's Trust.

instance, during the first few weeks of life, infants raised in an English-speaking environment can discriminate between the Thai *mp* sound and the English-language *p* sound; but by the time they are several months old, they lose this ability.

Early sounds   From the moment of birth, the infant can perceive speech sounds, discriminate among them, and produce sounds. These early sounds are not simply random noises. Regardless of their parents' language, the sounds infants make during their first year follow a highly ordered sequence: crying begins at birth, cooing (described as nonsyllabic, partially repetitive vowel sounds) starts at the end of the first month, and then babbling begins at around 6 months (Oller, 1980).

Babbling is an important milestone in language development. Initially it involves uttering simple consonant/vowel syllables and repeating them in succession, as in *ba ba ba ba, ma ma ma ma,* or *da da da da.* Eventually, "variegated babbling" (Oller, 1980) appears, which involves variations in the consonants and vowels repeated, as in *ba di* and *ba da.* Researchers do not yet know why infants babble, but they suggest that babbling helps develop the muscles of the sound-producing apparatus. Once infants come to associate certain movements of the throat, tongue, and lips with certain sounds, they will repeatedly practice this newly acquired skill (Menyuk, 1972). Recent evidence also suggests that there may be a relationship between babbling and later speech. Oller, Wienman, Doyle, and Ross (1976) found that the phonetic content of babbling varies from language to language, resembling the speech children make later in life. Weir (1966) reported that the pitch of the babbling varies in different countries, reflecting the pitch of the language the infants hear around them.

Researchers further note that all infants babble, even those who cannot hear others or themselves. Babbling in deaf infants diminishes after a while, because they cannot hear and thus are not reinforced to continue to babble or to progress in acquiring more sophisticated language skills. In fact, studies have shown that deaf and hard-of-hearing children have great difficulty learning to speak and, later on, have trouble with learning written vocabulary and grammar (Meadow, 1975). But if the hearing difficulty is diagnosed early in life, and if parents communicate with their deaf infants through sign language, they will develop the ability to sign at the same rate and in a similar manner as hearing infants develop the ability to speak (Schlesinger & Meadow, 1972; Goldin-Meadow, 1985). Deaf infants who are signed to from their earliest months appear to sign-babble; that is, they use rough gestures that are similar to signing gestures during the same period that hearing infants babble. Petitto and Marentette (1991) demonstrated this in their videotapes of five infants at ages 10, 12, and 14 months. Two infants were deaf children of deaf parents who used American Sign Language to communicate. When the researcher analyzed the infants' hand gestures and compared the two groups—those who were deaf and those who were not—it became apparent that the deaf infants used gestures that

The Role of Motherese in Language Acquisition

Anyone who has ever watched an adult speak to an infant knows that most adults modify their speech in addressing a baby. They use a special pattern of intonation and rhythm. This special way of speaking, which we can dub **motherese,** appears to be universal. That is, it exists in all cultures, regardless of the language spoken. Some universal features of motherese are a high pitch, an exaggerated range of pitch, or intonation, a slower rate of speech, and exaggerated facial expressions (Greiser & Kuhl, 1988). Does this have any special effect on the child's language? Certainly some parents feel strongly on this issue and make a special point *not* to use "baby talk." Still other parents use baby talk even when their children are grown.

Researchers have recently focused on the role of motherese in language acquisition. For example, Anne Fernald (1985) compared the speech of mothers and fathers to their babies in Italian, German, French, Japanese, British English, and American English. Regardless of the language spoken, parents addressed infants in a high pitch, using more intonation, shorter utterances, and longer pauses. Mothers, but not fathers, also used a wider range of pitch. American parents modified their speech the most, especially their intonation. Fernald (1985) also reported that American infants prefer the intonation pattern of their mothers over normal speech.

Some researchers advise against using motherese, contending that children would speak sooner and learn the rules of grammar faster if adults spoke to them in complex sentences (Gleitman, Newport, & Gleitman, 1984). But other researchers point out that adults' use of motherese plays an important role in enabling infants to communicate. The high pitch and exaggerated intonation are more likely to catch and maintain the infant's attention. The slower rate of speech, increased pauses, and greater range of intonation exaggerate the boundaries between words and phrases, thus marking the important elements of a sentence. Researchers

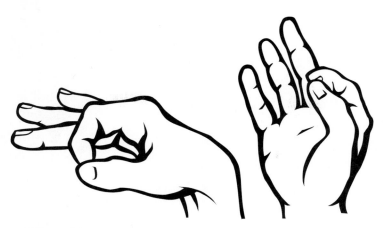

Figure 6.5 *When deaf infants are exposed to sign language they repeat these gestures and similar ones (each equivalent to a syllable); they can even babble in sign language: that is, they use the same gesture again and again.*

were similar to those used in sign language (see Figure 6.5). They also used a few of these gestures over and over again, much as the hearing infants use syllables, such as *ba ba ba,* in their babbling.

Unfortunately, for many infants, deafness often goes unnoticed in part because deaf infants can babble. As a result, parents assume the infants can hear and thus do

A CLOSER LOOK

suggest that these qualities of motherese give infants important cues to isolating grammatical units of language (Kemler-Nelson et al., 1989) and may serve as early language lessons.

Researchers also emphasize the importance of listening to the baby. In her early use of language, the infant is also hoping to be listened to. Being listened to is a reward. When the infant says, "See doggie?" she looks to see if she has had any effect on the adult. Is her mother looking at the dog? After all, that's what language is for—to communicate a message. One of the most important ways of facilitating language development, therefore, is to listen to the infant and to indicate that her communication did have an effect. "Yes, big doggie" or some similar response would provide such a cue and convey to the infant whether she was right in what she said. If the "doggie" the child points to is a horse, an appropriate reply, such as, "No, it's a horse," would correct her and expand her vocabulary (Dale, 1976). Thus the character of

the talking and listening relationship is also an important aspect in language acquisition.

Although this toddler doesn't yet speak, he can make his wishes known distinctly.

not provide experiences that would help the infants compensate for their disability. Child development professionals suggest, therefore, that even when infants babble, parents should look out for indications that they may have a hearing problem and note how they respond to loud noises. Although hearing infants may ignore loud noises, they will turn their head toward the source of sound and occasionally startle at a noise—evidence that they can hear. Since deaf infants never turn their heads or startle in reaction to noise, an alert parent or caretaker can spot the problem.

Communicating by sound and gesture After the babbling period, the infant progresses to a variety of short speech sounds, coupled with gestures, to express emotions and needs. Anyone who has spent any length of time with a 10- to 12-month-old infant is familiar with this phenomenon. They can whine or shriek and point to an object that they want. Or they can scream to show they are angry or do not want to comply with a demand, such as giving up a toy (Dore, 1978). Although some of their communicative expressions may be frustrating to interpret, others can be delightful, as when they convey surprise by raising their eyebrows and saying "oooh!" At this point in their lives infants may not have the ability to speak, but they certainly *can* communicate (Bates, O'Connell, & Shore, 1987)! Parents also note that even though these children cannot speak, they can understand much of what is said to them.

The First Words

True linguistic utterances—the first words—do not appear until around the end of the first year or the beginning of the second year. Parents are so eager for this milestone to occur that they often read meanings into the infant's babbling, assuming that they are actual words. It is difficult to establish exactly when words have meaning. When is *dada* a word designating father rather than just babbling *da da da da*? In fact, what is considered to be a first word is culturally defined. Whereas American parents would be quick to read meaning into what may be babbling—*da da da*—in the infant, in one African culture children are not considered to have language until they utter the word for *breast*.

Most researchers note that first words appear in the range of 10 to 13 months (McCarthy, 1954). To study this milestone, researchers give parents a vocabulary checklist and have them keep track of their children's vocabulary. This method is reliable when compared to observational measures of child language (Dale et al., 1989).

When the infant first acquires words, she uses them, as Bloom (1973) notes, one at a time. First words are further distinctive in their pronunciation and meaning. Typically, they are one or two syllables; often words such as *bottle* or *lamb* are likely to have different versions, such as *baba,* in which one syllable is simply duplicated, or *nam,* in which the child replaces consonants (Dale, 1976).

Sometime around the second year of life, many infants go through a transition from slow to rapid word learning. This marks the onset of the so-called **vocabulary spurt,** or **naming explosion.** Goldfield and Reznick (1990) tracked the way 18 infants acquired their first 75 words, beginning when the infants were just over 1 year old. Close to 75% of the children had a vocabulary spurt, and the majority of their newly acquired words were nouns. The remaining infants acquired the first 75 words more gradually and showed a varied vocabulary, including nouns, verbs, adjectives, and other word forms. Thus infants differ in their word-learning strategies; some focus on the names of things and tend to learn them rapidly, whereas others try to encode a wider range of experiences in their word learning, which results in a more gradual, but varied vocabulary growth.

Nelson (1973) found considerable uniformity in early vocabularies but noted that the infant's vocabulary is highly selective. It is likely to include items such as *mommy, milk,* and *ball* that play an important role in the infant's life. Nelson also pointed out that we can learn more about the selectivity of the infant's vocabulary by looking at what is omitted from each category as well as what is included. *Shoe* and *sock,* for example, are common. But *pants, sweater, diaper* are missing, even though a baby is just as likely to wear them as he is shoes and socks, perhaps even more so. The difference is that shoes and socks are items the infant can act on easily, whereas pants, sweaters, and diapers are not. That is, the infant can easily take off his shoe or sock but finds it harder to take off a sweater. Thus a crucial factor in what words are included in early vocabularies is whether the infant can act on an object (Dale, 1976). Other researchers point out that an infant's early vocabulary also includes words referring to specific categories rather than to higher-level generalities. For example, the infant is likely to include *flower* rather than *plant,* which is more general, and *doggie* rather than *animal* (Rosch et al., 1976).

Although there is considerable uniformity in early vocabularies, there are individual differences among infants; some infants use more words in one category than other infants do. Nelson (1981) contended that such individual differences may reflect the temperament and disposition of particular infants. An active infant may use such words as *go* or *sit* extensively, whereas a sociable infant may use *nice* and *bye-bye.* Despite these individual differences, each infant's vocabulary includes all the types of words discussed earlier.

The meaning of words   Just because an infant uses a word does not mean it has the same meaning to her as it does to an adult; many parents make this discovery, much to their chagrin. A father may be excited that his year-old infant finally says "Dada," but how disappointed he becomes when any strange male adult is greeted with "Dada" as well! This occurs with other words, too. First the infant learns to point to a dog and say "Doggie." Later, she may overgeneralize and call any four-legged animal "doggie," be it a cow, a horse, or a lamb. The infant is not making a mistake; rather, she is reasoning on the basis of her previous experience. It is reasonable for the infant to use the same word for objects that are related: "It is as though he were reasoning, 'I know about dogs, that thing is not a dog. I don't know what it's called, but it's like a dog' " (Bloom, 1975).

In addition, the way the infant uses overextensions is similar to the way adults use them; overextensions are usually based on an object's or action's perceptual properties. For example, adults may use the word *ball* or *ball-shaped* to indicate anything that is round (Clark, 1973), just as the infant may use the word *doggie* to describe any four-legged animal or the word *dance* to refer to any kind of turning-around or jumping up-and-down action (Rosch, 1975; Clark & Clark, 1977).

Holophrastic speech   Although the infant says his first words one at a time, individual words may be used as sentences. First words, according to Dale (1976), "appear to be attempts to express complex ideas, ideas that would be expressed in sentences by an adult. The term 'holophrastic speech' is often used to capture this idea of 'words that are sentences.' " For example, the infant may take a spoon and say "Me," meaning "I want to feed myself." Or the infant whose mother is about to wash his face may push her away and say, "Self," meaning "I want to do it myself." The infant is using one word but means something adults would use a sentence to express. He may also use some action such as pointing or pushing to make his intentions and desires clear.

Combining Words

At around 18 to 20 months of age, the infant begins to combine words. Obviously, the language of a 2-year-old is more limited and simpler than adult language. Infants use nouns, verbs, and adjectives, but omit auxiliary verbs, articles, and prepositions, much as you would omit them if you were sending a telegram. For this reason, researchers often describe early speech as **telegraphic speech.** A 2-year-old would say "See truck" rather than "Look at the truck." The topics are also limited to concrete aspects of the environment. That is, the infant will comment on an action ("Cookie all gone" or "Doggie bark"), or she will refer to objects she sees or possesses or that others possess: "My doggie," "Mommy room."

Once the infant acquires the ability to combine two words, she will progress during the preschool years to increasingly longer utterances, first combining three words, and later speaking in sentences (Brown, 1973). You will see in Chapter 9 that

Encouraging the child to participate in reading aloud (for example, asking questions about the story or pictures) enhances the development of vocabulary and language skills.

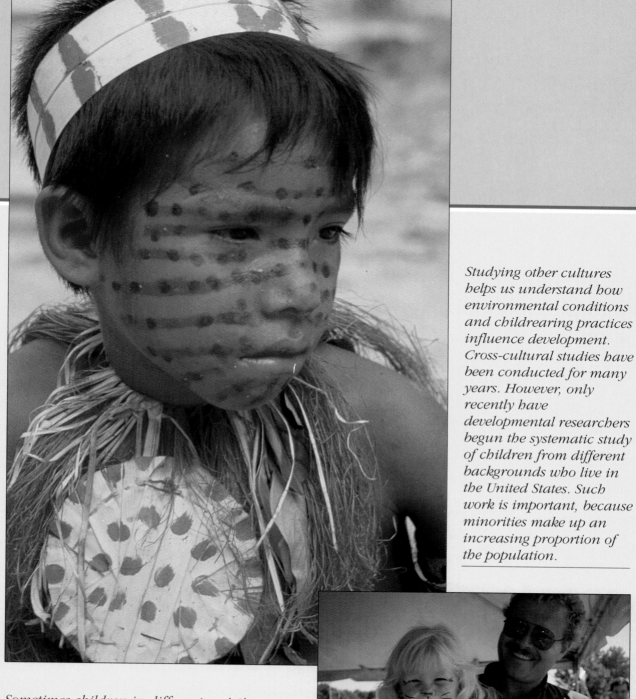

Studying other cultures helps us understand how environmental conditions and childrearing practices influence development. Cross-cultural studies have been conducted for many years. However, only recently have developmental researchers begun the systematic study of children from different backgrounds who live in the United States. Such work is important, because minorities make up an increasing proportion of the population.

Sometimes children in different societies may experience similar practices. In our society, children's faces are painted for fun at fairs and parties, but the custom is a serious matter for children in some other countries.

Children and Culture

Parents sometimes borrow effective child care practices from other societies. Many parents in technologically advanced countries now carry their babies cradled close to the chest or back as a matter of course.

Carrying the baby against the chest or back is a traditional practice in many societies. Benefits to the baby include early development of the trunk and thigh muscles, the security of closeness to the parent, and an opportunity to experience the surroundings. If parents need to work with their hands they are free to do so.

The Hopi use a cradle board to carry a swaddled baby, allowing for movement only of the head. But babies who are confined in this way develop motor skills at about the same rate as those whose movements are not restricted.

On a visit to a farm, this preschooler has an opportunity (no doubt a rare one) to milk a cow and learn where our food comes from.

Milking or otherwise gathering food is a daily chore for children in many cultures.

Although children in nontechnological societies have to gather and prepare food, care for younger siblings, and help with other work, like children the world over they can't resist taking a few minutes out for play.

No matter where they are or what they are doing, whether at play or in a formal educational setting, children interact with their peers. Through this contact they learn such social skills as how to get along with one another and to share, and they also learn about themselves. In our society, children are usually allowed to decide when to play in a group and when to spend time with just one special friend. In some other countries, including China, group activities are consistently emphasized.

regular and predictable progression in the child's language development continues and also that this language is not a simple version of adult speech. Instead, it is a language unique to the child, as she attempts to grasp the rules of structure and grammar and apply them to her speech.

New Ways Infants Are Growing Up Today

Teaching Babies to Read

Although a 2-year-old has yet to master the ability to speak in complete, well-formed sentences, some parents believe that infants can, and should, be taught to read and acquire other basic academic skills. These claims are receiving extensive media attention in part because the research on cognitive and language development has shown that infants are not helpless organisms living in a world of "booming, buzzing confusion." Rather they are individuals interested in many aspects of their environment and capable of organized intellectual behavior. Since infants are capable of learning at an early age, why not capitalize on this ability and teach them a variety of skills?

The temptation to nurture a talent and teach children at an early age is not new. Mozart, who learned to play the harpsichord by age 3, was taught by his hard-driving father. In the past only some parents attempted to pressure their children to acquire specific skills early in life; today, however, many parents are challenged to teach their babies to read, do math, play musical instruments, or speak a foreign language.

Parents are inundated with books, kits, and "how-to" courses on teaching babies and raising a superior child. Then they observe other parents and become concerned that if they do not actively teach their infant they will be inhibiting his intellectual potential. Michael and Denise, for example, love their 15-month-old son, Darrel, and, like most parents, want to do the best they can for him. Denise's 3-year-old nephew, Raymond, has been the center of attention at family gatherings when he gives a violin recital. Michael and Denise think that Darrel can be just as good, but they can't afford to purchase or rent the tiny violin (which has to be changed frequently as the child grows), nor can they afford the Suzuki lessons. Perhaps they can teach Darrel to read instead, so they have been looking into several kits that help parents teach their baby to read.

Should parents teach their babies?   Do you think Michael and Denise should be teaching their baby to read?

Babies, of course, can and do learn about the environment. The question is, Should they be taught? These "how-to" kits that Michael and Denise are looking into include flash cards that parents use to help infants memorize words. In an analysis of programs that promote reading in infancy and of empirical studies on precocious reading, Zigler and Lang (1985) point out that there is no conclusive evidence that parents or caretakers can teach infants to read—or that infants can actually learn to read. In addition, research indicates that before the child acquires the ability to read, he will first acquire prereading skills, which are the building blocks for later reading fluency, during the preschool years (Chall, 1983; Crowder, 1982). Whitehurst and colleagues (1988) found that parents do not necessarily have to use flash cards to "teach" their infant to read. Rather, they should read to their child and point out things in the book or ask questions about the story. Interacting in these ways lays the foundation for later reading and enhances the child's vocabulary and expressive language skills.

Direct teaching is often effective with older children. You will see in later chapters that the more a 10-year-old learns about a topic—say chess—the easier it is for him to recall related items (Chi & Koeske, 1983). During infancy, however, children need to have different types of experiences. By emphasizing academic instruction in infancy, we may interfere with the infant's development. David Elkind (1981; 1987), in his books *The Hurried Child* and *Miseducation,* notes that parents who focus their attention on the child's intellectual development may ignore her social and emotional needs and stifle her curiosity about the environment. Others note that "the overemphasis on training the [child's] mind has led to a distorted view of parental tasks. The parents' job has come to be viewed as little more than programming a computer" (Zigler & Cascione, 1980).

This overemphasis on training may also be harmful because it may take time away from other activities that infants and parents engage in naturally and through which they develop a close, loving relationship. You will see in Chapter 7 that in developing such a relationship with his caregivers, a baby learns that he is cared for and valued. Later in life as well, the child is better able to learn when he feels sure that his parents value his efforts. When parents spend time teaching their baby to read in the absence of evidence that he can learn to read, both the baby and the parents may feel frustrated if he does not learn to read; as a result, the infant may get the message that he is not pleasing his parents.

When parents and other adults play with and care for the baby, she learns that she can control her environment and that her actions make a difference. If she cries, her mother or father will pick her up, feed her, talk to her, or otherwise comfort her. When she turns over for the first time, takes her first step, or utters a word, her parents will clap their hands and cheer. This input seems to inspire the baby to further efforts. Although the infant cannot tell exactly how she is feeling, such experiences seem to give her a sense of effectiveness.

The infant also acquires this sense of personal effectiveness through play and the manipulation of objects, especially objects that respond to her actions (for example, a rubber duck that squeaks each time she squeezes it or a mobile that plays music when she pulls its string). Using these objects, the infant learns to associate her actions with specific outcomes (Watson & Ramey, 1972; Finkelstein & Ramey, 1977). The infant gains competence and a sense of mastery because she realizes that every time she squeezes the rubber duck, it squeaks. She can make it do something! An infant who feels competent is motivated to interact with people and objects she encounters and thereby acquire knowledge. An infant who is not given the opportunity to control his environment develops a sense of helplessness; he may believe that he cannot do much to alter his circumstances. He then stops his attempts to interact with the environment and loses his motivation to learn (Fincham & Cain, 1986; White, 1959; Turner, 1980).

Early experience and later life   Parents who feel pressured to teach their baby academic skills do not mean to harm the baby; on the contrary, their intentions are good. But they have the illusion that faster is always better and that the earlier children acquire academic skills, the more intelligent they are. In addition, parents have been encouraged to believe that infants at any age can be taught any skill; this is contrary to what we now know about human development. Recall from Chapter 2 that earlier in this century, J. B. Watson (1926) claimed that babies can be trained to achieve specific skills. He boasted:

Children whose parents do not pay attention to them may learn not to ask questions or otherwise interact with their parents.

Give me a dozen healthy infants, well-formed and my own specific world to bring them up in, and I'll guarantee to take any one at random and train him to become any type of specialist I might select—a doctor, lawyer, artist, merchant-chief and, yes, even into beggar-man and thief. . . .

Watson based his claim on the notion that development is a product of environmental input only and that the child's mind is a blank slate. However, newborns are born with the sensory and perceptual skills by which they gather information about the environment; cognitive growth is the result of an interaction between biological potential and environmental experiences.

Most researchers today note that both natural ability and the environment are significant in the child's development and that childrearing and educational practices should reflect a balance between the two. The question that remains is, If environment and experience are part of cognitive development, how much can, and should, we shape the environment and the child's experiences to optimize development?

Infants are natural learners. As long as they are in a nurturant environment and their caretakers respond to their needs and allow them to play and explore, they will extract from the environment the information they need at any given stage.

It is important, however, to determine conditions that may hinder this process and to discover why some infants do not learn at the same rate as their peers. Researchers have found that normal infants growing up in a perceptually and socially impoverished environment, such as at one time existed in some orphanages, are likely to suffer significant deficits in social, emotional, and intellectual development (Dennis, 1973) (see also Chapter 5). Such orphanages rarely had more than one adult caregiver for every eight or more infants. As a result, the infants did not have an opportunity for adult interaction and play; they simply laid in their cribs with nothing to look at but the ceiling. Dennis (1973) noted that the longer infants stayed in such unstimulating and unresponsive settings, the lower their IQ and the more retarded they were in language development. Dennis believed that this retardation occurred because the infants had nothing to look at or to manipulate, nor did they have the experience of being picked up, held, smiled at, and talked to.

The Role of Parents in Cognitive Development

Most infants, of course, grow up in a family where they are exposed to a great deal of environmental stimulation. In most homes the television set is on, there are people coming in and out of the house, and the baby is taken out of the crib and played with at different times. But even within such settings, some infants do not develop to their full intellectual potential.

In investigating why this occurs, researchers focused on the primary caregivers who mediate the infants' experiences. When caregivers prompt the infants' attention by handing them toys, pointing things out, and labeling objects, they encourage infants to become attentive (Bornstein, 1985). Studies also show that caregivers who hold, touch, smile at, and talk to their infants a great deal are more likely to have infants who are more advanced cognitively than those who do not receive such attention. Further, these cognitive advances persist beyond the first few years (Clarke-Stewart & Apfel, 1979; Yarrow, Rubenstein, & Pederson, 1975). This does not mean that talking to or holding the baby more often will cause the advanced cognitive skills to persist throughout the early childhood years. Rather, parents who engage in activities that enhance the child's competence during infancy are likely to continue similar activities as their child grows older (McCall, 1980). That is, parents who talk and listen to their infants and play with them are likely to respond similarly during the preschool and school-age years.

In turn, these children will interact more frequently with their parents, asking them questions and involving them in their play and other activities. Infants whose parents are not attentive soon learn not to attempt to interact with them or ask them questions. Therefore, researchers consider parental influence on cognitive development in terms of their behavior toward the child over time and in the context of the complex, reciprocal parent/child relationship. As Belsky, Lerner, and Spanier (1984) point out:

> . . . it would probably not appear to be the case that the intellectual brightness fostered by parents during infancy directly determines subsequent intelligence, but rather that a bidirectional and transactional process of parent-to-infant-to-parent-to-toddler-to-parent-to-preschooler effects characterize the connections that link together various developmental periods. . . . Primarily through such complex reciprocal pathways of influence . . . parental effects identified during infancy are connected to developmental outcomes and processes beyond the opening years of life.

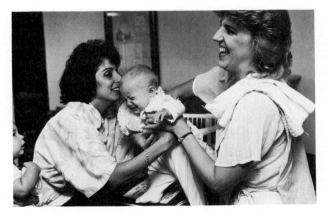

Some parents do not know how to interact positively with their child. A parent educator can come to the family's home to work with the parents and child. Many home visitation programs developed in recent years have proved to be effective in helping parents interact with their children.

Infants in Out-of-Home Group Care

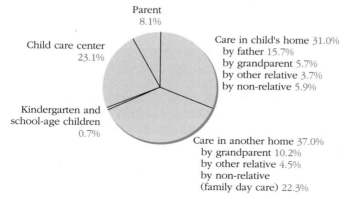

Child Care Arrangements Used by Parents of Children Age Five or Under

Parent
8.1%

Child care center
23.1%

Care in child's home 31.0%
by father 15.7%
by grandparent 5.7%
by other relative 3.7%
by non-relative 5.9%

Kindergarten and
school-age children
0.7%

Care in another home 37.0%
by grandparent 10.2%
by other relative 4.5%
by non-relative
(family day care) 22.3%

Figure 6.6 *Child care arrangements used by parents of children age 5 and under.*
Source: U.S. Bureau of the Census (1987). *Who's Minding the Kids?* Current Population Reports, series P–70, #9. Washington, D.C.: U.S. Government Printing Office.

Cognitive development depends on the active participation of adult caretakers. This finding raises some concerns in view of the recent social phenomenon of placing infants in out-of-home group care. Because of the increase in single-parent households and the need for both parents to work full-time, more women are in the work force and need to find suitable child care.

The child care issue is relevant to social and emotional development as well as cognitive and language development, and it affects older children as well. This is why we discuss child care in several chapters (see also Chapters 1, 7, 9, and 13). Infant day care, however, is of special concern for two reasons:

1. The shortage of child care facilities in this country (see Chapter 1) is especially evident in the area of infant day care.

2. Infants depend more on their caretaker; they are more vulnerable to adversity; and they cannot cope as well with internal or environmental discomfort or stress. Thus even the simple routines of infant care—feeding, bathing, diapering, and comforting—can affect the infant's physical safety and well-being and cognitive and emotional development (National Center for Clinical Infant Programs, 1988).

Over 50% of the mothers with an infant under age 1 are working (U.S. Department of Labor, 1987). Working parents place their infants in one of several types of child care arrangements. As you can see in Figure 6.6, these include a **family day-care home,** where an adult, usually a mother with young children, looks after a small group of children in her own home; a *child care center*; and the *infant's own home*, where the infant is cared for by a parent (in the case of parents who work different shifts), a relative, or a nonrelative.

Research Findings

There is a great deal of debate and controversy about whether infants should be raised by their parents or by other caretakers. The chief question is whether spending time away from both parents and being raised in a group setting harms the baby's cognitive and socioemotional development. Choosing an infant child-care site and even deciding to leave the infant there in the first place are difficult, anxiety-provoking decisions. Parents want to be sure that the child care situation will be conducive to their baby's development.

Unfortunately, the research findings are still inconclusive, especially when we look at studies on infants under 1 year who are in out-of-home child care. Some researchers claim that there are no negative effects associated with high-quality child care (Phillips et al., 1987). Others contend that the findings on infants in child care for 20 hours or more per week indicate that there is cause for concern, especially with regard to socioemotional development (Belsky, 1987). In part, the controversy stems from the fact that the studies are as yet imperfect and were conducted over a short period. A review of the literature notes that several problems plague the research in this area (National Research Council, 1990). First, most studies were conducted in high-quality child care centers, usually on or near a university campus. The only conclusion that can be reached on the basis of these studies is that as long as infants are in high-quality child care centers where they receive appropriate and nurturant care, they will not suffer any cognitive deficits. But the reality is that most infants are in family day-care homes. And so far researchers have not looked at the development of infants in such settings.

Second, the studies failed to consider the three factors that determine child development:

1. Factors within the infant, such as temperament and neurological integrity.
2. Factors in the immediate environment, such as the amount of family stress, interactions with parents, and the quality of care received in the day care setting (Gamble & Zigler, 1986).
3. Factors in the larger social environment, including the neighborhood and the broader culture (National Research Council, 1990).

Although these factors interact to influence developmental outcome, they are just now being considered in child care studies (Phillips, 1988). The new wave of studies will look at a sample of child care settings that represent the care children are likely to receive. For example, a new ten-site study sponsored by the National Institute of Child Health and Development will examine actual child care centers and their effects on children.

We are still awaiting the findings of these studies. Meanwhile, researchers have concluded that, in general and for infants over 12 months, child care is not inevitably and pervasively harmful; the quality of care infants receive is important to both their cognitive and socioemotional development, regardless of their socioeconomic background (National Center for Clinical Infant Programs, 1989). Panel members of the National Research Council (1990) state:

> There is no strong basis for our review [on the effects of child care on development] for urging parents toward or away from enrolling children in child care settings . . . rather, our review strongly directs attention to the issues of child care *quality* and its impact on children's development [p. 77].

The small group size and warm atmosphere of the family day care home are reasons many parents select this form of care for their children. Developmental psychologists agree that it is a good choice as long as the caregiver has time to interact with each of the children individually.

What Is Quality Care?

When researchers discuss quality care, they are referring to conditions existing in the child care setting: Do the infants have the opportunity to play with and interact with adults, or are they left alone in a crib all day? Do they receive adequate nutrition and health care? Are there enough caretakers so that each infant receives individual attention? How many children are in the group? How do the caregivers interact with each infant?

Researchers derive these questions from studies that have attempted to identify the dimensions of quality that foster child development. The findings reveal that there are several structural aspects of quality: group size, staff/child ratio, caregiver training, stability of care (a minimum staff turnover, which allows infants to form a relationship with their caregiver), and an unstructured daily routine that addresses the infants' developmental level.

The Reality of U.S. Child Care

Do infants in the United States receive quality care? The available research does not say with absolute certainty what kind of care American infants experience. But there are indications that many infants are in poor-quality settings. First, state regulations governing the operation of child care facilities vary from state to state. These regulations, addressing such health and safety issues as staff/child ratios and group size, and other quality indicators, represent minimum requirements—that is, a base below which the children's development is in jeopardy. Nevertheless, several states' regulations do not meet even this minimum. For example, a low staff/child ratio is a particularly important aspect of quality care for infants because they need individual attention. Although all states regulate this ratio, there are substantial variations in the acceptable standards. For example, developmental psychologists recommend a 1-to-3 staff/child ratio for infants under 12 months. However, California allows a 1-to-4 ratio and Georgia allows a 1-to-7 ratio. So, even though the state of Georgia licenses a particular child care facility, we could hardly regard it as safe, let alone of good quality. Just think, if a fire broke out, how could one provider remove seven infants from the building? Despite the inadequacy of these regulations, they affect many child care centers and family day-care homes (Morgan, 1987).

Second, observers estimate that 60% to 90% of all family day-care homes are unregulated; that is, they are operating "underground" (Kamerman & Kahn, 1987). These homes are the most common form of out-of-home care for infants and toddlers. Since the majority of these homes are unlicensed, we do not know what experiences infants have in them nor do we have any opportunity to intervene by giving family day-care providers training or other assistance.

Summary

In recent years researchers have shown that infants have the capacity for organized intellectual behavior, and that they use their sensory and perceptual skills to gather information and knowledge about the environment.

Studies on conditioning in infancy provide evidence of the infant's ability to learn. These studies have shown that infants can learn about predictive relationships in the environment through classical conditioning. Using reinforcement and reward, child psychologists can teach them to change the way they suck or to move their head in a certain way. Research has also shown that infants have the capacity for memory and that they can form categories at an early age.

There are three approaches to the study of intellectual behavior. In this chapter we looked at the information-processing approach and Jean Piaget's theory. While Piaget's theory is no longer the dominant view in the field, he was the first theorist to point out that the way infants and children think changes with age. They do not simply acquire more knowledge as they grow older.

According to Piaget, the individual undergoes four periods of cognitive development, each involving different cognitive structures. These structures are not physical entities, rather they are an interrelated group of actions, thoughts, and memories that the individual uses to make sense of the environment. A cognitive structure or way of understanding the world for a 9-month-old baby involves many strategies—or schemata, to use Piaget's expression. Using those schemata the infant explores the environment and manipulates objects in it. A cognitive structure for a 9-year-old involves the ability to classify objects.

Piaget has also shown that individuals are active organisms who constantly explore the environment and attempt to organize their experiences and adapt to their world. They accomplish this task by means of two complementary processes: assimilation and accommodation. Assimilation means interpreting external objects and events in terms of the way we think of them at the moment. By way of contrast, accommodation entails changing or expanding on what we already know.

During the first period of cognitive development, the sensorimotor period, which lasts from birth to age 2, infants undergo six stages during which they gradually acquire the understanding of object permanence—that is, the notion that objects continue to exist even though we cannot see, feel, or smell them. In the final stage, infants acquire the ability of mental representation, which means that they can retain an object's image in their mind. Because of this ability, infants can also begin to use a word to refer to an object or an event. Thus they begin to make tremendous progress in their ability to acquire language.

Language development progresses through a regular and predictable course, beginning at birth, as infants cry, coo, babble, and then utter their first word. After that point, their vocabulary increases. At about age 2 they begin to combine words and speak in two-word sentences. How do infants acquire the ability to talk and understand language? There are two different schools of thought on this issue; one emphasizes biological factors, the other experiential ones. Yet most researchers today agree that both heredity and environment play a role in language development. Although human beings are biologically equipped to learn language, they need experience for language development.

This is also true of cognitive development, which is governed by both maturation and the environment. Over the years child psychologists have disagreed about the relative importance of each factor. Sometimes psychologists have emphasized that learning occurs naturally as a result of maturation. At other times they have emphasized that babies' intelligence can grow as a result of stimulation.

At different times parents have been swayed by these schools of thought and have changed the way they raise their children. Many parents now feel pressured to teach their babies to read early and thus increase their intellectual potential and academic achievement. But there is no evidence that parents or caregivers can teach a baby to read, nor is there proof that precocious reading results in increased intelligence or later success in school. In fact, psychologists are concerned that parents who focus on intellectual growth may neglect the child's social and emotional needs. Parents should realize that both maturation and experience are important in development. Although infants can and do learn, we do not have to systematically teach them reading or mathematics during the infancy and preschool periods.

Experience plays an important role in cognitive development, as can be seen from studies of infants who grew up in the deprived setting of certain orphanages; these infants had significant mental and socioemotional deficits. Often one person cared for as many as eight infants. Thus there was no opportunity to give each infant the attention and stimulation needed.

Psychologists are concerned that infants who grow up in child care settings may suffer psychological harm. This issue is controversial, however, because studies of the effects of infant day care on development are inconclusive. Nevertheless, psychologists agree that infants and older children need to be in high-quality child care facilities. Quality care can be defined in part by the size of the group and the staff/child ratio, depending on the children's age and the staff's training.

7 Social and Emotional Development in Infancy

Even at birth, infants have an impressive array of capabilities. They possess far greater physiological and intellectual capacities than we had previously suspected, and they are social beings, born with the desire to be close to the people around them. Moreover, they are exquisitely well prepared to interact with and even influence their environment. Through interactions with their caregivers, infants grow in their capability to establish emotional ties with the people around them. From these relationships, infants derive a sense of security and the knowledge that they are loved. Researchers emphasize the importance of emotional security during infancy, noting that sound emotional growth proceeds from the relationships infants establish with their caregivers and influences all aspects of development. Emotionally well-developed infants display a zest for life, enjoy people, and are curious about their surroundings; they strive to encounter and learn from new experiences. But infants whose emotional health is weak show no interest in their surroundings and retreat from affective contact with people.

In this chapter we discuss the infant's capacities for developing into a feeling, loving individual and what may hinder this development. We consider the unique role of parents in offering the infant physical and emotional nurturance. We also study how an enduring and loving relationship, referred to as *attachment*, develops between the infant and another person. What is the significance of this first relationship? Do infants relate to their father in the same way as to their mother? What is essential for emotional security and optimal social development in infancy? Before answering these questions, we need to discuss infants' social predisposition and social and emotional development during the first few months of life because during this period infants and their caregivers form their first mutual ties and begin to learn about and from one another.

Early Social Development: Becoming Acquainted

Few areas of developmental psychology have expanded as rapidly in recent years or have captured the interest of psychologists and other professionals as much as the topic of early social development. Researchers have long recognized that newborns have an array of sensory and perceptual skills, and that shortly after birth they show an interest in the human face and seem to respond to their mother's voice and even prefer her smell. Building on this knowledge, we have sought to study infants as social beings and to document the emergence and development of their interactions with their mother and others who are important to them.

Much of the research emphasis on early social development is on the mother's role in the infant's social world. Researchers have studied the mother/infant relationship extensively, in part because the mother has always been seen as the primary caretaker. However, many research findings on the mother/infant relationship may also apply to the relationships between infants and others who play an important role in their life. This will become clear later in the chapter.

Although the mother/infant dyad is not the sole interpersonal interaction in early infancy, it is very important. Researchers have discovered numerous interesting findings about this relationship. For example, mother/infant interaction has been characterized as unidirectional in terms of the mother's effect on the infant; recently, however, we have found that infant and parent are partners in social interaction. Both contribute to it and are capable of influencing each other's behavior in a process of mutual adaptation (Tronick, 1989). Their interactions resemble a carefully choreographed dance in which both partners synchronize their steps, each taking turns and each modifying his or her behavior in accordance with that of the other. During these interactions mother and infant become increasingly attuned to each other's characteristics and needs. The infant learns the basic cues and conventions governing human social behavior and displays his ability to engage his mother in social interaction by inviting her to play and by maintaining and modulating the flow of a social exchange. The mother learns about her baby, what his behavioral cues mean, and what seems to comfort or distress him. She becomes increasingly confident of her ability to care for him and experiences pleasure and satisfaction when he appears happy, content, and responsive to her social overtures. By relating to and interacting with each other in mutually satisfying ways, mother and infant lay the foundation for a strong, enduring attachment.

Research on Mother/Infant Interactions

The loving relationship between mother and infant, and the *synchrony* (also referred to as *reciprocity* and *mutual modification of behavior*) that characterizes their interactions, are especially evident in their play. This synchrony depends on the infant's ability to signal her needs and her capacity to respond to her mother's behavior and on the mother's ability to perceive her infant's signals and respond appropriately.

Tuning in to one another   Daniel Stern (1977; 1985) spent many hours observing mothers and infants as they interacted, videotaping many of these interactions and later painstakingly analyzing the tapes. He explains the nature of positive mother/infant interaction by describing a few moments in the lives of a mother and her 3½-month-old son. The baby is working seriously at feeding from a bottle; he occasionally glances up at his mother, while she looks at him from time to time. At one point he notices his mother glance at him. He stops sucking and lets go of the nipple; his face eases into a faint suggestion of a smile. The mother, reacting to what she perceives as an overture for play, opens her eyes wider and raises her eyebrows. They look at each other. With eyes locked in a mutual gaze, mother and infant remain motionless for an instant until the mother breaks the silence by saying "Hey." At the same time she opens her eyes wider and throws her head in an upward motion. Stern (1977) writes:

> Almost simultaneously the baby's eyes widened, his eyes tilted up and, as his smile broadened . . . the mother said: "Well, Hello . . . heello . . . heeellooo" so that her pitch rose and the hellos became longer and more stressed on each successive repetition. With each phrase the baby expressed more pleasure and his body resonated almost like a balloon being pumped up, filling a little more with each breath.

After some easy social exchange of gazing at each other and taking turns to smile, vocalize, or otherwise make his or her delight known, the pace and excitement of the interaction increased to an even higher level. After a short while the infant, apparently not able to withstand quite so much excitement and stimulation and having satisfied his need for a few moments of play, broke his gaze; he turned away, his face averted and frowning, thus indicating his desire to terminate the interaction. Sensitive to the baby's cue, the mother ceased playing.

Other researchers have also documented this synchrony in the mother/infant interaction: the infant's ability to initiate a social exchange, and the mother's sensitivity in responding both to the infant's social overtures and then to his apparent desire to terminate the interaction (for example, Tronick & Cohn, 1989; Brazelton, Koslowski, & Main, 1974). However, this marvelous exchange between the baby and the mother does not occur all the time. Tronick and Cohn (1989) found that during the first year, this coordinated face-to-face interaction may occur in about 30% of their interaction time. Also, such animated and exciting face-to-face play sessions last only a few minutes. They are interspersed with periods of quiet, rest, the daily routines of care, and times when it is difficult for the infant or mother—or both—to be fully coordinated in their play and sensitive to each other (Tronick, 1989).

Also, although we highlight the positive aspect of the mother/infant interaction to convey current research findings, we do not mean to idealize the relationship. During the first few months of a baby's life, there are many moments of joy for both mother and infant, but there are also many moments of stress, tension, and frustration, as every parent awakened for 2:00 A.M. feedings can attest! Admittedly, the episodes of synchrony, when discussed in the research or observed on video, are very exciting, but in the daily life of mother and infant they may account for no more than 30 minutes each day (Thoman, 1978; Clarke-Stewart, 1973). In troubled families or in families where several children demand the mother's attention, these moments may add up to even less time (Zahn-Waxler, Cummings, & Radke-Yarrow, 1984). However, when mother and baby do have the opportunity to engage in face-to-face play, the interaction proceeds along the pattern described here, unless there are some disorders in their relationship.

Barriers to positive social interactions   Research on early mother/infant interactions has important implications since this early interaction lays the foundation for the attachment relationship between infant and mother. Some infants who fail to form secure attachments had mothers who were unable to provide sensitive care. Clinicians can now observe troubled parents and their babies to determine if the mother has difficulty reading the baby's signals and appropriately responding to them.

Disorders in early interactions between mother and baby can arise when the mother has difficulty taking care of the baby. Recall from Chapters 4 and 5 that frail, hypersensitive, and premature babies and babies who are unresponsive or difficult to calm experience difficulty adjusting to their environment. Such babies may influence their mothers negatively right from the beginning. It is very frustrating to take care of, and almost impossible to enjoy, a baby who cries continuously and who does not seem to respond to any soothing. Also, some babies may not be alert enough to be responsive to their mothers (Thoman, Korner, & Beason-Williams, 1977); other babies may be sensitive to being touched and thus resist being held. As a result, the mothers may feel rejected and helpless in their ability to effectively care for their infants.

The mother's characteristics can also present barriers to positive social interaction. Her sensitivity is a crucial aspect of the interaction pattern. She must be responsive when her infant communicates a desire to play. She must recognize that when the infant grimaces, yawns, averts her gaze, or begins to suck her thumb, she is signaling her desire to end the play session. Not all mothers, however, respond to their infant's signals appropriately. Mothers who are depressed or preoccupied with responsibilities and problems either at home or at work may not have the ability or the energy to respond to their baby and may not engage in these precious episodes of play (Tronick & Field, 1986). There can also be a mismatch in the mother/infant pair. For example, the baby may have a high threshold for stimulation and may want to engage in longer or more frequent play sessions than her mother is capable of. In

One way adults communicate with infants is through exaggerated facial expressions.

such a case, the mother may become exhausted and ultimately exasperated by the baby and angered by the demands the baby places on her (Tronick & Gianino, 1986; Gianino & Tronick, 1988).

On the other hand, some mothers seem to have more energy than their babies; they are reluctant to allow the baby to break eye contact and stop the interaction (Lewis, 1987; Hodapp & Mueller, 1982). Such mothers, referred to as intrusive, do not ease off when the babies avert their gaze. Instead, they try to continue to play with them. An intrusive mother would thus "chase" after her baby's eyes in an effort to reestablish eye contact, or she might increase the number and intensity of her vocalizations and other behaviors to get her baby's attention. These attempts are usually futile. Brazelton and his colleagues (1974) and Fafouti-Milenkovic and Uzgiris (1979) note that increasing the intensity of behaviors toward an already uninterested infant does not elicit eye contact and may serve to distress the baby. Tronick (1989) points out that by being intrusive, the mother deprives the infant of the opportunity to learn that through his actions and facial expressions he can communicate his needs and desires and thus regulate his world. A baby whose mother is continually intrusive or otherwise insensitive to his attempts to communicate eventually learns that he is not able to make his feelings known; as a result, he may stop trying.

Trust versus mistrust   The mother's sensitivity extends beyond her ability to respond to the baby's social overtures and need to play. She must also be able to respond lovingly and sensitively to the baby's physical needs. When she is able to do so, the infant develops a sense of basic trust, a sense that the world is a good, safe place.

Erik Erikson (1963), whose theory we discussed in Chapter 2, suggests that this basic sense of trust is a vital aspect of personality development and lays the foundation for later relationships the child will establish. As you will recall, he proposes that there are eight stages between birth and old age. Each stage involves a "crisis" that takes place in the encounters between the individual and others in the social setting. This crisis is not a tragic event, but rather a period in life when the individual attains a certain developmental stage. Erikson describes each crisis as an opposition between two characteristics; in infancy these are *trust* and *mistrust*. Infants develop a pervading sense of trust over a period of time during which their physical, social, and emotional needs are met in a loving, caring, and supportive manner, and when they have become accustomed to the caretaking routines of one or two special people. Although Erikson's notions are not supported by empirical research, they provide a framework for our understanding of the importance of the mother's sensitivity or that of any other caretaker. A sensitive and loving caretaker conveys to her baby that she enjoys him; she holds him close to her and gazes affectionately at him before and after leisurely feedings, showing reluctance to part from him. An insensitive or depressed caretaker, who is unable to care for her baby, or resentful at having to do so, exposes the baby to prolonged periods of negative emotions and tends to be abrupt in caring for the baby. Perhaps she may not hold him close to her body or she may terminate feedings as quickly as possible.

Mothers, or any other caretakers, are not always sensitive and loving, nor are they always insensitive and cold, in their interactions with their infants. Rather, most mothers, even if they are usually sensitive, may at times be abrupt with their babies, perhaps when they are in a hurry or depressed or frustrated. Similarly, usually insensitive mothers may at times display warmth in their interactions with their babies.

Depending on whether the relationship between baby and mother can be characterized as mostly positive or mostly negative, the infant, over time, will learn what to expect from her world—whether love, relaxation, and warmth or anger and coldness. On the basis of these experiences, the infant may learn that either she can trust others to respond sensitively to her needs and to care for her or she may come to feel she is not worthy of such care and thus may develop mistrust (Tronick, 1989).

The Baby's Social Predisposition

The way the mother and baby interact changes as the baby acquires more refined motor, cognitive, and social skills (Lewis, 1987). This alerts us to the fact that there is an interrelationship among the various aspects of development. For example, the synchronous pattern of mother/infant interaction during episodes of face-to-face play does not develop until infants are about 3 or 4 months old, when they have established a repertoire of vocalization and facial expressions that permit them to play with another person.

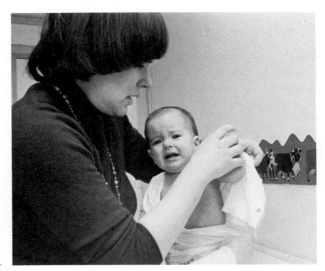

Many babies are responsive to their parents' care, but some infants are difficult to soothe and may negatively influence their parents from the beginning.

Communicating with the baby   Although the baby's ability to express himself in the social setting becomes increasingly more elaborate, from birth the infant attracts and is attracted to the people in his environment and begins to establish the skills needed for successful social interactions. By communicating with him, the infant's parents and other people in his life help him develop these skills.

One way adults communicate is through facial expressions (Papousek & Papousek, 1987; Stern, 1977; 1985). When adults interact with babies, they exaggerate their facial expressions; they raise their eyebrows and open their mouths in mock surprise, or they knit and lower their eyebrows in a frown. Their other expressions include smiles and a blank face. Exaggeration of facial expressions helps the infant attend to them, and the "faces" themselves communicate something to the infant. For example, the mock-surprise expression is a greeting, which invites the infant to join in social interaction. Indeed, this expression frequently gets the infant's attention. The smile maintains an interaction, and lets the infant know that the adult is interested in playing, whereas the frown or expressionless face signal that the adult is not interested in interacting (McCall, 1980; Stern, 1985).

Try these expressions next time you see a baby and you will see what we mean. You will soon realize that babies can discriminate among the facial expressions they observe. For example, they tend to look more often at expressions of joy than at expressions of anger (Malatessa & Izard, 1984). Also, infants seek out and use adult expressions as a guide to their own actions (Campos et al., 1983; Tronick, 1989).

Adults also vocalize in an exaggerated manner (Kaye, 1980), using nonsense words or squeals and squeaks, especially when addressing very young infants (Stern, 1977). Adults also tend to speak in a higher pitch and volume, and they punctuate with greater variations in sound level than usual. Adults in all cultures use this manner of speaking to a baby; it is often referred to as *baby talk* (Ruke-Dravina, 1977). It appears to be geared to the infants' sensory capacities (Sachs, 1977); apparently babies prefer to listen to this way of talking and have been observed to respond by increasing the pitch of their own vocalizations when they hear a high-pitched voice (Webster, Steinhardt, & Senter, 1972).

The baby communicates   Infants are capable of expressing themselves, a fact that became evident in our discussion on mother/infant interaction. They communicate through gestures (Fogel & Hannan, 1985), sound, and facial expressions (Izard, 1978). Gradually, infants learn to distinguish between expressions and behaviors, such as crying, that prompt the caretaker's attention and produce some kind of relief and comfort and those, such as moving their arms and legs, that may go unnoticed. That is, they discover by trial and error which expressions and behaviors are useful and which are not (Tronick, 1989).

Crying, of course, is one of the most potent ways for infants to communicate and engage their caretaker's attention, because their cry has an immediate effect on the people nearby. Wiesenfeld and Klorman (1978) found that mothers' heartbeats increased as they watched video recordings of an infant crying, especially when they watched recordings of their own babies crying.

Although most mothers are physiologically aroused by the baby's cry, they differ in their ability to ascertain why the infant is crying and in their ability to comfort the baby, as we discussed in Chapter 5. Some mothers also believe that if they respond immediately to crying they will spoil the baby, who will then use crying as a manipulative device. These mothers assume that to respond to crying reinforces it.

The infant's ability to establish eye contact is an important milestone in social development.

Some studies indicate that parents may be right. For example, Etzel and Gewirtz (1967) studied infants in laboratory situations and found that when caretakers ignore the crying but respond to other behaviors such as smiling, crying appears to decrease. However, other studies indicate that with babies younger than 6 months, the reverse is true. Ainsworth and her colleagues (Ainsworth, Bell, & Stayton, 1972) observed babies and mothers from the time the babies were 3 weeks old until they were 54 weeks old. The researchers found that mothers who did not immediately respond to crying had babies who cried more often than babies whose mothers picked them up right away. Also, the mother's responsiveness to the baby's crying during the first 3 months is related to the baby's crying at a later age. That is, 7-month-old babies who were observed to cry more than other babies were likely to have mothers who had been unresponsive to their cries when they were 3 months old. We might conclude that babies whose mothers respond to their cries soon learn that they do not need to cry a great deal to elicit their mother's attention. Should parents worry about spoiling their baby? Parents should attend to babies who are younger than 6 months when they cry; during infancy there will be ample opportunities for the infants to learn that they cannot always have their way, but initially, they have to learn that their crying does make a difference.

Another expressive behavior by which infants communicate and engage their parents' attention is the *gaze*. Even though infants cannot focus at birth, they are attracted to the human face and spend a great deal of time when they are feeding, for example, looking at their mother's face. In fact, although at first newborns can only see fuzzily at a distance, they can see close objects quite well. During feeding, the caretaker's face is close to the baby. "This may be," as McCall (1980) writes, "a way nature helps [the] parent and child to become important to one another."

Mothers look at their babies during feeding as well, but only occasionally, because they do not want to interrupt the feeding (Perry & Stern, 1976). Although baby and mother gaze at each other from the baby's birth, it is not until the baby is about 4 to 6 weeks old that they are able to actually establish eye contact. At this age the infant's visual motor system has developed to the extent that she is able to visually fixate on her mother's eyes; from that point on, the mother and infant can remain locked in a **mutual gaze** for increasingly long periods (Schaffer, Collins, & Parsons, 1977).

The ability to establish eye contact is an important milestone in social development. It vastly increases the infant's responsivity and makes the mother feel she is taking care of a real person. In addition, once she is able to establish eye contact, the mother realizes for the first time that the baby is looking at her. As a result, she becomes increasingly interactive with the baby and also more attached to him. This is evident in studies of blind infants. Fraiberg (1974) has shown that mothers of blind infants have trouble forming attachments to them. In fact, eye contact is so much a part of establishing an emotional bond that psychologists usually interpret a sighted infant's failure to establish eye contact with the mother as an early sign of disturbed mother/infant relations or of some other problem in development.

The Infant's Emotional Life

The baby is also adept at communicating emotions, expressing joy and delight by smiling and distress and fear by crying. Before describing these specific emotions, however, we need to discuss briefly the study of emotional development.

Researchers have long been interested in babies' emotional life and have attempted to ascertain the origins and course of such emotions as joy, fear, and anger. Psychologists' interest in the topic dates to Darwin's publication in 1872 of *The Expression of Emotions in Man and Animals*. During recent decades, researchers have concentrated more on cognitive development, but a renewed interest in emotional development has also emerged (Lewis & Michalson, 1983). Researchers have documented the stages of emotional development, beginning at birth (Greenspan & Greenspan, 1985; Sroufe, 1979), noting that infants' emotions and their ability to communicate their emotions are far more organized than previously thought (Tronick, 1989).

Several new research directions are emerging (Campos & Barrett, 1984), as scientists offer different explanations for emotional development during infancy. For the most part, however, we can trace all these concepts back to Katharine Bridges' (1932) classic studies. After observing a group of infants day after day for the first two years of life, Bridges theorized that babies are born with one basic emotional reaction: a *generalized excitement*. As they mature, this excitement differentiates into a general positive affect (delight) and a general negative affect (distress). These emotions are then differentiated into more specific emotional states such as elation and affection, and anger, disgust, and fear.

Sroufe (1979) makes a similar point, noting that as the baby matures, the full emotional panoply blossoms and the baby gradually becomes capable of expressing delight by smiling and distress by crying. Izard (1982) studied the facial expressions of 5- to 9-month-old infants by videotaping them at play with their mothers. Observers were later asked to view the tapes and identify the infants' expressions using the Facial Expression Scoring Manual (Izard, 1971). They identified a range of expressions, including joy, sadness, interest, and fear. Although we cannot ascertain what infants actually feel, this study indicates that early in life they have a range of emotional expressions similar to those of adults (see Table 7.1).

Smiling

Perhaps the most social and communicative of the infant's emotional expressions is the smile. Nothing entrances a parent or other adults more than this. As a parent, when you see your baby smile, you often feel it is a sign that the baby has come to know you and appreciate your loving care.

However, immediately after birth and for the first few weeks of life, babies are not necessarily smiling at their parents. Even blind infants smile during the first few months of life (Freedman, 1964; Fraiberg, 1974). Young, normal babies tend to smile most when they are not attentive to the parent, such as during states of irregular sleep and drowsiness; this suggests that there is a biological component to the smile. But experience is also important; babies in socially stimulating environments smile more frequently than babies deprived of social interactions. Blind infants, who are unable to see others respond to their smiles, begin to smile later than sighted infants (Fraiberg, 1974).

Stages of smiling   In the first year of life, there appear to be three stages of smiling. Soon after birth the spontaneous or *endogenous* (that is, internally triggered) smile occurs. These smiles appear during the first week of life when the baby is asleep. Emde and Robinson (1979) found that they occur during periods of increased brain wave activity. Wolff (1963) and Sroufe (1979) note that endogenous

TABLE 7.1   Range of Emotional Expressions During Infancy

Month	Pleasure-Joy	Wariness-Fear	Rage-Anger	Periods of emotional development
0	Endogenous smile	Startle/pain ↑ Obligatory	Distress due to: covering the face, physical restraint, extreme discomfort	Absolute stimulus barrier
1	Turning toward	Attention		Turning toward
2				
3	Pleasure		Rage (disappointment)	Positive affect
4	Delight Active laughter	Wariness		
5				
6				Active participation
7	Joy		Anger	
8				
9		Fear (stranger aversion)		Attachment
10				
11				
12	Elation	Anxiety Immediate fear	Angry mood, petulance	Practicing
18	Positive valuation of self-affection	Shame	Defiance	Emergence of self
24			Intentional hurting	
36	Pride, love		Guilt	Play and fantasy

Source: Handbook of Infant Development, edited by Joy D. Osofsky, Table 13.2, p. 473. Copyright © 1979 by John Wiley & Sons. Reprinted by permission of John Wiley & Sons, Inc.

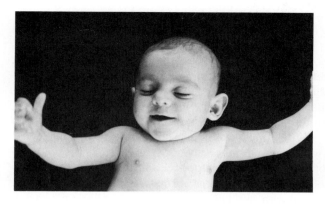

The endogenous or internally triggered smile does not signify conscious pleasure, but is associated with a relaxed, pleasant state.

smiles seem to be the result of a central nervous system activity. If the baby is startled, perhaps by some sudden noise, his level of excitation or arousal is raised. Later, when the baby relaxes below his threshold of arousal, the smile muscles relax, too, sometimes causing a tiny involuntary smile to appear. Although such a smile is associated with a relaxed and pleasant state, it does not signify conscious pleasure as do later smiles.

Soon after this stage the baby begins to smile at a nodding head, blinking lights, sounds, or anything else that has rhythm or repetition, and he does so when he is in an awake/alert state. This smile, called the *nonselective social smile,* is **exogenous,** meaning that something in the external world triggers it. The nonselective social smile occurs around the third or fourth week, most readily when the baby is watching a human face or when he hears his mother's voice. As the infant grows, this smile becomes increasingly social and instrumental; at about 5 to 6 months of age, the *selective social smile* emerges. During this stage, the infant smiles at familiar individuals; unfamiliar faces elicit no smile and may elicit crying.

Researchers are finding that infants are "social smilers," because they tend to smile at a friendly, attentive adult more readily than at one who is inattentive or withdrawn.

Theories of smiling Psychologists, too, are intrigued with the infant's smile. They want to know what makes the baby smile. There are several theoretical answers to this question.

The evolutionary theory of smiling emphasizes the smile's adaptive value. Babies are born with the ability to smile. Their smiles increase adults' interactions with them, thus ensuring fulfillment of their need to establish human relationships. Supporters of this theory note that the more attention we give babies when they smile, the more they will smile. There is some empirical evidence to support this contention. Jones and Raag (1989) found that infants smile more when adults are attentive and friendly than when they are inattentive or withdrawn. Gewirtz (1965) discovered that the development of smiling varies among infants depending on their childrearing setting. Infants who grow up in a normal family setting where they are frequently picked up, played with, and talked to when they smile, smile earlier and more frequently than infants raised in institutions where they are deprived of frequent interactions with caretakers.

Cognitive theorists recognize that the smile is a means of social communication, but they emphasize the cognitive bases of the infant's social behavior and emotional expressions (Kagan, 1984; 1978). They contend that the smile is an innate expression of the pleasure and joy infants experience when they master a cognitive task. This theoretical explanation predicts that infants will take longer to smile at a more complex visual stimulus than a simpler one, because they cannot assimilate a complex stimulus all at once into their cognitive framework. To test this hypothesis, Shultz and Zigler (1970) showed 3-month-old infants a doll (the stimulus), which was either stationary or swinging. The swinging doll was the more complex stimulus, because its contours were more difficult to define when it was moving. Although the infants smiled in both situations, they smiled more readily when the doll was stationary. In addition, the serious way the infants studied the more complex stimulus before smiling appeared to reflect their hard cognitive work in scanning and recognizing the swinging doll.

Fear

The infant is also capable of expressing fear. There is a developmental component to fear; children display different fears depending on their age. For example, toddlers associate fear with pain and are afraid of people who remind them of a painful experience (a doctor, for instance, who reminds them of receiving an injection). During the preschool years, children fear concrete objects such as lions and tigers, but they do not associate them with previous painful experiences; obviously, preschool children have had little firsthand contact with such animals. During the middle childhood years, children begin to fear failing in school, because they are able to think in an increasingly more logical manner; this suggests that there is a link between their fear and their cognitive status. This link between cognition and fear is also true of infants.

To illustrate the cognitive bases of fear, Kagan (1984) described a study in which infants ages 1 month and 7 months were shown a picture of a distorted human face. The 1-month-olds responded with interest to the bizarre face and rarely cried. The 7-month-olds cried and showed other signs of distress. The difference, according to Kagan, is that the older infants had a mental image of what a face should look like; they compared it with the distorted one and became distressed at the mismatch. The 1-month-olds did not yet have the cognitive abilities that would allow such comparisons and so were not disturbed.

Two fears especially evident during the first year of life are stranger anxiety and separation anxiety. **Stranger anxiety** refers to the infant's negative response to the approach of an unfamiliar adult. **Separation anxiety** refers to the crying, fretting, and other distressed behavior the infant exhibits when a parent or other significant adult leaves.

Fear of strangers   Researchers think that stranger anxiety is the baby's first really negative emotion. This fear is evident in a baby who watches a stranger's face for a few seconds, then frowns and breathes heavily, and finally turns away or starts to cry. In an early study, Morgan and Ricciuti (1969) observed infants 4 to 12 months of age. Each infant was sitting either on the mother's lap or several feet away from her when an unfamiliar adult approached. Infants younger than 8 months old were generally positive toward the stranger whether they were sitting on their mother's lap or not. But older infants who were not sitting on their mother's lap showed a much more negative reaction toward the stranger than their same-age counterparts who were sitting on their mother's lap. In several other studies researchers have found that stranger anxiety does not necessarily occur with all 8- to 12-month-old infants each time they see a stranger. Rather, the phenomenon is strongly influenced by their past experience with strangers (Rheingold & Eckerman, 1973; Brooks & Lewis, 1976; Sroufe, 1977) and by the particular situation they are in, such as whether the mother is present.

Quite early in life, infants are able to recognize their parents' emotional states and moods (Tronick, 1989; La Barbera et al., 1976), and they typically observe their mother's face when she sees a stranger approaching. If the mother smiles at or speaks positively to an unfamiliar adult, the baby often responds with less fear and negativity than if the mother speaks in a neutral tone (Feinman & Lewis, 1983). Known as **social referencing,** this ability to be influenced by other people's emotional expressions is considered an important factor in how infants and older children acquire the ability to manage their own emotional expressions and states (Jones & Raag, 1989; Lewis & Michalson, 1982).

At about one year, babies develop a fear of strangers, their first really negative emotion. This child is clearly apprehensive about meeting someone new.

Unfamiliar family members may also elicit wariness and distress. This can be upsetting, and these relatives may feel hurt or embarrassed by the infant's apparent rejection of their social overtures. They sometimes suspect that the parents may have taught the baby to reject or dislike them. However, it should comfort them to know that babies can also become distressed when they see their mother made up or dressed differently than usual or their father disguised in some way (for example, when he covers his face with shaving cream or dresses up like a clown or Santa Claus).

Psychoanalysts suggest that fear of strangers is related to the baby's love for the mother and fear of losing her (Spitz, 1965). Ethologists regard it as a response to an intuitive appraisal of a potentially dangerous situation or as an instinctual flight reaction to any strange stimulus (Freedman, 1965). Cognitive theorists, however, interpret stranger anxiety differently, suggesting that it represents extreme discrepancy from the schema the infant has for familiar people in her environment. That is,

A CLOSER LOOK

Social Referencing

Apparently, infants can discriminate among facial expressions denoting emotion (Bretherton, 1990); their understanding of other people's emotions and behaviors are subject to social influences. Lewis and Feiring (1981) explain that young children who observe their parents' interacting learn about some of their parents' emotions and about the nature of their relationship. In addition, the reactions of parents and others to people or situations can influence children's responses. Thus infants whose mothers greet strangers positively are also likely to respond to strangers in a positive way. In other words, infants can use another person's behavior to form an understanding of a social situation and how to respond to it. This is known as *social referencing*. Feinman and Lewis (1983) demonstrated it. They observed an infant's behavior under two conditions: (1) when her mother greeted an unfamiliar person positively and spoke warmly to the infant about that person; and (2) when the mother greeted and spoke to or about an unfamiliar person in a neutral tone. If the mother spoke positively to and about the stranger, the infant smiled at that person and offered her toys significantly more often than if the mother addressed and mentioned the stranger in a neutral tone.

Similar studies (Klinnert et al., 1983a; Jones & Raag, 1989) confirm these findings. The researchers note that the mother's emotional expressions help regulate the infant's behavior and that other adults' emotional expressions are also influential. For example, Klinnert and colleagues (1983b) posed the following scenario: An infant, his mother, and another adult are together in a room. Some unfamiliar object is then introduced into the room. If the other adult displays a look of happiness, the infant approaches and touches the object significantly more often than if the adult displays an expression of fear.

Infants can also use social referencing to make sense out of potentially dangerous situations. Sorce et al. (1981) used the visual cliff experiment to demonstrate this fact. As you will recall from Chapter 5, in this experiment infants showed their fear of the deep side of a cliff. Researchers found that if the visual cliff was constructed so that its deep side appeared very deep, the infants would not attempt to cross over it nor would they try to find out how their mothers felt about the cliff. But if the deep side of the visual cliff did not appear deep enough to clearly signal danger, the infants would look at their mother. If the mothers, who were on the other side of the cliff, were instructed to put on an expression of fear, none of the infants would cross the cliff. But when the mothers were instructed to pose a joyous expression, 15 out of the 19 infants crossed the cliff. The infants clearly used their mothers' facial affective information to make sense of an ambiguous situation and then decided whether to cross the visual cliff.

Social referencing studies yield valuable information on infant development and emphasize the importance of the social context for understanding emotional reactions (Tronick, 1989). According to Campos and Barrett (1984), this understanding provides direction for future research on emotional development.

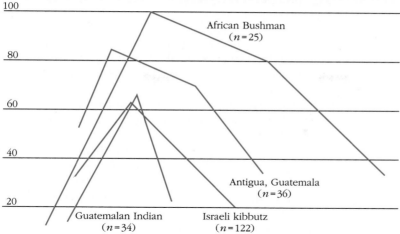

Percentage of Children Who Cried Following Maternal Departure (*n* = number of children)

African Bushman
(*n* = 25)

Antigua, Guatemala
(*n* = 36)

Guatemalan Indian
(*n* = 34)

Israeli kibbutz
(*n* = 122)

Figure 7.1 *Infants in every culture experience separation anxiety at about the same age.*

Source: *Infancy: Its Place in Human Development,* by Jerome Kagan, Richard B. Kearsley, and Philip R. Zelazo. Cambridge, Mass.: Harvard University Press. Copyright © 1978 by the President and Fellows of Harvard College. All rights reserved. Reprinted by permission of the publishers.

the baby's distress is due to her inability to assimilate the stranger's face (Kagan, 1976; 1984). This also explains her fear when she does not recognize her mother or father in disguise.

Separation anxiety Similarly, some researchers interpret separation anxiety in cognitive terms. Separation anxiety (or separation distress) refers to the infant's response to being separated from the mother or other primary caretaker. Such a response may be reduced bodily activity, fussiness, and loud crying. This anxiety begins around 5 or 6 months of age and increases gradually until its peak at about 13 months. Afterward, it declines, and the infant does not demonstrate as much distress at being separated from the primary caretaker. As you can see in Figure 7.1, separation anxiety also begins and peaks at about the same time for infants in other cultures.

Parents are familiar with separation anxiety and may find it stressful to leave their baby when he cries. How do we explain the phenomenon? Some researchers note that separation anxiety reflects the emergence of a new cognitive process— namely, object permanence, which we discussed in Chapter 6. After attaining object permanence, the baby can think about his mother even in her absence, but he cannot yet understand where she has gone or whether she will return, so he becomes anxious. Before attaining object permanence, however, the infant has no memory of his mother and therefore does not miss her (Bretherton, 1990). Separation anxiety declines with age, because the older the infant is, the more able he is to understand that although mommy is gone, she will return.

Establishing Relationships: Attachment

Separation anxiety also indicates, in part, the infant's attachment to her mother. Researchers define the **attachment** relationship, which is considered one of the most important of the infant's emotional experiences, as a strong and enduring bond—the feeling of love, if you will—that develops between the infant and persons she interacts with most frequently. We focus here on the infant's attachment to the mother, since much of the research on attachment does so. But infants have important relationships and attachments to other people as well. They interact with and grow to love their fathers, siblings, grandparents, and others who are important in their daily life (Lamb, 1981; Schaffer & Emerson, 1964).

To measure attachment scientifically, researchers have used the infant's behavior toward his parent as a gauge, studying the extent that the infant looks at his mother, orients his body toward her, smiles at her, clings to her, and becomes upset when she leaves him. They have found that attachment does not emerge suddenly but is acquired over a few months. Before the infant becomes attached, he needs to have sufficient exposure to his caretaker and the opportunity to become acquainted and familiar with her and to ascertain that she will respond to his needs.

John Bowlby (1969, 1973, 1980) first studied attachment; his work was followed by others like Ainsworth (1973), who identified several phases in the attachment process (see Table 7.2). During the first or preattachment phase, which lasts for the first several weeks of life, the baby does not discriminate among people and is as likely to be delighted with or comforted by someone else as by the mother. When the baby is about 3 months old, he enters the second phase of the attachment process; at this point he discriminates between familiar and unfamiliar people and responds differently to them. During this phase he smiles more at familiar people than at those he does not know. During the third phase, which begins at about 6 to 8 months of age, he exhibits preference for his mother and is said to have established an emotional bond with her. Maccoby (1980) notes the following signs that the infant is attached to the mother:

1. He will seek to be close to his mother and maintain physical contact with her, embracing her and holding his arms outstretched to be picked up.
2. He will sometimes cry or otherwise protest when the mother leaves his sight; and even when playing he will watch her.
3. In the presence of strangers, the infant will seem wary and uncomfortable, especially in unfamiliar situations.

This phase of the attachment process peaks at about 1 year of age. During the second year of life, the strong attachment to the mother begins to wane gradually, and the baby becomes increasingly sociable and at ease with others.

Individual Differences in Attachment

Attachment results in a feeling of emotional security in the infant, who grows up regarding her mother as a secure base or "an island of safety" from which she can venture forth and freely explore her surroundings (Bretherton & Waters, 1985). Although all infants usually develop attachments to their mother and to several other people as well, there are individual differences in the quality of the mother/infant relationship.

TABLE 7.2 Phases in the Attachment Process

Phase	Behavior	Age
Phase 1	Baby does not discriminate among people and is happy with, or accepts comfort from, familiar and unfamiliar people.	Birth to 2– 3 months
Phase 2	Baby begins to recognize and prefer familiar people; smiles more at familiar people.	2–3 months to 6–8 months
Phase 3	Baby has developed attachment to mother or other primary caregiver and will seek to be close to her; will cry when separated from her.	6–8 months to 30 months
Phase 4	Now feeling secure in the relationship with the primary caregiver, the baby is no longer distressed during separation from mother or primary caregiver.	30 months

Ainsworth developed a laboratory experiment to assess these differences. In this procedure, called the Strange Situation Procedure (Ainsworth & Wittig, 1969), the infant and parent stay in an unfamiliar room. Then a stranger enters the room. After introducing the child to the unfamiliar adult, the child is separated from the mother, first by leaving her with the stranger and then by leaving her completely alone. The mother returns after each of these brief separations.

Observing the infant's behavior in each situation, especially the behavior toward the mother during episodes of reunion, Ainsworth and her colleagues (1978) classified infants in terms of the security of their attachment relationship. They identified infants as *securely attached* if, at 12 to 18 months, they used their mother as a secure base from which to explore their surroundings and if they

At six months to a year old, infants become increasingly attached to their mothers, who find that leaving even for a few moments can result in crying or other protests.

seemed happy when she returned after a brief departure. According to Ainsworth, securely attached infants exhibited the healthiest pattern of attachment. They might be curious about the stranger and perhaps even temporarily hesitant, but they would soon warm up to him or her.

Some infants were identified as insecure in their attachment relationship. Infants who have formed *anxious attachments* tend to be distressed in an unfamiliar situation, even when their mother is with them. When their mother returns after brief episodes of separation, such infants are inclined to be angry and distressed, and to resist physical contact with her.

Other insecurely attached infants form *avoidant attachments*. They do not explore their surroundings as much as securely attached infants do. They tend to ignore their mother even when she is present, rarely show distress when briefly separated from her, and avoid interactions with her when she returns.

Michael Lamb (1984) notes that the way infants behave in this experiment is indicative of their prior social experiences. That is, some infants behave avoidantly because, on the basis of their past experiences, they expect to be rebuffed. Some infants who form anxious attachments and who resist physical contact do not know what to expect of adults whose past behavior has been unreliable and unpredictable.

Theories of Attachment

This interpretation of the antecedents of attachment is as yet speculative (Lamb, 1984). Nevertheless, researchers have observed individual differences in attachment in the home as well as the laboratory (Ainsworth et al., 1978). Why do infants become attached to their mother? What aspects of this relationship influence attachment in infants and determine whether their attachment will be secure or insecure? Psychologists' answers to these questions have changed in recent years. An earlier learning theory view held that infants become emotionally attached to their mother because she is a source of relief from discomfort and pain. Operant learning theorists such as Jacob Gewirtz (1965) claimed that initially the mother is nothing special, merely a neutral stimulus for the infant. But after repeatedly being associated with pleasurable events such as feedings, the mother takes on rewarding properties and becomes a desired object.

John Bowlby (1969; 1973; 1980) provides a more complete explanation of the nature and process of attachment. Drawing upon ethology, psychoanalytic theory, and Piaget's cognitive-developmental theory, Bowlby has contributed to our appreciation of the importance of the attachment relationship (Bretherton, 1990). He views attachment as a unique response that protects the young from harm, and he describes the attachment relationship in terms of a *behavioral system*. According to Bowlby (1969; 1973; 1980), the set goal of the attachment behavioral system is the infant's proximity to the caretaker. This goal is accomplished by the behavior of both infant and caretaker. Thus an attachment behavior is any behavior by the infant— such as smiling, crying, clinging, and so on—that initiates, maintains, or elicits proximity to the caretaker. Bowlby also believes that the infant's attachment behavior is innate, and is elicited by stimuli such as the mother herself or a frightening situation. In turn, the infant's behavior elicits protective responses from the mother.

Alan Sroufe and his colleagues have elaborated on Bowlby's explanation, emphasizing the affective component of the relationship. They explain the relationship in terms of the regulation of affect (Sroufe & Waters, 1977), noting that when the infant is securely attached he uses his mother or other caretaker as a ready source of comfort and security; this helps the infant enjoy his surroundings and explore them. Such feelings of security also help the infant develop social skills and enjoy social interactions with parents and others (Sroufe et al., 1984).

Influences on Attachment

Schaffer and Emerson (1964) also suggested that the infant has an innate need to be close to people, and they offered an explanation of what might influence the attachment process. After studying the development of attachment in a group of infants from the early weeks of life to 18 months, they found that infants differed in the age when they became attached to their caretaker and in the intensity level of their attachment. Some babies focused their attachment on one person while others were attached to several people. Additionally, the caretaker's responsiveness to the infant's crying and the amount of interaction with the infant had a relationship to attachment. That is, the infants did not simply become attached to the person who fed and cared for them. Rather, they became attached to the person who, in the context of many interactions over time, responded to their needs.

Several other researchers—notably Ricks (1982), Clarke-Stewart (1973), and Ainsworth and her colleagues (1972)—also noted that parent/infant interaction during the first few months and the parent's response to the infant's signals are important in the development of attachment. If the mother or any other primary caretaker is sensitive and responsive to the infant's social overtures, needs, and temperament, and adjusts his or her behavior accordingly, the infant will grow up feeling that the caretaker is accessible and responsive, and will form a secure attachment to the caretaker. These researchers found that babies developed anxious attachments if their mothers were slow to respond or were not affectionate toward them or unskilled at handling them. Infants developed avoidance attachments if their mothers did not like them or were indifferent to physical contact with them.

Although the mother's sensitivity is a factor in the development of attachment, the infant also plays an active role in developing the relationship (Malatesta et al., 1989). Remember that the infant is an active participant in his relationships and that his characteristics at times determine the ability of the mother or other adults to care for him. Thus in one study Waters, Vaughn, and Egeland (1980) found that infants who were unresponsive during the first few weeks were classified as insecurely attached at 12 months, perhaps because it was difficult for the parents to care for and interact with them.

However, Belsky, Lerner, and Spanier (1984) noted that since some parents were able to overcome the barriers to social interaction imposed by the infant's characteristics, other factors might play a role in the development of attachment. Crockenberg (1981) supported their contention; he found that highly irritable newborns developed insecure attachment, but not in every case. Rather, the attachment was insecure only when their mothers had little support from friends and relatives. Under such conditions, the mothers were apparently under psychological strain caused by having to care for an irritable, difficult baby without having any assistance. Lyons, Connell, Grunebaum, and Botein (1990) found that infants of depressed mothers who received home visitation and other family support services were twice as likely to be securely attached as infants of depressed mothers who did not receive such services.

Cultural Influences on Attachment

Researchers have also found that different childrearing practices may influence patterns of attachment. Although the studies are still inconclusive (Bretherton, 1990), they suggest that cultural beliefs influence the way parents interact with their children and affect the relationship between parent and infant. Grossman and his colleagues (1985), for example, studied 1-year-old infants from middle-class families in northern Germany. They found that whereas about 12% of middle-class American children are classified as insecurely attached, close to half the German infants (49%) were insecurely attached, exhibiting either anxious or avoidant attachments. According to Grossman and his colleagues, German mothers believe that babies should not be encouraged to cling or make demands on their parents; this is to help the children learn to become independent at an early age. As soon as babies can crawl, German mothers discourage bodily contact. Although they are sensitive and respond to their babies, they tend to do so differently than American mothers. For example, German mothers attempt to soothe a crying baby by giving her toys rather than by picking her up and hugging her.

On the other hand, infants of the !Kung San, a band of hunter-gatherers living in Africa's Kalahari Desert, spend their first year of life being carried by their mothers. When the children cry, their mothers respond immediately; and the majority of the infants are securely attached (Konner, 1977). Ugandan mothers also interact with their babies much more than American mothers. As Ainsworth (1967) found, Ugandan infants develop attachment earlier than American babies. Although there are differences in the attachment patterns of different cultures, researchers do not know yet if these variations are significant. They suggest that more research is needed on the factors influencing the attachment relationship (Lamb, 1982; Bretherton & Waters, 1985).

Importance of Attachment

Although more research is needed on the influences of attachment, experts agree that attachment is a crucial factor in many aspects of development.

Summarizing the research, Lamb (1978a; 1982) notes that through interactions with the mother an infant acquires security and a sense of trust in her reliability and predictability. This sense of security and basic trust becomes a fundamental aspect of the personality (Erikson, 1963). It is important to the development of autonomy and independence later in the child's life, ensuring that the infant will feel at ease exploring his surroundings and learning from them. Researchers (such as Bretherton, 1990; Belsky, Lerner, & Spanier, 1984) note that securely attached infants are more willing to venture forth and discover their world, thereby ensuring that they will learn by exploring the environment. They are also more socially mature and more inclined to establish social interactions with their age-mates.

Insecurely attached infants may be so concerned about ensuring their mother's presence and proximity that they have less opportunity to explore and to establish and maintain close relationships with others. Stayton, Hogan, and Ainsworth

An infant monkey clings to the cloth surrogate (from the original study by Harlow and Suomi).

(1971) found that securely attached infants are generally more competent in a variety of ways, and they are more capable of positively communicating their desires (using facial expressions, gestures, and vocalization).

In studies linking attachment in infancy with behavior during the preschool years, Pastor (1981) and Waters, Wippman, and Sroufe (1979) also found that preschoolers who were securely attached as infants displayed more competence. They were more self-directed, more interested in exploring their environment, and more likely to have good relationships with their peers than were preschoolers who were insecure in their attachments as infants. Studying the relationship between the quality of mother/infant attachment and infant competence in social relationships, Easterbrooks and Lamb (1979) found that securely attached infants were more friendly and more likely to interact with their peers.

Maternal deprivation and separation   Additional insights into the importance of attachment and its implications for later development are derived from studies that have looked into what happens when attachment does not occur; that is, when infants are deprived of the opportunity to interact with and form an attachment to their caretaker.

Harlow's studies   For ethical reasons, scientists cannot study the consequences of maternal deprivation through human experiments. But we have derived data from studies that manipulated the rearing conditions of animals.

These animal studies—most notably, a series of experiments by Harry Harlow and his colleagues—have illuminated the significance of the infant's interaction with his mother. In Harlow's initial experiments infant monkeys were separated from their mothers 6 to 12 hours after birth and raised in laboratory settings, where researchers gave them surrogate "mothers." These mothers were made either of heavy wire or of wood covered with terry cloth. In some experiments both surrogates were in the cage with the baby monkey, but only one had a nipple from which the baby could nurse. Some infant monkeys received nourishment from the wire surrogate, others from the cloth surrogate (Harlow & Zimmerman, 1959). Even the infant monkeys who received nourishment from the wire mothers spent the greatest amount of time clinging to the cloth mothers, suggesting that the contact comfort provided by the "mother" determined the monkey's degree of attachment (see

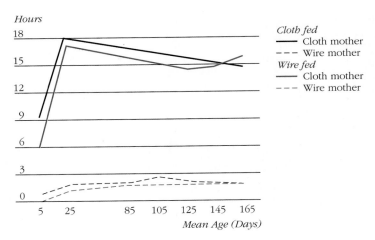

Figure 7.2 *Contact time to cloth and wire surrogate.*
Source: Adapted from *American Psychologist, 25,* 2; Figure 2, p. 162, by Harlow and Suomi. Copyright 1970 by the American Psychological Association. Reprinted by permission.

Figure 7.2). However, lactation was also a factor. Monkeys raised with two cloth surrogates, only one of which provided nourishment, clearly preferred to stay close to that surrogate (see Figure 7.3).

Although the contact comfort provided by the cloth mothers seemed to result in normal behavior in infancy, the monkeys raised with surrogates displayed bizarre behavior later in life. They were not able to mate easily, did not learn to communicate, and were not able to deal with fear. Those who eventually became mothers failed to nurse their babies and seemed to reject them (Harlow, 1971). Monkeys raised without any surrogate mother, cloth or wire, but only with other infant monkeys, also exhibited problems. They did not learn to explore or feel secure and spent most of the time clinging to each other (Harlow & Mears, 1979).

We also have evidence of the caretaker's importance in the infant's life from naturally occurring experiments, such as institutionalized infants or infants who grow up in isolation without warm human interaction, perhaps because of their parents' cruelty. Recall from Chapter 5 that Dennis (1973) found that infants raised in an orphanage that provided good physical care but no stimulation or opportunities for social interactions grew up with intellectual deficits. Tizard and her colleagues (Tizard & Rees, 1975; Tizard & Hodges, 1978) studied English infants raised in residential nurseries from birth until about age 2. They received good medical care, were fed well, and had toys to play with. Some of the children were adopted between the ages of 2 and 8. Tizard found that the longer the children stayed in the institution, the more difficulty they had establishing social relationships with their peers. The researchers noted that as infants, these children did not have an opportunity to establish a close relationship with any adult, because there was such a frequent staff turnover in the institution. Some children were cared for by 24 different nurses over a two-year period.

The problems of such children are due to the type of care they received, and not to the fact that they were institutionalized. Donatas, Maratos, Fafoutis, and Karangelis (1985) studied a Greek orphanage where infants received good physical care and individual attention from a limited number of caretakers. Most infants also had

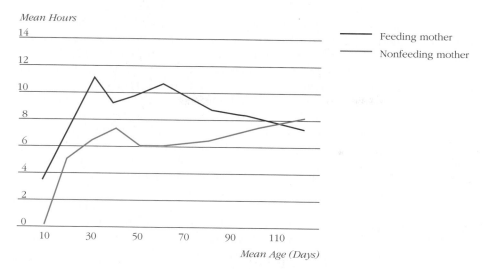

Mean Hours

Mean Age (Days)

——— Feeding mother
——— Nonfeeding mother

Figure 7.3 *Infant preference for lactating cloth surrogate.*
Source: Adapted from *American Psychologist, 25,* Figure 7, p. 164, by
Harlow and Suomi. Copyright 1970 by the American Psychological
Association. Reprinted by permission.

one primary caregiver who was responsible for them. Researchers found that the
infants became attached to their primary caregiver at about the same time as other
infants developed attachments.

Reversing the Negative Effects of Early Deprivation

Although infants suffer if they are deprived of a warm, nurturant relationship with a parent or caregiver, the negative effects of early deprivation can be reversed by giving them appropriate care. One of the most remarkable studies of developmental psychology proves this point. Harold Skeels (1942; 1966) studied 25 infants raised in an orphanage; these children received adequate physical care but no individual attention. Because the orphanage was overcrowded, 13 of the 25 infants were transferred to an institution for mentally retarded adults; there, a mentally retarded woman "adopted" an infant and gave the child individual attention. Skeels compared these two groups of infants: one group remained in the orphanage, while the other moved into a markedly more stimulating, socially responsive environment.

Thus Skeels had an opportunity to assess the impact of an improved social setting on development. The 12 infants remaining in the orphanage became the control group, and the 13 infants moved to the institution became the experimental group. Skeels first assessed the infants' mental status

when the transfer occurred. At that time the average age of the infants was 19 months. The control group had an average IQ of 86.7, whereas the average IQ of the experimental group was 64.3, placing them among the mentally retarded. Tested a year and a half later, however, the two groups reversed positions. The experimental group had gained an average of 28.5 IQ points, for an average IQ of 92.8. By contrast, the control group had lost 26.2 IQ points, declining to an average IQ of 60.5.

Skeels tested them again two and one-half years later in an attempt to find out whether the IQ gains of the experimental group would last. Eleven of the 13 subjects had been adopted during the interim; 2 remained institutionalized. Skeels found that the adopted children had an average IQ of 101.4, while the IQs of the 2 institutionalized children had dropped. After assessing the mental status of the 12 children in the control group who had remained institutionalized,

(continued)

Infants deprived of individual attention are apt to suffer physical and emotional consequences (Rutter, 1979a). But the consequences need not be permanent, if the infants eventually receive nurturant care (Tizard & Hodges, 1978). If they continue to be deprived of affection, however, they may exhibit delinquent and disturbed behavior later in life. This was the conclusion reached by John Bowlby (1980), who was asked by the World Health Organization to report on the mental health of homeless children. The assignment gave him an opportunity to study adolescents who had spent their infancy and childhood in institutions or foster homes. These adolescents, who had repeatedly moved from one institution or foster home to another, never had an opportunity to establish close, loving relationships with adults. Growing up without love, they were "affectionless"; that is, they were unable to care for others or to love.

Thus, while physical care and feeding are necessary, they are not sufficient for normal social and emotional development. Babies also need to have warmth and affection from a nurturant caretaker who is interested in them and who will cuddle them, smile at them, and laugh and play with them.

Consistency and continuity of care   It is immaterial whether infants receive loving care from their biological mother or another warm, sensitive adult (Schaffer, 1977). But two conditions are necessary for normal development. The care must be consistent and continuous. Consistency of care means that infants must have an

---

A CLOSER LOOK

(continued)

Skeels found that their average IQ was 66.1.

Perhaps even more revealing were the marked differences apparent in adulthood between the institutionalized subjects and those who had been adopted. Testing the subjects 21 years after the original study, Skeels found that the 11 subjects in the experimental group who had been adopted were in no way retarded and functioned as normal adults. Several had completed high school and attended college. Four control-group subjects, however, remained institutionalized. One had died. Only about half had attained a third-grade education.

Other studies mentioned in previous chapters (Dennis, 1973) and reviews of those studies (Clarke & Clarke, 1976) have indicated that we can alter the detrimental effects of early experiences. For example, Tizard and Hodges (1978) found that if institutionalized infants are adopted by age 2, they will be able to form attachments to their adoptive parents. But such children still are restless and find it difficult to establish peer relations when they reach age 8.

Let's recall that infant monkeys reared in isolation became socially inept and disturbed in their behavior. In attempts to rehabilitate such young monkeys, researchers paired them with normal monkeys of the same age. These

attempts failed, perhaps because the isolated monkeys were overwhelmed by the normal monkeys' social overtures. Trying to gradually ease the isolated monkeys to living with other animals, Suomi, Harlow, and McKinney (1972) paired monkeys that had been isolated for the first 6 months of their lives with normal 3-month-old monkeys. Since the normal monkeys' social behavior was not as sophisticated as that of the older monkeys, they did not overwhelm the isolated monkeys but served as "therapists" to them. Researchers placed an isolated monkey and a "therapist" monkey together for two hours a day three days a week. For two days a week the researchers subjected the isolated monkeys to "group therapy." This involved placing two pairs of isolated and "therapist" monkeys together. After 6 months of therapy, the isolated monkeys were rehabilitated to the extent that their behavior was similar to that of monkeys reared under normal circumstances. At 2 years of age, the previously isolated monkeys were completely recovered and able to conduct themselves successfully in all social situations. Other therapy studies with monkeys that had been isolated for 12 months (Harlow & Novak, 1973) were also successful. This proves that it is possible to reverse the negative effects of early deprivation.

opportunity to interact and become familiar with their caregiver over time. In an institution infants may experience frequent changes in caretakers and in the care they receive from them; as a result, they will not be able to rely on the predictability and responsivity of any one caretaker. Such infants often fail to form an attachment.

Infants must also have continuity of care; they must have a chance to establish a long-term relationship with their primary caregiver. Although they can withstand brief separations from the individual they are attached to, long-term separations are difficult for them to cope with (Rutter, 1979a). Initially they react to even short periods of separation by crying, screaming, or otherwise showing their distress. If the separations last a long time, they eventually stop crying and become apathetic. This is a way for them to withdraw emotionally from their environment.

DISCUSSION OF SOCIAL ISSUES

Foster Care

The importance of continuity of care is especially apparent in infants placed in foster care after forming specific attachments to their mother. According to Yarrow (1964), infants consigned to foster care after the age of 7 months showed severe emotional disturbances. This is because at that age they are sufficiently mature to feel attached to their mother, but cannot understand why that relationship, which is the most important part of their world, should be broken.

Observing that children need continuity in their interpersonal relationships in later childhood as well, psychologists have attempted to change policies governing the U.S. foster care system. Society has established this system to meet children's needs when their parents' behavior constitutes a serious risk for them (Provence, 1989; Cox & Cox, 1985). This situation can occur in families where a parent is physically abusive or fails to meet the child's physical and emotional needs. In such cases social agencies may intervene, remove the child from the home, and place him or her in a foster home.

One problem with our foster care system is that it is crisis-oriented. That is, social agencies often intervene only when the child's health and development are in imminent danger. In addition, some children have to remain in foster care for their entire childhood, although the system supposedly provides only temporary care until social workers can make decisions about permanent placements. Even worse, some children are moved from one foster home to another. A Children's Defense Fund survey (1978) found that 52% of children in foster care had been away from their families for two or more years, and that 18% of them had moved from one foster home to another two or three times.

During the last decade, researchers and children's advocates have publicized the inadequacy of our foster care system. According to the research, families whose children are in foster care have severe internal problems, too little access to necessary resources, and inadequate skills to manage their children (Weisbrod, Casale, & Faber, 1981). Instead of spending money on an inadequate and potentially harmful foster care system, researchers have proposed ways to channel public funds toward preventive services. These services would eliminate the need to remove children from their homes (Zigler & Finn, 1982). For example, the social agency might send a home visitor to a family on a regular basis to assess the parent/child relationship, to find out the parents' needs, and to offer support and education *before* the family situation becomes a threat to the child.

In addition, researchers have suggested ways to improve the foster care system. Public Law 96-272, known as the Adoption Assistance and Child Welfare Act of 1980, incorporates many of these suggestions. It is designed to ensure permanent families for children who must be removed from their homes and to pull together three elements: prevention of foster care placements, attempts to reunite foster children with their biological parents, and permanent adoptive families for children who cannot return home (Edna McConnell Clark Foundation, 1985). The law increases federal adoption aid and requires states to tighten their control over the foster care program and to ensure that each child in foster care receives consistency and continuity of care. Thus, society no longer regards a foster care arrangement as adequate unless it is a permanent living situation (Watson, 1982).

Of course, these basic changes in the system and the focus on giving the child an opportunity for adoption raise a number of unresolved issues regarding children's needs and parents' rights (Jones, 1985). But they have resulted in a better living situation for some children. According to a 1985 report to Congress by the U.S. Department of Health and Human Services, the number of children in foster care dropped from 500,000 in 1977 to 243,000 in 1982; the average time a child spent in the foster care system was reduced from 47 months in 1977 to 35 months in 1982. In effect, the foster care program has changed from a receiving and holding system for children unable to live with their parents to a system in which an increasing number of children are eligible for adoption and thus have an opportunity to become permanent members of a family.

Unfortunately not all states have made equal progress in their approach to foster care. Several obstacles have slowed the implementation of the act, such as the federal government's failure to appropriately monitor the states' efforts (Edna McConnell Clark Foundation, 1985). PL 96-272 is certainly an improvement over previous attempts to serve children and families in need. However, too many children still enter and remain in the foster care system (U.S. House Select Committee on Children, Youth, and Families, 1989; National Black Child Development Institute, 1989).

Infants of Working Mothers

Because attachment and the need for consistency and continuity of care are so important to infant development, questions have been raised about the social and emotional development of infants of working parents. This is an important research area; one out of every two infants a year old or younger needs some form of child care because the mother works (U.S. Department of Labor, 1987).

Whether to work is a sensitive question for many parents of young children. It is especially agonizing for parents of infants under a year old. Since the infant is so dependent on adult care, many parents fear that their baby will grow to love someone else. Some mothers find it difficult to decide to work while their children are very young (Belsky, Lerner, & Spanier, 1984). Many mothers who have to work or who do decide to work feel guilty leaving the baby in another person's care. The difficulty in finding suitable care and the expense of quality care further exacerbates the problem for many families (Zigler & Lang, 1990; Scarr, 1984).

Black Children in Foster Care

Although PL 96-272 resulted in a decrease in the number of children in the foster care system, black children still enter and remain in foster care in disproportionately large numbers. In addition, these children do not receive the services needed either to reunite them with their families or to make possible their adoption by new families.

Before making policy recommendations about black children in foster care, the National Black Child Development Institute (1989) collected comprehensive data from the public child welfare agencies in five major U.S. cities. Then, based on the data collected on 1003 children in the study group, the researchers compiled a profile on the black child in foster care.

A greater proportion of children below age 5 entered foster care in 1986 (the year the data were collected) than in previous years. The majority of these children (46%) came from single-parent families; in 41% of the cases, parents reportedly had a mental health problem, usually substance abuse. Inadequate housing and health care and extensive drug abuse characterized the child's family before foster care. Child abuse and neglect, including abandonment, were the primary reasons given for placement. The accompanying tables describe the family

(continued)

Primary Reasons for Children's Placement in Foster Care

Family factors	City					Total all cities
	Detroit	Houston	Miami	New York	Seattle	
Primary factors						
Abandonment	24%	20%	38%	15%	20%	21%
Neglect	68%	40%	70%	65%	32%	54%
Abuse	46%	51%	33%	21%	30%	38%
Voluntary	12%	9%	11%	41%	47%	22%
Parent-related factors						
Incarceration	7%	10%	15%	6%	26%	11%
Teen parent	5%	3%	6%	2%	5%	4%
Parent in foster care	2%	0%	0%	2%	1%	1%
Death of parent	7%	3%	5%	2%	6%	4%
Divorce or separation	8%	9%	0%	7%	2%	7%
Mental illness	21%	15%	7%	14%	7%	14%
Physical illness	3%	3%	3%	6%	5%	4%
Drug abuse in family	38%	18%	50%	52%	37%	36%
Alcoholism	22%	14%	19%	25%	26%	20%
Mental retardation	2%	4%	1%	3%	1%	3%
Environmental factors						
Poverty	23%	21%	28%	38%	13%	25%
Inadequate housing	36%	32%	16%	43%	3%	30%
Homelessness or in shelter	9%	8%	16%	14%	13%	11%
TOTAL NUMBER	219	311	98	243	121	992

Note: Multiple Responses-Percentage total for columns is greater than 100%.
Source: National Black Child Development Institute (1989). *Who will care when parents can't?* Washington, DC.

Does it harm the baby to be in care outside the home during the first year of life? Psychologists who have studied such infants disagree. Some researchers, such as Belsky (1986; 1987), contend that children who spend more than 20 hours a week in out-of-home care during their first year are more likely to be insecurely attached than home-reared infants. But other researchers (Chase-Landsdale & Owen, 1987) found no differences in attachment between infants over 6 months old in out-of-home care and infants reared at home. Phillips, McCartney, Scarr, and Howes (1987) argue that the effects of child care on infants have little to do with how early

---

FEATURE

(continued)

and child factors that contribute to children's placement in the foster care system.

Although social workers generally recommend foster care as a way to address children's needs and prevent more problems, the researchers found that the children's lives in foster care were not much better than at home. These children generally did not receive periodic health or educational assessment. Remember that the majority of children entering foster care are under 5 and at risk for developmental delays. In addition, many are also affected by other problems associated with parental substance

abuse. Despite these handicaps, most of these children do not receive psychological assessments or other specialized services needed to address their problems.

Often the reunification of the family is delayed because the parents do not receive appropriate remedial services. Although this study focused on black children, other children in foster care may also be inadequately served. Obviously, we need to make changes in child protection systems. In fact, the increasing numbers of children being born today to drug-abusing families make these changes urgent. What changes would you recommend?

Characteristics of Black Children in Foster Care

Child factors	City					Total population
	Detroit	Houston	Miami	New York	Seattle	
Emotional/behavioral problem of child	55%	66%	57%	66%	68%	62%
Mental retardation of child	9%	14%	17%	7%	2%	9%
Health or handicap of child	7%	13%	17%	4%	0%	7%
Child's antisocial behavior	3%	6%	29%	2%	31%	11%
Substance abuse of child	8%	5%	0%	3%	15%	7%
Boarded at hospital	6%	13%	11%	24%	2%	12%
Fetal alcohol syndrome	6%	5%	9%	2%	0%	4%
Child with AIDS	1%	5%	3%	3%	0%	2%
Child runaway	17%	22%	20%	14%	49%	24%
Child truancy	14%	6%	14%	13%	22%	14%
Other child factor	18%	13%	6%	10%	23%	15%
TOTAL NUMBER	88	64	35	91	65	343

Source: National Black Child Development Institute (1989). *Who will care when parents can't?* Washington, DC

One out of every two infants younger than one year has a mother in the work force.

in life they are in child care. What matters is the quality of their child care experiences.

In part, this lack of consensus is due to the lack of well-conceived, longitudinal studies. Some researchers also question the measures used in studying infants in child care, contending that they may not be valid. Recall that to assess attachment, we need to place the infant in a strange situation. Since infants who have spent months in child care have had considerable exposure to "strangers," the Strange Situation Procedure may not evoke in them typical attachment behaviors (Clarke-Stewart, 1989).

Also, researchers are beginning to realize that children in out-of-home care experience vastly different family lives. Some infants, for example, grow up in families that experience a great deal of stress; their parents may not be able to appropriately care for them, which may account for the infants' difficulty in establishing an attachment relationship. Reviewing the literature on infant child care, Gamble and Zigler (1986) found indications that (1) out-of-home care during the first year of life increases the likelihood of insecure parent/infant attachment in families experiencing significant life stresses, and (2) an insecure attachment in infancy makes the child more vulnerable to stresses encountered later in life.

A few studies have investigated the actual effects of maternal employment on the baby's development. These studies focus specifically on parent/infant interaction. Cohen (1978), for instance, observed the interactions of employed and nonemployed mothers and their infants in a laboratory setting. She found differences in the manner in which the mothers interacted with their infants during the first year of life. But when the same babies were 21 months old, she observed more positive interactions among nonemployed mothers and their infants. However, a greater proportion of the employed mothers were single and thus likely to be generally under more stress. Thus the stress may have accounted for the differences, rather than the mothers' employment status.

Other studies (Hock, 1980; Pistrang, 1984) indicate that some working mothers of young infants experience high levels of stress as they attempt to juggle work and family responsibilities. Especially if their babies are premature or difficult to care for, these mothers are less able to relate to the baby in a sensitive manner (Harwood, 1985; Crnic et al., 1983; 1984). Despite these difficulties and their possible negative effects on the babies, many mothers have to work for financial reasons (Louis Harris Associates, 1989). The only option for these parents is to place the infant in someone else's care.

Parental-leave policies Developmental psychologists and policymakers are concerned because out-of-home care for infants is the sole option available to many working couples and single parents. As we learned in Chapter 1, in most industrialized countries, parents of young infants are eligible for paid leaves of absence provided by law expressly so that parents can look after their babies if they so desire (Zigler & Frank, 1988; Kamerman & Kahn, 1988). In a study of European parental-leave policies, Allen (1985) found that in Sweden, West Germany, and France, parents have a choice between two kinds of arrangements for the care of the newborn. One parent can take advantage of a paid infant-care leave supported by the employer or a social insurance fund, or both parents can continue to work, in which case provisions for high-quality child care are made (see Figure 7.4).

In the United States, however, there are no national parental-leave policies—but not for lack of effort by many developmental psychologists and advocates for children and families. In fact, for several years, attempts have been made to pass family leave legislation that would require businesses to allow employees to take a leave of absence from work to care for a newborn, a newly adopted child, or a child (or other dependent, perhaps a parent) who is ill. Under this proposed law, employers would not be required to pay employees who are on leave but would have to guarantee their job (Finn-Stevenson & Trczinski, 1991).

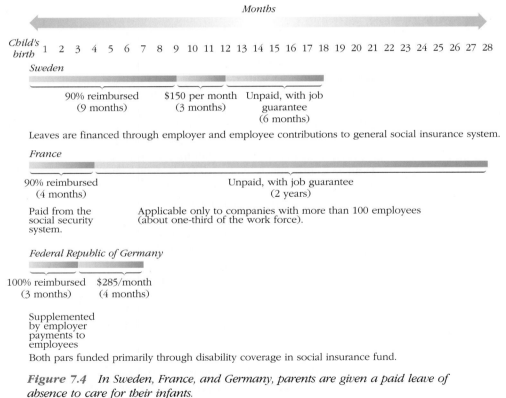

Figure 7.4 *In Sweden, France, and Germany, parents are given a paid leave of absence to care for their infants.*

Source: Adapted from "Durations of Funding Sources of Parental Leaves in Sweden, France, and the Federal Republic of Germany." Reprinted from *The Networker, 6, 4,* by permission of *The Networker* and Joseph P. Allen.

Although legislation calling for family leave has been introduced in Congress several times, it has yet to pass. Several states have made some progress in this regard, however. As you can see in Table 7.3 and Table 7.4, in states like Connecticut and New Jersey, employees who have a newborn, or whose baby or parent is seriously ill and needs constant care, can take a few weeks' leave. In states where such laws do not yet exist, some large corporations still have liberal leave policies (see Chapter 1). However, many individuals work for smaller businesses, and for them and their dependents, lack of a leave policy is a problem.

TABLE 7.3 Job Guaranteed Leave, Mandated Leave in the Public Sector, Maternity/Disability Leave

State	Length of leave	Coverage	Health benefit continuation	Eligibility requirement
Florida (effective date: 1979)	Up to 6 months' leave for women after birth; up to 4 months for adoption	State agencies: service, select exempt, & senior management employees	No	Not addressed
North Carolina (effective date: 2/1/88)	For period of physical disability	State agencies	Employee can choose to pay premium	Permanent full-time, part-time, trainee, and probationary employees
Parental (for birth or adoption—both parents eligible) and medical leave				
Pennsylvania (effective date: 12/15/86)	6 months	State and its agencies	No	Permanent employees
Family leave (for birth or adoption, or the serious illness of a child, spouse, or parent)				
North Dakota (effective date: 1/1/90)	4 months per year	State agencies	Discretionary, employee may be required to pay costs	1 year minimum at an average of 20 hours per week; leave prorated for part-time employees
Oklahoma (effective date: 8/20/89)	Unspecified	State agencies	Employee can choose to pay premium	6 months minimum
West Virginia (effective date: 7/7/89)	12 weeks per 12-month period	State employees, schools	Employer continues group health insurance; employee pays premium cost	12 consecutive weeks
Family and medical leave				
Connecticut (effective date: 7/1/88)	24 weeks in 2 years	State and its agencies	Employer pays	Permanent employees, 6 months minimum

Source: Finn-Stevenson, M., & Trczinski, E. (1991). *American Journal of Orthopsychiatry.*

TABLE 7.4 Mandated Leave in the Private and Public Sector, Maternity/Disability Leave

State	Length of leave	Minimum number of employees	Health benefit continuation	Eligibility requirement
California (effective date: 1/20/80)	Reasonable leave up to 4 months	5 or more employees	No	Not addressed
Hawaii (effective date: 11/15/82)	Reasonable leave	One or more employees	No	Not addressed
Iowa (effective date: 7/1/87)	Up to 8 weeks	4 or more employees	No	Not addressed
Kansas (effective date: 1/1/74)	Reasonable leave	4 or more employees	No	Not addressed
Louisiana (effective date: 9/1/87)	Reasonable leave up to 4 months; only 6 weeks' leave for normal pregnancy or childbirth (no job guarantee)	26 or more employees	No	Not addressed
Massachusetts (effective date: 10/17/72)	8 weeks for female employee for birth or adoption of a child under age 3	6 or more employees	No	3 consecutive months as a full-time employee or completion of probationary period
Montana (effective date: 9/14/84)	Reasonable leave	One or more employees	No	Not addressed
New Hampshire (effective date: 11/15/84)	For period of physical disability	6 or more employees	No	Not addressed
Oregon (effective date: 10/3/89)	For a reasonable period if such leave can be reasonably accommodated	25 or more employees	No	Not addressed
Tennessee (effective date: 1/1/88)	Up to 4 months	100 or more employees	Employee may be required to pay for benefit continuation	12 consecutive months as a full-time employee
Vermont (effective date: 7/1/89)	12 weeks (only covers women, but can include time after disability)	10 or more employees	Employee may be required to pay for benefit continuation	1 year minimum for an average of 30 hours per week
Washington (effective date: 10/28/73)	Reasonable period	8 or more employees	No	Not addressed
Parental leave (for birth or adoption—both parents eligible)				
Minnesota (effective date: 8/1/87)	6 weeks	21 or more employees	Employee can choose to pay premium	12 months minimum at 20 or more hours per week

TABLE 7.4 *(continued)*

State	Length of leave	Minimum number of employees	Health benefit continuation	Eligibility requirement
Parental leave (for birth or adoption—both parents eligible)				
Oregon (effective date: 1/1/88)	12 weeks per child	25 or more employees	No	90 days; temporary and seasonal workers excluded
Rhode Island (effective date: 7/1/87)	13 weeks within a 2-year period (includes leave for serious illness of a child)	50 or more employees (private); 30 or more (city, town, or municipal agency); state and its agencies	Employee pays during leave; employer refunds premium on employee's return	Not addressed
Washington (effective date: 9/1/89)	12 weeks within 24 months (includes leave for terminal illness of child)	100 or more employees	Employee can choose to pay premium	52 weeks at 35 or more hours per week
Family leave (for birth or adoption, or the serious illness of a child, spouse, or parent)				
New Jersey (effective date: 1990)	12 weeks within 24 months	100 or more employees (first year); 75 or more (second and third year); 50 or more thereafter	Employer pays	12 months minimum for at least 1000 hours in the 12 months before leave
Family and medical leave				
Connecticut (effective date: 7/1/90)	12 weeks combined within 24 months for both family and medical leave; increasing to 16 weeks by 1993	250 or more employees (first year); decreasing to 75 or more by 1993	No	12 months minimum for at least 1000 hours in the 12 months before leave
District of Columbia (effective date: 4/1/91)	16 weeks within 24 months for family leave; 16 weeks within 24 months for medical leave	50 or more for first three years; 20 or more thereafter		
Rhode Island (effective date: 7/12/90)	13 weeks combined within 24 months for both family and medical leave	50 or more employees (private); 30 or more (city, town, or municipal agency); state and its agencies	Employee pays during leave; employer refunds premium on employee's return	Not addressed

Source: Finn-Stevenson, M., & Trczinski, E. (1991). *American Journal of Orthopsychiatry.*

Relationships with Others

Infants and Their Fathers

Infants establish relationships with others in their social world, including their father, siblings, grandparents, aunts, and uncles. Since researchers are only now beginning to look beyond the mother/infant relationship, studies on other relationships are relatively scarce (Lewis, 1987).

The research on fatherhood is an example. Although developmental psychologists acknowledge that the father is physically present during infancy, they have only recently begun to investigate his role in the infant's life (Lamb, 1981; Parke, 1981).

Hodapp and Mueller (1982) suggest that there are at least three reasons for this general lack of research interest in the father. First, the mother has traditionally assumed the role of the primary caretaker. In accordance with sex-role stereotypes, this was considered appropriate. Second, researchers, influenced by the prevailing social climate, have concentrated on the mother's relationship with the infant. They have focused on breast-feeding and the hormonal changes associated with nurturance. Finally, both psychoanalytic and behavioral theories, which no longer dominate the field of developmental psychology, highlight the mother's role in the infant's life. But societal changes—along with the current emphasis among researchers on studying children within their entire social network (Bronfenbrenner, 1977; Belsky, Lerner, & Spanier, 1984; Weinraub, Brooks, & Lewis, 1977)—have resulted in a wave of studies on father/infant interactions. These studies have shown that babies interact with their fathers and also form an attachment to them (Lamb, 1981).

Because of the new interest in the father/infant relationship, researchers are beginning to acquire specific data about how fathers care for and play with their children, and how much time fathers and infants spend together. The research is new and therefore not yet entirely conclusive. It does appear, however, that although it is becoming increasingly socially acceptable for fathers to take some responsibility for their infant's care, the actual amount of time most fathers and infants spend together is still limited. In a review of this research, Parke (1981) notes that fathers do not spend as much time caring for their infants and playing with them as mothers do; in most families, the mother is totally responsible for the infant's care. Some fathers have never even changed diapers! Nevertheless, in some families the father takes the primary responsibility for childrearing while the mother works. Pruett (1987), who studied these fathers, notes that although they enjoy caring for their children, they feel that society in general has not yet accepted their nontraditional role.

When fathers do care for their infants, they appear to be as competent as mothers (Parke & O'Leary, 1976) and as sensitive to the babies' cues (Parke & Sawin, 1976). Also, the babies respond to their father's care. In comparing the amount of milk consumed by bottle-fed infants fed by the father and the mother, Parke and Sawin (1976) found that the babies consumed nearly identical amounts of milk. In another comparison of father/infant and mother/infant interactions, researchers discovered that when fathers and infants played together, their interactions followed the same attention/withdrawal pattern described in our discussion of the mother/infant interaction (Yogman et al., 1977).

A father may not spend as much time as the mother in the routine care of the baby, but research indicates that he is as capable of performing the job.

Whereas father/infant interactions are similar in structure to mother/infant interactions, and fathers and infants do form attachments (Lamb, 1978b; Schaffer & Emerson, 1964), important differences seem to characterize the father/infant relationship in general. First, many interactions occur in the context of play. Although most fathers interact less with their infants, the average father spends a greater percentage of his time with the baby in playful, highly arousing interaction (Parke, 1978; Lamb, 1978b; Belsky, Gilstrap, & Rovine, 1984). Moreover, the father is less likely to actually take care of the infant, although he is as able as the mother. When fathers interact with their babies, it is usually to play.

Second, there are differences between how fathers and mothers play with their infants. Yogman et al. (1977) found that fathers tend to be more physical in their interactions with their 2- to 3-month-old infants, and they tap the infants rhythmically or play poking games with them more. Mothers are more verbal; they tend to speak to their infants often and to engage them in vocal games. The differences between the interactions of fathers and mothers persist as the infants grow older. In studies of infants 7 to 13 months old (Lamb, 1977) and 15 to 30 months old (Clarke-Stewart, 1978a), researchers established that mothers are more likely to play peek-a-boo and pat-a-cake, whereas fathers engage in more physical rough-and-tumble games, especially with sons. Tiffany Field (1978) further notes that even fathers who are the primary caretakers engage in more physical play with their infants than mothers do. Male monkeys are also more likely than female monkeys to engage in physical play with their offspring (Suomi, 1977). This seems to suggest that males in general are predisposed to physical play.

Cross-cultural studies confirm these findings. Greenbaum and Landau (1982) observed middle- and lower-class Israeli parents interacting with infants 2, 7, and 11 months of age. Regardless of social class, mothers were more likely to engage in verbal interactions, whereas fathers tended to be physical in their interactions, even with very young babies. Studies on Israeli parents in a kibbutz, where both parents work and a caregiver looks after the child, also revealed the same differences between mothers' and fathers' interactions (Sagi et al., 1985).

The father's inclusion in the study of infancy does more than give researchers another interesting topic to observe. Pedersen, Anderson, and Cain (1980) and

Belsky (1981) point out that the study of the father's role is important because it emphasizes the *family system* comprised of mother, father, and baby, leading researchers to study joint parental influences on the infant. Alison Clarke-Stewart (1978a) suggests that there are complex reciprocal parent/child influences in mother-to-child-to-father-to-mother interaction. Her study reported that the mother's stimulating involvement with the baby promotes secure emotional development and enhances the child's intellectual status, which increases the father's interest and involvement in parenting. As a result, the mother is encouraged to become still more involved with the infant.

Belsky (1981) further points out that researchers are now also looking into the infant's effect on the husband/wife relationship. This study should also yield valuable insights into how the marital relationship affects parenting and thus the infant's development. These insights will be important for what they can reveal about early human development. Despite enormous upheavals in family life during the last decade, the mother-father-child family remains the primary context for the infant's first relationships and initial stages of development.

Peer Relations

The new research focus on studying infants within their broad social setting has had another interesting result: it has led to investigations of how infants relate to their age-mates. Of course, in the 1930s several studies were conducted on peer relations in infancy. But interest lapsed until the 1970s, when it was revived by the steadily increasing number of infants placed in some form of group care. Thus infant-to-infant interaction has become an important phenomenon that offers researchers an opportunity to study peer relations.

Recent studies suggest that infants are interested in and respond to other infants (Hartup, 1983). In fact, even at birth they respond to other neonates' cries, more so than to those of older children (Martin & Clark, 1982). At a slightly older age, infants seem to accept unfamiliar peers readily and are less fearful of them than of unfamiliar adults (Lewis & Brooks, 1974). But how do infants of the same age interact? Mueller and Vandell (1979) suggest that peer interactions in infancy follow a developmental sequence. Initially, infants younger than 3 months simply look at other infants. At 3 to 4 months of age, they try to touch each other and by 6 months they smile at one another. As infants mature and become more mobile, they approach and follow their age-mates. Hay, Nash, and Pedersen (1983) found that when 6-month-olds see each other for the first time, they tend to tug at or poke each other. They do not seem to mind such actions, however, because they usually do not fuss or withdraw from the situation.

True social exchanges between infants begin around 1 year of age and follow a developmental pattern (Mueller & Lucas, 1975). First, object-focused interactions occur; the infants seem more interested in an object they are playing with than with other infants. In playing with a pull-toy train, for example, one infant might pull and the other might toot, but neither one tries to interact with the other. Slightly older infants play contingency games in which one infant might say "da," and the other might laugh; they may repeat this sequence several times. (In contingency games one child acts while the other responds in some manner to the act.) Finally, when infants are approximately 20 months old, a stage of complementary interchanges occurs. Each child takes turns running and chasing the other child or offering and receiving toys in a reciprocal, coordinated manner.

Chapter 10 will show you that, as the children grow older, peer interactions become more complex and peers assume an increasingly large role in their lives.

Summary

Infants possess far greater physiological and intellectual capabilities than previously suspected. They are also social beings, born with the ability to attract people and the desire to be close to them, and they are well prepared to interact with and influence their caregivers by gazing at them, smiling, and then averting their gaze. Research on mother/infant interactions has shown that when mothers or other adults are communicating with a baby, they behave so that they accommodate the baby's capabilities.

As mother and baby communicate with and interact with each other, they become increasingly attuned to each other's characteristics and needs. The infant learns the basic cues and conventions governing human social behavior. The mother becomes increasingly confident of her ability to care for the baby and interpret his behavioral cues. By relating to and interacting with his mother in mutually satisfying ways, the infant acquires a sense of trust. He realizes that the world is a warm, safe place and that he can establish a strong, enduring attachment to his mother.

The infant's attachment to the mother, which occurs in phases, is strongest when the infant is about 8 months old. During that time she experiences stranger anxiety and separation anxiety. Researchers have also discovered individual differences in attachment. Some infants are securely attached; others display anxious and avoidant attachments indicative of disturbances in the mother/infant relationship. These problems may be due either to the baby's or to the mother's characteristics. They may also be due to life stresses experienced by the mother and a lack of support systems, such as family members, neighbors, or friends.

Researchers emphasize the importance of attachment, noting that it influences other aspects of development. They have found that baby monkeys deprived of an opportunity to become attached to an adult monkey exhibit bizarre behaviors later in life. Human infants also need an opportunity to establish a warm human relationship in order to develop normally. But this relationship does not have to be with their biological mother. What is important is that the infant experience consistency and continuity of care.

Infants placed in foster care often do not receive continuity of care, especially if the authorities place them in several foster homes during their childhood years. Infants of working mothers are also vulnerable, depending on the type of day care they receive and their mother's ability to give them sensitive care. Some psychologists have found that, although employed and nonemployed mothers generally interact with their infants in similar ways, the mother's employment is often associated with high levels of stress that may interfere with the mother/infant relationship.

The majority of the research on social and emotional development involves the infants' relationship with their mother, but infants also interact with others, most notably their father. Although just as capable of providing nurturant and sensitive care, fathers generally spend less time with their infants. Most often fathers play with their babies instead of providing routine care. Babies also play with other babies if they have an opportunity to do so.

IV The Preschool Years

T hink of one word that characterizes the preschool child. "Play" is probably the one that pops to mind. Preschoolers are always playing, it seems. Before the 1960s, researchers attached little importance to the preschool period; they saw the early childhood years as a time of frivolous play with little or no developmental value. We now realize that play is of crucial importance. It is the medium through which children gain much of their knowledge; it is their equivalent of work. Children strengthen their cognitive skills through play and become increasingly capable of understanding and dealing with the world around them.

8 Physical Development During the Preschool Years

Progress in Physical Growth and Motor Development

After she is able to walk, Emily goes on to develop a wide variety of fundamental motor skills. She and her age-mates can now climb, jump, and throw things—just for the sheer joy of knowing that they can do it. This progress in physical development also helps preschool children become increasingly independent, as they develop a sense of competence. They become more adept at feeding themselves and eventually acquire the muscular strength and coordination needed to undress and dress by themselves, to control their bowels and bladder, and to acquire such fine-motor skills as writing and drawing. During these years, they also begin to assert their individuality and think of themselves as more grown-up. Emily surprises her parents by refusing their help with dressing and other tasks, and she suddenly announces that she is no longer a baby!

In part, Emily's increased awareness is related to changes in her appearance and body proportions. During the preschool years, children lose some features that are characteristic of infants, such as bent legs and a protruding stomach, and their body proportions increasingly approach those of adults. Each individual's genetic blueprint governs these changes in physical growth and development. However, environmental factors such as adequate nutrition and health care are also fundamental aspects of growth and development. Many preschool children have access to health care and good nutrition, but many other preschoolers in this country do not. Although we have made progress in ensuring children's well-being through immunizations and other preventive health measures, the United States still lags far behind other nations in matters pertaining to children's health. Childhood deaths due to injuries, for example, are much higher in the United States than in other industrialized countries. These injuries—resulting primarily from motor vehicle crashes, fires, falls, and drowning—are not random; they occur in highly predictable patterns. If we know about the factors leading to childhood injuries, we can help prevent them. Before discussing these issues, let us first examine the course of normal physical growth and motor development.

Physical Growth

During the preschool years physical growth is not as rapid as during infancy, and some of the drama and excitement of seeing the child acquire new skills almost daily is gone. Yet if we compare the 2-year-old at the beginning of the preschool period with the 6-year-old he eventually becomes, we realize that the changes in physical development during this time are striking indeed. These changes facilitate his transition from infant to child, and they include weight and height gains, skeletal maturation, and brain growth.

Weight, height, and body proportions Gains in weight and height clearly show that growth in the preschool years is much slower than in infancy. During the first two years of life, infants quadruple their birth weight and more than double their height. But each year between the ages of 2 and 6, the average North American child only gains 4 to 5 pounds and grows about 3 inches (see Figures 8.1 and 8.2). Thus, by age 6, the child weighs, on the average, 45 pounds and measures about 43 inches. Of course, there are many variations in weight and height. Some 6-year-olds

can weigh as much as 50 pounds or as little as 35 pounds. Others are close to 50 inches tall or only slightly over 40 inches tall (National Center for Health Statistics, 1976).

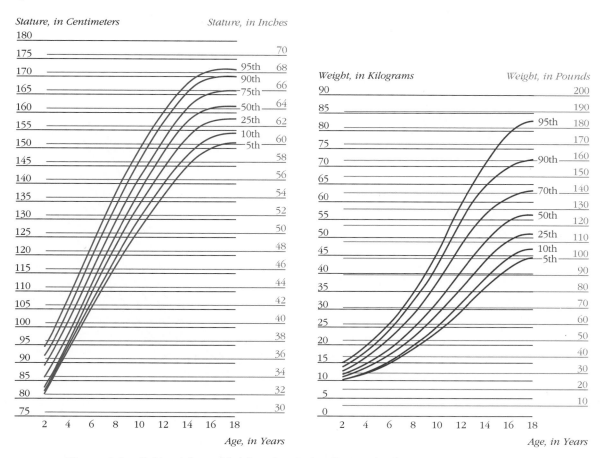

Figure 8.1 *Girls' weight and height gains during the preschool years.*

Source: Uncompiled data on height and weight gains by the National Center for Health Statistics, 1976, Washington, D.C.

Because of this slower rate of growth, children eat much less for their size than they did as infants, a fact that often alarms parents and prompts them to seek medical advice. However, there is nothing abnormal about the change in the amount of food the children consume. During the preschool period, and also during the middle childhood years when growth is also slow, they do not need as many calories to sustain growth. Later, during adolescence when growth once again speeds up, appetite changes as teenagers consume enormous quantities of food and put quite a dent in their parents' food budget (U.S. Department of Agriculture, 1982).

For preschool children, the gain in weight and especially in height is important, because they equate weighing more and growing taller with becoming older. But these gains are not as significant as the change in body proportions, which, in part, accounts for the remarkable transformation from infant to child. Between the ages of 2 and 3, children still have the protruding stomach, swayback, bent legs, and relatively large head characteristic of infancy. At that age, they are often referred to as *toddlers;* that is, they are no longer babies but not quite children either. Even-

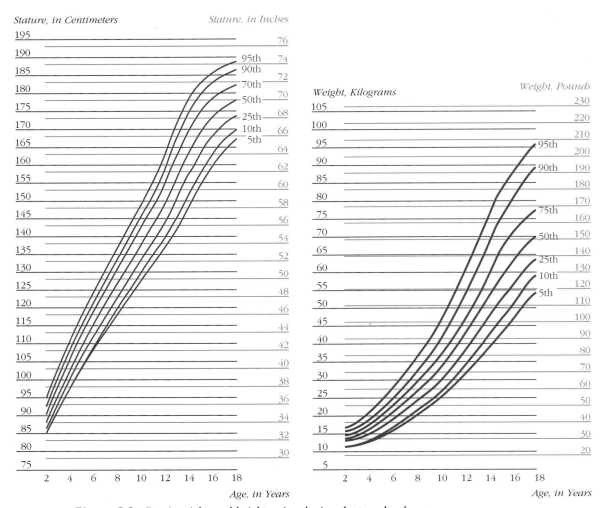

Figure 8.2 *Boys' weight and height gains during the preschool years.*
Source: Uncompiled data on height and weight gains by the National Center for Health Statistics, 1976, Washington, D.C.

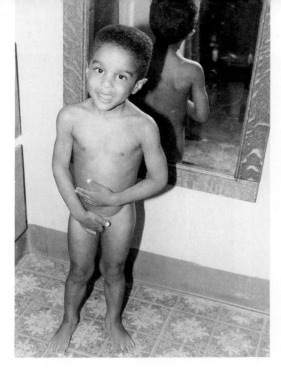

Between the ages of three and six the child loses baby fat, becoming taller and thinner. These physical changes are important, signaling that the child is no longer a baby.

tually, between the ages of 3 and 6, they lose their baby fat and become taller and thinner. At the same time, because of the increase in height, the size of the head lessens in proportion to body size, so you can see that they are also becoming more adultlike in their body proportions.

Skeletal maturity   Several internal changes also take place during this time. One change is related to skeletal maturity, which means that the bones become longer, thicker, and harder. During the prenatal period, skeletal development begins as cartilage, which is gradually replaced by bone in a process known as *ossification*. This process, which continues after birth and is not complete until late adolescence, occurs rapidly during the preschool period, enabling the child to participate in activities that require strength.

Physicians use the child's **bone age** (or **skeletal age**) to assess whether physical development is progressing normally. They can determine bone age by X-raying the child's hand and comparing the rate of ossification with ossification norms for the particular age. Knowledge of bone age is valuable for predicting the child's eventual height. This information is especially important in cases of children who are either too tall or too short, because then physicians must determine whether medical intervention is necessary. For example, a 4-year-old girl who is much taller than her peers may have the bone age of a 6- or 7-year-old; but her eventual height would be within the normal range. A 6-year-old boy who is very short may have the bone age of a 4-year-old, however, his eventual height would also be within the normal range. But some children need medical treatment or further assessment, because their bone X-rays reveal that their growth would be abnormal (Tanner et al., 1975). This usually means that they would be too short. Short stature is relatively rare, occurring in 1 out of 10,000 births and affecting more boys than girls. It can be caused by a growth hormone deficiency or a thyroid disorder in which the thyroid gland does not produce sufficient amounts of the hormone thyroxine.

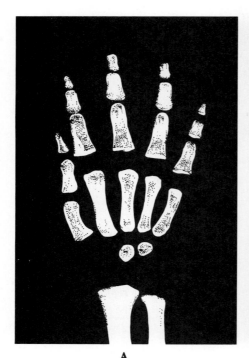
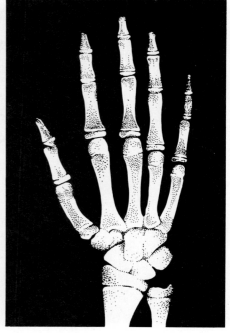

A   B

X-rays of the hands of two 14-year-old boys. The bone age of the hand on the left is 12 years; the bone age of the hand on the right is 16 years.

Tanner, J. M. (1978). *Foetus Into Man*, Cambridge, Mass.: Harvard University Press, p. 80, Fig.29.

Brain Development

Another important internal change that occurs during these years is the growth and maturation of the brain, which facilitates the acquisition of language skills and increases the child's ability to master increasingly more complex motor tasks.

During the prenatal period and infancy, brain growth is evident in the increase in brain weight. Much of this increase occurs before age 2, at which time the brain weighs 75% of its adult weight. During the preschool years, there is also a gain in brain weight. As a result, by the time the child is 5 years old, the brain has attained 90% of its adult weight; and by age 10, the brain is at 95% of its adult weight. However, these increases in brain weight are the result of different changes. During the prenatal period and early infancy, the number of brain cells increases rapidly; weight gains are due to the increased number of neurons, the brain's basic nerve cells. But subsequent weight gains during the preschool years reflect an increase in the size of neurons due to *myelination*—a process by which a white, fatty substance called myelin forms a sheath around nerve fibers. At the same time, the size of the *glial cells* that support the nerve cells also increases.

Lateralization   Myelination occurs within several functional centers within the brain. The brain is organized into right and left hemispheres. The right hemisphere controls the left part of the body, giving directions to the left ear, eye, hand, and leg. The left hemisphere controls the right side of the body, giving directions to the right ear, eye, hand, and leg (Tyler, 1974). These two hemispheres are not mirror images;

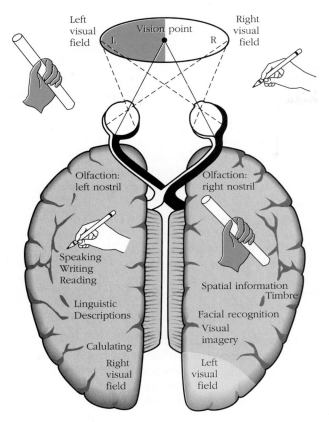

Figure 8.3 *Lateralization of the brain. The right hemisphere, which controls the left side of the body, contains the centers responsible for spatial information and visual imagery. The left hemisphere, which controls the right side of the body, contains the centers for receiving, processing, and producing language. Thus, the left hemisphere codes input of linguistic descriptions; the right hemisphere codes images.*

rather, each hemisphere contains "centers" that control different abilities and functions. The left hemisphere holds the brain centers responsible for receiving, processing, and producing language. The right hemisphere has the centers responsible for spatial information, either visual or tactile, and visual imagery (Tyler, 1974). Thus the left hemisphere codes input in terms of *linguistic descriptions,* whereas the right hemisphere codes *images.*

With age, one hemisphere (described as the dominant hemisphere) will increasingly control certain functions through the process of **lateralization** (Kolb & Wishaw, 1985). Lateralization of the brain is illustrated in Figure 8.3. Studies of the electrical brain patterns of infants reveal differences in functioning between the right and left hemispheres, indicating that lateralization actually begins during the early months of life (Kinsbourne & Hiscock, 1983).

Some researchers contend that people are predominantly left-brain or right-brain dominant. For example, an individual who is good at analyzing situations or problems may be left-brain dominant. Some observers claim that schools should design education on the basis of whether an individual is predominantly left- or right-brained. But according to Springer (1989), this claim is not warranted by research; she emphasizes that both the right and left hemispheres are used together most of the time. In fact, at times one hemisphere can fill in for the other. Some people with left-brain injuries who have lost their ability to speak (a left-brain function) still retain the ability to sing (a right-brain function). Taking advantage of this differentiation, scientists are trying to teach stroke victims to communicate by using the right brain's musical center.

This division of labor, so to speak, allows the brain to work efficiently, because an individual can master more skills if each part of the brain is responsible for a specific function or type of knowledge. Naturally, there are disadvantages as well, the main one being the brain's inability to compensate for loss or damage to one of its parts. Thus a victim of brain damage due to injury or stroke may lose the ability to speak, depending on the part of the brain that is damaged. If such an injury occurs before early adolescence, when the brain's speech center completes maturation, the right hemisphere might take over this function, permitting the individual to speak normally despite the injury (Lenneberg, 1967). This greater plasticity of the brain before early adolescence applies to other functional centers as well. During childhood, recovery from a variety of forms of brain damage is possible, provided one functional center can take over or compensate for the loss of the damaged center's functions.

Implications for language acquisition   The functional centers responsible for language skills begin to develop early in life. Their maturation, which takes several years to complete, is associated with **myelogenetic cycles,** during which myelination occurs to particular functional centers within the brain. The protective myelin sheath that coats the nerve fibers enhances their ability to send and receive impulses or signals. Lecours (1975) notes that three myelogenetic cycles seem to be associated with increased language ability. The first cycle, which involves the brainstem and starts before birth, is related to the infant's ability to produce sounds. The second cycle, which starts around birth and rapidly continues until about age 4, is related to the acquisition of language skills. The third myelogenetic cycle, which involves the upper cortex, is not complete until early adolescence.

Implications for motor development   Another change that contributes to brain maturation during the preschool years is the myelination of nerve fibers used to control voluntary movement. Myelination of these fibers is complete around age 3 or 4 (Tanner, 1978; Lecours, 1982); hence, the preschool child's increased capability to master the fine-motor skills needed to hold a pencil or tie shoelaces.

Development of Motor Skills

The development of the brain and the growth in height that occur during these years enable the child to experiment with a variety of motor movements and to acquire and gradually refine many motor skills (see Table 8.1). Two kinds of motor skills develop during early childhood: **gross-motor** skills, involving the use of large muscles, and **fine-motor** skills, involving the use of the small muscles of the hands and fingers. Becoming proficient in these skills is one of the child's most important tasks; and it usually occurs in the context of play. Since the acquisition of motor skills depends on physical growth and practice, the process occurs gradually. At the beginning of the preschool period, children are still quite clumsy, but by the time they reach school age, they are quite coordinated and become increasingly more graceful in their motor performance (Wickstrom, 1977; Skinner, 1979).

Because control of the large muscles develops first, gross-motor skills are easier for the young child to master, and progress can be quite impressive as long as the child has the opportunity to practice them (Skinner, 1979). Fine-motor skills depend on brain maturation and take longer to acquire because the preschool child lacks the muscular control needed to execute them. For this reason, 2- and 3-year-olds rarely sit still at a table or a desk; they prefer to run wildly across the room, climb a chair, or push large objects—activities requiring the use of large muscles. Even though they do not have complete control over their fine-motor muscles, they often enjoy painting or drawing. Also, they make many attempts to master such tasks as cutting paper with a pair of scissors or putting together pieces of a puzzle, often giving their full concentration to the task. Eventually, children develop proficiency in many fine-motor skills; by the time they reach school age, they have greater control over the manipulative tasks involved in dressing and undressing and can draw and even write with greater ease.

Children can practice and experiment with a variety of motor skills within the context of play (Hughes, 1991). Once they master a skill, they use it to become proficient in other tasks. For example, after learning how to hold a pencil, preschool children show a consistent, age-related progression from scribbles to recognizable forms such as circles and lines to representational figures. In other words, they begin by scribbling, but over the course of the preschool period, they begin to make pictures. Rhoda Kellogg (1970) notes that these changes in the ability to draw occur in other cultures as well and reflect brain maturation, which enables children to

This preschool girl is concentrating on using her fine motor skills.

TABLE 8.1 The Sequence and Emergence of Selected Motor Abilities (Left) and Manipulative Abilities (Right)

Movement pattern	Selected abilities	Approximate age of onset
Walking		
Walking involves placing one foot in front of the other while maintaining contact with the supporting surface.	Rudimentary upright unaided gait	13 months
	Walks sideways	16 months
	Walks backwards	17 months
	Walks upstairs with help	20 months
	Walks upstairs alone—follow step	24 months
	Walks downstairs alone—follow step	25 months
Running		
Running involves a brief period of no contact with the supporting surface.	Hurried walk (maintains contact)	18 months
	First true run (nonsupport phase)	2–3 years
	Efficient and refined run	4–5 years
	Speed of run increases	5 years
Jumping		
Jumping takes three forms: (1) jumping for distance; (2) jumping for height; and (3) jumping from a height. It involves a one- or two-foot takeoff with a landing on both feet.	Steps down from low objects	18 months
	Jumps down from object with both feet	2 years
	Jumps off floor with both feet	28 months
	Jumps for distance (about 3 feet)	5 years
	Jumps for height (about 1 foot)	5 years
Hopping		
Hopping involves a one-foot takeoff with a landing on the same foot.	Hops up to three times on preferred foot	3 years
	Hops from four to six times on same foot	4 years
	Hops from eight to ten times on same foot	5 years
	Hops distance of 50 feet in about 11 seconds	5 years
	Hops skillfully with rhythmical alteration	6 years
Galloping		
The gallop combines a walk and a leap with the same foot leading throughout.	Basic but inefficient gallop	4 years
	Gallops skillfully	6 years
Skipping		
Skipping combines a step and a hop in rhythmic alteration.	One-footed skip	4 years
	Skillful skipping (about 20 percent)	5 years
	Skillful skipping for most	6 years

have better control of their hands (see Figure 8.4). In studying children's art, Kellogg found that children go through four stages. Initially, in the *placement stage* they scribble; at about age 3 to 3½, they move to the *shape stage* and begin to create geometric shapes such as circles. Next comes the *design stage* from age 3½ to 4½, when they combine these shapes (for example, they'll draw a cross within a circle). Finally, at about age 4 or 5, they begin a *pictoral stage,* and their drawings appear to represent something: mom and dad, a younger brother, perhaps a house. As they get

TABLE 8.1 *(continued)*

Movement pattern	Selected abilities	Approximate age of onset
Reach, Grasp, Release		
Reaching, grasping and releasing involve making successful contact with an object, retaining it in one's grasp, and releasing it at will.	Primitive reaching behaviors	2–4 months
	Corralling of objects	2–4 months
	Palmar grasp	
Throwing		
Throwing involves imparting force to an object in the general direction of intent.	Body faces target, feet remain stationary, ball thrown with forearm extension only	2–3 years
	Same as above but with body rotation added	3.6–5 years
	Steps forward with leg on same side as the throwing arm	5–6 years
	Mature throwing pattern	6.6 years
	Boys exhibit more mature pattern than girls	6 years and over
Catching		
Catching involves receiving force from an object with the hands, moving from large to progressively smaller balls.	Chases ball; does not respond to aerial ball; responds to aerial ball with delayed arm movements	2 years 2–3 years
	Needs to be told how to position arms	2–3 years
	Fear reaction (turns head away)	3–4 years
	Basket catch using the body	3 years
	Catches using the hands only with a small ball	5 years
Kicking		
Kicking involves imparting force to an object with the foot.	Moves against ball; does not actually kick it	18 months
	Kicks with leg straight and little body movement (kicks *at* the ball)	2–3 years
	Flexes lower leg on backward lift	3–4 years
	Greater backward and forward swing with definite arm opposition	4–5 years
	Mature pattern (kicks *through* the ball)	5–6 years
Striking		
Striking involves imparting force to objects in an overarm, sidearm, or underhand pattern.	Faces object and swings in a vertical plane	2–3 years
	Swings in a horizontal plane and stands to the side of the object	4–5 years
	Rotates the trunk and hips and shifts body weight forward; mature horizontal patterns	5 years 6–7 years

Source: Motor Development and Movement Experiences for Young Children by D. L. Gallahue, p. 65, Table 3.1 and p. 66, Table 3.2. Copyright © 1976, reprinted by permission of John Wiley & Sons, Inc.

older, they add more details to their drawings. Of course, each child develops artistically at an individual pace, and by about age 5, some children develop a unique style of drawing (Gardner, 1980).

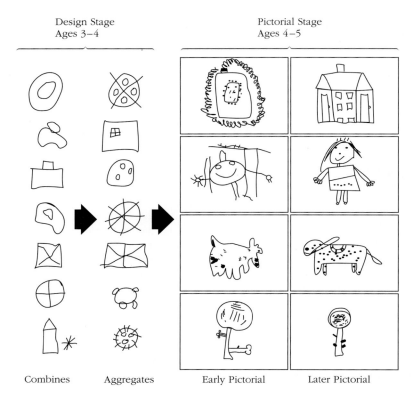

Design Stage
Ages 3–4

Pictorial Stage
Ages 4–5

Combines   Aggregates   Early Pictorial   Later Pictorial

Figure 8.4 *Sequential development in self-taught art. Note the development of the forms in these drawings by 3- to 5-year-olds.*
Source: Adapted from "Understanding Children's Art" by Rhoda Kellogg, May 1967, in *Psychology Today,* 1 (1), pp. 18–19. Reprinted with permission from Psychology Today Magazine. Copyright © 1967 Sussex Publishers, Inc.

In the development of gross-motor skills, a similar progression from simple to more complex use of a skill also occurs (Gallahue, 1982). For example, once children learn to skip, they experiment with skipping on one foot or on alternate feet; they often skip just for the sake of skipping. By school age, skipping becomes part of a variety of games they play with their peers. Thus, in motor development repetitive practice is an initial phase in the mastery of a skill. Once the skill is acquired, it is used for new purposes.

Although practice is important in motor development, young children today do not have sufficient opportunities to do so. The study of their physical activity is just now emerging. Although more research is needed, preliminary findings indicate that, especially among children in child care, youngsters do not engage in physical activities on a daily basis (Seefeldt, 1984). Poest, Williams, Witt, and Atwood (1989; 1990) report the results of observational studies of children in all-day child care and in nursery schools, which the children attended on a part-time basis. They found that children in child care had fewer opportunities to engage in large-muscle exercise, even in all-day child care centers that were well equipped for such activities. The researchers (Poest et al., 1989) suggest that parents and child care providers should plan motor activities for children; they should take the children on frequent outings where they will have opportunities for large-muscle development.

During the preschool period, children's drawing skills show consistent age-related progression from scribbles to recognizable shapes and representational figures.

Sex differences and similarities   Although boys and girls follow similar patterns in motor development during childhood, some underlying physical differences contribute to differences in motor skills performance. For example, on average, boys tend to be more muscular and to lose their baby fat sooner, and they continue to have less body fat during childhood and later life. On the other hand, girls generally mature more rapidly in bone ossification, and certain functional centers in their brains mature at an earlier age (Tanner, 1978). There is quite a bit of overlap at this age, however; some girls are taller and stronger than many boys their age. Since, on average, boys have the advantage in height and strength, they are usually better in such motor skills as throwing, catching, and hitting. Girls, however, are better at fine-motor skills, such as writing, drawing, and skipping, that require coordination and balance rather than strength (Tanner, 1978).

As with all types of skills, however, these sex differences may be related more to differences in the amount of practice and encouragement that adults give children to perform particular skills than to underlying physical differences (Sinclair, 1973). Our society tends to emphasize sex differences (Jacklin, 1989), and adults often treat children on the basis of sex-stereotyped expectations. For example, parents often buy different types of toys for boys and girls (Kacerguis & Adams, 1979), thus encouraging each sex to engage in different types of play. No matter what the reasons may be, boys and girls spend more time practicing those skills they are said to be better at (Harper & Sand, 1975).

Increased Competence in Self-Help Skills

Competency in movement and coordination enables the child to gain greater independence over feeding and other routine activities. Again, there is a progression in the development of self-help skills. At first, children learn to undress themselves; only later do they acquire the ability to dress since this is a more complicated task

One of the six-year-old's great accomplishments is learning to tie shoelaces.

requiring the fine-motor skills used to tie shoelaces or button a blouse. Acquiring the ability to dress is very important for preschool children, and one of the hallmarks of the 6-year-old's development is mastery of the task of tying shoelaces.

Toilet training   Toilet training is another developmental milestone attained during the early part of the preschool period, usually by the time the child is 3. There are individual and sex differences in toilet training: girls are generally toilet-trained at an earlier age, while boys are likely to wet their beds at night longer (Oppel, Harper, & Rider, 1968). Because differences in toilet training may be related to differences in the muscles' maturity, some child psychologists advise parents not to begin toilet training until children are physically mature enough to control the muscles allowing them to retain their feces and urine (McGraw, 1940).

LEARNING FROM OTHER CULTURES

Toilet Training

Other researchers, however, emphasize the cultural relativity of toilet-training readiness, contending that children in some societies achieve toilet training during the first year of life. DeVries and DeVries (1977) note that thanks to a conditioning approach employed by the East African Digo mother, the infant accomplishes night-and-day dryness by 5 to 6 months of age. Beginning when the baby is 2 to 3 weeks old, the mother gradually toilet-trains him by taking him outside the house and placing him in a special position facilitating elimination. The mother follows the procedure day and night each time she senses that her baby has to eliminate (for example, after feeding and before and after naps). While the baby is held in the elimination position, the mother makes a "shuus" sound; eventually, the infant associates the sound with voiding. If the infant voids on hearing the "shuus," the mother rewards him by hugging him, smiling at him, or feeding him. By 5 months of age, the infant learns to communicate his need to urinate by attempting to squat in the appropriate elimination position.

The Digo of East Africa have ideas about toilet training that are markedly different from ours, but they succeed at this undertaking when the child is very young.

The mother uses a similar procedure to teach the baby to move her bowels. Obviously, living conditions in East Africa may be conducive to early toilet training because the infant is not required to use a potty. In addition, the African baby's precocious motor development may also be a factor. All the same, the DeVries' study shows that parental attitudes and practices, as well as societal expectations, influence toilet training. The question is, When should children in our society begin toilet training? On the basis of his clinical practice, Brazelton (1962) recommends a child-oriented approach to toilet training, which should begin at about 18 months when the child is physiologically and psychologically ready. Thus the child is willing to participate in a relatively trouble-free training process. Unfortunately, some parents begin toilet training at an earlier age, normally when the child is only a year old, despite the fact that the later the toilet training begins, the faster the child learns. In addition, many parents scold and punish their child for not mastering toilet training, although it is unnecessary to upset him or to make an issue out of the process since

Toilet training is a gradual process. Even four- and five-year-olds have occasional accidents when they are tired or stressed.

most children become toilet-trained by age 3. Parents should realize that toilet-training is a gradual process; even when a 4- or 5-year-old child has been toilet trained, he is likely to have accidents when he is tired or unduly stressed (Stuart & Prugh, 1960).

Influences on Growth

During the preschool years, physical growth and the acquisition of motor skills follow a predictable course because physical development is largely governed by the genes. Yet there are variations in physical growth and development among children, in particular, differences in weight and height gain. It is not unusual for children to be taller or shorter than their peers. In most cases these variations reflect genetic differences. However, growth differences among children in different countries may also be attributed to differences in nutrition and health care (Miller, Fine, & Adams-Taylor, 1989). For example, when child experts compared a group of impoverished Guatemalan children with a group of relatively well-off American children, they found that the Guatemalans had developmental deficits due to their inferior health care and nutrition (Saco-Pollitt, Pollitt, & Greenfield, 1985). Thus environmental influence on growth is potentially significant.

Malnutrition

There is a close relationship between nutrition and growth and development; nutrients of the right kind and in adequate supply are critical for normal growth. Protein-energy undernutrition, a condition known to limit the potential for growth and development, affects 40% to 60% of children worldwide, and it occurs among American children as well (Lozoff, 1989). Many American children, especially among the poor, are also at risk for other nutritional disorders such as anemia, which results from iron deficiency (National Center for Children in Poverty, 1990; Lozoff, 1988). Many American children also go to bed hungry. A national study found that 5.5 million American children, or one in eight youngsters under 12, live in a household in which there is not enough to eat (Food Research & Action Center, 1991). Protein-energy undernutrition has deleterious effects on the central nervous system (Brozek & Schurch, 1984) and it interferes with the development of adaptive and intellectual capacities, especially if it occurs during the critical periods for brain growth (Birch & Gussow, 1970). Recent studies also suggest that infants who experience undernutrition are likely to have an attention-deficit disorder and poor memory later in their childhood years (Galler, Ramsey, & Solimanon, 1984). In addition, nutritional status affects behavior (Lozoff, 1989) and can result in a reduced ability to fight infectious diseases (Scrimshaw, Taylor, & Gordon, 1968).

Undernutrition during the preschool years also limits skeletal development, resulting in stunted physical growth (Jackson, 1966). This is the reason for the short stature of many children in developing countries where malnutrition is rampant (Meredith, 1978; 1984; Birch & Gussow, 1970). When preschool children experience only a moderate degree of malnutrition for brief periods, the stunting that occurs is usually overcome as soon as the nutritional deficiencies are corrected. However, there are limits to the child's ability to recover from malnutrition (Gyorgy, 1960).

Emotional factors   Although recovery from undernutrition depends partly on physical factors (that is, the extent and duration of malnourishment and the provision of adequate nourishment), emotional factors are also at work and can be even more influential. A classic study of children in two German orphanages illustrates the impact of emotional factors (Widdowson, 1951). Children in the first orphanage were given food supplements to enrich their deficient diets and consumed 20% more calories than children in a similar orphanage. Yet the children in the second orphanage grew more and gained more weight even though they did not receive more food. Observers attributed this outcome to the fact that at the time the food supplement was introduced, a new administrator took charge of the first orphanage. He was a strict disciplinarian, who often distressed the children with unjustified rebukes at mealtime. Interestingly, eight children who may have been the administrator's favorites were not subjected to this stress, and they did benefit from the food supplements. Possibly the stress agitated the other children and caused them to eat less or disturbed their digestive process. Tanner (1978) explains that in some children, stress causes a decrease in the brain's production of growth hormone, which prevents the children from growing.

Other studies attest to the relationship between recovery from nutritional deficiencies and emotional disorders. As Ernesto Pollitt and his colleagues note (Pollitt & Gilmore, 1977; Pollitt, Garza, & Liebel, 1984), it is difficult to separate the physiological effects of malnutrition from social and emotional factors because the selective characteristics of both child and parent affect the parent's caretaking and feeding activities. This, in turn, affects the child's growth. A study by Zeskind and Ramey (1978) underscored this point: Some malnourished children were given food supplements and participated in a supportive child care program involving interaction with other children and adults. These children improved more than a comparison group of malnourished children who were given food supplements but remained at home. Researchers suggest that because malnourished children are socially unresponsive, their mothers become less likely to interact with them, which may cause the children to continue their unresponsive behavior and the mothers to continue to withdraw from them. The group of children in the child care program received supportive interaction because the child care staff cared for them. As a result, their responsivity increased, preventing the cycle from repeating.

Failure to thrive and deprivation dwarfism   A disorder known as **deprivation dwarfism** further illustrates the effects of emotional factors on growth. In this condition, a child receives adequate nutrition but fails to grow normally because he is subjected to emotional abuse and neglect. (In other words, he is not given attention or nurturance and feels that he is not loved or wanted.) This emotional situation inhibits the secretion of adequate amounts of growth hormone (Patton & Gardner, 1963). Often, the pattern of emotional abuse begins in infancy; when it is diagnosed in an infant, it is referred to as **failure to thrive.** Failure to thrive may have physiological roots. For example, the infant may not grow because of a variety of medical problems such as digestive disorders. Physicians who treat these infants usually begin by looking for physiological problems. If they cannot find any and if the child continues to fail to grow, then they begin to look for emotional factors.

Deprivation dwarfism often entails a complex, self-sustaining relationship between parental attitude and the child's behavior. Mothers of these children have often experienced stressful events during their own childhood (Patton & Gardner, 1963) or they may have suffered from later disruptive events, such as a major illness, the death of another child, poverty, or the breakdown of their marriage (Barbero, 1975). Although the condition is related to mothering disorders, certain characteristics of the child may also be contributing factors. Researchers note that some children seem to be especially vulnerable: 20% to 40% of infants who fail to thrive were low-birth-weight babies (Parke & Collmer, 1975). You will recall from discussions in Chapter 4 that such infants are difficult to care for. Lack of responsivity in the infant—whether due to prematurity or other factors—is a contributing factor in establishing an unhappy relationship between mother and infant (Stern, 1985; Brazelton, 1973).

Failure to thrive due to emotional neglect is prevalent among low-income children. Lozoff (1989) notes that an estimated 6% of all children born at medical centers serving low-income families are diagnosed as failure to thrive. The condition is difficult to diagnose; but when a child fails to respond to hormone treatment, physicians suspect emotional maltreatment. Frasier and Rallison (1972) give the example of a preschool child who failed to grow even though she was given growth hormone. Suspecting that emotional factors might be responsible for the problem, the physicians suggested that the child leave the mother and stay with relatives. While she was with her relatives, the child's growth rate was twice what it had been at home. When she returned home, however, her growth rate slowed again. Other researchers (Patton & Gardner, 1963; Gardner, 1972) note that most infants and children suffering from retarded growth due to emotional neglect grow rapidly in the hospital but stop growing and even lose weight when they return home.

DISCUSSION OF SOCIAL ISSUES

Child Maltreatment

Besides emotional abuse, some children are also victims of physical abuse. Many children are mildly spanked from time to time and are not harmed by it. It becomes child abuse, however, when parents continually resort to physical punishment in interactions with their children or when punishment injures the children or threatens their lives (Gelles, 1978; Strauss, 1979; Strauss, Gelles, & Steinmetz, 1980; Gerbner, Ross, & Zigler, 1980). A surprisingly large number of parents assault, batter, or torture their children. Each year over 2000 children are killed by their parents or other caretakers, and over 2 million are badly beaten or otherwise abused (American Humane Association, 1989). As we have seen in previous chapters, child abuse may include any number of transgressions—from **acts of commission,** which refer to physical and sexual assault, to **acts of omission,** which include psychological abuse and neglect. Parents who fail to provide emotional comfort, food, clothing, and shelter are as guilty of abuse as those who physically assault their children (Parke & Collmer, 1975).

Developmental psychologists and other concerned professionals regard child abuse as one of the most difficult social problems to understand. How can parents, who have come to know and love their children, inflict harm on them, even kill them?

Although it is difficult to understand how the loving relationship between parents and child can sometimes take such a tragic turn, maltreatment of children has occurred in the past. Recall from Chapter 2 that in earlier eras children were forced to work long hours and were often abandoned by their parents. Recently, however, the physical abuse of children has become a problem worthy of society's concern. In part this is due to advancements in the use of X-rays, which have enabled physicians to discover and document the consequences of physical punishment and to identify children who are repeatedly abused. The X-rays show recent injuries as well as previous injuries in various stages of healing (Caffey, 1946; Kempe et al., 1962), thus providing forceful evidence of repeated abuse.

Causes of Child Abuse

What causes parents to abuse their children? The answer to this question is important, because once we understand the etiology of child abuse, we can take steps to prevent it. Researchers are just beginning to fathom some of its causes. No single factor accounts for abuse; rather, it is the result of many interrelated factors. Reviewing research on the etiology of child abuse, Belsky (1980) proposes that "child maltreatment is multiply determined by forces at work in the individual, in the family, in the community, and in the culture in which the individual and family are embedded."

Although we may regard child abuse as bizarre behavior, studies show that only about 10% of abusive parents suffer from mental disorders. On the basis of case studies and other research, scientists have said that parents who mistreat their children were mistreated by their parents or are subject to abuse, neglect, or abandonment by their spouses (Rutter, 1979b; Belsky, 1978; Kempe & Kempe, 1978). Many people believe that this history of parental maltreatment is a major reason for child abuse. However, having been abused does not inevitably mean an individual will abuse his or her child. Recent studies suggest that the cycle of abuse is found only in a limited number of families (Kaufman & Zigler, 1986).

Studies on abusive parents further reveal that they have unrealistic expectations of what babies and young children can do. They regard ordinary infant behavior, such as crying or dropping toys or other objects, as intentional wrongdoing, and they attribute children's failure to obey instructions to willful disobedience or even malice. These parents become upset, for example, when their 2-year-old is unable to sit still for a long time or when, unable to drink from a glass of milk, she spills it.

Abusive parents also lack effective child management techniques. Trickett and Kuczynski's (1986) study of lower-middle and working-class families found that although both abusive and nonabusive parents resort to physical punishment when children misbehave, abusive parents use physical punishment more often and utilize far harsher methods. The same study also found that abusive parents do not provide a reason for punishment but administer harsh beatings no matter what the transgression.

At times, the child's characteristics may trigger abuse. The research on the possibility that there are "abuse-provoking" child characteristics is, as yet, inconclusive (Ammerman, 1990). However, researchers suggest that some children may provoke frustration to the point that they elicit abuse. For example, parents are more likely to abuse a particularly troublesome child. Low-birth-weight babies who are hard to handle and to calm may be more likely to be abused than other infants (Egeland & Brunquette, 1979). Children demanding greater amounts of attention

Child Maltreatment Rates (per 1000 children), by Type of Maltreatment and Family Income, 1986

Type of maltreatment	Family income	
	Less than $15,000	$15,000 or more
All maltreatment	54.0	7.9
All abuse	19.9	4.4
Physical abuse	10.2	2.5
Sexual abuse	4.8	1.1
Emotional abuse	6.1	1.2
All neglect	36.8	4.1
Physical neglect	22.6	1.9
Educational neglect	10.1	1.3
Emotional neglect	6.9	1.5
Fatal injury	0.03	0.01
Serious injury/impairment	6.00	0.90
Moderate injury/impairment	30.90	5.50
Probable injury/impairment	5.40	0.90
Endangered	11.70	0.60

Source: Study of National Incidence and Prevalence of Child Abuse and Neglect by the U.S. Department of Health and Human Services, 1988, Washington, D.C.: Government Printing Office, p. 5–29.

(for example, mentally retarded or temperamentally difficult children) may also be more likely to be victims of abuse (Belsky, 1978).

Researchers have also found that child abuse often occurs when the parent is overburdened with the responsibilities and stresses of daily life. Abusive parents are often unemployed. They have to move frequently and have trouble establishing community ties or getting to know their neighbors. Thus, they have no relatives or close friends to turn to for help in times of stress (Garbarino, 1977). Researchers have found that several other factors also increase the likelihood of parental abusive behavior: alcohol abuse, legal problems, large family size, overcrowded and inadequate housing, or marital discord (Green, 1976; Steinmetz, 1977). In fact, as Albee (1980) and Garbarino (1977) point out, the more stressful the life conditions of the family, the more likely the occurrence of abuse. Thus, a great deal of child abuse frequently occurs among low-income families, because the stress of poverty creates a climate for abuse. As you can see in the table, the incidence of all types of child maltreatment is seven times greater among families earning less than $15,000 a year than among those with higher incomes (U.S. Department of Health and Human Services, 1988). Abuse is not confined to poor families; some middle-class parents also mistreat their children (Gil, 1970; 1976). Gauging the extent of abuse among middle-class families is difficult, however, because it is rarely reported.

Services That Prevent Child Abuse

In an effort to address the multiple causes of child abuse, researchers call for multidisciplinary, coordinated services that focus on the *prevention* of abuse as well as on the treatment of both parents and children. These services include therapeutic programs to raise the parents' low self-esteem and respite care programs where parents can leave their children at times of stress. Informal support groups and other services such as Parents Anonymous provide the nurturance and understanding that the parents have long needed. In addition, programs supporting family life (for example, ones that provide adequate child care services) can alleviate stress and thereby decrease the incidence of abuse (Zigler, 1980).

On the basis of these research recommendations, child welfare agencies in several states have developed family support and education initiatives designed to prevent child abuse. For instance, the Ounce of Prevention program is a collaborative effort of the Illinois Department of Children and Family Services and the Pittway Corporation. Its goal is to provide support services to families with young children, including parent education classes that focus on effective child-management techniques, child care programs, medical services, and job training. The community-based services are delivered in a variety of locations, such as churches, social service agencies, medical clinics, and schools. Since the program focuses on prevention, it is open to all families, regardless of income; but it serves primarily teenage parents, single parents, and low-income parents. Other similar family support services are available in Arkansas, Vermont, Oregon, and Iowa (Harvard Family Research Project, 1991). These programs include several different types of support services and an essential feature: program evaluation. That is, the staff continually monitor the programs to ensure that they meet families' needs (Weiss & Jacobs, 1988).

Although family support services are promising approaches to the prevention of child abuse, such efforts need to bring about changes in cultural attitudes toward violence, if they are to succeed on a large scale. American society is violent. The rate of violent crimes continues to rise and portrayals of violence on television are commonplace. Furthermore, we continue to condone physical punishment of children, making it difficult for parents to subscribe wholeheartedly to other methods of discipline. Gil (1970) notes that in 63% of the cases, child abuse develops out of disciplinary action taken by parents. Therefore, many prevention programs focus on teaching parents alternative methods of punishment. At the same time, however, school personnel in many states still have a right to use physical punishment in disciplining children. Although it does not appear to be directly related to child abuse, the message conveyed to parents is that the use of physical force against children is a preferred mode of punishment (Zigler, 1978). If teachers and principals find this an effective mode of resolving problems with children, why shouldn't parents?

Consequences of Child Abuse

Even this brief discussion shows that the prevention of child abuse is a difficult and multifaceted task (Bakan, 1979). We cannot overemphasize its importance, however, because the physical and psychological consequences of abuse can be very serious. Child abuse can result in physical handicaps and in severe neurological problems. Blows to the head can cause bleeding inside the skull, ultimately leading to brain damage. What is particularly surprising and disturbing is that infants, whose skull is much larger than their still-growing brain, can suffer brain hemorrhages simply by being shaken. Known as the **shaken-baby syndrome,** this form of abuse can cause brain damage, visual problems, and deficits in language and motor skills. What is frightening is how easily this can occur. Perhaps you have had a frustrating experience with a child and you felt that you could just hold his shoulders and shake him so he would listen to you. With older children, this may not cause a problem, but it can lead to severe injury in infants.

Besides the neurological consequences of abuse, abused children also suffer from disturbances in emotional and social development. Since they have learned from their home life that involvement with other people carries a great deal of pain, they may tend to be inhibited and socially unresponsive, often backing away when a friendly caregiver or another child approaches them (George & Main, 1979; Gaensbauer & Sands, 1979). Such children may also be overly compliant or display violent, aggressive behavior toward adults and peers (Herrenkohl & Herrenkohl, 1981). Some abused children are "hypervigilant" (Martin & Breezley, 1976), constantly looking for danger, scanning their environment, and ready to attack. A variety of underlying processes may also account for the behaviors. These children may also fail to develop the social skills required to engage in harmonious social interactions (Aber, 1982), or they may imitate the hostile interpersonal exchanges they have experienced.

Obesity

The problems associated with nutritional deprivation and failure-to-thrive cases are severe. At the opposite end of the spectrum is obesity, which also gives rise to physical and psychological problems; these problems, however, are not as life threatening. **Obesity,** which is an excess of body weight, is measured by skinfold thickness. A thickness of skin from the upper arm is pinched between two fingers and the thickness of the fold is measured. If the child's skinfold is thicker than that of 85% of the children the same age and sex, the child is considered obese. Obesity results from eating more food than the body uses for its basic energy needs and from expending less energy than the diet supplies. Associated problems include increased risk of high blood pressure, gall bladder disease, and adult onset of diabetes. All these conditions contribute to higher rates of heart disease and stroke. Social and psychological costs are also incurred. Obese children are sometimes victims of prejudice and may be teased or ignored by their peers.

Studies show that obese children are likely to grow up to be obese adolescents and adults. Abraham, Collins, and Nordsieck (1971) found that 86% of overweight boys and 80% of overweight girls were overweight as adults; in contrast, only 42% of average-weight boys and 18% of average-weight girls became overweight as adults. Although some researchers have long argued that the tendency to be overweight may be due to genetic factors, we have only recently received conclusive evidence to support this contention: studies of twins indicated that among twins with a tendency for obesity, even extreme caloric restrictions did not help in weight reductions, and among twins with a tendency to be relatively thin, overeating did not result in weight gain (Bouchard et al., 1990; Stunkard et al., 1990). Individuals who have a tendency to be thin apparently have an inherited tendency for the body to burn excess calories.

Although the tendency toward obesity is inherited, children gain weight because of inappropriate eating habits and other factors. In the United States and other affluent societies, the number of young overweight children appears to be increasing (Gortmaker et al., 1987; Winick, 1975; Mayer, 1968). How can we explain this? Researchers cite greater reliance on highly processed foods (U.S. Department of Agriculture, 1980), which are used even in school lunch and breakfast programs (Citizens' Commission on School Nutrition, 1991). Another contributing factor is the tendency to eat away from home and snack frequently. Both practices contribute significantly to the total calories consumed during the day. In addition, television advertising helps children form bad eating habits (Dietz & Gortmaker, 1985; Gallo, Connor, & Boehm, 1980), and simply sitting in front of the television contributes to a sedentary lifestyle that is characteristic of many children today.

American children as a group are exceedingly sedentary by world standards, even in comparison to the norms of past decades in this country (Bray, 1979). A sedentary lifestyle can affect the individual's general health. A review of studies of children's health reveals that the first signs of arteriosclerosis, or hardening of the arteries, are evident by age 5 (Institute of Aerobic Research, 1987). Regular exercise and a low-fat diet are necessary to stem the effects of this process (American Academy of Pediatrics, 1985); if left unchecked, it can lead to heart disease and stroke.

Educational policies may also be contributing to the increasingly sedentary lifestyle of American children. According to Janis and Bulow-Hube (1986), during the past ten years, the federal government has significantly reduced the amount of money spent for physical education. Thus many schools have few physical fitness programs. Preschool children are also less physically fit than they should be. Recall that, according to Poest and colleagues (1989; 1990), children in child care centers spend significantly less time in large-muscle and motor activities that promote cardiovascular health than do children in nursery school. Researchers suggest that the difference may be due to the fact that child care confines children to the classroom for a large part of the day, especially during the winter, and thus they do not have as much opportunity for extensive physical activity. But parents and teachers can make a difference here. The Poest team found that children of active parents are more active than other children, regardless of whether they are in child care or nursery school. And the same was true of children in child care centers or nursery schools where teachers encourage the children to engage in vigorous physical activity.

Health Care

Since illness can influence children's growth and development, they must have access to medical care. For example, a major illness lasting several months may slow their growth considerably. The mechanisms that affect growth vary from one illness to another. Sometimes changes in endocrine balance are involved; for instance, a change in the secretion of hormones from the adrenal gland retards growth (Tanner, 1978). However, as long as the child receives adequate medical care, he will experience a "catch-up period" after recovering from the illness. Since growth will then take place at twice its usual rate, he will eventually attain his normal height and weight (Tanner, 1978).

The preschool child is vulnerable to respiratory infections and a number of illnesses, such as German measles and the mumps. These diseases do not cause any discernible change in growth as long as the child is well nourished and receives adequate medical attention (Miller et al., 1960). Even a seemingly minor problem like an ear infection, when not properly treated, can cause deafness, which is an irreversible condition. In addition, immunizations, given at routine medical checkups, can prevent many childhood illnesses. Thus adequate health care can either prevent illnesses or minimize the complications that can arise.

Child health care in the United States   If someone asked you whether American children are in good health, you would probably say yes. Indeed, many children enjoy good health and access to medical care. Medical advances and increased attention to health promotion and disease prevention have contributed to the significant improvement in the health status of American children in recent decades (Kotelchuck & Richmond, 1982). Janis (1983) notes that increased public spending for children's health and welfare during the 1960s and 1970s increased the number of children's health services, causing a substantial decline in the number of children who became ill. In addition, national educational programs like Project Head Start provided referrals to medical care (North, 1979).

However, not all children have shared equally in this improvement in health status. Sharp disparities in health status and access to and use of health services persist. As one physician notes, "Poverty is the single most influential factor affecting the health status of children" (Shirley, 1982). Poor children are more likely to be

---

FEATURE

Immunizing Children

When Jason and Emily enroll in kindergarten, their parents will be asked for proof that they have received immunization vaccinations; 95% of school-age children are fully immunized against common childhood diseases such as measles, mumps, rubella, polio, diphtheria, pertussis (whooping cough), and tetanus. However, one-third of all American preschoolers are not immunized even though protection against disease is most crucial during infancy and early childhood (American Academy of Pediatrics, 1990b).

Since 1950, due to modern vaccination practices, the incidence of childhood diseases has dropped significantly; in fact, many parents think that these diseases are no longer a threat. This may help explain why parents have been lax about having their children immunized. Another part of the explanation may be the budget cut incurred by the Childhood Immunization Initiative Program. The result has been an increase in the incidence of major diseases that had ceased to exist for a time.

According to the American Academy of Pediatrics (1990b), measles outbreaks now occur among economically disadvantaged preschoolers. The *Morbidity and Mortality Weekly Report* for June 1, 1990, states that 17,850 measles cases were reported in 1989, a 423% increase over the 3,411 cases reported in 1988. Other diseases are also making a comeback. For example, there has been an 83% increase in the number of whooping cough cases among infants. All these cases could have been prevented through immunization. Immunization rates are higher for school-age children because most states require children to be fully immunized before they enter school. But during

infancy and early childhood, parents do not have to meet such requirements. To be effective, immunization vaccinations should be given on a regular schedule from the time the child is 2 months until age 14 to 16, as you can see in the following figure. Can you think of ways of enforcing the requirement of regular immunizations?

	DTP (Diptheria, Tetanus, Pertussis)	Polio	Tuberculosis test	Measles	Mumps	Rubella	Haemophilus–Conjugate	Tetanus–Diphtheria
2 months	✓	✓						
4 months	✓	✓						
6 months	✓							
1 year			✓					
15 months				✓	✓	✓	✓	
18 months	✓	✓						
4–6 years	✓	✓						
5–21 years				✓	✓	✓		
14–16 years								✓

exposed prenatally to drugs and the AIDS virus (National Center for Children in Poverty, 1990), to ingest lead, which can adversely affect their nervous system (Needleman et al., 1990), and to suffer nutritional deficits. Also, reductions (beginning in the 1980s) in the public funds available for children's services in general have affected health services as well.

Another factor contributing to the disparity in health care has to do with the Medicaid program. Medicaid is one way the United States ensures health care for poor children. Although the program is generally effective and encourages the poor to seek preventive health services for their children (Williams & Miller, 1991), its implementation varies from state to state. Because some states have a much stricter income-eligibility requirement than others, Medicaid covers only about two-fifths of poor children (Johns & Adler, 1989). Expert observers believe that about 7 million American children do not have access to the routine medical care needed for good health and disease prevention (National Association of Children's Hospitals and Related Institutions, 1989).

This vast difference in health status and access to health care services between rich and poor should concern students of developmental psychology. As we know, good health is essential for children to function well psychologically. It affects both their motivation to learn and their achievements. According to Birch (1972):

> The child who is apathetic because of malnutrition, whose experiences may have been modified by acute or chronic illness, whose learning abilities may have been affected by some "insult" to the central nervous system cannot be expected to respond to opportunities for learning in the same way as does a child who has not been exposed to such conditions. Increasing opportunity for learning, though entirely admirable in itself, will not overcome such biologic disadvantages.

In addition, research studies document that there is an unmistakable link between poor health and classroom failure, school absenteeism, and children's misconduct in the streets (Lewis & Balla, 1976). This combination often leads to a life of delinquency and crime.

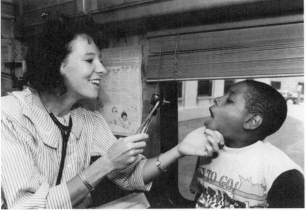

As part of the Children's Health Project in New York City, medical personnel make daily visits to shelters and welfare hotels, providing homeless children with complete medical examinations, tests, immunizations, and medication as needed.

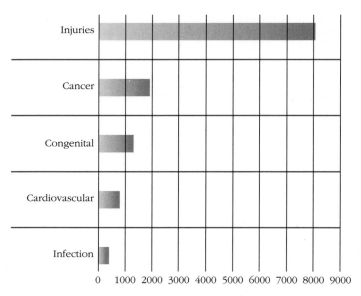

Figure 8.5 *Injuries claim the lives of more children than all major illnesses combined.*

Source: National Maternal and Health Clearinghouse, Washington, D.C., 1989.

Child health care in other countries Williams and Miller (1991) looked at children's health conditions in ten European countries—Belgium, Denmark, France, Germany, Ireland, the Netherlands, Norway, Spain, Switzerland, and the United Kingdom—in an effort to learn how to improve access to medical care in the United States. They found that all these countries had better infant and child survival rates than the United States. Also, more American children died of injuries, the majority of which tend to occur among 1- to 4-year-olds and among 15- to 19-year-olds. (We will discuss childhood injuries in the next section.) Additionally, they reported that the United States lags far behind European countries in immunizing preschool children. As Williams and Miller point out, it is almost unheard of "for a European preschool child to lack a regular source of [medical] care." In contrast, about 15% of U.S. children have no regular access to medical care. Further, about 16% to 34% of those who have access to medical care (according to their parents' statements) receive such care in a hospital emergency room; it is unlikely that in this setting they obtain such preventive care as immunization.

According to Williams and Miller (1991), European children receive health care in the home (through visiting nurses), in clinics, or in physicians' offices. Although variations may exist in the exact mixture of home, clinic, or physician services, all ten countries shared two important elements:

1. Health services are financed under national systems that ensure financial coverage for all children and require children to be registered with a health provider at birth.
2. By age 3 or 4, nearly all European children are enrolled in public preschools that "incorporate or are clearly linked with programs of health care" (p. 2).

This is how the European countries provide better oversight of their children's health. In contrast, the United States has no system for tracking children and

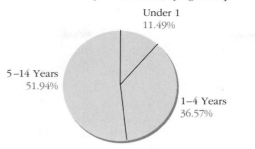

Accidental Mortality in Childhood, by Age Group

Under 1
11.49%

5–14 Years
51.94%

1–4 Years
36.57%

Figure 8.6   *Close to half of all injuries to children ages 1–14 occur during the preschool years.*
Source: Childhood Injury Prevention Project, by the Yale Bush Center in Child Development and Social Policy, New Haven, Connecticut. Based on 1986–1987 data.

ensuring their adequate health care. In fact, parents do not have to register children with any local agency until they are enrolled in elementary school. As a result, we miss out on opportunities to monitor the children's health, provide needed services, and educate parents on their children's health and well-being.

Childhood Injuries

Not being able to track American infants and preschool children and monitor their health has had troubling consequences, especially in the area of childhood injuries. Injuries are the leading cause of death among children ages 1 to 14 (see Figure 8.5), numbering close to 8000 deaths each year (National Safety Council, 1991). As you can see in Figure 8.6, nearly half these deaths occur among children ages 1 to 4 (Finn-Stevenson, Ward, & Stevenson, 1989). Children's injuries also account for about 30,000 permanent disabilities annually (Centers for Disease Control, 1990).

The annual costs of such injuries are estimated to exceed $7.5 billion (Centers for Disease Control, 1990), a figure that does not take into account the emotional and social toll on the children and their families. People often refer to fatal and disabling injuries as "accidents" because of the myth that they occur suddenly, are unpredictable, and are beyond anyone's control. But research has shown that injuries, like diseases, occur in highly predictable patterns and are, in fact, preventable (Committee on Trauma Research, 1985).

For most age groups, motor vehicle–related injuries are responsible for over half the deaths due to injuries. But for preschool children, motor vehicle trauma is second to injuries occurring at home (Centers for Disease Control, 1990). Researchers also point out that the kinds of injuries children are likely to sustain depend on their age. School-age children, for example, are victims of pedestrian and bicycle-related injuries (Rivara et al., 1989). Among preschoolers, fatal and disabling injuries occur as a result of fires, scalding, falls, drowning, choking, and, to a lesser degree, poisoning (Baker & Waller, 1989). Inadequate supervision is often the cause of such tragedies. For instance, in analyzing fatal house fires in a North Carolina community over one year, Gugelmann (1989) found that the parent or caregiver was absent or inattentive in 65% of the cases of children who had died from burns.

Preventing childhood injuries   Since 1980, when prevention of accidental injuries to children became one of several national health priorities (Select Panel for the

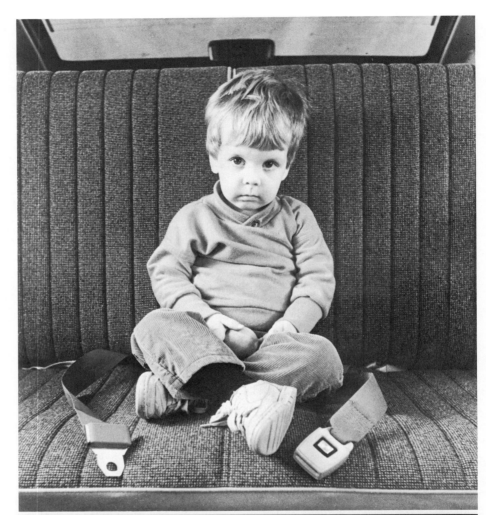

The most common form of child abuse.

Photo: Lance Photography

Society's perceptions of what constitutes intentional child abuse are changing, as are definitions of non-intentional injuries.

The leading child-killer in America isn't cancer, or Muscular Dystrophy, or any disease at all. It's adults. Adults who neglect children. . . by letting them ride unprotected in the car.

The National Safety Council says 81 percent of America's children ride totally unprotected. Bouncing on the back seat. Leaning over to talk with mom or dad. Waving from the window. Tiny missiles. . . waiting for launch through a wall of glass.

Each year, nearly 700 children under the age of five are killed in auto accidents. They deserve a chance to live. And you can give it to them. By strapping your children into car seats. Buckling them into safety belts. And setting a good example by buckling up yourself.

The leading child-killer in America is also the most curable. The cure is in your hands. Buckle it.

BUCKLE UP
It's more than a law.
It's a lifesaver.

Presented as a public service by
The Connecticut Safety Belt Coalition
and Aetna Life & Casualty

Promotion of Child Health, 1981), we have achieved some progress in preventing childhood deaths due to injuries. In part, this success has come about as a result of paying more attention to the problem and devoting more funds to research. Also, legislative initiatives have been especially effective in significantly reducing some types of injuries. For example, since Congress passed legislation requiring the installation of child-resistant bottle caps, children's deaths from aspirin poisoning have dropped by 60%. Many handicaps caused by lead poisoning were reduced after federal regulations banned the use of more than a trace of lead in household paints. (Yet lead poisoning still remains a major problem among low-income children who live in older homes.) Federal regulations have also required crib manufacturers to make narrower spaces between the slats; thus the number of infants who strangle because they get their head caught between the slats has decreased. Similarly, federal laws have required the manufacturers of pacifiers to make them large enough that they cannot be swallowed or drawn into the child's upper airways; this has virtually eliminated these kinds of deaths (Baker, 1981). New York City legislation mandating the installation of window guards on all high-rise residential buildings has resulted in a 50% decrease in the number of childhood deaths due to falls (Christophersen, 1989).

Despite this progress, the number of childhood deaths from injuries in the United States remains high, far exceeding that of other industrialized nations (Williams & Miller, 1991; World Health Organization, 1989). Given the enormous advances in our ability to prevent and treat numerous life-threatening diseases, why is our nation still unable to prevent so many childhood injuries?

In their analysis of U.S. childhood injury prevention policies, Margolin and Runyan (1983) suggest that these policies focus on only one aspect of a multifaceted problem, thus limiting the range of possible prevention options. For example, some observers suggest that injuries are due to parental ignorance. Many parents leave their children unattended or leave drugs and poisonous chemicals within easy reach. These observers recommend directing educational efforts at parents as a means of preventing childhood accidents.

Of course, such educational efforts are a necessary component of a childhood injury prevention policy, but by themselves, they may be ineffective. Dershewitz and Williamson (1977) and Dershewitz (1979) conducted a child-safety campaign to teach parents how to childproof their homes. They sent parents instructions and a booklet to help them implement the instructions. To ascertain if they had done so, the researchers conducted follow-up inspections in the parents' homes and in the homes of families that did not participate in the program. They found that program participants who thought that they had made their homes safe had as many household cleaning agents, prescription drugs, knives, and matches within reach of young children as did parents who had not participated in the program.

You can see, therefore, that alerting parents to the potential dangers in their homes and teaching them how to avoid childhood accidents do not guarantee that these accidents can be prevented. However, the timing of the educational effort may be a critical issue. Christophersen, Williams, and Barone (1988) gave the same educational intervention to two groups of parents: one group of expectant parents received the intervention as part of prenatal classes; the other group of parents already had toddlers. Both groups were taught about the importance of lowering water heater temperatures to prevent death and disability from hot-water scalds (the second leading cause of death among infants and preschoolers). Both groups were matched on demographic and other variables, and for both groups there were control groups that did not receive the educational message. Several months after the intervention, researchers interviewed the parents and found that a significant number of parents from the expectant parents group had, in fact, lowered the water heater temperature. But there was no difference among the parents of toddlers who had received the intervention and those who had not. When the researchers asked the subjects about following the advice, it became apparent that the expectant parents wanted to do everything right for their babies. In contrast, the toddlers' parents felt that since nothing had happened so far, their children must be safe. Thus, expectant parents appear to be receptive to educational approaches to prevention, at least to such initiatives as resetting the water heater temperature, which they need only do once.

When parents have to continually act with the child's safety in mind, educational approaches may not always work. This is painfully clear in the case of childhood automobile fatalities, which can be significantly reduced with seat belt use. Child auto-restraint laws, which legally require all young children to wear seat belts and caretakers to place and buckle infants in a car seat, have resulted in an increase of such practices. The American Academy of Pediatrics has given a high priority to educating parents about the use of car seats and seat belts beginning with the infant's trip home from the hospital (Christophersen & Sullivan, 1982). But some parents still do not realize the importance of the practice. At the relatively low speed of 15 to 30 miles per hour, an automobile crash can hurtle the child headfirst in the direction of the dashboard. Even parents who are aware of the risks frequently do not use child restraints because they find it inconvenient, uncomfortable, or costly, or because the children may be sleepy and beg to lie on the parent's lap (Margolin & Runyan, 1983). On such occasions parents who would otherwise insist that the children use the seat belt are tempted to let the children have the comfort they desire.

For these reasons, injury-control specialists suggest that as a means of childhood injury prevention, manufacturers should be required to install some automatic safety measures such as automatic seat belts or air bags that instantly inflate in the event of a crash. Newer cars may have some of these safety devices, but many parents still own cars that do not. And, despite widespread media campaigns on the importance of buckling children at all times, childhood deaths due to motor vehicle–related injuries continue to claim youngsters' lives.

Legal implications When unbuckled children die in car crashes, some states charge the parents with vehicular homicide. This recently occurred in Florida to Ramiro Rodriguez after his 3-year-old daughter died of head injuries suffered as a result of a car crash while he was driving. She was not wearing a seat belt as required by state law (Margolick, 1990). California brought a similar charge against a father, but it was later dropped. It is too early to tell if states will continue to enforce seat belt laws by holding parents accountable for their children's death. But the more information parents receive about protecting their children, the more likely our society is to change its perceptions about whether an injury is intentional (for example, a form of child abuse) or unintentional (that is, accidental) (Garbarino, 1988). Already organizations seeking to encourage the use of seat belts are distributing posters, which proclaim that the failure to use seat belts is the most prevalent form of child abuse. It is still too early to tell whether this form of parental education will change parental behavior. Do you think it is an effective approach? Are there any ramifications to broadening the definition of what constitutes child abuse and neglect?

Summary

In contrast to infancy when growth occurs at a dramatically rapid rate, physical growth during the preschool years is slower and more gradual. But still the child grows taller and gains weight. Also, significant changes occur in ossification (the process whereby the bones become longer, thicker, and harder), which contributes to skeletal growth and to involvement in activities requiring strength. These changes facilitate progress in the development of gross- and fine-motor skills. The child acquires control over the large muscles first, so gross-motor skills are easier to master. Fine-motor skills depend on brain maturation, so more muscular control is needed to execute them. Even though the young preschooler does not have complete control over fine-motor muscles, she attempts to use them and enjoys tasks— painting, drawing, cutting pieces of paper with scissors—that give her a chance to develop these muscles. Eventually, the child develops proficiency of many fine-motor skills and learns to dress and undress by herself as well as draw and write with greater ease.

Play provides the context within which the child develops fine- and gross-motor skills, but the acquisition of motor skills also depends on brain maturation. Another important aspect of brain maturation is related to brain specialization. The brain is divided into left and right hemispheres, which control opposite sides of the body and include different functional centers. The centers facilitating language skills are in the left hemisphere; during early childhood, these centers undergo myelination and increase in their ability to function. Hence, the child can acquire language skills at this time.

There are also environmental influences on growth—such as malnutrition, emotional factors, and health—that can result in stunting and can lead to growth disorders such as deprivation dwarfism or obesity. Despite the important influence of nutrition and health on physical growth and development, one out of eight American youngsters under 12 does not have enough to eat. Many American children, specifically those who are poor, do not receive adequate health care. Yet other industrialized countries have implemented specific initiatives to monitor children's health, which begin at birth and continue through childhood, and to provide adequate preventive health services. Perhaps studying child health care in other countries can help U.S. policymakers resolve the barriers that exist to adequate child health care in our nation. One major area needing substantial improvement is injury prevention; injuries are the number one cause of death among children ages 1 to 14.

Many American children are also victims of child abuse. No single factor accounts for abuse; it is the result of many factors. For example, abusive parents have unrealistic expectations of what young children can do and lack the ability to effectively discipline their children. Further, the child's characteristics may also contribute to abuse. Abuse is also more likely to occur in families that are overburdened with the responsibilities and stresses of daily life. Services for abusive parents focus on treatment and on prevention, by providing support to families and teaching parents about effective discipline techniques. The consequences of abuse are serious; in some cases, death or disabling injury results. In other cases the child is psychologically scarred and has difficulty establishing close relationships with peers.

9 Cognitive and Language Development During the Preschool Years

Preschool children are observant, and often imitate adult behavior.

When Eleanor comes to pick her daughter up from child care, she spends a few moments watching her play with her friends. It seems such a short time ago that Amy was a baby, unable to walk or talk. Now here she is, at age 4, leading a group of 4-year-olds in play. Amy is designating roles, telling one child he can be the gas station attendant and another that she can be the customer. Amy is the cashier. The three 4-year-olds reenact the gas station scene in detail; they don't mind that the car is imaginary, a garden hose is the gas pump, and a small piece of paper is the credit card!

When they are playing like this, Amy and her friends show their increased understanding of people and events in their environments. Pretend play helps children enhance their cognitive skills and allows them to interact and communicate with others.

In this chapter we discuss the role of play in cognitive development, the progress in cognitive and language development during early childhood, and ways that parents and educators can enhance this development. Our discussions of cognitive development explore Jean Piaget's theory and alternative explanations of cognitive development. In Chapter 6 we noted that Piaget underestimated children's cognitive skills at different ages; but his theory still has had a tremendous influence, because it shows that children actively participate in their learning. Piaget's theory has provided the grounds for developing preschool programs that emphasize the importance of play and has led to the development of preschool intervention programs. Longitudinal evaluations of such programs as Project Head Start have shown that providing preschool children with quality services can significantly alter their life paths. The documented benefits of early intervention programs have renewed national interest in **school readiness,** which refers to efforts to make preschool programs available to all low-income children so they will be "ready" for school and able to benefit from academic instruction. Now politicians and business leaders are also acknowledging the need for children to have stimulating experiences during early childhood and to explore their surroundings and interact with other children and adults. These experiences prepare children for later success in school.

When should we begin providing services to children—age 3, age 4, even earlier? Should we make services available to all children? Before answering these questions, let us look at how children acquire cognitive skills during early childhood.

Cognitive Development

Piaget's Theory: The Preoperational Period

According to Piaget, the preschool child is in the preoperational period of cognitive development. This period represents a transition in the child's mode of thinking; that is, the child has advanced beyond the restrictions imposed by a sensorimotor level of cognitive development, but he has not yet attained the skills necessary to think logically.

The answers that preschool children give to seemingly simple questions show that fantasy and reality are interchangeable. Their ideas are somewhat distorted and incomplete, suggesting that they cannot reason logically. Preschool children also tend to assume that others think as they do and share their views, feelings, and desires. This assumption clearly implies that they only partially understand the people around them.

Recent studies show that Piaget may have underestimated the cognitive capabilities of preschoolers. Although he focuses on the limitations inherent in the mode of thinking during early childhood (Flavell, 1985), children undergo important cognitive growth during the preoperational period, especially in the refinement of representational thought. Recall that at the end of the sensorimotor period, children can mentally represent objects and events. This new ability greatly expands their sphere of mental activities. Because their thinking is no longer tied to the present, preoperational children can think about past events, dwell on the future, and wonder what is going on right now somewhere else.

But they do not fully attain mental representation all at once. One-year-old infants who take their first few steps need to practice walking before they can fully master the task. In the same way, during the beginning of the preoperational period, children need to practice their new ability to mentally manipulate their experiences with the environment. They do so through their play and their interactions with adults and other children.

Symbolic functioning   Piaget explained that as young children practice their ability for representational thought, they acquire a symbolic mode of thinking, or **symbolic functioning.** Symbolic functioning is the child's ability to understand, create, and use symbols to represent something that is not present. It is a major distinction between the sensorimotor period and the preoperational period.

Ault (1977) notes that the degree of correspondence between an actual object—say, a hammer—and a symbolic representation of that object can vary from highly concrete to highly abstract. When we use a plastic toy hammer to represent a metal hammer, the degree of correspondence between the symbolic representation (toy hammer) and the actual object is highly concrete. When we evoke a picture of a hammer in our mind, the degree of correspondence between the symbolic representation (mental image of a hammer) and the actual object is slightly more abstract but still somewhat concrete. The mental image retains some features of the object it represents, such as color and shape. But a word made up of the letters *h-a-m-m-e-r* is a highly abstract symbolic representation of the object; it is an arbitrary representation of an object and bears no resemblance to the object.

Piaget called these abstract symbols **signs.** He noted that at first children mediate their thinking using concrete symbols; eventually they are able to mediate their thinking through signs such as words and distinguish between a word and what that word represents. Clearly, they must be able to call forth an image of a hammer and think about it as they use or hear the word *hammer,* even though no actual hammer may be present. As we saw in Chapter 8, many children are able to use some words correctly early in the second year of life. According to Piaget, however, words only become coherent abstract symbols during the preoperational period.

Piaget believed that three behaviors emerge during the early part of the preoperational period that reflect the preschool child's use of symbols to mediate thinking: deferred imitation, symbolic play, and sophisticated language skills. Deferred imitation, which we discussed in Chapter 6, is an imitation of a behavior some time after the child has observed that behavior. When preschool children observe the behavior of a parent, playmate, or TV actor, they form a mental representation of that behavior. Later, they can recall this mental representation and act out the behavior. For instance, after watching Batman on television, the child jumps off the edge of a chair, with arms outstretched, pretending to be the superhero.

Children's ability to imitate a behavior and to pretend to be someone or something else shows that they have a stable mental image of what they are pretending to be and that they can retain this image over time and recall it later. Recall that children can imitate activities that they observe even before they acquire the ability for symbolic functioning. Obviously, preschool children can never imitate every attribute of a person or object. Their imitations are usually individualized and not readily understood by others. For example, a 3-year-old running around the room waving his arms may be pretending to be an airplane, but an adult observing the child may think that he is pretending to be a bird or Batman. As he grows older,

A child who can initiate a behavior and pretend to be someone or something else is able to retain a mental image over time and recall it later.

however, his imitations become more closely related to what he is imitating; in pretending to be an airplane, he will hold his arms stretched out stiffly as if they were the wings of a plane, and he will hum to indicate its engine noise.

Symbolic functioning is also evident in the child's symbolic (or pretend) play. Piaget (1962) described many examples of symbolic play, noting that as children learn how objects are used, they engage in pretend activities reflecting these uses. Thus, a young preschool child may drink from an imaginary cup or brush her hair with an imaginary hairbrush (Garvey, 1977). At first, she directs such symbolic play toward herself, but eventually she will direct it toward others as well; she will play with a doll, pretending that the doll is drinking from an imaginary cup, or she will serve make-believe coffee to her friends.

Recent studies indicate that symbolic play becomes more complex and elaborate during the second year of life. As the photographs of the child and doll indicate, the child initially is the agent in pretend play. For example, he may put his head down and pretend to be asleep. Later on he may use another agent; for example, he may place a doll in a sleeping position (Watson & Fischer, 1977; 1980).

During the preschool period children become increasingly adept at using objects as if they were something else. For example, they may use sand to represent food or play with a broomstick as if it were a horse or with a cardboard box as if it were a truck. This symbolic play is a significant phase of cognitive growth. According to Piaget, symbolic play enables children to assimilate the objects they encounter in their experiences. For example, a child may transform a real horse into her mental construction of the world; in this way she eventually acquires the meaning of objects. Therefore, children should not be discouraged from indulging in a world of make-believe and should not be hurried through this stage. Through their manipulations of representational thought during symbolic play, they gradually attain a more mature mode of cognitive functioning. Other researchers also emphasize that preschool children's ability to play imaginatively is a precious characteristic. In essence, it may be the creativity and individuality we value in older children and adults (Singer & Singer, 1979b). As Flavell (1985) notes, preschool children know that a broomstick is not a horse. Yet they are able to mentally transform the broomstick in their play.

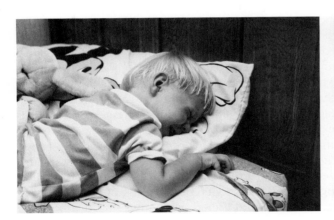

In the development of pretend play, this child first uses himself as the agent, putting his own head down in make-believe sleep. Later on, he will use another agent, pretending that the doll is asleep.

The symbolic mode of thinking is also apparent in their increasingly sophisticated use of words to represent objects, events, thoughts, and feelings, and to communicate effectively. Noting that language is a sign system, Piaget distinguished between signs and symbols. *Signs* have public meanings that society shares and understands and are thus used to communicate ideas. On the other hand, **symbols** are private; they are often understood only by the individual using them. Symbols may resemble what they signify. A short stick may resemble a knife, a spoon, or a screwdriver, depending on what the individual is pretending. Signs (most words) bear no resemblance to what they represent so children must slowly assimilate their meaning (Pulaski, 1980).

Children acquire language skills very rapidly during the preschool years. However, the first words they learn do not immediately serve as signs. Initially, to the child, the word *cat* seems to be no different than other properties of the animal, such as its soft fur or its meow. Only gradually does the child realize that the word *cat* is not part of the thing he knows, but rather a representation of it.

The development of concepts   Even when children realize that a word is actually an arbitrary representation, they still use words to refer to a specific object or event rather than to a class of similar objects or events. For example, the child may use the word *cat* to refer only to his cat, or the word *ball* to refer only to his ball. He soon realizes, however, that there are other cats and balls that are similar to his own cat and ball. Once he gains this insight, he can acquire knowledge at a much faster pace and organize his knowledge into concepts. A *concept* is a way of organizing information so that it is applicable to similar objects and events as well as specific ones. For example, the concept *dog* identifies a particular animal and refers also to all dogs. Once the child acquires the concept of dog, she can guess that when she sees a tiny poodle she has never seen before and is told that it is a dog, that this poodle must have similar characteristics to other dogs she knows. According to Piaget, the acquisition of concepts is a major step in cognitive growth because it greatly simplifies learning. As Bruner (1965) noted, if we had to "register" all the differences around us and had to respond to each object or event as unique, "we would soon be overwhelmed by the complexity of the environment."

Recent research suggests that children can acquire some simple concepts such as shape during the sensorimotor stage (Reznick, 1989). However, more abstract concepts, such as the concepts of number or space, are acquired very slowly. According to Piaget, children do not fully attain these concepts until the next period of cognitive development during the school-age years. During the preoperational stage, children acquire many concepts of objects such as a car, a house, or an apple; they can also refine or expand concepts acquired earlier. Armed with this new conceptual process, preschool children display their appreciation for the differences among objects and eagerly seek to classify them into different categories. This ability sets the motif for many popular games and routines.

Piaget maintained that preoperational children appear to be confused between a class of objects and its subclasses and have difficulty understanding that an object can be categorized in two different classes simultaneously. Piaget illustrated this point by showing children ten wooden beads; seven of the beads were white and three were blue. He then asked if there were more wooden beads or white beads. The children, focusing only on the subset, answered that there were more white beads. From this type of experiment, Piaget concluded that during the preoperational period, children can focus their attention—or **center**—on a single aspect of what they are asked to think about.

Piaget demonstrated this point in a classic series of experiments on conservation. Adults realize that a given quantity of liquid remains the same regardless of the shape of the container. That is, if the same amount of liquid is poured into two different containers—one tall and narrow, the other short and wide—each container has exactly the same amount of liquid despite the fact that the amounts do not *appear* to be the same. Preschool children, however, are more easily fooled by appearances, because they cannot understand the concept of **conservation**—that is, the notion that an amount remains the same (is conserved), even though the shape may change. They will not be able to understand the conservation of volume, weight, and other quantities until they reach school age (see Chapter 12).

Why do preschool children have problems understanding change? Piaget (1952) noted that two principles govern preoperational thinking and hinder task performance. The first principle is **irreversibility** of thought, which refers to children's inability to go forward and then backward in their thinking; thus, they have trouble understanding change. Because children can only move forward in their thinking, they have to reason on the basis of what they visualize now rather than thinking back to what they have just seen. Irreversibility of thought is apparent in their answers to questions. For example, if you ask a girl if she has a sister (and she does), she will say yes. But if you ask her if her sister has a sister, she will say no! About age 5 or 6, children acquire the ability to reverse—a major milestone in the development of logical thinking.

Distinguishing between appearance and reality   The second principle is children's tendency to center their attention on one aspect of a problem or situation and neglect other aspects. Hence, they are easily fooled by appearances (Flavell, 1985). This makes it difficult for them to distinguish between appearance and reality. For example, if you put a stick in a glass of water, the stick will appear to be distorted even though it is not (see Figure 9.1). This is difficult for young children to understand. Flavell and his colleagues (Flavell, Green, & Flavell, 1986) pretrained children to ensure that they understood the phrases "what it looks like" and "what it really and truly is." Then they were shown two glasses of milk, one with a colored filter in front of it and one without. At age 3 the children were unable to understand that the liquid in the glass with the filter in front of it was still milk, even though it looked like blue liquid. In another study children played with a black cat and then were shown the same cat with a mask on (see Figure 9.1); the 3-year-olds actually thought that the cat had become some ferocious animal and were afraid of it (De-Vries, 1969).

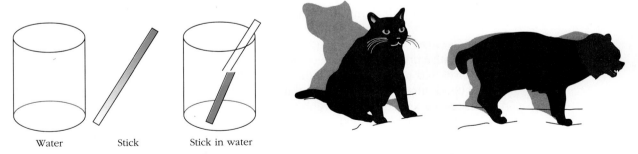

Water   Stick   Stick in water

Figure 9.1   *Three-year-olds have trouble distinguishing between reality and appearance. They can't understand that the stick is the same whether it's in or out of the water, or that the cat with a mask on is still a cat and not a wild animal.*

Practical applications We will return to these limitations on thinking in Chapter 12. But it may be useful to think about everyday experiences that illustrate preschool children's mode of thinking. Because they cannot distinguish between appearance and reality, some 2- and 3-year-olds may start crying if their father puts on a mask and pretends to be a clown. Then there is the 3-year-old who is in tears because he got a smaller piece of pie than his sister. Actually his piece is shorter and wider than hers, but no one is going to convince him that both pieces are the same size! These daily experiences usually help parents realize that it is useless to reason with the preschool child.

Examining how children understand relationships between events reveals another consequence of the mode of thinking of early childhood. Adults reason on the basis of deductive reasoning by attributing some aspects of a general situation to a particular situation. Or they may use inductive reasoning, by applying aspects of a particular situation to a more general context. But preschool children, who can only center on one aspect of an event, cannot use either of these types of reasoning. Rather, they use **transductive reasoning;** that is, they go from one particular to another particular, often ascribing cause-and-effect relationships to unrelated events. If a child falls, she blames the sidewalk; if she is hurt, she may blame a child who is not even near her at the time. Parents often think that she is being silly or even lying. However, this is merely her understanding of what happened. Transductive reasoning is not limited to preschool children. Adults often attribute cause-and-effect relationships to unrelated events. This is why you should never interpret correlational studies showing a relationship between two variables as meaning that one variable has caused a change in the other. Remember you are capable of understanding other possible, logical relationships, but the preschool child is not.

Egocentrism Another basic characteristic of the preoperational period is **egocentrism,** or children's tendency to interpret the environment from their point of view. Egocentrism in young children means that they see the world as revolving around them (hence the word *egocentric*). It snows so *they* can make a snowman; the grass grows so *they* can walk on it.

Since preschool children tend to understand life events in an egocentric way, it is hard for them to accept death, illness, and divorce. Often a preschool child blames himself for the death of a grandmother, or explains that she died because she didn't love him. A preschool child whose parents are separated or divorced may blame herself as well; she may think that her parents divorced because she did something to upset them.

Egocentric thought also prevents children from seeing another person's perspective, or putting themselves in another's place. It is not that they are selfish or insensitive. Rather, their understanding of the world is an integral aspect of the cognitive process. As they become increasingly capable of stepping away from themselves and recognizing that other people have different feelings and thoughts, they will advance in their ability to think and understand. Although egocentrism dominates preoperational children's thinking, it is present at every stage in development and even in adulthood to some extent (Elkind, 1978).

To demonstrate this basic inability to adopt another person's perspective or point of view, Piaget and Inhelder (1963) conducted an experiment in which 4- to 11-year-old children were shown a three-dimensional model of three mountains. The children were asked to walk around the model so they could see that the

Figure 9.2 *The three-mountain problem. Children are shown an exhibit of three mountains that look different from various positions, and asked to describe what the mountains look like from the perspective of a toy seated opposite.*

mountains looked different from various positions; then they were asked to sit on a chair facing one side of the model. A doll was placed on a chair facing another side of the model. Each child was asked to choose a picture that showed what the doll saw (see Figure 9.2). Invariably, children under age 6 thought the doll saw the same scene they did; children between the ages of 6 and 7 knew that the doll saw a different scene but were not sure which one. Older children between the ages of 9 and 11, however, selected the correct view from the doll's perspective. To choose the correct view for the doll, the children had to recognize that the doll, which was seated in a different position, had a different view of the mountains than they had. They also had to visualize that view of the mountains and then compare it with the pictures.

Some researchers maintain that this task is too difficult and is not a good gauge of the children's egocentrism. These researchers contend that egocentrism does not last throughout the preoperational period. In variations of the three-mountain experiment, they have shown that when the task is simplified, younger children are able to give the right answer. This finding indicates that the children are not egocentric in their thinking. Researchers have found, for example, that it is easier for children to give the right answer when they are able to rotate the model to indicate the doll's view (Huttenlocher & Presson, 1973). Borke (1975) modified the three-

Figure 9.3 *The farm-scene version of Piaget's three-mountain problem.*

mountain experiment so children were confronted with familiar farm scenes rather than mountains, and a Sesame Street character, Grover or Big Bird, that drove around the scene in a car (see Figure 9.3). From time to time, researchers stopped the car and asked the children what Grover's view of the scene looked like. Borke found that although 3-year-olds performed poorly on the three-mountain task, they did well on the farm-scene version. Thus, preschool children can display nonegocentric thinking as long as the elements of the experiment are familiar.

To identify the age at which egocentrism begins to decline, researchers devised numerous ways to gain insight into children's perspectives. In one study the child sits on the floor with his mother and another adult. One of the adults is asked to close her eyes. While the one adult's eyes are closed, the child chooses a toy that only he and the other adult know about. It is their secret. When 2- and 3-year-olds are asked if the other adult also knows about their toy, they answer yes; they are unable to recognize that another person's point of view may be different from their own. However, most 4-year-olds answer no, because they realize that only the adult who could see while they picked out the toy knows what was going on and therefore shares their secret (Marvin, Greenberg, & Mossler, 1976).

In addition, when 4-year-olds speak to infants, they modify their speech patterns so the infants can better understand them; they speak more clearly and slowly and repeat what they say (Shatz & Gelman, 1973), thus demonstrating that they are able to recognize and respond to the needs of their young listeners. In other words, they are not as egocentric as Piaget suggested.

Alternative Explanations of Cognition

New evidence that preschool children are more sophisticated in their thinking spurred researchers to find alternative explanations of cognitive development. As you learned in Chapter 8 on physical development, some researchers take a biological view of cognition and propose that maturational changes in the brain account for the cognitive changes that are evident during the preschool years (Friedman, Klivington, & Peterson, 1986). Some theorists believe that biological changes also account for children's rapid acquisition of language skills during this period.

A neo-Piagetian approach   Other researchers, referred to as *neo-Piagetians,* have sought to refine Piaget's theory. To illustrate their thinking, we will examine one question they ask: Is cognitive development domain-specific? Piaget maintained that cognitive stages of development cover broad domains of thought, and that children use the same cognitive structures across a wide range of tasks. Some neo-Piagetian researchers believe that cognitive skills appear in a stepwise progression but are more domain-specific than Piaget thought. In other words, children may do well on some tasks in some situations but not on other tasks or in other situations. We saw this earlier with the three-mountain experiment and the farm-scene version. According to the neo-Piagetians, cognitive skills are domain-specific because the amount of knowledge within the domain is critical. We all perform better on a familiar task, and children are no exception (Chi, 1978). We will return to this issue in Chapter 12, which covers cognitive development during middle childhood, and you will see that Piaget also acknowledged that the amount of knowledge children have is critical.

An emphasis on cultural context   Some researchers contend that the social environment influences cognitive development. Piaget emphasized the social environment's role to some extent, but several researchers have taken his view further, noting that adults create a context that supports children's learning of different behaviors (Topping, Crowell, & Kobayashi, 1989). What children learn may differ depending on their cultural background. You will see in Chapter 10 that depending on where they live, for example, children are exposed to different experiences, such as molding pottery, hunting animals, or weaving cloth, which influence what they learn and foster a higher level of performance on some tasks.

Information processing   Recall from Chapter 6 that some researchers describe cognition in terms of *information processing.* They contend that the cognitive limitations Piaget observed among preschoolers are not due to different mental processes, but to their limited capacity to process information.

For example, preschoolers have difficulty paying attention to a task for a long time. They can even lose their train of thought or interest in the middle of a task, becoming immediately engrossed in something else that captures their attention. This limited attention span means that they may fail to focus on details and thus are more prone to making errors (Small, 1990).

Memory Young children also have a limited capacity for memory, which is a fundamental aspect of cognition. For instance, in the three-mountain task children needed to remember what the mountains looked like from different vantage points.

Memory is present early in life. Even infants have a rudimentary capacity for memory; by age 2 children can remember single events. For example, they may remember receiving a specific toy from an aunt or uncle or a particular game they played with relatives on a previous visit. By age 4 they can remember more complex details and also a sequence of events. If you attempt to skip a page or two in a story you are reading to a 4-year-old, she will remind you that you are not adhering to the story as written! Studies have also shown that 4- and 5-year-olds can remember the sequence of a series of pictures or the way items are grouped on a supermarket shelf (Brown et al., 1983).

It is not easy to study memory capacity in young children because adults have difficulty interpreting what children mean. There are also questions about the reliability of children's memories since the memories depend on children's interpretation of the environment and events.

In an interesting study on memory, Nelson (1989) tape-recorded a child talking to himself at bedtime from the time he was 21 months old until age 3. She supplemented the data by asking mothers of several children to keep diaries of things their children remembered and by reviewing research studies on memory. Nelson concluded that memory of specific events, or **autobiographical memory,** generally begins at age 3 and increases with age, often lasting for many years. Further, preschoolers do not use any strategies for trying to remember. They remember events because the events made a strong impression. Hence they tend to remember unique events, such as a trip to the zoo, rather than day-to-day activities, such as going to the supermarket. Additionally, they are more likely to remember if adults discuss the events with them.

Young children also remember the words they hear. Language development occurs at such a rapid rate during the early childhood years that it often astonishes adults how easily children learn new words and grammatical rules. Keep in mind, however, that although preschoolers are budding linguists, some aspects of language are still difficult and they will not master them until they are older.

Language Development

Recall from Chapter 6 that toward the latter part of the second year of life, children begin to combine words instead of using one word at a time, and that gradually their sentences became longer. However, their speech was still telegraphic; that is, they spoke in very short sentences, using words as efficiently as possible, and including only those words essential to convey the message.

Language Acquisition

During early childhood, children acquire the ability to speak in longer sentences; they use an average of four or five words per sentence at age 4 and an average of six to eight words per sentence at age 5. Also, by age 5 they can speak in complex sentences and have a command of the tenses. For example, a 5-year-old can say something as linguistically complex as: "Yesterday we went to the house where Mary and John live because she forgot her sweater." Quite an accomplishment considering the very short sentences she used at age 2!

In part, the increase in the length of the sentences reflects their rapidly increasing vocabulary. Vocabulary growth is impressive. Studies estimate that by age

6, children know about 14,000 words (Carey, 1977). In addition, they are increasingly able to impose structure on language. This permits them to group words into meaningful chunks, such as phrases and clauses.

Preschool children seem to be able to correctly use difficult words such as *rivalry* or *decaffeinated* as long as someone explains the meanings. In fact, many children are fascinated by words, wanting to know the meaning of any new word and often picking up and using difficult words and profanity as well. Despite the young child's ability to acquire and use new words rapidly, some children develop an **idiolect;** that is, an idiosyncratic but generally very communicative vocabulary and way of using language. Although some aspects of the idiolect can be primitive, others can be quite creative, as when the child creates new words or changes verbs into nouns and nouns into verbs. A child tapped by a Woodstock doll was heard to exclaim: "Stop woodstocking me!" Another child invented the word *stocks* as a combination of both socks and stockings, using it to refer to either of them (Thompson & Chapman, 1977).

Immature cognitive processes still limit children's use of words, however. When asked to explain a word, a child may do so with an action, thus displaying egocentric thinking. For example, she may define the word *stone* as "something I pick up" or *hole* as "something I dig." In addition, some seemingly simple words are difficult for children to fully understand because of their abstract meaning. For example, children find it difficult to always use appropriately words conveying comparison, such as *little, big, near,* and *far.* The word *little,* for example, is meaningful only in relation to *big.* Thus a 4-year-old may refer to his baby brother as little but will get upset if he is referred to as little in comparison to an adult. As far as the child is concerned, babies are little, but he is big (deVilliers & deVilliers, 1978).

Learning the Rules of Grammar

Language growth is not simply the accumulation of words; knowledge of and the ability to use grammatical rules are also important accomplishments of the preschool years. These rules governing word order and word form lend meaning to words. Although at the beginning of early childhood, children have difficulty applying and comprehending the complex grammatical structures entailed in forming the passive voice or complex sentences, they can learn and apply basic grammatical rules, such as the appropriate word order in active sentences, negations, and questions.

Even very young children using one- or two-word sentences show an understanding of the basic grammatical rules of language in their use of gesture and intonations to give meaning to their thoughts (Brown, 1973). To illustrate this point, let us look at the way children ask questions. At the beginning of the preschool period, they often speak in sentences with a question mark: "Nice doggie?" Researchers are not sure why children speak in questions but speculate that they are looking for confirmation that someone is listening (Brown & Hanlon, 1970). Initially, their questions entail nothing more than raising their voice at the end of a sentence. Later, they place a question word such as *where* or *why* at the beginning of a sentence without further modifying the sentence in any way: "Where my mommy?" Only later in the preschool period do children apply the specific rule of placing a verb before the subject when asking a question: "Where *is* my mommy?"

Early in the preschool period, the verb *is* in the above example is actually absent, not merely misplaced. Is this because young preschool children don't know they have to use a verb? In other words, is their acquisition of syntax incomplete? Or is the missing verb the result of cognitive constraints that may limit their utterances to three words? This question is still under investigation, but it is difficult to answer by focusing on speech production. Therefore, current studies are looking at what children understand. In an early method of exploring language comprehension, researchers asked the children to "act out" a sentence. But this required them to understand the sentence and the task. Roberta Golinkoff and her colleagues developed a more sensitive method based on a preferential looking paradigm. The child listens to a sentence and simultaneously looks at one of two video presentations. Only one presentation matches the sentence. Using this method, the researchers can gain insight into the syntactic comprehension of infants as young as 12 months (Golinkoff et al., 1987).

Let us look at how such studies are conducted. The child is seated on her mother's lap in front of two large video screens. The mother is blindfolded, so she cannot help the child solve the task. A light between the two screens attracts the child's attention. The child then hears a sentence, accompanied by the two video events, only one of which matches the meaning of the sentence. To attract and maintain the child's attention, researchers use unusual events, such as "Look, the woman is kissing the keys." Or the videos portray familiar characters such as Big Bird or Cookie Monster. Using such studies, Golinkoff and her colleagues found that children as young as 13 months will consistently look at the video event matching the sentence they hear. Even more impressive, children as young as 17 months understand that the order of words in a sentence makes a difference in its meaning. This suggests that language learning occurs earlier and faster than we previously realized. Researchers continue to use this method to investigate children's understanding of clauses, passives, and other aspects of language previously thought to appear in later years.

Gradual grammatical progress is also evident in children's use of negatives. In English we construct a negative sentence by transforming a declarative sentence. That is, we can transform the sentence "The girl is eating her sandwich" into the negative by adding the word *not:* "The girl is not eating her sandwich." Initially, young children simply add the word *no* to an otherwise affirmative sentence: "No take this." Eventually, they learn the correct use of negation: "Don't take this." Children hear many different ways of negating, such as *don't* or *can't,* which are spoken within a sentence. But *no* is presented alone and is highly stressed. Although different languages have vastly different rules of negation, children in other parts of the world form early negative sentences the same way as English-speaking children, by simply placing the word *no* at the beginning of the sentence (Slobin, 1970). Bloom (1973) also found that as they grow, children use the word *no* differently; at first they use *no* to indicate absence or nonexistence as in "Daddy no here," indicating that their father is gone. Soon afterward they will begin to use *no* to indicate negation as in "No bed," meaning "I don't want to go to bed."

As you can see from this brief explanation of children's formation of questions and negations, the acquisition of grammar is a gradual process that progresses from the simple to the complex. Brown (1973), who conducted longitudinal studies on language development, further noted that many children acquire the rules of grammar in a remarkably regular order. Later studies have shown that there are individual differences (Bowerman, 1982; Nelson, 1981), but Brown's studies show that children do not begin language by imitating adult utterances. Brown illustrates this by the way children use **morphemes**—the smallest units of speech—to qualify and give more precise meanings to words. The *-ing* ending denoting the present progressive tense (as in "I am walk*ing*") is a morpheme. Other morphemes are the suffix -*ed,* which denotes the regular past tense, and the -*s* ending, which denotes the third-person singular of a verb or the plural. Brown identified 14 such morphemes, or qualifiers. He noted that although the rate at which children acquire these qualifiers differs from child to child, the order in which they are acquired is the same for most children. Thus children begin with the present progressive tense, or -*ing* ending, and eventually acquire other more complex qualifiers designating the plural or the past tense.

Once children learn a grammatical rule as it applies to one word, they generalize its use to other words, even words they are not familiar with. Jean Berko (1958) cited an experiment she conducted in an attempt to evaluate 4- to 7-year-old children's understanding of pluralization. She presented the children with a line drawing of a birdlike object and told them, "This is a Wug. Here is another Wug. Now there are two _____?" Children had to verbally fill in the blank. Berko repeated this experiment, using several other nonsensical words such as *bix* or *zat,* which required different plural endings. Although all the children made some errors, even the youngest often gave the correct plural endings, thus demonstrating that (1) they learned general rules for pluralization rather than individual words in their plural form, and (2) they can apply these general rules of language to novel situations.

Overregularization

Children apply the general rules of language in their use of other qualifiers as well. But when they first learn a rule, they tend to apply it to all words, thus adding quite a bit of charm to their speech. This characteristic of their language, known as **overregularization,** perplexes parents, for suddenly their children start to make mistakes in their speech and seem to resist correction. For example, children who have used the word *went* correctly often tend to switch and say *goed,* once they learn the -*ed* ending designating the past tense. Or they may apply the -*ed* rule to the irregular past and say *camed.* In the same way, once they learn the plural ending -*s,* even though they already know and use the words *mice* and *feet,* they may switch to *mouses* and *foots.* Some children go even further and say *footses* or *feets.* In all these cases, by applying general rules to all words, they are ignoring the irregularities and exceptions inherent in English.

A CLOSER LOOK

Learning the Meaning of Words

It is quite remarkable that children can pick up the regularities and structure of language without explicit instruction. Equally fascinating is how they learn the meaning of words. They probably pick up the words from adult speech. One function of motherese, as you may recall from Chapter 6, is to stress the important elements of a sentence. Parents also engage in labeling games, such as asking their children to name a picture they see in a storybook. But how does the child know that the word *kitty* refers to an animal and not the page of the storybook or the color of the animal? In other words, how do children induce what a word means?

Researchers note that the first words children learn are labels for objects such as *car, cat,* or *apple.* These words are at the basic level of a conceptual hierarchy. At the superordinate level are words representing category labels such as *animal* (rather than *cat* or *dog*). Subordinate-level words are specific labels such as *spaniel* or *Great Dane,* which describe a subset of the category *dog.* Children first learn the basic words *cat* or *dog;* only later do they learn *animal* or *Great Dane.* The first words children learn also apply to the

(continued)

Articulation

Children's ability to articulate often lags behind their vocabulary. Even after they acquire a large vocabulary, some young children have trouble pronouncing words correctly. In many cases this is because their motor control, especially for fine-tuned movements, takes longer to develop than their ability to learn the language. They tend to drop the first consonants of some words such as *spoon* (*'poon*). They often substitute consonants; so *doggie* may be pronounced *goggie*. They have difficulty articulating certain sounds such as *th;* as a result, *thick* is often pronounced *fick*. However, even though they may not pronounce the word correctly, they know how the word should be pronounced and will attempt to correct an adult who imitates their speech. One anecdote tells of a boy unable to pronounce *r* who often talked of *wabbits*. When an adult asked him about the *wabbits,* the child firmly stated, "Not wabbits, wabbits!"

When children learn to articulate a sound, they often apply it to many other words. A 3-year-old boy we know learned to pronounce the *th* sound correctly. For the first few days after learning it, he pronounced such words as *thick* and *thank you* correctly and clearly, but he also tended to say *thoday* for *today* and *Thommy* for *Tommy.*

Difficulty in articulating is normal. Eventually, the child will be able to articulate clearly and use correct grammar. Some children have minor lisps, but they can still be understood. However, if after age 6 the child still cannot speak clearly, parents should consult a speech therapist.

Egocentric and Socialized Speech

The functions of language also change as children grow older. Piaget (1955) characterized speech as either egocentric or socialized. In *egocentric speech* children either carry on a monologue, apparently deriving pleasure from the repetition of words, or they focus their speech largely on what they want. Many children engage in egocentric speech at the beginning of the preschool period, but the older the

---

A CLOSER LOOK

(continued)

whole object and not to an attribute. An attribute may be a descriptive word such as *furry* or *small* (Heibeck & Markman, 1987).

Researchers propose that children are biased, or predisposed, to assign meaning to new words in certain ways, and that certain principles guide the way children interpret labels (Markman 1989). For example, the *principle of uniqueness,* also referred to as the *no-synonym rule,* states every new word has a meaning. The first word learned is attached to an object as its basic-level meaning. All other words referring to the object must carry other meanings, usually some characteristic of the object (Markman 1989; Merriman & Bowman, 1989).

Ellen Markman's study (1989) illustrates this point. She showed a group of 3- and 4-year-olds some pewter tongs. The children did not know the words *tongs* or *pewter.* When shown the pewter tongs, they were told, "This is pewter." Later, she showed the children wooden tongs and a pewter cup and asked, "Which is pewter?" Most children chose the tongs; they had interpreted the new word to be the label for an unfamiliar object. Markham then showed another group of 3- and 4-year-olds a pewter cup. They were already familiar with the object (a cup). They were told: "This is pewter." Since they already knew the label for a cup, they interpreted the word *pewter* as describing something about the cup. When they were shown a ceramic cup, they denied that it was pewter.

When preschool children talk to infants they use simplified speech and short utterances, revealing their sensitivity to their young listeners' abilities. Thus they are not as egocentric as Piaget believed them to be.

child becomes, the more she needs to communicate her thoughts, intentions, and desires to others. As a result, speech begins to serve a more social function. In *socialized speech* the child demonstrates the ability to communicate effectively, because socialized speech includes an exchange of information between speaker and listener.

Learning to Communicate

As children grow, their ability to communicate increases. To communicate effectively, they need three skills:

1. The ability to engage the listener's attention.
2. The ability to display sensitivity to the listener's characteristics and feedback; that is, to speak so that the listener understands. In addition, children need to be able to determine if the listener actually understands the message.
3. The ability to listen, since communication is a reciprocal process that includes effective speaking and effective listening.

As most parents and caretakers can attest, preschool children demonstrate at least one of these communications skills—the ability to get the listener's attention. Two- and 3-year-olds want to be heard, and they attract attention by tugging at their mother's skirt, prodding their father with a finger, or literally placing their face directly in front of the face of their parent or other adult. It is very difficult not to pay attention to them.

Still they are unable to communicate fully. Recall that by age 4, children seem to be sensitive to their listener's characteristics and also adjust their speech, depending on the listeners. Shatz and Gelman (1973) found that when 4-year-olds are asked to tell a 2-year-old or other 4-year-olds about a toy, they are likely to talk differently to the 2-year-old, using simplified speech and shorter utterances. Furthermore, studies suggest that when they are playing with one another or simply talking to one another, preschoolers listen and respond appropriately to their peer's statements or questions (Wellman & Lempers, 1977). They do not always engage in a collective monologue. But this ability to communicate effectively is only rudimentary in the preschool child and is not always applied.

Language and thought   Indeed, preschoolers often have a tendency to overestimate the clarity of the message they are conveying. They may say, "I want my toy," but they do not realize that they need to clarify which toy they want. They expect the listener to know what they mean (Beal & Flavell, 1983). Because egocentric speech and thinking occur at about the same time in the child's development, researchers have wondered about the relationship between language development and cognitive development. For adults, language and thought are so indistinguishable that thinking often seems like talking or communicating with oneself. Of course, when preschool children are acquiring and using language, they are thinking. They remember words, and they associate a word with its meaning. They figure out grammatical rules about combining words and using sentences; and when they are speaking, they are using words to express their feelings and thoughts. The question is, Do children first have a thought and then try to express it in words, or does language shape their thoughts?

This is an important, although controversial, question, the answer to which differs according to one's theoretical approach. Piaget (1955), who took an interactionist approach, thought cognitive development occurred first and language followed. Since language reflects thought, according to Piaget, it cannot cause cognitive development. Rather, language is only possible given the development of cognition. Thus, language does not structure thought but is the vehicle for expressing it. To underscore this point, he explained that infants can solve problems and acquire basic concepts before they have acquired language skills. As the preschool years pass and linguistic ability increases, language begins to assume a greater role in children's thoughts and behavior. To illustrate this, Piaget asked children to crawl and then to describe what they were doing as they crawled. At age 3 children would crawl when he told them to, but they could not describe it, explaining that they moved both hands together and then both knees together. At age 5 or 6, however, children could accurately describe what they did as they crawled. Hence, Piaget pointed out that although young children have the necessary motor skills and vocab-

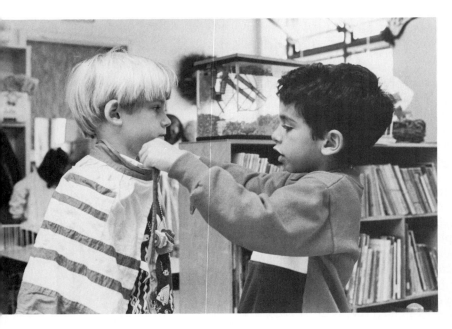

Once children start speaking fluently, they use language to organize and reorganize their experiences. Language enables them to acquire more and more information as well as to communicate better with others.

ulary, they do not acquire the cognitive skills necessary to understand and explain their behavior until later in the preschool years.

Other theorists, however, see language as taking on a far more significant and distinct role. The Russian psychologist Lev Vygotsky (1962) contended that with the beginning of symbolic thinking at about age 2, language comes to regulate children's thoughts and behavior. Unlike Piaget, Vygotsky did not think that egocentric speech implies a lack of awareness of other people's perspectives. Rather, he believed that egocentric speech has a specific function, which is self-regulation and self-guidance; that is, children use egocentric speech to direct their behavior. At first, this self-directing speech is external and audible to others, but over time audible speech declines and disappears. Vygotsky contends that it simply becomes internalized. However, he emphasizes that inner speech is actually a rapid sequence of ideas fleeting across the individual's mind; some ideas are translated into words, others into images. The important point here is that inner speech, just like egocentric speech, controls the child's behavior. For Vygotsky, language is an instrument of thought used "to plan, guide and monitor problem solving" (Frauenglass & Diaz, 1985, p. 357).

Many psychologists agree with Piaget that thinking occurs first and then is expressed in words, and many others agree with Vygotsky that language facilitates thinking. Still other researchers contend that initially children learn language, but eventually language facilitates learning. As Lois Bloom (1975) put it, during the preschool period children first learn to talk, and later they talk in order to learn. Bruner (1964), who sees language as a tool provided by culture, notes that language actually expands the child's mind. He explains that at first children understand the world only in terms of the actions they perform on it; but by age 3 when they start speaking fluently, they use language to organize and reorganize their experiences. Language enables them to acquire more and more information about their environment.

Getting Ready for School: Learning Environments

During early childhood, as children progress in their ability to think and talk, they become capable of organizing their knowledge into concepts. They become increasingly logical in their thinking and also acquire impressive language skills that enhance their ability to learn.

Preschool children do not need to be in a formal school setting to learn. Rather, learning occurs wherever they may be. Let us look at some of their major learning environments.

The Family

Preschoolers are naturally curious about their world, and they learn through their own discoveries what people and objects are like and how they behave. Parents play an important role in their children's understanding of the world, teaching them why they need to wash their hands before dinner, why they should be careful while crossing the street, and why they should be wary of strangers. There are many other ways that parents can enhance their children's learning.

Many children today start school or child care at an early age. From the earliest months of life, they are cared for by other caregivers at home and in out-of-home child care facilities. Nevertheless, the family is still the place where the child's learning takes place. And we encourage parents to think of themselves as their children's first teachers. By paying attention to their children and by sharing their daily discoveries, successes, failures, and concerns, parents can enhance their children's natural inclination to learn from their experiences. Parental activities that specifically encourage cognitive growth include reading to their children, playing with them, providing them with playthings, and taking them on special outings to the zoo, library, park, or the grocery store—or simply to play at a neighbor's house. Children whose parents interact with them in these ways are more likely to do well in elementary school (Entwisle & Alexander, 1990).

Longitudinal studies carried out in North Carolina attest to the importance of the home environment. The researchers found consistent correlation between the quality of family life and the level of cognitive achievement, noting that such specific aspects of the children's environment as parental attentiveness and the availability of playthings were "strongly related" to cognitive development (Bradley et al., 1989).

Child Care

Although the parents' interaction with their children is an important aspect of children's cognitive growth, many children do not have an opportunity to interact with their parents to a great extent. In many cases children grow up in single-parent families or in families where both parents work. In either case, parents are severely restricted in the time they can spend with their children and often have insufficient time and energy to attend to their needs for intellectual stimulation. Nancy Rubin (1984) points out that parents, specifically mothers, do not become as involved in their children's activities as they did in the past. Rather, they "manage" their children's time, coordinating but not participating in the various activities they engage in during the day.

Since the number of preschool children in some form of child care has quadrupled over the past two decades, the child care setting is another context within which they receive intellectual stimulation. In general, research suggests that children attending a well-run, quality child care center are not at a developmental disadvantage compared to children who spend most of their time at home (National Research Council, 1990). Clarke-Stewart (1982) points out that quality child care centers may even benefit some children who come from homes that do not provide them with opportunities for reading, playing, and getting along with peers—but only if the children are attending a quality child care center.

Choosing child care Amy has been in child care since she was 5 months old. Her mother Eleanor had felt that a family day care home would be appropriate. She found a provider nearby who was looking after two other children ages 3 and 4. Eleanor was fortunate to have found such a good setting; she read that it is better for infants to be in a small group and that they should have ample opportunity to interact with the provider on a one-to-one basis.

When Amy was 3, they moved to another part of town, and Eleanor had to make other child care arrangements. Amy was now old enough to benefit from socializing with other children in a child care center, but Eleanor was still worried about her physical safety and about the kinds of experiences she would have in child care. Eleanor visited several child care centers, before choosing one that she felt provided quality care.

Eleanor's task was not easy. Many parents know they have to choose quality care. The question is, What is good quality? Some parents focus on the curricular offerings of the center, feeling secure if their children receive some training in academic tasks that will prepare them for school. Research indicates, however, that quality child care is not determined by whether the child is exposed to academic training; rather, it has to do with the caretakers' behaviors and attitudes toward the child. According to the National Day Care Study (Ruopp et al., 1979) and a recent review of other studies (National Research Council, 1990), caretakers with training in early childhood education and child development spend more time with each child, comforting him, praising him, and providing him with guidance than do caretakers without such training. Children in centers where such caretakers are employed score better on standardized IQ tests, suggesting that just as parents can enhance the cognitive development of preschool children, the caregivers' behavior toward children is also important.

For many children, learning takes place in a child care center or family day care home.

Other studies suggest that frequent verbal interaction between caretaker and child also seems to be a key determinant of quality child care because it facilitates the child's language development and social and emotional development (McCartney et al., 1982; McCartney, 1984). In addition, a quality child care center should

1. employ a sufficient number of caregivers so that all children are supervised at all times and each child has ample opportunity to interact with an adult.
2. ensure that the number of children per class does not exceed 12 for 3-year-olds and 16 for older preschoolers.
3. provide a safe surrounding and a considerable variety of play materials—books, puzzles, paints, sandboxes, large-muscle equipment (Ruopp et al., 1979; National Research Council, 1990).
4. provide stability of care (Phillips, 1988). That is, the center should be staffed by caregivers who stay on the job over a relatively long period so the children have an

A CLOSER LOOK

Training Child Care Providers

Child development professionals have long recognized that the quality of care that young children receive from adult caretakers is the most important factor in their life. In reviewing several studies, the National Research Council (1990) found that young children in out-of-home care are likely to receive care that fosters their healthy development if:

1. The **staff/child ratio** in the caretaking situation is appropriate for the age of the children involved (1:3 for infants, 1:4 for toddlers, 1:8 for preschoolers)
2. The group size is appropriate, depending on the children's age (no larger than 6 for infants, 8 for toddlers, and 12 to 16 for preschoolers)
3. The caretakers responsible for the children's care have been trained in child development.

Unfortunately, public attitudes regarding child caretakers do not reflect the central role they play in children's lives or that they actually substitute for the children's family during a large part of the day. All too often they are regarded simply as babysitters. They earn low wages, have few, if any, fringe benefits, and are often not evaluated to ensure that they are capable of taking care of young children in groups. This results, in part, in a high turnover rate in the child care field. Observers estimate that the turnover rate averages 30% a year, compared with only 10% among other helping professionals (National Child Care Staffing Study, 1990). According to these same observers, caretakers in many child care centers have had no training in child care. How, then, can parents feel that they are entrusting their children to competent adults?

One way to improve the caretakers' public image and help parents evaluate the quality of care their children

receive is to provide proper training. As early as 1972 the Child Development Associate (CDA) Program took a step in this direction. Initiated with federal funds, the program trains and assesses caretakers and accredits those who have proved capable of taking care of children in groups (National Council for Early Childhood Professional Recognition, 1990).

The CDA program emphasizes the need to develop a reciprocal relationship between child and caretaker. Caretakers must understand the basic principles of child development, including the importance of play. The program uses competency-based training and assessment: it trains and assesses caretakers on the basis of their ability to work with young children and their ability to relate to each child individually. Individuals who complete the program receive the CDA credential, a certificate signifying that the individual has certain knowledge and skills and can apply them in the care of children.

The CDA program is an example of the work of child development researchers in an applied setting. It shows how research can help us make policy decisions that ultimately enhance children's lives. Indeed, research is an important aspect of the CDA program, which is based on knowledge of child development and the delineation of skills that are desirable in an individual who takes care of children. These skills, known as the CDA Competency Standards, include the ability to establish and maintain a safe, healthy learning environment and to promote the positive functioning of children in a group setting. Each skill is further defined in terms of the functions performed by caretakers. For example, in "promoting positive functioning of children in a group setting," caretakers must demonstrate that they can (1) help children

opportunity to get to know them and develop a relationship. Unfortunately, there is often frequent staff turnover in centers, where the staff stays on the job for only six months at most (Phillips, 1989; National Child Care Staffing Study, 1990).

Researchers also point out that since the care and socialization of children attending child care is really a joint effort between parents and caretakers, it is in the children's best interests for parents and caretakers to form a close relationship and for the parents to become involved in their children's child care experiences (Zigler & Turner, 1982). This aspect of programming is often referred to as *parent involvement*. In Amy's child care center, the staff encourage parents to stay and watch the children play or join in the play every once in a while. The staff also let parents know what kind of day the children have had and invite parents to participate in special activities. It is difficult for Eleanor to find the time to spend in child care, but her employer allows her to take a "personal" day off every few months.

A CLOSER LOOK

get along with one another, (2) provide a routine for the children, and (3) establish simple rules that children can understand (Ward, 1976). The CDA program evaluates caretakers on the basis of tasks performed on the job. These tasks ensure that children will receive the proper care needed for their development.

The CDA program is one example of several efforts to train and evaluate caretakers in such varied settings as child care centers and family day-care homes (National Association of Family Day Care Providers, 1989; Shuster, Finn-Stevenson, & Ward, 1990). All these programs provide a standard par-

ents can use in determining whether they are entrusting their children to caretakers who are sensitive to the children's needs and characteristics. In addition, the programs advance the public image of caretakers. Once Americans understand the skills and knowledge that are required to care for children, and once they realize that there are ways to train and accredit the people carrying out these important tasks, then members of the child care profession will receive the respect and recognition they deserve.

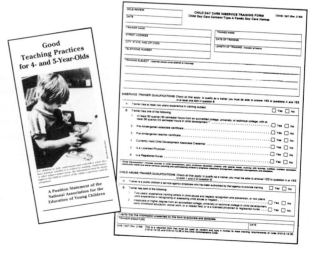

Studies show that child care providers who are trained in child development provide good-quality care.

Studies on Head Start, a program for economically disadvantaged preschool children, have shown that parent involvement and participation in children's activities benefit both the children and the parents. In addition, parent involvement facilitates the caregivers' ability to relate appropriately to the children (Powell, 1978).

Television: Its Educational Value

Children's learning environments also include television. Most homes have at least two TV sets, which are typically on when the children are home. Estimates of children's viewing time vary from 11 to 28 hours a week, but all of them indicate that children spend more time watching television than in any other activity except sleep (Huston, Watkins, & Kunkel, 1989). As we noted in Chapter 1, television is often a focal point of parental concern in large part because some kinds of content, notably violent and sexually oriented programming, are likely to induce unacceptable behaviors or dispositions. Parents are also concerned about television's role in selling products. However, researchers point out that television also plays an important role as an educator and a source of social learning.

In a review of studies on the topic, Huston, Watkins, and Kunkel (1989) note that programs designed to teach children can be effective, and that "the same mechanisms which generate adverse effects are also capable of producing positive outcomes" (p. 425). Programs containing prosocial content, for example, can be effective models for children's social learning (Collins & Getz, 1975). Programs such as Sesame Street can help children learn cognitive skills and concepts (Cook et al., 1975) and can enhance vocabulary (Rice et al., 1987). When compared with other forms of education, these programs are cost-effective as well, because they reach vast numbers of children simultaneously (Huston, Watkins, & Kunkel, 1989).

Part of the problem, however, is that educational programs make up only a small percentage of the programming and usually are aired only on public television stations (Kerkman et al., 1987). Also, the fact that children can simply switch to another channel and find a violent movie or a commercial diminishes the positive value of television as educator. Recently passed legislation (see Chapter 1) tries to build in some protection, such as limiting the advertising on programs likely to be watched by children.

Parents and other adults can help children benefit from watching television by watching with them and discussing the program (Singer & Singer, 1976). Mediating the child's television watching is important because young children have not developed what Greenfield (1984) terms **television literacy.** That is, they do not always know how to interpret the relationship between camera shots (sequences in which the camera is continuously on). Also, preschool children have trouble distinguishing between reality and fantasy; thus they have trouble understanding TV shows. When the "bad guy" is shot, they have difficulty understanding that the actor is not really dead (Dorr, 1983). As a result, they can become confused about what they are seeing unless someone explains it to them.

Preschool

Another aspect of children's learning environment is the preschool. Children who are not enrolled in child care are usually enrolled in a preschool program for several mornings a week.

The preschool (or nursery school) program is an important step toward preparing children for school because it provides an opportunity for children to learn to get along with peers and with an adult in a position of authority, as well as the opportunity to play with a variety of play materials and thereby progress in the attainment of cognitive skills.

Nursery schools, or preschools as they are often called, have been in the United States since about 1920. Many parents feel that by age 3 or 4, children should be in preschool where they can play with other children and learn the social skills that will prepare them for kindergarten and first grade. Historically, preschools offered a part-day program that children attended two or three times a week. Today, however, many preschools extend their day and enroll children for a longer period to accommodate parents' needs for child care. Therefore, it is difficult to distinguish between child care centers and preschools or nursery schools. Nevertheless, some people may regard child care as a caretaking facility that is open from 6 A.M. until 6 P.M. Nursery schools, on the other hand, provide a setting where the child can play with other children and become ready for formal schooling. For children not in child care, nursery schools represent the first opportunity to be with a group of other children. In nursery schools children experience about the same type of activities as in child care centers, except that the latter also include nap time and lunch.

There are many different types of preschools. Some focus on enabling children to develop social skills. Others focus on providing opportunities to learn to read and write and acquire other academic skills. Should parents choose a preschool on the basis of its curricular offerings? Developmental experts such as David Elkind (1987) suggest that teaching preschool children academic skills is not as important as giving them the opportunity to play, since at this age children learn through play.

No matter what their philosophies, preschools generally follow a similar routine. For example, there is a short period of group activities such as storytelling, in which children learn to pay attention to the teacher, and show-and-tell, in which they can talk about important happenings in their lives. Then there is a short break for juice and healthful snacks, during which time each child has the opportunity to develop such skills as pouring juice from the pitcher. In addition, children are often taken to different places of interest. In a quality preschool program the children also engage in free play, choosing from a number of different activities available in the art area, dress-up corner, housekeeping corner, or reading corner. Besides engaging in these activities, children become familiar with following a routine that is similar to what they will encounter in kindergarten. They also begin to learn how to write their names, recognize the letters of the alphabet, and pick out and name colors.

LEARNING FROM OTHER CULTURES

Preschools in the United States, Japan, and China

Parents in the United States were asked, What are the most important things for your child to learn in preschool? Close to 35% responded that they want their children to learn self-reliance and self-confidence. Over 30% of Japanese parents responded that they wanted their child to learn empathy and concern for others. Chinese parents cited cooperation and learning to be members of a group as the most important things that their child should learn in preschool.

These findings were derived from a study by Tobin, Wu, and Davidson (1989) that explored the relationship between society and child care by comparing preschools in the United States, Japan, and China. The preschools were matched for quality, social class of clientele, and geographical area. The researchers videotaped sessions in each preschool. Later on, administrators, teachers, parents, child development specialists, and university students were asked to explain the videotape made in their country and to make observations about the tapes made of the preschools in the other countries. The insiders' explanations were then compared with the reactions of observers from outside the culture. The group was also asked questions about the philosophy of preschool in their country, such as What are the three most important reasons for society to have a preschool? or What are the important things children should learn in preschool?

As we have seen, perceptions of the purpose of preschool differed depending on the culture. However, there were some commonalities. For example, parents in all three cultures considered learning communication skills an important aspect of preschool education. Nevertheless, how the skills were taught differed, reflecting societal differences in philosophy. American children were encouraged to use language to express their individual feelings and wishes. In Japan, where there is an overriding focus on teaching children empathy, children were taught that communication entails being an effective listener as well, so they were encouraged to listen to others. In China the emphasis in communication is placed on the speaker, as in our country. But Chinese children are encouraged to express the similarities between themselves and others in their group, rather than express their feelings and desires.

These differences in philosophy were also seen in the opinions about the role of preschool in the socialization of children. American preschools are traditionally seen as providing an opportunity for children to interact with their peers. This aspect of preschool is also noted in Japan and China, perhaps even more so. However, in the United States the underlying rationale is for children to acquire social skills, whereas in Japan parents are concerned that children will grow up to be selfish, and introducing them to other children in preschool is a way of preventing this. In China, where there is a policy encouraging parents to limit their families to one child only (see Chapter 1), the preschool is seen as an opportunity to prevent the child from becoming spoiled by the undivided attention of parents and grandparents.

In China there is also the perception that preschool is a place where the child can begin to develop a sense of nationalism. Children learn about their country, and they also learn academic skills that will help them become useful citizens.

There is a similar emphasis today on using preschool to prepare American children for later success in school and in life. Many parents believe that children need to learn academic skills in preschool. However, this view is somewhat tempered by developmental experts' warnings that children who are pressured to learn academic skills and to compete at an early age will be stressed (Elkind, 1987). Therefore, despite some focus on teaching academic skills, American preschools also offer children an opportunity for unstructured, free play. Chinese children do not have this opportunity. There is an emphasis on play in Japan, since the preschool years are seen as a time for children to relax before they enter an extremely rigorous and competitive educational system.

How do preschoolers spend their day in these three countries? In the United States the teacher plans the day, usually including periods for free play and for group activities such as show-and-tell and storytelling. Lunch or snack breaks are relatively informal and noisy, because the children are allowed to laugh, argue, talk to, or otherwise interact with one another.

Japanese children spend about 30 minutes on a workbook activity, followed by free play. When they are playing, the children are noisy and may argue and fight; the teacher does not interfere, even when one of the children comes to complain about another child. Instead the teacher encourages them to sort out their differences so they can learn to get along with one another. Lunch begins with a thank-you song, but then the children can be as noisy as they want while they eat.

In China the entire day is orderly. Even during lunch children are told to concentrate on their eating as much as they concentrate on their studying; quiet, serious behavior is reinforced. There is not much opportunity for play, and when the children do play, they are expected to play silently.

The preschool school experience benefits most children because it provides a transition from learning at home to learning in a more formal setting. By attending preschool, children learn to behave and interact with others in a group setting; they also have access to a variety of playthings and opportunities to play they may not encounter at home. All these factors facilitate the development of cognitive skills, readying children for school.

DISCUSSION OF SOCIAL ISSUES

Preschool Intervention Programs

Many children are ready to start school and to benefit from formal instruction by the time they are 6 years old. Unfortunately, some children enter school without the skills needed to cope with the school environment. These children, who are most often poor, fail to acquire the basic skills that would presumably give them equal opportunity to participate in and function within our society. Without an education they face a life of unemployment and hopelessness, and the cycle of poverty perpetuates itself.

To reverse this trend, educators, social scientists, and policymakers joined forces in the 1960s to mount the War on Poverty, a massive effort to eradicate social inequities in the United States. The War on Poverty included job-training programs and provisions for increasing welfare benefits. It also emphasized providing preschool education for disadvantaged children. By intervening during early childhood—a crucial time in development—and by providing learning experiences these children may not otherwise have, the program would foster school achievement and thus break the cycle of poverty.

Policymakers based their decision to concentrate on the preschool child as a strategy for social reform on the scientific evidence available at that time. This evidence pointed to the influence of early experiences on intelligence. On the basis of animal studies and other research, Hunt (1961), in his book *Intelligence and Experience,* argued that intelligence is in large measure an environmental product. He contended that we can promote a faster rate of intellectual development and higher levels of adult intelligence by "governing the encounters that children have with their environments, especially during the early years of their development." Benjamin Bloom (1964) stated that intellectual development reaches its peak growth rate during the early childhood years, and that by age 6, a significant portion of children's intellectual capacity has been developed. Thus, policymakers concluded that economically disadvantaged children, as a result of their lack of appropriate experiences in the home, must suffer from deficits that can only become greater as they grow older (Horowitz & Paden, 1973). First grade was already too late to change the path of educational failure; some intervention was needed during the preschool years to provide children with experiences that would stimulate their intellectual development and help them succeed in school.

Since that time, however, researchers have realized that intellectual development results from an interaction between biological and environmental factors, and that there is a limit to the malleability of intelligence. They have also concluded that intelligence, as well as any other trait, might be influenced by biological or environmental factors at other points in life besides the early childhood years. In Chapter 3 we reviewed the research indicating that the prenatal period is critical for physical development and the growth of the brain. We can also consider adolescence an important period in development. Feuerstein's studies (1980) suggest that in attempts to modify retardation that may result from a lack of experiences in the environment, adolescence is the most effective and critical time for intervention. Hence, although researchers and policymakers still believe in the importance of early intervention, these programs are no longer confined to early childhood. In addition, early intervention programs now focus on children's intelligence, their health, their nutritional status, and their motivation to learn and succeed. These factors are all important determinants of school achievement.

Project Head Start

Policymakers and educators have developed numerous early intervention programs since the 1960s. A description of each one is beyond the scope of this chapter, but we will focus on the most notable program—Project Head Start, one of the country's best-known "success stories." Head Start has survived for over 25 years, even though economic conditions have mandated budget cuts in other federally funded programs. And Congress has recently appropriated even more federal funds to make Head Start available to more children (Zigler & Muenchow, in press). Let us take a look at the history of the program and its accomplishments.

Project Head Start began in 1965 as a summer program for 4- and 5-year-olds whose socioeconomic status predicted poor performance in school. Eventually the program was extended to a full academic year and is now available to preschool children and, in some variations of the program, to parents and children from the prenatal period.

As with other early intervention programs, Head Start has had a tremendous impact on the lives of economically disadvantaged children and their parents, by setting in motion experiences that enhance the children's success in school and in life. Although Head Start is often synonymous with early childhood programs (Richmond, Stipek, & Zigler, 1979), not all intervention programs are the same. Programs

vary in their goals, methods of intervention, duration of services, and age of the participants. Furthermore, all Head Start programs are not the same. Project Head Start is actually a family of over 2000 programs that vary in type and quality of services they render. Some are center-based; others provide services in the home. Some are demonstration projects that provide a constellation of services to children and families beginning even before the birth of the child; others focus on providing services to parents and children only during the preschool years *(Head Start in the 1980s)*. But all these efforts share a commitment to enhancing the quality of life of children and families.

Project Head Start also differs from other early intervention efforts in that its planners did not focus on the deficits of economically disadvantaged children. Rather, they appreciated the fact that these children came from different, not necessarily inferior, cultural backgrounds. As a result, they adopted an approach that respected the varied backgrounds (Zigler & Valentine, 1979). This approach is reflected in the involvement of parents in all planning and administrative aspects of each program. Parent involvement has now become a standard aspect of most intervention programs for children and infants (Honing, 1988); but when Head Start began, this provision was a significant breakthrough from past practices in which paid professionals dictated the operation of children's services. Parent involvement in Head Start programs has proved to be successful for both parents and children. Children's intellectual performance increased largely because the parents, who had received responsibility for this program, began to feel better about themselves; their children, too, began to feel that they had more control over their lives and were more motivated to succeed in school (Coleman et al., 1966).

In addition, Head Start does not focus on promoting children's intellectual performance. From the beginning, Head Start was guided by the knowledge that the extent that children will succeed in school depends on how healthy they are, how they feel about themselves and others, how motivated they are to succeed, as well as on their mental and verbal skills (Zigler, 1973). Sick or hungry children are not likely to attend to academic tasks or benefit from any experiences provided; children who cannot relate positively to other children and adults in a position of authority are not likely to behave in a way that is conducive to learning in school.

The importance of Project Head Start extends beyond its impact on the lives of children and their families. Researchers have been involved in the policy process since Head Start's inception, which marked a turning point in the field of developmental psychology. Before Project Head Start, researchers regarded basic research and the accumulation of knowledge as their primary duties. Many researchers have since realized that they should direct their work toward solving social problems. By participating in the social policy process, they can help improve children's lives and also have an opportunity to learn more about their development and the processes that can enhance or inhibit that development (Zigler & Finn-Stevenson, 1992).

Evaluation of Early Intervention Programs

Participation in Head Start and other early intervention efforts has also helped researchers understand how to evaluate these programs and refine their methodologies for doing so.

Much of what the researchers learned about the evaluation of programs came from evaluating Project Head Start. Initially, they focused on the general question, Have children benefited from participation in the program? They used only IQ tests to determine the answer. If IQ scores increased, researchers thought the program was successful; if the IQ scores remained the same, the program had no effect on the children.

We question the evaluators' focus and their use of IQ tests as the only evaluation tool. First, by focusing only on benefits to the children, evaluators preempted the possibility of finding out if other members of the family had benefited. Subsequent studies revealed, in fact, that the positive effects of early intervention extend to parents and siblings as well (Lamb-Parker, Piotrkowski, & Peay, 1987; Gordon, 1979). Second, the use of the IQ scores yielded false optimism and later disenchantment with early intervention efforts (Zigler & Berman, 1983; Salkind, 1983: Bronfenbrenner, 1975). Early evaluations of Project Head Start revealed that although children's IQ scores initially increased, these gains later "faded out." The widely publicized Westinghouse Learning Corporation's (1969) evaluation revealed that even a full year of Head Start (as opposed to only the summer session) resulted in short-term gains in IQ, which tended to diminish during the early elementary grades. As a result, Head Start and other early intervention projects lost much of their initial popularity. Only a great deal of advocacy on the part of parents and professionals has kept them alive (Valentine & Zigler, 1983; Zigler & Muenchow, in press).

In retrospect, the evaluations of Head Start yielded important lessons. We now recognize that one problem stemmed from the fact that the program's goals were not stated clearly at the outset. For example, because parent participation was not included as a goal, researchers never evaluated this aspect of the program. Evaluators now recommend that when programs are developed, their goals should be clearly stated to facilitate their evaluation (Weiss, 1989).

We have also learned that the use of the IQ test as a criterion to measure the success or failure of a preschool program is inadequate. The IQ test is a good predictor of success in school, but it fails to measure how children feel about themselves and how healthy they are. Because these are also aspects of intervention, and because they influence school achievement, we should incorporate them into the evaluation (Zigler & Trickett, 1978).

Finally, we have realized that an important component of any evaluation is cost-effectiveness: How much does the program cost? How much would it have cost society if the children did not attend the program? This is an important question, because policymakers usually make funding decisions on the basis of costs and benefits (Travers & Light, 1982).

Follow-up evaluations of Head Start and other preschool intervention programs took a broader, more long-term approach to assessing their benefits and incorporating these principles. They found that children who attended these programs performed better in school than those who did not and were less likely to be in remedial education classes (Consortium of Longitudinal Studies, 1983; Lazar et al., 1982).

In one of the most widely publicized evaluations of a preschool intervention program (known as the Perry Preschool Program), for 19 years researchers followed children who had participated in the preschool program. Low-income children who had enrolled in the program achieved markedly greater success in school and their personal lives than did comparable children who had not received early childhood education. As young adults, participants were more likely to be gainfully employed, and fewer had dropped out of high school. In addition, they were less likely to receive public assistance and engage in criminal activities (Berrueta-Clement et al., 1984).

Preschool intervention has also proved cost-effective for society. Since the programs need to be of high quality, they are expensive (the Perry Preschool Program, for example, cost over $6000 per year per child). However, they are cheaper than providing remedial education and other programs later in the children's lives (Weikart, 1982). Several studies have shown that for every dollar spent on preschool intervention programs, society can save $4.75 in costs for remedial education, welfare, and crime later on (Committee on Economic Development, 1987).

Renewed Interest in School Readiness

These evaluation results made an impact on society. Impressed with the potential benefits of early intervention programs, educators, politicians, and business leaders are calling for increased spending for preschool programs in an effort to ensure "school readiness." In 1990 President George Bush and the National Governors' Association agreed to provide all eligible low-income preschoolers with the opportunity to attend a preschool program that would make them "ready" to benefit from formal schooling. Business leaders are interested in preschool programs because they recognize that the preparedness of the future work force depends on their experiences early in life (Committee on Economic Development, 1987).

State legislatures have also increased their funding for early childhood intervention programs; as a result, many schools have begun to open their doors to 3- and 4-year-olds. A national survey found that in 1989, 29 states passed legislation to fund preschool intervention programs, many of which were based in public schools (National Conference of State Legislators, 1989).

School Readiness: What Does It Mean?

It is important to give children a good start. But we need to clarify several points about school readiness in general and preschool intervention programs in particular:

1. Efforts to ensure children's success in school should also focus on programs that serve the family and child at birth or earlier. Recall that assaults to prenatal development can result in a range of developmental problems that will impede the child's ability to learn later in life. Regular prenatal care and adequate nutrition can prevent many of these problems. Further, services for infants and toddlers can either prevent or identify developmental problems at an early date.

2. Research documenting the benefits of early intervention has been based on high-quality programs. If high-quality services continue to be provided, children will benefit from the programs.

Summary

During the preschool years, significant advances occur in children's ability to think. There are several approaches to explaining these changes. Information-processing researchers explain the changes in terms of increases in memory. According to Jean Piaget, children in the preoperational period of cognitive development (ages 2 to 7) cannot reason; as a result, they make mistakes on seemingly simple cognitive tasks. For example, they cannot consistently classify objects according to their shape, color, or size until they are about 6 years old. Children usually fail such tasks because they can only center, or focus, on one aspect of the problem at a time and thus neglect other aspects. In addition, their thinking is governed by irreversibility; they do not have the flexibility to go back and forth in their reasoning. Since children cannot visualize what an object looks like, they reason on the basis of what they can see. Piaget also noted that children are egocentric in their thinking, understanding life only as it revolves around them. They are also egocentric in their language, despite the fact that they acquire impressive language skills during early childhood and learn and apply complex rules of language. Egocentrism begins to decline during the preschool years.

Because young children are egocentric in their thinking and their language, researchers ask, Is language related to thought? That is, do we think first and act later, or does language facilitate thinking? Piaget believed that language is possible only after the development of cognition; language does not structure thought, it is simply a vehicle for communicating it. But Bruner and Vygotsky, among others, disagree, noting that language expands the mind and regulates behavior.

Parents can facilitate their children's optimal cognitive development. Studies have shown that parents who respond to their children, encourage them to complete tasks independently, and provide them with intellectually stimulating experiences will enhance their cognitive growth. Just as parental behavior can enhance the child's mental development, the behavior of caregivers in a child care center also has an impact on child development.

Children learn in the context of their home and child care facility, and they also learn from television. Some children acquire cognitive skills through their nursery school experiences. Nursery school is an important transition between informal learning at home and more formal learning within the school setting. With this in mind, researchers, policymakers, and educators developed early childhood education programs for economically disadvantaged children. These programs—the most notable of which is Project Head Start—have had a positive impact on the lives of children and families. They have also brought about a turning point in developmental psychology and enhanced researchers' understanding of cognitive development. Researchers now realize that children's ability and motivation to learn depend on their health and the way they feel about themselves, as well as on their intellectual capacity.

10 Social and Emotional Development During the Preschool Years

The Social World

During the preschool years children make remarkable progress in physical development and in the acquisition of cognitive and language skills. This progress is paralleled by equally striking changes in social and emotional development. Whereas 2-year-olds begin early childhood primarily concerned with their own needs and desires and still dependent on their parents' care, by age 5 they are increasingly independent, masters of their environment, and able to recognize and accommodate the needs of others and to interact cooperatively with people in their social world.

Through interactions with those around them, children develop a sense of their own identity and abilities. They discover that the world holds endless opportunities for exploration and social interaction. As magical as the world may appear, however, children soon find that it is fraught with frustrations, fears, jealousies, and angers that they must learn to deal with.

A CLOSER LOOK

The Preschool Child: A Theoretical Perspective

Erica and John Lambert are at their wit's end. Allison has always been a good child and her sister Rebecca has also been cheerful and easy-going. But for several days, Rebecca, now almost 2½, is being very difficult. She refuses to change her clothes, eat when she is told to, or go to bed at a regular time. When the family is getting ready to leave the house, she sometimes refuses to get ready and bedtime has become a time of war between Rebecca and her parents. The Lamberts are wondering what happened to the sweet baby they had and what they may have done wrong.

Erik Erikson (1963)—the child psychologist whose theory we first discussed in Chapter 2—would describe the Lamberts' ordeal as perfectly natural. Rebecca is simply feeling her independence. Erikson described the emerging independence of young preschoolers as a function of the psychosocial crisis, **autonomy versus shame and doubt,** that occurs around age 2. He theorized that if children develop a healthy attitude toward being independent, they will acquire a sense of autonomy and gradually become self-sufficient. If, on the other hand, they are made to feel that their efforts toward independence are wrong, then shame and self-doubt will develop instead of autonomy.

Children can be extremely obstinate when they are making their first bid for autonomy. They want to do things for themselves and in their own way, often frustrating their parents and taxing their patience to the limit. Although the negativism of these children often results in difficult, rather stormy relations with their parents, this situation is relatively short-lived, because children eventually learn what they can and cannot do by themselves; and their parents come to feel comfortable about letting them assume greater self-reliance. The parents' tasks here are not easy. They must recognize their children's innate motivation toward independence and foster in them a sense of pride in their independent accomplishments by letting them do as much for themselves as they can. At the same time parents must also monitor their children's activities and impose limits on their behavior so they will understand what they cannot do as well. Erikson (1963) theorized that once children acquire a firm sense of what they can and cannot do and what they are not allowed to do, they will move on to the next psychosocial crisis, **initiative versus guilt.** During this stage, which occurs between the ages of 3 and 6, children gain increasing confidence as they discover ways to pursue activities on their own initiative. If such initiatives are successful, they will enjoy their accomplishments and acquire a sense of direction and purpose. Yet at times parents are too demanding of children this age, expecting them to be able to perform tasks well and belittling their efforts.

When parents are extremely demanding or when they are too rigid and prevent their children from trying to learn to accomplish tasks on their own, the children are overwhelmed by feelings of guilt that may inhibit any further attempts to pursue activities on their own initiative.

Erikson's description of preschool children is admittedly theoretical, but it provides a useful framework for understanding the emergence and development of personality and the potential influence of parents and others on children's personality.

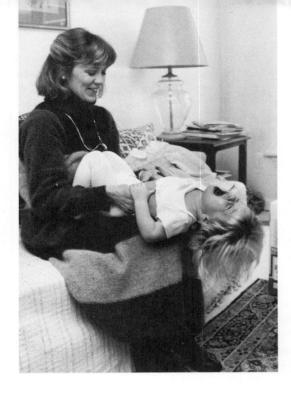

They also learn that as members of a family and society, they must abide by a set of rules, restrictions, and codes of social behavior. Although their parents assume a major role in teaching them how to become members of society, there are other influences on development. Children learn from their teachers, TV personalities, and others they encounter. Before discussing these influences on socialization, we explore the child's social world, which changes during the preschool years from one defined almost exclusively by the parents to one involving extensive and influential relations with siblings and peers. In the context of these social relations children acquire socially appropriate ways of behaving and evidence their emerging personality.

Expanding Family Relations

The changes in their social world occur against the background of children's increased independence and the developmental strides characteristic of the age. Children progress from clumsy coordination to increasingly refined motor skills. They attain wider intellectual awareness and a deepening understanding of symbols. They become increasingly able to talk and verbally communicate their feelings and desires. Also, having established a warm and trusting relationship with their parents during infancy, many children feel secure to explore their environment, meet new people, and enjoy the company of their parents, relatives, teachers, and playmates.

Always rushing and continuously on the move, preschool children are enthusiastically trying to find out as much as they can about the physical world. They wander off, touching and investigating every object in sight. Learning that they are quite capable of exploring the world by themselves, they acquire a sense of their own independence. They begin to regard themselves as individuals who exist separately from their parents and who can assert their will and desires. A preschool child may become enraged at any suggestion that she should stop playing to take a nap, and she seems to find pleasure in saying no many times a day. Frequently she chooses to do just the opposite of what her parents or other caretakers want her to do.

Interactions with the mother   Although preschool children are becoming increasingly independent, their relationship with their parents remains the primary focus of their interactions, and their attachment to the primary caregiver, usually the mother, continues to be strong. They enjoy spending time with their mother, talking to her, sharing toys with her, and drawing emotional support from her presence. When playing, they frequently check to see where mother is, and they are more likely to play quietly for long periods as long as they can see or hear their mother, or when they know where she is (Rheingold, 1973; Clarke-Stewart & Hevey, 1981). When 3-year-olds are asked to stay in an unfamiliar place, for example, researchers found that they are more likely to feel relaxed and to play if they can hear their mother's voice or see her on a television screen than when either of these conditions is not present (Adams & Passman, 1979).

Preschoolers depend on their mother's affection, often asking, especially after being scolded, "Do you love me, Mommy?" (Sears, Maccoby, & Leven, 1957). When they are under stress, or in a strange situation, such as the doctor's office or a new nursery school or child care center, they may have trouble leaving their mother. During the first few days, crying and refusing to let mother go is not unusual, even for children who have been eager to attend child care or nursery school. The older the children, however, the more able they are to tolerate relatively long periods of separation (Rheingold & Eckerman, 1971); they know from experience that the

The older children become, the better they tolerate physical distance from their mothers, and the more they accept increasingly long periods of separation.

separation will not be long. Also, their progress in physical and cognitive development enables them to concentrate on specific tasks for longer periods and master skills. As a result, they are less dependent on direct physical contact with the mother (Hartup, 1989).

Mothers also change in the way they interact with their children. They encourage independent behavior in preschoolers and become less tolerant of demands for attention, often telling them that they are old enough to stay away for a while (Maccoby, 1980). Also, during the preschool years mothers tend to be less involved in their children's specific activities, concentrating instead on verbally guiding them toward greater self-reliance (Heckhausen, 1987).

Interactions with the father   Although mothers relax their involvement with their preschool children somewhat, in households where the father is present, he comes to play a more prominent role in the children's life.

Recall from Chapter 7 that most fathers enjoy their children from birth and interact with them throughout infancy (Lamb, 1977). During the preschool period, however, fathers become increasingly involved in childrearing and are inclined to spend more time playing with and disciplining their children. In addition, children, especially boys, seem to prefer their father as a playmate, and they seek to play with him more often than with their mother (Lamb, 1981). The more time the father and child spend together, the stronger their relationship becomes, and the more the child recognizes that he has two parents to take care of his needs instead of just one. Children learn quickly to differentiate between their parents' characteristics and to direct some kinds of requests and concerns toward one and some toward the other. For example, a child who wants cookies before dinner is likely to ask the parent, mother or father, who is less concerned with her appetite at mealtime.

DISCUSSION OF SOCIAL ISSUES

Children of Divorce

Unfortunately, not all children have the opportunity to develop a close relationship with their father. One-fifth of all children under 5 in the United States are in single-parent families, 90% of these families are headed by women, in most cases as a result of divorce (U.S. Congress, 1989). Admittedly, in some instances both parents are awarded custody of the children. Nevertheless, data show that custody determinations still award most children to their mother and that about 9 out of 10 children live with their mother following divorce (Spanier & Glick, 1981). Eventually, 75% of divorced mothers and 80% of divorced fathers remarry, and the remarriages involve a series of transitions and household reorganizations that children have to adjust to (Hetherington, Stanley-Hagan, & Anderson, 1989). Regardless of whether the children remain in a single-parent family or come to live in an extended family, many only see their biological fathers for a few hours every week or every two weeks and usually under strained circumstances. The limited experiences they have with their father are quite different from the interactions other children have with their father in the context of daily family life.

For these children, the absence of a father usually means less social, emotional, and financial support and less help for the mother in decision making, childrearing, and household tasks (Hetherington & Camara, 1984). The absence of a father may also mean the loss of an effective disciplinarian and role model. In many

Many children see their divorced fathers only a few hours a week or month. Their time with each other is usually spent away from a home setting.

cases the father does not show any concern for or desire to be with the child. Mavis Hetherington and her colleagues (Hetherington, Cox, & Cox, 1976; 1978) found that during the first year after the divorce, fathers become emotionally detached from their children, and that fewer than half the fathers see their children as frequently as once a week, even though they live nearby. Furstenberg and colleagues (1983) reported similar findings, noting that although immediately following the divorce noncustodial fathers may spend more time with their children than they did before the divorce, this close contact rapidly diminishes. By the second year after the divorce, many fathers rarely see their children.

The father's emotional detachment is also evident in child support problems. The parent who does not have custody makes a monetary payment, known as **child support,** to the parent with custody (Espenshade, 1979). All states have some legal provisions binding the noncustodial parent to share in the expense of raising the child; the judge who presides over the divorce decides the exact amount (Weitzman, 1981a). However, the amount of support awarded is often inadequate to meet the child's needs (Weitzman, 1981b). Close to two-thirds of noncustodial fathers refuse to make any payment at all (U.S. Bureau of the Census, 1987c). The number of fathers who default on their obligation for child support has become so great that states have instituted a variety of measures to counteract the problem (Espenshade, 1979; Weitzman, 1981b); these efforts have met with only modest success. As a result, a large portion of ex-husbands still fail to pay child support (U.S. Bureau of the Census, 1987c). Although failure to pay child support often makes life very difficult for the mother and children (Hernandez, 1988), its direct emotional effects on the child must also be considered. Preschoolers may not be aware of the financial obligations of their father, but as they grow older they will realize that their father refuses to share in the cost of their care.

The arguing and conflict between parents that often precedes a divorce create a negative emotional climate that can undermine the child's psychological development (Kalter, 1977). Wallerstein and her colleagues (1988) found that preschool children experience a great deal of stress at the divorce of their parents. They have difficulty understanding divorce, and they think that once the father leaves the house, he is no longer part of the family. Their egocentrism also causes them to take the blame for the divorce and to feel rejected, abandoned, and unloved (Wallerstein & Kelly, 1980).

This negative impact is not inevitable; the effects of divorce on children and the extent to which they are able to cope with and adjust to the new situation are often affected by the quality of the parents' post-divorce relationship and the availability of social support. Several researchers have found that when ex-spouse relationships were harmonious—as revealed by high agreement on childrearing, positive attitudes toward the ex-mate, and low conflict following divorce—the child's functioning was less likely to be undermined (Hetherington, 1980; Wallerstein & Kelly, 1980; Raschke & Raschke, 1979). The resources available to support children in coping with divorce are also important. Children who have a good relationship with a grandparent, uncle, or older brother are more likely to cope with the stress associated with their parents' divorce and to evidence better social and personal functioning than children who do not have such a relationship (Hetherington, Cox, & Cox, 1981; Santrock et al., 1982; Zill, 1983).

Relations with Siblings

In families where there are two or more children, preschool children also have to learn to get along with younger or older brothers and sisters.

Researchers have focused on the negative aspect of sibling relations, noting that **sibling rivalry,** the conflict between brothers and sisters, is common. Allison has been an only child enjoying exclusive claim on her parents' attention. When Allison was 4, her sister Rebecca was born. Allison reacted negatively and expressed her jealousy in several direct ways. One day her mother found her trying to pinch the baby, which is not considered unusual. Other children in Allison's position find it hard to resist occasionally pinching, pushing, or otherwise harming the unwanted addition to the family. Making such remarks as "When are we going to bring the baby back to the hospital?" preschoolers also reveal their desire to see the baby gone. Allison also regressed in some learned skills, symbolizing her longing to be a baby again and enjoy the attention her new sister is receiving. She lost bowel control even though toilet training has been well established, and she asked if she could sleep with her parents. At the child care center, Allison kept asking the staff to pick her up and hold her as if she were a baby. This regressive behavior is usually short-lived, especially if parents are sensitive to the child's feelings and bestow their attention and affection on the older child as well as on the newborn.

The relationship of preschool children to older brothers and sisters also entails rivalry, as they come to resent the prerogatives of older children and to compete with them for parental affection and approval. The rivalry is especially apparent in same-sex sibling relationships (Minnett, Vandell, & Santrock, 1983), although it is not necessarily unique to them. Additionally, researchers increasingly realize that brothers and sisters also show positive behaviors in their interactions with one another (Lamb & Sutton-Smith, 1982). Abramovitch, Pepler, and Corter's study (1982) of the interaction of preschoolers with their older brothers and sisters found that siblings can be aggressive toward each other, but they also cooperate and act affectionately toward each other. Abramovitch and his colleagues (1986) also found that older siblings dominate the interaction; that is, they tend to be more antagonistic and more nurturant toward younger siblings. Younger siblings tend to imitate the behavior of their older brothers or sisters (Lamb, 1978c). Sutton-Smith and Rosenberg (1970) further noted that some siblings influence each other with regard to interests and skills. Thus, although sibling rivalry may be evident, especially during the preschool years, children also enjoy the company of their brothers and sisters and often exert a positive influence on each other.

Peer Relations

Friends and friendships   During the preschool years children also begin to spend more time with other children, playing with them and enjoying their company. Peer interactions do not necessarily begin in the early childhood period; even infants are often given the opportunity to play with others their own age (Lewis et al., 1975). During the preschool years, however, children's interest in and involvement with other children are continually expanding and changing. Children actively seek out their peers, preferring to play with children who are the same age and sex and who have the same energy level (Jacklin & Maccoby, 1978). Urberg and Kaplan (1989) investigated play behaviors in a naturally occurring context (preschool classroom). They found that girls were more likely to choose same-sex playmates, and that the older the children were, the more likely they were to choose same-sex playmates. However, the children did not seem to choose playmates on the basis of race. The children in this study were enrolled in a university laboratory preschool well known for its multiracial composition. In other studies, however, preschool children were found to prefer to play with children their own age, sex, and race (Lederberg et al., 1986; Finkelstein & Haskins, 1983).

At the beginning of the preschool period, the children simply play together. As they grow older, however, they become increasingly more sociable and begin to make friends (Lougee, Grueneich, & Hartup, 1977). Having a friend and being someone's friend are very important to preschool children. They frequently initiate social contact by asking, "Can I be your friend?" and they attempt to persuade each other to share toys by saying, "I'll be your friend." However, until the school-age years, they do not understand friendship as an enduring relationship. Whereas the older child views friendship as a relationship taking shape over time and regards friends as providers of intimacy and support, preschool children characteristically view their friends as momentary playmates (Rubin, 1980). That is, they consider the child they may be playing with at a particular time as a friend. Also, unlike the older child, preschool children focus on the physical attributes of their playmates rather than on psychological attributes such as interests or personality traits. When asked

In the preschool period, the child's interest in other children and involvement with them are continually expanding.

what sort of person makes a good friend, preschoolers are likely to answer "Someone who plays a lot" or "Someone who lives in Watertown" (Selman & Jaquette, 1977).

The value of peer relations   Although they are unable to conceive of friendship as an enduring relationship, children have interactions with each other that often are long-lasting and of vital importance. Researchers have shown that the opportunity to interact with children of the same age is necessary for normal social development. Children who do not play with age-mates miss out on important social learning experiences and are at considerable risk of becoming socially inept and uncertain of themselves in interpersonal situations later in life. These findings are derived from studies of children who have trouble establishing social relationships with other children and who are unable to initiate and maintain interactions with other children (Hartup, 1983). Researchers do not know whether these children became socially incompetent because they lacked contact with other children or if their lack of contact with other children caused them to become socially incompetent (Hartup, 1989). Research with young animals that have been raised without peers shows that they become socially inept, are unable to mate successfully, and may even subject themselves to serious danger by being aggressive toward or not knowing when to submit to dominant animals (Suomi & Harlow, 1975).

Furthermore, experimental and naturalistic studies have shown that when young animals (Harlow, 1961) and children (Freud with Dunn, 1951) grow up only in the company of their peers, they become extremely attached to one another. They also show disturbances in their development and are unable to effectively interact with others outside their group. When there is a balance between adult and peer interaction, however, peers can serve important functions, such as providing emotional support. Four-year-olds in an unfamiliar situation, for example, are more likely to roam about and explore their surroundings when there are other children present than when they are alone (Schwartz, 1972). Goldstein, Field, and Healy (1989), who measured the heart rate and cortisol levels of preschool children in different situations, noted that stress is reduced if the children are with a friend.

Relationships with peers also provide preschool children with a way to compare themselves to others of their own age. Researchers observing preschool children at play noted that they frequently make such statements as "My picture is better than yours" or "Let's see who can run faster—me or you" (Rubin, 1980). At first, such utterances may suggest that the world of childhood is extremely competitive. Corsaro (1980), however, proposes that these encounters reflect the children's emerging sense of self and need to define themselves through comparisons with others.

Making a related point, Rubin (1980) gives an example of the opportunity for comparisons that peer relations provide:

Steven: "You are bigger than me—right, Claudia?" *(Claudia and Steven then stand back to back, measuring themselves. Claudia is in fact taller than Steven.)*
Claudia: "We're growing up."
Steven: "Yeah. I'm almost as big as you, right? I'm gonna grow this big, right?" *(He stretches his arms far apart.)*
Claudia: "Me too."

Children are also valuable social resources for one another; they learn numerous social skills through their interactions, including how to approach another child and initiate an interaction and how to maintain the interaction (Hartup, 1983; Asher

& Hymel, 1981). From their parents, children learn how to get along in one sort of social hierarchy, the family; from their peers, they learn how to survive among equals in a wide range of social situations. In fact, peer-group interactions provide children with egalitarian social relationships, something that is impossible in children's relations with adults, who are bigger and more powerful (Hartup, 1978; Mueller & Vandell, 1979).

Play

Types of play   Peers help expand children's social horizons by making new behaviors possible, and they are also partners in play. One child defined play as "Fun stuff that kids do 'cause they like to do it" (quoted in Rubin, 1980). Many researchers agree with Garvey's (1977) definition of **play** as any pleasurable, spontaneous, and voluntary activity that is an end in itself and has no extrinsic goal. According to Hughes (1991), play has several essential characteristics: it is intrinsically motivated, freely chosen, pleasurable, and actively engaged in by participants.

We have long been interested in children's play. In one of the earliest studies on the topic, Mildred Parten (1932) found that children's play varies in the amount of social involvement; sometimes children enjoy the role of observer (she called this "onlooker play") and at other times they play alone or in groups. She observed 2- to 5-year-olds in nursery schools and, on the basis of her observations, identified four different kinds of play behaviors.

Solitary play: In solitary play the child is happily engrossed in playing alone with a toy or another object, and she makes no attempt to initiate a conversation or otherwise interact with any of the other children in the room. Although children of all ages engage in solitary play sometimes, it is characteristic of children ages 2 to 3 years.

Parallel play: Children 2 to 3 years of age also engage in parallel play. In this type of play, which is considered the first step toward playing in groups, the young preschool child still plays by himself, but he chooses to play close to another child and with a similar toy. However, the activities of the two children are unrelated; they are playing parallel to but not with each other.

Associative play: Slightly older children, ages 3 to 4, engage in associative play. They may borrow and lend toys, talk about the same activity, or follow one another, but there is no attempt to organize the group. Thus, although several children may

Typical preschoolers, these children enjoy playing together.

be engaged in the same activity—playing with cars or with dolls, for example—each plays as she wishes; no one tries to change what the others are doing.

Cooperative play: By the time they are 4 or 5, children spend most of their playtime in cooperative play. The activity engages everyone in the group and they all have a shared goal.

Influences on play   Parten's observations were so perceptive that we still use her categories of play as a framework for examining how children play (Hughes, 1991). More recent findings (Rubin, Watson, & Jambor, 1978) support her observation that as they grow older, children become more sociable in their play; the older preschoolers engage in more associative and cooperative play and in less solitary play. Although age is an important determinant of how children play, several other factors influence the amount of time they spend playing alone or with others.

Experience is one such factor. When first introduced to a play group, even some older preschoolers may be shy and avoid interacting with the other children. Although they may engage in solitary or parallel play, usually after a few play sessions they overcome their shyness and become increasingly playful, deriving pleasure from their interactions with playmates (Mueller & Brenner, 1977).

The *opportunity* for play is also important. When given the opportunity to play, most children automatically play, alone or with others (Sutton-Smith, 1974); play is, in effect, the "work" of childhood. Even in societies that require preschoolers to help with chores, children will find ways to integrate play into their work routines (see Table 10.1) (Whiting & Whiting, 1975). Hughes (1991) describes Harkness and Super's studies (1983) of Kenya, where children have responsibility for numerous chores but still play tag while watching cows or climb trees while supervising siblings. Children who are not given *space* to play in and *materials* to play with also do not play as much as children who have the space and toys (Frost & Sunderlin, 1985). Toys do not have to be expensive, because children are adept at using any household item, such as a broom or a cooking pot, as a plaything. It is important, however, to have enough toys or other objects for children to play with, because these are the focal point of interactions between preschoolers (see Table 10.2). They are required for social behaviors such as give-and-take, help attract playmates (Mueller & Vandell, 1979), and determine whether children will engage in positive or negative interactions with each other. In situations where there are few toys, frequent confrontations will occur.

TABLE 10.1   **The Amount of Time Children Play Varies from One Culture to Another. In Some Societies, Young Children Spend More Time Helping with Chores Than They Do Playing. However, the Appeal of Play Is So Great That Children Who Work Usually Manage to Incorporate Play into Their Routine Tasks**

Activity	Nyansongo, Kenya	Juxtlahuaca, Mexico	Tarong, Philippines	Taira, Okinawa	Khalapur, India	Orchard Town, United States
Play	17	49	48	76	31	52
Casual social interaction	43	37	31	11	46	30
Work	41	8	14	9	11	2
Learning	0	6	7	4	9	16

Source: Whiting, B. B., & Whiting, J. W. M. (1975). *Children of Six Cultures: A Psycho-Cultural Analysis.* Cambridge, MA: Harvard University Press; p. 48, table 11. Copyright © 1975 by the President and Fellows of Harvard College.

TABLE 10.2 General Characteristics of the Preschooler, and Appropriate Play Materials

Age	General characteristics	Appropriate play materials
2	Uses language effectively. Large muscle skills developing, but limited in the use of small muscle skills. Energetic, vigorous, and enthusiastic, with a strong need to demonstrate independence and self-control.	Large muscle play materials: Swing sets, outdoor blocks, toys to ride on, pull toys, push toys. Sensory play materials: Clay, fingerpaints, materials for water play, blocks, books, dolls and stuffed animals.
3	Expanded fantasy life, with unrealistic fears. Fascination with adult roles. Still stubborn, negative, but better able to adapt to peers than at age two. Early signs of product orientation in play.	Props for imaginative play (e.g., old clothes). Miniature life toys. Puzzles, simple board games, art materials that allow for a sense of accomplishment (e.g., paintbrushes, easels, marker pens, crayons).
4	Secure, self-confident. Need for adult attention and approval—showing off, clowning around, taking risks. More planful than threes, but products often accidental. Sophisticated small muscle control allows for cutting, pasting, sewing, imaginative block building with smaller blocks.	Vehicles (e.g., tricycles, Big Wheels). Materials for painting, coloring, drawing, woodworking, sewing, stringing beads. Books with themes that extend well beyond the child's real world.
5	Early signs of logical thinking. Stable, predictable, reliable. Less self-centered than at four. Relaxed, friendly, willing to share and cooperate with peers. Realistic, practical, responsible.	Cut-and-paste and artistic activities with models to work from. Simple card games (e.g., Old Maid), table games (e.g., Bingo), and board games (e.g., Lotto), in which there are few rules and the outcomes are based more on chance than on strategy. Elaborate props for dramatic play.

Source: From Hughes, Fergus P., *Children, Play, and Development.* Copyright © 1991 by Allyn and Bacon. Reprinted with permission.

Dramatic play   Play consists of any number of activities from which children derive pleasure: the manipulation of toys and other objects; rough-and-tumble play and physical games in which children run, jump, chase, or tickle one another; and verbal banter in which they enjoy the different rhythms and sounds of words. Children also engage in make-believe play. Make-believe, or pretend play, begins at around age 2 when children are capable of mental representation. Initially, they play by themselves pretending, for example, to feed a doll or brush their hair with an imaginary hairbrush. After age 3 they engage in make-believe play in cooperation with another child, although on occasion children who have no one to play with may play a sequence with an imaginary friend.

Sometimes called symbolic or **dramatic play,** make-believe play becomes gradually more elaborate and complex (see Table 10.3). By the time children are 4 or 5 years old, they engage in *sociodramatic play,* which is make-believe play about social situations. This type of play usually occurs in the context of a story or a specific plan of action focusing on a role identity. Popular role identities among preschool-

An increasing number of children in the U.S. attend early intervention programs, nursery school, or child care facilities. Although these settings may differ (for example, some are half-day programs, others are full-day), they provide similar opportunities: children can play with friends and acquire social skills; they can read books, play in sandboxes and work with paints; they are taken out on special excursions to the zoo or a nearby park.

Child Care

In many nontechnological societies, women as well as men work during the day. Even if their children are too young to help, they join the parents at the work site.

In our society, few parents have the option of taking their children to the workplace, except on rare occasions. Working parents place their children in some form of child care. A popular setting for infants and toddlers is family day care, where a woman, usually a mother herself, takes care of several children in her own home. Family day care can be a nurturing environment where children receive individual attention.

Child care centers are licensed by the state, and may be located in schools, churches, or offices. A licence merely confirms that the center has met minimal regulations; it does not indicate the quality of care. Child care services for infants and school-age children, are in critically low supply.

When choosing a child care center, parents should look for a safe physical environment as well as quality care. One positive feature is the opportunity for children to interact with one another.

Letting children choose their activities is important in preschool and school-age child care. Sometimes children want to be alone, reading or working on a puzzle. At other times they choose to play with friends in the housekeeping corner or sand box. Older children who are in before-and-after-school programs also need to be free to choose to play, practice music or sports, do their homework, or simply read.

The adult-child ratio is an important quality indicator. The younger the child, the smaller the ratio should be. When one caregiver takes care of more than ten preschoolers at a time, chances are she or he is simply managing and disciplining them rather than attending sensitively to the needs of each child. Parents should look for centers with caregivers who are trained in child development. Studies show that educated caregivers provide better quality care than those who have not studied child development.

ers are mother, father, baby, doctor, patient, firefighter, and police officer. The sequence of make-believe play begins with one child announcing, "Let's play house" and proceeding to assign different roles to those children who agree to play. "I'll be the mother. Lance, you be the father." It may also begin when a child has a plan and proposes, "Let's take a trip to the moon," in which case the children quickly improvise a spaceship and assign roles.

Sociodramatic play is important for the child's development. It provides children with the opportunity to rehearse adult roles and begin to understand them (Asher, 1978). It also helps them understand some of the events they experience in real life. By repeatedly reenacting some of these events (for example, the birth of a baby in the family), the children can eventually assimilate and come to terms with them. Such play provides an opportunity to try out activities usually forbidden by adults (Bruner, 1972). Sociodramatic play also enhances their cognitive skills (Smilanski, 1968); children who engage in dramatic play during the preschool years evidence creativity and imagination later in life (Vandenberg, 1980; Singer & Singer, 1979b; Sutton-Smith, 1974).

TABLE 10.3 Sequence of Symbolic Levels of Play. As Children Grow Older, Their Make-Believe Becomes More Complex and Dramatic.

		Examples
Sensorimotor Period Before Stage VI	1. Presymbolic scheme: The child shows understanding of object or meaning by brief gestures of recognition.	The child picks up a comb, touches it to his hair, drops it.
Stage VI	2. Autosymbolic scheme: The child pretends at self-related activities.	The child eats from an empty spoon.
Symbolic Stage 1	3. Single-scheme symbolic games: The child extends symbolism beyond his own actions:	
Type IA assimilative	A. Including other actors or receivers of action, like a doll or mother.	The child feeds mother or doll (A).
Type IB imitative	B. Pretending at activities of other people or objects like dogs, trucks, trains, and so on.	The child pretends to mop floor (B).
	4. Combinatorial symbolic games.	The child kisses doll, puts it to bed, puts spoon to its mouth. The child drinks from the bottle, feeds doll from bottle.
	5. Planned symbolic games: The child indicates verbally or nonverbally that pretend acts are planned before being executed:	The child picks up the play screwdriver, says "toothbrush," and makes the motions of brushing teeth.
Type IIA	A. Symbolic identification of one object with another.	The child picks up the bottle, says "baby," then feeds the doll and covers it with a cloth.
Type IIB	B. Symbolic identification of the child's body with some other person or object.	
Type IIIA	Combinations with planned elements, tending toward realistic scenes.	The child puts play foods in a pot, stirs them, then says "soup" before feeding the mother. She waits, then says "more?" offering the spoon to the mother.

Source: Fein, G. (1978). "Play Revisited." In M. E. Lamb (Ed.), *Social and Personality Development.* New York: Holt, Rinehart and Winston; p. 75, table 2. Copyright © by Holt, Rinehart and Winston. *Original source:* Nicholich, L. (1977). "Beyond Sensorimotor Intelligence: Assessment of Symbolic Maturity through Analysis of Pretend Play." *Merrill-Palmer Quarterly, 23* (2), 89–99. Copyright 1977 Wayne State University Press. Reprinted by permission of the publisher.

These children are engaged in make-believe play, which lets them rehearse adult roles.

Personality and Emotional Development

Relating to Others

Watching children play together, it becomes apparent that there are striking differences in personality. Some are boisterous and outgoing; others are more passive and shy. Some are cooperative, independent, and adventuresome; others are aggressive and disruptive. The child's personality—defined as his unique pattern of behavior, how he perceives things and reacts to them—depends on a complex interplay between heredity and environment. Children are born with certain personality characteristics, but their personality is shaped by the attitudes and reactions of adults.

Aggression One personality characteristic that becomes evident during the preschool years is aggression. Preschool children often display hostility and aggression toward one another, just as adults do. Most children use aggressive behavior to overcome resistance. But for some children aggression becomes a dominant theme in their social interactions.

Theories of aggression Psychologists have proposed various theories to explain aggression. They note that aggressive behavior is common to most species and thus has a biological component. Aggression is also a method of problem solving, and therefore it is subject to the influence of experience and learning (see Figure 10.1).

Theories of aggression differ in their emphasis on biological or psychological determinants and in those determinants they select as important in developing aggression and expressing it in the social setting (Feshbach & Feshbach, 1976). For example, psychoanalytic theorists like Freud (1930) believed that aggression is a biological instinct influenced by environmental factors. That is, children are born with an aggressive drive, but the manner in which they express aggression is learned. Ethologist Konrad Lorenz (1966) regarded aggression as an innate response to a particular stimulus. Learning theorists like Bandura (1962; 1967)

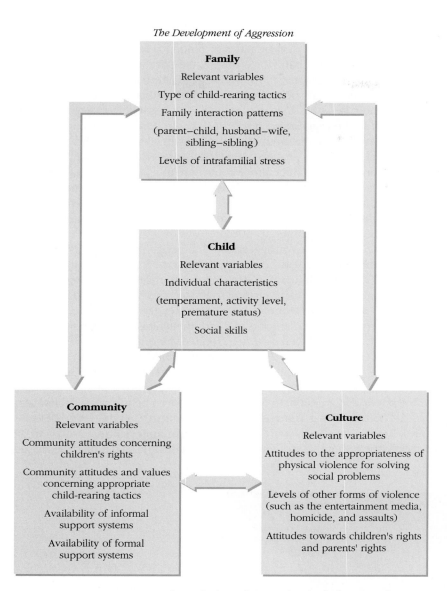

The Development of Aggression

Family

Relevant variables

Type of child-rearing tactics

Family interaction patterns

(parent–child, husband–wife, sibling–sibling)

Levels of intrafamilial stress

Child

Relevant variables

Individual characteristics

(temperament, activity level, premature status)

Social skills

Community

Relevant variables

Community attitudes concerning children's rights

Community attitudes and values concerning appropriate child-rearing tactics

Availability of informal support systems

Availability of formal support systems

Culture

Relevant variables

Attitudes to the appropriateness of physical violence for solving social problems

Levels of other forms of violence (such as the entertainment media, homicide, and assaults)

Attitudes towards children's rights and parents' rights

Figure 10.1 *An ecological view of aggression includes several variables involving the child, the family, the community, and the culture, all of which contribute to aggressive behavior.*
Source: Parke, R. D., and Slaby, R. G., "The Development of Aggression."
In P. H. Mussen, ed., *Handbook of Child Psychology,* Vol. 4, 1983, p. 559.
Copyright © 1983 John Wiley & Sons, Inc. Reprinted by permission of the publisher.

emphasize that early "training" in aggression is necessary, because aggression is a behavior learned through reinforcement and imitation. When children see their parents or others use physical force in their interactions with other people, or with each other, they too will use aggression as the primary means to resolve interpersonal problems.

On the basis of clinical experience with aggressive children and their families, Gerald Patterson (1982) proposes a *performance theory* of childhood aggression. He contends that aggressive and other maladaptive behaviors are learned, shaped, and maintained by forces operating in the social setting. That is, aggression originates in the behavior modeled by parents, among others, and is maintained by parental responses to the child (for example, the parents' mode of punishment).

However, Linda Dowdrey (1985) criticizes Patterson for failing to recognize children's contributions to social interactions, noting that some children are more malleable in their behavior than others and thus less likely to provoke physical punishment and other aggressive responses on the part of their parents. Indeed, many researchers believe that both biological and environmental factors play a role in shaping the development of aggression, and that several variables in the child, the family, the community, and the culture contribute to aggressive behavior (Parke & Slaby, 1983). Some children who are exposed to a great deal of violence at home or who are given little affection and attention (Feshbach, 1980; Feshbach & Feshbach, 1976) use hostility in their interactions with others. This behavior pattern is likely to last into later life (Huesmann et al., 1984).

Some researchers focus on aggression's immediate precursors, saying that it is a reaction to frustration (Dollard et al., 1939; Berkowitz, 1962). According to Parke and Slaby (1983), although not all frustrating experiences produce aggressive acts, preschoolers have many occasions to feel frustrated. Several times a day they ask for something and are told they cannot have it; or they try to do something and fail, suffering both frustration and affronts to their dignity. It is not surprising, therefore, that displays of aggressive behavior are frequent among preschoolers, especially early in the preschool period. However, young children are rarely deliberately aggressive. They may strike someone who interferes with what they are doing, but only to get an object or to remove an obstacle. As they grow older, they resort to deliberate physical aggression. In one study of children between the ages of 4 and 7, Hartup (1974) found that **instrumental aggression** (fighting over objects, for example) declines markedly with age, but **hostile aggression** (that is, an attack against someone rather than something) does not decline as rapidly. The frequency

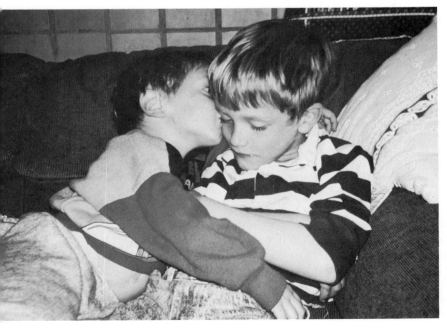

Even children as young as two-and-a-half are aware that others may be feeling unhappy.

of deliberate physical aggression reaches its peak in the preschool years. But if caretakers reprimand the children and tell them how they are expected to behave, they will learn to control their anger and to use other means of attack, notably, words and insults.

Altruism and empathy   Young children also display positive behaviors and are even capable of altruistic behavior. Altruism is an aspect of moral behavior involving a concern for the welfare of others; we can define **altruistic behavior** as a voluntary and intentional action that benefits another person and is not motivated by a desire to obtain external rewards (Eisenberg, 1982; Staub, 1975). A 3-year-old who sees another child cry and goes over to offer him a toy to play with is evidencing altruistic behavior.

Such acts of kindness toward others require **empathy,** the ability to feel another person's emotions vicariously. According to Piaget, the egocentrism of young children prevents them from being able to see others' perspectives and empathize with those around them. More recent research has shown, however, that although the ability to empathize increases with age, even 2 to 3-year-olds are capable of differentiating between happiness, sadness, and anger (Harter, 1979). Also, they are aware of and are able to respond to other people's feelings. As Borke (1971) maintained:

> Observations of young children interacting suggest that preschool children are not only aware that other people have feelings but [that they] also actively try to understand the feeling they observe. A two-and-a-half-year-old who holds a toy to a crying child certainly appears to be demonstrating an awareness that the other youngster is experiencing unhappy feelings.

The origins of empathy are unclear. Psychoanalysts suggest that empathy develops in the mother/infant relationship as the parent conveys her moods to the child by her tone of voice, facial expressions, and touch (Ekstein, 1978). Social learning theorists, on the other hand, contend that empathy is acquired through conditioning; cries of distress from another person evoke the unpleasant feelings that accompanied painful past experiences (Hoffman, 1976; 1978). For example, a child who cuts his finger feels pain and cries. When he sees another child cut herself, the sight of blood and her cries evoke the feeling of distress he had experienced earlier.

Although they disagree on the origins of empathy, researchers note that the way children respond to others' distress changes with age. These findings emerged from the research of Zahn-Waxler, Radke-Yarrow, and King (1979). They observed children in laboratory and naturalistic settings to see how they reacted when their mother hurt her elbow and showed her distress. They found that infants exhibited emotional arousal, such as crying or agitation. Gradually this behavior lessened, and by age 2 some children approached the mother, attempting to help or console her. They brought objects to her, made suggestions about what she could do, and verbalized their sympathy. When one method of consolation failed, they tried another. This suggests that they perceived the mother's distress as a problem to be solved. These and other observations (Dunn & Kendrick, 1979) of prosocial behaviors indicate that infants and young children are help-seeking creatures, who "freely offer their own attention, affection, sympathy, help, and possessions to others" (Rheingold & Hay, 1976). They can recognize when other people feel happy or sad. (In our society **prosocial behaviors** include sharing, helping, and cooperating with others.)

Many parents want to encourage these behaviors. Research indicates that there are strategies parents can use toward this goal, but not all strategies are equally effective. Eisenberg (1982) notes that when children see adults behave in prosocial ways, they are encouraged to do so as well. However, giving the child an *explicit reward,* such as a piece of candy or a new toy, does not promote prosocial behavior; instead, children may learn to exhibit prosocial behaviors only when they are likely to be rewarded.

The Emergence of the Self-Concept

With age, children learn about other people's feelings and about themselves, and they acquire a self-concept; that is, a subjective understanding and evaluation of their own personality, qualities, and capabilities. The self-concept is a personal picture made up of a range of impressions by which individuals distinguish themselves from others. These impressions depend on their own interpretation of their experiences in the social and physical environment and on the feedback they get from other people (Harter, 1983a & 1983b).

The development of the self-concept is a gradual process that continues throughout the life span and changes with age. For example, preschoolers think of themselves in relatively specific and concrete terms, often defining themselves by name ("I am Sharon") or in terms of frequent activities or behaviors ("I run fast" or "I watch television"). As they grow older and are more aware of their own thoughts and feelings, children think of themselves in terms of psychological traits, and they define themselves as "nice" or "friendly."

The self-concept includes the ability to define oneself, self-recognition (an awareness of oneself as a separate entity), and other components such as attitudes, motives, and values that together identify the individual as unique (Harter, 1983a). Although many components of the self-concept do not emerge until middle childhood, even 2-year-olds begin to acquire a sense of identity and realize that they are distinct from other people. Evidence of their emerging sense of self is found in their new ability to recognize themselves in the mirror or point to a picture of themselves and say "me" (Lewis & Brooks-Gunn, 1979) and in their excessive use of such linguistic terms as *me* and *mine* that refer specifically to themselves. In their strong desire to function autonomously and do things for themselves, they indicate that they have an awareness of themselves as separate individuals who can assert their own desires and wills.

Gender identity　Preschool children also show the development of a particularly important aspect of the self-concept, namely gender identity, as they grow in their ability to label themselves according to sex.

Gender identity refers to the child's awareness and acceptance of being either a boy or a girl. The awareness begins relatively early and is preceded by the child's ability to differentiate between the categories of male and female. Most children are able to differentiate between males and females by the time they are 2 years old, and by about 2½, they can identify their own gender and correctly answer the question, Are you a boy or a girl? (Huston, 1983; Thompson, 1975).

In an example of research on gender identity, Thompson (1975) showed children ages 2, 2½, and 3 pictures that appeared on a screen. The pictures were of men, women, boys, and girls. The children were asked to indicate which of the pictures were of a man, a lady, a girl, or a boy. They indicated their knowledge of gender by touching or pointing at the appropriate pictures. The children were also

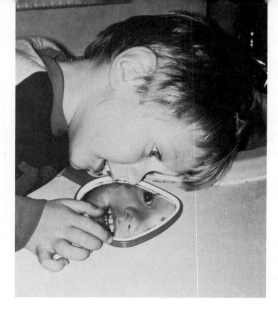

A young child's emerging sense of self is evident in her new ability to recognize her face in a mirror.

asked their own sex and then asked to pick out the picture that was of the same gender. Although children at age 2 could pick out the same-gender picture, they could not always identify the picture as that of a boy or a girl. At age 3, however, they could correctly identify which pictures were of a boy or a girl.

Other researchers note that not until age 3 can children identify their own gender and others'. Kohlberg (1966) described a little boy named Tommy, age 2½, who would go around the room saying, in reference to himself and his family, "I'm a boy, Daddy is a boy, Mommy is a boy, Joey is a boy." After being corrected, Tommy eliminated his mother from his list, but he still had trouble labeling people outside the family correctly. Kohlberg pointed out further that although by age 2½ or 3 the child knows his own gender, he does not yet accept the *stability and constancy of gender*. That is, he doesn't realize that gender is an anatomical reality that cannot be altered. He thinks that by putting on a wig and wearing a dress he can become a girl (meaning that he has not yet accepted the constancy of gender). He also does not realize that he cannot grow up to be Mommy and that his sister cannot grow up to be Daddy (Kohlberg, 1966). That is, he has not acquired the notion of the stability of gender. Not until ages 5 to 7 are children able to completely and accurately identify their gender and that of other people and realize that it cannot be changed.

Gender role During the preschool years, children also acquire **gender (sex) roles.** They adopt socially defined behaviors and attitudes associated with being a male or a female. Gender role is also an important aspect of development; it organizes the individual's behaviors and attitudes toward the self and others and influences the kinds of activities and occupations he or she will engage in as a child and later as an adult (Eccles & Hoffman, 1984).

It is important at the outset to distinguish between gender identity and gender role. The development of gender identity entails the ability to identify and accept one's gender and know that it will remain stable and constant throughout life. The development of gender role involves engaging in behaviors that are deemed culturally acceptable for one's gender. It is also the realization and acknowledgment that there are differences in the behaviors, abilities, and attitudes of males and females (Eisenberg, 1982).

The development of gender identity does not invariably mean that a child will behave in a sex-stereotyped way (Marcus & Overton, 1978). Allison, for example, may be aware of and satisfied with being a girl, but she does not play with dolls or engage in other activities that in our culture are typically considered feminine.

Since the 1970s, many changes have occurred in societal attitudes toward gender roles. Some women feel that the characteristics traditionally associated with the term *feminine* do not characterize them. Likewise, some men do not feel that the behaviors traditionally associated with the term *masculine* capture their characteristics. The term **androgynous** is often used to describe an individual—child or adult—who combines feminine and masculine characteristics. An androgynous girl, for example, would be nurturant (a traditionally feminine characteristic) yet aggressive and competitive in her relationship with peers (characteristics traditionally associated with masculinity). An androgynous boy may be assertive yet sensitive to other people's feelings (a traditionally feminine characteristic).

Researchers are also finding that young children may like some things that are traditionally associated with their gender, but still behave in a non-sex-stereotyped way. This point is made clear in a recent study by Maccoby and Jacklin (1990). They had parents of 4-year-olds rate their daughters on a scale of femininity, asking: Does your daughter like frilly clothes? Does she like to wear jewelry? The parents were also asked about their daughters' behaviors: Does your daughter prefer to play with boys? Does she get into fights? When she is pretend-playing, what roles does she choose? The girls rated the most feminine on the basis of their parents' answers tended to be tomboys; they played with boys, got into fights, and engaged in rough-and-tumble play.

Another term that has been used in reference to gender roles is **undifferentiated,** which describes an individual who does not behave in an especially feminine or masculine way.

These terms are useful, given the blurring of gender roles in our society and our inclination to assert our individuality rather than behave in any stereotyped way. As changes in gender roles continue, the characteristics that are associated with the

During the preschool years, children learn that certain activities and tasks are restricted to one sex or the other, and they adopt not only sex-typed behaviors but sex-typed attitudes as well.

terms *masculinity* and *femininity* are likely to change as well (Downs & Langlois, 1988).

Many of us may not believe that boys should grow up to be masculine and girls should be feminine. Nevertheless, children acquire sex-stereotyped behaviors, attitudes, and values beginning at a very young age (Smith & Daglish, 1977). Researchers have found that preschoolers are very rigid in adopting such behaviors. According to observers, they prefer to play with objects explicitly labeled as appropriate for their sex (Liebert, McCall, & Hanratty, 1971) or to engage only in activities deemed appropriate for their sex. This is true in other countries as well (Edwards & Whiting, 1980). Boys tend to choose rough-and-tumble activities and to play with trucks and airplanes more than girls, who often choose quieter activities, such as playing house or drawing and painting.

Damon (1977) also found that children from ages 4 to 7 are increasingly likely to believe that certain activities or tasks are restricted to one sex or the other, evidencing that they adopt sex-type attitudes as well. Damon (1977) established this by telling a group of children ages 4 to 7 a story about a boy named George who liked to play with dolls even though his parents told him not to, since only little girls play with dolls. The children were asked if George was right or wrong. Children older than 6 revealed their flexible attitudes toward sex-stereotyped behaviors by indicating that George had a right to do as he pleased. Children younger than 6, however, thought George was wrong; many indicated that George should be punished. Preschoolers are so rigid in their sex-typed behaviors and attitudes that it is as if they exaggerate their attitudes about what is appropriate for each sex in order to better understand their own identity (Maccoby, 1980). This may explain why, as children grow older and as their gender identity is stabilized, they are more flexible in their sex-typed behaviors and attitudes (Damon, 1977; Garrett, Ein, & Tremaine, 1977).

Explaining Sex Differences in Behavior

Sex differences in behavior continue to be evident throughout life. Of course, there are individual and sex differences among children and adults, and individuals may differ in the extent to which they display sex-stereotypic behaviors and attitudes. The question that has generated much debate in recent years is whether the behavioral differences between the sexes are biologically determined or learned. Psychologists agree that biological factors contribute to sex differences in behavior but environmental factors account for most of the reported sex differences.

Biological factors   Support for the view that biological factors are at play in sex differences in behavior is hard to come by, because it is difficult to specify a behavior that is strictly biologically determined. However, some studies have shown that male newborns are more physically active than females (Phillips, King, & DuBois, 1978). Although this temperamental difference exists at birth, it is difficult to separate biological from environmental factors; studies have shown that soon after birth mothers respond to the temperament of their child and interact differently with daughters than they do with sons (Lewis, 1974). So it may be the mothers' behavior that reinforces the increased levels of physical activity boys are born with. However, studies indicate that some traits, such as aggression, may have a biological basis since young male monkeys are also rougher in their play than their female counterparts (Harlow, 1962). Perhaps male aggressiveness may be accounted for in part by high levels of testosterone, the male hormone present in larger quantity in males than in females (Davis, 1964; Money & Ehrhardt, 1972). Indeed, many current studies attempting to find a link between biology and behavior focus on hormones. Researchers are finding that there are differences between the sexes in the quantities of certain hormones and that some types of hormones may be related to some traits (e.g., timidity) and moods in one sex but not in the other (Jacklin, 1989; Marcus et al., 1985).

Environmental factors   Although hormonal factors may be important in establishing certain behavioral dispositions, experience and child-rearing practices have an effect as well; they account for the acquisition of sex roles and for the child's awareness of gender. John Money and his colleagues made this point in a series of studies. In one study Money (1975) discussed a rare case of identical twin boys, one of whom lost his penis during circumcision at the age of 7 months. Growing up as a male without a penis would have given him psychological difficulties that might have been impossible to overcome. The decision was made to reassign him as a girl. The parents changed the child's name, hairstyle, and clothes and began treating him as a girl. When the twins were preschoolers, the mother reported how much more dainty the girl was than her brother. The girl was described as a tomboy and as bossy, but when asked whether she preferred to be a boy or a girl, she indicated a girl. During puberty the child underwent a series of surgical procedures and hormone treatments that made the sex reassignment complete.

In several other studies, Money, Hampson, and Hampson (1957) took advantage of similar naturally occurring experiments and studied children born with ambiguous genitals. In such cases the family decides—with the support of the physician and other professionals—to assign a sex to the child and raise him or her accordingly. Sometimes, as the child grows and the genitals develop normally, it becomes apparent that a mistake has been made. Money and his colleagues found that children raised from infancy as boys or as girls became aware of themselves and behaved as such, suggesting that rearing practices play an important role in the development of gender identity and gender roles. Furthermore, Money and his colleagues found that the first three years of life are a critical period for the development of gender identity. Children who were raised as a member of the wrong sex and then relabeled before age 2 or 3 developed a normal gender identity. Those who were relabeled after age 3 had trouble establishing a secure gender identity and adopting the gender role of their genetic sex.

Parents' role   Children learn about the behavioral differences between the sexes from the behavior of those around them, such as siblings, peers (Sheldon, 1989), teachers (Fagot, 1977), or media personalities (Sternglanz & Serbin, 1974). They also learn about sex-typed behaviors from other sources like books (Wirtenberg, Murez, & Alepektor, 1980). However, parents play a vital role in the acquisition of sex-typed behavior, especially during early childhood (Huston, 1983).

As we discussed earlier, sex-role attitudes and standards are changing. Nevertheless, most adults are still preoccupied with differences between the sexes (Jacklin, 1989). They have traditional, stereotyped conceptions of sex roles and behave accordingly (Eccles & Hoffman, 1984). For instance, American males are regarded as and expected to be assertive, independent, and dominant, whereas females are supposed to be submissive, warm, nurturant, and sensitive to interpersonal situations. Children learn these attitudes from the differences in behavior between their parents (Rosen & Aneshensel, 1978), and parents have different expectations of their sons and daughters (Rubin, Provenza, & Luria, 1974). They give boys and girls

Cross-cultural research indicates that in some societies girls are required to spend much of their time caring for younger children and thus develop nurturing behaviors. However, the studies do not explain why boys are not given child care tasks.

different toys to play with (Kacerguis & Adams, 1979) and treat them in ways that promote stereotypical functioning. Block (1982) studied more than 1000 families and found that sons were encouraged more than daughters to be competitive, achievement-oriented, independent, and to control their emotions ("Boys don't cry"). Daughters were encouraged to be warm, nurturant, and emotionally expressive.

Researchers have also found that the father plays an important role in sex-role development during the preschool years. In particular, the father's degree of masculinity seems to promote traditional sex roles in sons and in daughters (Hetherington, Cox, & Cox, 1978). Because the father's masculinity, not necessarily the mother's femininity, is associated with the girls' sex-role development, girls may acquire sex roles through a process of **reciprocal role learning.** That is, they learn how to behave as females by complementing their father's masculinity (Lamb & Urberg, 1978). The opposite is not true for boys, however. Boys tend to identify with and imitate their father's behavior, and those boys whose mothers are very feminine do not necessarily behave in a more masculine way.

Research on the father's role in the child's development also reveals that the preschool period may be critical for boys' sex-role development but not for girls'. Studies on the effects of paternal absence indicate that if fathers are absent due to divorce, desertion, or death before the sons are 5 years old, they grow up to be less traditionally masculine than do boys whose fathers are at home and attend to them during this period or who leave home after this period. These boys tend to be less aggressive and more dependent and to rely on greater use of verbal rather than physical aggression. Huston (1983) suggests that these less traditionally masculine behaviors may be due to the boys' lack of exposure to rough-and-tumble play and also to the fact that their mother is less likely to encourage independent behavior than mothers who have a male adult around to help them with childrearing. If the children of absent fathers have some other adult male living in the household (for example, an older brother or the mother's boyfriend), the effects of paternal absence are lessened (Lamb & Urberg, 1978).

Cross-cultural perspectives Cross-cultural studies provide yet another perspective on the issue. Whiting and Edwards (1988) studied children in 11 different cultures and found that they behave like the individuals (children or adults) with whom they interact the majority of the time. For example, in some cultures girls have responsibility for caring for younger siblings; because girls spend the majority of their time caring for children, they behave in nurturant ways. In other words, the siblings, and the task of child care, elicit nurturant behaviors in the girls. This notion deserves further exploration but does not explain, for example, why in some but not all cultures it is girls who are given child care responsibilities.

Theoretical Perspectives

Child development researchers have proposed several theoretical explanations of the processes by which children acquire gender identity and gender roles and other socially prescribed behaviors and attitudes. These explanations help guide the research. Although none of these theories offers an entirely satisfactory explanation (Jacklin, 1989; Katz, 1979), each has contributed to our understanding that several mechanisms play a part in the way children acquire socially acceptable behaviors.

The psychoanalytic theory Psychoanalytic theorists contend that the adoption of sex-typed attitudes and behaviors is the result of identification with the same-sex parent. **Identification** is the process in which the child responds to the attitudes and behaviors of another person by adopting them. Unlike imitation, however, identification is largely unconscious, meaning that the child is not aware she has taken on the characteristics she sees in others.

Freud's explanation of how children come to identify with the same-sex parent is rather controversial and differs for boys and girls. During infancy, the boy develops a unique attachment to his mother. He loves her and wants to possess her, but his father stands in his way. The boy grows to hate and fear his father. Because the child assumes that girls had their penises cut off, he becomes especially afraid that his father will discover his resentment and retaliate by castrating him. So he attempts to relieve his anxieties by pushing out of his consciousness his desire to be with his mother and his resentment toward his father. At the same time he identifies with and adopts his father's attitudes and behaviors, which enables him to feel safe. He believes that his father is unlikely to hurt someone like himself. Freud referred to the boy's anxieties as the *Oedipus conflict,* because he saw an analogy to the experiences of King Oedipus in Greek tragic drama.

Freud referred to girls' anxieties as the *Electra conflict,* also from an analogy to Greek drama. Girls notice that boys have penises, but they do not. They come to envy the boys' penises and devalue the mother for not having one. They also become angry at the mother for not allowing them to have a penis or for allowing them to be castrated. Therefore, they renounce their love for their mother and want to possess their father. At the same time they fear their resentment of their mother; to reduce their anxiety they identify with the mother and adopt her behaviors and attitudes.

As we indicated in Chapter 2, the psychoanalytic theory falls short in many respects; one of its major problems is the difficulty of testing it empirically (Zigler, Lamb, & Child, 1982). Whereas the psychoanalytic theory places a great deal of importance on the parent/child relationship, emphasizing the child's identification with the parents, many other theorists note that children also identify with and imitate the behavior of others.

Learning theory Social learning theorists think children acquire behaviors through the mechanisms of *reinforcement* and *punishment*. Socializers, such as parents, reinforce or reward their children for behaviors consistent with their gender role and punish them for engaging in inappropriate behaviors. If a young girl is rewarded by affection, approval, and praise when she carries out stereotypically female activities, such as helping her mother prepare a meal or wash the dishes, she is likely to repeat this or similar behaviors in the future. But if she is scolded for engaging in rough-and-tumble play or getting dirty playing with the parts of the car her father is working on, she will probably not repeat these activities.

Observational learning theorists emphasize that children learn by observation and imitation, and they do not always need to be rewarded or punished to acquire or extinguish a behavior. Further, children observe and imitate other socializers such as siblings, peers, teachers, neighbors, sports heroes, and TV personalities. Thus, when a girl sees in real life or on television that women usually stand around and watch men fix a car when it breaks down, she learns that fixing the car is an inappropriate activity for her.

Cognitive-developmental theory Cognitive-developmental theorists further elaborate on the role of imitation in acquiring gender roles; they emphasize that an awareness of gender precedes any attempt by children to imitate the behaviors of the same-sex people they encounter. Kohlberg (1966) proposed that the child's realization that he is a boy or that she is a girl (gender identity) stimulates the adoption of sex-typed gender role behaviors. As a result, children are active players in their own development. The reinforcement for imitating sex-typed behaviors comes from the children themselves.

Explaining that the adoption of sex-typed behaviors occurs in stages, Kohlberg noted that at first children observe anatomical and other differences in appearance. Based on these observations, they label themselves according to gender and regard themselves as boys or girls. This label helps children organize their social behavior because children value others who are like themselves. They begin to behave as such, reasoning, for instance: I am a girl; therefore I like to do girl things. The children then imitate the behaviors of same-sex models.

The appeal of this theory is that it points out that children do not simply imitate a behavior; they reason first. Although the development of gender identity and gender role depends, in part, on the child's cognitive status, there are shortcomings to the cognitive theory. It fails to explain why children acquire gender identity at an early age and why those children who have had to undergo sex reassignment after age 3 have problems establishing a stable gender identity. The theory also does not account for the fact that 1- and 2-year-olds who have not attained gender identity still exhibit sex-typed play activities (Etaugh, Collins, & Gerson, 1975).

A variation of the social learning and cognitive developmental theories is the **gender schema theory** (Bem, 1981; 1983; 1985). A schema is a series of ideas that help the child organize information. A schema may change and evolve as we acquire new information, and it may filter information when we decide what information to process (Jacklin, 1989). Children develop an idea of what men and women do and how they act, by watching people and noticing, for example, that women and men dress differently. They will then adapt their own behavior accordingly. Their gender schema develops from all sorts of information, even information that has nothing to do with gender; modes of behavior, properties of objects, attitudes, and feelings are examples of the information children are exposed to. The gender schema theory emphasizes that children are active participants in gender role development because they pick and choose from the information around them and construct their own gender schema. However, the people they interact with and society itself determine the information they will draw from. As Bem (1983) notes:

> Adults in the child's world rarely notice or remark upon how strong a girl is getting or how nurturant a little boy is becoming, despite their readiness to note precisely these attributes in the "appropriate" sex. [p. 604]

According to Jacklin (1989), the gender schema theory is a very new area of research, but it is likely to dominate the research agenda about gender socialization in the future. She notes that to date each theoretical perspective on how children adopt sex-role behaviors provides only a partial explanation of the processes involved. Taken together, however, the theories help us understand that parents and others in the children's lives play an important role in development. Their influence operates in three ways: as models for identification, as providers of rewards and punishment, and as models for imitation. The processes of identification, reward and punishment, and imitation function in children's acquisition of sex-role behaviors and in their adoption of other expectations, standards, and values of their family and social group. Also, they explain how children learn to behave in ways that their family and society sanction.

Socialization

The process by which children come to behave in socially acceptable ways and by which one generation shapes the behavior and personality of the younger generation is called **socialization.** One function of socialization is to ensure that there will be members of society capable of meeting the demands of the people. Thus we teach children what is necessary to coexist with others and to survive. Although children in all societies are taught how to behave in socially approved ways, the precise behaviors needed to survive differ from one society to another.

Socialization in the Family

Many influencing factors contribute to children's socialization: their parents' and siblings' demands, behaviors, values, and attitudes; the behaviors of other children and adults within their expanding social world; and the values espoused by the religious institutions and schools they attend. The family, however, is the core socialization agency (Maccoby & Martin, 1983). Depending on their socioeconomic status, culture, and religion, parents encourage children to adopt certain values, behaviors, and beliefs. Through their expectations, parents influence the extent to which children pursue their education and attain occupational success. During the preschool years, however, the main attributes of socialization are *self-control* and *social judgment*. Since young children have no innate sense of propriety and no knowledge of what is permissible and what is prohibited, they can learn only with guidance how to assess social situations and to form internal standards of conduct.

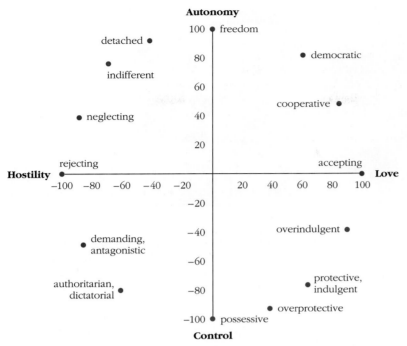

Figure 10.2 *An analysis of several different studies reveals that most parents' behavior can be described in terms of how hostile or loving they are, and how restrictive or permissive.*

Source: From "A Circumplex Model of Maternal Behavior," by Earl S. Schaefer, *Journal of Abnormal and Social Psychology, 59,* Fig. 4, p. 323.

For example, they must learn to regulate their behavior: they must accept and adopt the restrictions placed on them by their parents, and they must learn to be polite, wait their turn, be patient when they want something, and generally control their impulses. Children also need to adopt positively valued or prosocial behaviors.

Parental Care-Giving Practices

Parents are continually teaching their preschool children how to behave in socially appropriate ways, by imposing limits on their behavior and prompting them when to say please, thank you, and good-bye. Parents also convey social amenities, such as not interrupting people when they are talking (Maccoby & Martin, 1983).

Although all parents attempt to guide their children's behaviors, their methods differ greatly, and are not equally effective. Analyzing several classic studies, Schaefer (1959) found that most parents' behavior toward their children can be described in terms of how loving or hostile they are, and how permissive or restrictive (see Figure 10.2). Current studies support his findings. In a series of studies on parenting styles, Diana Baumrind (1967; 1968; 1971; 1975) found that parental care-giving practices are a major influence on the child's development. Welsely Becker (1964) and the Endsley team (1979) support Baumrind's findings. Baumrind identified three broad types of parents and the characteristics of the children that seemed to result from their childrearing methods.

Preschool children have no innate sense of propriety, and learn to regulate their behavior with guidance from their parents.

Authoritarian parents   One type of parent is authoritarian. These parents try to shape, control, and evaluate the child's behavior. According to Baumrind, authoritarian parents require their children to accept their word and authority, and they are likely to favor punitive and forceful disciplinary measures whenever the children's behaviors conflict with what the parent believes is correct. These parents want to control their children and tend to be cold in their interactions with them. Their children tend to be moodier, more apprehensive, and unhappier than other children. They are easily annoyed, sometimes hostile, and vulnerable to stress.

Permissive parents   The second type of parent is permissive. These parents attempt to interact with their children in a nonpunishing and accepting manner, and their relationship tends to be warm and friendly. They allow their children to govern their own behavior and do not provide guidance and direction. Although permissive parents are well meaning, their approach is inappropriate. Baumrind observed that although permissively reared children seem cheerful, perhaps as a result of the warmth their parents show them, they have no self-reliance, are frequently out of control, and have difficulty inhibiting their impulses.

However parents approach child rearing, they significantly influence their children's development. It is important to children that their parents show warmth toward them.

Authoritarian parents use punitive and forceful disciplinary measures. Their children tend to be more apprehensive and unhappy than other children.

Authoritative parents   The most nurturant and effective parents identified by Baumrind are the authoritative parents. These parents are warm in their interactions with their children and frequently use positive reinforcement to guide their behavior. However, they also use reprimand and punishment when the situation demands it. They are ready to exert direct control over their children and are unwilling to yield to unpleasant behaviors such as nagging and whining. They also encourage mature and independent behavior in their children. When they do discipline their children, they explain the rationale behind their actions. Their children are thus the most socially adept of all children. They are energetic and competent and cheerful and friendly in their relations with peers. They approach any experience with interest and curiosity.

It is tempting to interpret Baumrind's findings to mean that children's personality styles are the direct result of childrearing practices and the parents' characteristics. But since her findings are based on correlational data, the direction of the cause-and-effect relationship is obscure. Although guided and shaped by their parents, children also influence their parents' behavior. The reasonableness and effectiveness of authoritative parents could be due in part to the fact that their children are by nature socially competent and easy to discipline. In other words, the parents' behavior may be as much a response to their children's personality styles as the cause of them (Lamb, 1982).

Effective discipline techniques   Although parents differ in their effectiveness in disciplining their children and in the degree to which they are loving or hostile to them (Schaefer, 1959), a great deal of information is available to help parents become effective disciplinarians.

Parents need to discipline their children, because failure to restrain and discipline them may deprive them of opportunities to regulate their behavior and learn self-control and appropriate ways of interacting with others. To be truly effective, however, the discipline of preschoolers should foster self-regulation and social judgment without detracting from their initiative and self-confidence, and without generating either excessive compliance or rebellion. To these ends, parents should practice positive methods of discipline by establishing clear and appropriate rules that the children understand. They should also reinforce positive behaviors, thereby reducing the need for punishment.

However, as most of us who have children or work with them know, there are times when parents have to resort to punishing their children. Any punishment used should be instructive rather than merely punitive and should be directed toward the children's behavior rather than toward their essential worth as people (Parke, 1977). In a review of the research on punishment as a technique for controlling behavior in young children, Ross Parke (1976) acknowledged some limitations of the studies. But he noted that despite these limitations, researchers have concluded that punishment is an effective means of suppressing undesirable behaviors and encouraging the child to behave appropriately. However, Parke emphasized that to be effective, *timing* is crucial: "The longer the delay between the initiation of the act and the onset of punishment, the less effective the punishment." *Consistency* is also important. Parke cited a number of studies that have shown that parents of delinquent boys are more erratic in their disciplinary practices than parents of nondelinquent boys. At times the parents of delinquent boys punish their children for certain behaviors, and at other times they ignore the behaviors.

The nature of the relationship between the parent or other person administering punishment and the child being punished is also important. When this relationship is close and affectionate, the punishment is more effective than when the relationship is cold or impersonal. Additionally, the punishment is likely to be effective when the caretaker gives the child a clear reason for the punishment. Taking these factors into account, Belsky, Lerner, and Spanier (1984) explain that when a child is being punished by an angry parent or told in an angry and hostile manner to stop doing something, she will walk away feeling demeaned by the scolding. But when the caretaker tells the child in a controlled way to stop doing something and gives a reason, the child will understand what she did wrong and why it is unacceptable. Thus, she will gain insight that will guide her subsequent behavior.

Parents often feel that physical punishment is the most effective means of controlling behavior. Although this mode of punishment may be somewhat effective if appropriately administered (that is, when the timing of the punishment and other considerations are taken into account), Parke (1976, 1977) pointed out that physical punishment has undesirable consequences. Parents should consider employing other disciplinary techniques found to be effective. For example, Parke suggested that parents reinforce desired behavior by rewards and encouragement and ignore undesirable behavior. He further advised that "words, as well as deeds, can alter [the child's] physical behavior." Hence, there is no need for parents to resort to physical punishment as a means of controlling children's behavior. Feshbach and Feshbach (1976) offered similar advice, emphasizing the negative consequences of physical punishment and noting that parents who are hostile, coercive, and physically punitive often fail to adequately discipline their children and foster aggressive tendencies in their children. Why? First, physically punitive disciplinary practices function as a model of aggression the child is likely to imitate. Second, the frequent use of hostile disciplinary techniques demeans the child and teaches him that physical action in the form of aggression is a viable way to solve interpersonal disputes (Feshbach, 1980).

LEARNING FROM OTHER CULTURES

Influences on Socialization

As we noted earlier, the way parents socialize their children reflects the societal values and perceptions of what is needed to successfully function in the social world. For example, among hunting societies, such traits as strength and bravery are important. As a result, parents try to encourage these traits in their sons, because in these societies it is the men who hunt (Hoffman, 1984). In Japan, however, patience, conformity to rules, and emotional maturity are valued traits; so Japanese parents expect their preschoolers to be courteous and polite, to think about others' feelings, and to exercise self-control (Hess et al., 1980). Disciplinary techniques also depend on cultural values. In the United States, parents rely a great deal on physical punishment (Gil, 1970) and power assertion (for example, they probably will remind a child of rules he is expected to obey), but in other cultures parents tend to reason with the child and appeal to his emotions. Conroy, Hess, Azuma, and Kashiwagi (1980) note that Japanese mothers do not use physical punishment; instead, they appeal to the child's emotions, explaining to him, for example, that by misbehaving he is hurting his mother's feelings.

Minority-Group Children in the United States

How parents socialize their children also varies among American parents, depending on their cultural background. Our society is diverse, with several minority ethnic groups—blacks (or African Americans), Asian Americans, Hispanics, and American Indians—making up about one-third of the U.S. population (Spencer, 1990). Although in the minority, these ethnic groups—primarily made up of young families—are growing, and demographers predict that by the year 2000 they will constitute "a new majority" (McLoyd, 1990).

Minority parents have a unique system of beliefs and practices that may overlap, but will also substantially differ from those of other cultures (Laosa, 1981). Each ethnic group is not entirely homogeneous; there are differences depending on the family's economic status, how long the family has been in the United States, and, in some cases, the conditions preceding the family's immigration. Although minority children are likely to be affected by these factors and also by their parents' values and childrearing techniques, researchers have paid little attention to minority-group children.

In increasing numbers, however, developmental psychologists are recognizing the importance of studying children in the context of their family life and of emphasizing the strengths, rather than the deficits, associated with being a minority-group child. For example, Harrison and colleagues (1990) note that it is important for researchers to look at socially competent and academically successful minority-group children and ascertain how parents raise them and what values they instill in them. The research is still in its infancy, but in at least one study including a national sample of black children (Bowman & Howard, 1985), researchers found that the way in which parents prepare their children to deal with discrimination is a significant element in the children's motivation to succeed academically and aspire toward upward mobility. The parents who are successful emphasized ethnic pride, self-development, and awareness of racial barriers.

Harrison and colleagues (1990) further note that children are affected by some of the adaptive strategies minority families use to cope with the stress associated with living within the majority culture. One such mechanism is family extendedness. The researchers found that black children tend to live in an extended family, which may include a parent, grandparent, and other relatives; its function is to serve as a social support mechanism. The extended family is important to other ethnic groups as well and may reflect traditionally strong feelings of identification and loyalty to the family rather than an adaptive strategy. Native American families extend beyond the nuclear family and may be characterized as a cooperative including the mother, father, relatives, and others in the community and tribe (Burgess, 1980). Wilson and Gutierrez (1985) note that the extended family is a dominant feature among Asian Americans and Hispanics, in which relatives and nonrelatives often share households. Within the context of the extended family, minority parents would emphasize interdependence as a socialization goal and encourage children to think and behave in ways involving a cooperative way of life. They would try to instill such behaviors as social dependence on others and sharing as opposed to autonomy, self-reliance, and competitiveness.

The research on minority children will enhance our understanding of development, but we should be careful not to generalize from group data to individuals (Harrison et al., 1990). Nevertheless, as you consider the progress in social and cognitive development occurring during the childhood years, consider, too, that children's experiences will affect developmental outcome.

The Role of Television

Children also learn from the behavior of TV personalities. Television has a great deal of influence on children. It is a common and constant learning medium. Much of what the child sees on television can best be described as learning about people—how they behave, how they feel, and how they interact with one another. But the world of television is not like the real world, because television programs are produced to satisfy advertisers concerned with attracting people who can spend money, namely, middle-age people. Thus, relatively little attention is paid on television to portraying older people, who are very much a part of real life. In recent years TV programs have featured the divorced, single-parent family and the dual-career family. Nevertheless, researchers emphasize that the overall picture presented by television is still far from the real world, which may affect the preschool child. For example, crime is portrayed ten times more often on the screen than it occurs in real life (Gerbner, 1980).

Television violence   One concern is that television devotes a significant percentage of its programming to violence and aggression, and this is what children are exposed to. The Surgeon General's report on television violence (Pearl, Bouthilet, & Lazar, 1982) reveals that 80% of television programs surveyed contained at least one incident of overt physical aggression or a violent act. Despite continued efforts by children's advocates to reduce the amount of televised violence, it is becoming more intense and more widespread. It is evident in numerous programs and on music video channels. Often popular rock groups and singers are shown engaging in violence. A study by the National Coalition on Television Violence (1984) found that a large number of music videos contained sadistic violence in which the attacker took pleasure in committing senseless acts, such as choking people or knocking them unconscious.

Studies have shown that exposing children to such violence on television increases their aggression (Pearl, Bouthilet, & Lazar, 1982). In an early study demonstrating that children can learn aggression from television, Bandura (1969) set up an experimental procedure in which a group of children watched a TV program depicting violence. On later observing these children, he found that they were more likely to repeatedly hit a doll than children who did not watch the program. In another study Friedrich and Stein (1973) asked children to watch one of three types of programs—cartoons or other programs (such as Batman) depicting violence and aggression, programs depicting prosocial behaviors, and programs depicting neither violence nor prosocial behaviors—daily for four weeks. The children were observed for three weeks before watching the programs and for two weeks after watching them. After watching programs depicting violence, children were more likely to be intolerant in their interpersonal interactions and to disobey rules than the children who had watched other programs. Children observed to be aggressive before watching aggression and violence on television became more so afterward, whereas children who were not aggressive to begin with did not become more aggressive after watching the shows.

In another study Steuer, Applefield, and Smith (1971) selected pairs of preschoolers observed to exhibit about the same amount of aggressive behavior (kicking, hitting, etc.) while on a nursery school playground. One of the children in each pair was then shown violent TV programs each day for about two weeks. The other child in each pair was shown programs that did not include violence and aggression. Among all the pairs of children studied, the children who had watched the violent TV programs became more aggressive in their play than did the other children.

These negative effects on children may endure. Zuckerman and Zuckerman (1985) studied third graders' viewing habits, noting in particular the types of programs the children watched. Then they followed the children up to age 19. According to the researchers, the single most important factor predictive of aggressiveness at age 19 was the amount of violence these young adults had watched on television as children.

Television and prosocial behaviors   The capacity of television as a socializing agency is not limited to violence and aggression; thus television as a medium does

Significant improvements have been made in portraying minorities on television. This positive trend is likely to influence minority children's self-esteem and change societal attitudes.

not have to be harmful to children if parents direct them to appropriate programs (Daviss, 1989; Murray & Lonnborg, 1988). Some television programs, such as "Mr. Rogers' Neighborhood," attempt to teach prosocial behaviors. Mr. Rogers is a soft-spoken man who addresses himself to preschool children across the country. He discusses a number of topics with the children, encouraging them in his quiet manner always to be polite and helpful. His show has been found to increase sharing, helping, and cooperation among preschool children and to reduce the incidence of aggression they exhibit toward one another. Studies reviewed by Stein and Friedrich (1975) found that children who watched "Mr. Rogers' Neighborhood" became more self-controlled and more obedient than children who watched shows depicting aggression.

Television and minorities   Television producers have also made progress in recent years in offering a diversity of programs featuring minorities in a positive light (Adleson, 1991). "The Cosby Show" and "A Different World," for example, portray blacks within the context of the black family and in professional roles. Wilson and Gutierrez (1985), in their book *Minorities and the Media,* note that the change from portraying minorities as persons involved in crime or persons to be ridiculed to portraying them as socially influential and professional members of society encourages children and adults to change their views of minorities and contributes to positive self-esteem among minority-group children and encourages them to pursue higher education.

Although the effect of the family is of primary importance, child care centers and nursery schools also influence children's socialization.

Effects of Child Care on Socialization

Child care and nursery schools also influence children's socialization. In such settings children have an opportunity to interact with a number of children and adults, to learn to be cooperative and helpful in their interpersonal interactions, to wait their turn, and to conform to rules. Reviews of studies comparing children being raised at home to children in child care found that children in full-time child care centers are more cooperative in their interactions with peers (Clarke-Stewart & Fein, 1983). However, this is usually the case in high-quality child care centers and generally depends on the extent to which the caretakers discipline and provide direction for the children (Ruopp et al., 1979). In such centers children learn to obey rules and to interact effectively with adults and children in a group setting.

A casual observer may think that child care providers have to discipline the children all the time since they have so many youngsters to supervise. But in reality many child care providers do less disciplining than parents do (Cochran, 1977), perhaps because the care providers have less of an emotional investment in any one child. Ambron (1980) reported that some child care staff are more permissive, more tolerant of disobedience and aggression, and less inclined to set standards and directions for behavior than parents are.

Therefore, it is not surprising that just as some studies point to the positive effects of child care, other studies suggest that there may be negative effects as well. According to Ramey, MacPhee, and Yeats (1982), kindergarten teachers found children who had been enrolled in a child care program since infancy to be more hostile than their counterparts reared at home. Robertson (1982) cites similar findings indicating that some child care–reared children are aggressive toward their peers and have problems interacting with adults. He found that boys with child care histories were rated by their first-grade teachers as significantly more disobedient, quarrelsome, and uncooperative than children with no previous child care experience. Howes and Olenick (1986), however, note that the effects of child care vary depending on the quality of care provided and on the extent that the center encourages parent involvement. They further point out that negative effects associated with child care may reflect difficult conditions in the home. You can see that the question—Is child care harmful to children?—is difficult to answer and that more research is necessary (National Research Council, 1990). The child care experience may enrich the child's social world and open new avenues for learning and social interactions, but it can also have negative effects. Often the key is the staff because they determine the quality of care received (Phillips, 1988).

Summary

During the preschool years children become increasingly independent and show their mastery of the environment. They are more able to do things for themselves and to explore their surroundings, and they experience changes in their interactions with their parents. Children remain attached to their mother and enjoy being with her, but the father now assumes a more central role. Although the relationship they have with their father becomes very important to preschoolers, children of divorced parents often do not have the opportunity to develop a close relationship with their father.

Preschoolers' peer relationships provide the opportunity to develop social skills and to play. Play varies in the amount of social involvement, with younger preschoolers often playing alone and older preschoolers playing in groups. As they play together, striking differences in personality characteristics become obvious; some children are cooperative and independent whereas others are disruptive and aggressive. Aggression, in part a response to frustration, is common among young children. They eventually learn to contain their anger and become more cooperative in their interactions with others, often showing their ability to share and to help others in distress.

Peer relations also provide children with the opportunity to learn about other people's needs and emotions. And preschoolers also learn about themselves, developing a self-concept, which is an understanding and evaluation of their personality, qualities, and capabilities. They evidence their emerging self-concept in their adoption of gender identity.

Although biological factors contribute to sex differences in behavior, environmental factors account for most reported sex differences, as children learn from and imitate the behaviors of their siblings, peers, and adults. Parents, however, play a vital role in this respect. They influence the children's adoption of sex-typed behaviors and other aspects of personality as well. Researchers have found that when parents are reasonable and explain to children how they should behave and why, children are socially competent and happy. On the other hand, when parents are permissive, children have difficulty controlling their behavior in social situations. When parents are hostile, and resort to physical punishment, children are moody and unhappy and learn to behave aggressively as well.

Although physical punishment is potentially harmful to the child, many parents use this method of discipline, thereby conveying to their children that violence is an effective means of dealing with interpersonal difficulties. Children also learn about violence from what they see on television. Violence is continually portrayed on television, and researchers have shown that by imitating the behaviors of TV personalities, children begin to behave aggressively. However, television also has positive influences. Programs that provide models of prosocial behaviors help children learn how to cooperate with one another and to extend understanding and kindness to others.

V The Middle Childhood Years

11 Physical Development During Middle Childhood

12 Cognitive Development During Middle Childhood

13 Social and Emotional Development During Middle Childhood

When we look back over childhood memories, it seems as if the most vivid and happy ones come from the middle years: memories of pajama parties or skateboards, freeze tag or pick-up ball games, summer camp or just summertime. Except perhaps for a paper route or babysitting for younger brothers and sisters, most of us didn't have any major responsibilities during these years.

Sometimes called the school-age years, middle childhood starts at around age 6 and lasts through age 12. During this happy, troublefree time, however, we acquired an impressive array of physical skills and reached a new level of psychological development, which allowed us greater independence from adult care. We also began to form strong emotional ties with people outside the family, becoming increasingly self-sufficient. These years laid the groundwork for our independence and separation from our family.

11 Physical Development During Middle Childhood

Most adults quickly become aware of school-age children's self-sufficiency and interest in persons and activities outside the family. Children of this age are everywhere: on the playground and at the mall, pizza shop, or movies. This is especially true toward the latter part of the period when they are 11 or 12 years old. Although children in the middle childhood years are perhaps the most visible of all age groups, many of us pay surprisingly little attention to them—in part, because school and friends take up so much of their time (Collins, 1984). Also, the physical and psychological changes that occur do not attract adult attention; they are not as obvious as the changes that occurred during infancy and early childhood and will occur during adolescence (Ryan & Applegate, 1976; Shonkoff, 1984).

Although unobtrusive, developmental changes do indeed take place during these years, and they are accentuated when the children start school. They are exposed to many different people and must adapt to new social rules and expectations that inevitably affect their development. Between the time children enter school and adolescence, there are marked changes in their ability to learn, think, and remember. They grow in their capacity for knowledge of self and the social world so for the first time they are able to establish intimate friendships.

Progress in Physical Growth and Motor Development

In addition to acquiring cognitive and social skills, school-age children experience subtle but important changes in physical growth. Although physical development during this period is characterized by steady and sustained growth, substantial progress occurs in the maturation of higher cortical functions, resulting in refinements in brain structure (Combrink-Graham, 1991). Progress also occurs in children's ability to execute motor skills and master more complex, elaborate motor tasks (Shonkoff, 1984). Learning to swim, ski, and dance or play a musical instrument are among the skills children are able to master if given the opportunity.

The principles important for early physical development still characterize this stage of growth; however, physical growth and motor development begin to assume great personal significance. Children's attitudes about themselves become related in part to their concept of their body size and shape and their abilities. This change occurs because they are no longer egocentric in outlook during middle childhood. As they acquire the ability to think about what other people think, others' reactions to them become important. Although middle childhood can be happy and carefree for most children, some may be conscious of how they differ from others and of what other people think of them and can develop low self-esteem. In addition, variation in growth becomes very apparent. Thus there are great differences in height and rate of maturation among children of the same age. Not only do children of the same age grow at different rates but children today are also taller than they were in previous generations. They mature earlier as well, a phenomenon known as the *secular trend*. Several factors account for this phenomenon, and there are consequences associated with early maturation, especially for girls. Before discussing them, however, let us examine the progress in physical growth and motor development during middle childhood and the social significance of children's increased ability to perform a wide range of motor tasks.

During middle childhood, children explore new activities so avidly that sometimes they neglect their daily chores and responsibilities.

Motor Skills

We can observe progress in motor development through children's play behavior. School-age children seem to be forever racing around, climbing, jumping, hopping, or skipping. They are always in a hurry to get someplace. As a result, they tend to run more than they walk and frequently take to scooters, wagons, bicycles, or skates. Children put so much energy into their motor activities at this age that it often seems that if they could fly, they would. Indeed, they become more tired when sitting still than when running or engaging in a physical activity. Thus child experts recommend that teachers and parents provide children with active tasks (Katz & Chard, 1990).

During this period children improve in their control and coordination of fine-motor skills. When they first enter school, their writing is quite clumsy. But with increased maturity, their writing of letters, numbers, and words becomes progressively neater and smaller. They can now learn to play musical instruments, a feat requiring dexterity and control over the small muscles of the hands and fingers, and they can engage in sewing, knitting, or drawing pictures in minute detail—all activities requiring fine-motor control.

Gross-motor skills also improve, reflecting increased speed, power, coordination, agility, and balance, which are the basic components of motor fitness (Gallahue, 1982). On attaining greater speed and coordination, school-age children improve continuously on gross-motor skills previously acquired and learn many new skills. They run faster and show greater accuracy and distance in hopping and jumping. In addition, they are better able to throw, catch, and kick a ball (Corbin, 1973). Improvements in these basic motor skills enable school-age children to participate in team sports such as basketball, football, baseball, and soccer. In addition, they become increasingly able to learn and master rather complex tasks, such as dancing, swimming, roller skating, and playing tennis. Many children display an intense interest in acquiring and improving these skills. As McNassor (1975) observed:

Now that girls and boys participate in the same sports, researchers are finding that their abilities are equal.

This is a period when most children explore a new interest so intensely that daily chores or responsibilities are thoroughly neglected. Their need is to find out what they can do well and what they are really good at.

The extent of children's ability to acquire new motor skills and become adept at motor activities depends largely on opportunities for learning, encouragement, and practice (Tanner, 1970). Children who are not given the opportunity to learn to swim will not be able to swim. Having learned to swim, they need to practice to become proficient. And so it is with other motor skills. But opportunities to learn and practice are not enough; the ability to execute many of these skills also depends on genetic and physiological factors, such as body size, strength, and brain maturation (Tanner, 1970). In addition, the extent to which children develop their genetic potential for motor skills depends on their temperament, on certain aspects of their personality—such as energy level, venturesomeness, aggressiveness, and persistence (Ausubel, Sullivan, & Ives, 1980)—on their attitude toward their body build, and on their eagerness to participate in group functions and competition. Shy children or those with low self-esteem will have difficulty competing. Since motor skills are developed primarily in the context of the peer group, these children will miss the opportunity to acquire and develop such skills. It is important, however, for children to improve their motor skills because this progress enables them to become active members of their peer group. Children can participate in many social functions and sports such as summer camp, Boy Scouts or Girl Scouts, or Little League, thereby learning how to interact with other children and adults in a variety of settings. Or they can round up friends for a game of football or baseball, which provides a context for developing their social and physical skills and sharing their interests. Although many school-age children are interested in sports, just as many prefer to read, watch television, or simply talk to one another. Also, because the need for school-age child care programs far exceeds the supply, many children of working parents have no alternative but to stay home alone after school, thereby missing opportunities for play and sports activities.

Individual differences and similarities   A child who is good at some motor skills such as running or jumping is often good at other motor skills as well (Espenschade, 1960). Some children eventually become good, all-around athletes. There is a wide range of individual differences in the execution of motor skills and mastery of complex motor tasks. But boys and girls do not evidence many differences in their ability to acquire and execute motor skills—in large part because physical differences between the sexes are minimal during this period. As is true during the preschool years, however, boys tend to have greater strength, and girls tend to have better balance and coordination. Thus, the two groups have certain advantages in performing certain skills. In an early study of children ages 5 through 12, Keogh (1965) found that boys ran faster and for greater distances and were better at target throwing and grip strength. On the other hand, girls have an edge in gymnastics—specifically in beam walking, especially during the early part of middle childhood (Gallahue, 1982).

Yet, during this period, the sex of the child is not the determining factor in the mastery of skills. Rather, age is an important factor; both boys and girls improve their ability to execute motor skills as they grow older (Keogh, 1965). Practice is also very important in the mastery of skills. Now that more girls are participating in the same types of sports as boys (American Academy of Pediatrics, 1981), researchers are finding that the girls' ability to master these sports equals the boys' (Hall & Lee, 1984).

A CLOSER LOOK

Poor Physical Fitness: An Unhealthy Trend Among School-Age Children

When we imagine school-age children, we usually think of them running, jumping, sledding, or biking, faces flushed with the stimulation of the activity. Certainly, many school-age children enjoy participating in sports and other physical activities. In general, however, children today are less active than the children of 20 or 30 years ago.

Considering that children today spend an average of three hours a day in front of the TV, this is not surprising. In addition, other factors conspire to create a sedentary generation. Many children whose mothers work outside the home have to stay home alone and sometimes actually inside the home as a security measure. They are thus deprived of the opportunity to engage in many activities, including physical ones. The result is that children are not physically fit.

Physical fitness does not refer to athletic ability but rather to the optimal functioning of the heart, lungs, muscles, and blood vessels. To maintain physical fitness, you have to engage in exercises or sports that work four areas: muscle strength, muscle endurance, flexibility, and cardiovascular functioning. Not every physical activity works on the four areas. Tennis, basketball, swimming, and soccer, for example, enhance overall physical fitness, but sports such as baseball, which are popular among school children, do not. In baseball the child engages in relatively little physical activity because only one player moves at a time, and then only intermittently.

In a report of a national survey of 8000 children ages 10 to 18 conducted over a three-year period, researchers demonstrated that children today are less physically active and generally more obese than children in the 1960s. In addition, these findings indicated that (1) the children's heart/lung fitness lagged behind that of most middle-aged joggers, (2) more than half the children did not engage in any physical activities, and (3) most children did not learn anything at school about activities they can pursue to improve their physical fitness.

This study is one of several that attest to the startling facts about the health status of American children (see, for example, American Academy of Pediatrics, 1985; Reif, 1985).
(continued)

Physical Growth

Since physical growth during the school-age years proceeds at a slow but fairly even pace, children have an opportunity to develop interests, skills, and knowledge without being hampered by exhausting physical changes. They gain an average of 5 pounds a year during this period and grow approximately 2 ½ inches a year (National Center for Health Statistics, 1976). Other changes include increased skeletal and muscular growth, increased strength, and increased lung capacity. These changes help children grow stronger, go for longer periods without rest, and progress in motor development and in the acquisition of motor skills.

Changes in body proportions are also evident. By the time they enter school, children have lost the squat, chubby appearance characteristic of the early preschool period. During the school-age years, as they become taller and more slender, their body proportions seem more graceful and adultlike. In addition, they lose their deciduous teeth, which are replaced by permanent ones. This gradual process continues throughout middle childhood, resulting in changes in facial proportions as the child's jaw becomes increasingly larger.

A CLOSER LOOK

(continued)

These findings raise concerns; evidence shows that becoming physically fit is a habit learned in childhood that must be continued through the adult years (Select Panel for the Promotion of Child Health, 1981; Richmond, 1977). Even more alarming, studies have shown that the tendency toward such physical problems as cardiovascular disease can start as early as the first grade (American Academy of Pediatrics, 1985)! Reif (1985) found that among 7- to 12-year-old boys, body fat levels were on the average 2% to 5% above what is considered normal for optimal health, that 41% of U.S. children have high levels of cholesterol in their blood, and that 28% have higher than normal blood pressure. Furthermore, 98% of the children in Reif's study had *at least* one symptom that showed them to be at *major* risk for developing coronary heart disease later on.

This is a problem of national significance! But, there are easy solutions, if only we made them a priority. For example, in a model program tested in the Michigan school districts, children participated in a well-designed physical education program that required them to exercise regularly and take responsibility for choosing the type of foods they eat. The results were spectacular. The children's body fat measurements dropped an average of 16%, their blood cholesterol levels dropped 4%, and their blood pressure dropped 6% (Kuntzleman, 1983).

Developing such programs, however, does not ensure that they will be implemented in the schools. When there are fiscal constraints and budget cuts such as those most schools are experiencing, physical education courses are among the first to be eliminated from the curriculum. In fact, many schools have either eliminated or reduced physical education requirements during the past few years, a situation some observers cite as one contributing reason for our children's poor physical fitness (National Children and Youth Fitness Study, 1984).

Several times throughout this book we've noted how important it is to establish priorities in a climate of fiscal austerity and to develop and implement programs on the basis of these priorities. Schools today have increasing responsibilities and tasks and decreasing dollars to carry them out. Some people maintain that schools should not be held accountable for physical fitness. For them, the school's primary responsibility is teaching basic learning skills. Others argue that health is a fundamental aspect of development and that a sound body contributes to a sound mind. Indeed, they argue that providing children with the opportunities to improve their physical fitness actually *enhances* rather than detracts from their education.

What is your position? Assume that you are to speak before the Board of Education in your school district on the issue of more or fewer physical education courses in the coming year. What would your argument be? How would you attempt to convince the Board members to agree with you? What evidence would you present?

Individual differences   A wide range of individual differences in physical development are also apparent. Some of these differences have to do with activity level. Recall from previous chapters that differences in activity level are present in infancy and early childhood; some babies and young children seem more active, whereas others are quieter and calmer (Thomas & Chess, 1984; Thomas, Chess, & Birch, 1968).

Hyperactive and hypoactive children   During middle childhood, individual differences are accentuated, in part because the children are at school where they are required to sit still most of the time and attend to specific tasks for increasingly long periods. Most children have no problem with this. But in virtually every classroom, there are two or three children who cannot sit still and whose behavior is described as hyperactive, impulsive, irritable, moody, slow, and inattentive (Cohen, 1977). Henker and Whalen (1989) note that even their classmates describe hyperactive children as troublesome:

> [These] children can't sit still; they don't pay attention to the teacher; they mess around and get into trouble; they try to get others into trouble. . . . [p. 216]

Until recently, children exhibiting these behaviors were said to suffer from **hyperactive syndrome** or **minimal brain dysfunction (MBD).** Observers applied both terms indiscriminately to any child who was inattentive, impulsive, or hyperactive. Within the last decade, however, we have made significant advances in understanding these children, and researchers have coined the terms **attention deficit disorder (ADD)** or **attention deficit hyperactivity disorder (ADHD)** (American Psychiatric Association, 1987) to help explain the symptoms. Table 11.1 lists the criteria for diagnosing ADHD.

Activity levels differ even in early infancy. These differences are accentuated once the children are in school, where they are required to sit still for relatively long periods.

This is a relatively common disorder that occurs more frequently among boys; for every 4 boys characterized by hyperactivity and inattentiveness, there is only 1 girl with such behaviors (Cohen, 1977). These children move from one place to another, are unable to inhibit their actions, and are constantly diverted by sounds and objects. They are chaotic in their behavior, forget what they are told to do, and seem at a loss when asked to engage in sequentially ordered behaviors (for example, when they are asked to go outside and fetch something). Since these children evoke a great deal of anger and frustration in their parents and teachers, they are often scolded and punished (Cantwell, 1975). Their chaotic behavior contributes to stress in their parents (Fisher, 1990) and it annoys other children as much as it annoys adults. As a result, these children are not popular among their peers (Pelham & Bender, 1982).

Children with attentional problems may have a learning disability as well (see page 444). They may seem normal on the playground, at a birthday party, or at another unstructured setting. The disorder only becomes evident when they have to sit still. Most people are annoyed and angered by children who evidence hyperactivity because they are considerably more distracting than other children.

We also need to consider other children with attentional disorders who are hypoactive. **Hypoactivity,** a form of attentional behavior disturbance more common in girls, is characterized by less-than-normal activity levels and excessive daydreaming. While hypoactive children may be quiet and undistracting in their behavior, like hyperactive children they are unable to attend to specific tasks. The attentional deficits of hypoactive children, however, may go unnoticed for many years simply because they tend to be compliant in their behavior (Cohen, 1977).

Attentional disorders do not necessarily vanish with age. In over 50% of ADHD children, problems persist through adolescence and adulthood and may be evident

---

TABLE 11.1   Diagnosing Attention Deficit Hyperactivity Disorder

A. A disturbance of at least six months during which at least eight of the following are present.[a]
   1. Often fidgets with hands or feet or squirms in seat (in adolescents, may be limited to subjective feelings of restlessness)
   2. Has difficulty remaining seated when required to do so
   3. Is easily distracted by extraneous stimuli
   4. Has difficulty awaiting turn in games or group situations
   5. Often blurts out answers to questions before they have been completed
   6. Has difficulty following through on instructions from others (not due to oppositional behavior or failure of comprehension), e.g., fails to finish chores
   7. Has difficulty sustaining attention in tasks or play activities

   8. Often shifts from one uncompleted activity to another
   9. Has difficulty playing quietly
   10. Often talks excessively
   11. Often interrupts or intrudes on others, e.g., butts into other children's games
   12. Often does not seem to listen to what is being said to him or her
   13. Often loses things necessary for tasks or activities at school or at home (e.g., toys, pencils, books, assignments)
   14. Often engages in physically dangerous activities without considering possible consequences (not for the purpose of thrill-seeking), e.g., runs into street without looking.
B. Onset before the age of seven.
C. Does not meet the criteria for a Pervasive Developmental Disorder. (APA, 1987, pp. 53–54)

[a]A criterion is considered to be met only if the behavior is considerably more frequent than that of most people of the same mental age. The items are listed in descending order of discriminating power based on data from a national field trial of the *DSM-III-R* criteria for Disruptive Behavior Disorders.

Source: "Hyperactivity and attention deficits," by B. Henker and C. K. Whalen, *American Psychologist,* February 1989, pp. 216–223. Copyright 1989 by the American Psychological Association. Reprinted by permission.

in antisocial behavior, above-average rates of job changes, marital difficulties, and traffic accidents (Cantwell, 1986; Henker & Whalen, 1989).

In the past, school officials severely punished children with attentional problems, often expelling them from school (Ross & Ross, 1982). Although some ADHD children are still scolded for their behavior, we have increasingly recognized over the past three decades that these children need help. They cannot control their behavior, because they have problems in cognitive processing, attentional regulation, and motor control (Cohen, 1977; Shaywitz & Shaywitz, 1984). Researchers do not entirely understand or agree on the etiology of these problems. Some provide a biological explanation, arguing that prenatal and perinatal events (excessive radiation and maternal smoking during pregnancy, lack of oxygen or head trauma during birth) are to blame (Shaywitz & Shaywitz, 1984). Others note that there may be a genetic component to the disorder since ADHD children often have siblings or parents who experienced similar problems (Pauls et al., 1983). When studying adopted children diagnosed with ADHD, some researchers found that their biological, but not adoptive, parents showed evidence of attentional disorders (Wender, 1990). Food additives and allergies to certain foods have also been implicated as possible causes (Feingold, 1975), but the evidence has not yet been established.

Still other researchers provided a social explanation for ADHD, stressing that the hyperactive behavior is defined by the children's social environment (Conrad, 1976) and occurs in the context of their interactions with adults and peers. Thus, when children's behavior is socially deviant, the family or the school helps "create" the behavior by then labeling the child. Lambert and Hartsough (1984) note that the problem may stem from an interaction between the children's biological status and the social environment; children who are unable to modulate their activity and regulate their attention (a biological factor) tend to evoke anger in those around them (an environmental factor); as a result, their difficulties are exacerbated.

Controversies also surround treatment of the disorder, stemming largely from the practice of giving the children stimulant drugs like ritalin. These drugs paradoxically have a calming effect on children and are said to result in improved attentiveness, schoolwork, and social performance (Fish, 1971; Cohen, 1977). Wender (1990) notes that many experiments comparing these drugs with placebos have shown that the drugs produce moderate to dramatic improvements in the behavior of about 75% of ADHD children. According to Henker and Whalen (1989), physicians often recommend that the child on medication should change schools so he can try out his new social behaviors with peers and teachers who are unbiased by his previous history of disruptions.

Although effective for many ADHD children, the drugs have some side effects, such as interfering with physical growth. It is possible, however, to prevent this side effect by taking the children off the drugs for a time so that growth can resume. Other side effects may include diminished appetite and loss of weight. There are also concerns about drug dependency, since the child has to take the medication several times a day every day. Given the effectiveness of drug treatment, however, some physicians contend that we should perhaps regard it in much the same way as a diabetic patient's continuing need for insulin (Wender, 1990).

Further, the drugs, specifically ritalin, are sometimes overused. Some school officials may view the use of ritalin as a solution to a disorder in the classroom rather than as a treatment for attentional disorders. This situation came to light when analyses of ritalin consumption revealed that it was more frequently prescribed for children in some states than in others (Schmidt, 1987). Hence, we need to raise the following questions: Are teachers unnecessarily labeling children as hyperactive?

Are physicians freely prescribing the drug when parents and teachers complain about the child's behavior? Given these concerns, experts advise a diagnosis of ADHD before physicians prescribe any medication. Even when drugs are considered appropriate, they should not be prescribed indiscriminately. In addition, each child must be carefully evaluated and monitored after prescribing the drug (Fish, 1971; Cohen, 1977).

Besides drug treatment, physicians have advocated other treatment possibilities for use instead of or in conjunction with drugs. These include behavior modification techniques, psychotherapy, and physical education, which can help children acquire more coordination and mastery over their bodies and movements (Cohen, 1977; Shaywitz & Shaywitz, 1984). Since ADHD children learn better in quiet environments, another treatment suggestion is to change the school and home environment to eliminate as many distractions as possible (Cruikshank, 1977). Eliminating certain foods from the child's diet is another possibility (Feingold, 1975). In a dietary intervention study, Bonnie Kaplan and her colleagues (1989) selected 24 boys ages 3 ½ to 6 who were diagnosed as ADHD. The researchers eliminated food dyes, flavorings, preservatives, chocolate, and caffeine from the children's diets and noted behavioral improvements in close to half the group. Previous dietary intervention studies had not produced such behavioral changes in hyperactive children (Weiss, 1991; Wender, 1986), so additional studies must be conducted before any conclusions can be reached. It could well be that Kaplan's findings were due to a placebo effect.

Variations in growth Children differ in body build, just as adults do. Some are naturally tall and slender; others are short and chubby; and still others are skinny

---

FEATURE

Cultural Variations in Activity Levels: The Hispanic Child in School

Sociocultural factors influence the way we talk, gesture, move, and interact with others. You may have grown up in an ethnic culture where people use their hands to gesture when they speak, where animated discussions over everyday matters resemble arguments, or where intense emotional expression is considered the most healthy "normal" type of response to most situations. When teachers are not aware of such cultural differences, they may misinterpret behavior.

In fact, one problem with labeling children as hyperactive and prescribing medication for their supposed disorder is that teachers may fail to consider sociocultural variables. This is especially true for Hispanic children, who are at risk for biased referral because they are often suspected of presenting symptoms of ADHD. One study noted that Hispanics, who were all Puerto Rican in the sample, are more animated in their body movements and gestures, move their eyes more, and focus on the listener's face less than Anglo-Americans (Bauermeister et al., 1990). In addition, they react as a group more often rather than making

individualized responses. It is not unusual, for example, for three Hispanic children to answer a question at one time rather than take turns. These styles of interaction occur in the structured environment of the classroom, where they may be interpreted as apparent inattentiveness, impulsivity, and overactivity.

In fact, one study clearly demonstrated this possibility (Achenbach et al., 1990). The study sample consisted of demographically matched groups of children from the general U.S. population and from Puerto Rico, and used both Anglo-American and Puerto Rican teachers. In comparing the teacher ratings, the researchers found that Anglo-American teachers, but *not* the Puerto Rican teachers, rated the behaviors of the Puerto Rican children as distressing and in need of intervention.

Although more research on this issue is needed, it is apparent that what is considered normal in one cultural group may be considered an attentional disorder in another. You can see how important considering the child's sociocultural background is when making assessments.

Surprisingly, these girls are the same age.

and muscular. Children also grow at different rates. How fast they grow depends on their genetic inheritance, nutrition, and physical and emotional health (Tanner, 1970; Roberts, 1969). Even well-fed, healthy children differ in growth rates. Some children are fast growers; others are slow or average growers. These variations, especially noticeable in height, result in great differences among age-mates. If you enter a fifth-grade classroom and pick out the shortest and the tallest 10-year-olds, the difference may be so striking that it will be hard for you to believe they are the same age.

Variations in height among age-mates become evident when comparing children from different countries. Meredith (1969; 1971) found a 9- to 18-inch difference in height among 8-year-old children from different countries; the shortest children come from Southeast Asia and South America, the tallest from the United States and Europe.

Even more astounding are differences among children of different generations, a phenomenon referred to as the **secular trend.** This term describes the changes in physical growth over time found in large samples of populations (Roche, 1979). Secular change is measured for different aspects of growth, including the rate of sexual maturation and height. The age of sexual maturation for girls has decreased notably in the past few decades; that is, girls mature earlier today than in the past.

To determine the age of girls' sexual maturation in order to measure the secular trend, child experts take into account the onset of **menarche;** that is, the first menstrual period. The secular trend means that girls are becoming sexually mature at an increasingly younger age (see Figure 11.1), and that more girls are capable of sexual reproduction during childhood. Boys also reach sexual maturity at an earlier age, but the physiological and social implications of early maturation are not as significant for boys as for girls.

Other changes have also contributed to sexual experimentation among children in our society. The sexual revolution, spawned as a social protest on college campuses in the 1960s, has filtered down to high schools and junior high schools, even to elementary schools. Children engage in sex at a younger age and much more frequently (Ventura & Lewis, 1990). One disturbing consequence of earlier

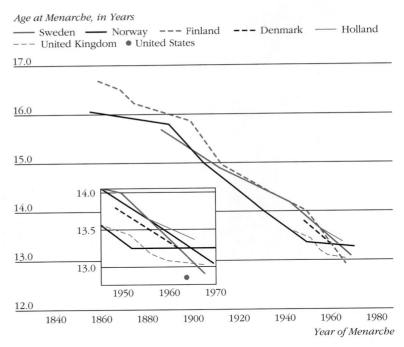

Age at Menarche, in Years

Figure 11.1 *The secular trend in age at menarche, 1860–1970.*

Source: Reprinted by permission of the publishers from *Foetus Into Man* by J. M. Tanner, Cambridge, Mass.: Harvard University Press, p. 152, Fig. 49. Copyright © 1978 by J. M. Tanner.

maturation and sexuality is that over 1 million young girls become pregnant each year (see Chapter 14). Many of these girls are only 10 to 14 years old (U.S. Department of Health and Human Services, 1983).

Children are also growing taller and achieving their adult height at an earlier age. In accord with the secular trend for stature (height), the average height of children also increased over the last several generations. This growth is especially evident during middle childhood. A study of British children noted that children between the ages of 6 and 12 are significantly taller than their counterparts in previous generations (Tanner, 1978). This phenomenon is also true for American children. Beginning about 100 years ago and for several decades thereafter, the height of American children between the ages of 6 and 15 has increased at the rate of about 1 inch per decade. After age 15, the secular trend is not quite so noticeable. This means that youngsters attain their adult height sooner (Meredith, 1976). The United States is not necessarily becoming a nation of tall people, but school-age children today on average are 4 inches taller than school-age children 40 years ago (Roche, 1979).

What caused these secular changes in height and in sexual maturation? Will they continue? Tanner (1978) noted that, due to improved health and nutrition, secular changes have been dramatic since the turn of the century. He described studies that posit a genetic explanation for these increases in height. Studies also indicate that secular changes have been leveling off (Roche, 1979) and seem to be about over.

Variations in height   Although school-age children are taller now than the children of previous generations, the gains in height during the middle childhood years are not as significant when compared to the gains during infancy or adolescence. In fact, as you can see in Figure 11.2, which depicts the average heights of children at different ages and the incremental changes in height from one age to the next, growth in height proceeds on a fairly even course throughout the childhood years until adolescence when a growth spurt occurs.

Some parents become concerned about their child's height and tend to use height (probably because it is the most obvious aspect of growth) as the criterion against which to evaluate progress in physical development (Tanner, 1978). For example, they may worry if one of their sons is shorter than the other (Goldstein & Peckham, 1976) or if their child is either much taller or much shorter than his or her age-mates.

Implications for psychological development   Variations in height are not a source of concern from a medical point of view, because physicians can give hormone treatment to very tall or very short children to correct the abnormality. Even if

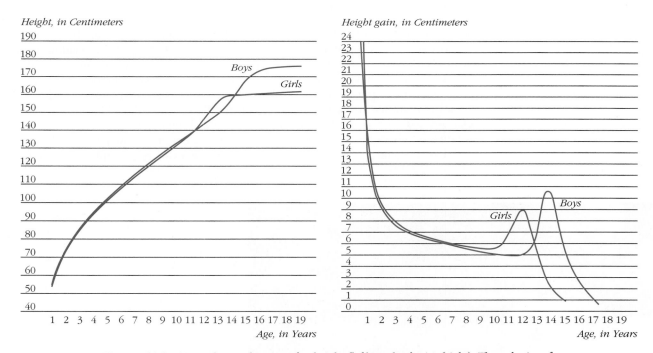

Figure 11.2   Typical growth curves for height (left) and velocity (right). The velocity of growth decreases from birth until puberty, when the adolescent growth spurt occurs. At all ages until adolescence, the average girl is shorter than the average boy. Because adolescence usually begins two years earlier for girls, they grow taller during early puberty. The average boy then surpasses the average girl in height. During the growth spurts of both sexes, boys' peak height velocity is greater than girls'.

Source: (right) Reprinted by permission of the publishers from *Foetus Into Man* by J. M. Tanner, Cambridge, Mass.: Harvard University Press, p. 14, Fig. 5. Copyright © 1978 by J. M. Tanner. (left) From Tanner, J. M., Whitehouse, R. H. and Takaishi, M. (1966), "Standards from birth to maturity for height, weight, height velocity and weight velocity: British children, 1965," *Archives of Disease in Childhood, 41,* pp. 454–471 and 613–635. Reprinted with permission.

During middle childhood, it is not unusual for boys of the same age to vary in height, but parents are concerned if their child is shorter than his peers.

the abnormality is not corrected, being too tall or too short is not a life-threatening or particularly serious medical condition. In our society, however, deviating from the norm is a source of concern to parents and can be emotionally traumatic for the children involved. In fact, being too small, too tall, or otherwise different (for example, being overweight or having protruding ears or a large nose) can be a source of embarrassment for many children during middle childhood. During this period, relationships with peers become important, and being regarded as different or feeling different detracts from a child's status in the peer group (Ausubel, Sullivan, & Ives, 1980). Some peers tend to tease, pick on, or even reject children who are

Children who differ from their peers in appearance tend to be laughed at. Although some children can ignore the teasing, many develop a negative body image.

somewhat different in physical appearance. Such children may come to realize that they are different and may dislike themselves as a result (Eveleth & Tanner, 1976).

Many children who are teased about their appearance eventually ignore the teasing, but some children cannot. Negative body images take root in their mind, and even years later they may retain a negative self-image (Cash & Pruzinski, 1990). Recent studies indicate that *when* children are teased the most makes a difference. Thompson (1990) found that long-lasting effects are most common among people who were teased sometime from age 8 to 16. This finding is not surprising; during these years, the child acquires a sense of self-worth. As you will see in Chapter 13, how other children and adults react to an individual influences his or her sense of self-worth. In studying people who were teased as children, Thompson (1990) found that they have high levels of dissatisfaction with their bodies, have low self-esteem, and tend to be depressed. Further, the more they were teased as children, the greater was their loss of self-esteem and the deeper their depression. Criticism can also have powerful effects on children's body image, especially when important people in their lives—parents, coaches, or teachers—criticize their appearance (Thompson, 1990).

Cash and Pruzinski (1990) note that negative body images also influence how people think and behave. Children who are self-conscious about their appearance may avoid social functions or refuse to participate in sports activities. It could also lead to a variety of eating disorders, such as bulimia and anorexia nervosa, which cause young women to continually diet and virtually starve themselves even when they are thin. Such women perceive themselves to be overweight. In part, this preoccupation with being thin is derived from our society's standards, which equate thinness with physical attractiveness. Apparently this concern begins at an early age. In a study of 500 girls ages 9, 10, and 11 in California (presented in testimony before the U.S. Congress, 1990b), researchers found that close to 50% were dieting even though only 17% were overweight. At a hearing before the U.S. House of Representatives Subcommittee on Regulation, Business Opportunities, and Energy (U.S. Congress, 1990b), researchers testified that nearly 7% of eighth- to tenth-grade girls take nonprescription diet pills. It is not clear whether parents encourage the girls to take the pills in order to lose weight, if the girls pressure parents to let them take diet pills, or if the girls purchase them without their parents' consent. What is clear is that there are dangers in taking diet pills, which can raise blood pressure and cause dizziness and, in some cases, strokes.

Health Issues

Obesity

Although some girls restrict their diet or even take weight-control pills because of a negative body image and preoccupation with weight, some children clearly need to change their eating habits and exercise more frequently because they are overweight. As we indicated in Chapter 8, obesity is becoming increasingly common among children and can seriously impact their physical and mental health. A report published in the *American Journal of Diseases of Children,* by Gortmaker, Dietz, Sobol, and Wehler (1987) indicates that in the 20-year period between 1960 and 1980, obesity among school-age children increased by 54% and among adolescents by about 40%.

If obese children derive a significant portion of their calories from junk foods, they may not get adequate nutrition; their unhealthy eating habits and lack of exercise will place them at high risk for developing health problems in later years. High blood pressure (or hypertension), for example, is associated with obesity. Among children, high blood pressure is not a public health concern, but physicians are finding that unless high blood pressure is treated in children, it may set the stage for hypertension and possibly heart disease later on (American Academy of Pediatrics, 1987).

Stress

It may seem odd to discuss hypertension in children, since we most often associate it with older adults, especially with persons who are impatient, highly competitive, and under a great deal of stress. Yet stress is a part of life for many children. Changes in family life—a divorce, two working parents who are always in a hurry, the disappearance of the extended family, and lack of support services such as child care—contribute to what Brazelton (1986) calls "an anxious atmosphere" for families and an inordinate amount of stress affecting parents and children as well.

Selye (1983) defined stress as "wear and tear" on the body because the response to stress involves extreme physiological changes, which, if prolonged, leave the body weakened and vulnerable to disease. He notes that although some stress can be beneficial and motivating, too much can lead to physical and mental illness. Sources of stress vary from culture to culture, and how much stress we can tolerate varies from person to person. For adults in our society, sources of stress may be life events—such as war, poverty, serious illness in a family member, or death—as well as such daily hassles as missing a train or being caught in a traffic jam. It is not so much these events, as the individual's response to them, that causes stress.

Children find a variety of experiences stressful. Some experiences—a test in school or temporary rejection by friends—are minor; others—such as the death of a parent or sibling or divorce—are major. The greater number of stressful events children experience, the less able they are to cope with stress (Rutter, 1979b). Some developmental experts express concern that children are exposed to too many pressures every day. Elkind (1981), in his book *The Hurried Child,* notes that children are growing up too fast and are learning too early, from real life and the media, about adult problems and issues. A child in a single-parent family, for example, often has to share her parent's concern about money or difficulties at work simply because there is no adult in the family in whom the parent can confide. Many children are pressured to achieve success at school or in sports, and some children are simply "overscheduled" with music, dancing, or other lessons, baseball, or band practice (Louv, 1990). Even summer camps take on a different role as parents place children in camps that offer recreation and an opportunity to learn an academic skill. The children get the message that they must continually strive to acquire or refine a skill.

For middle-class children, stress may emanate from divorce or too many pressures to succeed; however, for low-income children, poverty is a source of stress. Inner-city children, who may live in housing projects, are exposed to violence every day. These children, referred to as living in "urban combat" (Schuman, 1991), have numerous psychological problems, including depression, anxiety, behavior problems, and low self-esteem. Some develop a form of posttraumatic stress syndrome in which they repeatedly reenact a horrifying event they have witnessed (Garbarino, 1988).

Pedestrian injuries account for a significant number of deaths and disabilities among 5- to 9-year-olds. Contrary to popular misconceptions, these accidents occur in relatively traffic-free residential areas.

The physical effects of stress on children can range from minor to severe. A child might develop a stomachache on the morning she has to audition for a part in the school play, whereas another child may have sleep disturbances or headaches for a time after his parents' divorce. In a report prepared for the American Academy of Pediatrics, Michael Cohen (1987) notes that 5- to 15-year-olds have the greatest incidence of headaches, only a minority of which are caused by physiological problems such as visual difficulties, chronic infections, or tumors. The majority of childhood headaches are stress-related and caused by "peer pressure, school phobia, and family problems such as divorce" (Cohen, 1987, p. 1). Depression and susceptibility to illness are also among the effects of stress (Compas, 1989).

Injuries

Stress also leads to injuries, which—as we saw in Chapter 8—are the greatest cause of death and disability in childhood. Injuries account for approximately 51% of all deaths of children ages 5 to 9 and 58% of all deaths of children ages 10 to 14 (National Center for Health Statistics, 1987). Molloy (1987) notes that serious stresses within the family, such as financial problems and parental alcohol abuse, create an environment in which injuries to children are likely to occur. In a review of the research, Mare (1982) notes that several controlled studies have found a relationship between childhood injuries and adverse family life situations (marital disharmony, financial problems, and death or serious illness in the family). A similar relationship exists between childhood injuries and poverty; a greater proportion of children who die or are disabled as a result of injuries come from poor, stressed families (Baker & Waller, 1989).

The type of injuries children sustain vary by age. Toddlers and preschool children are at risk for suffocation, house fires, falls, and drowning; the number of deaths from pedestrian injuries is highest among elementary school children ages 5 to 9 (Gallagher, Finison, & Guyer, 1984; Rivara, 1985). Injuries sustained while riding a bicycle are prevalent among children ages 10 to 14 (Rivara, 1983).

Elementary-school children, ages 5 to 9, are relatively well coordinated, and they are acquiring a variety of motor skills that give them a greater degree of independence. Parents often let these children play unsupervised in the street or walk alone to school, usually becoming concerned about potential injuries only when the children are in high-traffic areas. Yet, the majority of pedestrian injuries occur in relatively traffic-free residential areas and in driveways and parking lots (Rivara & Barber, 1985).

Some parents perceive their children's skills to be greater than they really are; they feel comfortable that by the time the children are in kindergarten, they know how to be careful crossing streets. Although children may know how to cross a street, they have a limited ability to assess distance and localize sound. In addition, they are slower than adults at processing information and reacting accordingly and tend to act impulsively, often darting into the street without any thought to traffic (Avery & Avery, 1982).

Even when parents believe that their children are vulnerable to pedestrian injuries, they may leave them in situations where they may encounter traffic. Rivara and his colleagues (1989) made this point after surveying 2464 parents of 5- to 9-year-olds in a Seattle school district. Ninety-four percent of the parents surveyed did not believe that 5- to 6-year-olds could safely cross residential streets alone, yet 33% of the sample let their children walk alone to school. The researchers suggest that educating parents about the realities of pedestrian injuries should be part of any effort to prevent such injuries.

Educational programs are also necessary, albeit insufficient, to reduce the number of deaths and severe injuries sustained by children riding bicycles. Because head injuries predominate as a cause of death in bicycle-related crashes (National Center for Health Statistics, 1987), prevention strategies emphasize the use of bicycle helmets. But children and their parents may not always heed this advice. Just after a community instituted an educational awareness program emphasizing the importance of using bicycle helmets, Nakayama, Paseika, and Gardner (1990) reviewed hospital records of all children injured while riding a bicycle. They interviewed 230 injured children and their parents and found that the majority had not received the information about bicycle injury prevention. Thinking that just the fact that the children had been injured would inspire safe riding practices, the researchers called the parents of 82 of the children four months after the injury. Although some of the children were wearing a helmet after hospital discharge, 75% were not, and only 31% of the parents reported that they had instituted more stringent rules regarding bike riding. The researchers suggest that more comprehensive educational programs that reach a wider audience are necessary, as are legislative initiatives requiring children to wear helmets.

Health Care

With the exception of obesity, stress, and injuries, most children do not experience any major health problems during the school-age years. In this period dental and vision problems may become apparent, but they can be corrected. For the most part, children get mild illnesses lasting only a few days. However, 10% to 15% of school-age children have chronic illnesses. Physicians define these illnesses as conditions lasting at least three months and requiring extensive hospitalization or in-home health services (American Academy of Pediatrics, 1990a). Chronic illnesses among

Because head injuries are the predominant cause of death in bicycle crashes, children should always wear helmets while riding.

schoolchildren include potentially life-threatening conditions such as asthma and leukemia as well as severe allergies and migraine headaches (see Table 11.2). These children need access to specialized health services and require individual attention in school because they may be on medication that limits their alertness or diminishes their stamina. Public Law 94-142 (which we discuss in Chapter 12) guarantees

TABLE 11.2   Ten Leading Chronic Illnesses in Schoolchildren (1988–1989)

Illness/Disability	Known condition	New diagnosis	Total	Days lost
Asthma	21,214	2,239	23,453	17,872
Allergies (severe)	15,798	1,294	17,092	6,130
Heart conditions	5,296	611	5,907	1,811
Psychiatric disorders	4,495	726	5,221	7,982
Seizure disorders	4,077	268	4,345	1,636
Migraine headaches	2,043	301	2,344	3,115
Orthopedic disability	1,775	169	1,944	1,933
Diabetes	1,421	237	1,658	2,092
Substance abuse	896	619	1,515	6,513
Cerebral palsy	1,346	96	1,442	625

Source: Illinois Department of Public Health, "School Health Activities, 1988–1989."

children ages 3 to 18 with handicaps and chronic illnesses access to educational services in the least restrictive environment. According to the American Academy of Pediatrics (1990a), however, most schools are not well equipped to provide medications or to address medical emergencies varying from seizures to acute asthma attacks and serious bleeding episodes. As a result, many chronically ill children have to receive tutoring at home, rather than participate in regular school activities.

As you can see in Table 11.2, asthma is a leading health problem among American children and the most common reason for children missing school. About 2.5 million children in the United States have asthma, and their numbers are increasing (Kantrowitz, 1991). We don't know why the number of asthmatic children is increasing; some observers suggest that increased environmental pollution may be the reason. Boys, blacks, and urban children are especially at risk. With asthma, the child's airways contract and fill up with mucus. This reaction can happen in response to cold weather, infection, or exercise, or as a result of an allergy. The condition is often undiagnosed until it becomes acute, because parents and even pediatricians do not recognize the initial symptoms that may take the form of a persistent cold. Treatment for asthma includes giving allergy injections and educating the child to avoid cold weather and exercises that may trigger attacks. For some children, medication is prescribed to control the condition.

DISCUSSION OF SOCIAL ISSUES

Homeless Children

Homeless children also require special health attention at school. Ten years ago the U.S. homeless population consisted primarily of men who suffered largely from alcoholism or mental illness. Today families with children make up the fastest-growing segment of the homeless population (see table) and comprise more than half of the homeless population in several large cities (U.S. Conference of Mayors, 1989). Lack of affordable housing and cuts in federal spending for social services are cited as the reasons for this increase in the number of homeless families.

The homeless family's life is characterized by instability and discontinuity. Some families live with friends or relatives for a while, but eventually they move into the streets to live in a car, an abandoned building, or a shelter (Grant, 1989). In many cases the family is headed by the mother, who is burdened with numerous difficulties and, not surprisingly, is unable to care for her children.

Many cities attempt to help the homeless family with job training, child care, counseling, and transitional housing (U.S. Conference of Mayors, 1989), but for the children the experience of being homeless is often hard to leave behind. Homeless children suffer from a variety of emotional problems. In their review of the research, Axelson and Dail (1988) note that homeless preschool children suffered from sleep disorders and abnormal fears and that many had trouble controlling their aggression. Bassuk and Rubin (1987) found that homeless school-age children frequently experience anxiety and depression and require psychiatric counseling. Their school performance is also affected, since they are often bounced from school to school as their family moves around and they suffer from fatigue and malnutrition.

Demographic Characteristics of Homeless Women and Housed Women

Characteristic	Homeless (n = 194)	Housed (n = 193)[a]	P Value[b]
Maternal age			
Mean	29.2	29.4	.55
SE	0.5	0.6	
No. of children			
Mean	2.7	2.3	<.01
SE	0.1	0.1	
Maternal ethnicity, %			
Black	56.9	70.0	
Non-Latino white	29.7	15.0	
Latino	7.7	10.9	
Other	5.6	4.2	<.01
Maternal educational level, %			
0–11th grade	43	28	
High school diploma or some college	57	72	.01
Family structure, %			
Female head, single-parent	52.9	61.6	
Two-parent	47.1	38.4	.08
Among two-parent families couple together >1 year, %	83	62	<.01

[a]*n* varies slightly depending on the variable because of missing items.
[b]*P* value is reported for two-tailed *t* test for test of differences between means or x^2 for tests of proportions.

Source: D. L. Wood, et al. (1990). "Health of Homeless Children and Housed Poor Children." *Pediatrics, 86.* Reproduced by permission of *Pediatrics,* Vol. 86, © 1990 American Academy of Pediatrics.

In addition, homeless children suffer from inadequate health care and a variety of health problems. Wood, Valdez, Hayashi, and Shen (1990) studied 196 homeless children in ten Los Angeles shelters, comparing their health status with that of

poorly housed children. They found that the homeless children had more behavior problems in school than the poorly housed children; and the homeless children were more likely to evidence developmental delays. Their diets were frequently imbalanced because they had to rely heavily on fast foods and experienced repeated periods of food deprivation. Other studies indicate that homeless children do not receive immunization, and that they suffer from such chronic health problems as asthma, acute ear infections, and recurring diarrhea and dehydration (Grant, 1989).

What is being done to better the conditions of these children whose development is impaired by their circumstances? Much of the aid to the homeless involves providing shelter, food, and, in some cases, health care. The Stewart B. McKinney Homeless Assistance Act, which has augmented funding for these services in communities across America, may better the lives of some of these children. But the fact that we have so many children without homes in the United States is cause for grave concern. How should we, as a nation, deal with the complex and difficult issue of homelessness?

Summary

We have seen in this chapter that physical growth during middle childhood proceeds at a slow, steady pace. However, significant progress occurs in motor development, including increased control over fine-motor skills, as reflected by increases in speed, power, coordination, agility, and balance—the basic components of gross-motor fitness. School-age children are able to improve on skills they previously acquired and can also learn many new skills, such as playing a musical instrument, swimming, skiing, ballet dancing, or playing a variety of sports. Their ability to learn these skills depends on having opportunities for learning, practice, and encouragement. For example, children who are not given the opportunity to learn to swim will not be able to swim. Acquiring the ability to execute many motor skills is of great interest to school-age children. It is also important to their social development because it enables them to participate in social and sports functions and to interact with other children and adults in a variety of settings.

Children evidence wide differences in their motor skills. They also vary in physical growth and development. These variations become especially apparent during middle childhood, in part because they grow at different rates. Some are slow growers, whereas others are average or fast growers. Children today also seem to grow at a faster rate than previous generations, a phenomenon known as the secular trend. This trend also reveals that children attain sexual maturity earlier. As a result, some children are capable of sexual reproduction during the middle childhood years. One consequence is an increased number of children bearing children.

Children also reach adult height at an earlier age. Growth in height is an important aspect of physical development during the school-age years, even though there are no rapid incremental changes during this period. The great variations in height that occur at this time often concern many parents who focus on the possibility of growth disorders if their children are much taller or shorter than their peers. Yet most children do not have growth disorders. Some growth disorders, such as extreme tallness for girls or extreme short stature for either boys or girls, can be treated.

Being too tall or too short is not a particularly serious physiological condition, but it can affect socioemotional development. Being different can detract from children's status in their peer group. Some children who are teased about their appearance ignore the teasing, but others cannot. For these children, negative body images become rooted in their mind. Researchers are finding that such negative images can last through adulthood and cause depression and low self-esteem.

Obesity, stress, and injuries are major health concerns during the childhood years. Injuries account for 58% of deaths occurring among school-age children. Among 5- to 9-year-olds pedestrian injuries are prevalent, and among 10- to 14-year-olds deaths and disabilities are likely to occur as a result of bicycle-related injuries. Most school-age children are relatively healthy and become ill for only brief periods. They have dental and vision problems that are correctable. However, 10% to 15% are chronically ill with such conditions as asthma, which require the schools to be able to address these youngsters' special health needs.

Homeless children also need special health attention. Until about a decade ago, most of the homeless were alcoholic and mentally retarded men. Today, however, a growing number of the homeless are young families with children. Homeless children are likely to have poor health and nutrition and suffer a variety of emotional problems that prevent them from fully benefiting from the educational activities offered in school.

12 Cognitive Development During Middle Childhood

Almost everyone has a particularly vivid memory of the first day of school. It marked a real transition in life! Of course, some of us may have already experienced educational programs while attending a child care center, a nursery school, or a kindergarten. Some of these programs may even have taken place in a school building. All the same, our entrance into the first grade was a turning point. Our parents, our teachers, and we ourselves realized that we would now have to take intellectual tasks seriously; our formal education was beginning.

When children reach the age of 6 or 7, adults' expectations of them change. School-age children are expected to begin to assume adult roles. During the Middle Ages, as we saw in Chapter 2, children of this age were not regarded as dependents but were accepted as part of the community of men and women and expected to share in adult pastimes and responsibilities.

Is it really such a coincidence that we also expect more of school-age children? As you will learn in this chapter, significant developmental changes at this time make children amenable to the demands of school and to increased responsibility. They experience a wide range of physical and psychological changes. Most important, they acquire the mental ability to follow directions, engage in academic tasks, and profit from formal instruction.

Cognitive Development

Information-Processing Approach

Information-processing researchers explain that school-age children are able to profit from formal instruction due to their increased capacity to process information. Recall that, according to the information-processing approach, the human mind is like a computer. A computer's output or final product depends on its capacity, the kind of information it is "fed" (that is, the input), and the type of programming it has for organizing and retrieving this information. In the same way the basis

Progress in cognitive development allows school-age children to engage in increasingly complex tasks.

of cognitive performance and learning is the ability to receive (or encode), store, and later retrieve information; this is accomplished through basic cognitive processes such as attention and memory. During the middle childhood years, these processes are significantly enhanced.

Attention   Essential to our ability to process information is our ability to pay attention. The environment contains an array of stimuli that we must attend to selectively; otherwise, they will overwhelm us. **Selective attention** is the ability to focus on relevant aspects of the environment and to disregard irrelevant aspects. With age, children become increasingly more able to selectively attend to stimuli (Pick, Frankel, & Hess, 1975). They are also more able to control their attentional processes and concentrate on a specific task. That is, they are less easily distracted by irrelevant stimuli (Lane & Pearson, 1982) and more flexible in shifting their attention from one stimulus to another (Hale, 1979). To demonstrate this capability, Pick, Christy, and Frankel (1972) showed 8- and 12-year-old children colored wooden animals. The researchers questioned the children about the animals in a way that forced them to concentrate on one relevant aspect, such as color or shape, while ignoring all other aspects. The older children responded more quickly, which suggests that they are better able than younger children to attend to a relevant stimulus and shift their attention from one stimulus to another.

Older children are also able to attend to a particular task when specifically told to do so, such as when a teacher instructs them to pay attention or listen carefully (Hale et al., 1978; Pick, Frankel, & Hess, 1975). Also, they can concentrate on a particular task for increasingly longer periods. In contrast, preschoolers can only pay attention for a few minutes; as a result, they frequently leave the task and move on to something else that attracts their attention (Anderson & Levin, 1976). This ability to concentrate influences the length of the lessons children are taught in school. As they progress through the elementary grades, the lessons last for longer periods.

Memory   The ability to pay attention to a task also enhances children's capacity for memory, which is an important aspect of learning. Because children can draw on a store of memories of past experiences, they can build on what they already know. This aids their ability to solve problems and acquire new knowledge.

As we learned in previous chapters, the process of storing information involves three kinds of storage systems: sensory memory, short-term memory, and long-term memory. In *sensory memory,* we retain impressions for less than a second and then transfer them into our short-term memory, which retains them for a relatively short time. Some researchers use the term *working memory* to refer to short-term memory, whereas others distinguish between the two terms, claiming that short-term memory refers to performance on tasks that test for memory soon after the person acquires the information. In contrast, working memory is an aspect of short-term memory and represents information being attended to at a given time. Working memory is thus a temporary mechanism for coordinating and processing information from the environment (Small, 1990).

Working memory has a limited storage capacity. You would rely on working memory to remember a telephone number just long enough to take your eyes off the telephone directory and dial the number. But if you cannot find a telephone right away and do not have a pencil and paper on hand, you would be forced to remember the number a little longer. To do so, you would probably have to resort to some mental technique that facilitates your ability to remember. Most likely, you would repeat parts of the number over and over to yourself, either mentally or verbally—a technique known as **rehearsal**—and you would be able to remember the seven-digit telephone number. For a preschool child, however, this is difficult, perhaps because young children can remember fewer bits of information. (A bit, or piece, of information may be one digit in the telephone number.) But when children reach middle childhood, the capacity of their working memory increases to hold more bits of information. Children can even store the information in their memory while engaging in some other activity (White & Pillemer, 1979).

Memory-aiding devices: Also, school-age children are much more likely to use memory-aiding devices or *mnemonic strategies* than preschool children; people deliberately instigate these strategies to help themselves remember. Although preschool children can sometimes use these strategies, the quality and variety of their mnemonic strategies increase during the school-age years (Small, 1990).

Earlier we noted that when children want to remember something, they repeat the items to be remembered. Preschoolers use this strategy much less frequently than children in middle childhood (Weissberg & Paris, 1986). To aid their memory, children also use *organization,* the ability to group items to be remembered into groups or clusters of information. School-age children are better able to use this mnemonic strategy as well because they have acquired the ability to classify objects according to different categories (Moely & Jeffrey, 1974). For instance, if we show them the words *flute, hammer, bicycle, apple, violin, nail, boat,* and *orange,* they can remember more of them than preschool children because they can organize them according to category: musical instruments, tools, fruit, and modes of transportation.

This school-age girl understands how memory works and knows she needs time to memorize the pictures.

In addition, children and adults use *external aids* as a strategy for remembering. If you ask someone to recall a particular task, for example, he or she may write it down on a piece of paper or tie a string around a finger. Whereas some young children use such external devices, older children use them more often (Kreutzer, Leonard, & Flavell, 1975). Also, the older the children, the more likely they are to deliberately use a memory-aiding strategy to remember something (Brown, 1975).

Metamemory: To deliberately use a memory-aiding strategy, children must realize that it will help them remember. School-age children are aware of this fact because during middle childhood, they acquire **metamemory;** that is, an intuitive understanding of how memory works (Brown, 1975; Flavell, 1985). Then they realize that some situations require a planned strategy for remembering, and they know what techniques to use and when the information they are memorizing is sufficiently memorized (Kail, 1979). The older the children, the more they know the limitations of their capacity to remember. They also know when they need to commit something to memory. For example, when 5- to 8-year-olds were shown a set of ten pictures and asked to remember them, the 5-year-olds quickly scanned the pictures and said they remembered them, even though, when tested, they obviously did not. The 8-year-olds, however, carefully looked at the pictures before saying they remembered them; when they were tested, it was evident that they had indeed memorized the pictures (Flavell, Beach, & Chinsky, 1966).

Although this awareness about how memory works is especially evident during middle childhood, studies have shown that at age 5 children know something about memory and understand what it means to learn, to remember, and to forget (Kreutzer, Leonard, & Flavell, 1975). They also know that it is easier to remember fewer items than many items, that asking a friend to remember some of the information can ease the task of remembering, and that drawing the item may help as well (Wellman, 1985). However, they do not actually use this knowledge about memory until the school-age years (Small, 1990).

Accumulating knowledge: Another factor contributing to the improved memory capacity of school-age children is their increased knowledge base, or store of information, and their familiarity with the material. This is true with adults as well. Developmental psychologists, for instance, are likely to remember more of an article about children's development than an article about physics, in part because of their interest in the subject matter. Also, they bring more background knowledge to the article on children, which makes it easier for them to understand and remember the information. The same applies to children. Chi and Koeske (1983) found that children can remember twice as many items from a list of familiar things than from a list of unfamiliar items. When they know something, children may also evidence better capacity for memory than adults. Chi (1978) compared the memory ability of a group of 10-year-olds participating in a chess tournament with that of a group of college students. When the two groups were tested on their memory of chess arrangements, the 10-year-olds showed better memory than the college students, but when the groups were asked to remember a series of numbers that did not depend on prior knowledge, the college students outperformed the children. Thus, children's knowledge influences memory. The fact that children accumulate more knowledge with age helps explain their improved capacity for memory.

Piaget's Theory: The Concrete Operations Period

The information-processing approach explains the cognitive changes in middle childhood in quantitative terms by focusing, for example, on children's increased capacity for memory. Piaget, however, explained that *qualitative* changes occur between the ages of approximately 7 and 12 years. During these years, according to Piaget, children exhibit greater flexibility of thought and are able to think logically. Their thinking is no longer dominated by immediate visual impressions, as during the preoperational period of cognitive development.

Children can also now perform **mental operations.** They can mentally transform, modify, or otherwise manipulate what they see or hear according to logical rules. For example, they are able to verbalize and mentally manipulate numbers. Reversibility is the key here. As children learn to add, subtract, multiply, and divide, they are also aware that one mental activity such as adding, as in $2 + 2 = 4$, is related to another activity such as subtracting. By *reversing* the process, they are able to figure out that $4 - 2 = 2$. When children are able to mentally manipulate information in this way, their thinking is said to become *operational.* However, they can perform mental operations only on concrete and tangible objects or on signs of these objects (as in word problems) but not on hypothetical ideas. Hence, Piaget called this the **concrete operations period.** Not until the next stage of cognitive development, the formal operations period, will children be able to apply their mental abilities to abstract events and ideas.

Piaget noted that one of the most important aspects of operational thought is **reversibility,** which is the ability to perform mental inversions, or to mentally undo a sequence of actions. This new ability enhances children's ability to figure out mathematical problems. In addition, they can draw conclusions about observed outcomes on the basis of prior relationships, instead of on how things appear to be, as in the preoperational period. This evidences their sensitivity to distinctions between what seems to be and what really is (Flavell, 1985). If you take two short, wide glasses of milk and pour the milk from one glass into a tall, narrow glass, the preoperational child, relying on her immediate perception of a single feature—say, the height of the glass—concludes that the tall, narrow glass contains more milk than the short, wide glass. The concrete operations child, however, can mentally reverse the action and realizes that the amount of milk has not changed.

A related aspect of concrete operational thought is the ability to *decenter;* that is, to focus on multiple features of an object at the same time. Preoperational children can concentrate on only one feature at a time—say, the *height* of the glass of milk. Concrete operations children, however, can consider all relevant perceptual data and can simultaneously focus on both the height and the width of the glass. They also realize that one feature, such as the narrowness of the glass, makes up or compensates for another feature, the height, so that a shorter but wider glass holds the same amount of milk as the tall but narrow glass. This ability to recognize that a change in one feature is balanced by an equal and opposite change in another is known as **reciprocity** (see Figure 12.1).

Conservation   To study the emergence of concrete operational thinking, Piaget devised a number of problems that he discussed with children. He used some of these problems in his investigation of *conservation,* which refers to the ability to recognize that two equal quantities remain equal even if one of them is changed in some way, as long as nothing is added or taken away. As we saw in the example of the two glasses, concrete operational children are able to conserve liquid quantity. They recognize that when milk is poured from one container into another differently shaped container, the quantity of the milk has not changed (Figure 12.1). Besides the ability to conserve liquid quantity, concrete operational children gradually acquire the ability to conserve number, length, mass, area, weight, and volume

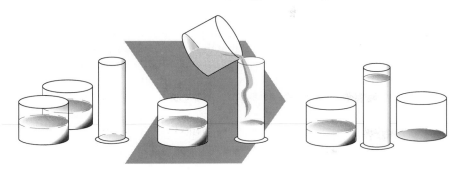

Figure 12.1 *A child in the concrete operations period no longer relies on immediate perceptions, as in the previous period of cognitive growth. The child knows that when the liquid from a short wide container is poured into a tall narrow container the amount of liquid does not change.*

of objects and substances. These abilities do not occur all at one time; they emerge in sequence (see Figure 12.2).

Piaget claimed that conservation emerges gradually over three stages. He demonstrated this in a classic experiment devised to investigate the ability to conserve the amount of substance (conservation of mass). In this experiment the researcher shows the child two balls made of equal amounts of clay; one ball is rolled into a long, thin sausage shape. The child is then asked if both pieces have the same amount of clay. Initially, at about age 4 or 5, the child may state that the sausage-shaped piece has more clay because it is longer.

At around age 6, she is not quite sure which piece has more clay. Or, when asked to predict what would happen if one ball was rolled into a sausage shape, she may guess correctly that the amount of clay in each would remain the same. Yet she cannot give an accurate reason for her answer. When one ball is actually rolled out into a sausage shape, she may change her mind when she sees the longer length, thinking that the sausage shape has more clay. In this stage the child still relies on immediate perceptions; not having the ability to reverse her mental images, she does not realize that the sausage-shaped piece may be rolled back into its original ball shape. Thus, she cannot make a mental reference to the initial state the clay was in or to the transformation that has taken place (see Figure 12.3).

Finally, at approximately age 7, the child is able to follow and remember the transformations the ball of clay has undergone and realizes that despite the change in shape, both pieces still have the same amount of clay. When asked for her reasoning, she may say, for example, "If you roll the piece back into a ball, you will see that they are the same," thus evidencing reversibility in her thinking. When she can give the correct answer and the correct reasoning behind it, she is able to conserve substance.

Unevenness of development   Children do not acquire conservation of all the properties of objects and substances at one time even though the principles and reasoning required in each case are the same. Rather, they first conserve number, then length, liquid quantity, mass, area, weight, and volume. Piaget referred to this phenomenon as **horizontal decalage.** *Decalage* is the French word for "gap";

since concepts vary in difficulty, children master some concepts earlier than others. At age 7, they may realize that the sausage-shaped piece of clay still has the same amount of clay as the ball of clay, but not that these two differently shaped pieces of clay also weigh the same. Whereas Piaget acknowledged that there is a decalage, or unevenness, in the understanding of conservation and other concepts, he did not think it was of great importance (Broughton, 1981).

Various Types Of Conservation

	Start with:	Then:	Ask the child:	Preoperational children usually answer:
Conservation of Liquids	Two equal glasses of liquid. 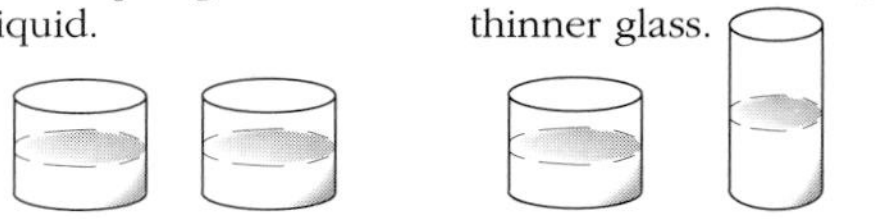	Pour one into a taller, thinner glass.	Which glass contains more?	The taller one.
Conservation of Number	Two equal lines of checkers. 	Lengthen the spaces between the checkers on one line.	Which line has more checkers?	The longer one.
Conservation of Matter	Two equal balls of clay. 	Squeeze one ball into a long, thin shape.	Which piece has more clay?	The long one.
Conservation of Length	Two sticks of equal length.	Move one stick.	Which stick is longer?	The one that is farther to the right.
Conservation of Volume	Two glasses of water with equal balls of clay inside.	Change the shape of one ball.	Which piece of clay will displace more water?	The long one.
Conservation of Area	Two identical pieces of cardboard on which are placed the same number of equally sized blocks. 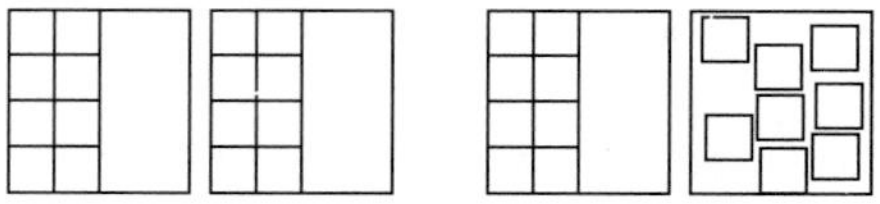	Rearrange blocks on one piece of cardboard.	Which has more cardboard covered up?	The one with the blocks not touching.

Figure 12.2 *A child in the concrete operations period knows that two equal quantities remain the same even when one of them is changed in some way. As you can see from their answers, preoperational children have not achieved this understanding.*

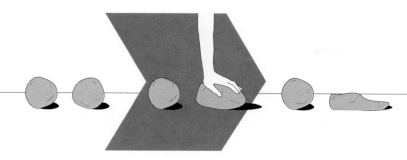

Figure 12.3 *Conservation of substance. During the preschool years, children are swayed by immediate perceptions and may say that a piece of clay rolled into a sausage shape is* larger *than a round piece of clay because it is* longer. *During middle childhood, children know that both pieces of clay are the same size.*

Other researchers have also wondered about this unevenness in the development of the ability to reason. Some believe it may arise from environmental influence (Pulos & Linn, 1981). For example, children have more experience with liquids (for instance, pouring milk and juice from a pitcher) than with other substances. Other researchers explain that when children learn to conserve one property of objects—say, liquidity—they do not generalize this knowledge to other properties. As a result, they have to go through the process of learning to conserve each property (Pinard, 1981).

Some researchers who elaborate on Piaget's theory by offering alternate explanations for the unevenness in development are known as neo-Piagetians. They incorporate much of Piaget's theory into their work. Instead of describing children as being in a particular stage of cognitive development, neo-Piagetians focus on specific behaviors, noting that during each stage of cognitive development children exhibit some behaviors that characterize that stage and others that characterize the previous stage or the next stage. In other words, some researchers claim that cognitive growth does not occur in stages all at once; we all have many abilities, each one at a different level of development (Fischer, 1983; Flavell, 1982). Some researchers find the stage description useful; others believe that it does not explain that each stage involves gradual, transitional changes that occur at different times, depending on the individual's particular abilities (Small, 1990; Flavell, 1985).

The concept of number Although children do not attain conservation of all properties of objects all at once, they accomplish it in much the same way as described earlier. Their ability to conserve enhances their understanding of concepts. For example, only concrete operations children can conserve number and fully understand that concept. Many parents believe that their preschool child understands the concept of number, since he can count from 1 to 10 in the correct order. Research indicates that preschoolers do have some knowledge of numbers (Gelman, 1982; Gelman & Meck, 1983). Yet their understanding of the concept of number is limited, as their failure on Piaget's number conservation tasks shows. The number conservation task is a simple experiment in which the researcher gives the child, for example, 6 glasses and 12 bottles and asks him to match an equal number of bottles with the glasses (see Figure 12.4). Instead of placing one bottle in front of each glass, a preschool child merely lengthens the row of glasses by increasing the space between each glass; he does not yet understand that each bottle has to correspond to each glass (one-to-one correspondence) for there to be an equal number of each.

According to Piaget, by the time children reach the concrete operations period, they understand one-to-one correspondence and are able to conserve number. Piaget and other investigators (for example, Ginsburg, 1977) demonstrated this point by showing the child two rows of checkers, one row of five black checkers and one row of five red checkers (see Figure 12.5). When the researcher places the checkers in each row one directly below the other so that both rows are of equal length, both the preoperational and the concrete operations child will agree that both rows have the same number of checkers. But if the researcher spreads the black checkers out so that row appears longer than the other row, a 4-year-old child will reason that there are now more black checkers "because the black row is longer" or "because the red row is all bunched up." At about age 5 or 6, the child

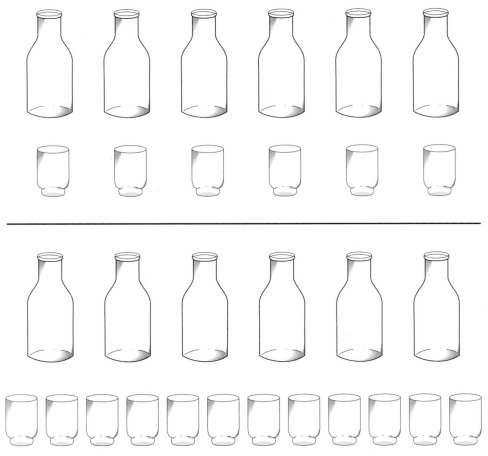

Figure 12.4 *When asked to match bottles with an equal number of glasses, a preschool child may simply lengthen the row of glasses. The school-age child understands that each bottle has to correspond to a glass.*

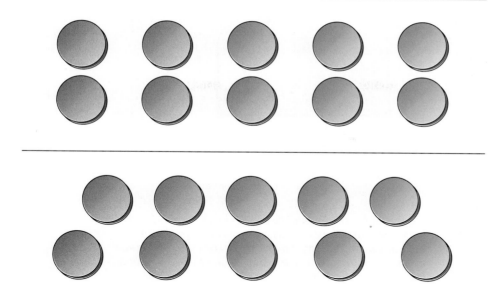

Figure 12.5 *Conservation of number.*

may answer correctly that there are the same number of checkers in both rows, but he justifies this correct answer by faulty reasoning.

By age 7, the child conserves number. He replies correctly that both rows have the same number of checkers, and he supports his answer by reasoning that nothing has been taken away or added—the checkers in one row were simply spread out a bit. In giving this reason, the child demonstrates his realization that certain properties of objects remain constant even when their outward appearance changes. He may also reason that while one of the rows is longer, the checkers in that row are more spread out than those in the other row. In this way he demonstrates his understanding that a *reciprocal relationship* exists between the two rows. That is, the length of one row is compensated for by the density of the other row, resulting in no net change in the number of objects. Or the child may explain that if the checkers were moved back to the way they were before, the number of checkers in each row would be the same. Thus he reveals the reversibility in his thinking; he can retrace the steps of the problem and think back to the original state the object was in.

Reversibility of thought is important in the mastery of conservation and also in academic activities. Its importance is demonstrated in arithmetic problems in which the child is required to find the solution to the question $6 \times 2 = ?$, for example, and also to perform the opposite operation, $12 \div 2 = ?$

Classification   To be able to understand and solve numerical problems, children need to understand one-to-one correspondence, conservation of number, "more than" and "less than," and the fact that one number is included in another. That is, the number 2 is part of the number 3, which, in turn, is included in the number 4. This is part of the concept of classification; it refers to **class inclusion,** or the ability

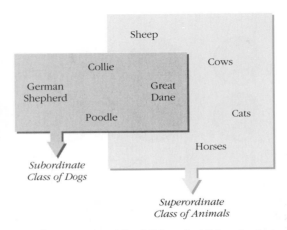

Figure 12.6 *During middle childhood, children begin to understand that there is a hierarchical relationship between subordinate and superordinate classes. For example, German shepherds, collies, and Great Danes belong to the subordinate class of dogs and to the superordinate class of animals.*

to understand that there is a hierarchical relationship between subordinate and superordinate classes. This understanding extends beyond numbers to all other objects children encounter: the wooden object with four legs and a top belongs to a subordinate class of tables and also a superordinate class of furniture; German shepherds, Great Danes, and collies belong to a subordinate class of dogs and also to a superordinate class of animals. Similarly, daisies and tulips, although different in type, still belong to one superordinate class of flowers (see Figure 12.6).

The ability to understand the hierarchical structure inherent in classification has far-reaching implications. It aids children's understanding of the social world and the multiple roles people play and enhances their ability to learn such subjects as geography, which entails an awareness that a large area such as a continent contains several smaller areas known as countries, which in turn contain even smaller areas, such as states, counties, cities, and towns.

Seriation   Another cognitive operation that, according to Piaget, emerges during the concrete operations period is **seriation,** or the ability to arrange objects in an orderly series. This ability demonstrates systematic, playful thinking by the child.

In seriation experiments the researcher gives the child a pile of sticks of various lengths and asks her to arrange them in ascending order from the shortest to the longest. The preoperational child cannot accomplish this task. At first, at about age 4, she picks out two sticks, puts the shorter of the two on one side and the longer one on the other side. She repeats this process, comparing only two sticks at a time and ending up with two groups of sticks of various lengths. She may be able to arrange some of the sticks in order of short, medium, and long, but she cannot arrange the whole pile of sticks into one series. When the researcher tells the 5- or 6-year-old to arrange the sticks in one ascending order in a staircase effect, she can arrange the sticks with their tops in ascending order like stairs, but she overlooks the irregular pattern at the bottom. However, by age 7, when she is in the concrete operations period, the child approaches the task systematically: she searches through the pile of sticks and picks out the shortest or longest one; then she picks

Figure 12.7 *The school-age child demonstrates systematic,*
planful thinking by arranging objects in an orderly series.

out the next shortest or longest in the series, and so on. Finally, she arranges all the sticks in ascending order without error (see Figure 12.7).

Even when we modify the experiment and give the children another set of sticks, they can, at the concrete operations stage, correctly insert each of the new sticks into the original set of sticks, again demonstrating that they realize that each new stick can be both shorter and longer than the original sticks (Ginsburg & Opper, 1988). Since seriation problems require children to understand that *A* is greater than *B*, *B* is greater than *C*, and *C* is greater than *D*, they can apply this knowledge to other tasks and engage in **transitive reasoning,** which is the ability to recognize a relationship between two objects by knowing their relationship to a third. Thus, if *A* is greater than *B* and *B* is greater than *C*, then *A* is greater than *C*, even though that relationship has not been described. At times, it may be difficult for concrete operations children to figure out relationships when we use such abstractions as the letters *A, B,* and *C.* However, when concrete examples are used, the child does not need to be told, for example, that Jim is smaller than Zack. Being told only that Jim is smaller than Tom and that Tom is smaller than Zack, he can *reason* that Jim is smaller than Zack. Piaget attributed this ability to engage in transitive thinking to changes in cognitive structures that occur during the concrete operations period. Other researchers propose that children's ability to remember may be the key here (Trabasso, 1975; Riley & Trabasso, 1974); when preoperational children are taught to memorize that Jim is smaller than Zack and so on, they are able to make the inference as well.

In numerous other challenges to Piaget's theory, researchers are finding that the manner in which Piaget presented the problems to the children could account for their erroneous answers. For example, with conservation of number, researchers have found that when they give children some training, and when they use a small number of objects in the experiment, children show one-to-one correspondence and can conserve number at age 3 or 4 (Gelman & Baillargeon, 1983). Yet researchers acknowledge that in preschoolers this competence is just beginning to emerge and used only in restricted settings (Gelman, 1982). Consider also the class inclusion problem in which it is not until the concrete operations period that children who are shown tulips and daisies are able to correctly answer the question, "Are there more tulips than there are flowers?" Other researchers contend that language may be a problem here. Researchers showed preoperational children some M & Ms and other candies. When they asked, "Are there more M & Ms or more of all candies?" the children answered the question correctly (cited in Siegel, 1978). In Piaget's presentation of the problem, the researcher asked the children, "Are there more tulips than there are flowers?" This question emphasizes tulips, leading the children to distinguish between tulips and flowers and thus arrive at an erroneous conclusion.

Environmental influences on the attainment of concrete operational thought   Although some researchers contend that language may be a problem with the Piagetian tasks, Piaget did not consider language an issue. He believed that as children acquire such operations as conservation, classification, and seriation, they develop new mental structures that provide the foundation for the next period of cognitive development. This is true of earlier developmental stages as well: children have to undergo the sensorimotor and preoperational periods before they can progress to the concrete operations stage; they do not skip any of the periods, and each period lays the groundwork for the next.

Although Piaget formulated his theory on the basis of observations and data accumulated by testing middle-class children of culturally homogeneous Western backgrounds, other researchers have conducted cross-cultural studies confirming the fact that children all over the world follow the same sequence of development. They proceed from the sensorimotor period to the preoperational period and then to the concrete operations period (Dasen, 1972; 1977). However, the rate at which children progress through one period and into the next differs among and within cultures. This is shown, for example, in studies using conservation tasks. In Mexico, where pottery making is a widespread skill, children from pottery-making families were found to conserve substance much earlier than children from families that did not make pottery. This is not surprising given the fact that these children have extensive experience working with clay (Price-Williams, Gordon, & Ramirez, 1969). Recall from previous discussions that Piaget regarded intelligence as the process of adapting to the environment, and that cognitive development depends on children's experiences and interactions with the environment. Depending on their experience, therefore, children from different backgrounds will vary in the rate that they acquire various cognitive concepts. The variations in the rate of development do not reflect differences in competence, but rather differences in the types of skills valued by the different cultural groups (Cole & Scribner, 1974).

Yet several cross-cultural studies found that in some cultures children ages 12 or 13 and some adults do not understand conservation. Greenfield (1966), for example, tested African Wolof children on conservation of liquid and found that only 50% of the 10- to 13-year-olds understood conservation. Dasen (1972) reviewed several other studies with similar findings. Do these findings mean that not all adults in all societies ever reach the concrete operations stage? Because this would seem incredible, investigators challenged the conclusions raised in these studies and attempted to ascertain the problems associated with conducting cross-cultural studies on conservation. They hypothesized that one problem was that the researchers who tested the children did not know the children's language well and were therefore unable to question the children appropriately. Nyiti (1982) tested children in Nova Scotia on conservation tasks. The children were from two different cultural backgrounds. One group was from English-speaking families of European descent; the other group was composed of Micmac Indian children who spoke their native language with their parents but English at school. The researchers tested the English-speaking children in English and the Micmac children both in English and their native language. When both groups of children were tested in English, the Micmacs appeared to lag behind the English speakers on conservation. But when the researcher tested the Micmac children in their native language, there were no differences between the two groups on understanding conservation. Therefore, the language used in testing situations impacts the findings of cross-cultural studies on conservation.

The role of training   Researchers have also attempted to find out whether children can be trained to achieve concrete operations. Several training studies have tried to determine whether intensive training can accelerate acquisition of classification or transitive reasoning (Winer, 1980), but many have focused on teaching conservation. Gelman (1969), for instance, hypothesized that children cannot conserve, because they are distracted by irrelevant cues. She set out to test this hypothesis, reasoning that if it is correct, then children trained to attend to relevant aspects of the objects would be able to conserve. Gelman's study attempted to determine the role of training in conservation and also to explore other alternatives to Piaget's explanation of children's ability to conserve during the school-age years. Could it be that they can conserve because they have better attention skills during this period and not because of changes in their cognitive structures?

First, Gelman chose a group of 5-year-old children who could not conserve (a condition she determined through testing). Then she gave them one of three types of training. Gelman gave children in a control group two sets of objects and rewarded them when they correctly identified the objects that were the same and those that were different. The purpose of the control group was to train children to pick out two objects that are the same (for example, two dolls) and two objects that are different (for example, a doll and a toy car). In this way the researchers could ensure that children do not fail conservation tasks simply because they do not know the meaning of *same* and *different*. She gave the second group of children two sets of objects and rewarded them when they differentiated between the objects along the dimensions required in number and length conservation tasks. In other words, Gelman trained them in conservation. She gave the third group of children the same two sets of objects as the second group but did not reward them for the correct answer. Thus, they had no idea if they had made the correct discrimination. Gelman found that children in the second group did well on number and length conservation tasks when tested two weeks after the training procedure, whereas the children in the other two groups did not. This suggests that by receiving feedback, preoperational children can be helped to attend to relevant dimensions and can be trained to conserve.

Critics of the study noted that since the children were 5 years old, they may have been close to attaining conservation anyway (Gardner, 1978). Yet several other studies demonstrated that training (Brainerd, 1974) or specific experiences such as observing others perform on similar tasks (Zimmermann & Lanaro, 1974; Murray, 1972) might accelerate children's acquisition of concepts.

Despite demonstrations that we can teach children to answer conservation problems correctly, we need to consider a number of other issues. Some researchers argue that accelerating mental growth, assuming it is possible to do so, might interfere with normal cognitive development. Wohlwill (1970), for example, noted that children eventually outgrow the reasoning of the preschool period. Yet this form of reasoning may remain useful later in life in the process of imaginative or creative acts. If we hurry children through the natural course of cognitive development, they may not fully incorporate the early processes of cognition into their cognitive apparatus, and as adults, they may not be as imaginative or creative as they would otherwise have been.

Piaget and Education

Piaget saw no value in training procedures. He contended that they only demonstrate artificial, verbally acquired responses. Piaget felt that until about age 7, children do not have the mental structures needed to grasp the notion of conservation. He argued that an important aspect of the progress in cognitive development occurring during the concrete operations period is physiological maturation; without the refinement and differentiation of the central nervous system, thinking could not become more elaborate. Interaction with adults and peers is also important. According to Piaget, at the core of the progress in cognitive growth is the child's self-initiated interaction with her physical surroundings. Thus, "each time one prematurely teaches a child something he could discover for himself, that child is kept from inventing it and consequently from understanding it completely" (Piaget, 1970).

Although Piaget was not particularly interested in applying his theory to classroom teaching, the educators who developed the concept of the *open classroom* have enhanced his notion that children learn through discovery. In the open classroom children choose from a variety of activity centers placed around the room and progress from one center to another at their own pace. In this way children of

Some children learn effectively in an open classroom (left); others may benefit more in a traditionally structured setting (right).

various abilities can learn together in the same classroom. The open classroom was widely encouraged during the late 1960s and 1970s (Silberman, 1970); however, researchers have found that although the open classroom may promote certain skills, such as creativity and social interaction, the traditional classroom is more effective for transmitting academic tasks (Bennett, 1976). Moreover, because of the individual differences that exist among children, one type of classroom may be more suitable for some children than for others. According to several researchers, some children, especially anxious ones, function well within the structured atmosphere of the traditional classroom, while others prefer an open classroom (Horowitz, 1979). The same finding is applicable to teachers, who may be more comfortable teaching in one setting than in another. For this reason many large school systems have a mix of traditional and open classrooms.

Language Development

Metalinguistic Awareness

During the school-age years, children develop an understanding of how memory works, which greatly enhances their ability to remember. They also develop an intuitive awareness of how language works, known as **metalinguistic awareness,** that emerges about age 5 and develops throughout middle childhood. This suggests that, although by the end of the preschool period children have acquired a substantial amount of knowledge about many aspects of language, further expansions in language development continue between the ages of 6 and 12. Metalinguistic awareness does not refer to the ability to *talk* about language; that is, whether children can talk about verbs, nouns, and clauses (this knowledge skill is known as **metalanguage**). Metalinguistic awareness refers to intuitions about language that enable children to know, for example, whether a sentence is correct or detect that an ambiguous sentence has two meanings.

It may not be a coincidence that metalinguistic awareness develops most rapidly during the elementary school years. After all, much of the elementary school curriculum helps children develop their language skills. They spend most of their time in school thinking about language, either implicitly or explicitly. Although some researchers suggest that the development of metalinguistic awareness is closely related to academic experiences during middle childhood, others suggest that metalinguistic awareness develops as a result of general cognitive development. Bialystock and Ryan (1985), for example, note that literacy and metalinguistic awareness involve two cognitive skills: the ability to focus attention on individual dimensions of language and the ability to access knowledge about language. Recall that middle childhood is a time when children acquire a great deal of knowledge about things, including language, and an enhanced ability to focus their attention.

Communicative competence Metalinguistic awareness is evident in two basic changes in children's understanding and use of language. One change is in their communicative competence. We can note this change in their ability to think about what they are being told and to judge whether the message conveyed is clear. Studies have demonstrated that children are not able to think about what they are being told until the school-age years. To prove this point, researchers gave children instructions for a game but left out a critical piece of information. This omission made playing the game impossible. First-graders were not aware of the inadequacy of the instructions, nor of the fact that they did not understand them. As a result, they attempted to play the game, only later realizing that they could not do so. Third-graders, on the other hand, noticed the problem with the instructions right away and did not even attempt to play the game (Markman, 1977).

School-age children's ability to understand complex grammatical sentences also reflects their communicative competence. They can master most simple grammatical rules during their preschool years, but the ability to access and use explicit knowledge about *syntax*—the underlying grammatical rules specifying the order and function of words in a sentence—develops throughout middle childhood as they become better able to understand the connections between words. For exam-

A CLOSER LOOK

Literacy and Metalinguistic Awareness

Educational experts agree that learning to read and write is the most important task children have during their first years of formal schooling. Children in the middle childhood years have to develop increasingly sophisticated literacy skills: they must learn how to understand a fairly long written text and how to express themselves clearly and correctly in writing.

Metalinguistics plays a big role in the way children learn to read and write. According to some researchers, children's literacy skills contribute to their developing metalinguistic awareness. For example, Flood and Menyuk (1983) report that poor readers also do poorly on such metalinguistic tasks as judging whether sentence structure is correct.

Another research study establishes this point (Smith et al., 1989). The researchers asked some second-graders to act out a series of sentences containing relative clauses. Some of the sentences were in nonstandard English and were rather hard to understand. For example, children were asked to react to the sentence "The man who the lady kissed held an umbrella." According to the researchers, a group of children who were poor readers made the same types of mistakes in judging the sentence as did a group of good readers. The researchers came to the following conclusion: the children's poor performance on grammatical judgment reflected the difficulty they were having in focusing on sentence structure.

Children learning to read must pay attention to both the phonological and semantic aspects of language. (The phonological aspects have to do with how we are able to read words, whereas the semantic aspects are concerned with how we understand the meaning of written words.) Bialystock (1988) and Bialystock and Nicholes (1989) have examined the following hypothesis: Younger children with less-developed metalinguistic ability have more difficulty selectively focusing their attention on either the sound or the meaning of words than do older children.

To test their hypothesis, the researchers gave a group of children ages 5 to 9 a stimulus word like *cat*. They then asked the children to match it on the basis of its sound (phonological properties) or its meaning (semantic properties). To make the task more difficult, the researchers added varying levels of distractions. All the children could focus on either of the properties if no distractions occurred at the same time; however, distractions made the task more difficult, especially for younger children, who could not focus their attention on either sound or meaning. Slightly older children adopted a strategy of default; they paid attention selectively only to sound. Only the oldest children could pay attention selectively to either sound or meaning.

How do children's literacy skills relate to their ability to communicate? Catherine Snow (1986) suggests that children develop two types of language skills: (1) *contextualized language skills,* for everyday informal communications, and (2) *decontextualized language skills,* for written and formal communications. What is the difference between these two kinds of skills? According to Snow, decontextualized language skills (for example, a prepared speech) require a greater awareness of the need to plan what we are going to say and how we want to say it. In everyday, informal communications, however, we receive many cues from other people, such as questions, looks, or gestures of approval or disapproval that may prompt us to adjust our communication accordingly.

In Snow's view, kindergartners with good prereading skills (that is, children knowing how to identify and isolate phonemes and identify letters) have greater decontextualized language skills than do children of the same age with poor prereading skills. For example, youngsters with good prereading skills can define words better and describe pictures more completely than their peers with less-developed prereading skills (Dickison & Snow, 1989). In other words, children with good prereading skills have a better sense of how language works.

ple, a 6-year-old who hears the sentence "John promised Mary to shovel the drive-way" is likely to think that Mary is going to do the shoveling. This is because the child thinks that the subject of a sentence is usually the noun preceding the verb (C. Chomsky, 1969). An 8-year-old, however, understands that John is going to do the shoveling.

During the school-age years children also acquire greater insight into differences between the meaning and structure of sentences. Before going to school, children speak in grammatically correct sentences but cannot judge whether the sentence is grammatically correct. When they are given a sentence and asked if it is correct, they don't understand the task, because they still cannot differentiate between the *meaning* of a sentence and its *structure*. If you asked them if the sentence "John Mary hit" is correct, they will answer that it is incorrect, because "it is wrong to hit." But they will not say anything about the structure of the sentence. Older children can differentiate between structure and meaning. If you ask third-graders if the sentence "The moon ate the cheese" is correct, they will answer, referring to the structure of the sentence, that it is correct.

School-age children also acquire a more precise meaning of words, and, unlike preschool children, do not confuse words. Preschool children often take the words *ask* and *promise* to mean "tell," so they interpret the sentence "John asked Bill what to do," to mean "John told Bill what to do" (C. Chomsky, 1969). Preschool children also confuse such words as *heavy, big,* and *strong*. When asked to judge objects that look alike but have different weights, preschool children may describe the heavier object as "bigger" or "stronger" because they confuse similar concepts. School-age children, on the other hand, are unlikely to confuse such concepts; they are capable of understanding the precise meanings of words and of using such words correctly.

Understanding metaphors   The second way in which language use changes during the middle childhood years is that it becomes increasingly nonliteral (Dent & Rosenberg, 1990). That is, children acquire the ability to understand that some words have a literal and a nonliteral meaning. This ability enables them to comprehend and appreciate metaphors and, like metalinguistic awareness, is an example of the relationship between language development and cognitive growth.

A metaphor relies on the use of a word or a phrase out of context to suggest an unexpected similarity. Preschool children may know the meaning of the words *sweet* and *bright* and can use them in their literal context: the chocolate is sweet; the light is bright. However, they have trouble comprehending the metaphors "He is a sweet child" or "She is a bright student." Asch and Nerlove (1960) found that pre-school children who correctly used the words *sweet* and *bright* to describe objects said that the same words could not be used to describe people. Children aged 7 or 8 acknowledged that such words can be applied to both objects and people, but only 10- and 11-year-olds were able to understand figures of speech and explain the relationship between the literal and nonliteral meanings of words.

Researchers have also found that although preschool children are creative in their own speech, often spontaneously producing metaphors such as "The bald man has a barefoot head," they have difficulty comprehending metaphorical speech. This may be because they are not really trying to speak metaphorically, but are simply trying to communicate effectively using their knowledge about the world to describe novel things. Gardner and Winner (1979) explained that in a figure of speech such as "After many years of working in jail, *the guard had become a hard rock that could not be moved,*" a link is made between the physical universe (a hard rock) and the universe of psychological traits (stubborn lack of feeling). To make sense of the statement, the similarity between physical and psychological inflexibility must be understood. According to these researchers, preschool children do not have this capacity. Instead of linking the two elements, most 5-year-olds, for example, misinterpret the meaning of the metaphor and explain that the guard piled rocks all day. By the time they are 8 years old, children have made significant progress: They recognize the basic intent behind the figure of speech, but they still do not appreciate the psychological trait at issue. They explain the metaphor as meaning that the guard has become angry or stupid, descriptions that allude to the intended negative connotation of the metaphor. But they fail to provide the precise psychological condition being described. Not until the latter part of middle childhood, age 10 or 11, can children offer accurate explanations of metaphors and be credited with genuine metaphoric comprehension. Then they can think of psychological traits in nonliteral and literal terms and can understand how a hard rock might bear a resemblance to being stubborn. They are also capable of thinking about the two meanings of the term simultaneously. By using their cognitive capacity for reversibility, they move back and forth mentally between the two meanings. In this way they can discover the link between the literal meaning and the idea conveyed by its use in a nonliteral context.

Other researchers suggest, however, that even 5-year-olds can make some meaning of metaphors referring to psychological phenomena (Waggoner & Palermo, 1989; Cacciari & Levorato, 1989). Interpreting metaphors involves two cognitive processes: (1) the ability to understand figurative language, and (2) the ability to create a meaning for the metaphor similar to that adults would create. Waggoner and Palermo (1989) found that 5-year-olds had no difficulty with the first task; they were able to understand figurative language and were not puzzled when faced with a sentence such as "Joe is a snorting bull." But they had difficulty with the second task, because their interpretations are different from those of adults. For example, adults interpreted "sinking ship" to mean sorrow, whereas young children consistently interpreted it to mean fear. If children are thinking about what it means to be in a sinking ship, it is not surprising that they interpret it as fear. As children grow older, they acquire more of the knowledge available to adults, and their interpretations become more similar.

Humor

To learn about comprehension of riddles, McGhee (1974) asked children to indicate which answer was funnier: a joking answer or a factual answer. To the question "Why did the old man tiptoe past the medicine cabinet?" the joking answer would be "So that he wouldn't wake up the sleeping pills." But the factual answer would be "Because he dropped a glass and didn't want to cut his foot." McGhee found that first-graders chose the factual answer as funny as often as they chose the joking answer, indicating that they did not understand what made the riddle funny; they were only guessing. Children in the second grade, however, showed a significant preference for the joking answer.

During the school-age years, children appreciate riddles and love to engage in plays on words and to tell jokes involving double meanings. To understand and appreciate these jokes, they must reclassify a key word—a feat they are not capable of until the concrete operations period. For example, to answer the riddle "What has an ear but cannot hear?" one must understand the two meanings of the word *ear* and reclassify the word according to another context—corn. That is, when children first hear the riddle, they focus on concepts that associate ears with hearing, but the surprising answer, if it is to be funny, requires them to quickly shift attention to another meaning of the word *ear*. The speed of reclassification is important because they must keep both meanings of the word in mind at the same time and shift their attention back and forth between them, using reversibility of thought, to find the riddle funny.

Other cognitive achievements, such as conservation, enable school-age children to appreciate such jokes as:

Waitress: Should I cut the pizza into eight slices for you?
Fat Woman: No, make it six. I could never eat eight. [McGhee, 1979].

They also laugh at absurd jokes, such as "Call me a cab. You're a cab" or "Order, order in the court! Ham and cheese on rye, Your Honor." To an adult, these jokes are not really humorous, but to school-age children, they are hilarious. Why? Zigler and his colleagues (Pinderhughes & Zigler, 1985; Zigler, Levine, & Gould, 1967) and McGhee (1976) indicate that we appreciate humor only when it offers a moderate amount of intellectual challenge. Many riddles and jokes based on incongruities of words and relationships are not very funny to most adults, because they are easy to understand; but they are amusing to school-age children because they are sufficiently difficult and challenging to surprise them.

Language-Minority Children

Bilingualism   The increased sophistication of school-age children in their understanding and use of language enhances their ability to profit from formal instruction. But for many children language presents a barrier to learning. For example, some children, referred to as *language-minority children,* often begin school unable to speak English. This presents a problem of how to teach them—in the mainstream English language (with or without additional language help) or in their native language with special English-language instruction until they can function in the regular classroom. This politically controversial issue has generated heated debates, but at its heart is a concern for education. Some argue that since the criterion for success in our educational system is the ability to be literate in English, we should teach language-minority children in mainstream English. Others contend that if these children are in mainstream English classrooms, they will not acquire basic academic skills and will fall behind their English-speaking peers. Before addressing these issues, we need to look at the different types of language-minority children.

Bilingual children   Children from a bilingual background grow up hearing and eventually speaking two languages. There are many different situations in which a child can become bilingual. Broadly speaking, there is "bilingualism as a first language" (Swain, 1972), in which children learn both languages at the same time; there is also bilingualism through learning two languages consecutively (second-language learners). Most research to date has focused on second-language learners; little systematic study has been done of children who learn two languages from infancy. However, researchers note that the situations in which children learn two languages from infancy can vary substantially, depending on the language of the parents, the language of the community, and the strategies the parents use to encourage bilingual development (Malakoff, 1988; Romaine, 1990).

When children are raised in a bilingual environment from infancy, they learn two separate grammatical systems and two separate vocabularies. This is quite an accomplishment, considering how complex it is to learn just one language. Initially, bilingual infants will mix both languages. But by age 2, they are aware that they are dealing with two languages; they begin to distinguish between two vocabularies and two grammatical systems (Vihmam, 1985) and will speak one language or the other, depending on the situation they are in. At age 3, one German/English youngster attending a U.S. preschool decided that it is "correct" to speak to all children in English and to all adults in German, no matter what language they spoke; when he returned to Germany, it took him several days before he spoke German to his German-speaking friends.

Once they have learned two languages, bilingual children often mix languages within a conversation, a paragraph, or even a sentence. This occurs with children who are bilingual from infancy, with second-language learners, and with bilingual adults. It may seem as if bilinguals cannot keep the languages straight and that the mixing of languages is random. However, they are really *switching* between the languages according to a set of grammatical and sociolinguistic rules. This is called **code-switching** and is governed by code-switching grammar. Take as an example, a child who may forget a word and "borrow" one from her other language (Voltera & Taeschner, 1978), including words from both languages in one sentence. This may be considered to be language confusion, but there is growing evidence that she is in fact code-switching. That is, she realizes and has deliberately chosen to borrow a word from the other language (Hakuta, 1987).

Although adults are intrigued by bilingual children, especially those who are bilingual from infancy, bilingualism was thought to be detrimental to children's cognitive and linguistic development. Recent studies reveal, however, that bilingual children appear to develop certain cognitive abilities earlier than their monolingual peers and they also show better performance on verbal and nonverbal IQ tests. Hakuta (1989) and Galambos and Goldin-Meadow (1990), found that bilingual children show earlier development and enhanced performance in metalinguistic ability. Recall that metalinguistic awareness, which develops during the school-age years, involves an ability to distinguish between the meaning and structure of language. This ability may develop earlier in bilingual children because of the insight into language that comes with speaking two different languages; knowing two separate vocabularies and grammatical systems gives these children, at an early age, an unconscious or intuitive understanding of language as a rule-governed system (Hakuta, 1989).

Bilingualism, however, is not always associated with a cognitive advantage. Lambert (1987) notes that there are two types of bilingualism, which vary depending on the values a society places on bilingualism. In one type the child's home language is the majority language and the second language is highly valued by the community, so being bilingual is regarded as an *additive*. The children are proud of their mastery of both languages, and they learn and maintain both of them. These children realize the cognitive gains associated with bilingualism. This type of bilingualism is usually found in middle-class families living in bilingual environments like Canada.

In another type of bilingualism, the home language is a minority language and the majority language is the language used in the community at large. Society may not value the home language, and being bilingual may be considered *subtractive*. The children are not proud of being bilingual and may prefer not to speak the home language. As a result, the community language will quickly replace the home language. It may be difficult to observe the cognitive benefits of bilingualism. These

An increasing number of children in the United States enter school unable to speak English. How to best educate these children is a controversial question.

children may experience problems if they reject the home language before their parents have learned to speak the majority language. Also, since it takes adults longer to acquire language proficiency, the parents may not be able to use figurative speech or tell language jokes. Thus, for a while the children may have to live in a linguistically impoverished environment. You can see, then, that when discussing bilingualism, we need to differentiate between the circumstances causing it.

Bilingual education   In the United States the largest proportion of bilingual children are second-language learners, and they are in a situation of *subtractive bilingualism*. Thus, they are under pressure to replace their minority language with English (Lindholm, 1989). These children learn their home or primary language from their parents and English from their playmates and others in the neighborhood or school. Society does not value their ability to speak two languages, they are often from poor families, and their parents may not have received much education. Taken together, these factors may contribute to the difficulties these children experience at school.

As noted earlier, the task of educating bilingual children is controversial. Although the debate focuses on how best to educate them, there is no debate over the ultimate goal of the education. No matter what approach the teachers may take, their aim is to mainstream children in monolingual English classrooms (Hakuta & Garcia, 1989). The question that arises in this connection is: When should we mainstream bilingual children, before or after they learn English? Some educators recommend mainstreaming the children in the regular English-speaking classroom, thus the children will have no distractions in their efforts to speak English. Others recommend teaching them content matter in their native language and giving them English-language instruction separately for the first few years. Afterward, the children should be gradually eased into the regular classroom. Critics contend that these children will not be able to profit from the instruction in a regular classroom for a while. As a result, they will lag far behind their English-speaking peers.

Bilingual programs focusing on native-language instruction typically involve teaching children content matter in their native tongue for half the day or a little longer. During the rest of the day, the teachers give them intensive English courses. The idea is that teaching children in their native language provides an important cognitive foundation for learning a second language and for academic learning in general (Hakuta & Garcia, 1989). Supporters contend that the knowledge and skills children learn in their native language will transfer to their understanding of English, after they master it. Thus, it is better for children to acquire literacy in their native language first (Hakuta, 1989; Snow, 1989). Recent research has demonstrated, for example, that children who learn to read and write in their native tongue first show better writing skills in English once they learn English than do children placed in English-speaking classrooms without having the opportunity to first acquire basic literacy skills (Snow, 1989). Proponents of this approach see these programs as ways of promoting the children's educational success once they learn English.

However, these findings are still preliminary; more research is needed to document which approach is better in teaching bilingual children (Hakuta, 1989; 1986; Padilla, 1989). To date, however, relatively few studies have evaluated the effectiveness of either approach, and these studies have been plagued with methodological flaws (Willig, 1985). One problem is that the studies usually focus only on which educational approach is more effective in teaching children English instead of looking at the effects of the two different approaches on overall academic development. With methodological improvements, our research on bilingualism may provide an important basis for policy decisions on how best to educate bilingual children.

This research is more important than ever, given the large influx of immigrants from Cuba, Puerto Rico, Latin America, and Asia. The children of these immigrants often find it hard to learn English, because even at school they can find many playmates who speak their native language. When placed in the same class with English-speaking children, these children do not perform well on academic tasks or IQ tests requiring proficiency in English. But if these children have lessons in their native language, will they ever learn English and function within our society as adults? You can appreciate the complexity of the issue of bilingual education. It is a problem for society as well as for schools. In response to the increasing numbers of non-English-speaking adults in many communities, some states require social and public services to use English and one other language, such as Spanish.

Nonstandard English   Some black children from low-income families share many problems faced by bilingual children. Although the black youngsters speak English, they often come to school after learning to use the language comfortably and informally in their homes only to discover that they cannot use this kind of language at school.

For a long time researchers and educators held that these black children have deficient language skills because they live in an impoverished linguistic environment. Summarizing some older dogmatic views about their language development, Dale (1976) noted that researchers argued that black children

> hear very little language, much of it ill formed. [They] cannot formulate complete sentences, and they do not know the names of common objects. They lack crucial concepts and they cannot produce or comprehend logical statements.

These conclusions were drawn from tests based on the standard English spoken by white, middle-class people. Researchers have now found that lower-class black children speak a nonstandard dialect of English called black English. Although not all blacks use **black English** (Labov, 1972), the term itself is useful because it highlights the fact that their language is different, not deficient. Indeed, once researchers began to focus on the characteristics of these children's language, they found that black children and adolescents are extremely verbal and that verbal games and the ability to use language flexibly and creatively are important status symbols. Yet black English is different from the English black children are likely to encounter at school. As such, it may be a handicap unless teachers are sensitive to these differences. Black English differs in its intonation patterns, vocabulary (DeStefano & Rentel, 1975), grammar, and pronunciation. These differences do not reflect a sloppy use of standard English, rather, black English is governed by its own set of grammatical rules (Labov, 1970). Thus, black children have to learn two sets of rules—one set for black English and one set for standard English.

Since standard English is the primary means of communication and instruction in schools, black children who use black English and bilingual children are at an academic disadvantage until they acquire proficiency in standard English. We also need to keep in mind, however, that differences in school performance are related to other aspects of development besides language.

The Child in School

The School as a Learning Environment

The school environment plays an important role in child development. Throughout much of middle childhood and adolescence, children spend a large portion of their time either attending school or performing school-related tasks. Thus, school inevitably influences their values, self-esteem, achievements and aspirations, and learning. Of course, learning occurs all the time and begins well before children start formal education. But the informal learning occurring outside school differs from the formal learning in school. Before entering school, children acquire concepts through experiences with many concrete instances; in the classroom, however, they are required to learn concepts set apart from their concrete referents. For example, they learn to add numbers, which are abstract, rather than to number items. Also, instead of observing others and then trying an activity as in preschool, they must follow specific verbal instructions about how to carry out certain tasks.

The verbal exchange children experience in school is also unique. Outside school they engage in conversations where everyone talks freely. In the classroom, however, the teacher dominates the exchange of information. For the most part, children are limited in what they can say. Generally they are expected to respond only to the teacher and to respond correctly (Meehan, 1979). This type of verbal exchange is an accepted characteristic of school life. The specific content may vary, but the basic format of the exchange remains constant regardless of the subject matter being taught or the age of the children (Litwak & Meyer, 1974).

Although teaching children in schools is a relatively new phenomenon (Cremin, 1976), adults have long regarded it as their right and responsibility to modify the thinking of the young and to transmit knowledge and values to them. For centuries, adults have taught their children informally in the context of everyday experiences. In some societies this kind of informal learning through direct observation and interaction with the adult community still takes place. Lave (1977), for example, studied the practice of apprenticeship, a form of learning and socialization (or, if you will, on-the-job training), in Liberia. Under this system children spend several years learning a trade such as sewing by working for and observing a seamstress or tailor. Initially, the apprentices run errands and do chores, but eventually they have an opportunity to practice the simple tasks related to the trade. In time, they will be able to work on their own (Greenfield & Lave, 1982).

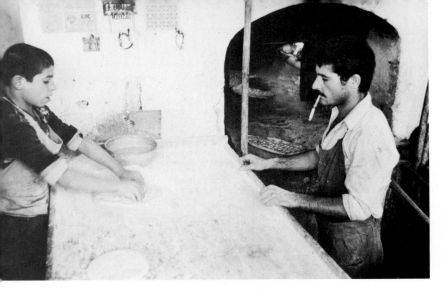

Whereas in our society children between the ages of 6 and 16 are legally required to attend school, in some societies children learn trades by observing and helping adults.

In complex societies like ours, education has moved away from everyday community life and has become increasingly more structured. We now delegate education to teachers within the formal school setting. For a time, only the children

A CLOSER LOOK

Children's Cognitive Style

Just as adults differ in temperament and approach to life, children, too, are not all alike in their cognitive style. By this we mean the way they perceive information in their environment and respond to it. Jerome Kagan (1965) pointed out that children's cognitive style plays a role in their academic performance. He divided children into two groups: those who are reflective in their approach to tasks and those who are impulsive.

To distinguish reflective children from impulsive ones in their approach to problem solving, Kagan devised the Matching Familiar Figures Test. This test contains, among other things, a number of pictures of a bear sitting in a chair. Although the pictures of the bear are basically identical, one differs in some minor detail. Kagan asked a group of children to point out which picture is different. To do so, of course, the children needed to pay close attention. According to Kagan, reflective children looked carefully at the pictures, compared them closely, and made relatively few errors in their responses. In contrast, impulsive youngsters quickly glanced at the pictures without paying attention to details, and almost always came up with wrong answers.

Is there a relationship between this difference in cognitive style and school performance? Debus (1970) reported that the impulsive child is generally at a disadvantage, because most academic tasks require children to give careful consideration to problems so they can answer questions accurately. Each classroom has impulsive children. Through training, however, their behavioral and cognitive patterns can be modified. For example, we can give them verbal descriptions of how they should respond to cognitive tasks, such as noticing tiny details in a picture. By reinforcing and modeling appropriate response styles, children can modify their approach to problems (Debus, 1970). We also need to keep in mind that impulsivity declines somewhat with age. Thus, the older the children, the more likely they are to become more reflective in their thinking.

Not surprisingly, researchers have noted that children tend to think either reflectively or impulsively about all sorts of situations. For example, at play impulsive children tend to run around the room and play with a toy for only a few minutes at a time. They then divert their attention to other toys. Reflective children take their time about choosing a toy and then play with it for a longer period. If you ask, "What is your favorite game?" impulsive children will be quick to answer. But reflective youngsters will take a few minutes to think before replying (Kagan & Kagan, 1970). Egeland (1974) found that impulsive children can be taught to wait before replying to questions so that they can consider all angles of a situation.

of the very rich had access to formal schooling. But about a century ago, in response to the Industrial Revolution, schooling in America and other nations became universally available and compulsory. Schools have since grown to serve more children, and children stay in school for a longer period of their lives.

Although children are increasingly attending school-based child care and early childhood programs beginning at age 3, formal schooling and academic instruction in most countries with compulsory education laws does not begin until sometime between the ages of 5 and 7. During this time, children undergo significant developmental changes that enable them to cope with the demands of the school milieu (White, 1965; 1970). They become better able to follow instructions, apply reasoning and memory skills to problem solving, and pay attention for increasingly longer periods. As a result, they are more able to concentrate on learning specific tasks.

Changes in social development also help school-age children profit from schooling. For example, they can now learn and function according to rules—an ability that is basic for all lasting social exchange. This ability makes formal education possible because most of what children learn in acquiring academic skills consists of rules. For instance, in learning to read they learn phonetic rules (for example, the letter *e* at the end of a word is sometimes silent); in learning to write, they learn spelling rules (for example, *i* comes before *e* except after *c*).

LEARNING FROM OTHER CULTURES

The Effects of Schooling on Cognitive Development

Child experts have long recognized that children's ability to profit from formal instruction depends on their attaining a certain level of cognitive and social maturity. Researchers have also wondered whether the school experience can enhance children's cognitive functioning. To this end, they have taken advantage of naturally occurring experiments made possible by the fact that schooling is neither compulsory nor universally available in many nontechnological societies. Hence, they can compare the cognitive abilities of samples of children who vary in their amount of schooling. Although there are some limitations to these cross-cultural studies (Rogoff & Morelli, 1989; Super, 1980), the results have shown that children attending school do better on some cognitive skills such as memory and classification than children with no schooling (Stevenson, 1982; Sharp, Cole, & Lave, 1979). This suggests that to some extent school experience influences cognitive ability. Researchers have also found that school experience enhances language development and increases children's *lexicons;* that is, the total number of words in their vocabulary (Olsen, 1978). Children who attend school are more proficient in their use of language than children from the same cultural background who do not attend school. Schoolchildren use a greater number of words to recount an experience and are more verbally explicit (Scribner, 1977). This finding is not surprising since language is a primary means of interaction and exchange of information in school.

In yet another study Sharp, Cole, and Lave (1979) asked adolescents which words they associated with the term *duck.* Those with at least one year of high school associated *duck* with other words in the same category—turkey, goose, or some other fowl. Those who had not attended school associated *duck* with such words as *swim,* which describes what ducks do. These adolescents knew that ducks are related to the fowl family (the researchers ascertained this through interviews), but they could not make the association in the abstract testing situation. Those with schooling, however, had experience making such associations in the abstract. As Rogoff and Morelli (1989) point out:

> People who have more schooling . . . may excel on many kinds of cognitive tests because not only the skills but also the social situations of testing resemble activities specifically practiced in school. [p. 344]

Learning Problems

Schooling also helps children acquire a considerable amount of knowledge that enhances their understanding of their world. Even more important, children learn such basic skills as reading, writing, and arithmetic, which are essential to functioning in adult life in our society. Once they acquire these skills, children can apply them in all kinds of situations in school and later in life.

Although by the time most children enter first grade, they are able to learn to read, write, and solve numerical problems, not all actually learn these skills. The U.S. Department of Education (1990) analyzed educational testing data compiled over the past two decades and surveyed more than 9 million children in the fourth, eighth, and twelfth grades. Their report noted the failure of many American children to acquire basic skills. The achievement levels of primary and secondary students are lower today than they were 20 years ago, despite society's demands for increasingly more skilled workers. This report added to the findings of several other studies, which gave an equally negative description of American children's scholastic achievements. Indications are that U.S. children's average achievement levels are low in relation to previous generations, and, perhaps even more disturbingly, in relation to their counterparts in other countries. This finding was established in a series of studies on first- and fifth-grade students in Japan, Taiwan, and the United States (Stevenson, 1983) and in Japan, China, and the United States (Stevenson et al., 1985).

These findings are of major concern. Children who do not succeed in school and fail to acquire basic skills will not successfully negotiate life as adults. We should also be concerned about the nation's future advances in technology, science, and industry. Without a well-educated work force, how can the United States maintain a leadership role among advanced technological societies and compete economically with other nations? These factors will undoubtedly affect the well-being of future generations.

Rising anxiety about children's school performance has produced numerous recommendations for educational reform, a complete discussion of which is beyond the scope of this book. Some reforms of the past decade have focused on teachers: increasing pay, instituting merit pay systems, mandating competency testing. Other reforms have focused on the child: making graduation requirements tougher, increasing the number of math and science courses required for graduation, ensuring school readiness (see Chapter 9).

Many state and local school districts have experimented with school reform, but the schools still operate essentially as they were designed to operate when, as an industrialized society, a high school diploma was not necessary to function successfully as an adult. Yet as Lays (1991) points out, our society has changed substantially and our economy needs an educated work force. Lays (1991) also notes that because of the global nature of politics, trade, business, and economics, brought on by advances in transportation and communication, our students need to study geography and languages. Also, societal changes, such as the increase in two-worker and single-parent families, have caused changes in family life. Do parents have the time to read to their children? Do they take the time to help children with their homework? After school, what happens to children whose parents work? These are questions we need to consider. Even this brief discussion shows how complex education reform is.

There are many reasons some children fail to achieve their learning potential. Prenatal factors and health and nutritional status can affect the ability to learn. In addition, the influence of the family, the peer group, and society, as well as various school practices, can help or hinder school achievement. For example, educators measure school performance on the basis of achievement tests devised to ascertain how much knowledge children have acquired in specific content areas, such as reading or mathematics, in relation to their age-mates. Although these tests are considered important and helpful in assessing children's school performance, their use brings into focus the differences among children. Inevitably, educators will categorize some children as good learners, others as average learners, and still others as poor learners. Children who do not score well on such tests are seen as failures. Worse yet, the children may see themselves as failures and lose their motivation to succeed in school.

FEATURE

Testing Young Children: Concerns and Precautions

Johnny is a 5-year-old in a small New England town. His parents recently registered him for kindergarten. However, the school principal tells them that Johnny is not "ready for kindergarten." Sue is a kindergartner in a St. Louis suburb. Her parents are told that she cannot progress into the first grade next fall. What has happened? Both children have "failed" their tests. Johnny is said to be "too immature" for kindergarten, whereas Sue, according to school officials, would not be able "to keep up with her peers." One unfortunate result might be that both sets of parents will feel that their children are intellectually inferior. Even worse, Johnny and Sue may come to believe it. Many families have similar experiences when they find out their children's test scores. When did testing children become popular with educators? Why? Are these tests valid?

The development of tests to assess children's educational progress dates back to the turn of the century. Recall from Chapter 2 that Binet and Simon wanted to develop a test that would help them determine children's developmental levels, so each child could be given appropriate education. Their efforts eventually led to the development of the intelligence quotient (IQ) measure. Since that time, social values and societal needs have given rise to an increased use of tests in schools and in other settings as well.

Before the 1950s standardized tests were typically administered to older students. Today they are given to increasingly younger children, and their use has spiraled. Children today take as many as 21 standardized tests over their school career (Perrone, 1990). You will see in Chapter 15 that IQ and other standardized tests are of value, but they have limitations as well and should not be used as the sole criterion for making decisions about education.

Other concerns are also associated with the use of standardized tests: These tests are used to assess the child and to gauge how good or bad the schools are. As a result, teachers and administrators, aware that test scores reflect their performance as well as the children's, spend increasing amounts of time helping their students prepare for them (Kamii & Kamii, 1990; Meisels, 1989).

Another major concern is the use of the tests with increasingly younger children such as Johnny and Sue. Standardized tests are being given to children to determine their readiness to enter or leave kindergarten. The National Association for the Education of Young Children (1988) has examined this issue. Its report lists the following types of standardized tests: (1) *achievement* tests measure what children have learned from instruction, (2) *readiness* tests assess children's skills so that teachers can plan appropriate

(continued)

Motivation for learning   Motivation is a basic ingredient in learning. Children are born with an intrinsic motivation to learn and to understand the world around them, an aspect of development that Robert White (1959) referred to as **competence motivation.** This motivation helps explain people's interest in their environment and their ability to persist in learning even difficult things, such as how to read and write, how to ride a bicycle, or how to swim.

Children's motivation for learning can increase or diminish over time depending, in part, on other people's reactions to their efforts. Harter and Zigler (1974) and Harter (1983b) note that children are motivated to learn from birth and make an independent effort to do so. Their efforts in turn produce either positive or negative reinforcement, both from their own perceptions of their performance and

FEATURE

(continued)

future activities, (3) *developmental screening* tests assess children's ability to acquire skills, and (4) *intelligence* tests measure intellectual performance.

The National Association for the Education of Young Children (NAEYC) does not advise educators to rely on the

Children are being tested at increasingly young ages, even though the tests are often poor predictors of how well the child will do in school.

results of standardized tests for three reasons. First, young children are not good test takers. For example, Sue may do poorly on a test because her inability to sit still may adversely influence her score. She may have "failed" her test because she cannot take the time to read and answer the questions, not because she cannot answer them correctly. Second, there may be wide variations in "normal" among young children who are still growing and learning rapidly. Third, test developers often ignore language and culture variations. As a result, there is no such thing as a culture-free test.

On the basis of these findings, the association concluded that these tests may give an inaccurate impression of a child's abilities. For example, a question may ask, "Where do people put their money?" The expected answer is "In a bank." But the family of a child living in poverty may not be able to save any money. Hence, the child would not be able to answer the question correctly, because she has never heard of a bank.

We will return to this issue in Chapter 15 when we discuss the testing of adolescents. For now, remember that we need to approach the whole subject of testing young children with great caution, because the tests are poor predictors of how they will do in school. Additionally, some of the most widely used tests, such as the Gesell test, have no established validity or reliability. Finally, research does not support the use of tests with children in kindergarten or prekindergarten. Yet, since an increasing number of children are in school-based programs at an early age, some schools do indeed use these tests. However, many national organizations, such as NAEYC and the National Association of State Boards of Education (1988), are advising educators to move away from tests and rely more on addressing the needs of individual children during the early childhood years.

from important adults' perceptions, such as parents and teachers. When the reinforcement is positive and children feel they have succeeded, they are motivated to continue to learn and they enjoy learning. When they are punished, they come to see themselves as failures. The motivation to learn decreases, and they avoid challenges, come to depend on adults more, and continue to fail as the cycle feeds on itself.

Reinforcement does not have to be tangible, however. It may be verbal approval or disapproval. The approval of important people—parents, relatives, and teachers—is usually a strong positive reinforcer. Indifference sometimes causes children to give up on learning the task at hand. After repeated failures, some children come to believe that they cannot overcome failure. This attitude, referred to as **learned helplessness,** inhibits learning. Children who feel helpless believe that they have no control over how they do in school, and so they do not even try. They tend to attribute their failure to achieve to bad luck, a bad teacher, or other factors beyond their control (Seligman, 1975).

Competence motivation varies, depending on the skill being learned. Children who may not be motivated to learn to read may be motivated to acquire proficiency in another skill, such as dancing, from which they derive a sense of competence and pleasure. Various aspects of development and events in their lives influence their motivation and determine which types of skills they will be motivated to acquire. For example, although many 7- and 8-year-old children have the cognitive skills to learn to add, subtract, or otherwise manipulate numbers, some are slower in their rate of development. Although these children may be able to learn arithmetic at a later age, they may become frustrated by their initial failures, and their motivation to study the subject matter may diminish.

Family influences   Parents and other adults also determine the child's motivation to learn because observational learning is an important aspect of motivation. When a child sees his parents read, he too wants to read. As a result, he will want to learn to read (Hess et al., 1982). The approval the child receives from parents or teachers when he attempts to learn a skill reinforces his motivation. Just as parental approval reinforces motivation, indifference can produce a feeling of inadequacy. In this case, the child may not only give up her efforts to learn the task, she may also be less willing to take up another task. Hence, researchers point out that the extent to which children are motivated to succeed in school often depends on a warm and encouraging family atmosphere during the school-age years (Laosa & Siegel, 1982). Such an atmosphere is important earlier in the child's life as well. Researchers have linked parents' involvement in their preschool child's activities and their tendency to respond to his questions and read to him to later success in school (Rich, 1985; Gottfried & Gottfried, 1984).

Several other studies indicate that the family's influence on the child's success at school begins even before first grade. Entwisle and Alexander (1990) considered a large sample of minority and majority kindergarten children in urban schools. They interviewed the parents just as the children began school when the researchers had no test scores or other objective information to base their opinions on. The parents were asked about their expectations of their children's math performance. The researchers found that children whose parents had high expectations of their ability to succeed scored higher on math reasoning scores than children whose parents did not expect them to succeed, and this finding held regardless of race. According to the researchers, parents tend to convey their high expectations to their children during the preschool years and encourage them to play number games. These parents also tend to be better educated. Also, white parents with high expec-

Research indicates that children are likely to succeed academically when their parents are involved in their education.

tations of their children encouraged them to go to the library, and they read to their children daily. Black parents with high expectations also engaged in such activities—although not to a statistically significant degree—and conveyed their expectations to their children. The researchers note that "The findings . . . emphasize that all parents should be alert to the important role they play in children's schooling before formal schooling even begins" (Entwisle & Alexander, 1990, p. 465).

Harold Stevenson (1983) also made this point. He found that American children's academic achievement in reading and arithmetic lags behind that of Japanese and Taiwanese children. Of significance is the fact that American children lag behind their age-mates in other countries in first grade as well as in the upper elementary grades. Stevenson suggests that the achievement problems of American children may stem from problems within the home. After looking at various factors that could have contributed to the differences in achievement, Stevenson asked, "Are American children less bright than other children? Are their parents less educated? Are their teachers less experienced?" None of these factors—intelligence, parental educational status, or teachers' experience and training—accounted for the lower achievement levels among American schoolchildren. But he did find some differences between American parents and parents in Taiwan and Japan in the way they interacted with their children and their expectations of them. For example, Japanese and Taiwanese mothers place more value on homework; they are more eager to help their children with academic tasks; and they realize, more so than American mothers, that they can help their children succeed in school.

Parental involvement The policy implications of these findings indicate that educators need to instill in parents the awareness that they are partners in their children's education and should participate in school activities. This is not an easy task. Historically, our society has viewed schools and families as having separate and distinct roles. We charge the schools with teaching children academic tasks, and we expect parents to shepherd the children's moral and social development (Cremin,

1976). Nevertheless, efforts to bring parents and schools together date back to the beginning of the century (Hammer & Turner, 1985). Two decades ago these efforts intensified when educators recognized that parent participation was a significant factor in the success of such early intervention programs as Head Start.

Since the inception of Project Head Start, the federal government has mandated that any federally funded program serving children must include a parent-involvement component. In addition, educators have developed numerous programs that specifically encourage parent participation in the school. For instance, Follow Through was designed to provide services to low-income, elementary schoolchildren and their parents in order to maintain and extend the academic gains made by these children as a result of participation in Head Start programs. Follow Through encouraged parents to participate in their children's education. Some parents joined the school system as volunteers or professionals; others were taught how to encourage their children to study and how to help them with homework. Other parents became involved in a policy advisory council through which they influenced the formulation of school policies and decisions. Educators found that through parent participation, the children's academic achievement increased (Rhine, 1981).

Although parental involvement began as an aspect of programs for economically disadvantaged children, educators are reporting that throughout the nation parents at all socioeconomic levels are increasingly taking an active role in their children's education, serving as volunteers in the schools and enhancing school/home relations to improve children's achievement (Rich, 1985). Williams (1985) reports that membership in parent/teacher organizations is increasing, and that the number of parents working as volunteers in schools doubled between 1980 and 1984. Many parents are finding that when they participate in a wide variety of school activities, their children improve in their attitudes toward learning (Rich, 1985). Researchers have discovered that there is a correlation between parent involvement and improved student achievement (Epstein, 1990), attendance at school, and reduction in suspension rates for disciplinary reasons (Thomas, 1980). However, more research is still needed on the effects of parent involvement.

The increased number of parents who participate in school activities is encouraging. Yet many educators feel that we are not including enough parents in the educational process. Numerous social factors impede parental involvement in the schools, including an increase in the numbers of working mothers and single-parent families; parents simply do not have the time to devote to school activities.

Anxiety   Another factor that may inhibit children's ability to succeed in school is anxiety; that is, children may fail to learn because they are too anxious or emotionally upset to pay attention in the classroom. Some learning problems of this kind are due to severe emotional disorders. Such emotional problems may also stem from the difficulties children encounter in learning. If this is the case, the school may become a negative experience (Gaudry & Spielberger, 1971). In many cases, however, the problem is related to a stressful situation in the children's life. Researchers are finding, for example, that a large percentage of elementary and secondary school students who have poor achievement records or who are often truant or suspended from school are from single-parent families (Harris & Associates, 1987; National Association of Elementary School Principals, 1980). In some single-parent families, both parents and children experience high levels of stress as a result of divorce or other conditions, such as poverty (National Center for Children in Poverty, 1990).

Learning disabilities   Learning problems can also have many other causes, such as a learning disability. Learning-disabled children are mistaken as mentally retarded, emotionally disturbed, or simply lazy. Their difficulties at school do not stem from poor intelligence or laziness or lack of motivation, however. In fact, learning-disabled children usually have an average or above-average intellectual potential, but their performance on relatively simple academic tasks, such as reading and writing, is severely inhibited by specific disabilities (Silver, 1989).

One type of learning disability is **dyslexia,** an impairment in the ability to read. Dyslexics, who make up 10% to 15% of the population (Shaywitz et al., 1990), often see letters upside down or reversed. For instance, a dyslexic may see *dyslexia* as *lybexia*. Although young children make similar errors, they eventually outgrow them; dyslexics do not. Therefore, they have difficulty with spelling and other reading-related tasks at school. In addition, some dyslexic children have impaired auditory perception; they cannot hear language sounds correctly. Others have frequent memory lapses so they cannot remember what words sound like. Needless to say, these children may also have speech problems, as well as trouble telling their left from their right, determining where they are in a room, organizing their work, and following multiple directions.

Until recently, educators thought that dyslexia was more likely to affect boys than girls. But a recent series of studies dispelled this myth. In one study, researchers followed 445 children from kindergarten through third grade (Shaywitz et al., 1990). Among these children, four times as many boys as girls were identified by their schools as dyslexic. However, when the researchers independently tested the students, they found equal numbers of boys and girls with dyslexia. This finding had not come to light previously, because much of the research on dyslexia was done on children identified by the schools as dyslexic. The Shaywitz study was the first to examine an unbiased group of subjects. Since most schools rely on the teacher's recommendations for testing children, many girls who need help have gone unnoticed. The referral bias may be evident in other learning or conduct problems, but more studies need to be done on this issue.

Although dyslexia is the best-known learning disability, it is only one of dozens of specific, education-related problems that we have recognized over the past few years. Others include **childhood aphasia,** the inability to speak or comprehend what is being said; **dyscalculia,** the inability to calculate numbers; and attention deficit hyperactivity disorder, which we discussed in Chapter 11. (ADHD is not a learning disability but may be present in some learning-disabled children.)

Learning disabilities have become a major educational concern in recent years, although we do not know exactly how many children are affected. Government officials, private organizations, and parents are requesting schools to provide the necessary services to identify and help these children (Chalfant, 1989). Researchers point out that whereas learning disabilities present problems in school, their effect is not confined to that problem. Hart-Johns and Johns (1982) note that some children have a mild learning disability that, in time, they might be able to compensate for. However, because of stresses and frustrations either in their initial failures to learn a task or some other stressful life event such as parental divorce, they are unable to overcome their disability. As a result, the problem becomes increasingly severe. Yet other researchers point to prenatal and perinatal factors relevant to learning disabilities (Brown, 1983) and to biological mechanisms underlying learning disorders. Analyzing data on twins, LaBuda and DeFries (1986) found that both identical twins are more likely to be dyslexic than both fraternal twins. Shelley Smith (1981) notes that when one identical twin has a learning disability, the other twin has the same disability in 90% of the cases. In addition, several individuals in the same family often have similar learning disabilities.

Researchers disagree on what causes learning disabilities, but they agree that it is not something children outgrow or completely overcome. With appropriate tutoring by teachers skilled at teaching learning-disabled children, these children can learn to compensate for the problem. The most successful educational approaches focus on the classroom. Learning-disabled children may not be able to read street signs or house and telephone numbers. Besides such difficulties, learning-disabled children also experience social and behavioral problems (Weissberg, Guare, & Lieberstein, 1989). Their peers often reject them (Bryan, 1974), and most people do not like them (Bryan & Bryan, 1978). Their teachers rate them as less cooperative, less attentive, less able to cope with new situations, less tactful, and less sensitive than other children (Bryan & McCrady, 1972).

Although in part these problems may grow out of the frustrations encountered by these students at school and their lowered self-esteem, they are also directly related to the learning disability. A learning-disabled child who cannot perceive words or numbers accurately on a page is also likely to misunderstand nonverbal communications (Silver, 1990). Therefore, in a social situation she is likely to say inappropriate things and to be regarded as insensitive. In addition, the learning-disabled child's inability to hear some words correctly makes her vulnerable to being seen as stubborn and unable to follow directions (Osman & Blinder, 1986), because she may do something different than what the words indicate. Or, because she is confused, she may not act at all.

Researchers do not agree on the cause of learning disabilities. Some contend that anxiety plays a large role in a problem's manifestation rather than in its causes. This is an important change in the way researchers and clinicians approach devel-

Dyslexia was once thought to affect more boys than girls, but new research shows that an equal number of boys and girls have this learning disability.

opmental problems: they now attempt to treat symptoms instead of trying to eliminate or figure out what caused them (Silver, 1990). Thus, educators have devised a broad educational therapy for learning-disabled children, which includes remediation of social skills, help with academic tasks, and individualized instructions that build on the children's strengths and focus on helping them identify effective strategies for learning and compensating for the disability. These experts also advise parents that when learning disabilities are identified early—even before children enter school—the children's ability to profit from therapy is enhanced. However, the professional help given must be appropriate to the particular disability. Not all teachers or parents are able to guide learning-disabled children in their effort to find and rely on different means of processing information (Chalfant, 1989)

DISCUSSION OF SOCIAL ISSUES

Mainstreaming

At one time educators isolated learning-disabled children, along with other children who have difficulty learning or who are deaf, blind, mentally retarded, or otherwise physically or mentally challenged. These children were taught in special classes. Concerns for them resulted in a law entitled the Education for All Handicapped Children Act (Public Law 94–142). Passed in 1975, it guarantees every handicapped child an appropriate public education individually tailored to meet his or her specific needs. The law mandates that each handicapped child will have an individualized plan for educational goals formulated in cooperation with parents and teachers, and that the child will be educated in "the least restrictive environment." Educators have interpreted this statement to mean **mainstreamed;** that is, teaching the handicapped child alongside her normal peers in a regular classroom. Although some children are so severely handicapped that they cannot be placed in a regular classroom, the majority of children who were in special education classes are now being mainstreamed for at least part of their school day. Whereas PL 94–142 focuses on older children who are handicapped or learning-disabled, another legislation, PL 99–457 (Part H), enacted a decade later, focuses on providing services to handicapped children under age 3.

Public Law 94-142 ensures that some children with disabilities are taught in the regular classroom.

Public Law 94–142 represents a major landmark in educational legislation and a significant attempt to use a law to bring about school reform (Gallagher, 1989). Since its passage, handicapped children have gained access to a major public school system. Their parents can now hold state and local education authorities accountable for providing some of the services necessary to raise and educate a handicapped child. Another important aspect of this legislation is its mandate for parent participation in developing an individualized educational program for their handicapped child. Some experts see this as a possible encouragement to parents of normal children to become involved in their children's education (Zigler & Muenchow, 1979; Kirk & Gallagher, 1986).

Most important, PL 94–142 is laudable in its intent, which is to benefit handicapped children and expand the education options available to them. By socializing with normal children and adults within the regular classroom setting, handicapped children will have the same opportunities for education that normal children do and will learn more social and academic skills than if they were in special education classes with other handicapped children (Birch, 1976; Salend, 1984). Advocates of mainstreaming contend that the practice will benefit handicapped children directly and will reduce the stigma of being educated in special education settings. Mainstreaming may also force our society to change its negative attitudes toward the handicapped. By interacting with handicapped children, normal children and adults will be better able to understand their needs, limitations, and strengths.

Although the intent of PL 94–142 is to benefit handicapped children, some people have vigorously debated its wisdom (Sarason, 1983; Zigler & Muenchow, 1979). Experts are equally divided about whether the law will prove beneficial to learning-disabled and handicapped children. Some experts contend that mainstreaming will not reduce educational opportunities for the handicapped. Learning-disabled, blind, deaf, or otherwise handicapped children need an opportunity to interact with normal children and to learn specific skills that will help them live and work as adults. For example, one deaf teacher explained that the special education he received in a school for the deaf was not restrictive in any way. Instead, it enabled him to acquire important skills; without these skills he would have been hopelessly lost in the hearing world (Greenberg & Doolittle, 1977).

Those who question the benefits inherent in mainstreaming wonder if regular classroom teachers are qualified for and capable of teaching handicapped and learning-disabled children (Chalfant, 1987). They argue that unless these children are taught by teachers trained to teach the handicapped and learning-disabled, it will be impossible to attain the individualized education program mandated by PL 94–142 (Turnbull, Strickland, & Hammer, 1978). Most teachers in regular classrooms are not trained to meet the specific needs of handicapped children and often do not have adequate support personnel to help them respond to the individual needs of all the children in the class (Sarason, 1983). Some school districts have available money to provide teachers with the support personnel and educational consultants needed to help them teach the handicapped, but many schools do not have such financing. Even those who regard PL 94–142 as an important breakthrough in educating the handicapped and who consider an integrated educational program potentially superior to a segregated special education program acknowledge that there are problems in translating the law into practice. They note that there is considerable variation in the amount of money made available to facilitate mainstreaming and in the way school districts define mainstreaming. Some schools do not provide handicapped children with an opportunity to be educated in a regular classroom; they simply count the time these children spend with normal children in the cafeteria or in the halls or on the playground during recess as time spent being main-streamed (Meyers, MacMillan, & Yoshida, 1980).

These problems are not unique. The implementation of any social policy involves overcoming obstacles. Unintended consequences surface that result in a discrepancy between the legislation's original intent and its subsequent outcome (Gallagher, 1989). This is because a policy, by definition, is a general guide for action. It specifies some general guidelines relevant to the achievement of a goal (Kahn, 1969), but these guidelines are subject to various interpretations that are not always congruent with the policy's intent or goal. Sometimes the legislation's central purpose is not clearly stated, leaving those in charge of implementing it to guess what the original intent was (Gallagher, 1989). Or the intent may be clear, but the legislators do not allocate enough funds for the schools to implement it. For these reasons, we need to analyze any social policy—even one that appears beneficial to children and families—in terms of its possible advantages and disadvantages. We must also evaluate the policy to ensure that it is being implemented in keeping with its original intent. This type of evaluation, called **process evaluation,** is used to verify whether the services mandated by the policy are delivered and how this takes place. Another type of evaluation, **outcome evaluation,** assesses the policy's impact and determines whether the services mandated have had positive effects. Both types of evaluation can yield valuable lessons about the program or policy that help minimize any discrepancy between the original intent and the outcome.

Another way to minimize this discrepancy is to ensure that the policy is for-mulated on the basis of knowledge gained from research about programs and expe-riences that enhance children's development and education. One problem with PL 94–142 is that legislators conceived it during the civil rights movement and in reaction to the way many minority children had been mislabeled as retarded. (Chap-ter 15 will give additional information on this point.) As a result, the legislators based PL 94–142 more on political and philosophical considerations than on sci-entific evidence concerning the merits of any particular educational placement for children with handicaps (Zigler & Muenchow, 1979). Evidence of the advantages of educating handicapped children with nonhandicapped children is inconclusive. In many cases researchers are finding that academically mainstreamed handicapped children fare no better or worse than handicapped children taught in special edu-cation classes (Budoff & Gottlieb, 1975; Gottlieb, 1981). In addition, whereas some note that mainstreamed handicapped children have a good self-image as a result of being in the regular classroom (Gleidman & Roth, 1980), others note that such children feel just as stigmatized by their normal peers as do handicapped children educated in a special classroom. For some handicapped children, self-image and academic performance may improve as a result of mainstreaming, but some may experience an inordinate amount of failure when they are in a regular classroom learning with children who are not limited by a disability.

How can we account for the mixed results reported by investigators concern-ing the effectiveness of PL 94–142? We may attribute these variations to a lack of sufficient funds (Sarason, 1983) and precise guidelines on how to implement main-streaming procedures (Salend, 1984). One major issue is that PL 94–142 provided a federal subsidy for special education, but it also "left considerable vote for financing through state subsidies to local tax levies" (Jacobson, 1990, p. 7). As a result, states and local districts vary in the amount of money they spend on mainstreaming. Now that PL 94–142 has been put into practice, a key issue facing educators is to deter-mine how the everyday experiences of handicapped children in integrated educa-tional settings affect their academic achievement, their self-esteem, and their moti-vation to learn and succeed. You can see how paramount the need for research is in the social policy process. All policies—even those that present opportunities to help children—carry the risk of making things worse, not better.

Summary

During middle childhood, children acquire numerous cognitive skills that help them profit from formal instruction in school. Information-processing researchers explain that increases in the ability to process information at this time make it easier for children to pay attention to a task for longer periods. School-age children also have more capacity for memory than preschoolers, and they become aware of how memory works, which increases their use of memory-aiding strategies.

The information-processing approach describes cognitive changes quantitatively, whereas Piaget stressed the qualitative changes that occur. According to Piaget, school-age children are in the concrete operations period of cognitive development. As a result, they can perform mental inversions (reversibility of thought) and draw conclusions about observed outcomes on the basis of prior relationships, rather than on the basis of how things appear. They can also decenter; that is, they can focus on multiple dimensions of an object at one time. These children can also classify objects and events in a series; this indicates that they are capable of systematic and planned thinking. Numerous researchers have criticized the way Piaget presented problems to children, because if his tasks are modified somewhat, younger children are able to accomplish them.

School-age children also have enhanced language skills. They understand how language works (metalinguistic awareness) and can understand and appreciate metaphors and jokes—skills that help them profit from instruction in school. But in the United States, an increasing number of bilingual children and minority children who speak nonstandard English are not acquiring academic skills.

In addition, many children have difficulty with such basic skills as reading, writing, and arithmetic. Although we often blame our educational system for schoolchildren's low levels of achievement, they may fail to learn because they lack motivation to do so. This lack of motivation may be due to an emotional problem or to conditions in their family life; it may reflect the fact their parents do not encourage them to learn; or they may be unable to learn as a result of some learning disability such as dyslexia. There are many reasons for learning problems; for example, children may be learning-disabled and may not accurately process information. Some learning-disabled children have difficulty with words, others with calculating numbers or concentrating on tasks.

Although in the past learning-disabled and other handicapped children were taught in special classrooms, Public Law 94–142 now requires school systems to mainstream these children into the regular classroom so they can learn along with normal children. The law's intent is to provide handicapped children with educational opportunities in the least-restrictive environment. However, since at times there is a discrepancy between the law's intent and its subsequent outcome, we do not know whether all mainstreamed handicapped children actually learn more than handicapped children who remain in special education. Now that PL 94–142 has been in practice for several years, researchers and educators have to determine how the daily experiences of handicapped children affect their academic achievement and their self-esteem.

13 Social and Emotional Development During Middle Childhood

The middle childhood years, between the ages of 6 and 12, are an exciting and happy time. Although children still need the protection and supervision of adults, they begin for the first time to extend their wings and to take off on their own. They become increasingly self-reliant and revel in their new-found feelings of independence. As they try to find out more about themselves and their abilities, they may take up hobbies and become engrossed in elaborate school projects. Or they may begin fairly destructive styles of behavior and engage in dangerous activities. They learn what they can and cannot do, and for the first time, they acquire a picture of themselves as unique individuals.

Children of this age group learn about themselves and about others in their world. Changes in their social and emotional development open up new horizons, propelling them toward greater social involvement. They expand their circle of friends and come increasingly under the influence of other people, particularly those they meet at school and on the playground.

Both boys and girls in the middle childhood period become more independent of the family and more dependent on their peers. By the end of this period, they tend to spend most of their spare time with a "best friend," who is a trusted confidant. They eventually become part of a peer group as well. The older they are, the more they tend to yield to peer pressure, choosing to do what their friends do. This development, as we will see, has both good and bad aspects.

Peer relations are important in middle childhood. For inner-city children whose lives are riddled with high-risk, even life-threatening situations, being with friends is especially important. However, some children do not have many opportunities to be with friends. Children whose parents work, for example, are alone at home after school, spending most of their time watching television. Although they may spend less time with friends than they would like to, peer relations still have a special significance.

Progress in Social and Emotional Development

Advances in Social Cognition: Role-Taking

Before discussing the changes in children's relationships with their peers, we need to understand why these changes take place. During the school-age years, children make enormous advances in social cognition—the ability to understand people and to think about social relations. They show that they can accurately infer other people's thoughts and feelings, while realizing that other people can do the same. Thus their thoughts and feelings are the object of other people's thinking (Selman, 1976). This new social awareness will lead them to wonder just how other people will react to their actions and ideas.

Advances in **role-taking,** or **perspective-taking,** make possible this ability to make inferences about others' psychological experiences. Role-taking refers to comprehending information about another person's internal experiences (see Chapter 10). There are several types of role-taking abilities, including the capacity to understand what another person sees (perceptual role-taking), how another person feels (affective role-taking), and what another person thinks (cognitive role-taking).

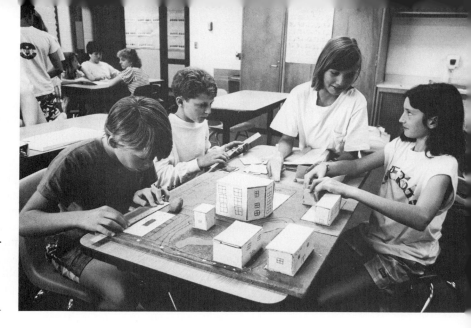

Children develop role-taking skills in their interactions with one another. They are increasingly aware that other children's thoughts and feelings may differ from their own.

Selman (1976, 1980) finds that children acquire role-taking gradually, progressing through a developmental sequence of levels. By telling children of different ages a story, and then asking them a series of questions about the story, Selman tested their understanding of people's personalities—their desires, feelings, expectations, and probable reactions. He distinguished four levels of role-taking between the ages of 4 and 12.

Level 0, Egocentric role-taking: Children do not yet distinguish between their own perspective and others'. They assume that other people's feelings and thoughts are more or less identical to their own.

Level 1, Subjective role-taking: Children realize that other people think or feel differently because they are in a different situation or have different kinds of information. They also realize that people may interpret the same event in different ways. However, children have difficulty thinking about their own and others' perspectives at the same time; and, they cannot put themselves in another person's position in order to judge what that person thinks or feels.

Level 2, Self-reflective role-taking: Children become aware that people think or feel differently because each person has her or his own particular values and interests. At this stage children realize that their perspective is not necessarily the only right or valid one. They can now put themselves in another person's place, realizing that the other person can do the same thing with regard to them. Thus, children begin to think about how others view them and to anticipate how others will react to their own actions and ideas.

Level 3, Mutual role-taking: Children are able to differentiate their perspective from someone else's and to think about their own point of view and another person's simultaneously.

Level 4, Societal or in-depth perspective: This is the last stage, occurring at about age 12 and continuing into adulthood. Individuals are able to take a generalized perspective of society and its laws, while realizing that people do not always understand each other's values. Thus, role-taking abilities will not necessarily resolve all disputes.

Selman (1980) notes that egocentrism begins to decline at age 4; by age 6, children become aware that others view things differently than they do; by age 10, they are beginning to be able to consider their own viewpoint and another person's simultaneously. However, some researchers disagree with the age levels Selman attaches to these developmental changes in role-taking ability. According to other experts, children younger than age 6 can grasp another person's perspectives. This was evident when the researchers observed children in their play interactions (Hoffman, 1976; Rubin & Pepler, 1980). Other researchers point out that an exact age cannot be associated with each level, because a given child's role-taking ability may fluctuate from one occasion to another (Maccoby, 1980). Some children can grasp another's perspective for a moment but may fail to maintain that perspective for longer periods. Also, children who understand the perspective of familiar people in familiar situations may be much less skillful in judging unfamiliar persons or situations (Flapan, 1968).

Finally, an important aspect of role-taking ability is social experience. No matter how old they are, children lacking the opportunity to interact with other children are less skilled at perspective-taking than children with extensive social experiences. Apparently peer interactions provide the opportunity children need to become acquainted with how others behave, think, and feel in different situations. Marida Hollos (1975) demonstrated this point by testing children in Norway and Hungary. She chose children who lived on farms, in villages, and in towns and tested their cognitive skills (using Piagetian tasks) and their role-taking ability. The children were of similar socioeconomic backgrounds, but they differed in the

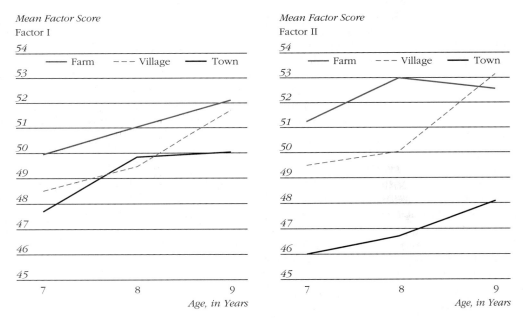

Figure 13.1 *(a) Children living on isolated farms are cognitively ahead of children who live in villages and towns; (b) however, without the opportunity to interact with children their own age, they lag behind in role-taking ability.*

Source: "Logical Operations and Role-Taking Abilities in Two Cultures: Norway and Hungary," by Marida Hollos in *Child Development 46,* p. 645, Figure 1. Copyright © 1975 by The Society for Research in Child Development, Inc.

amount of time they spent with peers. Farm children spent most of their time helping their parents or playing alone, whereas village children spent more time with other children, and children living in towns spent even more time with their peers.

The farm children outperformed the village and town children on Piagetian tasks, which measured their ability to think logically. However, they were not as good at grasping another person's perspective (see Figure 13.1). This study clearly illustrates that although the ability to think logically and acquire cognitive maturity may not be influenced by social interactions, they are indeed important to the ability to understand others and recognize that other people think and feel differently.

Just as social interactions enhance children's role-taking skills, their progress in role-taking enhances their interactions with other children and adults. Selman (1981) found that children who have difficulty getting along with their peers also have trouble initiating and maintaining friendships, because they are unable to grasp another person's perspective. When they are able to understand others' perspectives, they are better able to form friendships and also become better communicators. This is because effective communication depends on an assessment of what other people already know and what they need to know. Shatz (1983) summarizes several studies that reveal that if children ages 10 and older are asked to describe an object to a listener, they do not rely on information that only they would know. For example, they do not describe an object by saying, "It looks like my mommy's hat." Instead, they use examples likely to be familiar to the listener, such as "It looks like a flying saucer."

Role-taking also enhances empathy, the ability to understand and vicariously feel what another person is feeling. Empathy enables children to help others who may be in distress and enhances their ability to think about the effects of their own behavior on others (Eisenberg & Strayer, 1987). The capacity for empathy gradually becomes more refined during the school-age years. Recall from Chapters 7 and 10 that at a very young age, children are able to empathize with others in some situations. Even in infancy, they can identify emotions (Campos, 1983). But not until they are about 12 years old can they also infer how people think about other people's feelings. Dorothy Flapan (1968) showed 6-, 9-, and 12-year-old children movie scenes portraying feelings and motives within the context of family interactions and other social situations. In one scene a father punishes a girl but later takes her out to the circus to make up for the punishment. All the children were able to identify the emotions in the movie scene, but when the researcher asked them to describe what they had seen, it was evident that the younger children were not able to infer the emotions; they simply described the actions. For example, one 6-year-old described the movie scene as follows:

> Daddy was sitting in a chair . . . looking at the paper. And the little girl got out of bed and said, "Pa, will you kiss me good night?" And the daddy said "go to bed," and the little girl went to bed crying. And [the father] tore up the newspaper and threw it down on the floor and was ready to go out to the barn. [Flapan, 1968]

However, a 12-year-old gave the following description, revealing that he was able to infer thoughts and intentions and understand what the adults in the movie scene were thinking about and what the child was feeling:

> The father was reading the newspaper, but he was thinking about something else. He really couldn't read it. And the little girl was looking down and asked if her father didn't want to kiss her. The father wanted to say good night, but then he thought she did something bad so he said "No, go to bed." And the little girl was crying . . . . The

father tried to read the newspaper again, but couldn't read so he threw it away. He wanted to go up [to the girl] and say it wasn't that bad, but he decided he had better not so he went to his wife in the kitchen and said he was going out. [Flapan, 1968]

Moral Development

Progress in social cognition during middle childhood also enhances the ability to evaluate one's own behavior in relation to what other people think and feel. Hence, children grow in their ability to behave well and to reason about moral problems.

Every society has an unwritten moral code and explicit rules about its citizens' moral behavior. For example, we expect people to help others in distress; we also believe that people should be honest, even when they are able to steal and not get caught. If a clerk at the supermarket checkout counter makes a mistake and gives you change for $20 instead of for the $10 bill you handed her, you are expected to point out the error and return the proper amount to the clerk. If you don't, your conscience may bother you because you feel guilty about taking advantage of the situation. *Conscience* is a byproduct of our moral development; that is, it is the process by which we learn to accept standards of right and wrong as guides to our behavior.

The development of moral knowledge   Children are not born with a moral code or conscience; they acquire them gradually. Intent on discovering how this process occurs, child psychologists have long been asking the following questions: How do children learn the difference between right and wrong? What makes them feel they should be honest, even when no one can see them? How do youngsters learn to overcome the temptation to cheat? Child psychologists have come up with different answers, depending on their theoretical orientation.

Psychoanalysts, for example, focus on the emotional aspects of moral development. Noting that guilt is a major component of morality, psychoanalytic theorists point out that identification with the same-sex parent fosters moral growth. By resolving the Oedipus or Electra complex (see Chapter 10), a conscience is formed. As a result, boys and girls have feelings of anxiety over the thought of losing a parent's love and feelings of guilt over incestuous fantasies about the same-sex parent (Freud, 1965). These feelings of fear, anxiety, and guilt then generate moral sanctions that arise from within us; that is, from our conscience.

In contrast, social learning theorists contend that cultural experiences shape moral behavior and values through modeling and reinforcement. Both social learning theorists and psychoanalysts agree, however, that children acquire moral knowledge as a result of the influence of external forces, such as their parents.

Cognitive developmental theorists take a quite different position. They believe that moral reasoning develops progressively along with cognitive abilities. For example, both Jean Piaget (1932, 1965) and Lawrence Kohlberg (1969) contended that moral development is a function of cognitive growth.

Piaget was particularly interested in children's notions about rules. By studying how children thought about and followed the rules of a game, he felt that he could gain insight into their perceptions of morality. In playing marbles, for instance, children not only cooperate, they also have to deal with a number of moral issues such as *fairness* (who goes first), *reciprocity* (taking turns), and *justice* (yielding a marble if they lose). By analyzing how children play marbles, Piaget found that they did not begin to play by the rules until middle childhood. Preschool children perceive rules as sacred and unalterable, believing that they are absolute extensions of such authority figures as God or Daddy. But unlike school-agers, preschoolers may think of rules as something absolute and unchangeable, but when they are playing, they change the rules to suit themselves. Often they improvise new rules as the game progresses. Paley (1984) also found that preschoolers make up rules as they play, arbitrarily deciding, for example, that only boys can play Superman or that no girls are allowed in the spaceship. Thus, they can change the "rules" as they see fit.

School-age children, on the other hand, are very strict about following rules, especially during the early part of middle childhood, when they are about 7 or 8 years old. They will agree ahead of time to a set of rules for a game and will not change them unless there is a consensus. They consider it cheating to arbitrarily change the rules during a game. They play games by following the rules, and they expect adults to observe all other "rules" such as giving children an allowance every Friday or allowing them to stay up late on Saturday. Children often claim that it isn't fair if adults do not adhere to these precedents.

Piaget (1965) discovered that children cling to a rather rigid understanding of the concept of rules. For example, he asked 10-year-old Ben to invent a new rule for the game of marbles. After at first refusing to do so, Ben finally invented a rule. He claimed, however, that to adhere to the new rule would be cheating. Why? "Because I invented it," replied Ben. "It isn't a rule! It's a wrong rule because it's outside the rules. A fair rule is one that is in the game."

Gradually, however, school-age children acquire a more realistic notion of rules. By the end of elementary school, they reject the idea that rules are absolute. Instead, they reason that since the purpose of rules is to benefit all those involved, the participants can change and reformulate the rules through reasoning, discussion, and general agreement.

Children are not born with a moral code, but gradually come to accept standards of right and wrong as guides to behavior. Researchers have long been interested in their ethical development.

In studying moral development, Piaget also asked children questions about moral stories. He found that with age children change in their moral judgments. For example, Piaget presented children with two different stories. The first was about a boy who is called to dinner. While going into the dining room, he accidentally breaks 15 cups. In another story a boy climbs up on a chair to get some jam out of the cupboard. While trying to get the jam, he knocks over a cup and breaks it. In a variation of these stories, Piaget asked children to compare the two children, one of whom accidentally breaks 15 cups while helping his mother and the other who breaks one cup by throwing it across the room in anger. He then asked the children who is naughtier and who deserved more punishment. Children aged 5 to 10 said that the boy who broke more cups is naughtier since he broke a greater number of cups. That is, the children based their judgment of the act on its *consequences*. By age 11, however, children based their judgment on the *intentions* of the individual involved, saying that the boy who broke one cup was naughtier because he was intentionally engaged in an activity that led to breaking the cup.

Kohlberg's stages of moral development   Building on Piaget's observations, Kohlberg (1969, 1976) formulated a more comprehensive theory of moral development. He discovered that as children grow older, their way of understanding the social world and, consequently, of making moral judgments, changes. He proposed six (later revised to five) stages of moral development, each stage building upon the other and each associated with changes in cognitive structure. Kohlberg's theory groups these stages within three levels of moral thought—preconventional, conventional, and postconventional—that correspond roughly to the preoperational (2 to 7 years old), concrete operations (7 to 12 years old), and formal operations (12 years old to adulthood) periods of cognitive growth.

The Preconventional Level   At this lowest level of moral judgment, the **preconventional level,** children's emphasis is on avoiding punishment and getting a reward.

>   *Stage 1*   In Stage 1, which we might describe as *might makes right,* children value obedience to authority. They make moral decisions on the basis of possible physical consequences, such as punishment, that may result from an act. They follow rules to avoid being punished.

>   *Stage 2*   In Stage 2, *the instrumental relativist stage,* children try to take care of their own needs. They are motivated by an act's hedonistic consequences, believing, for instance, that the reason you should be nice to people is so they will be nice to you. A child in this stage might share her candy bar with another child, but only if that child will let her have something in return.

The Conventional Level   At the **conventional level,** children's emphasis is on social rules and on maintaining the expectations of their family, group, or nation.

>   *Stage 3*   We can characterize Stage 3 as *the good-girl and nice-boy orientation.* In this stage children consider a behavior to be right if it meets with the approval of other people. Approval is more important than any specific reward.

>   *Stage 4*   We can characterize Stage 4 by *the law-and-order orientation.* In this stage children emphasize the need to maintain social order and regard right behavior as doing one's duty and showing respect for authority.

The Postconventional or Autonomous Level   At the **postconventional or auton-omous level** people clearly try to define moral values and principles that have validity and application.

Stage 5   We can characterize Stage 5 by *the social contract or legalistic orientation*. In this stage people have a sense of obligation to law because of the social contract existing between people and society for the common good. Right actions are defined in terms of individual rights and of standards critically examined and agreed on by the whole society. Children are aware that these standards, or rules of society, exist for everyone's benefit and that people have established them by mutual agreement.

Stage 6   We can characterize Stage 6 by *the universal ethical principles orientation*. In this stage people acquire a sense of personal commitment to moral principles because of the rational recognition of universal concepts. We define right by decisions of the conscience in accord with self-chosen ethical principles. Since so few people ever reach this highest stage of moral development, Kohlberg (1978) combined it with Stage 5.

Kohlberg developed his theory of moral development on the basis of interviews with children and adults. He presented stories featuring a number of hypothetical moral dilemmas and then asked what the characters in the story should do and why. Table 13.1 is one example of such a dilemma.

Was stealing the drug an immoral or moral act? Kohlberg was not so much interested in the children's answer as he was in their justification or reasoning. For example, a child who is at Stage 3 might say that the husband should steal the drug because people will blame him for not saving his wife. Alternatively, the child might say that the husband should not steal the drug because he had already done everything he could legally and people would call him a thief if he stole. In both answers the child's justification showed that he considered moral behavior in terms of what other people might think.

In a longitudinal study of moral judgment, Colby, Kohlberg, and their colleagues (1983) found that human beings attain moral stages in the predicted order, and that no one skips a stage. Presenting moral dilemmas to children in various cultures, Kohlberg and others (Nisan & Kohlberg, 1982; Edwards, 1981; 1982; Turiel, Edwards, & Kohlberg, 1978) concluded that the developmental sequence of the stages of moral development is universal. Children in such diverse cultures as Turkey, Taiwan, India, Nigeria, and Central America, who obviously have different experiences and absorb different social values, generally progress through the stages in much the same way as American children. Some researchers, however, question the universality of moral development, suggesting that more research is needed to establish whether all children progress through the same stages of moral development.

Kohlberg's theory has had extensive influence among educators. His theory forms the basis for a procedure known as *value clarification,* in which researchers encourage children to think about their values through discussions of hypothetical dilemmas (Beyer, 1978). However, some researchers disagree with Kohlberg's contention that children construct a moral code in keeping with their cognitive capabilities, noting instead that children construct a moral code socially, through discussions and debates with others (Youniss, 1980).

In Europe, a woman was near death from a special kind of cancer. There was one drug that the doctors thought might save her. It was in the form of radium that a druggist in town had recently discovered. The drug was very expensive to make, but, even so, the druggist was charging 10 times what the drug cost him to make; he paid $200 for the radium and charged $2,000 for a small dose of the drug. The sick woman's husband, Heinz, went to everyone he knew to raise money for the drug, but could only raise $1,000, which is half of what the drug cost. He explained to the druggist that his wife was deathly ill and asked if he could sell the drug cheaper or let him pay for it later. The druggist refused, claiming that he discovered the drug and expects to make money from it. Desperate, Heinz broke into the druggist's store and stole the drug for his wife. Should Heinz have done that? Why?

TABLE 13.1 The Heinz dilemma. To illustrate the characteristics of each level of moral thought and the developmental changes in the child's reasoning about moral conflicts, Kohlberg presented children with stories featuring a number of hypothetical moral dilemmas. Then he asked the children what the characters in the stories should do and why. Here, their reasons for why Heinz should or should not have stolen the drug reflect their level of moral reasoning.

Stages	Pro	Con
Stage 1 Children are motivated to behave in order to avoid punishment.	Heinz should have stolen the drug. If he didn't and let his wife die, he would have been blamed for her death.	Heinz should not have stolen the drug because he could be caught and sent to jail and even if he gets away with it, his conscience would bother him and he would worry that the police would catch up with him.
Stage 2 Children are motivated to behave by the desire for benefit and reward.	If Heinz gets caught, he could give the drug back and wouldn't be punished much. Anyway, it wouldn't bother him to serve a sentence in jail since his wife is alive and will be there when he gets out of jail.	Heinz may not get much of a jail sentence for stealing the drug, but his wife may die anyway while he is in prison, so it wouldn't have helped him to steal the drug. If his wife dies, he shouldn't blame himself.
Stage 3 Right is defined according to what pleases other people and wins their praise.	No one will think that Heinz is bad for stealing the drug, but if he hadn't stolen the drug and let his wife die instead, his family would think of him as an inhuman husband.	Not only the druggist but everyone else will think that Heinz is a criminal and that he dishonored his family.
Stage 4 Right is regarded in terms of doing one's duty and showing respect for authority.	Heinz should not have been afraid to do anything that might save his wife because it's his duty to do so. If he didn't steal the drug and save her, he would have felt guilty.	When he was stealing the drug, Heinz was desperate and may not have realized that he was doing anything wrong. But after he is punished and jailed for his crime, he will feel guilty for his dishonesty and lawbreaking.
Stage 5 Right is defined in terms of standards that are agreed upon by the whole society.	If Heinz hadn't stolen the drug to save his wife, he would have lost other people's respect for him and his own self-respect.	By stealing the drug, Heinz lost the respect of everyone in the community and his own self-respect because he got carried away with emotion and forgot the long-term consequences of his action.
Stage 6 Right is defined by decisions of the conscience in accord with self-chosen ethical principles.	If he hadn't stolen the drug, Heinz would always have condemned himself afterward for not having lived up to his own standards of conscience.	Other people might not blame Heinz for having stolen the drug, but he would now condemn himself for not living up to his own conscience and standards of honesty.

Source: Stages in the Development of Moral Thought and Action, by L. Kohlberg, 1969. New York: Holt.

Numerous researchers have criticized Kohlberg's use of moral dilemmas that focus on breaking rules. Taking a different approach to the study of moral development, Damon (1977, 1980) used stories that depicted everyday occurrences instead of abstract stories. Damon also separated moral development into four different domains: positive justice (fairness), friendship, obedience to authority, and social rules and conventions. He believed that children develop moral concepts in each of these four areas. Turiel (1983) also notes that although children may recognize moral principles such as justice and fairness, they distinguish them from social conventions such as dress codes and rules of etiquette. When asked about school rules and policies, for example, 5- to 11-year-olds indicate that schools should prohibit hitting and other forms of moral transgressions. However, they can tolerate breaches of social conventions, such as undressing in the playground or talking back to the teacher (Turiel, Killen, & Helwig, 1987; Turiel, 1983).

In addition, some researchers have criticized Kohlberg for ignoring possible sex differences in children's answers to moral dilemmas and for basing his studies on males. Carol Gilligan (1982) finds that women base their moral decisions on different types of reasoning than men. For example, women are concerned with relationships and social responsibilities and use them in their moral reasoning, whereas men are concerned with legal issues and rules. Since Kohlberg's levels of moral development focus on rules, Gilligan contends that they are not valid for women. Although her research has also been subject to criticism (Walker, 1984), it provides an important perspective on issues involved in the study of moral development.

Moral behavior Researchers have further observed that children in middle childhood, as well as some older children and adults, often endorse moral standards they do not necessarily follow; children and adults do not always behave in ways that they think are best (Hoffman, 1984). Numerous factors besides moral reasoning—such as the behavior of others, our own personality characteristics, and the standards of society—can influence how people decide to behave in a given situation (Edwards, 1982). Most school-age children know that lying and cheating are wrong and can usually explain why they are wrong, thus showing that they are intellectually aware of the issues involved. But they still cheat at times, especially if they do not think they will be caught, and they lie about doing so (Ekman, 1989; Lewis, 1989).

We need to distinguish moral knowledge from moral behavior and to realize the two do not necessarily coincide. This fact has led some researchers to study how children come to accept standards of right and wrong as guides to behavior and how they behave accordingly. These researchers believe the ability to grasp another's perspective is an important influence on moral behavior (Selman, 1980). For example, a child may resist the temptation to steal her friend's watch because she realizes how her friend would feel if her watch was stolen. The ability to assume the perspective of others increases during the school-age years in the course of social interactions. These interactions help children understand more clearly how other people feel and think in numerous situations.

Perspective-taking ability is an important, but not dominant, influence on moral behavior. Observational learning, reinforcements, and punishments also play a role. Social learning theorists like Aronfreed (1968), for example, contended that children imitate the behavior of powerful, significant people in their lives; through observational learning, they learn specific moral behaviors such as sharing. Aronfreed also noted that social approval by significant people, such as parents, is one of the most powerful reinforcers of moral behavior. As children learn that their parents approve or disapprove of certain behaviors, they begin to think about their own behavior in line with the consequences they can expect for it.

Aronfreed outlined behavioral controls ranging from external to internal, noting that initially only external controls govern behavior. Children behave morally because they expect a reward for doing so and a punishment for behaving otherwise. With age, they learn about the different rules governing good behavior and develop internal controls, or a conscience. This motivates them to behave morally in order to avoid feeling guilty; they punish or reward themselves when they deviate from or conform to appropriate norms of behavior. According to Aronfreed, children are likely to develop strong internal controls if the parents—in their attempts to socialize their offspring—specify behaviors that lead to punishments or rewards and explain their reasoning.

Hoffman (1970; 1984) supports this view. His theory about the development of moral behavior focuses on the type of disciplinary strategies parents adopt. He distinguished two such strategies: punitive and inductive. **Punitive techniques** emphasize the personal consequences of breaking the rules; for example, "If you hit your little brother, I won't let you watch TV." **Inductive techniques** stress the effects of misbehavior on the victims of moral transgressions; parents explain to children that their actions are likely to have consequences: "If you hit your little brother, you will hurt him." Inductive techniques have proved to be more effective for teaching children to behave morally (Hoffman, 1970). The reason may be that when we explain the consequences of children's behavior, we encourage them to think about other people's feelings and to empathize with them (Hoffman, 1970; 1978).

Advances in Self-Concept

Through their actions and childrearing techniques, parents strongly influence children's morality and their adoption of standards of right and wrong as guides to behavior. Their influence extends beyond the development of morality to self-concept and self-esteem (Maccoby, 1984). Although parental influence begins early in life, the middle childhood years are particularly crucial. During these years, children become increasingly aware of themselves as unique individuals. They are also more able to consider the views of others and take them into their consideration of what they themselves are like.

Who am I?   Young children have only a rudimentary notion of the self. Early in the preschool period, they come to regard themselves as separate individuals who can exert their own will and desires. They also become aware of their gender identities and roles, recognizing themselves and behaving as boys or girls. During middle childhood, children gain an even more refined sense of their gender identities and gender roles and continue the process of differentiating themselves from others in their surroundings (Harter, 1983a). Gradually they discover more about themselves and acquire a picture of a unique, multifaceted self (Markus & Nurius, 1984; Damon & Hart, 1982). Whereas at the beginning of this period children may still define themselves in terms of age and physical characteristics, by age 11 they give a more complex description—one that includes comparisons with other children, such as "I ride a bike better than anyone around" (Keller, Ford, & Meachum, 1978).

With age, children's self-descriptions also include references to their inner thoughts and feelings and convey the fact that they are constantly changing

During the school-age years, children become aware of themselves as unique individuals and learn to appreciate their own capabilities.

(McGuire & McGuire, 1986). Montemayor and Eisen (1977) asked children to answer the question "Who am I?" They found that a 9-year-old may say, for example, "My name is Bruce, I have brown eyes, I am nine years old, and I have seven people in my family." An 11-year-old, on the other hand, may reply:

> I'm a human being. I'm a girl. I'm a truthful person. I'm not pretty. I do so-so in my studies . . . . I am a very good swimmer. I try to be helpful. I'm always ready to be friends with anybody. Mostly I'm good, but sometimes I lose my temper . . . . [Montemayor & Eisen, 1977]

How do I feel about myself? Children develop a more specific, multifaceted picture of themselves during the school-age years, and they begin to judge how worthy they are. Their opinion of their own worth is a vital part of their personality, affecting all aspects of behavior. The child with good self-esteem believes that he is a worthy individual who can achieve the goals he sets for himself. He feels that he likes the people around him and that they like him. The child with little self-esteem, on the other hand, is convinced that he is not worthy of anyone's affection, and that he is inadequate in comparison to others. Self-esteem is also an important gauge of mental health. Damon (1983) notes that children with low self-esteem tend to be depressed and anxious and to have difficulties in social situations. Self-esteem is important during childhood and later in life as well (Harter, 1983a).

Self-esteem develops gradually during middle childhood, becoming part of the complex network of attitudes and beliefs that make up the self-concept. Child experts often refer to self-esteem as the *evaluative component of the self-concept*. To measure self-esteem, researchers give children a list of phrases (for example, good at sports, sure of myself, have lots of friends) and ask them whether the statement describes them (Harter, 1983a).

Erik Erikson (1963) underscored the importance of the development of self-esteem during this period, noting that children then undergo the psychological crisis of **industry versus inferiority.** Erikson theorized that children who find and concentrate on areas they are good at and on things they can accomplish gain a sense that they can make and do things; that is, a sense of industry. They are ready and eager to move into the world of adulthood. Children who cannot find anything in which they are competent soon develop a sense of inferiority and regard themselves as insignificant in comparison to others.

Influences on Self-Esteem

Family influences   How children come to see themselves is largely, although not entirely, a function of their interactions with their parents. Coopersmith's (1967) study of the influences on self-esteem found that parental attitudes and childrearing practices tend to predict high or low self-esteem in children. He measured the self-esteem of 10- to 12-year-old boys, using his Self-Esteem Inventory, and also tested their parents' attitudes, using the Parent Attitudes Research Instrument and in-depth interviews. He found that parents of boys with high self-esteem often had the following attitudes and behavioral practices:

1. They were accepting, affectionate, and involved in their child's life; they treated his interests and problems as meaningful, and showed genuine concern for him.
2. They enforced rules carefully and consistently and set clear limits on what the child could and could not do, encouraging him to uphold high standards of behavior.
3. They used noncoercive discipline, such as denial of privileges; they typically explained to the child what he was being punished for and why his behavior was inappropriate.
4. They were democratic in their interactions with the child, considering his opinions and allowing him to participate in family plans, when appropriate.

When parents allow their children to express themselves and consider the children's opinions, they convey a clear sense of respect. As a result, the children regard themselves as worthy individuals.

Explaining these findings, Coopersmith noted that when parents consider their children's opinions and allow them to express themselves, they convey to the children that they think they are important and worthy individuals. As a result, the children come to regard themselves as such. In addition, Coopersmith emphasized how important it is for parents to set clear and realistic limits for their children; they need to be consistent in what they expect. This lessens the chance that the children will fail to meet parental standards of behavior. When the parents' standards are ambiguous, children do not know how to behave and have trouble monitoring, evaluating, and regulating their own behavior.

There are some methodological shortcomings to Coopersmith's study. For example, his sample is small and restricted to boys (Wylie, 1979). All the same, the research we examined in Chapter 10, which shows that authoritative parents have socially competent children, supports Coopersmith's conclusion that clear parental standards in childrearing lead to high self-esteem in their offspring. Keep in mind that the authoritative parents described in Baumrind's (1971) study have personal characteristics similar to those Coopersmith emphasized. Such parents are warm, rational, and receptive to their children's opinions and concerns. These parents also

A CLOSER LOOK

Self-Esteem in Minority-Group Children

According to child experts, the primary influences on children come from their parents. But there are also influences from the larger environment in which they live; that is, from siblings and relatives, the neighborhood and community, and from social institutions like the school (Bronfenbrenner, 1979). All these influences can affect self-esteem (Garbarino, 1982).

Minority-group children have to deal with different, and often conflicting, social values. Because our society frequently views these youngsters in terms of negative ethnic or racial stereotypes, they may develop a low self-esteem. For example, Yates (1987) reports a high rate of depression, intergenerational conflict, and behavioral problems among Native American children. In part he attributes these problems to low self-esteem and **maladaptive acculturation;** that is, these children have rejected either the dominant culture of the United States or their parents' original culture.

Because of a wide discrepancy between the two cultures, Native American children find it difficult to relate positively to their original culture and the dominant culture. For example, their families and tribes teach them to share things and to be loyal to the community rather than to themselves. Since this tradition discourages competition, they do not compete with other children in school. But teachers who do not share the Native American outlook may regard these children as lazy and unmotivated. These teachers may also fail to appreciate other traditional values, such as the need for harmony with nature and the orientation to the present rather than to the future. As a result, school officials may see these children as failures and reflect that attitude.

Other minority children—for example, blacks and Hispanics, especially from lower socioeconomic backgrounds—face similar problems (Garcia-Coll, 1990). Still, some of these children have managed to achieve adaptive acculturation and maintain their ethnic identity. Spencer and Markstrom-Adams (1990) point out the importance of keeping their ethnic identity because it gives these children a sense of belonging and group pride, which provides them, in turn, with the framework needed to acquire a sense of self-worth.

To discover if minority-group children have a sense of racial or ethnic identity, researchers present them with dolls (or pictures) that represent their group and the majority group. They then ask the children to choose the doll (or picture) they prefer. In one study Native American preschool and elementary children tended to choose the white doll (Beuf, 1977). This was also true of black children (Clark & Clark, 1987). A study with Native American children, however, yielded a different result: when researchers tested them in their tribal language, the children preferred the Native American doll (Corenblum & Annis, 1987).

What conclusions can we draw from these studies? None as yet, according to researchers, who recommend more research on issues associated with the development of minority children. As Spencer and Markstrom-Adams (1990) observe, researchers assumed that minority children who chose the white doll lacked identification with their own culture. However, perhaps these children were indicating their understanding of the power positions in the world around them.

firmly enforce rules when the situation calls for it. They demand high standards of behavior and achievement from their children. When necessary, they employ noncoercive discipline, and they explain to their children why they feel the need to punish them. More recent studies by Loeb, Horst, and Horton (1980) also show that parental warmth leads to high self-esteem in their children, whereas physical or psychological punishment (for example, the withdrawal of love and affection) leads to low self-esteem.

While parental attitudes and childrearing practices remain the most important influences on self-esteem, they are not alone in shaping children. Teachers and peers also can help children achieve a feeling of success. If teachers praise them for good work or good behavior in school, and if friends admire them for their skills and social presence, the children will probably feel better about themselves and accept themselves as worthy human beings.

The Social World of the School-Age Child

As we learned in previous chapters, the family is by no means the only influence on children. For instance, Chapter 9 reported how preschool children tend to adopt certain modes of behavior as a result of watching television and observing both other children and adults in child care centers or nursery schools. All the same, the family is the major socializing agent for this age. They spend most of their time with relatives and learn how people expect them to behave in the context of family life. The sphere of social contacts only opens up to a considerable extent during middle childhood. From this time forward others outside the family will assume a major role in shaping children's behavior (Maccoby, 1984). After they enter school, children gain new information about life; they meet new adult models and have

Children learn to behave in ways that are valued by teachers and friends as a result of increased contact with adult models and peers in school.

increased contact with their peers. They learn that they should behave in ways that are valued and approved by teachers and friends, as well as by parents. Thus, schools and peers become powerful agents of socialization.

Not surprisingly, the child at this point may have to deal with conflicting messages about how he should behave. The family, the school, and his peers may have different views. He learns, for example, that he can obtain the teacher's approval by behaving in class and getting good grades, but his friends will tease him about being a teacher's pet. When he is at home, he can offer his opinions, but at school he may not always be able to do so. Despite these and other often conflicting expectations, the child can gain much from his experiences at school and with his schoolmates. These experiences promote his social development and help him express himself appropriately in different social settings (Epps & Smith, 1984). Furthermore, he learns about different standards, values, and roles.

The School

Children's school experiences are extremely important because schools have norms of behavior that define the roles of both the children and the teachers. These norms come from the **academic curriculum,** which includes tasks children are expected to master, and from the **hidden curriculum** (Jackson, 1968), which refers to the mechanisms that maintain order and control in the classroom. These two curricula define the teacher's role as a classroom instructor, evaluator, and manager and the children's role as pupils who must learn their lessons and behave in an orderly and obedient manner. They need to learn how to respect authority and to conform to rules (Hess & Holloway, 1985).

As noted in Chapter 12, classroom structure (Schmuck & Schmuck, 1975) and other factors such as parent involvement (Stevenson, 1983; Rich, 1985) influence children's experiences in school. However, the extent to which children can succeed in school and have positive interactions with their teachers also depends on how quickly they learn the roles defined by both the academic and hidden curricula. Teachers, for example, prefer students who learn well, obey instructions, and are quiet in class. Some teachers have difficulty relating positively to students who are bright but nonconforming (Helton & Oakland, 1977). When asked what kind of students they prefer, most student teachers in one study (Feshbach, 1969) said that they prefer rigid, conforming, and orderly children, then dependent and acquiescent children, then flexible but untidy and nonconforming children, and finally, independent, assertive, and active children. This study also revealed that these would-be teachers equate the children's behavior with intellectual abilities. When asked which student is likely to get the highest grades and which they considered the brightest, most of them indicated the conforming child as the highest achiever and also the most intelligent.

The Influence of Teachers

Teachers' attitudes toward their students are important, because teachers assume a central role in the children's life, often determining to a large extent how they feel about being in school and how they feel about themselves. This is especially true during the first year or two of school, when the children are still getting used to the idea that their performance is under constant evaluation (Entwisle & Hayduk, 1978). Studying the changes in first-graders' social and motivational development, Stipek (1977) found that their experiences of success or failure are defined more by inter-

When their teachers are friendly and encouraging, children usually feel good about themselves and their school.

actions with their teachers than by their actual academic performance. As long as the children had a friendly and positively reinforcing teacher, they felt successful and good about themselves in school.

The teachers' powerful influence is hardly surprising. Most of us have fond memories of a teacher who had a significant role in shaping our lives—the teacher who responded to our needs, who acknowledged our feelings and ideas, and who inspired us toward greater academic involvement. Although teachers have always influenced students' academic skills, behavior, and values, researchers do not entirely understand how they do it. This is partly due to the fact that numerous methodological flaws have riddled these studies (Anderson, 1982). Nevertheless, some studies suggest that teachers who have a positive influence on their students rely heavily on praise and reasoning; they are able to create a warm and nurturant environment in the classroom (Gage, 1978; Brophy, 1983; U.S. Department of Education, 1986).

Teachers' expectations   The teacher's belief that children are capable is also an important factor in his or her ability to positively influence students. The U.S. Department of Education's review (1986) indicates that "teachers who set and communicate high expectations to all their students obtain greater academic performance from those students than teachers who set low expectations . . . students tend to learn as little—or as much—as their teachers expect" (p. 32).

The research on teachers' expectations dates back to a series of studies conducted by Rosenthal and his colleagues. They found that teachers' expectations affect their interactions with the children and the children's subsequent performance on academic tasks. In the original study, Rosenthal and Jacobsen (1966; 1968) gave a battery of intelligence tests to elementary school children, telling them that the test results would be communicated to their teachers. Selecting a number of students' names at random, the researchers told the teachers that, according to test results, these were the brightest children in the class. Some teachers were amazed, since the majority of these "bright" students had shown themselves to be average, at best. Nevertheless, accepting the test results, the teachers changed their attitudes toward those children and expected them to do extremely well in their studies. A follow-up study revealed that the IQs of these randomly selected children, formerly considered to be average, were now higher than those of their fellow students. The researchers suggested that the change in the children's performance probably resulted from the altered attitudes of the teachers. Believing the children to be highly capable, the teachers paid more attention to them.

Since this landmark study, other researchers have criticized Rosenthal and his colleagues on methodological grounds, partly because other studies failed to yield similar results (Cooper, 1979). Still, numerous researchers have conducted subsequent studies in an attempt to ascertain whether teachers' expectations can influence academic results (Wineberg, 1987). Although some researchers remain skeptical, others note that a rigorous reanalysis of the Rosenthal data, as well as data from several other studies (Good & Brophy, 1984; Purkey & Smith, 1983), indicate that, although many factors influence teachers' interactions with pupils, many teachers transmit their expectations to the children. Some pupils, like the students in Rosenthal's study, begin to behave in ways that validate those expectations, which sets into motion a self-fulfilling prophecy (Brophy, 1983). This sequence is especially true of children in the first and second grades.

How teachers communicate their expectations is not entirely known (Epps & Smith, 1984). Words are not essential, since they can convey their attitudes and expectations by tone of voice, facial expression, posture, and actions (for example, hugging a child). Chaikin, Sigler, and Derlega (1974) found that when teachers interact with children from whom they anticipate a superior academic performance, they engage in more positive nonverbal behaviors—smiling, leaning forward toward the student, making eye contact, and nodding their head—than when they interact with students from whom they expect inferior performance. On the other hand, some teachers give extra help to children of whom they have low expectations (Brophy, 1983).

In addition, children don't always interpret their teacher's behavior accurately. Lord, Kentaro, and Darley (1990) found that when teachers hugged one of two children with identical grades, their classmates assumed that the child who was hugged was the smarter of the two and had done better on the test. Acting on those assumptions, most children then chose the child who had been hugged when they had to choose a partner for a work activity.

Often teachers' expectations have little or no relationship to the children's actual abilities. According to some observers, certain teachers base their expectations on such irrelevant characteristics as race or social class, expecting less in the way of achievement from lower-class students (Minuchin & Shapiro, 1983), or gender, expecting boys rather than girls to succeed in math or science (Meece et al., 1982). Some teachers also form expectations of ability on the basis of the child's name. Harari and McDavid (1973) randomly assigned attractive names like *Lisa* and *David* and unattractive names like *Herbert* and *Gertrude* to a group of essays of similar quality. They then asked teachers to grade the essays. The teachers gave higher grades to essays attributed to the children with the attractive names.

A Society of Children

During middle childhood, children are influenced by their peers as well as their teachers. They spend more and more time with their peers and seek to be with them both in school and after school. Interaction with age-mates—talking to them, telling them secrets, squabbling with them, and engaging in other social activities (Medrich et al., 1982)—helps children prepare for the time when they become independent of their family. At the same time they learn about other people's perspectives (Selman, 1981), opinions, and values, and gain a perspective on themselves and on how others view them (Fine, 1980; Asher, 1978).

Children also become increasingly absorbed in their relations with their age-mates, becoming part of what social scientists refer to as a **society of children.** This social world has its own rituals, traditions, activities, and rules, as well as its own songs and games, that have been handed down from one generation of children to another. Child experts theorize that through the ages, school-age children have shared a world all their own. Children in many different countries often play similar games (Opie & Opie, 1969). Children also develop their own vocabulary, rules, and codes of behavior, many of which involve independence from adults (Opie & Opie, 1959). This society of children may ridicule or tease any child seen violating the codes. For example, a child observed being kissed by his parents may undergo humiliation at the hands of schoolmates who call him a baby.

Adults play no role in this world. They rarely take notice of it and may not even realize it exists. And children are reluctant to reveal what goes on in their world.

A CLOSER LOOK

Corporal Punishment

We have discussed the influence that teachers have on children. But did you realize that teachers can influence parents as well? Entwisle and Hayduk (1982) examined teacher, student, and parent expectations in three elementary schools. They found that middle-class parents, in particular, often change their expectations of their children's abilities on the basis of how their teachers graded them.

Viewing teachers as authorities in educational matters, some parents also adopt the teachers' techniques for disciplining children. This can be a positive influence when teachers are warm and nurturant and employ noncoercive punishment. By modeling appropriate ways of managing children, these teachers provide examples of alternatives to physical punishment. Unfortunately, some teachers can have a negative influence and sustain incorrect parental behavior.

Corporal punishment—spanking children or using other coercive methods—is often used allegedly to teach children to behave properly. Is it effective? Animal research indicates that intensive physical punishment can suppress an undesired behavior in an animal, but only for a time (Solomon, 1964). Physical punishment can injure a child or an animal, physically or emotionally. And, as we discussed in Chapter 10, it tends to heighten children's anger and aggression (Feshbach, 1980) and gives them an inappropriate model for ways to resolve problems with others (Parke, 1976). Patterson, DeBarsyshe, and Ramsey (1989) further note that coercive disciplining techniques can lead to antisocial behavior in childhood and delinquency in adolescence. Parents and teachers need to discipline children, but the use of physical punishment is not necessary. In fact, as we saw in Chap-ter 10, parents who refrain from coercive punishment are more likely to have well-behaved, socially competent children (Hoffman, 1990; Baumrind, 1971).

In spite of this information, many educators continue to regard physical punishment as a necessary tool for maintaining order in the classroom. While statistics on the topic are hard to obtain, experts estimate that close to 50% of American children are in schools where corporal punishment is permitted (National Committee for the Prevention of Child Abuse, 1989). Also, our legal system sanctions the use of physical punishment (Zigler & Hunsinger, 1977). To date, 27 states permit corporal punishment by teachers or other school personnel (Fathman, 1990), although the practice is now banned in 23 states. Schools are one of the few institutions where corporal punishment is still permitted; the practice is forbidden in the armed forces, federal prisons, and mental institutions (National Committee for the Prevention of Child Abuse, 1989).

There are indications that thousands of children from kindergarten to tenth grade are physically punished each school day, sometimes for trivial offenses such as forgetting school supplies or tardiness (Fathman, 1990). Who are these children? According to Hyman (1984) and Rose (1984), many are mentally retarded or physically handicapped, and punishments may be applied for such offenses as being too loud in class and not learning material as quickly as other children. Boys and minority children are particularly vulnerable. The National Coalition of Advocates for Students (1987) notes that in a survey of 16,000 public schools, blacks made up only 16% of the school population but accounted for 28% of corporal punishment cases.

They do not talk about what they do and tend to keep much of what goes on between them and their friends to themselves. As every parent of a school-age child knows, the older the child gets, the harder it becomes to obtain any information from her about her interactions with her friends. When asked, "Where did you go today?" or "What did you do with your friends?" she is likely to reply "Nowhere" or "Nothing."

Forming groups   The social world of children is particularly evident in the formation of groups. These groups have common goals, aims, and rules of social conduct, and they include a hierarchical structure that identifies each member's relationship to the others in the group. One member usually acts as the leader (Rubin, 1980; Sherif & Sherif, 1964).

Reviewing research on peer groups, Hartup (1984) concludes that relatively few studies have accumulated much information on the topic. Rubin (1980) points out that the nature of peer groups changes as children progress through middle childhood. When children are 6 or 7 years old, peer groups are nothing more than play groups; they have few rules and no structure or hierarchy to define roles and facilitate interaction among members. The groups form spontaneously and may include whoever happens to be nearby at the time. When the children are about 9, groups become more formal. The children now gather around shared interests and planned events; they form nature clubs, fan clubs, or secret societies with special rules, observations, passwords, and initiation rites. These groups have a core membership; each member must participate in the group's activities, and nonmembers are excluded. According to Rubin, children's participation in such groups does not always last long. The groups often break up shortly after celebrating the rituals involved in their creation.

Toward the latter part of middle childhood, peer groups become informal cliques of two or three individuals (Hallinan, 1980), who play an important role in the child's development. During these years, children begin the gradual process of leaving the safety of the family. Thus, their friends provide invaluable support. They also may begin to have a romantic interest in the opposite sex; in the context of a group of friends, they can exchange sexual information and get the reassurance and

Children everywhere enjoy spending time together in small groups.

Intense friendships are formed during the middle childhood years, when it is important for children to have a best friend to share the concerns of growing up.

support they need as they begin to deal with some of the concerns of growing up (Hartup, 1983; 1984). So taken are children with what they can learn from one another that they generally spend hours together, discussing any number of issues and constantly laughing and giggling.

Close friends   At this age children also have a strong affection for a few close friends in their group. Such intense friendships are not evident early in middle childhood. When they first start school, children still lack the ability to understand and empathize with other children and adults. They may describe their friends in terms of superficial qualities such as appearance or possessions. They may interact with one another as buddies, companions, or playmates, but not necessarily as close friends. By age 10 or 11, however, children evidence their maturing notion of friendship and come to regard a friend as someone who will stick up for them and whom they will defend in times of need (Berndt, 1982; Jacobson, 1975). They understand that friendships do not develop between people simply because they live nearby; for them, friendship means the ability to share inner thoughts and feelings (Youniss & Volpe, 1978).

As they grow older, children also begin to distinguish between a "friend" and a "best friend"; they become concerned with clearly defining who is and who is not their best friend. Gary Fine (1980) asked an 11-year-old boy who his best friends were. The boy "made a big production of the answer, thinking very carefully and then explaining why his best friends should be ranked in [a] particular order." Having questioned children on their notion of friendship, Fine (1980) found that among older school-age children an important criterion is the sharing of personal information—facts and feelings not known to other people. Through knowing so much about one another, about their fears and failings, about their hopes and aspirations, children become close friends. They provide one another with emotional support and an opportunity to understand some of the obligations of friendship. Children reveal their innermost feelings and thoughts to their friends, and they expect their friends to do the same. Youngsters of this age regard failure to do so as a violation of the obligations inherent in friendship (Youniss, 1980; Bigelow, 1977). Children also view trust as a basic tenet of friendship and consider the betrayal of a secret a serious breach in the relationship (Hinde, 1976). As a 12-year-old boy noted:

"Trust is everything in a friendship. You tell each other things that you don't tell anyone else, how you really feel about personal things" (Selman & Selman, 1979).

Peer acceptance   Age-mates who live in the same neighborhood or attend the same school or summer camp are likely to become friends and to cluster into groups of friends (Hartup, 1984). Although informal, these groups have obvious status hierarchies; leaders usually come to the fore and dominate much of what goes on within the group. Leaders are usually outgoing and energetic, witty and sociable, or have some specific skill—they may be good basketball players, for example (Hartup, 1970; 1983).

Group membership comes about in several different ways. Sometimes the leader will decide who will become a member of "his" or "her" group. At other times a group begins with an existing pair of friends, both of whom decide whether to include others in their activities. In a review of the research, Hartup (1983) points out that usually children tend to exclude a child who may seem to be odd or different in appearance, skills, or temperament; and they tend to accept children who are sociable, funny, or who get along with others.

Popular children   Psychologists have long examined peer-group formation and status ranking within groups, seeking to find out which children tend to be popular. Researchers have conducted observational studies to determine which children are often alone and which are sought out by others. They have also used a technique called **sociometry** (Hallinan, 1981), in which they typically ask children within an organized setting (for example, a classroom) to name the child or children who fit categories such as "best friend," "best liked by other children," or "least liked." On the basis of the answers, the researchers draw up a **sociogram,** or graphic representation of how each child in the group feels about the other children (see Figure 13.2). The sociogram helps determine which children are accepted by other chil-

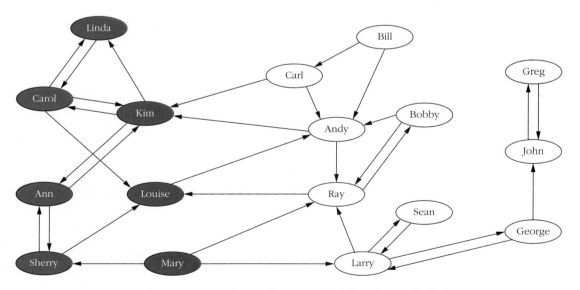

Figure 13.2   *This sociogram of a small group of children shows which child is the best liked and which child is the least liked.*

dren, which are accepted by few classmates, and which children no one accepts (Asher & Dodge, 1986). On the basis of this information, researchers then identify the attributes of popular and unpopular children.

Although no one quality makes a child popular, a number of qualities may contribute to an individual's popularity in various ways. Hartup (1970; 1983) and Dodge (1983) note that popular children are more outgoing, sociable, and friendly; they are also more socially sensitive and accepting of others, and more likely to cooperate with others. Putallaz's studies (1983) confirm the relationship between children's social skills and popularity.

Popularity is also related to IQ and academic achievement. Children prefer to be with moderately achieving children; they often stay away from those who are very intelligent and who aspire to do well in school as well as from those who do not do well academically. As indicated in Chapter 11, body build and other physical attributes such as good looks (Dodge, 1983) are also related to popularity; children with names other children rate as desirable are also likely to be popular, even when the names are ranked by a separate group of children who do not know the children personally (McDavid & Harari, 1966).

Although popularity is one factor children use to choose friends, other factors such as ethnic background and sex also come into play. Researchers have observed that children of like ethnic backgrounds sometimes tend to stick together; and they reject children who have friends outside their own ethnic group. For example, Janet Schofield (1980) reports a schoolgirl as saying: "They [the other black girls] get mad because you've made a white friend. . . . They say that blacks are supposed to have black friends and whites are supposed to have white friends."

There is also a tendency for children to separate themselves into groups of boys and girls, resulting in what researchers have labeled **sex cleavage** in peer relationships. Recall that even preschool children choose to play with age-mates of their own sex. This tendency intensifies as children grow older, peaking when they are about 10 years old so that girls play only with girls and boys play only with boys, except perhaps during some specific activities. Boys and girls also evidence sex differences in their patterns of interactions. Boys form relatively large groups, whereas girls are happy functioning in groups of about two, a tendency that persists in both sexes through adolescence (Elder & Hallinan, 1978).

Conformity Another characteristic of children at this time is their inclination to imitate one another and to conform to other children's behaviors. In an early study on peer conformity, Ruth Berenda (1950) found that 93% of the children between 7 and 10 years old in her study conformed to the judgment of the majority of their classmates rather than to that of their teacher. Other researchers have had similar results, noting that school-age children become increasingly likely to yield to peer pressure (Bixenstine, De Corte, & Bixenstine, 1976; Berndt, 1979) but not necessarily in all areas. When it comes to clothes, for example, they will do what their friends do. But in terms of basic values, they tend to follow their parents. When children are faced with conflicting advice—that of their parents or other adults and that of their peers—they side with their peers because they assume that "if everyone in my group is doing it, it must be right" (Rubin, 1980) and because they are anxious to gain and keep their friends' acceptance (Berndt, 1989).

A classic study by Muzafer Sherif and Carolyn Sherif (1964) demonstrated the pressure exerted by group members on one another to conform to the group's beliefs and norms. The researchers observed the ways in which social norms were established and enforced among two groups of 11- to 12-year-old boys at summer camp. Each group developed its own unique set of standards. For example, in one group the children came to value "being tough," a norm that apparently originated when the group leader accidentally hurt himself. He did not complain to any adult or to any of the group members but endured the pain and continued on with whatever tasks he had on hand. Perceiving his behavior as courageous, other group members began to act tough by cursing and bearing pain, characteristics that all the group members had to have. Members of the other group, on the other hand, came to value consideration of others; they even reflected this value in their insistence on the use of good language. In both groups, any member who did not uphold the group's standards for behavior and who did not do things "right" was either reprimanded or shunned by his peers. Thus, it did not take long for all the members to bring themselves in line with the group standards.

FEATURE

Social Skills Training

Have you ever noticed how some children get along with other children and adults and other children do not? Child development researchers believe that the problems some children experience in social relationships are due to their inability to understand how other people think and feel. To help children acquire the cognitive, emotional, and behavioral skills necessary to succeed in social relations, researchers have developed a number of promising programs.

For instance, Roger Weissberg designed the Yale/New Haven Social Problem Solving Project for children in middle schools (Caplan & Weissberg, 1989). Making use of such activities as role-playing, video and live modeling, and small-group discussions, children are taught to apply the following steps in responding to social problems:

1. Stop, calm down, and think before you act.
2. Describe the problem and how you feel about it.
3. Set a positive goal for yourself.
4. Think of lots of solutions.
5. Then go ahead and try the best plan of action.

Teachers engaged in the project also are trained to model adaptive ways of handling students' problems.

Evaluating the project, Weissberg and his colleagues concluded that: "[S]tudents who participated in 2 years of training showed significant gains, relative to students receiving no training, in their ability to generate more planful and cooperative solutions to hypothetical problems" (Elias & Weissberg, 1990, p. 182).

Working with preschoolers, Myrna Shure and George Spivak (1980) developed a program that teaches the children how to (1) find as many solutions as possible to social problems, (2) anticipate the consequences of their actions, and (3) be sensitive to the way other people might feel about a particular situation.

Shure and Spivak randomly divided the children into two groups. The experimental group received training in social skills and the control group did not. The researchers told both groups the same stories about a social situation or problem. For example, in one story a boy named Jim took another boy's ball without asking permission. The children were asked to answer such questions as: How would Jim's mother feel if she heard about her son? How would Jim's teacher feel?

Another story was about a girl named Susan who liked to play with a certain doll so much that she wouldn't give it up, even when another child wanted to have her turn with the doll. The children were asked, How does the girl who could not play with the doll feel?

The children's teachers rated the children in both groups before and after the experimental group had its training. The experimental-group children who were rated as poorly adjusted before the training sessions improved in their attitudes. Those who had no training showed no improvement. Thus it appears that children can be taught to negotiate successfully in their interactions with others and to think about how other people might feel.

The Family

Changes in the parent/child relationship   Although children become increasingly susceptible to peer pressure during middle childhood, they still remain very close to their parents and subject to their care and influence (Berndt, 1979; 1989). This is not to imply that the way parents and children interact remains the same. Indeed, researchers have found that parents spend about half as much time reading to, talking to, and playing with children ages 5 to 12 years as they do with children under 5 (Hill & Stafford, 1980). Different concerns arise as parents interact with school-age children. With preschoolers, parent/child interactions often focus on bedtime routines, temper, and fighting with siblings or peers. During middle childhood, however, new issues emerge, including responsibilities for household chores, payment for the chores (Newson & Newson, 1976), and their friends.

Maccoby (1984) also notes that parents spend less time supervising their children, expecting them to learn to monitor their own behavior; parents and children share responsibility for control of children's behavior. Maccoby refers to this shared responsibility as **coregulation,** noting that parents "exercise general supervisory control [over the school-age child] while [the child] begins to exercise moment to moment self-regulation" (p. 191). Coregulation exemplifies a cooperative arrangement between parents and children and, according to Maccoby (1984), it succeeds as long as there is clear communication; if children do not tell their parents where they are and what they are doing, or if parents are preoccupied or do not pay attention to their children, then the parents cannot help their children monitor their own behavior.

How children regard themselves is influenced in part by their interactions with their parents. Warm, nurturant relationships help children achieve independence and social competence.

Parents continue to play an important role during these years and later on as well (Collins, 1990). They exert an enormous influence on emerging self-esteem and provide guidance and support while allowing their children to do things on their own and to think for themselves (Hartup, 1979; Maccoby, 1984). Moreover, the children enjoy the company of their parents as much as they enjoy the company of peers (Youniss, 1980). They may sometimes resent some parental demands, but they recognize that they should obey (Maccoby, 1984). In addition, they are responsive to their parents' involvement in their activities and encouraged by it. Recall from Chapter 12 that the parental involvement in school life is an important factor in academic success. Parents who help their children and encourage them to do homework and who participate in school activities, such as parent/teacher conferences, have children who enjoy school more than other children and who score higher on achievement tests.

A warm, nurturant relationship between children and their parents is similarly important and helps the children achieve independence and social competence. Researchers have found that when parents are warm and accepting of their children, and when they appropriately discipline them and direct their behavior and activities, while recognizing their need for independence, the children are secure and sociable in their relations with other adults and children (Armentrout & Burger, 1972). Children who have a cool or hostile relationship with their parents, or whose parents are inattentive or hostile toward them, are more likely to lack social skills and engage in delinquent behavior (Rohner, 1975).

Realities of family life   The parents' impact on children's development is so crucial that it is important to consider some realities of contemporary life that may interfere with effective parenting.

First, in a large proportion of families both the mother and father work. As indicated in previous chapters, this is the result of the progressive influx of married women into the labor force. The greatest increase in recent years has occurred among married women with children. For example, U.S. government statistics indicate that about 45% of married women with children were in the labor force in 1975; by 1988 this figure had risen to 71% (U.S. Department of Labor, 1988b). Although many women work outside the home because they enjoy their careers, many others have to earn money to meet their family's financial needs. As Levitan and Conway (1990) note, in today's economy "most families need more than one income to make ends meet" (p. 11).

Research on the two-provider family has focused on the effects of the mothers' employment on their children's development and on the family's well-being. Researchers have conducted studies to determine the potential benefits and drawbacks of having two earners in the family. They found that although both the wife and husband may enjoy working and although the whole family may benefit from the money earned, the strains of having to meet the obligations of job and family are often too difficult for many individuals to handle (Piotrkowski, 1979; Baruch & Barnett, 1987). The Rapoports (1976), who outlined several problems faced by two-provider families, noted that working spouses experience *mental overload,* which can occur when the demands of job and family are contradictory and excessive and which lead to psychological strain. They also reported that often spouses in two-provider families have difficulty meeting the expectations of their family and friends as well as their obligations to them. These husbands and wives have little time in the evenings and on weekends for socializing and relaxed, entertaining family activities.

They must try to integrate and schedule childrearing to harmonize with the demands and expectations of their work. This is especially true of women. In dual-earner families fathers may share in household chores and childrearing to some degree, but in most of these families the mother handles most domestic tasks, whether she works full- or part-time and regardless of the demands of her job (Pleck, 1984). She has to remember what groceries the family needs and which children need new shoes or school supplies. She also has to determine what to do when she has to work and one of the children is sick.

The effects on children   How does being in a two-provider family affect children? The effects vary according to the children's age, which is one reason we discuss these matters in several chapters of this book. During infancy, children are totally dependent on their mother's care and are vulnerable to being separated from her during the day. But during middle childhood, they become more self-reliant. They still need the love, guidance, and support of their parents. But because their

Corporate Support of Family Life

When Sylvia Galvaro goes to work each morning, she drops her 11-year-old child at the before- and after-school child care program and takes her 3-year-old with her to the child care center in downtown Stamford. Sylvia is glad to have child care so close to work. Indeed, as director of public relations for a large corporation, she has been involved in efforts to convince her bosses that providing employee child care would mean less stressed, more productive workers and, ultimately, better business. The firm Sylvia works for could not support on-site child care; but over a five-year period, it formed a consortium of other businesses, and together, they paid for renovating a downtown building to make it suitable for child care and hiring a management firm to operate it. Employees pay for child care according to their income; and there are subsidies for those who cannot afford the full amount.

Our society was not prepared for the influx of women into the work force and does not have the support systems that families need if they are to function optimally both at home and at work. As a result, many employees like Sylvia have had to ask their employers for assistance. Businesses in general have been slow to respond to the needs of parents in the workplace. Corporations do not understand that their employees have other priorities besides their jobs, that they have family responsibilities as well (Zigler & Finn, 1982; Kanter, 1977). But as more and more women enter the work force, both employers and employees have had to investigate ways the business world can support family life (Schein,

1990; National Report on Work and Family, 1988; Trczinski & Finn-Stevenson, 1991), such as child care, part-time work, flex time, maternity and family leave, executive transfers, and spousal involvement in career planning.

Although the business world is not yet helping families on the scale that is required, some progress has been made. About 3000 U.S. corporations (up 50% from 1984) have either instituted on-site child care or have helped their employees locate child care. In some cases, the business also pays part of the employees' child care costs (Friedman, 1987).

Some companies allow flexible work schedules, permitting workers to determine when to start and finish their day (Steriel, 1979). Whereas the traditional work schedule is from 8:00 to 4:00 or 9:00 to 5:00, workers on flex time may start the day at 7:00 and finish at 3:00. Flex time enables them to schedule their time to minimize friction between family needs and work needs (Brett & Yogev, 1988; Kuhne & Blair, 1978). However, flex time does not always work out. With personnel working at different times, it is difficult to schedule meetings and to communicate with or supervise employees (Walton, 1979). Redesigning the workplace to accommodate the needs of families is not simple. But with the expectation that women will make up about half the work force, many corporate executives and business owners are realizing that work and family are not separate institutions, and ways have to be found to integrate them.

school and social activities take up a considerable amount of their time (Hill & Stafford, 1980), their parents' absence during the day does not necessarily have a negative influence. Furthermore, at this age children can understand why their mother has to work. All the same, many children express dissatisfaction because they miss the attention of their mothers, who often feel the same way. A national survey found that school-age children complained that their parents did not spend enough time with them (General Mills American Family Report, 1977). In the same survey mothers reported that their most precious commodity was time; they felt they had too little time to spend with their children. Several interview studies also noted mothers' concerns about not spending enough time with their children (Emmons et al., 1987; Baruch & Barnett, 1987).

Although some children may feel deprived of their parents' attention when both parents are working, studies reveal that maternal employment is generally associated with positive consequences for the children. Several researchers have found that daughters of working mothers show less stereotyped attitudes and expectations about appropriate behaviors for men and women than daughters whose mothers do not work (Zaslow, 1989; Lamb, 1982; Gold & Andres, 1978a). According to the researchers, maternal employment contributes to girls' academic and occupational competence later in life; daughters whose mothers work get good grades in school and often aspire to careers outside the home (Hoffman, 1974).

However, Eleanor Maccoby (1984) and Lois Hoffman (1989) point out that there are limitations to the research on the effects of maternal employment in part because only a small percentage of the studies are related to school-age children (most current studies focus on younger children). Many of the studies do not mention whether the mother is working full- or part-time.

Girls seem to benefit from having a working mother. But the same is not always true for boys, especially boys from working-class homes whose relationship with the father seems to be undermined by having a working mother (Lamb, 1982). Working-class families tend to hold the traditional view that men are responsible for providing economic support for their families (Greenberger et al., 1988). When the mothers in these families work, it is usually because the father has a low-paying job or is not working. Thus, the son may look down on his father because his mother has to work and because the father has failed in his obligation to the family. In a Canadian study of 223 10-year-olds (Gold & Andres, 1978b), boys of working-class families were nervous and evidenced disturbed relationships with their fathers; they were also disliked at school and had low math and language-achievement scores.

In middle-class homes, however, the mother's employment is not associated with particular strains on the father/son relationship. Some studies found no negative consequences at all on middle-class boys, but other studies found that middle-class boys whose mothers work have poor school achievement records (Gold & Andres, 1978a; Hoffman, 1989). This discrepancy in the research does not necessarily mean that either set of findings is correct. As Lamb (1982) points out, how maternal employment affects any child—boy or girl from a working-class or middle-class home—depends on many factors that vary from family to family. One important factor is how the mother herself feels about her work. Children whose mothers feel good about their work and who enjoy working are likely to benefit more than children whose mothers are dissatisfied with their roles in life. Indeed, satisfied mothers, whether they work or not, seem to have happy, well-adjusted children (Etaugh, 1974), whereas dissatisfied mothers, even if they do not work, seem to influence their children negatively (Hoffman, 1963).

Children in Self-Care

Latchkey Children

To what extent are mothers satisfied with their dual role as mothers and workers? This depends in part on the availability of adequate child care and on how children fare when their parents are working. Several studies and reviews of the research found that mothers become concerned and stressful when their children are unsupervised while they are at work (Hoffman, 1989; Emmons et al., 1987; Pilling & Pringle, 1978). Unfortunately, because of a lack of adequate child care facilities for school-age children, this is a reality for many mothers who may have to leave their children unattended for several hours each day before and after school (Zigler & Lang, 1990). It is difficult to ascertain exactly how many children are home alone, because parents are often embarrassed and tend to hide it. But according to reports, at least 2 to 4 million children between the ages of 6 and 13 stay home alone before and after school and during school vacations (Children's Defense Fund, 1990).

At one time people referred to these boys and girls as *latchkey children* because they often carry their house key on a string around their neck. Today, they are called *children in self-care*. These boys and girls, left to their own resources, suffer neglect during the critical hours of the day. They return from school at around 3:00, but their parents do not get home until 5:00 or 6:00, or even later in some cases. And these children are also alone for an hour or two each morning, if their parents leave for work early, and during school vacations.

Maternal employment in itself does not have a negative effect on children. However, difficulties may arise if children are left to care for themselves during critical hours of the day.

The effects of being left alone may vary depending on the child's age, whether the child has access to neighbors, and other factors. It is not surprising, therefore, that researchers disagree about the possible effects of being left alone before and after school. Some researchers argue that children left to their own resources acquire a sense of independence and early maturity; thus, being left alone before and after school might have beneficial effects (Korchin, 1981). In a series of relatively small studies, some researchers found no differences between supervised children and children in self-care with respect to their self-esteem and social adjustment (Rodman & Cole, 1987). But a recent national study comparing children who are supervised with those in self-care appears to have settled the controversy. This study (Richardson et al., 1989), which involved 5000 eighth-grade students, clearly indicated that children left unsupervised before and after school were more likely than supervised boys and girls to take drugs and abuse alcohol. Among the variables considered by the researchers, the presence or lack of supervision was the most predictive of drug and alcohol abuse.

Numerous other studies indicate that although school-age children are capable of taking care of their physical needs, they are still vulnerable to harm. In studies analyzing house fires, for example, researchers repeatedly find that as many as one out of six residential fires involves an unattended child (Baker & Waller, 1989; Smock, 1977). In some cases these children become victims of sexual assaults and other crimes, and they may encounter burglars (Finkelhor, 1979). Garbarino (1980) further notes that while children left alone in urban areas are vulnerable to the high crime rates associated with city neighborhoods, unattended children in rural areas also face problems as a result of their isolation.

Unattended children also often have to deal with emotional problems; many of them feel isolated, lonely, and afraid. Lynette and Thomas Long's study (1983) of children who have been or are now left alone while their parents work finds that because of their parents' concern for their safety, many children have to stay alone inside their homes. Since they cannot have other children with them, they do not have much opportunity to play with their peers. According to the Longs, most children are afraid of being left alone—a finding documented in other studies (Whitbread, 1982) and in an informal survey conducted by the editors of *Sprint,* a language arts magazine for 10- to 12-year-olds. The magazine editors asked children to respond to the question: "Think of a situation that is scary to you. How do you handle your fear?" Expecting to hear that the youngsters were afraid of snakes or of getting a poor report card, the editors were surprised when 70% of the respondents answered that they were most afraid of being left alone at home. How do they handle their fear? Some venture into the streets; those who do not like to leave their house or do not have permission to go outside entertain themselves by watching television, playing a musical instrument, or playing video games (School-Age Child Care Project, 1984).

School-Age Child Care

Many parents, who are well aware of their children's fears, express concern at having to leave them alone. Their concern increases when the children are on vacation or have to stay home all day because of sickness. Yet many parents are simply unable to take time off from their jobs to be at home with their children.

Unlike many of the social problems discussed in this book, there is an affordable solution to the problem of children in self-care. Instead of leaving these children alone at home, we can provide them with before- and after-school care pro-

In response to the child care crisis, many schools throughout the United States have implemented the School of the 21st Century program, which provides school-based care to children from infancy to age 12, and family support services.

grams. To do so, we would not need to make massive investments of public funds or to undertake the large-scale construction of new facilities. Wouldn't you agree that the logical place for such child care is the public school building (See Zigler, 1987; Zigler & Finn-Stevenson, 1989)? Schools in numerous communities are already providing the space, while the parents are paying for the personnel required to staff the programs. Because all the parents of enrolled children share in the payments, the cost is relatively low.

How do such programs get started? Some schools contract with community-based organizations to set up and operate the programs. Other schools provide school-age child care as a part of the comprehensive child care and family program known as the School of the 21st Century. Developed in response to the child care crisis, this program exists in school districts in several states; in fact, it has been the centerpiece of school reform legislation in certain states. In Kentucky, for example, the School Reform Act of 1990 mandates that schools provide school-age child care along with other family support services. In Hawaii schools must also provide before- and after-school programs to all children in need of child care. In Connecticut legislation has provided state funding for school-age child care programs implemented within the context of school-based Family Resource Centers.

In part, the actions of state legislators and educators in developing school-age child care programs stem from concerns about child development and reflect indications that parents want schools to extend their traditional mission to include child care. In a national survey of parents (Louis Harris Associates, 1989), 62% expressed the opinion that public schools should offer child care services. Although an increasing number of states are addressing this need, we need to develop many more programs to meet the demand.

Single-Parent Families

The need for after-school care is especially acute for single-parent families in which the only parent is almost always working. Currently, 1 out of every 4 children lives in a single-parent family (among blacks, it is 1 child out of 2) (National Center for Children in Poverty, 1990; U.S. Bureau of the Census, 1987b). Single-parent households occur as a result of divorce, separation, desertion, death, or out-of-state employment. Sometimes they come about through single-parent adoptions or because the mother is unmarried (Eiduson et al., 1982). Single-parent families also differ in their resources, motivation, and ability to function as a viable unit. Many such families may not be able to meet all the needs of the children and the parents.

Single-parent families do share some common characteristics, however. Women head about 90% of them, and most of these families are the outcome of divorce (Hetherington, Stanley-Hagan, & Anderson, 1989). As such, the families are in a state of transition when parents and children must adjust to changes in family relationships and responsibilities while learning to cope with the stress and pain of divorce.

School-age children are better able to cope with divorce than younger children. Schoolchildren are able to understand that they are not to blame for the family breakup. They are also more aware of their feelings and more open about admitting their sadness (Hetherington, Cox, & Cox, 1982). Nevertheless, they feel abandoned by their parents and are angry at their parents' decision to break up the family (Wallerstein & Kelly, 1980). They also evidence behavioral problems in school, often not performing as well academically as they did before the divorce (Guidubaldi et al., 1983). These children may also exhibit behavioral problems at home. This is especially true of boys, who tend to compete with the mother for the leadership role in the family, often challenging her authority over them and their siblings (Hetherington, Cox, & Cox, 1979). Although many of these problems persist for some time after the divorce (Guidubaldi et al., 1983), the negative effects of the divorce will diminish if the parents maintain a good relationship with each other and if the father remains involved in the day-to-day lives of his children (Hess & Camara, 1979).

Poverty

Another characteristic of many single-parent families is poverty. Several recent reports on poverty in the United States (National Center for Children in Poverty, 1990; U.S. Bureau of the Census, 1988; Bane & Ellwood, 1989) show that we have more poor children today than in the mid-1960s; in fact, poverty among families with children has grown deeper and more widespread in the last 20 years. About 13.9 million children—22.2% of Americans under the age of 18—are from poor families. If present trends continue, the number of children living in poverty in this country will increase.

What is the cause of this situation? Partly we can attribute it to the increase in the number of single-parent households, but there are other causes as well. For example, changes in the federal assistance programs for the poor have reduced the number of needy families eligible to receive food stamps and other government assistance (McLoyd, 1989; Garwood et al., 1989). These families still need help, but they can no longer receive it. In addition, our economy seems to have become less effective in reducing poverty. More and more families with children have fallen below the official poverty level. In 1968 the poorest families had an average of 91% of the income needed for their basic needs; in 1983 these families had only 60% of the income they needed. This means that the children and adults often had to go without food, health care, and other basic necessities.

Who are the poor children in America? According to the reports cited earlier, the poor child tends to come from a single-parent family and is likely to be Hispanic or black. Over one-third (38.2%) of all Hispanic children and close to one-half (46.7%) of all black children are poor and likely to remain so for a long time. Whereas for most white children, poverty is short-lived (about ten months) and associated with changes in their parents' marital status or family earnings, for the Hispanic or black child, poverty can last throughout childhood.

The effects of poverty are widespread; they include malnutrition, poor health care, and assaults on the child's emerging self-esteem (Isralewitz & Singer, 1986). This is especially true during the school-age years when children continually compare themselves to others in terms of looks, skills, achievement, and activities. Poor children have fewer possessions than other children, they may not be able to take sports or music lessons and thus they have fewer opportunities to develop their skills and abilities. As a result, they may regard themselves as inferior to others, a feeling that may hinder them later in life (Keniston, 1977).

It is not surprising, therefore, that research studies show that poor children are more likely to have mental health problems. Reviewing research on the effects on children of the family's loss of income, McLoyd (1989) notes that poor children are more depressed, lonely, and emotionally sensitive than better-off youngsters. In addition, poor children are less sociable, often fail in school, and tend to believe that they have little control over their future. They often blame their poor performance on external factors such as a bad teacher (Bryant, 1974). Their parents, too, feel that they have no control over their own or their children's future. Often these parents are unable to effectively rear their children. This does not mean that they care less for their children than other parents. It is simply that the conditions of life have so overburdened them that they have only a limited ability to provide the warmth, caring, and nurturance that children need (McLanahan, 1988).

Although poor children are more likely to be at developmental risk, the negative influences of poverty vary with its depth and duration, with the parents' physical and mental health, and with the availability of social support (National Center for Children in Poverty, 1990).

Helping Children Cope with Stress

How do these difficult conditions impact children? Many are latchkey children or members of single-parent households or are growing up in dire poverty. Thus, all too many of our children have to cope with severe life stresses. All the same, most youngsters manage to survive their difficult conditions. Somehow they find ways to compensate for their problems and even seem happy (Murphy & Moriarty, 1976).

Not all children are so fortunate, however. Many other children are unable to cope with their problems. They suffer from depression and may engage in bad behavior at home or in school. Numerous studies reveal the prevalence of childhood depression. An increasing number of children are sad and unhappy; many exhibit such withdrawal symptoms as boredom and difficulty in relating to other children or adults (Committee for the Institute of Medicine, 1989; Tuma, 1989). As Table 13.2 indicates, these symptoms often stem from chronic, stress-producing

A caring adult (parent, grandparent, teacher, or neighbor), can help children offset the negative effects of stress.

difficulties in their families, such as unemployment, marital discord, or divorce (Garrison, 1984; Tuma, 1989).

Rutter (1979b), who studied the effects of stress on children's emotional stability and mental health, identified several family variables strongly associated with

TABLE 13.2 Environmental Risk Factors and Children's Mental Health Problems

Environmental risk factor	Prevalence of risk factor in general population	Prevalence of disorders in child population[a]
Poverty and minority status	13.8 million[b]	11.8% > average[c]

Parental psychopathology
  Affective disorders of parents
	9%–25% females,
	  5%–12% males[d]
		40%[e]

Schizophrenic parent	0.2%–1%[d]	10 times the average[f]
Alcoholic parent	13%[d]	
Maltreatment	1 million[g]	
Teenage parenting (14–19-year-olds)	21%[h]	
Premature birth/low birthweight	6%–7% total live births[i]	3.7 million (1985)[j]
Parental divorce	20%[j]	
Major physical illness	⅓ to ½[k]	
Outpatient pediatrician visits	5%–12%[l]	

[a]All environmental risk factors are associated with high prevalence of mental health problems in children. Information in this column indicates more specific information about prevalence of mental health problems in children. [b]U.S. Congress (1985). [c]Gould, Wunsch-Hitzlg, & Dohrenwend (1981). [d]American Psychiatric Association (1987). [e]Ovaschel, Weissman, & Padian (1981). [f]Gottesman (1978). [g]U.S. Department of Health and Human Services (1981). [h]Sugar (1984). [i]National Center for Health Statistics (1987). [j]U.S. Department of Commerce (1982). [k]Wright (1975). [l]Schuman, Kramer, & Mitchell (1985).

Source: "Mental health services for children," by J.M. Tuma, *American Psychologist,* February 1989, pp. 188–199. Copyright 1989 by the American Psychological Association. Reprinted by permission.

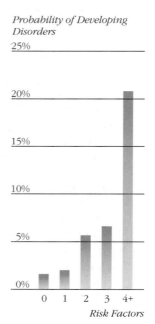

Probability of Developing
Disorders

Risk Factors

Figure 13.3 *Multiplicity of risk factors and child psychiatric disorders. The more risk factors children are subjected to, the higher the probability that they will develop psychiatric disorders.*
Source: From "Protective Factors in Children's Responses to Stress and Disadvantages," by M. Rutter, 1979, in *Primary Prevention of Psychopathology: Social Competence in Children,* edited by Martha Whalen Kent and Jon E. Rolf, pp. 49–74. By permission of University Press of New England. © 1979 by Vermont Conference on the Primary Prevention of Psychopathology.

behavioral and psychiatric disorders; they include severe marital discord, low social status, overcrowding or large family size, and maternal psychiatric disorders (see Figure 13.3). He found that children exposed to one of these risk factors were no more likely to develop psychiatric disorders than other children. But when the children experienced two or more risk factors simultaneously, for example, a bitter divorce battle and poverty after the divorce, their chances of developing a psychiatric problem more than doubled.

Since many children experience multiple stresses, why do some children have behavioral problems while others do not? Garmezy and Rutter (1983), who studied this issue, note that psychologists do not yet understand the sources of invulnerable children's strengths. Although the children's personality no doubt has much to do with their ability to withstand stress, other factors such as the influence of a caring adult—a parent, some other relative, a teacher, or a neighbor—can help offset the negative effects of stress, as can the children's ability to understand some of the problems confronting them and their parents. Rutter (1979) also notes that many children have the inner strength to fight the psychological problems arising from stress. To use and rely on this strength, they often need the help and support of just one close, understanding adult. It is apparent, therefore, that just as support services can help facilitate the lives of many parents (Albee, 1980), such services can also help children cope with the difficult realities of contemporary life.

Summary

During middle childhood, children experience tremendous advances in social cognition; that is, the ability to understand people and think about social relations. They become less egocentric and show an increasing ability to take another person's point of view. They thus become better able to infer another person's feelings and thoughts and also to recognize that other people are evaluating their behavior.

These advances in social cognition enable children to develop in their interactions with other children and adults and to reason about moral problems. Moral development—the process of learning to accept standards of right and wrong as guides to behavior—occurs gradually. According to Piaget, the child's cognitive growth influences moral development. Piaget found that as children grow, they develop an enhanced understanding of rules. They begin to obey rules, realizing that they are created to benefit everyone.

Elaborating on Piaget's work, Kohlberg proposed six (later revised to five) stages in moral development corresponding to the cognitive levels. He identified these levels by presenting children with moral dilemmas and studying their responses. Kohlberg was not interested in whether the children thought a particular action was right or wrong, only in the reasoning they used. Their justifications revealed how children think about right and wrong at different ages. Although many child experts consider Kohlberg's theory useful, others note that how a child or an adult thinks about a moral dilemma does not necessarily reflect how he or she actually behaves. In making a distinction between moral knowledge and moral behavior, researchers note that children learn how to behave by watching their parents. Youngsters acquire a conscience and begin to monitor their own behavior if their parents punish them for doing wrong and reward them for doing right.

During middle childhood, children also advance in developing their self-concept. They construct a more refined and complex picture of themselves as unique individuals, and they also develop self-esteem; that is, a judgment about how worthy they are. The child with good self-esteem believes she is a capable individual, and she is eager to learn and is willing to try to do many things. The child with low self-esteem believes he is inadequate and develops a sense of inferiority. How children feel about themselves usually reflects their parents' reactions to them. Children are also influenced by teachers and peers. Peer interactions in particular are important, enabling children to gradually acquire some independence from family life.

Although the child increasingly accepts her peers' suggestions, the relationship with her parents is still important; she remains responsive to their care and encouragement. Unfortunately, parents in many families are unable to provide appropriate care, because they are overwhelmed with responsibilities and stresses. This often occurs in families where both parents are working or in single-parent families. One problem that often arises is the lack of suitable before- and after-school care facilities, which means that many children are left alone for several hours each day. Unlike many other social problems, however, we could solve the problem of children in self-care inexpensively by creating special programs for them at school.

VI Adolescence

14 Physical Development During Adolescence

15 Cognitive Development During Adolescence

16 Social and Emotional Development During Adolescence

I f we had to decide what period of our life was the most challenging and complicated, most of us would probably say adolescence. During that time we went through many changes in the way we think, look, and behave. We moved from the secure and dependent life of a child to the insecure and independent life of an adult.

In preparing for adulthood, we had to establish our own identity; we tested who we were and what we could do. We also had to confront many questions that only we could answer and make many decisions only we could make. These answers and decisions are part and parcel of the adolescent experience. They could never be resolved all at once; in fact, some are resolved long after adolescence.

14 Physical Development During Adolescence

What Is Adolescence?

Puberty, the physiological event that culminates in sexual maturity, brings dramatic changes during the first years of adolescence. Adolescents rapidly become taller, their body proportions change, and they undergo sexual differentiation. Their sex organs enlarge to become capable of reproduction, and the secondary sex characteristics appear. These changes can also have a significant impact on adolescents' psychological development, because many adolescents are concerned over reaching sexual maturity.

Thus, adolescence is a challenging and difficult time for teenagers and their parents. Because some adolescents are prone to emotional outbursts, drastic changes in mood, and fits of acute depression, they often have a hard time getting along with their fathers and mothers.

Why are so many adolescents rebellious and moody? Is this the result of factors in our society? Or can we attribute this tendency to the biological changes of adolescence? We will attempt to answer these questions in this chapter, but keep in mind that researchers do not agree on the answers. In fact, some point out that for many young people adolescence is no more stressful than any of the other transitional periods in the life cycle. So before taking up the physical and psychological changes that occur, let us examine psychologists' views of this period. As you will see, they even disagree about what adolescence is and when it ends.

Adolescence as a Cultural Invention

It is not easy to define adolescence. Knowing when it begins is no problem because puberty marks this point as a rule. But when does adolescence end? When does the adolescent become an adult? There are several reasons for this difficulty in defining adolescence and deciding when it ends. First, adolescence is really a cultural invention. Only fairly recently has it been regarded as a separate period of life that is different from both childhood and adulthood. Recall from Chapter 2 that before the 17th century, the concept of adolescence did not exist. Society expected children to assume full adult responsibilities at an early age, and they were given the rights and freedoms adults enjoyed. Thus, when children started to work at age 7, they could also freely participate in adult games and pastimes.

The concept of childhood began to gain more meaning in the 17th century. However, adolescence as a special period of life did not become a reality until the late 18th century (Bakan, 1972). We can link several societal conditions to the emergence of this new concept of adolescence:

1. The increased need for specialized skills and training to satisfy the job requirements of an industrial society forced educators to expand the high school curriculum to meet these requirements (Elder, 1975).
2. On a more formal level, the concept of adolescence received support from three major social movements: compulsory education, child labor legislation, and special legal procedures developed for youth (Elder & Caspi, 1990; Bakan, 1972). These movements separated youths from adults and emphasized adolescents' dependence on adult care and guidance.
3. Recent developments have made adolescence an even longer period of life (Montemayor, Adams, & Gullotta, 1990). As noted in Chapter 11, children today become physically mature earlier and thus enter adolescence sooner. Some

Adolescence was not considered a special period of life until the late 18th century, when compulsory education, child labor legislation, and legal procedures developed specifically for young people highlighted the distinction between youth and adulthood.

observers point out that children also mature earlier in a sociocultural sense because they are exposed to the adult aspects of life much earlier than the previous generation (Elkind, 1981; Winn, 1983).

4. Because society today requires more and more education, adolescents remain dependent longer on parental care.

As a result, young people today do not assume adult roles and responsibilities as early as previous generations did. Hence the difficulty of determining just when adolescence ends. For our discussion, let us define adolescence as the time spanning the years between 12 and 18. Many of us define adolescence according to chronological age, so past age 18, we do not refer to an individual as an adolescent. However, since many individuals go on to college and remain dependent on their parents beyond the age of 18, adolescence may last well into the twenties.

The Passage to Adulthood

The duration of adolescence causes problems for some teens who have to live with a mature body but immature social and psychological characteristics, according to society. In addition, adolescents do not receive the psychological support needed to begin assuming adult roles. Some other societies do not have an adolescence. The child becomes an adult at a certain age, usually in conjunction with **puberty rites;** that is, ceremonies that mark the individual's assumption of new, more adult roles. Although fewer societies hold formal puberty rites, they do still exist in some societies. Puberty rites are frequently more complex for boys and include painful tests of endurance and courage. For girls, the ceremonies are related to matters pertaining to sex and marriage and center around the onset of menstruation (Conger, 1973). Worthman (1986), who studied the cultural environments and social expectations of adolescents in several societies, notes, for example, that the Kikuyu in Kenya mark the onset of puberty in girls with ceremonies serving as initiation rites.

These ceremonies and puberty rites have an important psychological function: they provide children with some notion of what society expects at this new stage of life and also help deflect anxiety (Powers, Hauser, & Kilmer, 1989). In our society, however, the passage from childhood to adulthood is longer, and the point at which the child is regarded as an adult is different for different purposes and in different places:

> All our own society has in a way of institutionalized patterns of recognizing the adolescent's increasing independence is a variety of laws, and these are often internally inconsistent. . . . For example, there are significant variations from state to state in the age at which a young person can drink alcohol, drive a car, marry, and own property. One of the ironies of our time is that until 1971, young people who were considered old enough to do most of the fighting for their elders . . . were not considered mature enough to vote. [Conger, 1973]

LEARNING FROM OTHER CULTURES

Sexual Scripts

Young Americans today are surrounded by sexual suggestions—in our advertisements, films, and TV programs. Riding on the subway or walking through the park, it's hard not to notice the large numbers of teenagers "smooching" or "heavy petting." More and more American teens engage regularly in sexual intercourse. As a result, many girls become pregnant at an early age. Educators, religious leaders, and parents have tried to prevent teen pregnancies by trying to delay teenage sexual activity, but they have not had much success. Some observers may blame the wealth of sexual stimuli contained in the media for the increased sexual activity among teens. Others, however, contend that since girls are becoming sexually mature so much earlier, we cannot realistically expect them to delay sexual activity until marriage (Frisch, 1974; 1978).

Whiting, Burbank, and Ratner (1986) point out that just as menarche marks the onset of female sexual maturity, a wedding legitimates sexual intercourse and motherhood. They refer to the interval between these two events as *maidenhood*. The accompanying table indicates that the duration of maidenhood differs from country to country. For example, it is only 1.8 years in Bangladesh, whereas in the United States it is 7.8 years. Obviously premarital pregnancy is not a problem in societies where early marriages occur. According to the researchers, even societies where a prolonged maidenhood is the rule can minimize premarital pregnancy by preparing a script for sexual activity. Its purpose would be to let boys and girls know what society expects of them and to give them a context within which they can have a sexual relationship.

How would this work out in practice? Whiting, Burbank, and Ratner (1986) studied the Kikuyu among whom maidenhood is relatively long (about five years). Although the Kikuyu do not permit sexual intercourse until marriage, they encourage premarital sex as long as the boy and girl avoid penetration. The Kikuyu expect boys and girls to sleep together and to change partners frequently, but only in the context of ceremonies that involve teaching girls how to sleep with a young man without getting pregnant—a practice known as *Ngweko*. The teachers are members of the next older group of girls. On the basis of their experience, the instructors tell the girls how to keep their pubic apron on while sleeping with their legs entwined with those of their partners. Boys receive similar instruction from male models.

Duration of Maidenhood and Ages at Menarche and Marriage

Country	Duration of maidenhood	Mean age of menarche	Mean age of marriage
Japan	11.8	12.9	24.7
Switzerland	10.7	13.1	23.8
Sweden	10.1	13.1	23.2
Hong Kong (Chinese)	9.5	12.8	22.3
Netherlands	9.8	13.4	23.2
England and Wales	9.8	13.0	21.8
Finland	9.6	13.2	22.8
France	9.3	13.2	22.5
Belgium	9.2	13.1	22.3
Norway	9.0	13.2	22.2
Denmark	9.0	13.2	22.2
New Zealand	8.7	13.0	21.7
Australia	8.5	13.2	21.7
Canada	8.6	13.1	21.7
Israel	8.2	13.2	21.4
Hungary	7.6	13.4	20.7
Singapore	7.8	12.7	20.5
United States	7.8	12.8	20.6
Czechoslovakia	6.9	14.2	21.1
Malaysian Chinese	6.4	14.2	20.6
Iraq	6.1	14.0	20.1
Turkey	6.0	13.2	19.2
Iran	5.8	13.3	19.1
Tunis	5.2	14.0	19.2
Pakistan	3.8	13.9	17.7
Bangladesh (Hindu)	2.7	15.9	18.6
India	2.4	14.4	16.8
Bangladesh (Muslim)	1.8	15.6	17.4

Source: Reprinted with permission from Jane B. Lancaster and Beatrix A. Hamburg, Editors. *School-Age Pregnancy and Parenthood: Biosocial Dimensions* (New York: Aldine de Gruyter). Copyright © 1986 by the Social Science Research Council.

Because the Kikuyu value sexual attractiveness highly and attach a higher bride price to it, they encourage girls to sleep frequently with boys. But both girls and boys clearly understand that they must not touch their partners' genitals. To do so would make them "polluted." Kikuyu adolescents realize that their parents and the elders would ostracize them if they failed to adhere to these rules.

Storm and Stress or Cultural Expectations?

Our inability as a society to arrive at a consensus about when adulthood begins means that adolescents, while undergoing changes that render them physically adults, must face the problem of assuming independence "not with the solidarity of the expectations of adult society, but with their apparent confusion and divisiveness" (Conger, 1973). Coupled with our society's failure to provide psychological support in the transition from childhood to adulthood, this uncertainty could well result in emotional difficulties. Thus, social observers have characterized adolescence as a time of deviation, rebelliousness (Eichorn, 1975), and emotional turmoil (Hall, 1904).

The behavioral difficulties of adolescents—some of whom are indeed rebellious, unruly, and overly emotional—have been the subject of theories and research for many years. Researchers once thought that these problems affected all adolescents, but this view is now changing (Powers, Hauser, & Kilmer, 1989). There is evidence that adolescence is an emotionally distressing period for some individuals. However, some questions remain: Do all adolescents experience emotional turmoil? Are these emotional problems related to cultural factors, or are they the outcome of biological changes occurring during adolescence?

G. Stanley Hall (1904) first named the phenomenon of *adolescence,* seeing it as a period signaling life beyond childhood but before the adoption of adult responsibilities. He believed that the adolescent's behavior is the outcome of biological determinants and described adolescence as a time of storm and stress during which young people experience vacillating and contradictory emotions. Many psychoanalytic theorists share this view, believing that we should regard as abnormal adolescents who do not have emotional problems and who are good and considerate toward their parents (Freud, 1968). However, Margaret Mead (1961; original publication, 1928) challenged this view, using evidence from her anthropological studies of adolescents in Samoa. She argued that adolescence does not have to be a time of stress. Indeed, because she found that in Samoa adolescence is a relatively trouble-free period, she asserted that the storm and stress associated with adolescence in our society has its roots in cultural not biological determinants.

Some researchers have questioned the validity of Mead's contentions because of methodological concerns with her research (Freeman, 1983). Still others have challenged the view that adolescence is an especially turbulent period because of biological forces. Kurt Lewin (1939) described the adolescent's behavior as similar to that of any person in a minority group. He noted that "to some extent behavior symptomatic for the marginal man [which Lewin defines as the underprivileged individual] can be found in the adolescent. He, too, is oversensitive, easily shifted from one extreme to the other . . . he knows he is not fully accepted by the adult." Bandura (1964) focuses on our expectations of adolescents, noting that:

> [I]f society labels adolescents as "teenagers" and expects them to be rebellious, unpredictable, sloppy, and wild in their behavior, and if this picture is repeatedly reinforced by the mass media, such cultural expectations may well force adolescents into the role of rebels.

Studies conducted in the last two decades further indicate that child psychologists have made too much of the stress of adolescence (Powers, Hauser, & Kilmer, 1989). Some researchers now note that although some adolescents are emotional, erratic, and rebellious, many others are calm and predictable. The point is that adolescence may not be any more or less stressful than other developmental periods (Collins, 1990; Adams, 1980). Several studies support this view. Offer and Offer (1975), who studied a group of adolescent boys, found that less than a third experienced a turbulent, crisis-filled adolescence; for the rest, adolescence was either a period of self-assurance and mutual respect between them and their parents or a period of relative calm coupled with some episodes of anger and frequent mood changes. Offer, Ostrov, Howard, and Atkinson (1988) examined adolescents' self-image in ten countries. They found that at least 73% of teens from the United States, Australia, Bangladesh, Hungary, Israel, Turkey, and West Germany have a good self-image and are emotionally healthy.

Even though the emotional turmoil of adolescence is not universal, the impact of physical growth and puberty is indeed significant for some individuals and can influence psychological development. Therefore, the question we need to ask ourselves is, What kind of physiological changes produce problems among some adolescents, and under what circumstances does this occur? In reading the following discussion about puberty's physical changes and psychological impact, keep in mind that many other cognitive and social changes transpire during adolescence as well. The cumulative effect of all these changes may cause emotional difficulties for many young people. Indeed, current studies take into account individual and sociocultural differences among teens, as well as the interaction among the physical, psychological, social, and cultural aspects of adolescence (Paikoff & Brooks-Gunn, 1990; Powers, Hauser, & Kilmer, 1989).

Physical Changes During Adolescence

Puberty

Physical changes marking the onset of adolescence occur in the context of puberty, the period of rapid growth that culminates in sexual maturity and reproductive capability (Roche, 1976). We can group these changes into two categories: those related to physical growth and the physique and those related to the development of sexual characteristics.

Hormonal secretions cause these physical and physiological changes. Hormones are chemical agents secreted into the bloodstream by the pituitary gland, often referred to as the master gland, which lies at the base of the skull. A portion of the brain called the hypothalamus signals the pituitary gland to produce hormones, which in turn stimulate other endocrine glands (the adrenal glands, ovaries, and testes) to produce and secrete sex hormones. As the sex hormones enter the bloodstream, changes in physical growth and sexual development occur (see Figure 14.1). The hormones, then, are a means of communication within the body, carrying messages from place to place and triggering changes in body function and structure (Petersen & Taylor, 1980).

There are several types of hormones. **Androgens,** from the Greek word for *man,* are the male sex hormones; **testosterone** is one type of male hormone. **Estrogen** is the female sex hormone. Although these hormones are designated as male or female, they are actually present in both sexes, but in differing amounts. During puberty, increased levels of androgens and estrogen in the bloodstream stimulate the events leading to sexual maturation and the development of male and female secondary sex characteristics (Paikoff & Brooks-Gunn, 1990). Even though the effects of hormones are particularly noticeable during puberty, they actually control growth throughout the prenatal period and childhood. In fact, high levels of sex hormones during the prenatal period cause sexual differentiation to occur early in prenatal development. During the first six weeks after conception, male and female embryos are identical. By about six weeks after conception, however, testosterone is produced in the male embryo, stimulating the development of male genitals. Throughout the prenatal period, both male and female fetuses have high levels of sex hormones, but at the end of this time the production of hormones is suppressed until about age 7 when hormonal levels begin to rise gradually. By age 10 to 12, hormone levels become very high and puberty begins. Once the hormones have triggered the biological events of puberty, the process is very rapid; most major changes occur within three years.

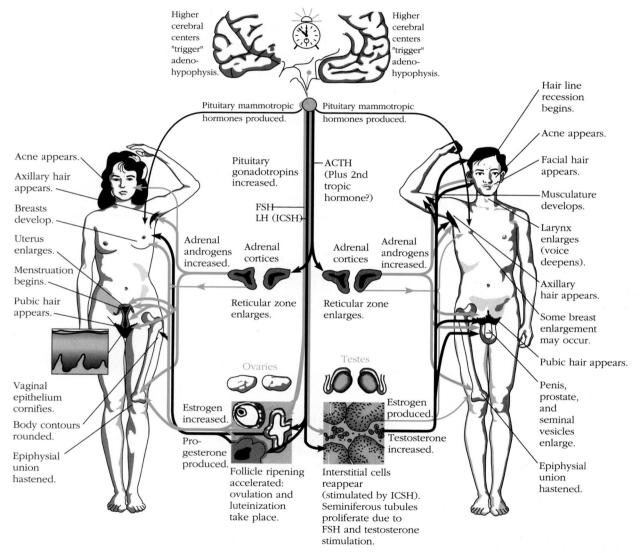

Figure 14.1 *At puberty, the production of hormones stimulates a number of physical changes, which affect many organs and functions.*

Source: Copyright © 1965, CIBA Pharmaceutical Company, Division of CIBA-GEIGY COLLECTION OF MEDICAL ILLUSTRATIONS, illustrated by Frank H. Netter, M. D. Reproduced by courtesy of CIBA-GEIGY Ltd., Basle, Switzerland. All rights reserved.

The Growth Spurt

During puberty, boys and girls undergo a period of rapid physical growth called the **growth spurt;** the whole body seems to shoot up and changes in body proportions and dimensions occur. Increased levels of human growth hormone are responsible for the overall increases in size associated with the growth spurt. The growth spurt begins with a weight gain, about 26 pounds in boys and 20 pounds in girls, that is largely due to the accumulation of fat around the legs, arms, abdomen, and buttocks (Malina, 1990; Malina, Bouchard, & Beunen, 1988; Tanner, 1978). After the initial weight gain, a spurt in height occurs, and some of the fat is redistributed.

The increase in height that occurs during the growth spurt is striking, especially for boys. The velocity of growth in height progressively declines after infancy; just before puberty it reaches its lowest point. When the growth spurt is at its peak, a boy typically grows 3½ inches during a 12-month period. In some boys growth is even more striking, as they gain as much as 4 inches in 6 months (Tanner, 1978). During childhood, however, gains in height are typically less than 2 inches a year on the average, so you can see how striking the change in boys' height is. For girls, the gain in height is also significant in relation to their height increases in previous years, but it is not usually as pronounced as in boys. Girls, however, begin their growth spurt two years ahead of boys. For girls, rapid growth typically begins at age 11, whereas for boys it begins around age 13 (Thissen et al., 1976). Thus, 11-year-old girls and 13-year-old boys are at a similar stage of physical development. Between the ages of 11 and 13, girls are usually several inches taller than boys their age.

There are also huge individual differences in the age at which the growth spurt begins, as you can see in Figure 14.2, which shows the growth spurt in five children of the same sex. These individual differences hold true for the other changes of puberty as well.

In early adolescence, a series of striking physical developments are triggered by the biological events of puberty. They include a growth spurt and changes both in body dimensions and in the proportion of muscle to fat.

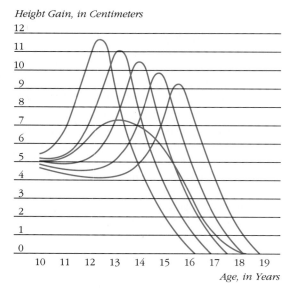

Height Gain, in Centimeters

Age, in Years

Figure 14.2 *Age of maturation in five boys. You can see that some boys enter puberty before they are 12 years old, and others do not begin to mature physically until they are nearly 16. The smooth middle curve represents an average.*

Source: Reprinted by permission of the publishers from *Changing Youth in a Changing Society: Patterns of Adolescent Development and Disorder,* by M. Rutter, 1980, Cambridge, MA: Harvard University Press; p. 9, Figure 1.1. Copyright © by the Nuffield Provincial Hospitals Trust.

Changes in Body Proportions

During the adolescent growth spurt, there are also changes in body parts and body proportions. Most noticeable is the growth of the hands, feet, and legs, which may take place at exaggerated rates and according to different timetables. Thus, at different times during puberty adolescents may feel awkward and clumsy and become concerned that their body will never catch up to their hands and feet, or that they are all legs (Beunen & Malina, 1988; Tanner, 1978).

There are also subtle changes that, collectively, contribute to the transformation of the individual from a child into an adult. The facial features characteristic of childhood disappear as the low forehead becomes wider, the mouth widens, and the lips become fuller. In addition to the changes in skeletal structure, there is a spurt of muscle growth and, as a result, a decrease in the amount of fat (Tanner, 1962). In both sexes muscular development occurs rapidly while height increases. For boys, however, muscular development is more rapid, and they gain more muscle tissue. The accumulation of fat slows down in both sexes. In some boys it can be so significant that it results in actual weight loss (Tanner, 1962). The acceleration in muscle development is also accompanied by an increase in strength. Because the differences between the sexes in the proportion of fat to muscle are significant, after adolescence boys become, and remain, much stronger than girls (Malina & Bouchard, 1990).

Other much less apparent aspects of the growth spurt include changes in the growth of the heart and the capacity of the lungs. Boys develop larger hearts and greater lung capacity relative to their size. In addition, the rate of the heartbeat gradually decreases during the growth spurt. This decrease is more pronounced in boys. Thus, toward the latter part of puberty and from then on, the heart rate for boys is slower (Eichorn, 1975). These changes, together with increased skeletal and muscular maturity, enable adolescents to engage in physical activities requiring endurance and to perfect the motor skills they developed during early and middle childhood. Many adolescents become involved in a variety of sports, and some become skilled athletes.

There are striking growth differences between adolescent boys and girls. In previous chapters on physical development during infancy and childhood, we could generalize about the growth of children without regard to sex since physical development is essentially similar during these years. During adolescence, however, sex differences in physical growth become pronounced. These differences extend in varying degrees to most aspects of growth. Men are larger than women, on the average, because they grow for an additional two years and because their growth is more vigorous; men differ from women in build because of differing rates of growth in different segments of the body (Stuart & Prugh, 1960). These sex differences in physical development may contribute, in part, to differences in behavior and motivation to pursue certain careers and activities. However, sex-typed behavior and motives are still influenced by a complex interaction among biological, cognitive, and sociocultural factors.

Increased Nutritional Needs

The increased rate of growth during puberty is coupled with a natural increase in appetite. Thus, adolescents often seem to consume enormous quantities of food

Appetite increases during the adolescent years, but many teens are undernourished due to poor dietary habits.

(Kemper, 1985). Apparently, metabolic changes alter the appetite to take care of growth needs (Stuart & Prugh, 1960). Although we can rely on the inherent adaptive mechanism of the human body to accommodate increased nutritional needs caused by the growth spurt, we cannot rely on adolescents to eat foods of the right quality. During puberty, they need more caloric intake and additional amounts of protein and specific minerals and vitamins, including calcium, iron, and vitamins A, B2, C, and D (U.S. Department of Agriculture, 1980). Adolescents eat more than they did as children; but since they derive a significant portion of their calories from fat, many are deficient in the required minerals and vitamins (Rees & Mahan, 1988; Select Panel for the Promotion of Child Health, 1981). They are most lacking in iron, and among girls who have started menstruating, iron deficiency anemia is very common. The undernourishment of teens does not go unnoticed; in a national survey of teachers, 70% indicated that poor health and undernourishment are problems for their students (Carnegie Foundation for the Advancement of Teaching, 1988).

It is obvious that adolescents need help in following a proper diet. Social and emotional factors often interfere with their ability to eat properly. These factors include misinformation about food values, participation in group activities that often occur during mealtimes, and increased frequency of eating at fast-food restaurants where foods are high in fat. However, as we have seen in previous chapters, a high-fat diet also characterizes the childhood years and is even prevalent in school lunch and food programs (Citizens' Commission on School Nutrition, 1991).

Eating Disorders

Additional problems can interfere with good nutrition, particularly in girls, whose increased nutritional needs occur at a time when they are more and more aware of their physical appearance. Many girls want to have the slender figures of fashion models.

This desire can take an extreme form of expression in **anorexia nervosa.** Anorexia nervosa is an eating disorder that occurs largely among young adolescent girls, although it is also found among young women and even boys. It is characterized by self-induced starvation, bizarre attitudes toward food, and a distorted body image (Thompson, 1990; Rollins & Piazza, 1978). Although anorexic girls are often severely emaciated, they believe they are fat and become preoccupied with dieting. Most victims of anorexia lose 25% or more of their normal body fat. They stop menstruating, become weak, and suffer muscle deterioration. From 5% to 15% of anorexics literally die of starvation (Goetz et al., 1977).

Anorexia, which means "lack of appetite" in Greek, seems to have reached epidemic proportions among young girls, although it was hardly a problem two to three decades ago. About 1% of adolescent girls, mostly from white, middle-class families, suffer from this disorder (Yates, 1990). Its cause is not known, but researchers are investigating the possibility that it is related to a psychological need. According to one theory, the anorexic expresses a strong desire to avoid becoming an adult. For this reason she refuses to eat since starvation can impede physical growth and the onset of puberty. Another theory is that anorexia involves either a rejection of the mother figure or the experience of being the daughter of an overly protective and controlling mother. By being anorexic, the girl demonstrates her ability to control at least one aspect of her own life (Stern et al., 1989; Landau, 1983). In addition, the problem may stem from a faulty body image shared by many adolescents. These young people embrace a societal ideal of feminine beauty as being very thin (Attie, Brooks-Gunn, & Peterson, 1990; Bruch, 1978). Magazine ads and televi-

This girl is in an advanced stage of anorexia. The literal meaning of anorexia is "without food."

sion continually project the image of a tall, thin, almost emaciated young woman, making it difficult for some adolescents to accept their own body type. However, these explanations are all theoretical and have not been supported by research data.

Anorexic girls suffer from depression (Yates, 1990). Researchers suspect that this does not reflect any particular personality trait associated with anorexia nervosa; in fact, its cause may be a lack of food (Garner, 1990).

Another eating disorder of teenage girls and young women is **bulimia** (a Greek word meaning "great hunger"), which is characterized by enormous eating binges followed by self-induced vomiting (Johnson et al., 1981). Both anorexia nervosa and bulimia can occur simultaneously (Yates, 1990). Both disorders are difficult to treat, although some strides have been made with psychotherapy (Casper, 1989) and behavior modification (Goetz et al., 1977; Geller et al., 1978). Without treatment of any kind, only half of anorexics and bulimics improve (Minuchin & Fishman, 1981; Minuchin, Rosman, & Baker, 1978), and the others suffer severe health problems that can culminate in death (Casper, 1989).

Sexual Maturation

The physiological event most often associated with puberty is sexual maturation, which includes a series of changes in the reproductive organs and the appearance of secondary sex characteristics. Although these developments usually follow a certain sequence, the sequence of sexual maturation is different in some people and there are individual differences in the age at which these changes occur (Brooks-Gunn, Petersen, & Eichorn, 1985). The first event associated with sexual maturation is an increased secretion of hormones by the pituitary gland, which causes the ovaries and testes to mature and to secrete sex hormones. Estrogen production rises in adolescent boys as well, but it is not cyclic and there is also a sharp increase in testosterone production. And in both sexes the adrenal gland greatly increases its production of androgens, which are responsible for the development of some secondary sex characteristics (Petersen & Taylor, 1980).

Reproductive organs   The increased level of hormones stimulates certain internal changes. In girls the uterus grows larger and the vaginal lining thickens. In boys the penis grows and thickens, and about a year later the scrotal sac enlarges. As these organs grow, the individuals become capable of reproduction. For girls, the physiological event signaling fertility is *menarche,* the first menstrual period. Boys reportedly achieve reproductive potential when **ejaculation**—the discharge of seminal fluid containing sperm—first occurs. However, menarche and ejaculation do not necessarily indicate reproductive capability; they are simply one in a series of events leading toward full sexual maturity. In fact, girls may not become fertile for six months to a year after menarche, since ovulation does not usually occur in the first several menstrual periods. In the same way, the ability to ejaculate does not mean that there are any sperm, or a sufficient concentration of live and mobile sperm in the seminal fluid, for the boy to be considered fertile. However, as you will see in the Discussion of Social Issues section, it is not safe to rely on the relative infertility of adolescents in puberty; some young girls before age 12 do, in fact, become pregnant.

Secondary sex characteristics   Hormonal secretion initiates several other changes in different parts of the body that further contribute to sex differentiation. One of these is the change in physique. By the end of puberty, most boys have wide shoulders and relatively narrow, slim hips. Girls have wider, more rounded hips and narrow shoulders.

Breasts   Another change contributing to obvious differences between boys and girls is the development of the breasts. In girls the growth of the breast "bud," which occurs when a small concentration of fat causes a slight rise of the breast, is one of the first signs that puberty has begun. From then on, the breasts develop gradually for several years; by the time most of the changes of puberty are over, girls attain their full breast growth. This gradual growth is quite difficult for girls to accept; once the breast bud appears, most girls cannot wait for their breasts to be large enough for them to wear a bra. Because breast development is a symbol of femininity in our society, girls whose breasts are not as developed tend to feel embarrassed and also worried that their breasts will remain small. However, there is often another reaction to breast development: not wanting it to occur. Some girls wear blousy clothing to hide their growing breasts and put off buying a bra. It is not unusual for girls to experience conflicting feelings, at times enjoying their physical maturation and at times refusing to acknowledge that they are in fact growing up.

Breast changes occur in boys, too. Their **areola**—the pigmented area around the nipple—grows in diameter, and their breasts become slightly larger. Many boys experience what they consider to be abnormal breast enlargement, but this development is usually temporary and subsides within a year or two (Roche, French, & Davilla, 1971).

Hair growth   During puberty, both boys and girls experience changes in hair growth. First of all, the hair on the head and body becomes darker and coarser. Next, hair begins to grow in regions of the body that were previously hairless, resulting in pubic, axillary (underarm), and facial hair. Boys also develop chest hair. At first, this hair is usually sparse and light in color; but as puberty continues, it becomes thicker and darker.

Voice   Adolescents' voices change during puberty, becoming lower as the larynx enlarges and the length of the vocal cords increases. In boys this change is quite pronounced and is referred to as the *breaking of the voice.* Until it actually occurs, boys tend to feel embarrassed and conscious of their high-pitched voices. Anticipating this change, many adolescent boys "practice" speaking in a lower voice when they are with their parents or other familiar people. The change of voice is often a gradual process that occurs rather late and after several other biological changes have taken place.

Acne   The increased production of androgens that stimulates sexual maturation leads to other conditions, such as acne, as well. **Acne** occurs when glands in the skin, stimulated by androgens, produce a fatty substance called **sebum.** The sebum mixes with the skin cells and forms a substance that can plug up pores, causing blackheads or whiteheads to form. If bacteria begin to grow in a sealed-off pore, infection may cause painful boils that can leave permanent scars.

Acne is very common, affecting over two-thirds of adolescents at some point (Stuart & Prugh, 1960). There is no evidence that poor eating habits or poor hygiene cause acne, although they may aggravate the condition once it is present (Stuart & Prugh, 1960). Genetics does play a role, however; children of acne sufferers are also likely to have acne (Sommer, 1978). Acne is often treated lightly as "part of growing up," and it usually clears up with time. But because adolescents are painfully aware of their inflamed faces, acne can cause significant psychological trauma. Embarrassed by pimples and marks, these young people may be afraid to date or participate in social situations out of fear that their peers will reject them. In severe cases medical treatment can relieve acne symptoms and minimize its lasting psychological and physical effects (Stuart & Prugh, 1960).

Hormonal effects on behavior   There is also some indication that hormones affect emotions and behavior, although the evidence is not conclusive. In girls the hormonal changes of puberty, which include cyclic increases in the levels of estrogen, may contribute to temporary mood changes and to an overall mood intensity. Some researchers have found, for example, that in the few days preceding menstruation, some girls are likely to be depressed (Kessel & Coppen, 1963). This condition, referred to as the *premenstrual syndrome* (PMS), can persist beyond adolescence; some women suffer a variety of emotional disturbances and fatigue during the premenstrual phase (Dalton, 1977). A decline in estrogen during that time in the menstrual cycle may cause PMS; however, vitamin deficiencies may also be part of the problem. According to some researchers, vitamin supplements and changes in dietary habits can alleviate PMS in many women (Lauersen & Stukan, 1983). Paikoff and Brooks-Gunn (1990) further point out that these mood changes may not be influenced by pubertal hormones; instead, they may reflect the influence of other physical and social changes.

In boys high levels of androgen secretion in puberty reportedly increase the **sex drive** (Money & Ehrhardt, 1972), which is the basic biological need to achieve sexual stimulation and satisfaction. Since both sexes secrete androgens, they may affect the sex drive in girls as well (Rutter, 1980).

Animal studies provide some interesting perspectives regarding the effects of hormones on behavior and the sex drive. According to this research, high levels of androgen secretions influence assertiveness, dominance, and the sex drive in both sexes. Joslyn (1973) reports that, after being injected with androgens, female rhesus monkeys became increasingly more aggressive and replaced males in the top position in the social hierarchy. Although this study shows the effects of androgens on behavior, Rutter (1980) points out that the association between hormone levels and behavior is a two-way street. Rose, Gordon, and Bernstein (1972) underscore this point. Their study showed that when adult male monkeys were in the company of receptive female monkeys, they displayed dominance and assertiveness and their hormone levels increased dramatically. When the same male monkeys were subjected to a sudden defeat by an all-male group of monkeys, their hormone levels fell. Researchers are now attempting to see if contextual factors have a role in the interplay between hormones and behavior (Olweus et al., 1988), but no conclusive data are available as yet. In animals, at least, hormones appear to influence behavior and social experience appears to influence hormone level.

Sexual activity among adolescents   Until recently psychologists generally believed the sex drive to be much stronger in males. Psychoanalysts, in particular, believed that since the male sex drive was stronger, their destiny was to be dominant and sexually aggressive, while females were to be sexually passive (Deutsch, 1945).

The prevalence of such beliefs led to the idea of the **double standard;** that is, a different set of rules for the sexual behavior of men and women. Some societal factors as well have led to the belief in the double standard. Since the male sex drive was allegedly so strong, society expected men to be sexually aggressive and to pursue as much sexual experience and gratification as possible. Women, on the other hand, were expected to have no interest in sex and to ward off sexual advances. However, attitudes toward sexuality in general among adolescents and adults became increasingly more permissive between 1920 and 1980 (Chilman, 1983). Equality between the sexes in all aspects of life became especially prevalent during the social revolution of the 1960s and 1970s. Many teenage girls believe that women desire sex as much as men and also enjoy sex as much as men. However, there are indications that the belief in the double standard still persists among some teens (Chilman, 1986). In an interview survey, Goodchilds and Zellman (1984) found that teens of both sexes believe that boys can be sexually aggressive and that girls must set the limits.

Although the number of sexually active teens has increased dramatically since the mid-1960s (Darling, Kellman, & VanDusen, 1984), boys still outnumber girls in sexual activity. In a report of the National Research Council, Hayes (1987) indicates that up to about the mid-1980s, 47.9% of 17-year-old boys and 64.0% of 18-year-old boys reported that they were sexually active; in contrast, 27.1% of 17-year-old girls and 44.0% of 18-year-old girls reported that they were sexually active. More recent data by the Centers for Disease Control indicate that there has been an increase in sexual activity among adolescent girls; 51.5% of 15- to 19-year-old women report having had premarital sexual intercourse.

This increase is especially apparent among 15-year-old girls (see Figure 14.3). The growth in sexual activity among adolescent girls has occurred despite the great emphasis by health officials and educators on efforts to prevent teenage pregnancies and to stop the spread of acquired immune deficiency syndrome (AIDS). In fact,

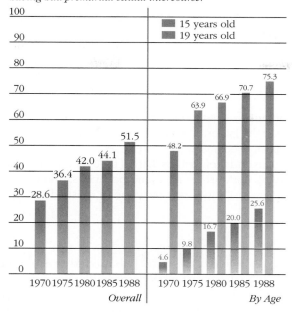

Percentage of women aged 15 to 19 years who reported having had premarital sexual intercourse.

- ■ 15 years old
- ■ 19 years old

Overall
1970: 28.6
1975: 36.4
1980: 42.0
1985: 44.1
1988: 51.5

By Age
15 years old — 1970: 4.6, 1975: 9.8, 1980: 16.7, 1985: 20.0, 1988: 25.6
19 years old — 1970: 48.2, 1975: 63.9, 1980: 66.9, 1985: 70.7, 1988: 75.3

Figure 14.3 *More than half of women aged 15 to 19 have had premarital sex.*

Source: The Waterbury Republican, p. 10c, January 5, 1991. Based on material from the *Morbidity and Mortality Weekly Report,* Centers for Disease Control, 1989, Atlanta, GA. Reprinted by permission.

numerous media programs continue to proclaim the dangerous consequences of sexual contacts in this age group. Have the teenagers received these behavioral messages? Has the focus on alerting teenagers to the dangers of sex actually encouraged them to engage in sex? Researchers do not know the answers. Yet we need to investigate the whole issue further in order to determine all the factors associated with teenage sexual activity. The consequences of early sex can be especially harmful to girls.

DISCUSSION OF SOCIAL ISSUES

Teenage Pregnancy and Childbearing

One of the consequences of increased sexual activity among adolescents is the alarming rise in teenage pregnancies. Each year one out of every ten teenage girls in America—about 1 million in all—becomes pregnant. In their review of the research, Earle (1990) and Furstenberg, Brooks-Gunn, and Chase-Landsdale (1989) point out several new trends:

1. About 50% of these pregnancies end in abortion.
2. The pregnancies and births are occurring to younger girls. In the United States girls under 15 are five times more likely to give birth than young women in other developed countries.
3. In the United States the number of girls between the ages of 10 and 15 who give birth is increasing, whereas the birth rate is decreasing among girls 16 to 19.
4. About 95% of the teenagers who do not have an abortion and decide to carry their pregnancy to term, keep the child.

In past generations most pregnant girls would have given the baby up for adoption or married the father. In contrast, teenage girls today often remain unmarried. Thus, the majority become single parents, even though they are usually unable to support themselves and their babies. Earle (1990) comments that "at a time when most teens are 'trying out' various roles and behaviors, [these] very young girls are saddled with . . . responsibilities that overwhelm most adults" (p. 3).

Poverty

Teenage pregnancy is believed to be the hub around which the cycle of poverty revolves. It is one of the major factors underlying the increase in young families in poverty (National Center for Children in Poverty, 1990). According to the Alan Guttmacher Institute (1981), most girls who terminate their pregnancy are white and from middle- or high-income families; many do well in their studies. In contrast, those who keep their baby tend to be poor, minority children and to have low academic records.

Teen pregnancy and parenthood usually have negative consequences for the mother and child. The mother is at risk for health problems and is often emotionally immature. A review by the National Research Council (see Hofferth & Hayes, 1987; Hayes, 1987) reports that teenage mothers frequently drop out of high school and then cannot find work, because they have no education. Thus, their life chances suffer as a result of childbearing.

What About the Father?

Not much information is available on adolescent fathers, because research on them is just beginning (Lamb & Elster, 1986). About 50% of children born to teenage girls have a teenage father; the other half are fathered by men over 20. The U.S. Department of Health and Human Services (1990) gives the following profile on unwed fathers aged 14 to 22: they are from all income and racial groups and tend to live with their parents. Most have poor school and work records. In many cases they do not acknowledge their parenthood out of ignorance, disbelief, or a refusal to accept financial responsibility for the baby (Furstenberg, Brooks-Gunn, & Morgan, 1987). Only about one-third of teenage mothers receive any emotional support from the fathers (Lamb & Elster, 1986).

Since most teenage fathers have little or no involvement with the pregnancy, childbearing, or childrearing, they seem to be less affected by the experience. One study (Marsiglio, 1986), however, noted that the baby's birth may interrupt the adolescent father's education, even if he does not marry the mother. Hispanic and white fathers are more apt to experience this negative effect than are black fathers (Marsiglio, 1986).

Effects on the Child

Children born to teenage parents are at risk, especially during infancy. They often have poor physical health, and their socioemotional and cognitive development may suffer (Centers for Disease Control, 1980). These problems may stem from a lack of proper prenatal care and inadequate nutrition (Hofferth & Hayes, 1987), particularly if the young mother is on her own. However, not all infants of teen parents are at risk for developmental problems. If the infant and mother live with other adults—say, family members—then the child will usually be better off (Baldwin & Cain, 1980).

Support Services and Systems

Young mothers who receive emotional support and counseling after the baby's birth are often able to continue their education. In addition, they have fewer problems and fewer repeat pregnancies than mothers who do not receive this help (Clewell, Brooks-Gunn, & Benasich, 1989; Badger, 1980). Schools, hospitals, and community health centers have developed numerous programs to help pregnant girls and young mothers. Some programs are also directed at teenage fathers (Marsiglio, 1986; Klinman & Kohl, 1984).

Although these programs are important and often effective, they are in short supply. Researchers and clinicians agree that more services are needed to address the needs of pregnant and parenting teens. The prevention of pregnancies should be a priority, according to the National Academy of Sciences (Hayes, 1987), which convened a panel of experts to review research on the issue. Prevention programs would focus on delaying sexual activity among teens by changing attitudes about early sexual involvement. These programs might also focus on teaching teens social and decision-making skills that would enable them to withstand peer pressure. Other prevention programs might include the provision of contraceptives and educating teens about their use. This latter recommendation is made in light of research suggesting that many sexually active children fail to use contraceptive methods because they are ignorant of the hazards and consequences of sexual intercourse (Furstenberg, 1976).

However, the use of contraceptives and sex education are controversial issues. Some people oppose them on the basis of moral and religious beliefs and on the grounds that they would promote, rather than prevent, sexual activity and result in more pregnancies (Dryfoos & Heisler, 1981).

Has the use of contraceptives been effective in reducing teen pregnancies? As yet we cannot give a satisfactory answer to this question (Vinouskis, 1988). Researchers point out, however, that the number of teen pregnancies declined during the 1970s when family planning services expanded substantially (Furstenberg, Brooks-Gunn, & Chase-Landsdale, 1989). In addition, despite high rates of sexual activity among adolescents in Western Europe, there are low rates of teenage pregnancy and childbearing in these countries (see Figure 14.4). Experts attribute this fact to the easy availability of contraceptives (Jones et al., 1985).

Although these findings are useful in providing some direction for prevention programs, their applicability to American teens remains to be established. We need to remember that teenagers are not a homogeneous population. Rather, they have diverse needs, beliefs, and values that must be considered; thus one approach to pregnancy prevention may be effective for some teens but not for others. As a society, our task is to focus on this problem, implement programs aimed at pre-

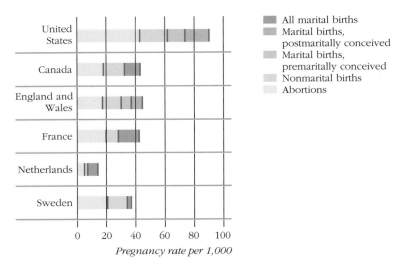

Figure 14.4 Percentage distribution of pregnancies and pregnancy rates by outcome, for women aged 15 to 19, 1980–1981.

Source: Reprinted with permission from Jones, E. F. *Teenage Pregnancy in Industrialized Countries.* Copyright © 1986, Yale University Press.

vention, and then evaluate them to determine which programs, or parts of programs, are effective (Zigler & Weiss, 1985). Only through continued experimentation and evaluation can we arrive at solutions to social problems.

Sexually transmitted diseases   We are also concerned about the trend toward greater sexual activity among teens because of the increase in sexually transmitted diseases. Teenage sexual activity is a significant risk factor for contracting AIDS (U.S. House of Representatives, 1987). AIDS (see also Chapter 5) is one of the most feared diseases because it is caused by a virus that destroys the body's immune system. Blood transfusions, shared needles, and sexual contact can transmit the virus. Although only 1% of all Americans infected with AIDS are adolescents, public health officials expect the number of adolescent victims to increase. This is because teenagers are ignorant about the transmission of the disease and fail to use effective contraceptives (Brooks-Gunn & Furstenberg, 1989). Sexually active teens who do not use contraceptives or who use contraceptives other than the condom have no protection against the transmission of AIDS (Task Force on Pediatric AIDS, 1989).

Sexually active teens are also at risk for contracting other common sexually transmitted diseases such as chlamydia and herpes. *Chlamydia,* which is caused by tiny bacteria infecting the reproductive tract, can affect both males and females.

Physicians can treat it with antibiotics, but if left untreated, chlamydia can cause scar tissue in the fallopian tubes and lead to infertility. Genital *herpes*, which causes sores and blisters, is difficult to treat and can be potentially dangerous. Women with herpes are eight times more likely to develop cervical cancer than those without herpes. If herpes is present in pregnant teens, their babies are exposed to the virus during birth and are at risk for brain damage (Cates & Rayh, 1985).

The Impact of Physical Changes on Psychological Development

Now that we have examined the physical and physiological changes of adolescence, let us look at the problems some individuals experience during this period, and the possible relationship these problems have to psychological growth and development.

The Timing of Puberty

First, let us consider the psychological impact of the timing of puberty. As shown earlier, individual variation in the rate of physical growth and development is most dramatic during adolescence. At the ages of 11, 12, and 13 in girls and 13, 14, and 15 in boys, variations in development are enormous, ranging from complete preadolescence to complete maturity; two children of the same age and sex may look and feel totally different, one resembling a child and the other looking very much like a young adult.

Early- and late-maturers   The age at which children reach puberty is not medically significant, but it does have an impact on how they feel about themselves. You may not remember how acutely aware you were of your growth and physical features during adolescence. Indeed, most adults forget how important feelings about sexuality and personal appearance are to adolescents. In fact, adolescents of both sexes are egocentric (see Chapter 15); they are concerned about their sexual maturation and physical growth. It is not surprising, therefore, to discover that whether the individual matures early or late has an impact on behavior. A series of investigations emanating from the California Growth Study and reviewed by Eichorn (1963) proved this point. This longitudinal study examined the physical and psychological characteristics of a large group of individuals.

The researchers found that for girls, maturing either early or late can be a source of great embarrassment and concern, which can affect the development of their self-concept. Early-maturing girls tend to feel embarrassed and isolated because none of their peers are at the same stage of development. Other children often tease them. However, these feelings are only temporary, for once other girls begin puberty, early-maturers become very popular among both girls and boys. Girls who mature late, on the other hand, tend to be more tense, to seek more attention, and to have low self-esteem. However, once these late-maturing girls start menarche, their feelings of low self-esteem diminish.

These boys are the same age but they are at different stages of development.

Boys who mature late also evidence negative feelings about themselves, but to a greater degree than girls. Early-maturing boys, however, tend to have positive self-esteem. In the California Growth Study these differences between early- and late-maturing boys were found to continue well into adulthood. When researchers tested early- and late-maturing males in their 30s, there were no longer any differences between the two groups in size and physical attractiveness, but there were some differences in their personality characteristics, social behavior, and occupational level. The early-maturers made a good impression and were cooperative, enterprising, sociable, and conforming. They were also more likely to be in supervisory positions. Late-maturers were more rebellious, touchy, and self-assertive; they more frequently sought the aid and encouragement of others.

More recent findings, while confirming the initial psychological impact of early and late maturation, shed some doubt on the long-term impact of the timing of puberty. Simmons and Blyth (1987), for example, followed a sample of 450 sixth-graders for five years. Classifying the students as early-, middle-, or late-maturers (on the basis of the presence of menses in girls and the growth in height in boys), the researchers found that, in seventh grade, early-maturing boys had higher levels of self-esteem than middle- or late-maturing boys. But when the researchers interviewed the boys again in the ninth and tenth grades, they found no differences between early-, middle-, and late-maturers.

Cultural variations   Although the physical events of puberty often significantly influence important personality traits such as self-esteem, the psychological impact of early and late maturing is largely determined by cultural forces (Lerner & Foch, 1987; Clausen, 1975). In the United States, where society tends to associate physical strength and size with masculinity, boys value these physical traits. It is not surprising, therefore, that early-maturing boys are more self-assured and independent than late-maturers, who are lacking in self-confidence. However, this is not necessarily the case in other countries. In Italy, for example, where society emphasizes family membership rather than physical size as a source of prestige, early or late maturation causes no differences in the boys' attitudes and behaviors (Mussen & Bouterline-Young, 1964).

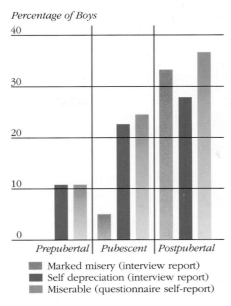

Percentage of Boys

Prepubertal | Pubescent | Postpubertal

■ Marked misery (interview report)
■ Self depreciation (interview report)
■ Miserable (questionnaire self-report)

Figure 14.5 *Researchers find that adolescence is associated with a marked increase in depression, especially among boys.*
Source: Reprinted by permission of the publishers from *Changing Youth in a Changing Society: Patterns of Adolescent Development and Disorder,* by M. Rutter, 1980, Cambridge, MA: Harvard University Press; p. 19, Figure 1.4. Copyright © by the Nuffield Provincial Hospitals Trust.

Depression During Adolescence

Besides the psychological problems associated with the timing of puberty, the experience of puberty itself is difficult for many adolescents. It entails having to adjust to physical growth and to many physiological changes, such as the first experience with menarche and ejaculation (Brooks-Gunn & Furstenberg, 1989).

Any period of adjustment to change involves stress, and early adolescence can be a time of stress for adolescents and their parents as well. This stress gives rise to a variety of behavioral and psychological problems. Offer (1969) noted that during early adolescence, quarrels between adolescents and their parents are very common, but they diminish toward late adolescence. Another study (Simmons, Rosenberg, & Rosenberg, 1973) found that between the ages of 11 and 14 adolescents evidence a poor self-concept, but by age 16 to 18 there is a marked improvement in the way they think of themselves. Poor self-concept is a problem particularly among adolescent girls. The American Association of University Women (1991) commissioned a survey of 3000 boys and girls from age 9 through 18. The researchers found that decreases in self-esteem among boys and girls occurred during early adolescence. Most boys recovered their sense of self-worth by the time they graduated from high school, but the majority of the girls did not.

Rutter (1980) notes that early adolescence is associated with a marked rise in the incidence of depression, especially among boys (see Figure 14.5). This depression has to do more with puberty than with chronological age. Prepubescent boys rarely show depressive feelings, but the percentage of boys who are rated depressed or who report feeling miserable rises significantly during puberty and remains high for some time afterward.

Depression is so severe for some adolescents that it becomes a psychological and physical health hazard. Depression can alienate the teenager from family and friends, and it inhibits the attainment of self-identity.

Besides the physiological changes of puberty, many other profound changes that occur during adolescence may contribute to stress, depression, and behavioral difficulties. These changes include the acquisition of self-identity and independence and the formation of close social and sexual relationships outside the family (Magnusson, Strattin, & Allen, 1985). In addition, adolescents often have to make important career and educational choices. Thus, many factors can affect the relationship between teenagers and their parents and bring on feelings of doubt and an inability to cope with stress and depression (Compas, 1987; Stern & Zevon, 1990).

Depression, which is broadly defined as a state of feeling extremely sad, involves a pervasive sense of loss, inactivity, fatigue, and difficulty in thinking and concentrating (Weiner, 1980). Many things can bring on depression, including divorce, death, peer rejection, failure in school or sports, illness, or physical injury. Thus, many individuals experience depression at various times during childhood, adolescence, and adulthood. Over the past two decades, however, there has been a significant increase in the incidence of depression among adolescents and younger children. Kazdin (1990) notes that between 2% and 7% of normal children show symptoms of depression; the prevalence of depression begins among very young children but increases substantially among adolescents.

For many adolescents and children, depression is so severe that it becomes a psychological and health hazard (Tuma, 1989). One danger is alienation from family and friends. Depression inhibits the individual from striving toward the attainment of self-identity and from making important career and educational choices. Depressed individuals also tend to just give up.

Adolescent Suicide

Depressed adolescents are emotionally vulnerable and often think of committing suicide. Adolescent suicide is not new. Terman (1914) wrote about the problem in the early part of this century, and statistics on adolescent suicide indicate that it was also a problem in the 1950s (National Center for Health Statistics, 1974). Today, however, self-destruction among youth has been increasing at a rapid rate. It is now the third leading cause of death among adolescents, after accidents and homicide

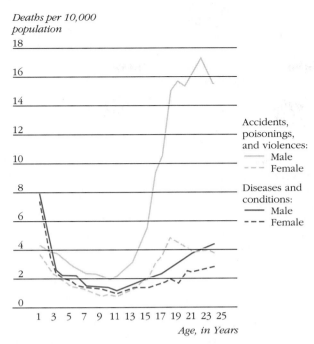

Deaths per 10,000 population

Accidents, poisonings, and violences:
—— Male
- - - Female

Diseases and conditions:
—— Male
- - - Female

Age, in Years

Figure 14.6   *The death rate for individuals between the ages of 15 and 24 years.*
Source: Select Panel for the Promotion of Child Health, 1981.

(Centers for Disease Control, 1990). In fact, accidents, homicides, and suicides account for three-quarters of adolescent deaths. The death rate for males by accidents, poisoning, and violence takes a sharp rise at about age 15 and peaks at about age 21 (see Figure 14.6).

The statistics on teen suicides do not give a complete picture of the extent of the problem (Brent et al., 1989); for every successful adolescent suicide, there are 50 to 100 attempts (Centers for Disease Control, 1989; Mishara, 1975). Researchers also note that because of the social stigma associated with suicide, many deaths attributed to accidents are actually suicides (Tishler, McKendry, & Morgan, 1981). In addition, there is the related phenomenon of suicide epidemics, or *suicide clusters,* in which one successful suicide triggers several other attempted or successful suicides by the victim's friends or other adolescents in the community (Davidson et al., 1989).

No single factor sufficiently explains adolescent suicide or its increase during the past two decades. Researchers have not yet isolated its causes, because their studies have produced conflicting results (Tishler, 1983). They do know, however, that there are multiple factors associated with the problem. For example, there appears to be a relationship between suicide and the advent of puberty (Garfinkel & Golombek, 1974). Poor school performance is also involved. In one study researchers found that 75% of those who attempted suicide had exceptionally low academic ratings, learning disabilities, a history of behavioral problems in school, and stressful home situations, such as a divorce or an alcoholic parent (Rohn et al., 1977). However, in another study Marks and Haller (1977) found that many adolescents who attempted suicide had a history of successful school experiences.

Cantor (1990) notes that media discussions of suicide may promote suicidal behaviors. Davidson and colleagues (1989) have studied two communities where suicide clusters occurred. In questioning parents of the teens who had committed suicide, they found that the following factors are associated with increased suicide risk:

1. Social disruptions resulting from frequent changes in residence, school, or parental figures.
2. Experience with violence or suicide, including attempting suicide or knowing someone who has committed suicide.
3. A previous arrest.
4. A previous hospitalization for psychiatric illness or substance abuse.
5. The loss of a girlfriend or a boyfriend during the preceding year.

Some personality traits relate to suicide. Cantor (1976) found that young women who attempted suicide had a low level of frustration tolerance and were likely to be in conflict with their parents. Other studies cited poor communication between parents and adolescents in conjunction with disruptions in family life (Garfinkel, Froese, & Hood, 1982). In addition, individuals suffering from depression during childhood and adolescence are more likely to commit suicide (Brent et al., 1989; Garfinkel & Golombek, 1974). The sex of the individual may also be a factor in the number of deaths due to suicide. More girls than boys (a ratio of 4 to 1) attempt suicide, but more boys than girls succeed in killing themselves because boys use more violent methods (Weissman, 1974).

We cannot interpret these findings to mean that any of these factors cause suicide. Yet it is easy to see that during the emotionally vulnerable period of adolescence, individuals experiencing emotional difficulties and a great deal of stress can be at risk of a similar tragedy. Suicide usually comes as a surprise to the victim's family and friends, but there are often some warning signals. Tishler (1983) points out that to prevent a suicide, physicians, teachers, parents, relatives, and friends need to know that there are certain precipitating events: the divorce or remarriage of the parents, the anniversary of a divorce or remarriage, a death in the family, or the suicide or death of a close friend. Besides watching out for the adolescent who experiences such difficulties, Tishler also advises monitoring any behavioral changes as a possible clue to the adolescent's suicidal intentions. Possible warning signals include a drastic change in personal appearance, frequent or continual complaints about aches and pains, changes in schoolwork and the daily routine, emotional outbursts, excessive use of alcohol or drugs, an overwhelming sense of guilt or shame, or talking about death.

Of course, many adolescents exhibit any or all of these behaviors and do not necessarily commit suicide. But family, friends, and others who come in contact with adolescents should still be aware of the possibility of suicide so they can help prevent the tragic and needless waste of human life by offering to help, by talking to the adolescent, or by alleviating the stress the young person may be experiencing.

Should schools implement suicide prevention programs? A recent study on school-based suicide prevention programs says no. The study (Shaffer et al., 1990), which involved an analysis of over 100 such programs, found that these programs are ineffective because they are based on the assumption that, given sufficient stress, there is a universal potential for suicide. As a result, they target prevention services to unselected groups of students. According to the study, this approach has the potential to trigger suicide among those at risk. Shaffer and his colleagues (1990) suggest that a more efficient means of preventing suicides among teens is to carefully observe individual students in order to ascertain any changes in their behavior and attitude.

Summary

Adolescence is a difficult period of life to define, due largely to the fact that it is a recent social invention that arose from the need to provide young people with extensive schooling in order to prepare them for life in a complex society. While adolescents in our society are not yet psychologically ready for adult life, they are physiologically ready to function as adults. This discrepancy between the cultural and physiological aspects of adolescence causes a great deal of emotional turmoil for some young people. At one time psychologists believed that all adolescents had emotional difficulties. Viewing emotional turbulence as an inevitable, biologically caused characteristic of adolescence, psychologists described this period as a time of storm and stress. Recent research reveals, however, that not all adolescents are emotionally troubled. Some do experience deep emotional difficulties, however, due in part to the physical changes brought on by puberty and also to social and emotional developments associated with adolescence.

Puberty, the physiological event culminating in sexual maturity, causes a series of physical and physiological changes. These developments include a growth spurt, changes in body dimensions, maturation of the sex organs, and the appearance of secondary sex characteristics. An increase in the levels of hormone secretion triggers these developments. Hormones can also cause acne and affect mood and behavior, most notably the sex drive.

The impact of puberty also extends beyond bodily changes. Adolescents are preoccupied with the process of sexual maturation and with their physical appearance. In addition, there is great variation in the age at which they begin puberty. Individuals who mature late or early are likely to be distressed by their physical development or lack of it; this distress can significantly affect boys' personalities.

The physical changes of puberty also cause a great deal of stress for teenagers who also have to adjust to internal and external changes. Thus, many adolescents exhibit behavioral difficulties, especially during early adolescence when puberty begins. They may also develop a negative self-concept and fits of depression. Associated with depression is the phenomenon of adolescent suicide. During the past 20 years, there has been a dramatic increase in teenage suicide. Today, suicide is the third leading cause of death among adolescents, after accidents and homicide.

Another social problem associated with adolescence is the increase in sexual activity and the phenomenon of children bearing children. About 1 million teenage girls become pregnant in the United States each year, and most decide to keep their babies rather than opt for adoption. Child psychologists are deeply concerned over the fact that pregnancy and parenthood are especially prevalent among girls under age 15 in the United States. Today these girls are five times more likely to become pregnant than their age-mates in other industrialized countries. Although we have learned a great deal about teenage parents and their offspring and about the consequences of early pregnancy and childbearing, we have not yet been able to develop adequate prevention programs. Yet we cannot overemphasize the importance of these programs. Without them, the problem of children having children will continue to severely compromise the lives of many teens and their babies.

15 Cognitive Development During Adolescence

Chapter 14 described the biological changes that occur during puberty. But these changes, no matter how important, are only part of the transformation from childhood to adulthood. Adolescents also develop a higher level of intellectual maturity; they can think ahead, consider hypotheses, entertain abstract ideas, and begin to speculate about the future and their role in it.

In explaining the changes that occur in the way adolescents think, we focus on Piaget's theory and information processing. We also discuss quantitative explanation of cognitive development known as the psychometric approach. This approach emphasizes individual differences in intellectual performance, as measured by the IQ test. Are intelligence tests valid? What is intelligence anyway? What factors influence individual differences in intellectual performance? These answers are important because IQ tests are used to make decisions about whether children are mentally retarded, normal, or gifted and about what kinds of school experiences they need. Before we consider the advantages and disadvantages of IQ tests, let us look at the characteristics of adolescent thought.

Intellectual Development

Research on Adolescent Thought

After reviewing the research on adolescent thought, Keating (1980) suggests that the adolescent's thinking differs from the child's thinking in five ways: First, adolescents can *think about abstract possibilities.* We can see this through an experiment in which a researcher at times conceals and reveals a poker chip, telling the young person: "The chip is either green *or* not green," and "The chip is green *and* it is not green." The experimenter then asks the child or adolescent whether each statement is true, false, or impossible to judge. When the chip is concealed, the child would reply that it is impossible to judge. The adolescent, however, would focus on what is being said to her, not on the chip. Since she knows that the statement, "The chip is green *and* it is not green" can never be true, she needs no physical evidence to arrive at the answer (Osherson, 1975).

Second, adolescents are capable of *thinking about hypotheses.* If you ask a younger child the hypothetical question, "If all dogs were pink and you had a dog, would your dog be pink, too?" he would laugh at the question. He would reject the suggestion that all dogs are pink and answer that this is not possible. He knows from his experience that all dogs are not pink, so he stops there and never attempts to consider the hypothetical question. In contrast, the adolescent can make a logical connection between the two statements in the question. She recognizes that if all dogs were pink then her dog would have to be pink too. This enables her to be flexible in her thinking and to consider all the actual and possible solutions to a problem.

Third, adolescents are capable of *thinking ahead* and planning. Although they may not always think before they act, they do so more often than younger children. This ability allows adolescents to approach problem solving in a systematic and efficient manner; they can integrate what they have learned in the past and consider all the possible combinations of relevant factors.

Fourth, adolescents are capable of *reflective thinking,* or thinking about the processes of thinking, and how to make them more efficient. They use various strategies to enhance their ability to learn and solve problems. Adolescents can also reflect on the process of thinking, which is referred to by information-processing researchers as **metacognition.** Just as children acquire metalinguistics (an intuitive awareness of how language works) and metamemory (which enables them to use memory-aiding devices to improve their capacity for memory), so adolescents become capable of thinking about their own cognitive processes, making them more efficient. They can thus analyze their own thoughts and judge whether they are appropriate for the task at hand. For example, if a 16-year-old anticipates that her parents won't let her go out of town with friends, she will formulate an argument to convince them otherwise, and before approaching them, she may go over the argument in her mind, to ascertain whether it is strong or weak. Related to reflective thinking is the adolescents' tendency to be preoccupied by thinking about themselves and to be egocentric. Also, adolescents tend to probe their own ideas about the nature of things. Mussen, Conger, and Kagan (1974) quote an adolescent as saying:

> I found myself thinking about my future and then I began to think about why I was thinking about my future, and then I began to think about why I was thinking about why I was thinking about my future.

Fifth, *the content of adolescent thought is broadened.* Adolescents think about many topics they have never considered before. Enhanced by their ability to think in the abstract, they can think about the world as it is and as it might become. For example, adolescents may construct their own elaborate political and economic theories or complex plans for the reorganization of society, or they may think through issues pertaining to social relations, morality, or religion:

> Topics of identity, society, existence, religion, morality, friendship, and so on are examined in detail and are contemplated with high emotion as well as increased cognitive capability. The spark for such consideration is not purely cognitive, of course; there are many lines of development converging with special significance for the adolescent. But . . . the cognitive skills applied to the task are much sharper, which makes the enterprise all the more exciting. [Keating, 1980]

Most researchers agree that for many American adolescents, thinking is generally characterized as we've just described. However, researchers disagree on their explanations of the cognitive changes that occur during adolescence.

A CLOSER LOOK

Adolescent Egocentrism

Although adolescents are capable of attaining what Jean Piaget called formal operational thought, some remain limited to the previous level of cognition, the concrete; they also become susceptible to *adolescent egocentrism.* This egocentrism is not, however, the same as the egocentrism of preschool children. Unlike very young children, adolescents realize that other people have their own unique thoughts. Nevertheless, adolescents tend to believe that they alone experience such intense emotions as love, anger, and hate. As a result, they often feel misunderstood.

According to Elkind (1978), adolescents fail to differentiate between the unique and the universal:

A young woman who falls in love for the first time is enraptured with the experience, which is entirely new and thrilling. But she fails to differentiate between what is new and thrilling to herself and what is new and thrilling to humankind. It is not surprising, therefore, that this young woman says to her mother, "But, Mother, you don't know how it feels to be in love."

Adolescents' preoccupation with their physical appearance is also a sign of egocentrism. Can you remember how, as an adolescent, you may have fantasized that everyone was watching how you looked and what you were wearing?
(continued)

Piaget's Theory

Recall from previous chapters that Jean Piaget described school-age children (ages 7 to 12) as being in the concrete operations stage. That is, they can think logically about things that are concrete and observable. But during adolescence, they move into the **formal operations period;** they can now think in the abstract and solve problems systematically.

This ability was evident in Keating's (1980) description of adolescent thought. Keating's ideas are based in part on Piaget's theory and on the tests Piaget and his colleagues devised to ascertain whether adolescents have reached formal operations.

Inhelder and Piaget (1958) developed a number of classic experiments that illustrate the gradual development of logic and test for the ability to engage in the scientific method of problem solving. That is, the adolescent systematically controls and observes the problem's variables in order to test for specific hypotheses.

In one Piagetian task, the chemistry problem, the researcher shows the child or adolescent five colorless, odorless liquids in test tubes. Four of the test tubes are

A CLOSER LOOK

(continued)
Adolescents create an imaginary audience for themselves, thinking that every time they walk into a room, everyone's eyes are on them either admiring or criticizing. This fixation helps explain why every tiny pimple or strand of hair that is out of place assumes such great importance.

Closely tied to this perception is the *personal fable* (Elkind, 1967). Adolescents believe that the reason everyone is interested in them is that they are unique and special. This can have positive consequences:

> The young person who feels that he or she is unique may strive to excel in music, literature, sports or other areas of endeavor. The sense of specialness can also be a source of personal strength and comfort in the face of many inevitable social, academic, and familial trials and tribulations of adolescence. [Elkind, 1967]

At the same time, the fable can have negative effects. An adolescent who regards himself as heroic or destined to great fame tends to have a *sense of indestructibility;* he believes that he is somehow magically protected from things that happen to other people. Such a belief can reinforce the excessive risk taking seen among many adolescents who believe nothing bad can befall them: they will never become addicted to drugs or alcohol; they will not get pregnant; and they will not die in an auto accident even though they often drive like maniacs.

Egocentrism does not disappear entirely; in fact, some adults still suffer from it. But around the age of 16, most teenagers begin to realize that other people do not focus especially on them because they have their own concerns. It gradually dawns on teenagers that they are not as unique or indestructible as they had imagined. Researchers point out that when adolescents begin to think about the future and to ponder their place in society, they will become willing to listen to other people and learn about their values, feelings, and thoughts. In this way adolescents overcome their egocentrism (Youniss, 1980).

Adolescents spend hours in front of the mirror, thinking that everyone will notice everything about them.

Figure 15.1 *In the chemistry problem, the experimenter has to find the correct combination of fluids to produce a yellow mixture.*

labeled 1, 2, 3, and 4, and the fifth is labeled *g*. The researcher then informs the subject that he can obtain a yellow mixture by adding a few drops of *g* to some combination of the other liquids. The subject's task is to find out the correct combination. During middle childhood, the child attempts to solve the problem through trial and error; he will add a few drops of *g* to each of the other test tubes and then give up. When prompted by the experimenter to continue, he will haphazardly combine the liquids, forgetting which he has already mixed and which he has not. The adolescent, however, proceeds to solve the problem along a preconceived plan of action; he anticipates the kind of information he will require to solve the problem. Knowing that he must try out all possible combinations, he will systematically add *g* to the four liquids. Then, he will pick up the test tube labeled 1 and combine it, along with *g*, with test tube 2, then with test tube 3, and then with 4, often keeping a log of what he has tried. Thus, if the experimenter asks what the adolescent had to do to obtain the yellow mixture, he can explain in detail what worked and what did not (see Figure 15.1).

In another task used by Piaget to test for formal operations, the experimenter gives the subject a pendulum created by suspending a weight from a string and allowing the weight to swing freely back and forth. The experimenter asks the subject which of four variables affects the rate at which the weight will swing: the force with which it is pushed, the amount of weight suspended from the string, the height from which the weight is released, or the length of the string. The experimenter then gives the subject a set of different weights and shows her how to change the weights and manipulate the other three variables so she can experiment with all the possible ways that might affect the rate at which the pendulum will swing (see Figure 15.2).

To find the answer to the problem, the concrete operations child will often push the weight at different speeds and say that it is only the force with which the weight is pushed that causes the weight to swing faster or slower. If she tries to manipulate the other variables, she does so haphazardly (Siegler, 1976; Inhelder &

Piaget, 1958). The formal operations adolescent, however, can think about each variable separately and systematically try out all possible manipulations, proceeding along a number of steps. First, she will set standards for each variable. Then she will hold constant three of the variables and vary a fourth so that she can see whether there is a change in the rate at which the weight swings. In successive steps she will continue to hold three variables constant while varying the standard of another variable. In doing so, she will demonstrate the ability to follow a planned strategy of problem solving and her inclination to test all possible hypotheses or their combinations.

Piaget explained that the adolescent's ability to think in the abstract is due to brain maturation and the increased opportunity for experimenting with various aspects of the environment. This interaction between biological and environmental factors is crucial. Since adolescents are neurologically ready for cognitive growth, changes must also occur in the environment. For example, adolescents should have the opportunity to engage in more demanding mental tasks. Since formal operations thought develops gradually during the adolescent years, young adolescents

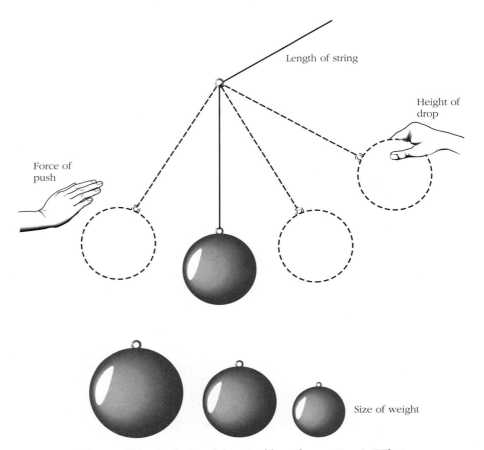

Figure 15.2 *In the pendulum problem, the question is "What causes the pendulum to swing quickly or slowly?" Adolescents, in the formal operations period of cognitive development, consider all possible factors: the size of the weight, the force of the push, the height of the drop, and the length of the string.*

can think in the abstract about some things but not others. We will return to this issue later in the chapter.

There are limitations to Piaget's theory. For example, some researchers say his tests focus on a view of the world that is dominated by abstract rules and do not take into account the practical intelligence used to solve everyday problems.

The Inadequacy of Piagetian Tests

Cross-cultural studies   Some researchers have used the pendulum experiment described in Figure 15.2 and other Piagetian tasks with adolescents in various cultures. According to their findings, everyone reaches the concrete operations stage but not everyone attains the formal operations stage as measured by Piagetian tasks. Individuals raised in nontechnical societies and without access to schooling do not acquire the ability for formal operations (Dasen, 1977; Laboratory of Comparative Human Cognition, 1983).

Other studies have shown that even in cultures with compulsory schooling, not everyone attains this final level of cognitive functioning (Keating, 1980; Niemark, 1975). Researchers who have critiqued or elaborated on Piaget's theory note that, in testing for formal operations, Piaget focused solely on scientific problems. As these researchers claim, adolescents apply their ability to think abstractly to other tasks besides those of a scientific nature. Thus, we need to raise some questions regarding these findings: Do some individuals fail to attain formal operations, or do the findings reflect the inadequacy of the tests used to measure formal operations? For example, anthropological evidence suggests that although individuals in nontechnological societies do not demonstrate the ability to think abstractly when tested on Piagetian experiments, they do think abstractly on tasks relevant to their own way of life. They are able to make and follow systematic plans and to consider all possible solutions to their daily problems. Cole (1981; 1983) provides support for these findings in extensive research conducted on cognitive development in the cross-

In high school, adolescents can formulate hypotheses and contemplate abstract ideas. In history, they can consider not only what the world is, but what it might have become if certain conditions had been different. In science, they can focus on complex theoretical issues.

cultural context. In addition, Kenny (1983) notes that some adolescents and adults are capable of formal operations only when performing certain tasks; this may be the result of motivational and environmental factors because the more knowledge people have, the more their abstract-reasoning capacity increases (Carey, 1988).

Fischer and Lazerson (1984) explain that an adolescent boy who has recently purchased a car and does not have much money to spend on car repairs will learn as much as he can about how the different parts of the car work. Then when his car breaks down, he is able to put this knowledge to use. Applying abstract mental skills, he will consider all possible reasons that the car does not start and will systematically test each of them. But this same adolescent may not be able to think abstractly when engaged in tasks related to physics or psychology. He may not have the interest or motivation to acquire more information about these subjects.

Individual and sex differences   You can see that accumulated knowledge is necessary if the adolescent is to use formal operations thinking. Does this mean that there are individual and sex differences in formal operations thinking? For example, we need to demonstrate formal operations thinking in such areas as engineering and science more than in other areas. Researchers have wondered if sex differences in formal operations may be the reason that more men traditionally work in these fields (Kaufman & Flaitz, 1987). Most studies Meehan (1984) reviewed on formal operations found no sex differences in performance on formal operations tasks. In the few studies where such differences existed, men generally performed better than women. Although these differences may be explained in terms of differing interests, some researchers suggest that they are the result of differences between the sexes in spatial abilities.

Some adolescents demonstrate formal operations thinking at an early age (Straham, 1983), whereas others have difficulty with such tasks even in late adolescence. People's interests and knowledge in part account for individual differences in formal operations thinking, but researchers also note that there are problems with Piaget's method for assessing formal operations. Clarifying the demands of the tasks helps elicit formal operations thinking in 85% of 13-year-olds and 95% of 17-year-olds, but does not help 10-year-olds (Danner & Day, 1977). Martornao (1977) used 10 Piagetian tasks to test for formal operations in 6th-, 8th-, 10th, and 12th-grade students. She found that formal operations thinking begins to emerge between 12 and 15 years of age. However, even 12th-graders in her study did not consistently demonstrate formal operations thinking across all 10 tasks, suggesting that each task assesses different skills. Piaget developed 15 tasks to test for formal operations, but most studies have relied on just a few of them. Also, as Small (1990) notes, it is not even clear that Piaget used all 15 tasks on any one individual.

Over the years Piaget changed his original assertion that the process of cognitive development is invariant and universal. He believed that the physiological maturation attained in adolescence—or at puberty, to be exact—is necessary to reach the formal operations stage. But a change in the environment is also necessary. Piaget admitted that people will remain in the concrete operations stage unless they interact with others who practice abstract and logical thinking or unless they have school or other experiences that encourage their abstract thinking skills (Piaget, 1972).

Information Processing

Piaget believed that qualitative changes in cognitive development account for formal operations thinking. Information-processing theorists, however, note that adolescents are better able to process information and have a better capacity to retain information that will help them solve problems efficiently. Scardamalia (1977), for example, varied Piaget's chemistry problem to include measures of working-memory capacity. She found that children could systematically work through the problem if the demands of the task were within their capacity for memory. The same children, however, were unable to solve the problem when its demands were beyond their capacity for memory. Sternberg (1977) makes the same observation, noting also that the adolescent's ability to store more information can aid in the ability to think and reason about hypotheses.

Intellectual Performance

Another approach to the study of cognitive development is the **psychometric approach** (mentioned briefly in Chapter 6), which focuses on individual differences in intellectual performance. The emphasis here is on how children of the same age differ in intelligence. The most common way of measuring differences in intelligence is through standardized intelligence tests that yield a score, known as the *intelligence quotient* or *IQ*. IQ is the basis for comparing a student's intellectual performance with that of other students. During adolescence, intellectual performance, as measured by IQ tests, improves; these improvements are related to improvements in the mental abilities the tests measure and in accumulated knowledge.

Individual differences in intellectual performance are impressively large. Those children with very low IQ scores are considered mentally retarded, while those with very high scores are considered gifted. Even within both groups significant individual variations exist; individuals with the same IQ may be very different in the way they behave and in what they accomplish. To understand the meaning of individual differences in intelligence, therefore, we must first consider the nature of intelligence.

A CLOSER LOOK

Children with Mental Retardation

Throughout history people have shown an interest in and been curious about individuals with mental retardation (Zigler & Hodapp, 1986). Yet the scientific study and understanding of what constitutes mental retardation is relatively recent. For example, not until the end of the 18th century did observers even understand the difference between mental retardation and emotional disorders (Syzmanski & Tanguay, 1980). Researchers today point out that mental retardation is more common and far easier to identify than other kinds of developmental psychopathology (Zigler, Lamb, & Child, 1982).

Children with mental retardation function intellectually at a level significantly below average. In some cases child experts can diagnose this condition either at birth or shortly afterward, but usually diagnosis occurs when the children reach school. In fact, although few children are diagnosed as having mental retardation before age 5, the number of cases increases rapidly during the school years (MacMillan, 1982). This should come as no surprise. Once children enter school, they are expected to perform a variety of intellectual tasks. Thus, it is easy to compare the performance of children with mental retardation against that of their age-mates.

Mental Retardation and IQ Tests
Psychologists identify children as having mental retardation on the basis of IQ test scores. For many years the consensus was that these children had IQ scores in the lowest one-third of the population. But in 1959 the American Association on Mental Deficiency (AAMD) decided that all persons whose *(continued)*

What Is Intelligence?

Over the years psychologists have proposed numerous definitions of intelligence. Although there appears to be no consensus on a precise definition, most agree that intelligence has two aspects: *intellectual potential* and *intellectual behavior* or performance. Unlike intellectual potential, intellectual performance can be observed and measured. Hebb (1972) called the two aspects of intelligence, *intelligence A* and *intelligence B*. Intelligence A refers to the child's innate potential to develop intellectual capacities, whereas intelligence B refers to the level of the child's intellectual functioning.

Cattell (1963) and Horn (1970) advanced the theory of fluid intelligence and crystallized intelligence. *Fluid intelligence* refers to basic, innate mental abilities,

---

A CLOSER LOOK

(continued)

IQ score was more than 1 standard deviation below the mean—that is, whose score was 84 or less—had mental retardation. Because of this decision, the number of Americans regarded as having mental retardation jumped from 5 million to more than 30 million! In 1973 the AAMD changed its criterion of mental retardation to include only those persons whose IQ was more than 2 standard deviations below the mean; that is, individuals whose score was less than 70. Given this new definition, psychologists would classify a child with an IQ of 70 as normal, even though before 1973 they would have regarded her as a child with mental retardation. Thus, you can see how important it is to avoid adherence to overly rigid cutoff points in deciding normal functioning. Using a definition of IQ score alone, the label of mental retardation becomes arbitrary and relative.

Other Criteria

Psychologists do consider other factors, such as personal and social functioning, in defining mental retardation. For example: What deficits do individuals display in their adaptive behavior? To what extent can they meet standards of personal independence and social responsibility for people in their age and cultural groups (American Psychiatric Association, 1987)?

Psychologists attempt to categorize children with mental retardation on the basis of the degree of their handicap. This differentiation indicates that not all children with mental retardation are totally incapacitated or socially incompetent, as people once thought. The great majority have only mild retardation; they can meet their personal needs, hold jobs, and run a household with minimal aid.

Take, for example, a 15-year-old boy with mental retardation. Depending on his ability to handle money, he might be placed in one of the following categories:

Mild mental retardation (IQ 55–69)   He can go to the store and purchase a number of items; he can make change correctly. He may eventually be able to earn a living, although he may need some help in managing his income.

Moderate mental retardation (IQ 40–54)   He can shop for several items and make minor purchases. He can handle bills and coins accurately.

Severe mental retardation (IQ 25–39)   He can go on simple errands, if he has a note to give to the store. He may be able to use a coin-operated machine. Although he understands that money has value, he may not know how to use it.

Profound mental retardation (IQ below 25)   He is incapable of any activity involving money.

Causes of Mental Retardation

Psychologists have identified two types of retardation:

Not all children with mental retardation are incapaciated; many have only mild retardation and can both meet their own personal needs and hold a job.

---

such as analytic ability, memory, and speed of thinking, that are relatively influenced by prior learning. *Crystallized intelligence* refers to what the individual knows; experience, cultural background, and education influence crystallized intelligence. Thus, two children with equal fluid intelligence may differ in crystallized intelligence depending on the kind of schools they attend and the other experiences they have had.

Although we do not fully understand the true nature of intelligence, most of us have some ideas about what intelligence is. In comparing popular ideas of intelligence with psychologists' notions of intelligence, Sternberg (1982) found that psychologists and others with no specialized training in human development believe that intelligence consists of three basic components: *verbal intelligence,* which

A CLOSER LOOK

1. *A known organic disorder* This group comprises about 30% of individuals with mental retardation; almost all have severe or profound mental retardation. Most of these individuals are diagnosed shortly after birth or during infancy. The cause of their disorder is usually any one of the large group of genetic or chromosomal anomalies discussed in Chapter 2.

2. *Cultural/familial retardation* This group comprises about 70% of individuals with mental retardation; their IQ scores are usually above 50 (Zigler & Cascione, 1984). Psychologists almost always classify them as having mild mental retardation. Because children in this group show no signs of abnormal genetic disorder or brain damage, psychologists usually cannot identify them as having mental retardation until they are in school. Apparently there is nothing wrong with them except that they are slow learners; they show little interest in school activities and have poor language and communication skills (Philips, 1980). Their behavior is immature, and each year they fall further behind their peers in academic achievement.

Although the cause of cultural/familial retardation is a mystery, psychologists generally agree that it results from a combination of environmental (cultural) and hereditary (familial) factors. They do not know, however, how much each factor contributes to the condition.

There are two schools of thought about mental retardation. Researchers adhering to the difference or defect perspective point out that whereas children with mental retardation suffer from some physiological impairment, those with cultural/familial mental retardation suffer from one of a small set of defects such as an impaired memory (Ellis, 1970) or attention deficiencies (Fisher & Zeaman, 1973); these defects are inherent in all individuals with mental retardation.

On the other hand, psychologists adhering to the developmental perspective believe that those with organic problems suffer from a faulty intellectual apparatus, whereas children with cultural/familial mental retardation go through the same developmental stages as do children of average or high intelligence. However, children with cultural/familial mental retardation differ in their rate of progress and in the ultimate intellectual ceiling they can achieve (Zigler & Balla, 1982).

Theorists adhering to the developmental perspective believe that children with cultural/familial mental retardation react to environmental influences like normal children. For this reason, the personality characteristics usually associated with children with mental retardation—rigidity, overdependency, and low expectations of success—are due to their life experiences rather than to defects associated with mental retardation (Zigler, Lamb, & Child, 1982). For example, children with cultural/familial mental retardation are likely to experience a great deal of failure because they are slower and less capable than normal children. A history of failure engenders certain behavior patterns among children with mental retardation as well as among normal youngsters. According to the theorists, these children expect to fail because of their repeated experience of failure. As a result, they settle for a low degree of success (Cromwell, 1963). These youngsters are also more apt to blame themselves for their lack of success.

Researchers point to experiments in which they asked a group of children with mental retardation and normal children to complete a task and then prevented them from doing so. When the researchers asked "Why didn't you complete the task?" normal children cited the handicap placed in their way. In contrast, children with mental retardation consistently attributed the failure to their own inadequacy (MacMillan, 1969; MacMillan & Keogh, 1971).

Although there is a great deal of information about children with mental retardation, many questions remain. Continuing research should help us devise ways to help these individuals and should also enhance our understanding of the range of development.

Using intelligence tests to evaluate students who may not do well academically is a highly controversial practice. A low score does not necessarily mean that the student is unintelligent: performance can be affected by lack of proficiency in English, a learning disability, low motivation, and even such seemingly simple factors as taking the test in an unfamiliar setting.

refers to a good vocabulary, verbal fluency, and comprehension; *problem-solving ability,* which refers to abstract thinking, reasoning skills, and the ability to see connections between ideas; and *practical intelligence,* which refers to the ability to identify and accomplish goals and to display an interest in the world at large. However, the question remains, How do we define an intelligent person? Is a person intelligent if we find her to be intelligent in all three components? In this case we may conclude that these intellectual components stem from a general intellectual source. Or, is a person considered intelligent on the basis of any one of the intellectual components? This would lead us to conclude that the three types of intelligence are separate and distinct from one another.

Early theorists regarded intelligence as a global or all-encompassing factor that influences the individual's abilities. Spearman (1904) proposed that intelligence is composed of two factors: general intelligence, or the *g factor,* which represents the general intellectual ability that is applied in all intellectual tasks, and the *s factor,* which refers to specific abilities required for particular tasks. The *s* factor accounts for the fact that some individuals are better at some skills than at others. For example, a student may perform well on verbal problems but not on math problems. Spearman claimed that intelligence tests should be designed to measure as much of the *g* factor as possible.

However, other psychologists have challenged this view. For a time there was some enthusiasm for the view that intelligence is made up of numerous independent mental abilities; psychologists argued that these abilities should be measured separately. Thurstone (1938) suggested that the intellect is made up of seven primary mental abilities: spatial perception, perceptual speed, verbal comprehension, numerical ability, memory, word fluency, and reasoning. After developing separate tests for each ability, he found that an individual's scores on these tests were often interrelated, which seemed to indicate the presence of a general factor for intelligence. Thus, the initial enthusiasm for differential aptitudes as measures of intelligence has waned, since these measures have not demonstrated greater utility than the single measure of intelligence proposed by earlier theorists. Some support for the multiple-intelligences concept still survives, however. For instance, Howard

Gardner (1983) believes there are at least seven intelligences, each following a somewhat different developmental path.

Measuring Intelligence

Validity, reliability, and standardization   Psychologists have developed different tests to measure intelligence that incorporate the assessment of those skills or abilities that make up intelligence. Although intelligence tests differ depending on the definition of intelligence, a common set of principles guides the construction of these tests.

First, the test must have *validity;* that is, it must measure what it proposes to measure. This is not as simple as it sounds. Since intelligence is difficult to define, how do we know that a test actually measures intelligence? This presents problems, as you will soon see.

Second, the test must have *reliability,* meaning that it is a consistent measuring device, yielding about the same results when the same individual is retested a short time later. Thus, using a test/retest method in which a group of individuals is tested twice, researchers can establish the test's reliability. There are other methods to determine reliability. Both validity and reliability are determined through field testing, in which the test is given to many children of different ages. After testing and retesting the children a number of times, researchers can eliminate some questions on the basis of the results of the field tests. Questions can be added or rewritten until researchers believe that the test is both valid and reliable. Validity and reliability are important in all tests, not just those that focus on intelligence (see also Chapter 2).

Finally, the test must be *standardized;* that is, standard items, procedures, and norms must be established. Standardization is an arduous process in which the test is administered to a group of children who are typical of those who will eventually take the test. Again, some questions will be rewritten or eliminated if it appears that differences in the children's responses are related to a particular characteristic. For example, if boys consistently fail to answer a particular question that most girls get right, that question would have to be rewritten or eliminated because it might reflect overall differences between boys and girls that are not attributable to their IQ. Standardization entails two important principles:

1. The larger the sample group of children used to standardize the test, the more applicable the test will be to all other children of similar circumstances.

2. The characteristics of the children in the standardization sample must be as similar as possible to those of the total population to be tested. That is, there should be the correct proportion of males to females, of urban dwellers to rural dwellers, of people residing in different parts of the country, and of various socioeconomic classes and ethnic backgrounds.

In 1972 researchers standardized the Stanford-Binet IQ test with samples of Americans from different backgrounds (Terman & Merrill, 1972). Problems had arisen with the test, in part because it had been standardized with white, middle-class, English-speaking Americans. Thus, it was not applicable to other ethnic and socioeconomic backgrounds.

There is also a question regarding the validity of the IQ test. Does it actually measure intelligence? In fact, since intelligence is a comprehensive term that includes different attributes, the IQ test may not be a good measure of intelligence.

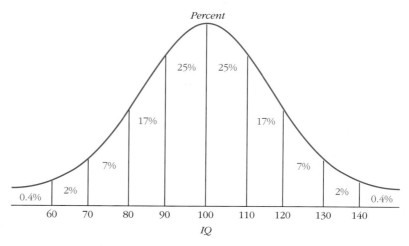

Figure 15.3   Distribution of IQ scores.

However, it is a reliable measure of intellectual performance. Researchers use the IQ test to evaluate students because it has been a good predictor of how well a child will do in school (Weinberg, 1989).

History of intelligence tests   A child's score on the IQ test is, in fact, a good predictor of the youngster's school success. This is not due to chance, however. Recall from Chapter 2 that two Frenchmen, Alfred Binet and Theophile Simon, developed early versions of the IQ test expressly for that purpose. At the turn of the century, the French government asked Alfred Binet to create a test that would identify mentally retarded or dull students so the school could offer them special instruction. Tests in use at the time measured such abilities as sensory acuity, eye/hand coordination, and reaction time, because people thought that intelligence had a physiological basis. These tests had no useful function, however, because French educators soon learned that performance on them had no relationship to how well children did in school nor to how intelligent their teachers thought them to be. Binet contended that a more useful measure of intelligence would incorporate the assessment of mental skills typically used in school. As a result, he devised items that measured such mental functions as memory, imagery, imagination, attention, and comprehension. He thought that these functions and several other specific abilities were related to one another and reflected some more basic intellectual ability.

At the turn of the century, Alfred Binet and Theophile Simon were asked by the French government to develop a test that would identify children who needed special instruction. Although they created the forerunner of the IQ test to prevent subjective judgments in assigning students to special classrooms, using IQ tests for this purpose is illegal in the United States.

Binet and Theophile Simon together constructed a test consisting of 30 items presented in ascending order of difficulty. Eventually, they devised a longer test that included different tasks for each age group, because older children could successfully complete more items. This test allowed Binet and Simon to determine the children's *mental age*. For example, a 5-year-old who could successfully complete a problem usually assigned to 7-year-olds would have a mental age (MA) of 7 even though his chronological (actual) age was 5. However, the mental age does not help us compare children of different ages. That is, a 10-year-old with an MA of 13 may know more than a 5-year-old with an MA of 7. Does that mean that the 10-year-old is more intelligent than the 5-year-old? A subsequent revision of the tests incorporating the views of William Stern (1911) resolved this problem. Stern developed the concept of the intelligence quotient, or IQ, which is essentially a comparison of the child's chronological age with his mental age. The IQ remains relatively constant with age. Stern derived the IQ on the basis of the following formula:

Figure 15.4 Examples of test items on the WISC-R. Wechsler Intelligence Scale for Children—Revised. Copyright © 1974 by The Psychological Corporation. Reproduced by permission. All rights reserved.

$$\frac{\text{Mental age (MA)}}{\text{Chronological age (CA)}} \times 100 = IQ$$

This formula allows us to compare the mental abilities of children at different ages: a 10-year-old with an MA of 13 has an IQ of 130 (13/10 × 100); the 5-year-old with an MA of 7 has an IQ of 140 (7/5 × 100). While the 10-year-old may know more than the 5-year-old, he has a lower IQ. Intelligence tests today are no longer based on this formula because more advanced statistical methods are used to calculate the IQ score, which is statistically adjusted with a standard deviation of 15 points. As a result, two-thirds of all people have IQs between 85 and 115, which is within the average or normal range (see Figure 15.3).

Binet and Simon's test was revised by Lewis Terman and his colleagues at Stanford University. Known as the Stanford-Binet test, it was standardized for use with American children. Like the French version, it relies heavily on the measurement of verbal abilities. Since this can be a problem with individuals lacking verbal skills, the test was revised accordingly. Also, David Wechsler (1958; 1974) developed other tests: the Wechsler Adult Intelligence Scale (WAIS), the Wechsler Intelligence Scale for Children (WISC), and the Wechsler Preschool and Primary Scale of Intelligence (WPPI). His tests yield three scores: the verbal IQ based on verbal abilities; the performance IQ; and a total, or overall, IQ score. Examples of the performance items on the WISC, revised, are given in Figure 15.4.

Here is an example of a performance problem: The researcher shows a child a picture of a car with a wheel missing and asks her to complete the picture. In another example, the researcher shows a child a maze and asks her to trace its route from start to home. As a general rule, the performance part of the tests is considered a valid indicator of the individual's intellectual aptitude, especially for children who are not native English speakers. Yet the verbal part of the tests is a better predictor of school success because most schoolwork is based on language skills.

What do IQ tests measure?   Although IQ tests are the most relied-on measure of intellectual performance, their use raises some problems. First, intelligence cannot be defined solely on the basis of school performance, because other cognitive abilities are important in other situations; and intelligence tests do not measure these other abilities. For example, they do not measure an individual's capacity to adapt to life circumstances (Sternberg, 1985; 1987). A child may have an IQ of 80, which is below normal. Although this child may not do well in school, she may be quite adept at holding her own among her friends and in her neighborhood. Like-wise, an adult with an IQ of 80 is quite capable of working and supporting a family. In both cases the individuals have shown that they are good at adapting to life circumstances.

Second, other factors that are important in educational achievement and career success are not reflected in the IQ score. We can see this by looking at correlational studies. IQ scores and academic success are correlated at about 0.60, and IQ scores and later occupational success are correlated at 0.50 (McCall, 1977). Since correlation coefficients range from 0.0 to 1.0, a correlation of 0.60 or 0.50 is quite good. However, if the IQ score reflected all the important factors involved in educational achievement and career success, the correlations would be perfect—1.0.

In fact, the IQ test does not measure intellectual *ability*; it measures intellectual *performance*. In general, intellectual performance is determined by a complex interaction among aptitude, achievement, and motivation (Zigler & Butterfield, 1968). Numerous factors influence intellectual performance, including intellectual potential, the amount of information or knowledge acquired, ability to read, and skill at taking tests. Even a seemingly simple factor—such as whether students feel comfortable in the test-taking situation—can have a significant effect on their performance (Zigler, Abelson, & Seitz, 1973). Researchers have found that when they test minority and disabled children in a familiar setting, the children do better than when tested in unfamiliar settings (Fuchs & Fuchs, 1986). In addition, the individual's cognitive style, or his way of responding to a task, may influence his ability to score well on an IQ test (see Chapter 12). Jerome Kagan (1965) notes that one of the most important differences in cognitive style is the tendency to either respond immediately in a hurried manner—an *impulsive style*—or slowly and deliberately—a *reflective style*. Reflectivity and impulsivity characterize many children and adults (see Chapter 12). When they are being tested, reflective individuals tend to approach the task slowly and carefully, making sure they get as many answers right as they can. Impulsive individuals, on the other hand, tend to make more mistakes, not because they are unable to answer correctly but because they scan the test questions hurriedly and are careless in their responses.

Finally, children's experiences can also influence their performance on the test. Many critics argue that IQ tests are culturally biased and give an unfair advantage to middle-class, white children (Oakland & Parmelee, 1985). Kagan (1972) noted that the tests usually include words and concepts that are common in middle-class homes but not in low-income homes. For example, a question on the test may be "What is the advantage of keeping money in the bank?" Low-income students whose families do not have enough money to meet their basic needs may not know the answer to this question because the issue never comes up at home. Another question might be "What would you do if you were sent to a store to buy a loaf of bread and the grocer said he didn't have any more?" The correct answer is "Go to another store." However, children in rural areas or neighborhoods where there is only one store would have to answer "Go home." Despite the fact that this is a reasonable answer for these children, given their circumstances and prior experiences, the test scorer would not give credit for such an answer. The issue of cultural bias in testing is also noted with respect to those children who are in cultures (the Native Americans, for example) that do not emphasize competition (see Chapter 13).

The consequences of using culturally biased tests are very serious. Minority-group and low-income students tend to score low on such tests; therefore, some educators label them slow learners or mentally retarded and place them in slow-paced educational programs or in special education classes. In studies conducted in California, Jane Mercer (1971; 1972) discovered that a disproportionate number of blacks and Mexican Americans were being placed in special education classes because of their low IQ scores. Yet when Mercer gave these children tests that measured their ability to adapt to life circumstances, she found that 90% of the blacks and 60% of the Mexican Americans passed, indicating that they are simply unfamiliar with words, objects, and strategies presented on the IQ test. After examining the issue, the California Federal District Court banned the use of IQ test scores as a major basis for placement in special education (in *Larry P.* v. *Wilson Riles,* 1979). The courts now require schools to use several criteria as a basis for deciding whether a child needs to be in a special education class. A child who scores low on an IQ test may indeed have mental retardation, but we cannot assume this on the basis of his IQ score. We need further investigations to determine why the child's score is low.

To reduce the influence of culture on test results researchers have devised a number of *culture-fair tests*. These tests include fewer verbal items; they assess children's intellectual performance by asking them to complete drawings, to fit irregularly shaped blocks into holes, or to copy designs with multicolored cubes. However, these tests still tend to favor some cultural experiences (Cole, 1985), because it has been difficult to develop a completely culture-fair test. Even if researchers devise a perfect test, it will never predict school performance, because successful school performance is also culturally biased. After all, schools encourage achievements and ways of performing that are considered valuable by the white, middle-class community.

A CLOSER LOOK

Socioeconomic Status and IQ

The controversy surrounding the use of the IQ test to evaluate students has to do with the cultural bias inherent in the test. Numerous studies have found that children from low-income homes tend to score, on the average, 10 to 15 points lower on IQ tests than children from middle-class families. In general, the higher a family's socioeconomic status, the higher the IQs of both parents and children. Remember, however, that the IQ differences are average differences for groups of people and have nothing to do with the intelligence of any one individual in any socioeconomic class. Furthermore, remember that socioeconomic status refers to income and not to cultural and ethnic background.

Researchers have developed several hypotheses to explain differences in IQ among socioeconomic levels. We have already seen that a cultural bias is inherent in the IQ test. Another explanation focuses on the motivational/emotional factors that affect people in different social classes. For example, a student from a low-income family may not be motivated to do well on a test or may not even want to take the test in the first place. That student's low IQ score does not necessarily indicate low intelligence; rather, it indicates a lack of motivation to do well on the test (Zigler & Seitz, 1982; Zigler & Butterfield, 1968). Usually children who are not motivated in test taking are also not motivated to succeed in school. Thus, there will be a correlation between their IQ score and their school performance.

In addition, low-income homes may provide poorer physical and cognitive environments. The lack of food and decent shelter, for example, can affect children's health and

(continued)

The Adolescent in School

So far we have examined the changes that occur in adolescent thought and the various approaches—Piagetian, information processing, and psychometric—that explain these changes. Now let us examine the adolescent's experiences in school.

A CLOSER LOOK

(continued)

inhibit their potential to succeed in school. Not having books to read or toys to play with can also inhibit their ability to develop cognitively.

Another hypothesis is that social-class differences in intellectual performance are related to genetic differences. Because representation in a low socioeconomic class is higher among some ethnic groups, most notably blacks, Jensen (1969) contended that the lower average IQ scores of low-income blacks are evidence of a genetic factor in intelligence, and that these blacks are intellectually inferior. However, most investigators consider the strong relationship between IQ and social class to be primarily environmental in nature (Weinberg, 1989). They point out, for example, that children from various ethnic backgrounds excel in different mental abilities. If we separate the groups along socioeconomic lines, the profiles of abilities for lower-class ethnic groups parallel the profiles of middle-class ethnic groups. However, lower-class ethnic groups score lower on all abilities, which suggests a greater socioeconomic disadvantage (Lesser, Fifer, & Clark, 1965).

Heredity and Environment

The notion that social class differences in IQ stem from genetic differences in intelligence is controversial because of the erroneous label it attaches to some ethnic groups and because of its many social and political implications. For instance, if we believe that intelligence is an inherited trait, then we would not strive to implement programs designed to improve the educational achievement of economically disadvantaged children. But if we believe that intelligence is affected by environmental factors, then we would contend that such programs are important.

In an effort to determine the relative contributions of heredity and the environment to intelligence, researchers have focused on studies using identical fraternal twins and on other studies using adopted children. Recall from Chapter 3 that these studies showed that both heredity and the environment affect intelligence, and that although genetic makeup determines intellectual potential, the extent to which this potential can be realized depends on environmental factors (Plomin, 1989). Even within the same family, environmental factors can affect children's IQs. For example, the IQs of siblings may differ according to birth order, family size, and the number of years between the children's births (Zajonc & Bargh, 1980; Zajonc, 1983). Later-born children tend to have a lower IQ than earlier-born children. One widely accepted explanation for this difference is that parents spend more time with their firstborn than with their later-born children. Researchers note, however, the influence of birth order is subtle and far less consequential than the impact of the parental attitudes, values, and behaviors evident to the child in the family environment (McCall, Applebaum, & Hogarty, 1973).

Sandra Scarr and Richard Weinberg (1976; 1977) clearly demonstrated that environmental factors account for some differences in intellectual performance among children from economically disadvantaged ethnic backgrounds. Studying IQ scores of black children adopted and raised by white, middle-class families, the researchers found that the younger the children were at the time of adoption, the closer they came to the average IQs of white, middle-class children. Scarr and Weinberg noted that their study does not refute the importance of heredity in intelligence. It does indicate, however, that individuals' IQ scores can be increased by 10 to 20 points by placing them in middle-class homes, and the earlier they are able to live under such circumstances, the better. In addition, recent data indicate that young black children generally have better achievement records than their counterparts of earlier generations. This development may be due to the compensatory educational programs the children receive during their preschool years and to the improved schooling and other social programs available since the late 1960s (Committee on Economic Development, 1987; Berrueta-Clement et al., 1984). Thus, intervention efforts can help improve the educational achievement of economically disadvantaged children. Also, young black children today may have better achievement records because their parents are better educated than previous generations of black parents.

Since adolescents can attain a more sophisticated level of cognitive functioning, they need a different kind of education. In the elementary grades children are taught the basic skills, with some emphasis on social studies and science; in high school, however, adolescents are exposed to more subjects and are expected to cover the material in greater depth. In addition, hypotheses and abstract notions now form part of schooling. The study of history, for example, includes a consideration of what has happened in the past and class discussions of what might have happened if different conditions had prevailed. Similarly, science and math lessons no longer focus on visible experiments and problems; instead they involve explanations and discussions of theoretical issues, such as the laws of physics or the principles of algebra and geometry. Most teachers do not abandon concrete examples altogether; rather they provide a variety of academic experiences, recognizing that many adolescents have the potential to reach formal operational thinking. An instructional mode that takes advantage of this fact is more challenging and stimulating (Elkind, 1983).

Unfortunately, all schools and all teachers do not provide this kind of high-quality intellectual stimulation and training. As a result, only some adolescents receive an education that helps them attain the formal operations stage. Dale (1970) pointed out that some high school students in science classes do not reach formal operational thought, because some high school science teachers emphasize rote learning rather than the active problem solving essential for cognitive growth.

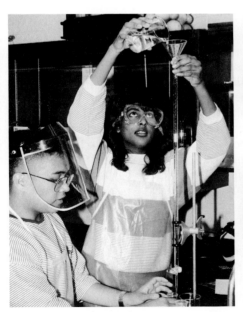 

For some students, their high school experience is determined by test scores. Some students are given opportunities to engage in intellectually stimulating activities and some are not.

Additionally, not all students pursue the same academic course. Students who are considered brighter than others are placed in an accelerated educational program. Some students take vocational courses and others are placed in middle or slow tracks. The conventional rationale underlying this almost universal practice of "tracking" students into fast or slow classes is to allow students to study at a realistic pace that will help them acquire useful training for their adult lives. Still some educators criticize tracking as unfair because it offers so-called bright students educational advantages that it denies to so-called slow youngsters. Goodlad's (1983) comprehensive study of public schools found that teachers in high-track classes spend more time on instruction and assign more homework than do teachers in middle- and low-track classes. Also the teachers in high-track classes focus on more difficult skills, whereas those in low-track classes encourage passivity and do not expect students to make full use of their abilities.

There is concern that tracking itself is not a good idea. Children in a slow track, for example, may be labeled "dummies," and they may see themselves as failures (Rutter, 1983). They may also be prevented from opportunities to learn from more advanced students. Furthermore, a child may not do well in school for a couple of years but may blossom later; if that child is in a slow track, he may not have the opportunity to change or may continually set low expectations for himself, thinking he cannot succeed. Rhona Weinstein (in press) developed an intervention program for low-achieving 9th-grade students. Teachers were trained to interact positively with the students and to convey positive expectations. Within a year, students who participated in the program improved their grades and their behavior.

There are also concerns about how children are placed in different tracks. As a rule, educators make these decisions on the basis of grades and earlier performance on batteries of tests. The tests may be IQ tests or achievement tests (see Chapter 12). Test scores reflect the norm; that is, the IQ test scores reflect the student's potential to succeed academically and the achievement test scores reflect what she has learned in relation to other students her age. Although students take such tests throughout their schooling, the test results are especially important in high school. At this point a student's record on the tests can determine the kind of courses she takes and even her future direction in life. In fact, test results can affect the way youngsters feel about themselves and the way others regard them.

As we noted earlier, there is a great deal of controversy about the use of tests to evaluate students. On the other hand, if the test scores accurately reflect intellectual ability, they can be useful to schools and teachers striving to help children reach their learning potential. Placing a child with a limited potential for intellectual growth in a high-track class where he would have to work far beyond his potential is unfair and dooms the child to certain failure. Similarly, it is a shame to place a student with high intellectual potential in a class that presents few, if any, opportunities to develop her potential. Still critics wonder if educators use test results to provide or to deny educational opportunities to children in the middle and low tracks. These critics also question the practice of making important decisions that may determine the future course of a student's life on the basis of test scores (Weinberg, 1989). Do such scores really indicate the individual's ability to succeed in school? If a student gets poor scores on these tests during his freshman year in high school, does that mean that he is not likely to succeed in college? On the basis of our previous discussion on the limitations and advantages of the IQ test, you can determine the answers to these questions.

High School Compensatory Education

Can we intervene and help students succeed in school? And if we can, when should we? Most educators and psychologists now agree that educational intervention efforts can improve the level of school achievement. Much of the focus has been on intervention during early childhood, or even earlier. As we discussed in Chapter 9, these programs have been very effective.

Intervention programs for low-income adolescents have focused on enhancing their education. These programs are usually offered to economically disadvantaged, academically capable students. Upward Bound and numerous other programs have given a variety of challenging opportunities to these youngsters. Yet the same programs have not been available to educationally deficient adolescents with low IQs (Stipek, 1979; Carnegie Council on Adolescent Development, 1989).

Why have we been reluctant to help teenagers with low IQ scores? This reluctance stems, in part, from a widely held belief that by the time youngsters reach adolescence, it is too late to overcome their educational handicaps. This opinion is based on the concept of the critical period of intervention, which has dominated U.S. educational policy for the past two decades. According to this belief, such students are doomed to educational failure unless their learning deficits are identified and overcome at an early age. Because both educators and social scientists share this view, they have not explored the possibility of intervening during adolescence.

However, direct evidence points to the fact that intervention programs can be successful, even during adolescence, which suggests that high school compensatory education programs may be beneficial. Reuven Feuerstein (1980) provides one line of evidence. He demonstrated that even adolescents with an IQ of 60 to 80 (which places them among the mentally retarded) are capable of significant increases in their mental abilities as long as they are not suffering from organic brain damage or damage to the central nervous system. Feuerstein believes that before adolescents can benefit from formal schooling, they have to master certain underlying cognitive skills: they need to be able to regulate their attention, to observe the stimuli they encounter, and to figure out and express the relationship between various aspects of their environment. To guide adolescents' experiences so they can acquire these skills, he developed a program of *mediated learning experiences,* in which adolescents learn to work closely with teachers who guide them in their interactions with the environment. In this way the youngsters can gradually adapt to new ways of perceiving the world and processing information.

Illiteracy in the United States

Feuerstein's program, which has been implemented in Israel and in selected schools in the United States and other countries, is expensive because of its emphasis on intensive, individualized instruction. Yet, along with other adolescent intervention initiatives (Carnegie Council on Adolescent Development, 1989), it is worthy of consideration in terms of potential savings in later costs to society. Imple-

Despite the widespread belief that by adolescence it is too late to help educationally deficient students, high school compensatory programs are effective. This teenager is learning to read with the help of a tutor.

mentation of this program in U.S. high schools would be especially valuable in light of the illiteracy problem in the United States. A significant number of high school students either drop out of school, or graduate without ever acquiring basic reading and writing skills. As a result, these young people are functionally illiterate (Fisher, 1976). According to several reports (Bennett, 1985; National Commission on Excellence in Education, 1983), 17 to 21 million English-speaking Americans cannot write a check, address an envelope, or read a sign in a store. Millions of other Americans cannot read proficiently; that is, they cannot read beyond the level of 9- or 10-year-olds. Yet they are often high school graduates (Irwin, 1986). For most of these people, their failure to acquire basic skills is deep-rooted and traceable to their inability to succeed in elementary school; some, however, come from non-English-speaking backgrounds and are not literate in either English or their native language. The need to help these people is paramount, for without the ability to read and write their chances for employment are minimal, and their ability to assume an independent way of life is in jeopardy.

The focusing of national attention on illiteracy has resulted in such highly publicized lawsuits as *Peter W. Doe* v. *The San Francisco Unified School District,* in which individuals sued the school systems for educational malfeasance, claiming that the schools failed to provide an adequate education. Some changes in educational standards have come about as a result of this attention. Some states now require seniors to demonstrate an adequate grasp of basic skills before they can graduate. Other states have passed laws abolishing "social promotions"; students below their grade level in reading and other basic skills cannot pass on to the next grade (Larson, 1977). The value of these measures is questionable, however. While they may prevent illiterates from graduating, there will still be a lot of illiterate youths.

Preventing Truancy and School Dropout

Illiteracy stems from a number of problems. For example, even though education is free and mandatory in this country, many children simply do not attend school. Reports on this issue (U.S. Bureau of the Census, 1983; National Education Association, 1984–1985) indicate that over 3 million children between the ages of 7 and 17 do not attend school, and that 1 million of them are between the ages of 7 and 15. In addition, these figures may be conservative because they are based only on Census Bureau data on nonenrollment. Interviews with school officials and community leaders reveal that the census data reflect only a partial count of how many children do not attend school. Often the parents of those truant children do not speak English and do not correctly answer the school enrollment questionnaire. Some parents may be afraid to admit that their children do not go to school.

Truant children are likely to be poor, nonwhite, and non-English-speaking. (A truant is a child or adolescent who stays away from school without parental or school permission.) Failure to go to school is especially prevalent among Hispanic children, many of whom eventually drop out of school. A report by the National Commission on Secondary Schooling for Hispanics (1984) states that 45% of Hispanic youths never complete high school, and that four out of ten of those who drop out of school do so before reaching the tenth grade. These findings carry significant implications for society at large, because Hispanic Americans are becoming a majority of the school population in our major cities and will be the country's largest minority group by the end of the century. The dropout rate among black youths is also a problem; 40% do not graduate from high school (Children's Defense Fund, 1990).

The societal costs of truancy and school dropout are enormous. The Carnegie Council on Adolescent Development (1989) estimates that, over their lifetime, each year's class of dropouts will cost the nation about $260 billion in lost earnings and foregone taxes. This is because the unemployment rate for school dropouts is more than twice that of high school graduates. In terms of this issue, we have found that more can be accomplished if we concentrate on prevention and attempt to reach children before they drop out of high school. Cairns, Cairns, and Neckerman (1989) note that students who are at risk for dropping out can be identified as early as the seventh grade; they are generally highly aggressive and do not do well in school. Can we reach out to such children and change the trajectory of their life experiences? Philanthropist and businessman Eugene Lang thinks so. He promised sixth-graders in East Harlem that he would pay their college tuition if they graduated from high school. He also let them know that he was available if they needed any advice or emotional support. Were they motivated to succeed? Over half went to college and nine more graduated from high school; this shows that when they have a goal to work toward as well as support, children will strive to succeed (Berger, 1989).

Many dropouts are absent from school on a regular basis several years before they reach high school. It is important, therefore, to take a close look at truancy. Several studies have identified some characteristics of truants, such as underdeveloped reading and academic skills, a negative self-concept, and a negative attitude toward school subjects. Many truants live in stressful family situations; they feel anxiety because of economic need; they lack personally satisfying experiences with other students or teachers; and they often face intense personal problems unrelated to the school experience (Kohler, 1976). These research findings clearly point to our obligation to respond to these students' needs in order to alleviate some of the pressures they are experiencing and to make learning experiences relevant for them (Walker, 1988; Rust, 1988). Nevertheless, some school officials see truancy as a crime. Although punitive approaches are understandable, they yield no positive results and may lead to further rebellion and, eventually, to their dropping out of school (Rogus, 1983).

Do Schools Make a Difference?

Several recent studies show that some secondary schools have been effective in reducing truancy and dropout rates and in increasing student achievement. Rogus (1983) has analyzed several of these studies, noting that the schools that proved successful in these efforts encouraged parental involvement and assigned homework on a regular basis.

Michael Rutter and his colleagues (1979) made similar points after conducting an extensive study on the effects of British secondary schools on student achievement. The researchers rejected standardized intelligence tests as indicators of academic progress, claiming that these tests did not directly test what the school attempted to teach. Instead, the researchers assessed the adolescents on five measures: knowledge of the subjects taught, behavior in school (e.g., violence), attendance, employment, and delinquency. They conducted their study in schools serving lower- and lower-middle-class populations in a large section of London. Lower-class children were of particular interest because they represent the population researchers often claim cannot be positively affected by school. Rutter and his colleagues found that individual differences among students existing at the beginning of the secondary school period correlated with achievement levels at the period's end. That is, high-achieving students tended to maintain their advantage. However, students in some schools—although judged to be truant, violent, or delinquent at the beginning of the period—significantly improved in their behavior and were far more able to succeed academically than were students in some other schools.

What accounted for these differences? According to the Rutter team, schools fostering good behavior and academic achievement in their students had the following characteristics:

1. The schools emphasized academics and assigned homework and similar activities.
2. Teachers spent more time interacting with the class as a whole, rather than with individual students.
3. Students enjoyed favorable conditions at school. For example, they could make free use of school facilities, had access to a telephone, and could get hot drinks.
4. Students could assume responsibilities and participate in a variety of activities.
5. The school population had continuity. This was evident from the number of years teachers were in the same school; many students were with the same group of adolescents during their secondary schooling.

Hill, Foster, and Gendler (1990) conducted a similar study of secondary schools in large American urban areas. The researchers compared successful schools (which were defined as schools where 80% of students graduated and 85% of seniors took college entrance tests) with regular schools (where 50% of students graduated and only 35% of seniors took college entrance tests). According to Hill and his colleagues, the successful schools emphasized student achievement and required all students to complete a basic curriculum. The less-effective schools did not place any burden on the students but let them define their own roles and curriculum. Thus, schools that set standards that they expect their students to meet are more likely to have successful students. These impressive findings indicate that some schools can, and do, make a difference in enhancing their students' achievements.

Summary

During adolescence youngsters attain a higher level of cognitive maturity, known to Piaget as formal operations thought. Adolescents are able to think abstractly about concrete matters and about ideas and hypothetical statements. They can approach problem solving in a scientific manner and systematically consider all possible solutions.

Using a number of scientific experiments to determine when children attain formal operations thought, researchers have discovered that although all children attain the previous level of cognitive development, not all are able to reach the formal operational level. This is the case in cultures like the United States. In addition, some people are able to think abstractly and systematically in some subjects but not in others, because the ability to think abstractly depends in part on their education and the extent of their interest in, and knowledge of, different topics. Whereas Piaget explained that the adolescent's ability to think in the abstract and solve problems systematically reflects qualitative changes in cognitive development, information-processing theorists argue that the change in adolescent thought reflects an increased ability to process and retain information.

Another explanation for cognitive change is the psychometric approach, which focuses on individual differences in intellectual performance. This is measured by the IQ test. Although the IQ test is a good predictor of school achievement, it should not be used to indicate an individual's intellectual ability; the test measures intellectual performance, not intellectual potential. Intellectual performance is influenced by the interaction of numerous factors, including innate intellectual ability, the ability to read, the ability to take tests, and emotional and motivational factors. For example, students who are anxious in the test situation are likely to get a low score even though they may be intellectually capable.

In addition, IQ tests are culturally biased. Low-income and minority students are unfamiliar with many words and concepts used on the tests. As a result, they tend to obtain lower scores, which causes some researchers to state, incorrectly, that these students are intellectually inferior. Studies have documented the fact that both genetic and environmental factors influence intelligence. For example, children adopted by middle-class families obtain IQ scores that are close to those obtained by middle-class individuals. Other studies have shown that young children from low socioeconomic backgrounds obtain higher IQ scores than their older siblings if they participate in compensatory education programs and other intervention efforts designed to increase the level of school achievement among low-income children. Although many educators and psychologists believe that such intervention efforts are successful only during early childhood, there is evidence that even adolescents with IQs as low as 60 or 80 (which place them among the mentally retarded) can be helped to learn cognitive skills and to increase their levels of school achievement. Enhancing the abilities of these adolescents is important because so many will either drop out of high school or graduate still unable to read or write. These youngsters are, in fact, illiterate.

16 Social and Emotional Development During Adolescence

Adolescents have the major task of establishing their own identity. They have to decide who their friends are, what lifestyle they want to adopt, and what kind of career they want as adults.

There is nothing new about the task of establishing an identity. Infants begin to define themselves as persons; that is, as individuals different from the physical environment in which they find themselves. In fact, by the end of middle childhood, they have a complex and multifaceted picture of who they are; they are aware of themselves as unique individuals with positive attributes, skills, thoughts, and feelings, and they are conscious of some of their failings.

When they become adolescents, however, they enter a time of many changes—in both physical and intellectual development. They have to redefine themselves in terms of who they are and of who they will become. This is a time when they reflect and focus their emotions, beliefs, attitudes, and desires (Harter, 1990). Adolescents struggle with questions such as, Who am I, really? What do I want to do with my life? What do I believe in? Of course, few are quite certain of the answers. When asked about herself, 17-year-old Sally would answer: "Who am I? I am a human being. I don't know who I am . . . I am a confused person" (Montemayor & Eisen, 1977).

The Search for a Personal Identity

In this chapter you will learn that the confusion Sally expresses is characteristic of many adolescents. Partly it stems from the fact that in our pluralistic society young people have numerous values and beliefs to choose from; they can adopt many possible lifestyles. Unlike young people in previous generations whose adult iden-

Teens decide early in high school whether to pursue an academic course that will lead to college or to set a vocational goal. Factors beyond the adolescent's control, such as economic constraints and parental expectations, can make this a difficult choice.

tity was primarily determined by family, community, and shared societal values and beliefs, adolescents today shoulder more of the burden of deciding who they are and what they would like to do in the future (Baumeister & Tice, 1986). This is a difficult task for adolescents because they are in a transitional phase. Early in the period, they may find the prospect of life as independent adults inviting and frightening. They may vacillate between their need for independence and their need for dependence. Sometimes they think of themselves as autonomous individuals and they expect others to think of them that way as well. At other times they need security and yearn for support and guidance. They are becoming acquainted with themselves as changing people. Their bodies are developing, and they experience intellectual challenges brought on by newly acquired cognitive skills that enable them to conceptualize the self more abstractly (Harter, 1990). At times they may feel superior and capable of an infinite number of tasks, often exaggerating the degree of their emancipation and becoming derisive and rebellious toward their parents. At other times they may feel helpless and vulnerable to the criticisms of those around them. Having to make major choices and decisions is difficult at any age. Given all the converging developmental factors during the early teenage years, you can appreciate how confusing the task is. For some adolescents, the transition from childhood to adulthood is a smooth process facilitated by nurturant, understanding parents and friends. For others, the journey is more difficult because they lack the security, guidance, and support they need as they attempt to establish a personal identity.

Theoretical Perspectives

The psychosocial theory of Erik Erikson   Erikson (1963; 1968) has had an extensive influence on current views of adolescence. He explains adolescents' quest for personal identity and answers to the questions of who they are and what they believe in as functions of the psychosocial crisis of **identity versus role confusion.** According to Erikson, having a sense of identity is as important and fundamental to human existence as food, security, and sexual satisfaction. Individuals, whether adolescents or adults, must have a sense of themselves—what their strengths and weaknesses are, what they believe in, and what they want to do in life. In Erikson's words, " . . . in the jungle of human existence, there is no feeling of being alive without a sense of identity" (1968).

Throughout childhood individuals gradually develop some sense of themselves as unique beings. Not until adolescence, however, does the quest for a personal identity become an all-consuming task, facilitated in part by their newly acquired cognitive skills. During this period, adolescents draw on the experiences they have had in the past and the kinds of identifications they have formed during infancy and childhood. Yet their sense of identity "includes but is more than the sum of successive identifications of those earlier years when the child wanted to be, and was often forced to become, like the people [s]he depended on" (Erikson, 1959). Now capable of thinking in the abstract and preparing for life as adults, adolescents think about their past and their future. Committing themselves to an ideology, a lifestyle, and a vocation, they establish a personal identity that is relatively stable and integrated into a coherent, consistent, and unique whole. With this identity they will gain a sense of the continuity of the self—a sense that no matter what they choose to do in life or what role they may assume, whether as worker, spouse, or parent, they will remain unique people with their own strengths and weaknesses and with a set of values, beliefs, and principles that will guide them through life.

Crisis and commitment A personal identity is not completely formed during adolescence. As with most aspects of growth and development, identity formation occurs gradually through countless experiences and numerous decisions. Many decisions affect the way adolescents form their personal identity and determine, in part, their adult life. But none of the decisions made during adolescence are irrevocable. There are still opportunities for growth after the adolescent period, and these opportunities may cause teenagers to redefine their choices (Waterman, 1985). Nevertheless, Erikson emphasizes that decisions made during adolescence profoundly affect the way individuals deal with their young adulthood, middle age, and old age and with options that are available in the future.

Erikson further points out that forming a personal identity is not an easy task. Take, for example, an adolescent girl undergoing an identity crisis while experiencing rapid physical growth and sexual maturation. In addition, she has to wrestle with questions about who she is and who she will become. Over the course of several years that may extend beyond adolescence, she will either resolve the crisis by committing herself to some decisions about her being and her future *(identity achievement)* or she will feel anxious and confused and become incapable of making decisions and choosing roles *(role confusion)*. Individuals who eventually achieve an identity will feel secure about themselves and aware of the kind of life they would like to lead. But adolescents who fail to establish an identity will remain confused about the future; they may become committed to the ideals of a close friend or someone they admire, instead of to their own.

Contemporary viewpoints Erikson based his theory on biographical case studies of famous individuals and of his own patients. Although these case studies are thought-provoking, they are difficult to apply to teens growing up today. Other researchers, however, have elaborated on Erikson's work. James Marcia (1966; 1980; 1988), for example, developed an interview that he initially administered to male college students, asking them questions about their occupational choice, religion, and political beliefs. On the basis of their answers, Marcia (1966) noted that identity formation is a gradual process that is difficult and fraught with pitfalls. He also discovered that the process involves four modes of resolution. Some adolescents become bewildered. Pressured by demands from their family and friends, and confused by the sheer number of possibilities open to them, they do not experience an increasing cohesion of identity (identity achievement). Instead, they undergo **identity diffusion** by either withdrawing from efforts to shape their identity or feeling ambivalent or unconcerned about making decisions. **Foreclosure,** or premature identity formation, can also occur when adolescents accept and incorporate, without question, the values of their family and society. Finally, instead of finding an identity and making commitments to what they believe in and what they want to do, some adolescents declare a *moratorium.* After wrestling for a time with the question of who they are and what their future holds, they defer resolution of the crisis. For some, a short moratorium gives them an opportunity to find out and examine available options. For others, however, the moratorium is long-lasting and destructive because they fail to make decisions about what they want to do and what they believe. As a result, they may remain undecided and without commitments throughout much of their adult life.

In general, as adolescents mature, they come closer to achieving an identity. According to Waterman (1985), the percentage of individuals who achieve identity increases from 5.2% in the pre–high school years, to 21.3% in the senior year of high school, to 39.7% in the senior year of college. Waterman (1985) also notes that some teens and young adults may achieve identity in one domain earlier than in others; that is, by their freshmen year in college, they may know what career they want to pursue, but they still may not be clear about their political beliefs.

The Social Context

The ease with which the individual establishes an identity for himself and decides on his eventual role as an adult partly depends on the society in which he lives (Baumeister & Tice, 1986). In primitive cultures the transition often entails a test of skills and willingness to endure pain; yet it is a relatively simple and quickly accomplished task (see Chapter 14). In these societies the individual does not have many choices to make. The society does not change much, if at all, from generation to generation, and its members hold essentially the same values and notions about what is expected of an adult. Because societal demands on the individual are relatively few and straightforward, the individual simply has to learn the skills and values of his elders and incorporate them as his own.

In complex societies like ours, identity formation is not as simple. Adolescents have a variety of values and social roles to choose from. In addition, social change occurs at an incredibly fast pace. Because of increasingly more sophisticated communication, transportation, and scientific techniques, individuals confront a future that is substantially different from what their parents had to deal with when they became adults. The decisions teenagers make during adolescence and young adulthood are not necessarily irrevocable, but they will have consequences for later life and so must be weighed carefully.

Adolescents have to make these decisions in light of their talents and capabilities, their family's economic resources, and the choices available. For example, Sally may want to go to college, but does she have the qualifications and skills to do so? Can she or her parents afford the cost? In addition, although our society prides itself on the great variety of choices available to individuals, the range of choices varies according to social class, ethnic background, and sex. Consider, for instance, vocational choices. Some jobs are open only to individuals with a certain background and skill. Also, although women have many more opportunities than ever before, they still face the prospect of sex discrimination in the workplace.

Vocational identity   Decisions about vocational roles and what we want to do as our life's work are essential aspects of every individual's identity. A job provides the means to an independent life, defines our place in society, and determines what kinds of people we associate with. It can also offer the personal satisfaction of being productive. It is hardly surprising, therefore, that adolescents spend much of their time thinking about what they would like to do when they grow up and about what they are capable of doing.

The decision as to what we will do as our life's work reflects our past and present academic achievements as well as our parents' aspirations for us. Some children grow up knowing that their parents expect them to go to college, to aspire to a career, and to value the security and responsibility of a job (Kohn, 1977). Throughout childhood, individuals learn about job values, attitudes, and career aspirations by observing their parents. But during adolescence they become capable of generating possibilities and reasoning about what they would like to do (Fischer, 1980). Some young people may take several years before arriving at a decision about their life's work. Others may become committed to a career early in life.

Even though adolescents may be undecided about what they want to do, they have to make a major decision early in their high school experience that will affect their later options. Do they want to pursue an academic course of study that will lead to college, or do they want to pursue a vocational course? Not all individuals choose the academic course; only half of middle-class adolescents and one-quarter of black adolescents attend college. Thus, many teens between the ages of 16 and 19 also have to find a job (National Commission on Youth, 1980). In some schools career-counseling services help teens decide about their future, but these services are often seriously understaffed and thus are not available to a significant number of teens (William T. Grant Foundation, 1988).

Many high school students also learn about work options by working part-time while attending school. A national survey found that three out of every four high school seniors worked 16 to 20 hours per week, and some worked over 30 hours per week (Bachman, 1982). Although work experience can help adolescents learn about getting and keeping a job and managing their time, jobs can also detract from schoolwork. Greenberger and Steinberg (1981) found that high school students who worked during the school year had a lower grade-point average than nonworking students, especially if the employed students worked more than 14 hours (for 10th graders) or more than 20 hours (for 11th graders) per week.

Youth unemployment   Although high school students seem to be able to find part-time employment, permanent employment is a different story. For them the question "What do I want to do with my life as an adult?" poses a dilemma not easily resolved by simply choosing an occupation. A national economic crisis, periodic economic depressions, and continually high rates of unemployment have had a devastating impact on youths seeking employment, especially blacks and Hispanics. According to statistics compiled by the U.S. Department of Labor, unemployment among 16- to 19-year-old whites is 15%, but for their black age-mates, unemployment is 43% (Bureau of Labor Statistics, 1985). The statistics are even more alarming for Hispanics; an estimated 59% drop out of school before completing the tenth grade and are without a job (Carnegie Council on Adolescent Development, 1989; Hirano-Nakanishi, 1984). These figures are conservative estimates because they only take into account teens who had already entered the job market and had a job at one time. Many more teens are not in school or in the labor force and, thus, are not counted among the unemployed even though they are not working and may be looking for a job.

The fact that minority youths are likely to be unemployed is a national concern. The Carnegie Council on Adolescent Development (1989) points out that by the year 2020, nearly half of all schoolchildren will be nonwhite. If minority youths continue to be jobless, our society will face enormous economic and social problems that "will directly affect our standard of living and democratic foundations" (p. 27).

The bleak picture of youth unemployment is due in part to shifts in the labor market. During the past two decades, many unskilled jobs have vanished as members of the baby-boom generation entered the labor force and displaced teens. In addition, as recently as 1990, federal minimum wage laws priced teens out of the market. As long as employers have to pay a minimum wage that is substantially higher than in the past, they will hire experienced workers. These factors, however, are only part of the picture. Another reason for youth unemployment is the high rate of illiteracy among young people; many leave school unprepared for the working world (William T. Grant Foundation, 1988; Gueron, 1984):

Adolescents undergo major bodily changes as they transform from children to adults. They mature sexually, they grow taller, and they acquire muscular strength. They can accomplish physical tasks that require skill and coordination as well as strength. Many teens, reveling in the independence brought on by their new abilities, feel there isn't anything they can't do.

Adolescence

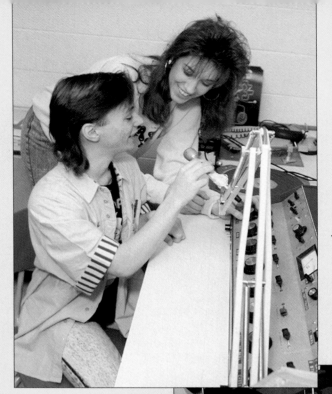

Adolescents gain a higher level of intellectual functioning. They can think in the abstract about different possibilities and they relish working with friends on a task. Many teens enjoy activities that challenge their physical strength, and also practice such skills as music with an intensity that lets them refine and excel in these areas as well.

Some teens become absorbed in mental tasks and find the challenge of difficult problems stimulating. They get together to develop a strategy for problem solving, and they enjoy debating, which requires them to formulate effective arguments.

Although the family remains important to adolescents, they spend more of their time with friends. Initially they form single-sex cliques. Later on, the cliques merge, so that by late adolescence boys and girls congregate in large crowds. They become comfortable with each other, develop close relationships, and begin dating.

Choosing friends is critical to the search for identity. Friends provide the emotional support adolescents need as they experience physiological and intellectual changes; they also help determine lasting values. For some adolescents, the influence of friends may result in drug dependency and crime. Although many teens complete high school, attend a senior prom, get a job, and eventually enroll in college or seek vocational training, some drop out of school at an early age and spend more and more of their time on the street.

Most teens work part time. If they spend too many hours on the job, their school performance may suffer. Nevertheless, part-time employment lets teens learn different skills and think about what they want to do in the future. Working also shows them what will be expected of them in the workplace.

In our society, teens (even those who are working) remain dependent on their parents, sometimes through their early adult years. In many other countries teens assume adult roles and responsibilities and, like this Brazilian girl, learn to fend for themselves and help support their family.

We have created an economy that seeks literate, technically trained and committed workers, while simultaneously we produce many young men and women who are functionally illiterate . . . and untrained in technical skills. [Carnegie Council on Adolescent Development, 1989, p. 29]

There is no easy solution to teenage unemployment because teens are competing for decreasing numbers of unskilled jobs with older, more experienced workers who have families to support. Any measure that would help provide jobs for teens might cause unemployment of other workers. Yet in an effort to stimulate business to hire unskilled, inexperienced youths, public and private agencies have proposed various programs, such as the establishment of a low "youth unemployment opportunity" wage for teens aged 19 or under, which would be in effect only during the summer. The rationale is that even short-term employment would give teenagers some paid work experience. However, many observers question its effects. Citing as an example a previous effort to help alleviate teen unemployment, a *New York Times* editorial (March 21, 1985) claims that in 1978 employers were allowed to write off 85% of the salary paid to low-income youths. Although the tax credit was of even greater benefit to employers than the savings on the proposed low wage, the program had no impact on overall teen unemployment.

Teens need educational and training programs to teach them basic skills and to prepare them for jobs. In the past such programs have proved to be useful and cost-effective (Carnegie Council on Adolescent Development, 1989; William T. Grant Foundation, 1988; Gueron, 1984). In fact, a number of evaluations of these educational and training programs indicate that their benefits far outweigh their costs (Opportunities for Success, 1985; Farkas, 1984). Why? Because many young people either drop out of school or graduate from high school unable to read or write beyond the fourth-grade level and so are severely limited in the kinds of jobs they can hold. Our recent economic crisis has resulted in shifts in the labor market and a marked decrease in the number of unskilled jobs. At the same time the federal government has eliminated many vocational training programs for fiscal reasons, and there is little likelihood that public funds will be available to reinstate such programs in the near future.

As a result, many teens are unable to get started on their vocation and feel hopelessness and despair. They realize that they are "all grown up [with] no place to

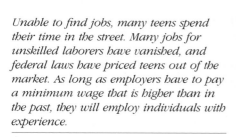

Unable to find jobs, many teens spend their time in the street. Many jobs for unskilled laborers have vanished, and federal laws have priced teens out of the market. As long as employers have to pay a minimum wage that is higher than in the past, they will employ individuals with experience.

go," to paraphrase the title of David Elkind's book on teens in our society (Elkind, 1984). In addition, many teens and young adults who graduate from high school are making their decisions about whether to go to college and what career to choose based on available job openings, rather than on their interests and aptitudes. Unable to find employment and unprepared for the job market even though they have college degrees, many young adults continue with their education as long as they or their parents can afford it. Although sometimes a higher degree or a change in the field of study may turn out to be a good choice, for a large number of young adults the tasks of establishing a place for themselves in the workplace and earning an independent living are simply postponed.

The Depression era   Adolescents of previous generations have also had to face the reality of social problems during the critical period of identity formation and to adapt to major social changes. Glen Elder (1980) showed that the larger social context in which people grow up has a significant impact on the course of human development, including the identity formed during adolescence. According to Elder (1980) and Feather (1980), the choices adolescents make and the values they adopt differ in times of war, peace, social unrest, prosperity, and economic depression. Elder gives an example of American adolescents who grew up during the 1920s and 1930s. During the 1920s, the nation experienced a social revolution in which there was a drastic shift from strict Victorian standards of behavior to far more liberal social norms. The whole society enjoyed an unleashing of new possibilities. This change especially affected young women, who, for the first time, were encouraged to think of their future in terms of education and a career. The Great Depression followed this prosperous, exuberant period; many people lost their jobs after the stock market crashed and thousands of families became poor. Many men, who had been raised to believe that their primary task was to support a family, suffered a loss of face and had trouble regaining their self-esteem and going back to work. Traditional family roles were thrown into disarray. By necessity, women assumed a more powerful role in the family; they went to work. Because the mothers were working, girls played a major role in household operations, and boys found jobs to help support the family.

The Oakland Growth Study, a longitudinal study conducted by the Berkeley Institute of Human Development, provides information on how the Depression affected some adolescents. The program, which began in 1931, included a series of studies and interviews of a group of children from the time they were 10 until they reached 19. Follow-up surveys tracked these individuals through the 1960s, when they became adults. The teenagers were old enough to play important roles in the household economy and to confront future prospects within the context of Depression realities. Elder (1974; 1980) analyzed the data from the Oakland Growth Study to find out how the Depression's social and economic changes affected individuals. He found that although many girls had expected to pursue an education in the 1920s, the Depression and the roles they had to assume within their family resulted in their marrying early and assuming traditional identities as homemakers (see Figure 16.1). This was especially so among adolescent girls whose families were hardest hit by the Depression.

Boys were also influenced by the Depression. They had to go out to work, and many benefited from these early experiences in the adult world. Adolescents from the poorest families showed a higher motivation to succeed than did those whose families were not as severely affected by the Depression. As adults, the boys and girls who lived through the Depression were family-centered and considered children to

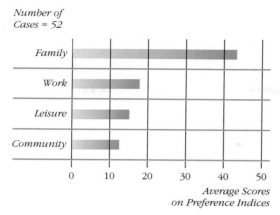

Number of
Cases = 52

Average Scores
on Preference Indices

Figure 16.1 *Although in the 1920s many girls expected to pursue an education, the Depression that followed resulted in their marrying earlier and preferring family activities.*
Source: *Children of the Great Depression: Social Changes in Life Experience*, by Glen H. Elder, Jr., p. 224. Copyright © 1974 by The Society for Research in Child Development, Inc.

be the most important aspect of a marriage. They emphasized the responsibilities of parenthood and stressed the value of dependability in their children. As Elder (1980) notes, "Personal aspects of Depression life are reflected in these preferences—the role of children in helping out [and] the importance of family support in times of need."

How does the present economic instability affect the identity and values of our youths? Unemployed teens have a sense of hopelessness about their future, and they wander aimlessly in the streets, sometimes resorting to crime (William T. Grant Foundation, 1988; Gueron, 1984). Other teens, however, are generally satisfied with life; according to several surveys, they are becoming increasingly conservative. During the 1960s and early 1970s—a period characterized by social and political unrest brought on by the Vietnam War and civil rights demonstrations—young people sought to change the world. Many seriously questioned and even repudiated their parents' values and attempted to create new values. In the 1980s, however, a large majority of young people had no difficulty accepting the kind of life society had to offer, and many said they adhered to such traditional values as hard work and close family ties (Gallup, 1986a). Although many factors accounted for this conservatism in the 1980s, the economy was an important factor. Since jobs were harder to find, hard work and parental support became more valuable.

Are youth in the 1990s different? Many still do not question the authority and values of adults. In an informal survey he conducted for a newspaper article, Oreskes (1990) quotes a 22-year-old college student as saying, "My teacher always told me to question authority. [I believe] you can question authority, but you can burden authority. Let them authoritate." Oreskes (1990) also cites a national survey

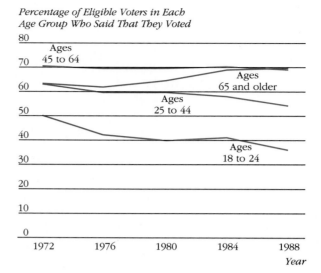

*Percentage of Eligible Voters in Each
Age Group Who Said That They Voted*

Figure 16.2 *Social apathy is reflected in the decreasing
percentage of 18- to 20-year-olds who say they vote.*
Source: "Profiles of Today's Youth: They Couldn't Care Less," by Michael
Oreskas, *The New York Times,* June 28, 1990, p. A1. Copyright © 1990 by
The New York Times Company. Reprinted by permission.

of young adults ages 18 to 29 who were found to be less likely to vote than young
adults in the early 1970s (see Figure 16.2) and less informed about public affairs.
However, the same survey found that young adults today are concerned about
threats to their health and feel a great deal of stress about their grades and their
ability to find a job.

Sex roles and sexual behavior The economy is only one aspect of social
change that significantly influences identity formation in adolescence. Our society
has also witnessed a sexual revolution that has had many consequences for traditional sex roles and sexual behavior. In the past boys learned that their adult responsibility would be to support a family, while girls learned that their roles would be as
wives and mothers. However, in recent years these traditional sex roles have
changed. Adolescents are realizing that, although differences in anatomy and physiology exist, as men and women they have an equal potential to assume any role
they want as long as they have the aptitude and the opportunity. Although changes in
attitudes toward sex roles have influenced adolescent boys and girls, these changes
have had the most impact on girls. As a result, girls feel differently about themselves,
their prospects in life, the value of their school performance, and the kinds of jobs
they seek (Rossi, 1977; Eccles, 1987). Many young women are no longer satisfied
with simply completing basic educational requirements and then quickly getting
married. Wanting to savor life and its opportunities, many women now defer marriage and parenthood until they have established their career.

The sexual revolution has also had the opposite effect for many other girls. As
noted in Chapter 14, one of the most obvious effects of the sexual revolution has
been increased sexual activity among adolescents. Of the 1 million teenage girls in
the United States who become pregnant each year, half carry their pregnancy to

The sexual revolution has affected teens and adults alike, changing their assumptions about traditional sex roles. Two or three decades ago, few girls would have tried to fix a car.

term. The overwhelming majority of these girls decide to keep their babies and, as a rule, remain single. Most, however, are unprepared for the responsibilities of parenthood.

Besides the poor health and poverty that characterize both the teenage mother and her baby, teenage parenthood has a devastating impact on the mother's education. In general, girls with lower academic aspirations are more likely to have sex during adolescence than those who are doing well at school (Hofferth & Hayes, 1987). Those who become pregnant and bear children during adolescence interrupt their education and tend to complete fewer years of schooling than their peers who become mothers later in life. Teenage mothers are also more likely to drop out of school (Earle, 1990; Furstenberg, Brooks-Gunn & Morgan, 1987; Card & Wise, 1978; Furstenberg, 1976). As researchers indicate, their life chances are severely compromised by early childbearing (Furstenberg, Brooks-Gunn & Chase-Lansdale, 1989).

Although the sexual revolution has created opportunities for some girls, such widespread problems as teenage pregnancy affect many, severely compromising their life chances.

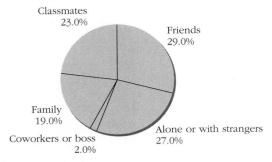

Figure 16.3 *Persons with whom adolescents spend time.*
Source: Being Adolescent: Conflict and Growth in the Teenage Years, by Mihaly Csikszentmihalyi and Reed Larson. Copyright © 1984 by Basic Books Inc. Reprinted by permission of Basic Books, a division of HarperCollins Publishers, Inc.

Fortunately, young people can quite often redefine their identity even though they may have gotten off to a difficult start. For example, some teenage mothers have benefited from support programs provided by numerous schools and hospitals. Thanks to child care and other programs, many young mothers have completed their education (Earle, 1990; Badger, 1980). Social policies that facilitate helpful programs of this kind can make a big difference in the lives of troubled adolescents.

Peers

Although broad social changes and social policies have important effects on the development of adolescents and their eventual course in life, family and friends also exert a great deal of influence. The choice of friends in particular is a major factor in the search for identity. Friends help determine lifestyle and values and provide emotional support as adolescents go through the slow process of disengaging from the family and establishing independent lives (Berndt & Perry, 1990; Ausubel, Montemayro, & Svajian, 1977). This process is never easy. Most adolescents are embarrassed at one time or another at some of their real or imagined social mistakes. They also experience times of joy and excitement as well as apprehension, such as when they are going out on a special date. Discussing such experiences with understanding friends who are also feeling similar emotions can make the difficulties much easier to handle and the happy moments even more exciting. It is not surprising, therefore, that studies reveal that a popular social activity among adolescents is talking to their peers (Berndt, 1982), and that adolescents spend most of their time with their peers (Csikszentmihalyi & Larson, 1984), as Figure 16.3 shows.

Friendships   Friends are important at an early age and are valuable and trusted confidants in the latter part of middle childhood as well. During adolescence, however, friends serve different functions. Berndt and Perry (1990), in a review of research on friendships during early adolescence, note that these relationships exhibit distinctive features:

1. Loyalty and faithfulness are important characteristics of a friend.
2. They avoid having an intense competition with close friends, aiming instead for equality through equal sharing.

3. They have more intimate friendships than do younger children. More often, adolescents view friendships as emotionally supportive relationships, describing friends as being understanding and sensitive. They express concern over losing a friend as well as joy over making a new friend.

Intimacy is an especially distinctive feature of friendships among girls. Douvan and Adelson (1966) pointed this out in their research, and more recent studies on friendships by Burhmester and Furman (1987) have confirmed this finding. Why is there such an emphasis on the security provided by friendship? Douvan and Adelson (1966) offered the following explanation:

> . . . the girl is seeking in the other some response or mirroring of herself, [and] she is in need of someone who is going through the same problems at the same time. In some sense, it could be argued that the early adolescent girl is dealing with her problems by [identifying with her friend]. . . . With so much invested in the friendship, it is no wonder that the girl is so dependent on it.

Coleman (1980) further points out that during early adolescence girls are becoming used to the physiological and physical changes they have undergone and are seeking the confidence of a friend who has undergone the same changes. In addition, by early and midadolescence, although many girls are sexually active, others are only beginning to date. Thus, a friend can provide much-needed emotional support in this new and exciting experience that may also prove frightening.

By late adolescence, physical maturation is complete. Adolescents are more at ease with themselves and have a better sense of their personal identity. During this stage, friendships become more relaxed, even though intimacy and loyalty are still important (Berndt & Perry, 1990; Youniss & Smollar, 1985). Since adolescents do not need their friends as much now, they are less anxious about being abandoned or betrayed. Instead, they value the *individuality* of their friends, often choosing them because of their personality and interests and what they can contribute to the relationship (Berndt, 1989).

Perhaps because they are generally two years behind girls in physiological maturity, boys have a different timetable for changes in the quality of their friendships. At age 13 or 14, for example, they exhibit the same attitudes toward friends that characterize girls at age 11 or 12. Are friendships as meaningful to boys as to girls? Reviewing studies on friendships of adolescent boys and girls, Coleman (1980) notes that friends are as important for boys as for girls. However, some research findings indicate that girls and boys differ somewhat in their expectations of friendship. Whereas girls generally say that they value sensitivity and empathy in a friend, boys do not mention these characteristics. Instead, they tend to discuss the value of friends in terms of common pursuits. A few studies have shown that boys also seem slightly less dependent on friends than girls and less anxious about having a friend (e.g., Coleman, 1974). Evidence for this finding is still rather sparse because only some studies find sex differences associated with friendships (Berndt & Perry, 1990). Nevertheless, this finding is not that surprising. As Coleman (1980) puts it:

> . . . for girls in our society, a stronger interpersonal orientation is expected; the capacity for intimacy and dependency are not only acceptable, they are highly valued, and there is no doubt that the processes of socialization all tend in this direction. For boys, however, the stress is placed on skills, achievement, and self-sufficiency.

Cliques and crowds Although individual friendships are important to the adolescent, they exist within the larger social structure of peer relationships (Berndt & Perry, 1990), which also include interactions with groups of 5 to 20 members (Cole-

By mid- to late adolescence, teens spend most of their time in a crowd of as many as 20 members that includes both sexes.

Friendship Patterns Among Black and White Adolescents

School desegregation policies provide an opportunity for children and adolescents to interact with peers of different racial and socioeconomic backgrounds. Can school integration help these students know one another better? As Epstein (1986) points out, children and adolescents in desegregated schools still have a tendency to select friends of the same race. In fact, a racial cleavage in friendship patterns seems to increase during early adolescence as all-black or all-white peer groups become models for young teens (Hartup, 1983; Asher, Singleton, & Taylor, 1985). All the same, most students in integrated schools report that they have at least one friend, but not necessarily a close friend, of a different race, but less than a third of these students see that friend outside school (DuBois & Hirsch, 1990).

Researchers have done much of their investigative work on black and white friendships in schools. DuBois and Hirsch went a step further by examining friendship patterns in the neighborhood as well. They selected an interracial junior high school where about 25% of the students were black and the rest were white. They then asked students to complete a questionnaire on where they lived, who their friends were, and how much value they attached to friendship. According to the researchers, cross-race friendships were more likely to occur among teens living in integrated neighborhoods than among those living in segregated ones. The researchers concluded that living close to people of a different race might counteract negative or stereotyped attitudes that hindered positive social contacts.

The researchers also found significant differences in friendship patterns of black and white adolescents. For example, more white girls than white boys said how much they valued the support and intimacy of a friendship. (This finding is consistent with other findings discussed in this chapter.) To the researchers' surprise, however, this gender difference was not apparent among blacks. Both black girls and black boys stated how much they valued the support of a close friend—someone they felt they could rely on for help, if necessary (see the accompanying table). How do we explain these differences? According to the researchers, as members of a minority group black adolescents have to face a number of race-related stressors. As a result, they have learned to rely on the support of their friends.

The researchers made another interesting point. Although the black and white adolescents in the study did not differ in the number of close friends, blacks reported a greater number of close neighborhood friends. They are more likely to have a close friend who does not attend the same school. According to researchers, the minority status of black adolescents in school may explain why they find friends in their neighborhood. It is also possible that neighborhood kinship and friendship networks are especially strong among blacks, and that black children in general are more attuned to the neighborhood than are white children.

Research on black and white friendship patterns is quite recent and requires additional study before any conclusions can be reached. Yet as DuBois and Hirsch (1990)

man, 1980). These groups, which tend to be closed to outsiders, are usually based on shared interests and change in size and other qualities depending on the age of the adolescents.

A classic study by an Australian researcher (Dunphy, 1963) documented the change in the nature of peer groups. Studying peer groups of adolescents and young adults aged 13 to 21, Dunphy found that early in adolescence these groups are single-sex *cliques* of about five members of the same socioeconomic background and age. Typically, members have the same values and interests and tend to be intolerant of anyone different. At about age 14, members of different cliques begin to interact; they tend to tease and embarrass members of opposite-sex groups. While adolescents are in high school, they belong to a clique of two or three friends of the same sex, but they may also be friendly with another clique of two or three teens of the opposite sex. Gradually the cliques merge, and by middle to late adolescence, teens spend most of their time in a *crowd* that may include as many as 20 members of both sexes. They congregate wherever they can—on street corners, in the park, in shopping malls, and at school—and spend as much time as possible together. Eventually, as young adults, they no longer feel comfortable in a crowd and function instead in groups of couples (see Figure 16.4).

A CLOSER LOOK

suggest, we cannot simply assume that research on friendship that has been traditionally conducted on studies with white middle-class children also applies to minority children. Today more researchers are attempting to look at children's development in the context of their family life and sociocultural background (McLoyd, 1990).

Percentage Breakdown of Peer-Support Items, by Race and Gender

	Talk with most school friends about personal problems[a]			
	Never/rarely	*Once a month*	*Once a week*	*Almost every day*
White boys	49.2 (32)	12.3 (8)	30.8 (20)	7.7 (5)
White girls	7.9 (6)	13.2 (10)	25.0 (19)	53.9 (41)
Black boys	25.0 (7)	21.4 (6)	28.6 (8)	25.0 (7)
Black girls	31.8 (7)	13.6 (3)	22.7 (5)	31.8 (7)

	Degree to which best school friend can be relied on for help when it is needed			
	Not very much of the time	*Some of the time*	*Most of the time*	*Whenever needed*
White boys	8.9 (9)	8.9 (9)	47.5 (48)	34.7 (35)
White girls	2.6 (3)	2.6 (3)	30.7 (35)	64.0 (73)
Black boys	10.0 (4)	10.0 (4)	20.0 (8)	60.0 (24)
Black girls	5.6 (2)	11.1 (4)	22.2 (8)	61.1 (22)

Note: Cell counts are provided in parentheses.
[a]This item was not administered to eighth-graders.

Source: DuBois, D. L., & Hirsch, B. J. (1990). School and neighborhood friendship patterns of blacks and whites in early adolescence. In *Child Development, 61,* 524–536. © 1990 The Society for Research in Child Development.

Although Dunphy studied adolescents of a different generation, studies confirm that adolescents today also segregate into groups. Brown and Lohr (1987), for example, note that adolescents in one midwestern high school belonged to one of five major cliques: the jocks (or athletically oriented teens), the populars, the normals, the druggies, and the nobodies. In other parts of the country, teens may use other names for their particular group.

Popularity and rejection Within cliques and crowds usually one or several adolescents stand out as leaders because others in the group admire them and consider them the most popular members. Coleman (1961) studied the individual's status within the peer group by interviewing high school students. Other researchers who interviewed students in subsequent generations (Sebald, 1981) replicated his findings. According to Coleman, boys and girls define popularity differently; boys admire other boys for their athletic ability or good looks, whereas girls admire other girls who have nice clothes and who are good-looking. For both boys and girls, however, popularity involves such personality factors as cheerfulness, friendliness, and a sense of humor. Adolescents, like younger children and adults, like to

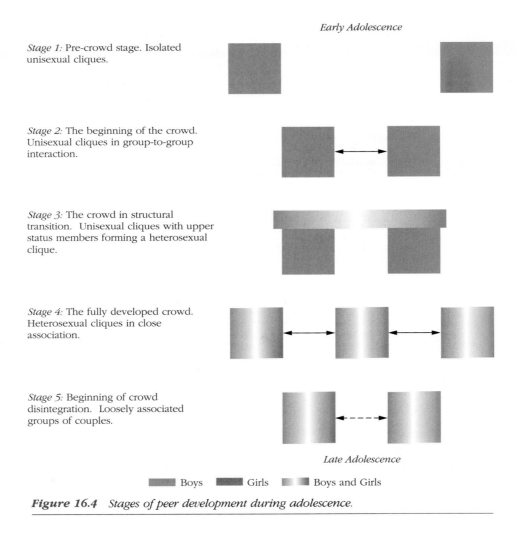

Figure 16.4 Stages of peer development during adolescence.

Some adolescents do not belong to a group, preferring instead to spend time by themselves.

be near people who are friendly, enthusiastic, and capable of initiating games and activities the entire group can enjoy.

Adolescents can also reject some of their peers. Often they will refuse to accept as friends or as part of the group individuals whom they consider socially awkward or unattractive. Thus, some adolescents do not belong to any group and have no friends. Researchers distinguish between *neglected* adolescents, who do not have friends but who are not necessarily disliked by their peers, and *rejected* adolescents. According to the researchers, rejected adolescents tend to be disruptive and aggressive and are generally disliked (Asher & Parker, 1990).

In studying neglected adolescents, Rosenberg (1975) found that these youngsters often have low self-esteem. They are afraid to approach their peers because they are certain that they will be rejected. There are many reasons for this low self-esteem because adolescence is a time of change. In addition, teenagers are able to realize that other people may have different opinions of them (Rosenberg, 1986; Harter, 1990). For example, a boy who is much shorter than his classmates or who does not perform well in school may feel inadequate (Rosenberg, 1965). By failing to befriend someone whom they perceive as different, other adolescents contribute to that person's poor self-esteem (Harter, 1983a). Recall from Chapter 13 that parents who are unresponsive and fail to take an interest in their children's activities end up raising children who feel inadequate and unworthy of anyone's attention.

Yet low self-esteem is not the only reason some adolescents are isolated. Often, intellectual or creative adolescents are also rejected because they are different. Thus, these gifted teens may spend much of their time alone or with adults unless they can find others like themselves with whom they can establish friendships.

Conformity   Since most adolescents are intimately associated with close friends or a group of friends, researchers thought that they were under pressure to conform, as was true in previous periods of development. In fact, adolescents do tend to dress and talk like their friends and to prefer the same music (Csikszentmihalyi & Larson, 1984). This further reinforces the stereotype of a "slavish conformity" (Coleman, 1980) as characteristic of adolescents. Yet other studies reveal that the need to conform is not uniformly high during adolescence but has a relationship to an individual's age and status in the peer group. During early adolescence, there is a

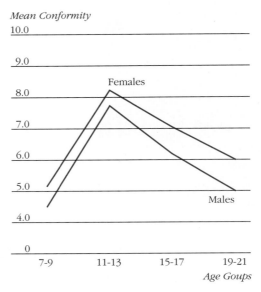

Mean Conformity

Figure 16.5 *There is a marked decrease in the need to conform to peers during middle to late adolescence.*
Source: *Handbook of Adolescent Psychology,* J. Adelson, editor, 1980, p. 422, Figure 7. Copyright © 1980 by John Wiley & Sons, Inc. Reprinted by permission of the publisher.

marked increase in adolescents' need to conform, which peaks at age 11 to 13. As adolescence progresses, however, there is a decrease in conformity (see Figure 16.5); teens aged 15 and over are not as susceptible to peer pressure as they were at a younger age (Berndt, 1979; Constanzo & Shaw, 1966).

Adolescents do not depend entirely on their peers to the exclusion of their parents. Instead, they tend to seek their peers' advice on how to dress for a particular occasion or on what courses to take in school. But for other issues, such as whether to take a part-time job or which college to attend, they solicit their parents' advice. These findings are reflected in Brittain's studies (1963; 1969), which analyzed adolescents' answers to hypothetical dilemmas concerning their relationships with parents and peers. More recent studies also support Brittain's findings. For instance, in a study of over a thousand 12- to 18-year-old urban and suburban adolescents, Smith (1976) found that although peers influence the choice of clothes and music, the family influences decisions on a variety of other, substantially more important issues regarding future goals and educational or vocational plans. In another study of adolescents and their parents in the United States and Denmark, researchers found that most adolescents are influenced by their parents in their thinking about life goals (Kandel & Lesser, 1972). Thus, although adolescents spend more time with their peers than with their parents, this shift in time commitments does not necessarily indicate a change from parental to peer influence (Berndt, 1979; Lerner & Spanier, 1980).

Is there, then, a generation gap between adolescents and their parents? Apparently not. As we have shown, adolescents understand their parents and are understood by them despite media projections to the contrary. However, teenagers whose parents are punitive or permissive to the point of neglect or who are themselves troubled and concerned about their marriage and the family's finances do conform to peer behavior rather than seek parental advice (Patterson, Bank, & Stoolmiller, 1990; Hartup, 1983). In such families the adolescent does not feel that her parents are supportive and nurturant; thus, she turns to her peers for advice.

Drug and Alcohol Abuse

Middle school kids who use drugs say they were turned on to them not only by dealers, but also by older teenage friends, older siblings and their friends, babysitters and adult relatives.

—Anne Schwarz Harritz and
Ann Brey Christensen [1987, p. 8]

Why do so many American adolescents take illegal drugs and drink alcohol? It's hard to come up with a simple all-encompassing answer. Some young people receive the message—partly from their friends, partly from the media, and partly from the example of adults around them—that it's "smart" and "grown-up" to consume alcohol or use marijuana, cocaine, or heroine. One encouraging sign is that adolescent drug use, which peaked in the 1970s, has been declining since 1979 (Johnson, O'Malley, & Bachman, 1988). All the same, American youngsters use and abuse drugs far more than adolescents in other industrialized societies (Newcomb & Bentler, 1989). Drugs are readily available in virtually all U.S. high schools and in an increasing number of elementary schools. Thus, younger children are also at risk for using drugs.

Alcohol, Marijuana, and Other Drugs

Alcohol is a legal drug found in many homes and throughout our society. It is the most popular drug with high school students, many of whom become problem drinkers. A survey of high school students found that 92.2% had used alcohol during their lifetime; 66.4% admitted using it during the previous month (Johnson, O'Malley, & Bachman, 1987). Marijuana is also popular; the same survey found that 50.2% of teens reported using it during their lifetime and 21% during the previous month (Johnson, O'Malley, & Bachman, 1987). As the table indicates, teens also take quite a lot of other drugs, including cocaine.

Researchers have discovered that some children and adolescents go through a number of stages in experimenting with drugs and alcohol. Some may start by drinking wine or beer; they may be alone or with companions. When slightly older, they begin to smoke cigarettes and drink hard liquor. Next, they may try marijuana. After using this very common drug, they almost inevitably progress to a combination of alcohol and hard drugs (Kandel, 1981).

Percentage of Drug Use Among High School Students. In a Survey of 16,300 High School Students, Johnson, O'Malley, and Bachman Asked Students If They Used These Drugs at Any Time, and Whether They Had Used Them During the Previous Month.

Drug	Lifetime	Past month
Alcohol	92.2%	66.4%
Cigarettes	67.2	29.4
Marijuana and hashish	50.2	21.0
Inhalents	18.6	3.5
Amyl and butyl nitrites	4.7	1.3
Hallucinogens	10.6	2.8
LSD	8.4	1.8
PCP	3.0	0.6
Cocaine	15.2	4.3
"Crack"	5.6	4.5
Other cocaine	14.0	4.1
Heroin	1.2	0.2
Other opiates	9.2	1.8
Stimulants	21.6	5.2
Sedatives	8.7	0.7
Barbiturates	7.0	1.4
Methaqualone	4.0	0.6
Tranquilizers	10.9	2.0

Source: National Trends in Drug Use and Related Factors Among American High School Students and Young Adults, 1975–1986, by L. D. Johnson, P. M. O'Malley, and J. Bachman, 1987. Rockville, MD: National Institute on Drug Abuse.

Effects of Drug and Alcohol Abuse

The widespread use of illegal substances can have devastating emotional and physical consequences for young minds and bodies. Many young people become addicted

(continued)

The Family

For most adolescents the family is an important source of influence regarding future goals and educational and vocational plans, and the family also eases the adolescent's transition from childhood to adulthood (Collins, 1990). Parents support their

FEATURE

(continued)

without realizing it. Excessive use of drugs and alcohol can subject adolescents to many dangers: It is the leading cause of fatal automobile accidents each year; it interferes with schoolwork; and it creates problems with family and friends (Albas, Albas, & McClusky, 1978; Brunswick, 1977). Research indicates that drugs and alcohol can have different effects, depending on the person's biological makeup, personality, and the extent to which he or she abuses these substances. Some adolescents can use drugs for a short time without suffering serious consequences, but others soon experience changes in their physiological and biochemical functions (Cohen, 1981) and in their social attitudes. Many young drug users, for example, lose all interest in social and academic activities; they often drop out of school and have bitter conflicts at home (Miller, 1981; Scarpitti & Datesman, 1980; Albas, Albas, & McClusky, 1978).

Their parents feel helpless because they can no longer control their children. Worried about their children's future, these parents experience anger, shame, and guilt, and they are not alone in their bewilderment. Educators, physicians, social workers, and policymakers are all uncertain about how to reduce the number of children and adolescents who become regular drug users. Despite the federal government's campaigns to cut off the flow of drugs, domestic and foreign drug producers continue to flood the market with a seemingly inexhaustible supply of illegal substances.

Preventive Means

Ideally, the best way to handle the problem would be through education to prevent drug use. In fact, many schools have launched drug and alcohol prevention courses in recent years, but the results have not been satisfactory (Bangert-Downs, 1988). One of the more promising courses teams up older children with younger ones in an effort to persuade elementary school pupils not to use drugs. Some such peer programs focus on assertiveness training and social skills, so children can learn to make decisions. They are taught to recognize how their decisions and actions can have long-term consequences for their future happiness (Tobler, 1986). To be successful, such programs need to begin before adolescence (Newcomb & Bentler, 1989).

Some states have raised the legal drinking age from 18 to 21, hoping to eliminate or reduce the problem of teenage drinkers and drivers. But since alcoholism among youngsters 18 and under continues to increase, it appears that this program is not always effective. Other states have instituted educational programs explaining the dangers of drug and alcohol abuse. Still other states have tried liberalizing laws governing the possession and use of marijuana; liberal policymakers hope that leniency with marijuana users will keep teenagers from progressing to hard drugs, but this view is controversial (Hanson, 1980).

Many school systems recommend punitive measures against all cases of drug and alcohol abuse. After surveying policies in secondary schools across the country, Schwartz (1984) reports that educators either suspend or expel all students caught using or possessing drugs as well as any students who voluntarily admit to drug use. However, this policy, it would appear, deprives teens of the very assistance they need.

How to Identify Teenage Drug Users

All individuals concerned with the adolescent drug problem agree that parents and educators must intervene quickly and decisively to stop youngsters suspected of alcohol and drug abuse. But it is not always easy to identify drug users, especially in the early stages. One problem is that they soon become experienced con artists who resort to all sorts of devices to conceal their addiction (Rees & Wilborn, 1983). We need to be alert to the following symptoms of extended drug use: (1) changing attitudes toward parents, (2) a decline in academic work, (3) the discovery that money or expensive items in the home are inexplicably missing, (4) severe mood swings, (5) dropping out of extracurricular activities, (6) new and perhaps unsavory friendships, (7) a decreased interest in the usual leisure activities, and (8) a tendency to spend an inordinate amount of time alone. These signs may appear either before or after the teen becomes addicted, and they are not typical of *all* teen drug abusers. However, they may help identify at least some endangered young people so we can help them before it is too late.

growing child by offering him advice and guidance as he attempts to find his place in life and by imparting their values and traditions (Hill & Holmbeck, 1986). Most adolescents believe that their parents are supportive of them (Offer, Ostrov, & Howard, 1981), and they tend to be responsive to their parents, accepting many of their values and following in their footsteps. They often choose friends from the same social class as their parents. Youngsters are as interested or disinterested in politics and religion as their parents are, often favoring the same presidential candidate and attending the same church or synagogue (Cooper & Ayers-Lopez, 1985). Also, they often choose occupational paths that reflect their parents' aspirations for them (Conger, 1973; Feather, 1980) and maintain a close attachment to their parents (Hill & Holmbeck, 1986).

Changes in family interactions   This is not to say that teens and parents always agree. On the contrary, in attempting to establish their own identity, adolescents may question their parents' ideologies; in fact, at times the teens' views may seem worlds apart from those of their parents. During early adolescence, most disagreements occur in connection with everyday matters such as performance of chores and appropriate dress. Toward the latter part of adolescence, conflicts about dating and alcohol and drug use are likely to occur (Carleton-Ford & Collins, 1988). In general, conflicts are often greatest when the adolescent is undergoing profound physical change (Collins, 1990). Indeed, most adolescents respect their parents and get along with them. Sorenson (1973) found that 88% of the teens he surveyed respected their parents; in a Gallup Poll survey (1986b) almost all adolescents said that they got along well with their parents. These findings reinforce a point made earlier in the chapter; in most families the generation gap is a myth evident only with respect to differences in dress, hairstyle, music, and manners of speech (Offer & Offer, 1975). When parents and teens get past these superficial differences and listen to each other's concerns, thoughts, and values, they find that they have much in common and can inform and influence one another (Hartup, 1983).

Researchers have found that the "generation gap" is a myth, evident only in differences in dress, hairstyle, musical taste, and manner of speech. When parents and teens get past these superficial distinctions, they realize that they have much in common.

Yet in establishing new patterns of authority and interaction during adolescence, especially early in the period, parents and teens have to adjust to the developmental changes the teenagers are undergoing (Collins, 1990). Reviewing research on interactions between parents and adolescents, John Hill (1980) notes that during this period parents are adjusting to "[a person] 'new' in stature, 'new' in approaching reproductive capability, 'new' in cognitive competence" in the house. Garbarino and Gilliam (1980) also note that while adolescents have to adjust to the physical, intellectual, and emotional changes they are experiencing, their parents also have to adjust to living with them. Parenting an adolescent is substantially different from parenting a child. Adolescents have far greater physical power; they can stimulate and influence family conflict (Patterson, Bank, & Stoolmiller, 1990); and they can leave the family, harm themselves and others, and embarrass their parents. This enhanced power, according to researchers, is often a destabilizing force unless parents and teens are flexible and willing to compromise.

Adolescents also become increasingly able to reason like adults, and they have a broader field of significant individuals in their life, most notably friends of the same and opposite sex, with whom parents must come to terms. In addition, the cost of raising children increases substantially during the adolescent years. According to U.S. Department of Agriculture (1982) figures, the yearly cost of maintaining a teenager is about 140% that of maintaining a young child. Garbarino (1986) notes that this drastically increased cost is stressful for many parents and can be the source of family conflict "particularly in families where the increased financial demands of adolescence are not matched by increased family income."

Given these changes, it is not surprising that surveys indicate that a majority of parents report that the adolescent years are the most difficult ones for childrearing (Pasley & Gecas, 1984). Parents have to adjust to an individual who is substantially different than she was in the past, and they have to adjust to the fact that she will one day leave the family and pursue an independent life. Their task is to guide their adolescent and offer the support and advice she needs while nurturing her quest for independence. This task is not easy, and it is exacerbated by the fact that in many families both the adolescent and the parents are changing and seeking to establish identities. Now that their child is ready to embark on an independent path in life, the parents may be contemplating their past and their future and redefining their existence in terms of the possibilities and limits confronting them (Levinson, 1978).

Parenting styles   The extent to which parents are able to adjust to their parenting tasks, and the approaches they use, have important effects on the adolescent's development. Diana Baumrind, who identified three distinct parenting styles and their effects on preschoolers (see Chapter 10), also reviewed the literature on parent/adolescent relationships. She found that although adolescents bring to the relationship their own personality and temperament, the parents' childrearing approaches and the way in which they react to their children definitely influence their personality and behavior (Baumrind, 1975; 1989; 1990).

Authoritative parents, according to Baumrind, show interest in their daughter's activities and are warm and supportive toward her. They give the teen consistent standards to abide by, but they are willing to grant her sufficient autonomy. They are flexible, often even willing to learn from the adolescent. Teens whose parents are authoritative are socially active and responsible, have high self-esteem, and evaluate their life possibilities; these young people are willing to commit themselves to certain values and goals.

Authoritarian parents are controlling. They expect their son to abide by numerous rules and are unwilling to adjust to his need for independence. Interactions are likely to be conflict-ridden. Adolescents of authoritarian parents have problems developing their own identity; they often prematurely withdraw from attempts to evaluate their life choices and make commitments.

Permissive parents are undemanding of their adolescent. They expect their daughter to be sufficiently mature to make major life decisions on her own, and they provide her with inconsistent rules, standards, and expectations, if any. Permissive parents often attempt to interact with her as though they were friends, and they resent her attempts to form attachments with peers. Adolescents of permissive parents feel rejected and confused by the lack of direction at home and resentful of their parents' attempts to be friendly. They often develop emotional and behavioral problems as a result of inadequate guidance and inconsistencies and leniency in their parents' attitudes. Generally, girls of permissive parents have emotional problems, including alienation and an attitude of helplessness, whereas boys develop behavioral problems (Duke, 1978).

Adolescent abuse Inappropriate parenting styles sometimes lead to abuse and neglect. In the past we limited our concern for the problems of abuse to infants and young children, perhaps because we assumed that by adolescence youngsters would no longer be helpless and vulnerable to abuse by adults. Recent studies reveal, however, that although adolescents are old enough to counteract abuse in certain respects, adolescent physical and emotional abuse is prevalent and related to inappropriate parenting styles and conflict between parents and teens.

Child experts have conducted only a few research studies and surveys of adolescent abuse, due in part to the tendency to concentrate public and professional emphasis on abuse and neglect of younger children. Although data from the available research are still inconclusive, we estimate that 650,000 adolescents are subject to abuse each year; these figures account for about 47% of the known cases of maltreatment of children aged 18 and under (U.S. Department of Health and Human Services, 1988). Since adolescents account for only 38% of the population under age 18, the fact that close to half the cases of abuse are of adolescents is significant.

Reviewing the research on the dynamics of adolescent maltreatment, Garbarino (1986) distinguishes between child and adolescent abuse, noting that teenagers are imperfect victims for abuse because they can and will strike back. This often creates potentially dangerous domestic quarrels involving mutual assault. He further points out that although many cases of child abuse are reported among low-income families, maltreatment of adolescents, although also occurring in families with financial difficulties, happens most frequently among middle- and upper-middle-class families. Garbarino cites the following characteristics of families in which adolescent abuse occurs: (1) the family is apt to contain a stepparent; (2) abused adolescents are less socially competent and are apt to exhibit more developmental problems than their nonabused peers; (3) families in which abuse occurs are often troubled by divorce; and (4) abusive parents are authoritarian parents. These parents are harsh and rigid in interacting with the adolescent. They are unable to understand his need for independence, and they cannot adjust to the fact that he is physically and mentally capable of challenging their authority.

Adolescents are subject to both physical and psychological abuse, which includes being terrorized, rejected, and isolated by their parents (Garbarino & Vondra, 1983). Often this maltreatment occurs to a greater degree than is true of younger children. A national survey on the severity of child abuse and neglect documents this point (Burgdorff, 1980). Burgdorff finds that children are more frequently physically abused than adolescents, whereas adolescents are more frequently psychologically abused.

DISCUSSION OF SOCIAL ISSUES

Runaway, Homeless, and Delinquent Youths

Adolescents subjected to abuse and neglect sometimes run away, only to find themselves homeless and in desperate situations. Some adopt a life of violence and crime. Although psychologists acknowledge the need for more research in this area, they are increasingly aware that maltreatment is at the root of many adolescent problems, including prostitution (Garbarino, 1986), and causes the subsequent problems of runaway, homeless, and delinquent youths (U.S. Congress, 1990a).

Runaways

Young people who run away from home have become a major national concern. About 500,000 adolescents do so each year. Ill equipped to fend for themselves, they are in many cases only 12 to 14 years old, which means they cannot legally hold a job. Even if they were capable of holding their own in the world, their opportunity to do so is slim because pimps and hustlers often latch onto them in city bus terminals or railroad stations, promising them food, shelter, and money. They then torture the runaways physically and emotionally, forcing them into submission and **putting them to work as prostitutes or in pornographic movies. This is true for both girls and boys. These young people suffer untold damage to their minds and bodies. They cannot escape their terrible situation; they are under constant surveillance and, in effect, held hostage by those who have taken them off the streets.**

Who are runaway youths? Why do they leave home? Jeffrey Artenstein (1990), a volunteer shelter supervisor at the Los Angeles Youth Network, notes in his book *Runaways: In Their Own Words* that 36% are fleeing from sexual or physical abuse and 44% leave because of other severe family problems. D'Angelo (1974) noted that teens who run away from home feel isolated and degraded while at home. The typical runaway episode stems from conflict or frustration in the parent/ teen relationship, including disagreements over appearance, friends, house rules, curfews, or level of expectation about school performance. Running away often reflects the adolescent's assumption of parental rejection and anger at their unwillingness to relax restrictions and enable her to assume some independence. Usually, the runaway episode is a spontaneous, impulsive act that may dramatically bring to a head the youth's desperate need for a flexible, responsive dialogue with the parents.

Some parents of runaways feel angered, concerned, and rejected by their teen's behavior, but many are overjoyed when their children contact them. Most are willing to do anything just to get their children back. Other parents, however, refuse to accept the youths back into their home, leaving them homeless. Only 50% of all runaways have the option to return to the family or be placed in foster care (Artenstein, 1990); in 25% of the cases, the youths remain homeless and have to live on the street (U.S. Congress, 1990a).

Homeless Youths

Some runaways become homeless, living in the streets; but there are also youths who are homeless. The family situation of youths who are homeless is substantially different from that of runaways. Homeless adolescents are rejected by their families. Sometimes the parents have flatly told them to leave home. According to reports submitted to the Judiciary Committee (U.S. Senate, 1980) at a hearing on homeless youths, these families are overburdened with financial responsibilities. Many of the parents have been divorced and suffer from low self-esteem. In many cases the divorced parent takes a new partner into the household. Subsequently the parent may become jealous of their child's more youthful sexuality. This can lead to sexual competition and an emotional situation full of family conflict. Often the teenager becomes an object of reprisal. In other cases the parent's lover may subject the adolescent to sexual and physical abuse. Unable to withstand this treatment, the youngster leaves home, knowing that her family is not eager to have her back.

There are also youths whose families are homeless. As we noted in Chapter 10, a growing number of families with children are now among the homeless. In fact, according to estimates submitted to the federal government, 68,000 children and teenagers aged 16 and under are members of homeless families (U.S. Congress, 1990a).

Numerous federal- and state-funded programs are available nationwide to help runaway and homeless youths. The National Runaway Switchboard helps teens

Approximately 500,000 adolescents run away each year, becoming vulnerable to pimps who use them for prostitution or pornography.

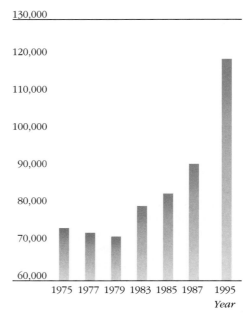

130,000

120,000

110,000

100,000

90,000

80,000

70,000

60,000

1975 1977 1979 1983 1985 1987   1995
Year

Figure 16.6 *Total juveniles in custody, 1975–1987, and 1995 projected.*
Source: U.S. House of Representatives (1990). *No Place to Call Home: Discarded Children in America.* Report of the Select Committee on Children, Youth, and Families. Washington, DC: U.S. Government Printing Office.

get in touch with their parents in the hope that the youngsters can go home. Youth shelters provide a safe, albeit temporary, place where the teens can get some food, sleep, and counseling. Often, however, the temporary shelter and counseling are not effective. Teens may be past the point where they are willing to listen to anyone and sometimes have unrealistic expectations of their capabilities and future. Although they are worried about a place to sleep and do not know where they will get their next meal, they are thinking that they can make it on their own, get a job, and buy a car. Many of them, however, don't make it and instead

> [end] up in the city workhouse or state penitentiary. . . . It's a bleak outlook for homeless kids who have no adult taking care of them and providing emotional support. They float around, latch onto someone, get married, are unemployed and continue the same cycle. [U.S. Senate, 1980]

Delinquent Youths

Similar situations characterize the lives of **juvenile delinquents,** or children 16 and under who commit offenses that would be considered criminal if they were adults. The Congressional (1990a) Select Committee on Children, Youth, and Families reports that the number of juveniles in custody rose from 74,270 in 1975 to 91,646 in 1987 (see Figure 16.6). In 1987, 60% of these delinquents were between the ages of 15 and 17; 21% were younger than 15. They were more likely to be male (79% of juvenile delinquents are male, 21% female); 52% of all delinquents were white, 34% were black, and 12% were Hispanic (Thomas, 1989). An analysis of custody rates, however, showed that the lowest representation was among whites

(249 per 100,000) and the highest was among blacks (839 per 100,000). Among Hispanics the rate was 460 per 100,000 (Thomas, 1989).

Delinquency, which is sometimes confused with minor behavior problems typical of adolescents (for example, stealing items from a grocery store), refers to a pattern of destructive behavior. It covers a wide range of violations of the law, including murder, assault, vandalism, and theft as well as promiscuity, truancy, and running away from home. The last three examples are considered crimes only when a minor commits them (Offer, Marhorn, & Ostrov, 1979); the minor is then designated as a "status offender."

When asked to report confidentially if they have broken any laws, most teens confess to one or more chargeable offenses, noting that they are guilty of minor crimes such as smoking marijuana or sexual intercourse with an underage girl (Gold & Petronio, 1980; Jessor & Jessor, 1977; Gold, 1970). However, not all crimes committed by adolescents are minor. According to statistics compiled by the U.S. Department of Justice (1985), 54% of all serious crimes such as murder, assault, and robbery are committed by youths aged 13 to 18; 31% of all general arrests nationally involve individuals aged 18 and under.

Developmental psychologists want to find out what causes an adolescent to progress from relatively minor delinquent acts to adopting delinquency and crime as a way of life. Delinquent youths have low self-esteem (Offer, Marhorn, & Ostrov, 1979); they are likely to have a history of school problems and be chronically unemployed (National Commission on Youth, 1980). Delinquents also have a lower IQ than average (an IQ of 92 as opposed to an average of 100) (Quay, 1987). In addition, they usually have been abused and neglected (Garbarino, 1986; Lewis et al., 1987). Having experienced abuse and disrespect from their parents during their teens and for much of their childhood, these adolescents learn aggression and exploitation as a means of negotiating life. They imitate their parents' behavior by exerting their strength on those who are less powerful. They terrorize women, the elderly, and defenseless men on the streets and are violent in school. As a result, an increasing number of teachers and students have become seriously concerned about their own safety at school. Several urban communities have full-time police officers on the school campus. Although this strategy is costly, school officials regard it as essential to maintain order (Gossnickle, Layne, & Tierney, 1988).

A report published by the U.S. Congress (1990a) points out that the drug trade has contributed significantly to violence among young people and to a nationwide spread of youth gangs. In the past gang turf wars entailed street fighting, today ". . . [gangs] deal with automatic weapons, Uzis and gang members with grenades" (p. 33).

Facilitating the Transition from Childhood to Adulthood

The serious problems confronting many young people—the poverty and despair associated with unemployment and teen parenthood, violence and crime, and the lack of a supportive family life—have existed for a long time and are becoming more prevalent each year. Child experts estimate that 7 million adolescents, or one out of every four, are at high risk for multiple behavior problems and school failure and that another 7 million are at moderate risk (Carnegie Council on Adolescent Development, 1989).

Several national groups have studied these problems in terms of their prevention. One such group (Carnegie Council on Adolescent Development, 1989), notes that we need to direct our prevention efforts at early adolescence:

> For many youths 10 to 15 years old, early adolescence offers opportunities to choose a path toward a productive and fulfilling life. For many others, it represents their last chance to avoid a diminished future. [p. 8]

We further recommend that the schools be used as the primary means for addressing the needs of youths, noting that we have to make changes in junior high, intermediate, and middle schools if our society is to recapture the millions of adolescents heading toward failure.

The focus on early adolescence and the use of the school as a focus of prevention efforts reflects numerous studies showing that early adolescence marks the "beginning of a downward spiral that leads some adolescents to academic failure and school drop out" (Eccles & Midgley, 1990, p. 134). Reviewing research on this topic, Eccles and Midgley (1990; 1989) note that part of the problem is that schools are not providing a developmentally appropriate educational environment for young teens. We "ghettoize" them into junior high schools that create an environment in which they are likely to act in accord with the negative stereotypes of adolescence.

The Carnegie Council on Adolescent Development (1989) notes that (1) schools need to become small communities for learning, where stable, close, and mutually respectful relationships can develop between students and adults; (2) teachers must be specifically trained in adolescent development; and (3) schools should provide health services to teens. Each school should have a health coordinator who can counsel and provide needed services.

The William T. Grant Foundation Commission on Work, Family, and Citizenship (1988) recommended in its report *The Forgotten Half: Non-College Youth in America* that we bridge the gap between school and work by preparing students for the world of work through monitored work experiences, internships, apprenticeships, and preemployment training for specific jobs. The commission and other study groups (e.g., the National Commission on Youth, 1980) further recommended that efforts be made to foster connections among all institutions serving adolescents—that is, the home, the school, and the workplace. These recommendations, if implemented, might indeed benefit young adolescents.

Perhaps more important we need to focus on the needs of both adolescents and their families. The problems teens experience stem only in part from their adolescent experience; these difficulties are also rooted in their experiences as children. As Erikson (1963) so eloquently stated, young people

> find an identity consonant with [their] own childhood . . . [and] by their responses and actions [they] tell the old whether life as presented by the old and as presented to the young, has meaning; it is the young who carry in them the power to confirm those who confirm them, and, joining the issues, to renew and regenerate, or to reform and rebel.

Summary

During adolescence, individuals must establish a personal identity and define themselves in terms of who they are and in terms of what they want to become. This is by no means an easy task. As adolescents undergo the psychosocial crisis of identity versus role confusion, they have to wrestle with the following questions: Who am I really? What do I want to do with my life? What do I believe in? They either resolve the crisis by committing themselves to some decisions about their being and their future, or they feel anxious and confused and become incapable of making decisions. Instead of resolving the crisis and achieving a sense of personal identity, some adolescents withdraw from efforts to shape an identity. Others adopt without question the values of their family and society. Some declare a moratorium; that is, they defer resolution of the crisis and make no decisions about what they believe and what they want to do.

The ease with which people establish an identity for themselves and decide on their eventual role as adults depends in part on their society. In a complex society like ours, identity formation is a difficult process; adolescents are faced with a variety of values and social roles to choose from. They have to make decisions about what they believe and what they want to do in life based on their interests and skills and on what society has to offer. This is especially true with regard to vocational decisions. For some adolescents, the question "What do I want to do when I grow up?" poses a dilemma. They cannot easily resolve the dilemma by choosing an occupation that appeals to them. The fact is that no matter what career they would like to follow, there are no jobs. As a result, an increasing number of youths aged 16 to 19 are unemployed and do not know what they will do in the future. However, this is not a unique situation. For example, adolescents during the Great Depression had to make decisions in the face of severe economic hardships. The social context in which people grow up is only one influence on the way their identities are formed. Family and friends also help shape how people view themselves and the plans they make for the future.

Friends, in particular, are important to adolescents; they provide emotional support as they begin the slow process of disengaging from the family and establishing an independent life. Although the adolescent girl spends as much time as she can with her friends, her parents remain an important influence. They are often most supportive of her, imparting to her their values and helping her make decisions about the future. As adolescents become increasingly independent, parents must adjust somewhat in their expectations and in their methods of discipline. Some parents are unable to make this adjustment and instead resort to abuse and neglect.

Until recently, researchers and policymakers were unaware of the extent of adolescent abuse. It has become increasingly clear, however, that some parents subject their adolescent youngsters to physical abuse, neglect, and isolation. Many abused adolescents become runaways. Some become homeless, and others adopt a life of delinquency and crime. Child experts have proposed numerous solutions to resolve some problems of young people and to stem the increasing number of runaway, homeless, and delinquent adolescents. Perhaps the most important change would be to institute improvements in the school system; another solution would be to support family life during adolescence and throughout childhood as well.

Glossary

Italic type designates terms appearing in a definition that are themselves defined in separate entries.

academic curriculum   What the child is expected to learn from instruction.

accommodation   In Piaget's theory an aspect of adaptation involving a change or expansion of cognitive view in response to new information from the environment.

achievement tests   Tests that measure what children learn from instruction.

acne   A skin problem caused by bacterial infection underneath the skin that leads to painful boils and potential scarring of the facial tissue. Although common among adolescents, acne can also strike older individuals.

acquired immune deficiency syndrome (AIDS)   The breakdown of the immune system caused by the *human immunodeficiency virus (HIV),* which leaves its victims vulnerable to fatal illness.

Action for Children's Television (ACT)   A group of parents who monitor television and try to change its impact on children.

acts of commission   In child abuse acts of physical force or violence against children.

acts of omission   In child abuse the emotional or physical neglect of children.

adaptation   Principle of functioning; the inherent tendency to adjust to the environment through the processes of *assimilation* and *accommodation.*

adenine   One of four nitrogenous bases comprising the chemical bonds that link the pair of intertwined coils within the *DNA* molecule. Adenine links only with *thymine.*

age of viability   The age at which fetal development is sufficiently advanced so that the baby will survive if born. The age of viability is estimated to be at the end of 28 weeks after conception, but with medical advances the age is periodically revised downward.

albinism   A hereditary condition characterized by white hair, pink eyes, and the absence of skin pigmentation. Albinism is transmitted by a recessive *allele;* it is therefore an observable characteristic only if the individual is *homozygous* for that trait.

alleles   The component parts of a *gene.* For any given gene, there are two alleles, one from the father and one from the mother.

alpha-fetoprotein screening   A test in which blood is drawn from a pregnant woman to ascertain whether the fetus is suffering from neural tube defects.

altruistic behavior   A voluntary, intentional action that benefits another person and is not motivated by a desire to gain approval or reward.

amniocentesis   A procedure to test for genetic abnormalities during pregnancy. It involves taking a sample of the *amniotic fluid* by inserting a needle through the abdomen into the *amniotic sac* in the uterus. This test can be done after the 10th week and is usually done between the 16th and 18th weeks. Results are obtained in approximately three weeks.

amnion   The inner membrane of the *amniotic sac,* which contains the *amniotic fluid.*

amniotic fluid   A liquid substance found within the *amniotic sac* that protects the *embryo* against physical shock and temperature change.

amniotic sac   A bag containing *amniotic fluid* in which the embryonic baby develops. It is formed by two membranes (the *chorion* and the *amnion*) that develop from cells on the outside of the fertilized egg.

androgens   Male sex hormones.

androgynous   An individual whose behavior combines both feminine and masculine characteristics.

anorexia nervosa   A severe eating disorder found most frequently among adolescent girls, characterized by self-induced starvation and may be accompanied by frequent purging. Anorexics have a distorted body image and a tremendous fear of being fat.

anoxia   A condition that results in the birth of children who suffer a severe lack of oxygen. Anoxia often leads to a variety of motor defects subsumed under the general term *cerebral palsy.*

Apgar Scoring System   A rating system used immediately after birth to assess the condition of the newborn infant.

apnea   Temporary cessation of breathing.

applied research   Research designed to meet society's needs for information or to be put to some immediate use.

areola   The pigmented area around the breast nipple.

artificialism   The childhood myth that everything is made by someone.

assimilation   In Piaget's theory the incorporation of new information into preexisting schemes.

attachment   The loving and enduring bond between the infant and the caregiver. Ainsworth has identified three types of attachments: secure, anxious, and avoidant.

attention deficit disorder (ADD)   A recently developed diagnostic category that applies to a relatively common disorder among children characterized by *hyperactivity* (or *hypoactivity*) and an inability to concentrate on or attend to specified tasks in an orderly manner; supercedes the labels *hyperactive syndrome* and *minimal brain dysfunction* to describe such children.

attention deficit hyperactivity disorder (ADHD)   See *attention deficit disorder.*

autobiographical memory   Memory of specific events.

autonomy versus shame and doubt   Erikson's second psychosocial crisis, occurring around age 2. Through this crisis, the toddler acquires either a basically healthy attitude toward independence, or fear and shame, which inhibit a healthy sense of self-sufficiency.

autosomes   The 22 pairs of chromosomes in each cell *nucleus,* possessed equally by the male and female, which determine traits other than gender; the 23rd chromosome pair determines gender.

autostimulation theory   Suggests that the high degree of *REM sleep* during the newborn period stimulates the development of the central nervous system.

axon   Wirelike extension of nerve-cell cytoplasm that transmits outgoing messages from the cell.

baby biographies   Day-to-day accounts of children's development.

basic research   Research motivated by the desire to expand human knowledge (as opposed to *applied research*).

birthing rooms   Comfortable, homey rooms where both labor and delivery take place often to the sound of soothing music and under dim lights.

black English   A nonstandard dialect of English spoken by low-income black children. It is governed by its own grammatical rules and should not be regarded as a simplified form of the standard dialect.

blended families   Families created by the divorce and remarriage of one or both partners; also known as *new extended families* and *reconstituted families.*

bone age   The rate of an individual's bone ossification as compared with norms for his or her particular age; can be used as an assessment tool to predict a skeletal feature such as eventual height; also known as *skeletal age.*

breech position   The baby's position in the womb that presents its legs or buttocks first.

bulimia   A severe eating disorder found most frequently among adolescent girls; characterized by enormous eating binges followed by self-induced vomiting.

canalization   The process by which some kinds of behaviors follow a prescribed genetic course. The less canalized the behavior, the easier it is to modify; highly canalized behaviors are difficult to alter.

capacitation   A process undergone by sperm that reach the outer end of the fallopian tube. As a result of capacitation, the successful sperm is able to dissolve the outer membrane surrounding the egg cell and penetrate into its center.

categorization   The ability to mentally organize information into related groupings.

cell   The smallest unit of living matter that is capable of independent functioning, made up of a *cell wall* containing *cytoplasm* and a *nucleus.* The human body is comprised of billions of cells, which have specialized functions.

cell wall   The outer membrane of the *cell,* which contains fluid called the *cytoplasm.*

(to) center   In Piaget's *preoperational period* the tendency to focus on one aspect of a problem or situation and neglect other properties that must be taken into account in order to arrive at the correct solution.

central nervous system   The bodily system comprised of the brain, brain stem, and spinal cord.

cephalocaudal sequence   Moving from head to toe; a principle governing physical growth.

cerebral palsy   A general term used to describe a variety of motor defects (such as paralysis of the limbs, tremors of the face or fingers, inability to use the vocal muscles) caused by brain damage due to a severe lack of oxygen before or during birth.

cesarean delivery   A surgical operation for removing a baby from the uterus through the abdominal wall.

childhood aphasia   Learning disability that involves the inability to speak or to comprehend what is being said.

childhood social indicators   Measures of changes or constancies in the conditions of children's lives and in their health, achievement, behavior, and well-being.

children in self-care   See *latchkey children.*

child support The monetary payment made by the parent who does not have custody of the child to the parent who does have custody.

cholinesterase An enzyme crucial for the transmission of neural impulses; it is synthesized in the nervous system.

chorion The outer membrane of the *amniotic sac,* which encloses the inner membrane (the *amnion*).

chorion biopsy A recently developed screening test for genetic abnormalities that can be conducted as early as the ninth week of pregnancy; it involves taking a sample of the chorion cells outside the fertilized egg for examination and biopsy; results are given within a few days.

chorionic villus sampling /See *chorion biopsy.*

chromatin Long, tiny fibers located within the *nucleus* of a cell, on which the *genes* are found.

chromosomes Name given to *chromatin,* after it was found that these fibers take stain very well and become highly visible under a microscope; from the Greek words "chromo" and "soma," meaning "color-body." There are 46 chromosomes in a normal human cell, each chromosome holding thousands of *genes.*

classical conditioning A type of learning, demonstrated by Pavlov, whereby an individual can be taught or conditioned to make a specific response to a neutral stimulus after the neutral stimulus is repeatedly paired with another stimulus that naturally elicited the specific response.

class inclusion An aspect of the concept of classification that refers to the ability to understand that there is a hierarchical relationship between subordinate and superordinate classes.

cloning A form of genetic engineering that involves asexual reproduction in which all offspring are identical.

cochlea The main hearing organ of the ear.

code-switching In bilingual children refers to their switching from one language to another, sometimes within one sentence.

cognition The act of knowing.

cognitive structures In Piaget's theory the structures of the mind that provide a framework for understanding the world.

competence motivation The child's intrinsic motivation to learn and understand the world.

concrete operations period Piaget's third stage of cognitive development, from approximately age 7 to 12, characterized by the ability to mentally manipulate tangible and concrete information according to logical rules.

conservation In Piaget's theory the fact that certain characteristics of an object remain the same despite superficial changes in appearance.

continuum of caretaking casualty The extent to which the effects of a *teratogen* will be manifested is often determined by experiences after birth.

continuum of reproductive casualty The range of variations in the degree to which the influence of a specific *teratogen* will culminate in abnormalities in the child.

conventional level Kohlberg's second level of moral judgment, wherein morality is based on social rules and on

living up to the expectations of the family, group, or nation.

coregulation Among parents and older school-age children, shared responsibility for monitoring children's behavior.

cretinism A syndrome caused by iodine deficiency in the mother; characterized by mental retardation and dwarfing in the offspring.

critical periods Specific developmental periods, during which environmental influences can play a crucial role in the extent to which an individual's *genotype* is expressed in his or her *phenotype;* times in the developmental process during which the organism is especially sensitive to a particular influence.

crossing over The random exchange of corresponding segments between pairs of *chromosomes* that may occur during *meiosis.*

cross-modal transfer of information Process involving the exchange of information among the senses.

cystic fibrosis A disorder of the exocrine glands transmitted as a recessive trait; the most common severe genetic disease of childhood in the United States.

cytoplasm The fluid contained within the *cell wall* and outside the *nucleus;* that part of the *cell* where the instructions originated by the *DNA* in the nucleus are ultimately carried out.

cytosine One of four nitrogenous bases comprising the chemical bonds that link the pair of intertwined coils within the *DNA* molecule. Cytosine links only with *guanine.*

decidua The thickened lining of the uterus into which the *zygote,* or fertilized egg, implants itself.

decrement of attention See *habituation.*

deep structure According to Chomsky, one of the two levels of the structure of language; the basic syntactical relationship between words.

dendrite Wirelike extension of nerve-cell cytoplasm that receives incoming impulses to the cell.

deprivation dwarfism A condition in which a child receives adequate nutrition but fails to grow normally because of emotional abuse and neglect.

DES (or **diethylstibestrol**) A synthetic hormone, prescribed between the late 1940s and early 1960s to women in the United States who were at risk of having a miscarriage. DES was found to cause delayed effects in female offspring, some of whom developed vaginal abnormalities and cervical cancer during maturity.

developmental screening tests Tests that assess children's ability to acquire skills.

dishabituation An observable phenomenon wherein interest in a familiar object will be reactivated if a comparable but slightly different object appears with it.

dizygotic twins A pair of individuals who develop simultaneously in the womb from two separate eggs; also known as *fraternal twins.*

DNA (or **deoxyribonucleic acid**) The component of the *chromosome* that controls the biological inheritance of all living things through a genetic code that directs the production of protein within the body and contains instructions about how the organism is to develop. DNA consists of a pair of intertwined coils of indefinite length comprised of sugar phosphate molecules; the cells are linked together by chemical bonds derived from the four bases—*adenine, thymine, cytosine,* and *guanine.*

dominance   Refers to the relationship between *alleles* within the *heterozygous gene.* One allele will dominate over the other in determining the *phenotype,* or observable characteristic, associated with a particular trait.

double standard   The two different sets of rules or expectations for sexual behavior for men and women.

Down's syndrome   A disorder that is caused by a mutation involving the 21st chromosome, which results in mental retardation, abnormalities affecting internal organs, and distinctive physical features.

dramatic play   Make-believe or pretend play; when it involves several children, also known as sociodramatic play.

dream sleep   See *REM sleep.*

dyscalculia   Learning disability involving the inability to calculate numbers.

dyslexia   Learning disability that involves an impairment in the ability to read.

ectoderm   One of the three layers into which the inner mass of the *zygote* differentiates during the *period of the embryo.* From the ectoderm develop the hair, nails, part of the teeth, the outer layers of the skin, skin glands, the nervous system, and sensory cells.

egocentrism   The belief that the world centers on one's own life; characteristic of the child in the *preoperational period.*

ejaculation   The discharge of seminal fluid containing sperm.

empathy   The capacity to experience another person's emotions vicariously.

endoderm   One of the three layers into which the inner mass of the *zygote* differentiates during the *period of the embryo.* From the endoderm develop the gastrointestinal tract, trachea, bronchi, eustachian tubes, glands, and other organs such as the lungs, pancreas, and liver.

endogenous   Internally triggered.

estrogen   The female sex hormone.

evolution   The process of change in life forms over time that is guided in a particular direction through natural selection and the survival of organisms whose genetic characteristics foster constructive adaptations to the environment.

exogenous   Externally triggered.

failure to thrive   Failure of infants to grow and develop in the absence of any physiological problem; usually the result of emotional abuse and neglect.

family day-care home   An environment where an adult, usually a mother of young children, looks after a small group of children in her own home.

fetal alcohol syndrome (FAS)   Withdrawal and other symptoms in a baby born to a mother who abused alcohol during pregnancy.

fine motor   See *motor.*

foreclosure   Premature identity formation during adolescence, characterized by an uncritical and unquestioning acceptance of the values of one's family and society as one's own.

formal operations period   According to Piaget, the fourth stage of cognitive development, from approximately age 12 to 18, characterized by the ability to think in the abstract and solve problems systematically.

fraternal twins   See *dizygotic twins.*

gametes   See *germ cells.*

gender identity   An aspect of the self-concept that refers to an individual's awareness and acceptance of being either male or female.

gender schema theory   Children acquire a notion of what it is like to be male or female by selectively watching how other people behave and then choosing information to develop their own gender schema.

gender (sex) roles   Socially defined behaviors and attitudes associated with being a male or a female.

gene   The unit of transmission of hereditary material, which is located on the *chromosomes.* Each chromosome holds thousands of genes, which are typically in pairs, one member of the pair contributed by the male and the other by the female. A gene can also be described as a complete chain of a multiple protein (a section of code from a start signal to a stop signal) along a *DNA* coil. See also *alleles.*

gene locus   The specific location of a particular *gene* on a *chromosome,* which is repeated on every chromosome of that type.

genetic engineering   A research activity that involves the manipulation of *genes.*

genotype   The individual's total genetic makeup, which, in interaction with the environment, can produce a wide range of possible *phenotypes.*

gentle birthing   A delivery method in which the baby is born in a dimly lit delivery room and then gently held in warm water as if he or she were still surrounded by the *amniotic fluid* in the uterus.

germ cells   The reproductive cells—that is, the sperm and the *ovum.* Contain 23 *chromosomes* each, versus *somatic,* or body, *cells,* which contain 46 chromosomes (23 pairs) each; also known as *gametes.*

germinal mutations   Changes in a *gene,* in the arrangements of the genes, or in the quantity of chromosomal material that affect the *gametes.*

gestational surrogacy   Placing sperm and egg cell of infertile couple in a petri dish in preparation for in vitro fertilization. Differs from *traditional surrogacy.*

glial cells   See *neuroglia.*

goodness of fit   A good match between children's temperament and the demands that are placed on the children.

gross motor   See *motor.*

growth spurt   A period of rapid physical growth that occurs in *puberty.*

guanine   One of four nitrogenous bases comprising the chemical bonds that link the pair of intertwined coils within the *DNA* molecule. Guanine links only with *cytosine*.

habituation   Refers to the individual's lack of interest in or reaction to a particular stimulus because it has become familiar through repeated exposure.

hemophilia   A sex-linked recessive disease often referred to as the "bleeding disease" because its victims lack a certain factor necessary for blood clotting and thus bleed excessively, either spontaneously or from cuts and bruises.

heritability ratio   A mathematical estimate of the proportion of trait variance having genetic causes; used to determine the relative importance of both heredity and the environment.

heterozygous   Having a *gene*-pair composition of two *alleles* that give different hereditary directions for the determination of a particular trait. In this case, one allele will dominate over the other. See also *dominance, recessiveness*.

hidden curriculum   Mechanisms for maintaining order in the classroom.

hierarchic integration   The integration of individual abilities into a complex behavior.

holophrastic speech   In children aged 1 to 1 ½, the use of one word to convey a thought or desire.

homozygous   Having a *gene*-pair composition of two *alleles* that give the same hereditary direction for the determination of a particular trait.

horizontal decalage   Piagetian term referring to the unevenness in children's understanding of concepts. For example, in *conservation* tasks, the child is first able to conserve number, then length, liquid quantity, and finally other properties of objects. "Decalage" is the French word for "gap."

hostile aggression   An attack against someone rather than something.

human immunodeficiency virus (HIV)   See *acquired immune deficiency syndrome*.

hyperactive syndrome   See *attention deficit disorder*.

hyperactivity   Attentional disorder involving the inability to settle down within structured situations that require concentrated attention to tasks.

hypoactivity   Attentional disturbance found more frequently in girls; characterized by less-than-normal activity levels and excessive daydreaming.

identical twins   See *monozygotic twins*.

identification   Unconscious mental process resulting in the adoption of another person's attitudes, behaviors, or values.

identity diffusion   Lack of consolidation of identity during adolescence; characterized by ambivalence or indifference about making decisions and a withdrawal of efforts to shape a personal identity.

identity versus role confusion   Erikson's psychosocial crisis of adolescence, involving the struggle for a personal sense of identity.

idiolect   In preschool children an idiosynchratic but generally communicative way of speaking involving, for example, combining parts of two words to create a new word.

inductive technique   In disciplining children refers to explaining the effects of their misbehavior.

industry versus inferiority   Erikson's psychosocial crisis of middle childhood, during which children either gain increasing confidence in their sense of competence and industry or manifest shrinking confidence in their abilities in comparison to others.

initiative versus guilt   Erikson's third psychosocial crisis, occurring between ages 3 and 6, during which children develop either an increasing sense of confidence in, and mastery of, their activities or increasing feelings of inadequacy and a lack of pleasure in, and motivation toward, accomplishing tasks on their own.

instrumental aggression   Fighting over objects in order to attain a desired goal.

intervillous space   In the uterine environment the space occupied by the *villi* (the fingerlike projections of the *placenta*), in which the vital exchange of substances and nutrients between the mother and the unborn baby occurs.

intrapair concordance   The similarity between twins.

irreversibility   Piaget's principle governing preoperational thinking that refers to children's inability to go forward and then backward in thinking, thus inhibiting the application of logical rules to solve problems or understand change.

juvenile delinquents   A statutory designation for children aged 16 and under who commit offenses that would be considered criminal if they were adults.

karyotype   A pictorial arrangement of *chromosomes* within a cell that have been grouped in pairs according to length and that can be studied to detect gross abnormalities.

Klinefelter's syndrome   A sex-chromosome abnormality in males characterized by an extra X *chromosome* (XXY instead of XY), which results in sterility, the development of many female characteristics, and a tendency to be tall and slim.

Lamaze   A method of preparing for childbirth that includes teaching expectant parents breathing techniques that will strengthen the uterine muscles.

language-acquisition device   According to Chomsky, a mental structure that enables infants to process sounds and patterns of speech and later triggers milestones of speech, including the capacity to understand the structure of language and the fundamental relationship between words.

lanugo   The growth of fine-textured hair covering the body of a newborn.

latchkey children   The large population of children who carry their housekey on a chain around their neck (because they return home each day after school to a house without adult supervision); also known as *children in self-care*.

lateralization   The process by which each of the two sides of the brain take control of certain mental functions.

learned helplessness   The belief that failure is not the result of one's own actions but rather is due to forces outside one's control.

learning readiness Children, or infants, learn with greater ease when they are developmentally ready to do so.

mainstreaming The educational practice of placing children with special needs alongside their normal peers in regular classrooms.

maladaptive acculturation Minority-group children's rejection of the majority culture or their family's culture.

maturation The orderly physiological changes that occur in all species over time and that appear to unfold according to a genetic blueprint.

meiosis A form of cell division involved in the production of the *gametes,* or germ cells. Each part of the *chromosome* pair migrates to opposite sides of the dividing *nucleus,* and the resultant cells then contain 23 single chromosomes (versus the 23 pairs within the somatic cells).

menarche The first menstrual period.

mental operations Mental manipulation of information, characteristic of Piaget's *concrete operations period.*

mesoderm One of three layers the inner mass of the *zygote* differentiates into during the *period of the embryo.* From this layer develop the muscles, skeleton, excretory and circulatory systems, and inner skin layer.

mesomorph A basic body type characterized by well-developed muscles, broad shoulders, and little or no evidence of excess body fat.

metacognition An intuitive understanding of the thinking process and how one acquires knowledge.

metalanguage The understanding of, and ability to talk about, various aspects of language such as nouns, verbs, clauses.

metalinguistic awareness An intuitive understanding of how language works.

metamemory An intuitive understanding of how memory works.

minimal brain dysfunction (MBD) See *attention deficit disorder.*

mitosis The process by which somatic (body) cells divide. It involves duplication of each of the 46 *chromosomes* within the cell *nucleus,* resulting in two identical sets of 46 chromosomes. The two sets of chromosomes then move to opposite sides of the cell, and the cell divides, to form two cells with identical chromosomes.

modifier genes *Genes* that influence the actions or observable characteristics of other genes.

monozygotic twins A pair of individuals who develop simultaneously in the womb from a single fertilized egg and have identical *genes;* also known as *identical twins.*

Moro reflex A reflex of infancy wherein the baby will throw its arms upward and clench its fingers in response to being suddenly dropped about 6 inches in midair.

morpheme Smallest unit of speech.

motherese Use of special intonation when speaking to infants. Involves high-pitch voice, slow speech, and exaggerated facial expressions.

motor Denotes muscular movement. *Gross motor* involves the use of the large muscles, *fine motor* involves the use of the small muscles of the hands and fingers.

mutant genes *Genes* that increase the rate of *mutations* in individuals who carry them.

mutation Change in a *gene,* in the arrangement of the genes, or in the quantity of chromosomal material.

mutual gaze In parent/infant interaction, gazing at one another for a time.

myelination A maturational process of the nervous system during which nerve fibers become coated with myelin, a protective fatty sheath that facilitates the transmission of neural signals.

myelogenetic cycles Periods during which *myelination* occurs in particular functional centers within the brain.

natural childbirth Childbirth in which the mother takes no medication during labor or takes it sparingly only at the final phase of delivery.

neuroglia Cells of the nervous system that feed and support the *neurons;* also known as *glial cells.*

neurons Nerve cells that receive and send impulses or signals.

new extended families See *blended families.*

new morbidity Term encompassing a wide range of behavioral and psychosocial factors that threaten the health of children.

nondisjunction An anomaly involving the 21st *chromosome* that is characterized by the presence of an extra chromosome, or part of a third chromosome, which leads to Down's syndrome. In this case, the individual will have 47 instead of the normal 46 chromosomes.

nucleus A special compact structure within the cell that contains genetic material and other structures that direct the manufacture and transport of substances within the cell.

obesity An excess of body weight, measured by skinfold thickness.

object permanence The cognitive capacity to understand that objects continue to exist even when they cannot be seen, touched, or smelled directly.

operant conditioning A type of learning whereby an individual is conditioned to make a specific response as a result of being rewarded whenever that response is initiated.

operator gene A type of *gene* that regulates protein synthesis in adjacent structural genes.

organization Piagetian principle of functioning that refers to the inherent tendency to organize experience by integrating two or more schemes into a more complex, higher-order scheme.

ossification The formation of solid bone.

outcome evaluation Evaluation used to assess the impact of a particular policy or program and determine whether it is beneficial. Usually conducted in conjunction with *process evaluation.*

overregularization The application of general rules of language to all words, including cases where the correct word form represents an exception to the rules.

ovum   The unfertilized egg cell of the female; also known as a germ cell or *gamete*.

parity   The number of births a woman has had.

perception   The interpretation of sensory experience into coherent signals.

period of the embryo   One of three periods that make up the development of the organism in utero. Lasts from the time of the *zygote's* attachment to the uterine wall (at about 2 weeks) until the first occurrence of the formation of solid bone *(ossification)* in the embryo (at about the 8th week). Marked by differentiation of important organs and can be a hazardous time for the embryo, since most miscarriages—involving an estimated 30% of embryos—occur during this time.

period of the fetus   One of three periods that make up the development of the organism in utero. Lasts from the beginning of the third month until birth and is marked by rapid muscular and central nervous system development.

period of the ovum   One of three periods that make up the development of the organism in utero. Lasts approximately two weeks from the moment of conception. During this time, the *zygote* establishes itself in the uterine wall and begins a physiologically dependent relationship with the mother that will continue throughout pregnancy.

perspective-taking   See *role-taking*.

phenocopy   An individual whose gene expression has been environmentally altered to mimic the observable characteristic, or *phenotype,* that is usually associated with another specific *genotype*.

phenotype   The observable characteristic of an individual or organism resulting from the interaction of the environment and the *genotype*.

phenylketonuria (PKU)   A hereditary condition caused by a recessive *gene* that leads to the absence of a certain enzyme needed to convert the protein phenylalanine, found in milk, into tyrosine, resulting in mental retardation.

phocomelia   The most dramatic and characteristic deformity in the offspring of mothers who ingested *thalidomide* during early pregnancy; limbs are absent, with the feet and hands attached to the torso like flippers.

physical fitness   Optimal functioning of the heart, lungs, muscles, and blood vessels.

placenta   An auxiliary structure that develops during the embryo period and allows for the passage of substances from the maternal bloodstream to that of the fetus, forming the vital link between the mother and the unborn baby on which the life of the fetus depends; also known as the afterbirth.

placental barrier   See *placenta*.

play   Any pleasurable, spontaneous, and voluntary activity that is an end in itself and has no extrinsic goal (Garvey, 1977). Several types have been distinguished: solitary, parallel, associative, cooperative, and *dramatic*.

pleiotropy   A single *gene* influencing more than one characteristic.

polygenetic inheritance   A trait that has as its source a constellation of *genes* acting together.

population gene pool   The collection of similar genetic characteristics in a particular part of the world or population.

postconventional level   Kohlberg's highest level of moral judgment, wherein morality is based on individually chosen moral values and ethical principles that have validity and application; also known as autonomous level.

pragmatic   Aspect of language referring to how we use language.

preconventional level   Kohlberg's lowest level of moral judgment, wherein emphasis is placed on avoiding punishment and getting a reward.

premature baby   The birth of a baby before the full term of 38 to 42 weeks in the uterus.

preoperational period   Piagetian period of cognitive growth beginning in the latter part of the second year of life and continuing to age 6 or 7; characterized by the acquisition of a prelogical symbolic mode of thinking that is dominated by egocentrism.

preparedness   See *canalization*.

preterm baby   See *premature baby*.

process evaluation   Evaluation used to verify whether, and under what circumstances, the services mandated by a policy are delivered and the manner in which a particular policy or program was implemented. Differs from but is usually accompanied by an *outcome evaluation*.

productive memory   The process of remembering an event or stimulus experienced previously, without the reappearance of that event or stimulus.

prosocial behaviors   Behaviors that are valued by society.

proximodistal direction   Moving from near to far; a principle governing physical growth.

psychometric approach   The measurement of intellectual behavior by standardized testing.

puberty   The period of rapid growth that culminates in sexual maturity and reproductive capability.

puberty rites   Ceremonies that mark the individual's assumption of new, more adult roles.

punitive technique   In disciplining children explaining the personal consequences of breaking a rule.

range of reaction   The array of possible variations in responsiveness that an individual will exhibit under different life experiences.

readiness tests   Tests that assess skills mastered by the child.

recall memory   To identify something when a physical stimulus is not present.

receptive language   Other conditions necessary for language development, such as listening attentively, discriminating among sounds, and understanding what is being said.

recessiveness   The relationship between *alleles* within the heterozygous *gene.* The recessive allele is subordinated to the dominant one and will not be expressed in the *phenotype;* however, it continues to be transmitted and thus may reappear as an observable characteristic in successive generations.

reciprocal role learning A theory of sex-role development in girls based on research suggesting that their femininity is associated more strongly with their fathers' masculinity than with their mothers' femininity.

reciprocity In mental operations the ability to recognize that a change in one feature of an object is balanced by an equal and opposite change in another feature of that object.

recognition memory Type of memory used to identify something previously known when a physical stimulus is present.

reconstituted families See *blended families.*

recovery of attention See *dishabituation.*

reflexes Specific, involuntary responses to stimuli.

regulator gene A *gene* that produces molecules that tell all genes when to turn on and off, thereby modifying the basic biochemical processes of the genes and resulting in individual differences.

rehearsal A memory-aiding technique involving mental or verbal repetition.

REM sleep (or **rapid eye movement sleep)** Stages of sleep during which the muscles of the eyeballs are in constant motion behind the eyelids. When awakened during REM sleep, adults often report that they had been dreaming.

reversibility The ability to go back and forth mentally, to perform mental inversions, or to mentally "undo" a sequence of actions, a hallmark of Piaget's *concrete operations period.*

RNA (or **ribonucleic acid)** That component of the *chromosome* that serves as a messenger to carry the directions, originated by the *DNA,* from the *nucleus* of the *cell* to its *cytoplasm.*

role-taking A cognitive skill that refers to the individual's ability to understand how another person perceives or feels in a certain situation; also known as *perspective-taking.*

rooming in A practice many hospitals currently offer that allows the mother and baby to stay in one room together rather than separating them after birth.

rooting reflex An adaptive reflex of infancy in which the baby will attempt to suck a finger that is touched gently to its mouth or cheek.

schema Piaget's strategies by which individuals understand the environment and make sense out of what they encounter. Schemata (plural of schema) evolve from simple innate reflexes to complex mental representations.

school readiness Efforts to ensure that children will enter school ready to profit from instruction. May include intervention programs for infants, home visitation programs for parents with children up to age 3, and early childhood education programs for disadvantaged children.

sebum A fatty substance produced by skin glands when stimulated by *androgens.*

secular trend The trend toward earlier sexual maturation and earlier attainment of adult height, observed by monitoring several generations.

selective attention The ability to focus on relevant aspects of the environment and disregard irrelevant aspects.

selective breeding A technique used in animal studies; mating animals that are similar in the degree to which a trait is manifested or not manifested in order to determine what traits are inherited.

semantics The linguistic representation of what we know about objects and events; the meaning of words and sentences.

sensation Sensory detection of a certain stimulus in the environment.

sensorimotor period Piaget's first period of cognitive development, which lasts from birth to age 2. The infant's interactions with the environment are governed by overt sensory and motor abilities, and learning takes place in the context of perceiving and acting on objects and people in the environment.

separation anxiety A fear of separation, especially evident during the first year of life; characterized by the infant's distressed behavior when separated from a parent or other significant caregiver.

seriation A cognitive achievement of the *concrete operations period* that involves the ability to arrange objects in an orderly series.

sex cleavage Tendency to separate into groups according to sex.

sex drive The basic biological need to achieve sexual satisfaction.

shaken-baby syndrome A form of infant physical abuse characterized by hemorrhages throughout the brain as a result of simply being shaken; can result in brain damage, visual problems, and deficits in language and motor skills.

sibling rivalry The conflict or competition existing between children within a family.

sickle-cell anemia A hereditary and ultimately fatal disease that attacks mostly blacks but also some Greeks and Italians, causing 100,000 deaths yearly. An individual who is *homozygous* for this *gene* produces abnormal hemoglobin that results in the distortion of the blood cells on their exposure to low oxygen levels, usually causing death at an early age.

signs According to Piaget, means of communication (for example, words) that have public meanings shared and understood by society but that bear no resemblance to that which they represent.

skeletal age See *bone age.*

social clock Chronological standards in each culture for appropriate behavior, so that individuals are "expected" to marry at a certain age, have children at another, and so on.

socialization The process by which children come to behave in socially acceptable ways and by which members of one generation shape the behavior and personality of members of the younger generation.

social referencing An ability or tendency to be influenced by other people's emotional expressions.

society of children The social world of children, which has its own rituals, traditions, activities, and social rules, handed down from one generation of children to another.

sociogram A graphic representation of how each child in a group feels about the other children.

sociometry A research technique used to establish children's social status and acceptability among their peers.

somatic cells Body cells that compose the muscles, bones, and various body systems. Somatic cells have 23 pairs of *chromosomes,* or 46 chromosomes in all.

somatic mutations Changes in a *gene,* in the arrangements of the genes, or in the quantity of chromosomal material that affect body cells after cell division has begun.

sonogram A detailed picture created by high-frequency sound waves. During pregnancy, a sonogram is used to determine the position of the fetus.

spina bifida A failure of the spinal column to close plus an abnormally small head and fluid in the brain.

stability and constancy of gender The understanding that one will always be male or female.

staff/child ratio The number of children per staff member in a child care center or *family day-care home.* Differs depending on the ages of the children; the younger the children, the lower the staff/child ratio should be.

startle reflex See *Moro reflex.*

state A point along a continuum of consciousness ranging from sleep to arousal.

stranger anxiety A fear of strangers, especially evident during the first year of life, characterized by the infant's negative response to the approach of unfamiliar people.

strange situation procedure Measures attachment in infancy.

structural gene A type of *gene* that guides the manufacture of material (protein) that goes into the structural organization of the cell.

subcortex Part of the brain consisting of the midbrain and hindbrain, which make up the brain stem.

sudden infant death syndrome (SIDS) Unexplained death of an infant; the most common cause of death for infants aged 6 weeks to a year; also known as crib death.

Supplemental Food Program for Women, Infants, and Children See *WIC.*

surface structure According to Chomsky, one of the two levels of the structure of language; the grammatical rules of language.

symbolic functioning The ability to understand, create, and use symbols to represent something that is not present. The acquisition of a symbolic mode of thinking is a major distinction between the child in the *preoperational period* and the child in the *sensorimotor period.*

symbols According to Piaget, representations or meanings that are personal and individualized, as distinguished from *signs,* which have shared public meanings.

syntax The underlying grammatical rules that specify the order and function of words in a sentence.

tabula rasa Literal meaning is "blank slate". Refers to past theory that the mind is a blank slate at birth; has been refuted.

Tay-Sachs disease A genetic disorder transmitted as a recessive trait, found almost exclusively among Jews of Eastern European descent; causes brain destruction, blindness, and eventually death at an early age.

telegraphic speech Speech characteristic of young children who use a minimal number of words to convey an idea.

television literacy The understanding of visual effects used on television.

temperament The individual's pattern of responding to the environment.

teratogen An environmental agent that can produce abnormalities in the developing fetus.

teratology The scientific study of abnormalities caused by environmental influences during the prenatal period; from the Greek word "teras" meaning "monster."

testosterone One of the male sex hormones.

thalidomide A drug that was formerly used as a sedative. Caused fetal abnormalities involving limb malformation if taken during the first three months of pregnancy; has a teratogenic effect.

thymine One of four nitrogenous bases comprising the chemical bonds that link the pair of intertwined coils within the *DNA* molecule. Thymine links only with *adenine.*

toxemia A common maternal disorder during pregnancy, caused by toxic substances in the mother's blood; results in the swelling of limbs and dysfunction of the kidneys and circulatory system in the mother and can lead to brain damage in the offspring.

traditional surrogacy When a woman "rents" her uterus to an infertile couple and is inseminated by the sperm of the man, later giving the child up for adoption by the couple. Differs from *gestational surrogacy.*

transductive reasoning Prelogical reasoning that links one particular event with another, often resulting in erroneous deductions regarding cause-and-effect relationships.

transitive reasoning The ability to recognize a relationship between two objects by knowing their relationship to a third object.

translocation A process of *mutation* in which part of the 21st *chromosome* becomes attached to another chromosome—a misarrangement that results in *Down's syndrome.*

transverse position The position of a baby in the womb who is lying crosswise across the uterus.

trust versus mistrust Erikson's first psychosocial stage, during which infants acquire either a sense that the world is a safe place to be in and that their needs will be met or a sense of mistrust of the people in the environment.

Turner's syndrome A sex-chromosome abnormality in females characterized by the absence of the sex chromosome X (XO instead of XX); results in short stature, incompletely developed breasts, sterility, and often short fingers and unusually shaped mouth and ears.

umbilical cord A cord that joins the embryo to the *placenta* at the abdomen (at the place of the future navel); the cord consists of arteries and veins carrying blood to and from the placenta.

undifferentiated In gender roles an individual who does not behave in an especially feminine or masculine way.

upper cortex The forebrain.

vernix caseosa The layer of greasy material that covers the skin of a newborn baby.

villi Fingerlike projections of the *placenta* that burrow into the lining of the uterus and come to lie in an area called the *intervillous space.*

visual acuity The ability to detect the separate parts of an object.

vocabulary spurt In language acquisition the period in early childhood when children experience an increase in the number of words they use; also known as naming explosion.

WIC The *Supplemental Food Program for Women, Infants, and Children,* a government-sponsored preventive health and nutrition program for pregnant women and young children.

zone of proximal development Vygotsky's notion that some tasks are easier for children to master when they receive guidance.

zygote The fertilized egg cell of the female.

References

ABEL, Z. L. (1980). Fetal alcohol syndrome: Behavioral teratology. *Psychological Bulletin, 87* (1), 29–50.

ABER, J. L. III. (1982). The socio-emotional development of maltreated children. Unpub. diss. Yale University, New Haven, CT.

ABRAHAM, S., COLLINS, G., & NORDSIECK, M. (1971). Relationship of childhood weight status to morbidity in adults. *Public Health Reports, 86,* 273–284.

ABRAMOVITCH, R., CORTER C., PEPLER, D., & STANHOPE, L. (1986). Sibling & peer interaction: A final follow-up and a comparison. *Child Development, 57,* 217–229.

ABRAMOVITCH, R., PEPLER, D., & CORTER, C. (1982). Patterns of sibling interaction among preschoolage children. In M. Lamb & B. Sutton-Smith, (Eds.), *Sibling relationships: Their nature and significance across the life-span.* Hillsdale, NJ: Erlbaum.

ACHENBACH, T. M., BIRD, H. R., CANINO, G., PHARES, V., GOULD, M. S., & RUBIO-STIPEC, M. (1990). Epidemiological comparisons of Puerto Rican and U.S. mainland children: Parent, teacher, and self-reports. *Journal of the American Academy of Child & Adolescent Psychiatry, 29,* 84–93.

ACREDOLO, L. P. & HAKE, J. L. (1982). Infant perception. In B. B. Wolman & G. Stricker, (Eds.), *Handbook of developmental psychology.* Englewood Cliffs, NJ: Prentice-Hall.

ADAMS, F. F. (1980). *Understanding adolescence: Current developments in adolescent psychology.* Boston: Allyn & Bacon.

ADAMS, L. M. & DAVIDSON, M. (1987). Present concepts of infant colic. *Pediatric Annals, 16,* 817–820.

ADAMS, R. E. & PASSMAN, R. H. (1979). Effects of visual and auditory aspects of mothers and strangers on the play and exploration of children. *Developmental Psychology, 15,* 269–274.

ADELSON, A. (1991). How television is cultivating new ways of looking at blacks. *New York Times,* February 7, C19, C24.

ADELSON, E. & FRAIBERG, S. (1974). Gross motor development in infants blind from birth. *Child Development, 45,* 114–126.

ADNOPOZ, J., GRIGSBY, R. S., & NAGLER, S. F. (1991). Multiproblem families and high-risk children and adolescents: Causes and management. In M. Lewis, (Ed.), *Child and adolescent psychiatry: A comprehensive textbook,* pp. 1059–1066. Baltimore, MD: Williams & Wilkins.

AHLBOM, A., ALBERT, E. N., FRASER-SMITH, A. C., GRODZINSKY, A. J., MARRON, M. T., MARTIN, A. O., PERSINGER, M. A., SHELANSKI, M. L., & WOLPOW, E. R. (1987). *Biological effects of power line field: New York state power lines project.* Final report of the scientific advisory panel. Albany, NY: State power lines project.

AINSWORTH, M. D. S. (1967). *Infancy in Uganda: Infant care and growth of love.* Baltimore, MD: Johns Hopkins University Press.

AINSWORTH, M. D. S. (1973). The development of infant-mother attachment. In B. Caldwell & H. Ricciuti, (Eds.), *Review of child development research* (Vol. 3). Chicago: University of Chicago Press.

AINSWORTH, M. D. S. (1980). Attachment and child abuse. In

G. Gerbner, C. Ross, & E. Zigler, (Eds.), *Child abuse: An agenda for action.* New York: Oxford University Press.

AINSWORTH, M. D. S., BELL, S. M., & STAYTON, D. J. (1972). Individual differences in the development of some attachment behaviors. *Merrill-Palmer Quarterly, 18,* 123–143.

AINSWORTH, M. D. S., BLEHAR, M., WATERS, E., & WALL, S. (1978). *Patterns of attachment: Observations in the strange situation and at home.* Hillsdale, NJ: Erlbaum.

AINSWORTH, M. D. S. & WITTIG, B. A. (1969). Attachment and exploratory behavior of one-year-olds in a strange situation. In B. M. Foss, (Ed.), *Determinants of infant behavior* (Vol. 4). London: Methuen.

ALAN GUTTMACHER INSTITUTE. (1981). *Teenage pregnancy: The problem that has not gone away.* New York: Author.

ALBAS, D., ALBAS, C., & McCLUSKY, K. (1978). Anomie, social class and drinking behavior of high school students. *Journal of Studies of Alcohol, 39,* 910–913.

ALBEE, G. W. (1980). Primary prevention and social problems. In G. Gerbner, C. J. Ross, & E. Zigler, (Eds.), *Child abuse: An agenda for action.* New York: Oxford University Press.

ALBEE, G. W. (1986). Toward a just society: Lessons from observations on the primary prevention of psychopathology. *American Psychologist, 41,* 891–898.

ALLEN, J. (1985, Summer). European parental leave policies. *The Networker, 6* (4), 5–6. (Available from the Bush Center in Child Development and Social Policy, Yale University, New Haven, CT).

ALS, H. (1981). Assessing infant individuality. In C. C. Brown, (Ed.), *Infants at risk: Assessment and intervention.* Skillman, NJ: Johnson & Johnson.

AMBRON, S. (1980). Casual models in early education research. In S. Kilmer, (Ed.), *Advances in early education and child care* (Vol. 2). Greenwich, CT: JAI Press.

AMERICAN ACADEMY OF PEDIATRICS. (1981). Nutritional aspects of obesity in infancy and childhood. *Pediatrics, 68,* 6, 880–893.

AMERICAN ACADEMY OF PEDIATRICS. (1982). The promotion of breastfeeding. *Pediatrics, 69,* 654–661.

AMERICAN ACADEMY OF PEDIATRICS. (1985). *Getting your child fit: Special report.* Elk Grove Village, IL: Author.

AMERICAN ACADEMY OF PEDIATRICS. (1987). Report to the Second Task Force on blood pressure control in children. *Pediatrics, 79* (1), 1–25.

AMERICAN ACADEMY OF PEDIATRICS. (1989). *Focus on crack babies: A fact sheet.* Elk Grove Village, IL: Author.

AMERICAN ACADEMY OF PEDIATRICS. (1990a). Children with health impairments in schools. *Pediatrics, 86* (4) 636–638.

AMERICAN ACADEMY OF PEDIATRICS. (1990b). *Immunizations: Protecting our children, the facts.* Elk Grove Village, IL: Author.

AMERICAN ACADEMY OF PEDIATRICS. (1990c). *Proceedings of a conference on cross-national comparisons of child health.* Elk Grove Village, IL: Author.

AMERICAN ACADEMY OF PEDIATRICS. (1991). *Facts about children with AIDS.* Elk Grove Village, IL: Author.

AMERICAN ASSOCIATION OF UNIVERSITY WOMEN. (1991). *Short-changing girls, short-changing America.* Washington, D.C.: Author.

AMERICAN HUMANE ASSOCIATION. (1989). *Highlights of official aggregate child neglect and abuse reporting, 1987.* Denver, CO: Author.

AMERICAN PSYCHIATRIC ASSOCIATION. (1987). *Diagnostic and statistical manual of mental disorder,* (3rd Ed.), rev. Washington, D.C.: Author.

AMERICAN PSYCHOLOGICAL ASSOCIATION. (1985). Psychologists warn of danger in TV violence. Position paper. Washington, D.C.: Author.

AMMERMAN, R. T. (1990). Etiological models of child maltreatment: A behavioral perspective. *Behavior Modification, 14* (3), 230–254.

ANASTASI, A. (1958). Heredity, environment, and the question "How?" *Psychological Review, 65,* 197–208.

ANDERSON, C. S. (1982). The search for school climate: A review of the research. *Review of Educational Research, 52,* 368–420.

ANDERSON, D. R. & LEVIN, S. R. (1976). Young children's attention to Sesame Street. *Child Development, 47,* 806–811.

ANDO, H. & YOSHIMURA, I. (1979). Effects of age on communication skills levels and prevalence of maladaptive behaviors in autistic and mentally retarded children. *Journal of Autism & Developmental Disorders, 9,* 83–94.

ANISFIELD, M. (in press). Neonatal imitation. *Developmental Review.*

ANNIS, L. (1978). *The child before birth.* Ithaca, NY: Cornell University Press.

ARIES, P. (1962). *Centuries of childhood.* London: Jonathan Cape.

ARLIN, P. (1984). *The Arlin test of formal reasoning.* E. Aurora, NY: Slosson Educational Publications.

ARMENTROUT, V. A. & BURGER, G. K. (1972). Children's reports of parental child-rearing behaviors at five grade levels. *Developmental Psychology, 7,* 44–48.

ARONFREED, J. (1968). *Conduct and conscience: The socialization of internal controls over behavior.* New York: Academic Press.

ARTENSTEIN, J. (1990). *Runaways in their own words: Kids talking about living on the street.* New York: Tor Books.

ASARNOW, R., ASARNOW, J., & STRANDBERG, R. (1989). Schizophrenia: A developmental perceptive. In D. Cicchetti, (Ed.), *The emergence of a discipline & Rochester Symposium on Developmental Psychopathology.* Hillsdale, NJ: Erlbaum.

ASCH, S. E. & NERLOVE, H. (1960). The development of double function terms in children: An exploratory investigation. In B. Kaplan & S. Wakner, (Eds.), *Perspectives in psychological theory: Essays in honor of Heinz Werner.* New York: International Universities Press.

ASHER, S. R. (1978). Children's peer relations. In M. E. Lamb, (Ed.), *Social and personality development.* New York: Holt, Rinehart & Winston.

ASHER, S. R. & DODGE, K. (1986). Identifying children who

are rejected by their peers. *Developmental Psychology, 22,* 444–449.

ASHER, S. R. & HYMEL, S. (1981). Children's social competence in peer relations: Sociometric and behavioral assessments. In J. D. Wine & M. D. Singe, (Eds.), *Social competence.* New York: Guilford Press.

ASHER, S. R. & PARKER, J. (1990). The significance of peer relationship problems in childhood. In B. H. Schneider, G. Attili, J. A. Nadel, & R. Weisberg, (Eds.), *Social competence in developmental perspective.* Amsterdam: Kluwer.

ASHER, S. R., SINGLETON, L. C., & TAYLOR, A. R. (1985). Acceptance versus friendship: A developmental study of black and white children's social relationships. Unpubl. study.

ASHMEAD, D. H. & PERLMUTTER, M. (1984). Infant memory in everyday life. In M. Perlmutter, (Ed.), *New directions in child development: Naturalistic approaches to children's memory.* San Francisco: Jossey-Bass.

ASLIN, R. (1987). Visual and auditory development in infancy. In J. D. Osofsky, (Ed.), *Handbook of infant development,* 2nd ed., New York: Wiley.

ATTIE, I., BROOKS-GUNN, J., & PETERSON, A. C. (1990). The emergence of eating problems: A developmental perspective. In M. Lewis & S. Miller, (Eds.), *Handbook of developmental psychopathology,* pp. 409–420. New York: Plenum.

AULT, R. L. (1977). *Children's cognitive development: Piaget's theory and the process approach.* New York: Oxford University Press.

AUSUBEL, D. P., MONTEMAYRO, R. R., & SVAJIAN, P. N. (1977). *Theory and problems of adolescent development,* 2nd ed. New York: Grune & Stratton.

AUSUBEL, D. P., SULLIVAN, E. V., & IVES, S. W. (1980). *Theory and problems of child development* (3rd Ed.). New York: Grune & Stratton.

AVERY, J. G. & AVERY, P. J. (1982). Scandinavian & Dutch lessons in childhood road traffic accident prevention. *British Medical Journal, 285,* 621–626.

AXELSON, L. & DAIL, P. (1988). The changing character of homeless in the United States. *Family Relations, 10,* 463–469.

BACHMAN, J. (1982). The American high school student: A profile. Paper presented at the conference on the American High School Today & Tomorrow. Berkeley, CA, June.

BADGER, E. (1980). Effects of a parent education program on teenage mothers and their offspring. In K. G. Scott, T. Field, & E. Robertson, (Eds.), *Teenage mothers and their offspring.* New York: Grune & Stratton.

BAECHER, C. M. (1983). *Children's consumerism: Implications for education.* Paper presented at the Bush Center in Child Development and Social Policy, Yale University, New Haven, CT.

BAER, A. S. (1977). *The genetic perspective.* Philadelphia: Saunders.

BAKAN, D. (1972). Adolescence in America. From idea to social fact. In J. Kagan & R. Cole, (Eds.), *Twelve to sixteen: Early adolescence.* New York: Norton.

BAKAN D. (1979). *Slaughter of the innocents.* San Francisco: Jossey-Bass.

BAKER, S. & WALLER, A. (1989). *Childhood injury: State-by-state mortality facts.* Washington, D.C.: National Maternal and Child Health Clearinghouse.

BAKER, S. P. (1981). Childhood injuries: The community approach to prevention. *Journal of Public Health Policy, 2* (3), 235–246.

BALDWIN, W. & CAIN, U. S. (1980). The children of teenage parents. *Family Planning Perspectives, 12* (1), 34–43.

BANDURA, A. (1962). Social learning through imitation. In M. R. Jones, (Ed.), *Nebraska symposium on motivation.* Lincoln: University of Nebraska Press.

BANDURA, A. (1964). The stormy decade: Fact or fiction? *Psychology in the School, 1,* 224–231.

BANDURA, A. (1967). The role of modeling processes in personality development. In W. W. Hartup & N. L. Smothergill, (Eds.), *The young child: Reviews of research.* Washington, D.C.: National Association for the Education of Young Children.

BANDURA, A. (1969). Social learning theory of identificatory processes. In D. A. Goslin, (Ed.), *Handbook of socialization theory and research.* Chicago: Rand McNally.

BANDURA, A. (1977). *Social learning theory.* Englewood Cliffs, NJ: Prentice-Hall.

BANDURA, A. (1986). *Social foundations of thought and action: A social cognitive theory.* Englewood Cliffs, NJ: Prentice-Hall.

BANE, M. J. (1976, Summer). Paying for childhood. *Working Papers for a New Society, 4* (2), 74–81.

BANE, M. J. & ELLWOOD, D. T. (1989). One-fifth of the nation's children: Why are they poor? *Science, 245,* 1047–1053.

BANGERT-DOWNS, R. L. (1988). The effects of school-based substance abuse education: A meta-analysis. *Journal of Drug Education, 18,* 243–264.

BANKS, M. S. & SALAPATEK, P. (1983). Infant visual perception. In Paul H. Mussen, (Ed.), *Handbook of child psychology.* Vol. 2, *Infancy and developmental psychobiology.* New York: Wiley.

BARBERO, G. (1975). Failure-to-thrive. In M. H. Klaus, T. Leger, & M. A. Trause, (Eds.), *Maternal attachment and mothering disorders: A roundtable.* Skillman, NJ: Johnson & Johnson.

BARKER, R. G. & WRIGHT, H. F. (1951). *One boy's day.* New York: Harper & Row.

BARKER, R. G. & WRIGHT, H. F. (1955). *Midwest and its children.* New York: Harper & Row. Reprinted in 1971 by Archon Books, Hamden, CT.

BAROANKAR, D. S. & SHAH, S. A. (1974). The XYY male—or syndrome? *Progress in Medical Genetics, 10,* 135–222.

BARRETT, D. E. (1982, May). An approach to the conceptualization and assessment of social-emotional functioning in studying nutrition-behavior relationships. *American Journal of Clinical Nutrition, 35* (5 Suppl.), 1220–1227.

BARRETT, D. E., RADKE-YARROW, M., & KLEIN, R. E. (1982). Chronic malnutrition and child behavior: Effects of early caloric supplementation on social and emotional functioning at school age. *Developmental Psychology, 18,* 541–556.

BARRY, R. J., & JAMES, A. L. (1978). Handedness in autistics, retardates, and normals of a wide range. *Journal of Autism & Childhood Schizophrenia, 8,* 315–323.

BARUCH, G. K. & BARNETT, R. C. (1987). Role quality and psychological well-being. In F. Crosby, (Ed.), *Spouse, parent, worker,* pp. 63–84. New Haven, CT: Yale University Press.

BASSUK, E. & RUBIN, L. (1987). Homeless children: A neglected population. *American Journal of Orthopsychiatry, 57,* 2.

BATES, E., O'CONNELL, B., & SHORE, C. (1987). Language and communication in infancy. In J. D. Osofsky, (Ed.), *Handbook of infant development* (2nd Ed.), pp. 149–203. New York: Wiley.

BATES, J. E. (1987). Temperament in infancy. In J. D. Osofsky, (Ed.), *Handbook of infant development* (2nd Ed.). New York: Wiley.

BAUERMEISTER, J., BERRIOS, V., JIMINEZ, A., ACEVEDO, L., & GORDON, M. (1990). Some issues and instruments for the assessment of attention deficit hyperactivity disorder in Puerto Rican children. *Journal of Clinical Child Psychology, 19,* 9–16.

BAUMEISTER, R. & TICE, D. (1986). How adolescence became the struggle for self: A historical transformation of psychological development. In J. Suls & A. Greenwald, (Eds.), *Psychological perspectives on the self* (Vol. 3), pp. 183–201. Hillsdale, NJ: Erlbaum.

BAUMESTER, D. & FURMAN, W. (1987). The development of companionship and intimacy. *Child Development, 58,* 1101–1113.

BAUMRIND, D. (1967). Child care practices anteceding three patterns of preschool behavior. *Genetic psychology monographs, 75,* 43–88.

BAUMRIND, D. (1968). Authorization vs. authoritative parental control. *Adolescence, 3,* 255–272.

BAUMRIND D. (1971). Current patterns of parental authority. *Developmental Psychology Monographs, 41* (1, Pt. 2).

BAUMRIND, D. (1975). Early socialization and adolescent competence. In S. Dragastin & G. H. Elder, Jr. (Eds.), *Adolescence in the life cycle.* New York: Wiley.

BAUMRIND, D. (1989). Parenting styles and adolescent development. In J. Brooks-Gunn, A. Lerner, & A. Petersen, (Eds.), *The encyclopedia of adolescence.* New York: Garland.

BAUMRIND, D. (1990). Effective parenting during the early adolescent transition. In P. Cowan, & E. M. Hetherington, (Eds.), *Advances in family research* (Vol. 2). Hillsdale, NJ: Erlbaum.

BEAL, C. R. & FLAVELL, J. H. (1983). Young speakers' evaluations of their listeners' comprehension in a referential communication task. *Child Development, 54,* 1, 148–153.

BECKER, H. J. & STERLING, C. W. (1987). Equity in school computer use: National data & neglected considerations. *Journal of Educational Computing Research, 3,* 289–311.

BECKER, W. C. (1964). Consequences of different kinds of parental discipline. In M. L. Hoffman & L. W. Hoffman, (Eds.), *Review of child development research* (Vol. 1). New York: Russell Sage.

BECKWITH, J., GELLER, L., & SARKAR, S. (1990). Letter to the editor. *Science, 250,* 191.

BEENTJES, J. W. & VANDERVOORT, T. H. (1988). Television's impact on children's reading skills. *Reading Research Quarterly, 23,* 389–413.

BELSKY, J. (1978). Three theoretical models of child abuse: A critical review. *International Journal of Child Abuse and Neglect, 2,* 37–49.

BELSKY, J. (1980). Child maltreatment: An ecological integration. *American Psychologist, 35,* 320–335.

BELSKY, J. (1981). Early human experience: A family perspective. *Developmental Psychology, 17,* 3–23.

BELSKY, J. (1986). Infant day care: A cause for concern. *Zero to Three, 6* (5), 1–9.

BELSKY, J. (1987). Risks remain. *Zero to Three, 7* (3), 22–24.

BELSKY, J., GILSTRAP, B., & ROVINE, M. (1984). The Pennsylvania infant and family development project: 1. Stability and change in mother-infant and father-infant interaction in a family setting at 1, 3, and 9 months. *Child Development, 55* (3), 692–705.

BELSKY, J., LERNER, R. M., & SPANIER, G. B. (1984). *The child in the family.* Reading, MA: Addison-Wesley.

BEM, S. L. (1981). Gender schema theory: A cognitive account of sex-typing. *Psychological Review, 88,* 354–364.

BEM, S. L. (1983). Gender schema theory and its implications for child development: Raising gender-aschematic children in a gender-schematic society. *Signs, 8,* 598–616.

BEM, S. L. (1985). Androgeny and gender schema theory: A conceptual and empirical integration. In T. B. Sonderegger, (Ed.), *Nebraska symposium on motivation, 1984: Psychology & gender.* Lincoln: University of Nebraska Press.

BENCH, J. (1978). The auditory response. In V. Stave, (Ed.), *Perinatal physiology.* New York: Plenum.

BENDER, B. G., LINDEN, M. G., & ROBINSON, A. (1987). Environmental and developmental risk in children with sex chromosome abnormalities. *Journal of the American Academy of Child and Adolescent Psychiatry, 26,* 499–503.

BENEDEK, R. S. & BENEDEK, E. D. (1977). Postdivorce visitation: A child's right. *Journal of the American Academy of Child Psychiatry, 16,* 256–271.

BENNETT, N. (1976). *Teaching styles and pupil progress.* Cambridge, MA: Harvard University Press.

BENNETT, W. J. (1985). Statement of William J. Bennett, Secretary of Education, before the Task Force on Literacy, U.S. Senate, Dec. 4.

BERENDA, R. W. (1950). *The influence of the group on the judgments of children.* New York: King's Crown Press.

BERG, W. K. & BERG, K. M. (1987). Psychophysiological development in infancy: Stare, startle, & attention. In J. D. Osofsky, (Ed.), *Handbook of infant development,* (2nd Ed.), pp. 238–317. New York: Wiley.

BERGER, J. (1989). East Harlem students clutch a college dream. *New York Times,* August 27, 1, 28.

BERKO, J. (1958). The child's learning of English morphology. *Word, 14,* 5–17.

BERKOWITZ, L. (1962). *Aggression: A social psychological analysis.* Englewood Cliffs, NJ: Prentice-Hall.

BERNDT, T. (1989). Obtaining support from friends in childhood and adolescence. In D. Belle, (Ed.), *Children's social networks and social supports,* pp. 308–331. New York: Wiley.

BERNDT, T. & ZIGLER, E. (1985). Developmental Psychology. In G. Kimble & K. Schlesinger, (Eds.), *Topics in the history of psychology* (Vol. 2). Hillsdale, NJ: Erlbaum.

BERNDT, T. J. (1979). Developmental changes in conformity to peers and parents. *Developmental Psychology, 15,* 608–616.

BERNDT, T. J. (1982). The features and effects of friendship in early adolescence. *Child Development, 53,* 1447–1460.

BERNDT, T. J. & PERRY, T. B. (1990). Distinctive features and effects of early adolescent friendships. In R. Montmayor, G. Adams, & T. Gullotta, (Eds.), *From childhood to adolescence: A transition period?,* pp. 269–290. New York: Russell Sage.

BERRUETA-CLEMENT, J., SCHWEINHART, L. J., BARNETT, W. S., EPSTEIN, A. S., & WEIKART, D. P. (1984). *Changed lives: Effects of the Perry Preschool Program on youths through age 19.* Ypsilanti, MI: High/Scope Press.

BERRY, H. K., BRUNNER, R. L., HUNT, M., WHITE, P. (1990). Valine, isoleucine, & leucine: A new treatment for phenylketonuria. *American Journal of Diseases in Children, 144,* 539–543.

BETTELHEIM, B. (1967). *The empty fortress: Infantile autism and the birth of the self.* New York: Free Press.

BEUF, A. H. (1977). *Red children in white America.* University Park: Pennsylvania State University Press.

BEUNEN, G. & MALINA, R. (1988). Growth and physical performance relative to the timing of the adolescent spurt. *Exercise and Sport Sciences Reviews, 16,* 503–540.

BEVAN, W. (1982). A sermon of sorts in three plus parts. *American Psychologist, 37* (12), 1302–1322.

BEYER, B. (1978). Conducting moral discussions in the classroom. In P. Scharf, (Ed.), *Readings in moral education.* Minneapolis: Winston.

BIALYSTOCK, E. (1988). Aspects of linguistic awareness in reading comprehension. *Applied Linguistic Research, 18,* 369–387.

BIALYSTOCK, E. & NICHOLES, A. (1989). Children's control over attention to phonological and semantic properties of words. *Journal of Psycholinguistic Research, 18,* 369–387.

BIALYSTOCK, E. & RYAN, E. B. (1985). Toward a definition of metalinguistics skill. *Merrill-Palmer Quarterly, 31,* 229–251.

BIGELOW, B. J. (1977). Children's friendship expectations: A cognitive developmental study. *Child Development, 48,* 246–253.

BINET, A. & SIMON, T. (1905). Methodes nouvelles pour le diagnostic du niveau intellectuel des anormaux. *L'annee psychologique, 11,* 191–244.

BIRCH, H. G. (1972). Health and the education of socially disadvantaged children. In U. Bronfenbrenner, (Ed.), *Influences on human development.* Hinsdale, IL: Dryden Press.

BIRCH, H. G. & GUSSOW, J. D. (1970). Disadvantaged children: Health, nutrition, and school failure. New York: Harcourt Brace & World.

BIRCH, J. W. (1976). Mainstreaming: Definition, development and characteristics. In J. B. Jordan, (Ed.), *Teacher, please don't close the door.* Reston, VA: Council for Exceptional Children.

BIXENSTINE, V., DeCORTE, M., & BIXENSTINE, B. (1976). Conformity to peer-sponsored misconduct at four age levels. *Developmental Psychology, 12,* 226–236.

BLACK, L. (1979). Developmental correlates of sleep apnea. Address delivered at the International Congress of Psychology of the Child, Paris, July 7.

BLASS, E., GRANCHROW, J., & STEINER, J. (1984). Classical conditioning in newborn humans 2–48 hours of age. *Infant Behavior and Development, 7,* 223–235.

BLAU, A. (1963). The psychogenetic etiology of premature births. *Psychosomatic Medicine, 25,* 201–211.

BLOCK, J. H. (1982). Another look at sex differentiation in the socialization behaviors of mothers and fathers. In J. Sherman & F. Denmark, (Eds.), *Psychology of women: Future of research.* New York: Psychological Dimensions.

BLOM, G. E., KEITH, J. G., & TOMBER, I. (1984). Child and family advocacy: Addressing the rights and responsibilities of child, family and society. In R. P. Boger, G. E. Blom, & L. E. Lezotte, (Eds.), *Child nurturance.* Vol. 4, *Child nurturing in the 1980s.* New York: Plenum.

BLOOM, B. S. (1964). *Stability and change in human characteristics.* New York: Wiley.

BLOOM, L. (1973). *One word at a time.* The Hague: Mouton.

BLOOM, L. (1975). Language development. In F. D. Horowitz, (Ed.), *Review of child development research* (Vol. 4). Chicago: University of Chicago Press.

BLOOM, L. & LAHEY, M. (1978). *Language development and language disorders.* New York: Wiley.

BLUM, K., NOBLE, E. P., SHERIDAN, P. J., MONTGOMERY, A., RITCHIE, T., JAGADEESWARAN, P., NOGAMI, H., BRIGGS, A. H., & COHN, J. B. (1990). Allelic association of human dopamine D_2 receptor gene in alcoholism. *Journal of American Medical Association, 263,* 2055–2060.

BOHANNON, J. & HIRSCH-PASEK, K. (1984). Do children say as they're told? A new perspective on motherese. In L. Feagans, C. Garvey, & R. Golinkoff (Eds.), *The origins and growth of communication,* pp. 176–195. Norwood, NJ: Ablex.

BOHANNON, J., MacWHINNEY, B., & SNOW, C. (1990). No negative evidence revisited: Beyond learnability or who has to prove what to whom. *Developmental Psychology, 26,* 221–226.

BOHANNON, J. & STANOWICZ, L. (1988). The issue of negative evidence: Adult responses to children's language error. *Developmental Psychology, 24,* 684–689.

BOHMAN, M., SIGVARDSSON, S., & CLONINGER, C. R. (1982).

Maternal inheritance of alcohol abuse. Cross-fostering analysis of adopted women. *Archives of General Psychiatry, 38,* 965–969.

BOLTON, P. (1983). Drugs of abuse. In D. F. Hawkins, (Ed.), *Drugs and pregnancy: Human teratogenesis and related problems.* Edinburgh: Churchill Livingston.

BOOHER, B. (1990). Rites of fertility: Hope for childless couples. *Duke, 76* (3), 12–16.

BORKE, H. (1971). Interpersonal perception of young children: Egocentrism or empathy? *Developmental Psychology, 5,* 263–269.

BORKE, H. (1975). Piaget's mountain revisited: Changes in the egocentric landscape. *Developmental Psychology, 11,* 240–243.

BORNSTEIN, M. H. (1985). How infant and mother jointly contribute to developing cognitive competence in the child. *Proceedings of the National Academy of Sciences, 82,* 7470–7473.

BORNSTEIN, M. & SIGMAN, M. (1986). Continuity in mental development from infancy. *Child Development, 57,* 251–274.

BOROVSKY, D., HILL, W., & ROVEE-COLLIER, C. (1987). Developmental changes in long-term memory. Paper presented at the meeting of the Society for Research in Child Development, Baltimore, April.

BOUCHARD T. C., HESTON, L., ECKERT, E., KEYES, M., & RESNICK, S. (1981). The Minnesota study of twins reared apart: Project description and sample results in the developmental domain. *Twin Research, 3,* 227–233.

BOUCHARD, T. C., TREMBLAY, A., DESPRIES, J. P., NADEAU, A., LUPIEN, P. J., THERIAULT, G., DUSSAULT, J., MOORJANI, S., PINAULT, S., & FOURNIER, G. (1990). The response to long-term overfeeding in identical twins. *New England Journal of Medicine, 322,* 21, 1477–1482.

BOUCHARD, T. J., JR., LYKKEN, D. T., MCGUE, M., SEGAL, N. L., & TELLEGEN, A. (1990). Sources of human psychological differences: The Minnesota study of twins reared apart. *Science, 250,* 223–228.

BOUCHARD, T. J., JR. & MCGUE, M. (1981). Familial studies of intelligence: A review. *Science, 212,* 1055–1059.

BOUKYDIS, C. F. Z. (1985). Perception of infant crying as an interpersonal event. In B. M. Lester & C. F. Z. Boukydis, (Eds.), *Infant crying: Theoretical and research perspectives.* New York: Plenum.

BOWER, T. G. R. (1974). *Development in infancy.* San Francisco: Freeman.

BOWER, T. G. R. (1977). *A primer of infant development.* San Francisco: Freeman.

BOWERMAN, M. (1982). Reorganizational processes in lexical and syntactic development. In E. Warner & L. R. Gleitman, (Eds.), *Language acquisition: The state of the art.* Cambridge, UK: Cambridge University Press, 51–77.

BOWLBY, J. (1951). *Maternal care and mental health.* Geneva: The World Health Organization.

BOWLBY, J. (1969). *Attachment and loss.* Vol. 1, *Attachment.* New York: Basic Books.

BOWLBY, J. (1973). *Attachment and loss.* Vol. 2, *Separation.* New York: Basic Books.

BOWLBY, J. (1980). *Attachment and loss.* Vol. 3, *Loss, sadness and depression.* New York: Basic Books.

BOWLBY, J. (1989). *Secure Attachments.* New York: Basic Books

BOWMAN, P. & HOWARD, C. (1985). Race-related socialization, motivation and academic achievement: A study of black youth in three generation families. *Journal of the American Academy of Child Psychiatry, 24,* 134–141.

BRACKBILL, Y. (1971). Cumulative effects of continuous stimulation on arousal level in infants. *Child Development, 42,* 17–26.

BRACKBILL, Y. (1979). Obstetrical medication and infant behavior. In J. Osofsky, (Ed.), *Handbook of infant development.* New York: Wiley.

BRACKBILL, Y., MCMANUS, K., & WOODWARD, L. (1985). *Medication in maternity: Infant exposure and maternal information.* Ann Arbor: University of Michigan Press.

BRADLEY, R., CALDWELL, B. M., ROCK, S. L., BARNARD, K., GRAY, C., HAMMOND, S., MITCHELL, S., SIEGEL, L., RAMEY, C., GOTTFRIED, A., & JOHNSON, D. (1989). Home environments and cognitive development in the first three years of life. *Developmental Psychology, 25,* 217–235.

BRAINERD, C. J. (1974). Training and transfer of transitivity conservation and class inclusion. *Child Development, 27,* 114–116.

BRAN, E. A. (1979). Strategies for the prevention of pregnancy in adolescents. *Advances in Planned Parenthood, 14,* 68–76.

BRAY, A., (Ed.). (1979). *Obesity in America.* Washington, D.C.: U.S. Department of Health, Education and Welfare, NIH Pub. No. 79-359.

BRAZELTON, T. B. (1961). Effects of maternal medication on the neonate and his behavior. *Journal of Pediatrics, 58,* 513–518.

BRAZELTON, T. B. (1962). Crying in infancy. *Journal of Pediatrics, 29,* 579–588.

BRAZELTON, T. B. (1973). *Neonatal behavioral assessment scale.* Clinics in developmental medicine (No. 50). Philadelphia: Spastics International Medical Publications, Lippincott.

BRAZELTON, T. B. (1976). Early mother-infant reciprocity. In V. C. Vaughn III & T. B. Brazelton, (Eds.), *The family—Can it be saved?* Chicago: Yearbook Medical Publishers.

BRAZELTON, T. B. (1986). Stress and families today. *Infant Mental Health Journal, 9* (1), 65–71.

BRAZELTON, T. B., ALS, H., TRONICK, E. & LESTER, B. M. (1979). Specific neonatal measures: The Brazelton neonatal behavior assessment scale. In J. D. Osofsky, (Ed.), *The handbook of infant development.* New York: Wiley.

BRAZELTON, T. B., KOSLOWSKI, B., & MAIN, M. (1974). The origins of reciprocity: The early mother-infant interactions. In M. Lewis & J. Rosenblum, (Eds.), *The origins of* behavior. New York: Wiley.

BRENT, D., KERR, M., GOLDSTEIN, C., BOZIGAR, J., WARTELLA, M., & ALLAN, M. J. (1989). An outbreak of suicides and suicidal behavior in a high school. *Journal of the American Academy of Child and Adolescent Psychiatry, 28,* 918–924.

BRETHERTON, I. (1990). Communication and internal working models. Their role in the development of attachment relationships. In R. A. Thompson and R. Dienstbier, (Eds.), *Socioemotional development.* Lincoln: University of Nebraska Press.

BRETHERTON, I. & WATERS, E. (1985). Growing points in attachment theory. *Monographs of the Society for Research in Child Development, 50* (12), Serial No. 209.

BRETT, J. M. & YOGEV, S. (1988). Restructuring work for families: How dual-earner couples with children manage. *Journal of Social Behavior and Personality, 3* (4), 159–174.

BRIDGES, K. (1932). Emotional development in early infancy. *Child Development, 3,* 324–341.

BRIM, O. G., JR. & ABELES, R. P. (1975). Work and personality in the middle years. *Social Science Research Council Items, 29,* 29–33.

BRITTAIN, C. V. (1963). Adolescent choices and parent-peer cross pressures. *American Sociological Review, 28,* 385–391.

BRITTAIN, C. V. (1969). A comparison of rural and urban adolescents with respect to peer versus parent compliance. *Adolescence, 13,* 59–68.

BRODY, J. E. (1990). A search to bar retardation in a new generation. *New York Times,* June 7, p. B9.

BRODY, L., ZELAZO, P., & CHAIKA, H. (1984). Habituation-dishabituation to speech in the neonate. *Developmental Psychology, 20,* 114–119.

BRONFENBRENNER, U. (1970). Who cares for America's children? Paper presented at the annual meeting of the National Association for the Education of Young Children.

BRONFENBRENNER, U. (1975). Is early intervention effective? In H. J. Leichter, (Ed.), *The family as educator.* New York: Teachers College Press.

BRONFENBRENNER, U. (1977). Toward an experimental ecology of human development. *American Psychologist, 32,* 513–531.

BRONFENBRENNER, U. (1979). Contexts of child rearing: Prospects and problems. *American Psychologist, 34* (10), 844–850.

BRONFENBRENNER, U. (1986). Ecology of the family as a context for human development: Research perspectives. *Developmental Psychology, 22,* 723–742.

BROOKS, J. & LEWIS, M. (1976). Infant's responses to strangers: Midget, adult, and child. *Child Development, 47,* 323–332.

BROOKS-GUNN, J. & FURSTENBERG, F. F., JR. (1989). Adolescent sexual behavior. *American Psychologist, 44,* 2, 249–257.

BROOKS-GUNN, J., PETERSEN, A. C., & EICHORN, D. (1985). The study of maturational timing effects on adolescence. *Journal of Youth and Adolescence, 14,* 3, 149–161.

BROPHY, J. E. (1983). Research on the self-fulfilling prophecy and teacher expectations. *Journal of Educational Psychology, 75,* 631–661.

BROUGHTON, J. M. (1981). Piaget's structural developmental psychology. Pt. III, Function and the problem of knowledge. *Human Development, 24,* 257–285.

BROWN, A. L. (1975). The development of memory: Knowing, knowing about knowing and knowing how to know. In H. W. Reese, (Ed.), *Advances in Child Development and Behavior* (Vol. 10), pp. 103–151. New York: Academic Press.

BROWN, A. L., BRANFORD, J. D., FERRARA, R. A., & CAMPIONE, J. C. (1983). Learning , remembering, and understanding. In P. H. Mussen, (Ed.), *Handbook of child psychology* (4th Ed.). Vol. 3, J. H. Flavell & E. M. Markman, (Eds.), *Cognitive development.* New York: Wiley.

BROWN, B. & LOHR, M. (1987). Peer-group affiliation and adolescent self-esteem: An integration of ego-identity and symbolic-interaction theories. *Journal of Personality and Social Psychology, 52,* 47–55.

BROWN, C. C., (Ed.) (1983). *Childhood learning disabilities and prenatal risk.* Skillman, NJ: Johnson & Johnson.

BROWN, J. V. & BAKEMAN, R. (1978). The at-risk infant in an at-risk population: The effects of prematurity on mother-infant interactions. Unpubl. manuscript. Atlanta: Georgia State University.

BROWN, R. (1973). *A first language.* Cambridge, MA: Harvard University Press.

BROWN, R. & HANLON, C. (1970). Derivational complexity and order acquisition. In J. R. HAYES, (Ed.), *Cognition and the development of language.* New York: Wiley.

BROZEK, J. & SCHURCH, B., (Eds.). (1984). *Malnutrition and behavior: Critical assessment of key issues.* Lausanne, Switzerland: Nestle Foundation.

BRUCH, H. (1978). *The golden cage: The enigma of anorexia nervosa.* Cambridge, MA: Harvard University Press.

BRUNER, J. S. (1964). The course of cognitive growth. *American Psychologist, 19,* 1–15.

BRUNER, J. S. (1965). Growth of mind. *American Psychologist, 20,* 1007–1019.

BRUNER, J. S. (1972). Nature and the uses of immaturity. *American Psychologist, 27,* 687–708.

BRUNSWICK, A. F. (1977). Health and drug behavior: A study of urban black adolescents. *Addictive Diseases, 3,* 197–214.

BRYAN, J. N. & BRYAN, T. H. (1978). *Understanding learning disabilities.* Sherman Oaks, CA: Alfred Publishing.

BRYAN, T. H. (1974). Peer popularity of learning disabled children. *Journal of Learning Disabilities, 7,* 261–268.

BRYAN, T. H. & MCCRADY, H. J. (1972). Use of a teacher rating scale. *Journal of Learning Disabilities, 5,* 199–206.

BRYANT, B. K. (1974). Locus of control related to teacher-child interpersonal relationships. *Child Development, 45,* 157–164.

BUDOFF, M. & GOTTLIEB, J. (1975). Special class EMR children mainstreamed: A study of an aptitude (learning potential x treatment interaction). *American Journal of Mental Deficiency, 81,* 1–11.

BUREAU OF BUSINESS PRACTICE. (1979). *Fair employment practice guidelines, 170,* 9–29.

BUREAU OF LABOR STATISTICS. (1985). U.S. Department of Labor. *Employment and earnings, January, 1985.*

BUREAU OF LABOR STATISTICS. (1990). U.S. Department of Labor. News Release USDL #89; data as of May 1989. Washington D.C.

BUREAU OF NATIONAL AFFAIRS. (1988). *BNA's Employee Relations Weekly,* May 16, 819.

BURGDORFF, K. (1980). *Recognition and reporting of child maltreatment: Findings from the National Incidence and Severity of Child Abuse and Neglect.* Prepared for the National Center on Child Abuse and Neglect, Washington, D.C., December.

BURGESS, B. J. (1980). Parenting in the Native American community. In M. D. Fantini & R. Cardenas, (Eds.), *Parenting in a multi-cultural society,* pp. 63–73. New York: Longman.

BURHMESTER, D. & FURMAN, W. (1987). The development of companionship and intimacy. *Child Development, 58,* 1101–1113.

BURNHAM, S. (1972, January 9). The heroin babies are going cold turkey. *The New York Times Magazine,* pp. 21–22, 24, 26.

BUSTILLO, M., BUSTER, J. E., FREEMAN, A. G., GORNBEIM, J. A., WHEELER, N., & MARSHALL, J. R. (1984). Nonsurgical ovum transfer as a treatment for intractable infertility: What effectiveness can we expect? *American Journal of Obstetrics and Gynecology, 149,* 371–375.

BUTLER, N. R., GOLDSTEIN, H., & ROSS, E. M. G. (1972). Cigarette smoking in pregnancy: Its influence on birth weight and perinatal mortality. *British Medical Journal, 4,* 573–575.

CACCIARI, C. & LEVORATO, M. C. (1989). How children understand idioms in discourse. *Journal of Child Language, 16,* 387–405.

CAFFEY, J. (1946). Multiple fractures in the long bones of children suffering from chronic subdural hematoma. *American Journal of Roentgenology, Radium Therapy, and Nuclear Medicine, 56,* 163–173.

CAIRNS, R. B., CAIRNS, B. D. & NECKERMAN, H. J. (1989). Early school dropout: Configurations and determinants. *Child Development, 60,* 1439–1452.

CAMARA, K. A. & RESNICK, G. (1989). Styles of conflict and cooperation between divorced parents: Effects on child behavior and adjustment. *American Journal of Orthopsychiatry, 59* (4), 560–575.

CAMPBELL, A. G. M. (1983). The right to be allowed to die. *Journal of Medical Ethics, 9,* 136–140.

CAMPBELL, A. G. M. & DUFF, R. S. (1979). Deciding the care of severely malformed or dying infants. *Journal of Medical Ethics, 5,* 65–67.

CAMPOS, J. (1983). The importance of affective communication in social referencing: A commentary on Feinman. *Merrill-Palmer Quarterly, 29,* 83–87.

CAMPOS, J., BARRETT, K., LAMB, M., GOLDSMITH, H., & STERNBERG, C. (1983). Socioemotional development. In P. H. Mussen, (Ed.), *Handbook of child psychology,* Vol 2, *Infancy and developmental psychology,* pp. 783–915. New York: Wiley.

CAMPOS, J. J. & BARRETT, K. C. (1984). A new understanding of emotions and their development. In C. E. Izard, J. Kagan, & R. B. Zajonc, (Eds.), *Emotions, cognition, and behavior.* New York: Cambridge University Press.

CAMPOS, J. J., LANGER, A., & KROWITZ, A. (1970). Cardiac responses on the visual cliff in pre-locomotor human infants. *Science, 170,* 196–197.

CANTOR, P. (1976). Personality characteristics found among youthful female suicide attempters. *Journal of Abnormal Psychology, 85,* 324–329.

CANTOR, P. (1990). Teen suicide and media responsibility. Paper presented at the Annual Convention of the American Psychological Association, Boston, August.

CANTWELL, D. (1975). *The hyperactive child: Diagnosis, management and research.* New York: Spectrum.

CANTWELL, D. P. (1986). Attention deficit disorder in adolescents. *Clinical Psychology Review, 6,* 237–247.

CAPARULO, B. K. & COHEN, D. J. (1977). Cognitive structures, language, and emerging social competence in autistic and aphasic children. *Journal of the American Academy of Child Psychiatry, 16,* 620–645.

CAPARULO, B. K. & COHEN, D. J. (1982). The syndrome of early childhood autism: Natural history, etiology, and treatment. In E. F. ZIGLER, M. E. LAMB, & I. L. CHILD, (Eds.), *Socialization and personality development* (2nd Ed.). New York: Oxford University Press.

CAPLAN, G. (1974). *Support systems and community mental health.* New York: Behavioral Publications.

CAPLAN, M. Z. & WEISSBERG, R. P. (1989). Promoting social competence in early adolescence: Developmental considerations. In D. H. Schneider, G. Attili, J. Nadel, & R. P. Weissberg, (Eds.), *Social competence in developmental perspective,* pp. 371–385. Boston: Kluwer Academic.

CARD, J. J. & WISE, L. L. (1978). Teenage mothers and teenage fathers: The impact of early childbearing on the parents' personal and professional lives. *Family Planning Perspective, 10,* 199.

CAREY, S. (1977). The child as a word learner. In M. Halle, J. Bressman, & G. Miller, (Eds.), *Linguistic theory and psychological reality.* Cambridge, MA: MIT Press.

CAREY, S. (1988). Are children fundamentally different kinds of thinkers and learners than adults? In K. Richardson & S. Sheldon, (Eds.), *Cognitive development in adolescence.* Hillsdale, NJ: Erlbaum.

CAREY, W. B. (1968). Maternal anxiety and infantile colic: Is there a relationship? *Clinical Pediatrics, 7,* 590–595.

CARLETON-FORD, S. & COLLINS, W. A. (1988). Family conflict. Dimensions, differential reporting and developmental differences. Paper presented at the annual meeting of the American Sociological Association, Chicago, August.

CARNEGIE COUNCIL ON ADOLESCENT DEVELOPMENT. (1989). *Turning points: Preparing American youth for the 21st century.* New York: Carnegie Corporation of New York.

CARNEGIE FOUNDATION FOR THE ADVANCEMENT OF TEACHING. (1988). *The condition of teaching. A state by state analysis. 1988.* Princeton, NJ: Princeton University Press.

CASH, T. & PRUZINSKI, T., (Eds.). (1990). *Body images.* Guilford, CT: Guilford Press.

CASPER, R. C. (1989). Psychodynamic psychotherapy in acute anorexia nervosa and acute bulimia nervosa. In A. H. Esman, (Ed.), *International annals of adolescent psychiatry,* Chicago: University of Chicago Press.

CATES, W., JR. & RAYH, J. L. (1985). Adolescents and sexually transmitted diseases: An expanding problem. *Journal of Adolescent Health Care, 6,* 1–5.

CATTELL, R. B. (1963). Theory of fluid and crystallized intelligence: A critical experiment. *Journal of Educational Psychology, 54,* 1–22.

CENTERS FOR DISEASE CONTROL. (1980). *Teenage childbearing and abortion patterns—United States, 1977, 29,* 157–159.

CENTERS FOR DISEASE CONTROL. (1989). *Statistical information.* Atlanta: Author.

CENTERS FOR DISEASE CONTROL. (1990). Childhood injuries in the United States. *American Journal of Diseases in Children, 144,* 627–646.

CENTERS FOR DISEASE CONTROL. (1990). Diabetes mellitus during pregnancy and the risks for specific birth defects: A population-based care-controlled study. *Pediatrics, 85* (1), 1–9.

CERNOCH, J. & PORTER, R. (1985). Recognition of maternal axillary odors by infants. *Child Development, 56,* 1593–1599.

CHAIKIN, A. L., SIGLER, E., & DERLEGA, V. J. (1974). Nonverbal mediators of teacher expectancy effects. *Journal of Personality and Social Psychology, 30* (1), 144.

CHALFANT, J. (1989). Learning disabilities: Policy issues and promising approaches. *American Psychologist, 44* (2), 392–398.

CHALFANT, J. C. (1987). Providing services to all students with learning problems: Implications for policy and programs. In S. Vaughn & C. Bos, (Eds.), *Research in learning disabilities,* pp. 239–251. Boston: Little, Brown.

CHALL, J. S. (1983). *Stages of reading development.* New York: McGraw-Hill.

CHASE, H. C. & BYRNES, M. E. (1983). Trends in prematurity: United States, 1967–1983. *Journal of Public Health Policy, 60.*

CHASE-LANDSDALE, L. & OWEN, M. (1987). Maternal employment in a family context: Effects on infant-mother and infant-father attachments. *Child Development, 58,* 1505–1512.

CHASNOFF, I. (1989). Drug use and women: Establishing standards of care. *Annals of the New York Academy of Sciences, 562,* 208–210.

CHASNOFF, I., LANDRESS, H., & BARRETT, M. (1990). The prevalence of illicit drug or alcohol use during pregnancy and discrepancies in mandatory reporting in Pinellas County, Florida. *New England Journal of Medicine,* April 26, 1202–1206.

CHESS, S. (1977). Follow-up report on autism in congenital rubella. *Journal of Autism and Childhood Schizophrenia, 1,* 69–81.

CHESS, S. & THOMAS, A. (1982). Infant bonding: Mystic and reality. *American Journal of Orthopsychiatry, 52* (2), 213–222.

CHI, M. (1978). Knowledge structures and memory development. In R. Siegler, (Ed.), *Childrens' thinking: What develops?* Hillsdale, NJ: Erlbaum.

CHI, M. T. H. & KOESKE, R. D. (1983). Network representation of a child's dinosaur knowledge. *Developmental Psychology, 19,* 29–39.

CHILD CARE ACTION CAMPAIGN. (1989). *Child care: The bottom line.* New York: Author.

CHILDREN'S DEFENSE FUND. (1978). *Children without homes. An examination of public responsibility to children in out-of-home care.* Study by J. Knitzer, M. Allen, & B. McGowan. Washington, D.C.: Author.

CHILDREN'S DEFENSE FUND. (1985). *A children's defense budget: An analysis of the president's FY 1986 budget and children.* Washington, D.C.: Author.

CHILDREN'S DEFENSE FUND. (1990). *A report card, briefing book, and action primer.* Washington, D.C.: Author.

CHILMAN, C. S. (1983). *Adolescent sexuality in a changing American society: Social and psychological perspectives for human services professions,* (2nd Ed.). New York: Wiley.

CHINESE MEDICAL JOURNAL. (1975) New Series Vol. 1, pp. 81–94. Child health care in new China, by Society of Pediatrics of the Chinese Medical Association, Peking, March.

CHING, C. C. (1982). Single-child families. *Studies in Family Planning* (United Nations), 115–118.

CHOMSKY, C. (1969). *The acquisition of syntax in children from 5 to 10.* Cambridge, MA: MIT Press.

CHOMSKY, N. (1968). *Language and mind.* New York: Harcourt Brace & World.

CHRISTOPHERSEN, E. R. (1989). Injury control. *American Psychologist, 44* (2), 238–241.

CHRISTOPHERSEN, E. R. & SULLIVAN, M. A. (1982). Increasing the protection of newborn infants in cars. *Pediatrics, 70,* 21–25.

CHRISTOPHERSEN, E. R., WILLIAMS, G., & BARONE, V. J. (1988). A comparison of the effectiveness of group health education messages between expectant parents and parents of toddlers. Unpubl. study.

CICCHETTI, D. (Ed.). (1989). *The emergence of a discipline. Rochester symposium developmental psychopathology* (Vol. 1.). Hillsdale, NJ: Erlbaum.

CITIZENS' COMMISSION ON SCHOOL NUTRITION. (1991). *White*

paper on school nutrition. Washington, D.C.: Center for Science in the Public Interest.

CLARK, E. V. (1973). What's in a word? On the child's acquisition of semantics in his first language. In T. E. Moore, (Ed.), *Cognitive development and the acquisition of language*. New York: Academic Press.

CLARK, H. & CLARK, E. (1977). *Psychology and language: An introduction to psycholinguistics*. New York: Harcourt Brace Jovanovich.

CLARK, K. & CLARK, M. (1987). Study on ethnic identification in black children. Paper presented at the annual convention of the American Psychological Association, New York, NY, August.

CLARKE, A. M. & CLARKE, A. D. B., (Eds.). (1976). *Early experience: Myth and evidence*. New York: Free Press.

CLARKE-STEWART, K. A. (1973). Interactions between mothers and their young children: Characteristics and consequences. *Monographs of the Society for Research in Child Development, 38* (Serial No. 153), 6–7.

CLARKE-STEWART, K. A. (1978a). And daddy makes three: The father's impact on mother and young child. *Child Development, 49,* 466–478.

CLARKE-STEWART, K. A. (1978b). Recasting the lone stranger. In J. Glick & K. A. Clarke-Stewart, (Eds.), *The development of social understanding*. New York: Gardner Press.

CLARKE-STEWART, K. A. (1982). *Day care*. Cambridge, MA: Harvard University Press.

CLARKE-SEWART, K. A. (1989). Infant day care: Maligned or malignant? *American Psychologist, 44* (2), 266–273.

CLARKE-STEWART, K. A. & APFEL, N. (1979). Evaluating parental effects on child development. In L. S. Shulman, (Ed.), *Review of research in education* (Vol. 6). Itasca, IL: Peacock.

CLARKE-STEWART, K. A. & FEIN, G. G. (1983). Early childhood programs. In P. H. Mussen, (Ed.), *Handbook of child psychology*. Vol. 2, *Infancy and developmental psychopathology*, pp. 917–1000. New York: Wiley.

CLARKE-STEWART, K. A. & HEVEY, C. M. (1981). Longitudinal relations in repeated observations of mother-child interactions from 1 to 2½ years. *Developmental Psychology, 17,* 127–149.

CLAUSEN, J. A. (1975). The social meaning of differential physical and sexual maturation. In S. E. Dragastin & G. H. Elder, (Eds.), *Adolescence in the life cycle: Psychological change and social context*. London: Halsted Press.

CLEWELL, B., BROOKS-GUNN, J., & BENASICH, A. (1989). Evaluating child-related outcomes of teenage parenting programs. *Family Relations, 38,* 201–209.

COCHRAN, M. M. (1977). A comparison of group care and family childrearing patterns in Sweden. *Child Development, 48,* 702–707.

COHEN, D. J. (1977). Minimal brain dysfunction: Diagnosis and therapy. In J. H. Masserman, (Ed.), *Current psychiatric therapies*. New York: Grune & Stratton.

COHEN, M. (1987). Stress: Most common cause of children's, teens' headaches. Paper presented at the annual meeting of the American Academy of Pediatrics, New Orleans, November.

COHEN, S. (1981). Adolescents and drug abuse: Biomedical consequences. In D. J. Lettier & J. P. Ludford, (Eds.), *Drug abuse and the American adolescent*. Rockville, MD: National Institute on Drug Abuse.

COHEN, S. E. (1978). Maternal employment and mother-child interaction. *Merrill-Palmer Quarterly, 24,* 189–197.

COLBY, A., KOHLBERG, L., GIBBS, J., & LIEBERMAN, M. (1983). A longitudinal study of mural development. *Monographs of the Society for Research in Child Development, 48,* Serial No. 200.

COLE, M. (1981). *The zone of proximal development: Where culture and cognition create each other*. Center for Human Information Processing, University of California at San Diego, Report No. 106.

COLE, M. (1983). Culture and cognitive development. In P. H. Mussen, (Ed.), *Handbook of child psychology*, (4th Ed.). Vol. 1, W. Kessen, (Ed.), *History, theory and methods*. New York: Wiley.

COLE, M. (1985). Mind as a cultural achievement: Implications for IQ testing. In E. Eisner, (Ed.), *Learning and teaching the ways of knowing*. Chicago: National Society for the Study of Education.

COLE, M., GAY, J., GLICK, J. A., & SHARP, D. W. (1971). *The cultural context of learning and thinking*. New York: Basic Books.

COLE, M. & SCRIBNER, S. (1974). *Culture and thought: A psychological introduction*. New York: Wiley.

COLEMAN, J. (1961). *The adolescent society*. New York: Free Press.

COLEMAN, J. C. (1974). *Relationships in adolescence*. Boston: Routledge & Kegan Paul.

COLEMAN, J. C. (1980). Friendship and the peer group in adolescence. In J. Adelson, (Ed.), *Handbook of adolescent psychology*. New York: Wiley.

COLEMAN, J. S., CAMPBELL, E., HOBSON, C., McPARTLAND, J., MOOD, A., WEINFIELD, F., & YORK, R. (1966). *Equality of educational opportunity*. Washington, D.C.: Government Printing Office.

COLEMAN, M. (1978). A report on the autistic syndrome. In M. Rutter & E. Schopler, (Eds.), *Autism: A reappraisal of concepts and treatment*. New York: Plenum.

COLLINS, W. A. (1984). Conclusion: The status of basic research on middle childhood. In W. A. Collins, (Ed.), *Development during middle childhood: The years from six to twelve*. Washington, D.C.: National Academy Press.

COLLINS, W. A. (1990). Parent-child relationship in the transition to adolescence: Continuity and change in interaction, affect, and cognition. In R. Montmayor, G. Adams, & T. Gullotta, (Eds.), *From childhood to adolescence: A transition period?* pp. 85–106. New York: Russell Sage.

COLLINS, W. A. & GETZ, S. K. (1975). Children's social responses following modeled reactions to provocation: The prosocial effects of television drama. *Journal of Personality, 44,* 488–500.

COMBRINK-GRAHAM, L. (1991). Development of school-age children. In M. Lewis, (Ed.), *Child and adolescent psychiatry: A comprehensive textbook*. Baltimore: Williams & Wilkins.

COMER, J. (1991). The black child in school. In M. Lewis, (Ed.), *Child and adolescent psychiatry: A comprehensive textbook*. Baltimore: Williams & Wilkins.

COMER, J. P. (1988). Educating poor minority students. *Scientific American, 259*, 5.

COMMITTEE FOR THE INSTITUTE OF MEDICINE. (1989). *Research on children and adolescents with mental, behavioral, and developmental disorders*. Washington, D.C.: National Academy Press.

COMMITTEE ON ECONOMIC DEVELOPMENT. (1987). *Children in need: Investment strategies for the educationally disadvantaged*. New York: Author.

COMMITTEE ON ECONOMIC DEVELOPMENT. (1988). *Social Security and National Savings*. New York: Author.

COMMITTEE ON TRAUMA RESEARCH. (1985). *Injury in America: A continuing public health problem*. Washington, D.C.: National Research Council, Institute of Medicine.

COMPAS, B. (1987). Coping with stress during childhood and adolescence. *Psychological Bulletins, 101*, 393–403.

COMPAS, B. (1989). Vulnerability and stress in childhood and adolescence. Paper presented at the meeting of the Society for Research in Child Development, Kansas City, MO, April.

CONDON, W. S. & SANDER, L. W. (1974). Neonate movement is synchronized with adult speech: Interactional participation and language acquisition. *Science, 183*, 99–101.

CONDRY, J., BENCE, P., & SCHEIB, C. (1987). Nonprogram content of children's television. *Journal of Broadcasting and Electronic Media, 32*, 255–270.

CONGER, J. J. (1973). *Adolescence and youth: Psychological development in a changing world*. New York: Harper & Row.

CONRAD, P. (1976). *Identifying hyperactive children and the medicalization of deviant behavior*. Lexington, MA: Lexington Books.

CONROY, M., HESS, D., AZUMA, H., & KASHIWAGI, K. (1980). Maternal strategies for regulating children's behavior. *Journal of Cross Cultural Psychology, 11*, 153–172.

CONSORTIUM OF LONGITUDINAL STUDIES. (1983). *As the twig is bent*. Hillsdale, NJ: Erlbaum.

CONSTANZO, P. & SHAW, M. (1966). Conformity as a function of age level. *Child Development, 37*, 967–975.

CONWAY, E. & BRACKBILL, Y. (1970). Delivery medication and infant outcome: An empirical study. *Monographs of the Society for Research in Child Development, 35* (137), 24–34.

COOK, T., APPLETON, H., CONNER, R., SHAFFER, A., TABKIN, C., & WEBER, S. (1975). *Sesame Street Revisited*. New York: Sage.

COOK-DEEGAN, R. (1990). *Mapping our genes*. Report by the Office of Technology Assessment. Washington, D.C.: Government Printing Office.

COOPER, C. & AYERS-LOPEZ, S. (1985). Family and peer systems in early adolescence. New models of the role of relationships in development. *Journal of Early Adolescence, 5*, 9–22.

COOPER, H. M. (1979). Pygmalion grows up: A model for teacher expectation, communication and performance influence. *Review of Educational Research, 49*, 389–410.

COOPER, R. M. & ZUBEK, J. P. (1958). Effects of enriched and restricted early environment on the learning ability of bright and dull rats. *Canadian Journal of Psychology, 12*, 159–164.

COOPERSMITH, S. (1967). *The antecedents of self-esteem*. San Francisco: Freeman.

CORAH, N. L., ANTHONY, E. J., PAINTER, P., STERN, J. A., & THURSTON, D. L. (1965). Effects of perinatal anoxia after seven years. *Psychological Monographs, 79*, 3.

CORBIN, C. B. (1973). *A textbook of motor development*. Dubuque, IA: W. C. Brown.

CORENBLUM, B. & ANNIS, R. C. (1987). Racial identity and preference in native and white Canadian children. *Canadian Journal of Behavioral Sciences, 19*, 254–265.

CORSARO, W. A. (1980). Friendship in the nursery school: Social organization in a peer environment. In S. R. Asher & J. M. Gottman, (Eds.), *The development of children's friendships*. New York: Cambridge University Press.

COUCHARD, T. J., JR. (1991). A twice told tale: Twins reared apart. In W. Grove & D. Cicchetti, (Eds.), *Thinking clearly about psychology: Essays in honor of Paul Everett Meehl*. Vol. 2, *Personality and psychopathology*. Chicago: University of Chicago Press.

COX, M. J. & COX, R. D. (1985). *Foster care: Current issues and practices*. Norwood, NJ: Ablex.

CRAIN, W. C. (1985). *Theories of development*. Englewood Cliffs, NJ: Prentice-Hall.

CREMIN, L. A. (1976). *Public education*. New York: Basic Books.

CRNIC, K. A., GREENBERG, M. T., RAGOZIN, A. S., ROBINSON, N. M., & BASHAM, R. B. (1983). Effects of stress and social support on mothers and premature and full-term infants. *Child Development, 54* (1), 209–217.

CRNIC, K. A., GREENBERG, M. T., ROBINSON, N. M., & RAGOZIN, A. S. (1984, April). Maternal stress and social support: Effects on mother-infant relationship from birth to eighteen months. *American Journal of Orthopsychiatry, 54* (2), 224–235.

CROCKENBERG, S. (1981). Infant irritability, mother responsiveness, and social support influences on the security of infant-mother attachment. *Child Development, 52*, 857–865.

CROMWELL, R. L. (1963). A social learning approach to mental retardation. In N. R. Ellis, (Ed.), *Handbook of mental deficiency*. NY: McGraw-Hill.

CRONBACH, L. J. (1975). Five decades of public controversy over mental testing. *American Psychologist, 30*, 1–14.

CROOK, C. K. & LIPSITT, L. P. (1976). Neonatal nutritive sucking: Effects of taste stimulation upon sucking rhythm and heart rate. *Child Development, 47,* 518–522.

CROWDER, R. D. (1982). *The psychology of reading.* New York: Oxford University Press.

CRUIKSHANK, W. M. (1977). *Learning disabilities in home, school, and community.* Syracuse, NY: Syracuse University Press.

CSIKSZENTMIHALYI, M., & LARSON, R. (1984). *Being adolescent: Conflict and growth in the teenage years.* New York: Basic Books.

CURTISS, S. (1977). *Genie.* New York: Academic Press.

DALE, L. (1970). The growth of systematic thinking: Replication and analysis of Piaget's first chemical experiment. *Australian Journal of Psychology, 22,* 227–286.

DALE, P., BATES, E., REZNICK, J. S., & MORISSET, C. (1989). The validity of a parent report instrument of child language at twenty months. *Journal of Child Language, 16,* 239–249.

DALE, P. S. (1976). *Language development: Structure and function* (2nd Ed.). New York: Holt, Rinehart & Winston.

DALTON, K. (1977). *The premenstrual syndrome and progesterone therapy.* London: Heinemann Medical.

DAMON, W. (1977). *The social world of the child.* San Francisco: Jossey-Bass.

DAMON, W. (1980). Patterns of change in children's social reasoning: A longitudinal study. *Child Development, 51,* 1010–1017.

DAMON, W. (1983). *Social and personality development: Infancy through adolescence.* New York: Norton.

DAMON, W. & HART, W. (1982). The development of self-understanding from infancy through adolescence. *Child Development, 53,* 841–869.

D'ANGELO, R. (1974). Families of sand: A report concerning the flight of adolescents from their families. Columbus: Ohio State University School of Social Work.

DANIELS, P. & WEINGARTEN, K. (1982). *Sooner or later.* NY: Norton.

DANNER, F. W. & DAY, M. C. (1977). Eliciting formal operations. *Child Development, 48,* 1600–1606.

DARLING, C. A., KELLMAN, D., & VANDUSEN, J. E. (1984). Sex in transition, 1900–1984. *Journal of Youth and Adolescence, 13,* 385–399.

DARWIN, C. (1958, originally published 1859). *On the origin of species.* NY: Penguin.

DASEN, P. R. (1972). Cross-cultural Piagetian research: A summary. *Journal of Cross-Cultural Psychology, 3* (1), 29–39.

DASEN, P. R. (Ed.) (1977). *Piagetian psychology: Cross-cultural contributions.* New York: Gardner Press.

DAVIDSON, L., ROSENBERG, M , MERCY, J., FRANKLIN, J., & SIMMONS, J. T. (1989). An epidemiologic study of risk factors in two teenage suicide clusters. *Journal of the American Medical Association, 262,* 2687–2692.

DAVIES, A., DEVAULT, S., & TALMADGE, M. (1971). Anxiety, pregnancy, and childbirth abnormalities. In H. Munsinger, (Ed.), *Readings in child development.* New York: Holt, Rinehart & Winston.

DAVIS, D. E. (1964). The physiological analysis of aggressive behavior. In E. Etkin, (Ed.), *Social behavior and organization among vertebrates.* Chicago: University of Chicago Press.

DAVIS, D. L. (1991). Fathers and fetuses. *New York Times,* March 1, A27.

DAVISS, B. (1989). T. V. as Boob. *Television and Families, 11* (2), 2–8.

DEBOLT, M. E., PASLEY, B. K., & KREUTZER, J. (1990). Factors affecting the probability of school dropout. *Journal of Adolescent Research, 5* (2), 190–205.

DEBUS, R. L. (1970). Effects of brief observation of model behavior on conceptual tempo of impulsive children. *Developmental Psychology, 2,* 22–32.

DECASPER, A. & SIGAFOOS, A. (1983). The intrauterine heartbeat: A potent reinforcer for newborns. *Infant Behavior and Development, 6,* 19–25.

DECASPER, A. & SPENCE, M. (1986). Prenatal maternal speech influences newborns' perceptions of speech sounds. *Infant Behavior and Development, 9,* 133–150.

DECASPER, A. J. & FIFER, W. P. (1980). Of human bonding: Newborns prefer their mothers' voices. *Science, 208,* 1174–1176.

DEFRIES, J. C., VANDENBERG, S. G., & MCCLEARN, G. E. (1976). The genetics of specific cognitive abilities. *Annual Review of Genetics, 10,* 179-207.

DEMENT, W. C. (1960). The effects of dream deprivation. *Science, 131,* 1705–1707.

DEMYER, W. (1975). Congenital anomalies of the central nervous system. In D. B. Tower, (Ed.), *The nervous system: The clinical neurosciences.* New York: Raven.

DENNIS, W. (1940). Infant reaction to restraint. *Transactions of the New York Academy of Science, 2,* 202–217.

DENNIS, W. (1960). Causes of retardation among institutional children: Iran. *Journal of Genetic Psychology, 96,* 47–59.

DENNIS, W. (1973). *Children of the creche.* New York: Appleton-Century-Crofts.

DENT, C. & ROSENBERG, L. (1990). Visual and verbal metaphors and developmental interactions. *Child Development, 61,* 983–994.

DERSHEWITZ, R. A. (1979). Will mothers use free household safety devices? *American Journal of Diseases of Children, 133,* 61–64.

DERSHEWITZ, R. A. & WILLIAMSON, J. W. (1977). Prevention of childhood household injuries: A controlled clinical trial. *American Journal of Public Health, 67,* 1148–1153.

DESTEFANO, J. S. & RENTEL, V. M. (1975). Language variation: Perspectives for teachers. *Theory into Practice, 14* (5), 328–337.

DEUTSCH, H. (1945). *The psychology of women: A psychoanalytic interpretation* (Vol. 2). New York: Grune & Stratton.

DEVILLIERS, J. G. & DEVILLIERS, P. A. (1978). *Language acquisition.* Cambridge, MA: Harvard University Press.

DEVRIES, M. W. & DEVRIES, M. R. (1977, August). The cultural relativity of toilet training readiness: A perspective from

East Africa. *Pediatrics, 60* (2), 170–177.

deVRIES, M. W. & SAMEROFF, A. J. (1984). Culture and temperament: Influences on infant temperament in three East-African societies. *American Journal of Orthopsychiatry, 54* (1), 83–96.

deVRIES, R. (1969). Constancy of genetic identity in the years three to six. *Monographs of the Society for Research in Child Development, 34* (Serial No. 127). Chicago: University of Chicago Press.

DICKISON, D. K. & SNOW, C. E. (1989). Interrelations among prereading and oral language skills in kindergartners from two social classes. *Early Childhood Research Quarterly, 2,* 1–25.

DICK-READ, G. (1972). *Childbirth without fear* (4th Ed.). New York: Harper & Row.

DIETZ, W. & GORTMAKER, S. (1985). Do we fatten our children at the television set? Obesity and television viewing in children and adolescents. *Pediatrics, 75,* 807–812.

DOBBIN, J. (1974). The later development of the brain and its vulnerability. In T. A. Davis & J. Dobbin, (Eds.), *Scientific foundations of pediatrics.* Philadelphia: Saunders.

DODGE, K. (1983). Behavioral antecedents of peer social status. *Child Development, 54,* 1386–1399.

DOLLARD, J., DOOB, L. W., MILLER, N. E., MOWRER, O. H., & SEARS, R. R. (1939). *Frustration and aggression.* New Haven: Yale University Press.

DONATAS, C., MARATOS, O., FAFOUTIS, M., & KARANGELIS, A. (1985). Early social development in institutionally reared Greek infants. *Monographs of the Society for Research in Child Development, 50* (Serial No. 209), 136–146.

DONOVAN, W. L. & LEAVITT, L. A. (1985). Physiology and behavior: Parents' response to the infant cry. In B. M. Lester & C. F. Z. Boukydis, (Eds.), *Infant crying: Theoretical and research perspectives.* New York: Plenum.

DORE, J. (1978). Conditions for the acquisition of speech. In J. MARKOVA, (Ed.), *The social context of language.* New York: Wiley.

DORR, A. (1983). No shortcuts in judging reality. In P. E. Bryant & S. Anderson, (Eds.), *Watching and understanding T. V.: Research on children's attention and comprehension.* New York: Academic Press.

DOUVAN, E. & ADELSON, J. (1966). *The adolescent experience.* New York: Wiley.

DOWD, M. (1983, Dec. 4). Many women in poll equate values of job and family life. *New York Times,* pp. 1, 66.

DOWDREY, L. (1985). Critical notice. (Review of *Coercive family process* by Gerald Patterson). *Journal of Child Psychology and Psychiatry, 26,* 5, 829–833.

DOWNS, A. & LANGLOIS, J. (1988). Sex typing: Construct and measurement issues. *Sex Roles, 18,* 87–100.

DRYFOOS, J. G. & HEISLER, T. (1981). Contraceptive services for adolescents: An overview. In F. Furstenberg, R. Lincoln, & J. Menken, (Eds.), *Teenage sexuality, pregnancy, and childbearing.* Philadelphia: University of Pennsylvania Press.

DUBOIS, D. L. & HIRSCH, B. J. (1990). School and neighborhood friendship patterns of blacks and whites in early adolescence. *Child Development, 61* (2), 524–536.

DUFF, R. (1979, July). Guidelines for deciding care of critically ill or dying patients. *Pediatrics, 64* (1), 17–23.

DUFF, R. (1981, March). Counseling families and deciding care of severely defective children: A way of coping with "medical Vietnam." *Pediatrics, 67* (3), 315–320.

DUKE, D. L. (1978). Why don't girls misbehave more than boys in school? *Journal of Youth and Adolescence, 7,* 114–158.

DUNKEL-SCHETTER, C., LOBEL, M., & SCRIMSHAW, S. (1990). Stress during pregnancy and infant prematurity. Paper presented at the annual convention of the American Psychological Association, Boston, August.

DUNN, J. & KENDRICK, C. (1979). Interactions between young siblings in the context of family relationships. In M. Lewis & L. Rosenblum, (Eds.), *The child and its family.* New York: Plenum.

DUNPHY, D. C. (1963). The social structure of urban adolescent peer groups. *Sociometry, 26,* 230–246.

EARLE, J. (1990). *Keeping pregnant and parenting teens in school.* Alexandria, VA: National Association of State Boards of Education.

EARLY, L., GRIESLER, P., & ROVEE-COLLIER, C. (1985). Ontogenetic changes in retention in early infancy. Paper presented at the meeting of the Society for Research in Child Development, Toronto, April.

EASTERBROOKS, M. & LAMB, M. (1979). The relationship between quality of infant-mother attachment and infant competence in initial encounters with peers. *Child Development, 50,* 380–387.

ECCLES, J. (1987). Gender roles and achievement patterns: An expectancy value perspective. In J. M. Reinisch, L. A. Rosenblum, & S. A. Sanders, (Eds.), *Masculinity/femininity.* New York: Oxford University Press.

ECCLES, J. & MIDGLEY, C. (1989). Stage/environment fit: Developmentally appropriate classrooms for early adolescents. In R. E. Ames & C. Ames, (Eds.), *Research on motivation in education* (Vol. 3). New York: Academic Press.

ECCLES, J. S. & HOFFMAN, L. W. (1984). Sex roles, socialization, and occupational behavior. In H. W. Stevenson & A. E. Siegel, (Eds.), *Child development research and social policy.* Chicago: University of Chicago Press.

ECCLES, J. S. & MIDGLEY, C. (1990). Changes in academic motivation and self-perception during early adolescence. In R. Montmayor, G. Adams, & T. Gullotta, (Eds.), *From childhood to adolescence: A transition period?,* pp. 134–155. New York: Russell Sage.

ECONOMIC POLICY COUNCIL. (1986). *Work and family life in the United States: A policy initiative.* New York: United Nations Association.

EDNA MCCONNELL CLARK FOUNDATION. (1985). *Keeping families together: The case for family preservation.* New York: Author.

EDWARDS, C. P. (1981). The development of moral reasoning in cross-cultural perspective. In R. H. Monroe, R. L. Monroe, & B. B. Whiting, (Eds.), *Handbook of cross-cultural human development.* New York: Garland Press.

EDWARDS, C. P. (1982). Moral development in comparative

cultural perspective. In D. A. Wagner & H. W. Stevenson, (Eds.), *Cultural perspectives on child development*. San Francisco: Freeman.

EDWARDS, C. P. & WHITING, B. B. (1980). Differential socialization of girls and boys in the light of cross-cultural research. In C. M. Super & S. Harkness, (Eds.), *Anthropological perspectives on child development*. San Francisco: Jossey-Bass.

EGELAND, B. (1974). Training impulsive children in the use of more efficient scanning techniques. *Child Development, 45,* 165–171.

EGELAND, B. & BRUNQUETTE, D. (1979). An at-risk approach to the study of child abuse: Some preliminary findings. *Journal of the American Academy of Psychiatry, 18,* 219–235.

EICHORN, D. H. (1963). Biological correlates of behavior. *Yearbook of the National Society for the Study of Education, 62,* 4–61.

EICHORN, D. H. (1975). Asynchronizations in adolescent development. In S. E. Dragastin & G. H. Elder, (Eds.), *Adolescence in the life cycle: Psychological change and social context.* Washington, D.C.: Hemisphere Publishing.

EICHORN, D. H. (1979). Physical development: Current foci of research. In J. D. Osofsky, (Ed.), *Handbook of infant development.* New York: Wiley.

EIDUSON, B., KORNFEIN, M., ZIMMERMAN, I., & WEISNER, T. (1982). Comparative socialization practices in traditional and alternative families. In M. E. Lamb, (Ed.), *Nontraditional families: Parenting and child development.* Hillsdale, NJ: Erlbaum.

EIMAS, P. (1985). The perception of speech in early infancy. *Scientific American, 204,* 66–72.

EIMAS, P. D., SIGUELAND, E. R., JUSCYZK, P., & VIGORITO, H. (1971). Speech perception in infants. *Science, 171,* 303–306.

EIMAS, P. D. & TARTTER, V. C. (1979). On the development of speech perceptions: Mechanisms and analogies. In H. W. Reese & L. P. Lipsitt, (Eds.), *Advances in child development and behavior.* New York: Academic Press.

EISENBERG, L. & KANNER, L. (1956). Early infantile autism. *American Journal of Orthopsychiatry, 26,* 556–566.

EISENBERG, N. (1982). Social development. In C. B. Kopp & J. B. Krakow, (Eds.), *The child: Development in a social context.* Reading, MA: Addison-Wesley.

EISENBERG, W. & STRAYER, J. (Eds.) (1987). *Empathy: A developmental perspective.* New York: Cambridge University Press.

EKMAN, P. (1989). *Why kids lie.* San Francisco: Scribner's.

EKSTEIN, R. (1978). Psychoanalysis, sympathy, and altruism. In L. Wispe, (Ed.), *Altruism, sympathy, and helping: Psychological and sociological principles.* New York: Academic Press.

ELDER, D. & HALLINAN, M. T. (1978). Sex differences in children's friendships. *American Sociological Review, 43,* 237–250.

ELDER, G. H., JR. (1974). *Children of the Great Depression.* Chicago: University of Chicago Press.

ELDER, G.H., JR. (1975). Adolescence in the life cycle: An introduction. In S. E. Dragastin & G. H. Elder, (Eds.), *Adolescence in the life cycle: Psychological change and social context.* Washington, D.C.: Hemisphere Publishing.

ELDER, G. H., JR. (1980). Adolescence in historical perspective. In J. Adelson, (Ed.), *Handbook of adolescent psychology.* New York: Wiley.

ELDER, G. H. & CASPI, I. (1990). Studying lives in a changing society. In A. I. Rubin, R. A. Zucker, S. Frank, & R. Emmons, (Eds.), *Study in persons and lives.* New York: Springer.

ELIAS, M. & WEISSBERG, R. (1990). School-based social competence promotion as a primary prevention strategy: A tale of two projects. *Prevention in Human Services, 7* (1), 177–185.

ELKIND, D. (1967). Egocentrism in adolescence. *Child Development, 38,* 1025–1034.

ELKIND, D. (1978). *The child's reality: Three developmental themes.* Hillsdale, NJ: Erlbaum.

ELKIND, D. (1981). *The hurried child: Growing up too fast too soon.* Reading, MA: Addison-Wesley.

ELKIND, D. (1983). Teenage thinking and the curriculum. *Educational Horizons, 61 (4),* 163–168.

ELKIND, D. (1984). *All grown up and no place to go: Teenagers in crisis.* Reading, MA: Addison-Wesley.

ELKIND, D. (1987). *Miseducation: Preschools at risk.* New York: Knopf.

ELLIS, N. R. (1970). Memory processes in retardates and normals. In N. R. Ellis, (Ed.), *International review of research in mental retardation.,* Vol. 4. New York: Academic Press.

EMDE, R., GAENSBAUER, T., & HARMON, R. (1976). Emotional expression in infancy: A behavioral study. *Psychological Issues Monograph Series, 10,* 1 (Serial No. 37). New York: International Universities Press.

EMDE, R. & ROBINSON, J. (1979). The first two months: Recent research in developmental psychobiology and the changing view of the newborn. In J. Noshpitz & J. Call, (Eds.), *Basic handbook of child psychiatry.* New York: Basic Books.

EMDE, R. N., HARMON, R. J., METCALF, D., KOENING, K. L., & WAGONFELD, S. (1971). Stress and neonatal sleep. *Psychosomatic Medicine, 33,* 491–497.

EMMONS, C. A., BIERNAT, M., TIEDGE, L. B., LANE, E. L., & WORTMAN, C. B. (1987). *Stress, support and coping among women professionals with preschool children.* Lansing, MI: Institute for Social Research.

ENDSLEY, R. C., HUTCHERS, M. A., GARNER, A. P., & MARTIN, M. J. (1979). Interrelationships among selected maternal behaviors, authoritarianism, and preschool children's verbal and nonverbal curiosity. *Child Development, 50* (2), 331–339.

ENTWISLE, D. & ALEXANDER, K. L. (1990). Beginning school math competence: Minority and majority comparisons. *Child Development, 61* (2), 454–471.

ENTWISLE, D. R. & HAYDUK, L. A. (1978). *Too great expectations: The academic outlook of young children.* Baltimore: Johns Hopkins University Press.

ENTWISLE, D. R. & HAYDUK, L. A. (1982). *Early schooling—*

Cognitive and affective outcomes. Baltimore: Johns Hopkins University Press.

EPPS, E. G. & SMITH, S. F. (1984). School and children: The middle childhood years. In A. W. Collins, (Ed.), *Development during middle childhood: The years from six to twelve.* Washington, D.C.: National Academy Press.

EPSTEIN, J. L. (1986). Friendship selection: Developmental and environmental influences. In E. C. Mueller & C. R. Cooper, (Eds.), *Process and outcome in peer relationships,* pp. 129–160. New York: Academic Press.

EPSTEIN, J. L. (1990). Effects of student achievement on teachers' practices and parent involvement. In S. Silvern, (Ed.), *Literacy through family, community and social interaction.* Greenwich, CT: JAI Press.

ERIKSON, E. (1959). Identity and the life cycle. *Psychological Issues, I.* (Monograph No. 1).

ERIKSON, E. (1963). *Childhood and society,* (2nd Ed.). New York: Norton.

ERIKSON, E. (1968). *Identity: Youth and crisis.* New York: Norton.

ERLENMEYER-KIMLING, L. & JARVIK, L. F. (1963, Dec. 13). Genetics and intelligence: A review. *Science, 142,* 1477–1479.

ESPENSCHADE, A. (1960). Motor development in children. In W. R. Johnson, (Ed.), *Science and medicine of exercise and sport.* New York: Harper & Row.

ESPENSHADE, T. J. (1979). The economic consequences of divorce. *Journal of Marriage and the Family, 41,* 615–625.

ETAUGH, C. (1974). Effects of maternal employment on children: A review of recent research. *Merrill-Palmer Quarterly, 20,* 71–98.

ETAUGH, C., COLLINS, G., & GERSON, A. (1975). Reinforcement of sex-typed behaviors of two-year-old children in a nursery school setting. *Developmental Psychology, 11,* 255.

ETZEL, B. C. & GEWIRTZ, J. L. (1967). Experimental modifications of caregiver maintained high-rate operant crying in a six-week and a 20-week old infant: Extinction of crying with reinforcement of eye contact and smiling. *Journal of Experimental Child Psychology, 5,* 303–317.

ETZIONI, A. (1977). Sex control, science, and society. In A. S. Baker, (Ed.), *Heredity and society: Readings in social genetics.* New York: Macmillan.

EVELETH, P. B. & TANNER, J. (1976). *Worldwide variations in human growth.* Cambridge, UK: Cambridge University Press.

FAFOUTI-MILENKOVIC, M. & UZGIRIS, I. C. (1979). The mother-infant communication system. In I. C. Uzgiris, (Ed.), *Social interaction and communication during infancy.* San Francisco: Jossey-Bass.

FAGOT, B. (1977). Consequences of moderate crossgender behavior in preschool children. *Child Development, 48,* 902–907.

FALBO, T. (1990). Population policy in context: The case of Chinese children. Presented at the 98th Annual Convention of the American Psychological Association, Boston, August.

FANTZ, R. L. (1961). The origin of form perception. *Scientific American, 204,* 66–72.

FANTZ, R. L. (1963). Pattern vision in newborn infants. *Science, 140,* 296–297.

FANTZ, R. L. (1966). Pattern discrimination and selective attention as determinants of perceptual development from birth. In A. H. Kidd & J. L. Rivoire, (Eds.), *Perceptual development in children.* New York: International Universities Press.

FARBER, S. L. (1981). *Identical twins reared apart.* New York: Basic Books.

FARKAS, G. (1984). *Post program impacts of the Youth Incentive Entitlement Pilot Project (YIEPP).* New York: Manpower Demonstration Research Corp.

FATHMAN, R. E. (1990). National Coalition to Abolish Corporal Punishment. Unpubl. study. Columbus, OH.

FEATHER, N. T. (1980). Values in adolescence. In J. Adelson, (Ed.), *Handbook of adolescent psychology.* New York: Wiley.

FEINGOLD, B. (1975). *Why your child is hyperactive.* New York: Random House.

FEINMAN, S. & LEWIS, M. (1983). Social referencing at ten months: A second-order effect on infants' responses to strangers. *Child Development, 54,* 878–887.

FENSON, L., CAMERON, M. S., & KENNEDY, M. (1988). Role of perceptual and conceptual similarity in category matching at age two years. *Child Development, 59,* 897–907.

FERNALD, A. (1985). Four-month-old infants prefer to listen to motherese. *Infant Behavior and Development, 8,* 181–195.

FERREIRA, A. J. (1969). *The prenatal environment.* Springfield, IL: Charles C Thomas.

FESHBACH, N. D. (1969). Student teacher preferences for elementary school pupils varying in personality characteristics. *Journal of Educational Psychology, 60,* 126–132.

FESHBACH, N. D., & FESHBACH, S. (1976). Children's aggression. In W. W. Hartup, (Ed.), *The young child: Reviews of research,* (2nd Ed., Vol. 2). Washington, D.C.: National Association for the Education of Young Children.

FESHBACH, S. (1980). Child abuse and the dynamics of human aggression and violence. In G. Gerbner, C. J. Ross, & E. Zigler, (Eds.), *Child abuse: An agenda for action.* New York: Oxford University Press.

FEUERSTEIN, R. (1980). *Instrumental enrichment: An intervention program for cognitive modifiability.* Baltimore: University Park Press.

FIELD, T. (1978). Interaction behaviors of primary versus secondary caretaker fathers. *Developmental Psychology, 14,* 183–184.

FIELD, T. (1980). Supplemental stimulation of preterm neonates. *Early Human Development, 3,* 301–314.

FIELD, T. (1983). Early interactions and interaction coaching of high risk infants and parents. In M. Perlmutter, (Ed.), *Development and policy concerning children with special needs.* Hillsdale, NJ: Erlbaum.

FIELD, T. (1987). Affective and interactive disturbances in

infants. In J. D. Osofsky, (Ed.), *Handbook of infant development*, (2nd Ed.), pp. 972–1005. New York: Wiley.

FIELD, T., WOODSON, R., GREENBERG, R., & COHEN, D. (1982). Discrimination and imitation of facial expressions by neonates. *Science, 218,* 179–182.

FINCHAM, F. & CAIN, K. (1986). Learned helplessness in humans: A developmental analysis. *Developmental Review, 6,* 301–333.

FINE, G. A. (1980). The natural history of preadolescent friendship groups. In H. Foot, A. Chapman, & J. Smith, (Eds.), *Friendship and social relations in children.* New York: Wiley.

FINEGAN, J. A., QUARRINGTON, B. J., HUGHES, H. E., MERVYN, J. M., HOOD, J. E., ZACHER, J. E., & BOYDEN, M. (1990). Child outcome following mid-trimester amniocentesis: Development, behavior, and physical status at age four years. *British Journal of Obstetrics and Gynaecology, 97,* 32–40.

FINKELHOR, D. (1979). *Sexually victimized children.* New York: Free Press.

FINKELSTEIN, N. W. & HASKINS, R. (1983). Kindergarten children prefer same-color peers. *Child Development, 54,* 502–508.

FINKELSTEIN, N. W. & RAMEY, C. T. (1977). Learning to control the environment in infancy. *Child Development, 48,* 806–819.

FINN, M. (1977). *The politics of nutrition education.* Unpubl. diss., Ohio State University, Columbus.

FINN-STEVENSON, M., EMMEL, B., & TRCZINSKI, E. (1988). *Issues of parental leave. Its practice, availability and feasibility in the State of Connecticut.* Study presented by the Connecticut Task Force on Work and Family. Hartford: Connecticut General Assembly.

FINN-STEVENSON, M. & TRCZINSKI, E. (1991). Parental and family leave policies: A state-by-state analysis and recommendation. *American Journal of Orthopsychiatry, 61* (4), 567–575.

FINN-STEVENSON, M., WARD, B., & STEVENSON, J. (1989). Injury prevention in child care facilities: An analysis of state regulations. Unpubl. report. Yale University Bush Center in Child Development and Social Policy, New Haven, CT.

FISCHER, K. & LAZERSON, A. (1984). *Human development.* New York: Freeman.

FISCHER, K. W. (1980). A theory of cognitive development: The control and construction of hierarchies of skill. *Psychological Review, 87,* 477–531.

FISCHER, K. W. (1983). Developmental levels as periods of discontinuity. In K. W. Fischer, (Ed.), *Levels and transitions in children's development.* San Francisco: Jossey-Bass.

FISH, B. (1971). The one child, one drug myth of stimulants in hyperkinesis: Importance of diagnostic categories in evaluating treatment. *Archives of General Psychiatry, 25,* 193–203.

FISHER. D. L. (1976). *Functional illiteracy and the schools: A reanalysis of several large-scale surveys.* Report to the U.S. Department of Health, Education and Welfare, National Institute of Education.

FISHER, M. (1990). Parenting stress and child with attention deficit hyperactivity disorder. *Journal of Clinical Child Psychology, 19* (4), 337–346.

FISHER, M. & ZEAMAN, D. (1973). An attention-retention theory of retardate discrimination learning. In N. R. Ellis, (Ed.), *International review of research in mental retardation,* Vol. 6. New York: Academic Press.

FISHMAN, B. & HAMEL, B. (1981, May). From nuclear to stepfamily ideology: A stressful change. *Alternative Lifestyles, 4* (2), 181–204.

FITZGERALD, H. E. & BRACKBILL, Y. (1976). Classical conditioning in infancy: Development and constraints. *Psychological Bulletin, 83,* 353–375.

FITZGERALD, T. A. (1974, Fall). Exploring childhood. *Colorado Audio-Visual Advance, 4* (3).

FITZGERALD, T. A. (1981, Spring). Exploring childhood in a private school. *Education for Parenthood Exchange, 7* (2).

FLAPAN, D. (1968). *Children's understanding of social interactions.* New York: Teachers College Press.

FLAVELL, J. (1977). *Cognitive development.* Englewood Cliffs, NJ: Prentice-Hall.

FLAVELL, J. (1985). *Cognitive development,* (2d Ed.). Englewood Cliffs, NJ: Prentice-Hall.

FLAVELL, J. H. (1982). On cognitive development. *Child Development, 53,* 1–10.

FLAVELL, J. H., BEACH, D., & CHINSKY, J. (1966). Spontaneous and verbal rehearsal in a memory task as a function of age. *Child Development, 37,* 283–299.

FLAVELL, J. H., GREEN, F. L., & FLAVELL, E. R. (1986). Development of knowledge about the appearance-reality distinction. *Monographs of the Society for Research in Child Development, 51* (1), (Serial No. 212).

FLOOD, J. & MENYUK, P. (1983). The development of metalinguistic awareness and its relation to reading achievement. *Journal of Applied Developmental Psychology, 4,* 65–80.

FOGEL, A. & HANNAN, E. (1985). Manual actions of 9–15 week-old human infants during face to face interactions with their mothers. *Child Development, 56,* 1271–1279.

FOLSTEIN, S. & RUTTER, M. (1978). Genetic influences and infantile autism. *Annual Progress in Child Psychiatry and Child Development,* 437–431.

FOOD RESEARCH & ACTION CENTER. (1991). *Community childhood hunger identification project: A survey of childhood hunger in the U.S.* Washington, D.C.: Author.

FORSYTH, B. W. C., LEVENTHAL, J. M., & MCCARTHY, P. L. (1985). Mothers' perceptions of problems of feeding and crying behaviors: A prospective study. *American Journal of Diseases of Children, 139,* 269–272.

FOUNDATION FOR THE STUDY OF INFANT DEATHS AND BRITISH PEDIATRIC RESPIRATORY GROUP. (1990). Monitoring and Sudden Infant Death Syndrome. London: Author.

FRAIBERG, S. (1968). Parallel and divergent patterns in blind and sighted infants. *Psychoanalytic Study of the Child, 19,* 5–7.

FRAIBERG, S. (1971). Intervention in infancy: A program for blind infants. *Journal of the American Academy of Child*

Psychiatry, 10, 381–405.

FRAIBERG, S. (1974). Blind infants and their mothers. In M. Lewis & L. A. Rosenblum, (Eds.), *The effect of the infant on its caregiver.* New York: Wiley.

FRAIBERG, S. (1977). *Insights from the blind: Comparative studies of blind and sighted infants.* New York: Basic Books.

FRANCIS, P., SELF, P., & HOROWITZ, F. (1987). The behavioral assessment of the neonate: An overview. In J. D. Osofsky, (Ed.), *Handbook of child development,* (2nd Ed.), pp. 723–779. New York: Wiley.

FRANKENBURG, W. K. (1981). Early screening for developmental delays and potential school problems. In C. C. Brown, (Ed.), *Infants at risk: Assessment and intervention.* Skillman, NJ: Johnson & Johnson.

FRASIER, S. D. & RALLISON, M. L. (1972). Growth retardation and emotional deprivation: Relative resistance to treatment with growth hormone. *Journal of Pediatrics, 80,* 603–605.

FRAUENGLASS, M. & DIAZ, R. (1985). Self-regulatory functions of children's private speech: A critical analysis of recent challenges to Vyotsky's theory. *Developmental Psychology, 21,* 357–364.

FRAZIER, T. M., DAVIS, G. H., GOLDSTEIN, H., & GOLDBERG, I. (1961). Cigarette smoking: A prospective study. *American Journal of Obstetrics and Gynecology, 81,* 988–996.

FREEDMAN, D. (1974). *Human infancy: An evolutionary perspective.* Hillsdale, NJ: Erlbaum.

FREEDMAN, D. G. (1964). Smiling in blind infants and the issue of innate versus acquired. *Journal of Child Psychology and Psychiatry, 5,* 171–184.

FREEDMAN, D. G. (1965). Hereditary control of early social behavior. In B. M. Foss, (Ed.), *Determinates of infant behavior* (Vol. 3). New York: Wiley.

FREEDMAN, D. G. (1971). Behavioral assessment in infancy. In G. A. B. Stoelinga & J. J. Van Der Werff Ten Bosch, (Eds.), *Normal and abnormal development of brain and behavior.* Leiden, The Netherlands: Leiden University Press.

FREEDMAN, D. G. & FREEDMAN, N. C. (1969). Behavioral differences between Chinese-American and European-American newborns. *Nature, 224,* 1227.

FREEDMAN, J. L. (1986). Television on violence and aggression: A rejoinder. *Psychological Bulletin, 100,* 364–371.

FREEMAN, D. (1983). *Margaret Mead and Samoa: The making and unmaking of an anthropological myth.* Cambridge, MA: Harvard University Press.

FREEMAN, E. W. (1980). Adolescent contraceptive use: Comparisons of male and female attitudes and information. *American Journal of Public Health, 70,* 790–797.

FREITAG, M. (1990). Thousands of children doing adults' work. *New York Times,* February 5, B1.

FREUD, A. (1968). Adolescence. In A. E. Winter & D. L. Angus, (Eds.), *Adolescence: Contempory studies.* New York: American Books.

FREUD, A., with DUNN, S. (1951). An experiment in group upbringing. *Psychoanalytic Study of the Child, 6,* 127–168.

FREUD, S. (1930; 2nd Ed., 1957). *Civilization and its discontents.* London: Hogarth.

FREUD, S. (1965). *The ego and the mechanism of defense.* C. Baines (Trans). New York: International University Press. (Original work published 1933.)

FRIEDMAN, D. (1987). *Family supportive policies: The corporate decision making process.* New York: The Conference Board.

FRIEDMAN, S., KLIVINGTON, K., & PETERSON, R. (1986). *The brain, cognition, and education.* New York: Academic Press.

FRIEDMAN, S. L., JACOBS, B. S., & WERTHMAN, M. W. (1978, Oct. 6–7). Information processing and temperament in preterm, full-term, and post-term infants at the neonatal period. Invited address, workshop on birth not at term: Constraints to optimal psychological development. Bethesda, MD: National Institute of Mental Health.

FRIEDMAN, S. L. & SIGMAN, M. (Eds.). (1980). *Preterm birth and psychological development.* New York: Academic Press.

FRIEDRICH-COFER, L. & HUSTON, A. C. (1986). Television violence and aggression: The debate continues. *Psychological Bulletin, 100,* 364–371.

FRIEDRICH, L. K. & STEIN, A. H. (1973). Aggressive and prosocial television programs and the natural behavior of preschool children. *Monographs of the Society for Research in Child Development, 38* (4), (Serial No. 151).

FRISCH, R. (1974). Body composition, hormones, and growth: Discussion. In M. M. Grumbach, G. D. Grave, & F. E. Mayer, (Eds.), *Control of the onset of puberty.* New York: Wiley.

FRISCH, R. (1978). Population, food intake, and fertility: There is historical evidence for a direct effect of nutrition on reproductive ability. *Science, 199,* 22–30.

FRODI, A. (1985). When empathy fails: Aversive infant crying and child abuse. In B. M. Lester & C. F. Z. Boukydis, (Eds.), *Infant crying: Theoretical and research perspectives.* New York: Plenum.

FROST, J. L. & SUNDERLIN, S. (1985). *When children play.* Wheaton, MD: Association for Children's Education International.

FUCHS, D. & FUCHS, L. S. (1986). Test procedure bias: A meta-analysis of examiner familiarity effects. *Review of Educational Research, 56,* 243–262.

FUCHS, F. (1980). Genetic amniocentesis. *Scientific American, 242,* 47–53.

FULLER, J. L. (1967). Experimental deprivation and later behavior. *Science,* 1645–1652.

FURSTENBERG, F. F., JR. (1976). *Unplanned parenthood: The social consequences of teenage childbearing.* New York: Free Press.

FURSTENBERG, F. F., JR. (1988). Child care after divorce and remarriage. In E. M. Hetherington & J. Arasteh, (Eds.), *Impact of divorce, single parenting, and step-parenting on children.* Hillsdale, NJ: Erlbaum.

FURSTENBERG, F. F., JR., BROOKS-GUNN, J., & CHASE-LANSDALE, L. (1989). Teenage pregnancy and childbearing. *American Psychologist, 44* (2), 313–320.

FURSTENBERG, F. F., JR., BROOKS-GUNN, J., & MORGAN, S. P. (1987). *Adolescent mothers in later life.* New York: Cambridge University Press.

FURSTENBERG, F. F., PETERSON, J. L., NORD, C. W., & ZILL, N. (1983). The life course of children of divorce: Marital disruption and parental contact. *American Sociological Review, 48* (5), 656–668.

GABEL, S. & ERICKSON, M. T. (Eds.) (1980). *Child development and developmental disabilities.* Boston: Little, Brown.

GAENSBAUER, T. J. & SANDS, K. (1979). Distorted affective communication in abused/neglected infants and their potential impact on caretakers. *Journal of the American Academy of Child Psychiatry, 18,* 236–250.

GAGE, N. L. (1978). *The scientific basis of the art of teaching.* New York: Teachers College Press.

GALAMBOS, S. J. & GOLDIN-MEADOW, S. (1990). The effects of learning two languages on levels of metalinguistic awareness. *Cognition, 34,* 1–56.

GALLAGHER, J. J. (1989). A new policy initiative: Infants and toddlers with handicapping conditions. *American Psychologist, 44* (2) 387–391.

GALLAGHER, S. S., FINISON, K., & GUYER, B. (1984). The incidence of injury among 87,000 Massachusetts children and adolescents: Results of the 1980–1981 statewide childhood injury prevention program surveillance system. *American Journal of Public Health, 74,* 1340–1346.

GALLAHUE, D. (1982). *Developmental experiences for children.* New York: Wiley.

GALLER, J., RAMSEY, F., & SOLIMANON, G. (1984). The influence of early malnutrition on subsequent behavioral development. In J. Galler, (Ed.), *Nutrition and behavior.* New York: Plenum.

GALLO, A., CONNOR, J., & BOEHM, W. (1980, Winter). Mass media food advertising. *National Food Review,* pp. 10–12.

GALLUP, G., JR. (1986a). Gallup Youth Survey (May–June 1985). Princeton, NJ: Gallup Organization.

GALLUP, G., JR. (1986b). Gallup Youth Survey (Aug.–Oct. 1985). Princeton, NJ: Gallup Organization.

GAMBLE, T. J. & ZIGLER, E. (1986). Effects of infant day care: Another look at the evidence. *American Journal of Orthopsychiatry, 56,* 26–42.

GARBARINO, J. (1977). The price of privacy: An analysis of the social dynamics of child abuse. *Child Welfare, 56,* 565–575.

GARBARINO, J. (1980). Latchkey children. *Vital Issues, 30* (3), 1–4 (whole issue). (Available from the Center for Information on America, Washington, CT 06793.)

GARBARINO, J. (1982). Sociocultural risk: Dangers to competence. In C. B. Koop & J. B. Krakow, (Eds.), *The child: Development in a social context.* Reading, MA: Addison-Wesley.

GARBARINO, J. (1986). Troubled youth, troubled families: The dynamics of adolescent maltreatment. In D. Cicchetti & V. Carlson, (Eds.), *Child maltreatment: Theory and research on the causes and consequences of child abuse and neglect.* **New York: Cambridge University Press.**

GARBARINO, J. (1988). Preventing childhood injury: Developmental and mental health issues. *American Journal of Orthopsychiatry, 58* (1), 25–45.

GARBARINO, J. (1989). Children and youth in dangerous environments: Coping with the consequences. Prepublication manuscript. Erikson Institute for Advanced Study in Child Development.

GARBARINO, J. & GILLIAM, G. (1980). *Understanding abusive families.* Lexington, MA: Lexington Books.

GARBARINO, J. & VONDRA, J. (1983). The psychological maltreatment of children and youth. Keynote presentation of the First International Conference on Psychological Abuse and Neglect, Indianapolis, August.

GARCIA-COLL, C. (1990). Developmental outcome of minority infants: A process-oriented look at our beginnings. *Child Development, 61* (2), 270–289.

GARDNER, B. & GARDNER, R. (1986). Discovering the meaning of primate signals. *British Journal for the Philosophy of Science, 37,* 477–495.

GARDNER, H. (1978). *Developmental psychology.* Boston: Little, Brown.

GARDNER, H. (1980). *Artful scribbles: The significance of children's drawings.* New York: Basic Books.

GARDNER, H. (1983). *Frames of mind.* New York: Basic Books.

GARDNER, H. & WINNER, E. (1979, May). The child is father to the metaphor. *Psychology Today, 12,* 81–91.

GARDNER, L. I. (1972). Deprivation dwarfism. *Scientific American, 227* (1), 76–82.

GARDNER, R. A. & GARDNER, B. T. (1980). Two comparative psychologists look at language acquisition. In K. E. Nelson, (Ed.), *Children's language* (Vol. 2). New York: Gardner.

GARFINKEL, B. D., FROESE, A., & HOOD, J. (1982). Suicide attempts in children and adolescents. *American Journal of Psychiatry, 139* (10), 1257–1261.

GARFINKEL, B. D. & GOLOMBEK, H. (1974). Suicide and depression in childhood and adolescence. *Canadian Medical Association Journal, 110,* 1278.

GARMEZY, M. (1985). Stress resistant children: The search for protective factors. In J. E. Stevenson, (Ed.), *Recent research in developmental psychopathology,* pp. 213–233. Oxford: Pergamon Press.

GARMEZY, N. & RUTTER, M., (Eds.). (1983). *Stress, coping, and development in children.* New York: McGraw-Hill.

GARNER, D. M. (1990). The association between bulimic symptoms and reported psychopathology. *International Journal of Eating Disorders, 9,* 1–15.

GARRAD, J. W. (1974). Breastfeeding: Second thoughts. *Pediatrics, 54,* 757.

GARRETT, C. S., EIN, P. L., & TREMAINE, L. (1977). The development of gender stereotyping of adult occupations in elementary school children. *Child Development, 48,* 507–512.

GARRISON, W. & EARLS, F. (1982). Preschool behavior problems and the multigenerational family: An island community study. *International Journal of Family Psychiatry, 2,* 195–207.

GARRISON, W. T. (1984). Inpatient psychiatric treatment of the difficult child: Common practices and their ethical implications. *Children and Youth Services Review, 6* (4), 353–365.

GARVEY, C. (1977). *Play.* Cambridge, MA: Harvard University Press.

GARWOOD, S. G., HARTMAN, A., PHILLIPS, D., & ZIGLER, E. (1989). As the pendulum swings: Federal agency programs for children. *American Psychologist, 44* (2), 434–440.

GAUDRY, E. & SPIELBERGER, C. (1971). *Anxiety and educational achievement.* Sydney: Wiley.

GAY, P. (1990). *The Freud reader.* New York: Norton.

GEDO, J. E. (1990). The roots of personality: Heredity and environment. *Harvard Mental Health Newsletter, 7* (1) 4–6.

GELLER, M. I., KELLEY, J. A., TRAXLER, W. T., & MARONE, F. J., JR. (1978). Behavioral treatment of an adolescent female's bulimic anorexia: Modification of immediate consequences and antecedent conditions. *Journal of Clinical Child Psychology, 7,* 138–142.

GELLES, R. (1978). Violence toward children in the United States. *American Journal of Orthopsychiatry, 48,* 580–592.

GELLIS, S. S. & HSIA, D. Y. (1959). The infant of the diabetic mother. *American Journal of Diseases of Children, 97,* 1.

GELMAN, R. (1969). Conservation acquisition: A problem of learning to attend to relevant attributes. *Journal of Experimental Child Psychology, 7,* 167–187.

GELMAN, R. (1982). Accessing one-to-one correspondence: Still another paper about conservation. *British Journal of Psychology, 73,* 209–220.

GELMAN, R. & BAILLARGEON, R. (1983). A review of some Piagetian concepts. In P. Mussen, (Ed.), *Handbook of child development.* Vol 3., *Cognitive development.* New York: Wiley.

GELMAN, R. & MECK, E. (1983). Preschoolers counting: Principles before skill. *Cognition, 13,* 343–359.

GENERAL MILLS AMERICAN FAMILY REPORT. (1977). *Raising children in a changing society.* Minneapolis: General Mills.

GEORGE, C. & MAIN, M. (1979). Social interactions of young abused children: Approach, avoidance, and aggression. *Child Development, 50,* 306–318.

GERBNER, G. (1980). Children and power on television: The other side of the picture. In G. Gerbner, C. J. Ross, & E. Zigler, (Eds.), *Child abuse: An agenda for action.* New York: Oxford University Press.

GERBNER, G., ROSS, C., & ZIGLER, E., (Eds.) (1980). *Child abuse: An agenda for action.* New York: Oxford University Press.

GEWIRTZ, J. L. (1965). The course of infant smiling in four childrearing environments in Israel. In B. M. Foss, (Ed.), *Determinants of infant behavior,* (Vol. 3). New York: Wiley.

GESELL, A. & ILG, F. L. (1942). *Infant and child in the culture of today.* New York: Harper.

GESELL, A. & THOMPSON, H. (1934). *Infant behavior: Its genesis and growth.* New York: McGraw-Hill.

GIANINO, A. & TRONICK, E. Z. (1988). The mutual regulation model: The infants' self and interactive regulation. Coping and defense. In T. Field, P. McCabe, & N. Schneiderman, (Eds.), *Stress and coping,* pp. 47–68. Hillsdale, NJ: Erlbaum.

GIBSON, E. J. & WALK, R. R. (1960). The "visual cliff." *Scientific American, 202,* 2–9.

GIL, D. G. (1970). *Violence against children.* Cambridge, MA: Harvard University Press.

GIL, D. G. (1976). Primary prevention of child abuse: A philosophical and political issue. *Journal of Pediatric Psychology, 1,* 54–57.

GILLIGAN, C. (1982). *In a different voice.* Cambridge, MA: Harvard University Press.

GINSBURG, H. (1977). *Children's arithmetic.* New York: Van Nostrand.

GINSBURG, H. & OPPER, S. (1988). *Piaget's theory of intellectual development,* (3rd Ed.). Englewood Cliffs, NJ: Prentice-Hall.

GLEIDMAN, J. & ROTH, W. (1980). *The unexpected minority: Handicapped children in America.* New York: Harcourt Brace Jovanovich.

GLEITMAN, L., NEWPORT, E., & GLEITMAN, H. (1984). The current status of the motherese hypothesis. *Journal of Child Language, 11,* 43–79.

GLICK, P. C. & LIN, S. (1986). Recent changes in divorce and remarriage. *Journal of Marriage and the Family, 48,* 737.

GOETZ, P. L., SUCCOP, R. A., REINHART, J. B., & MILLER, A. (1977). Anorexia nervosa in children: A follow-up study. *American Journal of Psychiatry, 47,* 597–603.

GOLD, D. & ANDRES, D. (1978a). Comparisons of adolescent children with employed and non-employed mothers. *Merrill-Palmer Quarterly, 24,* 243–254.

GOLD, D. & ANDRES, D. (1978b). Developmental comparisons between ten-year-old children with employed and nonemployed mothers. *Child Development, 49,* 75–84.

GOLD, M. (1970). *Delinquent behavior in an American city.* Pacific Grove, CA: Brooks/Cole.

GOLD, M. & PETRONIO, R. J. (1980). Delinquent behavior in adolescence. In J. Adelson, (Ed.), *Handbook of adolescent psychology.* New York: Wiley.

GOLDEN, G. S. (1984). The developmentally disabled child: Detection, assessment, referral, and treatment. *Child Care, 3* (1), 8–11.

GOLDFIELD, B. & REZNICK, J. S. (1990). Early lexical acquisition: Rate, content, and the vocabulary spurt. *Journal of Child Language, 17,* 171–183.

GOLDIN-MEADOW, S. (1985). Language development under atypical learning conditions. In K. E. Nelson, (Ed.), *Children's language,* (Vol. 5). Hillsdale, NJ: Erlbaum.

GOLDSMITH, H. & CAMPOS, J. (1982). Toward a theory of

infant temperament. In R. N. Emde & R. Harmon, (Eds.), *The development of attachment and affiliative systems*. New York: Plenum.

GOLDSTEIN, H. & PECKHAM, C. (1976). Birth weight, gestation, neonatal mortality and child development. In D. F. Roberts & A. M. Thompson, (Eds.), The biology of fetal growth. *Human Biology, 15,* 81–108.

GOLDSTEIN, J., FREUD, A., & SOLNIT, A. (1973). *Beyond the best interests of the child.* New York: Free Press.

GOLSDSTEIN, J., FREUD, A., & SOLNIT, A. (1979). *Before the best interests of the child.* New York: Free Press.

GOLDSTEIN, S., FIELD, T., & HEALY, B. (1989). Concordance of play behavior and physiology in preschool friends. *Journal of Applied Developmental Psychology, 10,* 337–351.

GOLINKOFF, R. M., HIRSCH-PASEK, K., CAULEY, K. M., & GORDON, L. (1987). The eyes have it: Lexical and syntactic comprehension in a new paradigm. *Journal of Child Language, 14,* 23–45.

GOOD, T. & BROPHY, J. (1984). *Looking in classrooms,* (3rd Ed.). New York: Harper & Row.

GOODCHILDS, J. D. & ZELLMAN, G. (1984). Sexual signalling and sexual aggression in adolescent relationships. In N. M. Malamuth & E. D. Donnerstein, (Eds.), *Pornography and sexual aggression.* New York: Academic Press.

GOODLAD, J. (1983). *A place called school.* New York: McGraw-Hill.

GORDON, E. W. (1979). Evaluation during the early years of Head Start. In E. Zigler & J. Valentine, (Eds.), *Project Head Start: A legacy of the War on Poverty.* New York: Free Press.

GORE, S. (1980). Stress buffering functions of social supports: An appraisal and clarification of research models. In B. S. Dohrenwend & B. P. Dohrenwend, (Eds.), *Stressful life events: Their nature and effects.* New York: Wiley.

GOREN, C., SARTY, J., & WU, P. Y. (1975). Visual following and pattern discrimination of face-like stimuli by new-born infants. *Pediatrics, 56,* 544–549.

GORSKI, P. A. (1984). Infants at risk. In M. J. Hanson, (Ed.), *Atypical infant development.* Baltimore: University Park Press.

GORTMAKER, S. L., DIETZ, W. H., SOBOL, A. M., & WEHLER, C. A. (1987). Increasing pediatric obesity in the United States. *American Journal of Diseases of Children, 141,* 535–540.

GOSSNICKLE, D., LAYNE, D., & TIERNEY, M. (1988 Spring). Policing school campuses. *School Safety,* 28–30.

GOTTFRIED, A. W. & GOTTFRIED, A. E. (1984). Home environment and mental development in young children. In A. W. Gottfried, (Ed.), *Home environment and early mental development: Longitudinal research.* New York: Academic Press.

GOTTLIEB, G. (1976). The roles of experience in the development of behavior and the nervous system. In G. Gottlieb, (Ed.), *Studies on the development of behavior and the nervous system,* (Vol. 3). New York: Academic Press.

GOTTLIEB, G. (1983). The psychobiological approach to developmental issues. In P. H. Mussen, (Ed.), *Handbook of child psychology* (4th Ed.). Vol. 2, M. Haith & J. J. Campos, (Eds.), *Infancy and developmental psychobiology.* New York: Wiley.

GOTTLIEB, J. (1981). Mainstreaming: Fulfilling the promise? *American Journal of Mental Deficiency, 86,* 115–126.

GOTTLIEB, M. & KRASNEGOR, N., (Eds.) (1985). *Measurement of audition and vision in the first years of prenatal life. A methodological overview.* Norwood, NJ: Ablex.

GRANT, R. (1989). *Assessing the damage: The impact of shelter experience on homeless young children.* New York: Association to Benefit Children.

GRATCH, G. & SCHATZ, J. A. (1987). Cognitive development: The relevance of Piaget's infancy books. In J. D. Osofsky, (Ed.), *Handbook of infant development,* (2nd Ed.), pp. 204–237. New York: Wiley.

GREEN, A. A. (1976). A psychodynamic approach to the study and treatment of child abusing parents. *Journal of Child Psychiatry, 15,* 414.

GREENBAUM, C. W. & LANDAU, R. (1982). The infant's exposure to talk by familiar people: Mothers, fathers, and siblings in different environments. In M. Lewis & L. Rosenblum, (Eds.), *The social network of the developing child.* New York: Plenum.

GREENBERG, J. & DOOLITTLE, G. (1977, Dec. 11). Can schools speak the language of the deaf? *New York Times Magazine,* 50–102.

GREENBERGER, E. (1989). Bronfenbrenner, et al., revisited: Maternal employment and the perception of young children. Paper presented at the 97th Annual Convention of the American Psychological Association, New Orleans, August.

GREENBERGER, E., GOLDBERG, W., CRAWFORD, T., & GRANGER, J. (1988). Beliefs about consequences of maternal employment for children. *Psychology of Women Quarterly, 12,* 35–59.

GREENBERGER, E. & STEINBERG, L. (1981). *The study of adolescent work.* Washington, D.C.: Department of Education.

GREENFIELD, P. & LAVE, J. (1982). Cognitive aspects of informal education. In D. A. Wagner & H. E. Stevenson, (Eds.), *Cultural perspectives on child development.* New York: Freeman.

GREENFIELD, P. M. (1966). On culture and conservation. In J. S. Bruner, R. P. Olver, & P. M. Greenfield, (Eds.), *Studies in cognitive development.* New York: Wiley.

GREENFIELD, P. M. (1984). *Mind and media: The effects of television, video games and computers.* Cambridge, MA: Harvard University Press.

GREENSPAN, S. & GREENSPAN, N. T. (1985). *First feelings: Milestones in the emotional development of your body and child.* New York: Viking.

GREISER, D. L. & KUHL, P. K. (1988). Maternal speech to infants in a tonal language: Support for universal prosodic features of motherese. *Developmental Psychology, 24,* 14–20.

GROSSMAN, K., GROSSMAN, K. E., SPANGLER, S., SUESS, G., & UNZNER, L. (1985). Maternal sensitivity and newborn orientation responses as related to quality of attachment in Northern Germany. In I. Bretherton & E. Waters, (Eds.), Growing points of attachment theory. *Monographs of the Society for Research in Child Development, 50,* 1–2, Serial No. 209.

GUERON, J. M. (1984). *Lessons from a job guarantee: The Youth Incentive Entitlement Pilot Project.* New York: Manpower Demonstration Research Corporation.

GUGELMANN, R. (1989). Personal factors influencing survival in housefires. A study completed in preparation for master's degree in maternal and child health. Chapel Hill: University of North Carolina at Chapel Hill.

GUIDUBALDI, J., PERRY, J. D., CLEMINSHAW, H. K., & McLOUGHLIN, C. S. (1983). The impact of parental divorce on children: Report of the nationwide NASP study. *School Psychology Review, 12* (3), 300–323.

GUNTHEROTH, W. G., LOHMANN, R., & SPIERS, P. S. (1990). Risk of Sudden Infant Death Syndrome in subsequent siblings. *Journal of Pediatrics, 116,* 4.

GYORGY, F. (1960). The late effects of early malnutrition. *American Journal of Clinical Nutrition, 8,* 344–345.

HAGLUND, B. & CNATTINGIUS, S. (1990). Cigarette smoking as a risk factor for Sudden Infant Death Syndrome: A population-based study. *American Journal of Public Health, 80* (1), 29–32.

HAITH, M. M. (1980). *Rules newborns look by.* Hillsdale, NJ: Erlbaum.

HAITH, M. M. (1986). Sensory and perceptual processes in early infancy. *Journal of Pediatrics, 109* (1), 158–171.

HAITH, M. M. (1990). Progress in understanding of sensory and perceptual processes in infancy. *Merrill-Palmer Quarterly, 36* (1), 1–27.

HAITH, M. M., BERGMAN, T., & MOORE, M. J. (1977). Eye contact and scanning in early infancy. *Science, 199,* 853–854.

HAKUTA, K. (1986). *Mirror of language: The debate on bilingualism.* New York: Basic Books.

HAKUTA, K. (1987). Degree of bilingualism and cognitive ability in mainland Puerto Rican children. *Child Development, 58,* 1372–1388.

HAKUTA, K. (1989). Language and cognition in bilingual children. In A. M. Padilla, H. H. Fairchild, & C. M. Valadez, (Eds.), *Bilingual education,* pp. 47–59. Newbury Park, CA: Sage.

HAKUTA, K. & GARCIA, E. (1989). Bilingualism and education. *American Psychologist, 44* (2), 374–379.

HALE, G. A. (1979). Development of children's attention to stimulus components. In G. A. Hale & M. Lewis, (Eds.), *Attention and cognitive development,* pp. 43–64. New York: Plenum.

HALE, G. A., TAWEEL, S. S., GREEN, R. Z., & FLAUGHER, J. (1978). Effects of instructions on children's attention to stimulus components. *Developmental Psychology, 14,* 499–506.

HALL, E. G. & LEE, A. M. (1984). Sex differences in motor performing of young children: Fact or fiction? *Sex Roles, 10,* 217–230.

HALL, G. S. (1904). *Adolescence: Its psychology and its rela-*

tions to physiology, anthropology, sociology, sex, crime, religion, and education.* New York: Appleton.

HALLIDAY, M. A. K. (1975). *Learning how to mean: Explorations in the development of language.* London: Arnold.

HALLINAN, M. (1981). Recent advances in sociometry. In S. Asher & J. Gottman, (Eds.), *The development of children's friendships.* New York: Cambridge University Press.

HALLINAN, M. T. (1980). Patterns of cliquing among youth. In H. C. Foot, A. J. Chapman, & J. R. Smith, (Eds.), *Friendship and peer relations in children.* New York: Wiley.

HAMMER, T. J. & TURNER, P. H. (1985). *Parenting in contemporary society.* Englewood Cliffs, NJ: Prentice-Hall.

HANSON, D. (1980). Drug education: Does it work? In F. R. Scarpitti & S. K. Datesman, (Eds.), *Drugs and the youth culture.* Beverly Hills CA: Sage.

HANSON, M. J. (1984a). Early intervention: Models and practices. In M. J. Hanson, (Ed.), *Atypical infant development.* Baltimore: University Park Press.

HANSON, M. J. (1984b). The effects of early intervention. In M. J. Hanson, (Ed.), *Atypical infant development.* Baltimore: University Park Press.

HARARI, H. & McDAVID, J. (1973). Teachers' expectations and name stereotypes. *Journal of Educational Psychology, 65,* 222–225.

HARKNESS, S. & SUPER, C. M. (1983). The cultural construction of child development: A framework for the socialization of affect. *Ethos, 11,* 221–231.

HARLOW, H. (1971). *Learning to love.* San Francisco: Albion.

HARLOW, H. & MEARS, C. (1979). *The human model: Primate perspectives.* New York: Wiley.

HARLOW, H. F. (1961). The development of affectional patterns in infant monkeys. In B. M. Foss, (Ed.), *Determinants of infant behavior.* London: Methuen.

HARLOW, H. F. (1962). The heterosexual affectional system in monkeys. *American Psychologist, 17,* 17–19.

HARLOW, H. F. (1963). The maternal affectional system. In B. M. Foss, (Ed.), *Determinants of infant behavior* (Vol. 3). New York: Wiley.

HARLOW, H. F. & NOVAK, M. A. (1973). A psychopathological perspective. *Perspectives in Biology and Medicine, 16,* 461–478.

HARLOW, H. F. & ZIMMERMAN, R. R. (1959). Affectional responses in the infant monkey. *Science, 130,* 431–432.

HARMAN, D. & BRIM, O. G., JR. (1980). *Learning to be parents: Principles, programs, and methods.* Beverly Hills CA: Sage.

HARPER, L. V. & SAND, K. M. (1975). Preschool children's use of space. Sex differences in outdoor play. *Developmental Psychology, 11,* 119–121.

HARPER, R. M., LEAKE, B., HOFFMAN, H., WALKER, D. V., HOPPENBROUWERS, T., HODGMAN, J., & STERNMAN, M. (1981). Periodicity of Sudden Infant Death Syndrome. *Science, 213,* 1030–1032.

HARRIS, L. & ASSOCIATES. (1987). *Strengthening the links between home and schools.* New York: Louis Harris Associates.

HARRISON, A. O., WILSON, M. N., PINE, C. J., CHAN, S. Q., &

BURIEL, R. (1990). Family ecology of ethnic minority children. *Child Development, 61* (2), 347–362.

HARRITZ, A. S. & CHRISTENSEN, A. B. (1987). *Kids, drugs and alcohol: A parent's guide to prevention and intervention.* White Hall, VA: Better Way Publications.

HART-JOHNS, M. & JOHNS, B. (1982). *Give your child a chance.* Reston, VA.: Reston Publishing Co.

HARTER, S. (1979). Children's understanding of multiple emotions: A cognitive-developmental approach. Paper presented at the Ninth Annual Symposium of the Jean Piaget Society, Philadelphia, May/June.

HARTER, S. (1983a). Developmental perspectives on the self-system. In P. H. Mussen, (Ed.), *Handbook of child psychology,* (4th Ed.). Vol. 4, E. M. Hetherington, (Ed.), *Socialization, personality and social development.* New York: Wiley.

HARTER, S. (1983b). Competence as a dimension of self-evaluation: Toward a comprehensive model of self-worth. In R. Leahy, (Ed.), *The development of the self.* New York: Academic Press.

HARTER, S. (1990). Processes underlying adolescent self-concept formation. In R. Montmayor, G. Adams, & T. Gullotta, (Eds.), *From childhood to adolescence: A transition period?* pp. 205–239. New York: Russell Sage.

HARTER, S. & ZIGLER, E. (1974). The assessment of effectance motivation in normal and retarded children. *Developmental Psychology, 10,* 169–180.

HARTUP, W. W. (1970). Peer interaction and social organization. In P. H. Mussen, (Ed.), *Carmichael's manual of child psychology.* New York: Wiley.

HARTUP, W. W. (1974). Aggression in childhood: Developmental perspectives. *American Psychologist, 29,* 336–341.

HARTUP, W. W. (1978). Perspectives on child and family interaction: Past, present and future. In R. M. Lerner & G. B. Spanier, (Eds.), *Child influences on marital and family interaction: A life-span perspective.* New York: Academic Press.

HARTUP, W. W. (1979). The social worlds of childhood. *American Psychologist, 34,* 944–950.

HARTUP, W. W. (1983). Peer relations. In P. H. Mussen, (Ed.), *Handbook of child psychology,* (4th Ed.). Vol. 4, E. M. Hetherington, (Ed.), *Socialization, personality, and social development.* New York: Wiley.

HARTUP, W. W. (1984). The peer context in middle childhood. In W. A. Collins, (Ed.), *Development during middle childhood: The years from six to twelve.* Washington, D.C.: National Academy Press.

HARTUP, W. W. (1989). Social relationships and their developmental significance. *American Psychologist, 44* (2), 120–126.

HARVARD FAMILY RESEARCH PROJECT. (1991). *Innovative states: Emerging family support and education programs.* Cambridge, MA: Author.

HARVEY, T. J. (1983). Statement of the Executive Director of the National Conference of Catholic Charities before the Select Committee on Children, Youth, and Families, Ninety-Eighth Congress (first session), Washington, D.C. July.

HARWAY, M. & LISS, M. (1988). Arab mothers in Morocco: Responsibilities without rights. In B. Birns & D. Hay, (Eds.), *The different faces of motherhood,* pp. 101–118. New York: Plenum.

HARWOOD, R. (1985). Summary: Work, parenting, and stress in the early postpartum months. In *Infant Care Leave Project: Summaries of research components.* Unpubl. manuscript, Bush Center in Child Development and Social Policy, Yale University, New Haven, CT.

HAY, D. F., NASH, A., & PEDERSEN, J. (1983). Interactions between 6 month old peers. *Child Development, 54,* 557–562.

HAYES, C. (1987). *Risking the future.* Vol. 1, *Adolescent sexuality, pregnancy and childbearing.* Washington, D.C.: National Academy Press.

HAYNES, H., WHITE, B. L., & HELD, R. (1965). Visual accommodations in human infants. *Science, 148,* 528–530.

HEBB, D. O. (1972). *Textbook of psychology.* Philadelphia: Saunders.

HECKHAUSEN, H. (1987). Balancing for weakness and challenges to developmental potential: A longitudinal study of mother-infant dyads in apprenticeship interactions. *Developmental Psychology, 23,* 762–770.

HECOX, K. & DEEGAN, D. M. (1985). Methodological issues in the study of auditory development. In M. Gottlieb & N. A. Krasnegor, (Eds.), *Measurement of audition and vision in the first year of prenatal life: A methodological overview,* pp. 367–389. Norwood, NJ: Ablex.

HEIBECK, T. & MARKHAM, E. (1987). Word learning in children: An examination of fast mapping. *Child Development, 58,* 1021–1034.

HELTON, G. B. & OAKLAND, T. D. (1977). Teachers' attitudinal responses to differing characteristics of school students. *Journal of Educational Psychology, 69,* 261–266.

HENDERSHOT, G. E. & PLACEK, P. (1981). *Predicting fertility.* Lexington, MA: D. C. Heath, Lexington Books.

HENDERSON, N. P. (1982). Human behavior and genetics. *Annual Review of Psychology, 33,* 403–440.

HENKER, B. & WHALEN, C. K. (1989). Hyperactivity and attention deficits. *American Psychologist, 44* (2), 216–223.

HERNANDEZ, D. J. (1988). Demographic trends and the living arrangements of children. In E. M. Hetherington & J. D. Arasteh, (Eds.), *Impact of divorce, single parenting, and step-parenting on children,* pp. 3–22. Hillsdale, NJ: Erlbaum.

HERRENKOHL, R. C. & HERRENKOHL, E. C. (1981). Some antecedents and developmental consequences of mild maltreatment. In R. Rigley & D. Cicchetti, (Eds.), *New directions for child development.* San Francisco: Jossey-Bass.

HESS, R., KASHINSAGI, K., AZUMA, H., PRICE, G. C., & DICKSON, W. P. (1980). Maternal expectations for mastery of developmental tasks in Japan and U.S. *International Journal of Psychology, 15,* 259–271.

HESS, R. D. & CAMARA, K. A. (1979). Post-divorce relationships as mediating factors in the consequences of divorce for children. *Journal of Social Issues, 35,* 79–96.

HESS, R. D. & HOLLOWAY, S. D. (1985). Family and school as educational institutions. In R. D. Parke, (Ed.), *Review of Child Development Research.* Vol. 7, *The Family.* Chicago: University of Chicago Press.

HESS, R. D., HOLLOWAY, S. D., PRICE, G. G., & DICKSON, W. P. (1982). Family environments and the acquisition of reading skills: Toward a more precise analysis. In L. M. Laosa & I. E. Sigel, (Eds.), *Families as learning environments for children.* New York: Plenum.

HETHERINGTON, E. M. (1980). Children and divorce. In R. Henderson, (Ed.), *Parent-child interaction: Theory, research and prospect.* New York: Academic Press.

HETHERINGTON, E. M. (1989). Children and social change: Social and behavioral problems. Section introduction. *American Psychologist, 44* (2), 265–266.

HETHERINGTON, E. M. & CAMARA, K. A. (1984). Families in transition: The processes of dissolution and reconstitution. In R. D. Parke, (Ed.), *The family: Review of child development research* (Vol. 7). Chicago: University of Chicago Press.

HETHERINGTON, E. M., COX, M., & COX, R. (1976). Divorced fathers. *The Family Coordinator, 25,* 417–428.

HETHERINGTON, E. M., COX, M., & COX, R. (1978). The aftermath of divorce. In J. H. Stevens, JR., & M. Mathews, (Eds.), *Mother-child father-child relations.* Washington, D.C.: National Association for the Education of Young Children.

HETHERINGTON, E. M., COX, M., & COX, R. (1979). The development of children in mother-headed families. In H. Hoffman & D. Reiss, (Eds.), *The American family: Dying or developing?* New York: Plenum.

HETHERINGTON, E. M., COX, M., & COX, R. (1981). Divorce and remarriage. Paper presented at the meeting of the Society for Research in Child Development, Boston.

HETHERINGTON, E. M., COX, M., & COX, R. (1982). Effects of divorce on parents and children. In M. Lamb, (Ed.), *Nontraditional families: Parenting and child development.* Hillsdale, NJ: Erlbaum.

HETHERINGTON, E. M., STANLEY-HAGAN, M. S., & ANDERSON, E. R. (1989). Marital transition: A child's perspective. *American Psychologist, 44* (2), 303–312.

HEWLETT, S. A. (1986). *A lesser life.* New York: Warner Books.

HEWSON, P., OBERKLAID, F., & MENAHEM, S. (1987). Infant colic, distress, and crying. *Clinical Pediatrics, 26,* 69–76.

HICKS, L. E., LANGHAM, R. A., & TAKENAKA, J. (1982). Cognitive and health measures following early nutritional supplementation: A sibling study. *American Journal of Public Health, 72* (10), 1110–1118.

HILL, C. R. & STAFFORD, F. P. (1980). Prenatal care of children: Time diary estimate of quantity, predictability and variety. *Journal of Human Resources, 15,* 219–239.

HILL, H. (1984). *WIC: A retrospective analysis of a success.* Unpublished manuscript, Bush Center in Child Development and Social Policy, Yale University, New Haven, CT.

HILL, J. P. (1980). The family. In M. Johnson, (Ed.), *Seventy-ninth yearbook of the National Society for the Study of Education.* Chicago: University of Chicago Press.

HILL, J. P. & HOLMBECK, G. (1986). Attachment and autonomy during adolescence. *Annals of Child Development, 3,* 145–189.

HILL, P. T., FOSTER, G. E., & GENDLER, T. (1990). *High schools with character: Alternatives to bureaucracy.* CA: Rand Corporation.

HINDE, R. A. (1976). On describing relationships. *Journal of Child Psychology and Psychiatry, 17,* 1–19.

HIRANO-NAKANISHI, M. (1984). *Hispanic school dropouts: Relevance of pre-high school attrition and delayed education.* Los Alamitos, CA: National Center on Bilingual Research.

HOCHSCHILD, A. (1989). *The second shift.* New York: Viking.

HOCK, E. (1980). Working and nonworking mothers and their infants: A comparative study of maternal caregiving characteristics and infant social behavior. *Merrill-Palmer Quarterly, 26* (2), 79–101.

HODAPP, R. & MUELLER, E. (1982). Early social development. In B. Wolman, (Ed.), *The handbook of developmental psychology.* Englewood Cliffs, NJ: Prentice-Hall.

HOFFERTH, S. L. & HAYES, D. (1987). *Risking the future,* (Vol. 2). Washington, D.C.: National Academy Press.

HOFFMAN, L. (1984). Work, family and the socialization of the child. In R. D. Parke, (Ed.), *Review of child development research* (Vol. 7), pp. 223–282. Chicago: University of Chicago Press.

HOFFMAN, L. W. (1963). Mother's enjoyment of work and effects on the child. In F. I. Nye & L. W. Hoffman, (Eds.), *The employed mother in America.* Chicago: Rand McNally.

HOFFMAN, L. W. (1974). Effects of maternal employment on the child: A review of the research. *Developmental Psychology, 10,* 204–228.

HOFFMAN, L. W. (1975). The value of children to parents and the decrease in family size. *Proceedings of the American Philosophical Society, 119* (6), 430–438.

HOFFMAN, L. W. (1989). Effects of maternal employment in the two-parent family. *American Psychologist, 44* (2), 283–292.

HOFFMAN, L. W. & HOFFMAN, M. L. (1963). The value of children to parents. In J. T. Fawcett, (Ed.), *Psychological perspectives on population.* New York: Basic Books.

HOFFMAN, M. L. (1970). Conscience, personality, and socialization techniques. *Human Development, 13,* 90–126.

HOFFMAN, M. L. (1976). Empathy, role-taking, guilt, and development of altruistic motives. In T. Lickona, (Ed.), *Moral development and behavior.* New York: Holt, Rinehart & Winston.

HOFFMAN, M. L. (1978). Empathy: Its development and prosocial implications. In C. B. Keasey, (Ed.), *1977 Nebraska Symposium on Motivation.* Lincoln: University of Nebraska Press.

HOFFMAN, M. L. (1990). Empathy and prosocial activism. In N. Eisenberg, J. Reykowski, & E. Staub, (Eds.), *Social and moral values,* pp. 65–86. Hillsdale, NJ: Erlbaum.

HOLDEN, C. (1980). Identical twins reared apart. *Science, 207,* 1323–1325, 1327–1328.

HOLLENBECK, A. & SLABY, R. (1979). Infant visual and vocal responses to television. *Child Development, 50,* 41–45.

HOLLOS, M. (1975). Logical operations and role-taking abilities in two cultures: Norway and Hungary. *Child Development, 46,* 638–649.

HONING, A. (1988). *Parent involvement in early childhood education.* Washington, D.C.: National Association for the Education of Young Children.

HONZIK, M. (1964). Personality consistency and change: Some comments on papers by Bayley, MacFarlane, Moss, Kagan, and Murphy. *Vita Humana, 7,* 139–142.

HONZIK, M. P. (1957). Developmental studies of parent-child resemblance in intelligence. *Child Development, 28,* 215–228.

HOOK, E. B. (1973). Behavioral implications of the human XYY genotype. *Science, 179,* 139–150.

HORN, J. L. (1970). Organization of data on life-span development of human abilities. In L. R. Goulet & P. B. Baltes, (Eds.), *Life-span developmental psychology: Research and theory.* New York: Academic Press.

HOROWITZ, F. D. & PADEN, L. Y. (1973). The effectiveness of environment programs. In B. Caldwell & H. N. Ricciuti, (Eds.), *Review of child development research.* Vol. 3, *Child development and social policy.* Chicago: University of Chicago Press.

HOROWITZ, R. A. (1979). Psychological effects of the "open classroom." *Review of Educational Research, 49,* 71–86.

HOUSE SELECT COMMITTEE ON CHILDREN, YOUTH AND FAMILIES (1989). *U.S. children and their families: Current conditions and recent trends, 1989.* Washington, D.C.: U.S. Government Printing Office.

HOWES, C. & OLENICK, M. (1986). Family and child care influences on toddlers' compliance. *Child Development, 57,* 202–216.

HUESMANN, L. R. & ERON, L. D., (Eds.). (1986). *Television and the aggressive child: A cross national comparison.* Hillsdale, NJ: Erlbaum.

HUESMANN, L. R., ERON, L. D., LEFKOWITZ, M. M., & WALDER, L. O. (1984). Stability of aggression over time and generations. *Developmental Psychology, 6,* 1120–1134.

HUGHES, F. P. (1991). *Children, play, and development.* Boston: Allyn & Bacon.

HUMPHREY, R. A. & HOCK, E. (1989). Infants with colic: A study of maternal stress and anxiety. *Infant Mental Health Journal, 10* (4), 263–272.

HUNT, J. McVICKER (1961). *Intelligence and experience.* New York: Ronald Press.

HUSTON, A. C. (1983). Sex typing. In P. H. Mussen, (Ed.), *Handbook of child psychology,* (4th Ed.). Vol. 4, E. M. Hetherington, (Ed.), *Socialization, personality, and social development.* New York: Wiley.

HUSTON, A. C., WATKINS, B., & KUNKEL, D. C. (1989). Public policy and children's television. *American Psychologist, 44* (2), 424–433.

HUSTON, A. C., WRIGHT, J. C., RICE, M. L., KERKMAN, D., & ST. PETERS, M. (1987). *The development of television viewing patterns in early childhood.* Paper presented at the meeting of the Society for Research on Child Development, Baltimore, April.

HUTT, S. J., HUTT, C., LENARD, H., BERNUTH, V., & MUNTJEWERFF, W. (1968). Auditory responsivity in the human neonate. *Nature, 318,* 888–890.

HUTT, S. J., LENARD, H. G., & PRECHTL, H. F. R. (1969). Psychophysiology of the newborn. In L. P. Lipsitt & H. W. Reese, (Eds.), *Advances in child development.* New York: Academic Press.

HUTTENLOCHER, J. & PRESSON, C. B. (1973). Mental rotation and the perspective problem. *Cognitive Psychology, 4,* 277–299.

HUTTENLOCHER, P. R. (1979). The nervous system. In V. Vaughan III, P. McKay, & R. Behrman, (Eds.), *Nelson: Textbook of pediatrics,* (11th Ed.). Philadelphia: Saunders.

HYMAN, I. (1984). Testimony before the Subcommittee on Juvenile Justice, Committee on the Judiciary, U.S. Senate, Ninety-Eighth Congress, 2nd Session, Oct. 17. Oversight on corporal punishment in schools and what is an appropriate range of discipline by school officials. (Serial No. J-98-146.)

ILLINGWORTH, R. S. (1985). Infantile colic revisited. *Archives of Disease in Childhood, 60,* 981–985.

INFANT HEALTH AND DEVELOPMENT PROGRAM. (1990). Enhancing the outcomes of low-birthweight premature infants. *Journal of the American Medical Association, 263,* 3035–3042.

INHELDER, B. & PIAGET, J. (1958). *The growth of logical thinking from childhood to adolescence.* New York: Basic Books.

INSTITUTE OF AEROBIC RESEARCH. (1987). *Get fit.* Dallas: Author.

INSTITUTE OF MEDICINE. (1988). *Prenatal care: Reaching mothers, reaching infants.* Washington, D.C.: National Academy Press.

IRWIN, P. M. (1986). Adult literacy issues, programs, and options, updated 01/06/86. Washington, D.C.: Education and Public Welfare Division, Congressional Research Service. Unpubl. manuscript.

ISRALEWITZ, R. & SINGER, M. (1986). Unemployment and its impact on adolescent work values. *Adolescence, 21,* 145–158.

IZARD, C. E. (1971). *The face of emotions.* New York: Appleton-Century-Crofts.

IZARD, C. E. (1978). On the ontogenesis of emotions and emotion cognition relationships in infancy. In M. Lewis & L. Rosenblum, (Eds.), *The development of affect.* New York: Plenum.

IZARD, C. E. (Ed.). (1982). *Measuring emotions in infants and children.* London: Cambridge University Press.

JACKLIN, C. N. (1989). Females and males: Issues of gender. *American Psychologist, 44* (2), 127–133.

JACKLIN, C. N. & MACCOBY, E. E. (1978). Social behavior at thirty-three months in same-sex and mixed-sex dyads. *Child Development, 49,* 557–569.

JACKSON, P. (1968). *Life in the classroom.* New York: Holt, Rinehart & Winston.

JACKSON, R. L. (1966). Effects of malnutrition on growth in the preschool child. In *Preschool child malnutrition. Primary deterrent to human progress.* Proceedings of the International Conference on Prevention of Malnutrition in the Preschool Child, Washington, D.C., Dec. 7–11, 1964. Washington, D.C.: National Academy of Sciences, National Research Council Publ. No. 1282.

JACOBS, P. A. (1968). Chromosome studies on men in a maximum security hospital. *Annals of Human Genetics, 31,* 339.

JACOBSON, D. (1975). Fair-weather friend: Label and context in middle-class friendship. *Journal of Anthropological Research, 31,* 225–234.

JACOBSON, D. J. (1979, May). Stepfamilies: Myths and realities. *Social Work, 24* (3), 202–207.

JACOBSON, J. (1990). Behavior modifications of technologies. Implications of changes in early childhood education statutes for behavioral analysis. *Psychology in Mental Retardation and Developmental Disabilities, 16* (1), 7–10.

JANIS, J. (1983). Health policy for children. In E. Zigler, S. Kagan, & E. Klugman, (Eds.), *Children, families and government: A perspective on American social policy.* New York: Cambridge University Press.

JANIS, J. M. & BULOW-HUBE, S. (1986). *Healthy children.* Downey: Los Angeles County Office of Education.

JASON, J. & VAN DER MEER, A. (1989). *Parenting your premature baby.* New York: Delta.

JENSEN, A. R. (1969). How much can we boost I.Q. and scholastic achievement? *Harvard Educational Review, 39,* 1–123.

JESSOR, R. & JESSOR, S. L. (1977). *Problem behavior and psychological development.* New York: Academic Press.

JOHN, E. M., SAVITZ, D. A., & SANDLER, D. P. (1991). Prenatal exposure to parents' smoking and childhood cancer. *American Journal of Epidemiology, 133,* 123–132.

JOHNS, L. & ADLER, G. S. (1989). Evaluation of recent changes in Medicaid. *Health Affairs, 8* (1), 171–181.

JOHNSON, C., STUCKEY, M., LEWIS, L., & SCHWARTZ, D. (1981). Bulimia: A descriptive survey of 509 cases. In P. Garfinkel, D. Gasner, & P. Darby, (Eds.), *Anorexia nervosa: A multidimensional perspective.* New York: Dorsey Press.

JOHNSON, J. R., KLINE, M., & TSCHANN, J. M. (1989). Ongoing post divorce conflict: Effects on children of joint custody and frequent access. *American Journal of Orthopsychiatry, 59* (4), 576–592.

JOHNSON, L. D., O'MALLEY, P., & BACHMAN, J. (1987). *National trends in drug use and related factors among American high school students and young adults—1975–1986.* Rockville, MD: National Institute on Drug Abuse.

JOHNSON, L. D., O'MALLEY, P., & BACHMAN, J. (1988). *National trends in drug use and related factors among American high school students and young adults. Through 1987.* Rockville, MD: National Institute on Drug Abuse.

JONES, C. & LOPEZ, R. (1988). *Direct and indirect effects on the infant of maternal drug abuse.* Washington, D.C.: Department of Health and Human Services/National Institutes of Health.

JONES, E., FORREST, J., GOLDMAN, N., HENSHAW, S., LINCOLN, R., ROSOFF, J., WESTOFF, C., & WULF, D. (1985). Teenage pregnancy in developed countries: Determinants and policy implications. *Family Planning Perspectives, 17* (2), 53–63.

JONES, K. L. & SMITH, D. W. (1973). Recognition of the fetal alcohol syndrome in early infancy. *Lancet, 2,* 999–1001.

JONES, L. (1985, Winter). Permanency and continuity: New issues in foster care planning. *The Networker, 6* (2), 4, 7. (Available from the Bush Center in Child Development and Social Policy, Yale University, New Haven, CT.)

JONES, S. S. & RAAG, T. (1989). Smile production in infants: The importance of a social recipient for the facial signal. *Child Development, 60,* 811–818.

JOSLYN, W. D. (1973). Androgen-induced social dominance in infant female rhesus monkeys. *Journal of Child Psychology and Psychiatry, 14,* 137–145.

KACERGUIS, M. A. & ADAMS, G. R. (1979). Implications of sex-typed childrearing practices, toys, and mass media materials in restricting occupational choices of women. *Family Coordinator, 28,* 368–375.

KADABA, L. S. (1990). Crack's costly legacy. *Boston Globe Magazine,* July 1, p. 3.

KAGAN, J. (1965). Impulsive and reflective children: Significance of conceptual tempo. In J. D. Krumholz, (Ed.), *Learning and the educational process.* Chicago: Rand McNally.

KAGAN, J. (1972). Case against I.Q. tests: Concept of intelligence. *Humanist, 32,* 7.

KAGAN, J. (1976). Emergent themes in human development. *American Scientist, 64* (21), 186–196.

KAGAN, J. (1978). On emotion and its development: A working paper. In M. Lewis & L. A. Rosenblum, (Eds.), *The development of affect.* New York: Plenum.

KAGAN, J. (1984). The idea of emotion in human development. In C. E. Izard, J. Kagan, & R. B. Zajonc, (Eds.), *Emotion, cognition, and behavior.* New York: Cambridge University Press.

KAGAN, J. & KAGAN, N. (1970). Individual variations in cognitive processes. In P. Mussen (Ed.), *Carmichael's manual of child psychology.* New York: Wiley.

KAHN, A. J. (1969). *Studies in social policy and planning.* New York: Russell Sage.

KAIL, R. V., JR. (1979). *The development of memory in children.* San Francisco: Freeman.

KALTER, N. (1977). Children of divorce in an outpatient psychiatric population. *American Journal of Orthopsychiatry, 51,* 85–100.

KAMERMAN, S. & KAHN, A. (1987). *Child care: Facing the hard choices.* Boston: Auburn.

KAMERMAN, S. & KAHN, A. (1988). *Mothers alone: Strategies for a time of change.* Dover, MA: Auburn House.

KAMII, C. & KAMII, M. (1990). Why achievement testing should stop. In C. Kamii, (Ed.), *Achievement testing in the early grades: The games grownups play,* pp. 15–38. Washington, D.C.: National Association for the Education of Young Children.

KANDEL, D. B. (1981). Drug use by youth: An overview. In D. J. Lettieri & J. P. Ludford, (Eds.), *Drug abuse and the American adolescent.* Rockville, MD: National Institute on Drug Abuse.

KANDEL, D. B. & LESSER, G. S. (1972). *Youths in two worlds.* San Francisco: Jossey-Bass.

KANNER, L. (1942). Autistic disturbances of affective contact. *Nervous Child, 2,* 217.

KANTER, R. M. (1977). *Work and family life in the United States: A critical review and agenda for research and policy.* New York: Russell Sage.

KANTROWITZ, B. (1991). The breath of life. *Newsweek* special edition (Summer), pp. 52–53.

KAPLAN, B. J., MCNICHOL, J., CONTE, R. A., & MOGHADAM, H. K. (1989). Dietary replacement in preschool-aged hyperactive boys. *Pediatrics, 83,* 7–17.

KATZ, A. J. (1979). Lone fathers: Perspectives and implications for family policy. *Family Coordinator, 28,* 521–528.

KATZ, L. & CHARD, S. (1990). *Engaging the minds of young children.* Norwood, NJ: Ablex.

KAUFMAN, J. & ZIGLER, E. (1986). Do abused children become abusive parents? Unpubl. manuscript, Yale University, New Haven, CT.

KAUFMANN, A. & FLAITZ, J. (1987). Intellectual growth. In V. B. Van Hasselt & M. Hersen, (Eds.), *Handbook of adolescent psychology.* New York: Pergamon Press.

KAYE, K. (1980). Why we talk "baby talk" to babies. *Journal of Child Language, 7,* 489–507.

KAZDIN, A. E. (1990). Childhood depression. *Journal of Child Psychology and Psychiatry, 31,* 121–160.

KEATING, D. P. (1980). Thinking processes in adolescence. In J. Adelson, (Ed.), *Handbook of adolescent psychology.* New York: Wiley.

KEEFE, M. R. (1988). Irritable infant syndrome: Theoretical perspectives and practice implications. *Advances in Nursing Science, 10,* 70–78.

KELLER, A., FORD, L. H., & MEACHUM, J. A. (1978). Dimensions of self-concept in preschool children. *Developmental Psychology, 14,* 483–489.

KELLOGG, R. (1967, May). Understanding children's art. *Psychology Today, 1* (1), 16–25.

KELLOGG, R. (1970). Understanding children's art. In P. Cramer (Ed.), *Readings in developmental psychology.* Del Mar, CA: CRM.

KEMLER-NELSON, D. G., HIRSH-PASEK, K., JUSCZYK, P. W., & CASSIDY, K. W. (1989). How prosodic cues in motherese might assist language learning. *Journal of Child Language, 16,* 55–68.

KEMPE, C., SILVERMAN, E., STEELE, B., DROEGEMUELLER, W., & SILVER, H. (1962). The battered child syndrome. *Journal of the American Medical Association, 181,* 17.

KEMPE, R. S. & KEMPE, H. C. (1978). *Child abuse.* Cambridge, MA: Harvard University Press.

KEMPER, H. C. G., (Ed.). (1985). *Growth, health and fitness of teenagers.* Basel: Karger.

KENISTON, K. (1977). *All our children: The American family under pressure.* New York: Harcourt Brace Jovanovich.

KENNY, S. L. (1983). Developmental discontinuities in childhood and adolescence. In K. Fischer, (Ed.), *Levels and transitions in children's development.* San Francisco: Jossey-Bass.

KEOGH, J. F. (1965). Motor performance in elementary school children. *Monographs.* Los Angeles: College of Education, University of California at Los Angeles.

KERKMAN, D., HUSTON, A., WRIGHT, J. C., & EAKINS, D. (1987). Children's programming, cable television and the free market. Paper presented at the meeting of the International Communication Association, Montreal.

KESSEL, N. & COPPEN, A. (1963). The prevalence of common menstrual symptoms. *Lancet, ii,* 61–64.

KESSEN, W. (1965). *The child.* New York: Basic Books.

KESSEN, W. & CAHAN, E. D. (1986). A century of psychology: From subject to object to agent. *American Scientist, 74* (11), 640–649.

KILBORN, P. T. (1990). For many women, one job isn't enough. *New York Times,* February 15, A1, A22.

KINNEY, T. R. & WARE, R. (1988). Advances in the management of sickle-cell disease. *Pediatric Consult, 7* (3), 1–6.

KINSBOURNE, M. & HISCOCK, M. (1983). Development of lateralization of the brain. In P. Mussen, (Ed.), *Handbook of child development.* Vol. 2, *Infancy and developmental psychobiology.* New York: Wiley.

KIRK S. & GALLAGHER, J. (1986). *Educating exceptional children.* Boston, MA: Houghton Mifflin.

KLAUS, J. H. & KENNEL, M. (1982). *Parent-infant bonding,* (2nd Ed.). St. Louis, MO: Mosby

KLAUS, M. H. & KENNELL, J. H. (1976). *Maternal-infant bonding.* St. Louis: Mosby.

KLERMAN, L. (1991). *Alive & well? A research and policy review of health programs for poor young children.* New York: National Center for Children in Poverty.

KLINMAN, D. G. & KOHL, R. (1984). *Fatherhood USA: Services and resources for and about fathers.* New York: Garland.

KLINNERT, M., CAMPOS, J., SORCE, J., EMDE, R., & SUEJDA, M. (1983a). Emotions as behavior regulators: Social referencing in infancy. In R. Plutchik & H. Kellerman, (Eds.), *Emotions in early development.* Vol. 2, *The emotions.* New York: Academic Press.

KLINNERT, M., EMDE, R., BUTTERFIELD, P., & CAMPOS, J. (1983b). Emotional communications from familiarized adults influences infants' behavior. Paper presented at the meeting of the Society for Research in Child Development, Boston.

KOCHANEK, T. T. (1988). Conceptualizing screening models for developmentally disabled and high-risk children and their families. *Zero to three, IX* (2), 16–20.

KOGAN, N. (1983). Stylistic variation in childhood and adolescence: Creativity, metaphor, and cognitive style. In P. H. Mussen, (Ed.), *Handbook of child psychology.* Vol. 3, J. H. Flavell & E. M. Markman, (Eds.), *Cognitive development.* New York: Wiley.

KOHLBERG, L. (1966). A cognitive developmental analysis of children's sex-role concepts and attitudes. In E. E. Maccoby, (Ed.), *The development of sex differences*. Stanford, CA: Stanford University Press.

KOHLBERG, L. (1969). Stage and sequence: The cognitive-developmental approach to socialization. In D. A. Goslin, (Ed.), *Handbook of socialization theory and research*. Chicago: Rand McNally.

KOHLBERG, L. (1976). Moral stages and moralization: The cognitive-developmental approach. In J. Lickona, (Ed.), *Moral development & behavior: Theory, research, & social issues*. NY: Holt, Rinehart & Winston.

KOHLBERG, L. (1978). Revisions in the theory and practice of moral development. In W. Damon, (Ed.), *New directions in child development: Moral development*. San Francisco: Jossey-Bass.

KOHLER, L. (1976). The student absentee. Paper presented at the annual convention of the American Association of School Administrators, Atlantic City, NJ, February 23.

KOHN, M. L. (1977). *Class and conformity: A study in values*, (2nd Ed.). Chicago: University of Chicago Press.

KOLATA, G. (1987). Tests of fetus rise sharply amid doubts. *New York Times*, Sept. 22, C1.

KOLATA, G. (1988). New treatments may aid women who have miscarriages. *New York Times*, Jan. 5, C5.

KOLATA, G. (1989). Understanding Down syndrome: A chromosome holds the key. *New York Times*, Dec. 5, C3.

KOLB, B. & WISHAW, I. (1985). *Fundamentals of human neuropsychology*, (2nd Ed.). New York: Freeman.

KONNER, M. (1977). Evolution in human behavior development. In P. H. Leiderman, S. Tulkin, & A. Rosenfeld, (Eds.), *Culture and infancy: Variations in human experience*. New York: Academic Press.

KOOP, C. (1984). *Report of the Surgeon General's workshop on breastfeeding and human lactation*. Washington, D.C.: Department of Health and Human Services.

KOPP, C. (1983). Risk factors in development. In P. H. Mussen (Ed.), *Handbook of child development*. Vol. 2, *Infancy and developmental psychology*. New York: Wiley.

KOPP, C. B. & KALER, S. R. (1989). Risk in infancy: Origins and complications. *American Psychologist, 49* (2), 224–230.

KOPP, C. B. & PARMELEE, A. H. (1979). Prenatal and perinatal influences on infant behavior. In J. D. Osofsky, (Ed.), *Handbook of infant development*. New York: Wiley.

KORCHIN, S. (1981, Feb. 16). Quoted in *Newsweek*, p. 97.

KORNER, A. F. (1971). Individual differences at birth: Implications for early experience and later development. *American Journal of Orthopsychiatry, 41*, 608–619.

KORNER, A. F. (1972). State as a variable, as obstacle and as mediator of stimulation in infant research. *Merrill-Palmer Quarterly, 18*, 77–94.

KORNER, A. F. (1990). Infant stimulation: Issues of theory and research. *Clinical Perinatology, 17*, 173–184.

KORNER, A. F., KRAEMER, H. C., HOFFNER, E., & COSPER, L. M. (1975). Effects of waterbed flotation on premature infants: A pilot study. *Pediatrics, 56* (3), 361–367.

KOTELCHUCK, M. & RICHMOND, J. B. (1982). Advocacy for child health: Past, present and future. In *Proceedings of the Conference on Better Health for Children: Action for the Eighties*, held at Harvard University School of Public Health, Cambridge, MA, April 17.

KOTELCHUCK, M., et al. (1981). *Final Report: 1980 Massachusetts Special Supplement Food Program for Women, Infants and Children Evaluation Project*. Submitted to Food and Nutrition Service, Department of Agriculture, Washington, D.C.

KOTELCHUCK, M., et al. (1984, Oct.). WIC participation and pregnancy outcomes: Massachusetts Statewide Evaluation Project. *American Journal of Public Health, 74*, 1084–1092.

KREUTZER, M., LEONARD, C., & FLAVELL, J. (1975). An interview study of children's knowledge about memory. *Monographs of the Society for Research in Child Development, 40* (1), (Serial No. 159).

KRISTOF, N. D. (1989). China rebuffs U.S. scrutiny of policy on family planning. *New York Times*, March 16, p. 1.

KRYGER, M. H., ROTH, T., & DEMENT, W. C. (1989). *Principles and practices of sleep medicine*. Harcourt Brace Jovanovich.

KUHNE, R. & BLAIR, C. (1978). Changing the work week. *Business Horizons, 21*, 2–4.

KUNTZLEMAN, C. T. (1983). *Feeling good*. Unpubl. report of a three-year project funded by the W. K. Kellogg Foundation. Spring Arbor, MI: Department of Health Services, Spring Arbor College

KYLE, J. E. (Ed.). (1987). *Children, families & cities: Programs that work at the local level*. Washington, D.C.: National League of Cities.

LaBARBERA, J. D., IZARD, C. E., VIETZE, P., & PARISI, S. A. (1976). Four and six-month-old infants' visual response to joy, anger, and neutral expressions. *Child Development, 47*, 535–538.

LABORATORY OF COMPARATIVE HUMAN COGNITION. (1983). Culture and cognitive development. In P. H. Mussen, (Ed.), *Handbook of child psychology*. Vol. 1, *History, theory and methods*. New York: Wiley.

LABOV, W. (1970). The logic of nonstandard English. In F. Williams, (Ed.), *Language and poverty*. Chicago: Markham.

LABOV, W. (1972). *Language in the inner city: Studies in the black English vernacular*. Philadelphia: University of Pennsylvania Press.

LaBUDA, M. C. & DeFRIES, J. C. (1986). Multiple regression analysis of twin data obtained from selected samples. *Journal of Genetic Epidemiology, 3* (6), 425–433.

LAMB, M. E. (1977). Father-infant and mother-infant interaction in the first year of life. *Child Development, 48*, 167–181.

LAMB, M. E. (1978a). Social interactions in infancy and the development of personality. In M. E. Lamb, (Ed.), *Social and personality development*. New York: Holt, Rinehart & Winston.

LAMB, M. E. (1978b). The father's role in the infant's social world. In J. H. Stevens, Jr. & M. Mathews, (Eds.), *Mother/child, father/child relationships*. Washington, D.C.: National Association for the Education of Young Children.

Lamb, M. E. (1978c). Interactions between eighteen-month-olds and their preschool age siblings. *Child Development, 49,* 51–59.

Lamb, M. E. (1981). The development of father-infant relationships. In M. E. Lamb, (Ed.), *The role of the father in child development,* (2nd Ed.). New York: Wiley.

Lamb, M. E. (1982). Early contact and maternal-infant bonding: One decade later. *Pediatrics, 70* (5), 763–768.

Lamb, M. E. (1984). Social and emotional development in infancy. In M. H. Bornstein & M. E. Lamb, (Eds.), *Developmental psychology: An advanced textbook.* Hillsdale, NJ: Erlbaum.

Lamb, M. E. & Elster, A. B. (Eds.). (1986). *Adolescent fatherhood.* Hillsdale, NJ: Erlbaum.

Lamb, M. E. & Sutton-Smith, B. (Eds.). (1982). *Sibling relationships: Their nature and significance across the lifespan.* Hillsdale, NJ: Erlbaum.

Lamb, M. E., & Urberg, K. A. (1978). The development of gender role and gender identity. In M. E. Lamb, (Ed.), *Social and personality development.* New York: Holt, Rinehart & Winston.

Lambert, N. M. & Hartsough, C. S. (1984). Contribution of predispositional factors to the diagnosis of hyperactivity. *American Journal of Orthopsychiatry, 54* (1), 97–109.

Lambert, W. E. (1987). The effects of bilingual and bicultural experiences on children's attitudes and perspectives. In P. Homer, M. Palij, & D. Aronson, (Eds.), *Childhood bilingualism: Aspects of linguistic, cognitive & social development,* pp. 197–221. Hillsdale, NJ: Erlbaum.

Lamb-Parker, F., Piotrkowski, C. S., & Peay, L. (1987). Head Start as a social support for mothers: The psychological benefits of involvement. *American Journal of Orthopsychiatry, 57* (2), 220–233.

Lampl, M. & Emde, R. (1983). Episodic growth spurts in infancy: A preliminary report on length, head circumference and behavior. In K. Fischer, (Ed.), *Levels and transitions in children's development.* San Francisco: Jossey-Bass.

Landau, E. (1983). *Why are they starving themselves? Understanding anorexia nervosa and bulimia.* New York: Julian Messner.

Lane, D. M. & Pearson, D. A. (1982). The development of selective attention. *Merrill-Palmer Quarterly, 28,* 317–337.

Laosa, L. (1981). Maternal behavior: Sociocultural diversity in modes of family interaction. In R. W. Henderson, (Ed.), *Parent-child interaction: Theory, research and prospects,* pp. 125–167. New York: Academic Press.

Laosa, L. M. & Siegel, I. E. (Eds.). (1982). *Families as learning environments for children.* New York: Plenum.

Largo, R. H. & Schinzel, A. (1985). Developmental and behavioral disturbances in 13 boys with fragile X syndrome. *European Journal of Pediatrics, 143,* 269–275.

Larrabee, E. (1960). Childhood in twentieth-century America. In E. Ginsberg, (Ed.), *The nation's children,* (Vol. 3). New York: Columbia University Press.

Larson, M. (1977). *Better skills for youth: Four proposals for federal policy.* Report to the National Institute of Education, Department of Health, Education & Welfare. Contract No. UEC-400-75-0078. Stanford Research Institute, Stanford.

Lauersen, N. & Stukan, E. (1983). *Premenstrual syndrome and you: What it is, how to recognize it, and how to overcome it.* New York: Simon & Schuster.

Lave, J. (1977). Tailor-made experiments. Evaluating the intellectual consequences of apprenticeship training. *Quarterly Newsletter of the Institute of Comparative Human Development, 1,* 1–3.

Lays, J. (1991). Educating Eddie. *State Legislatures, 17* (4), 20–22.

Lazar, I., Darlington, R., Murray, H., Royce, J., & Snipper, A. (1982). Lasting effects of early education: A report from the Consortium for Longitudinal Studies. *Monographs of the Society for Research in Child Development, 47* (213), Serial No. 195.

Leach, P. (1983). *Babyhood.* New York: Knopf.

Leboyer, F. (1975). *Birth without violence.* New York: Knopf.

Lecours, A. R. (1975). Myelogenetic correlates of the development of speech and language. In E. H. Lenneberg & E. Lenneberg, (Eds.), *Foundations of language development.* New York: Academic Press.

Lecours, A. R. (1982). Correlates of developmental behavior in brain maturation. In T. Bever, (Ed.), *Regressions in mental development.* Hillsdale, NJ: Erlbaum.

Lederberg, A., Chapin, S., Rosenblatt, V., & Vandell, D. (1986). Ethnic, gender and age preferences among deaf and hearing preschoolers. *Child Development, 57,* 375–386.

Lemna, W. K., Feldman, G. L., Kerem, B., Fernbach, S. D., Zekovich, E. P., O'Brien, W. E., Riordan, J. R., Collins, F. S., Tsui, L. C., & Beaudet, A. L. (1990). Mutation analysis for heterozygote detection and the prenatal diagnosis of cystic fibrosis. *New England Journal of Medicine, 322* (5), 291–296.

Lenke, R. R. & Levy, H. L. (1980). Maternal phenylketonuria and hyperphenylketonuria: An international survey of untreated and treated pregnancy. *New England Journal of Medicine, 303,* 1202–1208.

Lenke, R. R. & Levy, H. L. (1982). Maternal phenylketonuria—results of dietary therapy. *American Journal of Obstetrics and Gynecology, 142,* 548–553.

Lenneberg, E. (1967). *Biological foundations of language.* New York: Wiley.

Lepper, M. R. & Gurtner, J. (1989). Children and computers: Approaching the twenty-first century. *American Psychologist, 44* (2), 170–178.

Lerner, M. I., & Libby, W. J. (1976). *Heredity, evolution and society.* New York: Freeman.

Lerner, R. & Foch, T. (1987). *Biological-psychological interactions in early adolescence.* Hillsdale, NJ: Erlbaum.

Lerner, R. M. & Spanier, G. B. (1980). *Adolescent development: A life-span perspective.* New York: McGraw-Hill.

Lesser, G. S., Fifer, G., & Clark, D. H. (1965). Mental abilities of children from different social class and cultural groups.

Monographs of the Society for Research in Child Development, 30, (Serial No. 102).

LEVINSON, D. J. (1978). *The seasons of a man's life.* New York: Knopf.

LEVITAN, S. & CONWAY, E. (1990). *Families in flux: New approaches to meeting workforce challenges for child, elder, and health care in the 1990's.* Washington, D.C.: Bureau of National Affairs.

LEVITIN, T. E. (1979). Children of divorce: An introduction. *Journal of Social Issues, 35,* 4–9.

LEWIN, K. (1939). Field theory and experiment in social psychology: Concepts and methods. *American Journal of Sociology, 44,* 868–897.

LEWIS, D. O. & BALLA, D. A. (1976). *Delinquency and psychopathology.* New York: Grune & Stratton.

LEWIS, D. O., PINCUS, J., BARD, B., & RICHARDSON, E. (1987). Biopsychosocial characteristics of matched samples of delinquents and nondelinquents. *Journal of the American Academy of Child and Adolescent Psychiatry, 26,* 744–752.

LEWIS, M. (1974). State as an infant-environment interaction: An analysis of mother-infant interactions as a function of sex. *Merrill-Palmer Quarterly, 20,* 195–204.

LEWIS, M. (1984). Developmental principles and their implications for at-risk and handicapped infants. In M. J. Hanson, (Ed.), *Atypical infant development.* Baltimore: University Park Press.

LEWIS, M. (1987). Social development in infancy and early childhood. In J. D. Osofsky, (Ed.). *Handbook of infant development,* (2nd Ed.), pp. 419–555. New York: Wiley.

LEWIS, M. (1989). What do we mean when we say emotional development? In L. Cirrillo, B. Kaplan, & S. Wapner, (Eds.), *Emotions in ideal human development.* Hillsdale, NJ: Erlbaum.

LEWIS, M. & BROOKS, J. (1974). Self, other and fear: Infants' reactions to people. In M. Lewis & L. A. Rosenblum, (Eds.), *Origins of fear.* New York: Wiley.

LEWIS, M. & BROOKS-GUNN, J. (1979). *Social cognition and the acquisition of self.* New York: Plenum.

LEWIS, M. & FEIRING, C. (1981). Direct and indirect interactions in social relations. In L. Lipsitt, (Ed.), *Advances in infancy research* (Vol. 1). New York: Ablex.

LEWIS, M. & MICHALSON, L. (1982). The socialization of emotions. In T. Field & A. Fogel, (Eds.), *Emotions and early interaction.* Hillsdale, NJ: Erlbaum.

LEWIS, M. & MICHALSON, L. (1983). *Children's emotions and moods: Developmental theory and measurement.* New York: Plenum.

LEWIS, M., YOUNG, G., BROOKS, J., & MICHALSON, L. (1975). The beginning of friendship. In M. Lewis & L. A. Rosenblum, (Eds.), *Friendship and peer relations.* New York: Wiley.

LEWIS, T. L., MAURER, D., & KAY, D. (1978). Newborns' central vision: Whole or hole? *Journal of Experimental Psychology, 26,* 193–203.

LEWONTIN, R. C. (1982). *Human diversity.* San Francisco: Freeman.

LEWONTIN, R. C., ROSE, S., & KAMIN, L. (1984). *Not in our genes: Biology, ideology, and human nature.* New York: Pantheon.

LIEBERT, R. M., McCALL, R. B., & HANRATTY, M. A. (1971). Effects of sex-typed information on children's toy preferences. *Journal of Genetic Psychology, 119,* 133–136.

LIEDERMAN, P. H. (1983). Social ecology and child-birth: The newborn nursery as environmental stressor. In N. Garmezy & M. Rutter, (Eds.), *Stress, coping and development in children.* New York: McGraw-Hill.

LINDHOLM, K. J. (1989). Bilingual immersion education: Criteria for program development. In A. M. Padilla, H. H. Fairchild, & C. M. Valadez (Eds.), *Bilingual education,* pp. 75–86. Newbury Park, CA: Sage.

LIPS, H. M. (1988). *Sex and gender: An introduction.* Mt. View, CA: Mayfield.

LIPSITT, L. P. (1977). Taste in human neonates: Its effects on sucking and the heart rate. In J. M. Weiffenbach, (Ed.), *Taste and development: The genesis of sweet preference.* Washington, D.C.: Government Printing Office.

LIPSITT, L. P. (1986). Learning in infancy: Cognitive development in babies. *Journal of Pediatrics, 109* (1), 172–182.

LIPSITT, L. P. (1990a). Trophy children. *The Brown University Child Behavior and Development Letter.* Providence: Manissess Communications.

LIPSITT, L. P. (1990b). Learning and memory in infants. *Merrill-Palmer Quarterly, 36* (1), 53–66.

LIPSITT, L. P., ENGEN, T., & KAYE, H. (1963). Developmental changes in the olfactory threshold of the neonate. *Child Development, 34,* 371–376.

LIPTON, E. L., STEINSCHNEIDER, A., & RICHMOND, J. B. (1965). Swaddling, a child care practice: Historical, cultural, and experimental observations. *Pediatrics, 35* (3), 519–567.

LITWAK, E. & MEYER, H. J. (1974). *Schools, family, and neighborhood: The theory and practice of school-community relations.* New York: Columbia University Press.

LO, Y. M., PATEL, P., WAINSCOAT, J. S., SAMPIETRO, M., GILLMER, M. D., & FLEMING, K. A. (1989). Prenatal sex determination by DNA amplification from maternal peripheral blood. *Lancet, 2,* 1363–1365.

LOEB, R. C., HORST, L., & HORTON, P. J. (1980). Family interaction patterns associated with self-esteem in preadolescent boys and girls. *Merrill-Palmer Quarterly, 26,* 203–217.

LONG, L. & LONG, T. (1983). *The handbook for latchkey children and their parents.* New York: Arbor House.

LORD, C., SCHOPLER, E., & REVICKI, D. (1982). Sex differences in autism. *Journal of Autism and Developmental Disorders, 12,* 317–330.

LORD, C. G., KENTARO, U., & DARLEY, J. (1990). Developmental differences in decoding meanings of the appraisal actions of teachers. *Child Development, 61,* 191–200.

LORENZ, K. (1966). *On aggression.* New York: Harcourt Brace & World.

LORENZ, K. (1971). *Studies in animal and human behavior,* (Vol. II). Cambridge, MA: Harvard University Press.

LOTTER, V. (1978). Follow-up studies. In M. Rutter & E.

Schopler, (Eds.), *Autism: A reappraisal of concepts and treatment*. New York: Plenum.

LOUGEE, M. D., GRUENEICH, R., & HARTUP, W. W. (1977). Social interaction in same- and mixed-aged dyads of preschool children. *Child Development, 48,* 1353–1361.

LOUIS HARRIS ASSOCIATES (1989). *The Philip Morris, Inc. Family Survey II: Child care.* New York: Author.

LOUV, K. (1990). *Childhood's future.* Boston: Houghton Mifflin.

LOVE, H. D. & WALTHOD, J. E. (1977). Cerebral palsy. In *A handbook of medical, educational and psychological information for teachers of physically handicapped children.* Springfield, IL: Charles C Thomas.

LOWERY, G. H. (1978). *Growth and development of children,* (7th Ed.). Chicago: Year Book Medical Publishers.

LOZOFF, B. (1988). Behavioral alterations in iron deficiency. *Advances in Pediatrics, 35,* 331–360.

LOZOFF, B. (1989). Nutrition and behavior. *American Psychologist, 44* (2), 231–236.

LYONS, R., CONNELL, D., GRUNEBAUM, H., & BOTEIN, S. (1990). Infants at social risks: Maternal depression and family support services as mediators of infant development and security attachment. *Child Development, 61* (1), 85–98.

LYONS, R. D. (1983, July 18). Physical and mental disabilities doubled in twenty-five years. *New York Times,* A1, A10.

LYTTON, H. (1976). Do parents create or respond to differences in twins? *Developmental Psychology, 13* (5), 456–459.

MCANARNEY, E. & STEVENS-SIMON, C. (1990). Maternal psychological stress/depression and low birth weight. *American Journal of Diseases in Children, 144,* 789–792.

MCCALL, R. B. (1977). Childhood IQs as predictors of adult educational and occupational status. *Science, 197,* 482–493.

MCCALL, R., GREGORY, T., & MURRAY, J. P. (1984). Communicating developmental research results to the general public through television. *Developmental Psychology, 20,* 244–260.

MCCALL, R., LONNBORG, B., GREGORY, T., MURRAY, J. P., & LEAVITT, S. (1981). Communicating developmental research to the public: The Boys Town experience. *Newsletter of the Society for Research in Child Development,* Fall, 1–3.

MCCALL, R. B. (1980). *Infants: The new knowledge about the years from birth to three.* New York: Vintage.

MCCALL, R. B., APPLEBAUM, M. I., & HOGARTY, P. S. (1973). Developmental changes in mental performance. *Monographs of the Society for Research in Child Development, 38* (3), Serial No. 150.

MCCARLEY, R. W. (1989). The biology of dream sleep. In M. H. Kryger, T. Roth, & W. C. Dement (Eds.), *Principles and practices of sleep medicine.* San Diego: Harcourt Brace Jovanovich.

MCCARTHY, D. (1954). Language development in children. In L. Carmichael, (Ed.), *Manual of child psychology,* (2nd Ed.). New York: Wiley.

MCCARTNEY, K. (1984). Effects of quality day care environments on children's language development. *Developmental Psychology, 20* (2), 244–260.

MCCARTNEY, M., SCARR, S., PHILLIPS, D., GRAJEK, S., & SCHWARTZ, J. C. (1982). Environmental differences among day care centers and their effects on children's development. In E. Zigler & E. Gordon, (Eds.), *Day care: Scientific and social policy issues.* Boston: Auburn House.

MACCOBY, E. (1964). Effects of the mass media. In M. L. Hoffman & L. W. Hoffman, (Eds.), *Review of child development research,* (Vol. 1). New York: Russell Sage.

MACCOBY, E. (1980). *Social development: Psychological growth and the parent-child relationship.* New York: Harcourt Brace Jovanovich.

MACCOBY, E. (1984). Middle childhood in the context of the family. In W. A. Collins, (Ed.), *Development during middle childhood—The years from six to twelve.* Washington, D.C.: National Academy Press.

MACCOBY, E. E. & JACKLIN, C. N. (1990). Gender segregation in childhood. In H. Reese, (Ed.), *Advances in child development and behavior,* (Vol. 20). New York: Academic Press.

MACCOBY, E. E. & MARTIN, A. (1983). Socialization in the context of the family: Parent-child interaction. In P. H. Mussen, (Ed.), *Handbook of child psychology,* (4th Ed.). Vol. 4, E. M. Hetherington, (Ed.), *Socialization, personality and social behavior.* New York: Wiley.

MCDAVID, J. W. & HARARI, H. (1966). Stereotyping in names and popularity in grade school children. *Child Development, 37,* 453–459.

MACFARLANE, J. A. (1975). Olfaction in the development of social preferences in the human neonate. In M. A. Hofer, (Ed.), *Parent-infant interaction.* Amsterdam: Elsevier.

MCGHEE, P. E. (1974). Cognitive mastery and children's humor. *Psychological Bulletin, 81,* 721–730.

MCGHEE, P. E. (1976). Children's appreciation of humor—Test of cognitive congruency principle. *Child Development, 47* (2), 420–426.

MCGHEE, P. E. (1979). *Humor: Its origin and development.* New York: Freeman.

MCGILLICUDDY-DELISI, A. V. & SIGEL, I. (1982). Effects of the atypical child on the family. In L. A. Bond & J. M. Joffe, (Eds.), *Facilitating infant and early childhood development.* Hanover, NH: University Press of New England.

MCGRAW, M. B. (1940). Neural maturation as exemplified in achievement of bladder control. *Journal of Pediatrics, 16,* 580–589.

MCGUIRE, W. J. & MCGUIRE, C. V. (1986). Differences in conceptualizing self, versus conceptualizing other people in contrasting verb types used in natural speech. *Journal of Personality and Social Psychology, 51,* 1035–1043.

MCLANAHAN, S. (1988). The consequences of single parenthood for subsequent generations. *Focus, 2* (3), 16–21.

MCLOYD, V. C. (1989). Socialization and development in a changing economy. Effects of parental job and income loss on children. *American Psychologist, 44* (2), 293–302.

McLoyd, V. C. (1990). Minority children: Introduction to special issue. *Child Development, 61* (2), 263–266.

MacMillan, D. L. (1969). Motivational differences: Cultural-familial retardates vs. normal subjects on expectancy for failure. *American Journal of Mental Deficiency, 74,* 254–258.

MacMillan, D. L. (1982). *Mental retardation in school and society.* Boston, MA: Little, Brown.

MacMillan, D. L. & Keogh, B. K. (1971). Normal and retarded children's expectancy for failure. *Developmental Psychology, 4,* 343–348.

McNassor, D. (1975, April). The world of the preadolescent. *Childhood Education, 5,* 312–318.

Magnusson, D., Strattin, H., & Allen, V. L. (1985). Biological maturation and social development: A longitudinal study of some adjustment process from mid-adolescence to adulthood. *Journal of Youth and Adolescence, 14* (4), 267–283.

Malakoff, M. E. (1988). The effect of language of instruction on reasoning in bilingual children. *Applied Psycholinguistics, 9,* 17–38.

Malatessa, C. A. & Izard, C. E. (1984). The ontogenesis of human social signals: From biological imperative to symbol utilization. In N. A. Fox & R. J. Davidson, (Eds.), *The psychobiology of affective development,* pp. 161–206. Hillsdale, NJ: Erlbaum.

Malatesta, C. Z., Culver, C., Tesman, J., & Shepard, B. (1989). The development of emotional expression during the first two years of life. *Monographs of the Society for Research in Child Development, 54,* 1–2, Serial No. 219.

Malina, R. (1990). Physical growth and performance during the transitional years. In R. Montmayor, G. Adams, & T. Gullotta, (Eds.), *From childhood to adolescence: A transition period?* pp. 41–62. New York: Russell Sage.

Malina, R. & Bouchard, C. (1990). *Growth and physical activity.* Champaign, IL: Human Kinetics.

Malina, R., Bouchard, C., & Beunen, G. (1988). Human growth: Selected aspects of current research on well-nourished children. *Annual Review of Anthropology, 17,* 187–219.

Malina, R. M. (1982). Motor development in the early years. In S. G. Moore & C. R. Cooper, (Eds.), *The young child: Reviews of the research,* (Vol. 3). Washington, D.C.: National Association for the Education of Young Children.

Mandler, J. (1984). Representation and recall in infancy. In M. Moscovitch, (Ed.), *Infant memory.* New York: Plenum.

Mandler, J., Fivush, R., & Reznick, J. S. (1987). The development of contextual categories. *Cognitive Development, 2,* 339–354.

Marcia, J. E. (1966). Development and validation of ego identity status. *Journal of Personality and Social Psychology, 3* (5), 551–558.

Marcia, J. E. (1980). Identity in adolescence. In J. Adelson, (Ed.), *Handbook of adolescent psychology.* New York: Wiley.

Marcia, J. E. (1988). Common processes underlying ego identity, cognitive/normal development and individualization. In D. K. Lapsley & F. C. Power, (Eds.), *Self ego and liability.* New York: Springer-Verlag.

Marcus, D. E. & Overton, W. F. (1978). The development of cognitive gender constancy and sex-role preferences. *Child Development, 49,* 434–444.

Marcus, J., Maccoby, E., Jacklin, C., & Doering, C. (1985). Individual differences in mood: Their relation to gender and neonatal sex steroids. *Developmental Psychobiology, 18,* 327–340.

Mare, R. (1982). Socioeconomic effects on child mortality in the United States. *American Journal of Public Health, 72,* 539–547.

Margolick, D. (1990). Father is charged with crash after unbelted daughter dies. *New York Times,* Dec. 29, p. 1.

Margolin, L. & Farran, D. (1983, Fall). Consequences of unemployment. *The Networker, 4* (1), 1. (Available from the Bush Center in Child Development and Social Policy, Yale University, New Haven, CT).

Margolin, L. H. & Runyan, C. W. (1983). Accidental policy: An analysis of the problem of unintended injuries of children. *American Journal of Orthopsychiatry, 53* (4), 629–644.

Markman, E. (1986). Constraints children place on possible word meanings. Presented at R. Gelman, chair, constraints on learning and development of knowledge. Symposium held at the meeting of the Psychonomic Society, New Orleans.

Markman, E. (1989). *Categorization and naming in children: Problems of induction.* Cambridge, MA: MIT Press.

Markman, E. M. (1977). Realizing that you don't understand: A preliminary investigation. *Child Development, 48,* 986–992.

Marks, P. A. & Haller, D. L. (1977). Now I lay me down for keeps: A study of adolescent suicide attempts. *Journal of Clinical Psychology, 33,* 400–408.

Markus, H. J. & Nurius, P. S. (1984). Self-understanding and self-regulation in middle childhood. In A. W. Collins, (Ed.), *Development during middle childhood: The years from six to twelve.* Washington, D.C.: National Academy Press.

Marsiglio, W. (1986). Teenage fatherhood: High school accreditation and educational attainment. In B. Elster & M. Lamb, (Eds.), *Adolescent fatherhood.* Hillsdale, NJ: Erlbaum.

Martin, G. B. & Clark, R. D., III. (1982). Distress crying in neonates: Species and peer specificity. *Developmental Psychology, 18* (1), 3–9.

Martin, H. P. & Breezley, P. (1976). Personality of abused children. In H. P. Martin, (Ed.), *The abused child: A multi-disciplinary approach to developmental issues and treatment.* Cambridge, MA: Ballinger.

Martornao, S. (1977). A developmental analysis of performance on Piaget's formal operations tasks. *Developmental Psychology, 13,* 666–672.

Marvin, R. S., Greenberg, M., & Mossler, D. (1976). The

early development of conceptual perspective-taking: Distinguishing among multiple perspectives. *Child Development, 47,* 511–514.

MARX, J. L. (1978). Botulism in infants: A cause of sudden death? *Science, 201,* 799–801.

MASTERS, J. C. (1983). Models for training and research in child development and social policy. In G. Whitehurst, (Ed.), *Annals of child development,* (Vol. 1). Greenwich, CT: JAI Press.

MAXMEN, J. S. (1985). *The new psychiatry.* New York: Morrow.

MAYER, J. (1968). *Overweight: Causes, cost and control.* Englewood Cliffs, NJ: Prentice-Hall.

MEAD, M. (1928). *Coming of age in Samoa: A psychological study in primitive youth for Western civilization.* New York: Dell.

MEAD, M. (1961). *Coming of age in Samoa.* New York: Morrow.

MEADOW, K. P. (1975). The development of deaf children. In E. M. Hetherington, (Ed.), *Review of child development research,* (Vol. 5). Chicago: University of Chicago Press.

MEADOW, K. P. (1980). *Deafness and child development.* Berkeley: University of California Press.

MEDNICK, B. R., BAKER, R. L., & SUTTON-SMITH, B. (1979). Pregnancy and perinatal mortality. *Journal of Youth and Adolescence, 8* (3), 343–357.

MEDRICH, E., RUIZEN, J., RUBIN, V., & BUCKLEY, S. (1982). *The serious business of growing up: A study of children's lives outside of school.* Berkeley: University of California Press.

MEECE, J. L., PARSONS, J. E., KACZALA, C. H., GOFF, F. B., & FUTTERMAN, R. (1982). Sex differences in math achievement: Toward a model of academic choice. *Psychological Bulletin, 91,* 324–328.

MEEHAN, A. M. (1984). A meta-analysis of sex-differences in formal operational thought. *Child Development, 55,* 1110–1124.

MEHAN, H. (1979). What time is it, Denise? Asking known information questions in classroom discourse. *Theory into Practice, 18,* 285–294.

MEHLER, J., BERTONCINI, J., BARRIERE, M., & JASSIK-GERSCHENFELD, D. (1978). Infant recognition of mother's voice. *Perception, 7,* 491–497.

MEISELS, S. J. (1989). Can developmental screening tests identify children who are developmentally at risk? *Pediatrics, 83,* 578–585.

MELTZOFF, A. & MOORE, M. (1983). Newborn infants imitate adult facial gestures. *Child Development, 54,* 702–709.

MELTZOFF, A. N. & MOORE, M. K. (1977). Imitation of facial and manual gestures by human neonates. *Science, 198,* 75–78.

MENYUK, P. (1972). *Speech development.* Indianapolis: Bobbs-Merrill.

MERCER, J. (1972, Sept.). IQ: The lethal label. *Psychology Today,* 44–47.

MERCER, J. R. (1971). Sociocultural factors in labeling mental

retardates. *The Peabody Journal of Education, 48,* 188–203.

MEREDITH, A. V. (1969). Body size of contemporary groups of eight-year-old children studied in different parts of the world. *Monographs of the Society for Research in Child Development, 34,* Serial No. 1.

MEREDITH, A. V. (1971). Growth in body size: A compendium of findings on contemporary children living in different parts of the world. In H. W. Reese, (Ed.), *Advances in child development and behavior,* (Vol. 6). New York: Academic Press.

MEREDITH, A. V. (1976). Findings from Asia, Australia, Europe, and North America on secular change in mean height of children, youth and young adults. *American Journal of Physical Anthropology, 44,* 315–326.

MEREDITH, A. V. (1978). Research between 1960 and 1970 on the standing height of young children in different parts of the world. In H. W. Reese & L. P. Lipsitt, (Eds.), *Advances in child development and behavior,* (Vol. XII). New York: Academic Press.

MEREDITH, A. V. (1984). Body size of infants and children around the world in relation to socioeconomic status. In A. W. Reese, (Ed.), *Advances in child development and behavior,* (Vol. 18), pp. 81–145. Orlando: Academic Press.

MERRIMAN, W. E. & BOWMAN, L. L. (1989). The mutual exclusivity bias in children's word learning. *Monographs of the Society for Research in Child Development, 54* (3–4), Serial No. 220.

MEYERS, C. E., MACMILLAN, D. L, & YOSHIDA, R. K. (1980). Regular class placement of EMR students—From efficacy to mainstreaming: A review of issues and research. In J. Gottlieb, (Ed.), *Educating mentally retarded persons in the mainstream.* Baltimore: University Park Press.

MIKHAIL, M. (1979). *Images of Arab women.* Washington, D.C.: Three Continents Press.

MILLER, C. A., FINE, A., & ADAMS-TAYLOR, S. (1989). *Monitoring children's health: Key indicators* (2nd Ed.). Washington, D.C.: American Public Health Association.

MILLER, F. J. W., COURT, S. D. M., WALTON, W. S., & KNOW, E. G. (1960). *Growing up in Newcastle-Upon-Tyne: A continuing study of health and illness in young children within their families.* London: Oxford University Press.

MILLER, J. D. (1981). Epidemiology of drug use among adolescents. In D. J. Lettier & J. P. Ludford, (Eds.), *Drug abuse and the American adolescent.* Rockville, MD: National Institute on Drug Abuse.

MILLER, S. (1982). *Cognitive development: A Piagetian perspective, strategies and techniques of child study.* New York: Academic Press.

MILUNSKY, A. (1977). *Know your genes.* Boston: Houghton Mifflin.

MILUNSKY, A., JICK, H., JICK, S. S., BRUELL, C. L., MACLAUGHLIN, D. S., ROTHMAN, K. J., & WILLETT, W. (1989). Multivitamin/folic acid supplementation in early pregnancy reduces the prevalence of neural tube defects. *Journal of the Ameri-*

can *Medical Association, 262,* 2847–2852.

MINDEL, E. D. (1980). Auditory disorders. In H. J. Grossman & R. L. Stubblefield, (Eds.), *The physician and the mental health of the child.* Monroe, WI: American Medical Association.

MINNETT, A., VANDELL, D., & SANTROCK, J. (1983). The effects of sibling status on sibling interaction: Influence of birth order, age spacing, sex of child and sex of the sibling. *Child Development, 54,* 1064–1072.

MINTZ, S. & KELLOGG, S. (1988). *The domestic resolutions: A social history of American family.* New York: Free Press.

MINUCHIN, J., ROSMAN, B. L., & BAKER, L. (1978). *Psychosomatic families.* Cambridge, MA: Harvard University Press.

MINUCHIN, P. P. & SHAPIRO, E. K. (1983). The school as a context for social development. In P. H. Mussen, (Ed.), *Handbook of child psychology,* (Vol. 4). New York: Wiley.

MINUCHIN, S. & FISHMAN, H. C. (1981). *Family therapy techniques.* Cambridge, MA: Harvard University Press.

MIRINGOFF, M. L. (1989). *The index of social health 1989: Measuring the social well-being of the nation.* Tarrytown, NY: Fordham Institute for Innovation in Social Policy.

MISHARA, B. L. (1975). The extent of adolescent suicide. *Psychiatric Opinion, 12,* 32–37.

MISHELL. D. R., JR. & DAVAJAN, V., (Eds.). (1986). *Infertility, conception and reproductive economics.* Oxadell, NJ: Medical Economics Books.

MOELEY, B. & JEFFREY, W. E. (1974). The effect of organization training on children's free recall of category items. *Child Development, 45,* 1, 135–143.

MOEN, P. & DEMPSTER, M. C. (1987). Employed parents: Role strain, work time and preferences for working less. *Journal of Marriage and the Family, 49,* 579–590.

MOFFAT, M. (1989). *Coming of age in New Jersey.* New Brunswick, NJ: Rutgers University Press.

MOLLOY, P. J. (1987). Childhood injuries: The scope of the problem. *Public Health Currents, 27* (4), 1–28.

MOLNAR, G. E. (1979). Cerebral palsy: Prognosis and how to judge it. *Pediatric Annals, 8,* 596–605.

MONEY, J. (1975). Ablatiopenis: Normal male infant sex— reassigned as a girl. *Archives of Sexual Behavior, 4,* 65–72.

MONEY, J. & EHRHARDT, A. A. (1972). *Man and woman: Boy and girl: The differentiation and dimorphism of gender identity from conception to maturity.* Baltimore: Johns Hopkins University Press.

MONEY, J., HAMPSON, J. G., & HAMPSON, J. L. (1957). Imprinting and the establishment of gender role. *AMA Archives of Neurological Psychiatry, 77,* 333–336.

MONTEMAYOR, R. & EISEN, M. (1977). The development of self-conceptions from childhood to adolescence. *Developmental Psychology, 13,* 314–319.

MONTMAYOR, R., ADAMS, G., & GULLOTTA, T. (Eds.) (1990). *From childhood to adolescence: A transition period?* New York: Academic Press.

MOORE, K. (1982). *The developing human: clinically oriented embryology.* Philadelphia: Saunders.

MOORE, S. G. & COOPER, C. R. (1982). Personal and scientific sources of knowledge about children. In S. G. Moore & C. R. Cooper, (Eds.), *The young child: Review of research,* (Vol. 3). Washington, D.C.: National Association for the Education of Young Children.

MORGAN, G. (1987). *The national state of child care regulations, 1986.* Watertown, MA: Work/Family Directions.

MORGAN, G. & RICCIUTI, H. N. (1969). Infants' responses to strangers during the first year. In B. M. Foss, (Ed.), *Determinants of infant behavior,* (Vol. 4). New York: Wiley.

MOSS, H. S. (1967). Sex, age and state as determinants of mother-infant interaction. *Merrill-Palmer Quarterly, 13,* 19–36.

MOTOYAMA, E. K. (1966). Adverse effect of maternal hyperventilation on the foetus. *Lancet, 1,* 1966.

MUELLER, E. & BRENNER, J. (1977). The origins of social skills and interaction among playgroup toddlers. *Child Development, 48,* 854–861.

MUELLER, E. & LUCAS, F. A. (1975). A developmental analysis of peer interaction among toddlers. In M. Lewis & L. A. Rosenblum, (Eds.), *Friendship and peer relations.* New York: Wiley-Interscience.

MUELLER, E. & VANDELL, D. (1979). Infant-infant interaction. In J. D. Osofsky, (Ed.), *Handbook of infant development.* New York: Wiley.

MUENCHOW, S. & GILFILLAN, S. S. (1983). Social policy and the media. In E. Zigler, S. L. Kagan, & E. Klugman, (Eds.), *Children, families and government: Perspectives on American social policy.* New York: Cambridge University Press.

MULLER, E., HOLLIEN, H., & MURRAY, T. (1974). Perceptual responses to infant crying: Identification of cry types. *Journal of Child Language, 1,* 89–96.

MURPHY, D. P. (1947). *Congenital malformations.* Philadelphia: University of Pennsylvania Press.

MURPHY, L. B. & MORIARTY, A. E. (1976). *Vulnerability, coping and growth: From infancy to adolescence.* New Haven, CT: Yale University Press.

MURRAY, F. B. (1972). Acquisition of conservation through social interaction. *Developmental Psychology, 6,* 1–6.

MURRAY, J. P. (1980). *Television and youth: 25 years of research and controversy.* Boys Town, NE: Boys Town Center for the Study of Youth Development.

MURRAY, J. P. & LONNBORG, B. (1988). *Children and television: A primer for parents.* Boys Town, NE: Boys Town Press.

MUSSEN, P. H. & BOUTERLINE-YOUNG, H. (1964). Relationship between rate of physical maturing and personality among boys of Italian descent. *Vita Humana, 7,* 186–200.

MUSSEN, P. H., CONGER, J. J., & KAGAN, J. (1974). *Child development and personality.* New York: Harper & Row.

MUSTO, D. (1987). AIDS and panic: Enemies within. *Wall Street Journal,* April 28, p. 8.

NAEYE, R. L. (1982). Fetal hypoxia as cause of SIDS. In J. Tildon, R. Tyson, L. M. Roeder, & A. Steinschneider (Eds.), *Sudden infant death syndrome.* New York: Academic Press.

NAKAYAMA, D., PASEIKA, K., & GARDNER, M. (1990). How bicycle-related injuries change bicycling practices in children. *American Journal of Diseases in Children, 144,* 928–929.

NATIONAL ASSOCIATION OF CHILDREN'S HOSPITALS AND RELATED INSTITUTIONS. (1989). *Assuring children access to health care.* Alexandria, VA: Author.

NATIONAL ASSOCIATION FOR THE EDUCATION OF YOUNG CHILDREN. (1988). Testing children at a young age: Precautions. Position Statement. Washington, D.C.: Author.

NATIONAL ASSOCIATION OF ELEMENTARY SCHOOL PRINCIPALS. (1980). One-parent families and their children: The school's most significant minority. *Principal, 60,* 31–37.

NATIONAL ASSOCIATION OF FAMILY DAY CARE PROVIDERS. (1989). *Asking the right questions about information and referral.* Rochester, MN: Author.

NATIONAL ASSOCIATION OF STATE BOARDS OF EDUCATION. (1988). *Right from the start.* Alexandria, VA: Author.

NATIONAL BLACK CHILD DEVELOPMENT INSTITUTE. (1989). *Who will care when parents can't? A study of black children in foster care.* Washington D.C.: Author.

NATIONAL CENTER FOR CHILDREN IN POVERTY. (1990). *Five million children: A statistical profile of our poorest young children.* New York: Columbia University School of Public Health.

NATIONAL CENTER FOR CLINICAL INFANT PROGRAMS. (1988). *Who will mind the babies?* Washington, D.C.: Author.

NATIONAL CENTER FOR CLINICAL INFANT PROGRAMS. (1989). *Serving culturally diverse families of infants and toddlers with disabilities.* Washington, D.C.: Author.

NATIONAL CENTER FOR HEALTH STATISTICS. (1974). *U.S. Vital Statistics 1949–1973. Volume II: Mortality.* Washington, D.C.: Author.

NATIONAL CENTER FOR HEALTH STATISTICS. (1976). Uncompiled data on height and weight gains. Washington, D.C.: Author.

NATIONAL CENTER FOR HEALTH STATISTICS. (1987). *Monthly vital statistics report: Table 4. Infant deaths, and infant mortality rate and births and marriages, U.S. June 1984–June 1985.* Washington, D.C.: Author.

NATIONAL CENTER FOR HEALTH STATISTICS. (1990). Advance report: vital statistics of the U.S. Unpubl. data. Hyattsville, MD: Public Health Service.

NATIONAL CHILD CARE STAFFING STUDY. (1990). *Who cares for your child care teachers and the quality of care in America?* Final Report. Washington, D.C.: Child Care Employee Project.

NATIONAL CHILDREN AND YOUTH FITNESS STUDY. (1984). Washington, D.C.: Office for Disease Prevention and Health Promotion, Public Health Service.

NATIONAL COALITION OF ADVOCATES FOR STUDENTS. (1987). *A special analysis of 1984 elementary and secondary school civil rights survey data.* Boston: Author.

NATIONAL COALITION ON TELEVISION VIOLENCE (NCTV). (1984). *NCTV Music video report.* (Available from National Coalition on Television Violence. 1530 P Street NW, P.O. Box 12038, Washington, D.C. 20005.)

NATIONAL COMMISSION ON CHILDREN. (1990). *Opening the doors to America's children.* Washington, D.C.: Author.

NATIONAL COMMISSION ON EXCELLENCE IN EDUCATION. (1983). *A nation at risk.* Washington, D.C.: Government Printing Office.

NATIONAL COMMISSION ON SECONDARY SCHOOLING FOR HISPANICS. (1984). *Make something happen.* (Available from Hispanic Policy Development Project, 1001 Connecticut Avenue NW, Suite 310, Washington, D.C. 20036.)

NATIONAL COMMISSION ON YOUTH. (1980). *The transition of youth to adult: A bridge too long.* Boulder: Westview Press.

NATIONAL COMMISSION TO PREVENT INFANT MORTALITY. (1990). *Troubling trends: The health of America's next generation.* Washington, D.C.: Author.

NATIONAL COMMITTE FOR THE PREVENTION OF CHILD ABUSE (1989). *A future filled with healthy minds and bodies: A call to abolish corporal punishment in schools.* Prepared by A. Romano. Chicago: Author.

NATIONAL CONFERENCE OF STATE LEGISLATORS. (1989). *Childcare and early childhood education policy: A legislator's guide.* Denver: Author.

NATIONAL COUNCIL FOR EARLY CHILDHOOD PROFESSIONAL RECOGNITION. (1990). *Improving childcare through the Child Development Associate Program.* Washington, D.C.: Author.

NATIONAL EDUCATION ASSOCIATION. (1984–1985). *Estimates of school statistics.* Washington, D.C.: Author.

NATIONAL REPORT ON WORK AND FAMILY. (1988). *33 ways to ease work/family tensions: An employer's checklist.* Rockville, MD: Bureau of National Affairs.

NATIONAL RESEARCH COUNCIL. (1982). *Alternative dietary practices and nutritional abuses in pregnancy: Summary report.* Committee on Nutrition of the Mother and Preschool Child, Food and Nutrition Board, Commission on Life Sciences. Washington, D.C.: Author.

NATIONAL RESEARCH COUNCIL. (1990). *Who cares for America's children?* Washington, D.C.: Author.

NATIONAL SAFETY COUNCIL. (1991). *Injury fact book.* Chicago: Author.

NEEDLEMAN, A. L., SCHELL, A., BELLINGER, D., LEVITON, A., & ALFRED, E. N. (1990). Long-term effects of exposure to low levels of lead in childhood. An 11 year follow-up report. *New England Journal of Medicine, 322* (2), 83–88.

NELSON, K. (1973). Structure and strategy in learning to talk. *Monographs of the Society for Research in Child Development, 38* (1 & 2), Serial No. 149.

NELSON, K. (1981). Individual differences in language development: Implications for development and language. *Psychological Bulletin, 17,* 170–187.

NELSON, K. (1989). Remembering: A functional developmental perspective. In G. R. Goethels, C. M. Kelley, & B. R. Stephens (Eds.), *Memory: An interdisciplinary approach.* New York: Springer-Verlag.

NELSON, K. & ELLENBERG, J. (1979). Neonatal signs as predictors of cerebral palsy. *Pediatrics, 64,* 225–232.

NEWACECK, P., BURDETTI, P., & HALFON, N. (1986). Trends in

activity limiting chronic conditions among children. *American Journal of Public Health, 76* (2), 178–184.

NEWCOMB, M. D. & BENTLER, P. M. (1989). Substance use and abuse among children and teenagers. *American Psychologist, 44* (2), 242–248.

NEWMAN, H. H., FREEMAN, F. N., & HOLZINGER, K. J. (1937). *Twins: A study of heredity and the environment.* Chicago: University of Chicago Press.

NEWSON, J. & NEWSON, E. (1976). *Seven-year-olds in the home environment.* New York: Wiley.

NIELSON, A. C. (1988). *Nielson report on television.* Northbrook, IL: Author.

NIEMARK, E. D. (1975). Intellectual development during adolescence. In F. D. Horowitz, (Ed.), *Review of child development research,* (Vol. 4). Chicago: University of Chicago Press.

NISAN, M. & KOHLBERG, L. (1982). Universality & variation in moral judgment: A longitudinal and cross-section study in Turkey. *Child Development, 53,* 865–876.

NORTH, A. F. (1979). Health services in Head Start. In E. Zigler & J. Valentine, (Eds.), *Project Head Start: A legacy of the War on Poverty.* New York: Free Press.

NOVITSKI, E. (1977). *Human genetics.* New York: MacMillan.

NYITI, M. (1982). The validity of "cultural differences explanations" for cross-cultural variations in the rate of Piagetian cognitive development. In P. Wagner & H. Stevenson (Eds.), *Cultural perspectives in child development.* NY: W.H. Freeman.

OAKLAND, T. & PARMELEE, A. (1985). Mental measurement of minority group children. In B. Wolman, (Ed.), *Handbook of intelligence,* pp. 699–736. New York: Wiley.

O'BRIEN, T. & McMANUS, C. (1978). Drugs and the fetus: A consumer's guide by generic and brand name. *Birth and the Family Journal, 5,* 58–86.

OCKLEFORD, E. M., VINCE, M. A., LAYTON, C., & READ, M. R. (1988). Responses of neonates to parents and other voices. *Early Human Development, 18,* 27–36.

OFFER, D. (1969). *The psychological world of the teenager: A study of normal adolescent boys.* New York: Basic Books.

OFFER, D., MARHORN, R. C., & OSTROV, E. (1979). *The psychological world of the juvenile delinquent.* New York: Basic Books.

OFFER, D. & OFFER, J. (1975). *From teenage to young manhood.* New York: Basic Books.

OFFER, D., OSTROV, E., & HOWARD, K. I. (1981). *The adolescent: A psychological self-portrait.* New York: Basic Books.

OFFER, D., OSTROV, E., HOWARD, K. I., & ATKINSON, R. (1988). *The teenage world: Adolescents' self-image in ten countries.* New York: Plenum.

OFFICE OF TECHNOLOGY ASSESSMENT. (1986). *Children's mental health: Problems and services. A background paper.* Washington, D.C.: Government Printing Office.

OGBU, J. U. (1982). Socialization: A cultural ecological approach. In K. M. Borman, (Ed.), *The social life of children in a changing society.* Hillsdale, NJ: Erlbaum.

OLLER, J. W., WIENMAN, L. A., DOYLE, W. J., & ROSS, C. (1976). Infant babbling and speech. *Journal of Child Language, 3,* 1–11.

OLLER, K. (1980). The emergence of the sounds of speech in infancy. In G. Yeni-Komshian & C. Ferguson, (Eds.), *Child phonology,* (Vol. 1). New York: Academic Press.

OLSEN, D. R. (1978). The language of instruction. In S. Spiro, (Ed.), *Schooling and the acquisition of knowledge.* Hillsdale, NJ: Erlbaum.

OLWEUS, D., MATTSSON, A., SCHALLING, O., & LOW, A. (1988). Circulating testosterone levels and aggression in adolescent males: A causal analysis. *Psychosomatic Medicine, 50,* 261–272.

OPIE, I. & OPIE, P. (1959). *The lore and language of schoolchildren.* Oxford: Clarendon Press.

OPIE, I. & OPIE, P. (1969). *Children's games in the street and playground.* Oxford: Clarendon Press.

OPPEL, W. C., HARPER, P. A., & RIDER, R. V. (1968). The age of attaining bladder control. *Pediatrics, 42* (4), 614–626.

OPPORTUNITIES FOR SUCCESS. (1985, Aug.). *Cost effective programs for children.* Staff report of the Select Committee on Children, Youth and Families. Ninety-ninth Congress, 1st sess. Washington, D.C.: Government Printing Office.

ORESKES, M. (1990). Profiles of today's youth. *New York Times,* June 28, A1.

ORTHOPSYCHIATRY, 61, issue #4, pp. 567–575; Oct. 1991.

OSHERSON, D. N. (1975). *Logical abilities in children.* Vol. 3, *Reasoning in adolescence: Deductive inference.* Hillsdale, NJ: Erlbaum.

OSMAN, B. B. & BLINDER, H. (1986). *No one to play with: The social side of learning disabilities.* New York: Random House.

OSTREA, E. M. & CHAVEZ, C. J. (1979). Perinatal problems in maternal drug addiction: A study of 830 cases. *Journal of Pediatrics, 94,* 292–295.

PACKARD, V. (1972). *A nation of strangers.* New York: Simon & Schuster.

PACKARD, V. (1983). *Our endangered children: Growing up in a changing world.* Boston: Little, Brown.

PADILLA, A. M. (1989). Bilingual education: Issues and perspectives. In A. M. Padilla, H. H. Fairchild, & C. M. Valadez, (Eds.), *Bilingual education,* pp. 15–26. Newbury Park, CA: Sage.

PAGE, D. C., FISHER, E. M., McGILLIVRAY, B., & BROWN, L. G. (1990). Additional deletion in sex-determining region of human Y chromosome resolves paradox of X, + (Y;22) female. *Nature, 346,* 279–281.

PAIKOFF, R. L. & BROOKS-GUNN, J. (1990). Physiological processes: What role do they play during adolescence? In R. Montmayor, G. Adams, & T. Gullotta, (Eds.), *From childhood to adolescence: A transitional period?* pp. 63–84. New York: Russell Sage.

PALEY, V. G. (1984). *Boys and girls.* Chicago: University of Chicago Press.

PAPOUSEK, A. & PAPOUSEK, M. (1987). Intuitive parenting: A didactic counterpart to the infants' precocity in integrative capacities. In J. D. Osofsky, (Ed.), *Handbook of infant development,* (2nd Ed.), pp. 669–720. New York: Wiley.

PAPOUSEK, H. (1967). Conditioning during early postnatal development. In Y. Brackbill & G. G. Thompson, (Eds.), *Behavior in infancy and early childhood.* New York: Free Press.

PARKE, R. & PETERSON, J. L. (1981). Indicators of social change: Developments in the United States. *Accounting Organization and Society, 6,* 323–329.

PARKE, R. D. (1976). Some effects of punishment on children's behavior. In W. W. Hartup, (Ed.), *The young child: Reviews of the research,* (2nd Ed., Vol. 2). Washington, D.C.: National Association for the Education of Young Children.

PARKE, R. D. (1977). Punishment in children: Effects, side effects, and alternative strategies. In H. Horn & P. Robinson, (Eds.), *Psychological processes in early education.* New York: Academic Press.

PARKE, R. D. (1978). Children's home environments: Social and cognitive effects. In I. Altman & J. F. Wohlwill, (Eds.), *Children and the environment.* New York: Plenum.

PARKE, R. D. (1981). *Fathers.* Cambridge, MA: Harvard University Press.

PARKE, R. D. & COLLMER, C. W. (1975). Child abuse: An interdisciplinary analysis. In E. M. Hetherington, (Ed.), *Review of child development research,* (Vol. 5). Chicago: University of Chicago Press.

PARKE, R. D. & O'LEARY, S. (1976). Family interaction in the newborn period: Some findings, some observations and some unresolved issues. In K. Riegel & J. Meacham, (Eds.), *The developing individual in a changing world.* Vol. 2, *Social and environmental issues.* The Hague: Mouton.

PARKE, R., O'LEARY, S. E., & WEST, W. (1972). Mother-father-newborn interaction: Effects of maternal medication, labor, and sex of infant. *Proceedings of the American Psychological Association,* 85–96.

PARKE, R. & PETERSON, J. L. (1981). Indicators of social change: Developments in the U.S. *Accounting Organization and Society, 6,* 323–329.

PARKE, R. D. & SAWIN, D. B. (1976). The father's role in infancy: A re-evaluation. *Family Coordinator, 25,* 365–371.

PARKE, R. D. & SLABY, R. G. (1983). The development of aggression. In P. H. Mussen, (Ed.), *Handbook of child psychology,* (4th Ed.). Vol. 4, E. M. Hetherington, (Ed.), *Socialization, personality, and social development.* New York: Wiley.

PARTEN, M. B. (1932). Social participation among preschool children. *Journal of Abnormal and Social Psychology, 27,* 243–269.

PASLEY, K. & GECAS, V. (1984). Stresses and satisfactions of the parental role. *Personnel and Guidance Journal, 62,* 400–404.

PASTOR, D. C. (1981). The quality of mother-infant attachment and its relationship to toddler's initial sociability with peers. *Developmental Psychology, 17,* 326–335.

PATTERSON, F. G. (1980). Innovative uses of language by a gorilla: A case study. *Children's Language, 2,* 497–561.

PATTERSON, G. R. (1982). *Coercive family process.* Eugene, OR: Castalia Publishing.

PATTERSON, G. R., BANK, L., & STOOLMILLER, M. (1990). The preadolescent's contribution to disrupted family processes. In R. Montmayor, G. Adams, & T. Gullotta, (Eds.). *From childhood to adolescence: A transition period?* pp. 107–133. New York: Sage.

PATTERSON, G. R., DEBARSYSHE, B. & RAMSEY, E. (1989). A developmental perspective on anti-social behavior. *American Psychologist, 44* (2), 329–335.

PATTON R. G. & GARDNER, L. I. (1963). *Growth failure in maternal deprivation.* Springfield, IL: Charles C Thomas.

PAULS, D. L., SHAYWITZ, S. E., KRAMER, P. L., SHAYWITZ, B. A., & COHEN, D. J. (1983). Demonstration of vertical transmission of attention deficit disorders. *Annals of Neurology, 14,* 363–384.

PEARL, D., BOUTHILET, L., & LAZAR, S. J., (Eds.). (1982). Report by the Surgeon General on Television Violence. *Television and behavior: Ten years of scientific progress and implications for the eighties.* Washington, D.C.: Government Printing Office.

PEDERSEN , F. A., ANDERSON, B. J., & CAIN, R. L., JR. (1980). Parent-infant and husband-wife interactions observed at age 5 months. In F. A. Pedersen, (Ed.), *The father-infant relationship: Observational studies in the family setting.* New York: Praeger.

PEDIATRIC AIDS FOUNDATION. (1990). *Fact sheet on Pediatric AIDS.* Santa Monica: Author.

PEERY, J. C. & STERN, D. (1976). Gaze duration frequency distributions during mother-infant interactions. *Journal of Genetic Psychology, 129,* 45–55.

PELHAM, W. E. & BENDER, M. (1982). Peer relations in hyperactive children: Description and treatment. In K. Gadow & I. Slater, (Eds.), *Advances in learning and behavioral disabilities,* (Vol. 1), pp. 365–436. Greenwich, CT: JAI Press.

PERRONE, V. (1990). How did we get here? In C. Kamil, (Ed.), *Achievement testing in the early grades: The games grown-ups play,* pp. 1–14. Washington, D.C.: National Association for the Education of Young Children.

PETERSEN, A. C. & TAYLOR, B. (1980). The biological approach to adolescence: Biological change and psychological adaptation. In J. Adelson, (Ed.), *Handbook of adolescent psychology.* New York: Wiley.

PETITTI, D. B. & COLEMAN, C. (1990). Cocaine and the risk of low birthweight. *American Journal of Public Health, 80,* 1.

PETITTO, L. A. & MARENTETTE, P. F. (1991). Babbling in the manual mode: Evidence for the ontogeny of language. *Science, 251,* 1493–1496.

PHILIPS, I. (1980). The primary care physician and mental retardation. In H. Grossman & R. Stubblefield, (Eds.), *The physician and the mental health of the child.* Monroe, WI: American Medical Association.

PHILLIPS, D. (1988). Quality child care: Definitions. Paper presented at the A. L. Mailman Family Foundation, symposium on dimension of quality in programs for children, White Plains, NY, June 1.

PHILLIPS, D., (Ed.). (1989). *Quality in child care: What does the research tell us?* Washington, D.C.: National Association for the Education of Young Children.

PHILLIPS, D., MCCARTNEY, K., SCARR, S., & HOWES, C. (1987). Selective review of infant day care research: A cause for concern! *Zero to Three, 1* (3), 18–21.

PHILLIPS, S., KING, S., & DUBOIS, L. (1978). Spontaneous activities of female versus male newborns. *Child Development, 49* (3), 590–597.

PIAGET, J. (1932). *The moral judgment of the child.* New York: Harcourt Brace.

PIAGET, J. (1952). *The origins of intelligence in children.* New York: International Universities Press.

PIAGET, J. (1955). *The language and thought of the child.* New York: Meridian Books.

PIAGET, J. (1962). *Play, dreams, and imitation.* New York: Harcourt Brace & World.

PIAGET, J. (1965). *The child's conception of the world.* Totowa, NJ: Littlefield, Adams. (Original work published in 1929.)

PIAGET, J. (1970). Piaget's theory. In P. H. Mussen, (Ed.), *Carmichael's manual of child psychology.* New York: Wiley.

PIAGET, J. (1971). *The construction of reality in the child.* New York: Ballantine. (Original work published in 1954.)

PIAGET, J. (1972). Intellectual evolution from adolescence to adulthood. *Human Development, 15,* 1–12.

PIAGET, J. & INHELDER, B. (1963). *The child's conception of space.* F. J. Langdom & J. L. Lanzer (Trans.). London: Routledge & Kegan Paul.

PICK, A. D., CHRISTY, M. D., & FRANKEL, G. W. (1972). A developmental study of visual selective attention. *Journal of Experimental Child Psychology, 14,* 165–175.

PICK, A. D., FRANKEL, D. G., & HESS, V. (1975). Children's attention: The development of selectivity. In E. M. Hetherington, (Ed.), *Review of child development research,* (Vol. 5). Chicago: University of Chicago Press.

PILLING, D. & PRINGLE, M. (1978). *Controversial issues in child development.* New York: Schocken.

PINARD, A. (1981). *The concept of conservation.* Chicago: University of Chicago Press.

PINDERHUGHES, E. & ZIGLER, E. (1985). Cognitive and motivational determinants of children's humor responses. *Journal of Research in Personality, 19,* 185–196.

PINES, M. (1982, Feb.). Baby, you're incredible. *Psychology Today,* 48–53.

PIOTRKOWSKI, C. S. (1979). *Work and the family system: A naturalistic study of working class and lower-middle class families.* New York: Free Press.

PISTRANG, N. (1984, May). Women's work involvement and experience of new motherhood. *Journal of Marriage and the Family, 46* (2), 433–447.

PLECK, J. H. (1984). *Working wives and family well-being.* Beverly Hills, CA: Sage.

PLOMIN, R. (1986). *Development, genetics, and psychology.* Hillsdale, NJ: Erlbaum.

PLOMIN, R. (1988). The nature and nurture of cognitive abilities. In R. J. Sternberg, (Ed.), *Advances in psychology of human intelligence,* (Vol. 4.), pp. 1–33. Hillsdale, NJ: Erlbaum.

PLOMIN, R. (1989). Environment and genes: Determinants of behavior. *American Psychologist, 44* (2), 105–111.

PLOMIN, R. (1990). *Nature and nurture: An introduction to behavioral genetics.* Pacific Grove, CA: Brooks/Cole.

PLOMIN, R. & DANIELS, D. (1987). Why are children in the same family different from one another? *Behavioral and Brain Sciences, 10,* 1–16.

PLOMIN, R., DEFRIES, J. C., & FULKER, D. W. (1988). *Nature and nurture during infancy and early childhood.* New York: Cambridge University Press.

PLOMIN, R., DEFRIES, J. C., & MCCLEARN, G. E. (1989). *Behavioral genetics: A primer,* (2nd Ed.). New York: Freeman.

POEST, C. A., WILLIAMS, J. R., WITT, D., & ATWOOD, M. E. (1989). Physical activity patterns of preschool children. *Early Childhood Research Quarterly, 4,* 367–376.

POEST, C. A., WILLIAMS, J. R., WITT, D., & ATWOOD, M. E. (1990). Challenge me to move: Large muscle development in young children. *Young Children, 45* (5), 4–10.

POLLITT, E., GARZA, C., & LIEBEL, R. (1984). Nutrition and public policy. In H. W. Stevenson & A. E. Siegel, (Eds.), *Child development research and social policy,* (Vol. 1), pp. 421–470. Chicago: University of Chicago Press.

POLLITT, E. & GILMORE, M. (1977). Early mother-infant interaction and somatic growth. Paper presented at the Symposium on Disturbances of Early Parent-Infant Interaction: Symptoms and Origins, biennial meeting of the Society for Research in Child Development, New Orleans.

POLLITT, E. & THOMSON, C. (1977). Protein-calorie malnutrition and behavior: A view from psychology. In R. J. Wurtman, & J. J. Wurtman, (Eds.), *Nutrition and the brain,* (Vol. 2). New York: Raven.

POLLITT, K. (1990, March 26). Fetal rights: A new assault on feminism. *The Nation,* 409–414.

POWELL, D. (1978). The interpersonal relationship between parents and caregivers. *American Journal of Orthopsychiatry, 48,* 680–689.

POWERS, S., HAUSER, S. T., & KILMER, L. A. (1989). Adolescent mental health. *American Psychologist, 44* (2), 200–208.

PRECHTL, H. F. R. (1982). Assessment methods for the newborn infant: A critical evaluation. In P. Stratton, (Ed.), *Psychobiology of the human newborn.* New York: Wiley.

PRECHTL, H. F. R. & BEINTEMA, D. (1977). *The neurological examination of the full-term newborn infant,* (2nd Ed.), (Clinics in developmental medicine, No. 63). Philadelphia: Lippincott.

PRICE, R. H., COWEN, E. L., & LORION, R. P., (Eds.). (1988). *Fourteen ounces of prevention: A casebook for practition-*

ers. Washington, D.C.: American Psychological Association Press.

PRICE-WILLIAMS, D. R., GORDON, W., & RAMIREZ, M. (1969). Skill and conservation. *Developmental Psychology, 1,* 769.

PRITCHARD, J. & McDONALD, P. (1976). *Obstetrics.* New York: Appleton-Century-Crofts.

PROVENCE, S. (1989). Infants in institutions revisited. *Zero to Three, IX* (3), 1.

PRUETT, K. (1987). *The nurturing father.* New York: Warner Books.

PULASKI, M. A. S. (1980). *Understanding Piaget.* New York: Harper & Row.

PULOS, S. & LINN, M. C. (1981). Generality of the controlling variables scheme in early adolescence. *Journal of Early Adolescence, 1,* 26–37.

PURKEY, S. & SMITH, M. (1983). Effective schools: A review. *Elementary School Journal, 83* (4), 427–452.

PUTALLAZ, M. (1983). Predicting children's sociometric status from their behavior. *Child Development, 54,* 1417–1426.

QUAY, H. C. (1987). Intelligence. In. H. C. Quay, (Ed.), *Handbook of juvenile delinquency.* New York: Wiley.

QUIGLEY, M. E., SHEEHAN, K. L., WILKES, M. M., & YEN, S. S. (1979, March 15). Effects of maternal smoking on circulating catecholamine levels and fetal heart rates. *American Journal of Obstetrics and Gynecology, 133* (6), 685–690.

QUINN, P. O., SOSTEK, A. M., & DAVIT, M. K. (1978). The high-risk infant and his family. In P. R. Magrab, (Ed.), *Psychological management of pediatric problems.* Vol. 1, *Early life conditions and chronic diseases.* Baltimore: Baltimore University Press.

RAMEY, C., MacPHEE, D., & YEATS, K. O. (1982). Preventing developmental retardation: A general systems model. In L. Bond & J. Joffe, (Eds.), *Facilitating infant and early childhood development.* Hanover, NH: University Press of New England.

RAPHAEL, D. (1973). *The tender gift: Breastfeeding.* New York: Shocken Books.

RAPOPORT, R. & RAPOPORT, R. (1976). *Dual career families re-examined: New generations of work and family.* New York: Hoper Colophon.

RASCHKE, H. J. & RASCHKE, V. J. (1979, May). Family conflict and children's self-concepts: A comparison of intact and single-parent families. *Journal of Marriage and the Family,* 367–374.

REES, C. D. & WILBORN, B. L. (1983). Correlates of drug abuse in adolescents: A comparison of families of drug abusers with families of non-drug abusers. *Journal of Youth and Adolescence, 12* (1), 55–63.

REES, J. & MAHAN, M. (1988). Nutrition in adolescence. In S. R. Williams & B. S. Worthington-Roberts, (Eds.), *Nutrition throughout the life cycle.* St. Louis: Times Mirror/Mosby.

REESE, H. W. & LIPSITT, L. P., (Eds.). (1970). *Experimental child psychology.* New York: Academic Press.

REICHTER, R. J., & SCHOPLER, E., (Eds.). (1976). *Psychopathology and child development: Research and treatment.* New York: Plenum.

REIF, G. (1985). Fitness for youth. Unpublished report. Ann Arbor, MI: Department of Physical Education, University of Michigan.

REISCHAUER, R. (1987). *An analysis of the U.S. job market.* Washington, D.C.: Congressional Budget Office.

RESNICK, R. (1990). The elderly primagravida. *New England Journal of Medicine, 323,* 693.

REZNICK, J. S. (1989). Research on infant categorization. *Seminars in Perinatology, 13* (6), 458–466.

RHEINGOLD, H. (1973). Independent behavior of the human infant. In A. D. Pick, (Ed.), *Minnesota symposia on child psychology,* (Vol. 1). Minneapolis: University of Minnesota Press.

RHEINGOLD, H., GEWIRTZ, J. L., & ROSS, H. W. (1959). Social conditioning of vocalizations in the infant. *Journal of Comparative and Physiological Psychology, 52,* 68–73.

RHEINGOLD, H. L. & ECKERMAN, C. (1971). Departures from the mother. In H. R. Schaffer, (Ed.), *The origins of human social relations.* London: Academic Press.

RHEINGOLD, H. L. & ECKERMAN, C. O. (1973). Fear of the stranger: A critical examination. In H. W. Reese, (Ed.), *Advances in child development and behavior,* (Vol. 8). New York: Academic Press.

RHEINGOLD, H. L. & HAY, D. F. (1976). Sharing in the second year of life. *Child Development, 47,* 1148–1158.

RHINE, W. R., (Ed.). (1981). *Making schools more effective: New directions from Follow Through.* New York: Academic Press.

RICE, D. P. (1990). *The economic costs of alcohol, drug abuse and mental illness: 1985.* University of California at San Francisco: Institute for Health and Aging.

RICE, M. (1989). Children's language acquisition. *American Psychologist, 44* (2), 149–156.

RICE, M., HUSTON, A., TRUGLIO, R., & WRIGHT, J. (1987). Words from Sesame Street: Learning vocabulary while viewing. Unpubl. paper, University of Kansas, Lawrence.

RICE, R. D. (1977). Neurophysiological development in premature infants following stimulation. *Developmental Psychology, 13* (1), 69–76.

RICH, D. (1985). *The forgotten factor in school success: The family.* Washington, D.C.: Home and School Institute.

RICHARDSON, J. L., DWYER, K., McGUIGAN, K., HANSEN, W. B., DENT, C., JOHNSON, C., SUSSMAN, S. Y., BRANNON, B., & FLAY, B. (1989). Substance use among eighth-grade students who take care of themselves after school. *Pediatrics, 84* (3), 556–560.

RICHMOND, J. B. (1977). The needs of children. In J. H. Knowles, (Ed.), *Doing better and feeling worse: Health in the United States.* New York: Norton.

RICHMOND, J. B., STIPEK, D. J., & ZIGLER, E. (1979). A decade of Head Start. In E. Zigler & J. Valentine, (Eds.), *Project Head Start: A legacy of the War on Poverty.* New York: Free Press.

RICKS, M. (1982). The origins of individual differences in quality of attachment to the mother: Infant, maternal and familial variables. Paper presented at the International Conference on Infant Studies, Austin, March.

RIESEN, A. H. (1947). The development of visual perception in man and chimpanzee. *Science, 106,* 107–108.

RIESEN, A. H. (1958). Plasticity of behavior: Psychological aspects. In H. F. Harlow & C. N. Wolsey, (Eds.), *Biological and biochemical bases of behavior.* Madison: University of Wisconsin Press.

RIESER, J., YONAS, A., & WILKNER, K. (1976). Radical localization of odors by human newborns. *Child Development, 47,* 856–859.

RILEY, C. A. & TRABASSO, T. (1974). Comparatives, logical structures and encoding in a transitive inference task. *Journal of Experimental Child Psychology, 17,* 187–203.

RIVARA, F. P. (1983). Epidemiology of childhood injuries. *American Journal of Diseases of Children, 136,* 399–405.

RIVARA, F. P. (1985). Traumatic deaths of children in the United States: Currently available prevention strategies. *Pediatrics, 75,* 456–462.

RIVARA, F. P. & BARBER, M. (1985). Demographic analysis of childhood pedestrian injuries. *Pediatrics, 76,* 375–381.

RIVARA, F. P., BERGMAN, A. B., & DRAKE, A. C. (1989). Parental attitudes and practices toward children as pedestrians. *Pediatrics, 84,* 1017–1021.

RIVARA, F. P., MAIER, R. V., MUELLER, B. A., LUNA, G. A., DICKER, B. G., HERMAN, C. M., KENAGEY, J. W., COPASS, M. K., & CARRICO, C. J. (1989). Evaluation of potentially preventable deaths among pedestrian and bicyclist fatalities. *Journal of the American Medical Association, 261,* 566–570.

ROBERTS, D. F. (1969). Race, genetics and growth. *Journal of Biosocial Science, 1,* 43–67.

ROBERTSON, A. (1982). Day care and children's responsiveness to adults. In E. Zigler & E. Gordon, (Eds.), *Day care: Scientific and social policy issues.* Boston: Auburn House.

ROCHE, A. F. (1976). Growth after puberty. In E. Fuchs, (Ed.), *Youth in a changing world. Cross-cultural perspective on adolescence.* The Hague: Mouton.

ROCHE, A. F. (1979). Secular trends in human growth, maturation, and development. *Monographs of the Society for Research in Child Development, 44,* 3–4.

ROCHE, A. F., FRENCH, N. Y., & DAVILLA, G. H. (1971). Areolar size during pubescence. *Human Biology, 43,* 210–223.

RODMAN, H. & COLE, C. (1987). Latchkey children: A review of policy and resources. *Family Relations, 36,* 101–105.

RODMAN, H., PRATTO, D. J., & NELSON, R. S. (1985). Child care arrangements and children's functioning: A comparison of self-care and adult-care children. *Developmental Psychology, 21,* 413–418.

RODRIGUE, J. R., MORGAN, S. B., & GEFFKEN, G. (1990). Families of autistic children: Psychological functioning of mothers. *Journal of Clinical Child Psychology, 19* (4), 371–379.

ROESKE, N. C. A. (1980). The visually handicapped child. In J. H. Grossman & R. L. Stubblefield, (Eds.), *The physician and the mental health of the child.* Monroe, WI: American Medical Association.

ROFES, E., (Ed.). (1980). *The kids' book of divorce: By, for, and about kids.* New York: Vintage.

ROFFWARG, H. P., MUZIO, J. N., & DEMENT, W. C. (1966). Ontogenetic development of the human sleep-dream cycle. *Science, 152,* 604–619.

ROGOFF, B., GAUVAIN, M., & ELLIS, S. (1984). Development viewed in its cultural context. In M. Bornstein & M. Lamb, (Eds.), *Developmental psychology: An advanced textbook.* Hillsdale, NJ: Erlbaum.

ROGOFF, B. & MORELLI, G. (1989). Perspectives on children's development from cultural psychology. *American Psychologist, 44* (2), 343–348.

ROGUS, J. F. (1983). Education as a response to developmental needs: Preventing truancy and school dropout. In L. E. Arnold, (Ed.), *Preventing adolescent alienation.* Lexington, MA: Lexington Books.

ROHN, R. D., SARLES, R. M., KENNY, T. J., REYNOLDS, B. J., & HEALD, F. P. (1977). Adolescents who attempt suicide. *Journal of Pediatrics, 90,* 636–638.

ROHNER, R. (1975). Parental acceptance-rejection and personality: A universalistic approach to behavioral science. In R. Brislin et al., (Eds.), *Cross-cultural perspective on learning.* New York: Halsted Press.

ROLLINS, N. & PIAZZA, E. (1978). Diagnosis of anorexia nervosa. *Journal of Child Psychiatry, 17,* 126–137.

ROMAINE, S. (1990). *Bilingualism.* Oxford: Basil Blackwell.

ROSCH, E. (1975). Cognitive representations of semantic categories. *Journal of Experimental Psychology, 104,* 192–233.

ROSCH, E., MERVIS, C., GRAY, W. D., JOHNSON, D., & BOYES-BRAEM, P. (1976). Basic objects in natural categories. *Cognitive Psychology, 8,* 382–439.

ROSE, R. M., GORDON, T. P., & BERNSTEIN, I. S. (1972). Plasma testosterone levels in the male rhesus: Influences of sexual and social stimuli. *Science, 178,* 643–645.

ROSE, T. L. (1984). Current uses of corporal punishment in American public schools. *Journal of Educational Psychology, 76* (3), 427–441.

ROSEN, B. C. & ANESHENSEL, C. S. (1978). Sex differences in the educational-occupational expectation process. *Social Forces, 57,* 164–186.

ROSENBERG, M. (1965). *Society and the adolescent self-image.* Princeton, NJ: Princeton University Press.

ROSENBERG, M. (1975). The dissonant context of the adolescent self-concept. In S. E. Dragastin & G. H. Elder, (Eds.), *Adolescence in the life cycle.* Washington, D.C.: Hemisphere.

ROSENBERG, M. (1986). Self concept from middle childhood through adolescence. In J. Suls & A. G. Greenwald, (Eds.), *Psychological perspective on the self.* Hillsdale, NJ: Erlbaum.

ROSENTHAL, E. (1990). When a pregnant woman drinks. *New York Times Magazine,* February 4, p. 30.

ROSENTHAL, R. & JACOBSON, L. (1966). Teachers' expectancies: Determinants of pupils' IQ gains. *Psychological Reports, 19,* 115–118.

ROSENTHAL, R. & JACOBSON, L. (1968). *Pygmalion in the classroom.* New York: Holt, Rinehart & Winston.

ROSETT, H. L. & WEINER, L. (1985). *Alcohol and the fetus: A clinical perspective.* New York: Oxford University Press.

ROSS, D. M. & ROSS, S. A. (1982). *Hyperactivity: Research, theory and action,* (2nd Ed.). New York: Wiley.

ROSSI, A. (1977). Social trends in women's lives. In *Changing roles of women in industrial societies.* New York: Rockefeller Foundation Working Papers.

ROUSSEAU, J. J. (1911, originally published 1762). *Emile.* London: Dent.

ROVEE-COLLIER, C. (1987). Learning and memory in infancy. In J. D. Osofsky (Ed.), *Handbook of infant development,* pp. 98–148. New York: Wiley.

ROVEE-COLLIER, C. & FAGEN, J. (1981). The retrieval of memory in early infancy. In L. P. Lipsitt, (Ed.), *Advances in infancy research,* (Vol. 1), pp. 225–254. Norwood, NJ: Ablex.

ROVEE-COLLIER, C. K., SULLIVAN, M. W., ENRIGHT, M., LUCAS, D. & FAGAN, J. W. (1980). Reactivation of infant memory. *Science, 208,* 1159–1161.

RUBIN, J. Z., PROVENZA, F. J., & LURIA, Z. (1974). The eye of the beholder: Parents' views on sex of newborns. *American Journal of Orthopsychiatry, 44,* 512–519.

RUBIN, K. H., & PEPLER, D. J. (1980). The relationship of child's play to social-cognitive growth and development. In H. Foot, A. Chapman, & J. Smith, (Eds.), *Friendship and childhood relationships.* New York: Wiley.

RUBIN, K. H., WATSON, K. S., & JAMBOR, F. (1978). Free-play behaviors in preschool and kindergarten children. *Child Development, 49,* 534–536.

RUBIN, N. (1984). *The mother mirror: How a generation of women is changing motherhood in America.* New York: Putnam.

RUBIN, Z. (1980). *Children's friendships.* Cambridge, MA: Harvard University Press.

RUKE-DRAVINA, V. (1977). Modifications of speech addressed to young children in Latvian. In C. E. Snow & C. A. Ferguson, (Eds.), *Talking to children.* Cambridge, UK: Cambridge University Press.

RUOPP, R., TRAVERS, J., GLANTZ, F., & COELEN, C. (1979). *Children at the center.* Cambridge, MA: Abt Associates.

RUST, V. D. (1988). Education for young adolescents: The case of Europe and East Asia. Paper commissioned by the Task Force on Education of Young Adolescents, Carnegie Council on Adolescent Development. New York: Carnegie Corporation.

RUTTER, M. (1971). *Infantile autism: Concepts, characteristics, and treatment.* Edinburgh: Whitefriars Press.

RUTTER, M. (1979a). Maternal deprivation, 1972–1978: New findings, new concepts, new approaches. *Child Development, 50,* 283–305.

RUTTER, M. (1979b). Protective factors in children's responses to stress and disadvantages. In M. W. Kent & J. E. Rolf, (Eds.), *Primary prevention of psychopathology.* Vol. 3, *Promoting social competence and coping in children.* Hanover, NH: University Press of New England.

RUTTER, M. (1980). *Changing youth in a changing society.* Cambridge, MA: Harvard University Press.

RUTTER, M. (1983). School effects on pupil progress: Research findings and policy implications. *Child Development, 54,* 1–29.

RUTTER, M., MAUGHAN, B., MORTIMORE, J., & OUSTON, J. with A. SMITH (1979). *Fifteen thousand hours: Secondary schools and their effects on children.* Cambridge, MA: Harvard University Press.

RYAN, K., & APPLEGATE, J. (1976). The missed middle. *Ohio State University College of Education, Occasional Publications, 5,* 1.

RYDER, N. (1978). A model of fertility by planning status. *Demography, 15,* 433–458.

SACHS, J. (1977). The adaptive significance of linguistic input to prelinguistic infants. In C. E. Snow & C. A. Ferguson, (Eds.), *Talking to children.* Cambridge, UK: Cambridge University Press.

SACO-POLLITT, C., POLLITT, E., & GREENFIELD, D. (1985). The cumulative deficit hypothesis in light of cross-cultural evidence. *International Journal of Behavioral Development, 8* (1), 75–97.

SAGI, A., LAMB, M., LEWKOWICZ, K. S., SHOHAM, R., DVIR, R., & ESTES, D. (1985). Security of infant-mother, infant-father and metapelet attachments among kibbutz-reared Israeli children. In I. Bretherton & E. Waters, (Eds.), Growing points in attachment theory and research. *Monographs of the Society for Research in Child Development, 50* (1–2), Serial No. 209.

ST. JAMES-ROBERTS, I. (1989). Annotation: Persistent crying in infancy. *Journal of Child Psychiatry and Psychology, 30,* 189–195.

SALAPATEK, P. (1969). The visual investigation of geometric pattern by the one- and two-month-old infant. Paper presented at the Convention of the American Association for the Advancement of Science, Boston, December.

SALAPATEK, P. (1975). Pattern perception in early infancy. In L. B. Cohen & P. Salapatek, (Eds.), *Basic visual processes.* Vol. 1, *Infant perception: From sensation to cognition.* New York: Academic Press.

SALAPATEK, P. & KESSEN, W. (1966). Visual scanning of triangles by the human newborn. *Journal of Experimental Child Psychology, 3,* 155–167.

SALEND, S. J. (1984). Factors contributing to the development of successful mainstreaming programs. *Exceptional Children, 50* (5), 409–416.

SALKIND, N. J. (1983). The effectiveness of early intervention. In E. M. Goetz & K. E. Allen, (Eds.), *Early childhood education: Special environmental, policy, and legal considerations.* Gaithersburg, MD: Aspen Systems Corporation.

SAMEROFF, A. J. (1968). The components of sucking in the human newborn. *Journal of Experimental Child Psychology, 6,* 607–623.

SAMEROFF, A. J. (1975). Early influences on development: Fact or fancy? *Merrill-Palmer Quarterly, 21,* 275–301.

SAMEROFF, A. J. & CAVANAUGH, P. J. (1979). Learning in infancy: A developmental perspective. In J. Osofsky, (Ed.), *Handbook of infant development.* New York: Wiley.

SAMEROFF, A. J. & CHANDLER, M. J. (1975). Reproductive risk and the continuum of caretaking casualty. In F. D. Horowitz, (Ed.), *Review of child development research.* Chicago: University of Chicago Press.

SAMEROFF, A. J., SEIFER, R., ZAX, M. et al. (1987). Early indicators of developmental risk: The Rochester Longitudinal Study. *Schizophrenia Bulletin, 13,* 383–394.

SANTROCK, J. W., WARSHAK, R. A., & ELLIOTT, G. L. (1982). Social development and parent-child interaction in father custody and stepmother families. In M. Lamb, (Ed.), *Nontraditional families: Parenting and child development.* Hillsdale, NJ: Erlbaum.

SARASON, S. B. (1983). Public Law 94-142 and the formation of educational policy. In E. Zigler, S. L. Kagan, & E. Klugman, (Eds.), *Children, families, and government: Perspectives on American social policy.* New York: Cambridge University Press.

SCARDAMALIA, M. (1977). Information processing capacity and the problem of horizontal decalage: A demonstration using combinational reasoning tasks. *Child Development, 48,* 28–37.

SCARPITTI, F. R. & DATESMAN, S. K. (1980). *Drugs and the youth culture.* Beverly Hills, CA: Sage.

SCARR, S. (1968). Environmental bias in twin studies. *Eugenics Quarterly, 15,* 34–40.

SCARR, S. (1984). *Mother care/other care.* New York: Basic Books.

SCARR, S. & McCARTNEY, K. (1983). How people make their own environments. A theory of genotype-environment effects. *Child Development, 54,* 424–535.

SCARR, S. & WEINBERG, R. A. (1976). IQ test performance of black children adopted by white families. *American Psychologist, 31,* 726–791.

SCARR, S. & WEINBERG, R. A. (1977). Intellectual similarities within families of both adopted and biological children. *Intelligence, 3,* 31–39.

SCARR-SALAPATEK, S. (1975). Genetics and the development of intelligence. In F. Horowitz, (Ed.), *Review of child development research,* (Vol. 4). Chicago: University of Chicago Press.

SCARR-SALAPATEK, S. & WILLIAMS, M. L. (1973). The effects of early stimulation on low birth weight infants. *Child Development, 44,* 94–101.

SCHAEFER, E. S. (1959). A circumplex model of maternal behavior. *Journal of Abnormal and Social Psychology, 59,* 226–235.

SCHAFFER, H. R. (1977). *Mothering.* Cambridge, MA: Harvard University Press.

SCHAFFER, H. R., COLLINS, G. M., & PARSONS, G. (1977). Vocal interchange and visual regard in verbal and preverbal children. In H. R. Schaffer, (Ed.), *Studies on mother-infant interactions.* New York: Academic Press.

SCHAFFER, H. R. & EMERSON, P. E. (1964). Patterns of response to physical contact in early human development. *Journal of Child Psychology and Psychiatry, 5,* 1–13.

SCHEIN, V. E. (1990). The work-family interface: Challenging corporate convenience. Paper presented at the 98th Annual Convention of the American Psychological Association, Boston, August.

SCHLESINGER, H. S. & MEADOW, K. P. (1972). *Sound and sign: Childhood deafness and mental health.* Berkeley: University of California Press.

SCHMIDT, W. E. (1987). Sales of drugs are soaring for the treatment of hyperactivity. *New York Times,* May 5, C3.

SCHMUCK, R. & SCHMUCK, P. (1975). *Group processes in the classroom,* (2nd Ed.). Dubuque, IA: William C. Brown.

SCHNEIDER, K. (1990). Birth defects and pollution: Issue raised in Texas town. *New York Times,* April 15, p. 14.

SCHOFIELD, J. W. (1980). Complementary and conflicting identities: Images and interaction in an interracial school. In S. R. Asher & J. M. Gottman, (Eds.), *The development of children's friendships.* New York: Cambridge University Press.

SCHOOL-AGE CHILD CARE PROJECT (1984). *SACC Newsletter, 2* (2). Wellesley College, Center for Research on Women, Wellesley, MA 02181.

SCHOPLER, E. & DALLDORF, J. (1980). Autism: Definition, diagnosis, and management. *Hospital Practice, 15,* 64–73.

SCHOPLER, E. & MESIBOV, G. B. (1984). Professional attitudes toward parents. A forty-year progress report. In E. Schopler & G. B. Mesibov, (Eds.), *The effects of autism on the family.* New York: Plenum.

SCHORR, L. B. & SCHORR, D. (1988). *Within our reach: Breaking the cycle of disadvantage.* New York: Doubleday.

SCHOWALTER, J. E. & ANYAN, W. R., JR. (1979). *The family handbook of adolescence.* New York: Knopf.

SCHUMAN, M. (1991). Psychological help for children in urban combat. *New York Times,* February 21, B9.

SCHWARTZ, J. C. (1972). Effects of peer familiarity on the behavior of preschoolers in a novel situation. *Journal of Personality and Social Psychology, 24,* 276–284.

SCHWARTZ, S. (1984). A study of drug discipline policies in secondary schools. *Adolescence, 19* (4), 323–331.

SCRIBNER, S. (1976). Situating the experiment in cross-cultural research. In K. F. Riegel & J. A. Meacham, (Eds.). *The developing individual in a changing world.* Chicago: Aldine.

SCRIBNER, S. (1977). Modes of thinking and ways of speaking: Culture and logic reconsidered. In P. N. Johnson-Laird & P. C. Wason, (Eds.), *Thinking.* Cambridge, UK: Cambridge University Press.

SCRIMSHAW, N. S., TAYLOR, C. E., & GORDON, J. E. (1968). Interaction of nutrition and infection. *W. H. O. Monograph Series,* No. 57.

SEARLE, L. V. (1949). The organization of hereditary maze brightness and maze dullness. *Genetic Psychology Monographs, 39,* 279–325.

SEARS, R. R., MACCOBY, E. E., LEVIN, H. (1957). *Patterns of childrearing.* New York: Harper & Row.

SEBALD, H. (1981). Adolescents, concept of popularity and unpopularity. Comparing 1960 with 1976. *Adolescence, 16,* 187–193.

SEEFELDT, V. (1984). Physical fitness in preschool and elementary school-age children. *Journal of Physical Education, Recreation and Dance, 55* (9), 33–40.

SELECT PANEL FOR THE PROMOTION OF CHILD HEALTH (1981).

Better health for our children: A national strategy. Washington, D.C.: Government Printing Office.

SELF, P. A. & HOROWITZ, F. D. (1979). The behavioral assessment of the newborn: An overview. In J. D. Osofsky, (Ed.), *Handbook of infant development*. New York: Wiley.

SELIGMAN, M. E. P. (1975). *Helplessness: On depression, development, and death*. San Francisco: Freeman.

SELMAN, R. & SELMAN, A. (1979, Oct.). Children's ideas about friendship: A new theory. *Psychology Today, 13,* 70–80, 114.

SELMAN, R. L. (1976). Social cognitive understanding: A guide to educational and clinical practice. In T. Lickona, (Ed.), *Theory, research, and social issues*. New York: Holt, Rinehart & Winston.

SELMAN, R. L. (1980). *The growth of interpersonal understanding*. New York: Academic Press.

SELMAN, R. L. (1981). The child as a friendship philosopher. In S. R. Asher & J. M. Gottman, (Eds.), *The development of children's friendships*. Cambridge, UK: Cambridge University Press.

SELMAN, R. L. & JAQUETTE, D. (1977). Stability and oscillation in interpersonal awareness: A clinical-developmental analysis. In C. B. Keasey, (Ed.), *The Nebraska symposium on motivation,* (Vol. 25). Lincoln: University of Nebraska Press.

SELYE, H. (1983). The stress concept: Past, present, and future. In C. L. Cooper, (Ed.), *Stress research*. New York: Wiley.

SHAFFER, D., VIELAND, V., GARLAND, A., ROJAS, M., UNDERWOOD, M., & BUSNER, C. (1990). Adolescent suicide attempters. Response to suicide-prevention programs. *Journal of the American Medical Association, 264,* 3151–3155.

SHAPIRO, S. A. (1981). *Contemporary theories of schizophrenia: A review and synthesis*. New York: McGraw-Hill.

SHARP, D., COLE, M., & LAVE, C. (1979). Education and cognitive development: The evidence from experimental research. *Monographs of the Society for Research in Child Development, 44* (1–2), Serial No. 178.

SHATZ, M. (1983). Communication. In P. H. Mussen, (Ed.), *Handbook of child psychology.* Vol. 3, *Cognitive development*. New York: Wiley.

SHATZ, M. & GELMAN, R. (1973). The development of communication skills: Modifications in the speech of young children as a function of the listener. *Monographs of the Society for Research in Child Development, 38* (5), Serial No. 152.

SHAYWITZ, S. E., BENNETT, A., SHAYWITZ, B. A., FLETCHER, J. M., & ESCOBAR, M. D. (1990). Prevalence of reading disability in boys and girls: Results of the Connecticut Longitudinal Study. *Journal of the American Medical Association, 264,* 998–1002.

SHAYWITZ, S. E. & SHAYWITZ, B. A. (1984). Evaluation and treatment of children with attention deficit disorders. *Pediatrics in Review, 6* (4), 99–109.

SHELDON, A. (1989). Socialization of gender in preschool children through conversations with peers. Paper present-

ed at the meeting of the Society for Research in Child Development, Kansas City, MO.

SHELDON, E. B. & PARKE, R. (1975). Social science researchers are developing concepts and measures of change in society. *Science, 188,* 693–699.

SHERIF, M. & SHERIF, C. (1964). *Reference groups*. New York: Harper & Row.

SHERLOCK, R. (1979). Debate: Selective non-treatment of newborns. *Journal of Medical Ethics, 5,* 139–142.

SHIRLEY, A. (1982). Better health for children: What are the barriers? In *Proceedings of the Conference on Better Health for Children: Action for the Eighties,* held at Harvard University School of Public Health, Cambridge, MA, April 17.

SHONKOFF, J. P. (1984). The biological substrate and physical health in middle childhood. In W. A. Collins, (Ed.), *Development during middle childhood: The years from six to twelve*. Washington, D.C.: National Academy Press.

SHULTZ, T. R. & ZIGLER, E. (1970). Emotional commitants of visual mastery in infants: The effects of stimulus movement on smiling and vocalizing. *Journal of Experimental Child Psychology, 10,* 390–402.

SHURE, M. & SPIVAK, G. (1980). Interpersonal problem solving as a mediator of behavioral adjustment in preschool and kindergarten children. *Journal of Applied Developmental Psychology, 1,* 37–52.

SHUSTER, C., FINN-STEVENSON, M., & WARD, P., (Eds.). (1990). *Issue in family day care. Proceedings of the Round Table on Family Day Care*. New York: National Council of Jewish Women.

SIEGEL, A. W. & WHITE, S. H. (1982). The child study movement: Early growth and development of the symbolized child. *Advances in Child Development and Behavior, 17,* 233–285.

SIEGEL, L. S. (1978). The relationship of language and thought in the preoperational child: A reconsideration of non-verbal alternatives to Piagetian tasks. In L. S. Siegel & C. J. Brainerd, (Eds.), *Alternatives to Piaget: Critical essays on the theory*. New York: Academic Press.

SIEGLER, R. S. (1976). Three aspects of cognitive development. *Cognitive Psychology, 8,* 481–520.

SIGUELAND, E. (1968). Reinforcement patterns and extinction in human newborns. *Journal of Experimental Child Psychology, 6,* 431–442.

SILBERGELD, E., AKKERMAN, M., FOWLER, B. A., ALBUQUERQUE, E. X., & ALKONDON, M. (in press). Lead: Effects of male exposure on fertility and in-utero neurodevelopment.

SILBERMAN, C. (1970). *Crisis in the classroom: The remaking of American education*. New York: Random House.

SILVER, L. B. (1989). Psychological and family problems associated with learning disabilities: Assessment and intervention. *Journal of the American Academy of Child and Adolescent Psychiatry, 28,* 319–325.

SILVER, L. B. (1990). Learning disabilities. *Harvard Mental Health Letter, 7* (4), 3–8.

SIMMONS, R. & BLYTH, D. (1987). *Moving into adolescence*. New York: Aldine deGryter.

SIMMONS, R., ROSENBERG, F., & ROSENBERG, M. (1973). Disturbance in the self-image at adolescence. *American Sociological Review, 38,* 553–568.

SINCLAIR, C. (1973). *Movement of the young child: Ages two to six.* Columbus, OH: Merrill.

SINGER, D. G. & SINGER, J. L. (1976). Family television viewing habits and the spontaneous play of preschool children. *American Journal of Orthopsychiatry, 46,* 496–502.

SINGER, D. G. & SINGER, J. L. (1980). Television viewing and aggressive behavior in preschool children: A field study. *Forensic Pathology and Psychiatry, 347,* 289–303.

SINGER, J. L. (1981). *Cognitive and affective implications of television for the developing child.* Introduction. Revised draft submitted to the Committee to Update the Surgeon General's Committee Report on Television. New Haven, CT: Yale University.

SINGER, J. L. & SINGER, D. G. (1979a, March). Come back, Mister Rogers, come back. *Psychology Today, 12* (10), 56–60.

SINGER, J. L. & SINGER, D. G. (1979b). The value of the imagination. In B. Sutton-Smith, (Ed.), *Play and learning,* pp. 195–218. New York: Gardner Press.

SINGER, J. L. & SINGER, D. G. (1980). Television viewing, family style and aggressive behavior in preschool children. In M. Green, (Ed.), *Violence and the family: Psychiatric, sociological, and historical implications.* American Association for the Advancement of Science Symposium 47. Boulder: Westview Press.

SKEELS. H. M. (1942). A study of the differential stimulation on mentally retarded children: A follow-up report. *American Journal of Mental Deficiency, 46,* 340–350.

SKEELS, H. M. (1966). Adult status of children with contrasting early life experience: A follow-up study. *Monographs of the Society for Research in Child Development, 31* (3).

SKINNER, B. F. (1938). *The behavior of organisms.* New York: Appleton-Century-Crofts.

SKINNER, B. F. (1948). *Waldon two.* New York: Macmillan.

SKINNER, B. F. (1953). *Science and human behavior.* New York: Macmillan.

SKINNER, B. F. (1957). *Verbal behavior.* New York: Appleton-Century-Crofts.

SKINNER, B. F. (1987). Whatever happened to psychology as a science? *American Psychologist, 42,* 780–786.

SKINNER, L. (1979). *Motor development in the preschool years.* Springfield, IL: Charles C Thomas.

SKODAK, M. & SKEELS, H. (1949). A final follow-up of one hundred adopted children. *Journal of Genetic Psychology, 75,* 85–125.

SLOBIN, D. I. (1970). Universals of grammatical development in children. In G. B. Flores d'Arcais & W. J. M. Levett, (Eds.), *Advances in psycholinguistics.* New York: American Elsevier.

SLOMAN, J., BELLINGER, D. C., & KENTZEL, C. P. (1990). Infantile colic and transient developmental lag in the first year of life. *Child Development, 61* (1), 193–203.

SMALL, M. (1990). *Cognitive development.* San Diego: Harcourt Brace Jovanovich.

SMILANSKI, S. (1968). *The effects of sociodramatic play on disadvantaged preschool children.* New York: Wiley.

SMITH, P. K. & DAGLISH, L. (1977). Sex differences in parent and infant behavior in the home. *Child Development, 48,* 1250–1254.

SMITH, S. L. (1981). *No easy answers. The learning disabled child at home and at school.* New York: Bantam.

SMITH, S. T., MACARUSO, P., SHANKWEILER, D., & CRAIN, S. (1989). Syntactic comprehension in young poor readers. *Applied Psycholinguistics, 10,* 429–454.

SMITH, T. E. (1976). Push versus pull: Intrafamily versus peer group variables as possible determinants of adolescent orientation toward parents. *Youth and Society, 8,* 5–26.

SMOCK, S. M. (1977). *The children: The shape of child care in Detroit.* Detroit: Wayne State University Press.

SNOW, C. (1986). Definitions and definite noun phrases: Indicators of children's decontextualized language skills. *Journal of Research in Childhood Education, 1,* 37–48.

SNOW, C. E. (1989). Rationales for native language instruction: In A. M. Padilla, H. H. Fairchild, & C. M. Valadez, (Eds.), *Bilingual education,* pp. 60–74. Newbury Park, CA: Sage.

SOLOMON, R. L. (1964). Punishment. *American Psychologist, 19,* 239–253.

SOMMER, B. B. (1978). *Puberty and adolescence.* New York: Oxford University Press.

SONTAG, L. W. & WALLACE, R. F. (1935). The movement response of the human fetus to sound stimuli. *Child Development, 6,* 253–358.

SORCE, J., EMDE, R., CAMPOS, J. & KLINNERT, M. (1981). Maternal emotional signaling: Its effect on the visual cliff behavior of one-year-olds. Paper presented at the meeting of the Society for Research in Child Development, Boston, April.

SORENSON, R. C. (1973). *Adolescent sexuality in contemporary America: Personal values and sexual behavior, ages thirteen to nineteen.* New York: World.

SORRENTINO, C. (1990). The changing family: An international perspective. *Monthly Labor Reviews,* March, 41–58.

SPANIER, G. B. & GLICK, P. C. (1981). Marital instability in the United States: Some correlates and recent changes. *Family Relations, 31,* 329–338.

SPEARMAN, C. (1904). General intelligence objectively determined and measured. *American Journal of Psychology, 15,* 201–293.

SPELKE, E. (1976). Infant's intermodal perception of events. *Cognitive Psychology, 8,* 553–560.

SPENCER, M. B. (1990). Development of minority children. An introduction. *Child Development, 61* (2), 270–289.

SPENCER, M. B. & MARKSTROM-ADAMS, C. (1990). Identity processes among racial and ethnic minority children in America. *Child Development, 61* (2), 290–310.

SPITZ, R. A. (1965). *The first year of life.* New York: International Universities Press.

SPOCK, B. (1968). *Baby and child care.* New York: Hawthorn Books.

SPRINGER, S. (1989). Educating the two sides of the brain.

Separating fact from speculation. *American Educator, 13* (1), 32–37.

SROUFE, L. A. (1977). Wariness of strangers and the study of infant development. *Child Development, 48,* 731–746.

SROUFE, L. A. (1979). Socioemotional development. In J. D. Osofsky, (Ed.), *Handbook of infant development.* New York: Wiley.

SROUFE, L. A., SCHORK, E., MOTTI, F., LAWROSKI, N., & LaFRENIERE, P. (1984). Role of affect in social competence. In C. E. Izard, J. Kagan, & R. B. Zajonc, (Eds.), *Emotions, cognition and behavior.* New York: Cambridge University Press.

SROUFE, L. A. & WATERS, E. (1977). Attachment as an organizational construct. *Child Development, 48* (4), 1184–1199.

STAUB, E. (1975). To rear a prosocial child. In D. J. DePalma & J. M. Foley, (Eds.), *Moral development: Current theory and research.* Hillsdale, NJ: Erlbaum.

STAYTON, D. J., HOGAN, R., & AINSWORTH, M. D. S. (1971). Infant obedience and maternal behavior: The origins of socialization reconsidered. *Child Development, 42,* 1057–1069.

STEIN, A. H. & FRIEDRICH, L. K. (1975a). The effects of television content on young children. In A. D. Pick, (Ed.), *Minnesota Symposia on Child Psychology,* (Vol. 9). Minneapolis: University of Minnesota Press.

STEIN, A. H. & FRIEDRICH, L. K. (1975b). Impact of television on children and youth. In E. M. Hetherington, (Ed.), *Review of child development research,* (Vol. 5), pp. 183–256. Chicago: University of Chicago Press.

STEINMETZ, M. (1977). The use of force for resolving family conflict: The training ground for abuse. *Family Coordinator, 26,* 18–26.

STEINSCHNEIDER, A. (1975). Implications of the sudden infant death syndrome for the study of sleep in infancy. In A. D. Pick, (Ed.), *Minnesota Symposia on Child Psychology,* (Vol. 9). Minneapolis: University of Minnesota Press.

STERIEL, S. (1979). America's changing work ethic. *Editorial Research Reports, 22,* 903–920.

STERN, C. (1975). High points in human genetics. *American Biology Teacher, 32,* 144–149.

STERN, D. (1977). *The first relationship: Infant and mother.* Cambridge, MA: Harvard University Press.

STERN, D. (1985). *The interpersonal world of the infant: A view from psychoanalysis and development psychology.* New York: Basic Books.

STERN, M. & ZEVON, M. (1990). Stress, coping, and family environment: The adolescent's response to naturally occurring stressors. *Journal of Adolescent Research, 5* (3), 290–305.

STERN, S., NIXON, K., JONES, D., LAKE, M., NEMZER, E., & SANSONE, R. (1989). Family environment in anorexia nervosa and bulimia. *International Journal of Eating Disorders, 8,* 25–31.

STERN, W. (1911). The psychological methods of testing intelligence. G. M. Whipple (Trans.). Baltimore: Warwick & York.

STERNBERG, R. J. (1977). Component processes in analogical reasoning. *Psychological Review, 84,* 353–378.

STERNBERG, R. J. (1982, April). Who's intelligent? *Psychology Today,* 30–39.

STERNBERG, R. J. (1985). *Beyond IQ: A triarchic theory of human intelligence.* New York: Cambridge University Press.

STERNBERG, R. J. (1987). The uses and misuses of intelligence testing: Misunderstanding meaning. *Education Week, 28,* 22.

STERNGLANZ, S. H. & SERBIN, L. A. (1974). Sex role stereotyping in children's television programs. *Developmental Psychology, 10,* 710–715.

STEUER, F. B., APPLEFIELD, J. M., & SMITH, R. (1971). Televised aggression and the interpersonal aggression of preschool children. *Journal of Experimental Child Psychology, 11,* 442–447.

STEVENSON, H., STIGLER, J., LEE, S., LUCKER, G., KITAMURA, S., & ITSU, C. (1985). Cognitive performance and academic achievement of Japanese, Chinese and American children, *Child Development, 56,* 718–734.

STEVENSON, H. W. (1982). Influences of schooling on cognitive development. In D. A. Wagner & H. W. Stevenson, (Eds.), *Cultural perspectives on child development.* San Francisco: Freeman.

STEVENSON, H. W. (1983). Making the grade: School achievement in Japan, Taiwan, and the United States. *Annual Report,* Center for Advanced Study in Behavioral Sciences, Stanford University, Stanford, CA.

STEWART, M. A. & GATH, A. (1978). *Psychological disorders of children: A handbook for primary care physicians.* Baltimore: Williams & Wilkins.

STINSON, P. & STINSON, R. (1983). *The long dying of baby Andrew.* Boston: Atlantic Monthly Press (distributed by Little, Brown).

STIPEK, D. (1979). *The effectiveness of high schools in promoting intellectual achievement.* Working paper. New Haven, CT: Compulsory Education Project, Yale University Law School.

STIPEK, D. & McCROSKEY, J. (1989). Investing in children. Government and workplace policies for children. *American Psychologist, 44* (2), 416–423.

STIPEK, D. J. (1977). Changes during first grade in children's social-motivational development. Unpubl. doctoral diss., Yale University, New Haven, CT.

STRAHAM, D. (1983). The emergence of formal operations in adolescence. *Transcendence, 11,* 7–14.

STRAUSS, M., GELLES, R., & STEINMETZ, S. (1980). *Behind closed doors.* Garden City, NY: Doubleday.

STRAUSS, M. A. (1979). Family patterns and child abuse in a nationally representative American sample. *Child Abuse and Neglect, 3,* 213–225.

STRAUSS, M. E., LESSEN-FIRESTONE, J. K., STARR, R., & OSTREA,

E. M. (1975). Behavior of narcotics-addicted newborns. *Child Development, 46,* 887–893.

STREAN, L. P. & PEER, L. A. (1956). Stress as an etiological factor in the development of cleft palate. *Plastic and Reconstructive Surgery, 18,* 1–8.

STREISSGUTH, A. P., BARR, H. M., MARTIN, D. C., & HERMAN, C. S. (1980). Effects of maternal alcohol, nicotine, and caffeine use during pregnancy on infant mental and motor development at eight months. *Alcoholism: Clinical and Experimental Research, 4* (2), 152–164.

STREISSGUTH, A. P., LANDESMAN-DWYER, S., MARTIN, J. C., & SMITH, D. W. (1980, July 18). Teratogenic effects of alcohol in humans and laboratory animals. *Science, 209,* 353–361.

STUART, H. C. & PRUGH, D. G. (1960). *The healthy child: His physical, psychological and social development.* Cambridge, MA: Harvard University Press.

STUNKARD, A. J., HARRIS, J. R., PEDERSEN, N. L., & McCLEARN, G. E. (1990). The body-mass index of twins who have been reared apart. *New England Journal of Medicine, 322,* 1483–1487.

SULLIVAN, M., ROVEE-COLLIER, C., & TYNE, D. (1979). A conditioning analysis of infant long-term memory. *Child Development, 50,* 152–162.

SUOMI, S. J. (1977). Adult male-infant interactions among monkeys living in nuclear families. *Child Development, 48,* 1255–1270.

SUOMI, S. J. & HARLOW, H. F. (1975). The role and reason of peer friendships in rhesus monkeys. In M. Lewis & L. Rosenblum, (Eds.), *Friendship and peer relations.* New York: Wiley.

SUOMI, S. J., HARLOW, H. F., & McKINNEY, W. T. (1972). Monkey psychiatrists. *American Journal of Psychiatry, 128,* 41–46.

SUPER, C. M. (1980). Cognitive development: Looking across at growing up. In C. M. Super & S. Harkness, (Eds.), *Anthropological perspectives on child development* (New Directions for Child Development No. 8). San Francisco: Jossey-Bass.

SUPER, C. M. (1981). Behavioral development in infancy. In R. H. Munroe, R. L. Munroe, & B. B. Whiting, (Eds.), *Handbook of cross-cultural human development.* New York: Garland.

SUSSMAN, J. R. & LEVITT, B. (1989). *Before you conceive: The complete pregnancy guide.* New York: Bantam Books.

SUTTON-SMITH, B. (1974). The role of play in cognitive development. In R. E. Herron & B. Sutton-Smith, (Eds.), *Child's play.* New York: Wiley.

SUTTON-SMITH, B. & ROSENBERG, B. G. (1970). *The sibling.* New York: Holt, Rinehart & Winston.

SWAIN, M. (1972). *Bilingualism as a first language.* PhD. diss. University of California, Irvine.

SZYMANSKI, L. S. & TANGUAY, P. (1980). *Emotional disorders in mentally retarded persons.* Baltimore, MD: University Park Press.

TAFT, L. T. (1981). Intervention programs for infants with cerebral palsy: A clinician's view. In C. C. Brown, (Ed.), *Infants at risk: Assessment and intervention.* Skillman, NJ: Johnson & Johnson.

TAKANISHI, R. (1981). Graduate education for roles in child development and social policy. *UCLA Educator, 23,* 33–37.

TANNER, J. M. (1962). *Growth at adolescence,* (2nd Ed.). Oxford: Blackwell Scientific Publications.

TANNER, J. M. (1970). *Education and physical growth.* New York: International Universities Press.

TANNER, J. M. (1974). Variability of growth and maturity in newborn infants. In M. Lewis & L. Rosenblum, (Eds.), *The effect of the infant on its caregiver.* New York: Wiley.

TANNER, J. M. (1978). *Foetus into man: Physical growth from conception to maturity.* Cambridge, MA: Harvard University Press.

TANNER, J. M., WHITEHOUSE, R. H., MARSHALL, W. A., HEALY, M. J. R., & GOLDSTEIN, H. (1975). *Assessment of skeletal maturity and prediction of adult height.* London: Academic Press.

TASK FORCE ON PEDIATRIC AIDS. (1989). Task Force on Pediatric AIDS and Human Virus Infections. *American Psychologist, 44* (2), 258–264.

TELLER, D. Y. & BORNSTEIN, M. H. (1987). Infant color vision and color perception. In P. Salapatek & L. Cohen, (Eds.), *Handbook of infant perception.* Vol. 2, *From perception to cognition.* New York: Academic Press.

TERMAN, L. M. (1914). Recent literature on juvenile suicide. *Abnormal Psychology, 7,* 61.

TERMAN, L. M. (1916). *The measurement of intelligence.* Boston: Houghton Mifflin.

TERMAN, L. M. & MERRILL, M. A. (1972). *Stanford-Binet intelligence scale: Manual for the third revision.* Boston: Houghton Mifflin.

THELEN, E. & FISHER, D. M. (1982). Newborn stepping: An explanation for a "disappearing" reflex. *Developmental Psychology, 18* (5), 760–775.

THISSEN, D., BOCK, R. D., WAINER, H., & ROCHE, A. F. (1976). Individual growth in stature: A comparison of four growth studies in the U.S.A. *Annals of Human Biology, 3,* 529–542.

THODEN, C. J., JARVENPAA, A. L., & MICHELSSON, K. (1985). Sound spectrographic cry analysis of pain cry in prematures. In B. M. Lester & C. F. Z. Boukydis, (Eds.), *Infant crying: Theoretical and research perspectives.* New York: Plenum.

THOMAN, E. B. (1978). Individuality in the interaction process. In E. B. Thoman & S. Trotter, (Eds.), *Social responsiveness of infants.* Skillman, NJ: Johnson & Johnson.

THOMAN, E. B., KORNER, A. F., & BEASON-WILLIAMS, L. (1977). Modification of responsiveness to maternal vocalization in the neonate. *Child Development, 48,* 563–569.

THOMAS, A. & CHESS, S. (1977). *Temperament and development.* New York: Brunner/Mazel.

THOMAS, A. & CHESS, S. (1984). Genesis and evaluation of

behavioral disorders: From infancy to early adult life. *American Journal of Psychiatry, 141,* 1–9.

THOMAS, A. & CHESS, S. (1987). Commentary. In H. Goldsmith, A. Buss, R. Plomin, M. Rothbart, A. Thomas, S. Chess, R. Hinde & R. McCall, Roundtable, What is temperament? Four approaches. *Child Development, 58,* 505–529.

THOMAS, A., CHESS, S., & BIRCH, H. C. (1968). *Temperament and behavior disorders in children.* New York: New York University Press.

THOMAS, D. (1989). *Facts on children in custody.* Washington, D.C.: Department of Justice, Office of Juvenile Justice and Delinquency Prevention.

THOMAS, W. B. (1980). Parental and community involvement: R_X for better school discipline. *Phi Delta Kappan, 62,* 203–204.

THOMPSON, J. K., PENNER, L. A., & ALTABE, M. N. (1990). Procedures, problems, and progress in the assessment of body image. In T. F. Cash & T. Pruzinsky, (Eds.), *Body image: Development, deviance and change,* pp. 21–50. New York: Guilford Press.

THOMPSON, J. R. & CHAPMAN, R. S. (1977). Who is "Daddy" revisited: The status of two-year-olds' overextended words in use and comprehension. *Journal of Child Language, 4,* 359–379.

THOMPSON, R. A. (1990). Vulnerability in research: A developmental perspective on research risk. *Child Development, 61* 1–16.

THOMPSON, S. K. (1975). Gender labels and early sex-role development. *Child Development, 46,* 339–347.

THURSTONE, L. L. (1938). *Primary mental abilities.* Chicago: University of Chicago Press.

TISHLER. C. L. (1983). Making life meaningful for youth: Preventing suicide. In L. E. Arnold, (Ed.), *Preventing adolescent alienation.* Lexington, MA: Lexington Books.

TISHLER, C. L., McKENDRY, P. C., & MORGAN, K. C. (1981). Adolescent suicide attempts: Some significant factors. *Suicide and Life Threatening Behavior, 2,* 92.

TIZARD, B. & HODGES, J. (1978). The effects of early institutional rearing on the development of eight-year-old children. *Journal of Child Psychology and Psychiatry, 19,* 99–118.

TIZARD, B. & REES, J. (1975). The effect of early institutional rearing on the behavior problems and affectional relationship of four-year-old children. *Journal of Child Psychology and Psychiatry, 16,* 61–73.

TOBIN, J. J., WU, D. Y. H., & DAVIDSON, D. (1989). How three countries shape their children. *World Monitor,* April, 36–45.

TOBLER, N. S. (1986). Meta-analysis of 143 adolescent drug prevention programs: Quantitative and qualitative outcome results of program participants compared to a control or comparison group. *Journal of Drug Issues, 16,* 537–568.

TOPPING, D., CROWELL, O., & KOBAYASHI, V. (1989). *Thinking across cultures.* Hillsdale, NJ: Erlbaum.

TOWER, R., SINGER, D., SINGER, J. & BIGGS, A. (1979). Differential effects of television programming on preschoolers'

cognition, imagination and social play. *American Journal of Orthopsychiatry, 49* (2), 265–281.

TRABASSO, T. (1975). Representation, memory, and reasoning: How do we make transitive inferences? In A. D. Pick, (Ed.), *Minnesota Symposia on Child Psychology,* (Vol. 9). Minneapolis: University of Minnesota Press.

TRAVERS, J. R. & LIGHT, J. (Eds.). (1982). *Learning from experience: Evaluating early childhood demonstration programs.* Washington, D.C.: National Academic Press.

TRCZINSKI, E. & FINN-STEVENSON, M. (1991, May). A response to arguments against mandated parental leave: Findings from the Connecticut survey of parental leave policies. *Journal of Marriage and the Family, 53,* 445–460.

TRICKETT, P. & KUCZYNSKI, L. (1986). Children's misbehavior and parental discipline: Strategies in abusive and nonabusive parents. *Developmental Psychology, 22,* 113–123.

TRONICK, E. Z. (1989). Emotions and emotional communication in infants. *American Psychologist, 44* (2), 112–119.

TRONICK, E. Z. & COHN, J. F. (1989). Infant-mothers face-to-face interaction: Age and gender differences in coordination and the occurrence of miscoordination. *Child Development, 60,* 85–92.

TRONICK, E. Z. & FIELD, T. (1986). Maternal depression and infant disturbance. *New directions for child development,* (Vol. 34). London: Jossey-Bass.

TRONICK, E. Z. & GIANINO, A. (1986). Interactive mismatch and repair: Challenges to the coping infant. *Zero to Three, 6* (3), 1–6.

TUMA, J. (1989). Mental health services for children. *American Psychologist, 44* (2), 188–199.

TURIEL, E. (1983). Social regulations and domains of social concepts. In W. Damon, (Ed.), *Social cognition: New directions for child development.* Cambridge, UK: Cambridge University Press.

TURIEL, E., EDWARDS, C. P., & KOHLBERG, L. (1978). Moral development in Turkish children, adolescents and young adults. *Journal of Cross-Cultural Psychology, 9,* 75–86.

TURIEL, E., KILLEN, M., & HELWIG, C. C. (1987). Morality: Its structure, functions and vagaries. In J. Kagan & S. Lamb, (Eds.), *The emergence of morality.* Chicago: University of Chicago Press.

TURNBULL, A. P., STRICKLAND, B., & HAMMER, S. E. (1978). The individualized education program. Pt. 2, Translating law into practice. *Journal of Learning Disabilities, 11,* 18–23.

TURNER, E. K. (1956). The syndrome in the infant resulting from maternal emotional tension during pregnancy. *Medical Journal of Australia, 1,* 221–222.

TURNER, J. (1980). *Made for life: Coping, competence, and cognition.* New York: Methuen.

TYLER, T. J. (1974). *A primer of psychobiology: Brain and behavior.* San Francisco: Freeman.

TYRON, R. C. (1942). Individual differences. In F. A. Moss, (Ed.), *Comparative psychology.* Englewood Cliffs, NJ: Prentice-Hall.

U.S. BUREAU OF THE CENSUS. (1983). School enrollment—social and economic characteristics of students: October 1983. *Current Population Reports,* Series P–20, No. 394.

U.S. BUREAU OF THE CENSUS. (1984). Projections of population by age, sex and race: 1983 to 2080. *Population Estimates Projections,* Series P–25, No. 952. Washington, D.C.: Government Printing Office.

U.S. BUREAU OF THE CENSUS. (1987a). Fertility of American women: Through June 1986. *Current Population Reports,* Series P–20, No. 421. Washington D.C.: Government Printing Office.

U.S. BUREAU OF THE CENSUS. (1987b). Who's minding the kids? *Current Population Reports,* Series P–70, No. 9. Washington, D.C.: Government Printing Office.

U.S. BUREAU OF THE CENSUS. (1987c). Child support and alimony: 1985. *Current Population Reports,* Consumer Income Series P–60, No. 152. Washington, D.C.: Government Printing Office.

U.S. BUREAU OF THE CENSUS. (1988). Marital status and living arrangements: March 1987. *Current Population Reports,* Series P–20, No. 423. Washington, D.C.: Government Printing Office.

U.S. BUREAU OF THE CENSUS. (1989a). Household and family characteristics: March 1988. *Current Population Reports,* Series P–20, No. 437. Washington, D.C.: Government Printing Office.

U.S. BUREAU OF THE CENSUS. (1989b). Money income and poverty status in the U.S. *Current Population Reports,* Series P–60, No. 166. Washington, D.C.: Government Printing Office.

U.S. CONFERENCE OF MAYORS. (1989). *A status report on hunger and homelessness in America's cities: A 27-city survey.* Washington, D.C.: Author.

U.S. CONGRESS. (1989, Oct. 24). Select Committee on Children, Youth and Families. *Hearing summary: Caring for new mothers: Pressing problems, new solutions.* Washington, D.C.: Author.

U.S. CONGRESS. (1990a). *No place to call home: Discarded children of America.* Report #101–395 of the Select Committee on Children, Youth and Families. 101st Congress, 2nd sess., January 12. Washington, D.C.: Government Printing Office.

U.S. CONGRESS. (1990b). *Hearings of the subcommittee on regulations, business opportunities and energy.* Washington, D.C.: Government Printing Office.

U.S. CONGRESS, HOUSE SELECT COMMITTEE ON CHILDREN, YOUTH AND FAMILIES. (1989). *U. S. Children and their families: Current conditions and recent trends.* Washington, D.C.: Government Printing Office.

U. S. DEPARTMENT OF AGRICULTURE, SCIENCE AND EDUCATION ADMINISTRATION. (1980, Sept.). *Food and nutrient intake of individuals in one day in the U.S.: 1977–1978.* Nationwide food consumption survey, preliminary report No. 2.

U.S. DEPARTMENT OF AGRICULTURE. (1982). *Costs of raising children.* Washington, D.C.: Government Printing Office.

U.S. DEPARTMENT OF EDUCATION. (1986). *What works—research about teaching and learning.* Washington, D.C.: Government Printing Office.

U.S. DEPARTMENT OF EDUCATION. (1990). *National assessment of educational progress.* Washington, D.C.: Government Printing Office.

U.S. DEPARTMENT OF HEALTH, EDUCATION, AND WELFARE. (1979). *Smoking and health: A report of the surgeon general.* Washington, D.C.: Public Health Service.

U.S. DEPARTMENT OF HEALTH AND HUMAN SERVICES. (1983). *Monthly Vital Statistics Report: Final Natality Statistics, 29* (1), Suppl.

U.S. DEPARTMENT OF HEALTH AND HUMAN SERVICES. (1988). *Study of national incidence and prevalence of child abuse and neglect.* Children's Bureau, National Center on Child Abuse and Neglect. Washington, D.C.: Government Printing Office.

U.S. DEPARTMENT OF HEALTH AND HUMAN SERVICES. (1990). *Report of the young unwed fathers project.* Washington, D.C.: Author.

U.S. DEPARTMENT OF JUSTICE. (1985). *Uniform crime reports for the United States.* Washington, D.C.: Government Printing Office.

U.S. DEPARTMENT OF LABOR. (1987). Bureau of labor statistics. Over half of mothers with children under one in labor force. *Women and work.* Washington, D.C.: Government Printing Office.

U.S. DEPARTMENT OF LABOR. (1988a). Labor force participation among mothers of young children. *News.* Washington, D.C.: Author.

U.S. DEPARTMENT OF LABOR. (1988b). *Childcare: A workforce issue.* Washington, D.C.: Government Printing Office.

U.S. HOUSE OF REPRESENTATIVES. (1985). Committee on Ways and Means. *Children in poverty,* by the Congressional Research Service. Washington, D.C.: Government Printing Office.

U.S. HOUSE OF REPRESENTATIVES. (1987a). Report of the Select Committee on Children, Youth and Families. 98th Congress, 1st sess. *U.S. children and their families: Current conditions and recent trends,* p. 764. Washington, D.C.: Government Printing Office.

U.S. HOUSE OF REPRESENTATIVES. (1987b). Report of the Select Committee on Children, Youth and Families. *The crisis of homelessness: Effects on children and families.* Hearing report. Washington, D.C.: Government Printing Office.

U.S. SENATE. (1980). Report of the Committee on the Judiciary. Subcommittee on the Constitution, 96th Congress, 2nd sess. *Homeless youth: The saga of pushouts and throwaways in America.* Washington, D.C.: Government Printing Office.

URBERG, K. A. & KAPLAN, M. G. (1989). An observational study of race-age and sex-heterogeneous interactions in preschoolers. *Journal of Applied Developmental Psychology, 10,* 299–311.

VALENTINE, J. & ZIGLER, E. (1983). Head Start: A case study in the development of social policy for children and families. In E. Zigler, S. L. Kagan, & E. Klugman, (Eds.), *Children, families and government: Perspectives on American social policy.* New York: Cambridge University Press.

VANDENBERG, B. (1980). Play, problem-solving, and creativity.

In K. H. Rubin, (Ed.), *Children's play.* San Francisco: Jossey-Bass.

VANDENBERG, S. G. (1971). What do we know today about the inheritance of intelligence and how do we know it? In R. Canero, (Ed.), *Intelligence: Genetic and environmental influences.* New York: Grune & Stratton.

VASTA, R. (1979). *Studying children: An introduction to research methods.* San Francisco: Freeman.

VENTURA, S. & LEWIS, C. (1990). Report on teen birth statistics. Washington, D.C.: National Center for Health Statistics.

VIHMAN, M. (1985). Language differentiation by the bilingual infant. *Journal of Child Language, 12,* 297–324.

VINOUSKIS, M. A. (1988). *An epidemic of adolescent pregnancy: Some historical and policy considerations.* New York: Oxford University Press.

VOLTERA, V. & TAESCHNER, T. (1978). The acquisition and development of language by bilingual children. *Journal of Child Language, 5,* 311–326.

VYGOTSKY, L. (1962). *Thought and language.* Cambridge, MA: MIT Press. (Original work published in 1934).

WAGGENER, T. B., SOUTHALL, D. P., & SCOTT, L. A. (1990). Analysis of breathing patterns in a prospective population of term infants does not predict susceptibility to Sudden Infant Death Syndrome. *Pediatric Research, 27,* 2.

WAGGONER, J. E. & PALERMO, D. S. (1989). Betty is a bouncing bubble: Children's comprehension of emotion-descriptive metaphors. *Developmental Psychology, 25,* 152–163.

WALKER, D. F. (1988). Restructuring education for young adolescents: Possible guidelines for local curriculum reform. Paper commissioned by the Task Force on Education of Young Adolescents, Carnegie Council on Adolescent Development. New York: Carnegie Corporation.

WALKER, L. (1984). Sex differences in the development of moral reasoning: A critical review of the literature. *Child Development, 55* (3), 677–691.

WALLERSTEIN, J., CORBIN, S. (1991). The child and the vicissitudes of divorce. In M. Lewis (Ed.), *Child and adolescent psychiatry: A comprehensive textbook,* pp. 1108–1118. Baltimore: Williams & Wilkins.

WALLERSTEIN, J., CORBIN, S. B., & LEWIS, J. M. (1988). Children of divorce: A ten year study. In E. Hetherington & J. Arasteh, (Eds.), *Impact of divorce, single-parenting and step-parenting on children,* pp. 198–214. Hillsdale, NJ: Erlbaum.

WALLERSTEIN, J. S. & KELLY, J. B. (1979). Children and divorce: A review. *Social Work, 24,* 468–475.

WALLERSTEIN, J. S. & KELLY, J. B. (1980). *Surviving the breakup.* New York: Basic Books.

WALLIS, D. (1983, Sept. 26). The stormy legacy of Baby Doe. *Time,* 58.

WALTON, R. E. (1979, July–Aug.). Work innovations in the United States. *Harvard Business Review,* 91.

WARD, E. H. (1976). CDA: Credentialing for day care. *Voice for Children, 9* (5), 15.

WARNER, J. S. & WOOTEN, B. R. (1979). Human infant color vision and color perception. *Infant Behavior and Development, 2,* 241–274.

WASHBURN, S. L. & HAMBURG, D. (1965). The study of primate behavior. In I. Devore, (Ed.), *Primate behavior: Field studies of monkeys and apes.* New York: Holt, Rinehart & Winston.

WASSERMAN, R., DIBASIO, C. M., BOND, L. A., YOUNG, P., & COLLETT, R. (1990). Infant temperament and school age behavior: A pediatric practice. *Pediatrics, 85* (5), 801–807.

WATERMAN, A. S. (1985). Identity in the context of adolescent psychology. In A. S. Waterman, (Ed.), *Identity in adolescence: Processes and contents.* San Francisco: Jossey-Bass.

WATERS, E., VAUGHN, B. E., & EGELAND, B. (1980). Individual differences in infant-mother attachment relationships at age one: Antecedents in neonatal behavior in an urban, economically disadvantaged sample. *Child Development, 51,* 208–216.

WATERS, E., WIPPMAN, J., & SROUFE, L. A. (1979). Attachment, positive affect and competence in the peer group: Two studies in construct validation. *Child Development, 50* (3), 821–829.

WATSON, J. B. (1926). What the nursery has to say about instincts. In C. Murcheson, (Ed.), *Psychologies of 1925.* Worcester, MA: Clark University Press.

WATSON, J. B. (1928). *The psychological care of infant and child.* New York: Norton.

WATSON, J. S. & RAMEY, C. T. (1972). Reactions to contingent stimulation in early infancy. *Merrill-Palmer Quarterly, 18,* 219–227.

WATSON, K. (1982). A bold new model for foster care. *Public Welfare, 40* (2), 15.

WATSON, M. W. & FISCHER, K. (1977). A developmental sequence of agent use in late infancy. *Child Development, 48,* 828–835.

WATSON, M. W. & FISCHER, K. (1980). Development of social roles in elicited spontaneous behavior during the preschool years. *Developmental Psychology, 16,* 483–494.

WEBSTER, R. L., STEINHARDT, M. H., & SENTER, M. G. (1972). Changes in infants' vocalizations as a function of differential acoustic stimulation. *Developmental Psychology, 7* (1), 39.

WECHSLER, D. (1958). *The measurement and appraisal of adult intelligence,* (4th Ed.). Baltimore: Williams & Williams.

WECHSLER, D. (1974). *Manual for the Wechsler Intelligence Test for Children, revised.* New York: Psychological Corp.

WEIKART, D. P. (1982). Preschool education for disadvantaged children. In J. R. Travers & R. J. Light, (Eds.), *Learning from experience: Evaluating early childhood demonstration programs.* Washington, D.C.: National Academy Press.

WEINBERG, R. A. (1989). Intelligence and IQ: Landmark issues and great debates. *American Psychologist, 44* (2) 98–104.

WEINER, I. B. (1980). Psychopathology in adolescence. In J. Adelson, (Ed.), *Handbook of adolescent psychology.* New York: Wiley.

WEINRAUB, M., BROOKS, J., & LEWIS, M. (1977). The social

network: A reconsideration of the concept of attachment. *Human Development, 20,* 31–47.

WEINSTEIN, R. S. (in press). Expectations and high school: Teacher-researcher collaborations to prevent school failure. *American Journal of Community Psychology.*

WEIR, R. H. (1966). Some questions on the child's learning of phonology. In F. Smith & G. Miller, (Eds.), *The genesis of language: A psycholinguistic approach.* Cambridge, MA: MIT Press.

WEISBROD, J. A., CASALE, S., & FABER, S. (1981). *Family court disposition study.* New York: Vera Institute for Justice.

WEISS, G. (1991). Attention Deficit Hyperactive Disorder. In M. Lewis, (Ed.), *Child and adolescent psychiatry: A comprehensive textbook.* Baltimore: Williams & Wilkins.

WEISS, H. (1983). *Programs to strengthen families: A resource guide.* New Haven, CT: Bush Center in Child Development and Social Policy, Yale University.

WEISS, H. (1988). Family support and education programs: Working through ecological theories at human development. In H. B. Weiss & F. H. Jacobs, (Eds.), *Evaluating family programs.* New York: Aldine deGruyter.

WEISS, H. (1989). *Innovative states: Emerging family support and education programs.* Cambridge, MA: Harvard Family Research Project.

WEISS, H. & JACOBS, F., (Eds.) (1988). *Evaluating family programs.* New York: Aldine deGruyter.

WEISSBERG, J. & PARIS, S. (1986). Young children's remembering in different contexts. A reinterpretation of Istomina's study. *Child Development, 57,* 1123–1129.

WEISSBERG, R., GUARE, J., & LIEBERSTEIN, N. (1989). Learning disabled children. *Journal of Learning Disabilities, 23* (2), 115.

WEISSBLUTH, M. (1984). *Crybabies.* New York: Doubleday.

WEISSMAN, M. M. (1974). The epidemiology of suicide attempts, 1960–1971. *Archives of General Psychology, 30,* 737–739.

WEISZ, J. R. (1978). Transcontextual validity in developmental research. *Child Development, 49,* 1–12.

WEITZMAN, L. J. (1981a). *The marriage contract.* New York: Free Press.

WEITZMAN, L. J. (1981b). The economics of divorce: Social and economic consequences of property, alimony, and child support awards. *UCLA Law Review, 28,* 1181–1268.

WELLMAN, H. M. (1985). The child's theory of mind: The development of conceptions of cognition. In S. R. Yussen, (Ed.), *The growth of reflection in children,* pp. 169–206. New York: Academic Press.

WELLMAN, H. M. & LEMPERS, J. D. (1977). The naturalistic communicative capabilities of two-year-olds. *Child Development, 48,* 1052–1057.

WENDER, E. H. (1986). The food additive-free diet in the treatment of behavior disorders: A review. *Journal of Developmental and Behavioral Pediatrics, 7,* 35–42.

WENDER, P. H. (1990). Hyperactivity in children and adults. *Harvard Mental Health Letter, 7* (5), 4–7.

WERKER, J. & LALONDE, C. (1988). Cross-language speech perception: Initial capabilities and developmental change. *Developmental Psychology, 24,* 672–683.

WERNER, H. (1948). *Comparative psychology of mental development.* New York: International Universities Press.

WERTMANN, M. W. (1980). Medical constraints to optimal development of the preterm infant. In S. L. Friedman & M. Sigman (Eds.), *Preterm birth and psychological development.* New York: Academic Press.

WESSEL, M. A., COBB, J. C., JACKSON, E. B., HARRIS, G. S., & DETWILLER, A. C. (1956). Paroxysmal fussing in infancy, sometimes called "colic." *Pediatrics, 5* (1), 421–434.

WESTINGHOUSE LEARNING CORPORATION. (1969). *The impact of Head Start: An evaluation of the effects of Head Start on children's cognitive and affectional development.* Report to the Office of Economic Opportunity. Washington, D.C.: Learning House for Federal Scientific and Technical Information.

WESTON, D. R., IVINS, B., ZUCKERMAN, B., JONES, C., & LOPEZ, R. (1989). Drug exposed babies: Research and clinical issues. *Zero to Three, 9* (5), 1–7.

WHITBREAD, J. (1982). Who's taking care of the children? *Family Circle,* February, p. 88.

WHITE, B. L. (1967). An experimental approach to the effects of environment on early human behavior. In J. P. Hill, (Ed.), *Minnesota Symposia on Child Psychology,* (Vol. 1). Minneapolis: University of Minnesota Press.

WHITE, B. L. (1988). *Educating the infant and toddler.* Lexington, MA: Lexington Books.

WHITE, B. L. & HELD, R. (1966). Plasticity of sensorimotor development in human infants. In J. Rosenblith & W. Allinsmith, (Eds.), *The causes of behavior: Readings in child development and educational psychology.* Boston: Allyn & Bacon.

WHITE, R. W. (1959). Motivation reconsidered: The concept of competence. *Psychological Review, 66,* 297–333.

WHITE, S. & PILLEMER, D. (1979). Childhood amnesia and the development of a socially accessible memory system. In J. F. Kihlstrom & F. J. Evans, (Eds.), *Functional disorders of memory.* Hillsdale, NJ: Erlbaum.

WHITE, S. H. (1965). Evidence for a hierarchical arrangement of learning processes. In L. P. Lewis & C. C. Spiker, (Eds.), *Advances in child development and behavior,* (Vol. 2). New York: Academic Press.

WHITE, S. H. (1970). Some general outlines of the matrix of developmental change between five and seven years. *Bulletin of the Orton Society, 20,* 41–57.

WHITE, S. H. (1982). The idea of development in developmental psychology. In R. M. Lerner, (Ed.), *Developmental psychology: Historical and philosophical perspectives.* Hillsdale, NJ: Erlbaum.

WHITEHURST, G., FALCO, F., LONIGAN, J., FISCHEL, J., DEBARYSHE, B., VALDEZ-MENCHACA, M., & CAULFIELD, M. (1988). Accelerating language development through picture book reading. *Developmental Psychology, 24* (4), 552–559.

WHITING, B. & EDWARDS, C. P. (1988). *Children of different worlds: The formation of social behavior.* Cambridge, MA: Harvard University Press.

WHITING, B. B. & WHITING, J. W. M. (1975). *Children of six* cultures: A psycho-cultural analysis. Cambridge, MA: Harvard University Press.

WHITING, J. W. M., BURBANK, V. K., & RATNER, M. S. (1986). The duration of maidenhood across cultures. In J. B. Lancaster & B. A. Hamburg, (Eds.), *School-age pregnancy and parenthood: Biosocial dimensions,* pp. 273–302. New York: Aldine deGruyter.

WHITTAKER, J. K. & GARBARINO, J. (1983). *Social support networks: Informal helping in the human services.* New York: Aldine.

WHOL, T. (1963). Correlation of anxiety and hostility with adrenocortical function. *Journal of the American Medical Association, 183,* 113–114.

WICKSTROM, R. L. (1977). *Fundamental motor patterns,* (2nd Ed.). Philadelphia: Lea & Febiger.

WIDDOWSON, Z. M. (1951). Mental contentment and physical growth. *Lancet, 1,* 1316–1318.

WIEDER, S. (1989). Mediating successful parenting. *Zero to Three, 10* (1), 21–22.

WIESENFELD, A. R. & KLORMAN, R. C. (1978). The mother's psychological reactions to contrasting affective expressions by her own and unfamiliar infants. *Developmental Psychology, 14,* 294–304.

WILCOX, A. J., WEINBERG, C. R., O'CONNOR, J. F., BAIRD, D. D., SCHLATTERER, J. P., CANFIELD, R. E., ARMSTRONG, E. G., & NISULA, B. C. (1988). Incidence of early loss of pregnancy, *New England Journal of Medicine, 319,* 189–194.

WILLERMAN, L. & COHEN, D. (1989). *Psychopathology.* New York: McGraw-Hill.

WILLIAM T. GRANT FOUNDATION. (1988). *The forgotten half: Non-college youth in America.* Commission on Work, Family, and Citizenship, p. 49. New York: Author.

WILLIAMS, C. B. & MILLER, C. A. (1991). *Preventive health care for young children: A ten country study with analysis of relevance to U.S. policy.* Washington, D.C.: National Center for Clinical Infant Programs.

WILLIAMS, L. (1985, Jan. 16). Schools encourage active parent role. *New York Times,* C1, C10.

WILLIG, A. (1985). A meta analysis of selective studies on the effectiveness of bilingual education. *Review of Educational Research, 55,* 269–317.

WILSON, C. C. & GUTIERREZ, F. (1985). *Minorities and the media: Diversity and the end of mass communication.* Beverly Hills, CA: Sage.

WILSON, J. G. & FRASER, F. C. (Eds.). (1977). *Handbook of teratology.* New York: Plenum.

WINEBERG, S. (1987). The self-fulfillment of the self-fulfilling prophecy. *Educational Researcher, 16,* 28–36.

WINER, G. A. (1980). Class-inclusion reasoning in children: A review of the empirical literature. *Child Development, 51,* 309–328.

WINICK, M. (1975). *Childhood obesity.* New York: Wiley.

WINICK, M., BRASEL, J. A., & ROSSO, P. (1972). Nutrition and cell growth. In M. Winick, (Ed.), *Nutrition and development.* New York: Wiley.

WINN, M. (1983). *Children without childhood.* New York: Plenum.

WIRTENBERG, J., MUREZ, R., & ALEPEKTOR, R. A. (1980). *Characters in textbooks: A review of the literature.* Washington, D.C.: Commission on Civil Rights.

WITKIN, H. A., MEDNICK, S. A., SCHLUSINGER, R., BLACKESTROM, E., CHRISTIANSEN, K. O., GOODENOUGH, D. R., & HIRCHORN, K. (1976). Criminality in XYY and XXY men. *Science, 193,* 547–555.

WOHLWILL, J. F. (1970). The place of structured experience in early cognitive development. *Interchange, 1,* 13–27.

WOLFF, P. (1966), The causes, controls and organization of behavior in the neonate. *Psychological Issues, 5,* 1 (whole issue).

WOLFF, P. H. (1963). Observations on the early development of smiling. In B. M. Foss, (Ed.), *Determinants of infant behavior,* (Vol. 2). New York: Wiley.

WOLFF, P. H. (1971). Mother-infant relations at birth. In J. G. Howels, (Ed.), *Modern perspectives in international child psychiatry.* New York: Brunner/Mazel.

WOLFSON, R. J., AGHAMOHAMADI, A. M., & BERMAN, S. E. (1980). Disorders of the hearing. In S. Gabel & M. T. Erickson, (Eds.), *Child development and developmental disabilities.* Boston: Little, Brown.

WOOD, D. L., VALDEZ, R. B., HAYASHI, T., & SHEN, A. (1990). Health of homeless children and housed poor children. *Pediatrics, 86* (6), 858–866.

WORLD HEALTH ORGANIZATION. (1989). *Special tabulation of national mortality statistics.* Geneva: Author.

WORTHMAN, C. M. (1986). Developmental dysynchrony in normative experience: Kikuyu adolescents. In J. B. Lancaster & B. A. Hamberg, (Eds.), *School-age pregnancy and parenthood: Biosocial dimensions.* New York: Aldine deGruyter, 95–109.

WYLIE, R. (1979). *The self-concept.* Vol. 2, *Theory and research on selected topics.* Lincoln: University of Nebraska Press.

YARROW, L. J. (1964). Separation from parents during early childhood. In M. L. Hoffman & L. W. Hoffman (Eds.), *Review of child development research.* New York: Russell Sage.

YARROW, L. J. (1979). Historical perspectives and future directions in infant development. In J. Osofsky, (Ed.), *Handbook of infant development.* New York: Wiley.

YARROW, L. J., RUBENSTEIN, J. L., & PEDERSON, F. A. (1975). *Infant and environment.* New York: Halsted Press.

YATES, A. (1987). Current status and future directions of research on the American Indian child. *American Journal of Psychiatry, 144* (9), 1135–1142.

YATES, A. (1990). Current perspectives on eating disorders: Treatment, outcome and research directions. *Journal of American Academy of Child and Adolescent Psychiatry, 29,* 1–9.

YOGMAN, M., DIXON, S., TRONICK, E., ALS, H., & BRAZELTON, T. B. (1977). *The goals and structure of face-to-face interac-*

tion between infants and fathers. Paper presented at the biennial meeting of the Society for Research in Child Development, New Orleans.

YOUNG, J. G. & COHEN, D. J. (1979). The molecular biology of development. In J. D. Noshpitz, (Ed.), *Basic handbook of child psychiatry.* New York: Basic Books.

YOUNGER, B. (1990). Infants' detection of correlations among feature categories. *Child Development, 61,* 614–620.

YOUNGER, B. & COHEN, L. B. (1986). Developmental changes in infants' perception of correlation among attributes. *Child Development, 57,* 803–813.

YOUNISS, J. (1980). *Parents and peers in social development: A Sullivan-Piaget perspective.* Chicago: University of Chicago Press.

YOUNISS, J. & SMOLLAR, J. (1985). *Adolescent relations with mothers, fathers, and friends.* Chicago: University of Chicago Press.

YOUNISS, J. & VOLPE, J. (1978). A relational analysis of children's friendships. In W. Damon, (Ed.), *Social cognition.* San Francisco: Jossey-Bass.

ZAHN-WAXLER, C., CUMMINGS, R. J., & RADKE-YARROW, M. (1984). Young offspring in depressed parents: A population at risk for affective problems. In D. Cicchetti & K. Schneider-Rosen, (Eds.), *New directions for child development: Developmental approaches to childhood depression.* San Francisco: Jossey-Bass.

ZAHN-WAXLER, C. Z., RADKE-YARROW, M. R., & KING, R. A. (1979). Childrearing and children's prosocial initiations toward victims of distress. *Child Development, 50,* 319–330.

ZAJONC, R. B. (1983). Validating the confluence model. *Psychological Bulletin, 93,* 457–480.

ZAJONC, R. B. & BARGH, J. (1980, July). Birth order, family size, and decline of SAT scores. *American Psychologist, 35* (7), 662–668.

ZASLOW, M. J. (1989). Sex differences in children's response to maternal employment. Paper prepared for the National Research Council, Committee on Child Development Research and Social Policy. Washington, D.C.: National Research Council.

ZEITLIN, J. (1989). *Work and family responsibilities: Achieving a balance.* New York: Ford Foundation.

ZELAZO, P. R., ZELAZO, N. A., & KOLB, S. (1972). "Walking" in the newborn. *Science, 176,* 314–315.

ZESKIND, P. S. & RAMEY, C. T. (1978). Fetal malnutrition: An experimental study of its consequences on development in two caregiving environments. *Child Development, 49,* 1155–1162.

ZIGLER, E. (1963). Metatheoretical issues in developmental psychology. In M. Marx, (Ed.), *Theories in contemporary psychology.* New York: Macmillan.

ZIGLER, E. (1973). Project Head Start: Success or failure? *Learning, 1,* 43–47.

ZIGLER, E. (1978). Controlling child abuse in America: An effort doomed to failure. In R. Bourne & E. Newberger,

(Eds.), *Critical perspectives on child abuse.* Lexington, MA: Heath.

ZIGLER, E. (1980). Controlling child abuse: Do we have the knowledge and/or the will? In G. Gerbner, C. J. Ross, & E. Zigler, (Eds.), *Child abuse: An agenda for action.* New York: Oxford University Press.

ZIGLER, E. (1984). Review of Melton, G. B., *Child advocacy: Psychological issues and interventions. Book Reviews.* New York: Plenum.

ZIGLER, E., ABELSON, W., & SEITZ, V. (1973). Motivational factors in the performance of economically disadvantaged children on the Peabody Picture Vocabulary Test. *Child Development, 44,* 294–303.

ZIGLER, E. & BALLA, D. (Eds.). (1982). *Mental retardation: The developmental-difference controversy.* Hillsdale, NJ: Erlbaum.

ZIGLER, E. & BERMAN, W. (1983). Discerning the future of early childhood intervention. *American Psychologist, 38,* 894–906.

ZIGLER, E. & BUTTERFIELD, E. C. (1968). Motivational aspects of changes in IQ test performance of culturally deprived nursery school children. *Child Development, 39,* 1–14.

ZIGLER, E. & CASCIONE, R. (1980). On being a parent. In *Parenthood in a changing society.* Champaign: ERIC Clearinghouse on Elementary and Early Childhood Education, University of Illinois.

ZIGLER, E. & CASCIONE, R. (1984). Mental retardation: An overview. In E. S. Gollin, (Ed.), *Malformations of development: Biological sources and consequences.* New York: Academic Press.

ZIGLER, E. & FINN, M. (1981). From problem to solution: Changing public policy as it affects children and families. *Young Children, 36,* 31–36.

ZIGLER, E. & FINN, M. (1982). A vision of childcare in the 1980's. In L. A. Bond & J. M. Joffe, (Eds.), *Facilitating infant and early child development.* Hanover, NH: University Press of New England.

ZIGLER, E. F. (1987). A solution to the nation's child care crisis: The school of the Twenty-first Century. Paper presented at the eleventh annual Bush Luncheon in Social Policy, Yale University, New Haven, CT, September.

ZIGLER, E. F. & FINN-STEVENSON, M. (1989). Childcare in America: From problem to solution. *Educational Policy, 3,* 313–329.

ZIGLER, E. F. & FINN-STEVENSON, M. (1992). Applied developmental psychology. In M. Lamb & M. Bornstein, (Eds.), *Developmental psychology: An advanced textbook,* (3rd Ed.). Hillsdale, NJ: Erlbaum.

ZIGLER, E. F. & FRANK, M. (Eds.). (1988). *Infant love and infant care leave.* New Haven, CT: Yale University Press.

ZIGLER, E. F. & LANG, M. (1990). *Childcare choices: Balancing the needs of children, families and society.* New York: Macmillan.

ZIGLER, E. & HODAPP, R. M. (1986). Mental retardation. In J. O. Cavenar, (Ed.), *Psychiatry.* Philadelphia: Lippincott.

ZIGLER, E. & HUNSINGER, S. (1977). Supreme Court on spanking: Upholding discipline or abuse? *Young Children, 32,* 14–15.

ZIGLER, E., LAMB, M., & CHILD, I. (1982). *Socialization and personality development,* (2nd Ed.). New York: Oxford University Press.

ZIGLER, E. & LANG, M. E. (1985, Sept.–Oct.). The emergence of "superbaby": A good thing? *Pediatric Nursing, 11* (5), 337–341.

ZIGLER, E., LEVINE, J., & GOULD, L. (1967). Cognitive challenge as a factor in children's humor appreciation. *Journal of Personality and Social Psychology, 6,* 332–336.

ZIGLER, E. & MUENCHOW, S. (1979). Mainstreaming: The proof is in the implementation. *American Psychologist, 34* (2), 993–996.

ZIGLER, E. & MUENCHOW, S. (In press). *The story of Head Start.* New York: Basic Books.

ZIGLER, E. & SEITZ, V. (1982). Social policy and intelligence. In R. Sternberg, (Ed.), *Handbook of human intelligence.* New York: Cambridge University Press.

ZIGLER, E. & TRICKETT, P. E. (1978). IQ, social competence, and evaluation of early childhood intervention programs. *American Psychologist, 33,* 789–798.

ZIGLER, E. & TURNER, P. (1982). Parents and day care workers: A failed partnership? In E. Zigler & E. Gordon, (Eds.), *Day care: Scientific and social policy issues:* Boston: Auburn House.

ZIGLER, E. & VALENTINE, J. (1979). *Project Head Start: A legacy of the War on Poverty.* New York: Free Press.

ZIGLER, E. & WEISS, H. (1985). Family support systems: An ecological approach to child development. In R. N. Rapoport, (Ed.), *Children, youth, families: The action-research relationship.* Cambridge: Cambridge University Press.

ZILL, N. (1983). *Happy, healthy, and insecure.* New York: Doubleday.

ZILL, N., SIGAL, H., & BRIM, O. G., JR. (1983). Development of childhood social indicators. In E. Zigler, S. L. Kagan, & E. Klugman, (Eds.), *Children, families, and government: Perspectives on American social policy.* New York: Cambridge University Press.

ZIMMERMAN, B. J. & LANARO, P. (1974). Acquiring and retaining conservation of length through modeling and reversibility cues. *Merrill-Palmer Quarterly, 20,* 145–161.

ZUBIN, J. & SPRING B. (1977). Vulnerability—a new view of schizophrenia. *Journal of Abnormal Psychology, 86,* 103–126.

ZUCKERMAN, D. M. & ZUCKERMAN, B. S. (1985). Television's impact on children. *Pediatrics, 75,* 233–240.

ZUCKERMAN, M. (1979). *Sensation seeking: Beyond the optimal level of arousal.* Hillsdale, NJ: Erlbaum.

Name Index

Bem, 371, 372
Benasich, 509
Bence, 30
Bench, 179
Bender, 92, 394
Benedek, 23
Bennett, 427, 540
Bentler, 563, 564
Berenda, 474
Berg, 172
Berger, 541
Bergman, 181
Berkeley Institute of Human Development, 552
Berko, 327
Berkowitz, 362
Berman, 201, 342
Berndt, 472, 474, 476
Bernstein, 506
Berrueta-Clement, 343, 536
Berry, 83
Bettelheim, 112
Beuf, 465
Beunen, 499, 500
Bevan, 9
Beyer, 459,
Bialystock, 427, 428
Bigelow, 472
Binet, 44, 45, 56, 439, 532–533
Birch, 110, 167, 296, 305, 393, 447
Bixenstine, 474
Black, 169
Black Child Development Institute, National, 266–268
Blair, 478
Blass, 207
Blau, 138
Blinder, 445
Block, 369
Blom, 38
Bloom, 221, 229, 230, 326, 331, 340
Blum, 102
Blyth, 512
Boehm, 303
Bohannon, 222
Bohman, 102
Bolton, 132
Booher, 117, 118
Borke, 321, 322, 363
Bornstein, 180, 214, 215, 234
Borovsky, 210
Botein, 259
Bouchard, 105, 106, 107, 302, 499, 500
Boukydis, 177
Bouterline-Young, 512
Bouthilet, 379
Bower, 184, 185
Bowerman, 326
Bowlby, 44, 62, 63, 256, 258, 264
Bowman, 328, 378
Brackbill, 129, 130, 176, 207
Bradley, 332
Brainerd, 425
Brasel, 139
Bray, 303
Brazelton, 129, 174, 176, 244, 245, 295, 298, 402
Breezley, 302
Brendt, 556, 557, 562

Brenner, 357
Brent, 515, 516
Bretherton, 254, 255, 256, 258, 260
Brett, 478
Breuer, 48
Bridges, 249
Brim, 36, 154
Brittain, 562
Brody, 84, 179
Bronfenbrenner, 10, 27, 31, 63, 66, 274, 342, 465
Brooks, 253, 274, 276
Brooks-Gunn, 364, 497, 502, 504, 505, 507, 508, 509, 510, 513, 555
Brophy, 468, 469
Broughton, 418
Brown, 148, 230, 324, 325, 326, 327, 414, 444, 560
Brozek, 138, 296
Bruch, 502
Bruner, 318, 331, 344, 359
Brunquette, 299
Brunswick, 564
Bryan, 445
Bryant, 484
Budoff, 448
Bulow-Hube, 303
Burbank, 494
Burdetti, 198
Burgdorff, 568
Burger, 477
Burgess, 378
Burhmester, 557
Burnham, 131
Business Practices, Bureau of, 36
Bustillo, 119
Butler, 132
Butterfield, 534, 535
Byrnes, 141

Cacciari, 430
Caffey, 299
Cahan, 10
Cain, 137, 232, 275, 509
Cairns, 541
California Growth Study, 511, 512
Camara, 22, 351, 483
Cameron, 212, 213
Campbell, 197
Campos, 168, 183, 247, 249, 254, 455
Cantor, 516
Cantwell, 394, 395
Caparulo, 112, 113
Caplan, 33, 475
Card, 555
Carey, 176, 325, 526
Carleton-Ford, 565
Carnegie Council on Adolescent Development, 539, 541, 550, 551, 571, 572
Carnegie Foundation for the Advancement of Teaching, 502
Casale, 265
Cascione, 232, 529
Cash, 401
Casper, 503
Caspi, 492
Cates, 511
Cattell, 528

Cavanaugh, 207
CED, (Committee on Economic Development), 536
Census, United States Bureau of the, 12, 13, 14, 24, 25, 26, 235, 352, 483, 541
Cernoch, 184
Chaika, 179
Chaikin, 469
Chalfant, 444, 446, 447
Chall, 231
Chandler, 80, 126, 127, 138, 200
Chapman, 325
Chard, 389
Chase, 141
Chase-Lansdale, 268, 507, 509, 555
Chasnoff, 131, 136
Chavez, 131
Chess, 110, 113, 146, 163, 165, 167, 168, 393
Chi, 232, 323, 415
Child, 370, 527, 529
Child Abuse, National Committee for the Prevention of, 470
Child Care Action Campaign, 37
Child Care Staffing Study, National, 334, 335
Child Development, Society for Research in, 70, 193, 212, 213, 454, 553, 559
Child Health, Select Panel for the Promotion of, 307, 309, 392, 502
Children and Family Services, Illinois Department, 301
Children, National Commission on, 12, 16
Children in Poverty, National Center for, 12, 14, 18, 19, 34, 127, 141, 296, 305, 443, 483, 484, 508
Children's Defense Fund, 11, 13, 16, 20, 25, 33, 35, 141, 265, 481, 541
Children's Hospitals and Related Institutions, National Association, 305
Children, Youth, and Families, U.S. House Select Committee, 35, 142, 192, 266, 570
Children and Youth Fitness Study, National, 392
Chilman, 506
Chinese Medical Journal, 27
Ching, 27
Chinsky, 415
Chomsky, 223, 429
Christensen, 563
Christophersen, 309, 310
Christy, 413
Cicchetti, 110
Clark, 230, 276, 465, 536
Clark, Edna McConnell, Foundation, 266
Clarke, 264
Clarke-Stewart, 234, 244, 259, 269, 275, 276, 333, 350, 381
Clausen, 512
Clewell, 509
Clinical Infant Programs, National Center for, 35, 235, 236
Cloninger, 102
Cnattingius, 132, 169
Cochran, 381
Cohen, 111, 112, 113, 211, 269, 393, 394, 395, 396, 403, 564
Cohn, 244
Colby, 459

La Barbera, 253
Labor Statistics, United States Bureau of, 13, 14, 18, 24, 550
Labor, United States Department of, 13, 18, 235, 266, 477, 550
Labov, 434, 435
LaBuch, 444
Lahey, 221
La Leche League, 173
LaLonde, 224
Lamb, 146, 256, 258, 260, 261, 274, 275, 351, 353, 359, 369, 370, 375, 479, 508, 527, 529
Lambert, 395, 432
Lampl, 186
Lamb-Parker, 342
Lanaro, 425
Lancaster, 495
Landau, 275, 502
Landress, 136
Lane, 413
Lang, 38, 231, 266, 480, 541
Langer, 183
Langham, 143
Langlois, 367
Laosa, 377, 441
Largo, 92
Larrabee, 42, 44
Larson, 540, 556, 561
Lauersen, 505
Lave, 435, 437
Layne, 571
Lays, 438, 439
Lazar, 343, 379
Lazerson, 526
Leach, 160, 161
Leavitt, 177
Leboyer, 145
Lecours, 288
Lederberg, 354
Lee, 391
Lemna, 97
Lempers, 329
Lenard, 172
Lenke, 84
Lenneberg, 201, 223, 224, 288
Leonard, 415
Lepper, 29
Lerner, 90, 234, 259, 260, 266, 274, 376, 512, 562
Lesser, 536, 562
Leventhal, 176
Levin, 350, 413
Levine, 431
Levinson, 566
Levitan, 24, 25, 28, 36, 477
Levitin, 22
Levitt, 130, 131, 132, 135, 169
Levorato, 430
Levy, 84
Lewin, 496
Lewis, 180, 202, 245, 246, 249, 253, 254, 274, 276, 305, 354 364, 367, 397, 461, 571
Lewontin, 80, 111
Libby, 90
Liebel, 297
Lieberstein, 445
Liebert, 367

Liederman, 149
Light, 142, 343
Lin, 22
Linden, 92
Lindholm, 433
Linn, 419
Lippincott, 175
Lips, 90
Lipsitt, 180, 183, 184, 189, 207, 210
Lipton, 176
Liss, 153
Litwak, 435
Lo, 100
Lobel, 138
Locke, 6, 7, 39, 52
Loeb, 466
Lohmann, 169
Lohr, 560
Long, 20, 21, 481
Longitudinal Studies, Consortium of, 343
Lonnborg, 380
Lopez, 131
Lord, 113, 469
Lorenz, 62, 162, 360
Lotter, 113
Lougee, 354
Louv, 402
Love, 201
Lowery, 178
Lozoff, 296, 298
Lucas, 276
Luria, 368
Lyons, 198, 259
Lytton, 104

Maccoby, 31, 256, 350, 351, 354, 366, 367, 372, 373, 454, 462, 466, 476, 477, 479
MacFarlane, 184
MacMillan, 448, 527, 529
MacPhee, 381
MacWhinney, 222
Magnusson, 514
Mahan, 502
Main, 244, 302
Malakoff, 431
Malatessa, 247
Malatesta, 259
Malina, 193, 499, 500
Mandler, 211, 212
Maratos, 262
Marcia, 548
Marcus, 366, 368
Mare, 403
Marentette, 226
Margolick, 310
Margolin, 15, 309, 310
Marhorn, 571
Markman, 223, 328, 428
Marks, 515
Markstrom-Adams, 465
Markus, 462
Marsiglio, 508, 509
Martha's Vineyard Child Health Survey, 32
Martin, 276, 302, 372, 373
Martorano, 526
Marvin, 322
Marx, 169
Masters, 36

Maternal and Health Clearinghouse, National, 306
Maurer, 180
Maxmen, 110
Mayer, 302
Mayors, United States Conference of, 406
McAnarney, 138
McCall, 38, 181, 185, 225, 234, 247, 248, 367, 534, 536
McCall Children's Trust, 225
McCarley, 174
McCarthy, 176, 229
McCartney, 80, 85, 268, 334
McClearn, 105, 108
McClusky, 564
McCrady, 445
McCroskey, 10
McDavid, 469, 474
McDonald, 136
McGhee, 430–431
McGillicuddy, 127
McGraw, 46, 294
McGue, 106
McGuire, 463
McKendry, 515
McKinney, 264
McKinney, Homeless Assistance Act, 408
McLanahan, 484
McLoyd, 377, 483, 484, 559
McManus, 129, 130
McNassor, 389
Meachum, 462
Mead, 58, 59, 496
Meadow, 201, 226
Mears, 262
Meck, 419
Medicine, Committee for the Institute of, 11, 15, 484
Medicine, Institute of, 141
Mednick, 137
Medrich, 469
Meece, 469
Meehan, 435, 526
Mehler, 179
Meisels, 439
Meltzoff, 208, 221
Menahem, 176
Mendel, 81, 82
Mental Deficiency, American Association on, 527, 528
Menyuk, 226, 428
Mercer, 535
Meredith, 296, 397, 398
Merrill, 531
Merriman, 328
Mesibov, 113
Meyer, 435
Meyers, 448
Michalson, 249, 253
Michelsson, 149
Midgley, 572
Miller, 215, 296, 303, 305, 306, 309, 564
Milunski, 89, 92, 96, 97, 139
Mindel, 201
Minnett, 353
Mintz, 12
Minuchin, 469, 503
Miringoff, 11
Mishara, 515

Stanford-Binet Test, 45, 531, 533
Stanley-Hagan, 13, 22, 351, 483
Stanowicz, 222
State Boards of Education, National Association of, 343, 440
State Legislators, National Conference of, 343
Staub, 363
Stayton, 248, 260
Stein, 31, 379, 380
Steinberg, 550
Steiner, 207
Steinhardt, 247
Steinmetz, 298, 300
Steinschneider, 169, 176
Steriel, 478
Sterling, 29
Stern, 90, 208, 224, 243, 247, 248, 298, 502, 514, 532
Sternberg, 527, 529, 534
Sternglanz, 368
Steuer, 379
Stevenson, 307, 437, 438, 442, 467
Stevens-Simon, 138
Stewart, 112
Stinson, 197
Stipek, 9, 340, 467, 539
St. James-Roberts, 176
Stoolmiller, 563, 566
Straham, 526
Strandberg, 111
Strattin, 514
Strauss, 131, 298
Strayer, 455
Strean, 138
Streissguth, 132, 133, 134
Strickland, 447
Stuart, 176, 296, 501, 502, 505
Stukan, 505
Stunkard, 302
Sugar, 485
Sullivan, 210, 310, 390, 400
Sunderlin, 357
Suomi, 262, 263, 264, 275, 355
Super, 196, 357, 437
Sussman, 130, 131, 132, 135, 169
Sutton-Smith, 137, 353, 357, 359
Swain, 431
Syzmanski, 527

Taeschner, 432
Taft, 203
Takaishi, 399
Takanishi, 9
Takenaka, 143
Tanguay, 527
Tanner, 123, 147, 162, 189, 285, 288, 293, 297, 303, 390, 397, 398, 399, 401, 499, 500
Tartter, 179
Taylor, 296, 497, 504, 558
Technology Assessment, Office of, 11
Television Violence, National Coalition on, 379
Teller, 180
Terman, 45, 514, 531, 533
Thelen, 172
Thissen, 499
Thoden, 149

Thoman, 244
Thomas, 110, 146, 163, 165, 167, 168, 393, 443, 570, 571
Thompson, 45, 71, 325, 364, 401, 502
Thomson, 139
Thurstone, 530
Tice, 547, 549
Tierney, 571
Timiras, 187
Tishler, 515, 516
Tizard, 262, 264
Tobin, 338
Tobler, 564
Tomber, 38
Topping, 323
Tower, 32
Trabasso, 423
Trauma Research, Committee on, 307
Travers, 142, 343
Trczinski, 36, 270, 271, 273, 478
Tremaine, 367
Trickett, 299, 343
Tronick, 243–247, 249, 253, 254
Tschann, 23
Tuma, 12, 484, 485, 486, 514
Turiel, 459, 461
Turnbull, 447
Turner, 138, 232, 335, 443
Tyler, 287
Tyne, 210
Tyron, 103

University Women, American Association of, 513
Urberg, 354, 369
Uzgiris, 245

Valdez, 407
Valentine, 341, 342
Vandell, 276, 353, 356, 357
Vandenberg, 107, 108, 359
Van der Meer, 149
Van der Voort, 32
VanDusen, 506
Vasta, 47, 68, 69
Vaughn, 259
Ventura, 397
Vihmam, 432
Vinouskis, 509
Volpe, 472
Voltera, 432
Vondra, 567
Vygotsky, 56, 331, 344

Waggener, 169
Waggoner, 430
Walden Two, 53
Walk, 182
Walker, 461, 542
Wallace, 124
Waller, 307, 403, 481
Wallerstein, 22, 23, 352, 353, 483
Wallis, 197
Walthod, 201
Walton, 478
Ward, 307, 335
Ware, 95

Warner, 180
Warshak, 23
Washburn, 80
Wasserman, 168
Waterman, 548
Waters, 256, 259, 260, 261
Watkins, 30, 31, 336
Watson, 46, 52, 53, 232, 233, 266, 317, 357
Ways and Means, United States House Committee, 143
Webster, 247
Wechsler, 533
Wehler, 401
Weikart, 343
Weinberg, 45, 532, 536, 538
Weiner, 134, 514
Weingarten, 28
Weinman, 226
Weinraub, 274
Weinstein, 538
Weir, 226
Weisbrod, 265
Weiss, 33, 301, 342, 396, 510
Weissberg, 414, 445, 475
Weissbluth, 176
Weissman, 485, 516
Weisz, 63
Weitzman, 352
Welfare Association, American, 15
Wellman, 329, 415
Wender, 395, 396
Werker, 224
Werner, 56, 57, 193
Wertmann, 150
Wessel, 176
West, 130
Westinghouse Learning Corporation, 342
Weston, 131
Whalen, 393, 394, 395
Whitbread, 481
White, 31, 43, 45, 177, 180, 184, 185, 232, 414, 437, 440
Whitehouse, 399
Whitehurst, 231
Whiting, 357, 367, 370, 494
Whittaker, 33
Whol, 138
Wickstrom, 289
Widdowson, 297
Wieder, 154
Wiesenfeld, 247
Wilborn, 564
Wilcox, 120
Wiley, 562
Wilkner, 184
Willerman, 111
Williams, 147, 183, 292, 305, 306, 309, 443
Williamson, 309
Willig, 434
Wilson, 126, 378, 380
Wineberg, 469
Winer, 425
Winick, 139, 302
Winn, 493
Winner, 429
Wippman, 261
Wirtenberg, 368
Wise, 555
Wishaw, 287

Subject Index

American Association on Mental Deficiency (AAMD), 527–528
American Journal of Diseases of Children, 401
American Psychological Association, 8
American Sign Language, 226
Amniocentesis, 99, 100–101
Amnion, 118
Amniotic fluid, 99, 118, 179
Amniotic sac, 99, 118, 123
Amyl, 563
Anal retentive personality, 50
Anal zone, 49
Androgens, 125, 497, 504, 505, 506. *See also* Hormones
Androgynous, 366
Anemia, 97, 125, 296, 502
Animal studies (on heredity and behavior), 61–64, 102–103
Anorexia nervosa, 401, 502–503
Anoxia, 147
Anxiety
    and childbirth, 144–145
    gender role, 370
    and learning disabilities, 443–446
    maternal, prenatal development, 138
    and moral development, 456
    separation, 253, 255–256, 350–351
    stranger, 253, 254–255
Anxious attachments, 258, 259
Apgar scoring system, 144, 174
Aphasia, 444
Apnea, 148
Appearance
    adolescents, concerns, 521–522
    older children, concerns, 401
Applied research, 64
Apprenticeship, 572
Area conservation, 416, 417, 418
Areola, 504
Arteriosclerosis, 303
Articulation, 328
Articulatory system, 224
Asbestos, 128
Aspirin, 125
Aspirin, poisoning, 309
Assault, 571
Assimilation, behavior, 217–218
Associative play, 356–357
Asthma, 405, 406
Attachment, mother-infant, 62–63, 242–243, 256–265
    communication between, 243, 247–249
    cultural factors, 260
    definition of, 242, 256
    effects of child care, 269
    importance of, 260–265
    individual differences in, 256–258
    influences on, 259
    theories of, 258–259
Attention
    deficiencies, 529
    measures of, 214
    older children, 413
Attention, deficit disorder (ADD), 296, 393–396
Attention deficit hyperactivity disorder (ADHD), 393–396, 444
Attention, selective, 413

Attrition, 68
Atypical development, 125, 126, 196–203. *See also* Autism; Down's syndrome; Mental retardation; Schizophrenia
Audience, imaginary, 522
Authoritarian parents, 374, 567
Authoritative parents, 375, 465, 566
Autism, 111–113
Autobiographical memory, 324
Automobile safety, 310
Autonomous level, 459. *See also* Postconventional level
Autonomy, 50, 566
Autonomy vs. shame and doubt, 50, 348
Autosomes, 90
Autostimulation theory, 175
Aversive conditioning, 207
Avoidant attachments, 258
Axons, 189

Babbling, 222–228
Babies. *See* Infants
Baby biographies, 8, 44
Baby boom, 23–24, 28, 44, 550
Baby Doe, 196–197
Baby Jane Doe, 197
"Baby talk," 226, 247
Barbiturates, 563
Basic research, 64
Basic skills, problems with learning, 438–439. *See also* Academic performance
Behavior
    adaptive, 216–217
    aggressive, 29–30, 65–67, 302, 360–363, 561
    destructive, 571
    and divorce, 483
    environmental factors and, 54
    genetic approach, 61
    heredity and, 102–112
    hormonal effects on, 505–506
    modification of, 462
    multiple causes, 71
    norms of, 71–72
    patterns of mental retardation, 529
    problems with, 445, 465, 483, 484–486, 496, 513–514, 515, 567
    regressive, 353
    stages of, 46
Behavioral system, 258
Behaviorism, 52–54
Behaviorists, 52
Berkeley Institute of Human Development, 552
Bilingualism, 431–435
Binet-Simon tests, 45, 532, 533. *See also* IQ tests
Biological factors
    of adolescence, 496
    and aggression, 360–362
    in language development, 223–224
    and learning disabilities, 444
    in sex-typed behavior, 367–368
Biological theory of personality. *See* Psychoanalytic theory
Birth
    breech, 145, 147
    delivery options, 144–145

evaluating the newborn, 144
process of, 143–147
rate of, 23–25, 44
social aspects, 150–155
transverse, 145
See also Childbirth
Birthing, gentle, 144–145
Birthing rooms, 145–146
Black Child Development Institute, National, 267–268
Black English, 434–435
Blacks
    drop-out rate, 541
    family income and, 15
    foster care, children in, 267–268
    friendship patterns, 558–559
    infant mortality, 140–141
    and IQ tests, 535, 536
    poverty and, 484
    sickle-cell anemia, 94, 96–97
    single-parent families, 12, 483
    and unemployment, 550
    vocational choices of, 550
Blended families. *See* Stepfamilies
Blind infants, 200–201, 249, 250. *See also* Smiles, infant
Blood cholesterol levels, 392
Blood pressure, 302, 392
Blood relative, 81
Body cells (somatic cells), 87–88
Body proportions, 186-187, 392, 499–501
Bonding, mother-infant, 146. *See also* Attachment, mother-infant; Imprinting
Bone Age, 285–286
Boys
    and depression, 513
    and The Depression, 552–553
    and divorce parents, 483
    effect of parents on, 479
    friendships and, 557
    physical changes in, 499, 500, 501
    as prostitutes, 568
    puberty rites, 493
    reproductive organs, 504
    self-esteem of, 464–465, 512, 513
    See also Sex-typed behavior
Brain
    damage, 131, 133, 137, 147, 201, 223, 288, 301, 539
    development of, 139, 189–191, 282, 286–288
    hemispheres of, 286–288
    imaging, 48
    maturation, 524
Breast development, 504
Breast-feeding, 172–173
Breech position, 145, 147
Bulimia, 401, 503
Butyl nitrites, 563

Caffeine, 125, 132
California Growth Study, 511, 512
Canalization, 80
Cancer, 306
Cancer, cervical, 511
Capacitation, 117
Cardiovascular, 306
Cardiovascular disease, 392

Enzymes, 117, 128
Epigenetic theories, 48
Epistemology, genetic, 56–57
Equality, 556
Equilibrium, 218
Estrogens, 125, 497, 504, 505. *See also* Hormones
Ethics, 70, 197, 198. *See also* Moral judgment
Ethnic group diseases, 96–97. *See also* Cultural factors
Ethnic identity, 465
Ethnological research, 62–63
Evolutionary theory, 8, 93, 252
Excitement, generalized, 249
Exercise, 303
Exocrine glands, 97
Exogenous smile, 251
Experimental
  method, 65–66
  research and studies, 8–9
  See also Field experiments; Natural experiments
Expressions of Emotions in Man and Animals, The, (Darwin), 249
Expressive language, 224
External aids, memory, 415
Extinction, 54
Extroverted, 110
Eye contact, 248–249

Face-to-face play, 244, 245, 246
Facial proportions, 392, 500
Failure to thrive, 297–298, 302
Fairness, 456, 461
Faithfulness, 556
Fallopian tube, 116, 117, 118, 119, 511
Families
  and adolescents, 564–565, 569, 571
  annual earnings, 16
  changes in, 12–31, 44, 552–553
  current realities of, 477–479
  distribution of children, 13
  divorce, effects of, 22–23
  homeless, 569
  influence of, 252, 441–442, 464–466
  interaction with television, 336
  isolation of, 12
  poverty and, 17–19
  and preschoolers, 331–332, 349–350
  as socializing agent, 372–373, 466
  social support, 12, 478
  support programs, 32–33
  types of, 454–455, 477–478, 483
  welfare, living on, 15
  See also Parents; Stepfamilies
Family day-care home, 235
Family Resource Centers, 482
Family Support Act, 34
Family Support Service (FSS), 35
Family system, 276
Fathers
  adolescents as, 508
  and infant relationships, 274–276
  interactions of, with older children, 351
  and older child relationships, 479
  of premature infants, 148–149
  role in birth defects, 132
  See also Parents

Fear, 53, 252–255, 456, 481
Feeding, infant, 248
Feminine, 366–367
Femininity, 367, 369
Fertility, 504
Fertilization, 87, 116–119. *See also* Conception
Fetal Alcohol Syndrome (FAS), 133–134, 135
Fetal development, 118–123, 498
Fetus, 87, 90, 92, 99–101, 118, 121–128, 130–139, 498
Field experiments, 66
Figurative, language, 430
Fine motor, skills, 64, 288, 289, 293, 389
Fires, 481
Flexible work time, 478
Fluid intelligence, 528–529
Follow Through, 443
Food allergies, 395. *See also* Diet, Nutrition
Foreclosure, 548
Forgotten Half: Non-College Youths in America, The, 572
Formal operational thinking, 57, 521
Formal operations stage
  of cognitive development, 215, 416
  vs. concrete operations, 522–525, 526
  definition of, 522
  individual differences, 526–527
  nonuniversality of, 525–526
  quality of education and, 537
  testing for, 522–525
Formula, IQ tests, 532–533
Foster care, 35, 265–266, 267, 568
Foster homes, 264, 265
Foundling homes, 42. *See also* Orphanages
Fragile X Syndrome, 92
Fraternal (dizygotic) twins, 104, 107
Friends
  between black and white adolescents, 558–559
  making of, 455, 472, 474
  at various stages, 354–355, 472, 556–557
Friendships, 461, 556–559
Frustration, preschool, 362

Gall bladder, 302
Games, infant-infant, 276. *See also* Play
Gametes, 87–88, 92
Gang turf wars, 571
Gaze, 248
Gender
  identity, 364–365, 368, 371, 462
  role, 365–367, 368, 371, 462
  stability and constancy of, 365
  See also Sex-typed behavior
Gender schema theory, 371–372
Gene locus, 87
General intelligence (g factor), 530
Generation gap, 562, 565
Generativity vs. stagnation, 50, 52
Genes
  chemical nature of, 85–87
  complex activity, 84–85
  defective, 84, 86, 90
  definition of, 81, 86
  mutations of, 92, 94
  types of, 86
  See also Heredity; Environmental factors

Genetic
  behavioral approach, 61
  behavior influence, 54
  cognitive development and, 57, 108
  counseling, 96–97
  defects, 81–85
  detecting disorders, 98–100
  diseases, 94
  engineering, 98, 101
  vs. environmental factors, 536
  mental disorders, 110–113
  mental retardation, 529
  prenatal problems, 137–138
  research, 95
  screening, 98
  transmission of information, 81
  variability, 89–90
  See also Heredity; Environmental factors
Genital period, 50
Genotypes, 78–80, 83, 126
German measles, 303
Germ cells. *See* Gametes
Germinal mutations, 92
Gesell test, 440
Gestational age, 200
Gestational surrogacy, 120
Gestures, 226, 228, 247
Girls
  and The Depression, 552–553
  effects of parents on, 479
  friendships and, 474, 557
  nutritional needs of, 502–503
  physical changes in, 499, 500, 501
  puberty rites, 493
  reproductive organs, 504
  self-esteem of, 511, 513
  sex roles of, 554
  See also Sex-typed behavior
Glandular secretions, 53
Glial cells, 189, 286
Gonorrhea, 125
"Good-girl and nice-boy" stage, 458
Goodness of fit, 168
Government
  child care assistance, 34
  family support, 34–36
  social programs, 9
Grammar, acquisition of, 325–327, 428
Grasping, 216, 217, 218, 220. *See also* Reflexes, infant
Gross motor, skills, 64, 288, 289, 292, 389
Groups. *See* Cliques; Crowds; Peer groups
Growth
  of adolescents, 499–501
  of infants, 186–192
  of preschoolers, 296–298, 360–372
  rates, 186–192, 396–398, 499
  during school-age years, 392–401
  spurts, 139, 499, 500, 501, 502
  See also Physical development
Guanine, 86, 87
Guilt, 51, 348, 456, 462, 564

Habituation, 178, 214
Haemophilus, 304
Hair growth, 505
Hallucinogens, 563
Handicapped children, 446–449
Hashish, 563

Head Start, 9, 67, 304, 314, 336, 340–342, 443
Health, 303, 401–404
Health care
   of children, 303–307, 484
   of the homeless, 407–408
   in middle childhood, 404–406
Health and Human Services, U. S. Department of, 266
Hearing aids, 201
Hearing problems
   impaired, 444
   of infants, 179–180, 201, 226–228
Heart conditions, 405
Heart disease, 302, 303
Height, 282–285, 397, 398, 399, 499
Hemoglobin, 94
Hemophilia, 90–91
Heredity
   and behavior, 102–112
   diseases, 94
   and environment, 78–98, 536
   and intelligence, 105–109, 536
   of personality traits, 109–112
   physical effects of, 8, 505
Heritability ratio, 106–107, 111
Heroin, 125, 131, 563
Herpes, 125, 510
Heterozgotes, 81–83, 94, 96
Hidden curriculum, 467
Hierarchic integration, 57, 193
High school
   dropouts from, 540–542
   social issues and, 536–543
Hispanics
   activity levels, 396
   drop-out rate, 541
   family income and, 15
   infant mortality, 141
   and IQ tests, 535
   poverty and, 484
   and unemployment, 550
   See also Minority groups
Historical events (longitudinal), 68
HIV (Human Immunodeficiency Virus), 191
Holophrasic speech, 230
Homeless children, 264, 305, 406–408, 568–570
Homelessness, 34
Homework, 542
Homozygotes, 81–83, 91, 94
Honesty. See Moral development
Horizontal decalage, 417–418
Hormones, 125, 138, 303, 367–368, 497–498, 499, 504–506. See also Sexual maturation
Hostile aggression, 362–363
Human Genome Project, 95
Humor, 430–431
Huntington disease, 85
Hurried Child, The, 232, 402
Hyperactive syndrome, 393
Hyperactivity, 393–396
Hypertension (high blood pressure), 402
Hypervigilant, 302
Hypnosis, 48
Hypoactivity, 394
Hypothalamus, 497

Hypothesis, 47, 520, 522, 524, 525, 526, 535, 536, 537

Id, 48–49, 50
Identical (monozygotic) twins, 104, 107
Identification, 370
Identity
   achievement, 548
   crisis, 548
   diffusion, 548
   formation, 548, 549, 552–553, 554
   personal, 546–568
   vs. role, 50, 51, 547
   search, 556–563
Idiolect, 325
Illiteracy
   functional, 539–540
   and jobs, 550–551
Illnesses, childhood, 303, 304
Illnesses, chronic, 404–406
Images, 287
Imagination, 31
Imitation
   by children, 461
   deferred, 316–317
   by infants, 208–209, 220–221
   by preschoolers, 316–317
   sex-typed behaviors, 371
Immunization, 303, 304, 305, 306
Immunization Initiative Program, Childhood, 304
Imprinting, 62
Impulsivity, 436, 534
Inattentiveness, 393, 394
Incompetence, social, 355
Independence, 51, 348–350, 470, 476, 477, 481, 496, 514, 566, 567, 568
In-depth perspective, 453
Indestructibility, sense of, 522
Individuality, 162–169, 557
Inductive reasoning, 320
Inductive techniques, 462
Industry vs. inferiority, 50, 51, 464
Infancy, 42
Infant Health and Development Programs, 70
Infant Health and Development Study, 150
Infanticide, 42
Infants
   AIDS, born with, 191–192
   attachment to parents, 51, 242, 256–273
   breast-feeding, 172–173
   characteristics of, 161–177
   cognitive development of, 205–221, 234–239
   communication skills, 247–249
   Darwin's studies of, 8
   dependence and competency in, 169–174
   development of, 232–233
   "difficult babies," 79–80, 164
   disabled and handicapped, 196–203
   emotional development, 249–255
   growth rates, 186–192
   interaction among, 276–277
   language development, 221–231
   low birth weight of, 147–150
   mortality rates, 140–143

physical development, 158–203
   premature, 12, 147–150, 168, 174, 176, 183
   reflexes of, 8, 169–172, 192
   risks to, 200
   sensory and perceptual development of, 178–185
   social development, 242–255
   states of, 172–174
   as superbabies, 184–185
Infants and Toddlers with Handicapping Conditions, Services for, 199
Infertile, 116–120
Infertility, 117–120, 511
Influenza, 125
Information-processing, 56, 57–58, 214–215, 323, 412–413, 520–521, 526–527
Inhalants, 563
Inheritance, laws of, 81–84. See also Heredity
Initiative vs. guilt, 50, 51, 348
Injuries
   childhood, 306, 307–310
   in older children, 403–404
   prevention of, 307–310
   types of, 403
Insecurity, 44
Insemination, 118, 119
Instinctive drives, 50
Institutions, 262–265
Instrumental. See Conditioning, operant
Instrumental aggression, 362–363
Instrumental relativist stage, 458
Integration, 558
Integrity
   and continuity, 35
   vs. despair, 50, 52
Intellectual development, adolescents, 520–527
Intellectual performance, 527–535
Intelligence, 45, 55, 105–109
   A and B, 528–529
   definition of, 528–531
   factors affecting, 535–536
   measuring of, 531–532
   mental abilities, 530, 536
   See also Heredity
Intelligence and Experience (Hunt), 340
Intelligence tests. See IQ tests; Wechsler intelligence tests
Interdependence, 378
Internship, 572
Intervention programs, 339–344, 538, 539
Intervillous space, 122
Intimacy vs. isolation, 50, 51
Intrapair concordance, 104
Introverted, 110
In utero, 118, 123, 136, 139
Invariant sequence, 45
In vitro fertilization, 118–119, 120
Iodine, 127, 129
IQ (intelligence quotient), 32, 45, 147, 233, 263–264, 527–528, 531–536, 539, 571
IQ tests
   bilinguals and, 432
   description of, 440

effect of Early Intervention Programs, 150
factors affecting results of, 147, 468–469, 534–536
heredity and, 105–108
history of, 45, 532–533
limits on accuracy of, 45
measuring intelligence, 527
mental retardation, identifying, 527–528
effect of preschool programs on, 333, 343
problems with, 531, 534
and socioeconomic status, 535–536
in "tracking" students, 538
value of, 439
See also Cognitive development;
Isolation, 481, 561, 567, 568

Jaundice, 147
Jobs. *See* Vocational, identity;
Unemployment, of youths
Job training programs, 551
Jokes, 430–431
Junk foods, 402
Justice, 456, 461
Juvenile delinquents. *See* Delinquent youths

Karyotype, 91–92
Klinefelter's syndrome, 91, 93

Laboratory, research, 66
Laboratory schools. *See* Research, centers for
Labor laws, child, 43–44, 492, 493
La Leche League, 173
Lamaze method, 144–145
Language acquisition device (LAD), 223
Language development
    bilingualism, 431–435
    and the brain, 286–288
    cross-cultural and, 59–60
    in the disabled, 201
    in infants, 221–231
    in middle childhood, 427–435, 437
    milestones in, 224–228
    of minorities, 431–435
    in preschoolers, 318, 324–331
    theories of, 221–224
    See also Verbal
Language-minority children, 431
Language structure, 223–224
Lanugo, 162
Latchkey children, 20–21, 480–481, 484
Latency period, 49–50
Lateralization, 286–287
"Law and order stage," 458
Lead poisoning, 15, 128, 305, 309
Learned helplessness, 441
Learning
    at different stages, 206–212
    disabilities, 444–446
    environments, 331–339
    formal vs. informal, 435–438
    motivations for, 440–441
    problems with, 438–439
    theories of, 52–55, 222–223, 371
    in the womb, 124
    See also Conditioning
Learning readiness, 209

Leaves of absence, 36, 270–273
Legalistic orientation, 459
Length conservation, 416, 417, 418
Leukemia, 92, 405
Lexicons, 437
Life, beginning of, 87–88
Linguistic descriptions, 287
Liquid conservation, 416–417, 418
Literacy skills, 428
"Lively fours," 46
Logic, 319
Longitudinal research, 68
Long-term memory, 413
Low-achieving students, 538
Low-birth weight, 12, 130, 131, 132, 134, 135, 137, 138, 141, 143, 147–150, 168, 298, 299, 300, 485. *See also* Prematurity
Loyalty, 556, 557
LSD, 125, 131, 563
Lying, 461

Maidenhood, 494, 495
Mainstreaming, 433, 446–449
Make-believe. *See* Dramatic play
Maladaptive acculturation, 465
Malaria, 94
Malnutrition, 139, 296–297, 305, 484. *See also* Diet
Maltreatment. *See* Abuse; Neglect
Marijuana, 125, 130, 131, 563, 564, 571
Marriage, 493, 494, 495
Martha's Vineyard Child Health Survey (Garrison and Earls), 32
Masculine, 366–367
Masculinity, 367, 369
Matching Familiar Figures Test, 436
Maternity leaves, 19, 173, 271–273, 478. *See also* Leaves of absence
Matter conservation, 418
Maturation
    Brain, 286–293
    Gesell's theory of, 45–46
    physiological, 194
    rates of, 194, 397, 398, 492–493, 511–512
    See also Sexual maturation
Maturational readiness, 46
Maturational theories, 45–46
Measles, 304
Mediated learning experiences, 539
Medicaid, 34, 305
Medical
    care, 303–307
    technology, 197–198
Meiosis, 88, 89, 93
Memory
    aids to, 414
    as cognitive process, 55, 57–58, 214–215, 323–324, 413–415
    effect on, 296
    impaired, 444, 529
    in infants, 209–211
    knowledge accumulating and, 415
Menarche, 397, 398, 494, 495, 504, 511, 513. *See also* Puberty
Menstruation, 493, 502, 504, 505. *See also* Menarche

Mental abilities. *See* IQ (intelligence quotient); IQ tests; Intelligence
Mental age (MA), 532–533
Mental disorders
    in children, 11
    factors of, 12
    genetic link, 110–113
    poverty, affect of, 15
    prevention of, 33
    treatment of, 48
Mental health problems, 484, 485
Mental operations, 416
Mental overload, 477
Mental retardation, 527–529, 535
    categorization of, 528
    causes of, 528–529
    genetic defects, 82
    and IQ tests, 527–528
    mislabeling of, 444
    radiation, 92
    teratogens and, 126, 128
    See also Atypical development
Mesoderm, 122
Metabolism, disorder, 97
Metacognition, 521
Metalanguage, 427–428
Metalinguistic awareness, 427, 432, 521
Metaphorical speech, 429
Metaphors, 429–430
Metamemory, 415, 521
Methadone, 125, 131
Methaqualone, 563
Middle childhood
    cognitive development in, 410–449
    emotional development in, 450–487
    language development in, 427–435, 437
    moral development in, 456–461
    motor development, 389–391
    physical development in, 387–409
    and school, 435–446
    social development in, 450–487
Midwest and its Children (Barker and Wright), 63
"Might makes right," 458
Migraine, 405
Minimal brain dysfunction (MBD), 393
Minimum wage laws, 550
Minorities in the Media, 380
Minority groups
    in IQ testing, 534–535, 536
    and language development, 431–435
    self-esteem in, 465
    socialization, 377–378
    study of, 60–61
    and teen pregnancies, 508
    television, influence of, 380
    and unemployment, 550
    See also Blacks; Hispanics
Miscarriage, 90, 120, 128, 129, 130, 136, 137
Miseducation, 232
Mitosis, 88–89
Mnemonic device, 414
Modifier genes, 85
Monkeys, experiments, 61, 63, 64, 261–262, 264, 275, 506
Moral, 43
    behavior, 461–462
    development, 456–461

Reinforcement, 54, 371, 375, 440–441, 456, 461
Rejection, 560–561, 569
Relationships
    establishing, 51–52
    infants, 256–265, 274–276
REM (rapid eye movement) sleep, 174–176
Repeat testing, 68
Representational thought, 220, 315
Reproductive cells. *See* Gametes
Reproductive system, 117, 504–505
Research
    application of, to practice, 71–72
    case histories, 69–70
    centers for, 46
    child care, 35
    child development, 6–8, 35, 42–44, 63–72
    cultural factors, 58–61
    enhancing family life, 17
    genetic, 95
    methods of, 64–70
    vs. personal knowledge, 63
    reliability, 65
    types of, 64
    See also Child development, research in
Retractive-inhibitive, 185
Retrospective research, 69
Reversibility, 416–417, 421, 430, 431
Reward, 53–54, 55, 208, 364, 371, 462
RH factor, 137–138
Riddles, 430–431
Risk-taking, 522
Ritalin, 395
RNA (ribonucleic acid), 87
Role confusion, 51, 548
Role identities, 358–359, 368–369, 462, 548–549
Role-taking, 452–456
"Rooming in," 145–146
Rooting reflex, 170
Rubella, 125, 136, 201, 304
Rules, concept of, 456–457, 470
Runaways, 568–569
Runaways: In Their Own Words, 568

Schema (schemata), Piagetian, 216–218, 220
Schizophrenia, 110–111
Scholastic achievement, 438
Schooling, compulsory, 43
School readiness, 314, 343–344
School Reform Act of 1990, 482
School of the 21st Century, 37–38, 482
Schools
    adolescents in, 536–543
    child care at, 481–482
    compulsory, 525
    effect on achievement, 542–543
    effect on cognitive development, 437–438, 536–538
    improvements of, in assisting youths, 572
    intellectual performance in, 538
    as a learning environment, 435–446
    performance in. *See* Academic performance
    physical fitness, and, 303, 392
    preparation for, 331–339

punishment in, 470
    as a socializing agent, 467
    violence in, 571
    See also Child care; Education; High school
Scribbling, 289, 290, 293
Seat belts, 310
Sebum, 505
Secondary Schooling for Hispanics, National Commission, 541
Secular trend, 388, 397, 398
Securely attached, 257–258, 260–261
Security
    and infant attachment, 256, 257, 260–261
    as purpose of friends, 557
Sedatives, 563
Seeing, 218. *See also* Reflexes, infant
Segregate, groups, 560
Seizures, 405
Selective breeding, 103
Selective social smile, 251
Self-care children, 20, 480–486. *See also* Latchkey children
Self-concept
    in adolescents, 511, 513, 541
    evaluative component of. *See* Self-esteem
    of handicapped children, 445, 448
    influences on, 462–464
    in preschoolers, 364–367
    See also Gender identity
Self-control, 7, 372–373
Self-discipline, 7
Self-esteem
    of adolescents, 566
    of boys, 464, 465, 512, 513
    of delinquent youths, 571
    development of, 51, 463–464
    of friendless adolescents, 561
    of girls, 511, 513
    influences on, 388, 390, 401, 464–466, 477, 484
    of learning-disabled children, 445
    in minorities, 465
Self-Esteem Inventory, 464
Self-help, skills, 293–294
Self-identity, 514
Self-image, 401, 448
Self-reflective role-taking, 453
Self-worth, 401, 513
Semantics, language, 221, 428
Senses, interconnection, 185
Sensorimotor period, 57, 215, 216–221, 315, 318, 359, 424
Sensory capabilities, 178–185, 247
Sensory memory, 413
Sensory skills, infant, 8
Sentences
    preschoolers, 324–325, 326
    school-age children, 428–429
Separation anxiety, 253, 255–256, 350–351
Seriation, 422–424
"Sesame Street," 31, 336
Sex
    chromosomes, 84–87, 90–92
    cleavage, 474
    drive, 505–506
    education, 509–510
    hormones, 497–498, 504
    roles, 554–555

stereotyped, 293
    See also Gender
Sex differences
    in formal operations stage, 526
    in friendships, 557
    in interactions, 474
    in moral development 461
    in motor skills, 293, 294, 391
    in physical characteristics, 504–505
    in physical growth, 501
    in sex drive, 505–506
Sex-typed behavior
    of adolescents, 506, 554–556
    and biological factors, 367–368
    environmental factors, 368
    and the parental role, 368–369
    in preschoolers, 365–372
    theories on, 370–372
Sexual abuse, 300, 568, 569
Sexual activity, 494, 506–507, 554, 557
Sexual assault, 481
Sexual development. *See* Sexual maturation
Sexual diseases, 510–511
Sexual feelings, desires, 49–50
Sexual identity. *See* Gender identity
Sexual intercourse
    by adolescents, 494, 506
    by children, 397
Sexual maturation
    during puberty, 49, 50, 492, 494, 497–498, 503–505
    rate of, 397, 398, 511–512
Sexual revolution, 397, 506, 554, 555
Shaken baby syndrome, 301
Shapes, memory of, 211
Shape stage, drawing, 290
Sharing, 458, 461
Short-term memory, 413
Sibling relationships, 353–354
Sibling rivalry, 353
Sickle-cell anemia, 94–95, 96–97
Sight. *See* Visual acuity, newborn
Sign language, 224, 226, 227
Signs, Piagetian, 316, 318
Single children, 27
Single-parents, 12, 483. *See also* Parents
Skeletal development, 282, 285, 296–297, 500, 501
Skills, practice of, 289, 292, 293, 390
"Slavish conformity," 561
Slow learners, 535
Smell, sense of, 183–185
Smiles, infant, 249–252
Social apathy, 554
Social class, 535–536
Social cognition, 452
Social competence, 476, 477
Social contract stage, 459
Social development
    of adolescents, 544–573
    of infants, 242–255
    in middle childhood, 450–487
    of preschoolers, 348–359, 372–382
Social factors, 10, 12
Social indicators, childhood, 10–12, 24–25, 35

Text Photo Credits

Part I. 2, Gale Zucker.   **Chapter 1. 4,** Gale Zucker; **6,** Library of Congress; **7,** (top) Michael Siluk; (bottom) The Bettmann Archive; **8,** (top) Library of Congress; (bottom) The Bettmann Archive; **20,** (right) Courtesy, Dr. Frank I. Moore; (left) Gail Meese/Meese Photo Research; **21,** (top) Gail Meese/Meese Photo Research; (bottom) Skjold Photos; **27,** Robert E. Murowchick/Photo Research, Inc.; **29,** Cathy Watterson.   **Chapter 2. 40,** UPI/Bettmann; **48,** Courtesy, National Library of Medicine; **50,** Courtesy, Harvard University Archive; **54,** Courtesy, B.F. Skinner; **56,** Albert Bandura; **57,** Courtesy, APA Monitor; **60,** Edward Tronick/Anthro Photo; **61,** Cleo Freelance Photo; **63,** UPI/Bettmann; **67,** Virginia Blaisdell.   **Part II. 74,** Omikron/Photo Researchers, Inc.   **Chapter 3. 76,** Paul Conklin; **82,** The Bettmann Archive; **91,** Leonard Lessin/Photo Researchers, Inc.; **93,** Michael Siluk; **94,** (left) K.R. Porter/Photo Researchers, Inc.; (right) Omikron/Photo Researchers, Inc.; **104,** Gail Meese/Meese Photo Research.   **Chapter 4. 114,** Gale Zucker; **120,** Ed Lettau/Photo Researchers, Inc.; **122,** Petit Format/Nestle/Science Source/Photo Researchers, Inc.; **123,** James Stevenson/Science Photo Library/Photo Researchers, Inc.; **127,** Martha McBride/Unicorn Stock Photos; **129,** AP/Wide World Photos; **132,** Allen Zak; **134,** (all) Fetal Alcohol Syndrome Research Fund; **139,** Reuters/Bettmann; **141,** Virginia Blaisdell; **146,** Tom Tucker/Science Source; **148,** Ed Lettau/Photo Researchers, Inc.; **152,** Larry Hamill; **154,** Gail Meese/Meese Photo Research.   **Part III. 156,** Loren Fogelman.   **Chapter 5. 158,** Loren Fogelman; **161,** Gale Zucker; **171,** (all photos) Cathy Watterson except (bottom left) Allen Zak; **183,** Gale Zucker; **191,** Reuters/Bettmann; **195,** (left) Edward Tronick/AnthroPhoto; (right) Gail Meese/Meese Photo Research; **202,** Gale Zucker.   **Chapter 6. 204,** Gale Zucker; **209,** (left) Cathy Watterson; (right) Gail Meese/Meese Photo Research; **211,** Cathy Watterson; **227,** Paul Conklin; **228,** Art Phaneuf; **230,** Cathy Watterson; **233,** Allen Zak; **237,** Grace Davies/Envision; **234,** Cathy Watterson.   **Chapter 7. 240,** Gale Zucker; **245,** Cathy Watterson; **246,** Jim West; **248,** Jim Bradshaw; **251,** (top) Gale Zucker; (bottom) Cleo Freelance Photo; **253,** Cleo Freelance Photo; **257,** Gail Meese/Meese Photo Research; **261,** Harlow Primate Lab/University of Wisconsin; **269,** Gail Meese/Meese Photo Research; **275,** Michael Siluk.   **Part IV. 278,** Norman Prince.   **Chapter 8. 280,** Gale Zucker; **283,** Gail Meese/Meese Photo Research; **285,** Jeanetta Holliman; **291,** Gail Meese/Meese Photo Research; **293,** (top) Gail Meese/Meese Photo Research; (bottom) Cathy Watterson; **294,** Dr. Martin W. De Vries; **295,** Cathy Watterson; **305,** Steve Berman/The Children's Health Fund/The N.Y. Children's Health Project; **305,** Steve Berman/The Children's Health Fund/The N.Y. Children's Health Project.   **Chapter 9. 312,** Gail Meese/Meese Photo Research; **314,** Virginia Blaisdell; **316,** Cathy Watterson; **317,** (both) Cathy Watterson; **329,** Skjold Photos; **330,** Gale Zucker; **332,** Jim Bradshaw; **333,** (left) Jim West; (right) Robert Pleban; **335,** (both) Gail Meese/Meese Photo Research; **341,** Gale Zucker.   **Chapter 10. 346,** Jim Bradshaw; **349,** Paul Conklin; **350,** Gail Meese/Meese Photo Research; **352,** Art Phaneuf; **354,** Gail Meese/Meese Photo Research; **356,** Michael Siluk; **360,** Cathy Watterson; **362,** Gail Meese/Meese Photo Research; **365,** Gail Meese/Meese Photo Research; **366,** (both) Gale Zucker; **369,** Robert Finken; **374,** (top) Paul Conklin; (bottom) Gail Meese/Meese Photo Research; **375,** Cathy Watterson; **380,** Courtesy, NBC/Carsey-Werner Co; **381,** Gail Meese/Meese Photo Research.   **Part V.**

384, Cleo Freelance Photography.   **Chapter 11. 386,** Gale Zucker; **389,** Virginia Blaisdell; **390,** Gail Meese/Meese Photo Research; **393,** Mike Voss; **397,** Cleo Freelance Photo; **400,** (top) Jim West; (bottom) Cathy Watterson; **403,** Gail Meese/Meese Photo Research; **405,** Gail Meese/Meese Photo Research; **407,** Gale Zucker.   **Chapter 12. 410,** Jim Bradshaw; **412,** Mike Penney; **414,** Robert Finken; **426,** (left) Gail Meese/Meese Photo Research; (right) Michael Siluk; **436,** Chris Walter/Anthro-Photo; **433,** Robert Finken; **442,** Gail Meese/Meese Photo Research; **445,** Gail Meese/Meese Photo Research; **446,** Michael Siluk; **440,** Michael Siluk.   **Chapter 13. 450,** Paul Conklin; **453,** Mike Penney; **457,** Gail Meese/Meese Photo Research; **463,** Jim Bradshaw; **464,** Cleo Freelance Photo; **466,** Mike Penney; **468,** Pat Watson; **471,** (left) Gale Zucker; (right) Larry Hamill; **472,** Paul Conklin; **476,** Gail Meese/Meese Photo Research; **480,** Gail Meese/Meese Photo Research; **482,** Courtesy, School of the 21st Century Program, Leadville, Colorado; **485,** Gail Denham.   **Part VI. 488,** Michael Siluk.   **Chapter 14. 490,** Michael Siluk; **493,** The Bettmann Archive/Lewis Hine; **499,** Gail Meese/Meese Photo Research; **501,** Gail Meese/Meese Photo Research; **503,** Susan Rosenberg/Photo Researchers, Inc.; **512,** Mike Penney; **514,** Gail Denham.   **Chapter 15. 518,** Envision/MacDonald Photo; **522,** Michael Siluk; **525,** Mike Penney; **528,** Karen Osborne/United Methodist Children's Home; **530,** Ulrich Tutsch; **532,** The Bettmann Archive; **537,** (both) Ulrich Tutsch; **541,** Gail Meese/Meese Photo Research.   **Chapter 16. 544,** Michael Siluk; **546,** (left) Michael Siluk; (right) Ulrich Tutsch; **551,** Catherine Green; **555,** (top) Gail Meese/Meese Photo Research; (bottom) Allen Zak; **558,** Gail Meese/Meese Photo Research; **561,** Michael Siluk; **565,** Gail Meese/Meese Photo Research; **569,** Gail Meese/Meese Photo Research.

Four-Color Photo Credits

Prenatal Life and Birth: 1, (top) © Petit Format/Nestle/Science Source; (bottom) Photo Researchers, Inc.; **2,** (top) Edward Tronick/Anthro-Photo; (middle) Jay Foreman, Unicorn Stock Photos; (bottom) Alexander Tsiaras/Photo Researchers, Inc.; **3,** (top) S.I.U./Science Source/Photo Researchers, Inc.; (middle) S.I.U./Science Source/Photo Researchers, Inc.; (bottom) Larry Hamill; **4,** (top) Lila Abulughod/Anthro-Photo; (bottom) Larry Hamill.   **Children and Culture: 1,** (top) Borys Malkin/Anthro-Photo; (bottom) Gail Meese/Meese Photo Research; **2,** (top) Cathy Watterson; (middle) Joel Halpern/Anthro-Photo; (bottom) James Chisholm/Anthro-Photo; **3,** (top) Gail Meese/Meese Photo Research; (middle) B. Worley/Anthro-Photo; (bottom) Edward Tronick/Anthro-Photo; **4,** (top) Paul Conklin; (bottom right) Gale Zucker; (bottom left) Cleo Photo   **Child Care: 1,** (top) Gale Zucker; (bottom) Paul Conklin; **2,** (top) Edward Tronick/Anthro-Photo; (bottom) Cathy Watterson; **3,** (top) Paul Conklin; (middle) Gail Meese/Meese Photo Research; (bottom) Joan Bushno/Unicorn Stock Photos; **4,** (top) Gail Meese/Meese Photo Research; (middle) Gale Zucker; (bottom) Paul Conklin.   **Adolescence: 1,** Ralph W. Hennen; **2,** (top) D & I MacDonald/Atlanta Stock Associates; (middle and bottom) Paul Conklin; **3,** (top) Mary Elenz-Tranter; (middle right) Paul Conklin; (middle left and bottom) Gale Zucker; **4,** (top) Tony Griffiths/Unicorn Stock Photos; (bottom) Ulrike Welsch.

TO THE OWNER OF THIS BOOK:

We hope that you have found *Children in a Changing World: Development and Social Issues, Second Edition,* useful. So that this book can be improved in a future edition, would you take the time to complete this sheet and return it? Thank you.

Instructor's name: _____

Department: _____

School and address: _____

_____

1. The name of the course in which I used this book is: _____

_____

2. My general reaction to this book is: _____

_____

_____

3. What I like most about this book is: _____

_____

_____

4. What I like least about this book is: _____

_____

_____

5. Were all of the chapters of the book assigned for you to read?   Yes   No

   If not, which ones weren't? _____

6. Do you plan to keep this book after you finish the course?   Yes   No

   Why or why not? _____

_____

7. On a separate sheet of paper, please write specific suggestions for improving this book and anything else you'd care to share about your experience in using the book.

Optional:

Your name: ______________________________ Date: ____________________

May Brooks/Cole quote you, either in promotion for *Children in a Changing World* or in future publishing ventures?

Yes: ________ No: ________

Sincerely,
Edward F. Zigler
Matia Finn Stevenson

FOLD HERE

NO POSTAGE
NECESSARY
IF MAILED
IN THE
UNITED STATES

BUSINESS REPLY MAIL

FIRST CLASS PERMIT NO. 358 PACIFIC GROVE, CA

POSTAGE WILL BE PAID BY ADDRESSEE

ATT: Edward F. Zigler & Matia Finn Stevenson

Brooks/Cole Publishing Company
511 Forest Lodge Road
Pacific Grove, California 93950-9968

FOLD HERE